D0956436

Oxford English Mini Dictionary

SEVENTH EDITION

Edited by
Catherine Soanes

OXFORD
UNIVERSITY PRESS

OXFORD

UNIVERSITY PRESS

Great Clarendon Street, Oxford OX2 6DP

Oxford University Press is a department of the University of Oxford.
It furthers the University's objective of excellence in research, scholarship,
and education by publishing worldwide in

Oxford New York

Auckland Cape Town Dar es Salaam Hong Kong Karachi
Kuala Lumpur Madrid Melbourne Mexico City Nairobi
New Delhi Shanghai Taipei Toronto

With offices in

Argentina Austria Brazil Chile Czech Republic France Greece
Guatemala Hungary Italy Japan Poland Portugal Singapore
South Korea Switzerland Thailand Turkey Ukraine Vietnam

Oxford is a registered trade mark of Oxford University Press
in the UK and in certain other countries

Published in the United States
by Oxford University Press Inc., New York

First edition 1981
Second edition 1988
Third edition 1991
Revised third edition 1994
Fourth edition 1995
Fifth edition 1999
Revised fifth edition 2003
Sixth edition 2004
Seventh edition 2007

British Library Cataloguing in Publication Data

Data available

Library of Congress Cataloging in Publication Data

Data available

Typeset in OUP Argo by SPI Publisher Services, Pondicherry, India
Printed in Italy by Legoprint S.p.A.

ISBN 978-0-19-921365-8

10 9 8 7 6 5 4 3 2

Introduction

The seventh edition of the *Oxford English Mini Dictionary* belongs to the family of dictionaries based on the *Oxford Dictionary of English* (ODE). It aims to provide wide-ranging, up-to-date, and compact coverage of the core vocabulary of current English in a highly portable format.

Definitions are written in a clear and accessible style using straightforward language, with the most common meanings of words placed first in individual entries. A fresh, open layout and design makes the dictionary especially easy to use. Special notes throughout the text give extra help and guidance on difficult spellings, on words that are easily confused with each other, and on tricky points of usage. Pronunciations are given for words which might cause problems, using a simple respelling system.

New to the dictionary is a central supplement that includes a quick-reference guide to grammar terms, lists of common misspellings and confusable words, and a handy word games section giving, for example, lists of three-letter words containing *x* or *z*.

Small enough to fit into a bag, backpack, or briefcase, the *Oxford English Mini Dictionary* is an ideal quick-reference text for anyone requiring an informative, robust, and user-friendly guide to the English language of today.

Guide to the dictionary

Pronunciation (given for difficult words)

Headword ·········· **buoy** /boy/ n. a floating object
used to mark an area of water. •v. ·········· Part of speech

Sense number ········· **1** keep afloat. **2** (**be buoyed up**)
be cheerful and confident. ·········· Typical use

Spelling note ·········· ! Remember: *u* before *o* in b*u*oy
and b*u*oyant.

Plural forms

gas n. (pl. **gases** or US **gasses**) **1** an
air-like substance which expands ·········· Label showing
to fill any available space. **2** gas where term is
Verb used as a fuel. **3** US informal petrol, used
inflections ·········· •v. (**gassing, gassed**) **1** harm or
kill with gas. **2** informal chatter.

Compounds □ **gas chamber** a room filled with
and phrases poisonous gas to kill people. **gas** ·········· Label showing
(in alphabetical **mask** a mask used as protection how term is
order) ·········· against poisonous gas. ■ **gassy** used
adj.

Adjective
inflections

Derivatives **sad** adj. (**sadder, saddest**) feeling
(in alphabetical or causing sorrow: *a sad story.*
order) ·········· ■ **sadden** v. **sadly** adv. **sadness** n. ·········· Example of
use

Different spelling
of headword **bosun** (or **bo'sun**) var. of
(both allowed) ·········· BOATSWAIN. Cross-reference
to another
dictionary entry

Label showing **fortissimo** adv. Music very loudly.
subject the
entry deals with

Pronunciations

Pronunciations are given for words which might cause problems. The part of the pronunciation printed in bold is the syllable that is stressed.

List of symbols

vowels	examples	vowels	examples	vowels	examples
a	as in **cat**	ew	as in **few**	u	as in **cup**
ah	as in **calm**	i	as in **pin**	uh	as in **the**
air	as in **hair**	I	as in **eye**		first part
ar	as in **bar**	o	as in **top**		of **ago**
aw	as in **law**	oh	as in **most**	uu	as in **book**
ay	as in **say**	oi	as in **join**	y	as in **cry**
e	as in **bed**	oo	as in **soon**	yoo	as in **unit**
ee	as in	oor	as in **poor**	yoor	as in
	meet	or	as in **corn**		**Europe**
eer	as in **beer**	ow	as in **cow**		
er	as in **her**	oy	as in **boy**		

consonants	examples	consonants	examples	consonants	examples
b	as in **bat**	m	as in **man**	t	as in **top**
ch	as in **chin**	n	as in **not**	th	as in **thin**
d	as in **day**	ng	as in **sing, finger**	th	as in **this**
f	as in **fat**			v	as in **van**
g	as in **get**	nk	as in **thank**	w	as in **will**
h	as in **hat**			y	as in **yes**
j	as in **jam**	p	as in **pen**	z	as in **zebra**
k	as in **king**	r	as in **red**		
kh	as in **loch**	s	as in **sit**	zh	as in **vision**
l	as in **leg**	sh	as in **shop**		

Abbreviations used in the dictionary

adj.	adjective	Naut.	Nautical
abbrev.	abbreviation	N. Engl.	northern English
adv.	adverb	offens.	offensive
Austral.	Australian	past part.	past participle
aux. v.	auxiliary verb	pl.	plural
Chem.	Chemistry	pl. n.	plural noun
comb. form	combining form	possess. pron.	possessive pronoun
conj.	conjunction	prep.	preposition
derog.	derogatory	pres. part.	present participle
esp.	especially	pron.	pronoun
exclam.	exclamation	Sc.	Scottish
fem.	feminine	sing.	singular
Geom.	Geometry	usu.	usually
Gk. Myth	Greek Mythology	v.	verb
hist.	historical	var.	variant
Math.	Mathematics	vars.	variants
n.	noun		

Abbreviations that are in common use (such as cm, RC, US, and USA) appear in the dictionary itself.

Note on trademarks and proprietary status

This dictionary includes some words which have, or are asserted to have, proprietary status as trademarks or otherwise. Their inclusion does not imply that they have acquired for legal purposes a non-proprietary or general significance, nor any other judgement concerning their legal status. In cases where the editorial staff have some evidence that a word has proprietary status this is indicated in the entry for that word by the label trademark, but no judgement concerning the legal status of such words is made or implied thereby.

a *adj.* **1** used when mentioning someone or something for the first time; the indefinite article. **2** one single. **3** per: *twice a week.*

@ *symb.* 'at', used: **1** to show cost or rate per unit. **2** in Internet addresses between the user's name and the domain name: *john.smith@oup.com.*

AA *abbrev.* **1** Alcoholics Anonymous. **2** Automobile Association.

aardvark *n.* an African mammal with a long snout.

aback *adv.* (**taken aback**) surprised and disconcerted.

abacus *n.* a frame with rows of wires along which beads are slid, used for counting.

abandon *v.* **1** leave permanently. **2** give up. •*n.* lack of inhibition. ■ **abandonment** *n.*

abandoned *adj.* wild or uncontrolled.

abase *v.* humiliate or degrade. ■ **abasement** *n.*

abashed *adj.* embarrassed or ashamed.

abate *v.* become less severe or widespread. ■ **abatement** *n.*

abattoir /a-buh-twar/ *n.* a slaughterhouse.

abbey *n.* a building occupied by a community of monks or nuns.

abbot *n.* (*fem.* **abbess**) the head of an abbey.

abbreviate *v.* shorten a word or phrase. ■ **abbreviation** *n.*

abdicate *v.* **1** give up the throne. **2** fail to carry out a duty. ■ **abdication** *n.*

abdomen *n.* the part of the body containing the digestive organs. ■ **abdominal** *adj.*

abduct *v.* kidnap. ■ **abduction** *n.* **abductor** *n.*

aberrant *adj.* not normal or acceptable.

aberration *n.* a departure from what is normal or acceptable.

abet *v.* (**abetting, abetted**) encourage or help in wrongdoing. ■ **abettor** *n.*

abeyance *n.* (**in abeyance**) in temporary disuse.

abhor *v.* (**abhorring, abhorred**) detest.

abhorrent *adj.* disgusting; hateful. ■ **abhorrence** *n.*

abide *v.* **1** (**abide by**) accept or obey a rule or decision. **2** (**cannot abide**) dislike greatly.

abiding *adj.* lasting; enduring.

ability *n.* (*pl.* **abilities**) **1** the power to do something. **2** talent.

abject *adj.* **1** wretched. **2** completely without pride. ■ **abjectly** *adv.*

abjure *v.* renounce a belief, claim, etc.

ablaze *adj.* burning fiercely.

able *adj.* **1** capable of doing something. **2** talented. ■ **ably** *adv.*

ablutions *pl. n.* the act of washing yourself.

a

abnegation n. the giving up of something wanted.

abnormal adj. not normal. ∎ **abnormality** n. **abnormally** adv.

aboard adv. & prep. on board.

abode n. a house or home.

abolish v. put an end to a law or custom. ∎ **abolition** n.

abominable adj. causing disgust. ∎ **abominably** adv.

abominate v. hate; detest. ∎ **abomination** n.

aboriginal adj. existing in a land from its earliest times. •n. (**Aboriginal**) a member of one of the original peoples of Australia.

Aborigine /ab-uh-ri-ji-nee/ n. an Australian Aboriginal.

abort v. 1 carry out the abortion of a fetus. 2 end before complete, because of a problem.

abortion n. the deliberate ending of a human pregnancy.

abortionist n. derog. a person who carries out abortions.

abortive adj. unsuccessful.

abound v. be plentiful.

about prep. & adv. 1 concerning. 2 here and there within a place. 3 nearly. □ **about-turn** a complete change of direction or policy.

above prep. & adv. 1 at a higher level than. 2 more than. □ **above board** lawful and honest.

abracadabra exclam. said by magicians when performing a trick.

abrasion n. 1 scraping or wearing away. 2 an area of scraped skin.

abrasive adj. 1 rough and used for polishing or cleaning. 2 harsh or hurtful.

abreast adv. 1 side by side. 2 (**abreast of**) up to date with.

abridge v. shorten a book, account, etc. ∎ **abridgement** n.

abroad adv. away from your home country.

abrogate v. cancel or abolish. ∎ **abrogation** n.

abrupt adj. 1 sudden. 2 curt. ∎ **abruptly** adv. **abruptness** n.

abscess n. a swelling containing pus.

! Remember the s and c: abscess.

abscond v. leave quickly and secretly.

abseil /ab-sayl/ v. climb down a rock face using a rope fixed at a higher point.

absence n. 1 the state of being absent. 2 (**absence of**) lack of.

absent adj. not present. •v. (**absent yourself**) stay away. □ **absent-minded** forgetful; inattentive.

absentee n. a person who is absent from something. ∎ **absenteeism** n.

absinthe /ab-sinth/ n. a green liqueur.

absolute adj. 1 complete. 2 not limited. ∎ **absolutely** adv.

absolution n. formal forgiveness of a person's sins.

absolutism n. the principle of government with unrestricted power. ∎ **absolutist** n. & adj.

absolve v. formally clear of guilt, blame, or sin.

absorb v. 1 soak up liquid. 2 understand information. 3 hold the attention of someone. 4 reduce in effect or strength.

absorbent adj. able to soak up liquid.

absorption n. the process of absorbing.

abstain v. **1** stop yourself from doing something. **2** choose not to vote. ∎ **abstainer** n. **abstention** n.

abstemious adj. limiting your intake of food or alcohol.

abstinence n. the avoidance of doing or indulging in something.

abstract adj. **1** relating to ideas or qualities; not physical. **2** (of art) not representing things pictorially. ∙v. take out or remove. ∙n. a summary of a book or article. ∎ **abstraction** n.

abstruse adj. hard to understand.

absurd adj. completely illogical or ridiculous. ∎ **absurdity** n. **absurdly** adv.

abundant adj. **1** plentiful. **2** having plenty of something. ∎ **abundance** n. **abundantly** adv.

abuse v. **1** use badly or wrongly. **2** treat cruelly. **3** insult. ∙n. **1** cruel treatment or misuse. **2** insulting language.

abusive adj. **1** very insulting. **2** cruel and violent. ∎ **abusively** adv.

abut v. (**abutting**, **abutted**) be next to or touching.

abysmal adj. very bad.

abyss n. a very deep hole.

AC abbrev. alternating current.

a/c abbrev. account.

acacia /uh-kay-shuh/ n. a tree or shrub with yellow or white flowers.

academic adj. **1** of education or study. **2** not related to a real situation; theoretical. ∙n. a teacher or scholar in a university or college. ∎ **academically** adv.

academician n. a member of an academy.

academy n. (pl. **academies**) **1** a place for training in a special field. **2** a society of artists or scientists.

accede /uhk-seed/ v. agree to a demand or request.

accelerate v. begin to move more quickly. ∎ **acceleration** n.

accelerator n. a foot pedal which controls a vehicle's speed.

accent n. **1** a way of pronouncing a language. **2** emphasis. **3** a written mark guiding pronunciation. ∙v. **1** (**accented**) spoken with an accent. **2** emphasize.

accentuate v. make more noticeable. ∎ **accentuation** n.

accept v. **1** say yes to. **2** take as true. **3** resign yourself to. ∎ **acceptance** n.

acceptable adj. satisfactory. ∎ **acceptability** n. **acceptably** adv.

access n. **1** a way in. **2** the right or opportunity to use something or see someone. ∙v. obtain data from a computer.

accessible adj. able to be reached, used, or understood. ∎ **accessibility** n. **accessibly** adv.

accession n. **1** the gaining of a position or rank. **2** an addition to a library or museum collection.

accessory n. (pl. **accessories**) **1** a thing added as a supplement or decoration. **2** a person who helps in a crime.

accident n. **1** an unpleasant incident that happens unexpectedly. **2** an incident that happens by chance.

accidental adj. happening by chance. ∎ **accidentally** adv.

acclaim v. praise enthusiastically. ∙n. enthusiastic praise. ∎ **acclamation** n.

a

acclimatize (or **-ise**) *v.* get used to new conditions. ■ **acclimatization** *n.*

accolade *n.* a thing given as a special honour or reward.

accommodate *v.* **1** provide lodging or space for. **2** adapt to.

> ! Double *c*, double *m*: accommodate.

accommodating *adj.* willing to do as asked.

accommodation *n.* a place to live.

accompany *v.* (**accompanying**, **accompanied**) **1** go with. **2** play musical backing for an instrument or voice. ■ **accompaniment** *n.* **accompanist** *n.*

accomplice *n.* a person who helps another commit a crime.

accomplish *v.* **1** succeed in doing or achieving. **2** (**accomplished**) highly skilled.

accomplishment *n.* **1** a skill or special ability. **2** something achieved successfully.

accord *v.* be consistent with. • *n.* agreement in opinion. □ **of your own accord** willingly.

accordance *n.* (**in accordance with**) in a way conforming with.

according *adv.* (**according to**) **1** as stated by. **2** following or agreeing with.

accordingly *adv.* **1** appropriately. **2** therefore.

accordion *n.* a musical instrument with bellows and keys or buttons.

accost *v.* approach and speak to.

account *n.* **1** a description of an event. **2** a record of money spent and received. **3** a credit arrangement with a bank or firm. • *v.* (**account for**) explain. □ **on account of** because of.

accountable *adj.* responsible for actions and expected to explain them. ■ **accountability** *n.*

accountant *n.* a person who keeps or inspects financial accounts. ■ **accountancy** *n.*

accoutrement /uh-koo-truh-muhnt/ *n.* an extra item of dress or equipment.

accredited *adj.* officially authorized.

accretion *n.* growth or increase by a gradual build-up.

accrue *v.* (**accruing**, **accrued**) collect or accumulate. ■ **accrual** *n.*

accumulate *v.* **1** acquire more and more of. **2** increase. ■ **accumulation** *n.*

> ! Two *c*'s and one *m*: accumulate.

accumulator *n.* **1** a rechargeable electric battery. **2** a series of bets with the winnings from each placed on the next.

accurate *adj.* with no errors. ■ **accuracy** *n.* **accurately** *adv.*

accusative *n.* the grammatical case used for the object of a verb.

accuse *v.* charge with committing an offence or crime. ■ **accusation** *n.* **accuser** *n.*

accustom *v.* make or be used to.

ace *n.* **1** a playing card with a single spot. **2** *informal* an expert. **3** *Tennis* a serve that an opponent cannot return.

acerbic /uh-ser-bik/ *adj.* sharp and direct. ■ **acerbity** *n.*

acetate /a-si-tayt/ *n.* a synthetic textile fibre.

acetic acid /uh-see-tik/ *n.* the acid that gives vinegar its taste.

acetone /a-si-tohn/ *n.* a colourless liquid used as a solvent.

acetylene /uh-set-i-leen/ n. a gas which burns with a bright flame.

ache n. a continuous dull pain. •v. have an ache.

achieve v. succeed in doing by effort or skill. ■ **achievable** adj. **achievement** n. **achiever** n.

Achilles heel n. a weak point.

Achilles tendon n. the tendon connecting calf muscles to the heel.

acid n. a substance that turns litmus red, neutralizes alkalis, and dissolves some metals. •adj. **1** sour. **2** unkind; cutting. □ **acid rain** rain made acidic by pollution. **acid test** a decisive test of something. ■ **acidic** adj. **acidity** n. **acidly** adv.

acknowledge v. **1** accept the truth of. **2** confirm receipt of. **3** show recognition of. ■ **acknowledgement** n.

acme /ak-mi/ n. the height of achievement or excellence.

acne n. a skin condition causing red pimples.

acolyte /ak-uh-lyt/ n. an assistant or follower.

acorn n. the oval nut of the oak tree.

acoustic adj. **1** of sound. **2** not electrically amplified. •n. (**acoustics**) the aspects of a room that affect the way sound is carried.

acquaint v. **1** make aware of. **2** (**be acquainted with**) know slightly.

acquaintance n. **1** a person you know slightly. **2** knowledge or familiarity.

acquiesce v. accept without protest. ■ **acquiescence** n. **acquiescent** adj.

acquire v. buy or get.

acquisition n. **1** something acquired. **2** the act of acquiring.

acquisitive adj. eager to acquire things. ■ **acquisitiveness** n.

acquit v. (**acquitting, acquitted**) **1** declare to be not guilty **2** (**acquit yourself**) behave in a particular way. ■ **acquittal** n.

acre n. a unit of land area equal to 4,840 sq. yds (0.405 hectare). ■ **acreage** n.

acrid adj. unpleasantly bitter.

acrimonious adj. angry and bitter. ■ **acrimony** n.

acrobat n. a performer of spectacular gymnastic feats.

acrobatic adj. involving spectacular gymnastic feats. •n. (**acrobatics**) acrobatic feats.

acronym n. a word formed from the first letters of other words, e.g. Aids.

across prep. & adv. from one side to the other of.

acrostic n. a poem or puzzle in which certain letters in each line form a word or words.

acrylic adj. (of a fabric, paint, etc.) made from acrylic acid (an organic acid).

act v. **1** do something. **2** have an effect. **3** behave. **4** (**acting**) temporarily doing another's duties. **5** perform in a play or film. •n. **1** a thing done. **2** a law made by a parliament. **3** a section of a play or opera. **4** a set performance or performing group.

actinium n. a radioactive chemical element.

action n. **1** the process of doing something. **2** a thing done. **3** a lawsuit. **4** armed conflict.

actionable adj. giving cause for legal action.

activate v. cause to act or work. ■ **activation** n. **activator** n.

active adj. **1** energetic; lively. **2** functioning. **3** Grammar (of a verb) having as its subject the person or thing doing the action. ■ **actively** adv.

activist n. a person campaigning for political change. ■ **activism** n.

activity n. (pl. **activities**) **1** the state of being active. **2** an action or pastime.

actor n. (fem. **actress**) a person who acts in a play or film.

actual adj. existing in fact. ■ **actuality** n.

actually adv. in truth; really.

actuary n. (pl. **actuaries**) a person who calculates insurance risks.

actuate v. **1** activate. **2** motivate.

acumen n. shrewdness.

acupuncture n. the insertion of needles into the skin as a medical treatment. ■ **acupuncturist** n.

acute adj. **1** serious or severe. **2** sharp-witted. **3** (of an angle) less than 90°. □ **acute accent** the accent (´). ■ **acutely** adv. **acuteness** n.

AD abbrev. Anno Domini (used in dates counted from the traditional date of Jesus's birth).

adage /ad-ij/ n. a saying expressing an accepted truth.

adagio /uh-dah-ji-oh/ adv. Music in slow time.

adamant adj. refusing to change your mind.

Adam's apple n. the lump of cartilage at the front of the neck.

adapt v. make or become suitable for a new use or purpose. ■ **adaptation** n.

adaptable adj. able to adapt or be adapted. ■ **adaptability** n.

adaptor (or **adapter**) n. a device for connecting several electric plugs to one socket.

add v. **1** join to or put with something else. **2** put together numbers to find their total value. **3** say as a further remark.

addendum n. (pl. **addenda**) an extra item added to a book.

adder n. a poisonous snake.

addict n. a person addicted to something.

addicted adj. **1** dependent on a substance. **2** devoted to an activity. ■ **addiction** n. **addictive** adj.

addition n. **1** the act of adding. **2** a thing added.

additional adj. added; extra. ■ **additionally** adv.

additive n. a substance added to improve or preserve something.

addled adj. muddled or confused.

address n. **1** the details of a building's location or a person's home. **2** a speech. **3** a string of characters identifying a destination for email. •v. **1** write an address on. **2** speak to. **3** begin to deal with. ■ **addressee** n.

adduce v. refer to as evidence.

adenoids pl. n. a mass of tissue between the back of the nose and the throat. ■ **adenoidal** adj.

adept adj. very skilled or able.

adequate adj. satisfactory or acceptable. ■ **adequacy** n. **adequately** adv.

adhere v. **1** stick firmly. **2** follow or support. ■ **adherence** n. **adherent** n.

adhesion n. the process of adhering.

adhesive n. a sticky substance. •adj. sticky.

ad hoc *adj. & adv.* created or done for a particular purpose only.

adieu /uh-dyoo/ *exclam.* goodbye.

ad infinitum *adv.* endlessly.

adipose *adj.* (of body tissue) fatty.

adjacent *adj.* near or next to.

adjective *n.* a word adding information about a noun. ■ **adjectival** *adj.*

adjoin *v.* be next to.

adjourn *v.* break off a meeting until later. ■ **adjournment** *n.*

adjudge *v.* declare to be.

adjudicate *v.* 1 make a formal judgement. 2 judge a competition. ■ **adjudication** *n.* **adjudicator** *n.*

adjunct *n.* an additional part.

adjust *v.* 1 alter slightly. 2 adapt to a new situation. ■ **adjustable** *adj.* **adjustment** *n.*

adjutant *n.* an army officer assisting with administrative work.

ad-lib *v.* (**ad-libbing, ad-libbed**) speak without preparing first. • *adv. & adj.* spoken without preparation.

administer *v.* 1 organize or put into effect. 2 give or apply a drug or remedy.

administrate *v.* manage the business affairs of. ■ **administration** *n.* **administrative** *adj.* **administrator** *n.*

admirable *adj.* deserving respect. ■ **admirably** *adv.*

admiral *n.* a naval officer of the highest rank.

admire *v.* 1 greatly respect. 2 look at with pleasure. ■ **admiration** *n.* **admirer** *n.*

admissible *adj.* acceptable or valid. ■ **admissibility** *n.*

admission *n.* 1 entry to or permission to enter somewhere. 2 a confession.

admit *v.* (**admitting, admitted**) 1 confess to be true. 2 allow to enter. 3 accept as valid.

admittance *n.* admission to a place.

admittedly *adv.* it must be admitted that.

admixture *n.* a mixture.

admonish *v.* reprimand firmly. ■ **admonition** *n.*

ad nauseam *adv.* to a boringly excessive extent.

ado *n.* trouble; fuss.

adobe /uh-doh-bi/ *n.* clay used as a building material.

adolescent *adj.* developing from a child into an adult. • *n.* an adolescent boy or girl. ■ **adolescence** *n.*

adopt *v.* 1 legally bring up another's child as your own. 2 choose a course of action. ■ **adoption** *n.*

adoptive *adj.* related by adoption.

adorable *adj.* lovable or charming.

adore *v.* love or like very much. ■ **adoration** *n.*

adorn *v.* make more attractive; decorate. ■ **adornment** *n.*

adrenal /uh-dree-n'l/ *adj.* of the **adrenal glands**, a pair of glands above the kidneys.

adrenalin (or **adrenaline**) *n.* a hormone produced by the adrenal glands in response to stress.

adrift *adj. & adv.* 1 drifting. 2 no longer attached.

adroit *adj.* clever or skilful.

adsorb *v.* (of a solid) hold a gas or liquid as a thin film on its surface.

adulation *n.* excessive admiration. ■ **adulatory** *adj.*

adult *n.* a fully grown person. • *adj.* fully grown. ■ **adulthood** *n.*

adulterate *v.* make poorer in quality by adding another substance. ■ **adulteration** *n.*

a

adulterer n. a person who has committed adultery.

adultery n. sex with someone other than your husband or wife. ■ **adulterous** adj.

advance v. 1 move or put forward. 2 make progress. 3 pay money as a loan or before it is due. •n. 1 a forward movement. 2 an improvement. 3 a loan. 4 (**advances**) romantic or sexual approaches. ■ **advancement** n.

advanced adj. 1 far on in progress or life. 2 not basic; complex.

advantage n. something that puts you in a favourable position. □ **take advantage of** 1 exploit. 2 make good use of. ■ **advantageous** adj.

advent n. 1 an arrival. 2 (**Advent**) the time before Christmas.

adventure n. an exciting and daring experience. ■ **adventurer** n. **adventurous** adj.

adverb n. a word adding information about an adjective, verb, or other adverb. ■ **adverbial** adj.

adversary n. (pl. **adversaries**) an opponent. ■ **adversarial** adj.

adverse adj. harmful; unfavourable. ■ **adversely** adv.

❗ Don't confuse **adverse** with **averse**, which means 'opposed to'.

adversity n. (pl. **adversities**) difficulty; misfortune.

advertise v. describe a product, service, etc. in the media to increase sales, or a job vacancy to encourage applications. ■ **advertiser** n.

advertisement (or informal **advert**) n. a notice or display advertising something.

advice n. recommendations about future action.

advisable adj. prudent or sensible. ■ **advisability** n.

advise v. 1 recommend a course of action. 2 inform. ■ **adviser** (or **advisor**) n. **advisory** adj.

advocate n. 1 a person who recommends a policy. 2 a person arguing a case on another's behalf. •v. recommend. ■ **advocacy** n.

adze n. a tool like an axe, with an arched blade.

aegis /ee-jiss/ n. protection or support.

aeon /ee-on/ (US **eon**) n. a very long period of time.

aerate v. bring air into.

aerial n. a structure for transmitting or receiving radio or television signals. •adj. 1 existing or taking place in the air. 2 by or from aircraft.

aerobatics pl. n. spectacular feats by aircraft in flight. ■ **aerobatic** adj.

aerobics pl. n. vigorous exercises intended to increase oxygen intake. ■ **aerobic** adj.

aerodrome n. a small airfield.

aerodynamics n. the science concerned with the movement of objects through the air. ■ **aerodynamic** adj.

aerofoil n. a curved structure, such as a wing, designed to give an aircraft lift.

aeronautics n. the study or practice of travel through the air. ■ **aeronautical** adj.

aeroplane n. a powered flying vehicle with fixed wings.

aerosol n. a substance sealed in a container under pressure and released as a fine spray.

aerospace → after

aerospace n. the technology and industry concerned with flight.

aesthete /eess-theet/ (US **esthete**) n. a person who appreciates art and beauty.

aesthetic /ess-thet-ik/ (US **esthetic**) adj. 1 concerned with beauty. 2 pleasant in appearance. •n. 1 the aesthetic qualities of something. 2 (**aesthetics**) the philosophical study of beauty. ■ **aesthetically** adv.

aetiology /eet-i-ol-uh-ji/ (US **etiology**) n. the cause of a disease or condition.

afar adv. far away.

affable adj. good-natured and friendly. ■ **affability** n. **affably** adv.

affair n. 1 an event or series of events. 2 a person's responsibility or concern. 3 a love affair.

affect v. 1 make a difference to. 2 pretend to feel, have, etc.

! Don't confuse **affect** and **effect**: affect mainly means 'make a difference to', as in the changes will affect everyone.

affectation n. artificial and pretentious behaviour.

affected adj. false and intended to impress.

affection n. fondness or liking.

affectionate adj. loving. ■ **affectionately** adv.

affidavit n. a written statement sworn on oath to be true.

affiliate v. link a person or group to a larger organization. ■ **affiliation** n.

affinity n. (pl. **affinities**) 1 a natural liking or understanding. 2 a close relationship between similar people or things.

affirm v. state firmly or publicly. ■ **affirmation** n.

affirmative adj. agreeing with or to a statement or request.

affix v. attach or fasten. •n. a prefix or suffix.

afflict v. cause pain or suffering to. ■ **affliction** n.

affluent adj. wealthy. ■ **affluence** n.

afford v. 1 have enough money or time for. 2 give or provide. ■ **affordable** adj.

afforestation n. the planting of an area with trees to form a forest.

affray n. a fight or violent behaviour.

affront n. an insult. •v. insult; offend.

Afghan n. a person from Afghanistan. •adj. of Afghanistan.

aficionado /uh-fi-shuh-nah-doh/ n. (pl. **aficionados**) an enthusiastic fan of an activity.

afield adv. to or at a distance.

afloat adj. & adv. 1 floating. 2 out of debt or difficulty.

afoot adj. & adv. going on.

aforementioned adj. mentioned previously.

afraid adj. frightened. □ **I'm afraid** I regret.

afresh adv. in a new or different way.

African adj. of Africa or its people. •n. an African person.

Afrikaans n. a language of southern Africa.

Afrikaner n. an Afrikaans-speaking white person in South Africa.

aft adv. & adj. at or towards the rear of a ship or aircraft.

after prep. 1 later than. 2 behind. 3 pursuing. •conj. & adv. in the time following an event. □ after-

a

birth the placenta discharged from the womb after a birth. **after-effect** an effect that occurs some time after its cause. **aftermath** the results of an unpleasant event. **afternoon** the time between noon and evening. **aftershave** a scented lotion used after shaving. **afterthought** a thought of or added later. **afterwards** at a later time.

again adv. once more; another time.

against prep. **1** in opposition to. **2** in or into contact with.

agar /ay-gah/ n. a substance obtained from seaweed, used as a thickener in foods.

agate /ag-uht/ n. a form of quartz with bands of colour.

age n. **1** the length of life or existence. **2** a period of history. **3** informal a very long time. •v. (**ageing** or **aging**, **aged**) grow or cause to appear older.

aged adj. **1** /ayjd/ of a specified age. **2** /ay-jid/ old.

ageism n. prejudice on the grounds of age. ■ **ageist** adj.

ageless adj. not ageing or appearing to age.

agency n. **1** an organization providing a particular service. **2** action or intervention.

agenda n. a list of items to be dealt with, esp. at a meeting.

agent n. **1** a person who provides a particular service. **2** a person or thing producing an effect.

agent provocateur /a-zhon pruh-vo-kuh-**ter**/ n. a person who tempts others to do something illegal.

agglomerate v. collect into a mass. ■ **agglomeration** n.

aggrandize (or **-ise**) v. increase the power or status of. ■ **aggrandizement** n.

aggravate v. **1** make worse. **2** informal annoy. ■ **aggravation** n.

aggregate n. a whole formed by combining several elements. •adj. formed or calculated by combining several items. •v. combine into a whole. ■ **aggregation** n.

aggression n. hostile or violent behaviour or attitudes.

aggressive adj. showing aggression. ■ **aggressively** adv.

! Double g, double s: aggressive.

aggressor n. a person or country that begins hostilities.

aggrieved adj. having a grievance.

aghast adj. filled with horror.

agile adj. able to move quickly and easily. ■ **agility** n.

agitate v. **1** worry; disturb. **2** campaign to arouse public concern. **3** stir briskly. ■ **agitation** n. **agitator** n.

AGM abbrev. annual general meeting.

agnostic n. a person who believes it is not possible to know whether or not God exists. ■ **agnosticism** n.

ago adv. before the present.

agog adj. eager and expectant.

agonize (or **-ise**) v. **1** worry greatly. **2** (**agonizing**) very painful or worrying.

agony n. (pl. **agonies**) extreme suffering.

agoraphobia n. abnormal fear of open or public places. ■ **agoraphobic** adj. & n.

agrarian adj. of agriculture.

agree v. (**agreeing**, **agreed**) **1** have the same opinion. **2** be willing to do something suggested. □ **agree with 1** be consistent with. **2** be good for.

agreeable adj. **1** pleasant. **2** willing to agree. ■ **agreeably** adv.

agreement n. **1** the sharing of opinion. **2** an arrangement agreed between people.

agriculture n. the science or practice of farming. ■ **agricultural** adj.

agronomy n. the science of soil management and crop production.

aground adj. & adv. (of a ship) on the bottom in shallow water.

ague /ay-gyoo/ n. old use an illness involving fever and shivering.

ahead adv. further forward.

ahoy exclam. Naut. a call to attract attention.

aid n. & v. help.

aide n. an assistant to a political leader. □ **aide-de-camp** a military officer who assists a senior officer.

Aids n. acquired immune deficiency syndrome, a disease caused by the HIV virus, which breaks down the sufferer's defences against infection.

aikido /I-kee-doh/ n. a Japanese martial art.

ail v. cause suffering to.

aileron n. a hinged flap on an aircraft's wing.

ailing adj. in poor health.

ailment n. a minor illness.

aim v. **1** point or direct towards. **2** try to achieve. •n. a purpose or intention.

aimless adj. without purpose. ■ **aimlessly** adv.

ain't contr. informal **1** am not; are not; is not. **2** has not; have not.

air n. **1** the mixture of gases surrounding the earth. **2** an impression. **3** (**airs**) an affected and condescending manner. **4** a tune. •v. **1** express an opinion publicly. **2** expose to fresh or warm air. □ **airbag** a car safety device that fills with air in a collision to protect the driver. **airborne 1** carried by air. **2** (of an aircraft) flying. **air conditioning** a system that cools the air in a building or vehicle. **aircraft** a machine capable of flight. **aircraft carrier** a warship acting as a base for aircraft. **airfield** an area where aircraft can take off and land. **air force** the branch of the armed forces using aircraft. **air gun** a gun using compressed air to fire pellets. **airlift** an act of transporting supplies by aircraft. **airline** a company providing flights for public use. **airliner** a passenger aircraft. **airlock 1** an air bubble stopping the flow in a pipe or pump. **2** an airtight compartment. **airmail** mail carried overseas by air. **airman** a member of an air force. **airplane** US an aeroplane. **airport** an airfield with facilities for passengers and goods. **air raid** an attack by aircraft. **airship** a large aircraft filled with gas that is lighter than air. **airspace** the part of the air above a country. **airstrip** a strip of ground where aircraft can take off and land. **airtight** not allowing air to enter or escape. **airwaves** the radio frequencies used for broadcasting. **airway 1** a passage for air into the lungs. **2** a regular route for aircraft. **airworthy** (of an aircraft) safe to fly. ■ **airless** adj.

a

airy *adj.* (**airier, airiest**) **1** well ventilated. **2** casual; dismissive. ▪ **airily** *adv.* **airiness** *n.*

aisle *n.* a passage between rows of seats or between shelves in a shop.

ajar *adv. & adj.* (of a door) slightly open.

aka *abbrev.* also known as.

akimbo *adv.* with hands on the hips and elbows turned outwards.

akin *adj.* related; similar.

alabaster *n.* a white translucent mineral.

à la carte *adj.* (of a menu) having separately priced dishes.

alacrity *n.* eager enthusiasm.

alarm *n.* **1** fear and anxiety. **2** a warning sound or device. **3** a warning of danger. ▪ *v.* frighten or disturb.

alarmist *n.* a person who exaggerates a danger, causing unnecessary alarm.

alas *exclam.* an expression of sorrow.

albatross *n.* a very large seabird.

albeit *conj.* though.

albino *n.* (*pl.* **albinos**) a person or animal without pigment in the skin and hair.

album *n.* **1** a blank book for photos, stamps, etc. **2** a collection of recordings issued as a single item.

albumen *n.* egg white.

alchemy *n.* a medieval form of chemistry, concerned with trying to turn other metals into gold. ▪ **alchemist** *n.*

alcohol *n.* **1** drinks containing an intoxicating liquid, such as wine, beer, and spirits. **2** this liquid.

alcoholic *adj.* of alcohol. ▪ *n.* a person addicted to drinking alcohol. ▪ **alcoholism** *n.*

alcopop *n.* a ready-mixed fizzy drink containing alcohol.

alcove *n.* a recess in a wall.

al dente /al den-tay/ *adj. & adv.* (of food) cooked so as to be still firm when bitten.

alder *n.* a tree of the birch family, which bears catkins.

alderman *n. hist.* a member of an English county or borough council.

ale *n.* beer.

alert *adj.* quick to notice and respond. ▪ *v.* warn of a danger or problem. ▪ *n.* **1** a watchful state. **2** a warning.

A level *n.* (in the UK except Scotland) the higher of the two main levels of the GCE exam.

alfalfa *n.* a plant used as fodder for livestock.

alfresco *adv. & adj.* in the open air.

algae /al-jee, al-gee/ *pl. n.* simple plants with no true stems or leaves.

algebra *n.* a branch of mathematics using letters and symbols to represent quantities. ▪ **algebraic** *adj.*

algorithm *n.* a step-by-step procedure for calculations.

alias *adv.* also called. ▪ *n.* a false identity.

alibi *n.* evidence that a person was elsewhere when a crime was committed.

alien *adj.* **1** foreign. **2** unfamiliar. **3** extraterrestrial. ▪ *n.* **1** a foreigner. **2** a being from another world.

alienate *v.* **1** cause to feel isolated. **2** lose the support or sympathy of. ▪ **alienation** *n.*

alight *v.* **1** get off a train or bus. **2** (of a bird) land on. ▪ *adj. & adv.* on fire.

align v. **1** bring into the correct position. **2** ally yourself. ■ **alignment** n.

alike adj. similar. • adv. in a similar way.

alimentary canal n. the passage along which food passes through the body.

alimony n. financial support for a wife or husband after separation or divorce.

alive adj. **1** living; existing. **2** lively. **3** (**alive to**) aware of.

alkali n. a substance that turns litmus blue and neutralizes acids. ■ **alkaline** adj.

all adj. the whole quantity or extent of. • pron. everything or everyone. • adv. completely. □ **all clear** a signal that danger is over. **all out** using all your effort. **all right 1** unhurt. **2** satisfactory.

allay v. reduce fear or concern.

allegation n. an unproven accusation.

allege v. claim without proof. ■ **alleged** adj. **allegedly** adv.

allegiance n. loyal support.

allegory n. (pl. **allegories**) a story, picture, etc. with a hidden meaning. ■ **allegorical** adj. **allegorically** adv.

allegro /uh-lay-groh/ adv. Music briskly.

alleluia var. of HALLELUJAH.

allergen n. a substance causing an allergic reaction.

allergic adj. having or caused by an allergy.

allergy n. (pl. **allergies**) a condition causing an unfavourable bodily reaction to certain substances.

alleviate v. lessen pain or distress. ■ **alleviation** n.

alley n. (pl. **alleys**) **1** a narrow street. **2** a long, narrow area for tenpin bowling or skittles.

alliance n. a relationship formed between countries or groups for a joint purpose.

allied adj. joined by an alliance.

alligator n. a large reptile similar to a crocodile.

alliteration n. the occurrence of the same letter or sound at the start of adjacent words. ■ **alliterative** adj.

allocate v. allot or assign. ■ **allocation** n.

allot v. (**allotting, allotted**) give or share out.

allotment n. **1** a small plot of land rented for cultivating vegetables etc. **2** an allotted share.

allotrope n. each of the physical forms in which a chemical element can exist.

allow v. **1** let someone do something. **2** provide; set aside. **3** admit. **4** (**allow for**) take into account. ■ **allowable** adj.

allowance n. **1** a permitted amount. **2** a sum of money paid regularly. □ **make allowances** be lenient because of mitigating circumstances.

alloy n. a mixture of two or more metals. • v. mix metals to make an alloy.

allspice n. a spice made from the fruit of a Caribbean tree.

allude v. (**allude to**) mention briefly or indirectly. ■ **allusion** n. **allusive** adj.

allure n. attractiveness or charm.

alluring adj. attractive; tempting.

alluvium n. a fertile mix of clay, silt, etc. left by flood water. ■ **alluvial** adj.

ally n. (pl. **allies**) a person or country that cooperates with another. •v. (**allying**, **allied**) **1** (**ally yourself with**) support. **2** (**allied to/with**) combined with.

alma mater n. a person's former school, college, or university.

almanac n. **1** a calendar giving important dates and information about the sun, tides, etc. **2** a yearbook on a particular topic.

almighty adj. **1** all-powerful. **2** informal huge.

almond n. an edible oval nut.

almost adv. very nearly.

alms /ahmz/ pl. n. hist. charitable donations to the poor. □ **almshouse** a house providing accommodation for the poor.

aloe n. a tropical plant with fleshy leaves.

aloft adv. up in or into the air.

alone adj. & adv. **1** on your own. **2** only.

along prep. & adv. **1** moving or extending on. **2** in company with others.

alongside prep. close to the side of.

aloof adj. unfriendly; distant. ■ **aloofness** n.

alopecia /a-luh-pee-shuh/ n. abnormal hair loss.

aloud adv. in an audible voice.

alpaca n. a long-haired South American llama.

alpha n. the first letter of the Greek alphabet (A, α). •adj. dominant within a group.

alphabet n. an ordered set of letters representing the sounds of a language. ■ **alphabetical** adj. **alphabetically** adv. **alphabetize** (or **-ise**) v.

alpine adj. of high mountains.

already adv. **1** before this time. **2** sooner than expected.

Alsatian n. a German shepherd dog.

also adv. in addition.

altar n. a table used in religious services. □ **altarpiece** a painting behind an altar.

alter v. make or become different. ■ **alteration** n.

altercation n. a noisy dispute.

alternate v. occur in turn repeatedly. •adj. **1** every other. **2** (of two things) repeatedly following and replacing each other. □ **alternating current** an electric current that reverses direction many times a second. ■ **alternately** adv. **alternation** n.

alternative adj. **1** available as another choice. **2** unconventional. •n. an available option. ■ **alternatively** adv.

alternator n. a dynamo that generates an alternating current.

although conj. in spite of the fact that.

altimeter n. an instrument in an aircraft showing altitude.

altitude n. height above sea level or ground level.

alto n. (pl. **altos**) the highest adult male or lowest female singing voice.

altogether adv. **1** completely. **2** in total. **3** on the whole.

altruism n. unselfishness. ■ **altruist** n. **altruistic** adj.

aluminium n. a lightweight silvery-grey metal.

always adv. **1** at all times. **2** forever.

Alzheimer's disease /alts-hy-merz/ n. a disease which affects the functioning of the brain.

AM *abbrev.* amplitude modulation.

am see **BE**.

a.m. *abbrev.* before noon.

amalgam *n.* **1** a blend. **2** an alloy of mercury with another metal.

amalgamate *v.* combine or unite. ∎ **amalgamation** *n.*

amass *v.* collect or accumulate.

amateur *n.* a person who does something as a pastime rather than as a profession.

amateurish *adj.* unskilful.

amatory *adj.* relating to love.

amaze *v.* astonish. ∎ **amazement** *n.*

Amazon *n.* a very tall, strong woman.

ambassador *n.* a diplomat representing their country abroad.

amber *n.* **1** a hard yellowish substance used in jewellery. **2** a yellowish colour.

ambidextrous *adj.* able to use either hand equally well.

ambience *n.* a place's atmosphere.

ambient *adj.* surrounding.

ambiguous *adj.* having more than one meaning. ∎ **ambiguity** *n.* **ambiguously** *adv.*

ambit *n.* scope or extent.

ambition *n.* a strong desire to achieve something.

ambitious *adj.* **1** determined to succeed. **2** intended to reach a high standard and so difficult to achieve. ∎ **ambitiously** *adv.*

ambivalent *adj.* having mixed feelings. ∎ **ambivalence** *n.*

amble *v.* walk at a leisurely pace.

ambrosia *n.* something delicious.

ambulance *n.* a vehicle equipped to carry sick or injured people.

ambush *n.* a surprise attack by people lying in wait. • *v.* make a surprise attack.

ameba US = **AMOEBA**.

ameliorate *v.* make better. ∎ **amelioration** *n.*

amen *exclam.* so be it (used at the end of a prayer).

amenable *adj.* cooperative.

amend *v.* make minor changes or improvements to. □ **make amends** make up for a wrongdoing. ∎ **amendment** *n.*

amenity *n.* (*pl.* **amenities**) a useful or desirable feature of a place.

American *adj.* of America or the USA. • *n.* an American person. □ **American football** a kind of football played with an oval ball.

Americanism *n.* a word or phrase originating in the USA.

amethyst /am-uh-thist/ *n.* a violet or purple precious stone.

amiable *adj.* friendly or likeable. ∎ **amiability** *n.* **amiably** *adv.*

amicable *adj.* friendly. ∎ **amicably** *adv.*

amid (or **amidst**) *prep.* in the middle of.

amino acid *n.* any of the organic compounds which form proteins.

amiss *adj.* not quite right. □ **take amiss** be offended by.

amity *n.* friendly relations between people or countries.

ammeter *n.* an instrument for measuring electric current.

ammonia *n.* a strong-smelling gas which can be used to make a cleaning fluid.

ammonite *n.* a fossilized spiral shell of an extinct sea animal.

ammunition *n.* a supply of bullets and shells.

a

amnesia n. loss of memory. ■ **amnesiac** adj.

amnesty n. (pl. **amnesties**) a pardon for crimes against the state.

amniocentesis n. a test for possible abnormality in a fetus, involving the removal of some amniotic fluid.

amniotic fluid n. the fluid surrounding a fetus before birth.

amoeba /uh-mee-buh/ (US **ameba**) n. (pl. **amoebas** or **amoebae**) a single-celled organism that can change its shape.

amok (or **amuck**) adv. (**run amok**) be out of control.

among (or **amongst**) prep. 1 surrounded by. 2 included in. 3 shared by; between.

amoral adj. not concerned about right or wrong.

amorous adj. showing sexual desire.

amorphous adj. without definite shape.

amount n. 1 the total of something. 2 a quantity. • v. (**amount to**) 1 add up to. 2 be equivalent to.

amp n. informal an amplifier.

ampere /am-pair/ n. a basic unit of electric current.

ampersand n. the sign & (= and).

amphetamine n. a drug used as a stimulant.

amphibian n. an animal such as a frog, able to live both on land and in water.

amphibious adj. living in or suited for both land and water.

amphitheatre n. a round open building with tiers of seats surrounding a central area.

ample adj. 1 quite enough; plentiful. 2 large. ■ **amply** adv.

amplify v. (**amplifying, amplified**) 1 make a sound or electrical signal stronger. 2 explain in more detail. ■ **amplification** n. **amplifier** n.

amplitude n. great size or extent.

ampoule n. a small sealed capsule containing liquid for injection.

amputate v. cut off a limb. ■ **amputation** n.

amuck var. of AMOK.

amulet n. something worn as protection against evil.

amuse v. 1 cause to laugh. 2 make time pass pleasantly for. ■ **amusement** n. **amusing** adj.

an adj. the form of 'a' used before vowel sounds.

anabolic steroid n. a synthetic hormone used to build up muscle.

anachronism n. something which seems to belong to another time. ■ **anachronistic** adj.

anaconda n. a large South American snake.

anaemia /uh-nee-mi-uh/ (US **anemia**) n. a shortage of red cells or haemoglobin in the blood. ■ **anaemic** adj.

anaerobic adj. not using oxygen from the air.

anaesthetic /an-iss-thet-ik/ (US **anesthetic**) n. a drug or gas that stops you feeling pain.

anaesthetist /uh-neess-thuh-tist/ (US **anesthetist**) n. a medical specialist who gives anaesthetics. ■ **anaesthetize** (or -**ise**) v.

anagram n. a word or phrase formed by rearranging the letters of another.

anal /ay-n'l/ adj. of the anus.

analgesic n. a pain-relieving drug.

analogous adj. comparable.

analogue adj. using a variable physical effect, e.g. voltage, to represent information, rather than a digital display. • n. a comparable thing.

analogy n. (pl. **analogies**) **1** a comparison. **2** a partial similarity.

analyse (US **analyze**) v. **1** examine in detail. **2** psychoanalyse. ■ **analyst** n.

analysis n. (pl. **analyses**) **1** a detailed examination or study. **2** psychoanalysis.

analytical (or **analytic**) adj. of analysis. ■ **analytically** adv.

anarchist n. a person who believes that government should be abolished. ■ **anarchism** n.

anarchy n. complete disorder due to lack of government or control. ■ **anarchic** adj.

anathema /uh-na-thuh-muh/ n. something hated.

anatomize (or **-ise**) v. examine in detail.

anatomy n. (pl. **anatomies**) **1** the scientific study of the structure of the body. **2** a detailed analysis. ■ **anatomical** adj. **anatomically** adv.

ancestor n. a person from whom someone is descended. ■ **ancestral** adj.

ancestry n. (pl. **ancestries**) a person's ancestors.

anchor n. a heavy metal object for mooring a ship to the sea bottom. • v. **1** moor with an anchor. **2** fix firmly. ◻ **anchorage** a place where ships may anchor. **anchorman** a presenter of a live TV or radio programme.

anchovy n. (pl. **anchovies**) a small strong-tasting fish.

ancient adj. **1** of the very distant past. **2** very old.

ancillary adj. **1** providing support. **2** extra.

and conj. used to connect words, clauses, or sentences.

andante /an-dan-tay/ adv. Music in moderately slow time.

androgynous /an-dro-ji-nuhss/ adj. partly male and partly female.

android n. a robot with a human appearance.

anecdotal adj. (of a story) not backed up by facts.

anecdote n. a short, entertaining true story.

anemia US = **ANAEMIA**.

anemometer /an-i-mom-i-ter/ n. an instrument for measuring wind speed.

anemone /uh-nem-uh-ni/ n. a plant with red, purple, or white flowers.

anesthesia etc. US = **ANAESTHESIA** etc.

aneurysm /an-yuu-ri-z'm/ n. a swelling of the wall of an artery.

anew adv. **1** in a different way. **2** again.

angel n. **1** a spiritual being acting as a messenger of God. **2** a beautiful or good person. ■ **angelic** adj.

angelica n. the candied stalks of a plant, used in cake decoration.

angelus n. a Roman Catholic prayer said at morning, noon, and sunset.

anger n. a strong feeling of displeasure. • v. make angry.

angina /an-jy-nuh/ (or **angina pectoris**) n. pain in the chest caused by an inadequate blood supply to the heart.

angle n. **1** the space between two lines or surfaces that meet. **2** a position from which someone or something is viewed. **3** a point of view. • v. **1** place in a slanting position. **2** present from a certain point of view. **3** fish with a rod and line. **4** try to get by hinting. ■ **angler** n.

Anglican adj. of the Church of England. • n. a member of the Church of England. ■ **Anglicanism** n.

anglicize (or **-ise**) v. make English in character.

Anglo- comb. form English or British.

Anglo-Saxon n. **1** a Germanic inhabitant of England between the 5th century and the Norman Conquest. **2** the Old English language.

angora n. soft fabric made from the hair of a long-haired goat or rabbit.

angry adj. (**angrier**, **angriest**) feeling or showing anger. ■ **angrily** adv.

angst n. great anxiety.

angstrom n. a unit of measurement for wavelengths.

anguish n. severe pain or distress. ■ **anguished** adj.

angular adj. having angles or sharp corners.

anhydrous adj. containing no water.

aniline /an-i-leen/ n. an oily liquid used in making dyes, drugs, and plastics.

animal n. **1** a living being with sense organs, that can move of its own accord. **2** a mammal, as opposed to a bird, reptile, fish, or insect.

animate v. **1** bring life or energy to. **2** make drawings into an animated film. • adj. alive. ■ **animator** n.

animated adj. **1** lively. **2** (of a film) made using animation.

animation n. **1** liveliness. **2** the technique of filming a sequence of drawings to give the appearance of movement.

animism n. the belief that all natural things have a soul.

animosity n. hatred or strong dislike.

animus n. animosity.

anion n. an ion with a negative charge.

aniseed n. the seed of the **anise plant**, used as a flavouring.

ankle n. the joint connecting the foot with the leg.

anklet n. a chain or band worn round the ankle.

annals pl. n. a historical record of events year by year.

anneal v. toughen metal or glass by heating and slow cooling.

annex v. **1** take possession of another country's territory. **2** add or attach. • n. (or **annexe**) a building attached or near to a main building. ■ **annexation** n.

annihilate v. destroy completely. ■ **annihilation** n.

anniversary n. (pl. **anniversaries**) the date on which an event took place in a previous year.

annotate v. add explanatory notes to. ■ **annotation** n.

announce v. make a public statement about. ■ **announcement** n. **announcer** n.

annoy v. make slightly angry. ■ **annoyance** n.

annual adj. yearly. • n. **1** a plant living for a year or less. **2** a book published once a year. ■ **annually** adv.

annuity n. (pl. **annuities**) a fixed sum of money paid each year.

annul v. (**annulling, annulled**) declare a legal contract to be invalid. ■ **annulment** n.

annular adj. ring-shaped.

Annunciation n. the announcement by the angel Gabriel to the Virgin Mary that she was to be the mother of Jesus.

anode n. an electrode with a positive charge.

anodized (or **-ised**) adj. (of metal) coated with a protective layer by electrolysis.

anodyne adj. bland and inoffensive. • n. a painkilling drug.

anoint v. smear or rub with oil as part of a religious ceremony.

anomaly n. (pl. **anomalies**) something differing from what is standard or normal. ■ **anomalous** adj.

anon adv. old use soon.

anonymous adj. having a name that is not publicly known. ■ **anonymity** n. **anonymously** adv.

anorak n. a waterproof jacket with a hood.

anorexia (or **anorexia nervosa**) n. a disorder in which a person refuses to eat because they want to be thinner. ■ **anorexic** adj. & n.

another adj. & pron. **1** one more. **2** a different.

answer n. **1** something said or written in reaction to a question or statement. **2** the solution to a problem. • v. **1** give an answer. **2** (**answer for**) be responsible for. **3** meet a need. ■ **answering machine** a machine which answers phone calls and records callers' messages.

answerable adj. having to account for something.

ant n. a small insect that lives with many others in an organized group. □ **anteater** a mammal that feeds on ants and termites.

antacid adj. (of a medicine) reducing excess acid in the stomach.

antagonism n. open hostility.

antagonist n. an opponent or enemy. ■ **antagonistic** adj.

antagonize (or **-ise**) v. make someone hostile.

Antarctic adj. of the region around the South Pole.

ante n. a stake put up by a poker player before receiving cards.

antecedent n. **1** a thing that comes before another. **2** (**antecedents**) a person's ancestors. • adj. previous.

antechamber n. an anteroom.

antedate v. precede in time.

antediluvian adj. **1** very old-fashioned. **2** of the time before the biblical Flood.

antelope n. a swift deer-like animal.

antenatal adj. before birth; during pregnancy.

antenna n. (pl. **antennae**) **1** an insect's feeler. **2** (pl. also **antennas**) an aerial.

anterior adj. at or nearer the front.

anteroom n. a small room leading to a main one.

anthem n. **1** a song chosen by a country to express patriotic feelings. **2** a piece of music to be sung in a religious service.

anther n. the part of a flower's stamen that contains pollen.

anthology n. (pl. **anthologies**) a collection of poems or other pieces of writing or music.

a

anthracite n. hard coal that burns with little flame and smoke.

anthrax n. a serious disease of sheep and cattle, able to be transmitted to humans.

anthropoid adj. of apes that resemble humans, e.g. chimpanzees.

anthropology n. the study of human origins, societies, and cultures. ■ **anthropological** adj. **anthropologist** n.

anthropomorphic adj. treating a god, animal, or object as if they were human. ■ **anthropomorphism** n.

anti- prefix **1** opposed to. **2** preventing or relieving.

antibiotic n. a medicine that kills bacteria.

antibody n. (pl. **antibodies**) a protein produced in the blood in reaction to harmful substances.

anticipate v. **1** be aware of and prepared for a future event. **2** expect or look forward to. ■ **anticipation** n. **anticipatory** adj.

anticlimax n. a disappointing end to exciting events.

anticlockwise adv. & adj. in the opposite direction to the rotation of the hands of a clock.

antics pl. n. silly or playful behaviour.

anticyclone n. an area of high atmospheric pressure around which air slowly circulates.

antidote n. a medicine taken to counteract a poison.

antifreeze n. a liquid added to water to prevent it from freezing.

antigen n. a harmful substance which causes the body to produce antibodies.

anti-hero n. a central character in a story, film, etc. who is either ordinary or unpleasant.

antihistamine n. a drug used in treating allergies.

antimacassar n. a cloth used to protect the back of a chair from dirt.

antimony n. a silvery-white metallic element.

antioxidant n. a substance that counteracts oxidation.

antipasto n. (pl. **antipasti**) an Italian hors d'oeuvre.

antipathy n. (pl. **antipathies**) strong dislike. ■ **antipathetic** adj.

antiperspirant n. a substance that reduces sweating.

antiphonal adj. sung or recited alternately between two groups.

Antipodes /an-ti-puh-deez/ pl. n. Australia and New Zealand. ■ **Antipodean** adj. & n.

antiquarian adj. relating to the collection of antiques or rare books.

antiquated adj. old-fashioned or outdated.

antique n. an old and valuable object. •adj. valuable because of its age.

antiquity n. (pl. **antiquities**) **1** the distant past. **2** an object from the distant past.

anti-Semitism n. prejudice against Jews. ■ **anti-Semitic** adj.

antiseptic adj. preventing the growth of microorganisms that cause disease or infection. •n. an antiseptic substance.

antisocial adj. **1** acting in a way that is unacceptable to others. **2** avoiding the company of other people.

antithesis n. (pl. **antitheses**) a person or thing that is the direct opposite of another. ■ **antithetical** adj.

antitoxin n. a substance that neutralizes a toxin.

antler n. each of a pair of branched horns on a male deer.

antonym n. a word opposite in meaning to another.

anus /ay-nuhss/ n. the opening through which solid waste leaves the body.

anvil n. an iron block on which metal is hammered and shaped.

anxiety n. (pl. **anxieties**) an anxious feeling or state.

anxious adj. 1 worried or uneasy. 2 very eager. ■ **anxiously** adv.

any adj. & pron. 1 one or some. 2 whichever or whatever you choose. □ **anybody** anyone.

anyhow 1 anyway. 2 in a careless way. **anyone** any person or people. **anything** a thing of any kind. **anyway** 1 used to emphasize something just said or to change the subject. 2 nevertheless. **anywhere** 1 in or to any place. 2 any place.

AOB abbrev. any other business.

aorta /ay-or-tuh/ n. the main artery carrying blood from the heart.

apace adv. quickly.

apart adv. 1 separated by a distance. 2 into pieces. □ **apart from** except for.

apartheid /uh-par-tayt/ n. the former official system of racial segregation in South Africa.

apartment n. 1 a flat. 2 a set of private rooms in a large house.

apathy n. lack of interest or enthusiasm. ■ **apathetic** adj.

ape n. an animal like a monkey but without a tail, e.g. a chimpanzee. • v. imitate.

aperitif n. an alcoholic drink taken before a meal.

aperture n. an opening, esp. one letting in light.

apex n. the top or highest point.

aphasia /uh-fay-zi-uh/ n. inability to understand or produce speech due to brain damage.

aphid /ay-fid/ n. a small insect feeding on the sap of plants.

aphorism /af-uh-ri-z'm/ n. a short clever phrase which makes a true point.

aphrodisiac /af-ruh-diz-i-ak/ n. a food, drink, or drug that arouses sexual desire.

apiary n. (pl. **apiaries**) a place where bees are kept. ■ **apiarist** n.

apiece adv. for or by each one.

aplomb /uh-plom/ n. calm self-confidence.

apocalypse n. 1 an event involving great destruction. 2 (**the Apocalypse**) the final destruction of the world, as described in the biblical book of Revelation. ■ **apocalyptic** adj.

Apocrypha n. those books of the Old Testament not accepted as part of Hebrew scripture.

apocryphal adj. (of a story) widely circulated but unlikely to be true.

apogee /ap-uh-jee/ n. 1 the highest point. 2 the point in the moon's orbit furthest from the earth.

apologetic adj. admitting and showing regret for a wrongdoing. ■ **apologetically** adv.

apologist n. a person who defends something controversial.

a

apologize (or **-ise**) v. express regret for a wrongdoing.

apology n. (pl. **apologies**) **1** an expression of regret for a wrongdoing. **2** (**an apology for**) a very poor example of.

apoplectic adj. **1** furious. **2** dated of apoplexy.

apoplexy n. (pl. **apoplexies**) **1** extreme anger. **2** Med., dated a stroke.

apostasy /uh-poss-tuh-si/ n. abandonment of a belief or principle.

apostate /ap-uh-stayt/ n. a person who abandons a belief or principle.

apostle n. **1** (**Apostle**) each of the twelve chief disciples of Jesus. **2** an enthusiastic supporter of an idea or cause. ■ **apostolic** adj.

apostrophe /uh-poss-truh-fi/ n. a punctuation mark (') used to indicate either possession or the omission of letters or numbers.

apothecary n. (pl. **apothecaries**) old use a person who prepared and sold medicines.

apotheosis /uh-po-thi-oh-siss/ n. (pl. **apotheoses**) the highest level of something.

appal v. (**appalling**, **appalled**) **1** dismay or horrify. **2** (**appalling**) very bad.

apparatus n. equipment for a particular activity or purpose.

apparel n. clothing.

apparent adj. **1** clearly seen or understood. **2** seeming real, but not necessarily so. ■ **apparently** adv.

apparition n. a ghost.

appeal v. **1** make a serious or earnest request. **2** be attractive or interesting. **3** refer a decision to a higher court. •n. **1** an act of

appealing. **2** attractiveness or interest.

appear v. **1** become visible. **2** seem. ■ **appearance** n.

appease v. pacify someone by agreeing to their demands. ■ **appeasement** n.

appellation n. a name or title.

append v. add to the end of a document.

appendage n. a thing attached to something larger or more important.

appendectomy n. (pl. **appendectomies**) the surgical removal of the appendix.

appendicitis n. inflammation of the appendix.

appendix n. (pl. **appendices** or **appendixes**) **1** a small tube of tissue attached to the large intestine. **2** a section of additional information at the end of a book.

appertain v. relate to.

appetite n. **1** desire for food. **2** a liking or inclination.

appetizer (or **-iser**) n. something eaten or drunk to stimulate the appetite.

appetizing (or **-ising**) adj. stimulating the appetite.

applaud v. show approval, esp. by clapping. ■ **applause** n.

apple n. a round fruit with crisp flesh.

appliance n. a machine for use in the home.

applicable adj. relevant; appropriate. ■ **applicability** n.

applicant n. a person who applies for something.

application n. **1** a formal request. **2** the act of applying something. **3** continued effort. **4** a computer program designed for a particular purpose.

applicator n. a device for inserting or spreading something.

applied adj. practical rather than theoretical.

appliqué /uh-plee-kay/ n. needlework in which fabric shapes are attached to a fabric background.

apply v. (applying, applied) 1 request formally. 2 bring into operation. 3 be relevant. 4 spread on a surface. 5 (apply yourself) concentrate on a task.

appoint v. give a job or role to. ■ **appointee** n.

appointment n. 1 an arrangement to meet. 2 a job.

apportion v. share out.

apposite /ap-puh-zit/ adj. very appropriate.

apposition n. Grammar a relationship in which a word or phrase is placed next to another so as to qualify or explain it (e.g. my friend Sue).

appraise v. assess the quality or value of. ■ **appraisal** n.

appreciable adj. considerable. ■ **appreciably** adv.

appreciate v. 1 recognize the value of. 2 understand fully. 3 be grateful for. 4 rise in value. ■ **appreciation** n. **appreciative** adj.

apprehend v. 1 arrest a suspect. 2 understand.

apprehension n. 1 worry or anxiety. 2 understanding.

apprehensive adj. worried or anxious. ■ **apprehensively** adv.

apprentice n. a person learning a trade. ■ **apprenticeship** n.

apprise v. inform.

approach v. 1 come near to. 2 make a proposal or request to.

3 start to deal with. •n. 1 a way of dealing with something. 2 the act of approaching. 3 a way leading to a place.

approachable adj. easy to talk to.

approbation n. approval.

appropriate adj. suitable; proper. •v. 1 take and use without permission. 2 set money aside for a purpose. ■ **appropriately** adv. **appropriation** n.

approval n. 1 a favourable opinion of someone or something. 2 official acceptance.

approve v. 1 regard as good or acceptable. 2 officially approve as satisfactory.

approximate adj. almost but not completely accurate. •v. be very similar to. ■ **approximately** adv. **approximation** n.

APR abbrev. annual percentage rate.

après-ski n. social activities after skiing.

apricot n. an orange-yellow fruit like a small peach.

April n. the fourth month.

a priori adj. & adv. using known facts to decide what an unknown outcome will be.

apron n. 1 a garment worn to protect the front of clothes from dirt. 2 an area on an airfield for manoeuvring or parking aircraft. 3 a strip of stage extending in front of the curtain.

apropos /a-pruh-poh/ prep. (apropos of) with reference to.

apse n. a recess with a domed or arched roof at the end of a church.

apt adj. 1 appropriate. 2 (apt to) tending to. ■ **aptly** adv.

aptitude n. a natural ability.

aqualung n. a piece of equipment enabling divers to breathe under-water.

aquamarine n. a bluish-green precious stone.

aquaplane v. (of a vehicle) slide uncontrollably on a wet surface.

aquarium n. (pl. **aquaria** or **aquariums**) a water-filled glass tank for keeping fish in.

aquatic adj. taking place or living on or in water.

aqueduct n. a structure carrying water across country.

aqueous /ay-kwee-uhss/ adj. of or containing water.

aquifer n. a body of rock that holds water or through which water flows.

aquiline adj. **1** (of a nose) narrow and curved. **2** like an eagle.

Arab n. a member of a people of the Middle East and North Africa. ▪ **Arabian** n. & adj.

arabesque n. **1** a ballet posture in which one leg is extended back-wards and the arms are out-stretched. **2** an ornamental design of intertwined lines.

Arabic n. the language of the Arabs. • adj. of the Arabs. ▫ **Arabic numerals** the numerals 0, 1, 2, 3, etc.

arable adj. (of land) suitable for growing crops.

arachnid n. a creature of a class including spiders and scorpions.

arbiter n. **1** a person who settles a dispute. **2** a person whose taste or opinions are influential.

arbitrary adj. not seeming to be based on a reason or plan. ▪ **arbitrarily** adv.

arbitrate v. officially settle a dispute. ▫ **arbitration** n.

arbitrator n. a person appointed to settle a dispute.

arboreal adj. of or living in trees.

arboretum n. (pl. **arboretums** or **arboreta**) a place where trees are grown for study and display.

arbour (US **arbor**) n. a place or seat in a garden shaded by trees or climbing plants.

arc n. **1** a curve forming part of the circumference of a circle. **2** a curving movement through the air. **3** a glowing electrical dis-charge between two points.

arcade n. **1** a covered passage with arches along one or both sides. **2** a covered walk with shops along the sides.

arcane adj. secret and mysterious.

arch n. **1** a curved structure sup-porting a bridge, roof, or wall. **2** the inner side of the foot. • v. form an arch. • adj. playfully knowing. ▫ **archway** a passage-way under an arch.

arch- comb. form chief, main: arch-enemy.

archaeology (US **archeology**) n. the study of ancient history by examining objects dug up from the ground. ▪ **archaeological** adj. **archaeologist** n.

archaic adj. belonging to former or ancient times.

archaism n. an old or old-fashioned word or phrase.

archangel n. an angel of high rank.

archbishop n. a bishop of the highest rank.

archdeacon n. a senior Christian priest.

archer n. a person who shoots with a bow and arrows. ▪ **arch-ery** n.

archetype /ar-ki-typ/ n. **1** a typical example. **2** an original model. ■ **archetypal** adj.

archipelago /ar-ki-pel-uh-goh/ n. (pl. **archipelagos** or **archipelagoes**) a group of many islands.

architect n. a person who designs buildings.

architecture n. **1** the design and construction of buildings. **2** the style of a building. ■ **architectural** adj.

architrave n. the frame round a doorway or window.

archive /ar-kyv/ n. a collection of documents, data, etc. kept for historical purposes.

archivist /ar-ki-vist/ n. a person in charge of archives.

Arctic adj. of the regions around the North Pole.

! Remember the c: Arctic.

ardent adj. enthusiastic or passionate. ■ **ardently** adv.

ardour (US **ardor**) n. enthusiasm or passion.

arduous adj. difficult and tiring.

are see BE.

area n. **1** a part of a place, object, or surface. **2** the extent or measurement of a surface. **3** a subject.

arena n. **1** a level area surrounded by seating, for sports and other events. **2** an area of activity.

aren't contr. are not.

argon n. an inert gas, present in small amounts in the air.

argot /ar-goh/ n. jargon or slang.

arguable adj. **1** able to be supported by reasons. **2** open to disagreement. ■ **arguably** adv.

argue v. **1** exchange conflicting views heatedly. **2** give reasons for an opinion.

argument n. **1** a heated exchange of conflicting views. **2** a set of reasons given in support of an opinion.

! No e in the middle: argument, not argue-.

argumentative adj. apt to argue.

aria n. a solo in an opera.

arid adj. dry; parched. ■ **aridity** n.

arise v. (**arising**, **arose**; past part. **arisen**) **1** start to exist or be noticed. **2** occur as a result of. **3** get up.

aristocracy n. (pl. **aristocracies**) the highest social class, consisting of people with hereditary titles. ■ **aristocrat** n. **aristocratic** adj.

arithmetic n. the use of numbers in calculation. ■ **arithmetical** adj. **arithmetically** adv.

ark n. **1** (in the Bible) the ship built by Noah to escape the Flood. **2** a chest housing the holy scrolls in a synagogue.

arm n. **1** each of the two upper limbs of the body. **2** a side part of a chair. **3** a branch or division of an organization. **4** (**arms**) weapons. • v. **1** supply with weapons. **2** make a bomb ready to explode. ◻ **armchair** an upholstered chair with side supports for a person's arms. **armpit** the hollow under the arm at the shoulder.

armada n. a fleet of warships.

armadillo n. (pl. **armadillos**) a mammal of South America, with a body covered in bony plates.

Armageddon n. **1** (in the Bible) the last battle between good and

a

evil before the Day of Judgement.
2 a huge and destructive conflict.

armament (or **armaments**) n.
military weapons.

armature n. the rotating coil of a
dynamo or electric motor.

armistice n. a truce.

armorial adj. of coats of arms.

armour (US **armor**) n. **1** metal
coverings formerly worn to protect the body in battle. **2** the
tough metal layer covering a military vehicle or ship. ■ **armoured**
adj. **armourer** n.

armoury (US **armory**) n. (pl. **ar-
mouries**) a store or supply of
weapons.

army n. (pl. **armies**) **1** an organized military force for fighting on
land. **2** a large number.

aroma n. a pleasant smell. ■ **aromatic** adj.

aromatherapy n. the use of
aromatic oils for healing. ■ **aro-
matherapist** n.

arose past of ARISE.

around adv. & prep. **1** on every
side. **2** in or to many places
throughout an area. • adv. **1** so as
to face in the opposite direction.
2 approximately.

arouse v. **1** bring about a feeling
or response. **2** excite someone
sexually. **3** awaken.

arpeggio /ar-pej-ji-oh/ n. (pl.
arpeggios) the notes of a musical
chord played in succession.

arraign /uh-rayn/ v. call before a
court to answer a criminal charge.
■ **arraignment** n.

arrange v. **1** put into order. **2** organize. **3** adapt music for different
instruments or voices.
■ **arrangement** n.

arrant adj. utter; complete.

array n. **1** a display or wide range.
2 an arrangement. **3** literary elaborate clothing. • v. (**be arrayed**)
1 be arranged impressively. **2** be
clothed.

arrears pl. n. money owed that
should already have been paid.

arrest v. **1** seize and take into
custody. **2** stop or delay.
3 (**arresting**) attracting attention.
• n. **1** the act of arresting someone.
2 a sudden stop.

arrival n. **1** the process of arriving.
2 a person or thing that has
arrived.

arrive v. **1** reach a destination.
2 (of a moment) come about.
3 (**arrive at**) reach a conclusion or
decision.

arriviste /ar-ri-veest/ n. usu.
derog. a person who has recently
become rich or risen in status.

arrogant adj. behaving in an unpleasantly superior way.
■ **arrogance** n. **arrogantly** adv.

arrogate v. take or claim for yourself without justification.

arrow n. **1** a stick with a sharp
pointed head, shot from a bow.
2 a sign shaped like this, showing
direction.

arrowroot n. a powdery starch
used as a thickener in cookery.

arsenal n. a store of weapons and
ammunition.

arsenic n. a brittle grey element
with many highly poisonous compounds.

arson n. the criminal act of deliberately setting fire to property.
■ **arsonist** n.

art n. **1** the expression of creative
skill in a visual form. **2** paintings,
drawings, and sculpture. **3** (**the
arts**) creative activities such as
painting, music, and drama. **4** a

skill. □ **artwork** illustrations to be included in a publication.

artefact (US **artifact**) n. a man-made object.

arteriosclerosis /ar-teer-i-oh-skluh-**roh**-siss/ n. thickening of the walls of the arteries.

artery n. (pl. **arteries**) **1** any of the tubes carrying blood from the heart around the body. **2** an important transport route. ■ **arterial** adj.

artesian well n. a well in which water comes to the surface through natural pressure.

artful adj. clever in a cunning way. ■ **artfully** adv.

arthritis n. painful inflammation and stiffness of the joints. ■ **arthritic** adj. & n.

arthropod n. an animal with a segmented body, such as an insect, spider, or crab.

artichoke n. a round vegetable with fleshy green leaves.

article n. a particular object. **2** a piece of writing in a newspaper or magazine. **3** a clause in a legal document.

articulate adj. fluent and clear in speech. • v. **1** pronounce or express clearly. **2** (**articulated**) having sections connected by a flexible joint or joints. ■ **articulately** adv. **articulation** n.

artifact US = **ARTEFACT**.

artifice n. the clever use of tricks so as to deceive.

artificial adj. **1** made as a copy of something natural. **2** not sincere. □ **artificial insemination** the insertion of semen through a syringe into the vagina or womb. **artificial intelligence** the performance by computers of tasks normally requiring human intelli-

gence. ■ **artificiality** n. **artificially** adv.

artillery n. **1** large guns used in warfare. **2** a branch of an army using artillery.

artisan n. a skilled worker who makes things by hand.

artist n. **1** a person who paints or draws. **2** a person who performs any of the creative arts. ■ **artistry** n.

artiste /ar-**teest**/ n. a professional singer or dancer.

artistic adj. **1** having creative skill. **2** of art or artists. ■ **artistically** adv.

artless adj. sincere and straight-forward. ■ **artlessly** adv.

arty (**artier**, **artiest**) informal displaying a pretentious interest in the arts.

as adv. used in comparisons to refer to extent or amount. • conj. **1** while. **2** in the way that. **3** because. **4** even though. • prep. **1** in the role of. **2** while; when.

asafoetida /ah-suh-**fee**-ti-duh/ n. a strong-smelling resin used in Indian cookery.

asap abbrev. as soon as possible.

asbestos n. a fibrous mineral used in fire-resistant materials.

asbestosis n. a serious lung disease caused by inhaling asbestos dust.

ASBO abbrev. antisocial behaviour order.

ascend v. go up; climb or rise.

ascendant adj. rising in power or status. ■ **ascendancy** n.

ascension n. **1** the act of ascending. **2** (**the Ascension**) the ascent of Jesus into heaven.

ascent n. **1** an act of ascending. **2** an upward slope.

a

ascertain v. find out. ■ **ascertainable** adj.

ascetic /uh-set-ik/ adj. choosing to live without pleasures or luxuries. •n. an ascetic person. ■ **asceticism** n.

ASCII abbrev. Computing American Standard Code for Information Interchange.

ascorbic acid n. vitamin C.

ascribe v. (**ascribe to**) consider to be caused by. ■ **ascription** n.

aseptic adj. free from harmful bacteria.

asexual adj. without sex or sexual organs. ■ **asexually** adv.

ash n. **1** the powder remaining after something has been burned. **2** a tree with a silver-grey bark. □ **ashtray** a small container for tobacco ash and cigarette ends.

ashamed adj. feeling shame.

ashen adj. very pale, esp. from shock.

ashlar n. masonry made of large square-cut stones.

ashore adv. to or on the shore.

ashram n. a Hindu religious retreat or community.

Asian adj. of Asia or its people. •n. an Asian person.

Asiatic adj. of Asia.

aside adv. to one side. •n. a remark made so that only certain people will hear.

asinine adj. very silly.

ask v. **1** say so as to get an answer or some information. **2** make a request. **3** invite someone. **4** expect or demand.

askance adv. with a suspicious or disapproving look.

askew adv. & adj. not straight or level.

asleep adj. & adv. in or into a state of sleep.

asp n. a small viper.

asparagus n. a vegetable consisting of the shoots of a tall plant.

aspect n. **1** a part or feature of a matter. **2** an appearance or quality. **3** the direction in which a building faces.

aspen n. a poplar tree.

asperity n. harshness of manner.

aspersions pl. n. critical remarks.

asphalt n. a tar-like substance used in surfacing roads or roofs.

asphyxia n. deprivation of oxygen, leading to unconsciousness or death.

asphyxiate v. die or kill by deprivation of oxygen. ■ **asphyxiation** n.

aspic n. a savoury jelly made with meat stock.

aspidistra n. a plant with broad tapering leaves.

aspirant n. a person with ambitions to do or be something.

aspirate v. pronounce with an h.

aspiration n. a hope or ambition.

aspire v. have ambitions.

aspirin n. a medicine that relieves pain and reduces fever.

ass n. **1** a donkey. **2** informal a stupid person.

assail v. attack violently. ■ **assailant** n.

assassin n. a person who assassinates someone.

assassinate v. murder a political or religious leader. ■ **assassination** n.

assault n. a violent attack. •v. make an assault on.

assay n. a test of metal for quality. •v. test a metal.

assemblage n. 1 a collection or gathering. 2 something made of pieces fitted together.

assemble v. 1 come or bring together. 2 construct by fitting parts together.

assembly n. (pl. **assemblies**) 1 a group of people gathered together. 2 a body of people with law-making powers. 3 the assembling of parts.

assent n. agreement. •v. agree.

assert v. 1 state confidently. 2 (**assert yourself**) be confident and forceful. 3 make others recognize your rights. ■ **assertion** n. **assertive** adj.

assess v. evaluate the value, importance, or quality of. ■ **assessment** n. **assessor** n.

asset n. 1 a useful or valuable thing or person. 2 (**assets**) property owned by a person or company.

assiduous adj. very careful and thorough. ■ **assiduity** n. **assiduously** adv.

assign v. 1 give a task or duty to. 2 provide with a value, date, etc.

assignation n. a secret arrangement to meet.

assignment n. a task assigned to someone.

assimilate v. 1 take in and understand information. 2 absorb into a larger group. ■ **assimilation** n.

assist v. help or support. ■ **assistance** n.

assistant n. a person employed to help someone more senior.

assizes n. hist. a county court.

associate v. 1 connect in the mind. 2 frequently meet or have dealings with. 3 (**associate yourself with**) be involved with. •n. a work partner or colleague.

association n. 1 a group of people organized for a joint purpose. 2 a connection or link.

assonance n. the rhyming of vowel sounds.

assorted adj. of various sorts.

assortment n. a varied collection.

assuage /uh-swayj/ v. 1 lessen an unpleasant feeling. 2 satisfy a desire.

assume v. 1 accept as true without proof. 2 take responsibility or control. 3 begin to have.

assumption n. a thing assumed to be true.

assurance n. 1 an assertion or promise. 2 self-confidence. 3 life insurance.

assure v. 1 tell confidently. 2 make certain.

assured adj. 1 confident. 2 certain; guaranteed. ■ **assuredly** adv.

astatine /ass-tuh-teen/ n. a very unstable radioactive chemical element.

asterisk n. a symbol (*) used as a pointer to a note.

! Remember: aster**isk**, not -*ix*.

astern adv. behind or towards the rear of a ship or aircraft.

asteroid n. a small rocky planet orbiting the sun.

asthma /ass-muh/ n. a medical condition causing difficulty in breathing. ■ **asthmatic** adj. & n.

astigmatism n. a defect in the eye preventing proper focusing. ■ **astigmatic** adj.

astonish v. surprise greatly. ■ **astonishment** n.

astound v. shock or greatly surprise.

a

astral adj. of the stars.

astray adv. away from the correct course.

astride prep. & adv. with a leg on each side of.

astringent adj. **1** causing body tissue to contract. **2** sharp or severe. • n. an astringent lotion. ■ **astringency** n.

astrology n. the study of the supposed influence of stars and planets on human affairs. ■ **astrologer** n. **astrological** adj.

astronaut n. a person trained to travel in a spacecraft.

astronomical adj. **1** of astronomy. **2** informal very large. ■ **astronomically** adv.

astronomy n. the science of stars, planets, and the universe. ■ **astronomer** n.

astrophysics n. the study of the physical nature of stars and planets. ■ **astrophysicist** n.

astute adj. good at making accurate judgements. ■ **astutely** adv.

asunder adv. literary apart.

asylum n. **1** protection from danger, esp. for those who leave their country for political reasons. **2** dated an institution for mentally ill people.

asymmetrical (or **asymmetric**) adj. lacking symmetry. ■ **asymmetrically** adv. **asymmetry** n.

at prep. used to express: **1** location, arrival, or time. **2** a value, rate, or point on a scale. **3** a state or condition. **4** direction towards.

atavistic adj. inherited from the earliest humans. ■ **atavism** n.

ate past of EAT.

atheism n. the belief that God does not exist. ■ **atheist** n.

atherosclerosis n. damage to the arteries caused by a build-up of fatty deposits.

athlete n. **1** a person who is good at sports. **2** a person who takes part in athletics. □ **athlete's foot** a form of ringworm affecting the feet.

athletic adj. **1** fit and good at sport. **2** of athletics. • n. (**athletics**) track and field sports. ■ **athletically** adv. **athleticism** n.

Atlantic adj. of the Atlantic Ocean.

atlas n. a book of maps or charts.

atmosphere n. **1** the gases surrounding the earth or another planet. **2** the quality of the air in a place. **3** an overall tone or mood. **4** a unit of pressure. ■ **atmospheric** adj.

atoll n. a ring-shaped coral reef or chain of islands.

atom n. **1** the smallest particle of a chemical element. **2** a very small amount. □ **atom bomb** a bomb deriving its power from the fission of atomic nuclei. ■ **atomic** adj.

atomize (or **-ise**) v. convert into very fine particles or droplets. ■ **atomizer** n.

atonal /ay-toh-n'l/ adj. not written in any musical key.

atone v. (**atone for**) make amends for. ■ **atonement** n.

atrium n. (pl. **atria** or **atriums**) **1** a central hall rising through several storeys. **2** each of the two upper cavities of the heart. **3** an open central court in an ancient Roman house.

atrocious adj. **1** horrifyingly wicked. **2** very bad. ■ **atrociously** adv.

atrocity n. (pl. **atrocities**) a very wicked or cruel act.

atrophy *v.* (**atrophying, atrophied**) (of part of the body) waste away. •*n.* the condition or process of atrophying.

attach *v.* 1 fasten or join. 2 regard as important. 3 (**attached to**) very fond of.

attaché /uh-tash-ay/ *n.* a person on an ambassador's staff. □ **attaché case** a small briefcase for documents.

attachment *n.* 1 an extra part attached to something. 2 a computer file sent with an email.

attack *v.* 1 take violent action against. 2 criticize fiercely. 3 (in sport) try to score goals or points. •*n.* 1 an act of attacking. 2 a sudden spell of an illness. ■ **attacker** *n.*

attain *v.* succeed in doing. ■ **attainable** *adj.* **attainment** *n.*

attar *n.* a scented oil made from rose petals.

attempt *v.* try. •*n.* an effort.

attend *v.* 1 be present at. 2 (**attend to**) deal with or pay attention to. 3 accompany. ■ **attendance** *n.*

attendant *n.* 1 an employee providing help in a public place. 2 an assistant. •*adj.* accompanying.

attention *n.* 1 special care, notice, or consideration. 2 a straight standing position in military drill.

attentive *adj.* 1 paying attention. 2 considerate; helpful. ■ **attentively** *adv.* **attentiveness** *n.*

attenuate *v.* make thin or weaker. ■ **attenuation** *n.*

attest *v.* 1 provide proof of. 2 declare to be true. ■ **attestation** *n.*

attic *n.* a space or room inside the roof of a building.

attire *n.* clothes. •*v.* (**be attired**) be dressed.

attitude *n.* 1 a way of thinking. 2 a posture of the body. 3 *informal* self-confident or hostile behaviour.

attorney *n.* (*pl.* **attorneys**) 1 a person who acts for another in legal matters. 2 *esp. US* a lawyer.

attract *v.* 1 cause to come somewhere or do something. 2 cause to like or admire. 3 draw closer by an unseen force. ■ **attraction** *n.*

attractive *adj.* 1 pleasing in appearance. 2 arousing interest. ■ **attractively** *adv.* **attractiveness** *n.*

attribute *v.* (**attribute to**) regard as belonging to or caused by. •*n.* a quality or feature. ■ **attributable** *adj.* **attribution** *n.*

attributive *adj. Grammar* (of an adjective) coming before the word that it describes.

attrition *n.* gradual wearing down.

attune *v.* (**be attuned**) be receptive to and able to understand.

atypical *adj.* not typical. ■ **atypically** *adv.*

aubergine /oh-ber-zheen/ *n.* a purple vegetable.

auburn *n.* a reddish-brown colour.

auction *n.* a public sale where articles are sold to the highest bidder. •*v.* sell at an auction.

auctioneer *n.* a person who conducts auctions.

audacious *adj.* daring. ■ **audaciously** *adv.* **audacity** *n.*

audible *adj.* able to be heard. ■ **audibly** *adv.*

audience *n.* 1 a group of listeners or spectators. 2 a formal meeting with an important person.

audio *n.* sound or the reproduction of sound. □ **audio tape**

a

magnetic tape on which sound can be recorded. **audio-visual** using both sight and sound.

audit n. an official inspection of an organization's accounts. •v. (**auditing, audited**) make an audit of. ■ **auditor** n.

audition n. a test of a performer's ability for a particular part. •v. test or be tested by an audition.

auditorium n. (pl. **auditoriums** or **auditoria**) the part of a theatre or hall in which the audience sits.

auditory adj. of hearing.

au fait /oh fay/ adj. (**au fait with**) having good knowledge of.

auger /aw-ger/ n. a tool for boring holes.

augment v. increase. ■ **augmentation** n.

au gratin /oh gra-tan/ adj. cooked with a topping of breadcrumbs or grated cheese.

augur /aw-ger/ v. be an omen.

augury /aw-gyoo-ri/ n. (pl. **auguries**) a sign of what will happen.

August n. the eighth month.

august /aw-gust/ adj. inspiring respect.

auk n. a black and white seabird.

aunt n. the sister of your father or mother or the wife of your uncle.

au pair n. a foreign girl employed to look after children and help with housework.

aura n. the atmosphere surrounding a place or person.

aural /aw-ruhl/ adj. of the ear. ■ **aurally** adv.

aureole n. a halo.

au revoir /aw ruh-**vwar**/ exclam. goodbye.

aurora borealis /aw-raw-ruh bo-ri-**ay**-liss/ n. bands of light seen in the sky near the North Pole; the Northern Lights.

auspices pl. n. (**under the auspices of**) with the support or protection of.

auspicious adj. suggesting that there is a good chance of success. ■ **auspiciously** adv.

austere adj. **1** severe or strict. **2** very simple or plain. ■ **austerity** n.

Australasian adj. of Australasia, a region made up of Australia, New Zealand, and islands of the SW Pacific.

Australian n. a person from Australia. •adj. of Australia.

authentic adj. known to be real; genuine. ■ **authentically** adv. **authenticity** n.

authenticate v. prove to be authentic. ■ **authentication** n.

author n. **1** a writer of a book etc. **2** the inventor of a plan or idea. ■ **authorial** adj. **authorship** n.

authoritarian adj. demanding strict obedience to authority.

authoritative adj. **1** reliably true or accurate. **2** commanding and self-confident. ■ **authoritatively** adv.

authority n. (pl. **authorities**) **1** the power to give orders and make others obey. **2** a person or group with official power. **3** official permission. **4** a trusted expert.

authorize (or **-ise**) v. give official permission for. ■ **authorization** n.

autism /aw-ti-z'm/ n. a mental condition in which a person has communication difficulties. ■ **autistic** adj. & n.

auto- *comb. form* self; own.

autobiography *n.* (*pl.* **autobiographies**) an account of a person's life written by that person. ■ **autobiographical** *adj.*

autocracy *n.* (*pl.* **autocracies**) government in which one person has total power.

autocrat *n.* a ruler with total power. ■ **autocratic** *adj.*

autocue *n. trademark* a device displaying a presenter's script on a television screen, unseen by the audience.

autodidact /aw-toh-dy-dakt/ *n.* a self-taught person.

autograph *n.* a celebrity's signature. • *v.* write an autograph on.

autoimmune *adj.* (of disease) caused by antibodies produced to counteract substances naturally present in the body.

automate *v.* convert a process or facility to operate automatically. ■ **automation** *n.*

automatic *adj.* 1 operating without human control. 2 done without conscious thought. ■ **automatically** *adv.*

automaton *n.* (*pl.* **automata** or **automatons**) a robot.

automobile *n.* US a car.

automotive *adj.* of motor vehicles.

autonomous *adj.* self-governing or independent. ■ **autonomy** *n.*

autopilot *n.* a device for keeping an aircraft on course automatically.

autopsy *n.* (*pl.* **autopsies**) a post-mortem.

autumn *n.* the season between summer and winter. ■ **autumnal** *adj.*

auxiliary *adj.* giving help and support. • *n.* (*pl.* **auxiliaries**) an auxiliary person or thing. □ **auxiliary verb** a verb used to form tenses of other verbs (e.g. be).

avail *v.* (**avail yourself of**) make use of. • *n.* use or benefit.

available *adj.* able to be used or obtained. ■ **availability** *n.*

avalanche *n.* a mass of snow and ice falling down a mountainside.

avant-garde /a-von gard/ *adj.* (in the arts) new and experimental.

avarice *n.* greed for wealth. ■ **avaricious** *adj.*

avenge *v.* take revenge for. ■ **avenger** *n.*

avenue *n.* 1 a broad road. 2 a way of achieving something.

aver *v.* (**averring**, **averred**) declare to be the case.

average *n.* 1 the result obtained by adding several amounts together and then dividing the total by the number of amounts. 2 a usual amount or level. • *adj.* 1 being an average. 2 usual or ordinary.

averse *adj.* (**averse to**) strongly disliking.

> **!** Don't confuse **averse** with **adverse**, which means 'harmful or unfavourable'.

aversion *n.* a strong dislike.

avert *v.* 1 turn your eyes away. 2 prevent an unpleasant event.

avian *adj.* of birds. □ **avian flu** = BIRD FLU.

aviary *n.* (*pl.* **aviaries**) a large enclosure for keeping birds in.

aviation *n.* the activity of operating and flying aircraft. ■ **aviator** *n.*

avid *adj.* very interested or enthusiastic. ■ **avidly** *adv.*

a

avionics n. electronics used in aviation.

avocado n. (pl. **avocados**) a pear-shaped tropical fruit.

avocet n. a wading bird with a long upturned bill.

avoid v. keep away or refrain from. ■ **avoidable** adj. **avoidance** n.

avoirdupois /av-war-dyoo-pwah/ n. a system of weights based on a pound of 16 ounces.

avow v. declare. ■ **avowal** n.

avuncular adj. kind and friendly towards a younger person.

await v. wait for.

awake v. (**waking, awoke**; past part. **awoken**) stop sleeping. •adj. not asleep.

awaken v. **1** stop sleeping. **2** stir up a feeling.

award v. give officially as a prize or reward. •n. **1** something awarded. **2** the act of awarding.

aware adj. having knowledge of something. ■ **awareness** n.

awash adj. covered or flooded with water.

away adv. **1** to or at a distance. **2** until disappearing. **3** constantly. •adj. (of a match) played at the opponents' ground.

awe n. great respect mixed with fear. •v. fill with awe.

awesome adj. inspiring awe.

awful adj. **1** very bad or unpleasant. **2** used for emphasis: an awful lot. ■ **awfully** adv.

awhile adv. for a short time.

awkward adj. **1** hard to do or deal with. **2** causing or feeling embarrassment. **3** inconvenient. **4** clumsy. ■ **awkwardly** adv.

awl n. a pointed tool for making holes.

awning n. a sheet of canvas on a frame, used for shelter.

awoke past of AWAKE.

awoken past part. of AWAKE.

AWOL /ay-wol/ adj. absent without leave.

awry /uh-ry/ adv. & adj. away from the expected course or position.

axe (US **ax**) n. a chopping tool with a heavy blade. •v. ruthlessly cancel or dismiss.

axiom n. a statement regarded as obviously true. ■ **axiomatic** adj.

axis n. (pl. **axes**) **1** an imaginary line around which an object rotates. **2** a fixed line against which points on a graph are measured.

axle n. a rod on which wheels turn.

ayatollah n. a religious leader in Iran.

aye exclam. old use or dialect yes.

azalea /uh-zay-li-uh/ n. a shrub with brightly coloured flowers.

Aztec n. a member of an American Indian people ruling Mexico before the Spanish conquest in the 16th century.

azure /az-yuur/ n. a bright blue colour.

BA abbrev. Bachelor of Arts.

baa v. (**baaing, baaed**) (of a sheep or lamb) bleat.

babble v. talk rapidly in a foolish or confused way. • n. foolish or confused talk.

babe n. **1** a baby. **2** informal an attractive young woman.

babel n. a confused mixture of voices.

baboon n. a large monkey.

baby n. (pl. **babies**) **1** a very young child or animal. **2** a timid or childish person. • adj. small or very young. ■ **babyish** adj.

babysit v. (**babysitting, babysat**) look after a child while the parents are out. ■ **babysitter** n.

baccalaureate /ba-kuh-lor-i-uht/ n. an exam taken to qualify for higher education.

baccarat /bak-kuh-rah/ n. a gambling card game.

bacchanalian /bak-kuh-nay-li-uhn/ adj. (of a party) drunken and wild.

bachelor n. **1** an unmarried man. **2** a holder of a first degree from a university.

bacillus /buh-sil-luhss/ n. (pl. **bacilli**) a rod-shaped bacterium.

back n. **1** the rear surface of a person's body, or the upper part of an animal's body. **2** the side or part furthest from the front. **3** a defending player in a team game. • adv. **1** at or towards the rear. **2** in or into a previous time, position, or state. **3** in return. • v. **1** give sup-

port to. **2** move backwards. **3** bet money on. **4** (**back on to**) (of a building) have its back facing. • adj. **1** at or towards the back. **2** of the past. □ **backbencher** a member of parliament who does not hold a government or opposition post. **back down** give in. **back out** withdraw from a commitment. **back-pedal** reverse a previous action or opinion. **back up 1** support. **2** Computing make a spare copy of data or a disk. ■ **backer** n.

backbiting n. spiteful talk about an absent person.

backbone n. the spine.

backchat n. informal cheeky replies.

backdate v. make valid from an earlier date.

backdrop (or **backcloth**) n. a painted cloth at the back of a theatre stage.

backfire v. **1** produce an undesired effect. **2** (of an engine) make a bang due to fuel igniting wrongly.

backgammon n. a board game played with counters and a dice.

background n. **1** the back part of a scene or picture. **2** the circumstances that explain or influence something.

backhand n. a stroke played with the back of the hand turned forwards.

backhanded adj. indirect or ambiguous.

backhander n. **1** a backhand stroke. **2** informal a bribe.

b

backing n. 1 support. 2 music or singing accompanying a pop singer.

backlash n. an angry reaction.

backlog n. a build-up of work.

backpack n. a rucksack. ■ **backpacker** n.

backside n. informal the buttocks.

backslide v. revert to previous bad behaviour.

backstage adv. & adj. behind the stage in a theatre.

backstroke n. a swimming stroke performed on the back.

backtrack v. 1 retrace your steps. 2 reverse your opinion.

backward adj. 1 towards the back. 2 having made less than normal progress. ▪ adv. (or **backwards**) 1 towards the back or back towards the start. 2 in reverse. ■ **backwardly** adv. **backwardness** n.

backwash n. waves flowing outwards behind a ship.

backwater n. 1 a stretch of stagnant water on a river. 2 a place unaffected by progress.

backwoods pl. n. a remote area.

bacon n. salted or smoked meat from a pig.

bacteria pl. n. (sing. **bacterium**) a group of microscopic organisms, many of which cause disease. ■ **bacterial** adj. **bacteriologist** n. **bacteriology** n.

> **!** **bacteria** should always be used with a plural verb, e.g. the bacteria were multiplying.

bad adj. (**worse**, **worst**) 1 poor in quality. 2 unpleasant. 3 severe; serious. 4 wicked. 5 harmful. 6 injured, ill, or diseased. 7 (of food) decayed. ■ **badness** n.

bade past of BID².

badge n. a small flat object worn to show membership or rank.

badger n. a large nocturnal mammal with a black-and-white striped head. ▪ v. pester.

badly adv. (**worse**, **worst**) 1 in an unacceptable way. 2 severely. 3 very much. □ **badly off** poor.

badminton n. a game with rackets in which a shuttlecock is hit across a high net.

baffle v. puzzle. ■ **bafflement** n.

bag n. 1 a flexible container with an opening at the top. 2 (**bags of**) informal plenty of. 3 informal an unpleasant woman. ▪ v. (**bagging**, **bagged**) 1 put in a bag. 2 informal manage to get.

bagatelle n. 1 a board game in which balls are hit into numbered holes. 2 something unimportant.

bagel /bay-g'l/ n. a ring-shaped bread roll with a heavy texture.

baggage n. luggage.

baggy adj. (**baggier**, **baggiest**) hanging in loose folds.

bagpipes pl. n. a musical instrument with pipes sounded by wind squeezed from a bag.

baguette /ba-get/ n. a loaf of French bread.

bail n. 1 the release of an accused person on condition that a sum of money is left with the court, which will be returned as long as the person attends their trial. 2 money paid for this reason. 3 each of two crosspieces resting on the stumps in cricket. ▪ v. 1 free an accused person on payment of bail. 2 (or **bale**) scoop water out of. □ **bail** (or **bale**) **out** 1 make an emergency parachute jump from an aircraft. 2 rescue from difficulty.

bailey n. the outer wall of a castle.

bailiff n. a person who delivers writs and seizes property for non-payment of fines or debts.

bailiwick n. an area of authority or interest.

bairn n. Sc. & N. Engl. a child.

bait n. food put on a hook or in a trap to catch fish or other animals. • v. **1** taunt or tease. **2** put bait on or in.

baize n. thick green material used to cover billiard tables.

bake v. cook or harden by dry heat.

baker n. a person whose trade is making bread and cakes. □ **baker's dozen** a group of thirteen. ■ **bakery** n.

baksheesh n. (in eastern countries) a tip or bribe.

balaclava n. a woollen hat covering the head and neck.

balalaika n. a Russian musical instrument like a guitar.

balance n. **1** an even distribution of weight. **2** a situation in which elements are in the correct proportions. **3** a device for weighing. **4** the difference between credits and debits in an account. **5** an amount still owed after paying part of a debt. • v. **1** be or put in a steady position. **2** compare.

balcony n. (pl. **balconies**) **1** an enclosed platform projecting from the outside of a building. **2** the highest level of seats in a theatre or cinema.

bald adj. **1** having no hair on the head. **2** (of a tyre) with the tread worn away. **3** without details. ■ **baldly** adv. **baldness** n.

balderdash n. nonsense.

balding adj. going bald.

bale (see also **bail**) n. a large bundle of cloth, paper, or hay. • v. make into bales.

baleful adj. menacing. ■ **balefully** adv.

balk US = BAULK.

ball n. **1** a rounded object used in games. **2** a throw or kick of the ball in a game. **3** a rounded part or thing. **4** a formal social gathering for dancing. □ **ball bearing** a ring of small metal balls reducing friction between moving parts of a machine, or one of these balls.

ballcock n. a valve controlling the water level in a cistern. **ballpoint pen** n. a pen with a tiny ball as its writing point. **ballroom** n. a large room for formal dancing.

ballad n. **1** a poem or song telling a story. **2** a slow sentimental song.

ballast n. **1** heavy material carried by a ship to keep it stable. **2** coarse stone used as the base of a railway or road.

ballerina n. a female ballet dancer.

ballet n. an artistic dance form performed to music. ■ **balletic** adj.

ballistics n. the science of missiles and firearms. □ **ballistic missile** a missile which is fired into the air and falls under gravity on to its target.

balloon n. **1** a small inflatable rubber bag used as a toy. **2** (or **hot-air balloon**) a large bag filled with hot gas to make it rise, with a basket for carrying passengers. • v. swell or increase.

ballot n. a way of voting secretly by means of paper slips placed in a box. • v. (**balloting**, **balloted**) ask for a secret vote from.

ballyhoo n. informal a fuss.

balm n. **1** a scented ointment. **2** something that soothes or heals.

balmy adj. (of the weather) pleasantly warm.

baloney n. informal nonsense.

balsa n. lightweight wood from a tropical American tree.

balsam n. a scented resin used in perfumes and medicines.

baluster n. a short pillar forming part of a series supporting a rail.

balustrade n. a railing supported by balusters.

bamboo n. a giant tropical grass with hollow stems.

bamboozle v. informal cheat or deceive.

ban v. (**banning, banned**) forbid officially. •n. an official order forbidding something.

banal /buh-**nahl**/ adj. predictable and unoriginal. ▪ **banality** n.

banana n. a curved yellow fruit.

band n. 1 a piece of material used for fastening, strengthening, etc. 2 a stripe or strip. 3 a range of values or frequencies within a series. 4 a group of musicians. 5 a group of people with a shared aim or feature. •v. form a group.
□ **bandstand** a covered circular platform for a band playing music. **bandwagon** an activity or cause that has suddenly become popular. ▪ **banded** adj.

bandage n. a strip of material for tying round a wound. •v. tie a bandage round.

bandanna (or **bandana**) n. a square of cloth tied round the head or neck.

B. & B. abbrev. bed and breakfast.

bandit n. a member of a gang of armed robbers.

bandy adj. (of a person's legs) curved outwards at the knees. •v. (**bandying, bandied**) mention

frequently or casually. □ **bandy words** exchange angry remarks.

bane n. a cause of great distress or annoyance.

bang n. 1 a sudden loud, sharp noise. 2 a sharp blow. •v. 1 hit or put down noisily. 2 make a bang. • adv. informal exactly: bang on time.

banger n. informal 1 a sausage. 2 an old car. 3 a loud explosive firework.

bangle n. a bracelet made of rigid material.

banish v. 1 send into exile. 2 get rid of; drive away. ▪ **banishment** n.

banisters (or **bannisters**) pl. n. the upright posts and handrail at the side of a staircase.

banjo n. (pl. **banjos**) a guitar-like musical instrument with a circular body.

bank n. 1 an organization that keeps customers' money and provides other financial services. 2 the land alongside a river. 3 a stock or supply. 4 a long, high slope or mass. 5 a row of similar objects. v. 1 put money in a bank. 2 (**bank on**) rely on. 3 form into a mound or mass. 4 (of an aircraft) tilt sideways when turning.
□ **bank holiday** a public holiday. **banknote** a piece of paper money. ▪ **banker** n.

bankrupt adj. officially declared not to have enough money to pay debts. •n. a bankrupt person. •v. make bankrupt. ▪ **bankruptcy** n.

banner n. a strip of cloth with a slogan or design, hung up or carried on poles.

banns pl. n. an announcement in church of a forthcoming marriage.

banquet n. an elaborate formal meal for many people.

banquette /bang-ket/ n. a padded bench along a wall.

banshee n. (in Irish legend) a female spirit whose wailing warns of a death.

bantam n. a small chicken. □ **bantamweight** a weight in boxing between flyweight and featherweight.

banter n. friendly teasing. • v. tease in a friendly way.

Bantu n. (pl. **Bantu** or **Bantus**) a member of a large group of indigenous African peoples.

! Bantu is a very offensive word in South African English, esp. when used to refer to individual people.

bap n. a soft bread roll.

baptism n. a Christian ceremony in which a person is sprinkled with or dipped in water as a sign of purification and entry to the Church. ■ **baptismal** adj.

Baptist n. a member of a Protestant group believing that only adults should be baptized.

baptize (or **-ise**) v. **1** perform baptism on. **2** give a name or nickname to.

bar n. **1** a long rigid bar of wood, metal, etc. **2** a counter, room, etc. where alcohol is served. **3** a barrier. **4** one of the short units into which a piece of music is divided. **5** (**the Bar**) barristers or their profession. **6** a unit of atmospheric pressure. • v. (**barring**, **barred**) **1** fasten with a bar or bars. **2** forbid or prevent. • prep. except for. □ **bar code** a row of printed stripes identifying a product and its price, readable by a computer. **barman** (or **barmaid**) a person serving drinks in a pub or bar.

barb n. **1** a backward-pointing part of fish hook etc. **2** a spiteful remark.

barbarian n. an uncivilized or cruel person.

barbaric adj. **1** savagely cruel. **2** not civilized. ■ **barbarity** n.

barbarous adj. barbaric. ■ **barbarism** n.

barbecue n. **1** an outdoor meal at which food is grilled over an open fire. **2** a structure or device for grilling food outdoors. • v. cook on a barbecue.

barbed adj. **1** having a barb or barbs. **2** spiteful. □ **barbed wire** wire with clusters of sharp points along it.

barber n. a men's hairdresser.

barbiturate n. a sedative drug.

bard n. literary a poet.

bare adj. **1** not clothed. **2** lacking the usual covering or contents. **3** only just enough. • v. uncover or reveal. ■ **bareback** on horseback without a saddle. **barefaced** done openly and without shame. ■ **barely** adv.

bargain n. **1** a thing bought at a low price. **2** an agreement where each party does something for the other. • v. **1** discuss the terms of an agreement. **2** (**bargain for/on**) expect.

barge n. a long flat-bottomed boat used on canals and rivers. • v. **1** move forcefully. **2** (**barge in**) burst in on rudely.

baritone n. a man's singing voice between tenor and bass.

barium n. a white metallic element.

bark n. **1** the sharp cry of a dog. **2** the outer layer of a tree. • v. **1** give a bark. **2** say suddenly or fiercely.

3 scrape the skin off your shin accidentally.

barley n. a type of cereal plant with bristly heads. □ **barley sugar** a sweet made of boiled sugar.

bar mitzvah n. a religious ceremony in which a Jewish boy aged 13 takes on the responsibilities of an adult.

barmy adj. (**barmier, barmiest**) informal mad.

barn n. a large farm building used for storing grain etc.

barnacle n. a shellfish which fixes itself to objects under water.

barney n. (pl. **barneys**) informal a noisy quarrel.

barometer n. an instrument that measures atmospheric pressure, used in weather forecasting. ■ **barometric** adj.

baron n. **1** a man belonging to the lowest rank of the nobility. **2** a powerful businessman. ■ **baronial** adj.

baroness n. **1** a baron's wife or widow. **2** a woman with the rank of baron.

baronet n. a man who holds a title below that of baron. ■ **baronetcy** n.

baroque n. an ornate style of architecture, art, and music of the 17th and 18th centuries. • adj. ornate in style.

barque /bark/ n. a sailing ship.

barrack v. shout insults at a performer or speaker. • pl. n. (**barracks**) buildings for housing soldiers.

barracuda n. a large, predatory tropical sea fish.

barrage n. **1** a continuous artillery attack. **2** a large number of questions or complaints. **3** an artificial barrier across a river.

barre n. a horizontal bar used for support in ballet exercises.

barrel n. **1** a cylindrical container with flat ends. **2** a tube forming part of a gun, pen, etc. □ **barrel organ** a small organ playing a set tune when a handle is turned.

barren adj. **1** (of land) not fertile. **2** unable to bear young. **3** empty or lifeless. ■ **barrenness** n.

barricade n. a makeshift barrier. • v. block or defend with a barricade.

barrier n. an obstacle that prevents movement, access, or progress.

barring prep. except for; if not for.

barrister n. a lawyer qualified to argue a case in court.

barrow n. **1** a two-wheeled handcart used by street traders. **2** an ancient burial mound.

barter v. exchange goods or services for other goods or services. • n. trading by bartering.

basal /bay-s'l/ adj. forming or belonging to a base.

basalt /ba-sawlt/ n. a dark volcanic rock.

base n. **1** the lowest or supporting part of something. **2** the main place where a person works or stays. **3** a centre of operations. **4** a main element to which others are added. **5** a substance able to react with an acid to form a salt and water. **6** the number on which a system of counting is based. **7** Baseball each of the four points that must be reached in turn to score a run. • v. **1** (**base on**) use something as the foundation for. **2** put at a centre of operations. • adj. bad or immoral. □ **baseball**

a team game played with a bat and ball on a circuit of four bases, which a batter must run around to score.

baseless adj. not based on fact; untrue.

basement n. a room or floor below ground level.

bash informal v. hit hard. •n. **1** a heavy blow. **2** a party.

bashful adj. shy. ■ **bashfully** adv. **bashfulness** n.

BASIC n. a high-level computer programming language.

basic adj. **1** forming an essential foundation; fundamental. **2** consisting of the minimum needed or offered. •n. (**basics**) essential facts or principles. ■ **basically** adv.

basil n. a herb used in cookery.

basilica n. a large church with two rows of columns and a curved end.

basilisk n. a mythical reptile whose gaze or breath was deadly.

basin n. **1** a round open container for food or liquid. **2** a circular valley. **3** an area drained by a river. **4** an enclosed area of water for mooring boats.

basis n. (pl. **bases**) **1** the foundation of a theory or process. **2** a way in which things are done: *they met on a regular basis.*

bask v. lie in the sun for pleasure.

basket n. a container for carrying things, made from strips of cane or wire. □ **basketball** a team game in which goals are scored by throwing a ball through a hoop.

Basque n. **1** a member of a people living in the western Pyrenees in France and Spain. **2** the language of the Basques.

bas-relief n. a carving with figures standing out slightly from the background.

bass¹ /bayss/ n. **1** the lowest male singing voice. **2** the deep, low-frequency output of a radio or audio system. •adj. of the lowest pitch in music.

bass² /bass/ n. (pl. **bass** or **basses**) an edible fish related to the perch.

bassoon n. a large bass woodwind instrument.

bastard n. **1** old use or derog. an illegitimate child. **2** informal an unpleasant person.

bastardize (or **-ise**) v. make less good by adding new elements.

baste v. **1** pour fat or juices over meat during cooking. **2** sew together temporarily with loose stitches.

bastion n. **1** a stronghold of a principle or activity. **2** a projecting part of a fortification.

bat n. **1** an implement for hitting the ball in sports. **2** a flying mammal active at night. •v. (**batting**, **batted**) **1** (in sport) take the role of hitting the ball. **2** hit with the flat of the hand. □ **batsman** a player who bats in cricket.

batch n. a quantity of goods produced or dispatched at one time.

bated adj. (**with bated breath**) in great suspense.

> ! The spelling is *bated*, not *baited*.

bath n. **1** a large tub filled with water for washing the body. **2** an act of washing in a bath. **3** (also **baths**) a public swimming pool. •v. wash in a bath. □ **bathroom** a room with a bath, washbasin, toilet, etc.

bathe v. **1** soak or wipe gently with liquid. **2** take a swim. •n. a swim. ■ **bather** n.

b

b

bathos /bay-thoss/ n. (in literature) a change from a serious mood to something trivial or ridiculous.

batik /ba-teek/ n. a method of producing designs on cloth by waxing the parts not to be dyed.

batman n. dated (in the armed forces) an officer's personal attendant.

baton n. 1 a thin stick used to conduct an orchestra or choir. 2 a short stick passed from runner to runner in a relay race.

battalion n. an army unit forming part of a brigade.

batten n. a long wooden or metal strip for strengthening or securing something. • v. hit hard and repeatedly. □ **battering ram** a heavy object swung or rammed against a door to break it down.

batter n. 1 a mixture of flour, eggs, and milk or water, used in cooking. 2 a player who bats in baseball.

battery n. (pl. **batteries**) 1 a device containing an electrical cell or cells, used as a source of power. 2 a set of small cages for the intensive rearing of poultry. 3 Law the crime of physically attacking another person. 4 a group of heavy guns.

battle n. 1 a fight between organized armed forces. 2 a long and difficult struggle. • v. fight or struggle with determination. □ **battleaxe** 1 a large axe used in ancient warfare. 2 informal an aggressive woman. **battlefield** the scene of a battle. **battlement** a parapet with gaps for firing through. **battleship** a large, heavily armoured warship.

batty adj. (**battier**, **battiest**) informal mad.

bauble n. a small, showy trinket or decoration.

baulk (US **balk**) v. 1 (**baulk at**) hesitate to accept. 2 thwart or hinder.

bauxite n. a clay-like rock from which aluminium is obtained.

bawdy adj. (**bawdier**, **bawdiest**) referring to sex in an amusing way. ■ **bawdiness** n.

bawl v. 1 shout. 2 weep noisily.

bay n. 1 a broad curved inlet of the sea. 2 a shrub whose leaves are used in cookery. 3 a window area that projects outwards from a wall. 4 an area with a particular purpose: a loading bay. • v. (of a dog) howl loudly. • adj. (of a horse) reddish-brown. □ **bay window** a window projecting out from a wall.

bayonet n. a long blade fixed to a rifle. • v. (**bayoneting**, **bayoneted**) stab with a bayonet.

bazaar n. 1 a market in a Middle Eastern country. 2 a sale of goods to raise funds.

bazooka n. a short-range rocket launcher used against tanks.

BBC abbrev. British Broadcasting Corporation.

BC abbrev. before Christ (used to indicate that a date is before the Christian era).

be v. (sing. present **am**; **are**; **is**; pl. present **are**; 1st & 3rd sing. past **was**; 2nd sing. past & pl. past **were**; pres. part. **being**; past part. **been**) 1 exist; be present. 2 happen. 3 have a specified state, nature, or role. • aux. v. used to form tenses of other verbs.

beach n. an area of sand or pebbles at the edge of the sea. • v. bring on

to a beach from the water.
□ **beachcomber** a person who searches beaches for things of value. **beachhead** a fortified position on a beach taken by landing forces.

beacon n. **1** a fire lit on a hill as a signal. **2** a light acting as a signal for ships or aircraft.

bead n. **1** a small piece of glass, stone, etc., threaded in a string with others. **2** a small drop of liquid. ■ **beaded** adj.

beadle n. hist. a parish officer who dealt with minor offenders.

beady adj. (of eyes) small, round, and observant.

beagle n. a small breed of hound.

beak n. **1** a bird's horny projecting jaws. **2** informal a magistrate.

beaker n. **1** a tall plastic cup. **2** a glass container used in laboratories.

beam n. **1** a long piece of timber or metal used as a support in building. **2** a ray of light or particles. **3** a radiant smile. **4** the width of a ship. • v. **1** transmit a radio signal. **2** shine brightly. **3** smile radiantly.

bean n. **1** an edible seed growing in long pods on certain plants. **2** the seed of a coffee or cocoa plant.

bear[1] v. (**bearing**, **bore**; past part. **borne**) **1** carry. **2** support a weight. **3** (**bear yourself**) behave in a particular way. **4** tolerate. **5** give birth to a child. **6** produce fruit or flowers. **7** take a specified direction. □ **bear down on** approach in a purposeful way. **bear out** support or confirm. **bear up** remain cheerful in adversity. **bear with** be patient with. ■ **bearable** adj. **bearer** n.

bear[2] n. a large mammal with thick fur. □ **bearskin** a tall furry cap worn by certain troops.

beard n. a growth of hair on a man's chin. • v. boldly confront an important person. ■ **bearded** adj.

bearing n. **1** a way of standing, moving, or behaving. **2** relevance. **3** a device allowing two parts to rotate or move in contact with each other. **4** direction or position in relation to a fixed point. **5** (**your bearings**) awareness of where you are.

beast n. **1** a large animal. **2** a very cruel or wicked person.

beastly adj. informal very unpleasant. ■ **beastliness** n.

beat v. (**beating**, **beat**; past part. **beaten**) **1** hit repeatedly. **2** defeat or outdo. **3** move or throb rhythmically. **4** stir cooking ingredients vigorously. • n. **1** an act of beating. **2** a main accent in music or poetry. **3** an area patrolled by a police officer. □ **beat up** attack violently.

beatific /bee-uh-**tif**-ik/ adj. very happy. ■ **beatifically** adv.

beatify /bi-at-i-fy/ v. (**beatifying**, **beatified**) (in the RC Church) declare a dead person to be in a state of bliss, the first step towards canonization.

beatitude /bi-at-i-tyood/ n. blessedness.

beautician n. a person whose job is to give beauty treatments.

beautiful adj. **1** very pleasing to the senses. **2** excellent. ■ **beautifully** adv.

beautify v. (**beautifying**, **beautified**) make beautiful.

beauty n. (pl. **beauties**) **1** the quality of being very pleasing to the senses. **2** a beautiful woman. **3** an excellent example.

b

b

beaver n. a large rodent that lives partly in water. •v. (**beaver away**) informal work hard.

becalmed adj. (of a sailing ship) unable to move through lack of wind.

because conj. for the reason that.

beck n. (**at someone's beck and call**) doing whatever someone asks.

beckon v. make a summoning gesture.

become v. (**becoming**, **became**; past part. **become**) **1** begin to be. **2** turn into. **3** (**become of**) happen to. **4** suit or be appropriate to.

becquerel n. a unit of radioactivity.

bed n. **1** a piece of furniture for sleeping on. **2** an area of ground where flowers are grown. **3** a flat base or foundation. •v. (**bedding**, **bedded**) (**bed down**) sleep in an improvised place. □ **bedclothes** sheets, blankets, etc. **bedpan** a container used as a toilet by a bedridden person. **bedridden** confined to bed due to illness or old age. **bedrock 1** a layer of solid rock under soil. **2** the central principles on which something is based. **bedroom** a room for sleeping in. **bedsit** (or **bedsitter**) a rented room combining a bedroom and living room. **bedsore** a sore caused by lying in bed in one position for a long time. **bedspread** a decorative bed covering. **bedstead** the framework of a bed.

bedding n. bedclothes.

bedevil v. (**bedevilling**, **bedevilled**; US **bedeviling**, **bedeviled**) cause continual trouble to.

bedlam n. a noisy, confused scene.

Bedouin /bed-oo-in/ n. (pl. **Bedouin**) an Arab living as a nomad in the desert.

bedraggled adj. untidy.

bee n. a winged insect which makes wax and honey. □ **beehive** a structure in which bees are kept. **beeswax** wax produced by bees to make honeycombs, used in polishes etc. **make a beeline for** hurry straight to.

beech n. a large tree with grey bark.

beef n. meat from a cow, bull, or ox. •v. (**beef up**) informal make stronger or larger. □ **beefburger** a fried or grilled cake of minced beef. **beefeater** a warder in the Tower of London.

beefy adj. informal muscular or strong.

been past part. of BE.

beep n. a short, high-pitched sound made by electronic equipment or a car's horn. •v. make a beep. ■ **beeper** n.

beer n. an alcoholic drink made from malt and hops.

beet n. a plant with a fleshy root, grown as food and for making into sugar.

beetle n. an insect with hard, shiny covers over its wings.

beetroot n. the edible dark red root of a kind of beet.

befall v. (**befalling**, **befell**; past part. **befallen**) happen to.

befit v. (**befitting**, **befitted**) be appropriate for.

before prep., conj., & adv. **1** during the time preceding. **2** in front of. **3** rather than.

beforehand adv. in advance.

befriend v. become a friend to.

befuddled adj. muddled or confused.

beg v. (**begging, begged**) 1 ask humbly for something. 2 ask for food or money as charity.

beget v. (**begetting, begot**; past part. **begotten**) literary 1 cause. 2 father a child.

beggar n. a person who lives by begging for food or money. ■ **beggarly** adj.

begin v. (**beginning, began**; past part. **begun**) 1 carry out or experience the first part of an action or activity. 2 come into being. 3 have as its starting point. ■ **beginner** n. **beginning** n.

begonia n. a plant with brightly coloured flowers.

begrudge v. 1 feel envious that someone possesses something. 2 give reluctantly.

beguile v. charm or trick.

behalf n. (**on behalf of**) 1 in the interests of. 2 as a representative of.

behave v. 1 act in a certain way. 2 (also **behave yourself**) act in a polite or acceptable way.

behaviour (US **behavior**) n. a way of behaving. ■ **behavioural** adj.

behead v. execute someone by cutting off their head.

behemoth /bi-hee-moth/ n. something very large, esp. an organization.

behest n. (**at the behest of**) at the request or order of.

behind prep. & adv. 1 at or to the back of. 2 less advanced than others. 3 in support of. 4 responsible for an event or plan. 5 late in doing something. •n. informal the buttocks.

behold v. (**beholding, beheld**) old use see or observe.

beholden adj. owing something in return for a favour.

behove v. (**it behoves someone to do**) it is right or necessary for someone to do.

beige n. a pale fawn colour.

being n. 1 existence. 2 the nature of a person. 3 a living creature.

belabour (US **belabor**) v. attack.

belated adj. coming late or too late. ■ **belatedly** adv.

belay v. secure a rope by winding it round something.

belch v. 1 noisily expel wind from the stomach through the mouth. 2 give out smoke or flames with great force. •n. an act of belching.

beleaguered adj. 1 in difficulties. 2 under siege.

belfry n. (pl. **belfries**) the place in a bell tower in which bells are housed.

belie v. (**belying, belied**) 1 fail to give a true idea of. 2 show to be untrue.

belief n. 1 a feeling that something exists or is true. 2 a firmly held opinion. 3 trust or confidence. 4 religious faith.

believe v. 1 accept that something is true or someone is telling the truth. 2 (**believe in**) have faith in the truth or existence of. 3 think or suppose. 4 have religious faith. ■ **believer** n.

belittle v. dismiss as unimportant.

bell n. 1 a metal cup that sounds a clear musical note when struck. 2 a device that buzzes or rings to give a signal.

belladonna n. a drug made from deadly nightshade.

belle n. a beautiful woman.

bellicose adj. eager to fight.

belligerent adj. **1** aggressive. **2** engaged in a war.
■ **belligerence** n. **belligerently** adv.

bellow v. **1** give a deep roar of pain or anger. **2** shout very loudly. •n. a deep shout or noise.

bellows pl. n. a device used for blowing air into a fire.

belly n. (pl. **bellies**) **1** the abdomen. **2** a person's stomach.
■ **bellyful** n.

belong v. **1** (**belong to**) be the property of. **2** (**belong to**) be a member of. **3** be in the right place or category. **4** feel at ease in a particular situation.

belongings pl. n. personal possessions.

beloved adj. dearly loved.

below prep. & adv. at a lower level than.

belt n. **1** a strip of material worn round the waist. **2** a continuous band in machinery that connects two wheels. **3** a strip or encircling area. •v. **1** fasten with a belt. **2** informal hit very hard. **3** (**belt up**) informal be quiet. □ **below the belt** unfair.

belying pres. part. of **BELIE**.

bemoan v. complain about.

bemused adj. confused; bewildered. ■ **bemusement** n.

bench n. **1** a long seat for more than one person. **2** a long work table. **3** (**the bench**) the office of judge or magistrate. □ **benchmark** a standard against which things may be compared.

bend v. (**bending, bent**) **1** make or become curved. **2** lean or curve the body downwards. **3** change a rule to suit yourself. •n. a curve or turn. ■ **bendy** adj.

beneath prep. & adv. **1** extending or directly underneath. **2** of lower status or worth than.

benediction n. the speaking of a blessing.

benefactor n. a person who gives money or other help.
■ **benefaction** n.

benefice n. an arrangement by which a Christian priest is paid and given accommodation in return for their duties.

beneficent adj. doing or resulting in good. ■ **beneficence** n.

beneficial adj. favourable or advantageous. ■ **beneficially** adv.

beneficiary n. (pl. **beneficiaries**) a person who benefits from something.

benefit n. **1** advantage or profit. **2** a payment made by the state to someone in need. •v. (**benefiting, benefited** or **benefitting, benefitted**) **1** receive an advantage; profit. **2** bring advantage to.

benevolent adj. well meaning and kindly. ■ **benevolence** n.

benighted adj. lacking understanding of cultural, intellectual, or moral matters.

benign adj. **1** kindly. **2** (of a tumour) not malignant.

bent past & past part. of **BEND**. •adj. **1** informal dishonest; corrupt. **2** (**bent on**) determined to do. •n. a natural talent.

benzene n. a liquid hydrocarbon found in coal tar and petroleum.

bequeath v. leave property to someone by a will.

bequest n. a legacy.

berate v. scold angrily.

bereaved v. (**be bereaved**) be deprived of a relation or friend through their death. ■ **bereavement** n.

bereft adj. **1** (**bereft of**) without. **2** lonely and abandoned.

beret /be-ray/ n. a flat round cap with no peak.

bergamot /ber-guh-mot/ n. an oily substance found in some oranges, used as a flavouring.

beriberi n. a disease caused by a lack of vitamin B1.

berk n. informal a stupid person.

berry n. (pl. **berries**) a small round juicy fruit without a stone.

berserk adj. out of control with anger etc.

berth n. **1** a place for a ship to moor. **2** a bunk on a ship or train. • v. moor in a berth.

beryl n. a transparent pale green, blue, or yellow gem.

beryllium n. a lightweight grey metallic element.

beseech v. (**beseeching**, **besought** or **beseeched**) ask in a pleading way.

beset v. (**besetting**, **beset**) trouble or worry continuously.

beside prep. **1** at the side of. **2** compared with. **3** (or **besides**) as well as. • adv. (**besides**) as well. □ **beside yourself** frantic with worry.

besiege v. **1** surround with armed forces. **2** overwhelm with requests etc.

besmirch v. damage someone's reputation.

besom /bee-zuhm/ n. a broom made of twigs tied round a stick.

besotted adj. infatuated.

besought past & past part. of BESEECH.

bespeak v. (**bespeaking**, **bespoke**; past part. **bespoken**) be evidence of.

bespoke adj. made to a customer's requirements.

best adj. **1** of the highest quality. **2** most suitable or sensible. • adv. **1** to the highest degree or standard. **2** most suitably or sensibly. • n. (**the best**) that which is of the highest quality. □ **best man** a man chosen by a bridegroom to assist him at his wedding.

bestial adj. savagely cruel. ■ **bestiality** n.

bestir v. (**bestirring**, **bestirred**) (**bestir yourself**) rouse yourself to action.

bestow v. award an honour, gift, etc.

bestride v. (**bestriding**, **bestrode**; past part. **bestridden**) stand astride over.

bet v. (**betting**, **bet** or **betted**) **1** risk money against someone else's on the outcome of an unpredictable event. **2** informal feel sure. • n. an act of betting or the money betted.

beta blocker /bee-tuh/ n. a drug used to treat high blood pressure and angina.

betake v. (**betaking**, **betook**; past part. **betaken**) (**betake yourself to**) go to.

bête noire /bet nwar/ n. (pl. **bêtes noires**) a person or thing that you particularly dislike.

betide v. literary happen or happen to.

betimes adv. literary early.

betoken v. be a sign of.

betray v. **1** act treacherously towards your country by helping an enemy. **2** be disloyal to. **3** reveal unintentionally. ■ **betrayal** n. **betrayer** n.

betrothed adj. engaged to be married. ■ **betrothal** n.

b

better adj. **1** more satisfactory or suitable. **2** recovered from illness or injury. •adv. **1** in a better way. **2** to a greater degree. •n. (**your betters**) people who are more important than you. •v. **1** improve on. **2** (**better yourself**) improve your social status. □ **better off** in a more favourable position. **get the better of** defeat.

between prep. & adv. **1** at, across, or in the space or period separating two things. **2** indicating a connection or relationship. **3** shared by; together with.

betwixt prep. & adv. old use between.

bevel n. an edge cut at an angle. •v. (**bevelling, bevelled;** US **beveling, beveled**) cut a bevel on.

beverage n. a drink.

bevy n. (pl. **bevies**) a large group.

bewail v. express great regret or sorrow over.

beware v. be aware of danger.

bewilder v. puzzle or confuse. ■ **bewilderment** n.

bewitch v. **1** cast a spell over. **2** attract and delight.

beyond prep. & adv. **1** at or to the further side of. **2** outside the range or limits of. **3** happening or continuing after.

bezel n. a groove holding the glass cover of a watch in place.

bhaji /bah-ji/ n. an Indian dish of vegetables fried in batter.

bi- comb. form **1** two. **2** twice.

biannual adj. occurring twice a year.

bias n. **1** a feeling for or against someone or something that is not based on fair judgement. **2** a direction diagonal to the grain of a fabric.

biased adj. having a bias; prejudiced.

bib n. **1** a piece of material fastened under a child's chin to protect its clothes. **2** the upper front part of an apron or pair of dungarees.

Bible n. **1** the Christian or Jewish scriptures. **2** (**bible**) informal an authoritative book. ■ **biblical** adj.

bibliography n. (pl. **bibliographies**) **1** a list of the books referred to in a written work. **2** a list of books on a particular subject. ■ **bibliographer** n. **bibliographic** adj.

bibliophile n. a person who collects books.

bicarbonate of soda n. a soluble powder used in baking.

bicentenary n. (pl. **bicentenaries**) a 200th anniversary. ■ **bicentennial** n. & adj.

biceps n. (pl. **biceps**) a large muscle in the upper arm.

bicker v. argue about trivial things.

bicycle n. a two-wheeled vehicle propelled by pedals. •v. ride a bicycle.

bid[1] v. (**bidding, bid**) **1** offer a price for. **2** try to get or do. •n. an act of bidding. ■ **bidder** n. **bidding** n.

bid[2] v. (**bidding, bid** or **bade;** past part. **bid**) **1** say hello or goodbye to. **2** old use command.

biddable adj. obedient.

bide v. (**bide your time**) wait patiently for an opportunity.

bidet /bee-day/ n. a low basin for washing the genitals.

biennial adj. **1** taking place every other year. **2** (of a plant) living for two years.

bier /beer/ n. a platform on which a coffin is placed before burial.

bifocal adj. (of a lens) made in two sections, one for distant and one for close vision. • n. (**bifocals**) glasses with bifocal lenses.

big adj. (**bigger**, **biggest**) 1 large in size, amount, or extent. 2 very important or serious. 3 (of a sibling) older.

bigamy n. the crime of marrying someone who already married to another person. ■ **bigamist** n. **bigamous** adj.

bigot n. a prejudiced and intolerant person. ■ **bigoted** adj. **bigotry** n.

bijou /bee-zhoo/ adj. (of a place) small and elegant.

bike n. a bicycle or motorcycle. • v. ride a bike. ■ **biker** n.

bikini n. (pl. **bikinis**) a woman's two-piece swimsuit.

bilateral adj. 1 involving two parties. 2 having two sides. ■ **bilaterally** adv.

bilberry n. a small blue edible berry.

bile n. 1 a fluid produced by the liver. 2 anger.

bilge n. 1 the bottom of a ship's hull. 2 informal nonsense.

bilingual adj. speaking or expressed in two languages.

bilious adj. feeling sick.

bill n. 1 a written statement of charges for goods or services. 2 a draft of a proposed law. 3 a programme of entertainment at a theatre or cinema. 4 an advertising poster. 5 US a banknote. 6 a bird's beak. • v. 1 list in a programme. 2 send a statement of charges to. □ **billboard** a hoarding for advertising posters.

billhook a pruning tool with a curved blade.

billabong n. Austral. a branch of a river forming a stagnant pool.

billet n. a private house where soldiers live temporarily. • v. (**be billeted**) (of a soldier) stay in a private house.

billet-doux /bil-li-doo/ n. (pl. **billets-doux**) a love letter.

billiards n. a game played on a table with pockets at the sides and corners, into which balls are struck with a cue.

billion n. 1 a thousand million. 2 (**billions**) informal very many. ■ **billionth** adj.

billionaire n. a person owning money and property worth at least a billion pounds or dollars.

billow v. 1 (of smoke, cloud, etc.) roll outward. 2 fill with air and swell out. • n. a large rolling mass of cloud, smoke, etc.

bimbo n. (pl. **bimbos**) informal an attractive but unintelligent woman.

bin n. 1 a container for rubbish. 2 a large storage container. • v. (**binning**, **binned**) throw away.

binary adj. 1 composed of or involving two things. 2 of a system of numbers with two as its base, using the digits 0 and 1.

bind v. (**binding**, **bound**) 1 firmly tie, wrap, or fasten. 2 hold together in a united group or mass. 3 place under a legal obligation. 4 (**bind over**) (of a court of law) require someone to do something. 5 enclose the pages of a book in a cover. 6 trim the edge of material with a fabric strip. • n. informal a difficult situation.

binding n. 1 a covering holding the pages of a book together.

b

2 fabric in a strip, used for trimming material. •*adj.* (of an agreement) involving a legal obligation.

binge *n. informal* a bout of uncontrolled eating or drinking. •*v.* eat or drink uncontrollably.

bingo *n.* a game in which players mark off on a card numbers called at random.

binocular *adj.* using both eyes. •*n.* (**binoculars**) an instrument with a separate lens for each eye, for viewing distant objects.

binomial *n.* an algebraic expression consisting of two terms linked by a plus or minus sign.

biochemistry *n.* the study of the chemical processes that occur within living things. ∎ **biochemical** *adj.* **biochemist** *n.*

biodegradable *adj.* able to be decomposed by bacteria or other living organisms.

biodiversity *n.* the variety of living things in an environment.

biography *n.* (*pl.* **biographies**) an account of a person's life written by someone else. ∎ **biographer** *n.* **biographical** *adj.*

biology *n.* the scientific study of living organisms. ∎ **biological** *adj.* **biologist** *n.*

bionic *adj.* (of an artificial body part) electronically powered.

biopsy *n.* (*pl.* **biopsies**) an examination of tissue taken from the body.

biorhythm *n.* a recurring cycle in the functioning of an organism.

biotechnology *n.* the use of microorganisms in industry and medicine.

bipartisan *adj.* involving two political parties.

bipartite *adj.* involving two separate groups.

biped /by-ped/ *n.* an animal that walks on two feet.

biplane *n.* an aircraft with two pairs of wings, one above the other.

birch *n.* a slender tree with thin, peeling bark.

bird *n.* **1** an egg-laying animal with feathers and wings, usu. able to fly. **2** *informal* a young woman or girlfriend.

bird flu *n.* a severe type of influenza that affects birds and can also be fatal to humans.

birdie *n.* (*pl.* **birdies**) *Golf* a score of one stroke under par at a hole.

biro *n.* (*pl.* **biros**) *trademark* a ballpoint pen.

birth *n.* **1** the emergence of a baby or other young from its mother's body. **2** the beginning of something. **3** a person's ancestry. ◻ **birth control** the use of contraceptives. **birthday** the anniversary of the day on which a person was born. **birthmark** an unusual mark on the body which is there from birth. **birthright** a right or privilege possessed from birth.

biscuit *n.* a small, flat, crisp cake.

bisect *v.* divide into two parts.

bisexual *adj.* sexually attracted to both men and women. •*n.* a bisexual person. ∎ **bisexuality** *n.*

bishop *n.* **1** a senior member of the Christian clergy. **2** a chess piece that can move diagonally.

bishopric *n.* the position or diocese of a bishop.

bismuth *n.* a reddish-grey metallic element.

bison *n.* (*pl.* **bison**) a shaggy-haired wild ox.

bistro n. (pl. **bistros**) a small, inexpensive restaurant.

bit n. **1** a small piece or quantity. **2** a short time or distance. **3** the mouthpiece of a horse's bridle. **4** a tool for boring or drilling. **5** Computing the smallest unit of information, expressed as either 0 or 1. □ **a bit** rather; slightly.

bitch n. **1** a female dog. **2** informal a spiteful or unpleasant woman. •v. informal make spiteful comments. ■ **bitchiness** n. **bitchy** adj.

bite v. (**biting, bit**; past part. **bitten**) **1** cut into with the teeth. **2** (of a tool, tyre, etc.) grip a surface. **3** take effect, with unpleasant consequences. •n. **1** an act of biting or a piece bitten off. **2** informal a quick snack.

biting adj. **1** (of wind) very cold. **2** sharply critical.

bitter adj. **1** having a sharp taste; not sweet. **2** resentful. **3** (of a conflict) intense and full of hatred. **4** intensely cold. •n. bitter-tasting beer. ■ **bitterly** adv. **bitterness** n.

bittern n. a marshland bird with a booming call.

bitumen n. a black sticky substance obtained from petroleum. ■ **bituminous** adj.

bivalve n. a mollusc with a shell divided into two parts, e.g. a mussel.

bivouac n. a temporary camp without tents. •v. (**bivouacking, bivouacked**) stay in a bivouac.

bizarre adj. very strange or unusual.

blab v. (**blabbing, blabbed**) informal reveal a secret.

black adj. **1** of the very darkest colour. **2** relating to people with dark-coloured skin. **3** (of coffee or tea) without milk. **4** marked by disaster or despair. **5** (of humour) presenting distressing situations in comic terms. **6** hostile. •n. **1** black colour. **2** a black person. •v. **1** make black. **2** (**black out**) faint. □ **black eye** an area of bruising round the eye. **black economy** unofficial and untaxed business activity. **black hole** a region in space with a gravitational field so strong that no matter or radiation can escape. **black magic** magic involving the summoning of evil spirits. **black market** illegal trading in officially controlled goods. **black pudding** a sausage containing dried pig's blood. **black sheep** a person seen as a disgrace to their family. ■ **blackness** n.

blackball v. prevent from joining a club.

blackberry n. the dark edible fruit of a prickly shrub.

blackbird n. a bird with black feathers and a yellow beak.

blackboard n. a dark board for writing on with chalk.

blackcurrant n. a small round edible black berry.

blacken v. **1** become or make black. **2** damage someone's reputation.

blackguard /blag-gerd/ n. dated a dishonest or unprincipled man.

blackhead n. a lump of oily matter blocking a pore in the skin.

blackleg n. derog. a person who continues working when fellow workers are on strike.

blacklist n. a list of people seen as unacceptable or untrustworthy.

blackmail n. the demanding of money from someone in return for not revealing information that could disgrace them. •v. blackmail on. ■ **blackmailer** n.

b

blackout n. **1** a sudden failure of electric lights. **2** a short loss of consciousness. **3** an official restriction on the publishing of news. **4** a period when all lights must be turned out during an enemy air raid.

blacksmith n. a person who makes and repairs iron objects.

bladder n. a bag-like organ in the abdomen which stores urine for excretion.

blade n. **1** the flat cutting edge of a knife or other tool or weapon. **2** the broad flat part of an oar, leaf, etc. **3** a long narrow leaf of grass.

blame v. hold responsible for a fault or wrong. •n. responsibility for a fault or wrong. ■ **blameless** adj. **blameworthy** adj.

blanch v. **1** become white or pale. **2** immerse vegetables briefly in boiling water.

blancmange /bluh-**monzh**/ n. a jelly-like dessert made with milk.

bland adj. lacking interesting qualities or features.

blandishments pl. n. flattery intended to persuade.

blank adj. **1** not marked or decorated. **2** not understanding or reacting. •n. **1** an empty space. **2** a cartridge containing gunpowder but no bullet. •v. (**blank out**) hide or block out. □ **blank verse** poetry that does not rhyme.

blanket n. **1** a warm covering made of woollen material. **2** a thick mass or layer. •v. (**blanketing**, **blanketed**) cover with a thick layer.

blare v. make a loud, harsh sound. •n. a blaring sound.

blarney n. charming or flattering talk.

blasé /**blah**-zay/ adj. unimpressed with something through over-familiarity.

blaspheme v. speak irreverently about God or sacred things. ■ **blasphemous** adj. **blasphemy** n.

blast n. **1** an explosion, or the rush of air spreading out from it. **2** a strong gust of wind. **3** a loud note of a horn or whistle. •v. **1** blow up with explosives. **2** (**blast off**) (of a rocket etc.) take off. **3** produce loud music or noise.

blatant adj. open and unashamed. ■ **blatantly** adv.

❗ The ending is -*ant*, not -*ent*: blat**ant**.

blather v. chatter foolishly.

blaze n. **1** a large or fierce fire. **2** a bright light or display of colour. **3** an outburst. **4** a white stripe on an animal's face. •v. burn or shine fiercely or brightly. □ **blaze a trail** **1** mark out a path. **2** pioneer something.

blazer n. a jacket worn by schoolchildren or sports players as part of a uniform.

blazon v. display or describe prominently.

bleach v. lighten by chemicals or sunlight. •n. a chemical used to bleach or sterilize things.

bleak adj. **1** barren and exposed. **2** dreary and unwelcoming. **3** (of a situation) not hopeful. ■ **bleakly** adv. **bleakness** n.

bleary adj. (**blearier**, **bleariest**) (of the eyes) dull and unfocused. ■ **blearily** adv.

bleat v. **1** (of a sheep or goat) make a weak, wavering cry. **2** speak or complain feebly. •n. a bleating sound.

bleed v. (**bleeding, bled**) **1** lose blood from the body. **2** draw blood or fluid from. **3** *informal* drain of money or resources.

bleep n. a short high-pitched sound made by an electronic device. •v. make a bleep. ■ **bleeper** n.

blemish n. a small mark or flaw. •v. spoil the appearance of.

blench v. flinch suddenly.

blend v. **1** mix and combine. **2** (**blend in**) merge so as to be unnoticeable. •n. a mixture.

blender n. an electric device for liquidizing food.

bless v. **1** make holy. **2** ask God to protect. **3** (**be blessed with**) be fortunate in having.

blessed adj. **1** holy. **2** bringing welcome pleasure or relief.
■ **blessedly** adv.

blessing n. **1** God's protection, or a prayer asking for this. **2** something for which you are very grateful. **3** a person's approval or support.

blew past of BLOW.

blight n. **1** a plant disease. **2** a cause of harm. •v. spoil or harm.

blind adj. **1** unable to see. **2** lacking awareness or judgement. **3** concealed, closed, or blocked off. •v. **1** make blind. **2** prevent from thinking clearly. •n. a screen for a window. □ **blindfold** a piece of cloth used to cover a person's eyes. ■ **blindly** adv. **blindness** n.

blink v. **1** shut and open the eyes quickly. **2** shine unsteadily. •n. an act of blinking.

blinkered adj. having a limited point of view.

blinkers pl. n. a pair of flaps attached to a bridle to prevent a horse from seeing sideways.

blip n. **1** a short high-pitched sound. **2** a flashing point of light on a radar screen. **3** a temporary change in an otherwise steady situation.

bliss n. perfect happiness.
■ **blissful** adj. **blissfully** adv.

blister n. **1** a small bubble on the skin filled with watery liquid. **2** a similar bubble on a surface. •v. form blisters.

blithe adj. casually indifferent.
■ **blithely** adv.

blitz n. **1** a sudden military attack. **2** *informal* a sudden and concentrated effort. •v. make a sudden attack on.

blizzard n. a severe snowstorm.

bloat v. cause to swell with fluid or gas.

bloater n. a salted smoked herring.

blob n. **1** a drop of a thick liquid. **2** a roundish mass.

bloc n. a group of allied countries with similar political systems.

block n. **1** a solid piece of material with flat surfaces on each side. **2** a large building divided into flats or offices. **3** a group of buildings bounded by four streets. **4** an obstacle. •v. prevent movement, flow, or progress in. □ **blockbuster** *informal* a very successful film or book. **block capitals** plain capital letters.

blockade n. an act of sealing off a place to prevent goods or people from entering or leaving. •v. set up a blockade of.

blockage n. an obstruction.

blog n. a weblog. •v. (**blogging, blogged**) keep a weblog.
■ **blogger** n.

bloke n. *informal* a man.

blonde *adj.* (or **blond**) **1** (of hair) fair. **2** having fair hair. • *n.* a woman with blonde hair.

blood *n.* **1** the red liquid circulating in the arteries and veins. **2** family background. • *v.* initiate in an activity. □ **bloodbath** a massacre. **blood-curdling** horrifying. **bloodhound** a large dog used in tracking scents. **bloodless** without violence or killing. **bloodshed** the killing or wounding of people. **bloodshot** (of eyes) red from dilated blood vessels. **blood sport** a sport involving the killing of animals. **bloodstream** the blood circulating in the body. **bloodthirsty** taking pleasure in killing or violence.

bloody *adj.* (**bloodier, bloodiest**) **1** covered in blood. **2** involving much violence or cruelty. • *v.* (**bloodying, bloodied**) cover or stain with blood. □ **bloody-minded** *informal* deliberately uncooperative.

bloom *v.* **1** produce flowers. **2** be very healthy. • *n.* **1** a flower. **2** the state or period of blooming. **3** a healthy glow in the complexion.

bloomers *pl. n.* **1** women's long baggy knickers. **2** *hist.* women's loose-fitting trousers.

blossom *n.* a flower or a mass of flowers on a tree. • *v.* **1** produce blossom. **2** develop and flourish.

blot *n.* **1** a spot of ink. **2** a thing that spoils something good. • *v.* (**blotting, blotted**) **1** dry with an absorbent material. **2** mark or spoil. **3** (**blot out**) hide or cover.

blotch *n.* a large irregular mark. ■ **blotchy** *adj.*

blouse *n.* a woman's top with buttons down the front.

blouson /bloo-zon/ *n.* a short loose-fitting jacket.

blow *v.* (**blowing, blew**; *past part.* **blown**) **1** (of wind) move. **2** send out air through pursed lips. **3** play a wind instrument. **4** break open with explosives. **5** burst or burn out through pressure or overheating. **6** *informal* spend money recklessly. **7** *informal* waste an opportunity. • *n.* **1** an act of blowing. **2** a stroke with the hand or a weapon. **3** a shock or disappointment. □ **blowfly** a large fly which lays its eggs in meat. **blowout** the release of air or gas from a tyre, oil well, etc. **blowtorch** (or **blowlamp**) a portable device producing a hot flame, for burning off paint. **blow up 1** explode. **2** enlarge an image. ■ **blowy** *adj.*

blowsy (or **blowzy**) *adj.* (of a woman) plump and untidy.

blub *v.* (**blubbing, blubbed**) *informal* sob noisily.

blubber *n.* the fat of whales and seals. • *v. informal* sob noisily.

bludgeon *n.* a heavy stick used as a weapon. • *v.* **1** hit with a bludgeon. **2** bully into doing something.

blue *adj.* **1** of the colour of the sky on a sunny day. **2** *informal* sad or depressed. **3** *informal* indecent or pornographic. • *n.* **1** blue colour or material. **2** (**blues**) slow sad music of black American origin. **3** (**the blues**) sadness or depression. □ **bluebell** a plant with blue bell-shaped flowers. **bluebottle** a large bluish fly. **blue-collar** of manual work. **blueprint 1** a technical drawing or plan. **2** a model or prototype. **bluestocking** a serious intellectual woman. **out of the blue** *informal* unexpectedly. ■ **blueness** *n.* **bluish** *adj.*

bluff v. try to make someone believe that you know or will do something. • n. **1** an act of bluffing. **2** a steep cliff. • adj. frank and direct.

blunder n. a clumsy mistake. • v. **1** make a blunder. **2** move clumsily.

blunderbuss n. hist. a gun with a short, wide barrel.

blunt adj. **1** lacking a sharp edge or point. **2** frank and direct. • v. make or become blunt. ■ **bluntly** adv.

blur v. (blurring, blurred) make or become less distinct. • n. something perceived indistinctly. ■ **blurry** adj.

blurb n. a short description written to promote a book, film, etc.

blurt v. say suddenly and without thinking.

blush v. become red-faced through shyness or embarrassment. • n. an act of blushing.

blusher n. a cosmetic used to give a rosy tinge to the cheeks.

bluster v. **1** talk loudly or aggressively but with little effect. **2** blow in gusts. • n. loud and empty talk. ■ **blustery** adj.

boa n. **1** a large snake which crushes its prey. **2** a thin stole of feathers or fur.

boar n. (pl. boar or boars) **1** a wild pig with tusks. **2** a male pig.

board n. **1** a long, thin, flat piece of sawn wood. **2** a rectangular piece of stiff material used as a surface. **3** the decision-making body of an organization. **4** the provision of regular meals in return for payment. • v. **1** get on a ship, aircraft, etc. **2** receive meals and accommodation in return for payment. **3** cover or seal with pieces of wood. ◻ **boarding house** a private house providing meals and accommodation for paying guests. **boarding school** a school in which the pupils live during term time. **boardroom** a room in which a board of directors meets. **on board** on or in a ship, aircraft, etc. ■ **boarder** n.

boast v. **1** talk about yourself with excessive pride. **2** possess an impressive feature. • n. an act of boasting. ■ **boastful** adj. **boastfully** adv.

boat n. a vehicle for travelling on water. ■ **boating** n.

boater n. a flat-topped straw hat.

boatswain /boh-s'n/ n. a ship's officer in charge of equipment and crew.

bob v. (bobbing, bobbed) move quickly up and down. • n. **1** a bobbing movement. **2** a short hairstyle that hangs evenly all round. ◻ **bobsleigh** a sledge used for racing down an ice-covered run.

bobbin n. a reel for holding thread.

bobble n. a small ball made of strands of wool.

bode v. (bode well/ill) be a sign of a good or bad outcome.

bodge v. informal make or repair badly.

bodice n. **1** the part of a dress above the waist. **2** a woman's sleeveless undergarment.

bodily adj. of the body. • adv. by taking hold of a person with force.

bodkin n. a thick, blunt needle.

body n. (pl. bodies) **1** the physical structure of a person or animal. **2** the main part. **3** a mass or collection. **4** a group organized for a particular purpose. ◻ **bodyguard** a person paid to protect an important person. **bodywork** the metal outer shell of a vehicle.

Boer → bone

Boer n. a member of the Dutch people who settled in southern Africa.

boffin n. informal a scientist.

bog n. **1** an area of soft, wet ground. **2** informal a toilet. • v. (**be/ get bogged down**) be prevented from progressing. ■ **boggy** adj.

bogey n. (pl. **bogeys**) **1** Golf a score of one stroke over par at a hole. **2** (or **bogy**) a cause of fear or alarm.

boggle v. informal be astonished or baffled.

bogus adj. not genuine or true.

Bohemian adj. artistic and un-conventional.

boil v. **1** (of a liquid) reach a temperature at which it bubbles and turns to vapour. **2** cook in boiling water. • n. **1** the process of boiling. **2** an inflamed pus-filled swelling.

boiler n. a device for heating water.

boisterous adj. noisy, lively, and high-spirited.

bold adj. **1** confident and brave. **2** (of a colour or design) strong or vivid. **3** (of printing) in thick, dark type. ■ **boldly** adv. **boldness** n.

bole n. a tree trunk.

bolero n. (pl. **boleros**) **1** /buh-lair-oh/ a Spanish dance. **2** /bol-uh-roh/ a woman's short open jacket.

boll n. the rounded seed capsule of plants such as cotton.

bollard n. a short thick post.

bolshie (or **bolshy**) adj. informal hostile and uncooperative.

bolster n. a long, firm pillow. • v. support or strengthen.

bolt n. **1** a metal pin that screws into a nut, used to fasten things. **2** a sliding bar used to fasten a door or window. **3** a flash of light-

ning. **4** a roll of fabric. • v. **1** fasten with a bolt. **2** run away. **3** eat food quickly. □ **bolt-hole** a place where a person can escape to and hide.

bomb n. **1** a device intended to explode and cause damage. **2** (**the bomb**) nuclear weapons. **3** (**a bomb**) informal a large sum of money. • v. **1** attack with bombs. **2** informal move very quickly. **3** informal fail badly. □ **bombshell** a great surprise or shock.

bombard v. **1** attack with bombs or other missiles. **2** direct a flow of questions or information at. ■ **bombardment** n.

bombardier n. a rank of non-commissioned artillery officer.

bombast n. pompous language with little meaning. ■ **bombastic** adj.

bomber n. **1** an aircraft that drops bombs. **2** a person who plants bombs.

bona fide /boh-nuh **fy**-di/ adj. genuine.

bonanza n. a situation creating wealth or success.

bond n. **1** a force or feeling that links people. **2** a thing used for fastening. **3** (**bonds**) ropes or chains used to restrain someone. **4** an agreement with legal force. **5** a certificate issued by a government or a public company promising to repay money lent to it at a fixed rate of interest. • v. **1** join securely. **2** form a relationship based on shared feelings etc.

bondage n. the state of being a slave or prisoner.

bone n. any of the pieces of hard material making up the skeleton in vertebrates. • v. **1** remove the bones from meat or fish. **2** (**bone**

up on) *informal* study a subject intensively.

bonfire *n.* a large open-air fire.

bongo *n.* (*pl.* **bongos**) each of a pair of small drums held between the knees.

bonhomie /bon-uh-mee/ *n.* good-natured friendliness.

bonnet *n.* **1** a hat with strings that tie under the chin. **2** the hinged cover over the engine of a vehicle.

bonny *adj.* (**bonnier, bonniest**) *Sc. & N. Engl.* attractive and healthy-looking.

bonsai /bon-sy/ *n.* the art of growing miniature ornamental trees.

bonus *n.* **1** a sum of money added to wages for good performance. **2** an unexpected extra benefit.

bon voyage /bon voy-yahzh/ *exclam.* have a good journey.

bony *adj.* (**bonier, boniest**) **1** containing or resembling bones. **2** very thin, with the bones showing.

boo *exclam.* **1** said suddenly to surprise someone. **2** said to show disapproval. •*v.* (**booing, booed**) shout 'boo'.

boob *informal n.* an embarrassing mistake. •*v.* make such a mistake.

booby *n.* (*pl.* **boobies**) *informal* a stupid person. ▫ **booby prize** a prize given to the person who comes last in a contest. **booby trap** an object containing a hidden explosive device.

boogie *v.* (**boogieing, boogied**) *informal* dance to pop music.

book *n.* **1** a written or printed work consisting of pages bound in a cover. **2** a main division of a literary work. **3** (**books**) a set of records or accounts. •*v.* **1** reserve accommodation, a ticket, etc.

2 engage a performer for an event. **3** officially note the name of someone who has broken a law or rule. ▫ **bookcase** a cabinet containing shelves for books. **bookkeeping** the keeping of records of financial transactions. **booklet** a small thin book. **bookmaker** a person who takes bets and pays out winnings. **bookmark 1** a strip of card or leather to mark a place in a book. **2** a record of the address of a computer file, website, etc. enabling quick access by the user. **bookworm** *informal* a person who loves reading. ■ **booker** *n.* **booking** *n.*

bookie *n. informal* a bookmaker.

boom *n.* **1** a loud, deep sound. **2** a period of rapid economic growth. **3** a pivoted beam at the foot of a sail. **4** a movable arm carrying a microphone or film camera. **5** a beam forming a barrier across a harbour mouth. •*v.* **1** make a loud, deep sound. **2** experience rapid economic growth.

boomerang *n.* a curved flat piece of wood that can be thrown so as to return to the thrower.

boon *n.* a very useful thing.

boor *n.* a rough, bad-mannered person. ■ **boorish** *adj.*

boost *v.* help or encourage. •*n.* a source of help or encouragement.

booster *n.* **1** a dose of a vaccine that increases or renews the effect of an earlier one. **2** the part of a rocket or spacecraft giving acceleration after lift-off.

boot *n.* **1** an item of footwear covering the foot and ankle or lower leg. **2** a space at the back of a car for luggage. **3** (**the boot**) *informal* dismissal from a job. •*v.*

1 kick hard. **2** start a computer and make it ready to operate.

b bootee n. a baby's woollen shoe.

booth n. **1** an enclosed compartment allowing privacy when telephoning etc. **2** a stall or stand for selling goods etc. at a fair or market.

bootleg adj. made or distributed illegally. ■ **bootlegger** n. **bootlegging** n.

booty n. valuable stolen goods.

booze informal n. alcoholic drink. • v. drink alcohol. ■ **boozer** n. **boozy** adj.

bop v. (**bopping**, **bopped**) informal dance to pop music.

borax n. a white mineral used in making glass.

border n. **1** a boundary between two countries etc. **2** a decorative band around the edge of something. **3** a flower bed along the edge of a lawn. • v. **1** form a border around or along. **2** (**border on**) come close to. □ **borderline** between two states or categories.

bore¹ v. **1** make someone feel weary and unenthusiastic being dull. **2** make a hole with a drill or other tool. • n. **1** a dull person or activity. **2** the hollow part inside a gun barrel. ■ **boredom** n. **boring** adj.

bore² past of BEAR¹.

boric acid n. a substance made from boron, used as an antiseptic.

born adj. **1** existing as a result of birth. **2** having a particular natural ability. □ **born-again** newly converted to Christianity or a particular cause.

borne past part. of BEAR¹.

boron n. a chemical element used in making steel.

borough n. a town with a corporation and privileges granted by a royal charter.

borrow v. take and use something belonging to someone else and return it later. ■ **borrower** n.

borstal n. hist. a prison for young offenders.

bosom n. a woman's breasts or chest. • adj. (of a friend) very close.

boss n. **1** a person in charge of an employee or organization. **2** a knob at the centre of a shield etc. • v. informal give orders in a domineering way. □ **boss-eyed** cross-eyed.

bossy adj. (**bossier**, **bossiest**) informal tending to give orders. ■ **bossily** adv. **bossiness** n.

bosun (or **bo'sun**) var. of BOATSWAIN.

botany n. the study of plants. ■ **botanical** adj. **botanist** n.

botch v. informal do badly or carelessly.

both adj. & pron. two people or things regarded together.

bother v. **1** take the trouble to do something. **2** worry, disturb, or upset. • n. **1** trouble and fuss. **2** (**a bother**) a cause of trouble or fuss. ■ **bothersome** adj.

bottle n. a container with a narrow neck, for storing liquids. • v. **1** put in bottles. **2** (**bottle up**) hide your feelings. □ **bottleneck** a narrow part of a road where congestion occurs.

bottom n. **1** the lowest or furthest point, part, or position. **2** the buttocks. • adj. in the lowest or furthest position. □ **the bottom line** informal the most important factor. ■ **bottomless** adj.

botulism n. a dangerous form of food poisoning.

boudoir /boo-dwar/ *n.* a woman's bedroom or small private room.

bouffant /boo-fon/ *adj.* (of hair) standing out from the head in a rounded shape.

bougainvillea /boo-guhn-**vil**-li-uh/ *n.* a tropical plant with brightly coloured bracts.

bough *n.* a large branch.

bought past & past part. of **BUY**.

boulder *n.* a large rock.

boulevard *n.* a wide street.

bounce *v.* 1 move quickly up from a surface after hitting it. 2 move up and down repeatedly. 3 *informal* (of a cheque) be returned by a bank when there is not enough money in an account to meet it. • *n.* 1 an act of bouncing. 2 lively self-confidence. ■ **bouncy** *adj.*

bouncer *n.* a person employed by a nightclub to control or keep out troublemakers.

bound¹ *v.* 1 move with leaping strides. 2 form the boundary of. 3 restrict. • *n.* 1 a leaping movement. 2 a boundary or limit. • *adj.* going towards somewhere. □ **bound to** certain to. **out of bounds** beyond permitted limits.

bound² past & past part. of **BIND**.

boundary *n.* (*pl.* **boundaries**) a line marking the limits of an area.

boundless *adj.* unlimited.

bounteous *adj.* old use bountiful.

bountiful *adj.* 1 plentiful. 2 giving generously.

bounty *n.* (*pl.* **bounties**) 1 *literary* generosity, or something given in large amounts. 2 a reward for killing or capturing someone.

bouquet *n.* 1 a bunch of flowers. 2 the scent of a wine or perfume.

bourbon /ber-buhn/ *n.* an American whisky made from maize and rye.

bourgeois /boor-zhwah/ *adj.* of the middle class, esp. in being conventional.

bourgeoisie /boor-zhwah-**zee**/ *n.* the middle class.

bout *n.* 1 a period of illness or intense activity. 2 a wrestling or boxing match.

boutique *n.* a small shop selling fashionable clothes.

bovine *adj.* 1 of cattle. 2 sluggish or stupid.

bow¹ /rhymes with **go**/ *n.* 1 a knot tied with two loops and two loose ends. 2 a weapon for shooting arrows. 3 a rod with horsehair stretched along its length, for playing a violin etc. □ **bow-legged** having legs that curve outwards at the knee.

bow² /rhymes with **cow**/ *v.* 1 bend the head or upper body as a sign of respect. 2 bend under a heavy weight. 3 give in to pressure. • *n.* 1 an act of bowing. 2 (or **bows**) the front of a ship.

bowdlerize (or -**ise**) *v.* remove indecent or offensive material from a text.

bowel *n.* 1 the intestine. 2 (**bowels**) the innermost parts of something.

bower *n.* a shady place under trees.

bowl *n.* 1 a round, deep dish or basin. 2 a rounded, hollow part of an object. 3 (**bowls**) a game in which heavy wooden balls are rolled as close as possible to a small white ball. 4 a ball used in the game of bowls. • *v.* 1 roll a round object along the ground. 2 move rapidly and smoothly. 3 *Cricket* throw the ball towards the wicket. 4 (**bowl over**) knock down.

b

5 (bowl over) *informal* impress or astonish.

bowler *n.* **1** Cricket a member of the fielding side who bowls. **2** a player at bowls. **3** a hard black felt hat with a rounded top.

box *n.* **1** a straight-sided container with a lid. **2** an enclosed area reserved for a group of people in a theatre, sports ground, etc. **3 (the box)** *informal* television. **4** a shrub with small glossy leaves. •*v.* **1** put in a box. **2** fight with the fists as a sport. □ **box office** the place at a theatre or cinema where tickets are sold. ■ **boxing** *n.*

boxer *n.* **1** a person who boxes as a sport. **2** a dog with a brown coat and pug-like face. □ **boxer shorts** men's underpants resembling shorts.

boy *n.* a male child. □ **boyfriend** a person's regular male romantic or sexual partner. ■ **boyhood** *n.* **boyish** *adj.*

boycott *v.* refuse to have dealings with or trade with. •*n.* an act of boycotting.

bra *n.* a woman's undergarment worn to support the breasts.

brace *n.* **1** a strengthening or supporting part. **2 (braces)** a pair of straps that pass over the shoulders and fasten to trousers to hold them up. **3** a wire device used to straighten the teeth. **4** (*pl.* **brace**) a pair. •*v.* **1** make stronger or firmer with a brace. **2 (brace yourself)** prepare for something difficult.

bracelet *n.* an ornamental band or chain worn on the arm.

bracing *adj.* fresh and invigorating.

bracken *n.* a tall fern.

bracket *n.* **1** each of a pair of marks ( ) [ ] { } < > used to enclose

words or figures. **2** a category. **3** a right-angled support projecting from a wall. •*v.* (**bracketing**, **bracketed**) **1** enclose in brackets. **2** put in the same category.

brackish *adj.* (of water) slightly salty.

bract *n.* a leaf with a flower in the angle where it meets the stem.

brag *v.* (**bragging**, **bragged**) boast.

braggart *n.* a boastful person.

braid *n.* **1** threads woven into a decorative band. **2** a plait of hair. •*v.* **1** plait hair. **2** trim with braid.

Braille *n.* a written language for blind people, using raised dots.

brain *n.* **1** an organ of soft tissue in the skull, the centre of the nervous system. **2** intellectual ability. □ **brainchild** a person's idea or invention. **brainstorm** **1** a moment in which you are unable to think clearly. **2** a group discussion to produce ideas. **brainwash** pressure someone into accepting an idea or belief. **brainwave** a sudden clever idea.

brainy *adj.* (**brainier**, **brainiest**) *informal* clever.

braise *v.* fry food lightly and then stew it slowly in a closed container.

brake *n.* a device for slowing or stopping a moving vehicle. •*v.* slow or stop a vehicle with a brake.

bramble *n.* a blackberry bush or similar shrub.

bran *n.* pieces of grain husk separated from flour after milling.

branch *n.* **1** a part of a tree growing out from the trunk. **2** a river, road, or railway growing out from a main one. **3** a division of a larger group. •*v.* **1** divide into one or more branches. **2 (branch out)** embark on new activities.

brand n. **1** a type of product made by a company under a particular name. **2 (or brand name)** a name given to a product by its maker. **3** a mark burned on livestock with hot metal. •v. **1** describe as being bad in a particular way. **2** give a brand name to. **3** mark with hot metal. □ **brand new** completely new.

brandish v. wave something as a threat or in anger or excitement.

brandy n. (pl. **brandies**) a strong alcoholic spirit made from wine or fermented fruit juice.

brash adj. aggressively self-confident. ■ **brashness** n.

brass n. **1** a yellow alloy of copper and zinc. **2** a brass memorial plaque. **3** brass wind instruments forming a section of an orchestra.

brasserie /brass-uh-ri/ n. (pl. **brasseries**) an inexpensive French or French-style restaurant.

brassica n. a plant of the cabbage family.

brassiere /braz-i-er/ n. a bra.

brassy adj. (**brassier, brassiest**) **1** like brass. **2** tastelessly showy.

brat n. informal a badly behaved child.

bravado n. confidence that is intended to impress.

brave adj. having or showing courage. •v. face unpleasant conditions with courage. •n. dated an American Indian warrior. ■ **bravely** adv. **bravery** n.

bravo exclam. well done!

bravura n. great skill and enthusiasm.

brawl n. a noisy fight or quarrel. •v. take part in a brawl.

brawn n. physical strength. ■ **brawny** adj.

bray v. (of a donkey) make a loud, harsh cry. •n. the cry of a donkey.

brazen adj. bold and shameless. •v. (**brazen it out**) endure an awkward situation without seeming ashamed. ■ **brazenly** adv.

brazier n. a portable heater holding lighted coals.

Brazil nut n. a large three-sided nut from a South American tree.

breach v. **1** make a hole in. **2** break a rule or agreement. •n. **1** a gap made in a wall or barrier. **2** an act of breaking a rule or agreement. **3** a quarrel or disagreement.

bread n. **1** food made of flour, water, and yeast mixed together and baked. **2** informal money. □ **breadwinner** a person who earns money to support their family. **on the breadline** very poor.

breadth n. **1** the distance from side to side of something. **2** wide range.

break v. (**breaking, broke; past part. broken**) **1** separate into pieces as a result of a blow or strain. **2** stop functioning or working. **3** interrupt a sequence or course. **4** fail to obey a rule or agreement. **5** beat a record. **6** soften a fall. **7** suddenly make or become public. **8** (of a boy's voice) deepen at puberty. **9** (of the weather) change suddenly. •n. **1** a pause, gap, or short rest. **2** an instance of breaking, or the point where something is broken. **3** a sudden rush or dash. **4** a chance. □ **break down 1** stop functioning. **2** lose control of your emotions. **breakdown 1** a failure or collapse. **2** a careful analysis.

b

break in 1 force entry to a building. **2** make a horse used to being ridden. **breakneck** dangerously fast. **break out 1** start suddenly. **2** escape. **breakthrough** a sudden important development or success. **break up** (of a gathering or relationship) end. **breakwater** a barrier built out into the sea to protect a coast etc. from waves. ■ **breakable** adj.

breakage n. the action of breaking something.

breaker n. a heavy wave that breaks on the shore.

breakfast n. the first meal of the day.

bream n. (pl. **bream**) a freshwater fish.

breast n. **1** either of the two organs on a woman's chest which produce milk after pregnancy. **2** a person's or animal's chest. □ **breastbone** the bone down the centre of the chest. **breaststroke** a swimming stroke in which the arms are pushed forwards and swept back while the legs are kicked out.

breath n. **1** air taken into or sent out of the lungs. **2** an act of breathing in or out. **3** a slight movement of air. □ **breathtaking** astonishing or impressive. ■ **breathless** adj.

breathalyser (US trademark **Breathalyzer**) n. a device for measuring the amount of alcohol in a driver's breath. ■ **breathalyse** (US **-yze**) v.

breathe v. **1** take air into the lungs and send it out again. **2** say quietly.

breather n. informal a brief pause for rest.

bred past & past part. of **BREED**.

breech n. the back part of a rifle or gun barrel. □ **breech birth** a birth in which the baby's buttocks or feet are delivered first.

breeches pl. n. short trousers fastened just below the knee.

breed v. (**breeding**, **bred**) **1** (of animals) mate and produce offspring. **2** keep animals for the young that they produce. **3** produce or cause. •n. **1** a particular type within a species of animals. **2** a type. ■ **breeder** n.

breeding n. upper-class good manners.

breeze n. a gentle wind. □ **breeze block** a lightweight building block. ■ **breezy** adj.

brethren pl. n. fellow Christians or members of a group.

breve /breev/ n. Music a note twice as long as a semibreve.

brevity n. **1** concise and exact use of words. **2** shortness of time.

brew v. **1** make beer. **2** make a drink of tea or coffee. **3** begin to develop. •n. something brewed. ■ **brewer** n.

brewery n. (pl. **breweries**) a place where beer is made.

briar (or **brier**) n. a prickly shrub, esp. a wild rose.

bribe v. dishonestly pay someone to help you. •n. something offered in an attempt to bribe. ■ **bribery** n.

bric-a-brac n. various objects of little value.

brick n. a small rectangular block of fired clay, used in building. •v. block or enclose with a wall of bricks. □ **brickbat** a critical remark. **bricklayer** a person who builds structures with bricks.

bridal adj. of a bride or a newly married couple.

bride n. a woman at the time of her wedding. □ **bridegroom** a man at the time of his wedding.

bridesmaid a girl or woman who accompanies a bride at her wedding.

bridge n. 1 a structure providing a way across a river, road, etc. 2 the platform on a ship from which the captain directs its course. 3 the upper bony part of the nose. 4 the part on a stringed instrument over which the strings are stretched. 5 a card game played between two pairs of players. • v. be or make a bridge over. □ **bridgehead** a strong position gained by an army inside enemy territory.

bridle n. the harness used to control a horse. • v. 1 put a bridle on. 2 show resentment or anger. □ **bridleway** (or **bridle path**) a path for horse riders or walkers.

brief adj. 1 lasting a short time. 2 using few words. 3 (of clothes) not covering much of the body. • n. 1 a set of instructions about a task. 2 a summary of the facts in a case given to a barrister to argue in court. 3 (**briefs**) short underpants. • v. instruct someone about a task. □ **briefcase** a flat case for carrying documents. ■ **briefly** adv.

briefing n. a meeting for giving information or instructions.

brier var. of BRIAR.

brig n. a sailing ship with two masts.

brigade n. 1 a large army unit forming part of a division. 2 a particular group: *the anti-smoking brigade.*

brigadier n. the army rank above colonel.

brigand n. a member of a gang of bandits.

bright adj. 1 giving out or filled with light. 2 (of colour) vivid. 3 intelligent. 4 cheerfully lively. 5 (of prospects) good. ■ **brighten** v. **brightly** adv. **brightness** n.

brilliant adj. 1 very bright or vivid. 2 very clever or talented. 3 *informal* excellent. ■ **brilliance** n. **brilliantly** adv.

brim n. 1 the projecting edge of a hat. 2 the lip of a cup, bowl, etc. • v. (**brimming, brimmed**) be full to the point of overflowing.

brimstone n. *old use* sulphur.

brindle (or **brindled**) adj. (of an animal) brownish with streaks of grey or black.

brine n. water containing dissolved salt. ■ **briny** adj.

bring v. (**bringing, brought**) 1 carry or take to a place. 2 cause to be in a particular position or state. 3 begin legal action. □ **bring about** cause to happen. **bring off** achieve. **bring on** cause to occur. **bring out** 1 produce and launch. 2 emphasize a feature. **bring up** 1 rear a child. 2 raise for discussion.

brink n. 1 the edge of land before a steep slope or an area of water. 2 the point just before a new situation. □ **brinkmanship** the pursuing of a dangerous course of action to the limits of safety before stopping.

brisk adj. 1 active and energetic. 2 practical and efficient. ■ **briskly** adv.

brisket n. meat from the breast of a cow.

bristle n. a short, stiff hair. • v. 1 (of hair or fur) stand upright away from the skin. 2 react angrily.

b

3 (bristle with) be covered with. ∎ **bristly** adj.

British adj. of Great Britain.

Briton n. a British person.

brittle adj. hard but easily broken.

broach v. **1** raise a subject for discussion. **2** pierce a container.

broad adj. **1** larger than usual from side to side; wide. **2** large in area or range. **3** without detail. **4** (of an accent) very strong. □ **broadband** a telecommunications technique which uses a wide range of frequencies, enabling messages to be sent simultaneously. **broad bean** a large flat green bean. **broad-minded** not easily shocked. **broadsheet** a large-sized newspaper. **broadside 1** a fierce critical attack. **2** hist. a firing of all the guns from one side of a ship. ∎ **broaden** v. **broadly** adv.

broadcast v. (**broadcasting**, **broadcast**) **1** transmit by radio or television. **2** make generally known. • n. a radio or television programme. ∎ **broadcaster** n.

brocade n. a rich fabric woven with a raised pattern.

broccoli n. a vegetable with heads of small green or purplish flower buds.

> ! Two c's, one l: broccoli.

brochure n. a booklet containing information about a product or service.

broderie anglaise /broh-duh-ri ong-glayz/ n. open embroidery on white cotton or linen.

brogue n. **1** a strong shoe with perforated patterns in the leather. **2** a strong regional accent.

broil v. US grill meat or fish.

broke past of **BREAK**. • adj. informal having no money.

broken past part. of **BREAK**. • adj. (of a language) spoken with many mistakes. □ **brokenhearted** overwhelmed with grief.

broker n. a person who buys and sells on behalf of others. • v. arrange a deal or plan. ∎ **brokerage** n.

brolly n. (pl. **brollies**) informal an umbrella.

bromide n. a compound of bromine, used in medicine.

bromine n. a dark red liquid chemical element.

bronchial adj. of the tubes leading to the lungs.

bronchitis /brong-ky-tiss/ n. inflammation of the bronchial tubes.

bronco n. (pl. **broncos**) a wild or half-tamed horse of the western US.

brontosaurus n. a huge plant-eating dinosaur.

bronze n. **1** a yellowish-brown alloy of copper and tin. **2** a yellowish-brown colour. **3** an object made of bronze. • v. make suntanned.

brooch n. an ornament fastened to clothing with a hinged pin.

brood n. a family of young animals born or hatched at one time. • v. **1** think deeply about an unpleasant subject. **2** (of a bird) sit on eggs to hatch them.

broody adj. **1** (of a hen) wishing to hatch eggs. **2** informal (of a woman) wanting to have a baby. **3** thoughtful and unhappy.

brook n. a small stream. • v. tolerate or allow.

broom n. **1** a long-handled brush for sweeping. **2** a shrub with yellow flowers. □ **broomstick** the handle of a broom, on which witches are said to fly.

Bros *abbrev.* brothers.

broth *n.* thin soup or stock.

brothel *n.* a house where men visit prostitutes.

brother *n.* **1** a man or boy in relation to other children of his parents. **2** a male colleague or friend. **3** (*pl.* also **brethren**) a male fellow Christian or member of a religious order. □ **brotherhood 1** the relationship between brothers. **2** comradeship. **3** a group linked by a shared interest. **brother-in-law** (*pl.* **brothers-in-law**) the brother of a person's wife or husband, or the husband of a person's sister. ■ **brotherly** *adj.*

brought past & past part. of BRING.

brow *n.* **1** the forehead. **2** an eyebrow. **3** the highest point of a hill. □ **browbeat** intimidate.

brown *adj.* **1** of the colour of rich soil. **2** suntanned. • *n.* brown colour. • *v.* make or become brown. • *v.* **browned off** *informal* annoyed or dissatisfied. ■ **brownish** *adj.*

browse *v.* **1** read or look at something in a leisurely way. **2** look at information on a computer. **3** (of an animal) feed on leaves, twigs, etc.

browser *n.* **1** a person or animal that browses. **2** a computer program for navigating the Internet.

bruise *n.* an area of discoloured skin on the body, caused by a blow. • *v.* cause a bruise on.

bruiser *n.* *informal* a tough, aggressive person.

brunch *n.* a meal combining breakfast and lunch.

brunette *n.* a woman or girl with dark brown hair.

brunt *n.* the chief impact of something bad.

brush *n.* **1** an implement with a handle and a block of bristles or wire. **2** an act of brushing. **3** a brief encounter with something bad. **4** a fox's tail. **5** undergrowth and shrubs. • *v.* **1** clean, smooth, or apply with a brush. **2** touch lightly. **3** (**brush off**) dismiss curtly. **4** (**brush up**) work to regain a former skill.

brusque /bruusk/ *adj.* abrupt or offhand. ■ **brusquely** *adv.*

Brussels sprout *n.* a green vegetable like a very small cabbage.

brutal *adj.* savagely violent. ■ **brutality** *n.* **brutally** *adv.*

brutalize (or **-ise**) *v.* **1** make brutal by frequent exposure to violence. **2** treat in a cruel way.

brute *n.* a violent or cruel person or a large, uncontrollable animal. • *adj.* involving physical strength rather than reason: *brute force.* ■ **brutish** *adj.*

BSc *abbrev.* Bachelor of Science.

BSE *abbrev.* bovine spongiform encephalopathy, a fatal brain disease in cattle.

BST *abbrev.* British Summer Time.

bubble *n.* **1** a thin sphere of liquid enclosing a gas. **2** a gas-filled sphere in a liquid, glass, etc. • *v.* **1** (of a liquid) contain rising bubbles. **2** (**bubble with**) be filled with. ■ **bubbly** *adj.*

bubonic plague *n.* a form of plague passed on by rat fleas.

buccaneer *n.* **1** *hist.* a pirate. **2** a recklessly adventurous person.

buck *n.* **1** the male of some animals, e.g. deer and rabbits. **2** *US & Austral.* a dollar. **3** *old use* a fashionable young man. • *v.* **1** (of a horse) jump with the back arched. **2** resist or go against. **3** (**buck up**)

b

informal make or become more cheerful. □ **buck teeth** teeth that stick out. **pass the buck** *informal* shift responsibility to someone else

bucket *n.* an open container with a handle, for carrying liquids. • *v.* (**bucketing, bucketed**) *informal* rain heavily.

buckle *n.* a flat frame with a hinged pin, used as a fastener. • *v.* **1** fasten with a buckle. **2** crumple under pressure. **3** (**buckle down**) tackle a task with determination.

bucolic /byoo-**kol**-ik/ *adj.* of country life.

bud *n.* a growth on a plant which develops into a leaf or flower. • *v.* (**budding, budded**) form a bud or buds.

Buddhism *n.* a religion based on the teachings of Buddha. ■ **Buddhist** *n.* & *adj.*

budding *adj.* beginning and showing signs of promise.

buddleia *n.* a shrub with lilac or white flowers.

buddy *n.* (pl. **buddies**) *US informal* a friend.

budge *v.* move slightly.

budgerigar *n.* a small Australian parakeet.

budget *n.* **1** an estimate of income and spending for a set period. **2** the amount of money available for a purpose. • *v.* (**budgeting, budgeted**) plan to spend a particular amount. ■ **budgetary** *adj.*

budgie *n.* (pl. **budgies**) a budgerigar.

buff *n.* **1** a yellowish-beige colour. **2** *informal* an expert on a particular subject. • *v.* polish.

buffalo *n.* (pl. **buffalo** or **buffaloes**) **1** a wild ox. **2** the North American bison.

buffer *n.* **1** (**buffers**) shock-absorbing devices on a railway track or railway vehicle. **2** a person or thing that lessens the impact of harmful effects.

buffet[1] /boo-**fay**, buf-**fay**/ *n.* **1** a meal in which guests serve themselves. **2** a counter at which snacks are sold.

buffet[2] /**buff**-it/ *v.* (**buffeting, buffeted**) (esp. of wind or waves) hit repeatedly.

buffoon *n.* a ridiculous but amusing person. ■ **buffoonery** *n.*

bug *n.* **1** *informal* a germ, or an illness caused by one. **2** a small insect. **3** a microphone used for secret recording. **4** an error in a computer program or system. • *v.* (**bugging, bugged**) **1** hide a microphone in. **2** *informal* annoy. □ **bugbear** a cause of worry or irritation.

buggery *n.* anal sex.

buggy *n.* (pl. **buggies**) **1** a folding pushchair. **2** a small open-topped motor vehicle.

bugle *n.* a brass instrument like a small trumpet. ■ **bugler** *n.*

build *v.* (**building, built**) **1** construct by putting parts together. **2** (**build up**) increase over time. • *n.* bodily proportions. ■ **builder** *n.*

building *n.* a structure with a roof and walls. □ **building society** an organization that pays interest on members' investments and lends money for mortgages.

built-in *adj.* included as part of a larger structure.

built-up *adj.* covered by many buildings.

bulb *n.* **1** the rounded base of the stem of some plants. **2** a glass ball giving light in an electric lamp.

bulbous *adj.* round or bulging.

bulge *n.* a rounded swelling. •*v.* swell or stick out.

bulimia /buu-lim-i-uh/ *n.* a disorder marked by bouts of overeating, followed by fasting or vomiting. ■ **bulimic** *adj. & n.*

bulk *n.* 1 the mass or size of something large. 2 the greater part. 3 a large mass or shape. □ **bulkhead** a partition in a ship or aircraft. **in bulk** (of goods) in large quantities.

bulky *adj.* (**bulkier, bulkiest**) large and unwieldy.

bull *n.* 1 an adult male of the cattle family. 2 a male whale, elephant, etc. 3 a bullseye. 4 an official order issued by the pope. □ **bulldog** a powerful dog with a flat wrinkled face. **bulldozer** a tractor with a device for clearing ground. **bullfighting** the sport of baiting and killing a bull. **bullseye** the centre of the target in archery and darts.

bullet *n.* a small missile fired from a gun.

bulletin *n.* a short official statement or summary of news.

bullion *n.* gold or silver in bulk or bars.

bullish *adj.* aggressively confident.

bullock *n.* a castrated bull.

bully *n.* (*pl.* **bullies**) a person who intimidates weaker people. •*v.* (**bullying, bullied**) intimidate.

bulrush *n.* a tall waterside plant with a long brown head.

bulwark *n.* 1 a defensive wall. 2 a ship's side above deck level.

bum *n. informal* 1 a person's bottom. 2 *US* a lazy or worthless person.

bumble *v.* act or speak in an awkward or confused way.

bumblebee *n.* a large hairy bee.

bumf (or **bumph**) *n. informal* printed information.

bump *n.* 1 a light blow or collision. 2 a projection on a level surface. •*v.* 1 knock or run into. 2 travel with a jolting movement. 3 (**bump into**) meet by chance. ■ **bumpy** *adj.*

bumper *n.* a bar across the front or back of a vehicle to reduce damage in a collision. •*adj.* exceptionally large or successful.

bumpkin *n.* an unsophisticated country person.

bumptious *adj.* irritatingly self-important.

bun *n.* 1 a small cake or bread roll. 2 a tight coil of hair at the back of the head.

bunch *n.* 1 a number of things held or grouped together. 2 *informal* a group of people. •*v.* collect into a bunch.

bundle *n.* a group of things tied or wrapped up together. •*v.* 1 tie or roll up in a bundle. 2 *informal* push or carry forcibly.

bung *n.* a stopper for a container. •*v.* 1 (**bung up**) block up. 2 *informal* put or throw casually.

bungalow *n.* a one-storeyed house.

bungee jumping *n.* the sport of leaping from a high place, attached by an elastic cord around the ankles.

bungle *v.* perform a task incompetently. •*n.* a mistake or failure. ■ **bungler** *n.*

bunion *n.* a painful swelling on the big toe.

bunk *n.* a narrow bed on a ship etc. □ **do a bunk** *informal* run away.

bunker *n.* 1 a container for storing fuel. 2 an underground shelter for use in wartime. **3** a hollow filled with sand on a golf course.

b bunkum n. informal nonsense.

bunny n. (pl. **bunnies**) informal a rabbit.

Bunsen burner n. a small gas burner used in laboratories.

bunting n. **1** a small songbird. **2** decorative flags.

buoy /boy/ n. a floating object used to mark an area of water. •v. **1** keep afloat. **2** (**be buoyed up**) be cheerful and confident.

> ! Remember: u before o in buoy and buoyant.

buoyant adj. **1** able to float. **2** cheerful. ∎ **buoyancy** n.

burble v. **1** make a continuous murmuring noise. **2** speak at length in a confused way.

burden n. **1** a heavy load. **2** a cause of hardship or distress. •v. **1** load heavily. **2** cause hardship or distress to. ∎ **burdensome** adj.

bureau /byoor-oh/ n. (pl. **bureaux** or **bureaus**) **1** a writing desk with a sloping top. **2** US a chest of drawers. **3** an office or organization providing a service. **4** a government department.

bureaucracy /byuu-**rok**-ruh-si/ n. (pl. **bureaucracies**) **1** excessively complicated administrative procedure. **2** a system of government in which most decisions are taken by unelected officials.

bureaucrat n. a government official, esp. one who follows guidelines rigidly. ∎ **bureaucratic** adj.

burgeon /ber-juhn/ v. grow or increase rapidly.

burger n. a hamburger.

burgher /ber-guh/ n. old use a citizen of a town or city.

burglar n. a person who breaks into a building to steal its contents. ∎ **burglary** n. **burgle** v.

burgundy n. (pl. **burgundies**) **1** a red wine. **2** a deep red colour.

burial n. the burying of a dead body.

burlesque n. a comically exaggerated imitation.

burly adj. (**burlier**, **burliest**) (of a man) large and strong.

burn v. (**burning**, **burned** or **burnt**) **1** (of a fire) flame or glow while using up a fuel. **2** harm or destroy by fire. **3** feel a strong desire or emotion. **4** (**burn out**) become exhausted through overwork. •n. **1** an injury caused by burning. **2** Sc. a stream.

burner n. a part of a cooker, lamp, etc. that gives out a flame.

burning adj. **1** intense. **2** important and urgent.

burnish v. polish by rubbing.

burp v. & n. informal (make) a belch.

burr n. **1** a strong pronunciation of the letter r. **2** a prickly seed case that clings to clothing and fur.

burrow n. a hole dug by a small animal to live in. •v. **1** dig a burrow. **2** hide underneath or search inside something.

bursar n. a person who manages the financial affairs of a college or school.

bursary n. (pl. **bursaries**) a grant for study.

burst v. (**bursting**, **burst**) **1** break suddenly and violently apart. **2** be very full. **3** move or be opened suddenly and forcibly. **4** suddenly do something as a result of strong emotion. • *n.* 1 an instance of bursting. 2 a sudden brief outbreak.

bury *v.* (**burying**, **buried**) 1 put underground. 2 place a dead body in the earth or a tomb. 3 conceal or cover. 4 (**bury yourself**) involve yourself deeply in something.

bus *n.* (*pl.* **buses**) a large vehicle carrying customers along a fixed route. • *v.* (**busing**, **bused** or **bussing**, **bussed**) transport or travel in a bus.

busby *n.* (*pl.* **busbies**) a tall fur hat worn by certain troops.

bush *n.* 1 a shrub. 2 (**the bush**) wild or uncultivated country. □ **bushbaby** a small African mammal with large eyes.

bushel *n.* 1 a measure of capacity equal to 8 gallons (36.4 litres). 2 *US* a measure of capacity equal to 64 US pints (35.2 litres).

bushy *adj.* (**bushier**, **bushiest**) 1 growing thickly. 2 covered with bushes.

business *n.* 1 a person's regular occupation. 2 commercial activity. 3 a commercial organization. 4 work to be done or matters to be attended to. 5 a person's concern. □ **businesslike** efficient and practical. **businessman** (or **businesswoman**) a person who works in commerce.

busk *v.* play music in the street for voluntary donations. ■ **busker** *n.*

bust *n.* 1 a woman's breasts. 2 a sculpture of a person's head, shoulders, and chest. • *v.* (**busting**, **busted** or **bust**) *informal* burst or break. □ **bust-up** *informal* a quarrel or fight. **go bust** *informal* become bankrupt.

bustle *v.* move energetically or noisily. • *n.* 1 excited activity. 2 *hist.* a pad or frame worn under a skirt to puff it out.

busy *adj.* (**busier**, **busiest**) 1 having a great deal to do. 2 occupied with an activity. 3 full of activity. • *v.* (**busying**, **busied**) (**busy yourself**) keep occupied. □ **busybody** an interfering person. ■ **busily** *adv.*

but *conj.* 1 nevertheless. 2 on the contrary. • *prep.* except; apart from. • *adv.* only.

butane *n.* a flammable gas used in liquid form as a fuel.

butch *adj.* *informal* aggressively masculine.

butcher *n.* 1 a person who cuts up and sells meat. 2 a person who kills brutally. • *v.* 1 slaughter or cut up an animal for food. 2 kill brutally. ■ **butchery** *n.*

butler *n.* the chief male servant of a house.

butt *v.* 1 hit with the head or horns. 2 (**butt in**) interrupt. • *n.* 1 the thicker end of a weapon or tool. 2 a cigarette stub. 3 a cask for holding liquid. 4 an object of criticism or ridicule.

butter *n.* a yellow fatty substance made by churning cream. • *v.* 1 spread with butter. 2 (**butter up**) *informal* flatter. □ **butter bean** a large flat edible bean. **buttercup** a plant with yellow cup-shaped flowers. **buttermilk** the liquid left after butter has been churned. **butterscotch** a sweet made with butter and brown sugar.

butterfly *n.* 1 an insect with two pairs of large wings. 2 a swimming stroke in which both arms are raised out of the water together.

buttock n. either of the two round fleshy parts of the body that form the bottom.

button n. **1** a disc sewn on to a garment to fasten it. **2** a knob pressed to operate equipment. • v. fasten with buttons.

buttonhole n. **1** a slit in a garment through which a button is pushed to fasten it. **2** a flower worn in a lapel buttonhole. • v. informal stop and detain in conversation.

buttress n. a projecting support built against a wall. • v. support or strengthen.

buxom adj. (of a woman) plump and large-breasted.

buy v. (**buying**, **bought**) **1** get in return for payment. **2** informal accept the truth of. • n. a purchase. ■ **buyer** n.

buzz n. **1** a low continuous sound. **2** an atmosphere of excitement and activity. **3** informal a thrill. • v. **1** make a low continuous sound. **2** be full of excitement or activity. **3** (**buzz off**) informal go away. □ **buzzword** informal a specialist word that has become fashionable.

buzzard n. a large bird of prey.

buzzer n. an electrical device that buzzes as a signal.

by prep. **1** through the action of. **2** indicating the end of a period. **3** beside. **4** past and beyond.

5 during. • adv. so as to go past. □ **by and by** before long. **by and large** on the whole.

bye exclam. informal goodbye. • n. **1** the moving of a competitor straight to the next round in the absence of an opponent. **2** Cricket a run scored from a ball not hit by the batsman.

by-election n. an election held during a government's term of office to fill a vacant seat.

bygone adj. belonging to the past.

by-law (or **bye-law**) n. a rule made by a local authority.

byline n. a line in a newspaper naming the writer of an article.

bypass n. **1** a road passing round a town. **2** an operation to help the circulation of blood by directing it through a new passage. • v. go past or round.

by-product n. a product produced in the making of something else.

byre n. a cowshed.

bystander n. a person who is at an event but does not take part.

byte n. a unit of information stored in a computer, equal to eight bits.

byway n. a minor road.

byword n. **1** a notable example. **2** a saying.

C (or **c**) *n.* the Roman numeral for 100. •*abbrev.* **1** Celsius or centigrade. **2** cents. **3** (**c.**) century or centuries. **4** (**c** or **ca.**) circa. **5** (©) copyright.

cab *n.* **1** a taxi. **2** the driver's compartment in a truck, bus, or train.

cabal /kuh-**bal**/ *n.* a secret political group.

cabaret /**kab**-uh-ray/ *n.* entertainment held in a nightclub.

cabbage *n.* a round vegetable with green or purple leaves.

cabby *n.* (pl. **cabbies**) *informal* a taxi driver.

caber *n.* a tree trunk thrown in a Scottish Highland sport.

cabin *n.* **1** a compartment on a ship or in an aircraft. **2** a small hut.

cabinet *n.* **1** a cupboard with drawers or shelves. **2** (**Cabinet**) a committee of senior government ministers. □ **cabinetmaker** a skilled joiner who makes furniture.

cable *n.* a thick rope of wire or fibre, esp. for carrying electricity or telecommunication signals. □ **cable car** a small carriage hung from a moving cable for travelling up and down a mountain. **cable television** a system transmitting programmes by cable.

cabriolet /kab-ri-oh-lay/ *n.* a car with a roof that folds down.

cacao /kuh-kah-oh/ *n.* the seeds from which cocoa and chocolate are made.

cache *n.* a hidden store of things.

cachet /ka-shay/ *n.* the state of being respected or admired; prestige.

cackle *n.* a noisy clucking cry or laugh. •*v.* make a cackle.

cacophony /kuh-**koff**-uh-ni/ *n.* (pl. **cacophonies**) a harsh mixture of sounds. ■ **cacophonous** *adj.*

cactus *n.* (pl. **cacti** or **cactuses**) a plant with thick fleshy stems bearing spines but no leaves.

cad *n. dated* a dishonourable man. ■ **caddish** *adj.*

cadaver *n.* a corpse.

cadaverous *adj.* very pale and thin.

caddie (or **caddy**) *n.* (pl. **caddies**) a person who carries a golfer's clubs. •*v.* (**caddying**, **caddied**) work as a caddie.

caddy *n.* (pl. **caddies**) a small tin or box.

cadence *n.* **1** the rise and fall of a person's voice. **2** the close of a musical phrase.

cadenza *n.* a difficult solo passage in a musical work.

cadet *n.* a young trainee in the armed services or police.

cadge *v. informal* ask for or get something without paying or working for it.

cadmium *n.* a silvery-white metallic element.

cadre /kah-der/ *n.* a small group of people trained for a particular purpose or at the centre of a political organization.

caecum /see-kuhm/ (US **cecum**) n. (pl. **caeca**) a pouch at the junction of the small and large intestines.

Caesarean /si-zair-i-uhn/ (US **Cesarean**) n. an operation for delivering a child by cutting through the wall of the mother's abdomen.

caesium /see-zi-uhm/ (US **cesium**) n. a soft silvery metallic element.

cafe /ka-fay/ n. a small restaurant selling light meals and drinks.

cafeteria n. a self-service restaurant.

cafetière /ka-fuh-tyair/ n. a coffee pot with a plunger to push the grounds to the bottom.

caffeine n. a stimulant found in tea and coffee.

caftan var. of **KAFTAN**.

cage n. a structure of bars or wires for confining animals. •v. enclose in a cage.

cagey (or **cagy**) adj. informal cautiously reluctant to speak. ■ **cagily** adv.

cagoule n. a light hooded waterproof jacket.

cahoots pl. n. (**in cahoots**) informal making secret plans together.

caiman (or **cayman**) n. an American reptile like an alligator.

cairn n. a mound of stones built as a memorial or landmark.

cajole v. persuade by using flattery.

Cajun /kay-juhn/ adj. of the French-speaking community of Louisiana.

cake n. **1** an item of soft sweet food made from baking a mixture of flour, fat, eggs, and sugar.

2 a flat compact mass of something. •v. (of a thick substance) cover and form a crust on.

calamine n. a pink powder used to make a soothing lotion.

calamity n. (pl. **calamities**) a sudden disastrous event. ■ **calamitous** adj.

calcify v. (**calcifying**, **calcified**) harden by a deposit of calcium salts.

calcium n. a soft grey metallic element.

calculate v. **1** work out using mathematics. **2** intend to have a particular effect. ■ **calculation** n.

calculating adj. craftily planning things to your own advantage.

calculator n. an electronic device for mathematical calculations.

calculus n. the branch of mathematics dealing with rates of variation.

caldron US = **CAULDRON**.

Caledonian adj. of Scotland.

calendar n. a chart showing the days, weeks, and months of a year.

calf n. (pl. **calves**) **1** a young cow, bull, elephant, etc. **2** the back of a person's leg below the knee.

calibrate v. check the accuracy of an instrument by comparing the readings with those of a standard. ■ **calibration** n.

calibre (US **caliber**) n. **1** quality or ability. **2** the diameter of a bullet, shell, or the inside of a gun barrel.

calico n. plain cotton cloth.

californium n. a radioactive metallic element.

caliper (or **calliper**) n. **1** (or **calipers**) a measuring instrument with two hinged legs. **2** a metal support for a person's leg.

caliph /kay-lif/ n. hist. the chief Muslim ruler.

calk US = CAULK.

call v. 1 shout to attract attention. 2 ask to come somewhere. 3 telephone. 4 name or describe as. 5 pay a brief visit. 6 announce an event. •n. 1 an act of calling. 2 a brief visit. 3 a bird or animal's cry. 4 (**call for**) demand or need for. □ **call centre** an office which handles large numbers of phone calls for an organization. **call for** require. **call off** cancel. **call on** turn to for help. ■ **caller** n.

calligraphy n. decorative handwriting. ■ **calligrapher** n.

calling n. 1 a profession or occupation. 2 a vocation.

callisthenics (US **calisthenics**) pl. n. gymnastic exercises.

callous adj. insensitive and cruel. •n. (or **callus**) a patch of hardened skin. ■ **calloused** adj. **callousness** n.

callow adj. inexperienced and immature.

calm adj. 1 not nervous, angry, or excited. 2 peaceful and undisturbed. •n. a calm state or period. •v. make or become calm. ■ **calmly** adv. **calmness** n.

calorie n. (pl. **calories**) 1 a unit for measuring how much energy food will produce. 2 a unit of heat.

calorific adj. of heat or calories.

calumny n. (pl. **calumnies**) slander.

calve v. give birth to a calf.

calves pl. of CALF.

Calvinism n. the form of Protestantism following the teachings of John Calvin. ■ **Calvinist** n.

calypso n. (pl. **calypsos**) a West Indian song on a topical theme.

calyx n. (pl. **calyces** or **calyxes**) the ring of leaves (sepals) covering a flower bud.

cam n. a projecting part on a wheel or shaft changing rotary into to-and-fro motion. □ **camshaft** a shaft with one or more cams attached.

camaraderie n. trust and friendship.

camber n. a slight upward curve on a horizontal surface, esp. a road.

cambric n. a light linen or cotton fabric.

camcorder n. a combined video camera and video recorder.

came past of COME.

camel n. a large mammal of desert countries, with either one or two humps on the back.

camellia n. a shrub with showy flowers.

cameo n. (pl. **cameos**) 1 a piece of jewellery with a head carved in relief on a differently coloured background. 2 a small role played by a well-known actor.

camera n. a device for taking photos or recording moving images. □ **in camera** Law with the press and public excluded.

camiknickers pl. n. a woman's one-piece undergarment combining a camisole and knickers.

camisole n. a woman's loose-fitting undergarment for the upper body.

camomile (or **chamomile**) /kam-uh-myl/ n. a plant with white and yellow flowers.

camouflage n. 1 clothing etc. used to make soldiers and military equipment blend in with the surroundings. 2 an animal's natural appearance which allows it to blend in with its surroundings. •v. hide by means of camouflage.

camp n. **1** a place where soldiers, refugees, etc. live temporarily in tents or huts. **2** a complex of buildings for holidaymakers. **3** the supporters of a particular party or viewpoint. •v. live in tent while on holiday. •adj. informal exaggeratedly effeminate or theatrical. □ **camp bed** a folding portable bed. ■ **camper** n.

campaign n. **1** a series of military operations in a particular area. **2** an organized course of action to achieve a goal. •v. work towards a goal. ■ **campaigner** n.

campanology n. the art of bell-ringing.

camphor n. a strong-smelling substance used esp. in insect repellents.

campus n. (pl. **campuses**) the grounds and buildings of a university or college.

can¹ aux. v. (past **could**) be able or allowed to.

can² n. a cylindrical metal container. •v. (**canning**, **canned**) preserve in a can.

Canadian n. a person from Canada. •adj. of Canada.

canal n. **1** an artificial waterway. **2** a tubular passage in a plant or animal.

canapé /kan-uh-pay/ n. a small piece of bread or pastry with a savoury topping.

canard n. an unfounded rumour.

canary n. (pl. **canaries**) a bright yellow finch with a tuneful song.

cancan n. a lively high-kicking stage dance.

cancel v. (**cancelling**, **cancelled**; US **canceling**, **canceled**) **1** decide that a planned event will not happen. **2** end an agreement. **3** (**cancel out**) have an equal but opposite effect on. **4** mark a ticket to show that it has been used. ■ **cancellation** n.

cancer n. **1** a disease caused by uncontrolled growth of abnormal cells. **2** a harmful tumour resulting from this. ■ **cancerous** adj.

candela n. the basic unit of luminous intensity.

candelabrum (or **candelabra**) n. (pl. **candelabra**) a large branched candlestick.

candid adj. truthful and straightforward. ■ **candidly** adv.

candidate n. a person applying for a job, nominated for election, or taking an exam. ■ **candidacy** n.

candied adj. (of fruit) preserved in sugar.

candle n. a stick of wax with a central wick which is burnt to give light. □ **candlestick** a holder for a candle.

candour (US **candor**) n. frankness.

candy n. (pl. **candies**) US sweets. □ **candyfloss** a mass of spun sugar on a stick.

cane n. **1** the hollow stem of tall reeds, grasses, etc. **2** a stick used as a support or to beat someone. •v. beat with a cane.

canine /kay-nyn/ adj. of dogs. •n. a pointed tooth next to the incisors.

canister n. a cylindrical container.

canker n. **1** a fungal disease of plants. **2** a disease in animals causing open sores.

cannabis n. a drug obtained from the hemp plant.

cannelloni pl. n. rolls of pasta with a savoury filling.

cannibal n. a person who eats human flesh. ■ **cannibalism** n.

cannibalize → cape

cannibalize (or **-ise**) v. use a machine as a source of spare parts for others.

cannon n. (pl. **cannon** or **cannons**) a large heavy gun. • v. bump heavily into.

cannonade n. continuous heavy gunfire.

cannot contr. can not.

canny adj. (**cannier, canniest**) shrewd. ■ **cannily** adv.

canoe n. a narrow boat with pointed ends, propelled with a paddle. • v. (**canoeing, canoed**) travel in a canoe. ■ **canoeist** n.

canon n. **1** a general rule or principle. **2** the authentic set of works of an author or artist. **3** a member of the clergy of a cathedral. ■ **canonical** adj.

canonize (or **-ise**) v. officially declare a dead person to be a saint. ■ **canonization** n.

canoodle v. informal kiss and cuddle.

canopy n. (pl. **canopies**) a cloth covering held up over a throne or bed. ■ **canopied** adj.

cant n. **1** insincere talk. **2** the language of a particular group.

can't contr. cannot.

cantaloupe n. a small melon with orange flesh.

cantankerous adj. bad-tempered and uncooperative.

cantata n. a musical work for accompanied solo voices and chorus.

canteen n. **1** a restaurant in a workplace, school, etc. **2** a case of cutlery.

canter n. a horse's pace between a trot and a gallop. • v. move at a canter.

cantilever n. a girder fixed at only one end, used in bridge construction.

canto n. (pl. **cantos**) a section of a long poem.

canton n. a political division of a country, esp. Switzerland.

canvas n. (pl. **canvases** or **canvasses**) **1** a strong coarse cloth. **2** an oil painting on canvas.

canvass v. **1** visit someone to seek their vote in an election. **2** question someone to find out their opinion. ■ **canvasser** n.

canyon n. a deep gorge.

cap n. **1** a soft hat with a peak. **2** a lid or cover. **3** an upper limit on spending or borrowing. **4** a case of explosive powder for a toy gun. • v. (**capping, capped**) **1** put a cover on. **2** provide a fitting end to. **3** put a limit on. **4** (**be capped**) be chosen as a member of a national sports team.

capable adj. **1** having the ability to do something. **2** competent and efficient. ■ **capability** n. **capably** adv.

capacious adj. roomy.

capacitance n. the ability to store electric charge.

capacitor n. a device used to store electric charge.

capacity n. (pl. **capacities**) **1** the maximum amount that something can contain or produce. **2** the ability to do something. **3** a role or position: *employed in a voluntary capacity.*

caparison v. (**be caparisoned**) be dressed in rich decorative coverings.

cape n. **1** a short cloak. **2** a coastal promontory.

caper¹ v. skip about in a lively way. • n. *informal* a light-hearted or dishonest activity.

caper² n. an edible pickled flower bud.

capillarity (or **capillary action**) n. the force which acts on a liquid in a narrow tube to push it up or down.

capillary n. (pl. **capillaries**) a very small blood vessel or tube.

capital n. 1 the chief city of a country or region. 2 wealth that is owned, invested, lent, or borrowed. 3 a capital letter. 4 the top part of a pillar. • adj. 1 (of a letter) large and used to begin sentences and names. 2 involving the death penalty. 3 *informal, dated* excellent.

capitalism n. a system in which a country's trade and industry are controlled by private owners. ■ **capitalist** n. & adj.

capitalize (or **-ise**) v. 1 (**capitalize on**) take advantage of. 2 convert into or provide with financial capital. 3 write as or with a capital letter. ■ **capitalization** n.

capitation n. a fee or tax of an equal amount per person.

capitulate v. give in to an opponent or demand. ■ **capitulation** n.

capon /kay-pon/ n. a castrated domestic cock fattened up for eating.

cappuccino /kap-puh-chee-noh/ n. (pl. **cappuccinos**) coffee made with frothed milk.

caprice /kuh-preess/ n. a sudden change of mood.

capricious adj. prone to sudden changes of mood. ■ **capriciously** adv.

capsicum n. a sweet pepper.

capsize v. (of a boat) overturn.

capstan n. a broad revolving post used to wind a cable.

capsule n. 1 a small soluble gelatin case containing medicine. 2 a small case or container.

captain n. 1 the person in command of a ship or civil aircraft. 2 the naval rank above commander. 3 the army rank above lieutenant. 4 the leader of a team. • v. be the captain of. ■ **captaincy** n.

caption n. 1 a title or explanation printed with a picture etc. 2 a piece of text appearing with a film or television broadcast.

captious adj. prone to petty fault-finding.

captivate v. attract and hold the interest of.

captive n. a person who is held prisoner. • adj. unable to leave or choose: *a captive audience.* ■ **captivity** n.

captor n. a person who captures another.

capture v. 1 take or get by force. 2 take prisoner. 3 record accurately in words or pictures. 4 cause data to be stored in a computer. • n. the act of capturing.

car n. 1 a motor vehicle for a small number of people. 2 a railway carriage. □ **carport** an open-sided shelter for a car.

carafe /kuh-raf/ n. a glass flask for serving wine or water.

caramel n. 1 sugar or syrup heated until brown. 2 a toffee made with sugar and butter. ■ **caramelize** (or **-ise**) v.

carapace n. the hard upper shell of a tortoise, lobster, etc.

carat n. 1 a measure of the purity of gold. 2 a unit of weight for precious stones.

caravan n. 1 a vehicle equipped for living in, able to be towed by a vehicle or a horse. 2 a group of people with vehicles or animals who are travelling together. ■ **caravanning** n.

caraway n. a spice made from the seeds of a plant.

carbine n. an automatic rifle.

carbohydrate n. an energy-producing substance (e.g. sugar and starch) found in food.

carbolic (or **carbolic acid**) n. a disinfectant.

carbon n. a chemical element with two main pure forms (diamond and graphite), found in all organic compounds. □ **carbon copy** 1 a copy made with carbon paper. 2 a person or thing identical to another. **carbon dating** a way of finding out the age of an object by measuring how much radioactive carbon is in it. **carbon dioxide** a gas produced by burning carbon and also by breathing. **carbon monoxide** a poisonous flammable gas. **carbon paper** thin paper coated with carbon, used to make a copy of a document.

carbonate n. a compound containing carbon and oxygen together with a metal.

carbonated adj. (of a drink) fizzy because it contains dissolved carbon dioxide.

carborundum n. a very hard black substance used for grinding and polishing.

carboy n. a large round bottle with a narrow neck, used for holding acids.

carbuncle n. 1 a severe abscess. 2 a garnet cut in a round shape.

carburettor (US **carburetor**) n. a device in an engine that mixes air with the fuel.

carcass (or **carcase**) n. 1 the dead body of an animal. 2 the structural framework or remains of something.

carcinogen /kar-sin-uh-juhn/ n. a substance that can cause cancer. ■ **carcinogenic** adj.

carcinoma /kar-si-noh-muh/ n. (pl. **carcinomas**) a cancerous tumour.

card n. 1 thick, stiff paper or thin cardboard. 2 a piece of card printed with information, greetings, etc. 3 a rectangle of plastic containing information readable by a computer: *a credit card.* 4 a playing card. 5 (**cards**) a game played with playing cards. • v. comb wool with a toothed instrument. □ **cardboard** stiff paper made from paper pulp. **card sharp** a person who cheats at cards.

cardamom n. a spice used in cooking.

cardiac adj. of the heart.

cardigan n. a knitted jumper with buttons down the front.

cardinal n. a leading Roman Catholic clergyman. • adj. most important; chief. □ **cardinal number** a number expressing quantity (1, 2, 3, etc.), rather than order.

cardiograph n. an instrument recording heart movements.

cardiology n. the branch of medicine concerned with the heart. ■ **cardiologist** n.

care n. 1 special attention to avoid damage, risk, or error. 2 the provision of welfare and protection. 3 a cause for anxiety, or a worried feeling. • v. 1 feel concern or interest. 2 feel affection or liking.

3 (**care for/to do**) like to have or be willing to do. **4** (**care for**) look after.

careen v. (of a ship) tilt to one side.

career n. an occupation undertaken for a long period of a person's life. •v. move swiftly in an uncontrolled way.

careerist n. a person intent on progressing in their career.

carefree adj. free from anxiety or responsibility.

careful adj. **1** taking care to avoid harm or trouble. **2** showing thought and attention. ∎ **carefully** adv.

careless adj. not giving enough attention to avoiding harm or mistakes. ∎ **carelessly** adv. **carelessness** n.

carer n. a person who cares for a sick, elderly, or disabled person.

caress v. touch or stroke gently or lovingly. •n. a gentle or loving touch.

caretaker n. a person employed to look after a public building.

careworn adj. showing signs of prolonged worry.

cargo n. (pl. **cargoes** or **cargos**) goods carried on a ship, aircraft, or truck.

Caribbean adj. of the Caribbean Sea and its islands.

❗ One r, two bs: Caribbean.

caribou n. (pl. **caribou**) US a reindeer.

caricature n. a portrayal in which a person's characteristics are comically exaggerated. •v. make a caricature of. ∎ **caricaturist** n.

caries /kair-eez/ n. decay of a tooth or bone.

carillon /ka-ril-lyuhn/ n. a set of bells sounded by an automatic mechanism.

carmine n. vivid crimson.

carnage n. the killing of a large number of people.

carnal adj. of sexual urges and activities. ∎ **carnally** adv.

carnation n. a garden plant with pink, red, or white flowers.

carnelian (or **cornelian**) n. a dull red or pink semi-precious stone.

carnival n. a public festival involving a procession and music.

carnivore n. an animal that eats meat. ∎ **carnivorous** adj.

carob n. a chocolate substitute made from the pod of an Arabian tree.

carol n. a Christmas hymn or song. •v. (**carolling**, **carolled**; US **caroling**, **caroled**) **1** sing carols. **2** sing or say happily.

carotene n. an orange or red substance found in carrots, tomatoes, etc.

carotid artery /kuh-rot-id/ n. either of the two main arteries carrying blood to the head.

carouse /kuh-rowz/ v. drink alcohol and enjoy yourself.

carousel n. **1** a merry-go-round at a fair. **2** a conveyor system for baggage at an airport.

carp n. (pl. **carp**) an edible freshwaterfish. •v. complain continually.

carpel n. the female reproductive organ of a flower.

carpenter n. a person who makes wooden objects and structures. ∎ **carpentry** n.

carpet n. **1** a floor covering of thick woven fabric. **2** a thick, soft layer. •v. (**carpeting**, **carpeted**) **1** cover with a carpet. **2** informal reprimand severely. □ **carpet-bomb** bomb an area intensively.

carpus n. (pl. **carpi**) the group of small bones in the wrist. ■ **carpal** adj.

carriage n. **1** a horse-drawn passenger vehicle. **2** a passenger vehicle in a train. **3** the carrying of goods from one place to another. **4** a person's way of standing or moving. □ **carriage clock** a portable clock with a handle on top. **carriageway** the part of a road intended for vehicles.

carrier n. **1** a person or thing carrying something. **2** a company that transports goods or people. □ **carrier bag** a plastic or paper shopping bag.

carrion n. the decaying flesh of dead animals.

carrot n. **1** a tapering orange root vegetable. **2** an incentive.

carry v. (**carrying**, **carried**) **1** move or take somewhere. **2** support the weight of. **3** assume responsibility. **4** have as a feature or result. **5** (of a sound or voice) be heard from a distance. **6** approve a proposal by a majority of votes. **7** (**carry yourself**) stand and move in a specified way. □ **be/get carried away** lose self-control. **carry off 1** succeed in doing. **2** take away by force. **carry on** continue. **carry out** perform a task.

cart n. an open, wheeled vehicle for carrying loads. • v. **1** transport in a cart. **2** informal carry with difficulty. □ **carthorse** a large, strong horse. **cartwheel** a sideways handspring with the arms and legs extended.

carte blanche /kart blahnsh/ n. complete freedom to act as you wish.

cartel n. a group of manufacturers or suppliers formed to keep prices high.

cartilage n. firm, flexible tissue forming part of the skeleton of vertebrates.

cartography n. map-drawing. ■ **cartographer** n.

carton n. a cardboard container.

cartoon n. **1** a humorous drawing. **2** an animated film made from a sequence of drawings. ■ **cartoonist** n.

cartridge n. **1** a container holding film, ink, etc., for inserting into a mechanism. **2** a casing containing a charge and a bullet for a gun. □ **cartridge paper** thick drawing paper.

carve v. **1** cut into a hard material to form an object or design. **2** cut cooked meat into slices. ■ **carving** n.

carvery n. (pl. **carveries**) a restaurant where cooked joints are carved as required.

Casanova n. a man known for seducing many women.

casbah n. var. of KASBAH.

cascade n. **1** a waterfall. **2** a mass of something falling or hanging down. • v. fall or flow in large quantities.

case n. **1** an instance of a particular situation. **2** a lawsuit. **3** a set of arguments supporting one side of a debate or lawsuit. **4** a container. **5** a suitcase. **6** a form of a noun, adjective, or pronoun expressing its role in a sentence. • v. enclose in a case.

casement n. a window hinged at one side.

cash n. money in coins or notes. • v. **1** give or obtain notes or coins for a cheque. **2** (**cash in on**) informal take advantage of. **3** (**cash in**) convert an insurance policy or savings account into money. □ **cashpoint** *trademark* a machine dispensing cash when a special card is inserted.

cashew *n.* an edible kidney-shaped nut.

cashier *n.* a person who pays out and receives money in a shop, bank, etc. •*v.* dismiss from the armed forces.

cashmere *n.* very fine soft wool.

casing *n.* a protective cover.

casino *n.* (*pl.* **casinos**) a public building or room for gambling.

cask *n.* a large barrel for storing alcoholic drinks.

casket *n.* **1** a small ornamental box for valuables. **2** *esp. US* a coffin.

cassava *n.* the starchy root of a tropical American tree, used as food.

casserole *n.* **1** a covered dish for cooking food slowly. **2** a kind of stew cooked slowly. •*v.* cook in a casserole.

cassette *n.* a sealed case containing audio tape, videotape, etc.

cassock *n.* a long garment worn by some Christian clergy and members of church choirs.

cassowary *n.* (*pl.* **cassowaries**) a large flightless bird, native to New Guinea.

cast *v.* **1** throw forcefully. **2** direct the eyes or thoughts towards something. **3** cause light or shadow to appear on something. **4** register a vote. **5** give a part to an actor or allocate parts in a play or film. **6** leave aside or discard. **7** shape molten metal in a mould. **8** make a magic spell. •*n.* **1** the actors in a play or film. **2** an object made by casting molten metal.

3 (or **plaster cast**) a bandage stiffened with plaster of Paris to support and protect a broken limb. **4** appearance or character. □ **casting vote** an extra vote used by a chairperson to decide an issue when votes on each side are equal.

cast iron a hard alloy of iron and carbon cast in a mould. **cast-iron** firm and unchangeable. **cast-off** a discarded garment.

castanets *pl. n.* two small curved pieces of wood, clicked together in the hand to accompany Spanish dancing.

castaway *n.* a shipwrecked person.

caste *n.* each of the Hindu social classes.

castellated *adj.* having battlements.

castigate *v.* reprimand severely. ■ **castigation** *n.*

castle *n.* a large medieval fortified building.

castor (or **caster**) *n.* **1** a small swivelling wheel fixed to the legs or base of a piece of furniture. **2** a small container with a perforated top for sprinkling salt, sugar, etc. □ **castor oil** oil from the seeds of an African shrub, used as a laxative. **castor sugar** white sugar in fine granules.

castrate *v.* remove the testicles of. ■ **castration** *n.*

casual *adj.* **1** relaxed and unconcerned. **2** lacking care or thought. **3** not regular; occasional: *casual work*. **4** happening by chance. **5** informal. ■ **casually** *adv.*

casualty *n.* (*pl.* **casualties**) a person killed or injured in a conflict or accident.

casuistry *n.* the use of clever but false reasoning. ■ **casuist** *n.*

cat *n.* **1** a small furry mammal kept as a pet. **2** a wild animal related to this. ◻ **catcall** a whistle of disapproval. **catgut** material used for the strings of musical instruments, made of the dried intestines of sheep or horses. **catkin** a spike of small flowers hanging from a willow etc. **catnap** a short nap. **catseye** *trademark* each of a series of reflective studs marking the lanes of a road. **cat's paw** a person used by another to perform an unpleasant task. **catsuit** a woman's close-fitting one-piece garment. **catwalk** a narrow platform along which models walk to display clothes.

cataclysm *n.* a violent upheaval or disaster. ■ **cataclysmic** *adj.*

catacomb /kat-uh-koom/ *n.* an underground cemetery with recesses for tombs.

catafalque *n.* a decorated wooden support for a coffin.

catalepsy *n.* a medical condition involving loss of consciousness and the body becoming rigid. ■ **cataleptic** *adj. & n.*

catalogue (*US* catalog) *n.* **1** a list of items arranged in order. **2** a publication containing details of items for sale. •*v.* (**cataloguing, catalogued**; *US* **cataloging, cataloged**) list in a catalogue.

catalyse *v.* cause or speed up a reaction by acting as a catalyst. ■ **catalysis** *n.*

catalyst *n.* **1** a person or thing that causes something to happen. **2** a substance that speeds up a chemical reaction while remaining unchanged itself.

catalytic converter *n.* a device in a vehicle's exhaust system for converting pollutant gases into less harmful ones.

catamaran *n.* a boat with twin parallel hulls.

catapult *n.* a forked stick with an elastic band attached, for shooting small stones. •*v.* throw forcefully.

cataract *n.* **1** a cloudy area on the lens of the eye, causing blurred vision. **2** a large waterfall.

catarrh /kuh-tar/ *n.* excessive mucus in the nose or throat.

catastrophe /kuh-tass-truh-fi/ *n.* a sudden great disaster. ■ **catastrophic** *adj.* **catastrophically** *adv.*

catatonia /kat-uh-toh-ni-uh/ *n.* a medical condition involving periods of unconsciousness or overactivity. ■ **catatonic** *adj.*

catch *v.* (**catching, caught**) **1** seize and hold something moving. **2** capture. **3** be in time to board a vehicle or see a person etc. **4** surprise someone in the act of doing something. **5** hear or understand. **6** become infected with. •*n.* **1** an act of catching. **2** a device for fastening a window etc. **3** a hidden problem. **4** an amount of fish caught. ◻ **catch on** *informal* **1** become popular. **2** understand. **catch out** discover that someone has done something wrong. **catchphrase** a well-known phrase. **catch-22** a difficult situation from which there is no escape because it involves conflicting conditions. **catch up** **1** succeed in reaching a person ahead. **2** do tasks that should have been done earlier. **catchword** a word or phrase frequently used to sum something up.

catching *adj.* infectious.

catchment area *n.* **1** the area from which a hospital's patients or a school's pupils are drawn. **2** the area from which rainfall flows into a river or lake.

catchy *adj.* (**catchier, catchiest**) (of a tune) appealing and easy to remember.

catechism /kat-i-ki-z'm/ *n.* a summary of the principles of Christian religion in the form of questions and answers.

catechize (or **-ise**) *v.* teach by using a catechism.

categorical (or **categoric**) *adj.* completely clear and direct. ■ **categorically** *adv.*

categorize (or **-ise**) *v.* place in a category. ■ **categorization** *n.*

category *n.* (*pl.* **categories**) a class of people or things with shared characteristics.

cater *v.* **1** (**cater for**) provide food and drink. **2** (**cater for/to**) provide with what is needed or required. ■ **caterer** *n.*

caterpillar *n.* **1** the larva of a butterfly or moth. **2** (or **caterpillar track** or **tread**) *trademark* a steel band passing round the wheels of a vehicle for travel on rough ground.

caterwaul /kat-er-wawl/ *v.* wail or howl.

catharsis *n.* the release of pent-up emotions. ■ **cathartic** *adj.*

cathedral *n.* the principal church of a diocese.

Catherine wheel *n.* a rotating firework.

catheter *n.* a tube inserted into the bladder etc. to remove fluid.

cathode *n.* an electrode with a negative charge. ☐ **cathode ray tube** a vacuum tube in which beams of electrons produce a luminous image on a fluorescent screen.

catholic *adj.* **1** including a wide range of things. **2** (**Catholic**) Roman Catholic. •*n.* (**Catholic**) Roman Catholic. ■ **Catholicism** *n.*

cation /kat-I-uhn/ *n.* an ion with a positive charge.

cattery *n.* (*pl.* **catteries**) a place where cats are kept while their owners are away.

cattle *pl. n.* cows, bulls, and oxen.

catty *adj.* spiteful.

Caucasian /kaw-kay-zh'n/ *adj.* **1** of peoples from Europe, western Asia, and parts of India and North Africa. **2** white-skinned.

caucus *n.* (*pl.* **caucuses**) **1** a meeting of a political party's policy-making committee. **2** a group with shared concerns within a larger organization.

caught past & past part. of **CATCH**.

caul *n.* a membrane enclosing a fetus in the womb.

cauldron (*US* **caldron**) *n.* a large metal cooking pot.

cauliflower *n.* a vegetable with a large white flower head.

caulk (*US* **calk**) *n.* a waterproof substance for filling cracks and joins.

causal *adj.* of or being a cause. ■ **causally** *adv.* **causality** *n.*

causation *n.* the causing of an effect. ■ **causative** *adj.*

cause *n.* **1** a person or thing that produces an effect. **2** a reason for doing something. **3** a principle or movement to support. •*v.* make happen. ☐ **cause célèbre** (*pl.* **causes célèbres**) a matter causing great public interest.

causeway *n.* a raised road across low or wet ground.

caustic *adj.* **1** able to burn by chemical action. **2** sarcastic. ☐ **caustic soda** sodium hydroxide.

cauterize (or **-ise**) v. burn the area around a wound to stop bleeding or prevent infection.

caution n. 1 care taken to avoid danger or mistakes. 2 a formal warning given for a minor offence. •v. 1 warn. 2 give a caution to.

cautionary adj. acting as a warning.

cautious adj. careful to avoid danger or mistakes. ■ **cautiously** adv.

cavalcade n. a procession.

cavalier adj. showing a lack of proper concern. •n. (**Cavalier**) a supporter of Charles I in the English Civil War.

cavalry n. (pl. **cavalries**) soldiers who formerly fought on horseback.

cave n. a natural hollow in a hill or cliff, or underground. •v. 1 (**cave in**) collapse. 2 (**cave in**) give in to demands. 3 (**caving**) exploring caves as a sport.

caveat /ka-vi-at/ n. a warning.

cavern n. a large cave.

cavernous adj. huge or gloomy.

caviar n. the pickled roe of the sturgeon.

cavil v. (**cavilling**, **cavilled**; US **caviling**, **caviled**) raise petty objections. •n. a petty objection.

cavity n. (pl. **cavities**) 1 a hollow space within a solid object. 2 a decayed part of a tooth.

cavort v. jump around excitedly.

caw v. (of a rook or crow) make a harsh cry.

cayenne n. a hot red powder made from dried chillies.

cayman var. of CAIMAN.

CB abbrev. 1 Citizens' Band. 2 Companion of the Order of the Bath.

CBE abbrev. Commander of the Order of the British Empire.

cc (or **c. c.**) abbrev. 1 carbon copy. 2 cubic centimetres.

CCTV abbrev. closed-circuit television.

CD abbrev. compact disc.

CD-ROM n. a compact disc used in a computer as a read-only device for data.

cease v. come or bring to an end. □ **ceasefire** a temporary truce. **ceaseless** never stopping.

cecum US = CAECUM.

cedar n. a coniferous tree with aromatic wood.

cede v. give up power or territory.

cedilla n. a mark ( ) written under the letter c to show that it is pronounced like an s.

ceilidh /kay-li/ n. a social event with Scottish or Irish folk music and dancing.

ceiling n. 1 the top surface of a room. 2 an upper limit.

celandine n. a small yellow-flowered plant.

celebrant n. a person who performs a religious ceremony.

celebrate v. mark an important occasion by doing something special. ■ **celebration** n. **celebratory** adj.

celebrated adj. famous.

celebrity n. (pl. **celebrities**) 1 a famous person. 2 fame.

celeriac n. a vegetable with a large edible root.

celerity n. literary speed.

celery n. a vegetable with crisp stalks.

celestial adj. of heaven or the sky.

celiac n. US = COELIAC.

celibate adj. not marrying or having sex. ■ **celibacy** n.

cell n. 1 a small room for a prisoner, monk, or nun. 2 the smallest unit of a living organism. **3** a small political group. **4** a device for producing electricity by chemical action or light.

cellar *n.* **1** an underground storage room. **2** a stock of wine.

cello /chel-loh/ *n.* (*pl.* **cellos**) a large bass instrument of the violin family. ■ **cellist** *n.*

cellophane *n. trademark* a thin transparent wrapping material.

cellphone *n.* a mobile phone.

cellular *adj.* **1** of or made up of cells. **2** (of a mobile phone system) using a number of short-range radio stations.

cellulite *n.* fat that builds up under the skin, causing a dimpled effect.

celluloid *n.* transparent plastic formerly used for cinema film.

cellulose *n.* a substance in plant tissues, used to make plastics and textiles.

Celsius *n.* a scale of temperature on which water freezes at 0˚ and boils at 100˚.

Celt /kelt/ *n.* a member of an ancient European people or their descendants. ■ **Celtic** *adj.*

cement *n.* a powdery substance made from lime and clay, used to make mortar and concrete. •*v.* **1** fix with cement. **2** strengthen.

cemetery *n.* (*pl.* **cemeteries**) a large burial ground.

cenotaph *n.* a memorial to members of the armed forces killed in a war.

censer *n.* a container for burning incense.

censor *n.* an official who examines books, films, etc. and bans anything considered offensive or a threat to security. •*v.* ban un-

acceptable parts of a book, film, etc. ■ **censorship** *n.*

❗ Don't confuse **censor** with **censure**.

censorious *adj.* very critical.

censure *v.* criticize strongly. •*n.* strong disapproval or criticism.

census *n.* (*pl.* **censuses**) an official count of a population.

cent *n.* a 100th of a dollar, euro, or other decimal currency unit.

centaur *n.* a mythical creature with a man's upper body and a horse's lower body and legs.

centenarian *n.* a person who is 100 or more years old.

centenary *n.* (*pl.* **centenaries**) the 100th anniversary of an event.

centennial *n.* a centenary.

center US = CENTRE.

centigrade *adj.* measured by the Celsius scale of temperature.

centilitre (US **centiliter**) *n.* a 100th of a litre.

centimetre (US **centimeter**) *n.* a 100th of a metre.

centipede *n.* an insect-like creature with many legs.

central *adj.* **1** in or near the centre. **2** very important. ◻ **central heating** heating conducted from a boiler through pipes and radiators. **central nervous system** the brain and spinal cord in vertebrates. ■ **centrally** *n.* **centrally** *adv.*

centralize (or **-ise**) *v.* bring under the control of a central authority. ■ **centralism** *n.* **centralization** *n.*

centre (US **center**) *n.* **1** a point in the middle of something. **2** a place devoted to a particular activity. **3** a point from which something spreads or to which something is directed. •*v.* (**centring**, **centred**)

US **centering, centered** 1 place in the centre. 2 (**centre on/around**) have as a major concern. □ **centrefold** the two middle pages of a magazine.

centrifugal force n. a force which appears to cause something moving round a centre to fly outwards.

centrifuge n. a machine with a rapidly rotating container, used to separate substances.

centurion n. a commander in the ancient Roman army.

century n. (pl. **centuries**) 1 a period of 100 years. 2 a batsman's score of 100 runs in cricket.

cephalopod n. a mollusc of a group including octopuses and squids.

ceramic adj. made of clay hardened by heat. •n. (**ceramics**) the art of making ceramic objects.

cereal n. 1 a grass producing an edible grain, e.g. wheat. 2 a breakfast food made from this.

cerebellum n. (pl. **cerebellums** or **cerebella**) the part of the brain at the back of the skull.

cerebral adj. 1 of the cerebrum. 2 intellectual. □ **cerebral palsy** a medical condition involving difficulty in controlling the muscles.

cerebrum n. (pl. **cerebra**) the main part of the brain.

ceremonial adj. of ceremonies. ■ **ceremonially** adv.

ceremonious adj. done in a grand and formal way. ■ **ceremoniously** adv.

ceremony n. (pl. **ceremonies**) 1 a formal occasion celebrating an event. 2 the set procedures followed at certain formal occasions. □ **stand on ceremony** insist on formal behaviour.

cerise /suh-**reess**/ n. a pinkish red colour.

certain adj. 1 able to be relied on to happen or be the case. 2 feeling sure. 3 specific but not directly stated.

certainly adv. 1 definitely. 2 yes.

certainty n. (pl. **certainties**) 1 the state of being certain. 2 something that is certain.

certifiable adj. able or needing to be officially declared insane.

certificate n. an official document recording a fact or event. ■ **certification** n.

certify v. (**certifying**, **certified**) 1 declare in a certificate. 2 officially declare insane.

certitude n. a feeling of certainty.

cerulean /si-**roo**-li-uhn/ adj. deep blue.

cervical /ser-vi-k'l, ser-vy-k'l/ adj. of the cervix. □ **cervical smear** a specimen of cells taken from the neck of the womb and examined for signs of cancer.

cervix n. (pl. **cervices**) the narrow passage forming the lower end of the womb.

Cesarean US = CAESAREAN.

cesium US = CAESIUM.

cessation n. an act of stopping.

cession n. the giving up of rights or territory by a state.

cesspool (or **cesspit**) n. an underground tank or covered pit for liquid waste and sewage.

cetacean /si-**tay**-sh'n/ n. a sea mammal of a group including whales and dolphins.

cf. abbrev. compare.

CFC abbrev. chlorofluorocarbon, a gas used in fridges and aerosols and harmful to the ozone layer.

chador n. a piece of cloth worn by Muslim women around the head and upper body.

chafe v. **1** make sore or wear away by rubbing. **2** warm by rubbing. **3** become impatient because of restrictions.

chafer n. a large flying beetle.

chaff n. husks of grain separated from the seed. • v. tease.

chaffinch n. a pink-breasted finch.

chagrin n. annoyance or shame at having failed.

chain n. **1** a series of connected metal links. **2** a connected series, set, or sequence. • v. fasten or restrain with a chain. □ **chain reaction** a series of events, each caused by the previous one. **chainsaw** a power-driven saw with teeth set on a moving chain.

chair n. **1** a seat for one person, with a back and four legs. **2** the person in charge of a meeting or an organization. • v. be in charge of a meeting. □ **chairlift** a series of chairs on a moving cable, for carrying passengers up and down a mountain. **chairman** (or **chairwoman**) a person in charge of a meeting or organization. **chairperson** a person in charge of a meeting.

chaise longue /shayz long/ n. (pl. **chaises longues**) a sofa with a backrest at only one end.

chalcedony n. a type of quartz.

chalet /sha-lay/ n. **1** a wooden house with overhanging eaves, found in the Alps. **2** a small cabin used by holidaymakers.

chalice n. a goblet.

chalk n. **1** a white soft limestone. **2** a similar substance made into

sticks, used for drawing or writing. ■ **chalky** adj.

challenge n. **1** a demanding task or situation. **2** an invitation to take part in a contest or to prove something. • v. **1** dispute or query something. **2** call on someone to fight or do something difficult. ■ **challenger** n. **challenging** adj.

chamber n. **1** a large room for formal or public events. **2** an enclosed space or cavity. **3** each of the houses of a parliament. **4** (**chambers**) rooms used by a barrister. **5** old use a bedroom. □ **chambermaid** a woman who cleans rooms in a hotel. **chamber music** classical music played by a small group of musicians. **chamber pot** a bowl kept in a bedroom and used as a toilet.

chamberlain n. hist. an officer who managed the household of a monarch or noble.

chameleon /kuh-mee-li-uhn/ n. a small lizard that changes colour according to its surroundings.

chamfer /cham-fer/ v. (**chamfering**, **chamfered**) cut an angled edge on.

chamois n. (pl. **chamois**) **1** /sham-wah/ a mountain antelope of southern Europe. **2** /sham-mi/ a piece of soft leather for cleaning windows etc.

chamomile var. of **CAMOMILE**.

champ v. munch noisily. □ **champ at the bit** be very impatient.

champagne n. a white sparkling French wine.

champion n. **1** the winner of a contest. **2** a person who argues or fights for a cause. • v. strongly support. ■ **championship** n.

chance n. **1** a possibility of something happening. **2** an opportunity. **3** occurrence without any obvious plan or cause. •v. **1** happen or do something by chance. **2** informal do something risky. ◻ **on the off chance** just in case.

chancel n. the part of a church near the altar.

chancellor n. **1** a senior state or legal official. **2** the head of the government in some European countries. **3** (or **Chancellor of the Exchequer**) (in the UK) the chief finance minister. ■ **chancellorship** n.

Chancery n. (in the UK) a division of the High Court of Justice.

chancy adj. informal risky.

chandelier n. a large hanging light with branches for several light bulbs or candles.

chandler n. a dealer in supplies for ships.

change v. **1** make or become different. **2** exchange for another. **3** move from one to another. **4** exchange a sum of money for the same sum in a different currency or smaller units. •n. **1** an act of changing. **2** money returned as the balance of a sum paid. **3** coins as opposed to banknotes. ◻ **changeling** a child believed to have been exchanged by fairies for the parents' real child. **changeover** a change from one system etc. to another. ■ **changeable** adj. **changeless** adj.

channel n. **1** a band of frequencies used in radio and television transmission. **2** a means of communication. **3** a passage along which liquid flows. **4** a stretch of water joining two seas. •v. (**channelling**, **channelled**; US **channeling**, **channeled**) direct towards a purpose or by a particular route.

chant n. a repeated rhythmic phrase, shouted or sung. •v. say, shout, or sing rhythmically.

chaos n. complete disorder and confusion. ■ **chaotic** adj. **chaotically** adv.

chap n. informal a man.

chapatti n. (pl. **chapattis**) (in Indian cookery) a flat round piece of unleavened bread.

chapel n. **1** a small building or room for Christian worship. **2** a part of a large church with its own altar.

chaperone n. **1** a person who accompanies and looks after another person or people. **2** dated an older woman in charge of an unmarried girl at social occasions. •v. go with and look after.

chaplain n. a member of the clergy attached to a chapel in a private house or an institution, or to a military unit. ■ **chaplaincy** n.

chapped adj. (of the skin) cracked and sore.

chapter n. **1** a main division of a book. **2** the governing body of a cathedral or other religious community.

char v. (**charring**, **charred**) blacken by burning. •n. informal **1** a woman employed to clean a house. **2** tea.

charabanc /sha-ruh-bang/ n. an early form of bus.

character n. **1** the distinctive qualities of a person or thing. **2** strong personal qualities. **3** a person's good reputation. **4** a person in a novel, play, or film. **5** informal an eccentric or amusing person. **6** a printed or written letter or symbol. ■ **characterless** adj.

characteristic n. a quality typical of a person or thing. •adj. typical of a particular person or thing. ■ **characteristically** adv.

characterize (or **-ise**) v. 1 describe the character of. 2 be typical of. ■ **characterization** n.

charade /shuh-rahd/ n. 1 an absurd pretence. 2 (**charades**) a game of guessing a word or phrase from acted clues.

charcoal n. a black form of carbon made by burning wood slowly.

charge v. 1 ask an amount as a price. 2 formally accuse someone of something. 3 rush forward, esp. in attack. 4 entrust with a task. 5 store electrical energy in a battery. 6 fill with. • n. 1 a price asked. 2 a formal accusation against someone. 3 responsibility for care or control. 4 a person or thing entrusted to someone's care. 5 a rush forward. 6 electricity existing naturally in a substance. 7 energy stored in a battery. 8 a quantity of explosive. □ **charge card** a credit card issued by a shop. ■ **chargeable** adj.

chargé d'affaires /shar-zhay da-fair/ n. (pl. **chargés d'affaires**) an ambassador's deputy.

charger n. 1 a device for charging a battery. 2 a cavalry horse.

chariot n. a two-wheeled horse-drawn vehicle, used in ancient warfare and racing. ■ **charioteer** n.

charisma /kuh-riz-muh/ n. the power to inspire admiration or enthusiasm in other people. ■ **charismatic** adj.

charitable adj. 1 of charity or charities. 2 tolerant in judging others. ■ **charitably** adv.

charity n. (pl. **charities**) 1 an organization set up to help people in need. 2 the giving of money or help to people in need. 3 tolerance in judging others.

charlatan n. a person falsely claiming to have a skill.

charm n. 1 the power to delight or fascinate others. 2 a small ornament worn on a bracelet. 3 an object or saying believed to have magic power. • v. 1 delight greatly. 2 influence someone by using your charm. 3 (**charmed**) unusually lucky as if protected by magic. ■ **charmer** n.

charming adj. very pleasant, attractive, or likeable.

charnel house n. hist. a building in which corpses or bones were kept.

chart n. 1 a table, graph, or diagram. 2 a map for navigation. 3 (**the charts**) a weekly listing of the current best-selling pop records. • v. plot or record on a chart.

charter n. 1 an official document granting or setting out rights. 2 a document setting out an organization's functions. 3 the hiring of an aircraft, ship, or vehicle. • v. 1 hire an aircraft, ship, or vehicle. 2 grant a charter to. □ **charter flight** a flight by an aircraft chartered for a specific journey.

chartered adj. (of an accountant, engineer, etc.) qualified as a member of a professional body that has a royal charter.

chary adj. cautiously reluctant.

chase v. 1 pursue so as to catch. 2 try to get. • n. 1 an act of chasing. 2 (**the chase**) hunting as a sport.

chaser n. informal a strong alcoholic drink taken after a weaker one.

chasm n. a deep crack in the earth.

chassis /shas-si/ n. (pl. **chassis** /shas-siz/) the base frame of a vehicle.

chaste adj. 1 not having sex at all or not having sex outside marriage. 2 simple and undecorated. ∎ **chastity** n.

chasten v. cause to feel subdued or ashamed.

chastise v. reprimand severely. ∎ **chastisement** n.

chat v. (**chatting**, **chatted**) talk in an informal way. • n. an informal conversation. □ **chat room** an area on the Internet where users can email each other. ∎ **chatty** adj.

chateau /sha-toh/ n. (pl. **chateaux** or **chateaus**) a large French country house or castle.

chatelaine /sha-tuh-layn/ n. dated a woman in charge of a large house.

chattel n. a personal possession.

chatter v. 1 talk informally about unimportant matters. 2 (of teeth) click together. • n. 1 informal talk. 2 a series of short high-pitched sounds. □ **chatterbox** informal a person who chatters.

chauffeur n. a person employed to drive a car.

chauvinism n. 1 extreme or unreasonable support for your own country. 2 the belief held by some men that men are superior to women. ∎ **chauvinist** n. & adj. **chauvinistic** adj.

cheap adj. 1 low in price. 2 charging low prices. 3 low in price and quality. 4 worthless because achieved in a regrettable way. □ **cheapskate** informal a miserly person. ∎ **cheapen** v. **cheaply** adv. **cheapness** n.

cheat v. 1 act dishonestly or unfairly to gain an advantage. 2 deprive of something by unfair or dishonest means. • n. a person who cheats.

check v. 1 examine the accuracy or quality of. 2 make sure that something is the case. 3 stop or slow the progress of. 4 Chess move a piece to a square where it directly attacks the opposing king. • n. 1 an act of checking. 2 a control or restraint. 3 a pattern of small squares. 4 US a restaurant bill. 5 US = **CHEQUE**. • adj. (or **checked**) having a pattern of small squares. □ **check in** register at a hotel or airport. **checkmate** Chess a position from which a king cannot escape. **checkout** a point at which goods are paid for in a shop. **check out** pay a hotel bill before leaving. **checkpoint** a barrier where security checks are carried out on travellers. **check-up** a medical examination.

checkers US = **CHEQUERS**.

Cheddar n. a firm smooth cheese.

cheek n. 1 either side of the face below the eye. 2 rude or disrespectful remarks or behaviour. • v. informal speak rudely to.

cheeky adj. (**cheekier**, **cheekiest**) cheerfully disrespectful. ∎ **cheekily** adv. **cheekiness** n.

cheep n. a shrill cry made by a young bird. • v. make a cheep.

cheer v. 1 shout for joy or to praise or encourage. 2 (**cheer up**) make or become less miserable. • n. 1 a shout of joy, encouragement, or praise. 2 cheerfulness; optimism.

cheerful adj. 1 happy and optimistic. 2 bright and pleasant. ∎ **cheerfully** adv. **cheerfulness** n.

cheerless adj. gloomy; depressing.

cheers exclam. informal **1** expressing good wishes before drinking. **2** thank you. **3** goodbye.

cheery adj. (**cheerier**, **cheeriest**) happy and optimistic. ■ **cheerily** adv. **cheeriness** n.

cheese n. a food made from the pressed curds of milk. □ **cheesecake** a rich sweet tart made with cream and soft cheese. **cheesecloth** thin, loosely woven cotton cloth. **cheese-paring** meanness with money. ■ **cheesy** adj.

cheetah n. a large swift spotted cat of Africa and Asia.

chef n. a professional cook.

chef d'oeuvre /shay-dervr/ n. (pl. **chefs d'oeuvre**) a masterpiece.

chemical adj. of chemistry or chemicals. ▪ n. an artificially prepared or purified substance. ■ **chemically** adv.

chemise /shuh-meez/ n. a woman's loose-fitting dress or petticoat.

chemist n. **1** a person authorized to dispense medicines prescribed by a doctor. **2** a shop where medicines, toiletries, etc. are sold. **3** a scientist who studies chemistry.

chemistry n. **1** the scientific study of the nature of substances and how they react with each other. **2** attraction or interaction between two people.

chemotherapy /kee-moh-the-ruh-pi/ n. the treatment of cancer with drugs.

chenille /shuh-neel/ n. a fabric with a velvety pile.

cheque (US **check**) n. a written order to a bank to pay a stated sum from an account. □ **cheque**

card a card issued by a bank guaranteeing payment of cheques.

chequered adj. **1** marked with chequers. **2** marked by periods of varied fortune.

chequers (US **checkers**) n. **1** a pattern of alternately coloured squares. **2** (**checkers**) US the game of draughts.

cherish v. **1** protect and care for lovingly. **2** remember, esp. with pleasure.

cheroot n. a cigar with both ends open.

cherry n. (pl. **cherries**) **1** a small, round red fruit with a stone. **2** a bright deep red colour.

cherub n. **1** (pl. **cherubim** or **cherubs**) a type of angel, shown in art as a chubby child with wings. **2** (pl. **cherubs**) a beautiful or innocent-looking child. ■ **cherubic** adj.

chervil n. a herb with an aniseed flavour.

chess n. a board game for two players, the aim being to put the opponent's king into checkmate.

chest n. **1** the front of a person's body between the neck and the stomach. **2** a large strong box. □ **chest of drawers** a piece of furniture consisting of a set of drawers.

chestnut n. **1** an edible brown nut. **2** the tree producing chestnuts. **3** a deep reddish-brown colour. **4** a reddish-brown horse. **5** (**old chestnut**) a joke or story that has been repeated too often.

chevron n. a V-shaped symbol.

chew v. bite and work food between the teeth. ■ **chewy** adj.

chiaroscuro /ki-ah-ruh-skoor-oh/ n. the treatment of light and shade in drawing and painting.

chic /sheek/ *adj.* elegant and fashionable. •*n.* stylishness and elegance.

chicane /shi-**kayn**/ *n.* a sharp double bend on a motor-racing track.

chicanery *n.* trickery.

chick *n.* a newly hatched young bird.

chicken *n.* **1** a domestic fowl kept for its eggs or meat. **2** *informal* a coward. •*v.* (**chicken out**) *informal* be too scared to do something. •*adj. informal* cowardly. □ **chicken feed** *informal* a very small sum of money. **chickenpox** a disease causing itchy red pimples.

chickpea *n.* a yellowish seed eaten as a vegetable.

chicory *n.* a plant with edible leaves and a root which can be used instead of coffee.

chide *v.* scold or rebuke.

chief *n.* **1** a leader or ruler. **2** the head of an organization. •*adj.* **1** most important. **2** highest in rank.

chiefly *adv.* mainly; mostly.

chieftain *n.* the leader of a people or clan.

chiffon *n.* a light, see-through fabric.

chignon /**sheen**-yon/ *n.* a coil of hair arranged on the back of a woman's head.

chihuahua /chi-**wah**-wuh/ *n.* a very small smooth-haired dog.

chilblain *n.* a painful swelling on a hand or foot caused by cold weather.

child *n.* (*pl.* **children**) **1** a young human being. **2** a son or daughter. □ **childbirth** the act of giving birth to a child. ■ **childhood** *n.* **childless** *adj.*

childish *adj.* **1** silly and immature. **2** like a child.

childlike *adj.* innocent or simple.

chill *n.* **1** an unpleasant feeling of coldness. **2** a feverish cold. •*v.* **1** make cold. **2** frighten. **3** *informal* relax. •*adj.* chilly.

chilli (US **chili**) *n.* (*pl.* **chillies**) a small hot-tasting pepper.

chilly *adj.* (**chillier**, **chilliest**) **1** unpleasantly cold. **2** unfriendly.

chime *n.* **1** a tuneful ringing sound. **2** a bell or a metal bar used in a set to ring when struck. •*v.* **1** make a tuneful ringing sound. **2** (**chime in**) interrupt with a remark.

chimera /ky-**meer**-uh/ *n.* **1** an unrealistic idea or hope. **2** *Gk Myth.* a female monster with a lion's head, a goat's body, and a serpent's tail.

chimney *n.* (*pl.* **chimneys**) a vertical pipe taking smoke and gases up from a fire or furnace. □ **chimney breast** a projecting part of an inside wall surrounding a chimney. **chimney pot** a pipe at the top of a chimney.

chimp *n. informal* a chimpanzee.

chimpanzee *n.* an African ape.

chin *n.* the part of the face below the mouth.

china *n.* **1** a fine white ceramic material. **2** objects made of china.

chinchilla *n.* a small squirrel-like South American rodent.

chine *n.* a joint of meat containing part of an animal's spine.

Chinese *n.* (*pl.* **Chinese**) **1** the language of China. **2** a person from China. •*adj.* of China.

chink *n.* **1** a narrow opening. **2** a thin beam of light. **3** a high-pitched ringing sound. •*v.* make a high-pitched ringing sound.

chinos /chee-nohz/ pl. n. casual trousers made from a smooth cotton fabric.

chintz n. a shiny cotton fabric used for furnishings.

chip n. **1** a small piece cut or broken off from something hard. **2** a strip of deep-fried potato. **3** a microchip. **4** a counter used in gambling. •v. (**chipping**, **chipped**) **1** cut or break a chip from something hard. **2** (**chip in**) informal make a contribution. □ **a chip on your shoulder** informal a long-held grievance. **chipboard** board made of compressed wood chips.

chipmunk n. a striped burrowing squirrel.

chipolata n. a small sausage.

chippings pl. n. fragments of stone or wood.

chiropody /ki-rop-uh-di/ n. medical treatment of the feet.
■ **chiropodist** n.

chiropractic /ky-roh-prak-tik/ n. a system of complementary medicine based on manipulation of the joints. ■ **chiropractor** n.

chirp v. (of a small bird) make a short, high-pitched sound. •n. a chirping sound.

chirpy adj. informal cheerful and lively.

chisel n. a tool with a long blade for shaping wood or stone. •v. (**chiselling**, **chiselled**; US **chiseling**, **chiseled**) cut or shape with a chisel.

chit n. **1** a disrespectful young woman. **2** an official note recording money owed.

chivalrous adj. (of a man) polite and gallant towards women.
■ **chivalrously** adv.

chivalry n. **1** an honourable code of behaviour which medieval knights were expected to follow. **2** polite behaviour by a man towards women.

chives pl. n. a herb with thin onion-flavoured leaves.

chivvy v. (**chivvying**, **chivvied**) nag or pester.

chloride n. a compound of chlorine with another substance.

chlorinate v. treat water with chlorine.

chlorine n. a green gaseous chemical element.

chloroform n. a liquid used as a solvent and formerly as an anaesthetic.

chlorophyll n. a green pigment in plants which allows them to convert sunlight into energy.

chock n. a wedge or block placed against a wheel to prevent it from moving. □ **chock-a-block** informal crammed full.

chocolate n. **1** a dark brown food made from roasted cacao seeds, eaten as a sweet, or made into a drink. **2** a sweet covered with chocolate.

choice n. **1** an act of choosing. **2** the right or ability to choose. **3** a range from which to choose. **4** something chosen. •adj. of very good quality.

choir n. **1** an organized group of singers. **2** the part of a church used by a choir.

choke v. **1** prevent someone from breathing by blocking their throat. **2** have trouble breathing. **3** fill or clog up. •n. a valve controlling the flow of air into a petrol engine.

choker n. a close-fitting necklace.

cholera n. an infectious disease causing severe vomiting and diarrhoea.

choleric adj. irritable.

cholesterol n. a substance in most body tissues, believed to cause disease of the arteries if present in excessive levels in the blood.

chomp v. munch noisily.

choose v. (**choosing, chose**; past part. **chosen**) pick out as being the best of the available alternatives.

choosy adj. (**choosier, choosiest**) informal very careful in making a choice.

chop v. (**chopping, chopped**) **1** cut into pieces with a knife or axe. **2** hit with a short, downward stroke. **3** end something or reduce it by a large amount. • n. **1** a thick slice of meat, usu. including a rib. **2** a downward cutting blow.

chopper n. **1** a short large-bladed axe. **2** informal a helicopter.

choppy adj. (of the sea) having many small waves.

chopstick n. each of a pair of thin sticks used as eating utensils in China and Japan.

chop suey n. a Chinese-style dish of meat fried with vegetables.

choral adj. sung by a choir.

chorale n. a simple, stately hymn tune.

chord n. a group of three or more notes sounded together.

chore n. a routine or boring task.

choreograph /ko-ri-uh-grahf/ v. compose the sequence of steps and moves for a dance. ■ **choreographer** n. **choreography** n.

chorister n. a member of a choir.

chortle v. laugh loudly.

chorus n. (pl. **choruses**) **1** the refrain of a song. **2** a group of singers or dancers in a musical or opera.

3 something said at the same time by many people. • v. (of a group) say the same thing at the same time.

chose past of **CHOOSE**.

chosen past part. of **CHOOSE**.

choux pastry /shoo/ n. light pastry, used for eclairs.

chow n. **1** informal food. **2** a Chinese breed of dog with a tail curled over its back.

chowder n. thick soup containing fish, seafood, etc.

chow mein /mayn/ n. a Chinese-style dish of fried noodles with shredded meat etc.

Christ n. the title given to Jesus.

christen v. name a baby at baptism.

Christendom n. literary the worldwide body of Christians.

Christian adj. of or believing in Christianity. • n. a believer in Christianity. □ **Christian name** a forename.

Christianity n. the religion based on the teaching and works of Jesus.

Christmas n. the annual Christian festival celebrating Jesus's birth, held on 25 December.

chromatic adj. **1** (of a musical scale) rising or falling by semitones. **2** of or produced by colour.

chromatography n. a technique for separating a mixture by passing it through a material in which the components move at different rates. ■ **chromatographic** adj.

chrome n. a hard shiny coating made from chromium.

chromium n. a hard white metallic element.

chromosome n. a thread-like structure in a cell nucleus, carrying the genes.

chronic adj. 1 (of an illness etc.) lasting a long time. 2 having a chronic illness or habit. 3 informal very bad. ■ **chronically** adv.

chronicle n. a record of historical events. •v. record a series of events. ■ **chronicler** n.

chronological adj. following the order in which things occurred. ■ **chronologically** adv.

chronology n. the arrangement of events in order of occurrence.

chronometer n. an instrument measuring time.

chrysalis n. (pl. **chrysalises**) 1 an insect pupa, esp. of a butterfly or moth. 2 the hard case enclosing a pupa.

chrysanthemum n. a garden plant with bright flowers.

chubby adj. (**chubbier, chubbiest**) plump and rounded.

chuck v. 1 informal throw carelessly. 2 touch playfully under the chin. •n. 1 a device holding something in a lathe or a tool in a drill. 2 a cut of beef from the neck to the ribs.

chuckle v. laugh quietly. •n. a quiet laugh.

chuff v. (of a steam engine) move with a regular puffing sound.

chuffed adj. informal pleased.

chug v. (**chugging, chugged**) (of a vehicle) move slowly with muffled regular sounds.

chum n. informal a close friend. ■ **chummy** adj.

chump n. informal a foolish person.

chunk n. 1 a thick, solid piece. 2 a large amount. ■ **chunky** adj.

church n. 1 a building for public Christian worship. 2 (**Church**) a particular Christian organization.

3 (**the Church**) Christians as a whole. □ **churchwarden** either of two people elected by an Anglican congregation to oversee church property. **churchyard** an enclosed area surrounding a church.

churlish adj. rude or bad-tempered. ■ **churlishly** adv.

churn v. 1 (of liquid) move about vigorously. 2 (**churn out**) produce quickly and in large quantities. 3 shake milk or cream in a machine to make butter. •n. 1 a machine for making butter by shaking milk or cream. 2 a large metal milk can.

chute n. a sloping channel for moving things to a lower level.

chutney n. (pl. **chutneys**) a spicy pickle made of fruit or vegetables with vinegar and sugar.

CIA abbrev. (in the US) Central Intelligence Agency.

ciabatta /chuh-bah-tuh/ n. a flat Italian bread made with olive oil.

cicada /si-kah-duh/ n. a chirping insect like a grasshopper.

cicatrix n. (pl. **cicatrices**) a scar.

CID abbrev. (in the UK) Criminal Investigation Department.

cider n. an alcoholic drink made from fermented apple juice.

cigar n. a cylinder of tobacco in tobacco leaves for smoking.

cigarette n. a cylinder of finely cut tobacco in paper for smoking.

cinch n. informal a very easy task.

cinder n. a piece of partly burnt coal or wood.

cine adj. of film-making.

cinema n. 1 a theatre where films are shown. 2 the production of films as an art or industry. ■ **cinematic** adj.

cinematography n. the art of camerawork in film-making. ■ **cinematographer** n.

cinnamon n. a spice made from the bark of an Asian tree.

cipher (or **cypher**) n. 1 a code. 2 an unimportant person or thing.

circa prep. approximately.

circle n. 1 a round flat shape whose edge is at the same distance from the centre all the way round. 2 a group with shared interests, friends, etc. 3 a curved upper tier of seats in a theatre. • v. 1 move or be placed all the way around. 2 draw a line round.

circlet n. a circular band worn on the head.

circuit n. 1 a roughly circular route. 2 a motor-racing track. 3 a system of components forming a complete path for an electric current. 4 a series of sporting events.

circuitous /ser-kyoo-i-tuhss/ adj. (of a route) long and indirect.

circuitry n. electric circuits.

circular adj. 1 having the shape of a circle. 2 (of an argument) false because it uses as evidence the point to be proved. • n. a letter or leaflet sent to a large number of people.

circulate v. 1 move continuously through a closed system or area. 2 pass from place to place or person to person.

circulation n. 1 movement around something, esp. the continuous movement of blood round the body. 2 the number of copies sold of a newspaper or magazine. 3 the public availability of something.

circumcise v. cut off the foreskin or clitoris of. ■ **circumcision** n.

circumference n. 1 the boundary of a circle. 2 the distance around something.

circumflex n. the accent (ˆ).

circumlocution n. the use of many words where fewer would do.

circumnavigate v. sail all the way around. ■ **circumnavigation** n.

circumscribe v. restrict; limit.

circumspect adj. cautious; sensible.

circumstance n. 1 a fact or condition connected with an event or action. 2 events that are beyond your control.

circumstantial adj. (of evidence) suggesting but not proving something.

circumvent v. evade a difficulty.

circus n. (pl. **circuses**) a travelling show with acrobats, trained animals, and clowns.

cirque n. a steep-sided hollow on a mountain.

cirrhosis /si-roh-siss/ n. a liver disease.

cirrus /si-ruhss/ n. (pl. **cirri**) a high wispy cloud.

cistern n. a water storage tank connected to a toilet.

citadel n. a fortress overlooking a city.

citation n. 1 a quotation from a book or author. 2 an official mention of a notable act.

cite v. quote a book or author as evidence for an argument.

citizen n. 1 a person legally recognized as a member of a country. 2 an inhabitant of a town or city. ■ **citizenship** n.

citrus n. (pl. **citruses**) a fruit of a group including lemons, oranges, etc. ■ **citric** adj.

c

city *n.* (*pl.* **cities**) **1** a large town, esp. one created by charter and containing a cathedral. **2** (**the City**) the part of London that is a centre of finance and business.

civet /siv-it/ *n.* **1** a cat native to Africa and Asia. **2** a strong perfume obtained from its glands.

civic *adj.* of a city or town.

civil *adj.* **1** of civilians. **2** polite. **3** (of a court) dealing with personal legal matters. □ **civil engineer** an engineer who designs roads, bridges, etc. **civil servant** a member of the civil service. **civil service** the departments that carry out the work of the government. **civil war** a war between people of the same country. ■ **civilly** *adv.*

civilian *n.* a person not in the armed services or the police force.

civility *n.* (*pl.* **civilities**) politeness.

civilization (or **-isation**) *n.* **1** an advanced stage of social development. **2** the process of achieving this. **3** a civilized nation or area.

civilize (or **-ise**) *v.* **1** bring to an advanced stage of social development. **2** (**civilized**) polite and good-mannered.

CJD *abbrev.* Creutzfeldt–Jakob disease, a fatal brain disease.

cl *abbrev.* centilitre.

clack *v.* make a sharp sound like that of one hard object hitting another. •*n.* a clacking sound.

clad *adj.* clothed.

cladding *n.* a covering or coating on a structure or material.

claim *v.* **1** state as being the case, without giving proof. **2** request as your right. **3** cause loss of life. •*n.* **1** a statement that something is true. **2** a request for something to

which you have a right. ■ **claimant** *n.*

clairvoyant *n.* a person claiming the power to see into the future. ■ **clairvoyance** *n.*

clam *n.* a shellfish with a hinged shell. •*v.* (**clam up**) *informal* refuse to talk.

clamber *v.* climb with difficulty.

clammy *adj.* damp and sticky.

clamour (US **clamor**) *n.* **1** a loud confused noise. **2** a strong protest or demand. •*v.* make a clamour. ■ **clamorous** *adj.*

clamp *n.* a device for holding something tightly. •*v.* **1** fasten or hold tightly. **2** fit a clamp to the wheel of a car to immobilize it. **3** (**clamp down**) take strict action to prevent something.

clan *n.* a group of related families.

clandestine *adj.* done secretly.

clang *n.* a loud metallic sound. •*v.* make a clang.

clanger *n.* *informal* a mistake.

clangour (US **clangor**) *n.* a continuous clanging sound.

clank *n.* a sharp sound like that of pieces of metal hitting each other. •*v.* make a clank.

clap *v.* (**clapping**, **clapped**) **1** strike the palms of the hands together repeatedly, esp. to applaud. **2** slap on the back. •*n.* **1** an act of clapping. **2** a sharp sound of thunder. □ **clapped-out** *informal* worn out. **claptrap** nonsense.

clapper *n.* the striking part of a bell. □ **clapperboard** hinged boards struck together at the start of filming to synchronize picture and sound machinery.

claret *n.* a dry red wine.

clarify *v.* (**clarifying**, **clarified**) **1** make easier to understand.

2 melt butter to separate out the impurities. ■ **clarification** n.

clarinet n. a woodwind instrument. ■ **clarinettist** n.

clarion call n. a clear demand for action.

clarity n. clearness.

clash v. **1** come into violent conflict. **2** disagree. **3** look or sound unpleasant together. **4** (of events) occur inconveniently at the same time. •n. an act of clashing.

clasp v. **1** grasp tightly with your hand. **2** place your arms tightly around. **3** fasten with a clasp. •n. **1** a device with interlocking parts used for fastening. **2** an act of clasping.

class n. **1** a group of things having a common characteristic. **2** a group having the same social status. **3** a group of students taught together. **4** a lesson. **5** informal impressive stylishness. •v. put in a category. □ **classroom** a room in which a class of students is taught. ■ **classless** adj. **classy** adj. (informal).

classic adj. **1** of recognized high quality. **2** typical. •n. **1** a work of art recognized as being of high quality. **2** (**Classics**) the study of ancient Greek and Latin culture, literature, etc. ■ **classicism** n. **classicist** n.

classical adj. **1** of ancient Greek or Latin culture etc. **2** (of music) written in the formal European tradition. ■ **classically** adv.

classified adj. **1** (of newspaper or magazine advertisements) organized in categories. **2** (of information or documents) officially secret.

classify v. (**classifying**, **classified**) **1** arrange a group in classes.

2 put in a category. ■ **classifiable** adj. **classification** n. **classifier** n.

clatter n. a loud rattling sound like that of hard objects hitting each other. •v. make a clatter.

clause n. **1** a distinct part of a sentence, with its own verb. **2** a part of a treaty, law, or contract.

claustrophobia n. extreme fear of being in an enclosed place. ■ **claustrophobic** adj.

clavichord n. an early keyboard instrument.

clavicle n. the collarbone.

claw n. **1** a horny nail on an animal's or bird's foot. **2** the pincer of a shellfish. •v. scratch or tear at with claws or hands.

clay n. sticky earth used for making bricks and pottery. □ **clay pigeon** a disc of baked clay thrown up as a target for shooting.

clean adj. **1** free from dirt or harmful substances. **2** not obscene or immoral. •v. make clean. ■ **cleaner** n. **cleanliness** /klen-li-nuhss/ n. **cleanly** adv.

cleanse v. make thoroughly clean or pure.

clear adj. **1** easy to see, hear, or understand. **2** leaving or feeling no doubt. **3** transparent. **4** free of obstructions or anything unwanted. •v. **1** make or become clear. **2** get past or over. **3** prove innocent. **4** give official approval to. □ **clear off** informal go away. **clear out** empty. **clear up 1** (of an illness) become cured. **2** solve or explain. **clearway** a main road on which vehicles are not allowed to stop. ■ **clearly** adv.

clearance n. **1** the act of clearing. **2** official authorization. **3** space allowed for one thing to pass another.

clearing n. an open space in a forest.

cleat n. **1** a projection for attaching a rope. **2** a projection on the sole of a shoe.

cleavage n. **1** the space between a woman's breasts. **2** a marked difference or division.

cleave v. (**cleaving**, **clove** or **cleft** or **cleaved**; past part. **cloven** or **cleft** or **cleaved**) **1** divide or split in two. **2** (**cleave to**) stick to.

cleaver n. a tool for chopping meat.

clef n. Music a symbol on a stave showing the pitch of the notes.

cleft adj. split. •n. a split or crack. □ **cleft lip** (or **palate**) a split in the upper lip (or roof of the mouth), present from birth.

clematis n. a climbing plant with showy flowers.

clemency n. kind or merciful treatment.

clement adj. (of weather) mild.

clementine n. a variety of tangerine.

clench v. close your fist or hold your teeth or muscles together tightly.

clerestory /kleer-stor-i/ n. (pl. **clerestories**) an upper row of windows in a large church.

clergy n. the priests and ministers of a religion, esp. those of the Christian Church. ■ **clergyman** (or **clergywoman**) n.

cleric n. a priest or religious leader.

clerical adj. **1** of office work. **2** of the clergy.

clerk n. an office worker who carries out administrative work, keeps accounts, etc.

clever adj. **1** quick to understand and learn. **2** skilled at doing something.

cliché /klee-shay/ n. an overused phrase or idea. ■ **clichéd** adj.

click n. **1** a short, sharp sound. **2** an act of pressing a button on a computer mouse. •v. **1** make a click. **2** press a computer mouse button. **3** informal become friendly.

client n. a person using the services of a professional person or organization.

clientele /klee-on-tel/ n. clients or customers.

cliff n. a steep rock face on the coast. □ **cliffhanger** a story or event that is exciting because its outcome is uncertain.

climate n. **1** the general weather conditions in an area over a long period. **2** a trend or general attitude. ■ **climatic** adj.

climax n. **1** the most intense, exciting, or important point. **2** an orgasm. •v. reach a climax. ■ **climactic** adj.

climb v. go or come up to a higher position. •n. **1** an act of climbing. **2** a route up a mountain etc. ■ **climber** n.

clime n. literary a region in terms of its climate.

clinch v. settle conclusively. •n. **1** a tight hold in a fight. **2** an embrace.

cling v. (**clinging**, **clung**) (**cling to/on to**) **1** hold on tightly to. **2** stick to or depend on. ■ **clingy** adj.

clinic n. a place where medical treatment or advice is given.

clinical adj. **1** of the treatment of patients. **2** efficient and unemotional. ■ **clinically** adv.

clink n. a sharp ringing sound. •v. make a clink.

clinker n. the stony remains of burnt coal.

clip n. **1** a device for holding objects together or in place. **2** an act of cutting. **3** an excerpt of a film or broadcast. **4** *informal* a sharp blow. • v. (**clipping, clipped**) **1** fasten with a clip. **2** cut with shears or scissors. **3** hit sharply.

clipper n. **1** (**clippers**) a tool for clipping. **2** *hist.* a fast sailing ship.

clipping n. **1** a piece clipped off. **2** a newspaper cutting.

clique /cleek/ n. a small group who tend to exclude non-members.

clitoris n. the small sensitive organ just in front of the vagina.

cloak n. a loose sleeveless outer garment. • v. cover or hide. □ **cloakroom 1** a room where coats and bags may be left. **2** a room containing a toilet.

clobber *informal* n. clothing and personal belongings. • v. hit hard.

cloche /klosh/ n. a cover for protecting tender plants.

clock n. an instrument that shows the time. • v. (**clock in/out** or **on/off**) register your arrival at or departure from work. □ **clockwise** moving in the direction of the hands of a clock. **clockwork** a mechanism with a spring and toothed gearwheels, used to drive a clock etc.

clod n. a lump of earth.

clog n. a shoe with a thick wooden sole. • v. (**clogging, clogged**) block up.

cloister n. a covered passage round a courtyard in a convent, monastery, etc.

cloistered adj. **1** having a cloister. **2** protected from the problems of daily life.

clone n. an animal or plant created from the cells of another, to which it is genetically identical. • v.

1 create as a clone. **2** make an identical copy of.

close adj. **1** near in space or time. **2** very similar. **3** very affectionate or friendly. **4** careful and thorough. **5** humid or airless. • v. **1** move so as to cover an opening. **2** bring two parts of something together. **3** bring or come to an end. **4** (**close on/in on**) gradually surround or get nearer to. • adv. so as to be very near. • n. **1** the end of a period or an activity. **2** a street closed at one end. **3** the grounds of a cathedral. □ **closed-circuit television** a television system in which signals are sent by cable to a restricted set of monitors. **close-up** a photo or film sequence taken at close range. ■ **closely** adv. **closeness** n.

closet n. a cupboard or wardrobe. • adj. secret. • v. (**closeting, closeted**) shut yourself in a private place, esp. to talk to someone.

closure n. **1** the act of closing. **2** a feeling that an upsetting experience has been resolved.

clot n. **1** a thick mass of a semi-liquid substance, esp. blood. **2** *informal* a foolish person. • v. (**clotting, clotted**) form into clots. □ **clotted cream** very thick cream.

cloth n. (pl. **cloths**) **1** fabric made from a soft fibre such as cotton. **2** a piece of cloth for a particular purpose. **3** (**the cloth**) Christian clergy.

clothe v. **1** provide with clothes. **2** (**be clothed in**) be dressed in.

clothes pl. n. things worn to cover the body.

clothing n. clothes.

cloud n. **1** a mass of condensed watery vapour floating in the sky.

2 a mass of smoke, dust, etc. **3** a state or cause of gloom or anxiety. • v. **1** become full of clouds. **2** make less clear. **3** become sad or gloomy. □ **cloudburst** a sudden fall of heavy rain. ■ **cloudy** adj.

clout informal n. **1** a heavy blow. **2** influence. • v. hit hard.

clove[1] n. **1** the dried bud of a tropical tree, used as a spice. **2** any of the segments making up a bulb of garlic.

clove[2] past of **CLEAVE**. □ **clove hitch** a knot used to fasten a rope round a pole etc.

cloven past part. of **CLEAVE**. □ **cloven hoof** the divided hoof of animals such as cattle, sheep, etc.

clover n. a flowering plant having leaves with three lobes. □ **in clover** in ease and luxury.

clown n. an entertainer who does comical tricks. • v. behave in a silly or playful way. ■ **clownish** adj.

cloying adj. excessively sweet or sentimental.

club n. **1** a group who meet for a particular activity. **2** an organization providing benefits for members. **3** a nightclub with dance music. **4** a heavy stick used as a weapon. **5** a stick with a thick head, used to hit the ball in golf. **6** (**clubs**) a suit of playing cards, represented by a black clover leaf. • v. (**clubbing, clubbed**) **1** (**club together**) combine with others to do something. **2** go to nightclubs. **3** beat with a club. ■ **clubber** n.

cluck v. (of a hen) make a short, low sound. • n. a clucking sound.

clue n. a fact that helps solve a mystery or problem.

clueless adj. unable to understand or do something.

clump n. **1** a cluster of trees or plants. **2** a mass or lump. • v. **1** form into a clump. **2** tread heavily. ■ **clumpy** adj.

clumsy adj. (**clumsier, clumsiest**) **1** awkward in movement or performance. **2** difficult to use. ■ **clumsily** adv. **clumsiness** n.

clung past & past part. of **CLING**.

cluster n. a small close group of similar things. • v. form a cluster.

clutch v. hold tightly. • n. **1** a tight hold. **2** a mechanism in a vehicle for connecting the engine with the axle and wheels. **3** a group of eggs laid at one time. **4** a brood of chicks.

clutter v. fill with an untidy assortment of things. • n. things lying about untidily.

cm abbrev. centimetres.

Co. abbrev. **1** company. **2** county.

c/o abbrev. care of.

co- prefix joint; jointly.

coach n. **1** a long-distance bus. **2** a sports instructor or trainer. **3** a private tutor. **4** a railway carriage. **5** a horse-drawn carriage. • v. train or teach as a coach.

coagulate /koh-ag-yoo-layt/ v. (of a liquid) become semi-solid or solid. ■ **coagulant** n. **coagulation** n.

coal n. a black rock burnt as fuel. □ **coalfield** a large area rich in underground coal. **coal tar** a thick black liquid made from coal.

coalesce v. form into a mass or whole.

coalition n. a temporary alliance, esp. one enabling political parties to form a government.

coarse adj. **1** rough in texture. **2** consisting of large particles. **3** rude or vulgar. □ **coarse fish**

any freshwater fish other than salmon and trout. ■ **coarsen** v.

coast n. land next to or near the sea. •v. move easily without using power. □ **coastguard** an organization or person that keeps watch over coastal waters. **coastline** the land along a coast. ■ **coastal** adj.

coaster n. a small mat for a glass.

coat n. **1** a long outer garment with sleeves. **2** an animal's covering of fur or hair. **3** a covering layer. •v. cover with a layer. □ **coat of arms** a design on a shield as the emblem of a family or institution.

coating n. a covering layer.

coax v. **1** persuade gently. **2** manipulate carefully.

coaxial /koh-ak-si-uhl/ adj. (of a cable) having two wires, one wrapped around the other but separated by insulation.

cob n. **1** the central part of an ear of maize. **2** a round loaf. **3** a hazelnut.

cobalt n. a silvery-white metallic element.

cobble n. a small round stone used to surface roads. •v. (**cobble together**) roughly assemble from available parts. ■ **cobbled** adj.

cobbler n. a person whose job is mending shoes.

cobra n. a poisonous snake native to Africa and Asia.

cobweb n. a spider's web.

cocaine n. a drug used as an illegal stimulant.

coccyx /kok-siks/ n. the bone at the base of the spine.

cochineal /koch-i-neel/ n. red food colouring.

cock n. **1** a male chicken or game bird. **2** a firing lever in a gun. •v. **1** tilt or bend. **2** set a gun ready for firing. **3** (**cock up**) informal do

badly; ruin. □ **cock-a-hoop** very pleased.

cockade n. a rosette worn on a hat as a badge.

cockatoo n. a crested parrot.

cockerel n. a young domestic cock.

cockeyed adj. informal **1** crooked. **2** impractical.

cockle n. an edible shellfish.

cockney n. (pl. **cockneys**) **1** a person from the East End of London. **2** the dialect or accent used in this area.

cockpit n. **1** a compartment for the pilot in an aircraft. **2** the driver's compartment in a racing car.

cockroach n. a beetle-like insect.

cocksure adj. arrogantly confident.

cocktail n. **1** a mixed alcoholic drink. **2** a mixture.

cocky adj. (**cockier, cockiest**) too self-confident. ■ **cockily** adv. **cockiness** n.

cocoa n. a drink made from powdered cacao seeds, mixed with hot milk.

coconut n. the large brown seed of a tropical palm, with edible white flesh.

cocoon n. a silky case protecting a chrysalis. •v. surround or cover in a protective way.

cod n. (pl. **cod**) a large edible sea fish.

coda n. the final part of a musical composition.

coddle v. treat in an overprotective way.

code n. **1** a system of words, figures, or symbols used to represent something, esp. for secrecy. **2** a sequence of numbers dialled to connect a phone line with another exchange. **3** a set of laws or rules. **4** instructions for a computer program. ∎v. convert into a code.

codeine n. a painkilling drug.

codex n. (pl. **codices** /koh-di-seez/ or **codexes**) an ancient manuscript in book form.

codicil n. an addition or alteration to a will.

codify v. (**codifying**, **codified**) organize laws or rules into a system.

co-education n. the education of pupils of both sexes together. ∎ **co-educational** adj.

coefficient n. a quantity which is placed before another which it multiplies (e.g. 4 in $4x^2$).

coelacanth /seel-uh-kanth/ n. a large sea fish.

coeliac disease /seel-i-ak/ (US **celiac**) n. a disease in which the small intestine fails to digest and absorb food.

coerce v. force into doing something. ∎ **coercion** n. **coercive** adj.

coeval adj. contemporary.

coexist v. exist together, esp. harmoniously. ∎ **coexistence** n.

C. of E. abbrev. Church of England.

coffee n. a hot drink made from the seeds of a tropical shrub.

coffer n. **1** a small chest for holding valuables. **2** (**coffers**) financial resources.

coffin n. a box in which a dead body is buried or cremated.

cog n. a wheel or bar with projections on its edge, which engage with projections on another wheel or bar.

cogent adj. logical and convincing. ∎ **cogency** n. **cogently** adv.

cogitate v. think deeply. ∎ **cogitation** n.

cognac /kon-yak/ n. French brandy.

cognition n. the gaining of knowledge through thought and the senses. ∎ **cognitive** adj.

cognizance (or **-isance**) n. knowledge or awareness. ∎ **cognizant** adj.

cognoscenti /kon-yuh-shen-ti/ pl. n. people well informed about a particular subject.

cohabit v. live together and have a sexual relationship without being married. ∎ **cohabitation** n.

cohere v. hold firmly together; form a whole.

coherent adj. **1** logical and consistent. **2** articulate. ∎ **coherence** n. **coherently** adv.

cohesion n. the state of being coherent. ∎ **cohesive** adj.

cohort n. **1** a large group of people. **2** a tenth part of an ancient Roman legion.

coiffure /kwah-fyoor/ n. a hairstyle.

coil n. **1** a length of something wound in a spiral. **2** a contraceptive device placed in the womb. ∎v. form or arrange into a coil.

coin n. a flat metal disc used as money. ∎v. **1** invent a new word. **2** make coins.

coinage n. **1** coins of a particular type. **2** a currency. **3** a newly invented word.

coincide v. **1** happen at the same time or place. **2** be the same or similar.

coincidence n. **1** a remarkable instance of things happening together by chance. **2** the fact of things being the same or similar. ∎ **coincidental** adj.

coir /koy-uh/ n. coconut fibre.

coitus *n.* sexual intercourse.
■ **coital** *adj.*

coke *n.* **1** a solid fuel made by heating coal in the absence of air. **2** *informal* cocaine.

col *n.* the lowest point between two peaks of a mountain ridge.

colander *n.* a bowl with holes in it, used for draining food.

cold *adj.* **1** at a low temperature. **2** not feeling or showing emotion. **3** without preparation. •*n.* **1** cold weather or surroundings. **2** an infection causing a streaming nose and sneezing. □ **cold-blooded 1** (of reptiles and fish) having a body temperature varying with that of the environment. **2** heartless and cruel. **cold sore** an inflamed blister near the mouth. **cold turkey** *informal* the unpleasant effects caused by the abrupt withdrawal of an addictive drug. **cold war** the state of hostility between the Soviet Union and its allies and Western nations after the Second World War. ■ **coldly** *adv.* **coldness** *n.*

coleslaw *n.* a salad of shredded raw cabbage and carrots in mayonnaise.

coley *n.* an edible sea fish.

colic *n.* severe abdominal pain. ■ **colicky** *adj.*

collaborate *v.* work together on an activity. ■ **collaboration** *n.* **collaborative** *adj.* **collaborator** *n.*

collage /kol-lahzh/ *n.* a form of art in which various materials are arranged and stuck to a backing.

collagen *n.* a protein forming the main component of connective tissue.

collapse *v.* **1** fall down suddenly. **2** fail and come to a sudden end. •*n.* an instance of collapsing.

collapsible *adj.* able to be folded down.

collar *n.* **1** a band of material round the neck of a garment. **2** a band put round the neck of a dog or cat. •*v.* *informal* seize or arrest.

collate *v.* collect and combine documents or information. ■ **collation** *n.*

collateral *n.* something promised if you cannot repay a loan. •*adj.* additional but less important.

colleague *n.* a person that you work with.

collect *v.* **1** bring or come together. **2** call for and take away. **3** buy or find items of a particular kind as a hobby. **4** (**collected**) calm. ■ **collectable** (or **collectible**) *adj.* & *n.* **collection** *n.* **collector** *n.*

collective *adj.* **1** done by or relating to all the members of a group. **2** taken as a whole. □ **collective noun** a noun that refers to a group of people or things (e.g. *staff*, *herd*).

college *n.* an establishment providing higher education or specialized training. ■ **collegiate** *adj.*

collide *v.* hit accidentally when moving.

collie *n.* a breed of sheepdog with long hair.

colliery *n.* (*pl.* **collieries**) a coal mine.

collision *n.* an instance of colliding.

colloquial *adj.* (of language) used in ordinary conversation. ■ **colloquialism** *n.* **colloquially** *adv.*

collude v. cooperate secretly for a dishonest or underhand purpose. ■ **collusion** n.

cologne /kuh-lohn/ n. a light perfume.

colon n. 1 a punctuation mark (:). 2 the main part of the large intestine. ■ **colonic** adj.

colonel /ker-nuhl/ n. the army rank above lieutenant colonel.

colonial adj. of a colony or colonialism.

colonialism n. the practice of gaining control over other countries and occupying them with settlers. ■ **colonialist** n. & adj.

colonize (or **-ise**) v. 1 establish a colony in. 2 take over for your own use. ■ **colonist** n. **colonization** n.

colonnade n. a row of columns supporting a roof.

colony n. (pl. **colonies**) 1 a country under the control of another and occupied by settlers from there. 2 a group of one nationality or race living in a foreign place. 3 a community of animals or plants of one kind.

color etc. US = **COLOUR** etc.

coloration (or **colouration**) n. natural colouring.

coloratura n. elaborate ornamentation of a vocal melody, e.g. in opera.

colossal adj. very large. ■ **colossally** adv.

colossus n. (pl. **colossi**) a very large or important person or thing.

colostomy n. (pl. **colostomies**) an operation in which the colon is shortened and the cut end diverted to an opening in the abdominal wall.

colour (US **color**) n. 1 the appearance that an object has, resulting from the way it reflects or gives out light. 2 one of the parts into which light can be separated. 3 the natural shade of the skin. •v. 1 give a colour to. 2 blush. 3 influence or affect. □ **colourblind** unable to distinguish between certain colours.

colourant (US **colorant**) n. a dye.

coloured (US **colored**) adj. 1 having a colour or colours. 2 offens. not having white skin.

colourful (US **colorful**) adj. 1 full of colours. 2 lively and exciting. ■ **colourfully** adv.

colouring (US **coloring**) n. 1 visual appearance in terms of colour. 2 a substance used to colour something.

colourless (US **colorless**) adj. 1 without colour. 2 dull.

colt n. a young male horse.

column n. 1 an upright pillar. 2 a long line of people or vehicles. 3 a vertical division of a page. 4 a regular article in a newspaper or magazine.

columnist n. a journalist who writes a column in a newspaper or magazine.

coma n. deep and prolonged unconsciousness.

comatose adj. in a coma.

comb n. 1 an object with a row of narrow teeth for tidying the hair. 2 a chicken's fleshy crest. •v. 1 tidy the hair with a comb. 2 search thoroughly.

combat n. fighting, esp. between armed forces. •v. (**combating**, **combated**) take action against. ■ **combatant** n. **combative** adj.

combe (or **coomb**) /koom/ n. a short valley.

combination n. 1 something made up of distinct elements.

2 the act of combining things. □ **combination lock** a lock opened using a specific sequence of letters or numbers.

combine v. join or mix together. •n. a group acting together for a commercial purpose. ■ **combine harvester** a farming machine that reaps and threshes in one operation.

combustible adj. able to catch fire.

combustion n. **1** burning. **2** rapid chemical combination with oxygen, involving the production of heat.

come v. (**coming, came**; past part. **come**) **1** move towards or into a place. **2** arrive at. **3** happen. **4** achieve a specified position. □ **come about** happen. **come across 1** give a particular impression. **2** find by chance. **comeback 1** a return to fame or popularity. **2** a quick reply. **come by** manage to get. **comedown** informal a loss of status. **come into** inherit. **come off** succeed. **come out** (of a fact) become known. **come round 1** recover consciousness. **2** be persuaded. **come to** recover consciousness. **come up** occur. **comeuppance** informal deserved punishment.

comedian n. (fem. **comedienne**) an entertainer whose act is intended to make people laugh.

comedy n. (pl. **comedies**) an amusing film, play, or other entertainment.

comely adj. old use attractive.

comestibles pl. n. food.

comet n. a mass of ice and dust with a long tail, moving around the solar system.

comfort n. **1** a state of ease and relaxation. **2** consolation for grief or anxiety. **3** (**comforts**) things giving comfort. •v. make less unhappy. ■ **comforter** n.

comfortable adj. **1** giving or enjoying comfort. **2** free from financial worry. ■ **comfortably** adv.

comfy adj. (**comfier, comfiest**) informal comfortable.

comic adj. **1** causing laughter. **2** of comedy. •n. **1** a comedian. **2** a children's magazine with comic strips. □ **comic strip** a sequence of drawings telling an amusing story. ■ **comical** adj. **comically** adv.

comma n. a punctuation mark (,).

command v. **1** give an order. **2** be in charge of (a military unit). **3** be in a position to receive. •n. **1** an order. **2** authority. **3** a group of officers in control of a unit or operation. **4** the ability to use or control something.

commandant /kom-muhn-dant/ n. an officer in charge of a force or institution.

commandeer v. officially take possession of.

commander n. **1** a person in command. **2** the navy rank below captain.

commandment n. a divine rule.

commando n. (pl. **commandos**) a soldier trained for carrying out raids.

commemorate v. honour the memory of. ■ **commemoration** n. **commemorative** adj.

commence v. begin. ■ **commencement** n.

commend v. **1** praise publicly. **2** recommend. ■ **commendable**

adj. **commendably** *adv.* **commendation** *n.*

commensurable *adj.* measurable by the same standard.

commensurate *adj.* corresponding or in proportion.

comment *n.* a remark expressing an opinion or reaction. •*v.* express an opinion or reaction.

commentary *n.* (*pl.* **commentaries**) **1** a broadcast report of an event as it happens. **2** a discussion of a situation. **3** a set of notes on a text.

commentate *v.* provide a commentary on an event. ■ **commentator** *n.*

commerce *n.* the activity of buying and selling.

commercial *adj.* **1** concerned with commerce. **2** intended to make a profit. •*n.* a television or radio advertisement. ■ **commercially** *adv.*

commercialize (or **-ise**) *v.* manage in a way intended to make a profit. ■ **commercialization** *n.*

commiserate *v.* express sympathy or pity. ■ **commiseration** *n.*

commission *n.* **1** an instruction, command, or duty. **2** a formal request for something to be designed or made. **3** a group given official authority to do something. **4** payment to an agent for selling something. **5** the position of officer in the armed forces. •*v.* **1** order the production of. **2** bring into working order. **3** (**commissioned**) having the rank of military officer. □ **out of commission** not in working order.

commissionaire *n.* a uniformed door attendant at a hotel, theatre, etc.

commissioner *n.* **1** a member of a commission. **2** a representative of the highest authority in an area.

commit *v.* (**committing, committed**) **1** do something wrong or illegal. **2** allocate to a particular use. **3** (**commit yourself**) promise to do something. **4** put in a safe place. **5** send to prison or a psychiatric hospital.

commitment *n.* **1** dedication to a cause, activity, etc. **2** a promise. **3** an obligation.

! Two *m*s, but only one *t* in the middle: commit**ment**.

committal *n.* the sending of someone to prison or a psychiatric hospital, or for trial.

committee *n.* a group of people appointed for a particular function by a larger group.

! Double *m*, double *t*: committee.

commode *n.* a seat with a concealed chamber pot.

commodious *adj.* roomy and comfortable.

commodity *n.* (*pl.* **commodities**) **1** an article that can be bought and sold. **2** something valuable.

commodore *n.* **1** the naval rank above captain. **2** the president of a yacht club.

common *adj.* **1** occurring, found, or done often; not rare. **2** ordinary. **3** shared. **4** not well mannered or tasteful. •*n.* a piece of open land for public use. □ **common denominator** a number that can be divided exactly by all the numbers below the line in a set of fractions. **common law** English law developed from custom and judges' decisions. **the Common Market** the European Union. **common room** a room in a school or college for students or staff to use outside teaching hours. **common sense** good sense in practical matters. **commonwealth 1 (the Commonwealth)** an association of the UK and independent states formerly under British rule. **2** an independent state. ■ **commonly** *adv.*

commoner *n.* an ordinary person as opposed to an aristocrat.

commonplace *adj.* ordinary. •*n.* a cliché.

commotion *n.* noisy confusion or disturbance.

communal *adj.* shared or done by a group. ■ **communally** *adv.*

commune *n.* a group of people living together and sharing possessions and responsibilities. •*v.* communicate mentally or spiritually.

communicable *adj.* (of a disease) able to be passed on to others.

communicant *n.* a person who receives Holy Communion.

communicate *v.* **1** share or exchange information. **2** pass on or convey an emotion, disease, etc. ■ **communicator** *n.*

communication *n.* **1** the act of communicating. **2** a letter or message. **3 (communications)** means of travelling or sending information.

communicative *adj.* willing to talk or give information.

communion *n.* **1** the sharing of thoughts and feelings. **2 (or Holy Communion)** the Christian service at which bread and wine are made holy and shared.

communiqué /kuh-myoo-ni-kay/ *n.* an official announcement.

communism *n.* **1** a political system in which all property is owned by the community. **2** a system of this kind based on Marxism. ■ **communist** *n.* & *adj.*

community *n.* (*pl.* **communities**) **1** a group of people living together in one place or sharing a religion, race, etc. **2 (the community)** the people of an area as a group.

commute *v.* **1** travel regularly between your home and place of work. **2** reduce a judicial sentence to a less severe one. ■ **commuter** *n.*

compact *adj.* **1** closely and neatly packed together. **2** having all the necessary parts fitted into a small space. •*v.* compress. •*n.* **1** a small flat case for face powder. **2** a formal agreement. □ **compact disc** a small disc on which digital information is stored.

companion *n.* **1** a person that you spend time or travel with. **2** a thing intended to complement another. □ **companionway** a staircase from a ship's deck down to a lower deck. ■ **companionship** *n.*

companionable *adj.* friendly.

company *n.* (*pl.* **companies**) **1** a commercial business. **2** the fact of being with others. **3** a division of an infantry battalion. **4** a group of actors, singers, or dancers.

comparable *adj.* able to be compared; similar. ■ **comparably** *adv.*

comparative *adj.* **1** involving or measured by comparison. **2** (of an adjective or adverb) expressing a higher degree of a quality (e.g. braver). ■ **comparatively** *adv.*

! **comparative**, not -itive.

compare v. **1** assess the similarity between. **2** be similar to. ■ **comparison** n.

compartment n. a separate section of a structure or container.

compass n. **1** a device showing the direction of magnetic north. **2** a hinged instrument for drawing circles. **3** range or scope.

compassion n. pity and concern. ■ **compassionate** adj.

compatible adj. **1** able to exist or be used together. **2** (of two people) well suited to each other. **3** consistent. ■ **compatibility** n.

compatriot n. a fellow citizen of a country.

compel v. (**compelling, compelled**) force to do something.

compelling adj. attracting much attention or admiration.

compendious adj. giving much information in a concise way.

compendium n. (pl. **compendiums** or **compendia**) **1** a collection of facts on a subject. **2** a collection of similar items.

compensate v. **1** give a payment to reduce the bad effect of loss, injury, etc. **2** (**compensate for**) reduce something bad by having an opposite effect. ■ **compensation** n.

compère /kom-pair/ n. a person who introduces the acts in a variety show. • v. act as a compère for.

compete v. try to gain or win something by defeating others.

competent adj. **1** having the necessary skill or knowledge. **2** satisfactory. ■ **competence** n. **competently** adv.

competition n. **1** the act of competing. **2** an event in which people compete. **3** the people that you are competing with.

competitive adj. **1** involving competition. **2** keen to be more successful than others. ■ **competitively** adv. **competitiveness** n.

competitor n. a person or organization that competes.

compile v. produce a book, record, etc. by assembling material from other sources. ■ **compilation** n. **compiler** n.

complacent adj. smugly self-satisfied. ■ **complacency** n. **complacently** adv.

complain v. **1** express dissatisfaction. **2** (**complain of**) state that you are suffering from a symptom.

complainant n. Law a plaintiff.

complaint n. **1** an act of complaining. **2** a minor illness.

complaisant adj. willing to please others.

complement n. **1** a thing that completes or improves something. **2** the full number required. • v. add to in a way that improves. ■ **complementary** adj.

! Don't confuse **complement** and **compliment**, which means 'politely congratulate or praise'.

complete adj. **1** having all necessary parts. **2** finished. **3** to the greatest degree. • v. **1** make complete. **2** fill in a form. ■ **completely** adv. **completion** n.

complex adj. **1** consisting of many parts. **2** hard to understand. • n. **1** a group of buildings. **2** an interlinked system. **3** a set of repressed feelings affecting behaviour. ■ **complexity** n.

complexion n. 1 the condition of the skin of a person's face. 2 the general character of something.

compliant adj. 1 meeting rules or standards. 2 excessively obedient. ∎ **compliance** n.

complicate v. make more intricate or confusing.

complicated adj. involving many connected parts or confusing aspects.

complication n. 1 a difficulty. 2 a new medical condition which makes treatment of an existing one more complicated.

complicity n. involvement in wrongdoing. ∎ **complicit** adj.

compliment n. an expression of praise or admiration. •v. politely congratulate or praise.

! Don't confuse **compliment** with **complement**, which means 'add to in a way that improves'.

complimentary adj. 1 praising or approving. 2 free of charge.

comply v. (**complying, complied**) 1 do what is requested or ordered. 2 meet specified standards.

component n. a part of a whole.

comport v. (**comport yourself**) behave in a particular way.

compose v. 1 make up a whole. 2 create music or poetry. 3 arrange in an orderly or artistic way. 4 (**composed**) calm and controlled. ∎ **composer** n.

composite adj. made up of various parts.

composition n. 1 the way in which something is made up. 2 a work of music, literature, or art. 3 a thing composed of various elements.

compositor n. a typesetter.

compost n. decayed organic material used as a fertilizer.

composure n. calmness.

compote n. fruit cooked in syrup.

compound n. 1 a thing made up of two or more elements. 2 a large open area enclosed by a fence. •adj. made up of several parts. •v. 1 make up a whole. 2 make worse.

comprehend v. understand.

comprehensible adj. able to be understood.

comprehension n. the ability to understand.

comprehensive adj. including all or nearly all. •n. a secondary school in which pupils of all abilities are educated together. ∎ **comprehensively** adv.

compress v. 1 force into a smaller space. 2 squeeze together. •n. a pad to reduce inflammation or stop bleeding. ∎ **compression** n. **compressor** n.

comprise v. 1 be made up of. 2 make up a whole.

compromise n. an agreement reached by each side making concessions. •v. 1 make concessions so as to settle a dispute. 2 cause embarrassment or risk by unthinking behaviour.

compulsion n. 1 pressure to do something. 2 an irresistible urge.

compulsive adj. 1 resulting from or acting on an irresistible urge. 2 irresistibly exciting.

compulsory adj. required by law or a rule.

compunction a feeling of guilt or shame.

compute v. calculate a figure or amount. ∎ **computation** n. **computational** adj.

computer n. an electronic device for storing and processing information.

computerize (or **-ise**) v. convert to a system controlled by or stored on computer.

comrade n. a fellow member or soldier. ■ **comradeship** n.

con informal v. (**conning, conned**) deceive or trick. • n. a deception.
□ **pros and cons** see **PRO**.

concatenation n. a connected series.

concave adj. having an outline or surface that curves inwards.

conceal v. prevent from being seen or known. ■ **concealment** n.

concede v. 1 admit to be true. 2 give up an advantage or right. 3 admit defeat in a contest.

conceit n. 1 excessive pride in yourself. 2 a complicated metaphor. ■ **conceited** adj.

conceivable adj. able to be imagined or understood. ■ **conceivably** adv.

conceive v. 1 become pregnant. 2 imagine.

concentrate v. 1 focus all your attention. 2 gather together in one place. 3 (**concentrated**) (of a solution) strong. • n. a concentrated substance.

concentration n. 1 the ability to concentrate. 2 a great deal of things gathered in one place. 3 the amount of a substance in a solution or mixture. □ **concentration camp** a camp for holding political prisoners.

concentric adj. (of circles) having the same centre.

concept n. an abstract idea.
■ **conceptual** adj. **conceptualize** (or **-ise**) v.

conception n. 1 the act of conceiving. 2 a concept.

concern v. 1 be about. 2 affect or involve. 3 make anxious. • n. 1 anxiety. 2 a matter of interest or importance. 3 a business.

concerned adj. anxious.

concerning prep. about.

concert n. a public musical performance.

concerted adj. done jointly or in a determined way.

concertina n. a small musical instrument with bellows and buttons. • v. (**concertinaing, concertinaed**) compress in folds like those of a concertina.

concerto /kuhn-cher-toh/ n. (pl. **concertos** or **concerti**) a musical composition for an orchestra and a solo instrument.

concession n. 1 a thing given up to settle a dispute. 2 a reduction in price. 3 a right to use land for a specific purpose.

conch n. a shellfish with a spiral shell.

conciliate v. try to bring the sides in a dispute together. ■ **conciliation** n. **conciliatory** adj.

concise adj. giving information clearly and in few words. ■ **concisely** adv. **concision** n.

conclave n. a private meeting.

conclude v. 1 end. 2 reach an opinion by reasoning. 3 formally settle an agreement.

conclusion n. 1 an ending. 2 an opinion reached by reasoning.

conclusive adj. decisive or convincing. ■ **conclusively** adv.

concoct v. 1 prepare a dish from ingredients. 2 invent a story or plan. ■ **concoction** n.

concomitant adj. accompanying or associated with something.

concord n. agreement; harmony.

concordance n. an index of the important words in a written work.

concourse n. a large open area in a public building.

concrete n. a building material made from gravel, sand, cement, and water. • adj. **1** existing in a physical form; not abstract. **2** definite. •v. cover with concrete.

concubine n. (in some societies) a woman who lives with a man but has lower status than his wife or wives.

concur v. (**concurring**, **concurred**) agree.

concurrent adj. existing or happening at the same time. ■ **concurrence** n. **concurrently** adv.

concussion n. temporary unconsciousness or confusion caused by a blow on the head. ■ **concussed** adj.

condemn v. **1** express strong disapproval of. **2** sentence to a punishment. **3** force to endure. **4** declare unfit for use. ■ **condemnation** n.

condensation n. water from humid air collecting as droplets on a cold surface.

condense v. **1** make more concentrated. **2** change from a gas or vapour to a liquid. **3** express in fewer words.

condescend v. **1** behave as if you are better than others. **2** do something you regard as being beneath your dignity. ■ **condescending** adj. **condescension** n.

condiment n. a seasoning for food.

condition n. **1** state as regards appearance, fitness, etc. **2** (conditions) circumstances. **3** a situation that must exist before something else is possible. •v. **1** influence. **2** bring into a desired condition. **3** train or accustom.

conditional adj. depending on one or more conditions being met. ■ **conditionally** adv.

conditioner n. a substance for improving the condition of hair or fabric.

condolence n. an expression of sympathy.

condom n. a rubber sheath worn on the penis during sex to prevent conception or infection.

condominium n. US a building containing a number of individually owned flats.

condone v. accept or forgive an offence or wrong.

condor n. a large South American vulture.

conducive adj. (**conducive to**) contributing or helping towards.

conduct n. **1** behaviour. **2** management or direction. •v. **1** organize and carry out. **2** direct the performance of an orchestra etc. **3** guide or lead. **4** transmit heat or electricity.

conduction n. the transmission of heat or electricity directly through a substance. ■ **conductive** adj. **conductivity** n.

conductor n. **1** a person who conducts an orchestra or choir. **2** a material or device that conducts heat or electricity. **3** a person who collects fares on a bus.

conduit n. **1** a channel for liquid. **2** a tube protecting electric wiring.

cone n. **1** an object which tapers from a circular base to a point. **2** the dry fruit of a conifer.

coney n. (pl. **coneys**) a rabbit.

confection n. **1** an elaborate sweet dish. **2** an elaborately constructed thing.

confectionery n. sweets and chocolates. ■ **confectioner** n.

confederacy n. (pl. **confederacies**) an alliance of states.

confederate adj. joined by an agreement or treaty. •n. an accomplice.

confederation n. an alliance of states or groups.

confer v. (**conferring**, **conferred**) **1** grant a title, degree, etc. **2** have discussions.

conference n. a formal meeting for discussion.

confess v. **1** admit to a crime etc. **2** acknowledge reluctantly. **3** formally declare your sins to a priest. ■ **confession** n.

confessional n. an enclosed stall in a church for hearing confessions.

confessor n. a priest who hears confessions.

confetti n. bits of coloured paper thrown over a bride and groom.

confidant n. (fem. **confidante**) a person that you confide in.

confide v. tell someone about a secret or private matter.

confidence n. **1** faith, certainty, or trust. **2** the belief that you are able to do things well. □ **confidence trick** an act of cheating someone by gaining their trust.

confident adj. feeling confidence. ■ **confidently** adv.

confidential adj. to be kept secret. ■ **confidentiality** n. **confidentially** adv.

configuration n. a particular arrangement of parts. ■ **configure** v.

confine v. **1** (**confine to**) keep within certain limits. **2** (**be confined to**) be unable to leave somewhere due to illness etc. •n. (**confines**) boundaries.

confinement n. **1** the state of being confined. **2** dated the time of childbirth.

confirm v. **1** establish the truth of. **2** make definite. **3** (**confirmed**) firmly established in a habit etc. **4** (**be confirmed**) undergo the rite of confirmation.

confirmation n. **1** the act of confirming. **2** the rite at which a baptized person is admitted as a full member of the Christian Church.

confiscate v. officially seize property. ■ **confiscation** n.

conflagration n. a large fire.

conflate v. combine into one.

conflict n. **1** a serious disagreement. **2** an armed struggle. **3** a difference of opinions etc. •v. be different or in opposition.

confluence n. the junction of two rivers.

conform v. comply with rules, standards, or conventions. ■ **conformity** n.

conformist n. a person who behaves in a conventional way.

confound v. **1** surprise or bewilder. **2** prove wrong.

confront v. **1** meet an opponent face to face. **2** deal with or force to face a problem. ■ **confrontation** n.

confuse v. **1** make bewildered. **2** make less easy to understand. **3** mistake one for another. ■ **confusion** n.

confute v. prove wrong.

conga n. a dance performed in single file.

congeal v. become semi-solid.

congenial adj. suited or pleasing to your tastes.

congenital adj. present from birth.

conger eel n. a large sea eel.

congested adj. **1** very crowded. **2** abnormally full of blood. **3** blocked with mucus. ■ **congestion** n.

conglomerate n. **1** a corporation formed by a merger of separate firms. **2** something consisting of a number of distinct things. ■ **conglomeration** n.

congratulate v. express good wishes or praise at the happiness or success of. ■ **congratulation** n. **congratulatory** adj.

congregate v. gather in a crowd.

congregation n. people gathered for religious worship.

congress n. **1** a formal meeting between delegates. **2** (**Congress**) a national law-making body, esp. of the USA. ■ **congressional** adj.

congruent adj. **1** in agreement or harmony. **2** (of geometrical figures) identical in form. ■ **congruence** n.

conical adj. cone-shaped.

conifer n. an evergreen tree bearing cones. ■ **coniferous** adj.

conjecture n. & v. (make) a guess.

conjoin v. join.

conjugal adj. of marriage.

conjugate v. give the different forms of a verb. ■ **conjugation** n.

conjunction n. **1** a word used to connect words or clauses (e.g. *and, if*). **2** an instance of two or more events occurring together.

conjunctivitis n. inflammation of the membrane connecting the eyeball and eyelid.

conjure v. **1** cause to appear as if by magic. **2** call to the mind.

conjuror (or **conjurer**) n. a performer of seemingly magical tricks.

conk informal v. (**conk out**) (of a machine) break down. • n. a nose.

conker n. the fruit of the horse chestnut tree.

connect v. **1** join or bring together. **2** (**be connected**) be related in some way. ■ **connective** adj. **connector** n.

connection n. **1** a link or relationship. **2** (**connections**) influential friends or relatives. **3** a train, bus, etc. that arrives in time for passengers to catch another.

connive v. (**connive at/in**) secretly allow something wrong. ■ **connivance** n.

connoisseur /kon-nuh-ser/ n. an expert judge in matters of taste.

connote v. (of a word) suggest in addition to its main meaning. ■ **connotation** n.

conquer v. **1** take control of by military force. **2** overcome a problem. ■ **conqueror** n. **conquest** n.

conscience n. a person's sense of right and wrong.

conscientious adj. careful and thorough in carrying out your work or duty. □ **conscientious objector** a person who refuses to serve in the armed forces for moral reasons.

conscious adj. **1** awake and responsive. **2** aware. **3** intentional. ■ **consciously** adv. **consciousness** n.

conscript v. summon for compulsory military service. • n. a conscripted person. ■ **conscription** n.

consecrate v. make or declare sacred. ■ **consecration** n.

consecutive adj. following in unbroken sequence. ■ **consecutively** adv.

consensual adj. involving consent.

consensus n. general agreement.

! consensus, not -cen-.

consent n. permission or agreement. •v. 1 give permission. 2 agree to do.

consequence n. 1 a result or effect. 2 importance.

consequent adj. resulting. ■ **consequential** adj. **consequently** adv.

conservancy n. (pl. **conservancies**) an organization helping to preserve natural resources.

conservation n. 1 preservation of the natural environment. 2 preservation and repair of historical sites etc. ■ **conservationist** n.

conservative adj. 1 opposed to change. 2 (in politics) favouring free enterprise and private ownership. 3 (**Conservative**) of the British Conservative Party. 4 (of an estimate) deliberately low. •n. 1 a conservative person. 2 (**Conservative**) a member of the Conservative Party. ■ **conservatism** n. **conservatively** adv.

conservatory n. (pl. **conservatories**) a room with a glass roof and walls, attached to a house.

conserve v. protect from harm or overuse. •n. jam.

consider v. 1 think carefully about. 2 believe or think. 3 take into account.

considerable adj. great in amount or importance. ■ **considerably** adv.

considerate adj. careful not to harm or inconvenience others. ■ **considerately** adv.

consideration n. 1 careful thought. 2 a fact taken into account when making a decision. 3 thoughtfulness. 4 a payment or reward.

considering prep. taking into account.

consign v. 1 put aside or in an unpleasant situation. 2 deliver.

consignment n. a batch of goods sent.

consist v. (**consist of**) be composed of.

consistency n. (pl. **consistencies**) 1 being consistent. 2 the thickness of a liquid.

consistent adj. 1 regular; unchanging. 2 in agreement. ■ **consistently** adv.

console v. comfort in a time of grief etc. •n. 1 a panel containing a set of controls. 2 a machine for playing computerized video games. ■ **consolation** n.

consolidate v. 1 make stronger or more secure. 2 combine. ■ **consolidation** n.

consommé /kuhn-som-may/ n. a clear soup.

consonant n. a letter of the alphabet representing a sound in which the breath is completely or partly obstructed. •adj. (**consonant with**) in agreement with.

consort n. a wife or husband. •v. (**consort with**) associate with.

consortium n. (pl. **consortia** or **consortiums**) an association of several companies.

conspicuous adj. 1 clearly visible. 2 attracting notice. ■ **conspicuously** adv.

...ble or effort. ■ **conveniently** *...v.*

nvent *n.* a building occupied by a community of nuns.

...nvention *n.* **1** a way in which something is usually done. **2** socially acceptable behaviour. **3** an agreement between countries. **4** a conference. ■ **conventional** *adj.* **conventionally** *adv.*

converge *v.* come to or towards the same point. ■ **convergence** *n.* **convergent** *adj.*

conversant *adj.* (**conversant with**) having knowledge of.

conversation *n.* an informal talk between people. ■ **conversational** *adj.*

converse *v.* hold a conversation. · *n.* the opposite. · *adj.* opposite. ■ **conversely** *adv.*

convert *v.* **1** change in form, character, or function. **2** change money or units into others of a different kind. **3** change your religious faith. · *n.* a person who has changed their religious faith. ■ **conversion** *n.*

convertible *adj.* able to be converted. · *n.* a car with a folding or detachable roof.

convex *adj.* having an outline or surface that curves outwards.

convey *v.* **1** transport or carry. **2** communicate an idea or feeling.

conveyance *n.* **1** the act of conveying. **2** a means of transport. **3** the legal transfer of ownership of property. ■ **conveyancing** *n.*

conveyor belt *n.* a continuous moving band for transporting objects.

convict *v.* officially declare guilty of a criminal offence. · *n.* a convicted person serving a prison sentence.

conviction *n.* **1** an instance of being convicted of a criminal offence. **2** a firm belief. **3** strong belief in something.

convince *v.* **1** cause to feel certain that something is true. **2** persuade to do.

convincing *adj.* **1** able to convince. **2** (of a victory) decisive.

convivial *adj.* friendly and lively.

convocation *n.* a large assembly of people.

convoluted *adj.* **1** very complex. **2** intricately folded or twisted. ■ **convolution** *n.*

convolvulus *n.* a twining plant with trumpet-shaped flowers.

convoy *n.* a group of ships or vehicles travelling together under armed protection.

convulse *v.* **1** suffer convulsions. **2** (**be convulsed**) laugh uncontrollably. ■ **convulsive** *adj.*

convulsion *n.* **1** a sudden uncontrolled movement of the body. **2** (**convulsions**) uncontrollable laughter.

coo *v.* (of a pigeon or dove) make a soft murmuring sound. · *n.* a cooing sound.

cook *v.* **1** prepare food by heating ingredients. **2** (**cook up**) *informal* invent a story. · *n.* a person who cooks.

cooker *n.* an appliance for cooking food.

cookery *n.* the practice or skill of cooking.

cookie *n.* (*pl.* **cookies**) *US* a sweet biscuit.

cool *adj.* **1** fairly cold. **2** unfriendly or unenthusiastic. **3** calm. **4** *informal* fashionably attractive or impressive. · *v.* make or become cool. · *n.* low temperature. □ **ke...** (**or lose**) **your cool** *informal* st...

conspiracy *n.* (*pl.* **conspiracies**) a secret plan by a group to do something unlawful.

conspire *v.* **1** jointly make secret plans to commit a wrongful act. **2** (of events) seem to act together to cause something bad. ■ **conspirator** *n.* **conspiratorial** *adj.*

constable *n.* a police officer of the lowest rank.

constabulary *n.* (*pl.* **constabularies**) a police force.

constant *adj.* **1** occurring continuously. **2** unchanging. **3** faithful. · *n.* a number or quantity that does not change its value. ■ **constancy** *n.* **constantly** *adv.*

constellation *n.* a group of stars.

consternation *n.* anxiety or dismay.

constipation *n.* difficulty in emptying the bowels. ■ **constipated** *adj.*

constituency *n.* (*pl.* **constituencies**) an area or group of voters that elects a representative to a law-making body.

constituent *adj.* being a part of a whole. · *n.* **1** a voter in a constituency. **2** a constituent part.

constitute *v.* **1** be a part of a whole. **2** be or be equivalent to.

constitution *n.* **1** the principles by which a state is governed. **2** composition or formation. **3** a person's physical or mental state.

constitutional *adj.* of or in accordance with a constitution. · *n.* *dated* a walk taken for exercise.

constrain *v.* **1** force. **2** restrict.

constraint *n.* **1** a restriction. **2** strict control of your behaviour.

constrict *v.* **1** make or become narrower or tighter. **2** restrict. ■ **constriction** *n.* **constrictor** *n.*

construct *v.* build or put together. · *n.* an idea or theory containing various elements. ■ **constructor** *n.*

construction *n.* **1** the process of constructing. **2** a building or other structure. **3** an interpretation.

constructive *adj.* useful or helpful. ■ **constructively** *adv.*

construe *v.* interpret in a specific way.

consul *n.* an official representative of a state in a foreign city. ■ **consular** *adj.*

consulate *n.* the place where a consul works.

consult *v.* seek information or advice from. ■ **consultation** *n.* **consultative** *adj.*

consultant *n.* a specialist consulted for professional advice. ■ **consultancy** *n.*

consume *v.* **1** eat or drink. **2** use up. **3** (of a fire) destroy. **4** fill the mind of.

consumer *n.* a person who buys or uses goods or services.

consummate *v.* /kon-syuu-mayt/ make a marriage or relationship complete by having sex. · *adj.* /kuhn-sum-muht/ highly skilled. ■ **consummation** *n.*

consumption *n.* **1** the process of consuming. **2** *dated* tuberculosis. ■ **consumptive** *adj.* & *n.* (*dated*).

contact *n.* **1** physical touching. **2** communication. **3** a person who may be asked for information or help. **4** an electrical connection. · *v.* get in touch with. □ **contact lens** a plastic lens placed on the surface of the eye to correct visual defects.

contagion *n.* the spreading of a disease by close contact. ■ **contagious** *adj.*

contain v. **1** have or hold within. **2** control or restrain.

container n. **1** an object for holding something. **2** a large metal box for transporting goods.

containment n. the limitation of something harmful.

contaminate v. pollute. ∎ **contamination** n.

contemplate v. **1** look at thoughtfully. **2** think about. ∎ **contemplation** n. **contemplative** adj.

contemporaneous adj. existing or occurring at the same time.

contemporary adj. **1** living or occurring at the same time. **2** of or happening in the present. •n. (pl. **contemporaries**) a person of the same age or living at the same time as another.

contempt n. **1** the feeling that someone or something is worthless. **2** disobedience or disrespect to a court of law. ∎ **contemptuous** adj. **contemptuously** adv.

contemptible adj. deserving contempt.

contend v. **1** struggle to deal with a difficulty. **2** struggle to achieve. **3** assert. ∎ **contender** n.

content adj. happy or satisfied. •n. **1** (also **contents**) what is contained in something. **2** the material in a piece of writing rather than its form or style. **3** happiness or satisfaction. •v. satisfy or please. ∎ **contented** adj. **contentment** n.

contention n. **1** disagreement. **2** an assertion.

contentious adj. causing disagreement or controversy.

contest n. a competitive event. •v. **1** participate in a competition or

election. **2** challenge or dispute. ∎ **contestant** n.

context n. **1** the circumstances surrounding an event etc. **2** the parts that precede and follow a word or passage and clarify its meaning. ∎ **contextual** adj.

contiguous adj. adjacent or touching. ∎ **contiguity** n.

continent[1] n. **1** any of the world's main land masses. **2** (**the Continent**) the mainland of Europe. ∎ **continental** adj.

continent[2] adj. **1** able to control the bowels and bladder. **2** self-restrained. ∎ **continence** n.

contingency n. (pl. **contingencies**) a possible future event.

contingent n. a distinct group of people within a larger group. •adj. (**contingent on**) dependent on.

continual adj. happening repeatedly or often. ∎ **continually** adv.

continue v. **1** keep doing. **2** keep existing or happening. **3** carry on in the same direction. **4** start again. ∎ **continuation** n. **continuity** n.

continuous adj. without interruptions or gaps. ∎ **continuously** adv.

continuum n. (pl. **continua**) a continuous sequence in which the elements change gradually.

contort v. twist or bend out of normal shape. ∎ **contortion** n.

contortionist n. an entertainer who contorts their body.

contour n. **1** an outline. **2** a line on a map joining points of equal height.

contra- prefix against; opposite.

contraband n. smuggled goods.

contraception n. the use of contraceptives.

contraceptive n. a device or drug that prevents pregnancy. •adj. preventing pregnancy.

contract n. a legally binding agreement. •v. **1** make or become smaller or shorter. **2** make or arrange by a contract. **3** catch a disease. ∎ **contractual** adj. **contractor** n.

contractile adj. able to contract or produce contraction.

contraction n. **1** the process of contracting. **2** a shortening of the muscles of the womb during childbirth. **3** a shortened form of a word or words.

contradict v. deny the truth of a statement by saying the opposite. ∎ **contradiction** n. **contradictory** adj.

contraflow n. a flow of traffic in a direction opposite to and alongside the usual flow.

contralto n. (pl. **contraltos**) the lowest female singing voice.

contraption n. a strange machine or device.

contrapuntal adj. of or in counterpoint.

contrary adj. **1** opposite in nature, direction, or meaning. **2** /kuhn-**trair**-i/ inclined to do the opposite of what is desired. •n. (**the contrary**) the opposite.

contrast n. the state of being noticeably different when compared. •v. **1** differ noticeably. **2** compare so as to note differences.

contravene v. break a law, treaty, etc. ∎ **contravention** n.

contretemps /kon-truh-ton/ n. (pl. **contretemps**) a minor disagreement.

contribute v. **1** give so as to help achieve or provide something.

2 help to cau[...]
contributor n[...]

contrite adj. s[...]
wrong. ∎ **contr**[...]

contrivance n[...]
or scheme. **2** the[...]

contrive v. **1** pla[...]
fully. **2** manage to[...]

contrived adj. arti[...]
false.

control n. **1** the pow[...]
ence or limit somethi[...]
means of limiting or re[...]
something. **3** a standar[...]
checking the results of a[...]
ment. •v. (**controlling**, [...]
led) **1** have power over. **2**[...]
regulate. ∎ **controllable** a[...]
controller n.

controversial adj. causing[...]
troversy. ∎ **controversially** a[...]

controversy n. (pl. **controve**[...]
sies) public debate about a ma[...]
which arouses conflicting opin[...]
ions.

contusion n. a bruise.

conundrum n. a puzzle or problem.

conurbation n. a large urban area where several towns have merged together.

convalesce v. regain health after illness. ∎ **convalescence** n. **convalescent** adj. & n.

convection n. transference of heat within a fluid caused by the tendency of warmer material to rise. ∎ **convector** n.

convene v. come or bring together for a meeting. ∎ **convener** (or **convenor**) n.

convenience n. **1** freedom from effort or difficulty. **2** a useful thing. **3** a public toilet.

convenient adj. **1** fitting in with needs or plans. **2** involving little (or fail to stay) calm. ■ **coolly** adv. **coolness** n.

coolant n. a fluid used for cooling machinery.

coolie n. (pl. **coolies**) dated an unskilled labourer in some Asian countries.

coomb var. of **COMBE**.

coop n. a cage for poultry. •v. (**coop up**) confine in a small space.

cooper n. a person who makes or repairs casks and barrels.

cooperate v. 1 work together to achieve something. 2 comply with a request. ■ **cooperation** n.

cooperative adj. 1 involving co-operation. 2 willing to help. 3 (of a business) owned and run jointly by its members. •n. a cooperative business. ■ **cooperatively** adv.

co-opt v. appoint to a committee by the invitation of existing members.

coordinate v. 1 organize the different elements of an activity so that it works efficiently. 2 match or harmonize well. •n. 1 each of the numbers used to indicate the position of a point. 2 (**coordinates**) matching items of clothing. ■ **coordination** n. **coordinator** n.

coot n. a black waterbird.

cop informal n. a police officer. •v. (**copping, copped**) 1 catch or arrest. 2 (**cop out**) avoid doing something that you ought to do.

cope v. deal effectively with something difficult.

copier n. a copying machine.

coping n. the top layer of a brick or stone wall.

copious adj. abundant; plentiful. ■ **copiously** adv.

copper n. 1 a red-brown metallic element. 2 (**coppers**) coins made of copper or bronze. 3 a reddish-brown colour. 4 informal a police officer. □ **copper-bottomed** thoroughly reliable. **copperplate** neat slanting handwriting.

coppice n. a small wood in which the trees are regularly cut back to ground level.

copse n. a small group of trees.

copulate v. have sex. ■ **copulation** n.

copy n. (pl. **copies**) 1 a thing made to look like another. 2 a single example of a book, record, etc. 3 matter to be printed in a newspaper etc. •v. (**copying, copied**) 1 make a copy of. 2 imitate. □ **copyright** the exclusive right to publish or record a work. **copywriter** a person who writes advertisements or publicity material.

coquette n. a woman who flirts. ■ **coquetry** n. **coquettish** adj.

coracle n. a small wicker boat.

coral n. 1 a hard substance consisting of the skeletons of certain sea animals. 2 a pinkish-red colour.

cor anglais /kor ong-glay/ n. (pl. **cors anglais**) a woodwind instrument of the oboe family.

corbel n. a stone or wooden support projecting from a wall.

cord n. 1 thin string or rope made from several twisted strands. 2 an electric flex. 3 corduroy. □ **cordless** (of an electrical appliance) working without connection to a mains supply.

cordial adj. 1 warm and friendly. 2 deeply felt. •n. a fruit-flavoured drink. ■ **cordiality** n. **cordially** adv.

cordite n. a smokeless explosive.

cordon n. a line or circle of police, soldiers, etc. forming a barrier. •v.

(**cordon off**) close off by means of a cordon.

cordon bleu /kor-don bler/ adj. Cookery of the highest class.

corduroy n. thick cotton fabric with velvety ribs.

core n. **1** the tough central part of some fruits. **2** the central or most important part. • v. remove the core from a fruit.

co-respondent n. the person named in a divorce case as having committed adultery with the respondent.

corgi n. (pl. **corgis**) a short-legged breed of dog.

coriander n. a herb used in cookery.

cork n. **1** a light substance obtained from the bark of a tree. **2** a bottle stopper made of cork. • v. **1** seal with a cork. **2** (**corked**) (of wine) spoilt by a decayed cork. □ **corkage** a charge made by a restaurant for serving wine brought in by a customer. **corkscrew** a device for pulling corks from bottles.

corm n. an underground storage organ of some plants.

cormorant n. a large black seabird.

corn n. **1** wheat, oats, or maize; grain. **2** a small painful area of thickened skin on the foot. □ **cornflour** fine flour made from maize. **cornflower** a blue-flowered plant.

cornea n. the transparent layer forming the front of the eye.

cornelian var. of CARNELIAN.

corner n. **1** a place or angle where sides or edges meet. **2** a free kick or hit taken from a corner of the field in football or hockey. • v. **1** force into a situation from which

it is hard to escape. **2** go round a bend in a road. **3** control a market by dominating the supply of a commodity. □ **cornerstone** a vital part; a foundation.

cornet n. **1** a brass instrument like a small trumpet. **2** a cone-shaped wafer holding ice cream.

cornice n. a decorative moulding round the wall of a room below the ceiling.

cornucopia n. an abundant supply of good things.

corny adj. (**cornier, corniest**) informal sentimental or unoriginal.

corolla n. the petals of a flower.

corollary n. (pl. **corollaries**) **1** a direct consequence. **2** a proposition that follows logically from another.

corona n. (pl. **coronae**) the gases surrounding the sun or another star.

coronary adj. of the arteries which supply the heart. • n. (pl. **coronaries**) a blockage of the flow of blood to the heart.

coronation n. the ceremony of crowning a monarch.

coroner n. an official who holds inquests into violent, sudden, or suspicious deaths.

coronet n. a small crown.

corpora pl. of CORPUS.

corporal n. the army rank below sergeant. • adj. of the human body. □ **corporal punishment** physical punishment, e.g. caning.

corporate adj. **1** of a business corporation. **2** shared by or of all members of a group.

corporation n. **1** a large company or a group of companies as a unit. **2** a group of people elected to govern a town.

corporeal adj. of the body; physical.

corps /kor/ n. (pl. **corps**) **1** a military unit. **2** a group of people involved in a particular activity.

corpse n. a dead body.

corpulent adj. fat.

corpus n. (pl. **corpora** or **corpuses**) a collection of written works.

corpuscle n. a blood cell.

corral n. US a pen for livestock. •v. (**corralling**, **corralled**) put or keep in a corral.

correct adj. **1** free from error; true. **2** following accepted social standards. •v. **1** put right. **2** mark errors in a text. ■ **correction** n. **correctly** adv. **correctness** n.

corrective adj. designed to correct something undesirable.

correlate v. have or bring into a dependent relationship. ■ **correlation** n.

correspond v. **1** be similar or equivalent. **2** exchange letters.

correspondence n. **1** letters sent or received. **2** a close link or similarity.

correspondent n. **1** a journalist reporting on a particular subject. **2** a person who writes letters.

corridor n. **1** a passage in a building or train, with doors leading into rooms or compartments. **2** a strip of land linking two other areas.

corroborate v. confirm or support. ■ **corroboration** n.

corrode v. (of metal etc.) wear or be worn away slowly by chemical action. ■ **corrosion** n. **corrosive** adj.

corrugated adj. shaped into alternate ridges and grooves. ■ **corrugation** n.

corrupt adj. **1** willing to act dishonestly in return for money etc. **2** evil or immoral. **3** (esp. of computer data) full of errors. •v. make corrupt. ■ **corruption** n.

corsair n. old use a pirate.

corset n. a tight-fitting undergarment worn to shape or support the body.

cortège /kor-tezh/ n. a funeral procession.

cortex n. (pl. **cortices**) the outer layer of a bodily organ, esp. of the brain.

cortisone n. a hormone used to treat inflammation and allergy.

corvette n. a small warship.

cos abbrev. cosine.

cosh n. a heavy stick or bar used as a weapon. •v. hit with a cosh.

cosine n. (in a right-angled triangle) the ratio of the side adjacent to an acute angle to the hypotenuse.

cosmetic adj. **1** intended to improve the appearance. **2** superficial. •n. a cosmetic substance for the face and body.

cosmic adj. of the universe.

cosmology n. the science of the origin and development of the universe. ■ **cosmological** adj. **cosmologist** n.

cosmonaut n. a Russian astronaut.

cosmopolitan adj. **1** made up of people from many different countries. **2** familiar with many different countries.

cosmos n. the universe.

Cossack n. a member of a people of Russia and Ukraine noted for their horsemanship.

cosset v. (**cosseting**, **cosseted**) look after with excessive kindness.

cost v. (**costing, cost**) **1** be obtainable for a specific price. **2** involve the loss of. **3** (**costing, costed**) estimate the cost of. • n. what something costs.

co-star n. a performer appearing with another of equal importance.

costermonger n. dated a person who sells fruit and vegetables in the street.

costly adj. (**costlier, costliest**) **1** expensive. **2** causing suffering or loss.

costume n. **1** a set of clothes typical of a country or historical period. **2** clothes worn by an actor or performer.

cosy (US **cozy**) adj. (**cosier, cosiest**) **1** comfortable, warm, and secure. **2** not difficult or demanding. • n. (pl. **cosies**) a cover to keep a teapot hot. ■ **cosily** adv. **cosiness** n.

cot n. a child's bed with high barred sides. □ **cot death** the unexplained death of a baby in its sleep.

coterie /koh-tuh-ri/ n. a small exclusive group.

cottage n. a small house in the country. □ **cottage cheese** soft, lumpy white cheese. **cottage industry** a business or manufacturing activity carried on in the home.

cotton n. **1** soft white fibres round the seeds of a tropical plant. **2** cloth or thread made from these fibres. • v. (**cotton on**) informal understand. □ **cotton wool** fluffy cotton material for wiping the skin.

cotyledon /ko-ti-lee-duhn/ n. the first leaf growing from a seed.

couch n. a sofa. • v. express in a particular way. □ **couch potato**

informal a person who watches a lot of television.

couchette /koo-shet/ n. a railway carriage with seats convertible into beds.

cougar /koo-ger/ US a puma.

cough v. **1** send out air from the lungs with a sudden sharp sound. **2** (**cough up**) informal give money reluctantly. • n. **1** an act of coughing. **2** an illness causing coughing.

could past of **can**[1].

couldn't contr. could not.

coulomb n. a unit of electric charge.

council n. **1** a group meeting regularly for debate and administration. **2** a group elected to govern a town or region. □ **council tax** a UK tax charged on households by local authorities. ■ **councillor** n.

counsel n. **1** advice. **2** (pl. **counsel**) a barrister. • v. (**counselling, counselled**; US **counseling, counseled**) **1** advise. **2** professionally advise someone with personal or psychological problems. ■ **counsellor** n.

count v. **1** find the total number of. **2** say numbers in order. **3** include. **4** regard as being. **5** be important. **6** (**count on**) rely on. • n. **1** an act of counting. **2** a total. **3** a point to consider. **4** a charge against an accused person. **5** a foreign nobleman. □ **countdown 1** the counting of seconds backwards to zero to launch a rocket. **2** the final moments before a significant event.

countenance n. a person's face or expression. • v. allow.

counter n. **1** a long flat surface over which goods are sold or across which business is conducted. **2** a small disc used in board games. •v. speak or act against. •adv. (**counter to**) in the opposite direction or in opposition to.

counter- prefix **1** opposing or done in return. **2** corresponding.

counteract v. reduce or prevent the effects of.

counter-attack n. an attack made in response to an attack. •v. make a counter-attack.

counterbalance n. a weight or influence that balances or neutralizes another. •v. have an equal but opposite effect on.

counterfeit adj. not genuine; forged. •n. a forgery. •v. imitate fraudulently.

counterfoil n. the part of a cheque, ticket, etc. kept as a record by the person issuing it.

countermand v. cancel an order.

counterpane n. a bedspread.

counterpart n. a person or thing that corresponds to another.

counterpoint n. **1** the technique of combining musical melodies. **2** a contrasting idea or thing.

counterproductive adj. having the opposite of the desired effect.

countersign v. sign a document already signed by another person.

countersink v. (**countersinking**, **countersunk**) insert a screw or bolt so that the head is level with the surface.

countertenor n. the highest male adult singing voice.

counterterrorism n. political or military activities designed to prevent terrorism.

countess n. **1** the wife or widow of a count or earl. **2** a woman with the rank of count or earl.

countless adj. too many to be counted.

countrified adj. characteristic of the country or country life.

country n. (pl. **countries**) **1** a nation with its own government. **2** areas outside large towns and cities. □ **countryman** (or **countrywoman**) **1** a person from your country. **2** a person living in the country. **country music** (or **country and western**) popular music from the rural southern US. **countryside** the land of a rural area.

county n. (pl. **counties**) each of the main administrative areas into which some countries are divided.

coup /koo/ n. (pl. **coups** /kooz/) **1** (or **coup d'état** /koo day-**tah**/) a sudden violent seizure of power from a government. **2** a successful move.

coup de grâce /koo duh **grahss**/ n. (pl. **coups de grâce**) a final blow or shot given to kill a wounded person or animal.

coupe /koo-pay, koop/ n. a two-door car with a fixed roof and a sloping back.

couple n. **1** two people or things of the same sort. **2** two people who are married or romantically involved. **3** informal a small number. •v. **1** connect or combine. **2** have sex.

couplet n. two successive rhyming lines of verse.

coupling n. a connecting device.

coupon n. **1** a voucher entitling the holder to something. **2** a detachable order form.

courage n. the ability to control fear when facing danger or pain. ■ **courageous** adj. **courageously** adv.

courgette /koor-*zhet*/ n. a small vegetable marrow.

courier /kuu-ri-er/ n. **1** a person employed to deliver things quickly. **2** a person employed to assist a group of tourists.

course n. **1** a direction taken or intended. **2** the way something progresses. **3** (or **course of action**) a procedure adopted. **4** one of the stages of a meal. **5** a series of lessons. **6** a series of treatments. **7** an area for racing, golf, etc. • v. **1** flow. **2** (**coursing**) hunting hares with greyhounds. □ **of course 1** as expected. **2** yes.

court n. **1** the judge, jury, and law officers who hear legal cases. **2** the place where a law court meets. **3** an area for playing tennis, squash, etc. **4** a courtyard. **5** the home, advisers, and staff of a sovereign. • v. **1** try to win the support of. **2** risk danger etc. **3** *dated* try to win the love of. □ **courtship** the act or period of courting someone. **court shoe** a woman's shoe with a low-cut upper and no fastening. **court martial** (*pl.* **courts martial**) a court trying offences against military law. **courtyard** an open area enclosed by walls or buildings.

courteous /ker-ti-uhss/ adj. polite. ■ **courteously** adv.

courtesan /kor-ti-zan/ n. a prostitute with upper-class clients.

courtesy n. (*pl.* **courtesies**) **1** polite behaviour. **2** a polite action.

courtier n. a sovereign's companion or adviser.

courtly adj. dignified and polite.

couscous /kuuss-kuuss/ n. a North African dish of steamed semolina.

cousin n. (or **first cousin**) a child of your uncle or aunt. □ **second cousin** a child of your parent's first cousin.

couture /koo-*tyoor*/ n. the design and making of fashionable clothes. ■ **couturier** n.

cove n. a small bay.

coven /kuv-uhn/ n. a group of witches who meet regularly.

covenant n. a formal agreement, esp. one to make regular payments to a charity.

cover v. **1** put something over or in front of to protect or hide. **2** spread or extend over. **3** deal with or report on. **4** travel a specified distance. **5** be enough to pay for. **6** protect by insurance. **7** (**cover up**) try to hide a mistake or crime. **8** (**cover for**) temporarily take over the job of. • n. **1** something that covers or protects. **2** protection by insurance. ■ **coverage 1** the treatment of a subject by the media. **2** the extent to which something is covered. **covering letter** an explanatory letter enclosed with goods. **coverlet** a bedspread. **cover-up** an attempt to hide a mistake or crime.

covert adj. done secretly. • n. a thicket in which game can hide. ■ **covertly** adv.

covet v. (**coveting**, **coveted**) long to possess something belonging to someone else. ■ **covetous** adj.

covey /kuv-i/ n. (*pl.* **coveys**) a small flock of game birds.

cow n. **1** a mature female animal of cattle and of the elephant or whale. **2** *informal, derog.* a woman. • v. intimidate. □ **cowboy 1** a man on horseback who herds cattle in the western US. **2** *informal* a dishonest or unqualified tradesman.

coward → crane

coward n. a person who lacks courage. ■ **cowardly** adj. **cowardice** n.

cower v. crouch or shrink back in fear.

cowl n. 1 a loose hood on a monk's robe. 2 a covering for a chimney.

cowling n. a removable cover for an engine.

cowrie n. a shellfish with a glossy shell.

cowslip n. a wild plant with small yellow flowers.

cox n. a person who steers a rowing boat.

coxcomb n. old use a vain man.

coxswain /kok-suhn/ n. = cox.

coy adj. 1 pretending to be shy or modest. 2 reluctant to give details about something. ■ **coyly** adv.

coyote /koy-oh-ti/ n. a North American wolf-like wild dog.

coypu n. a large beaver-like South American rodent.

cozy US = cosy.

crab n. a ten-legged shellfish.

crab apple n. a small, sour apple.

crabbed adj. 1 (of writing) hard to read. 2 (or **crabby**) bad-tempered.

crack n. 1 a line where something has broken but not separated. 2 a sudden sharp noise. 3 a sharp blow. 4 informal a joke. 5 informal an attempt. 6 a strong form of cocaine. • v. 1 break without separating. 2 give way under pressure. 3 make a sudden sharp sound. 4 hit hard. 5 (of a voice) suddenly change in pitch. 6 informal solve. • adj. very good or skilful. ◻ **crackdown** a series of severe measures against something. **crack down on** informal take severe measures against.

crackpot informal eccentric or impractical. **crack up** informal suffer an emotional breakdown.

cracker n. 1 a paper tube making a sharp noise when pulled apart. 2 an explosive firework. 3 a thin, dry biscuit.

crackers adj. informal mad.

crackle v. make a series of slight cracking noises. • n. a crackling sound. ■ **crackly** adj.

crackling n. the crisp fatty skin of roast pork.

cradle n. 1 a baby's bed on rockers. 2 a place where something originates. 3 a supporting framework. • v. hold or support gently.

craft n. 1 an activity involving skill in making things by hand. 2 skill. 3 (pl. **craft**) a ship or boat. • v. make skilfully.

craftsman n. a worker skilled in a craft. ■ **craftsmanship** n.

crafty adj. (**craftier**, **craftiest**) clever at deceiving people; cunning. ■ **craftily** adv. **craftiness** n.

crag n. a steep or rugged rock face. ■ **craggy** adj.

cram v. (**cramming**, **crammed**) 1 force into too small a space. 2 fill to overflowing. 3 study hard for an exam.

cramp n. painful involuntary tightening of a muscle. • v. 1 restrict. 2 (**cramped**) very small or crowded.

crampon n. a spiked plate fixed to a boot for climbing on ice.

cranberry n. a small sour red berry.

crane n. 1 a tall machine for lifting and moving heavy objects. 2 a long-legged wading bird. • v. stretch out your neck to see something.

cranium n. (pl. **craniums** or **crania**) the skull.

crank n. **1** a right-angled part of an axle or shaft for converting linear to circular motion. **2** an eccentric person. • v. turn a crankshaft or handle. □ **crankshaft** a shaft driven by a crank.

cranky adj. informal eccentric or strange.

cranny n. (pl. **crannies**) a crevice.

craps n. a gambling game played with two dice.

crash v. **1** (of a vehicle) collide violently with something. **2** (of an aircraft) fall from the sky and hit the land or sea. **3** move loudly and forcefully. **4** Computing fail suddenly. • n. **1** an instance of crashing. **2** a sudden loud noise. • adj. rapid and concentrated. □ **crash helmet** a helmet worn to protect the head. **crash-land** (of an aircraft) land roughly in an emergency.

crass adj. very thoughtless and stupid.

crate n. **1** a wooden box for transporting goods. **2** a container divided into sections for holding bottles. • v. pack in a crate.

crater n. a large hollow in the ground or forming the mouth of a volcano.

cravat n. a man's scarf worn tucked inside a shirt.

crave v. **1** feel a strong desire for. **2** old use ask for. ■ **craving** n.

craven adj. cowardly.

crawl v. **1** move forward on the hands and knees or with the body on the ground. **2** move along very slowly. **3** (**be crawling with**) be crowded with. **4** informal be very submissive or friendly so as to gain favour. • n. **1** a crawling movement

or pace. **2** an overarm swimming stroke. ■ **crawler** n.

crayfish n. a shellfish like a small lobster.

crayon n. a stick of coloured chalk or wax, used for drawing. • v. draw with a crayon or crayons.

craze n. a widespread but short-lived enthusiasm for something.

crazy adj. (**crazier, craziest**) **1** mad. **2** informal very enthusiastic or fond. **3** very foolish. □ **crazy paving** paving made of irregular flat stones. ■ **crazily** adv. **craziness** n.

creak v. make a harsh, high sound. • n. a creaking sound. ■ **creaky** adj.

cream n. **1** the thick fatty part of milk. **2** a thick liquid substance. **3** the very best of a group. **4** a pale yellowish-white colour. • v. **1** mash a cooked vegetable with milk or cream. **2** (**cream off**) take away the best of. ■ **creamy** adj.

crease n. **1** a line or ridge made on paper or cloth by folding or pressing. **2** a line on a cricket pitch marking the position of the bowler etc. • v. make or develop creases in.

create v. **1** bring into existence. **2** cause to happen. ■ **creation** n. **creator** n.

creative adj. involving the use of imagination to create something. ■ **creatively** adv. **creativity** n.

creature n. a living being.

crèche /kresh/ n. a day nursery.

credence n. belief that something is true.

credentials pl. n. **1** qualifications or qualities indicating a person's suitability for something. **2** documents proving qualifications etc.

credible adj. able to be believed. ■ **credibility** n. **credibly** adv.

credit n. **1** a system allowing customers to pay at a later date for goods or services supplied. **2** public recognition or praise. **3** a source of pride. **4** (**credits**) a list of the contributors to a film or television programme, displayed at the end. **5** an entry in an account recording a sum received. • v. (**crediting, credited**) **1** (**credit with**) attribute something to. **2** believe. **3** add money to an account. □ **credit card** a plastic card allowing the holder to make purchases on credit.

creditable adj. deserving praise. ■ **creditably** adv.

creditor n. a person or company to whom money is owed.

credulous adj. too ready to believe things. ■ **credulity** n.

creed n. **1** a system of religious belief. **2** a set of beliefs or principles.

creek n. **1** an inlet in a shoreline. **2** US a stream.

creep v. (**creeping, crept**) **1** move slowly and cautiously. **2** progress or develop gradually. • n. **1** informal an unpleasant person. **2** slow and gradual movement.

creeper n. a plant that grows along the ground or another surface.

creepy adj. (**creepier, creepiest**) informal frightening or disturbing.

cremate v. burn a corpse to ashes. ■ **cremation** n.

crematorium n. (pl. **crematoria** or **crematoriums**) a building where the dead are cremated.

crenellated adj. having battlements. ■ **crenellations** pl. n.

Creole /kree-ohl/ n. **1** (in the Caribbean) a person of mixed European and black descent. **2** a descendant of French settlers in the southern US. **3** a combination of a European language and an African one.

creosote n. a dark brown oil used as a wood preservative.

crêpe n. **1** /krayp/ a fabric or a type of rubber with a wrinkled surface. **2** /krep/ a thin pancake.

crept past & past part. of **CREEP**.

crepuscular adj. resembling twilight.

crescendo n. (pl. **crescendos** or **crescendi**) a gradual increase in loudness.

crescent n. a narrow curved shape tapering to a point at each end.

cress n. a salad vegetable with small leaves.

crest n. **1** the top of a hill or wave. **2** a tuft of feathers or a growth of skin on a bird's or animal's head. **3** a plume of feathers on a helmet. **4** a design above a shield on a coat of arms. □ **crestfallen** sad and disappointed. ■ **crested** adj.

cretin n. informal a stupid person. ■ **cretinous** adj.

crevasse n. a deep open crack in a glacier.

crevice n. a narrow opening in a rock or wall.

crew[1] n. **1** the people working on a ship, aircraft, etc. **2** a group working together. • v. act as a member of a crew. □ **crew cut** a very short haircut. **crew neck** a close-fitting round neckline.

crew[2] past of **CROW**.

crib n. **1** a child's cot. **2** informal a list of facts, often used to cheat in a test. **3** a rack for animal fodder. • v. (**cribbing, cribbed**) informal copy dishonestly.

cribbage n. a card game.

crick n. a painful stiff feeling in the neck or back. •v. cause a crick in.

cricket n. **1** an open-air team game played with a bat, ball, and wickets. **2** an insect like a grasshopper. ■ **cricketer** n.

cried past & past part. of **CRY**.

crime n. **1** an act that is illegal and can be punished by law. **2** illegal actions.

criminal n. a person who has committed a crime. •adj. of a crime or a crime. ■ **criminality** n. **criminally** adv.

criminology n. the study of crime. ■ **criminologist** n.

crimp v. press into ridges.

crimson n. a deep red colour.

cringe v. **1** cower in fear. **2** feel embarrassment or disgust.

crinkle v. form small creases. •n. a small crease. ■ **crinkly** adj.

crinoline n. a petticoat stiffened with hoops, formerly worn to make a long skirt stand out.

cripple n. old use or offens. a person unable to walk properly through disability or injury. •v. **1** make unable to walk properly. **2** severely damage.

crisis n. (pl. **crises**) a time of severe difficulty or danger.

crisp adj. **1** firm, dry, and brittle. **2** cold and bracing. **3** brisk and decisive. •n. a thin slice of fried potato. □ **crispbread** a thin, crisp biscuit made from rye or wheat. ■ **crisply** adv. **crispness** n. **crispy** adj.

criss-cross adj. with a pattern of crossing lines. •v. form a criss-cross pattern on.

criterion n. (pl. **criteria**) a standard by which something may be judged.

! The singular form is **criterion** and the plural form is **criteria**. Don't use **criteria** as a singular, as in a further criteria needs to be considered.

critic n. **1** a person who points out faults. **2** a person who assesses literary or artistic works.

critical adj. **1** expressing disapproving comments. **2** assessing a literary or artistic work. **3** having a decisive importance. **4** at a point of danger or crisis. ■ **critically** adv.

criticism n. **1** expression of disapproval. **2** the assessment of literary or artistic works.

criticize (or **-ise**) v. **1** express disapproval of. **2** assess a literary or artistic work.

critique n. a critical assessment.

croak n. a deep hoarse sound, like that made by a frog. •v. make a croak. ■ **croaky** adj.

crochet /kroh-shay/ n. a handicraft in which yarn is made into a fabric by means of a hooked needle. •v. make in this way.

crock n. **1** an earthenware pot. **2** informal a feeble old person.

crockery n. china or earthenware plates, cups, etc.

crocodile n. **1** a large tropical reptile living partly in water. **2** informal a line of schoolchildren walking in pairs. □ **crocodile tears** false sorrow.

crocus n. (pl. **crocuses**) a small spring-flowering plant.

croft n. a small rented farm in Scotland. ■ **crofter** n.

croissant /krwass-on/ n. a crescent-shaped flaky bread roll.

crone n. an ugly old woman.

crony n. (pl. **cronies**) informal a close friend or companion.

crook n. **1** informal a criminal. **2** a hooked staff. **3** the inner bend at the elbow. •v. bend a finger.

crooked adj. **1** not straight. **2** informal dishonest. ■ **crookedly** adv.

croon v. hum, sing, or speak in a soft, low voice. ■ **crooner** n.

crop n. **1** a plant grown for food or other use. **2** a harvest from this. **3** a very short hairstyle. **4** a riding crop. **5** a pouch in a bird's throat where food is prepared for digestion. •v. (**cropping, cropped**) **1** cut or bite off very short. **2** (**crop up**) occur unexpectedly. **3** produce a crop.

cropper n. (**come a cropper**) informal fall or fail heavily.

croquet /kroh-kay/ n. a game in which balls are hit through hoops with a mallet.

croquette /kroh-ket/ n. a small roll or cake of vegetables etc. fried in breadcrumbs.

crosier var. of CROZIER.

cross n. **1** a mark, object, or shape formed by two intersecting lines or pieces (+ or ×). **2** a mixture of two things. **3** a hybrid animal or plant. **4** a pass of the ball across the field in football. •v. **1** go or extend across. **2** pass in an opposite or different direction. **3** place crosswise. **4** oppose the wishes of. **5** draw a line or lines across. **6** mark a cheque so that it must be paid into a named account. **7** pass the ball across the field in football. **8** cause to interbreed. •adj. annoyed. □ **at cross purposes** misunderstanding one another. **crossbow** a mechanical bow with a wooden support. **cross-breed**

produce an animal by interbreeding. **cross-check** verify figures etc. by an alternative method. **cross-dressing** the wearing of clothing typical of the opposite sex. **cross-examine** question a witness called by the other party in a court of law. **cross-eyed** having one or both eyes turned inwards. **crossfire** gunfire crossing another line of fire. **cross reference** a reference to another part in the same book. **crossroads** a place where roads cross each other. **cross section 1** a surface exposed by cutting across something. **2** a representative sample. **crosswise** (or **crossways**) **1** in the form of a cross. **2** diagonally. **crossword** a puzzle consisting of a grid of squares into which intersecting words are written according to clues. ■ **crossly** adv. **crossness** n.

crossing n. **1** a place where roads or railway lines cross. **2** a place to cross a road or railway line.

crotch n. the part of the body between the legs.

crotchet n. a musical note having the value of half a minim.

crotchety adj. irritable.

crouch v. bend the knees and bring the upper body forward and down. •n. a crouching position.

croup n. **1** inflammation of the throat in children, causing coughing and breathing difficulties. **2** the rump of a horse.

croupier /kroo-pi-ay/ n. the person in charge of a gambling table at a casino.

crouton /kroo-ton/ n. a small piece of fried or toasted bread used as a garnish.

crow n. **1** a large black bird. **2** the cry of a cock. •v. (**crowing,**

crowed or **crew) 1** (of a cock) make its loud shrill cry. **2** express gloating triumph.

crowbar n. an iron bar with a flattened end, used as a lever.

crowd n. a large group of people gathered together. • v. **1** fill a space almost completely. **2** move or gather in a crowd.

crown n. **1** a monarch's ceremonial headdress. **2** (**the Crown**) the monarchy or reigning monarch. **3** the top or highest part. **4** an artificial covering for a tooth. • v. **1** formally place a crown on the head of a new monarch. **2** rest on or form the top of. **3** be the climax of. □ **Crown prince** (or **Crown princess**) the heir to a throne.

crozier (or **crosier**) n. a bishop's hooked staff.

crucial adj. very important to the success or failure of something. ■ **crucially** adv.

crucible n. a container in which metals are melted.

crucifix n. a model of a cross with a figure of Jesus on it.

crucifixion n. **1** an act of crucifying someone. **2** (**the Crucifixion**) the killing of Jesus in this way.

cruciform adj. cross-shaped.

crucify v. (**crucifying, crucified**) **1** put to death by nailing or binding to a cross. **2** informal criticize severely.

crude adj. **1** in a natural or unprocessed state. **2** rough or simple. **3** coarse or vulgar. ■ **crudely** adv. **crudity** n.

crudités /kroo-di-tay/ pl. n. mixed raw vegetables to dip into a sauce.

cruel adj. (**crueller, cruellest** or **crueler, cruelest**) **1** taking pleasure in others' suffering. **2** causing

pain or suffering. ■ **cruelly** adv. **cruelty** n.

cruet n. a set of containers for salt, pepper, etc. for use at the table.

cruise v. **1** travel around slowly, esp. by ship. **2** travel at a moderate economical speed. • n. a voyage on a ship taken as a holiday.

cruiser n. **1** a fast warship. **2** a motorboat with a cabin.

crumb n. **1** a small fragment of bread etc. **2** a tiny amount.

crumble v. break or fall apart into small fragments. • n. a baked pudding made with fruit and a crumbly topping. ■ **crumbly** adj.

crummy adj. informal bad or unpleasant.

crumpet n. **1** a flat soft cake eaten toasted. **2** informal sexually attractive women.

crumple v. **1** crush so as to become creased. **2** collapse.

crunch v. **1** crush noisily with the teeth. **2** move with a noisy grinding sound. • n. **1** a crunching sound. **2** (**the crunch**) informal the crucial point. ■ **crunchy** adj.

crusade n. **1** (**the Crusades**) a series of medieval Christian military expeditions to recover the Holy Land from the Muslims. **2** a campaign for a cause. • v. take part in a crusade. ■ **crusader** n.

crush v. **1** press so as to squash, crease, or break up. **2** defeat completely. • n. **1** a crowded mass of people. **2** informal an infatuation.

crust n. a hard outer layer, esp. of bread.

crustacean /kruss-**tay**-sh'n/ n. a hard-shelled animal such as a crab, usu. living in water.

crusty adj. (**crustier, crustiest**) **1** having a crust. **2** irritable.

crutch n. **1** a stick with a cross-piece used as a support by a lame person. **2** the crotch.

crux n. the most important point under discussion.

cry v. (**crying, cried**) **1** shed tears. **2** shout or scream loudly. **3** (**cry off**) informal fail to keep to an arrangement. • n. (pl. **cries**) **1** a period of crying. **2** a shout or scream. **3** an animal's call.

cryogenics n. the study of very low temperatures. ■ **cryogenic** adj.

crypt n. an underground room or vault in a church.

cryptic adj. mysterious or obscure in meaning. ■ **cryptically** adv.

cryptogram n. a document written in code.

cryptography n. the art of writing or solving codes.

crystal n. **1** a transparent mineral, esp. quartz. **2** a piece of a solid substance with symmetrical flat sides. **3** very clear glass.

crystalline adj. **1** of or like a crystal. **2** very clear.

crystallize (or **-ise**) v. **1** form crystals. **2** make or become definite and clear. **3** (**crystallized**) (of fruit) preserved in sugar. ■ **crystallization** n.

CS gas n. tear gas used in the control of riots.

cu. abbrev. cubic.

cub n. the young of a fox, bear, lion, etc.

cubbyhole n. a small space or room.

cube n. **1** a three-dimensional shape with six equal square faces. **2** the product of a number multiplied by itself twice. • v. **1** cut into cubes. **2** find the cube of a number. □ **cube root** the number

which produces a given number when cubed. ■ **cubic** adj.

cubicle n. a small area partitioned off in a large room.

cubism n. a style of painting in which objects are shown as geometric shapes. ■ **cubist** n. & adj.

cuckold n. a man whose wife has been unfaithful.

cuckoo n. a bird that lays its eggs in the nests of other birds.

cucumber n. a long, green fruit eaten in salads.

cud n. food that cattle etc. bring back from the first stomach to the mouth for further chewing.

cuddle v. **1** hug lovingly. **2** lie or sit close. • n. an affectionate hug.

cuddly adj. pleasantly soft or plump.

cudgel n. a short thick stick used as a weapon. • v. (**cudgelling, cudgelled; US cudgeling, cudgeled**) beat with a cudgel.

cue n. **1** a signal for action, esp. to an actor to enter or to begin their speech. **2** a long rod for hitting the ball in snooker etc. • v. (**cueing** or **cuing, cued**) **1** give a signal to. **2** use a cue to hit a ball.

cuff n. **1** the end part of a sleeve. **2** a blow with an open hand. • v. hit with an open hand. □ **cufflink** a device for fastening together the sides of a shirt cuff. **off the cuff** informal without preparation.

cuisine /kwi-zeen/ n. a style of cooking.

cul-de-sac n. (pl. **cul-de-sacs**) a street closed at one end.

culinary adj. of cooking.

cull v. **1** kill certain animals to reduce numbers. **2** select from a wide range.

culminate v. reach a climax. ■ **culmination** n.

culottes pl. n. women's wide-legged knee-length trousers.

culpable adj. deserving blame. ■ **culpability** n.

culprit n. a person responsible for an offence.

cult n. **1** a small, unconventional religious group. **2** a system of religious beliefs and practices. **3** something popular among a group.

cultivate v. **1** prepare and use land for crops. **2** grow plants or crops. **3** try to develop a quality. **4** try to win the friendship or support of. **5** (**cultivated**) well educated and having good taste. ■ **cultivation** n. **cultivator** n.

culture n. **1** the arts, customs, etc. of a nation or group. **2** the arts and intellectual achievements as a whole. **3** cells or bacteria grown for scientific study. •v. **1** grow cells etc. for study. **2** (**cultured**) well educated and having good taste. ■ **cultural** adj. **culturally** adv.

culvert n. a drain under a road.

cum prep. combined with: *a study-cum-bedroom.*

cumbersome adj. heavy and awkward to carry or use.

cumin n. a spice made from the seeds of a plant.

cummerbund n. a sash worn around the waist.

cumulative adj. increasing by successive additions. ■ **cumulatively** adv.

cumulus /kyoo-myuu-luhss/ n. (pl. **cumuli**) cloud forming rounded masses on a flat base.

cuneiform /kyoo-ni-form/ n. an ancient writing system using wedge-shaped characters.

cunning adj. **1** skilled at deception. **2** skilful or clever. •n. craftiness. ■ **cunningly** adv.

cup n. **1** a small curved drinking container with a handle. **2** a cup-shaped trophy with a stem. •v. (**cupping**, **cupped**) form the hands into a curved shape.

cupboard n. a piece of furniture or small recess with a door, used for storage.

cupidity n. greed for money etc.

cupola n. a small dome.

cur n. a mongrel dog.

curare /kyuu-**rah**-ri/ n. a paralysing poison obtained from plants.

curate n. a member of the clergy who assists a parish priest. ■ **curacy** n.

curator n. a keeper of a museum or other collection.

curb v. control or limit. •n. **1** a control or limit. **2** *US* = **KERB**.

curd n. (or **curds**) n. a soft, white substance formed when milk coagulates.

curdle v. (of a liquid) form lumps.

cure v. **1** make well again. **2** get rid of a disease, problem, etc. **3** preserve by salting, drying, or smoking. •n. **1** a remedy. **2** the healing of someone who is ill. ■ **curable** adj. **curative** adj.

curfew n. **1** a regulation requiring people to remain indoors between specified hours. **2** the time when this begins.

curie n. a unit of radioactivity.

curio n. (pl. **curios**) an unusual and interesting object.

curiosity n. (pl. **curiosities**) **1** a strong desire to know something. **2** a curio.

curious adj. **1** eager to know something. **2** strange; unusual. ■ **curiously** adv.

curl v. form a curved or spiral shape. •n. something in the shape of a spiral or coil. ■ **curly** adj.

curler n. a roller around which hair is wound to curl it.

curlew n. a wading bird with a long curved bill.

curlicue n. a decorative curl or twist.

curling n. a game like bowls played on ice.

curmudgeon n. a bad-tempered person.

currant n. **1** a dried grape. **2** a shrub producing edible berries.

currency n. (pl. **currencies**) **1** a system of money used in a country. **2** the state or period of being current.

current adj. **1** happening or being used now. **2** in general use. •n. **1** a body of water or air moving in a particular direction. **2** a flow of electricity. □ **current account** a bank account from which money may be withdrawn at any time. ■ **currently** adv.

curriculum n. (pl. **curricula** or **curriculums**) a course of study. □ **curriculum vitae** an outline of a person's qualifications and previous jobs. ■ **curricular** adj.

curry n. (pl. **curries**) a dish cooked in a hot, spicy sauce. •v. (**currying, curried**) **1** (**curried**) made as a curry. **2** (**curry favour**) try to win favour by flattery. □ **curry comb** a rubber device for grooming horses.

curse n. **1** an appeal to a supernatural power to harm a person or thing. **2** a cause of harm or misery. **3** a swear word. •v. **1** use a curse

against. **2** (**be cursed with**) be afflicted with. **3** use swear words.

cursive adj. (of writing) written with the characters joined.

cursor n. a movable indicator on a computer screen.

cursory adj. hasty and so not thorough. ■ **cursorily** adv.

curt adj. rudely brief. ■ **curtly** adv.

curtail v. reduce or restrict. ■ **curtailment** n.

curtain n. a piece of material hung as a screen, esp. at a window.

curtsy (or **curtsey**) n. (pl. **curtsies** or **curtseys**) a woman's respectful greeting, made by bending the knees. •v. (**curtsying, curtsied**) perform a curtsy.

curvaceous adj. having an attractively curved shape.

curvature n. the fact of being curved.

curve n. a line which gradually turns from a straight course. •v. form a curve. ■ **curvy** adj.

curvilinear adj. contained by or consisting of curved lines.

cushion n. **1** a stuffed bag for sitting or leaning on. **2** a means of protection against impact etc. •v. **1** soften the effect of an impact on. **2** reduce the bad effects of.

cushy adj. (**cushier, cushiest**) informal easy and undemanding.

cusp n. **1** a pointed end where two curves meet. **2** a point of change between different states.

cussed /kuss-id/ adj. informal awkward or annoying.

custard n. a sweet sauce made with milk and eggs or flavoured cornflour.

custodian n. a guardian or keeper.

custody n. **1** protective care. **2** imprisonment. ■ **custodial** adj.

custom n. **1** a traditional way of behaving or doing something. **2** regular dealings by customers. **3** (**customs**) duties charged on imported goods.

customary adj. usual. ■ **customarily** adv.

customer n. a person buying goods or services from a shop etc.

customize (or **-ise**) v. modify to suit a person or task.

cut v. (**cutting**, **cut**) **1** open or wound with a sharp implement. **2** make, divide, or remove in this way. **3** reduce. **4** go across or through. **5** move to another shot in a film. **6** divide a pack of cards. •n. **1** an act of cutting. **2** an incision or wound. **3** a reduction. **4** a style in which a garment or the hair is cut. **5** a piece of meat cut off. **6** informal a share. □ **cut off** isolated. **cut-throat** ruthless and fierce.

cute adj. **1** charmingly pretty; sweet. **2** US informal clever. ■ **cutely** adv. **cuteness** n.

cuticle n. the skin at the base of a nail.

cutlass n. a short curved sword.

cutlery n. knives, forks, and spoons.

cutlet n. **1** a lamb or veal chop from behind the neck. **2** a flat cake of minced meat, nuts, etc., covered in breadcrumbs and fried.

cutter n. **1** a person or thing that cuts. **2** a fast patrol boat or sailing boat.

cutting n. **1** an article cut from a newspaper. **2** a piece cut from a plant to grow a new one. **3** a passage cut through high ground for a railway etc. •adj. hurtful. □ **the**

cutting edge the most advanced stage.

cuttlefish n. a sea animal like a squid.

CV abbrev. curriculum vitae.

cwt abbrev. hundredweight.

cyan /sy-uhn/ n. a greenish-blue colour.

cyanide n. a highly poisonous compound.

cyber- comb. form of information technology, the Internet, etc.

cybernetics n. the science of systems of communication and control in machines and living things.

cyberspace n. the hypothetical environment in which communication over computer networks occurs.

cyclamen n. a plant with pink, red, or white flowers.

cycle n. **1** a recurring series of events. **2** a bicycle. **3** a series of musical or literary works composed around a theme. •v. ride a bicycle. ■ **cyclist** n.

cyclic (or **cyclical**) adj. occurring in cycles.

cyclone n. **1** a violent wind rotating round a central area. **2** a violent tropical storm. ■ **cyclonic** adj.

cyclotron n. a machine for accelerating charged atomic or subatomic particles in a spiral path.

cygnet n. a young swan.

cylinder n. an object with straight parallel sides and circular ends. ■ **cylindrical** adj.

cymbal n. a musical instrument consisting of a round brass plate struck against another or hit with a stick.

cynic n. a person who believes that people's motives are always selfish. ■ **cynical** adj. **cynically** adv. **cynicism** n.

cynosure /sin-uh-zyoor/ n. a centre of attention.

cypher var. of CIPHER.

cypress n. an evergreen tree.

cyst n. an abnormal sac or cavity in the body, containing fluid.

cystic adj. **1** of cysts. **2** of the bladder or the gall bladder. □ **cystic fibrosis** a hereditary disorder which often results in respiratory infection.

cystitis n. inflammation of the bladder.

cytology n. the study of the structure and function of cells. ■ **cytological** adj.

czar var. of TSAR.

Dd

D n. the Roman numeral for 500.

dab v. (**dabbing, dabbed**) **1** press lightly with something absorbent. **2** apply with light, quick strokes. •n. a small amount lightly applied. □ **dab hand** informal an expert in a particular activity.

dabble v. **1** splash around gently in water. **2** take part in an activity in a casual way.

dace n. (pl. **dace**) a small freshwater fish.

dacha /da-chuh/ n. a Russian country cottage.

dachshund n. a dog with a long body and very short legs.

dad (or **daddy**) n. informal a person's father.

daddy-long-legs n. informal a long-legged flying insect.

dado /day-doh/ n. (pl. **dados**) the lower part of a wall decorated differently from the upper part.

daffodil n. a plant having yellow flowers with a trumpet-shaped centre.

daft adj. informal silly; foolish.

dagger n. a short pointed knife, used as a weapon.

daguerreotype /duh-ger-ruh-typ/ n. an early kind of photograph.

dahlia /day-li-uh/ n. a garden plant with brightly coloured flowers.

daily adj. & adv. every day or every weekday. •n. (pl. **dailies**) informal a daily newspaper.

dainty adj. (**daintier, daintiest**) delicately small and pretty. ■ **daintily** adv. **daintiness** n.

daiquiri /da-ki-ri/ n. (pl. **daiquiris**) a cocktail containing rum and lime juice.

dairy n. (pl. **dairies**) a building where milk and milk products are produced.

dais /day-iss/ n. a low platform for a lectern or throne.

daisy n. (pl. **daisies**) a small flower with many white petals.

dale n. a valley.

dally v. (**dallying, dallied**)
1 waste time. 2 (**dally with**) have a casual relationship with. ■ **dalliance** n.

Dalmatian n. a large white dog with dark spots.

dam n. 1 a barrier built across a river to hold back water. 2 the female parent of an animal. •v. (**damming, dammed**) build a dam across.

damage n. 1 physical harm reducing the value or usefulness of something. 2 harmful effects. 3 (**damages**) money paid to compensate for a loss or injury. •v. cause harm to.

damask n. a fabric with a pattern woven into it.

dame n. 1 (**Dame**) the title of a woman awarded a knighthood. 2 US informal a woman.

damn v. 1 (**be damned**) be condemned by God to eternal punishment in hell. 2 strongly criticize. •exclam. informal expressing anger. •adj. (or **damned**) informal used to emphasize anger. ■ **damnation** n. & exclam.

damnable adj. very bad or unpleasant.

damp adj. slightly wet. •n. moisture. •v. 1 make damp. 2 (**damp down**) control a feeling or situation. ■ **dampness** n.

dampen v. 1 make damp. 2 make less strong or intense. ■ **dampener** n.

damper n. 1 a pad for silencing a piano string. 2 a metal plate regulating the air flow in a chimney.

damsel n. old use a young woman.

damson n. a small purple plum-like fruit.

dance v. 1 move rhythmically to music. 2 move in a quick and lively way. •n. 1 a series of steps and movements performed to music. 2 a social gathering at which people dance. ■ **dancer** n.

dandelion n. a weed with large yellow flowers.

dandle v. gently bounce a young child on your knees.

dandruff n. flakes of dead skin from the scalp.

dandy n. (pl. **dandies**) a man who is too concerned with looking stylish and fashionable. ■ **dandified** adj.

Dane n. a person from Denmark. ■ **Danish** adj. & n.

danger n. 1 the possibility of suffering harm or of experiencing something unpleasant. 2 a cause of harm.

dangerous adj. likely to cause harm or problems.
■ **dangerously** adv.

dangle v. 1 hang so as to swing freely. 2 offer an incentive.
■ **dangly** adj.

dank adj. damp and cold.

dapper adj. (of a man) neat and smart in appearance.

dapple v. mark with small patches of colour, light, etc. ■ **dapple grey** (of a horse) grey with darker ring-shaped markings.

dare v. 1 have the courage to do. 2 challenge to do. •n. a challenge to do something brave or risky. □ **daredevil** a recklessly daring person.

daring adj. 1 willing to do dangerous things. 2 involving danger. •n. adventurous courage.
■ **daringly** adv.

dark adj. 1 with little or no light. 2 of a deep colour. 3 (of skin, hair, or eyes) brown or black. 4 depressing or gloomy. 5 evil or sin-

ister. **6** mysterious. • *n.* **1 (the dark)** the absence of light.
2 night. **dark horse** a person about whom little is known.
darkroom a darkened room for developing photos. ■ **darken** *v.* **darkly** *adv.* **darkness** *n.*

darling *n.* **1** an affectionate form of address. **2** a lovable or popular person. • *adj.* **1** much loved.
2 charming.

darn *v.* mend knitted material by weaving yarn across it. • *adj.* (or **darned**) *informal* damn.

dart *n.* **1** a small pointed missile.
2 (darts) an indoor game in which darts are thrown at a dartboard.
3 a sudden run. **4** a tapered tuck in a garment. • *v.* run suddenly.
□ **dartboard** a circular target used in the game of darts.

dash *v.* **1** run or travel in a great hurry. **2** hit or throw with great force. **3** destroy. • *n.* **1** an act of dashing. **2** a small amount added.
3 style and confidence. **4** a horizontal stroke (-) in writing.
□ **dashboard** the instrument panel in a vehicle.

dashing *adj.* (of a man) attractive, stylish, and confident.

dastardly *adj. dated* wicked and cruel.

data *n.* **1** facts or statistics used for reference or analysis. **2** information processed by a computer.
□ **database** a set of data held in a computer.

> **!** Although **data** is the plural of Latin **datum**, in everyday English use it is usually treated as a singular noun, taking a singular verb, as in *the data was analysed*.

date *n.* **1** the day of the month or year as specified by a number.
2 the day or year of an event's

occurrence. **3** a social or romantic appointment. **4** a sweet, dark brown, oval fruit. • *v.* **1** establish the date of. **2** mark with a date.
3 (date back to) originate from.
4 (dated) old-fashioned.
5 *informal* go on regular dates with. ■ **to date** until now.
■ **datable** (or **dateable**) *adj.*

dative *n.* (in certain languages) the case of nouns and pronouns indicating the indirect object.

datum *n.* (*pl.* **data**) a piece of information.

daub *v.* smear with a thick substance. • *n.* **1** a smear. **2** an unskilful painting.

daughter *n.* a girl or woman in relation to her parents.
□ **daughter-in-law** (*pl.* **daughters-in-law**) the wife of a person's son.

daunt *v.* intimidate or discourage.

dauntless *adj.* fearless and determined.

dauphin /doh-fan/ *n. hist.* the eldest son of the King of France.

davit *n.* a small crane on a ship.

dawdle *v.* move slowly.

dawn *n.* **1** the first appearance of light in the morning. **2** the beginning of something. • *v.* **1** (of a day) begin. **2** come into existence.
3 (dawn on) become evident to.

day *n.* **1** a period of 24 hours. **2** the time between sunrise and sunset.
3 a particular period, esp. of the past. □ **daybreak** dawn. **day-dream** a series of pleasant distracting thoughts. **daylight 1** the natural light of the day. **2** dawn.

daze *v.* stun or bewilder. • *n.* a dazed state.

dazzle *v.* **1** (of a bright light) blind temporarily. **2** amaze with an impressive quality. • *n.* blinding brightness.

dB *abbrev.* decibels.

DC *abbrev.* direct current.

DDT *abbrev.* an insecticide.

deacon *n.* **1** a Christian minister ranking below a priest. **2** (in some Protestant Churches) a lay officer assisting a minister. ■ **deaconess** *n.*

dead *adj.* **1** no longer alive. **2** (of a body part) numb. **3** without activity or excitement. **4** not functioning or current. **5** complete: *dead silence.* • *adv.* **1** completely, exactly, or directly. **2** *informal* very. □ **dead end** a road or passage that is closed at one end. **dead heat** a result in a race in which competitors finish at exactly the same time. **deadline** the latest time or date for completing something. **deadlock** a situation in which no progress can be made. **deadlocked** in a deadlock. **deadpan** expressionless. ■ **deaden** *v.*

deadly *adj.* (**deadlier, deadliest**) **1** causing death. **2** complete; total. • *adv.* very: *deadly serious.* □ **deadly nightshade** a plant with poisonous black berries.

deaf *adj.* **1** unable to hear. **2** (**deaf to**) unwilling to listen to. ■ **deafen** *v.* **deafness** *n.*

deal *v.* (**dealing, dealt**) **1** (**deal out**) distribute. **2** trade in a product. **3** buy and sell illegal drugs. **4** give out cards to players of a game. • *n.* **1** an agreement. **2** a way of being treated: *a fair deal.* □ **a big deal** *informal* an important thing. **deal a blow to** hit or be harmed by. **deal with 1** take action to put right. **2** cope with. **3** have as a subject. **a good (or great) deal** a large amount. ■ **dealer** *n.*

dean *n.* **1** the head of the governing body of a cathedral. **2** the head of a university department etc.

dear *adj.* **1** much loved. **2** expensive. • *n.* a lovable person. • *adv.* at a high cost. • *exclam.* used in expressions of surprise or dismay. ■ **dearly** *adv.*

dearth /derth/ *n.* a scarcity or lack.

death *n.* **1** the act or fact of dying. **2** the state of being dead. **3** the end of something. □ **deathtrap** a dangerous building, vehicle, etc. **death-watch beetle** a beetle whose larvae bore into wood. ■ **deathly** *adj.* suggesting death.

debacle /day-bah-k'l/ *n.* a complete failure or disaster.

debar *v.* (**debarring, debarred**) ban from doing something.

debase *v.* lower in quality or value. ■ **debasement** *n.*

debatable *adj.* open to discussion.

debate *n.* **1** a formal discussion. **2** an argument. • *v.* **1** discuss. **2** consider.

debauchery *n.* excessive behaviour involving sex, alcohol, or drugs. ■ **debauched** *adj.*

debenture *n.* a certificate issued by a company acknowledging that it has borrowed money on which interest is being paid.

debilitate *v.* severely weaken. ■ **debilitation** *n.*

debility *n.* (*pl.* **debilities**) physical weakness.

debit *n.* **1** an entry in an account recording a sum owed. **2** a payment made or owed. • *v.* (**debiting, debited**) (of a bank) take money from a customer's account.

debonair *adj.* (of a man) confident, stylish, and charming.

debrief v. question in detail about a completed mission.

debris /deb-ree/ n. scattered rubbish or broken pieces.

debt n. **1** a sum of money owed. **2** the state of owing something. **3** gratitude for a favour.

debtor n. a person who owes money.

debunk v. reveal a belief to be false.

debut /day-byoo/ n. a person's first appearance in a role. • v. make a debut.

debutante /deb-yuh-tahnt/ n. a young upper-class woman making her first formal appearance in society.

decade n. a period of ten years.

decadent adj. immoral and interested only in pleasure. ■ **decadence** n.

decaffeinated adj. with the caffeine removed or reduced.

decagon n. a plane figure with ten straight sides and angles.

decamp v. leave suddenly or secretly.

decant v. pour liquid from one container into another to remove sediment.

decanter n. a container into which wine etc. is decanted.

decapitate v. behead. ■ **decapitation** n.

decathlon n. an athletic contest involving ten events.

decay v. **1** rot. **2** become worse or weaker. • n. the state or process of decaying.

decease n. death.

deceased adj. recently dead.

deceit n. behaviour intended to mislead or deceive. ■ **deceitful** adj. **deceitfully** adv.

deceive v. **1** cause to believe something false. **2** give a misleading impression. ■ **deceiver** n.

decelerate v. slow down. ■ **deceleration** n.

December n. the twelfth month.

decent adj. **1** following accepted moral standards. **2** of an acceptable quality. **3** informal kind or generous. ■ **decency** n. **decently** adv.

decentralize (or **-ise**) v. transfer from central to local control.

deception n. **1** the act of deceiving. **2** a thing that deceives.

deceptive adj. misleading. ■ **deceptively** adv.

decibel n. a unit for measuring the intensity of sound.

decide v. **1** think about and choose. **2** settle a matter or contest.

decided adj. definite; clear. ■ **decidedly** adv.

deciduous adj. (of a tree) shedding its leaves annually.

decimal adj. of a system of numbers based on the number ten. • n. a fraction in the decimal system, with figures either side of a full point. ☐ **decimal place** the position of a digit to the right of a decimal point. **decimal point** a full point placed after the figure representing units in a decimal.

decimate v. kill or destroy a large proportion of. ■ **decimation** n.

decipher v. **1** succeed in understanding. **2** convert from code into normal language.

decision n. **1** a choice made after consideration. **2** the ability to decide quickly.

decisive adj. **1** very important for the outcome of a situation. **2** able to decide quickly. ■ **decisively** adv. **decisiveness** n.

deck n. **1** a floor of a ship or bus. **2** a pack of cards. **3** a player or recorder for discs or tapes. •v. decorate. □ **deckchair** a folding canvas chair.

declaim v. speak or recite in a dramatic way. ■ **declamation** n. **declamatory** adj.

declare v. **1** announce openly or formally. **2** state that you have income or goods on which tax or duty is payable. ■ **declaration** n.

declassify v. (**declassifying**, **declassified**) officially declare to be no longer secret.

declension n. the changes in the form of a noun, pronoun, or adjective that identify its grammatical case, number, and gender.

decline v. **1** become smaller, weaker, or worse. **2** politely refuse. •n. a gradual loss of strength, numbers, or value.

declivity n. (pl. **declivities**) a downward slope.

decoction n. a concentrated liquid produced by heating or boiling.

decode v. **1** convert a coded message into understandable language. **2** convert audio or video signals from analogue to digital. ■ **decoder** n.

décolletage /day-kol-i-**tahzh**/ n. a low neckline on a woman's dress or top.

decompose v. decay. ■ **decomposition** n.

decompress v. **1** reduce air pressure in or on. **2** expand compressed computer data to its normal size. ■ **decompression** n.

decongestant n. a medicine that relieves a blocked nose.

deconstruct v. reduce to basic elements so as to interpret differently. ■ **deconstruction** n.

decontaminate v. remove dangerous substances from. ■ **decontamination** n.

decor /day-kor/ n. the furnishing and decoration of a room.

decorate v. **1** add ornamentation to make more attractive. **2** apply paint or wallpaper to. **3** give an award or medal to. ■ **decorator** n.

decoration n. **1** the act of decorating or the way something is decorated. **2** a decorative thing. **3** a medal or award.

decorative adj. making something look attractive. ■ **decoratively** adv.

decorous adj. polite and restrained. ■ **decorously** adv.

decorum /di-kor-uhm/ n. polite and socially acceptable behaviour.

decoy n. **1** a real or imitation animal used to lure game. **2** a person or thing used to mislead or trap. •v. lure by a decoy.

decrease v. make or become smaller or fewer. •n. **1** the amount by which something decreases. **2** the act of decreasing.

decree n. an official order with the force of law. •v. order officially.

decrepit adj. worn out or weakened because of age or neglect. ■ **decrepitude** n.

decriminalize (or -**ise**) v. cease to treat as illegal.

decry v. (**decrying**, **decried**) publicly declare to be wrong.

dedicate v. **1** give time or effort to. **2** address a book to a person as a tribute. **3** (**dedicated**) used or intended for one purpose only. ■ **dedication** n.

deduce v. reach a conclusion on the basis of available information. ■ **deducible** adj.

deduct v. subtract. ■ **deductible** adj.

deduction n. 1 the act of deducting. 2 an amount deducted. 3 the act of deducing. ■ **deductive** adj.

deed n. 1 an action performed deliberately. 2 a legal document.

deem v. consider to be.

deep adj. 1 extending or situated far down or in from the top or surface. 2 low-pitched. 3 (of colour) dark. 4 very intense or extreme. 5 difficult to understand. ■ **deepen** v. **deeply** adv.

deer n. (pl. **deer**) a hoofed animal, the male of which usu. has antlers. □ **deerstalker** a cap with peaks in front and behind and ear flaps.

deface v. spoil the appearance of.

de facto /day fak-toh/ adj. existing, whether legally accepted or not.

defame v. damage the good reputation of. ■ **defamation** n. **defamatory** adj.

default n. 1 failure to do something required by law. 2 an option adopted by a computer program when no alternative is specified. •v. fail to fulfil a legal obligation. □ **by default** because of a lack of opposition or positive action. ■ **defaulter** n.

defeat v. 1 win a victory over. 2 cause to fail. •n. an act of defeating or the state of being defeated.

defeatist n. a person who accepts failure too readily. ■ **defeatism** n.

defecate v. discharge waste matter from the bowels. ■ **defeca-tion** n.

defect n. an imperfection. •v. abandon your country or cause for an opposing one. ■ **defection** n. **defector** n.

defective adj. imperfect or faulty.

defence (US **defense**) n. 1 the act of defending. 2 protective military measures or resources. 3 attempted justification. 4 the case presented by the person being accused or sued in a lawsuit. ■ **defenceless** adj.

defend v. 1 protect from attack. 2 attempt to justify. 3 act as a lawyer for the defendant. ■ **defender** n.

defendant n. a person sued or accused in a court of law.

defensible adj. able to be defended.

defensive adj. 1 intended for defence. 2 anxious to challenge criticism. ■ **defensively** adv.

defer v. (**deferring**, **deferred**) 1 put off to a later time. 2 (**defer to**) give in to. ■ **deferment** n. **deferral** n.

deference n. polite respect. ■ **deferential** adj. **deferentially** adv.

defiance n. open disobedience. ■ **defiant** adj. **defiantly** adv.

deficiency n. (pl. **deficiencies**) 1 a lack or shortage. 2 a fault or shortcoming.

deficient adj. 1 not having enough of a specified thing. 2 inadequate.

deficit n. 1 the amount by which something falls short. 2 an excess of money spent over money earned.

defile v. 1 make dirty. 2 desecrate. •n. a narrow gorge or mountain pass.

define v. **1** describe the exact nature of. **2** give the meaning of a word. **3** mark out the limits of.

definite adj. **1** clearly stated or decided. **2** certain. **3** known to be true or real. **4** having exact physical limits. □ **definite article** the word the. ▪ **definitely** adv.

❗ -ite, not -ate: definite.

definition n. **1** a statement of the meaning of a word or the nature of something. **2** sharpness of outline.

definitive adj. **1** settling something finally with authority. **2** the most accurate of its kind. ▪ **definitively** adv.

deflate v. **1** let air or gas out of a tyre etc. **2** make less confident. **3** reduce price levels in an economy. ▪ **deflation** n. **deflationary** adj.

deflect v. turn aside. ▪ **deflection** n.

deflower v. literary have sex with a woman who is a virgin.

defoliate v. remove the leaves from. ▪ **defoliation** n.

deforest v. clear of trees. ▪ **deforestation** n.

deform v. change or spoil the shape of. ▪ **deformed** adj.

deformity n. (pl. **deformities**) **1** a deformed part. **2** the state of being deformed.

defraud v. obtain money from by deception.

defray v. provide money to pay a cost.

defrock v. officially remove a Christian priest from their job.

defrost v. **1** remove ice from. **2** thaw frozen food.

deft adj. quick and skilful. ▪ **deftly** adv.

defunct adj. no longer existing or functioning.

defuse v. **1** make a situation less tense or difficult. **2** remove the fuse from an explosive device.

❗ Don't confuse **defuse** with **diffuse**, meaning 'spread over a wide area'.

defy v. (**defying**, **defied**) **1** openly resist or refuse to obey. **2** challenge to do.

degenerate v. become worse or weaker. • adj. immoral. • n. an immoral person. ▪ **degeneracy** n. **degeneration** n.

degrade v. **1** cause to lose self-respect. **2** make worse. **3** cause to break down chemically. ▪ **degradation** n.

degree n. **1** the extent to which something happens or is present. **2** a unit for measuring angles. **3** a stage in a scale, e.g. of temperature. **4** a qualification awarded by a university.

dehumanize (or **-ise**) v. deprive of good human qualities.

dehydrate v. **1** cause to lose a large amount of moisture. **2** remove water from food to preserve it. ▪ **dehydration** n.

deify /day-i-fI/ v. (**deifying**, **deified**) worship as a god. ▪ **deification** n.

deign /dayn/ v. (**deign to do**) condescend to do.

deity /day-i-ti/ n. (pl. **deities**) a god or goddess.

déja vu /day-zhah voo/ n. a feeling of having already experienced the present situation.

dejected adj. sad and in low spirits. ▪ **dejection** n.

delay v. **1** make late or slow. **2** postpone. • n. **1** the time that someone or something is delayed. **2** the act of delaying.

delectable adj. delightful or delicious. ■ **delectably** adv.

delectation n. pleasure and delight.

delegate n. **1** a person sent to represent others. **2** a member of a committee. •v. give a task or responsibility to a subordinate.

delegation n. **1** a group of delegates. **2** the act of delegating.

delete v. cross out or remove something written or stored in a computer's memory. ■ **deletion** n.

deleterious adj. harmful.

deliberate adj. **1** done on purpose. **2** careful and unhurried. •v. consider carefully and at length. ■ **deliberately** adv. **deliberation** n.

delicacy n. (pl. **delicacies**) **1** the quality of being delicate. **2** a tasty, expensive food.

delicate adj. **1** very fine in quality or structure. **2** easily broken or damaged. **3** prone to illness. **4** requiring tact and discretion. ■ **delicately** adv.

delicatessen n. a shop selling unusual or foreign prepared foods.

delicious adj. **1** very pleasant to eat or drink. **2** delightful. ■ **deliciously** adv.

delight v. **1** please greatly. **2** (**delight in**) take great pleasure in. •n. great pleasure, or a cause of this.

delightful adj. very pleasing. ■ **delightfully** adv.

delineate v. describe or indicate precisely. ■ **delineation** n.

delinquent adj. tending to commit crime. •n. a delinquent person. ■ **delinquency** n.

delirious adj. **1** suffering from delirium. **2** very excited or happy. ■ **deliriously** adv.

delirium n. a disturbed state of mind occurring esp. during a fever.

deliver v. **1** bring and hand over to the intended person. **2** provide something promised. **3** give a speech. **4** aim a blow. **5** save or set free. **6** assist in a baby's birth.

deliverance n. the process of being saved or set free.

delivery n. (pl. **deliveries**) **1** the act of delivering. **2** something delivered. **3** the manner of giving a speech.

dell n. a small valley.

delphinium n. a tall garden plant with blue flowers.

delta n. an area where the mouth of a river has split into several channels.

delude v. deceive or mislead.

deluge n. **1** a severe flood or heavy fall of rain. **2** a large number of things arriving at the same time. •v. **1** overwhelm with many things. **2** flood.

delusion n. a mistaken belief or impression. ■ **delusional** adj.

deluxe adj. of a high quality.

delve v. **1** search within. **2** (**delve into**) research thoroughly.

demagogue n. a political leader appealing to popular desires and prejudices. ■ **demagogic** adj.

demand n. **1** a firm request. **2** (**demands**) urgent or difficult requirements. **3** consumers' desire for a product or service. •v. **1** ask for firmly. **2** need a quality etc.

demanding adj. requiring much skill or effort.

demarcation n. **1** the fixing of boundaries. **2** a dividing line.

demean v. lower the dignity of.

demeanour (US **demeanor**) n. outward behaviour or bearing.

demented adj. **1** having dementia. **2** informal wild or irrational.

dementia n. a serious mental disorder.

demerara sugar n. light brown sugar.

demi- prefix half.

demilitarize (or **-ise**) v. remove military forces from. ■ **demilitarization** n.

demise n. **1** death. **2** the end or failure of something.

demo informal n. (pl. **demos**) a demonstration. •v. (**demos, demoing, demoed**) demonstrate something.

demob v. (**demobbing, de-mobbed**) informal demobilize.

demobilize (or **-ise**) v. release from military service. ■ **demobilization** n.

democracy n. (pl. **democracies**) **1** a form of government in which the people vote for representatives to govern on their behalf. **2** a state governed in this way. ■ **democrat** n. **democratic** adj. **democratically** adv.

demography n. the statistical study of human populations. ■ **demographic** adj.

demolish v. pull or knock down a building. ■ **demolition** n.

demon n. an evil spirit or devil. • adj. forceful or skilful. ■ **demoniac** adj. **demonic** adj. **demonically** adv.

demonize (or **-ise**) v. portray as wicked or threatening.

demonstrable adj. clearly apparent or able to be proved. ■ **demonstrably** adv.

demonstrate v. **1** clearly show to exist or be true. **2** show and explain how something works. **3** take part in a public demonstration. ■ **demonstrator** n.

demonstration n. **1** an act of demonstrating. **2** a public meeting or march to express an opinion on an issue.

demonstrative adj. **1** showing your feelings openly. **2** demonstrating something. ■ **demonstratively** adv.

demoralize (or **-ise**) v. dishearten.

demote v. move to a less senior position. ■ **demotion** n.

demur v. (**demurring, de-murred**) show reluctance. ☐ **without demur** without hesitating or objecting.

demure adj. modest and shy. ■ **demurely** adv.

demystify v. (**demystifying, demystified**) make easier to understand.

den n. **1** a wild animal's lair. **2** informal a person's private room.

denationalize (or **-ise**) v. privatize a nationalized industry.

deniable adj. able to be denied.

denial n. **1** a statement denying something. **2** refusal to accept something unpleasant.

denier /den-yer/ n. a unit for measuring the fineness of yarn.

denigrate v. criticize unfairly. ■ **denigration** n.

denim n. **1** a hard-wearing cotton twill fabric. **2** (**denims**) denim jeans.

denizen n. an inhabitant.

denomination n. **1** a recognized branch of a Church or religion. **2** the face value of a banknote, coin, etc. ■ **denominational** adj.

denominator n. the number below the line in a fraction.

denote v. **1** be a sign of. **2** (of a word) have as a main meaning. ■ **denotation** n.

denouement /day-noo-mon/ n. the final outcome of a play, film, etc.

denounce v. publicly declare to be wrong or evil.

dense adj. **1** closely packed together. **2** thick in texture. **3** informal stupid. ■ **densely** adv.

density n. (pl. **densities**) the degree to which something is dense.

dent n. a slight hollow made by a blow or pressure. • v. **1** mark with a dent. **2** have a bad effect on.

dental adj. of the teeth or dentistry.

dentine n. the hard tissue forming the main part of a tooth.

dentist n. a person qualified to treat conditions affecting the teeth and gums. ■ **dentistry** n.

denture n. a removable plate or frame holding a false tooth or teeth.

denude v. make bare or empty.

denunciation n. the act of denouncing.

deny v. (**denying**, **denied**) **1** state that something is not true. **2** refuse to admit. **3** prevent from having something wanted.

deodorant n. a substance which prevents unpleasant bodily odours.

deodorize (or **-ise**) v. prevent an unpleasant smell in.

depart v. **1** leave. **2** (**depart from**) do something different from what is usual.

departed adj. dead.

department n. a section of a large organization. □ **department store** a large shop selling many types of goods. ■ **departmental** adj. **departmentally** adv.

departure n. **1** the act of leaving. **2** a change from usual procedure.

depend v. (**depend on**) **1** be determined by. **2** rely on.

dependable adj. reliable. ■ **dependability** n.

dependant (or **dependent**) n. a person who relies on another for financial support.

dependency n. (pl. **dependencies**) **1** a country or province controlled by another. **2** the state of being dependent.

dependent adj. **1** relying on for support or survival. **2** (**dependent on**) determined by. • n. var. of DEPENDANT. ■ **dependence** n.

depict v. represent in a picture or in words. ■ **depiction** n.

depilatory adj. used to remove unwanted hair.

deplete v. reduce the number or quantity of. ■ **depletion** n.

deplorable adj. shockingly bad. ■ **deplorably** adv.

deplore v. strongly disapprove of.

deploy v. **1** bring or move into position for military action. **2** use effectively. ■ **deployment** n.

depopulate v. reduce the population of. ■ **depopulation** n.

deport v. expel a foreigner from a country. ■ **deportation** n.

deportment n. the way a person stands and walks.

d

depose v. remove from power.

deposit n. **1** a sum of money paid into an account. **2** a first instalment in buying something. **3** a returnable sum paid to cover possible loss of or damage to something rented. **4** a layer of a substance that has accumulated. • v. (**depositing, deposited**) **1** put down. **2** store for safe keeping. **3** pay as a deposit. **4** lay down a layer of a substance. □ **deposit account** a bank account paying interest. ■ **deposition** n. **depositor** n.

depository n. (pl. **depositories**) a place where things are stored.

depot /dep-oh/ n. **1** a place for storing goods. **2** a place where vehicles are housed.

deprave v. corrupt morally. ■ **depravity** n.

deprecate v. express disapproval of. ■ **deprecation** n. **deprecatory** adj.

depreciate v. **1** reduce in value over time. **2** dismiss as unimportant. ■ **depreciation** n.

depredation n. a harmful or damaging act.

depress v. **1** make very unhappy. **2** make less active. **3** push down. ■ **depressant** n. & adj.

depression n. **1** a mental state involving great unhappiness and hopelessness. **2** a long economic slump. **3** a sunken place or hollow. **4** an area of low pressure which may bring rain. ■ **depressive** adj.

deprive v. prevent from having or using something. ■ **deprivation** n.

depth n. **1** the distance from the top or surface down, or from front to back. **2** detailed thought or study. **3** intense quality. **4** (**the**

depths) the deepest, lowest, or inmost part. □ **depth charge** a device designed to explode under water.

deputation n. a group of people sent to represent others.

depute v. delegate authority or a task to someone.

deputize (or **-ise**) v. act as a deputy for someone.

deputy n. (pl. **deputies**) a person appointed to act on behalf of another.

derail v. **1** make a train leave the tracks. **2** obstruct a process. ■ **derailment** n.

deranged adj. insane. ■ **derangement** n.

deregulate v. remove regulations from. ■ **deregulation** n.

derelict adj. left to fall into ruin.

dereliction n. **1** the state of being derelict. **2** (**dereliction of duty**) failure to do your duty.

deride v. ridicule.

de rigueur /duh ri-ger/ adj. necessary for social acceptance.

derision n. scornful ridicule. ■ **derisive** adj. **derisively** adv.

derisory adj. ridiculously small or inadequate.

derivative adj. imitating another artist, writer, etc.; not original. • n. something derived from another source.

derive v. (**derive from**) **1** obtain from. **2** arise or originate from. ■ **derivation** n.

dermatitis n. inflammation of the skin.

dermatology n. the branch of medicine concerned with skin disorders. ■ **dermatologist** n.

derogatory adj. critical or disrespectful.

derrick n. **1** a crane with a pivoted arm. **2** the framework over an oil well.

dervish n. a member of a Muslim religious group, some orders of which are known for their wild rituals.

desalinate v. remove salt from seawater. ▪ **desalination** n.

descant n. a melody sung or played above a basic melody.

descend v. **1** move, slope, or lead down. **2** (**descend to**) do something shameful. **3** make an attack or unexpected visit. **4** (**be descended from**) have as an ancestor.

descendant n. a person descended from another.

descent n. **1** an act of descending. **2** a downward slope. **3** a person's origin or nationality.

describe v. **1** give a detailed account of. **2** mark out or draw a shape.

description n. **1** a spoken or written account. **2** the act of describing. **3** a sort or kind. ▪ **descriptive** adj. **descriptively** adv.

descry v. (**descrying**, **descried**) literary catch sight of.

desecrate v. treat something sacred with violent disrespect. ▪ **desecration** n.

desegregate v. end racial segregation in. ▪ **desegregation** n.

deselect v. reject an existing MP as a candidate in a forthcoming election. ▪ **deselection** n.

desert v. **1** leave someone without help or support. **2** leave a place, making it seem empty. **3** illegally leave the armed forces. •n. a waterless, empty area of land with few plants. ▪ **deserter** n. **desertion** n.

deserts /di-zerts/ pl. n. the reward or punishment that someone deserves.

deserve v. be worthy of a reward or punishment. ▪ **deservedly** adv.

deserving adj. worthy of favourable treatment or help.

déshabillé /day-za-bee-yay/ n. the state of being partly dressed.

desiccate v. remove the moisture from. ▪ **desiccation** n.

desideratum n. (pl. **desiderata**) something needed or wanted.

design n. **1** a plan or drawing showing how something is to be made. **2** a decorative pattern. **3** purpose or deliberate planning. •v. **1** produce a design for. **2** intend for a purpose. ▪ **designer** n.

designate v. **1** officially give a status or name to. **2** appoint to a job. •adj. appointed to a post but not yet having taken it up. ▪ **designation** n.

designing adj. cunning and deceitful.

desirable adj. **1** wished for as being attractive, useful, or necessary. **2** sexually attractive. ▪ **desirability** n.

desire n. **1** a strong feeling of wanting something. **2** strong sexual appetite. •v. **1** strongly wish for or want. **2** want sexually.

desirous adj. strongly wishing for.

desist v. stop doing.

desk n. **1** a piece of furniture for working on. **2** a counter in a hotel, airport, etc. **3** a section of a news organization. □ **desktop 1** a computer suitable for use at a desk. **2** the working area of a computer screen.

desolate *adj.* **1** bleak and empty. **2** very unhappy. •*v.* make very unhappy. ■ **desolation** *n.*

despair *n.* complete lack of hope. •*v.* lose or be without hope.

despatch var. of DISPATCH.

desperado *n.* (pl. **desperadoes** or **desperados**) a reckless and dangerous criminal.

desperate *adj.* **1** feeling or involving despair. **2** done when all else has failed. **3** very serious. ■ **desperately** *adv.* **desperation** *n.*

! desperate, not -parate.

despicable *adj.* deserving hatred and contempt. ■ **despicably** *adv.*

despise *v.* feel hatred or disgust for.

despite *prep.* in spite of.

despoil *v.* literary steal valuable possessions from.

despondent *adj.* sad and dispirited. ■ **despondency** *n.* **despondently** *adv.*

despot *n.* a ruler with total power, esp. a cruel one. ■ **despotic** *adj.* **despotism** *n.*

dessert *n.* the sweet course eaten at the end of a meal. □ **dessert-spoon** a spoon between a tablespoon and a teaspoon in size.

destabilize (or **-ise**) *v.* make unstable.

destination *n.* the place to which someone or something is going.

destined *adj.* **1** intended for a particular purpose. **2** bound for a particular destination.

destiny *n.* (pl. **destinies**) **1** the events that will happen to a person. **2** the power believed to control future events; fate.

destitute *adj.* very poor. ■ **destitution** *n.*

destroy *v.* **1** end the existence of something by badly damaging it. **2** kill an animal in a painless way.

destroyer *n.* **1** a person or thing that destroys. **2** a small, fast warship.

destruction *n.* the destroying of something. ■ **destructive** *adj.*

desuetude /dess-wi-tyood/ *n.* disuse.

desultory /dess-uhl-tuh-ri/ *adj.* lacking enthusiasm or purpose. ■ **desultorily** *adv.*

detach *v.* **1** disconnect and remove. **2** (**detach yourself from**) distance yourself from. ■ **detachable** *adj.*

! Only one t: detach, not -tatch.

detached *adj.* **1** separate or disconnected. **2** not involved; objective.

detachment *n.* **1** the state of being uninvolved. **2** a group of troops etc. sent on a separate mission.

detail *n.* **1** a small individual item or fact. **2** small items or facts as a group. **3** a small detachment of troops or police officers. •*v.* **1** describe fully. **2** order to undertake a task.

detain *v.* **1** keep from going somewhere. **2** keep in custody. ■ **detainment** *n.*

detainee *n.* a person who is kept in custody.

detect *v.* **1** discover the presence of. **2** investigate a crime. ■ **detection** *n.* **detector** *n.*

detective *n.* a person whose job is to investigate crimes.

détente /day-tahnt/ *n.* the easing of hostility between countries.

detention *n.* **1** the state of being detained in custody. **2** the punishment of being kept behind at school.

deter v. (**deterring, deterred**) discourage from action.

detergent n. a chemical substance used for cleaning.

deteriorate v. become gradually worse. ■ **deterioration** n.

determinant n. a determining factor.

determination n. **1** persistence in the face of difficulty. **2** the act of establishing something exactly.

determine v. **1** cause to occur in a particular way or be of a specific type. **2** firmly decide. **3** establish by research or calculation.

determined adj. persisting even in the face of difficulty.

deterrent n. a thing that deters or is intended to deter. ■ **deterrence** n.

detest v. dislike intensely. ■ **detestable** adj. **detestation** n.

dethrone v. remove a monarch from power.

detonate v. explode or cause to explode. ■ **detonation** n. **detonator** n.

detour n. a long or roundabout route.

detoxify v. (**detoxifying, detoxified**) remove harmful substances from.

detract v. (**detract from**) cause to seem less valuable or impressive.

detractor n. a critic of someone or something.

detriment n. harm or damage. ■ **detrimental** adj. **detrimentally** adv.

detritus /di-try-tuhss/ n. debris or waste material.

deuce n. the score of 40 all in a game in tennis.

Deutschmark /doych-mark/ n. the former basic unit of money in Germany.

devalue v. reduce the value or worth of. ■ **devaluation** n.

devastate v. **1** destroy or ruin. **2** (**be devastated**) be overwhelmed with shock or grief. ■ **devastation** n.

devastating adj. **1** very destructive. **2** very distressing. **3** informal very impressive or attractive.

develop v. (**developing, developed**) **1** become or make larger or more advanced. **2** start to exist, experience, or possess. **3** convert land to a new purpose. **4** treat a film with chemicals to make a visible image. ■ **developer** n.

development n. **1** the action of developing. **2** a new product, idea, or phase. **3** an area with new buildings on it.

deviant adj. different from what is considered normal. • n. a deviant person. ■ **deviance** n.

deviate v. depart from an established course or normal standards. ■ **deviation** n.

device n. **1** a piece of equipment with a particular purpose. **2** a plan or method.

devil n. **1** (**the Devil**) (in Christian and Jewish belief) the most powerful evil spirit. **2** an evil spirit. **3** a very cruel person. **4** a mischievous person. **5** informal a specified type of person: the poor devil. □ **devil-may-care** cheerful and reckless. **devil's advocate** a person who expresses an opinion so as to provoke debate. ■ **devilish** adj.

devilment n. mischief.

devilry n. **1** wickedness. **2** mischief.

devious adj. **1** cunning and underhand. **2** (of a route) indirect. ■ **deviously** adv. **deviousness** n.

devise v. plan or invent.

devoid adj. (**devoid of**) completely lacking in.

devolution n. the transfer of power by central government to local or regional governments.

devolve v. **1** transfer power to a lower level. **2** (**devolve on/to**) (of responsibility) pass to.

devote v. (**devote to**) give time or resources to.

devoted adj. very loving or loyal.

devotee n. **1** an enthusiast. **2** a follower of a particular religion or god.

devotion n. **1** great love or loyalty. **2** religious worship. **3** (**devotions**) prayers. ■ **devotional** adj.

devour v. **1** eat greedily. **2** (of a force) destroy completely. **3** read quickly and eagerly.

devout adj. **1** deeply religious. **2** earnestly sincere. ■ **devoutly** adv.

dew n. drops of condensed moisture forming on cool surfaces at night. ■ **dewy** adj.

dewlap n. a fold of loose skin hanging from an animal's throat.

dexterity n. skill in performing tasks. ■ **dexterous** (or **dextrous**) adj.

dextrose n. a form of glucose.

dhal (or **dal**) n. (in Indian cookery) cooked split pulses.

diabetes n. an illness in which a lack of insulin results in a failure to absorb sugar and starch properly. ■ **diabetic** adj. & n.

diabolical adj. **1** (or **diabolic**) of or like the Devil. **2** informal very bad. ■ **diabolically** adv.

diadem n. a jewelled crown.

diagnose v. identify the nature of an illness or problem by examining the symptoms.

diagnosis n. (pl. **diagnoses**) the identification of an illness or problem by examining the symptoms. ■ **diagnostic** adj.

diagonal adj. **1** (of a line) joining opposite corners of a rectangle or square. **2** slanting. •n. a diagonal line. ■ **diagonally** adv.

diagram n. a simplified drawing showing the appearance or structure of something. ■ **diagrammatic** adj.

dial n. **1** a disc marked to show the time or to indicate a measurement. **2** a disc with numbered holes on a phone, turned to make a call. **3** a disc turned to select a setting on a radio, cooker, etc. •v. (**dialling, dialled**; US **dialing, dialed**) call a phone number.

dialect n. a local form of a language. ■ **dialectal** adj.

dialectic (or **dialectics**) n. the investigation of the truth of opposing opinions by logical discussion. ■ **dialectical** adj.

dialogue (US **dialog**) n. **1** conversation as a feature of a book, play, etc. **2** a discussion.

dialysis n. (pl. **dialyses**) the use of a machine to purify the blood of a person whose kidneys do not work properly.

diamanté /dy-uh-mon-tay/ adj. decorated with artificial diamonds.

diameter n. a straight line passing from side to side through the centre of a circle or sphere.

diametrical adj. **1** (of opposites) complete. **2** of a diameter. ■ **diametrically** adv.

diamond n. **1** a very hard, clear precious stone. **2** a figure with four sides of equal length forming two opposite acute angles and two opposite obtuse angles. **3** (**diamonds**) one of the four suits in a pack of cards. □ **diamond wedding** the 60th anniversary of a wedding.

diaper n. US a baby's nappy.

diaphanous /dy-af-fuh-nuhss/ adj. delicate and semi-transparent.

diaphragm /dy-uh-fram/ n. **1** a layer of muscle between the lungs and the stomach. **2** a thin contraceptive cap fitting over the cervix.

diarrhoea /dy-uh-ree-uh/ (US **diarrhea**) n. a condition involving frequent liquid bowel movements.

diary n. (pl. **diaries**) a book for keeping a daily record of events, or for noting appointments. ■ **diarist** n.

diaspora /dy-ass-puh-ruh/ n. the dispersion of a people from their homeland, esp. that of the Jews from Israel.

diatribe n. a vehement verbal attack.

dice n. (pl. **dice**; sing. also **die**) a small cube with faces bearing from one to six spots, used in games of chance. • v. **1** cut food into small cubes. **2** (**dice with**) take great risks with.

dicey adj. (**dicier, diciest**) informal difficult or risky.

dichotomy /dy-kot-uh-mi/ n. (pl. **dichotomies**) a division or contrast between two things. ■ **dichotomous** adj.

dicky adj. informal not strong, healthy, or working reliably.

dictate v. **1** state or order with authority. **2** control or determine. **3** speak words to be typed or written down. • n. an order or command. ■ **dictation** n.

dictator n. a ruler with total power over a country. ■ **dictatorial** adj. **dictatorship** n.

diction n. **1** a person's way of pronouncing words. **2** the choice and use of words in literature.

dictionary n. (pl. **dictionaries**) a book that lists the words of a language and gives their meaning, or their equivalent in a different language.

dictum n. (pl. **dicta** or **dictums**) **1** a formal announcement. **2** a saying.

did past of **DO**.

didactic adj. intended to teach or give moral guidance.

diddle v. informal cheat or swindle.

didgeridoo n. an Australian Aboriginal wind instrument in the form of a long wooden tube.

didn't contr. did not.

die v. (**dying, died**) **1** stop living. **2** (**die out**) become extinct. **3** become less loud or strong. **4** (**be dying for/to do**) informal be very eager for or to do. • n. **1** (pl. **dies**) a device for cutting or moulding metal or for stamping a design. **2** sing. of **DICE**. □ **diehard** a person who stubbornly supports something in spite of change or opposition.

dieresis US = **DIAERESIS**.

diesel n. **1** an internal-combustion engine in which the heat of compressed air is used to ignite the

d

fuel. **2** a form of petroleum used to fuel diesel engines.

diet n. **1** the food that a person or animal usually eats. **2** a limited range or amount of food, adopted to lose weight or for medical reasons. **3** a law-making assembly in certain countries. • v. (**dieting, dieted**) keep to a special diet to lose weight. • adj. with reduced fat or sugar content. ■ **dieter** n. **dietary** adj.

dietetics n. the study of diet and its effects on health. ■ **dietetic** adj.

dietitian (or **dietician**) n. an expert on diet and nutrition.

differ v. **1** be unlike. **2** disagree.

difference n. **1** a way in which people or things are not the same. **2** a disagreement or dispute. **3** the remainder left after one value is subtracted from another.

different adj. **1** not the same as another or each other. **2** separate. **3** new and unusual. ■ **differently** adv.

differential adj. involving a difference. • n. **1** an agreed difference in wage rates. **2** a gear allowing a vehicle's wheels to revolve at different speeds when cornering.

differentiate v. **1** recognize as different. **2** cause to appear different. ■ **differentiation** n.

difficult adj. **1** needing much effort or skill to do, deal with, or understand. **2** hard to please.

difficulty n. (pl. **difficulties**) **1** the state of being difficult. **2** a difficult situation; a problem.

diffident adj. lacking self-confidence. ■ **diffidence** n. **diffidently** adv.

diffract v. cause a beam of light to be spread out as a result of passing through a narrow opening or across an edge. ■ **diffraction** n.

diffuse v. **1** spread over a wide area. **2** (of a gas or liquid) become mingled with a substance. • adj. **1** spread out over a large area. **2** not clear or concise. ■ **diffusely** adv. **diffuser** n. **diffusion** n.

! Don't confuse **diffuse** with **defuse**, which means 'make a situation less tense'.

dig v. (**digging, dug**) **1** break up and turn over or move earth. **2** remove or make by digging. **3** push or poke sharply. **4** (**dig into/through**) search in. **5** (**dig out/up**) discover facts. • n. **1** an act of digging. **2** an archaeological excavation. **3** a sharp push or poke. **4** informal a critical remark. **5** (**digs**) informal lodgings. ■ **digger** n.

digest v. **1** break down food in the body so that it can be easily absorbed. **2** reflect on and absorb information. • n. a summary or collection of information. ■ **digestible** adj. **digestion** n. **digestive** adj.

digit n. **1** any of the numerals from 0 to 9. **2** a finger, thumb, or toe.

digital adj. **1** of information represented as a series of binary digits, as in a computer. **2** involving computer technology. **3** (of a clock) showing the time by displaying numbers electronically. **4** (of a camera) producing images that can be stored in a computer and displayed on screen. ■ **digitally** adv.

digitalis /di-ji-tay-liss/ n. a heart stimulant made from foxgloves.

digitize (or **-ise**) v. convert pictures or sound into a digital form.

dignified adj. showing dignity.

dignify v. (**dignifying**, **dignified**) make impressive or worthy of respect.

dignitary n. (pl. **dignitaries**) a high-ranking or important person.

dignity n. (pl. **dignities**) **1** the state of being worthy of respect. **2** a calm or serious manner. **3** pride in yourself.

digress v. depart from the main subject temporarily. ■ **digression** n.

dike var. of DYKE.

diktat n. a decree imposed by someone in power.

dilapidated adj. in a state of disrepair or ruin. ■ **dilapidation** n.

❗ dil-, not del-: dilapidated.

dilate v. make or become wider or more open. ■ **dilation** n.

dilatory /di-luh-tri/ adj. **1** slow to act. **2** causing delay.

dilemma n. a situation in which a difficult choice has to be made.

dilettante /di-li-tan-tay/ n. (pl. **dilettanti** or **dilettantes**) a person who dabbles in a subject for enjoyment.

diligent adj. careful and conscientious. ■ **diligence** n. **diligently** adv.

dill n. a herb.

dilly-dally v. (**dilly-dallying**, **dilly-dallied**) informal dawdle or be indecisive.

dilute v. **1** make a liquid thinner or weaker by adding water etc. **2** reduce the forcefulness of. •adj. (of a liquid) diluted. ■ **dilution** n.

dim adj. (**dimmer**, **dimmest**) **1** not bright or well lit. **2** indistinct. **3** informal stupid. •v. (**dimming**, **dimmed**) make or become dim. ■ **dimly** adv. **dimness** n.

dime n. US a 10-cent coin.

dimension n. **1** a measurable extent, such as length, breadth, or height. **2** an aspect or feature. ■ **dimensional** adj.

diminish v. make or become smaller, weaker, or less.

diminuendo adv. & adj. Music with a decrease in loudness.

diminution n. a reduction.

diminutive adj. very small. •n. a shortened informal form of a name.

dimmer n. a device for varying the brightness of an electric light.

dimple n. a small depression, esp. in the cheeks when someone smiles. •v. form or show dimples.

din n. a prolonged loud and unpleasant noise. •v. (**dinning**, **dinned**) (**din into**) teach someone something by constant repetition.

dinar /dee-nar/ n. the basic unit of money of Serbia, Montenegro, and some Middle Eastern and North African countries.

dine v. eat dinner.

diner n. **1** a person who dines. **2** US a small roadside restaurant.

dinghy n. (pl. **dinghies**) **1** a small open sailing boat. **2** a small inflatable rubber boat.

dingle n. literary a wooded valley.

dingo n. (pl. **dingoes** or **dingos**) a wild Australian dog.

dingy /din-ji/ adj. (**dingier**, **dingiest**) gloomy and drab. ■ **dinginess** n.

dinky adj. (**dinkier**, **dinkiest**) informal attractively small and neat.

dinner n. **1** the main meal of the day. **2** a formal evening meal. ◻ **dinner jacket** a man's jacket worn for formal evening occasions.

dinosaur n. an extinct prehistoric reptile, often of enormous size.

dint n. (**by dint of**) by means of.

diocese /dy-uh-siss/ n. a district for which a bishop is responsible. ■ **diocesan** adj.

diode n. a semiconductor device with two terminals, allowing the flow of current in one direction only.

dioxide n. an oxide with two atoms of oxygen to one of a metal or other element.

dioxin /dy-ok-sin/ n. a highly poisonous organic compound.

dip v. (**dipping, dipped**) 1 (**dip in/ into**) put or lower briefly in or into. 2 move or slope downwards. 3 (of a level or amount) temporarily drop. • n. 1 an act of dipping. 2 a thick sauce in which pieces of food are dipped before eating. 3 a brief swim. 4 a brief downward slope.

diphtheria n. a serious infectious disease causing inflammation of the throat.

diphthong n. a compound vowel sound (as in *coin*).

diploma n. a certificate awarded on completing a course of study.

diplomacy n. 1 the profession or skill of managing international re-lations. 2 skill and tact in dealing with people.

diplomat n. an official representing a country abroad.

diplomatic adj. 1 of diplomacy. 2 tactful. ■ **diplomatically** adv.

dipper n. a small diving bird.

dipsomania n. alcoholism. ■ **dipsomaniac** n.

diptych /dip-tik/ n. a painting on two hinged panels, forming an altarpiece.

dire adj. 1 very serious or urgent. 2 *informal* very bad.

direct adj. 1 going straight from one place to another. 2 with nothing or no one in between. 3 frank. 4 clear and explicit. • adv. in a direct way or by a direct route. • v. 1 aim towards. 2 tell or show someone the way. 3 control the operations of. 4 supervise and control a film, play, etc. 5 give an order to. □ **direct current** electric current flowing in one direction only. **direct debit** an arrange-ment with a bank to transfer money regularly from an account to a third party. **direct object** the person or thing directly affected by the action of a transitive verb. **direct speech** the actual words of a speaker quoted in writing.

direction n. 1 a course along which someone or something moves. 2 a point to or from which someone or something faces. 3 control or management. 4 (**dir-ections**) instructions. ■ **direct-ional** adj.

directive n. an official instruction.

directly adv. 1 in a direct way. 2 exactly in a specified position. 3 immediately. • conj. as soon as.

director n. 1 a person in charge of an organization or activity. 2 a member of the board managing a business. 3 a person who directs a film, play, etc. ■ **directorial** adj.

directorate n. 1 the board of dir-ectors of a company. 2 a section of a government department in charge of a particular activity.

directory n. (pl. **directories**) 1 a book listing names, addresses, and phone numbers. **2** a computer file listing other files.

dirge n. a mournful song or piece of music.

dirigible n. an airship.

dirk n. a short dagger.

dirndl n. a full, wide skirt.

dirt n. **1** a substance causing something not to be clean. **2** soil. **3** *informal* scandalous or damaging information.

dirty adj. (**dirtier**, **dirtiest**) **1** covered or marked with mud, dust, etc. **2** obscene. **3** dishonest or unfair. • v. (**dirtying**, **dirtied**) make dirty. ■ **dirtiness** n.

disability n. (pl. **disabilities**) **1** a physical or mental condition that limits a person's movements, senses, or activities. **2** a disadvantage.

disable v. **1** limit someone in their movements, senses, or activities. **2** put out of action. ■ **disablement** n.

disabled adj. having a physical or mental disability.

disabuse v. persuade someone that a belief is mistaken.

disadvantage n. something causing a problem or reducing the chances of success. • v. **1** put in an unfavourable position. **2** (**disadvantaged**) having less money and fewer opportunities than most people. ■ **disadvantageous** adj.

disaffected adj. discontented and no longer loyal. ■ **disaffection** n.

disagree v. **1** have a different opinion. **2** be inconsistent. **3** (**disagree with**) make slightly unwell. ■ **disagreement** n.

disagreeable adj. **1** unpleasant. **2** bad-tempered.

disallow v. declare to be invalid.

disappear v. cease to be visible or to exist. ■ **disappearance** n.

disappoint v. fail to fulfil the hopes of. ■ **disappointment** n.

disapprobation n. strong disapproval.

disapprove v. consider to be wrong or bad. ■ **disapproval** n.

disarm v. **1** take weapons away from. **2** (of a country or force) reduce its armed forces or weapons. **3** win over a hostile person. ■ **disarmament** n.

disarrange v. make untidy.

disarray n. disorder or confusion.

disassociate var. of **DISSOCIATE**.

disaster n. **1** a sudden event causing great damage or loss of life. **2** a sudden misfortune.

disastrous adj. **1** causing great damage. **2** *informal* very unsuccessful. ■ **disastrously** adv.

disavow v. deny any responsibility or support for. ■ **disavowal** n.

disband v. (of an organized group) break up.

disbar v. (**disbarring**, **disbarred**) expel a barrister from the Bar.

disbelieve v. be unable to believe. ■ **disbelief** n.

disburse v. pay out money from a fund. ■ **disbursement** n.

disc (US **disk**) n. **1** a flat, thin, round object. **2** (**disk**) a device on which computer data is stored. **3** a layer of cartilage separating vertebrae in the spine. **4** a compact disc or record. □ **disc jockey** a DJ.

discard v. get rid of something useless or unwanted.

discern v. **1** recognize or become aware of. **2** see or hear with difficulty. ■ **discernible** adj.

discerning adj. having or showing good judgement. ■ **discernment** n.

discharge v. 1 dismiss or allow to leave. 2 send out a liquid, gas, etc. 3 fire a gun or missile. 4 fulfil a responsibility. •n. 1 the act of discharging. 2 a substance discharged.

disciple n. 1 one of the original followers of Jesus. 2 a follower of a teacher, leader, etc.

disciplinarian n. a person who enforces strict discipline.

disciplinary adj. of discipline.

discipline n. 1 the training of people to obey rules or a code of behaviour. 2 controlled behaviour resulting from this. 3 a branch of academic study. •v. 1 train to be obedient or self-controlled. 2 punish for an offence.

disclaim v. deny responsibility for or knowledge of.

disclaimer n. a statement disclaiming responsibility.

disclose v. reveal. ■ **disclosure** n.

disco n. (pl. **discos**) a club or party at which people dance to pop music.

discolour (US **discolor**) v. make or become stained or otherwise changed in colour. ■ **discoloration** n.

discomfit v. (**discomfiting, discomfited**) make uneasy or embarrassed. ■ **discomfiture** n.

discomfort n. 1 slight pain. 2 slight anxiety or embarrassment.

disconcert v. unsettle; upset.

disconnect v. 1 break the connection of or between. 2 detach an electrical device from a power supply. ■ **disconnection** n.

disconsolate adj. very unhappy.

discontent n. unhappiness or dissatisfaction. ■ **discontented** adj. **discontentment** n.

discontinue v. stop doing, providing, or making. ■ **discontinuation** n.

discontinuous adj. having intervals or gaps. ■ **discontinuity** n.

discord n. 1 lack of agreement or harmony. 2 lack of harmony between musical notes sounding together.

discordant adj. 1 (of a sound) harsh and unpleasant. 2 not in agreement.

discotheque n. a disco.

discount n. a deduction from the usual price. •v. 1 reduce the price of. 2 disregard because unlikely.

discourage v. 1 cause to lose enthusiasm or confidence. 2 try to persuade not to do something. ■ **discouragement** n.

discourse n. 1 written or spoken communication or debate. 2 a formal discussion of a topic. •v. speak or write authoritatively about a topic.

discourteous adj. rude and inconsiderate. ■ **discourteously** adv. **discourtesy** n.

discover v. 1 find. 2 gain knowledge or become aware of. 3 be the first to find or observe.

discovery n. (pl. **discoveries**) 1 the act of discovering. 2 a person or thing discovered.

discredit v. (**discrediting, discredited**) 1 harm the good reputation of. 2 cause to seem false or unreliable. •n. loss or lack of reputation.

discreditable adj. bringing discredit; shameful.

discreet adj. careful to keep something secret or to avoid causing embarrassment. ■ **discreetly** adv.

> ! Don't confuse **discreet** with **discrete**.

discrepancy n. (pl. **discrepancies**) a difference between things expected to be the same.

discrete adj. separate and distinct.

discretion n. **1** the quality of being discreet. **2** freedom to decide.

discretionary adj. done or used according to a person's judgement.

discriminate v. **1** recognize a difference. **2** treat differently and unfairly on grounds of race, sex, etc. ■ **discrimination** n. **discriminatory** adj.

discriminating adj. having good taste or judgement.

discursive adj. moving from subject to subject.

discus n. (pl. **discuses**) a heavy disc thrown in athletic contests.

discuss v. **1** talk about so as to reach a decision. **2** talk or write about in detail.

discussion n. **1** conversation or debate. **2** a detailed written treatment of a topic.

disdain n. a feeling of scornful superiority. • v. treat with disdain. ■ **disdainful** adj. **disdainfully** adv.

disease n. an illness. ■ **diseased** adj.

disembark v. leave a ship, aircraft, or train. ■ **disembarkation** n.

disembodied adj. (of a sound) coming from a person who cannot be seen.

disembowel v. (**disembowelling, disembowelled**; US **disemboweling, disemboweled**) cut out the internal organs of.

disempower v. make less powerful or confident.

disenchant v. disillusion. ■ **disenchantment** n.

disenfranchise v. deprive of the right to vote.

disengage v. release or detach. ■ **disengagement** n.

disentangle v. free from being tangled.

disestablish v. deprive a national Church of its official status.

disfavour (US **disfavor**) n. disapproval or dislike.

disfigure v. spoil the appearance of. ■ **disfigurement** n.

disgorge v. cause to pour out.

disgrace n. **1** the loss of the respect of others. **2** a shamefully bad person or thing. • v. bring disgrace on. ■ **disgraceful** adj. **disgracefully** adv.

disgruntled adj. angry or dissatisfied. ■ **disgruntlement** n.

disguise v. **1** change in appearance or nature to prevent recognition. **2** hide a feeling. • n. **1** a means of disguising yourself. **2** the state of being disguised.

disgust n. revulsion or strong disapproval. • v. cause disgust in. ■ **disgusting** adj.

dish n. **1** a shallow container for cooking or serving food. **2** a particular kind of prepared food. **3** a shallow concave object. • v. **1** (**dish out/up**) put food on to plates before a meal. **2** (**dish out**) distribute or provide. □ **dishwasher** a machine for washing dishes.

disharmony n. lack of harmony.

dishearten v. cause to lose determination or confidence.

dishevelled (US **disheveled**) adj. untidy in appearance.

dishonest adj. not honest, sincere, or trustworthy. ■ **dishonestly** adv. **dishonesty** n.

dishonour (US **dishonor**) n. a state of shame or disgrace. • v. **1** bring dishonour to. **2** fail to keep an agreement.

dishonourable (US **dishonorable**) adj. bringing shame or disgrace.

dishy adj. (**dishier**, **dishiest**) informal sexually attractive.

disillusion v. cause to realize that a belief is mistaken or unrealistic. • n. disappointment from realizing that a belief is mistaken or unrealistic. ■ **disillusionment** n.

disincentive n. a factor discouraging a particular action.

disinclination n. unwillingness.

disinclined adj. reluctant; unwilling.

disinfect v. use disinfectant to destroy bacteria. ■ **disinfection** n.

disinfectant n. a chemical liquid that destroys bacteria.

disinformation n. information intended to mislead.

disingenuous adj. not sincere. ■ **disingenuously** adv.

disinherit v. prevent from inheriting.

disintegrate v. break up into small parts. ■ **disintegration** n.

disinter v. (**disinterring**, **disinterred**) dig up something buried.

disinterest n. **1** impartiality. **2** lack of interest.

disinterested adj. not influenced by personal feelings; impartial.

! Don't confuse **disinterested** with **uninterested**, which means 'not interested'.

disjointed adj. lacking logical or coherent connection.

disjunction n. a difference between things expected to be similar.

disk US & Computing = **DISC**.

diskette n. a floppy disk.

dislike v. find unpleasant. • n. the feeling that someone or something is unpleasant.

dislocate v. **1** displace a bone from its proper position. **2** disrupt. ■ **dislocation** n.

dislodge v. remove from the usual position.

disloyal adj. not loyal or faithful. ■ **disloyalty** n.

dismal adj. **1** gloomy or depressing. **2** informal very bad. ■ **dismally** adv.

dismantle v. take to pieces.

dismay n. distress resulting from an unpleasant surprise. • v. cause to feel dismay.

dismember v. tear or cut the limbs from. ■ **dismemberment** n.

dismiss v. **1** order or allow to leave. **2** order an employee to leave a job. **3** treat as unworthy of consideration. ■ **dismissal** n.

dismissive adj. treating something as unworthy of consideration. ■ **dismissively** adv.

dismount v. get off a bicycle or horse.

disobedient adj. not obedient. ■ **disobedience** n.

disobey v. fail or refuse to obey.

disorder n. **1** untidiness or disorganization. **2** the disruption of peaceful and law-abiding behaviour. **3** an illness. ■ **disordered** adj. **disorderly** adj.

disorganized (or **-ised**) adj. not properly planned or arranged. ■ **disorganization** n.

disorientate (or **disorient**) v. cause someone to lose their bearings. ■ **disorientation** n.

disown v. refuse to have anything further to do with.

disparage v. speak critically of. ■ **disparagement** n.

disparate adj. very different in kind. ■ **disparity** n.

dispassionate adj. unemotional and impartial. ■ **dispassionately** adv.

dispatch (or **despatch**) v. **1** send to a destination, esp. for a purpose. **2** deal with a task quickly. **3** kill. •n. **1** the act of dispatching. **2** an official report on military affairs. **3** a report by a journalist abroad. **4** promptness and efficiency.

dispel v. (**dispelling, dispelled**) make a doubt or feeling disappear.

dispensable adj. not essential.

dispensary n. (pl. **dispensaries**) a room where medicines are dispensed.

dispensation n. **1** permission to be exempt from a rule. **2** a religious or political system.

dispense v. **1** distribute to a number of people. **2** prepare and supply medicine. **3** (**dispense with**) get rid of or manage without. ■ **dispenser** n.

disperse v. **1** go or send in different directions. **2** spread over a wide area. ■ **dispersal** n. **dispersion** n.

dispirited adj. disheartened or depressed. ■ **dispiriting** adj.

displace v. **1** move from the proper or usual position. **2** take over the role of. **3** force someone to leave their home. ■ **displacement** n.

display v. **1** present for viewing, esp. in an attractive way. **2** show something. •n. **1** a public performance or show. **2** a thing or things displayed.

displease v. annoy or upset.

displeasure n. annoyance.

disport v. (**disport yourself**) old use enjoy yourself freely.

disposable adj. **1** intended to be thrown away after use. **2** (of income) available for use as required.

disposal n. the act of disposing. □ **at someone's disposal** available for someone to use as and when they wish.

dispose v. **1** (**dispose of**) get rid of. **2** (**be disposed to**) be inclined to do or think. **3** (**disposed**) having a specified attitude. **4** arrange in a particular position.

disposition n. **1** a person's character. **2** a tendency. **3** the arrangement of something.

dispossess v. take land or property from. ■ **dispossession** n.

disproportionate adj. relatively too large or too small. ■ **disproportionately** adv.

disprove v. prove to be false.

disputation n. debate or argument.

disputatious adj. fond of arguing.

dispute v. **1** argue about. **2** question the truth of. **3** compete for. •n. an argument or disagreement. ■ **disputable** adj.

d

d

disqualify v. (**disqualifying, disqualified**) prevent from performing an activity or taking a job because of unsuitability or a breach of rules. ■ **disqualification** n.

disquiet n. anxiety or unease. •v. make anxious or uneasy.

disquisition n. a long or complex discussion of a subject.

disregard v. pay no attention to. •n. lack of attention.

disrepair n. a poor condition due to neglect.

disreputable adj. not respectable.

disrepute n. the state of having a bad reputation.

disrespect n. lack of respect. ■ **disrespectful** adj. **disrespectfully** adv.

disrobe v. undress.

disrupt v. interrupt the normal operation of an activity or process. ■ **disruption** n. **disruptive** adj.

dissatisfied adj. not content or happy. ■ **dissatisfaction** n.

dissect v. cut up a body or plant so as to study its internal parts. ■ **dissection** n.

dissemble v. hide or disguise your feelings.

disseminate v. spread widely. ■ **dissemination** n.

dissension n. disagreement within a group.

dissent v. disagree with a widely held or official view. •n. disagreement. ■ **dissenter** n.

dissertation n. a long essay.

disservice n. a harmful action.

dissident n. a person opposing official policy. ■ **dissidence** n.

dissimilar adj. not similar; different. ■ **dissimilarity** n.

dissimulate v. hide or disguise your feelings. ■ **dissimulation** n.

dissipate v. **1** disperse. **2** waste money etc. **3** (**dissipated**) indulging too much in physical pleasures. ■ **dissipation** n.

dissociate v. **1** disconnect or separate. **2** (**dissociate yourself from**) declare that you are not connected with. ■ **dissociation** n.

dissolute adj. indulging too much in physical pleasures.

dissolve v. **1** disperse in a liquid so as to form a solution. **2** close down or end an assembly or agreement. **3** give way to strong emotion. ■ **dissolution** n.

dissonant adj. lacking harmony. ■ **dissonance** n.

dissuade v. persuade not to do. ■ **dissuasion** n.

distaff n. a stick on to which wool or flax is wound for spinning. □ **distaff side** the female side of a family.

distance n. **1** the length of the space between two points. **2** the state of being distant. **3** a far-off point or place. **4** the full length of a race. •v. (**distance yourself**) become less friendly or supportive.

distant adj. **1** far away. **2** at a specified distance. **3** far apart in resemblance or relationship. **4** aloof. ■ **distantly** adv.

distaste n. dislike.

distasteful adj. unpleasant or offensive.

distemper n. **1** a kind of paint for walls. **2** a disease of dogs.

distend v. swell because of internal pressure. ■ **distension** n.

distil (US **distill**) v. (**distilling, distilled**) **1** purify a liquid by heating it so that it vaporizes and then condensing the vapour.

2 make whisky etc. in this way.
3 extract the most important aspects of. ■ **distillation** n.

distiller n. a person or company that manufactures spirits. ■ **distillery** n.

distinct adj. **1** noticeably different. **2** clearly perceptible.
■ **distinctly** adv. **distinctness** n.

distinction n. **1** a difference or contrast. **2** outstanding excellence. **3** a special honour or award.

distinctive adj. characteristic of a person or thing and distinguishing them from others. ■ **distinctively** adv. **distinctiveness** n.

distinguish v. **1** recognize or treat as different. **2** manage to see or hear. **3** be a characteristic of. **4** (**distinguish yourself**) do something very well. ■ **distinguishable** adj.

distinguished adj. **1** successful and highly respected. **2** dignified in appearance.

distort v. **1** pull or twist out of shape. **2** misrepresent.
■ **distortion** n.

distract v. draw away the attention of.

distraction n. **1** a thing that distracts someone's attention. **2** an entertainment. **3** mental agitation.

distraught adj. very worried and upset.

distress n. extreme anxiety, pain, or hardship. •v. cause distress to.

distribute v. **1** hand or share out. **2** (**be distributed**) be spread over an area. **3** supply goods to retailers. ■ **distribution** n. **distributive** adj.

distributor n. **1** an agent who supplies goods to retailers. **2** a device in a petrol engine for passing electric current to the spark plugs.

district n. a particular area of a town or region.

distrust n. lack of trust. •v. have little trust in. ■ **distrustful** adj.

disturb v. **1** interrupt the activity, rest, etc. of. **2** move from the normal place. **3** make anxious. **4** (**disturbed**) having emotional or mental problems.

disturbance n. **1** the interruption of a normal or settled condition. **2** a breakdown of peaceful behaviour.

disunited adj. not united. ■ **disunity** n.

disuse n. the state of not being used. ■ **disused** adj.

ditch n. a narrow trench for drainage. •v. informal get rid of.

dither v. be indecisive.

ditto n. (in lists) the same thing again.

ditty n. (pl. **ditties**) a short, simple song.

diuretic n. a drug that causes more urine to be excreted.

diurnal adj. of or in the daytime.

diva /dee-vuh/ n. a famous female singer.

Divali var. of **DIWALI**.

divan n. **1** a bed consisting simply of a base and mattress. **2** a sofa without a back or arms.

dive v. **1** plunge head first into water. **2** swim under water. **3** move quickly downwards or under cover. •n. **1** an act of diving. **2** informal a disreputable nightclub or bar. ■ **diver** n.

diverge v. separate and go in a different direction. ■ **divergence** n. **divergent** adj.

diverse adj. widely varied.

d

d

diversify v. (**diversifying, diversified**) 1 make or become more varied. 2 (of a company) expand its range of products or markets. ■ **diversification** n.

diversion n. 1 the act of diverting. 2 an alternative route avoiding a closed road. 3 something intended to distract attention. 4 a recreational activity.

diversity n. (pl. **diversities**) 1 the state of being varied. 2 a range of different things.

divert v. 1 change the direction or course of. 2 distract. 3 amuse or entertain.

divest v. (**divest of**) deprive of.

divide v. 1 separate into parts. 2 share out. 3 cause to disagree. 4 find how many times one number contains another. •n. a wide difference between two groups.

dividend n. 1 a sum of money paid to a company's shareholders out of its profits. 2 (**dividends**) benefits.

divider n. 1 a screen dividing a room. 2 (**dividers**) a measuring compass.

divination n. the use of supernatural means to find out about the future.

divine adj. 1 of God or a god. 2 informal excellent. •v. discover by intuition. ■ **divinely** adv. **diviner** n.

divinity n. (pl. **divinities**) 1 the state of being divine. 2 a god or goddess.

divisible adj. capable of being divided.

division n. 1 the act of dividing. 2 each of the parts into which something is divided. 3 a partition. ■ **divisional** adj.

divisive adj. causing disagreement.

divisor n. a number by which another is to be divided.

divorce n. the legal ending of a marriage. •v. 1 legally end your marriage with. 2 (**divorce from**) separate from.

divorcee n. a divorced person.

divot n. a piece of turf cut out of the ground.

divulge v. reveal information.

Diwali n. a Hindu festival with lights, held in October and November.

DIY n. the activity of doing your own home decoration and repairs.

dizzy adj. (**dizzier, dizziest**) having a sensation of spinning around. ■ **dizzily** adv. **dizziness** n.

DJ n. 1 a person who introduces and plays recorded pop music on the radio or at a club. 2 a dinner jacket.

djellaba /jel-luh-buh/ n. an Arab cloak.

DNA n. deoxyribonucleic acid, a substance carrying genetic information.

do v. (**does, doing, did**; past part. **done**) 1 carry out an action or task. 2 act or perform. 3 work on. 4 make or provide. 5 be suitable or acceptable. •aux. v. used in questions, for emphasis, or to avoid repeating a verb just used. •n. (pl. **dos** or **do's**) a party. □ **do away with** informal put an end to. **do-gooder** a well-meaning but interfering person. **do in** informal 1 kill. 2 tire out. **dos and don'ts** rules of behaviour. **do up** 1 fasten or wrap. 2 informal renovate.

Dobermann (or **Dobermann pinscher**) n. a large breed of dog with powerful jaws.

docile adj. quiet and easy to control. ■ **docilely** adv. **docility** n.

dock n. **1** an enclosed area of water for the loading, unloading, and repair of ships. **2** the enclosure in a court for a person on trial. **3** a weed with broad leaves. • v. **1** come or bring into a dock. **2** (of a spacecraft) join with another craft in space. **3** deduct money from a person's wages. **4** cut short an animal's tail. □ **dockyard** an area where ships are repaired and built.

docker n. a person who loads and unloads ships.

docket n. a document accompanying goods, listing the contents etc.

doctor n. **1** a person qualified to practise medicine. **2** a person holding a doctorate. • v. **1** change information so as to deceive. **2** add a harmful ingredient to.

doctorate n. the highest degree awarded by a university. ■ **doctoral** adj.

doctrinaire adj. very strict in applying beliefs.

doctrine n. a set of beliefs or principles held by a religious, political, or other group. ■ **doctrinal** adj.

document n. a piece of written, printed, or electronic matter providing information or evidence. • v. record in written or other form. ■ **documentation** n.

documentary n. (pl. **documentaries**) a film or television or radio programme giving a factual report. • adj. consisting of documents.

dodder v. be slow and unsteady. ■ **doddery** adj.

dodecagon n. a plane figure with twelve sides.

dodge v. **1** avoid by a sudden quick movement. **2** avoid in a cunning way. • n. an act of dodging. ■ **dodger** n.

dodgem n. a small electric car driven at a funfair with the aim of bumping other such cars.

dodgy adj. informal **1** dishonest. **2** risky. **3** not good or reliable.

dodo n. (pl. **dodos** or **dodoes**) a large extinct bird.

doe n. a female deer, hare, or rabbit.

does 3rd person sing. present of DO.

doesn't contr. does not.

doff v. remove your hat when greeting someone.

dog n. **1** a domesticated meat-eating mammal. **2** the male of this, or of a fox or wolf. • v. (**dogging**, **dogged**) follow or affect persistently. □ **dog collar** informal a white upright collar worn by Christian clergy. **dog-eared** having turned-down corners. **dogfish** a small shark. **dog rose** a wild rose. **dogsbody** informal a person given menial tasks. **in the doghouse** informal in disgrace. ■ **doggy** adj.

doge n. hist. the chief magistrate of Venice or Genoa.

dogged /dog-gid/ adj. persistent. ■ **doggedly** adv.

doggerel n. badly written verse.

doggo adv. (**lie doggo**) informal remain still and quiet to avoid being found.

dogma n. a set of principles intended to be accepted without question.

dogmatic adj. firmly putting forward your opinions and unwilling to accept those of others.

■ **dogmatically** adv. **dog-matism** n.

doily n. (pl. **doilies**) a small ornamental lace or paper mat.

doldrums pl. n. (**the doldrums**) a state of inactivity or depression.

dole n. informal unemployment benefit. •v. (**dole out**) distribute.

doleful adj. mournful. ■ **dolefully** adv.

doll n. a child's toy in the form of a small human figure. •v. (**be dolled up**) informal be dressed in smart or fancy clothes.

dollar n. the basic unit of money of the US and various other countries.

dollop n. informal a mass of something soft.

dolmen n. a prehistoric tomb with a large flat stone laid on upright ones.

dolour (US **dolor**) n. literary great sorrow. ■ **dolorous** adj.

dolphin n. a small whale with a beak-like snout.

dolt n. a stupid person.

domain n. **1** an area controlled by a ruler or government. **2** an area of activity. **3** a part of the Internet with addresses sharing a common suffix.

dome n. a rounded roof with a circular base. ■ **domed** adj.

domestic adj. **1** of a home or family. **2** (of an animal) tame and kept by humans. **3** of or inside a country; not foreign. •n. a person employed to do household tasks. ■ **domestically** adv.

domesticate v. tame an animal and keep it as a pet or for farm produce. ■ **domestication** n.

domesticity n. home life.

domicile n. the country in which a person lives permanently. •v. (**be domiciled**) be living in a particular place.

dominant adj. most important or influential. ■ **dominance** n.

dominate v. **1** have a very strong influence over. **2** be the most important or noticeable person or thing in. ■ **domination** n.

domineering adj. arrogant and overbearing.

dominion n. **1** supreme power or control. **2** a ruler's territory.

domino n. (pl. **dominoes**) any of the small oblong pieces marked with 1–6 pips in each half, used in the game of **dominoes**.

don n. a university teacher. •v. (**donning, donned**) put on an item of clothing.

donate v. **1** give to a good cause. **2** give blood or an organ for use in treating another person. ■ **donation** n.

done past part. of **DO**.

donkey n. (pl. **donkeys**) a long-eared mammal of the horse family. □ **donkey jacket** a heavy jacket with waterproof material across the shoulders. **donkey's years** informal a very long time.

donor n. a person who donates something.

don't contr. do not.

donut US = **DOUGHNUT**.

doodle v. draw absent-mindedly. •n. a doodled drawing.

doom n. death or another terrible fate. •v. (**be doomed**) be fated to fail or be destroyed. □ **doomsday** the last day of the world's existence.

door n. a movable barrier at the entrance to a building, room, etc. □ **doorway** an entrance with a door.

dope informal n. **1** an illegal drug. **2** a stupid person. •v. give a drug to.

dopey (or **dopy**) adj. informal **1** half-asleep. **2** stupid.

doppelgänger /dop-puhl-gang-er/ n. a ghost or double of a living person.

dormant adj. temporarily inactive with physical functions slowed down.

dormer n. an upright window set into a sloping roof.

dormitory n. (pl. **dormitories**) a bedroom for a number of people in a school etc.

dormouse n. (pl. **dormice**) a small mouse-like rodent with a bushy tail.

dorsal adj. of or on the back.

dosage n. the size of a dose.

dose n. **1** a quantity of a medicine taken at one time. **2** an amount of radiation received at one time. •v. give a dose of medicine to.

doss v. informal **1** sleep in rough or makeshift conditions. **2** spend time idly. ■ **dosser** n.

dossier n. a collection of documents about a person or subject.

dot n. a small round mark. •v. (**dotting**, **dotted**) **1** mark with a dot or dots. **2** scatter over an area. □ **dot-com** a company doing business on the Internet. **on the dot** informal exactly on time.

dotage n. the period of life when a person is old and weak.

dote v. (**dote on**) be excessively fond of. ■ **doting** adj.

dotty adj. informal slightly mad or eccentric.

double adj. **1** consisting of two equal or similar parts or things. **2** of twice the usual size. **3** for use by two people. •adv. twice as much. •n. **1** a double quantity or thing. **2** a person who looks exactly like another. **3** (**doubles**) a game with two players on each side. •v. **1** make or become double. **2** fold or bend over on itself. **3** have two uses or roles. **4** (**double back**) go back in the direction you came from. □ **at the double** very fast. **double bass** the largest and lowest-pitched instrument of the violin family. **double-breasted** (of a coat) having an overlap at the front and two rows of buttons. **double chin** a roll of flesh below a person's chin. **double cream** thick cream with a high fat content. **double-cross** betray. **double dealing** deceitful behaviour. **double-decker** a bus with two levels. **double Dutch** incomprehensible speech. **double entendre** /doo-b'l on-ton-druh/ a word or phrase with two meanings, one of which is rude. **double glazing** two sheets of glass in a window, designed to reduce heat loss. **double take** a second reaction to something unexpected, just after your first one. ■ **doubly** adv.

doublet n. hist. a man's short close-fitting jacket.

doubloon n. hist. a Spanish gold coin.

doubt n. a feeling of uncertainty. •v. **1** feel uncertain about. **2** disbelieve or mistrust. ■ **doubter** n.

doubtful adj. **1** uncertain. **2** not probable. ■ **doubtfully** adv.

doubtless adv. very probably.

douche /doosh/ n. a jet of water applied to part of the body.

dough n. a thick mixture of flour and liquid, for baking into bread or pastry. □ **doughnut** (US **donut**) a small fried cake or ring of sweetened dough. ■ **doughy** adj.

doughty /dow-ti/ adj. brave and resolute.

dour adj. stern or gloomy.

douse v. 1 drench with liquid. 2 extinguish a fire.

dove n. 1 a bird with a cooing call. 2 a person favouring a policy of peace and negotiation. □ **dovecote** a shelter for domesticated pigeons.

dovetail v. fit together neatly. • n. a wedge-shaped joint interlocking two pieces of wood.

dowager n. a widow holding a title that belonged to her late husband.

dowdy adj. not smart or fashionable.

dowel n. a headless peg for holding together components.

down adv. 1 to, in, or at a lower place or level. 2 to a smaller amount or size. 3 in or into a weaker or worse position or condition. 4 from an earlier to a later point. • prep. 1 from a higher to a lower point of. 2 at a point further along. • adj. 1 directed or moving downwards. 2 unhappy. 3 (of a computer system) out of action. • v. informal drink quickly. • n. 1 soft fine feathers or hairs. 2 a gently rolling hill. □ **down and out** homeless and without money. **downbeat** 1 gloomy. 2 relaxed and low-key. **downcast** 1 (of eyes) looking downwards. 2 dejected. **downfall** a loss of power or status. **downgrade** move to a lower rank or level. **downhearted** sad or discouraged. **downhill** 1 towards the foot of a slope. 2 into a worsening situation. **downmarket** cheap and of poor quality. **downpour** a heavy fall of rain. **downright** utter; completely as described. **downsize** reduce the number of employees in a company. **downstairs** on or to a lower floor. **downstream** in the direction in which a stream or river flows. **down-to-earth** practical and realistic. **downtown** esp. US in, to, or towards the central area of a city. **downtrodden** oppressed. **down under** informal Australia and New Zealand. ■ **downward** adj. & adv. **downwards** adv.

download v. copy data from one computer system to another. • n. a downloaded computer file.

Down's syndrome n. a congenital disorder causing physical abnormalities and below-average intellectual ability.

downy adj. covered with fine soft hair or feathers.

dowry n. (pl. **dowries**) property or money brought by a bride to her husband on their marriage.

dowse /dowz/ v. search for underground water or minerals with a stick which supposedly moves when these are present.

doxology n. (pl. **doxologies**) a prayer praising God.

doyen n. (fem. **doyenne**) the most respected or prominent person in a particular field.

doze v. sleep lightly. • n. a short, light sleep. ■ **dozy** adj.

dozen n. 1 (pl. **dozen**) a group of twelve. 2 (**dozens**) a lot.

Dr abbrev. (as a title) Doctor.

drab adj. (**drabber, drabbest**) dull and uninteresting.

drachma n. the former basic unit of money in Greece.

draconian adj. very harsh or strict.

draft n. 1 a preliminary version of a piece of writing. 2 a written order to a bank to pay a specified sum. 3 US military conscription. 4 US = **DRAUGHT**. • v. 1 prepare a draft of. 2 select someone for a purpose.

drafty US = **DRAUGHTY**.

drag v. (**dragging, dragged**) 1 pull along with effort. 2 trail along the ground. 3 (of time) pass slowly. 4 (**drag out**) prolong unnecessarily. 5 search the bottom of a lake etc. with hooks or nets. 6 move an image across a computer screen using a mouse. • n. 1 informal a boring or annoying person or thing. 2 informal women's clothes worn by a man. 3 informal an inhalation of smoke from a cigarette. 4 the force exerted by air or water to slow down a moving object. □ **dragnet** a net drawn through water to trap fish.

dragon n. a mythical monster that can breathe out fire. □ **dragonfly** a long-bodied insect with two pairs of wings.

dragoon v. force into doing something. • n. a member of certain British regiments.

drain v. 1 make empty or dry by removing liquid. 2 (of liquid) run off or out. 3 exhaust the strength or resources of. 4 drink the entire contents of. • n. 1 a channel or pipe carrying off surplus liquid. 2 a thing that uses up a resource or strength. □ **drainage** n.

drake n. a male duck.

dram n. a small drink of spirits.

drama n. 1 a play. 2 plays as a literary form. 3 an exciting series of events.

dramatic adj. 1 of drama. 2 sudden and striking. 3 exciting or impressive. ■ **dramatically** adv.

dramatist n. a person who writes plays.

dramatize (or **-ise**) v. 1 present a novel etc. as a play. 2 cause to seem more exciting or serious. ■ **dramatization** n.

drank past of **DRINK**.

drape v. arrange loosely on or round something. • pl. n. (**drapes**) US long curtains.

drapery n. (pl. **draperies**) fabric hanging in loose folds.

drastic adj. having a strong or far-reaching effect. ■ **drastically** adv.

draught (US **draft**) n. 1 a current of cool air indoors. 2 an act of drinking or breathing in. 3 old use a medicinal drink. 4 (**draughts**) a game played on a chequered board. • adj. 1 (of beer) served from a cask. 2 (of an animal) used for pulling loads. □ **draughtsman** a person who makes detailed technical plans or drawings. ■ **draughty** adj.

draw v. (**drawing, drew**; past part. **drawn**) 1 produce a picture or diagram by making lines and marks on paper. 2 pull a vehicle. 3 move in a specified direction. 4 pull curtains shut or open. 5 arrive at a point in time. 6 take out. 7 attract to a place. 8 reach a conclusion. 9 finish a contest or game with an even score. 10 take in a breath. • n. 1 a game that ends with the scores even. 2 a random selection of names or numbers for prizes etc. 3 a very attractive or interesting person or thing. □ **drawback** a disadvantage. **drawbridge** a bridge hinged at one end so that it can be raised.

d

draw on use as a resource. **draw out 1** make something last longer. **2** encourage to talk. **drawstring** a string that can be pulled to close an opening. **draw up 1** come to a halt. **2** prepare a plan or document.

drawer n. **1** a storage compartment that slides horizontally in and out of a desk or chest. **2** (**drawers**) dated knickers or underpants.

drawing n. a picture made with a pencil or pen. □ **drawing pin** pin for fastening paper to a surface. **drawing room** a formal sitting room.

drawl v. speak slowly with prolonged vowels. •n. a drawling accent.

drawn past part. of **DRAW**. •adj. looking strained from illness or exhaustion.

dray n. a low cart without sides.

dread v. fear greatly. •n. great fear or anxiety.

dreadful adj. very bad or serious. ■ **dreadfully** adv.

dreadlocks pl. n. a Rastafarian hairstyle with the hair twisted into tight ringlets.

dream n. **1** a series of images and feelings occurring in the mind during sleep. **2** an ambition or wish. •v. (**dreaming, dreamed** or **dreamt**) **1** have dreams while asleep. **2** think of as possible. **3** (**dream up**) invent. ■ **dreamer** n. **dreamless** adj.

dreamy adj. **1** tending to daydream. **2** seeming pleasantly unreal.

dreary adj. (**drearier, dreariest**) dull, bleak, and depressing. ■ **drearily** adv. **dreariness** n.

dredge v. scoop up mud and objects from the bed of a river etc. ■ **dredger** n.

dregs pl. n. **1** the last drops of liquid and any sediment left in a container. **2** the most worthless parts.

drench v. wet thoroughly.

dress v. **1** put on clothes. **2** (**dress up**) dress in smart clothes or in a special costume. **3** decorate in an attractive way. **4** clean and cover a wound. •n. **1** a woman's garment that covers the body and extends down over the legs. **2** clothing. □ **dress circle** the first level of seats in a theatre. **dress rehearsal** a final rehearsal, in full costume, before a real performance.

dressage /dress-ahzh/ n. controlled movements performed by a horse at the rider's command.

dresser n. **1** a sideboard with shelves above for crockery. **2** a person who dresses in a particular way.

dressing n. **1** a sauce for a salad. **2** a protective covering for a wound. □ **dressing-down** informal a severe reprimand. **dressing gown** a long robe worn after getting out of bed or bathing. **dressing table** a table with a mirror, used while applying make-up.

dressy adj. (of clothes) smart or formal.

drew past of **DRAW**.

drey n. a squirrel's nest.

dribble v. **1** (of a liquid) fall slowly in drops or a thin stream. **2** let saliva run from the mouth. **3** (in sport) take the ball forward with slight touches. •n. a thin stream of liquid.

dried past & past part. of **DRY**.

drier var. of **DRYER**.

drift v. 1 be carried slowly by a current of air or water. 2 go slowly or aimlessly. • n. 1 a drifting movement. 2 the general meaning of someone's remarks. 3 a mass of snow piled up by the wind.
□ **driftwood** pieces of wood floating on the sea or washed ashore.

drifter n. a person who moves aimlessly from place to place.

drill n. 1 a tool or machine for boring holes. 2 training in military exercises. 3 (**the drill**) informal the correct procedure. 4 a strong twilled cotton fabric. • v. 1 bore a hole with a drill. 2 give training or instruction to.

drily (or **dryly**) adv. in a humorously ironic way.

drink v. (**drinking**, **drank**; past part. **drunk**) 1 swallow liquid. 2 consume alcohol. • n. 1 a liquid for drinking. 2 alcohol. ■ **drinker** n.

drip v. (**dripping**, **dripped**) fall or let fall in small drops. • n. 1 a small drop of a liquid. 2 a device for slowly passing a substance into a patient's body through a vein. 3 informal a weak person. □ **drip-dry** (of a garment) able to dry without creases if hung up when wet.

dripping n. fat melted from roasting meat.

drive v. (**driving**, **drove**; past part. **driven**) 1 operate a vehicle. 2 carry in a vehicle. 3 carry or urge along. 4 compel to do something. 5 provide the energy to keep a machine in motion. • n. 1 a car journey. 2 a short private road leading to a house. 3 a natural urge. 4 an organized effort to

achieve something. 5 determination. ■ **driver** n.

drivel n. nonsense.

drizzle n. light rain falling in fine drops. • v. rain lightly. ■ **drizzly** adj.

droll adj. strange and amusing.

dromedary n. (pl. **dromedaries**) an Arabian camel, with one hump.

drone v. 1 make a low humming sound. 2 (**drone on**) speak tediously and at length. • n. 1 a low humming sound. 2 a male bee.

drool v. 1 let saliva dribble. 2 (**drool over**) informal show great pleasure or desire for.

droop v. bend or hang down limply. ■ **droopy** adj.

drop v. (**dropping**, **dropped**) 1 fall or let fall. 2 make or become lower or less. 3 give up a course of action. 4 set down a passenger or load. • n. 1 a small rounded mass of liquid. 2 a small drink. 3 an act of dropping. 4 an abrupt fall or slope. □ **drop by/in** pay a casual visit. **drop off** fall asleep. **dropout** a person who lives an alternative lifestyle or has given up a course of study. **drop out** stop participating.

droplet n. a very small drop of a liquid.

dropper n. a glass tube for measuring out liquid.

droppings pl. n. animal dung.

dross n. rubbish.

drought /drowt/ n. a very long period of little or no rainfall.

drove past of **DRIVE**. • n. 1 a large number of people. 2 a flock of animals being herded along.

drown v. 1 die or kill through submersion in water. 2 make inaudible by being much louder.

drowse v. be half asleep; doze.

drowsy adj. sleepy. ■ **drowsily** adv. **drowsiness** n.

drubbing n. informal a thorough defeat.

drudge n. a person made to do hard or dull work. ■ **drudgery** n.

drug n. **1** a substance used as a medicine. **2** an illegal substance taken for its stimulating or other effects. •v. (**drugging, drugged**) give or add a drug to. □ **drugstore** US a pharmacy also selling toiletries etc.

Druid n. a priest in the ancient Celtic religion.

drum n. **1** a percussion instrument with a skin stretched across a frame, sounded by being struck. **2** a cylindrical container or part. •v. (**drumming, drummed**) **1** play on a drum. **2** make a continuous rhythmic noise. **3** (**drum into**) teach by constant repetition. **4** (**drum up**) try to get support or business. □ **drumstick 1** a stick used for beating a drum. **2** the lower part of a cooked chicken's leg. ■ **drummer** n.

drunk past part. of **DRINK**. •adj. strongly affected by alcohol. •n. (or **drunkard**) a person who is drunk or often drunk. ■ **drunken** adj. **drunkenly** adv. **drunkenness** n.

dry adj. (**drier, driest**) **1** free from moisture or liquid. **2** serious and boring. **3** (of humour) subtle and usu. ironic. **4** (of wine) not sweet. •v. (**drying, dried**) **1** make or become dry. **2** preserve by evaporating the moisture from. **3** (**dry up**) (of a supply) decrease and stop. □ **dry-clean** clean a garment with a chemical. **dry ice** white mist produced artificially as a theatrical effect. **dry rot** a fungus causing wood decay. **dry run** a rehearsal. ■ **dryness** n.

dryer (or **drier**) n. a machine or device for drying something.

dryly var. of **DRILY**.

dual adj. consisting of two parts. □ **dual carriageway** a road with two or more lanes in each direction. ■ **duality** n.

dub v. (**dubbing, dubbed**) **1** give an unofficial name to. **2** knight someone. **3** provide a film with a soundtrack in a different language from the original.

dubbin n. a grease for softening and waterproofing leather.

dubiety n. doubt or uncertainty.

dubious adj. **1** doubtful or hesitant. **2** probably not honest. **2** of uncertain value. ■ **dubiously** adv.

ducal adj. of a duke.

ducat /duk-uht/ n. a former European gold coin.

duchess n. **1** a duke's wife or widow. **2** a woman holding a rank equivalent to duke.

duchy n. (pl. **duchies**) the territory of a duke or duchess.

duck n. (pl. **duck** or **ducks**) **1** a waterbird with a broad bill and webbed feet. **2** a female duck. **3** a batsman's score of nought in cricket. •v. **1** lower yourself quickly to avoid being hit or seen. **2** push someone under water. **3** informal avoid a duty. □ **duckboards** wooden slats forming a path over mud. **duckling** n.

duct n. **1** a tube or passageway for air, cables, etc. **2** a tube in the body through which fluid passes.

ductile adj. (of a metal) able to be drawn out into a thin wire. ■ **ductility** n.

dud n. informal a thing that fails to work properly.

dude n. US informal a man.

dudgeon n. (**in high dudgeon**) angry or resentful.

due adj. **1** expected at a certain time. **2** needing to be paid or given; owing. **3** owed or deserving something. **4** proper or required. •n. **1** (**someone's due/dues**) what someone deserves or is owed. **2** (**dues**) fees. •adv. directly: due south. □ **due to 1** caused by. **2** because of.

duel n. **1** hist. a fight between two people to settle a point of honour. **2** a contest between two parties. •v. (**duelling, duelled**; US **dueling, dueled**) fight a duel.

duet n. a musical composition for two performers.

duff informal adj. worthless or false. •v. (**duff up**) beat up.

duffel coat n. a thick hooded overcoat.

duffer n. informal an incompetent or stupid person.

dug past & past part. of **DIG**. •n. an udder or teat.

dugong n. an Asian sea mammal.

dugout n. a low or underground shelter.

duke n. **1** the highest rank of nobleman in Britain and certain other countries. **2** hist. a male ruler of a small independent state. ■ **dukedom** n.

dulcet adj. (of a sound) sweet and soothing.

dulcimer n. a musical instrument with strings struck with hand-held hammers.

dull adj. **1** lacking interest. **2** lacking brightness. **3** slow to understand. •v. make or become dull. ■ **dullness** n. **dully** adv.

dullard n. a stupid person.

duly adv. as is required or expected.

dumb adj. **1** offens. unable to speak. **2** silent. **3** US informal stupid. •v. (**dumb down**) informal make easier to understand. □ **dumb-bell** a short bar with weighted ends, used for exercise.

dumbfound astonish greatly.

dumdum n. a soft-nosed bullet that expands on impact.

dummy n. (pl. **dummies**) **1** a model of a human being. **2** a model of something used as a substitute. **3** a plastic teat for a baby to suck on. **4** informal a stupid person. □ **dummy run** a practice or trial.

dump n. **1** a site where rubbish or waste is left. **2** informal an unpleasant or dull place. **3** a temporary store of weapons or provisions. •v. **1** get rid of. **2** put down carelessly. □ **down in the dumps** informal unhappy.

dumpling n. a ball of dough cooked in a stew.

dumpy adj. short and stout.

dun n. a greyish-brown colour.

dunce n. a person slow at learning.

dune n. a mound of drifted sand.

dung n. animal excrement.

dungarees pl. n. a garment consisting of trousers held up by shoulder straps.

dungeon n. an underground prison cell.

dunk v. dip food into a drink or soup before eating it.

duo n. (pl. **duos**) **1** a pair of people or things. **2** a duet.

duodenum /dyoo-uh-dee-nuhm/ n. (pl. **duodenums**) the part of the small intestine next to the stomach. ■ **duodenal** adj.

dupe v. deceive or trick. •n. a duped person.

duple *adj.* (of rhythm) having two main beats to the bar.

duplex *n.* US a building divided into two flats.

duplicate *adj.* **1** exactly like something else. **2** having two corresponding parts. • *n.* an exact copy. • *v.* **1** make or be an exact copy of. **2** multiply by two. **3** do again unnecessarily. ■ **duplication** *n.* **duplicator** *n.*

duplicity *n.* deceitful behaviour. ■ **duplicitous** *adj.*

durable *adj.* **1** hard-wearing. **2** (of goods) able to be kept. ■ **durability** *n.*

duration *n.* the time during which something continues.

duress *n.* threats or violence used to force a person to do something.

during *prep.* **1** throughout. **2** at a point in the course of.

dusk *n.* the darker stage of twilight.

dusky *adj.* darkish in colour.

dust *n.* fine, dry particles of earth or other matter. • *v.* **1** remove dust from the surface of. **2** cover lightly with a powdered substance. □ **dustbin** a large container for household rubbish. **dustman** a man employed to empty dustbins. **dustpan** a container into which dust and waste can be swept. ■ **dusty** *adj.*

duster *n.* a cloth for dusting furniture.

Dutch *adj.* of the Netherlands. • *n.* the language of the Netherlands. □ **Dutch courage** confidence gained from drinking alcohol. **go Dutch** share the cost of a meal equally.

dutiable *adj.* on which duty must be paid.

dutiful *adj.* obedient and conscientious. ■ **dutifully** *adv.*

duty *n.* (*pl.* **duties**) **1** a moral or legal obligation. **2** a task required as part of your job. **3** a tax on the import, export, or sale of goods. □ **on** (or **off**) **duty** doing (or not doing) your regular work.

duvet /doo-vay/ *n.* a thick quilt used instead of a top sheet and blankets.

DVD *abbrev.* digital versatile disc.

dwarf *n.* (*pl.* **dwarfs** or **dwarves**) **1** a mythical short human-like being. **2** an unusually short person. • *v.* cause to seem comparatively small.

dwell *v.* (**dwelling**, **dwelt** or **dwelled**) **1** live in or at a place. **2** (**dwell on**) think at length about. ■ **dweller** *n.*

dwelling *n.* a place where someone lives.

dwindle *v.* gradually become smaller or weaker.

dye *n.* a substance used to colour something. • *v.* colour with dye.

dying *pres.* part. of **DIE**.

dyke (or **dike**) *n.* **1** a barrier built to prevent flooding from the sea. **2** a drainage ditch.

dynamic *adj.* **1** constantly changing or active. **2** full of energy and new ideas. **3** *Physics* of forces producing motion. ■ **dynamically** *adv.*

dynamics *n.* **1** the study of the forces involved in movement. **2** forces which stimulate change.

dynamism *n.* the quality of being dynamic.

dynamite *n.* a kind of high explosive.

dynamo *n.* (*pl.* **dynamos**) a machine for converting mechanical energy into electrical energy.

d
e

dynasty n. (pl. **dynasties**) a series of related rulers or powerful people. ■ **dynastic** adj.

dysentery n. a disease causing severe diarrhoea.

dysfunctional adj. **1** not operating properly. **2** unable to deal with normal social relations.
■ **dysfunction** n.

dyslexia n. a disorder involving difficulty in reading. ■ **dyslexic** adj. & n.

dyspepsia n. indigestion.
■ **dyspeptic** adj.

Ee

E abbrev. **1** East or Eastern. **2** (€) euro or euros. **3** informal the drug Ecstasy. □ **E-number** a code number given to food additives.

each adj. & pron. every one of two or more, regarded separately. • adv. to, for, or by every one of a group.

eager adj. strongly wanting to do or have. ■ **eagerly** adv. **eagerness** n.

eagle n. a large bird of prey. □ **eagle-eyed** very observant.

ear n. **1** the organ of hearing. **2** an ability to recognize and appreciate music or language. **3** the seed-bearing head of a cereal plant. □ **eardrum** a membrane in the ear which vibrates in response to sound waves. **earmark** choose for a purpose. **earphones** devices worn on the ears to listen to radio, recorded sound, etc. **earring** a piece of jewellery worn on the ear. **earwig** a small insect with pincers at its rear end. **within** (or **out of**) **earshot** near enough (or too distant) to be heard.

earl n. a British nobleman ranking above a viscount. ■ **earldom** n.

early adj. (**earlier, earliest**) & adv. **1** before the expected time. **2** near the beginning of a period or sequence.

earn v. **1** be given money or reward in return for work or merit. **2** (of money invested) gain as interest. ■ **earner** n. **earnings** pl. n.

earnest adj. very serious. □ **in earnest 1** more intensely than before. **2** in a serious or sincere way. ■ **earnestly** adv.

earth n. **1** (or **Earth**) the planet we live on. **2** soil. **3** electrical connection to the ground. **4** a fox's den. • v. connect an electrical device to earth. □ **earthquake** a sudden violent movement in the earth's crust. **earthwork** a large defensive bank of soil. **earthworm** a worm that burrows in the soil.

earthen adj. made of earth or fired clay. □ **earthenware** pottery made of fired clay.

earthly adj. **1** of the earth or human life. **2** informal used for emphasis: no earthly reason.

earthy adj. **1** like soil. **2** treating sex or bodily functions in a direct way. ■ **earthiness** n.

ease n. **1** lack of difficulty or effort. **2** freedom from problems. v. **1** make or become less severe or intense. **2** move carefully or gradually.

easel n. a frame on legs for holding an artist's work.

easily adv. **1** without difficulty. **2** definitely.

east n. **1** the direction in which the sun rises. **2** the eastern part of a place. • adj. & adv. **1** towards or facing the east. **2** (of a wind) from the east. ■ **easterly** adj. & adv. **eastward** adj. & adv. **eastwards** adv.

Easter n. the Christian festival celebrating the resurrection of Jesus.

eastern adj. situated in or facing the east.

easterner n. a person from the east of a region.

easy adj. (**easier, easiest**) **1** achieved without great effort. **2** free from worry or problems. □ **easy chair** a comfortable chair. **easy-going** relaxed and open-minded.

eat v. (**eating, ate**; past part. **eaten**) **1** chew and swallow food. **2** (**eat away**) erode or destroy. **3** (**eat up**) use up resources. ■ **eatable** adj. **eater** n.

eatery n. (pl. **eateries**) informal a restaurant or cafe.

eau de cologne /oh duh kuh-lohn/ = **COLOGNE**.

eaves pl. n. the overhanging edge of a roof.

eavesdrop v. (**eavesdropping, eavesdropped**) secretly listen to a conversation. ■ **eaves-dropper** n.

ebb n. the movement of the tide away from the land. • v. **1** (of the

tide) move away from the land. **2** gradually lessen. □ **at a low ebb** in a weakened or depressed state.

ebony n. **1** heavy dark wood from a tropical tree. **2** a deep black colour.

ebullient adj. cheerful and full of energy. ■ **ebullience** n.

EC abbrev. European Community.

eccentric adj. **1** unconventional and rather strange. **2** not concentric. • n. an eccentric person. ■ **eccentrically** adv. **eccentricity** n.

ecclesiastical adj. of the Christian Church or its clergy.

echelon /esh-uh-lon/ n. a level in an organization, profession, etc.

echo n. (pl. **echoes**) **1** a repetition of sound caused by the reflection of sound waves. **2** a reflected radio or radar beam. • v. **1** (of a sound) reverberate or be repeated as an echo. **2** be similar to. **3** repeat someone's words.

eclair /i-klair/ n. a long cake of choux pastry filled with cream.

éclat /ay-klah/ n. an impressive or successful effect.

eclectic adj. using ideas from a wide range of sources.

eclipse n. **1** an occasion when one planet, the moon, etc. blocks out the light from another. **2** a sudden loss of significance or power. • v. **1** (of a planet etc.) block the light from or to another. **2** make less significant or powerful.

eco-friendly adj. not harmful to the environment.

E. coli /ee koh-ly/ n. a bacterium which can cause severe food poisoning.

ecology n. the study of the relationships of living things to one

economic adj. **1** of economics or the economy of a country. **2** profitable.

economical adj. **1** giving good value in relation to outlay. **2** careful in the use of money or resources. ∎ **economically** adv.

economics n. the study of the production, consumption, and transfer of wealth. ∎ **economist** n.

economize (or **-ise**) v. spend less.

economy n. (pl. **economies**) **1** the state of a country in terms of the production and consumption of goods and services and the supply of money. **2** careful management of resources.

ecosystem n. a biological community of interacting living things and their environment.

ecru n. a light beige colour.

ecstasy n. (pl. **ecstasies**) **1** intense happiness. **2** (**Ecstasy**) an illegal drug. ∎ **ecstatic** adj. **ecstatically** adv.

> ! No x: -cs- at the beginning and s at the end: ecstasy.

ectopic pregnancy n. a pregnancy in which the fetus develops outside the womb.

ecumenical adj. representing or promoting unity among the different Christian Churches.

eczema /eks-muh/ n. a condition causing dry, itchy patches on the skin.

eddy n. (pl. **eddies**) a circular movement of water. • v. (**eddying**, **eddied**) move in eddies.

edelweiss /ay-duhl-vyss/ n. an alpine plant.

edema US = **OEDEMA**

edge n. **1** the outside limit of an object or area. **2** the sharpened side of a blade. **3** a slight advantage. **4** an intense or exciting quality. • v. **1** provide with an edge. **2** move gradually and carefully. □ **edgeways** (or **edgewise**) with the edge uppermost or towards the viewer. **on edge** tense or irritable.

edging n. a decorative border.

edgy adj. (**edgier**, **edgiest**) tense or irritable. ∎ **edgily** adv. **edginess** n.

edible adj. fit to be eaten.

edict n. an official order.

edifice n. a large and impressive building.

edify v. (**edifying**, **edified**) improve the mind or character of. ∎ **edification** n.

edit v. (**editing**, **edited**) **1** prepare written material for publication. **2** prepare material for a film or broadcast.

edition n. **1** a version of a published written work. **2** all the copies of a book etc. issued at one time.

editor n. **1** a person in charge of a newspaper or magazine. **2** a person who edits material for publication or broadcast.

editorial adj. of the editing of material. • n. a newspaper article giving an opinion on a topical issue.

educate v. give intellectual or moral instruction to.

education n. **1** the process of teaching, training, or learning. **2** the theory of teaching. ∎ **educational** adj. **educationally** adv.

Edwardian adj. of the reign of King Edward VII (1901–10).

e

EEC *abbrev.* European Economic Community.

eel *n.* a snake-like fish.

eerie *adj.* (**eerier, eeriest**) strange and frightening. ■ **eerily** *adv.*

efface *v.* **1** rub off or cause to disappear. **2** (**efface yourself**) make yourself appear inconspicuous.

effect *n.* **1** a change produced by an action or other cause; a result. **2** the state of being operative or effective. **3** (**effects**) personal belongings. **4** (**effects**) the lighting, sound, or scenery used in a play or film. •*v.* bring about a result.

> ! Don't confuse **affect** and **effect**: **affect** is a verb which chiefly means 'make a difference to'.

effective *adj.* **1** producing an intended result. **2** operative. **3** existing in fact, though not formally acknowledged as such. ■ **effectively** *adv.* **effectiveness** *n.*

effectual *adj.* effective. ■ **effectually** *adv.*

effeminate *adj.* (of a man) having characteristics regarded as typical of a woman. ■ **effeminacy** *n.*

effervescent *adj.* **1** fizzy. **2** lively and enthusiastic. ■ **effervesce** *v.* **effervescence** *n.*

effete *adj.* **1** weak; feeble. **2** (of a man) effeminate.

efficacious *adj.* effective. ■ **efficacy** *n.*

efficient *adj.* working productively with no waste of money or effort. ■ **efficiency** *n.* **efficiently** *adv.*

effigy *n.* (*pl.* **effigies**) a model of a person.

efflorescence *n.* a high stage of development.

effluent *n.* liquid waste or sewage.

effluvium *n.* (*pl.* **effluvia**) an unpleasant or harmful smell or discharge.

effort *n.* **1** a determined attempt. **2** the physical or mental energy needed to do something. ■ **effortless** *adj.*

effrontery *n.* insolence or disrespect.

effusion *n.* an outpouring of feeling.

effusive *adj.* expressing pleasure or approval in an unrestrained way. ■ **effusively** *n.*

e.g. *abbrev.* for example.

egalitarian *adj.* believing in the principle of equal rights for all. •*n.* an egalitarian person. ■ **egalitarianism** *n.*

egg *n.* **1** an oval or round object laid by a female bird, reptile, etc., and containing a cell which can develop into a new organism. **2** an ovum. •*v.* (**egg on**) urge to do something foolish. ■ **egghead** *informal* a very studious person. **eggplant** *US* an aubergine. ■ **eggy** *adj.*

ego *n.* (*pl.* **egos**) **1** a person's sense of their own value. **2** the part of the mind responsible for a person's sense of identity.

egocentric *adj.* self-centred.

egotism (or **egoism**) *n.* the quality of being very conceited or self-centred. ■ **egotist** *n.* **egotistic** *adj.* **egotistical** *adj.*

egregious /i-gree-juhss/ *adj.* very bad.

egress *n.* **1** the act of going out. **2** a way out.

Egyptian *n.* a person from Egypt. •*adj.* of Egypt.

Egyptology n. the study of ancient Egypt. ■ **Egyptologist** n.

Eid /eed/ (or **Id**) n. **1** the Muslim festival marking the end of the fast of Ramadan. **2** the Muslim festival marking the end of the annual pilgrimage to Mecca.

eider n. a large northern sea duck. □ **eiderdown** a quilt filled with down or other soft material.

eight adj. & n. one more than seven; 8. ■ **eighth** adj. & n.

eighteen adj. & n. one more than seventeen; 18. ■ **eighteenth** adj. & n.

eighty adj. & n. (pl. **eighties**) ten less than ninety; 80. ■ **eightieth** adj. & n.

einsteinium n. an unstable radioactive element.

eisteddfod /I-steth-vod/ n. a Welsh festival with music and poetry competitions.

either conj. & adv. **1** as the first of two alternatives specified. **2** indicating a link with a previous statement. •adj. & pron. **1** one or the other of two. **2** each of two.

ejaculate v. **1** eject semen from the penis. **2** dated say suddenly. ■ **ejaculation** n.

eject v. force or throw out. ■ **ejection** n. **ejector** n.

eke v. (**eke out**) **1** use sparingly. **2** make a living with difficulty.

elaborate adj. with many carefully arranged parts. •v. **1** develop in detail. **2** add detail to something said. ■ **elaborately** adv. **elaboration** n.

élan n. energy and flair.

elapse v. (of time) pass.

elastic adj. **1** able to return to normal size or shape after being stretched or squeezed. **2** flexible.

•n. elastic cord or fabric. ■ **elasticated** adj. **elasticity** n.

elated adj. very happy and excited. ■ **elation** n.

elbow n. the joint between the forearm and the upper arm. •v. hit or push with the elbow. □ **elbow grease** informal vigorous cleaning. **elbow room** informal enough space to move in.

elder adj. of a greater age. •n. **1** a person older than you. **2** a senior figure in a community. **3** a shrub with white flowers and small dark berries (**elderberries**).

elderly adj. old.

eldest adj. oldest.

elect v. **1** choose for a public position by voting. **2** choose to do. •adj. elected but not yet in office.

election n. **1** a procedure whereby a person is elected. **2** the act of electing.

electioneering n. campaigning to be elected to a political position.

elective adj. **1** of or chosen by election. **2** chosen by the person concerned.

elector n. a person entitled to vote in an election. ■ **electoral** adj.

electorate n. the people entitled to vote in an election.

electric adj. **1** of, using, or producing electricity. **2** very exciting. •n. (**electrics**) the electric wiring in a house or vehicle. □ **electric chair** a chair for executing convicted criminals by electrocution.

electrical adj. of, using, or producing electricity. ■ **electrically** adv.

electrician n. a person who installs and repairs electrical equipment.

e

electricity n. 1 a form of energy resulting from charged particles. 2 the supply of electric current to a building.

electrify v. (**electrifying, electrified**) 1 charge with electricity. 2 convert to use electrical power. 3 (**electrifying**) very exciting. ■ **electrification** n.

electroconvulsive adj. (of the treatment of mental illness) using electric shocks applied to the brain.

electrocute v. injure or kill by electric shock. ■ **electrocution** n.

electrode n. a conductor through which electricity enters or leaves something.

electrolysis n. 1 the separation of a liquid into its chemical parts by passing an electric current through it. 2 the removal of hair roots by means of an electric current.

electrolyte n. a liquid or gel that an electric current can pass through.

electromagnet n. a metal core made into a magnet by passing electric current through a surrounding coil.

electromagnetic adj. of electric currents and magnetic fields. ■ **electromagnetism** n.

electromotive adj. producing an electric current.

electron n. a subatomic particle with a negative charge, found in all atoms. □ **electron microscope** a powerful microscope using electron beams instead of light.

electronic adj. 1 having parts such as microchips and transistors that control and direct electric currents. 2 of electrons or electronics. 3 carried out by computer. ■ **electronically** adv.

electronics n. 1 the study of electrons or electronic devices. 2 electronic circuits or devices.

electroplate v. coat a metal object with another metal using electrolysis.

elegant adj. 1 graceful and stylish. 2 pleasingly clever but simple. ■ **elegance** n. **elegantly** adv.

elegy n. (pl. **elegies**) a sad poem, esp. a lament for a dead person. ■ **elegiac** adj.

element n. 1 a basic part. 2 a substance that cannot be chemically changed or broken down into other substances. 3 earth, water, air, and fire, formerly believed to make up all matter. 4 a trace. 5 (**the elements**) the weather, esp. when bad. 6 a part that gives out heat in an electric device. □ **in your element** in a situation in which you are happy or relaxed. ■ **elemental** adj.

elementary adj. of the most basic aspects of a subject.

elephant n. a very large mammal with a trunk and tusks.

elephantine adj. huge or clumsy.

elevate v. raise to a higher position or level.

elevation n. 1 the act of elevating. 2 height above a given level. 3 one side of a building.

elevator n. US a lift in a building.

eleven adj. & n. one more than ten; 11. ■ **eleventh** adj. & n.

elevenses pl. n. informal a mid-morning snack.

elf n. (pl. **elves**) an imaginary small being with magic powers.

elfin adj. (of a person) small and delicate.

elicit v. (**eliciting**, **elicited**) draw out a response.

elide v. omit a sound or syllable when speaking. ■ **elision** n.

eligible adj. **1** satisfying the conditions to do or receive something. **2** desirable as a wife or husband. ■ **eligibility** n.

eliminate v. get rid of. ■ **elimination** n.

elite n. a group regarded as the best in a particular sphere or organization.

elitism n. **1** the belief that a society should be run by an elite. **2** the superior attitude associated with an elite. ■ **elitist** adj. & n.

elixir n. a magical potion.

Elizabethan adj. of the reign of Queen Elizabeth I (1558–1603).

elk n. a large deer.

ellipse n. a regular oval.

ellipsis n. (pl. **ellipses**) **1** the omission of words in speech or writing. **2** a set of dots indicating this.

elliptical adj. **1** with a word or words omitted. **2** oval.

elm n. a tall deciduous tree with rough leaves.

elocution n. the skill of speaking clearly.

elongate v. make or become longer.

elope v. run away secretly to get married. ■ **elopement** n.

eloquence n. fluent or persuasive speaking or writing. ■ **eloquent** adj. **eloquently** adv.

else adv. **1** in addition. **2** different; instead. □ **elsewhere** in or to another place. **or else** otherwise; if not.

elucidate v. explain. ■ **elucidation** n.

elude v. **1** cleverly escape from or avoid. **2** fail to be understood or achieved by.

elusive adj. hard to find or achieve.

elver n. a young eel.

elves pl. of **ELF**.

emaciated adj. abnormally thin and weak. ■ **emaciation** n.

email (or **e-mail**) n. **1** the sending of electronic messages from one computer user to another. **2** a message sent by email. •v. send a message by email.

emanate v. (**emanate from**) come or spread out from. ■ **emanation** n.

emancipate v. free from legal, social, or political restrictions. ■ **emancipation** n.

emasculate v. **1** make weaker or less effective. **2** deprive a man of his male role or identity. ■ **emasculation** n.

embalm v. treat a corpse to preserve it from decay.

embankment n. a wall or bank built to prevent flooding or to carry a road or railway.

embargo n. (pl. **embargoes**) an official ban, esp. on trade with a particular country. •v. (**embargoing**, **embargoed**) ban officially.

embark v. **1** board a ship or aircraft. **2** (**embark on**) begin a new course of action. ■ **embarkation** n.

embarrass v. cause to feel awkward or ashamed. ■ **embarrassment** n.

❗ Two r's, two s's: embarrass.

embassy n. (pl. **embassies**) the official residence or offices of an ambassador.

embattled adj. **1** facing many problems. **2** surrounded by enemy forces.

embed (or **imbed**) v. (**embedding, embedded**) fix firmly in a surrounding mass.

embellish v. **1** decorate. **2** add extra details to a story. ■ **embellishment** n.

ember n. a piece of burning wood or coal in a dying fire.

embezzle v. steal money placed in your trust. ■ **embezzlement** n. **embezzler** n.

embittered adj. bitter or resentful.

emblazon v. conspicuously display a design on something.

emblem n. a design or symbol as a badge of a nation, group, etc.

emblematic adj. representing a quality or idea.

embody v. (**embodying, embodied**) **1** give a tangible or visible form to. **2** include. ■ **embodiment** n.

embolden v. make braver.

embolism n. obstruction of an artery by a clot or an air bubble.

emboss v. make a raised design on.

embrace v. **1** hold closely in your arms. **2** include or contain. **3** willingly accept or support a change etc. •n. an act of embracing.

embrocation n. a liquid rubbed on the body to relieve aches.

embroider v. **1** sew decorative needlework patterns on. **2** embellish a story. ■ **embroidery** n.

embroil v. involve in a conflict or difficult situation.

embryo n. (pl. **embryos**) an unborn or unhatched baby or animal in the early stages of development.

embryonic adj. **1** of an embryo. **2** in a very early stage of development.

emend v. correct and revise written material. ■ **emendation** n.

emerald n. **1** a green precious stone. **2** a bright green colour.

emerge v. **1** come out into view. **2** (of facts) become known. **3** survive a difficult period. ■ **emergence** n. **emergent** adj.

emergency n. (pl. **emergencies**) a serious and unexpected situation requiring immediate action.

emeritus adj. retired but retaining a title as an honour.

emery board n. a strip of wood or card coated with a rough substance and used as a nail file.

emetic adj. causing vomiting.

emigrate v. leave your own country and settle permanently in another. ■ **emigrant** n. **emigration** n.

émigré /em-i-gray/ n. a person who has emigrated.

eminence n. **1** the quality of being distinguished and respected. **2** an important person.

eminent adj. **1** distinguished. **2** obvious. ■ **eminently** adv.

emir n. a Muslim ruler.

emirate n. the territory of an emir.

emissary n. (pl. **emissaries**) a person sent on a special diplomatic mission.

emit v. (**emitting, emitted**) **1** give out heat, gas, etc. **2** make a sound. ■ **emission** n.

emollient adj. **1** softening or soothing the skin. **2** attempting to avoid conflict.

emolument n. a salary or fee.

emotion n. **1** a strong feeling, e.g. anger. **2** instinctive feeling as contrasted with reasoning.

emotional adj. **1** of the emotions. **2** arousing or showing emotion. ■ **emotionally** adv.

emotive adj. arousing strong feeling.

empathize (or **-ise**) v. understand and share the feelings of another.

empathy n. the ability to empathize.

emperor n. the male ruler of an empire.

emphasis n. (pl. **emphases**) **1** special importance or value given to something. **2** stress on a word in speaking.

emphasize (or **-ise**) v. give special importance to.

emphatic adj. showing or giving emphasis. ■ **emphatically** adv.

emphysema n. a condition that affects the lungs, causing breathlessness.

empire n. **1** a large group of countries under a single ruler or authority. **2** a large business organization controlled by one person or group.

empirical adj. based on observation or experience rather than theory. ■ **empirically** adv. **empiricism** n. **empiricist** n.

emplacement n. a platform for a gun or battery of guns.

employ v. **1** give work to someone and pay them for it. **2** make use of. ■ **employee** n. **employer** n. **employment** n.

emporium n. (pl. **emporia** or **emporiums**) a large shop selling a variety of goods.

empower v. **1** authorize. **2** give strength and confidence to. ■ **empowerment** n.

empress n. **1** a female ruler of an empire. **2** an emperor's wife or widow.

empty adj. (**emptier**, **emptiest**) **1** containing nothing; not filled or occupied. **2** having no real meaning. •v. (**emptying**, **emptied**) make or become empty. •n. (pl. **empties**) informal an empty bottle or glass. ■ **emptiness** n.

emu n. a flightless Australian bird similar to an ostrich.

emulate v. try to equal or be better than. ■ **emulation** n. **emulator** n.

emulsify v. (**emulsifying**, **emulsified**) combine liquids into an emulsion. ■ **emulsifier** n.

emulsion n. **1** a mixture of two liquids in which particles of one are evenly distributed in the other. **2** a type of paint for walls. **3** a light-sensitive coating for photographic film.

enable v. provide with the ability or means to do something.

enact v. **1** make a bill or other proposal law. **2** act out a role or play. ■ **enactment** n.

enamel n. **1** a glossy coloured coating for metal or pottery. **2** the hard outer covering of a tooth. **3** a paint that dries to give a hard shiny coat. •v. (**enamelling**, **enamelled**; US **enameling**, **enameled**) coat or decorate with enamel.

enamoured (US **enamored**) adj. (**enamoured of/with**) full of love or admiration for.

encamp v. settle in a camp.

encampment n. a place where a camp is set up.

encapsulate v. express clearly and briefly.

e

encase v. enclose or cover in a case.

encephalitis n. inflammation of the brain.

enchant v. **1** delight. **2** put under a spell. ■ **enchanter** n. **enchantment** n. **enchantress** n.

encircle v. form a circle round.

enclave n. a small territory surrounded by a foreign country.

enclose v. **1** surround on all sides. **2** place in an envelope with a letter.

enclosure n. **1** an enclosed area. **2** a document etc. placed in an envelope with a letter.

encode v. convert into a coded form. ■ **encoder** n.

encomium n. (pl. **encomiums** or **encomia**) a formal expression of praise.

encompass v. **1** include. **2** surround.

encore /ong-kor/ n. an extra item at the end of a concert, as called for by the audience. •exclam. again!

encounter v. unexpectedly meet or be faced with. •n. **1** an unexpected meeting. **2** a confrontation.

encourage v. give confidence, hope, or support to. ■ **encouragement** n.

encroach v. (**encroach on**) gradually intrude on territory, rights, etc. ■ **encroachment** n.

encrust v. cover with a hard crust. ■ **encrustation** n.

encrypt v. convert into code. ■ **encryption** n.

encumber v. be a burden to. ■ **encumbrance** n.

encyclical n. a letter sent by the pope to all Roman Catholic bishops.

encyclopedia (or **encyclopaedia**) n. a book or set of books giving information on many subjects. ■ **encyclopedic** adj.

end n. **1** the final part. **2** the furthest part. **3** the stopping of a state or situation. **4** a person's death or downfall. **5** a goal or desired result. •v. **1** come or bring to an end. **2** (**end up**) eventually reach a particular state or place. □ **make ends meet** earn just enough money to live on.

endanger v. **1** put in danger. **2** (**endangered**) in danger of becoming extinct.

endear v. cause to be loved or liked.

endearment n. a word or phrase expressing affection.

endeavour (US **endeavor**) v. try hard to achieve. •n. **1** a serious attempt to achieve something. **2** hard work.

endemic adj. (of a disease) regularly found in a particular group or area.

ending n. an end or final part.

endive n. a salad vegetable with bitter leaves.

endless adj. having or seeming to have no end or limit. ■ **endlessly** adv.

endocrine adj. (of a gland) producing and discharging hormones etc. directly into the blood.

endorphin n. a painkilling chemical compound produced in the brain.

endorse v. **1** declare approval of. **2** sign a cheque on the back. **3** record an offence on a driving licence. ■ **endorsement** n.

endow v. **1** provide with property or a permanent income. **2** (**be**

endowed with) possess a quality or asset. ■ **endowment** n.

endure v. **1** experience and cope with prolonged pain or difficulty. **2** last for a long time. ■ **endurable** adj. **endurance** n.

enema n. a medical procedure in which fluid is injected into the rectum to empty it.

enemy n. (pl. **enemies**) a person or group opposed or hostile to another.

energetic adj. showing or involving great energy. ■ **energetically** adv.

energize (or **-ise**) v. give energy and enthusiasm to.

energy n. (pl. **energies**) **1** the strength and vitality required to keep active. **2** power derived from physical or chemical resources to provide light, heat, etc.

enervate v. cause to feel drained of energy. ■ **enervation** n.

enfant terrible /on-fon te-ree-bluh/ n. (pl. **enfants terribles**) a person who behaves in a controversial or unconventional way.

enfeeble v. weaken.

enfold v. envelop or surround.

enforce v. **1** ensure a law etc. is obeyed. **2** force to happen. ■ **enforceable** adj. **enforcement** n.

enfranchise v. give the right to vote to. ■ **enfranchisement** n.

engage v. **1** involve someone's interest or attention. **2** (**engage in/with**) become involved in. **3** employ someone. **4** move part of a machine into an operating position. **5** begin to fight with.

engaged adj. **1** occupied. **2** in use. **3** having formally agreed to marry.

engagement n. **1** a formal agreement to get married. **2** an appointment. **3** involvement. **4** a battle.

engaging adj. charming.

engender v. give rise to.

engine n. **1** a machine that converts power into motion. **2** a railway locomotive.

engineer n. **1** a person qualified in engineering. **2** a person who controls an engine on an aircraft or ship. • v. **1** design and build. **2** arrange for something to occur.

engineering n. the study of the design, building, and use of engines, machines, and structures.

English n. the language of England, used in many varieties throughout the world. • adj. of England.

engorged adj. swollen.

engrave v. **1** carve a design on a hard surface. **2** (**be engraved on** or **in**) be fixed in the mind. ■ **engraver** n. **engraving** n.

engross v. absorb all the attention of.

engulf v. surround or cover completely.

enhance v. increase the quality, value, or extent of. ■ **enhancement** n.

enigma n. a mysterious person or thing. ■ **enigmatic** adj. **enigmatically** adv.

enjoin v. instruct or urge to do.

enjoy v. **1** take pleasure in. **2** (**enjoy yourself**) have a pleasant time. **3** possess and benefit from. ■ **enjoyable** adj. **enjoyment** n.

enlarge v. **1** make or become larger. **2** (**enlarge on**) say more about. ■ **enlargement** n.

enlighten v. give greater knowledge and understanding to. ■ **enlightenment** n.

enlist v. 1 join the armed services. 2 ask for someone's help in doing something. ■ **enlistment** n.

enliven v. make more interesting or lively.

en masse /on mass/ adv. all together.

enmesh v. involve in complicated circumstances.

enmity n. (pl. **enmities**) hostility.

ennoble v. give greater dignity to.

ennui /on-wee/ n. boredom and lethargy.

enormity n. (pl. **enormities**) 1 (the enormity of) the extreme seriousness of something bad. 2 great size or scale.

enormous adj. very large.

enough adj., pron., & adv. as much or as many as is necessary or desirable.

enquire v. 1 ask for information. 2 investigate.

enquiry n. (pl. **enquiries**) 1 an act of enquiring. 2 an official investigation.

enrage v. make very angry.

enrapture v. delight greatly.

enrich v. 1 improve the quality or value of. 2 make wealthier. ■ **enrichment** n.

enrol (US enroll) v. (**enrolling, enrolled**) officially register as a member or student. ■ **enrolment** n.

en route /on root/ adv. on the way.

ensconce v. establish comfortably or securely.

ensemble /on-som-b'l/ n. 1 a group of performers. 2 a group of items viewed as a whole.

enshrine v. preserve in a form that ensures protection and respect.

ensign n. a ship's flag.

enslave v. cause to lose freedom of choice or action. ■ **enslavement** n.

ensnare v. trap or gain control over.

ensue v. happen afterwards or as a result.

en suite /on sweet/ adj. (of a bathroom) leading directly off a bedroom.

ensure v. make certain that something will occur or be so.

entail v. involve as a necessary part or result.

entangle v. 1 make tangled. 2 involve in complicated circumstances. ■ **entanglement** n.

entente /on-tont/ n. a friendly understanding between states.

enter v. 1 come or go into. 2 begin to be involved in or do. 3 register as a participant in. 4 record information in a book, computer, etc.

enteritis n. inflammation of the intestines.

enterprise n. 1 a business or company. 2 a large project. 3 the ability to initiate new projects.

enterprising adj. showing initiative and resourcefulness.

entertain v. 1 provide with amusement or enjoyment. 2 offer hospitality to. 3 consider. ■ **entertainer** n. **entertainment** n.

enthral (US enthrall) v. (**enthralling, enthralled**) fascinate and hold the attention of.

enthrone v. ceremonially install a new monarch on a throne. ■ **enthronement** n.

enthuse v. fill with or express great enthusiasm.

enthusiasm n. great enjoyment and interest. ■ **enthusiastic** adj. **enthusiastically** adv.

enthusiast n. a person who is full of enthusiasm for something.

entice v. attract by offering something desirable. ■ **enticement** n.

entire adj. with no part left out. ■ **entirely** adv.

entirety n. (**the entirety**) the whole.

entitle v. 1 give a right to. 2 give a title to a book etc. ■ **entitlement** n.

entity n. (pl. **entities**) a thing existing independently from other things.

entomb v. 1 place in a tomb. 2 bury or completely cover.

entomology n. the study of insects. ■ **entomological** adj. **entomologist** n.

entourage /on-toor-ahzh/ n. the people accompanying an important person.

entrails pl. n. intestines.

entrance[1] n. 1 a door, gate, etc. for entering. 2 an act of entering. 3 the right or opportunity to enter.

entrance[2] v. fill with wonder and delight.

entrant n. a person who joins or takes part in something.

entrap v. (**entrapping, entrapped**) 1 catch in a trap. 2 trick into committing a crime. ■ **entrapment** n.

entreat v. ask earnestly or anxiously. ■ **entreaty** n.

entrée /on-tray/ n. 1 the main course of a meal. 2 the right to enter a place or social group.

entrench v. establish firmly. ■ **entrenchment** n.

entrepreneur /on-truh-pruh-ner/ n. a person who is successful in setting up businesses. ■ **entrepreneurial** adj.

entropy n. a quantity expressing how much of a system's thermal energy is unavailable for conversion into mechanical work.

entrust v. make responsible for doing or caring for.

entry n. (pl. **entries**) 1 an act of entering. 2 an entrance. 3 an item in a list etc.

entwine v. wind or twist together.

enumerate v. mention items one by one. ■ **enumeration** n.

enunciate v. pronounce or state clearly. ■ **enunciation** n.

envelop v. (**enveloping, enveloped**) wrap up or surround completely.

envelope n. a flat paper container for a letter etc., with a sealable flap.

enviable adj. desirable and so arousing envy. ■ **enviably** adv.

envious adj. feeling or showing envy. ■ **enviously** adv.

environment n. 1 the surroundings in which a person, animal, or plant lives. 2 the natural world. ■ **environmental** adj. **environmentally** adv.

> ! Don't forget the n: envir**on**ment.

environmentalist n. a person seeking to protect the environment. ■ **environmentalism** n.

environs pl. n. the surrounding area.

envisage v. 1 see as a possibility. 2 imagine.

envoy n. a messenger or representative.

envy n. (pl. **envies**) discontented longing aroused by another person's possessions etc. • v. (**envying, envied**) feel envy of.

enzyme n. a substance produced by a living organism and assisting in chemical processes.

eon US = AEON.

epaulette n. an ornamental shoulder piece on a uniform.

ephemera pl. n. items of short-lived interest or use.

ephemeral adj. lasting only for a short time.

epic n. a long poem, book, or film about heroic people or covering a long period of time. • adj. heroic or on a grand scale.

epicene adj. characteristic of both sexes or neither sex.

epicentre (US **epicenter**) n. the point on the earth's surface directly above the origin of an earthquake.

epicure n. a person who enjoys good food and drink. ■ **epicurean** n. & adj.

epidemic n. a widespread occurrence of an infectious disease in a community.

epidemiology n. the study of the spread and control of diseases. ■ **epidemiologist** n.

epidermis n. the outer layer of the skin.

epidural n. an anaesthetic injected into the space around the spinal cord, esp. during childbirth.

epiglottis n. a flap of cartilage that covers the larynx during swallowing.

epigram n. a short witty saying. ■ **epigrammatic** adj.

epilepsy n. a disorder of the nervous system causing convulsions and loss of consciousness. ■ **epileptic** adj. & n.

epilogue n. a short concluding section of a book or play.

Epiphany n. the Christian festival (6 January) commemorating Jesus's appearance to the Magi.

episcopal adj. of or governed by bishops.

episcopalian n. a supporter of government of a Church by bishops.

episode n. 1 an event occurring as part of a sequence. 2 each part of a serialized story or programme. ■ **episodic** adj.

epistemology n. the branch of philosophy that deals with knowledge. ■ **epistemological** adj.

epistle n. a letter. ■ **epistolary** adj.

epitaph n. words written in memory of a person who has died.

epithet n. a descriptive word or phrase.

epitome /i-pit-uh-mi/ n. a perfect example.

epitomize (or **-ise**) v. be a perfect example of.

epoch n. a long and distinct historical period.

eponymous adj. (of a person) giving their name to something.

equable adj. 1 even-tempered. 2 not varying greatly.

equal adj. 1 the same in quantity, size, value, or status. 2 evenly balanced. 3 (**equal to**) able to deal with. • n. a person or thing that is equal to another. • v. (**equalling, equalled**; US **equaling, equaled**) 1 be equal to. 2 match or rival. ■ **equality** n. **equally** adv.

equalize (or **-ise**) v. **1** make or become equal. **2** level the score in a match by scoring a goal. ■ **equalization** n. **equalizer** n.

equanimity n. evenness of temper.

equate v. consider one thing as equal to another.

equation n. a statement that the values of two mathematical expressions are equal.

equator n. an imaginary line around the earth at equal distances from the North and South Poles. ■ **equatorial** adj.

equerry n. (pl. **equerries**) a male officer of a royal household acting as an attendant to a member of the royal family.

equestrian adj. of horse riding. ■ **equestrianism** n.

equidistant adj. at equal distances.

equilateral adj. having all sides the same length.

equilibrium n. (pl. **equilibria**) a balanced state.

equine adj. of or like a horse.

equinox n. the time or date (twice each year) when day and night are of equal length. ■ **equinoctial** adj.

equip v. (**equipping, equipped**) supply with what is needed.

equipment n. the items needed for a particular purpose.

equitable adj. treating everyone equally; fair. ■ **equitably** adv.

equitation n. horse riding.

equity n. **1** fairness and impartiality. **2** (**equities**) stocks and shares not paying a fixed amount of interest. **3** the value of a mortgaged property after all charges and debts have been paid.

equivalent adj. equal in value, amount, meaning, etc. •n. a person or thing equivalent to another. ■ **equivalence** n.

equivocal adj. unclear in meaning. ■ **equivocally** adv.

equivocate v. deliberately use language that can be interpreted in different ways. ■ **equivocation** n.

era n. a long and distinct historical period.

eradicate v. remove or destroy completely. ■ **eradication** n.

erase v. rub out or remove all traces of. ■ **erasable** adj. **eraser** n. **erasure** n.

ere /air/ prep. & conj. old use before (in time).

erect adj. **1** rigidly upright. **2** (of a body part) enlarged and rigid. •v. build. ■ **erection** n.

erectile adj. able to become erect.

erg n. a unit of work or energy.

ergo adv. therefore.

ergonomics n. the study of people's efficiency in their working environment. ■ **ergonomic** adj.

ermine n. **1** a stoat. **2** the stoat's white winter fur.

erode v. gradually wear away. ■ **erosion** n.

erogenous adj. sensitive to sexual stimulation.

erotic adj. of sexual desire or excitement. ■ **erotically** adv.

erotica n. erotic literature or art.

eroticism n. the quality of being erotic.

err v. **1** make a mistake. **2** do wrong.

errand n. a short journey to deliver or collect something.

errant adj. doing something wrong.

e

erratic *adj.* happening or acting in an irregular way. ■ **erratically** *adv.*

erratum *n.* (*pl.* **errata**) an error in a printed work.

erroneous *adj.* incorrect.

error *n.* **1** a mistake. **2** the state of being wrong.

ersatz *adj.* used as a poor-quality substitute.

erstwhile *adj.* former.

erudite *adj.* knowledgeable or learned. ■ **erudition** *n.*

erupt *v.* **1** (of a volcano) throw out lava etc. **2** express emotion in a sudden and noisy way. ■ **eruption** *n.*

escalate *v.* increase in intensity or extent. ■ **escalation** *n.*

escalator *n.* a moving staircase.

escalope *n.* a thin slice of meat coated in breadcrumbs and fried.

escapade *n.* a daring and adventurous act.

escape *v.* **1** get free from. **2** succeed in avoiding. **3** fail to be noticed or remembered by. • *n.* an act or means of escaping. ■ **escapee** *n.* **escaper** *n.*

escapement *n.* a mechanism regulating the movement of a clock or watch.

escapism *n.* indulging in enjoyable activities so as to ignore unpleasant realities. ■ **escapist** *n.* & *adj.*

escapologist *n.* an entertainer whose act involves breaking free from ropes, handcuffs, etc. ■ **escapology** *n.*

escarpment *n.* a steep slope at the edge of an area of high ground.

eschew *v.* deliberately avoid doing.

escort *n.* **1** a person, vehicle, or group accompanying another to protect or honour them. **2** a person accompanying a member of the opposite sex to a social event. • *v.* accompany as an escort.

escritoire /ess-kri-twar/ *n.* a writing desk with drawers.

escudo *n.* (*pl.* **escudos**) the former basic unit of money of Portugal.

escutcheon *n.* a shield bearing a coat of arms.

Eskimo *n.* (*pl.* **Eskimo** or **Eskimos**) a member of a people inhabiting northern Canada, Alaska, Greenland, and eastern Siberia.

! Many of the peoples traditionally called **Eskimos** now prefer to call themselves **Inuit**; **Inuit** is the official term in Canada.

esophagus *US* = **OESOPHAGUS**.

esoteric *adj.* intended for or understood by only a few people with specialized knowledge.

ESP *abbrev.* extrasensory perception.

espadrille *n.* a canvas shoe with a plaited fibre sole.

espalier *n.* a tree trained to grow against a wall.

especial *adj.* special; particular.

especially *adv.* **1** in particular. **2** to a great extent.

Esperanto *n.* an artificial international language.

espionage *n.* spying.

esplanade *n.* a promenade.

espouse *v.* support or adopt a cause or way of life. ■ **espousal** *n.*

espresso *n.* (*pl.* **espressos**) strong black coffee made by forcing steam through ground coffee.

esprit de corps n. pride and loyalty uniting a group.

espy v. (**espying, espied**) catch sight of.

Esq. abbrev. Esquire, a polite title placed after a man's surname.

essay n. **1** a piece of writing on a particular subject. **2** an attempt. • v. attempt. ∎ **essayist** n.

essence n. **1** the quality which makes something what it is. **2** a concentrated extract obtained from a plant etc.

essential adj. **1** absolutely necessary. **2** central to something's nature. • n. (**essentials**) **1** essential things. **2** the basic elements. ▫ **essential oil** a natural oil extracted from a plant. ∎ **essentially** adv.

establish v. **1** set up on a firm or permanent basis. **2** make accepted by others. **3** find out facts.

establishment n. **1** the act of establishing. **2** an organization. **3** (**the Establishment**) the group in society who control policy and resist change.

estate n. **1** a large house with extensive grounds. **2** a residential or industrial area planned as a unit. **3** the money and property owned by a person at the time of their death. ▫ **estate agent** a person who sells and rents out houses etc. for clients. **estate car** a car with a large storage area behind the seats and a rear door.

esteem n. respect and admiration. • v. respect and admire.

esthete etc. US = AESTHETE etc.

estimable adj. worthy of great respect.

estimate v. roughly calculate the amount, value, etc. of. • n. **1** a rough

calculation. **2** a written statement of the likely price for work to be carried out. ∎ **estimation** n.

estranged adj. **1** no longer close to or friendly with someone. **2** (of a person's husband or wife) no longer living with them. ∎ **estrangement** n.

estrogen US = OESTROGEN.

estuary n. (pl. **estuaries**) the mouth of a large river where it becomes affected by tides. ∎ **estuarine** adj.

et al. abbrev. and others.

etc. abbrev. et cetera.

et cetera adv. and other similar things.

etch v. **1** produce a picture by engraving a metal plate with acid. **2** fix clearly in the mind. ∎ **etching** n.

eternal adj. lasting forever. ∎ **eternally** adv.

eternity n. (pl. **eternities**) **1** unending time. **2** informal a very long period of time.

ether n. **1** a liquid used as an anaesthetic and solvent. **2** the upper regions of the air.

ethereal adj. **1** very delicate and light. **2** heavenly or spiritual.

ethic n. **1** a moral principle. **2** (**ethics**) the study of moral principles.

ethical adj. **1** of moral principles. **2** morally correct. ∎ **ethically** adv.

ethnic adj. of a group of people sharing a common origin, culture, or language. ▫ **ethnic cleansing** the expelling or killing of members of one ethnic or religious group in an area by those of another. ∎ **ethnically** adv. **ethnicity** n.

ethnology n. the study of the characteristics of different peoples. ∎ **ethnologist** n.

ethos n. the characteristic spirit of a culture, era, or community.

ethylene n. a flammable hydrocarbon gas.

etiolated adj. (of a plant) pale and weak due to a lack of light.

etiquette n. the rules of polite behaviour in a society.

etymology n. (pl. **etymologies**) an account of a word's origins and development. ■ **etymological** adj.

EU abbrev. European Union.

eucalyptus n. an evergreen Australasian tree important for its oil.

Eucharist n. **1** the Christian ceremony commemorating the Last Supper, in which consecrated bread and wine are consumed. **2** this bread and wine.

eugenics n. the science of improving a population by controlled breeding.

eulogy n. (pl. **eulogies**) a speech or piece of writing praising someone. ■ **eulogize** (or **-ise**) v.

eunuch n. a castrated man.

euphemism n. a less direct word used instead of an offensive one. ■ **euphemistic** adj. **euphemistically** adv.

euphonious /yoo-foh-ni-uhss/ adj. sounding pleasant. ■ **euphony** n.

euphoria n. great happiness. ■ **euphoric** adj.

Eurasian adj. **1** of mixed European and Asian parentage. **2** of Europe and Asia.

eureka exclam. a cry of joy on discovering something.

eurhythmics pl. n. physical exercises to music.

euro n. the basic unit of money in twelve states of the European Union.

European n. a person from Europe. • adj. of Europe or the European Union. □ **European Union** an economic and political association of certain European countries.

Eustachian tube /yoo-stay-sh'n/ n. a passage between the ear and the throat.

euthanasia n. the painless killing of a person with an incurable illness.

evacuate v. **1** send from a place of danger to somewhere safer. **2** empty the bowels. ■ **evacuation** n. **evacuee** n.

evade v. avoid doing, dealing with, etc.

evaluate v. assess the amount or value of. ■ **evaluation** n. **evaluator** n.

evanescent adj. quickly fading. ■ **evanescence** n.

evangelical adj. **1** of a tradition within Protestant Christianity which emphasizes biblical authority and salvation through personal faith in Jesus. **2** of the teaching of the gospel. **3** passionately supporting something. ■ **evangelicalism** n.

evangelist n. **1** a person who tries to convert others to Christianity. **2** the writer of one of the four Gospels. ■ **evangelism** n. **evangelistic** adj.

evaporate v. **1** turn from liquid into vapour. **2** disappear. ■ **evaporation** n.

evasion n. the act of evading.

evasive adj. intended to avoid something. ■ **evasively** adv. **evasiveness** n.

eve n. the day or period immediately before an event.

even adj. 1 level. 2 equal in number, amount, or value. 3 regular or balanced. 4 (of a number) exactly divisible by two. •v. make or become even. •adv. used for emphasis: *even less*. ■ **evenly** adv. **evenness** n.

evening n. the period of time at the end of the day.

evensong n. (in the Anglican Church) an evening service.

event n. 1 a thing that happens. 2 a public or social occasion. 3 a contest forming part of a sports competition.

eventful adj. marked by exciting events.

eventual adj. occurring at the end of a process or period. ■ **eventually** adv.

eventuality n. (pl. **eventualities**) a possible event.

ever adv. 1 at any time. 2 always. □ **evergreen** a plant having green leaves throughout the year. **everlasting** lasting forever or a very long time. **evermore** forever.

every adj. 1 each without exception. 2 happening at specified intervals: *every three months*. 3 all possible: *every effort was made*. □ **everybody** every person. **everyday** 1 daily. 2 ordinary. **everyone** every person. **everything** 1 all things. 2 the most important thing. **everywhere** in or to all places.

evict v. legally force to leave a property. ■ **eviction** n.

evidence n. 1 information indicating whether something is true or valid. 2 information presented in a law court to support a case. •v.

be evidence of. □ **in evidence** noticeable.

evident adj. clear or obvious. ■ **evidently** adv.

evil adj. 1 very immoral and wicked. 2 very unpleasant. •n. 1 extreme wickedness. 2 something harmful or undesirable. ■ **evilly** adv.

evince v. show or indicate.

eviscerate v. disembowel.

evoke v. 1 bring a feeling or image to the mind. 2 obtain a response. ■ **evocation** n. **evocative** adj.

evolution n. 1 the process by which different kinds of living organism develop from earlier forms. 2 gradual development. ■ **evolutionary** adj.

evolve v. 1 develop gradually. 2 (of an organism) develop by evolution.

ewe n. a female sheep.

ewer n. a large jug.

ex n. *informal* a former spouse or partner.

exacerbate v. make something bad worse. ■ **exacerbation** n.

exact adj. 1 correct in all details. 2 precise. •v. 1 demand and obtain. 2 inflict revenge. ■ **exactness** n.

exacting adj. demanding much effort or skill.

exactitude n. exactness.

exactly adv. 1 in an exact way. 2 used to express agreement.

exaggerate v. make something seem larger, better, etc. than in reality. ■ **exaggeration** n.

exalt v. 1 praise highly. 2 raise to a higher rank.

exaltation n. extreme happiness.

exam n. an examination.

examination n. 1 a detailed inspection. 2 a formal test of knowledge or ability.

examine v. 1 inspect closely. 2 test the knowledge or ability of. ■ **examinee** n. **examiner** n.

example n. 1 a thing typical of its kind or illustrating a general rule. 2 a person or thing worthy of being copied. □ **make an example of** punish as a warning to others.

exasperate v. greatly irritate. ■ **exasperation** n.

excavate v. 1 make a hole by digging. 2 remove earth from an area to find buried remains. ■ **excavation** n. **excavator** n.

exceed v. 1 be greater than. 2 go beyond the limit of.

exceedingly adv. extremely.

excel v. (**excelling**, **excelled**) 1 be very good at. 2 (**excel yourself**) perform exceptionally well.

Excellency n. a form of address for certain high officials of state.

excellent adj. very good. ■ **excellence** n. **excellently** adv.

except prep. not including. •v. exclude.

! Don't forget the c in **except** and related words.

excepting prep. except for.

exception n. a person or thing that is excluded or does not follow a rule. □ **take exception to** object to.

exceptionable adj. causing disapproval or offence.

exceptional adj. 1 not typical; unusual. 2 unusually good. ■ **exceptionally** adv.

excerpt n. a short extract from a film, book, etc.

excess n. 1 an amount more than necessary, allowed, or desirable. 2 (**excesses**) outrageous behaviour. •adj. exceeding a limit.

excessive adj. too much. ■ **excessively** adv.

exchange v. give something and receive another thing. •n. 1 an act of exchanging. 2 a short conversation. 3 the changing of money for its equivalent in another currency. 4 a building used for trading. 5 a centre where phone lines are connected. ■ **exchangeable** adj.

exchequer n. a national treasury.

excise n. a tax on certain goods. •v. cut out. ■ **excision** n.

excitable adj. easily excited. ■ **excitability** n. **excitably** adv.

excite v. 1 make very enthusiastic and eager. 2 arouse sexually. 3 give rise to. ■ **excitation** n.

excitement n. 1 great enthusiasm and eagerness. 2 a cause of this.

exclaim v. cry out suddenly.

exclamation n. a sudden cry or remark. □ **exclamation mark** a punctuation mark (!) indicating an exclamation. ■ **exclamatory** adj.

exclude v. 1 prevent from being a part of something. 2 choose not to include for consideration. ■ **exclusion** n.

exclusive adj. 1 restricted to the person, group, or area concerned. 2 high-class and expensive. 3 excluding something. •n. a story published in only one newspaper etc. ■ **exclusively** adv. **exclusivity** n.

excommunicate v. officially bar from the sacraments and services of a Church. ■ **excommunication** n.

excoriate v. **1** criticize severely. **2** remove part of the skin. ■ **excoriation** n.

excrement n. waste matter discharged from the bowels.

excrescence n. an abnormal growth on an animal or plant.

excreta n. waste discharged from the body.

excrete v. discharge waste material from the body. ■ **excretion** n. **excretory** adj.

excruciating adj. **1** very painful. **2** very embarrassing or tedious.

excursion n. a short journey taken for pleasure.

excuse v. **1** justify or defend a fault or offence. **2** release from a duty. **3** forgive. •n. a reason put forward to justify a fault or offence. ■ **excusable** adj.

ex-directory adj. not listed in a phone directory at your own request.

execrable adj. very bad or unpleasant.

execrate v. loathe. ■ **execration** n.

execute v. **1** carry out a plan, order, etc. **2** perform an action. **3** kill a condemned person as a legal punishment. ■ **execution** n. **executioner** n.

executive n. **1** a senior manager or managerial group in an organization. **2** (**the executive**) the branch of a government responsible for putting plans or laws into effect. •adj. having the power to put plans, actions, or laws into effect.

executor n. a person appointed to carry out the terms of a will.

exemplar n. a typical example or model.

exemplary adj. **1** giving a good example to others. **2** serving as a warning.

exemplify v. (**exemplifying**, **exemplified**) be or give a typical example of. ■ **exemplification** n.

exempt adj. free from a requirement or duty imposed on others. •v. make exempt. ■ **exemption** n.

exercise n. **1** physical activity carried out to improve health and fitness. **2** a task set to practise or test a skill. **3** the use of a power, right, etc. •v. **1** use a power, right, etc. **2** do physical exercise. **3** worry or puzzle.

exert v. **1** apply a force, influence, or quality. **2** (**exert yourself**) make an effort. ■ **exertion** n.

exfoliate v. rub the skin with a rough substance to remove dead cells. ■ **exfoliation** n.

ex gratia /eks gray-shuh/ adv. & adj. (of payment) given as a gift or favour rather than a legal requirement.

exhale v. **1** breathe out. **2** give off vapour or fumes. ■ **exhalation** n.

exhaust v. **1** tire out. **2** use up resources completely. •n. **1** waste gases discharged from an engine. **2** the device through which waste gases are discharged. ■ **exhaustible** adj. **exhaustion** n.

exhaustive adj. covering all aspects fully. ■ **exhaustively** adv.

exhibit v. **1** put on public display. **2** display a quality. •n. an object on public display. ■ **exhibitor** n.

exhibition n. **1** a public display in an art gallery, museum, etc. **2** a display of a skill or quality.

exhibitionism n. behaviour intended to attract attention. ■ **exhibitionist** n.

e

exhilarate v. make very happy or lively. ■ **exhilaration** n.

! *-arate* not *-erate*: exhilarate.

exhort v. strongly urge to do something. ■ **exhortation** n.

exhume v. dig up a buried corpse.

exigency n. (pl. **exigencies**) an urgent need or demand. ■ **exigent** adj.

exiguous adj. very small.

exile n. **1** the state of being barred from your native country. **2** a person who lives in exile. •v. send into exile.

exist v. **1** be real or present. **2** live. ■ **existence** n. **existent** adj.

existential adj. of existence or existentialism.

existentialism n. a philosophical theory emphasizing individuals' freedom to choose their own actions. ■ **existentialist** n. & adj.

exit n. **1** a way out. **2** an act of leaving. •v. (**exiting**, **exited**) go out of or leave a place.

exodus n. a mass departure of people.

ex officio adv. & adj. as a result of a person's position or status.

exonerate v. declare free from blame. ■ **exoneration** n.

exorbitant adj. (of a price) unreasonably high. ■ **exorbitantly** adv.

exorcize (or **-ise**) v. drive out an evil spirit from a person or place. ■ **exorcism** n. **exorcist** n.

exotic adj. **1** coming from or characteristic of a distant foreign country. **2** strikingly colourful or unusual. ■ **exotically** adv. **exoticism** n.

expand v. **1** make or become larger. **2** (**expand on**) give a fuller

account of. ■ **expandable** adj. **expansion** n.

expanse n. a wide continuous area.

expansive adj. **1** covering a wide area. **2** friendly and communicative. ■ **expansively** adv.

expatiate /ik-spay-shi-ayt/ v. (**expatiate on**) speak or write in detail about.

expatriate n. a person who lives outside their native country.

expect v. **1** regard as likely to happen. **2** regard as likely to do or be something. **3** require or demand as a person's duty. ■ **expectation** n.

expectant adj. **1** filled with anticipation. **2** pregnant. ■ **expectancy** n. **expectantly** adv.

expectorant n. a cough medicine which helps to bring up phlegm.

expectorate v. cough or spit out phlegm.

expedient adj. helping to achieve something, though possibly unfair or immoral. •n. a means of achieving something. ■ **expediency** n.

expedite v. hasten the progress of.

expedition n. a journey made for a particular purpose. ■ **expeditionary** adj.

expeditious adj. quick and efficient. ■ **expeditiously** adv.

expel v. (**expelling**, **expelled**) **1** force to leave a school, organization, or place. **2** force out.

expend v. spend or use up a resource.

expendable adj. able to be sacrificed or abandoned to achieve an objective.

expenditure n. **1** the spending of money etc. **2** the amount of money spent.

expense n. **1** the cost of something. **2** (**expenses**) money spent in the course of doing a job etc. **3** something on which money must be spent.

expensive adj. costing a lot of money.

experience n. **1** practical involvement in an activity, event, etc. **2** knowledge or skill gained over time. **3** an event which affects someone. • v. **1** undergo or be affected by. **2** feel an emotion.

experienced adj. having knowledge or skill gained over time.

experiment n. **1** a scientific procedure to find out or prove something. **2** a new course of action with an uncertain outcome. • v. **1** perform a scientific experiment. **2** try out new things. ■ **experimental** adj. **experimentally** adv. **experimentation** n.

expert n. a person having great knowledge or skill in a particular field. • adj. having or involving great knowledge or skill. ■ **expertly** adv.

expertise n. great skill or knowledge in a particular field.

expiate v. make amends for. ■ **expiation** n.

expire v. **1** cease to be valid. **2** die. **3** breathe out air.

expiry n. the end of the period for which something is valid.

explain v. make clear by giving a detailed description. **2** give a reason for. ■ **explanation** n. **explanatory** adj.

expletive n. a swear word.

explicable adj. able to be explained.

explicit adj. clear, detailed, and unambiguous. ■ **explicitly** adv.

explode v. **1** burst or shatter violently. **2** suddenly express emotion. **3** increase suddenly. **4** show a belief to be false.

exploit v. **1** make use of someone unfairly. **2** make full use of a resource. • n. a daring act. ■ **exploitative** adj. **exploitation** n.

explore v. **1** travel through an unfamiliar area so as to learn about it. **2** examine or discuss in detail. ■ **exploration** n. **exploratory** adj. **explorer** n.

explosion n. **1** an act of exploding. **2** a sudden increase.

explosive adj. able or likely to explode. • n. an explosive substance.

exponent n. **1** a promoter of an idea. **2** a person who does a particular thing skilfully. **3** a raised figure beside a number indicating how many times the number is to be multiplied by itself.

exponential adj. **1** (of an increase) becoming more and more rapid. **2** a mathematical exponent. ■ **exponentially** adv.

export v. send goods etc. to another country for sale. • n. **1** an exported item. **2** the act of exporting. ■ **exportation** n. **exporter** n.

expose v. **1** uncover and make visible. **2** show the true nature of. **3** (**exposed**) unprotected from the weather. **4** (**expose to**) make vulnerable to. **5** subject photographic film to light.

e

exposé /ik-spoh-zay/ *n.* a report in the media revealing shocking information.

exposition *n.* **1** a full account and explanation of a theory. **2** a large exhibition.

expostulate *v.* disagree strongly. ■ **expostulation** *n.*

exposure *n.* **1** the state of being exposed. **2** the act of exposing. **3** the quantity of light reaching a photographic film.

expound *v.* explain a theory in detail.

express *v.* **1** convey a feeling etc. by words or gestures. **2** squeeze out liquid or air. •*adj.* **1** operating or delivered very quickly. **2** stated clearly. •*adv.* by express delivery. •*n.* a fast train that stops at few stations. □ **expressway** *US* an urban motorway. ■ **expressly** *adv.*

expression *n.* **1** the act of expressing. **2** a look on someone's face. **3** a word or phrase.

expressionism *n.* a style of art seeking to express feelings rather than represent objects realistically. ■ **expressionist** *n.* & *adj.*

expressive *adj.* effectively conveying a thought or feeling. ■ **expressively** *adv.*

expropriate *v.* take property for public use. ■ **expropriation** *n.*

expulsion *n.* the act of expelling.

expunge *v.* remove completely.

expurgate *v.* remove unsuitable matter from a text. ■ **expurgation** *n.*

exquisite *adj.* **1** very beautiful and delicate. **2** highly refined. **3** intensely felt. ■ **exquisitely** *adv.*

extant *adj.* still existing.

extemporize (or **-ise**) *v.* improvise.

extend *v.* **1** make larger or longer. **2** reach or continue to. **3** stretch out part of the body. **4** offer. ■ **extendable** (or **extendible**) *adj.*

extension *n.* **1** the act of extending. **2** a part added to enlarge or lengthen something. **3** an additional period of time. **4** an extra phone on the same line as the main one.

extensive *adj.* large in area, amount, or scope. ■ **extensively** *adv.*

extent *n.* **1** the area covered by something. **2** size or scale. **3** the degree to which something is true.

extenuating *adj.* making an offence less serious by partially excusing it.

exterior *adj.* of the outside. •*n.* an outer surface or structure.

exterminate *v.* destroy completely. ■ **extermination** *n.* **exterminator** *n.*

external *adj.* of or on the outside. ■ **externally** *adv.*

externalize (or **-ise**) *v.* express a thought etc. in words or actions.

extinct *adj.* **1** (of a species etc.) having no living members. **2** (of a volcano) not having erupted in recorded history. ■ **extinction** *n.*

extinguish *v.* **1** put out a fire or light. **2** put an end to. ■ **extinguisher** *n.*

extirpate *v.* destroy completely. ■ **extirpation** *n.*

extol *v.* (**extolling**, **extolled**) praise enthusiastically.

extort *v.* obtain by force or threats. ■ **extortion** *n.*

extortionate *adj.* (of a price) much too high.

extra adj. added to an existing or usual amount. • adv. **1** to a greater extent than usual. **2** in addition. • n. **1** an additional item. **2** a person employed as one of a crowd in a film.

extra- prefix **1** outside. **2** beyond the scope of.

extract v. **1** remove with care or effort. **2** obtain from someone unwilling. **3** separate out a substance by a special method. • n. **1** a short passage taken from a book, film, etc. **2** the concentrated active ingredient of a substance. ■ **extractor** n.

extraction n. **1** the act of extracting. **2** ancestry or ethnic origin.

extra-curricular adj. done in addition to the normal curriculum.

extradite v. hand over an accused person for trial in the country where the crime was committed. ■ **extradition** n.

extramarital adj. occurring outside marriage.

extramural adj. for students who are not full-time members of an educational establishment.

extraneous adj. unrelated to the subject.

extraordinary adj. **1** very unusual or remarkable. **2** (of a meeting) held for a special reason. ■ **extraordinarily** adv.

extrapolate /ik-strap-uh-layt/ v. use a fact or conclusion valid for one situation and apply it to a different one. ■ **extrapolation** n.

extrasensory perception n. the supposed ability to perceive things by means other than the known senses.

extraterrestrial adj. of things coming from beyond the earth or its atmosphere.

extravagant adj. **1** spending or using more than is necessary or can be afforded. **2** exceeding reasonable limits. ■ **extravagance** n. **extravagantly** adv.

extravaganza n. a lavish and spectacular entertainment.

extreme adj. **1** to the highest degree. **2** highly unusual. **3** very severe or serious. **4** not moderate. **5** furthest from the centre or a given point. • n. **1** either of two things that are as different from each other as possible. **2** the most extreme degree. ■ **extremely** adv.

extremist n. a person holding extreme views. ■ **extremism** n.

extremity n. (pl. **extremities**) **1** the furthest point or limit. **2** (**extremities**) the hands and feet. **3** extreme hardship.

extricate v. free from a difficulty. ■ **extrication** n.

extrinsic adj. not part of something's basic nature; coming from outside.

extrovert n. a lively, sociable person.

extrude v. thrust or force out. ■ **extrusion** n.

exuberant adj. lively and cheerful. ■ **exuberance** n.

exude v. **1** discharge slowly and steadily. **2** display a quality clearly.

exult v. show or feel triumphant joy. ■ **exultant** adj. **exultation** n.

eye n. **1** the organ of sight. **2** something compared to an eye in shape, position, etc. • v. (**eyeing**, **eyed**) look at closely or with interest. □ **eyeball** the round part of the eye within the eyelids. **eyebrow** the strip of hair on the ridge above the eye socket. **eyelash** each of the hairs on the edges

e

of the eyelids. **eyelet** a small round hole through which a lace can be threaded. **eyelid** either of the two folds of skin which cover the eye when closed. **eyeshadow** a cosmetic applied to the skin around the eyes. **eyesight** the ability to see. **eyesore** a very ugly thing. **eyewitness** a person who has seen something happen. **see eye to eye** be in full agreement.

eyrie /eer-i/ n. an eagle's nest.

Ff

F abbrev. Fahrenheit.

FA abbrev. Football Association.

fable n. a story with a moral or based on myth.

fabled adj. 1 famous. 2 mythical.

fabric n. 1 cloth. 2 the basic structure of a building, system, etc.

fabricate v. 1 invent false information. 2 make a product. ■ **fabrication** n.

fabulous adj. 1 very great. 2 informal excellent. 3 mythical. ■ **fabulously** adv.

facade n. 1 the front of a building. 2 a misleading outward appearance.

face n. 1 the front of the head. 2 a facial expression. 3 a surface. 4 an aspect. • v. 1 have the face or front towards. 2 confront. 3 put a facing on. □ **facecloth** a small cloth for washing the face. **faceless** remote and impersonal. **facelift** an operation to tighten the skin of the face. **lose** (or **save**) **face** suffer (or avoid) humiliation.

facet n. 1 one of the sides of a cut gem. 2 an aspect.

facetious adj. treating serious issues with inappropriate humour. ■ **facetiously** adv. **facetiousness** n.

facia var. of FASCIA.

facial adj. of the face. • n. a beauty treatment for the face.

facile adj. lacking careful thought.

facilitate v. make easy or easier. ■ **facilitation** n. **facilitator** n.

facility n. (pl. **facilities**) 1 a building, service, etc. provided for a purpose. 2 a natural ability or skill.

facing n. 1 a piece of material sewn to an inside edge of a garment to strengthen it. 2 an outer layer on a wall.

facsimile n. an exact copy of a document.

fact n. a thing known to be true. □ **the facts of life** information about sexual matters. **in fact** in reality.

faction n. a small group within a larger one that disagrees with some of its beliefs. ■ **factional** adj. **factious** adj.

factitious adj. not genuine.

factor n. 1 a circumstance contributing to a result. 2 a level on a scale of measurement: a high sun protection factor. 3 a number that divides into another number exactly. • v. (**factor in**) consider when making a decision.

factory n. (pl. **factories**) a building where goods are made or assembled in large numbers.

factotum n. an employee who does a wide variety of tasks.

factual adj. based on or containing facts. ■ **factually** adv.

faculty n. (pl. **faculties**) 1 a mental or physical power. 2 a department or group of related departments in a university.

fad n. 1 a craze. 2 a fussy like or dislike. ■ **faddy** adj.

fade v. 1 gradually disappear. 2 lose colour.

faeces /fee-seez/ (US **feces**) pl. n. excrement. ■ **faecal** adj.

fag n. informal 1 a cigarette. 2 a tiring or boring task.

faggot n. 1 a ball of seasoned chopped liver, baked or fried. 2 a bundle of sticks tied together.

Fahrenheit n. a scale of temperature on which water freezes at 32° and boils at 212°.

faience /fy-ahns/ n. painted glazed earthenware.

fail v. 1 be unsuccessful in a task or exam. 2 neglect to do. 3 stop working properly. 4 become weaker. 5 let down. • n. a mark too low to pass an exam.

failing n. a character weakness. • prep. if not.

failure n. 1 lack of success. 2 an unsuccessful person or thing. 3 an act of failing.

fain adv. old use gladly.

faint adj. 1 not clearly perceived. 2 slight. 3 about to faint. • v. lose consciousness briefly. • n. a brief loss of consciousness. □ **fainthearted** timid. ■ **faintly** adv.

fair adj. 1 treating people equally. 2 just or appropriate. 3 quite large.

4 quite good. 5 light in colour. 6 (of weather) fine and dry. • adv. in a fairway. • n. 1 a funfair. 2 an event held to sell or promote goods. □ **fairground** an outdoor area where a funfair is held. **fairway** a part of a golf course between a tee and a green. ■ **fairness** n.

fairing n. a streamlining structure added to a vehicle, boat, etc.

fairly adv. 1 justly. 2 quite.

fairy n. (pl. **fairies**) a small imaginary being with magical powers. □ **fairy godmother** a person who helps someone in difficulty. **fairy lights** small decorative electric lights.

fait accompli /fayt uh-kom-pli/ n. a thing that has been done and cannot be altered.

faith n. 1 complete trust or confidence. 2 strong religious belief. 3 a system of religious belief.

faithful adj. 1 loyal. 2 true to the facts or the original. ■ **faithfully** adv. **faithfulness** n.

faithless adj. disloyal.

fake adj. not genuine. • n. a fake person or thing. • v. 1 make a copy in order to deceive. 2 pretend to have.

fakir n. a Muslim or Hindu holy man who lives by asking for money or food.

falcon n. a fast-flying bird of prey.

falconry n. the keeping and training of birds of prey. ■ **falconer** n.

fall v. (**falling**, **fell**; past part. **fallen**) 1 move downwards quickly and without control. 2 collapse to the ground. 3 hang or slope down. 4 become less or lower. 5 become. 6 be captured or defeated. • n. 1 an act of falling. 2 a thing which has fallen. 3 (**falls**) a waterfall. **4** a drop in size or number. **5** *US* autumn. □ **fall for** *informal* **1** begin to love. **2** be tricked by. **fallout** airborne radioactive debris. **fall out** quarrel. **fall through** fail.

fallacy *n.* (*pl.* **fallacies**) **1** a mistaken belief. **2** unsound reasoning. ■ **fallacious** *adj.*

fallible *adj.* capable of making mistakes. ■ **fallibility** *n.*

Fallopian tube *n.* either of two tubes connecting the ovaries to the uterus.

fallow *adj.* (of farmland) not planted with crops.

false *adj.* **1** not true or correct. **2** fake; artificial. **3** mistaken. ■ **falsely** *adv.* **falsity** *n.*

falsehood *n.* **1** the state of being untrue. **2** a lie.

falsetto *n.* (*pl.* **falsettos**) a high-pitched voice used by male singers.

falsify *v.* (**falsifying, falsified**) alter so as to mislead. ■ **falsification** *n.*

falter *v.* **1** lose strength or momentum. **2** move or speak hesitantly.

fame *n.* the state of being famous. ■ **famed** *adj.*

familial *adj.* of a family.

familiar *adj.* **1** well known. **2** often encountered. **3** (**familiar with**) having knowledge of. **4** friendly. • *n.* a spirit believed to accompany a witch. ■ **familiarity** *n.* **familiarly** *adv.*

familiarize (or **-ise**) *v.* give knowledge or understanding to. ■ **familiarization** *n.*

family *n.* (*pl.* **families**) **1** a group consisting of parents and their children. **2** a group related by blood or marriage. **3** a person's

children. **4** a group of related things.

famine *n.* a time of severe food shortages.

famished *adj. informal* very hungry.

famous *adj.* **1** known about by many people. **2** *informal* excellent. ■ **famously** *adv.*

fan *n.* **1** a device creating a cooling current of air. **2** an enthusiastic admirer or supporter. • *v.* (**fanning, fanned**) **1** drive a current of air towards. **2** strengthen a feeling etc. **3** (**fan out**) spread out from a central point. □ **fan belt** a belt driving the fan that cools a vehicle's engine.

fanatic *n.* **1** a person who holds extreme political or religious opinions. **2** *informal* a person who is very enthusiastic about a hobby etc. ■ **fanatical** *adj.* **fanatically** *adv.* **fanaticism** *n.*

fancier *n.* a person who keeps or breeds a particular type of animal.

fanciful *adj.* **1** imaginary. **2** unusual or creative. ■ **fancifully** *adv.*

fancy *v.* (**fancying, fancied**) **1** *informal* want or want to do. **2** *informal* find sexually attractive. **3** think. • *adj.* (**fancier, fanciest**) elaborate or highly decorated. • *n.* (*pl.* **fancies**) **1** a brief feeling of attraction. **2** imagination. **3** an unfounded belief. □ **fancy dress** a costume representing a famous person, animal, etc., worn for a party.

fandango *n.* (*pl.* **fandangoes** or **fandangos**) a lively Spanish dance.

fanfare *n.* a short tune played on trumpets to announce someone.

fang n. 1 a long sharp tooth. 2 a snake's tooth which injects poison.

fantasia n. a musical composition based on several tunes.

fantasize (or **-ise**) v. imagine something desirable. ■ **fantasist** n.

fantastic adj. 1 hard to believe. 2 strange or exotic. 3 informal excellent. ■ **fantastically** adv.

fantasy n. (pl. **fantasies**) 1 a pleasant imagined situation. 2 the imagining of things that do not exist. 3 fiction involving magic and adventure.

far adv. 1 at, to, or by a great distance. 2 by a great deal. •adj. 1 distant. 2 extreme. □ **the Far East** China, Japan, and other countries of east Asia. **far-fetched** exaggerated or unlikely.

farad n. the basic unit of electrical capacitance.

farce n. 1 a comedy involving ridiculous situations. 2 an absurd event. ■ **farcical** adj. **farcically** adv.

fare n. 1 a charge for travel on public transport. 2 a range of food. •v. perform in a specified way.

farewell exclam. old use goodbye. •n. an act of leaving.

farm n. an area of land and buildings used for growing crops and rearing animals. •v. 1 grow crops or keep animals as a living. 2 (**farm out**) give work to others to do. ■ **farmer** n.

farrago /fuh-**rah**-goh/ n. (pl. **farragos** or **farragoes**) a confused mixture.

farrier n. a person who shoes horses.

farrow n. a litter of pigs. •v. give birth to piglets.

farther, **farthest** vars. of **FURTHER**, **FURTHEST**.

farthing n. a former UK coin, worth a quarter of an old penny.

fascia (or **facia**) /**fay**-shuh/ n. 1 a signboard on a shopfront. 2 a vehicle's dashboard. 3 a detachable cover for a mobile phone.

fascinate v. interest or charm greatly. ■ **fascination** n.

fascism /**fash**-i-z'm/ n. a right-wing system of government with extreme nationalistic beliefs. ■ **fascist** n. & adj.

fashion n. 1 a popular trend, esp. in dress. 2 the production and marketing of new styles of clothing. 3 a way of doing something. •v. make or shape.

fashionable adj. in or adopting a currently popular style. ■ **fashionably** adv.

fast adj. 1 moving or able to move very quickly. 2 happening at high speed. 3 (of a clock etc.) ahead of the correct time. 4 firmly fixed. •adv. 1 quickly. 2 firmly or securely. •v. go without food. •n. a period of fasting.

fasten v. 1 close or do up securely. 2 fix or hold in place. ■ **fastener** n.

fastidious adj. 1 attentive to detail. 2 very concerned about cleanliness. ■ **fastidiously** adv. **fastidiousness** n.

fastness n. a secure place well protected by natural features.

fat n. 1 an oily substance found in animals. 2 this, or a similar substance made from plants, used in cooking. •adj. (**fatter**, **fattest**) 1 having too much fat. 2 informal large. ■ **fatness** n. **fatten** v. **fatty** adj.

fatal adj. causing death or disaster. ■ **fatally** adv.

fatalism n. the belief that all events are decided in advance by a supernatural power. ■ **fatalist** n. **fatalistic** adj.

fatality n. (pl. **fatalities**) a death caused by an accident or disease, or occurring in war.

fate n. **1** a power believed to control all events. **2** the unavoidable events or outcome of a person's life. • v. (**be fated**) be destined to happen in a particular way.

fateful adj. having important, often unpleasant, consequences.

father n. **1** a male parent. **2** a founder or originator. **3** a title of certain priests. • v. be the father of. □ **father-in-law** (pl. **fathers-in-law**) the father of a person's husband or wife. **fatherland** a person's native country. ■ **fatherhood** n. **fatherly** adj.

fathom n. a measure of the depth of water, equal to 1.8 m. • v. understand.

fatigue n. **1** tiredness. **2** brittleness in metal etc. caused by repeated stress. **3** (**fatigues**) loose-fitting military clothing. • v. make very tired.

fatuous adj. silly and pointless. ■ **fatuously** adv.

fatwa n. an authoritative ruling on a point of Islamic law.

faucet n. US a tap.

fault n. **1** a defect or mistake. **2** responsibility for a mistake etc. **3** a break in the layers of rock of the earth's crust. • v. criticize for being unsatisfactory. ■ **faultless** adj. **faulty** adj.

faun n. a Roman god with a man's body and a goat's horns, tail, and legs.

fauna n. the animals of a particular region or period.

faux pas /foh pah/ n. (pl. **faux pas**) an embarrassing social blunder.

favour (US **favor**) n. **1** approval or liking. **2** a kind or helpful act. **3** favouritism. • v. **1** regard or treat with favour. **2** work to the advantage of.

favourable (US **favorable**) adj. **1** expressing approval or agreement. **2** advantageous or helpful. ■ **favourably** adv.

favourite (US **favorite**) adj. preferred to all others. • n. **1** a favourite person or thing. **2** the competitor expected to win.

favouritism (US **favoritism**) n. unfairly generous treatment of one person or group.

fawn n. **1** a young deer in its first year. **2** a light brown colour. • v. try to please by flattery and being very attentive.

fax n. **1** a copy of a document which has been scanned and sent electronically. **2** a machine for sending and receiving faxes. • v. send by fax.

faze v. informal unsettle.

FBI abbrev. (in the US) Federal Bureau of Investigation.

FC abbrev. Football Club.

fealty n. hist. loyalty sworn to a feudal lord.

fear n. an unpleasant emotion caused by the threat of danger, pain, etc. • v. **1** be afraid of. **2** (**fear for**) be anxious about.

fearful adj. **1** showing or causing fear. **2** informal very great. ■ **fearfully** adv.

fearless adj. feeling no fear; brave. ■ **fearlessly** adv.

fearsome adj. frightening.

feasible → feldspar

feasible *adj.* **1** able to be done. **2** likely. ■ **feasibility** *n.* **feasibly** *adv.*

feast *n.* **1** a large meal marking a special occasion. **2** an annual religious celebration. • *v.* **1** have a feast. **2** eat heartily.

feat *n.* an act requiring great courage, skill, or strength.

feather *n.* any of the structures covering a bird's body, consisting of a shaft fringed with fine strands. □ **featherweight** a weight in boxing between bantamweight and lightweight. **feather your nest** make money, esp. at someone's expense. ■ **feathered** *adj.* **feathery** *adj.*

feature *n.* **1** a distinctive element or aspect. **2** a part of the face. **3** a special newspaper or magazine article. **4** the main film showing at a cinema. • *v.* **1** have as a feature. **2** have an important part in.

febrile *adj.* **1** feverish. **2** overactive and excitable.

February *n.* the second month.

❗ *-ruary*, not *-uary*: February.

feces US = **FAECES**.

feckless *adj.* irresponsible and weak in character.

fecund *adj.* fertile. ■ **fecundity** *n.*

fed past & past part. of **FEED**. □ **fed up** *informal* annoyed or bored.

federal *adj.* of a system in which several states unite under a central authority but are independent in internal affairs. ■ **federalism** *n.* **federalist** *n.* & *adj.* **federally** *adv.*

federate *v.* unite as a federation.

federation *n.* **1** a group of states united on a federal basis. **2** a group organized like a federation.

fedora *n.* a soft hat with a curled brim.

fee *n.* a sum payable for professional services or to be allowed to do something.

feeble *adj.* **1** weak. **2** not convincing. ■ **feebleness** *n.* **feebly** *adv.*

feed *v.* (**feeding**, **fed**) **1** give food to. **2** eat. **3** supply with material, power, etc. **4** pass gradually through a confined space. • *n.* **1** an act of feeding. **2** food for domestic animals. □ **feedback 1** comments about a product or a person's performance. **2** the return of part of the output of an amplifier to its input, causing a whistling sound.

feeder *n.* **1** a thing that feeds or supplies something. **2** a minor route linking outlying districts with the main route.

feel *v.* (**feeling**, **felt**) **1** be aware of or examine by touch. **2** give a sensation when touched. **3** experience an emotion or sensation. **4** have a belief or opinion. • *n.* **1** an act of touching. **2** the sense of touch. **3** an impression. **4** (**a feel for**) a sensitive appreciation of.

feeler *n.* **1** a long slender organ of touch in some animals. **2** a suggestion made to gauge opinion.

feeling *n.* **1** an emotional state or reaction. **2** (**feelings**) the emotional side of a person's character. **3** the ability to feel. **4** the sensation of touching or being touched. **5** a belief or opinion.

feet pl. of **FOOT**.

feign *v.* pretend.

feint *n.* a pretended attack in boxing or fencing. • *v.* make a feint. • *adj.* (of paper) printed with faint ruled lines.

feisty /fy-sti/ *adj.* spirited and lively.

feldspar (or **felspar**) *n.* a white or red mineral.

felicitations pl. n. congratulations.

felicitous adj. well chosen or appropriate.

felicity n. (pl. **felicities**) **1** great happiness. **2** an apt and pleasing feature.

feline adj. of a cat or cats. •n. an animal of the cat family.

fell[1] past of **FALL**.

fell[2] v. cut or knock down. •n. a hill or high moor in northern England.

fellow n. **1** a man or boy. **2** a person in the same situation as another. **3** a thing like another. **4** a member of a learned society or governing body of a college.

fellowship n. **1** friendliness and companionship. **2** a group with a shared interest. **3** the position of a fellow of a college or society.

felon n. a person who has committed a serious crime. ■ **felonious** adj.

felony n. (pl. **felonies**) (in the US and formerly also in English Law) a serious crime.

felspar var. of **FELDSPAR**.

felt[1] n. cloth made by rolling and pressing damp wool.

felt[2] past & past part. of **FEEL**.

female adj. **1** of the sex that can bear offspring or produce eggs. **2** (of a plant or flower) having a pistil but no stamens. **3** (of a fitting) made hollow to allow insertion of another part. •n. a female person, animal, or plant.

feminine adj. **1** having qualities associated with women. **2** female. ■ **femininity** n.

feminism n. a movement supporting equal rights for women. ■ **feminist** n. & adj.

femme fatale /fam fuh-**tahl**/ n. (pl. **femmes fatales**) an attractive and seductive woman.

femur n. (pl. **femurs** or **femora**) the thigh bone. ■ **femoral** adj.

fen n. a low-lying marshy or flooded area of land.

fence n. **1** a barrier made of wire or wood enclosing an area. **2** informal a dealer in stolen goods. •v. **1** surround with a fence. **2** practise the sport of fencing. ■ **fencer** n.

fencing n. **1** the sport of fighting with blunted swords. **2** fences or material for fences.

fend v. **1** (**fend for yourself**) provide for yourself. **2** (**fend off**) defend yourself from.

fender n. **1** a low frame around a fireplace. **2** an object hung over a ship's side to cushion it against impact. **3** US the mudguard or wing of a vehicle.

feng shui /feng shoo-i, fung shway/ n. an ancient Chinese system of designing buildings and arranging objects to ensure a favourable flow of energy.

fennel n. an aniseed-flavoured vegetable and herb.

fenugreek n. a spice made from the seeds of a plant.

feral adj. wild.

ferment v. **1** undergo fermentation. **2** stir up unrest. •n. unrest or excitement.

fermentation n. the chemical breakdown of a substance by bacteria, yeast, etc.

fern n. a flowerless plant with feathery fronds.

ferocious adj. very fierce or violent. ■ **ferociously** adv. **ferocity** n.

ferret n. a domesticated polecat.
• v. (**ferreting**, **ferreted**) search for in a place or container.

ferric (or **ferrous**) adj. of or containing iron.

Ferris wheel n. a funfair ride consisting of a large upright revolving wheel.

ferrule n. a metal cap which protects the end of a stick etc.

ferry n. (pl. **ferries**) a boat for transporting passengers and goods. • v. (**ferrying**, **ferried**) carry by ferry or other transport.

fertile adj. 1 producing abundant vegetation or crops. 2 able to conceive young or produce seed. 3 productive or inventive. ■ **fertility** n.

fertilize (or **-ise**) v. 1 introduce sperm or pollen into an egg or plant. 2 add a substance to soil to make it more fertile. ■ **fertilization** n. **fertilizer** n.

fervent adj. very passionate. ■ **fervently** adv.

fervid adj. fervent.

fervour (US **fervor**) n. passionate feeling.

fester v. 1 become septic. 2 (of ill feeling) become worse.

festival n. 1 a day or period of celebration. 2 a series of concerts, films, etc.

festive adj. of a festival.

festivity n. 1 joyful celebration. 2 (**festivities**) activities or events celebrating a special occasion.

festoon v. decorate with chains of flowers etc. • n. a decorative chain of flowers etc.

feta n. a salty Greek cheese.

fetch v. 1 go for and bring back. 2 sell for a particular price. 3 (**fetching**) attractive.

fete /fayt/ n. an outdoor event to raise funds for a particular cause. • v. honour or entertain lavishly.

fetid (or **foetid**) adj. smelling very unpleasant.

fetish n. 1 an object worshipped for its supposed magical powers. 2 sexual desire in which pleasure is gained from a particular object. ■ **fetishism** n. **fetishist** n.

fetlock n. the joint of a horse's leg between the knee and the hoof.

fetter v. 1 limit the freedom of. 2 restrain with chains or shackles. • n. 1 (**fetters**) restrictions. 2 a shackle.

fettle n. condition: in fine fettle.

fettuccine /fet-tuh-**chee**-ni/ pl. n. pasta made in ribbons.

fetus (or **foetus**) n. (pl. **fetuses**) an unborn mammal. ■ **fetal** adj.

feud n. a long, bitter dispute. • v. take part in a feud.

feudalism n. the social system in medieval Europe, in which people worked and fought for a lord in return for land. ■ **feudal** adj.

fever n. 1 an abnormally high body temperature. 2 nervous excitement. ■ **fevered** adj. **feverish** adj.

few adj., pron., & n. 1 (**a few**) a small number of. 2 not many.

> ! There's a difference between **fewer** and **less**. Use **fewer** with plural nouns, as in eat fewer cakes; use **less** with nouns referring to things that can't be counted, as in there is less blossom on this tree.

fey adj. 1 unworldly and vague. 2 able to see into the future.

fez n. (pl. **fezzes**) a flat-topped conical red hat worn by some Muslim men.

ff. abbrev. following pages.

fiancé n. (fem. **fiancée**) a person to whom you are engaged to be married.

fiasco n. (pl. **fiascos**) a ridiculous or humiliating failure.

fiat n. an official order.

fib n. a trivial lie. •v. (**fibbing, fibbed**) tell a fib. ■ **fibber** n.

fibre (US **fiber**) n. 1 each of the strands forming plant or animal tissue, cloth, or minerals. 2 a substance formed of fibres. 3 roughage in food. 4 strength of character. □ **fibreglass** a reinforced plastic material containing glass fibres. **fibre optics** the use of glass fibres to send information in the form of light. ■ **fibrous** adj.

fibroid adj. consisting of fibrous tissue. •n. a benign fibroid tumour in the womb.

fibula n. (pl. **fibulae** or **fibulas**) the outer of the two bones between the knee and the ankle.

fickle adj. changeable in your loyalties.

fiction n. 1 literature describing imaginary events and people. 2 an invented story. ■ **fictional** adj.

fictitious adj. imaginary or invented.

fiddle informal n. 1 a violin. 2 an act of fraud. •v. 1 handle restlessly or nervously. 2 falsify expenses etc. ■ **fiddler** n.

fiddly adj. informal complicated and awkward.

fidelity n. 1 faithfulness. 2 accuracy in a copy or reproduction.

fidget v. (**fidgeting, fidgeted**) make small movements through nervousness or impatience. •n. a person who fidgets. ■ **fidgety** adj.

fiduciary Law adj. held or given in trust. •n. (**fiduciaries**) a trustee.

fief /feef/ n. 1 a person's area of operation or control. 2 hist. a piece of land held under the feudal system. ■ **fiefdom** n.

field n. 1 an enclosed area of land for crops or grazing animals. 2 a piece of land used for a sport. 3 a subject of study or area of activity. 4 an area within which a force has an effect: a magnetic field. 5 the participants in a race etc. •v. 1 select to play in a game or to stand in an election. 2 try to deal with. 3 Cricket & Baseball try to catch or stop the ball after it has been hit. □ **field day** a good opportunity to do something. **field events** athletic sports other than races. **field marshal** the highest rank of army officer. **fieldwork** practical research done outside a laboratory or office. ■ **fielder** n.

fiend n. 1 an evil spirit. 2 a very cruel person. 3 informal an enthusiast: an exercise fiend.

fiendish adj. 1 very cruel. 2 informal very difficult. ■ **fiendishly** adv.

fierce adj. 1 violent or aggressive. 2 powerful. ■ **fiercely** adv. **fierceness** n.

fiery adj. (**fierier, fieriest**) 1 consisting of or like fire. 2 quick-tempered or passionate.

fiesta n. (in Spanish-speaking countries) a religious festival.

fife n. a small high-pitched flute.

fifteen adj. & n. one more than fourteen; 15. ■ **fifteenth** adj. & n.

fifth adj. & n. next after fourth.

fifty adj. & n. (pl. **fifties**) ten less than sixty; 50. □ **fifty-fifty** with equal shares or chances. ■ **fiftieth** *adj. & n.*

fig *n.* a soft, sweet fruit with many seeds.

fight *v.* (**fighting, fought**) **1** take part in a violent physical struggle. **2** take part in a war or contest. **3** try hard to stop, overcome, or achieve. •*n.* an act of fighting.

fighter *n.* **1** a person who fights. **2** a military aircraft designed for attack.

figment *n.* a thing that exists only in the imagination.

figurative *adj.* not using words literally. ■ **figuratively** *adv.*

figure *n.* **1** a number or numerical symbol. **2** a person's body shape. **3** a well-known person. **4** a geometric shape. **5** a diagram or drawing. •*v.* **1** play an important part. **2** US *informal* think; suppose. □ **figurehead 1** a leader without real power. **2** a carved statue at the front of a sailing ship. **figure of speech** a word or phrase used in a non-literal sense. **figure out** *informal* understand.

figurine *n.* a statuette.

filament *n.* **1** a slender thread. **2** a fine wire giving off light in an electric light bulb.

filbert *n.* a hazelnut.

filch *v. informal* steal.

file *n.* **1** a folder or box for keeping loose papers. **2** a set of computer data stored under a single name. **3** a line of people or things one behind another. **4** a tool with a rough surface for smoothing. •*v.* **1** place in a file. **2** present so as to be officially dealt with. **3** walk one behind the other. **4** smooth with a file.

filial *adj.* of a son or daughter.

filibuster *n.* prolonged speaking which obstructs progress in a law-making assembly.

filigree *n.* ornamental work of fine gold or silver wire.

filings *pl. n.* small particles rubbed off by a file.

fill *v.* **1** make or become full. **2** block up a hole etc. **3** appoint a person to a vacant post. **4** occupy time. •*n.* (**your fill**) as much as you want or can bear. □ **fill in 1** complete a form. **2** give information to. **3** act as a substitute. **fill out** put on weight.

filler *n.* something used to fill a gap or to increase bulk.

fillet *n.* a boneless piece of meat or fish. •*v.* (**filleting, filleted**) remove the bones from a fish.

filling *n.* a substance used to fill something. •*adj.* (of food) making you feel full. □ **filling station** a petrol station.

fillip *n.* a stimulus or boost.

filly *n.* (*pl.* **fillies**) a young female horse.

film *n.* **1** a thin flexible strip of light-sensitive material for photos or motion pictures. **2** a story or event recorded by a camera and shown in a cinema or on television. **3** a thin layer covering a surface. •*v.* make a film of.

filmy *adj.* (of fabric) thin and almost transparent.

filo *n.* Greek pastry in the form of very thin sheets.

filter *n.* **1** a device or substance for holding back solid particles in a liquid or gas passing through it. **2** a screen which absorbs some of the light passing through it. •*v.* **1** pass through a filter. **2** move gradually in or out.

filth n. **1** disgusting dirt. **2** obscene language or material. ■ **filthy** adj.

filtrate n. a filtered liquid. ■ **filtration** n.

fin n. **1** a flattened part projecting from the body of a fish, dolphin, etc., used for swimming and balancing. **2** a projection on an aircraft, rocket, etc. to improve stability.

final adj. **1** coming at the end; last. **2** allowing no dispute. • n. **1** the last game in a tournament, deciding the overall winner. **2** (**finals**) exams at the end of a degree course. ■ **finality** n. **finally** adv.

finale /fi-nah-li/ n. the last part of a piece of music or entertainment.

finalist n. a competitor in a final.

finalize (or **-ise**) v. complete a plan or agreement.

finance n. **1** the management of money. **2** money to support an enterprise. **3** (**finances**) the money held by an organization etc. • v. fund. ■ **financial** adj. **financially** adv.

financier n. a person who manages the finances of large organizations.

finch n. a small bird with a short bill.

find v. (**finding**, **found**) **1** discover. **2** learn. **3** declare a verdict. **4** reach a state or point. • n. a valuable or interesting discovery. □ **find out** discover information. ■ **finder** n.

finding n. a conclusion reached after an inquiry etc.

fine adj. **1** of very high quality. **2** satisfactory. **3** in good health. **4** (of the weather) bright and free from rain. **5** thin. **6** consisting of small particles. **7** delicate or complex. **8** subtle. • n. a sum of money to be paid as a punishment. • v. make someone pay a fine. □ **with a fine-tooth comb** (or **fine-toothed comb**) with a very thorough search or examination. ■ **finely** adv. **fineness** n.

finery n. showy clothes.

finesse n. delicate skill, esp. in handling situations.

finger n. **1** each of the four jointed parts attached to either hand (five, if the thumb is included). **2** a small measure of alcohol in a glass. • v. touch or feel with the fingers. □ **fingerboard** a flat strip on the neck of a stringed instrument, against which the strings are pressed to vary the pitch. **fingerprint** a mark made by the pad of a person's finger, used for identification.

finial n. an ornament at the end of a gable etc.

finicky adj. **1** fussy. **2** detailed and fiddly.

finish v. **1** bring or come to an end. **2** eat or drink the whole or the remainder of. **3** reach the end of a race etc. **4** (**finish off**) kill or completely defeat. **5** complete or put the final touches to. • n. **1** an end or final stage. **2** the way in which a manufactured article is finished.

finite /fy-nyt/ adj. limited.

Finn n. a person from Finland. ■ **Finnish** n. & adj.

fiord var. of **FJORD**.

fir n. an evergreen coniferous tree.

fire n. **1** the light, heat, etc. produced when something burns. **2** an instance of destructive burning. **3** wood or coal that is burning. **4** a gas or electric heater. **5** passion. **6** the firing of guns. • v. **1** a bullet, missile, etc. from a gun or other weapon. **2** *informal* dismiss from a job. **3** stimulate. **4** supply fuel to. **5** bake pottery in a kiln. □ **firearm** a rifle, pistol, or shotgun. **firebrand** a passionate supporter of a cause. **firebreak** a strip of open space to stop a fire from spreading. **fire brigade** a team of people employed to put out fires. **fire engine** a vehicle carrying firefighters and their equipment. **fire escape** a staircase or ladder used to escape from a burning building. **firefighter** a person whose job is to put out fires. **firefly** a kind of beetle which glows in the dark. **fireman** a male firefighter. **fireplace** a recess at the base of a chimney for a domestic fire. **fireside** the area round a fireplace. **firewall** a part of a computer system that blocks unauthorized access. **firework** a device containing chemicals that explode to produce spectacular effects. **firing squad** a group of soldiers ordered to shoot a condemned person.

firm *adj.* **1** not giving way under pressure. **2** solidly in place. **3** (of a grip etc.) steady and strong. **4** showing determination and strength of character. **5** fixed or definite. • *v.* make firm. • *n.* a business organization. ■ **firmly** *adv.* **firmness** *n.*

firmament *n.* the heavens; the sky.

first *adj. & n.* **1** coming before all others in time, order, or importance. **2** before doing something else. □ **at first** at the beginning. **first aid** emergency medical help given before full treatment. **first class** excellent. **first-degree** (of burns) causing only reddening of the skin. **first-hand** directly from the original source. **first name** a personal name. **first-rate** excellent. ■ **firstly** *adv.*

firth *n.* a narrow inlet of the sea, esp. in Scotland.

fiscal *adj.* of government revenue.

fish *n.* (pl. **fish** or **fishes**) **1** a cold-blooded animal with gills and fins, living in water. **2** the flesh of fish as food. • *v.* **1** try to catch fish. **2** take out of water or a container. **3** (**fish for**) try to get by subtle means. □ **fisherman** a person who catches fish for a living or for sport. **fishmonger** a person selling fish for food. **fishnet** an open mesh fabric.

fishery *n.* (pl. **fisheries**) a place where fish are reared for food, or caught in numbers.

fishy *adj.* **1** of or like fish. **2** *informal* arousing suspicion.

fissile *adj.* **1** able to undergo nuclear fission. **2** (of rock) easily split.

fission *n.* the act of splitting, esp. of an atomic nucleus with the release of much energy.

fissure *n.* a long, narrow crack.

fist *n.* a tightly closed hand. □ **fisticuffs** fighting with the fists. ■ **fistful** *n.*

fit *adj.* (**fitter**, **fittest**) **1** of a suitable quality, standard, or type. **2** in good health. • *v.* (**fitting**, **fitted**) **1** be the right shape and size for. **2** be able to occupy a particular position or space. **3** fix into place. **4** provide with. **5** try clothing on and alter it. • *n.* **1** the way something fits. **2** a sudden attack of violent, uncontrolled movements. **3** a sudden outburst of feeling, coughing, etc. ■ **fitness** *n.*

fitful *adj.* not steady or continuous. ■ **fitfully** *adv.*

fitment n. a fixed item of furniture.

fitter n. 1 a person who assembles or installs machinery. 2 a person who fits clothes.

fitting n. 1 a small part attached to furniture or equipment. 2 (**fittings**) items fixed in a building but removable when the owner moves. 3 an occasion of a garment being fitted. · adj. appropriate. ■ **fittingly** adv.

five adj. & n. one more than four; 5.

fiver n. informal a five-pound note.

fix v. 1 attach or position securely. 2 repair. 3 decide or settle on. 4 make arrangements for. 5 make permanent. 6 (**fix on**) direct the eyes etc. steadily toward. 7 informal influence a result etc. dishonestly. · n. 1 an act of fixing. 2 informal a difficult situation. 3 informal a dose of an addictive drug. □ **fix up 1** organize. 2 informal provide with. ■ **fixer** n.

fixate v. (**fixate on** or **be fixated on**) be obsessed with.

fixation n. an obsession.

fixative n. a substance used to fix or protect something.

fixity n. the state of being permanent.

fixture n. 1 a piece of equipment etc. which is fixed in position. 2 (**fixtures**) articles attached to a house that remain where the owner moves. 3 a sports event on a particular date.

fizz v. produce bubbles of gas with a hissing sound. · n. 1 the quality of being fizzy. 2 informal a fizzy drink.

fizzle v. 1 make a weak hissing sound. 2 (**fizzle out**) end feebly.

fizzy adj. (**fizzier**, **fizziest**) (of a drink) containing bubbles of gas.

fjord (or **fiord**) /fyord, fee-ord/ n. a long, narrow inlet of the sea between high cliffs, esp. in Norway.

fl. abbrev. 1 floruit, used to indicate when a historical figure lived or was most active. 2 fluid.

flab n. informal excess fat on the body.

flabbergasted adj. informal very surprised.

flabby adj. (**flabbier**, **flabbiest**) fat and floppy. ■ **flabbiness** n.

flaccid /flass-id/ adj. soft and limp.

flag n. 1 a piece of cloth attached to a pole or rope as a symbol or signal. 2 a flagstone. · v. (**flagging**, **flagged**) 1 mark for attention. 2 (**flag down**) signal to a driver to stop. 3 become tired or less enthusiastic. □ **flagship 1** an admiral's ship. 2 the most important product of an organization.

flagstone a large paving stone.

flagellate v. whip. ■ **flagellation** n.

flagon n. a large bottle or jug for wine, cider, etc.

flagrant adj. very obvious and unashamed. ■ **flagrantly** adv.

flail v. move around wildly. · n. a tool or machine used for threshing grain.

flair n. 1 a natural ability or talent. 2 stylishness.

flak n. 1 anti-aircraft fire. 2 strong criticism.

flake n. a small, flat, thin piece of something. · v. 1 come off in flakes. 2 separate into flakes. 3 (**flake out**) informal fall asleep or drop from exhaustion. ■ **flakiness** n. **flaky** adj.

flambé /flom-bay/ v. (**flambéing**, **flambéed**) cover food with spirits and set it alight briefly.

flamboyant adj. **1** very confident and lively. **2** brightly coloured or decorated. ■ **flamboyance** n. **flamboyantly** adv.

flame n. **1** a glowing stream of burning gas produced by something on fire. • v. **1** give off flames. **2** (of the face) go red. **3** informal send insulting email to. □ **old flame** informal a former lover.

flamenco n. a Spanish style of singing and dancing.

flamingo n. (pl. **flamingos** or **flamingoes**) a pink wading bird with long legs.

flammable adj. easily set on fire.

flan n. an open pastry or sponge case with a filling.

flange n. a projecting flat rim. ■ **flanged** adj.

flank n. **1** a side, esp. of the body between the ribs and hip. **2** the left or right side of a group. • v. be on either side of.

flannel n. **1** a soft fabric with a raised surface. **2** (**flannels**) trousers made of flannel. **3** a facecloth. **4** informal evasive and meaningless talk.

flannelette n. a cotton fabric like flannel.

flap v. (**flapping**, **flapped**) **1** move up and down or from side to side. **2** informal be agitated. • n. **1** a piece of something attached on one side only to cover an opening. **2** a single flapping movement. **3** informal a panic.

flapjack n. a thick biscuit made with oats.

flare n. **1** a burst of flame or light. **2** a device producing a very bright flame as a signal or marker. **3** a gradual widening towards the hem of a garment. **4** (**flares**) trousers which widen from the knees down. • v. **1** blaze suddenly. **2** suddenly become intense or violent. **3** gradually widen at one end.

flash v. **1** shine with a bright but brief or irregular light. **2** move or send swiftly. **3** display briefly, repeatedly, or obviously. • n. **1** a sudden brief burst of bright light. **2** a camera attachment producing a flash of light. **3** a sudden or brief occurrence. **4** a coloured patch on a uniform. • adj. informal stylish or expensive in a showy way. □ **flashback** a scene in a film or novel set in a time earlier than the main story. **flash flood** a sudden local flood. **flash in the pan** a sudden but brief success. **flashlight** an electric torch. **flashpoint** a point at which anger or violence flares up.

flashing n. a strip of metal sealing the joins of a roof.

flashy adj. (**flashier**, **flashiest**) attractive in a showy or cheap way. ■ **flashily** adv.

flask n. **1** a bottle with a narrow neck. **2** a vacuum flask.

flat adj. (**flatter**, **flattest**) **1** level and even. **2** not sloping. **3** not lively or interesting. **4** no longer fizzy. **5** (of a battery) having used up its charge. **6** (of a price) fixed. **7** definite and firm. **8** (of musical sound) below true pitch. **9** (of a note) lower by a semitone than a specified note. • adv. **1** so as to be flat. **2** informal definitely; absolutely. • n. **1** a flat part or area. **2** a musical note that is a semitone lower than a specified note, or a sign indicating this. **3** a set of rooms forming an individual home within a larger building. □ **flatfish** a sea fish with a flattened body and both eyes on the upper side.

f

flatmate a person with whom you share a flat. **flat out** as fast or as hard as possible. ∎ **flatly** adv. **flatness** n. **flatten** v.

flatter v. **1** compliment insincerely. **2** (**be flattered**) feel honoured. **3** make someone appear attractive. ∎ **flatterer** n. **flattery** n.

flatulent adj. having too much gas in the intestines or stomach. ∎ **flatulence** n.

flaunt v. display obviously.

! Don't confuse **flaunt** with **flout**, which means 'openly fail to follow a rule'.

flautist n. a flute player.

flavour (US **flavor**) n. **1** the distinctive taste of a food or drink. **2** a particular quality. •v. give flavour to. ∎ **flavourless** adj.

flavouring (US **flavoring**) n. a substance used to flavour food or drink.

flaw n. **1** a mark or fault that spoils something. **2** a weakness or mistake. ∎ **flawed** adj. **flawless** adj.

flax n. a blue-flowered plant grown esp. for making cloth.

flaxen adj. (of hair) pale yellow.

flay v. **1** strip the skin from. **2** criticize harshly.

flea n. a small jumping bloodsucking insect. ▢ **flea market** a street market selling second-hand goods. **fleapit** informal a run-down cinema.

fleck n. a very small patch or particle. •v. mark with flecks.

fledged adj. (of a young bird) having wing feathers large enough for flight.

fledgling (or **fledgeling**) n. a young bird that has just learned to fly.

flee v. (**fleeing**, **fled**) run away.

fleece n. **1** the wool coat of a sheep. **2** a soft, warm fabric with a pile, or a jacket made from this. •v. informal swindle. ∎ **fleecy** adj.

fleet n. **1** a group of ships, vehicles, or aircraft travelling together or having the same owner. **2** a navy. •adj. fast and nimble.

fleeting adj. passing quickly; brief. ∎ **fleetingly** adv.

flesh n. **1** the soft substance in the body consisting of muscle and fat. **2** the soft part of a fruit or vegetable. **3** (**the flesh**) the physical aspects of the body. •v. (**flesh out**) make more detailed. ▢ **in the flesh** in person. ∎ **fleshly** adj.

fleshy adj. (**fleshier**, **fleshiest**) **1** plump. **2** soft and thick.

fleur-de-lis (or **fleur-de-lys**) /fler-duh-lee/ n. (pl. **fleurs-de-lis**) a design of a lily with three petals.

flew past of FLY.

flex v. bend a limb or joint. **2** tighten a muscle. •n. an insulated cable for carrying electric current. ∎ **flexion** n.

flexible adj. **1** able to bend easily. **2** easily changed; adaptable. ∎ **flexibility** n. **flexibly** adv.

flexitime n. a system allowing flexible working hours.

flibbertigibbet n. a frivolous person.

flick v. move, hit, or remove with a quick light movement. •n. **1** a sudden quick movement. **2** (**the flicks**) informal the cinema.

flicker v. **1** shine or burn unsteadily. **2** appear briefly. **3** make small, quick movements. •n. **1** a flickering movement or light. **2** a brief occurrence.

flier var. of FLYER.

flight n. **1** the act of flying. **2** a journey through air or space. **3** the path of something through the air. **4** the act of running away. **5** a group of flying birds or aircraft. **6** a series of steps. **7** the tail of an arrow or dart. □ **flight deck 1** the cockpit of a large aircraft. **2** the deck of an aircraft carrier. **flightless** unable to fly.

flighty adj. unreliable and frivolous.

flimsy adj. (**flimsier**, **flimsiest**) **1** fragile. **2** light and thin. **3** unconvincing. ■ **flimsily** adv. **flimsiness** n.

flinch v. **1** make a quick, nervous movement from fear or pain. **2** (**flinch from**) avoid through fear or anxiety.

fling v. (**flinging**, **flung**) throw or move forcefully. • n. **1** a short period of enjoyment. **2** a short sexual relationship.

flint n. **1** a hard grey rock. **2** a piece of flint or a metal alloy, used to produce a spark. □ **flintlock** an old type of gun. ■ **flinty** adj.

flip v. (**flipping**, **flipped**) **1** turn over, throw, or move with a sudden, quick movement. **2** informal lose self-control. • n. a flipping movement. • adj. flippant. □ **flip-flop** a sandal with a thong passing between the big and second toes.

flippant adj. not showing proper seriousness or respect. ■ **flippancy** n. **flippantly** adv.

flipper n. **1** a sea animal's broad, flat limb used in swimming. **2** each of two flat rubber attachments worn on the feet for underwater swimming.

flirt v. **1** behave as if trying to attract someone sexually but without serious intentions. **2** (**flirt**

with) show a casual interest in. • n. a person who flirts. ■ **flirtation** n. **flirtatious** adj.

flit v. (**flitting**, **flitted**) move quickly and lightly.

flitter v. move quickly here and there.

float v. **1** rest or move on the surface of a liquid. **2** move or be held up in the air. **3** put forward a suggestion. **4** offer the shares of a company for sale. • n. **1** a thing designed to float on water. **2** a vehicle carrying a display in a procession. **3** a sum of money for minor expenses or giving change. ■ **floaty** adj.

floatation var. of FLOTATION.

flocculent adj. like tufts of wool.

flock n. **1** a number of birds or animals together. **2** a large number or crowd. **3** a Christian congregation. **4** wool or cotton refuse used as stuffing. • v. gather or move in a flock. □ **flock wallpaper** wallpaper with a raised pattern made from powdered cloth.

floe n. a sheet of floating ice.

flog v. (**flogging**, **flogged**) **1** beat with a whip or stick. **2** informal sell.

flood n. **1** an overflow of a large amount of water over dry land. **2** an overwhelming quantity or amount. **3** the rising of the tide. • v. **1** cover with flood water. **2** (of a river) overflow its banks. **3** arrive in very large numbers.

floodlight n. a large lamp with a broad, powerful beam. • v. (**floodlighting**, **floodlit**) light up with floodlights.

floor n. **1** the lower surface of a room. **2** a storey of a building. **3** (**the floor**) the right to speak in a debate. • v. **1** provide with a floor. **2** informal knock down. **3** informal baffle. □ **floor show** an entertainment in a nightclub or restaurant.

flooring n. material for a floor.

floozy (or **floozie**) n. (pl. **floozies**) informal a woman who has many sexual partners.

flop v. (**flopping, flopped**) **1** hang loosely. **2** sit or lie down heavily. **3** informal fail totally. • n. **1** a flopping movement. **2** informal a total failure.

floppy adj. not firm or rigid. □ **floppy disk** a flexible disk for storing computer data.

flora n. (pl. **floras** or **florae**) the plants of an area or period.

floral adj. of flowers.

floret n. **1** each of the small flowers of a composite flower. **2** each of the flowering stems of a head of cauliflower or broccoli.

florid adj. **1** red or flushed. **2** over-elaborate.

florin n. a former British coin worth two shillings.

florist n. a person who sells flowers. ■ **floristry** n.

floss n. **1** soft thread used to clean between the teeth. **2** silk embroidery thread. • v. clean the teeth with floss.

flotation (or **floatation**) n. the act of floating, esp. of a company's shares.

flotilla n. a small fleet.

flotsam n. wreckage floating on the sea. □ **flotsam and jetsam** useless or discarded objects.

flounce v. move in an angry or impatient way. • n. **1** a flouncing movement. **2** a wide frill.

flounder v. **1** have difficulty doing something. **2** stagger clumsily in

mud or water. • n. a small edible flatfish.

flour n. a powder produced by grinding grain, used to make bread etc. ■ **floury** adj.

flourish v. **1** grow vigorously. **2** be successful. **3** wave about in a noticeable way. • n. **1** a bold or exaggerated gesture. **2** an ornamental curve in handwriting. **3** a fanfare.

flout v. openly fail to follow a rule etc.

> ! Don't confuse **flout** with **flaunt**, which means 'display obviously'.

flow v. **1** move steadily and continuously in a stream. **2** move or proceed smoothly. **3** hang loosely. • n. **1** a steady, continuous stream. **2** the act of flowing. □ **flow chart** a diagram showing the sequence of stages in a process.

flower n. **1** the part of a plant from which the seed or fruit develops, usu. brightly coloured. **2** the best of a group. • v. **1** produce flowers. **2** develop fully and well.

flowery adj. **1** full of flowers. **2** (of speech or writing) elaborate.

flown past part. of **FLY**.

flu n. influenza.

fluctuate v. vary irregularly. ■ **fluctuation** n.

flue n. a pipe that takes smoke and gases away from a chimney, heater, etc.

fluent adj. **1** speaking or writing in a clear and natural way. **2** smoothly graceful. ■ **fluency** n. **fluently** adv.

fluff n. a soft mass of fibres or down. • v. **1** make fuller and softer by shaking or patting. **2** informal fail to do properly. ■ **fluffiness** n. **fluffy** adj.

fluid n. a liquid or gas. • adj. **1** able to flow easily. **2** not stable. **3** graceful. □ **fluid ounce** one twentieth of a pint (approx. 0.028 litre). ■ **fluidity** n.

fluke n. **1** a lucky chance occurrence. **2** a parasitic worm.

flume n. **1** an artificial water channel. **2** a water slide.

flummery n. empty talk or compliments.

flummox v. informal baffle.

flung past & past part. of FLING.

flunk v. informal fail an exam.

flunkey (or **flunky**) n. (pl. **flunkeys** or **flunkies**) **1** a uniformed male servant. **2** a person who does menial work.

fluorescent adj. **1** giving off bright light when exposed to radiation such as ultraviolet light. **2** vividly colourful. ■ **fluoresce** v. **fluorescence** n.

fluoridate v. add fluoride to. ■ **fluoridation** n.

fluoride n. a compound of fluorine added to water supplies or toothpaste to reduce tooth decay.

fluorine n. a poisonous yellow gas.

fluorite (or **fluorspar**) n. a colourless mineral.

flurry n. (pl. **flurries**) **1** a swirling mass of snow, leaves, etc. **2** a sudden spell of activity or excitement.

flush v. **1** become red; blush. **2** clean or remove by passing large quantities of water through. **3** force into the open. • n. **1** a blush. **2** a rush of emotion. **3** an act of flushing. **4** (in poker) a hand of cards all of the same suit. • adj. **1** level with another surface. **2** informal having plenty of money.

fluster v. agitate or confuse.

flute n. **1** a wind instrument consisting of a tube held sideways with holes along it **2** a tall, narrow wine glass.

fluted adj. decorated with a series of grooves.

flutter v. **1** fly unsteadily by flapping the wings quickly and lightly. **2** move with a light trembling motion. **3** (of the heart) beat irregularly. • n. **1** a state of nervous excitement. **2** a fluttering movement. **3** informal a small bet.

fluvial adj. of rivers.

flux n. **1** continuous change. **2** a bodily discharge. **3** a substance mixed with a solid to lower the melting point.

fly¹ v. (**flies**, **flying**, **flew**; past part. **flown**) **1** (of a winged creature or aircraft) move through the air. **2** control the flight of or transport in an aircraft. **3** move quickly through the air. **4** go or move quickly. **5** flutter in the wind. **6** (of a flag) be displayed on a flagpole. **7** (**fly into**) suddenly become angry. **8** (**fly at**) attack. **9** old use run away. • n. (pl. **flies**) **1** (also **flies**) an opening at the crotch of a pair of trousers, closed with a zip or buttons. **2** a flap of material covering the opening of a tent. □ **flying buttress** a buttress slanting upwards from a separate support. **flying fish** a tropical fish with wing-like fins for gliding above the water. **flying saucer** a disc-shaped flying craft supposedly piloted by aliens. **flying squad** a division of a police force capable of reaching an incident quickly. **fly-tipping** the illegal dumping of waste.

fly² n. (pl. **flies**) a two-winged flying insect. □ **flyblown** contaminated by contact with flies.

fly in the ointment a minor irritation that spoils something. **fly on the wall** an unnoticed observer. **flyweight** a weight in boxing below bantamweight.

flyer (or **flier**) n. 1 a person or thing that flies. 2 a small advertising leaflet.

FM abbrev. frequency modulation.

foal n. a young horse or related animal. •v. give birth to a foal.

foam n. 1 a mass of small bubbles. 2 a substance containing many small bubbles. 3 lightweight spongy rubber or plastic. •v. form or produce foam. ▪ **foamy** adj.

fob n. 1 a chain attached to a watch. 2 a tab on a key ring. •v. (**fobbing, fobbed**) (**fob off**) try to deceive into accepting excuses or something inferior.

focaccia /fuh-kach-uh/ n. a flat Italian bread made with olive oil.

focal adj. of a focus.

fo'c's'le var. of FORECASTLE.

focus n. (pl. **focuses** or **foci**) 1 the centre of interest or activity. 2 sharp visual definition. 3 the point at which an object must be situated for a lens or mirror to produce a clear image of it. 4 a point where rays or sound waves etc. meet. •v. (**focusing, focused** or **focussing, focussed**) 1 bring into focus. 2 adjust the focus of. 3 (**focus on**) concentrate on. □ **focus group** a group assembled to assess a new product, policy, etc. ▪ **focuser** n.

fodder n. food for animals.

foe n. an enemy.

foetid var. of FETID.

foetus var. of FETUS.

fog n. a thick mist. •v. (**fogging, fogged**) 1 become covered with mist. 2 confuse. ▪ **foghorn** a

device making a loud, deep sound as a warning to ships in fog. ▪ **foggy** adj.

fogey (or **fogy**) n. (pl. **fogeys** or **fogies**) an old-fashioned person.

foible n. an odd habit or minor eccentricity.

foil v. prevent from succeeding or doing something. •n. 1 a thin flexible sheet of metal. 2 a person or thing emphasizing another's qualities by contrast. 3 a light, blunt-edged fencing sword.

foist v. (**foist on**) impose an unwelcome person or thing on.

fold v. 1 bend something over on itself so that one part of it covers another. 2 be able to be folded into a flatter shape. 3 clasp in your arms. 4 informal go out of business. 5 mix an ingredient gently into another. •n. 1 a folded part. 2 a line produced by folding. 3 a pen for sheep.

folder n. a folding cover or wallet for loose papers.

foliage n. leaves.

folic acid n. a vitamin found esp. in green vegetables, liver, and kidney.

folio n. (pl. **folios**) 1 a sheet of paper folded once to form four pages of a book. 2 a book made up of folios.

folk pl. n. 1 (or **folks**) informal people in general. 2 (**your folks**) informal your family. 3 (or **folk music**) music in the traditional style of a country or community. □ **folklore** the traditional beliefs and stories of a community.

folksy adj. traditional and homely. ▪ **folksiness** n.

follicle n. a small cavity containing a hair root. ▪ **follicular** adj.

follow → footing

follow v. **1** go or come after. **2** go along a route. **3** be or happen as a result or consequence. **4** act according to an instruction or example. **5** accept as a leader, guide, etc. **6** understand or pay attention to. **7 (follow up)** investigate further. □ **follow suit** do the same as someone else. ■ **follower** n.

following prep. coming after or as a result of. • n. a group of supporters. • adj. next in time or order.

folly n. (pl. **follies**) **1** foolishness. **2** a foolish act. **3** an ornamental building with no practical purpose.

foment v. stir up conflict.

fond adj. **1 (fond of)** having an affection or liking for. **2** affectionate. **3** (of a hope) unlikely to be fulfilled. ■ **fondly** adv. **fondness** n.

fondant n. a paste of sugar and water, used to make sweets and as icing.

fondle v. stroke lovingly.

fondue n. a dish of melted cheese etc. into which pieces of food are dipped.

font n. **1** a large stone bowl in a church holding water for baptism. **2** (or **fount**) a set of type of a particular size and design.

fontanelle n. a soft area between the bones of the skull in a baby or fetus.

food n. any substance that people or animals eat or that plants absorb to stay alive. □ **foodstuff** n. a substance used as food.

fool n. **1** a foolish person. **2** a cold dessert made of puréed fruit and cream. • v. **1** trick or deceive. **2 (fool about/around)** act in a joking or silly way. ■ **foolery** n.

foolhardy adj. recklessly bold. ■ **foolhardiness** n.

foolish adj. silly or unwise. ■ **foolishly** adv. **foolishness** n.

foolproof adj. unable to go wrong or be wrongly used.

foolscap n. a large size of paper.

foot n. (pl. **feet**) **1** the part of the leg below the ankle. **2** the bottom of something vertical. **3** the end of a bed. **4** a unit of length equal to 12 inches (30.48 cm). **5** a basic unit of metre in poetry. • v. informal pay a bill. □ **foot-and-mouth disease** a disease of cattle and sheep, caused by a virus. **footbridge** a bridge for pedestrians. **footfall** the sound of footsteps. **foothill** a low hill at the base of a mountain. **foothold 1** a place where you can put a foot down securely when climbing. **2** a secure position as a basis for progress. **footlights** a row of spotlights along the front of a stage. **footloose** free to do as you please. **footman** a uniformed manservant. **footnote** a note printed at the bottom of a page. **footpath** a path for walkers. **footprint** the mark left by a foot or shoe on the ground. **footsore** having sore feet from much walking. **footstep** a step taken in walking. **footstool** a low stool for resting the feet on when sitting. **footwear** shoes, boots, etc. **footwork** the manner of moving the feet in dancing and sport.

footage n. part of a cinema or television film.

football n. **1** a team game involving kicking a ball, esp. in the UK soccer or (in the US) American football. **2** a large ball used in football. ■ **footballer** n.

footing n. **1** a secure grip with the feet. **2** the basis on which something is established or operates.

footling *adj.* trivial.

fop *n.* a man who is too concerned about his clothes and appearance. ∎ **foppish** *adj.*

for *prep.* **1** relating to. **2** in favour or on behalf of. **3** because of. **4** so as to get, have, or do. **5** in place of. **6** in the direction of. **7** over a period or distance. • *conj.* literary because.

forage *v.* search for food etc. • *n.* fodder.

foray *n.* **1** a sudden attack. **2** a brief attempt to become involved in a new activity.

forbear *v.* (**forbearing, forbore;** *past part.* **forborne**) stop yourself from doing.

forbearing *adj.* patient or tolerant. ∎ **forbearance** *n.*

forbid *v.* (**forbidding, forbade;** *past part.* **forbidden**) **1** refuse to allow. **2** order not to do.

forbidding *adj.* appearing unfriendly or threatening.

force *n.* **1** physical strength or energy. **2** violence or pressure used to achieve something. **3** influence or power. **4** an organized group of soldiers, police, etc. **5** *Physics* a measurable influence causing movement. • *v.* **1** make someone do something against their will. **2** use improper means to achieve. **3** achieve by effort. □ **forcemeat** chopped meat used as a stuffing. **in force 1** in great strength or numbers. **2** in effect.

forceful *adj.* powerful and confident. ∎ **forcefully** *adv.* **forcefulness** *n.*

forceps *pl. n.* pincers used in surgery.

forcible *adj.* done by force. ∎ **forcibly** *adv.*

ford *n.* a shallow place in a river where it can be crossed. • *v.* cross at a ford.

fore *adj.* in or at the front. □ **to the fore** in or to a prominent position.

forearm *n.* the arm from the elbow to the wrist. • *v.* (**be forearmed**) be prepared in advance for danger.

forebear *n.* an ancestor.

foreboding *n.* a feeling that something bad will happen.

forecast *v.* predict a future event. • *n.* a prediction. ∎ **forecaster** *n.*

forecastle (or **fo'c's'le**) /fohk-s'l/ *n.* the front part of a ship below the deck.

foreclose *v.* take possession of a property because the occupant has failed to keep up the mortgage payments. ∎ **foreclosure** *n.*

forecourt *n.* an open area in front of a building.

forefather *n.* an ancestor.

forefinger *n.* the finger next to the thumb.

forefoot *n.* (*pl.* **forefeet**) an animal's front foot.

forefront *n.* the leading position.

foregather *v.* assemble.

forego var. of FORGO.

foregoing *adj.* preceding.

foregone conclusion *n.* a predictable result.

foreground *n.* the part of a view or picture nearest to the observer.

forehand *n.* (in tennis etc.) a stroke played with the palm of the hand facing forwards.

forehead *n.* the part of the face above the eyebrows.

foreign *adj.* **1** of a country or language other than your own. **2** coming from outside. **3** (**foreign**

to) not known to or typical of. ■ **foreigner** n.

> ! -eign, not -iegn: foreign.

foreknowledge n. awareness of something before it happens.

foreleg n. an animal's front leg.

forelock n. a lock of hair just above the forehead.

foreman (or **forewoman**) n. **1** a worker who supervises others. **2** a person who is head of a jury and speaks on its behalf.

foremost adj. highest in importance or position. •adv. in the first place.

forename n. a first name.

forensic adj. **1** of the use of scientific methods to investigate crime. **2** of a court of law.

foreplay n. sexual activity preceding intercourse.

forerunner n. a person or thing coming before and influencing someone or something else.

foresee v. (**foreseeing, foresaw**; past part. **foreseen**) be aware of beforehand. ■ **foreseeable** adj.

foreshadow v. be a sign or warning of.

foreshore n. the part of a shore between the highest and lowest levels reached by the sea.

foreshorten v. **1** portray an object as closer than it really is. **2** end something prematurely.

foresight n. the ability to predict future events.

foreskin n. the roll of skin covering the end of the penis.

forest n. a large area covered thickly with trees. ■ **forested** adj.

forestall v. prevent or delay by taking action first.

forestry n. the science or practice of planting and managing forests. ■ **forester** n.

foretaste n. a sample of something that lies ahead.

foretell v. (**foretelling, foretold**) predict.

forethought n. careful planning for the future.

forever adv. **1** for all future time. **2** continually.

forewarn v. warn in advance.

foreword n. an introduction in a book.

forfeit v. lose property or a right as a penalty for wrongdoing. •n. a penalty for wrongdoing. ■ **forfeiture** n.

forge v. **1** make or shape a metal object by heating and hammering. **2** make a fraudulent copy of. **3** move forward gradually or steadily. •n. **1** a blacksmith's workshop. **2** a furnace for heating metal. ■ **forger** n. **forgery** n.

forget v. (**forgetting, forgot**; past part. **forgotten**) **1** fail or be unable to remember. **2** no longer think of. **3** (**forget yourself**) behave inappropriately. □ **forget-me-not** a plant with small blue flowers. ■ **forgettable** adj.

forgetful adj. tending not to remember. ■ **forgetfully** adv. **forgetfulness** n.

forgive v. (**forgiving, forgave**; past part. **forgiven**) stop feeling angry or resentful towards or about. ■ **forgivable** adj. **forgiveness** n.

forgo (or **forego**) v. (**forgoing, forwent**; past part. **forgone**) go without something you want.

fork n. **1** a small pronged implement for lifting or holding food. **2** a large pronged tool for digging or lifting. **3** a point where a road divides into two parts. **4** either of two such parts. •v. **1** divide into two parts. **2** take one route or the other at a fork. **3** dig or lift with a fork. **4** (**fork out**) *informal* pay money. ■ **forklift truck** a vehicle with a forked device for lifting and carrying loads. ■ **forked** *adj.*

forlorn *adj.* **1** sad and alone. **2** unlikely to succeed or be achieved. ■ **forlornly** *adv.*

form n. **1** shape or arrangement. **2** a way in which a thing exists. **3** a type. **4** a document with blank spaces for information. **5** the current standard of a sports player or team. **6** a person's mood or state of health. **7** a school class or year. **8** the way something is usually done. •v. **1** create. **2** constitute. **3** establish or develop. ■ **formless** *adj.*

formal *adj.* **1** suitable for official or important occasions. **2** officially recognized. **3** having a recognized form, rules, etc. ■ **formalize** (or **-ise**) v. ■ **formally** *adv.*

formaldehyde /for-mal-di-hyd/ n. a gas used in solution as a preservative and disinfectant.

formalin n. a solution of formaldehyde in water.

formalism n. excessive concern with rules and outward form.

formality n. (*pl.* **formalities**) **1** a thing done to follow customs or rules. **2** correct and formal behaviour.

format n. **1** the way something is arranged. **2** the shape and size of a book etc. **3** a structure for the processing, storage, etc. of computer data. •v. (**formatting**, **formatted**) put into a format.

formation n. **1** the act of forming. **2** a structure or arrangement.

formative *adj.* influencing development.

former *adj.* **1** having been previously. **2** in the past. **3** referring to the first of two things mentioned.

formerly *adv.* in the past.

formic acid n. an acid in the fluid discharged by some ants.

formidable *adj.* causing fear or respect. ■ **formidably** *adv.*

formula n. (*pl.* **formulae** or **formulas**) **1** a set of symbols showing chemical constituents or expressing a mathematical relationship. **2** a fixed form of words used in particular situations. **3** a list of ingredients. **4** a classification of racing car.

formulaic *adj.* **1** containing a set form of words. **2** following a rule or style too closely.

formulate v. **1** create methodically. **2** express precisely. ■ **formulation** n.

fornicate v. have sex outside marriage. ■ **fornication** n. **fornicator** n.

forsake v. (**forsaking**, **forsook**; *past part.* **forsaken**) **1** abandon. **2** give up.

forsooth *adv.* *old use* indeed.

forswear v. (**forswearing**, **forswore**; *past part.* **forsworn**) agree to give up or do without.

forsythia /for-sy-thi-uh/ n. a shrub with bright yellow flowers.

fort n. a fortified building.

forte /for-tay/ n. a thing for which someone has a particular talent. •*adv.* *Music* loudly.

forth *adv.* **1** forwards or into view. **2** onwards in time.

forthcoming *adj.* **1** about to happen or appear. **2** willing to reveal information.

forthright *adj.* direct and outspoken.

forthwith *adv.* without delay.

fortify *v.* (**fortifying, fortified**) **1** strengthen against attack. **2** invigorate or encourage. **3** increase the alcoholic content or nutritional value of. ■ **fortification** *n.*

fortissimo *adv. Music* very loudly.

fortitude *n.* courage when facing pain or trouble.

fortnight *n.* a period of two weeks. ■ **fortnightly** *adj. & adv.*

fortress *n.* a fortified building or town.

fortuitous *adj.* **1** happening by chance. **2** lucky. ■ **fortuitously** *adv.*

fortunate *adj.* lucky. ■ **fortunately** *adv.*

fortune *n.* **1** chance as a force affecting people's lives. **2** luck. **3** (**fortunes**) the success or failure of a person or undertaking. **4** a large amount of money. □ **fortune-teller** a person who predicts future events in people's lives.

forty *adj. & n.* (*pl.* **forties**) ten less than fifty; 40. □ **forty winks** *informal* a short sleep. □ **fortieth** *adj. & n.*

forum *n.* a meeting or opportunity for an exchange of views.

forward *adv. & adj.* **1** in the direction you are facing or moving. **2** towards a successful end. **3** ahead in time. **4** in or near the front. •*adj.* too familiar or confident. •*n.* an attacking player in a sport. •*v.* send a letter etc. on to a further destination. ■ **forwards** *adv.*

forwent past of **FORGO**.

fossil *n.* the remains of a prehistoric plant or animal that have become hardened into rock. □ **fossil fuel** a fuel such as coal, formed from the remains of animals and plants. ■ **fossilize** (or **-ise**) *v.*

foster *v.* **1** encourage the development of. **2** bring up a child that is not your own.

fought past & past part. of **FIGHT**.

foul *adj.* **1** having a disgusting smell or taste. **2** very bad. **3** against the rules or decent. **4** polluted. •*n.* an action that breaks the rules of a sport. •*v.* **1** make foul or dirty. **2** (in sport) commit a foul against. **3** (**foul up**) make a mistake with. **4** entangle or jam. ■ **foully** *adv.*

found[1] past & past part. of **FIND**.

found[2] *v.* **1** establish an institution. **2** (**be founded on**) be based on. **3** melt and mould metal to make an object.

foundation *n.* **1** the lowest weight-bearing part of a building. **2** an underlying basis. **3** the act of founding an institution. **4** an institution. **5** a cream applied as a base for other make-up.

founder *n.* a person who founds an institution etc. •*v.* **1** (of a plan etc.) fail. **2** (of a ship) sink.

foundling *n.* an infant abandoned by its parents.

foundry *n.* (*pl.* **foundries**) a workshop or factory for casting metal.

fount *n.* **1** a source. **2** *literary* a spring or fountain. **3** var. of **FONT** (sense 2).

fountain *n.* **1** a decorative structure pumping out a jet of water. **2** a source. □ **fountainhead** a source. **fountain pen** a pen with a container supplying ink to the nib.

four adj. & n. one more than three; 4. □ **four-poster** a bed with four posts supporting a canopy. **foursome** a group of four people.

four-wheel drive a vehicle with a system providing power directly to all four wheels. ■ **fourfold** adj. & adv.

fourteen adj. & n. one more than thirteen; 14. ■ **fourteenth** adj. & n.

fourth adj. & n. next after third. **2** a quarter. ■ **fourthly** adv.

fowl n. **1** a bird kept for its eggs or meat, e.g. a hen. **2** birds as a group.

fox n. an animal with a bushy tail and a reddish coat. ·v. informal baffle or deceive. □ **foxglove** a tall plant with bell-shaped flowers. **foxhole** a hole in the ground used by troops as a shelter. **foxhound** a hound trained to hunt foxes in packs. **foxtrot** a ballroom dance with slow and quick steps. ■ **foxy** adj.

foyer /foy-ay/ n. a large entrance hall in a hotel or theatre.

fracas /fra-kah/ n. (pl. **fracas**) a noisy disturbance or quarrel.

fraction n. **1** a number that is not a whole number. **2** a very small part or amount. ■ **fractional** adj. **fractionally** adv.

fractious adj. **1** bad-tempered. **2** difficult to control.

fracture n. **1** a crack or break. **2** the cracking or breaking of something. ·v. break or break up.

fragile adj. **1** easily broken or damaged. **2** delicate or vulnerable. ■ **fragility** n.

fragment n. **1** a small part broken off. **2** an incomplete part. ·v. break

into fragments. ■ **fragmentary** adj. **fragmentation** n.

fragrance n. **1** a pleasant, sweet smell. **2** a perfume or aftershave.

fragrant adj. having a pleasant, sweet smell.

frail adj. **1** weak. **2** fragile. ■ **frailty** n.

frame n. **1** a rigid structure surrounding a picture etc. or supporting something. **2** a person's body. **3** a conceptual structure. **4** a single picture in a series forming a cinema or video film. **5** a single game of snooker. ·v. **1** put or form a frame around. **2** develop a plan etc. **3** informal produce false evidence against. □ **frame of mind** a particular mood. **framework** a supporting structure.

franc n. the basic unit of money of Switzerland (formerly also of France and Belgium).

franchise n. **1** authorization to use or sell a company's products. **2** the right to vote in public elections. ·v. grant a franchise to.

francium n. a radioactive metallic element.

frank adj. **1** honest and direct. **2** open or undisguised. ·v. mark a letter etc. to indicate that postage has been paid. ■ **frankly** adv. **frankness** n.

frankfurter n. a smoked sausage.

frankincense n. a scented gum burnt as incense.

frantic adj. **1** wildly agitated. **2** hurried and confused. ■ **frantically** adv.

fraternal adj. like a brother.

fraternity n. (pl. **fraternities**) **1** a group with a common interest. **2** friendship and support in a group.

fraternize (or **-ise**) v. be on friendly terms. ■ **fraternization** n.

fratricide n. the killing of your brother or sister. ■ **fratricidal** adj.

fraud n. **1** the crime of deceiving someone to get money or goods. **2** a person who deceives others by falsely claiming to be something. ■ **fraudster** n. **fraudulence** n. **fraudulent** adj.

fraught adj. **1** (**fraught with**) filled with something undesirable. **2** anxious or stressful.

Fräulein /froy-lyn/ n. a title for a young German woman.

fray v. **1** (of a fabric or rope) unravel or become worn at the edge. **2** (of a person's nerves or temper) show the effects of strain. •n. a battle, fight, or other conflict.

frazzle n. informal an exhausted state. ■ **frazzled** adj.

freak n. **1** informal a person obsessed with a particular interest. **2** an abnormal person, animal, or plant. •v. (**freak out**) informal react in a wild, excited, or shocked way. ■ **freakish** adj. **freaky** adj.

freckle n. a small light brown spot on the skin. ■ **freckled** adj. **freckly** adj.

free adj. (**freer, freest**) **1** not under the control of anyone else. **2** not confined, obstructed, or fixed. **3** not busy or being used. **4** (**free of/from**) not containing or affected by. **5** costing nothing. **6** (**free with**) giving without restraint. •adv. at no cost. •v. set free. □ **free fall** downward movement under the force of gravity. **freehand** drawn by hand without a ruler etc. **freehold** permanent ownership of land or property with the freedom to sell it when you wish. **free house** a pub not

controlled by a brewery. **freelance** **1** self-employed and working for different companies. **2** (or **freelancer**) a freelance worker. **freeloader** informal a person who takes advantage of other people's generosity. **the free market** a system in which prices are determined by unrestricted competition between private companies. **free radical** a highly reactive molecule with one odd electron not paired up in a chemical bond. **free-range** (of farming) in which animals are kept in conditions where they may move around freely. **freestyle** having few restrictions on the technique to be used. **freeway** US a dual carriageway. **freewheel** ride a bicycle without pedalling. **free will** the power to act according to your own wishes. ■ **freely** adv.

freebie n. informal a thing given free of charge.

freedom n. **1** the right to act or speak freely. **2** the state of being free. **3** a special honour or right granted by a city.

Freemason n. a member of an organization established for mutual help, which holds secret ceremonies. ■ **Freemasonry** n.

freesia n. a plant with scented flowers.

freeze v. (**freezing, froze**; past part. **frozen**) **1** change from a liquid to a solid as a result of extreme cold. **2** become blocked or rigid with ice. **3** be very cold. **4** preserve by storing at a very low temperature. **5** become motionless. **6** keep or stop at a fixed level or in a fixed state. •n. **1** an act of freezing. **2** a period of very cold weather. □ **freeze-dry** preserve by freezing and removing the ice in a vacuum.

freezer n. a refrigerated cabinet for preserving food at very low temperatures.

freight n. goods transported in bulk. •v. transport goods.

freighter n. a large ship or aircraft designed to carry freight.

French adj. of France. •n. the language of France. □ **French fries** chips. **French horn** a brass instrument with a coiled tube. **French polish** a kind of wood polish producing a high gloss. **French windows** a pair of glazed doors in an outside wall.

frenetic adj. fast, energetic, and disorganized. ■ **frenetically** adv.

frenzy n. (pl. **frenzies**) uncontrolled excitement or wild behaviour. ■ **frenzied** adj.

frequency n. (pl. **frequencies**) **1** the rate at which something occurs. **2** the state of being frequent. **3** the number of cycles per second of a sound, light, or radio wave. **4** the particular waveband at which radio signals are transmitted.

frequent adj. **1** occurring or done many times at short intervals. **2** doing something often. •v. visit a place often. ■ **frequently** adv.

fresco n. (pl. **frescoes** or **frescos**) a painting done on wet plaster on a wall or ceiling.

fresh adj. **1** new or different. **2** (of food) recently made or obtained. **3** recently created. **4** (of water) not salty. **5** (of the wind) cool and fairly strong. **6** pleasantly clean and cool. **7** lively. **8** informal overfamiliar. □ **freshman** (or **fresher**) a first-year college or university student. **freshwater** of or found

in fresh water. ■ **freshen** v. **freshener** n. **freshly** adv. **freshness** n.

fret v. (**fretting**, **fretted**) be anxious or restless. •n. each of the ridges on the fingerboard of a guitar etc.

fretful adj. anxious or irritated. ■ **fretfully** adv.

fretsaw n. a narrow saw used for fretwork.

fretwork n. decorative patterns cut in wood.

friable adj. easily crumbled.

friar n. a member of certain religious orders of men.

friary n. (pl. **friaries**) a building occupied by friars.

fricassée /fri-kuh-say/ n. a dish of pieces of meat in a white sauce.

friction n. **1** the resistance encountered by one surface when moving over another. **2** the action of one surface rubbing against another. **3** conflict or disagreement.

Friday n. the day before Saturday.

fridge n. an appliance for keeping food and drink cold.

fried past & past part. of **FRY**.

friend n. **1** a person that you like and know well. **2** a supporter of a cause or organization. ■ **friendship** n.

❗ *-ie-*, not *-ei-*: friend.

friendly adj. (**friendlier, friendliest**) **1** kind and pleasant to others. **2** not harmful to a specified thing. •n. (pl. **friendlies**) a game not forming part of a serious competition. ■ **friendliness** n.

frieze n. a band of decoration around a wall.

frigate n. a kind of fast warship.

fright n. **1** a sudden strong feeling of fear. **2** a shock.

frighten v. make afraid.
■ **frightening** adj.

frightful adj. **1** very unpleasant, serious, or shocking. **2** informal very bad. ■ **frightfully** adv.

frigid adj. **1** very cold. **2** (of a woman) unable to be sexually aroused. ■ **frigidity** n.

frill n. **1** a strip of gathered or pleated material used as a decorative edging. **2** (frills) unnecessary extra features. ■ **frilled** adj. **frilly** adj.

fringe n. **1** a decorative edging of threads on clothing etc. **2** the front part of someone's hair that hangs over the forehead. **3** the outer part of something. •adj. not part of the mainstream. •v. give or form a fringe to. □ **fringe benefit** a benefit received in addition to regular wages.

frippery n. (pl. **fripperies**) a showy or unnecessary ornament.

frisbee n. trademark a plastic disc for skimming through the air as an outdoor game.

frisk v. **1** pass the hands over to search for hidden weapons or drugs. **2** skip or move playfully.

frisky adj. (**friskier**, **friskiest**) playful and lively.

frisson /free-son/ n. a sudden shiver of excitement.

fritter v. waste time or money on trivial things. •n. a piece of food coated in batter and deep-fried.

frivolous adj. **1** not having any serious purpose or value. **2** not treating things seriously.
■ **frivolity** n. **frivolously** adv.

frizz v. (of hair) form into a mass of tight curls. •n. a mass of tight curls. ■ **frizzy** adj.

frock n. a dress. □ **frock coat** a man's long, double-breasted coat.

frog n. a tailless amphibian with long hind legs for leaping.
□ **frogman** a diver with a rubber suit, flippers, and breathing equipment. **frogmarch** force someone to walk while pinning their arms from behind. **frogspawn** a mass of frogs' eggs surrounded by transparent jelly.

frolic v. (**frolicking**, **frolicked**) play or move about in a cheerful, lively way. •n. a playful action.

from prep. **1** indicating the starting point, source, or cause. **2** indicating separation, removal, or prevention.

fromage frais /from-**ahzh** fray/ n. a smooth soft cheese.

frond n. the leaf or leaf-like part of a palm, fern, etc.

front n. **1** the part of an object that faces forward or that is normally seen first. **2** the position directly ahead. **3** the furthest position reached by an army. **4** the forward edge of an advancing mass of air. **5** a particular situation. **6** a false appearance or way of behaving. **7** a cover for secret activities. •adj. of or at the front. •v. **1** have the front towards. **2** place or be at the front of. **3** provide with a specified front. **4** be the leader or presenter of. ■ **frontage 1** the front of a building. **2** a strip of land next to a street or waterway. **frontbencher** a member of the cabinet or shadow cabinet, who sits in the front seats in the House of Commons. **front line** the part of an army closest to the enemy. **front runner** the leader in a competition. ■ **frontal** adj. **frontally** adv.

frontier n. **1** a border separating two countries. **2** the extreme limit of settled land.

frontispiece n. an illustration facing the title page of a book.

frost n. **1** small white ice crystals on surfaces. **2** cold weather when frost forms. •v. cover with frost.

frostbite n. injury to body tissues caused by exposure to extreme cold. ■ **frostbitten** adj.

frosted adj. (of glass) having a semi-transparent textured surface.

frosting n. US icing.

frosty adj. (**frostier, frostiest**) **1** very cold with frost forming on surfaces. **2** cold and unfriendly. ■ **frostily** adv. **frostiness** n.

froth n. a mass of small bubbles. •v. form or contain froth. ■ **frothy** adj.

frown v. **1** wrinkle the forehead in disapproval or thought. **2** (**frown on**) disapprove of. •n. a frowning expression.

frowsty adj. warm and stuffy.

frowzy (or **frowsy**) adj. scruffy and dingy.

froze past of FREEZE.

frozen past part. of FREEZE.

fructose n. a sugar found in honey and fruit.

frugal adj. **1** sparing with money or food. **2** (of a meal) plain and cheap. ■ **frugality** n. **frugally** adv.

fruit n. **1** an edible fleshy part of a plant that contains seed. **2** the seed-bearing part of any plant. **3** the result of work or activity. •v. produce fruit. ▢ **bear fruit** have good results. **fruit machine** a coin-operated gambling machine.

fruiterer n. a person who sells fruit.

fruitful adj. producing a lot of fruit or good results. ■ **fruitfully** adv. **fruitfulness** n.

fruition n. the fulfilment of a plan or project.

fruitless adj. failing to achieve the desired results. ■ **fruitlessly** adv.

fruity adj. (**fruitier, fruitiest**) **1** like or containing fruit. **2** (of a voice) deep and rich. ■ **fruitiness** n.

frump n. a dowdy woman. ■ **frumpy** adj.

frustrate v. **1** prevent from progressing or succeeding. **2** cause to feel dissatisfied. ■ **frustration** n.

fry[1] v. (**frying, fried**) cook in hot fat or oil. •n. (**fries**) chips. ▢ **frying pan** a shallow pan used for frying. ■ **fryer** n.

fry[2] pl. n. young fish.

ft abbrev. foot or feet.

fuchsia /fyoo-shuh/ n. a plant with drooping pink flowers.

fuddled adj. unable to think clearly.

fuddy-duddy n. (pl. **fuddy-duddies**) informal an old-fashioned and pompous person.

fudge n. **1** a soft sweet made of sugar, butter, and milk. **2** an attempt to present an issue in a vague way. •v. present in a vague way.

fuel n. **1** material burnt to produce heat or power. **2** something that stirs up emotion. •v. (**fuelling, fuelled**; US **fueling, fueled**) **1** supply with fuel. **2** stir up strong feeling.

fug n. informal a warm, stuffy atmosphere. ■ **fuggy** adj.

fugitive n. a person who has escaped from captivity or is in hiding.

fugue /fyoog/ n. a musical composition in which a short melody is successively repeated by different voices or instruments.

fulcrum n. the point of support on which a lever turns.

fulfil (US **fulfill**) v. (**fulfilling, fulfilled**) 1 achieve something desired or promised. 2 meet a requirement. 3 **fulfil yourself** fully develop your abilities. ■ **fulfilment** n.

full adj. 1 holding as much or as many as possible. 2 (**full of**) having a lot of. 3 complete. 4 rounded. 5 (of flavour etc.) strong or rich. • adv. 1 directly. 2 very. □ **full back** (in football) a defender who plays at the side. **full-blooded** wholehearted and enthusiastic. **full-blown** fully developed. **full moon** the moon when its whole disc is illuminated. **full-scale** (of a model etc.) of the same size as the thing represented. **full stop** a punctuation mark (.) used at the end of a sentence or an abbreviation. **full time 1** the end of a sports match. 2 (**full-time**) working for the whole of the available time. ■ **fully** adv. **fullness** n.

fulminate v. protest strongly. ■ **fulmination** n.

fulsome adj. 1 excessively flattering. 2 large in size or quantity.

fumble v. 1 use the hands clumsily. 2 deal with clumsily. • n. an act of fumbling.

fume n. a strong-smelling gas or vapour. • v. 1 send out fumes. 2 feel great anger.

fumigate v. disinfect with chemical fumes. ■ **fumigation** n.

fun n. light-hearted pleasure, or something that provides it. □ **funfair** a gathering of rides, sideshows, etc. for entertainment. **make fun of** mock.

function n. 1 a purpose or natural activity of a person or thing. 2 a large or formal social event. 3 *Math.* a quantity whose value depends on the varying values of others. • v. 1 work or operate. 2 (**function as**) fulfil the purpose of.

functional adj. 1 of a function. 2 practical and useful. 3 working or operating. ■ **functionality** n. **functionally** adv.

functionary n. (pl. **functionaries**) an official.

fund n. 1 a sum of money for a special purpose. 2 (**funds**) financial resources. 3 a large stock. • v. provide with money.

fundamental adj. of basic importance. • n. a basic rule or principle. ■ **fundamentally** adv.

fundamentalism n. strict following of the basic teachings of a religion. ■ **fundamentalist** n. & adj.

funeral n. a ceremony in which a dead person is buried or cremated. □ **funeral director** an undertaker.

funerary adj. of or used for a funeral.

funereal adj. solemn or mournful.

fungicide n. a chemical that destroys fungus. ■ **fungicidal** adj.

fungus n. (pl. **fungi**) an organism without leaves or flowers that grows on other plants or on decaying matter (e.g. a mushroom). ■ **fungal** adj.

funicular adj. (of a railway) operating by cable up and down a steep slope.

funk n. a style of dance music with a strong rhythm.

funky adj. (**funkier, funkiest**) informal **1** having a strong dance rhythm. **2** stylish and modern.

funnel n. **1** a tube with a wide top for pouring liquid or powder into small openings. **2** a chimney on a ship or steam engine. •v. (**funnelling, funnelled**; US **funneling, funneled**) move through a funnel or narrow space.

funny adj. (**funnier, funniest**) **1** causing amusement. **2** strange. □ **funny bone** informal the part of the elbow over which a very sensitive nerve passes. ■ **funnily** adv.

fur n. **1** the short, soft hair of some animals. **2** the skin of an animal with fur on it. **3** a deposit formed by hard water on the inside of a kettle etc. ■ **furred** adj. **furriness** n. **furry** adj.

furious adj. **1** very angry. **2** intense or energetic. ■ **furiously** adv.

furl v. roll up neatly and securely.

furlong n. an eighth of a mile.

furlough /fer-loh/ n. a time when you have permission to leave your work.

furnace n. an enclosed chamber for heating material to very high temperatures.

furnish v. **1** provide with furniture. **2** supply or provide.

furnishings pl. n. furniture and fittings.

furniture n. the movable objects used to make a room or building suitable for living or working in.

furore /fyoo-ror-i/ (US **furor**) n. an outbreak of public anger or excitement.

furrier n. a person who deals in furs.

furrow n. **1** a long, narrow trench cut in the ground. **2** a deep wrinkle on the face. •v. make a furrow in.

further adv. (or **farther**) **1** at, to, or over a greater distance. **2** at or to a more advanced stage. **3** in addition. •adj. **1** (or **farther**) more distant in space. **2** additional. •v. help the progress of. □ **further education** education below degree level for people above school age.

furtherance n. the advancement of a plan or interest.

furthermore adv. in addition.

furthest (or **farthest**) adj. & adv. at or to the greatest distance.

furtive adj. secretively trying to avoid notice. ■ **furtively** adv.

fury n. (pl. **furies**) **1** extreme anger. **2** violent intensity.

furze n. gorse.

fuse v. **1** combine to form a whole. **2** melt something so as to join it with something else. **3** (of an electrical appliance) stop working when a fuse melts. **4** fit with a fuse. •n. **1** a strip of wire that melts and breaks an electric circuit if the current reaches an unsafe level. **2** a length of material lit to explode a bomb or firework. **3** a device in a bomb controlling the timing of the explosion. ■ **fusible** adj.

fuselage /fyoo-zuh-lahzh/ n. the main body of an aircraft.

Fusilier /fyoo-zi-leer/ n. a soldier of certain regiments.

fusillade /fyoo-zi-**layd**/ n. a series of shots fired at the same time or one after the other.

fusion n. the act of fusing, esp. of atomic nuclei with the release of much energy.

fuss n. 1 unnecessary excitement or activity. 2 a vigorous protest. • v. show unnecessary concern.

fussy adj. (fussier, fussiest) 1 hard to please. 2 full of unnecessary detail. ■ **fussily** adv. **fussiness** n.

fustian n. a thick twilled cotton.

fusty adj. 1 smelling stale or damp. 2 old-fashioned.

futile adj. pointless. ■ **futility** n.

futon /**foo**-ton/ n. a padded mattress that can be rolled up.

future n. 1 time still to come. 2 what may happen in time still to come. 3 a prospect of success. • adj. existing or occurring in the future.

futuristic adj. with very modern technology or design.

fuzz n. a frizzy mass of hair or fibre.

fuzzy adj. (fuzzier, fuzziest) 1 frizzy. 2 blurred; not clear. ■ **fuzzily** adv. **fuzziness** n.

Gg

G (or **g**) abbrev. 1 giga-. 2 grams. 3 gravity.

gab v. (gabbing, gabbed) informal talk at length. ■ **the gift of the gab** the ability to speak fluently and persuasively.

gabble v. talk quickly and indistinctly.

gaberdine (or **gabardine**) n. a smooth, hard-wearing cloth for making raincoats.

gable n. the triangular upper part of a wall at the end of a ridged roof. ■ **gabled** adj.

gad v. (gadding, gadded) (**gad about/around**) informal go from place to place enjoying yourself. ■ **gadabout** n.

gadfly n. a fly that bites livestock.

gadget n. a small mechanical device. ■ **gadgetry** n.

Gaelic /**gay**-lik, **ga**-lik/ n. a language spoken in parts of Ireland and western Scotland.

gaff n. a hooked stick for landing large fish.

gaffe n. an embarrassing blunder.

gaffer n. informal 1 a boss. 2 an old man.

gag n. 1 a piece of cloth put over a person's mouth to silence them. 2 a joke. • v. (gagging, gagged) 1 put a gag on. 2 choke or retch.

gaga adj. informal senile.

gage US = GAUGE.

gaggle n. 1 a flock of geese. 2 informal a disorderly group.

gaiety n. the state of being light-hearted and cheerful.

gaily adv. 1 cheerfully. 2 thoughtlessly. 3 colourfully.

gain v. 1 obtain or secure. 2 reach. 3 (**gain on**) come closer to someone or something pursued. 4 increase in weight, speed, etc. 5 (of a clock) become fast. • n. 1 a thing gained. 2 an increase in wealth or value.

gainful adj. paid; profitable.
■ **gainfully** adv.

gainsay v. (**gainsaying, gainsaid**) deny or contradict.

gait n. a way of walking.

gaiter n. a covering for the ankle and lower leg.

gala n. 1 a social occasion with entertainment. 2 a swimming competition.

galaxy n. (pl. **galaxies**) 1 a system of millions or billions of stars. 2 (**the Galaxy**) the galaxy including the sun and the earth.
■ **galactic** adj.

gale n. 1 a very strong wind. 2 an outburst of laughter.

gall /gawl/ n. 1 bold and disrespectful behaviour. 2 annoyance or resentment. 3 a sore made by rubbing. 4 an abnormal growth on plants and trees. • v. annoy or irritate. □ **gall bladder** an organ beneath the liver, storing bile. **gallstone** a small hard mass forming in the gall bladder.

gallant adj. 1 brave. 2 charming and attentive. ■ **gallantry** n.

galleon n. hist. a large sailing ship.

gallery n. (pl. **galleries**) 1 a building for displaying works of art. 2 an upstairs sitting area in a hall, theatre, etc. 3 a long room or passage.

galley n. (pl. **galleys**) 1 a small kitchen in a ship or aircraft. 2 hist. a sailing ship with several banks of oars.

Gallic adj. of France or the French.

gallium n. a soft metallic element.

gallivant v. informal go from place to place enjoying yourself.

gallon n. a measure for liquids, equal to eight pints (4.55 litres).

gallop n. 1 a horse's fastest pace. 2 a ride on a horse at a gallop. • v. (**galloping, galloped**) 1 go at the pace of a gallop. 2 go fast.

gallows pl. n. a structure with a noose for hanging criminals.

galore adj. in abundance: there were prizes galore.

galoshes pl. n. rubber overshoes.

galvanize (or **-ise**) v. 1 shock or excite into action. 2 (**galvanized**) (of iron or steel) coated with zinc.

gambit n. an action or remark intended to gain an advantage.

gamble v. 1 play games of chance for money. 2 bet money. 3 risk in the hope of gaining something. • n. a risky action. ■ **gambler** n.

gambol v. (**gambolling, gambolled**; US **gamboling, gamboled**) run or jump about playfully.

game n. 1 an activity done for amusement or sport. 2 a period of play, ending in a final result. 3 wild mammals or birds hunted for sport or food. • adj. eager and willing. • v. gamble for money. □ **gamekeeper** a person employed to breed and protect game. **gamesmanship** the tactic of winning games by making an opponent feel less confident. ■ **gamely** adv.

gamete n. a reproductive cell.

gamine adj. (of a girl) having a mischievous, boyish charm.

gamma rays pl. n. electromagnetic radiation of shorter wavelength than X-rays.

gammon n. cured ham.

gammy adj. informal painful or injured.

gamut n. the whole range or scope.

gamy (or **gamey**) adj. (of meat) having the strong flavour or smell of game when it is high.

gander n. 1 a male goose. 2 informal a look.

gang n. an organized group, esp. of criminals or manual workers. •v. (**gang up**) join together against someone.

gangling (or **gangly**) adj. tall, thin, and awkward.

ganglion n. (pl. **ganglia** or **ganglions**) 1 a mass of nerve cells. 2 a swelling on a tendon.

gangplank n. a movable plank used to board or leave a ship.

gangrene n. the death of body tissue. ■ **gangrenous** adj.

gangster n. a member of a gang of violent criminals.

gangway n. 1 a passage between rows of seats. 2 a movable bridge linking a ship to the shore.

gannet n. 1 a large seabird. 2 informal a greedy person.

gantry n. (pl. **gantries**) an overhead structure supporting heavy equipment.

gaol var. of JAIL.

gap n. 1 a break or hole. 2 a space or interval. □ **gap year** a break taken by a student between school and university or college education. ■ **gappy** adj.

gape v. 1 be or become wide open. 2 stare with the mouth open wide in amazement.

garage n. 1 a building for storing a vehicle. 2 a place which sells fuel or which repairs and sells vehicles.

garb n. clothing. •v. (**be garbed**) be clothed.

garbage n. rubbish.

garble v. confuse or distort a message etc.

garden n. 1 an area next to a house, with a lawn or flowers. 2 (**gardens**) a public park. •v. work in a garden. ■ **gardener** n.

gargantuan adj. enormous.

gargle v. wash the throat with a liquid that is kept there by slowly breathing out through it.

gargoyle n. a grotesque face or figure carved on the gutter of a building.

garish /gair-ish/ adj. unpleasantly bright and showy. ■ **garishly** adv.

garland n. a wreath of flowers and leaves. •v. decorate with a garland.

garlic n. the bulb of a plant of the onion family, used in cookery. ■ **garlicky** adj.

garment n. an item of clothing.

garner v. gather or collect.

garnet n. a red semi-precious stone.

garnish v. decorate food. •n. a decoration for food.

garret n. an attic.

garrison n. a group of troops in a fortress or town. •v. provide with a garrison.

garrotte (US **garrote**) v. strangle with a wire or cord. •n. a wire or cord used for garrotting.

garrulous adj. very talkative.

garter n. a band worn around the leg to keep up a stocking or sock.

gas n. (pl. **gases** or US **gasses**) 1 an air-like substance which expands to fill any available space. 2 gas used as a fuel. 3 US informal petrol. •v. (**gassing**, **gassed**) 1 harm or kill with gas. 2 informal chatter.

g

□ **gas chamber** a room filled with poisonous gas to kill people. **gas mask** a mask used as protection against poisonous gas. ■ **gassy** *adj.*

gaseous *adj.* of or like a gas.

gash *n.* a long deep cut. •*v.* make a gash in.

gasket *n.* a sheet or ring of rubber sealing a joint in an engine etc.

gasoline *n. US* petrol.

gasp *v.* draw in breath suddenly or with difficulty. •*n.* a sudden quick breath.

gastric *adj.* of the stomach.

gastro-enteritis *n.* inflammation of the stomach and intestines.

gastronomy *n.* the art of cooking and eating good food. ■ **gastronomic** *adj.*

gastropod *n.* a mollusc such as a snail or slug.

gate *n.* **1** a hinged barrier across an opening in a wall, fence, etc. **2** an exit from an airport building to an aircraft. **3** the number of people paying to attend a sports event. □ **gatecrash** go to a party without an invitation. **gateway 1** an opening closed by a gate. **2** a means of access.

gateau *n.* (*pl.* **gateaus** or **gateaux**) a cake with layers of cream or fruit.

gather *v.* **1** come or bring together. **2** increase in speed, force, etc. **3** understand to be the case. **4** collect plants or fruit for food. **5** pull fabric into folds by drawing thread through it. •*n.* (**gathers**) a gathered part of a garment.

gathering *n.* an assembled group.

gauche /gohsh/ *adj.* socially awkward.

gaucho /gow-choh/ *n.* (*pl.* **gauchos**) a South American cowboy.

gaudy *adj.* (**gaudier, gaudiest**) tastelessly bright or showy. ■ **gaudily** *adv.* **gaudiness** *n.*

gauge (*US gage*) *n.* **1** an instrument for measuring the amount or level of something. **2** a measure of thickness, size, etc. **3** the distance between the rails of a railway track. •*v.* estimate, measure, or judge.

❗ *gau-*, not *gua-*: gauge

gaunt *adj.* lean and haggard.

gauntlet *n.* a glove with a long wide cuff. □ **run the gauntlet** go through an intimidating crowd or experience. **throw down the gauntlet** set a challenge.

gauze *n.* **1** a thin transparent fabric. **2** a fine wire mesh. ■ **gauzy** *adj.*

gave past of **GIVE**.

gavel *n.* a small hammer used by an auctioneer or judge to call for attention or order.

gavotte *n.* a French dance of the 18th century.

gawky *adj.* awkward and ungainly.

gawp *v. informal* stare in a stupid or rude way.

gay *adj.* **1** homosexual. **2** *dated* light-hearted and carefree. **3** *dated* brightly coloured. •*n.* a homosexual person.

gaze *v.* look steadily. •*n.* a steady look.

gazebo /guh-zee-boh/ *n.* (*pl.* **gazebos**) a garden shelter with open sides.

gazelle *n.* a small antelope.

gazette *n.* a journal or newspaper.

gazetteer *n.* a list of place names.

gazump v. informal offer or accept a higher price for a house after a lower price has already been accepted.

GB abbrev. **1** Great Britain. **2** (or **Gb**) gigabytes.

GBH abbrev. grievous bodily harm.

GCE abbrev. General Certificate of Education.

GCSE abbrev. General Certificate of Secondary Education.

GDP abbrev. gross domestic product.

gear n. **1** (**gears**) a set of toothed wheels that connects the engine to the wheels of a vehicle and controls its speed. **2** a particular setting of gears. **3** informal equipment or clothing. • v. **1** adapt for a purpose. **2** adjust the gears in a vehicle. **3** (**gear up**) prepare. ◻ **gearbox** a set of gears with its casing. **in** (or **out of**) **gear** with a gear (or no gear) engaged.

gecko n. (pl. **geckos** or **geckoes**) a tropical lizard.

geek n. informal **1** an awkward or unfashionable person. **2** an obsessive enthusiast. ■ **geeky** adj.

geese pl. of **GOOSE**.

Geiger counter /gy-ger/ n. a device for measuring radioactivity.

geisha /gay-shuh/ n. (pl. **geisha** or **geishas**) a Japanese hostess trained to entertain men.

gel /jel/ n. **1** a jelly-like substance. • v. (**gelling**, **gelled**) **1** (of jelly etc.) set or become firmer. **2** take definite form. **3** style the hair with gel.

gelatin (or **gelatine**) n. a clear substance used to make jelly, glue, etc. ■ **gelatinous** adj.

geld v. castrate.

gelding n. a castrated horse.

gelignite n. a high explosive made from nitroglycerine.

gem n. **1** a precious stone. **2** an outstanding person or thing.

gender n. **1** the state of being male or female (with reference to social or cultural differences). **2** each of the classes into which nouns are placed in some languages, usu. masculine, feminine, and neuter.

gene n. a distinct sequence of DNA by which offspring inherit parental characteristics.

genealogy n. (pl. **genealogies**) **1** a line of descent from an ancestor. **2** the study of lines of descent. ■ **genealogical** adj. **genealogist** n.

genera pl. of **GENUS**.

general adj. **1** affecting or concerning all or most people or things. **2** involving only the main features; not detailed. • n. the army rank above lieutenant general. ◻ **general anaesthetic** an anaesthetic causing a loss of consciousness. **general election** an election of parliamentary representatives from the whole country. **general practitioner** a doctor treating patients in a local community. **in general** mainly; as a whole. ■ **generally** adv.

generality n. (pl. **generalities**) **1** a general statement. **2** the state of being general.

generalize (or **-ise**) v. **1** make a general statement. **2** make generally available or applicable. ■ **generalization** n.

generate v. create or produce. ■ **generative** adj.

generation n. **1** all of the people born and living at about the same time. **2** the average period in which a person grows up and has children. **3** a single stage in a family's descent. **4** production or creation. ■ **generational** adj.

generator n. a machine for generating electricity.

generic adj. **1** of a whole class or group. **2** (of goods) having no brand name. ■ **generically** adv.

generous adj. **1** giving freely. **2** kind. **3** large or plentiful. ■ **generosity** n. **generously** adv.

genesis n. the origin of something.

genetic adj. of genes or genetics. • n. (**genetics**) the study of heredity and inherited characteristics. □ **genetically modified** containing genetic material artificially altered to produce a desired characteristic. **genetic engineering** the alteration of an animal's or plant's characteristics by manipulating its DNA. **genetic fingerprinting** the analysis of DNA to identify individuals. ■ **genetically** adv. **geneticist** n.

genial adj. friendly and cheerful. ■ **geniality** n. **genially** adv.

genie n. a spirit in Arabian folklore.

genital adj. of reproductive organs. • pl. n. (**genitals** or **genitalia**) the external reproductive organs.

genitive n. the grammatical case showing possession.

genius n. (pl. **geniuses**) **1** exceptional natural ability. **2** a very intelligent or able person.

genocide n. the deliberate killing of many people from a particular ethnic group or nation.

genre /zhon-ruh/ n. a style of art or literature.

genteel adj. affectedly polite and refined.

gentian /jen-sh'n/ n. a plant with deep blue flowers.

Gentile n. a person who is not Jewish.

gentility n. polite and refined behaviour.

gentle adj. **1** kind and mild. **2** not harsh or severe. ■ **gentleness** n. **gently** adv.

gentleman n. **1** a courteous or honourable man. **2** a man of good social position. ■ **gentlemanly** adj.

gentrify v. (**gentrifying, gentrified**) renovate a district so that it conforms to middle-class taste.

gentry n. people of the class next below the nobility.

genuflect v. lower the body as a sign of respect by bending one knee. ■ **genuflection** n.

genuine adj. truly what it is said to be. ■ **genuinely** adv.

genus n. (pl. **genera**) a category in the classification of animals and plants.

geodesic /jee-oh-**dess**-ik/ adj. of a method of construction based on the shortest possible lines between points on a curved surface.

geography n. **1** the study of the earth's physical features and human activity as it relates to these. **2** the arrangement of the features of a place. ■ **geographer** n. **geographical** (or **geographic**) adj. **geographically** adv.

geology n. **1** the study of the earth's physical structure and substance. **2** the geological features of a district. ■ **geological** adj. **geologically** adv. **geologist** n.

geometric adj. **1** of geometry. **2** (of a design) featuring regular lines and shapes. ■ **geometrical** adj. **geometrically** adv.

geometry n. the branch of mathematics dealing with points, lines, surfaces, and solids.

Georgian adj. of the time of Kings George I–IV (1714–1830).

geothermal adj. of or produced by the internal heat of the earth.

geranium n. a flowering garden plant.

gerbil n. a small domesticated rodent.

geriatric adj. of old people. • n. **1** an old person. **2** (**geriatrics**) the branch of medicine dealing with the care of old people.

germ n. **1** a microorganism causing disease. **2** a part of an organism capable of developing into a new one. **3** an early stage of development.

German n. **1** a person from Germany. **2** the language of Germany, Austria, and parts of Switzerland. • adj. of Germany. □ **German measles** rubella. **German shepherd** a large breed of dog often used as guard dogs.

germane adj. relevant.

Germanic adj. **1** of the language family including English, German, Dutch, and the Scandinavian languages. **2** of Germans or Germany.

germanium n. a grey crystalline element.

germinate v. (of a seed) begin to grow. ■ **germination** n.

gerontology n. the study of old age and old people.

gerrymander v. alter the boundaries of an electoral constituency so as to favour one party.

gerund n. a noun formed from a verb, in English ending in -ing.

Gestapo n. the German secret police under Nazi rule.

gestation n. **1** the growth of a baby in the womb. **2** the development of an idea over time.

gesticulate v. gesture in place of or to emphasize speech. ■ **gesticulation** n.

gesture n. **1** a movement of part of the body to convey a meaning. **2** an action done to convey feelings or intentions. • v. make a gesture.

get v. (**getting, got**) **1** come to have or hold; receive. **2** succeed in achieving. **3** experience or suffer. **4** fetch. **5** reach a specified state or place. **6** begin to be or do. **7** travel by a form of transport. **8** catch or thwart. □ **get across** manage to communicate. **getaway** an escape. **get by** manage to survive or do something. **get off** informal escape punishment. **get on 1** make progress. **2** be friendly. **3** informal grow old. **get over** recover from. **get round** persuade. **get-together** a social gathering. **get-up** informal an outfit.

geyser n. a hot spring intermittently sending a jet of water and steam into the air.

ghastly adj. **1** very frightening or horrible. **2** informal very unpleasant. **3** very pale. ■ **ghastliness** n.

ghee n. clarified butter used in Indian cooking.

gherkin n. a small pickled cucumber.

ghetto n. (pl. **ghettos** or **ghettoes**) a part of a city occupied by people of a particular race, nationality, etc.

g

ghost *n.* **1** an apparition of a dead person. **2** a faint trace. □ **ghost town** a town with no inhabitants. **ghost writer** a person who writes a book for someone else who is named as the author. ■ **ghostly** *adj.*

ghoul *n.* **1** an evil spirit. **2** a person excessively interested in death or disaster. ■ **ghoulish** *adj.*

GI *n.* (*pl.* **GIs**) a private soldier in the US army.

giant *n.* **1** an imaginary being of superhuman size. **2** an unusually large person, animal, or plant. • *adj.* very large.

gibber *v.* speak rapidly and unintelligibly.

gibberish *n.* unintelligible speech or writing.

gibbet *n. hist.* a gallows.

gibbon *n.* a long-armed SE Asian ape.

gibe var. of **JIBE**.

giblets *pl. n.* the liver, heart, etc. of a chicken or other bird.

giddy *adj.* (**giddier, giddiest**) **1** having a feeling of whirling and being about to fall. **2** not interested in serious things. ■ **giddily** *adv.* **giddiness** *n.*

gift *n.* **1** a thing given without payment. **2** a natural talent. • *v.* **1** give as a gift. **2** (**gifted**) having exceptional talent.

gig *n.* **1** *informal* a live performance by a musician. **2** *esp. hist.* a light two-wheeled horse-drawn carriage.

gigabyte *n.* Computing a unit of information equal to one thousand million bytes.

gigantic *adj.* very large.

giggle *v.* laugh in a nervous or silly way. • *n.* a nervous or silly laugh. ■ **giggly** *adj.*

gigolo /jig-uh-loh/ *n.* (*pl.* **gigolos**) a man paid by a woman to be her escort or lover.

gild *v.* cover thinly with gold. ■ **gilding** *n.*

gilet /zhi-lay/ *n.* a light sleeveless padded jacket.

gill /jil/ *n.* a quarter of a pint.

gills /gilz/ *pl. n.* **1** the organ with which a fish breathes. **2** the plates on the underside of a mushroom.

gilt *adj.* covered thinly with gold. • *n.* a thin layer of gold on a surface. □ **gilt-edged** (of an investment) very safe.

gimcrack /jim-krak/ *adj.* showy but poorly made.

gimlet /gim-lit/ *n.* a small tool with a screw-tip for boring holes.

gimmick *n.* something intended to attract attention. ■ **gimmicky** *adj.*

gin *n.* an alcoholic spirit flavoured with juniper berries.

ginger *n.* **1** a hot spice made from the root of a SE Asian plant. **2** a light reddish-yellow colour. □ **gingerbread** cake flavoured with ginger. ■ **gingery** *adj.*

gingerly *adv.* cautiously.

gingham /ging-uhm/ *n.* cotton cloth with a checked pattern.

gingivitis /jin-ji-vy-tiss/ *n.* inflammation of the gums.

ginseng *n.* the root of an east Asian and North American plant, used in some medicines.

Gipsy var. of **GYPSY**.

giraffe *n.* a large African animal with a very long neck and legs.

gird *v. literary* encircle with a belt or band.

girder *n.* a large metal beam.

girdle *n.* **1** a belt. **2** a corset. • *v.* encircle.

girl n. **1** a female child. **2** a young woman. □ **girlfriend** n. **1** a person's regular female romantic or sexual partner. **2** a woman's female friend. ■ **girlhood** n. **girlish** adj. **girly** adj. & n.

giro n. (pl. **giros**) a system of electronic credit transfer involving banks, post offices, etc.

girth n. **1** the measurement around the middle of something. **2** a band attached to a saddle and fastened around a horse's belly.

gist /jist/ n. the general meaning of a speech or text.

give v. (**giving, gave**; past part. **given**) **1** cause to have, get, or experience. **2** do an action or make a sound. **3** state information. **4** bend under pressure. •n. the ability to bend under pressure. □ **give and take** willingness to compromise on both sides. **give away** reveal something secret. **giveaway** informal **1** something that reveals the truth. **2** a free gift. **give in** admit defeat. **give off/out** send out a smell, heat, etc. **give out** stop operating. **give rise to** make happen. **give up 1** stop making an effort. **2** stop doing regularly. **3** hand over. **give way 1** collapse. **2** allow other traffic to go first.

given adj. **1** specified or stated. **2** (**given to**) inclined to. •prep. taking into account. •n. an established fact. □ **given name** a first name.

gizmo n. (pl. **gizmos**) informal a gadget.

gizzard n. a muscular part of a bird's stomach for grinding food.

glacé /gla-say/ adj. preserved in sugar.

glacial adj. **1** of ice and glaciers. **2** very cold.

glaciation n. the formation of glaciers.

glacier n. a slowly moving mass of ice.

glad adj. (**gladder, gladdest**) **1** pleased; delighted. **2** causing happiness. ■ **gladden** v. **gladly** adv. **gladness** n.

glade n. an open space in a forest.

gladiator n. a man trained to fight at public shows in ancient Rome. ■ **gladiatorial** adj.

gladiolus n. (pl. **gladioli**) a tall plant with brightly coloured flowers.

glamorize (or **-ise**) v. make something undesirable seem attractive.

glamour (US **glamor**) n. an attractive and exciting quality. ■ **glamorous** adj.

> ! **glamorous** drops the u of **glamour**.

glance v. **1** look briefly. **2** hit and bounce off at an angle. •n. a brief look.

gland n. an organ of the body which produces a particular chemical substance. ■ **glandular** adj.

glare v. **1** stare angrily. **2** shine with a dazzling light. **3** (**glaring**) very obvious. •n. **1** an angry stare. **2** dazzling light.

glass n. **1** a hard transparent substance. **2** a glass drinking container. **3** (**glasses**) a pair of lenses in a frame that rests on the nose and ears, used to correct eyesight. **4** a mirror. □ **glass ceiling** an imaginary barrier to progress in a profession. **glasshouse** a greenhouse. ■ **glassy** adj.

g

glaucoma /glaw-koh-muh/ n. a condition causing gradual loss of sight.

glaze v. 1 fit or cover with glass. 2 cover with a glaze. 3 (of the eyes) lose brightness and animation. •n. a shiny surface or coating.

glazier n. a person whose job is to fit glass into windows.

gleam v. shine brightly with reflected light. •n. 1 a faint or brief light. 2 a brief or faint sign of a quality.

glean v. 1 collect from various sources. 2 *hist.* gather leftover grain after a harvest. ■ **gleanings** pl. n.

glee n. great delight. ■ **gleeful** *adj.* **gleefully** *adv.*

glen n. a narrow valley.

glib *adj.* articulate but insincere or shallow. ■ **glibly** *adv.*

glide v. 1 move with a smooth, quiet motion. 2 fly without power or in a glider. •n. an act of gliding.

glider n. a light aircraft with no engine.

glimmer v. shine faintly with a wavering light. •n. 1 a faint or wavering light. 2 a faint sign of a quality.

glimpse n. a brief or partial view. •v. see briefly or partially.

glint v. give out small flashes of light. •n. a small flash of light.

glisten v. (of something wet) shine or sparkle.

glitch n. *informal* a sudden problem or fault.

glitter v. 1 sparkle. 2 (**glittering**) impressively successful. •n. 1 sparkling light. 2 tiny pieces of sparkling material for decoration. ■ **glittery** *adj.*

glitz n. *informal* superficial glamour. ■ **glitzy** *adj.*

gloaming n. *literary* twilight.

gloat v. be smug or pleased about your own success or another's failure.

global *adj.* 1 worldwide. 2 of or affecting an entire group.
□ **global warming** the gradual increase in the temperature of the earth's atmosphere due to increased levels of carbon dioxide etc. ■ **globally** *adv.*

globalization (or **-isation**) n. the process by which businesses start to operate globally. ■ **globalize** v.

globe n. 1 a spherical object. 2 a spherical model of the earth with a map on the surface.

globetrotter n. *informal* a person who travels widely. ■ **globetrotting** v. & *adj.*

globule n. a small round drop. ■ **globular** *adj.*

glockenspiel /glok-uhn-shpeel/ n. a musical instrument consisting of metal bars struck with hammers.

gloom n. 1 partial or total darkness. 2 depression or despair. ■ **gloomily** *adv.* **gloomy** *adj.*

glorify v. (**glorifying, glorified**) 1 represent as admirable or important, esp. without justification. 2 praise and worship God. ■ **glorification** n.

glorious *adj.* 1 having or bringing glory. 2 beautiful or splendid. ■ **gloriously** *adv.*

glory n. (pl. **glories**) 1 fame and honour. 2 beauty or splendour. 3 a beautiful or splendid thing. 4 praise and worship of God. •v. (**glorying, gloried**) (**glory in**) take great pride or pleasure in.

gloss n. **1** the shine on a smooth surface. **2** a type of paint that dries to a shiny finish. **3** a translation or explanation. •v. **1** (**gloss over**) give only brief or misleading details about. **2** translate or explain a word etc. ■ **glossy** adj.

glossary n. (pl. **glossaries**) a list of words and their meanings.

glottis n. the part of the larynx made up of the vocal cords and the opening between them. ■ **glottal** adj.

glove n. a covering for the hand with separate parts for each finger.

glow v. **1** give out steady light. **2** have a warm or flushed look. **3** look very happy. •n. a glowing state. ■ **glow-worm** a kind of beetle that gives out light.

glower /glow-er/ v. scowl. •n. a scowling expression.

glucose n. a simple sugar which is an important energy source.

glue n. a sticky substance used for joining things. •v. (**gluing** or **glueing**, **glued**) join with glue.

glum adj. (**glummer**, **glummest**) sad or miserable. ■ **glumly** adv.

glut n. an excessive supply. •v. (**glutting**, **glutted**) supply to excess.

gluten n. a substance containing protein, found in cereal grains.

glutinous adj. like glue; sticky.

glutton n. **1** a greedy person. **2** a person who is eager for something challenging. ■ **gluttonous** adj. **gluttony** n.

glycerine (US **glycerin**) n. a thick liquid used in cosmetics etc.

glycerol n. glycerine.

GM abbrev. genetically modified.

gm abbrev. grams.

GMT abbrev. Greenwich Mean Time.

gnarled adj. knobbly or twisted.

gnash v. grind your teeth together.

gnat n. a small biting fly.

gnaw v. **1** bite at persistently. **2** cause persistent anxiety or pain.

gnome n. an imaginary being like a tiny man.

gnomic adj. clever but difficult to understand.

gnostic adj. of or having mystical knowledge.

GNP abbrev. gross national product.

gnu /noo/ n. a large heavy antelope.

GNVQ abbrev. General National Vocational Qualification.

go v. (**goes**, **going**, **went**; past part. **gone**) **1** move to or from a place. **2** pass into or be in a particular state. **3** extend. **4** end, disappear, or be used up. **5** (of time) pass. **6** take part in an activity. **7** have a particular outcome. **8** function. **9** match. **10** fit into or be regularly kept in. **11** make a specified sound. •n. (pl. **goes**) informal **1** an attempt. **2** a turn to do something. **3** energy. □ **go-ahead** informal permission to proceed. **go back on** fail to keep a promise. **go-between** an intermediary or negotiator. **go-cart** (or **go-kart**) a small lightweight racing car. **go for 1** choose. **2** attack. **go-getter** informal an energetic and enterprising person. **go into** investigate. **go off 1** explode. **2** (of food) become stale or bad. **3** informal begin to dislike. **go into** investigate. **go out 1** stop shining or burning. **2** have a

g

regular romantic relationship. **go round** be enough for everyone.

goad v. provoke to action. •n. **1** a stimulus to action. **2** a pointed stick for driving cattle.

goal n. **1** (in football, rugby, etc.) a framework into or over which the ball has to be sent to score. **2** an act of scoring. **3** an aim or desired result. □ **goalkeeper** (in football, hockey, etc.) a player whose role is to keep the ball out of the goal. **goalpost** either of the two upright posts of a goal.

goalie n. informal a goalkeeper.

goat n. an animal with horns, often kept for milk.

goatee n. a small pointed beard.

gob n. informal a person's mouth.

gobble v. **1** eat hurriedly and noisily. **2** (of a turkey) make a swallowing sound in the throat.

gobbledegook n. informal complicated and unintelligible language.

goblet n. a drinking glass with a foot and a stem.

goblin n. a mischievous ugly elf.

goby n. (pl. **gobies**) a small sea fish.

God n. **1** (in Christianity and some other religions) the creator and supreme ruler of the universe. **2** (**god**) a superhuman being or spirit. □ **God-fearing** earnestly religious.

godchild n. a person in relation to a godparent.

god-daughter n. a female godchild.

goddess n. a female god.

godfather n. **1** a male godparent. **2** the male leader of an illegal organization.

godforsaken adj. (of a place) remote or unattractive.

godhead n. **1** (**the Godhead**) God. **2** divine nature.

godly adj. very religious.

godmother n. a female godparent.

godparent n. a person who promises to be responsible for a child's religious education.

godsend n. a very helpful or welcome thing.

godson n. a male godchild.

goes 3rd person sing. present of **GO**.

goggle v. stare with wide open eyes. •n. (**goggles**) close-fitting protective glasses.

going n. the condition of the ground as suitable for horse racing or walking. •adj. **1** existing or available. **2** (of a price) current. □ **going concern** a thriving business.

goitre /goy-ter/ n. a swollen neck resulting from an enlarged thyroid gland.

gold n. **1** a yellow precious metal. **2** a deep yellow colour. **3** articles made of gold. □ **gold-digger** informal a woman who forms relationships with men purely for financial gain. **goldfish** a small orange carp often kept in ponds and tanks. **gold leaf** gold beaten into a very thin sheet. **gold rush** a rush of people to a place where gold has been discovered. **goldsmith** a person who makes gold articles.

golden adj. **1** made of or like gold. **2** very happy and prosperous. **3** excellent. □ **golden handshake** informal a payment given on redundancy or early retirement. **golden jubilee** the 50th

anniversary of an important event.
golden wedding the 50th anniversary of a wedding.

golf *n.* an outdoor game in which a small ball is struck with a club into a series of small holes. ■ **golfer** *n.*

golliwog *n.* a soft doll with a black face and fuzzy hair.

gonad *n.* a bodily organ producing gametes; a testis or ovary.

gondola *n.* a boat with high-pointed ends and a single oar, used on canals in Venice.

gondolier *n.* a person who propels a gondola.

gone past part. of **go**.

gong *n.* **1** a metal disc that makes a resonant sound when struck. **2** *informal* a medal or award.

gonorrhoea /gon-uh-**ree**-uh/ (*US* **gonorrhea**) *n.* a sexually transmitted disease.

goo *n. informal* a sticky or slimy substance. ■ **gooey** *adj.*

good *adj.* (**better**, **best**) **1** having the right qualities; of a high standard. **2** morally right, polite, or obedient. **3** enjoyable or satisfying. **4** appropriate. **5** (**good for**) of benefit to. **6** thorough. •*n.* **1** morally right behaviour. **2** something beneficial. **3** (**goods**) products, freight, or possessions. □ **for good** forever. **good faith** honest or sincere intentions. **good-for-nothing** worthless. **Good Friday** the Friday before Easter Sunday, commemorating the Crucifixion of Jesus. **goodwill** friendly feeling. **make good** compensate for loss or damage. ■ **goodness** *n.*

goodbye *exclam.* used to express good wishes when parting or ending a conversation.

goodly *adj. dated* considerable in size or quantity.

goody *n.* (or **goodie**) (*pl.* **goodies**) *informal* **1** a good person in a story etc. **2** (**goodies**) pleasant things to eat. □ **goody-goody** a person who behaves well to impress others.

goofy *adj. informal* having front teeth that stick out. **2** *US* silly.

goose *n.* (*pl.* **geese**) **1** a large waterbird with webbed feet. **2** a female goose. □ **gooseflesh** (or **goose pimples**) small raised bumps on the skin caused by cold or fear. **goose step** a marching step with the legs kept straight.

gooseberry *n.* **1** an edible berry with a hairy skin. **2** *informal* a third person in the company of two lovers.

gopher *n.* a burrowing American rodent.

gore *n.* **1** blood from a wound. **2** a triangular part of a garment, sail, etc. •*v.* pierce with a horn or tusk.

gorge *n.* a narrow valley or ravine. •*v.* eat greedily.

gorgeous *adj.* **1** beautiful. **2** *informal* very pleasant.

gorgon *n.* **1** *Gk Myth.* each of three sisters able to turn people to stone. **2** an intimidating woman.

gorilla *n.* a large powerful African ape.

gormless *adj. informal* stupid.

gorse *n.* a yellow-flowered prickly shrub.

gory *adj.* **1** involving bloodshed. **2** covered in blood.

goshawk /**goss**-hawk/ *n.* a short-winged hawk.

gosling *n.* a young goose.

gospel *n.* **1** the teachings of Jesus. **2** (**Gospel**) any of the first four books of the New Testament. **3** something absolutely true. **4** a style of black American religious singing.

gossamer n. a fine piece of cobweb. ∙adj. very fine or flimsy.

gossip n. **1** casual talk about other people. **2** a person who likes gossiping. ∙v. (**gossiping**, **gossiped**) engage in gossip.

got past & past part. of **GET**.

Gothic adj. **1** of the style of architecture common in western Europe in the 12th–16th centuries. **2** very gloomy or horrifying.

gouache /goo-**ash**/ n. **1** a method of painting using watercolours thickened with glue. **2** paint of this kind.

gouge v. cut out roughly. ∙n. a chisel with a concave blade.

goulash n. a rich Hungarian stew of meat and vegetables.

gourd n. a hard-skinned fruit of a climbing plant, esp. used as a container.

gourmand n. a person who enjoys eating.

gourmet /**gor**-may/ n. a person knowledgeable about good food.

gout n. a disease causing swollen painful joints.

govern v. **1** conduct the policy and affairs of a state etc. **2** control or influence. ■ **governance** n. **governor** n.

governess n. a woman employed to teach children in a private household.

government n. **1** the group of people who govern a state. **2** the system by which a state is governed. ■ **governmental** adj.

gown n. **1** a long dress. **2** a protective garment. **3** a loose cloak worn by lawyers, academics, etc.

GP abbrev. general practitioner.

grab v. (**grabbed**, **grabbing**) seize suddenly and roughly. ∙n. a sudden attempt to seize.

grace n. **1** elegance of movement. **2** polite respect. **3** (**graces**) attractive qualities. **4** a period allowed to do something. **5** a short prayer of thanks for a meal. **6** the unearned favour of God. ∙v. **1** honour by your presence. **2** make more attractive. ■ **graceless** adj.

graceful adj. having or showing grace or elegance. ■ **gracefully** adv.

gracious adj. polite, kind, and pleasant. ■ **graciously** adv.

gradation n. **1** a scale of successive stages. **2** a stage in a such a scale.

grade n. **1** a level of rank or quality. **2** a mark indicating the quality of a student's work. **3** US a class in school. ∙v. arrange in or allocate to grades. □ **make the grade** informal succeed.

gradient n. **1** a slope. **2** the degree to which ground slopes.

gradual adj. **1** taking place in stages over time. **2** (of a slope) not steep. ■ **gradually** adv.

graduate n. a person awarded a first academic degree. ∙v. **1** successfully complete a degree or course. **2** arrange or mark according to a scale. ■ **graduation** n.

graffiti n. writings or drawings on a surface in a public place.

❗ double f, one t: graffiti.

graft n. **1** a shoot from one plant inserted into another to form a new growth. **2** a piece of living body tissue transplanted surgically. **3** informal hard work.

• v. **1** insert or transplant as a graft. **2** informal work hard.

Grail n. (in medieval legend) the cup or bowl used by Jesus at the Last Supper.

grain n. **1** cultivated cereal used as food. **2** a single seed of a cereal. **3** a small, hard particle. **4** a unit of weight. **5** the arrangement of fibres in wood etc. □ **against the grain** conflicting with your instinct. ■ **grainy** adj.

gram (or **gramme**) n. one thousandth of a kilogram.

grammar n. **1** the whole system and structure of a language. **2** knowledge and use of the rules of grammar. **3** a book on grammar.

| ! -ar, not -er: gramm**ar**. |

grammatical adj. following the rules of grammar. ■ **grammatically** adv.

gramophone n. dated a record player.

grampus n. (pl. **grampuses**) a dolphin-like sea animal.

gran n. informal a person's grandmother.

granary n. (pl. **granaries**) a storehouse for grain.

grand adj. **1** large and impressive. **2** ambitious in scale. **3** highest in importance or rank. **4** informal excellent. • n. informal a thousand dollars or pounds. □ **grand piano** a large piano with a horizontal body and strings. **grand slam** the winning of all the major championships in a sport in the same year. **grandstand** the main stand at a sports ground. ■ **grandly** adv.

grandad n. informal a person's grandfather.

grandchild n. a child of a person's son or daughter.

granddaughter n. the daughter of a person's son or daughter.

grandeur n. **1** splendour and impressiveness. **2** high rank or social status.

grandfather n. the father of a person's father or mother. □ **grandfather clock** a clock in a tall wooden case.

grandiloquent adj. using long words in a pompous way.

grandiose adj. large and ambitious and intended to impress.

grandma n. informal a person's grandmother.

grandmother n. the mother of a person's father or mother.

grandpa n. informal a person's grandfather.

grandparent n. a grandmother or grandfather.

grandson n. the son of a person's son or daughter.

grange n. a country house with farm buildings attached.

granite n. a very hard grey rock.

granny (or **grannie**) n. (pl. **grannies**) informal a person's grandmother. □ **granny flat** a self-contained part of a house suitable for an elderly relative.

grant v. **1** agree to give or allow. **2** give formally or legally. **3** admit to be true. • n. a sum of money given from public funds for a particular purpose. □ **take for granted 1** fail to appreciate. **2** assume to be true.

granulated adj. in the form of granules.

granule n. a small particle or grain. ■ **granular** adj.

g

grape *n.* a green or purple berry, used for making wine. □ the **grapevine** the spreading of information through talk or rumour.

grapefruit *n.* a large round yellow citrus fruit.

graph *n.* a diagram showing the relation between variable quantities.

graphic *adj.* 1 of visual art, esp. drawing and the design of printed material. 2 giving vivid details. •*n.* 1 a pictorial image or symbol on a computer screen. 2 (**graphics**) the use of designs or pictures to illustrate books etc. □ **graphic equalizer** a device for controlling the strength and quality of selected frequency bands.
■ **graphically** *adv.*

graphite *n.* a form of carbon.

graphology *n.* the study of handwriting as a guide to character. ■ **graphologist** *n.*

grapnel (or **grappling hook**) *n.* a device with iron claws, for dragging or grasping.

grapple *v.* 1 wrestle. 2 (**grapple with**) struggle to deal with.

grasp *v.* 1 seize and hold firmly. 2 understand fully. 3 (**grasping**) greedy. •*n.* 1 a firm grip. 2 understanding.

grass *n.* 1 a short plant with long narrow leaves. 2 ground covered with grass. 3 *informal* cannabis. 4 *informal* an informer. •*v.* 1 cover with grass. 2 *informal* act as an informer. □ **grasshopper** a jumping insect that makes a chirping sound. **grass roots** the ordinary people in an organization or society. ■ **grassy** *adj.*

grate *v.* 1 shred food by rubbing it on a grater. 2 make an unpleasant scraping sound. 3 have an irritat-ing effect. •*n.* a metal frame keeping fuel in a fireplace.

grateful *adj.* thankful and appreciative. ■ **gratefully** *adv.*

! **grateful**, not **greatful**.

grater *n.* a device having a surface covered with sharp-edged holes, used for grating food.

gratify *v.* (**gratifying, gratified**) 1 give pleasure or satisfaction. 2 satisfy a wish. ■ **gratification** *n.*

grating *n.* a grid of metal bars over an opening.

gratis *adv. & adj.* free of charge.

gratitude *n.* the feeling of being grateful.

gratuitous *adj.* without reason or purpose. ■ **gratuitously** *adv.*

gratuity *n.* (*pl.* **gratuities**) a tip given to a waiter etc.

grave *n.* a hole dug to bury a corpse. •*adj.* 1 giving cause for alarm or concern. 2 solemn. □ **gravestone** a stone slab marking a grave. **graveyard** a burial ground. ■ **gravely** *adv.*

grave accent /grahv/ *n.* the accent (`).

gravel *n.* small stones used for paths etc.

gravelly *adj.* 1 made of gravel. 2 rough-sounding.

gravitas *n.* a serious and dignified manner.

gravitate *v.* be drawn towards.

gravitation *n.* movement towards a centre of gravity. ■ **gravitational** *adj.*

gravity *n.* 1 the force that attracts a body towards the centre of the earth. 2 seriousness. 3 solemnity.

gravy *n.* (*pl.* **gravies**) a sauce made from the fat and juices from cooked meat.

gray US = GREY.

graze v. **1** eat grass in a field.
2 injure by scraping the skin.
3 touch lightly in passing. •n. a
grazed area on the skin.

grease n. a fatty or oily substance.
•v. smear or lubricate with grease.
□ **greasepaint** make-up used by
actors. ■ **greasy** adj.

great adj. **1** considerably above
average in size, intensity, ability,
quality, or importance. **2** informal
excellent. **3** (**great-**) (of a family
relationship) one generation removed in ancestry or descent.
□ **greatcoat** a heavy overcoat.
Great Dane a dog of a very large
short-haired breed. ■ **great-
ness** n.

greatly adv. very much.

grebe n. a diving bird.

Grecian adj. of ancient Greece.

greed n. **1** a strong and selfish desire for wealth or power. **2** a desire
to eat more food than is necessary. ■ **greedily** adv. **greedy** adj.

Greek n. **1** a person from Greece.
2 the ancient or modern language
of Greece. •adj. of Greece.

green adj. **1** of a colour like that of
grass. **2** covered with grass.
3 (**Green**) concerned with protecting the environment. **4** inexperienced or naive. •n. **1** green
colour. **2** a piece of grassy public
land. **3** (**greens**) green vegetables. **4** (**Green**) a supporter of a
Green political party. □ **green
belt** an area of open land round a
city, on which building is
restricted. **green card** (in the US)
a permit allowing a foreigner to
live and work permanently in the
US. **green fingers** informal skill in
growing plants. **greenfly** a green
aphid. **greengage** a sweet

greenish plum-like fruit. **green-
grocer** a person selling fruit and
vegetables. **green light** permission to go ahead with a project.
Green Paper a preliminary report
of government proposals.
■ **greenish** adj. **greenness** n.

greenery n. green leaves or
plants.

greenhouse n. a glass building
for protecting plants from cold
weather. □ **greenhouse effect**
the tendency of atmospheric
temperature to rise because
certain gases absorb infrared
radiation from the earth. **greenhouse gas** a gas that contributes to the greenhouse
effect.

greet v. **1** meet with friendliness or
expressions of welcome. **2** react to
in a particular way.

greeting n. **1** a word or sign of
welcome. **2** (**greetings**) a formal
expression of good wishes.

gregarious adj. **1** fond of company. **2** living in flocks or colonies.

gremlin n. a mischievous sprite
regarded as responsible for mechanical faults.

grenade n. a small bomb thrown
by hand.

grenadier n. hist. a soldier armed
with grenades.

grew past of GROW.

grey (US **gray**) adj. **1** of a colour
like that of ash. **2** (of weather)
cloudy and dull. •n. a grey colour.
•v. (of hair) turn grey. □ **grey area**
a situation that does not fit easily
into existing categories. **greyhound** a swift, slender breed of
dog used in racing. **grey matter**
informal intelligence. ■ **greyish**
adj. **greyness** n.

g

grid n. 1 a framework of parallel or crossed bars. 2 a network of crossed lines forming a series of squares. 3 a network of cables or pipes. □ **gridiron** 1 a metal grid for grilling food. 2 a field for American football. **gridlock** a traffic jam affecting linked streets.

griddle n. an iron plate for cooking food.

grief n. deep sorrow.

grievance n. a cause for complaint.

grieve v. suffer or cause grief.

grievous adj. very severe or serious. □ **grievous bodily harm** the offence of deliberately inflicting serious physical injury. ■ **grievously** adv.

griffin (or **gryphon**) n. a mythical creature with an eagle's head and wings and a lion's body.

griffon n. a small dog like a terrier.

grill n. 1 a device on a cooker for directing heat downwards. 2 food cooked using a grill. •v. 1 cook with a grill. 2 informal interrogate.

grille n. a grating.

grim adj. (**grimmer, grimmest**) 1 very serious or gloomy. 2 depressing or unappealing. ■ **grimly** adv. **grimness** n.

grimace n. a twisted facial expression, showing disgust, pain, or amusement. •v. make a grimace.

grime n. ingrained dirt. ■ **grimy** adj.

grin v. (**grinning, grinned**) smile broadly. •n. a broad smile.

grind v. (**grinding, ground**) 1 crush into small particles or powder. 2 sharpen or smooth by friction. 3 rub together gratingly. 4 (**grind down**) treat harshly. •n. hard dull work. □ **grindstone** a

revolving disc for sharpening or polishing.

grip v. (**gripping, gripped**) 1 hold firmly. 2 hold the attention of. •n. 1 a firm hold. 2 understanding. 3 a part by which something is held.

gripe v. informal grumble. •n. 1 informal a trivial complaint. 2 pain in the stomach.

grisly adj. (**grislier, grisliest**) causing horror or disgust.

grist n. grain to be ground. □ **grist to the mill** useful experience or knowledge.

gristle n. tough inedible tissue in meat. ■ **gristly** adj.

grit n. 1 particles of stone or sand. 2 courage and determination. •v. (**gritting, gritted**) spread grit on an icy road. □ **grit your teeth** resolve to do something difficult. ■ **grittiness** n. **gritty** adj.

grizzle v. informal cry fretfully.

grizzled adj. grey-haired.

grizzly bear n. a large American brown bear.

groan v. make a deep sound of pain or despair. •n. a groaning sound.

grocer n. a person selling food and household goods.

grocery n. (pl. **groceries**) 1 a grocer's shop. 2 (**groceries**) items of food sold in a shop.

grog n. spirits mixed with water.

groggy adj. dazed and unsteady. ■ **groggily** adv.

groin n. 1 the area between the abdomen and the thigh. 2 a curved edge formed by two intersecting roof arches. 3 US = GROYNE.

grommet n. 1 a protective metal ring or eyelet. 2 a tube implanted in the eardrum to drain the ear.

groom v. **1** brush and clean the coat of an animal. **2** prepare or train for a particular activity. •n. **1** a person employed to take care of horses. **2** a bridegroom.

groove n. **1** a long, narrow channel. **2** a spiral track in a record. **3** a fixed routine. ■ **grooved** adj.

grope v. try to find or reach by feeling with the hands.

gross adj. **1** unattractively large. **2** very obvious and unacceptable. **3** informal very unpleasant. **4** vulgar. **5** (of income etc.) before tax has been deducted. **6** (of weight) including contents or other variable items. •v. produce or earn as gross profit. •n. (pl. **gross**) twelve dozen. ■ **grossly** adv.

grotesque /groh-tesk/ adj. ugly or distorted. •n. a grotesque figure or image. ■ **grotesquely** adv.

grotto n. (pl. **grottoes** or **grottos**) a small cave.

grouch n. informal **1** a grumpy person. **2** a complaint. ■ **grouchy** adj.

ground[1] n. **1** the solid surface of the earth. **2** land of a specified kind. **3** an area of land or sea with a specified use. **4** (**grounds**) enclosed land surrounding a large house. **5** (**grounds**) good reasons for doing something. **6** (**grounds**) coffee dregs. •v. **1** ban from flying. **2** (be grounded in/on) have as a basis. □ **groundbreaking** pioneering. **groundnut** a peanut. **ground rent** rent paid by a building's owner to the owner of the land on which it stands. **ground rules** basic rules controlling something. **groundsheet** a waterproof sheet used as the floor of a tent. **groundsman** a person employed to look after a sports ground. **groundswell** a build-up of public opinion. **groundwork** preliminary work.

ground[2] past & past part. of **GRIND**.

grounding n. basic training or instruction.

groundless adj. not based on any good reason.

group n. **1** a number of people or things classed or classed together. **2** a band of pop musicians or singers. •v. place in or form a group or groups.

grouse n. **1** (pl. **grouse**) a game bird. **2** a complaint. •v. grumble.

grout n. a paste for filling gaps between tiles. •v. fill gaps with grout.

grove n. a group of trees.

grovel v. (**grovelling**, **grovelled**; US **groveling**, **groveled**) **1** crouch or crawl on the ground. **2** act humbly to obtain forgiveness or favour.

grow v. (**growing**, **grew**; past part. **grown**) **1** (of a living thing) develop and get bigger. **2** increase over time. **3** cultivate a crop. **4** become gradually: we grew braver. □ **grown-up** an adult. **grow on** gradually start to appeal to. **grow up** become an adult. ■ **grower** n.

growl v. (of a dog) make a low hostile sound in the throat. •n. a growling sound.

growth n. **1** the process of growing. **2** something that has grown or is growing. **3** a tumour.

groyne (US **groin**) n. a low wall built out into the sea to prevent erosion.

grub n. **1** the larva of an insect. **2** informal food. •v. (**grubbing**, **grubbed**) dig shallowly in soil.

g

grubby adj. (**grubbier, grubbiest**) dirty. ∎ **grubbiness** n.

grudge n. a long-lasting feeling of resentment or dislike. • v. 1 be unwilling to give or allow. 2 resent. ∎ **grudgingly** adv.

gruel n. thin porridge.

gruelling (US **grueling**) adj. very tiring.

gruesome adj. causing disgust or horror.

gruff adj. 1 (of a voice) rough and low. 2 abrupt in manner. ∎ **gruffly** adv.

grumble v. 1 complain in a bad-tempered way. 2 rumble. • n. a complaint.

grumpy adj. bad-tempered and sulky. ∎ **grumpily** adv.

grunge n. a style of rock music with a raucous guitar sound. ∎ **grungy** adj.

grunt v. make a low, short sound. • n. a grunting sound.

gryphon var. of **GRIFFIN**.

G-string n. skimpy knickers consisting of a narrow strip of cloth attached to a waistband.

guano /gwah-noh/ n. the excrement of seabirds, used as fertilizer.

guarantee n. 1 a formal promise to do something. 2 a promise that a product will remain in working order for a stated period. 3 an undertaking to pay or do something on behalf of someone if they fail to do it. • v. give a guarantee for.

guarantor n. a person that gives a guarantee.

guard v. 1 watch over so as to protect or control. 2 take precautions. • n. 1 a person or group guarding or keeping watch. 2 a protective device. 3 a state of vigilance. 4 an official in charge of a train.

guarded adj. cautious.

guardian n. 1 a defender or protector. 2 a person legally responsible for someone unable to manage their own affairs. ∎ **guardianship** n.

guava /gwah-vuh/ n. a tropical fruit.

gudgeon n. 1 a small freshwater fish. 2 a pivot or socket.

guerrilla (or **guerilla**) n. a member of a small independent group fighting against the government or regular forces.

guess v. estimate or suppose without enough information to be sure. • n. an estimate. □ **guesswork** guessing.

guest n. 1 a person invited to someone's house or to a social occasion. 2 an invited speaker or performer. 3 a person staying at a hotel. □ **guest house** a kind of small hotel.

guffaw n. a loud laugh. • v. laugh loudly.

guidance n. advice or information to solve a problem.

guide n. 1 a person who advises or shows the way to others. 2 an aid to deciding something. 3 a book of information. 4 a structure or mark to direct the movement or position of something. • v. 1 act as a guide to. 2 (**guided**) directed by remote control or internal equipment. □ **guidebook** a book of information about a place.

guideline n. a general rule or principle.

guild n. 1 a medieval association of craftsmen or merchants. 2 an association of people for a common purpose.

guilder n. the former basic unit of money of the Netherlands.

guile n. clever but deceitful behaviour. ■ **guileless** adj.

guillemot /gil-li-mot/ n. a seabird with a narrow pointed bill.

guillotine n. 1 a machine for beheading people. 2 a machine for cutting paper or metal. • v. execute by guillotine.

guilt n. 1 the fact of having committed an offence. 2 a feeling of having done something wrong. ■ **guiltless** adj.

guilty adj. (**guiltier, guiltiest**) 1 responsible for a wrongdoing. 2 having or showing guilt. ■ **guiltily** adv.

guinea n. a former British coin worth 21 shillings.

guinea pig n. 1 a small domesticated rodent. 2 a person or thing used as a subject for experiment.

guise n. an external form, appearance, or manner.

guitar n. a stringed musical instrument. ■ **guitarist** n.

gulch n. US a narrow ravine.

gulf n. 1 a large area of sea partly surrounded by land. 2 a deep ravine. 3 a wide difference in opinion or circumstances.

gull n. a long-winged seabird.

gullet n. the passage by which food passes from the mouth to the stomach.

gullible adj. easily deceived. ■ **gullibility** n.

gully n. (pl. **gullies** or **gulleys**) a channel or ravine formed by running water.

gulp v. 1 swallow food or drink quickly or in large mouthfuls. 2 swallow noisily from strong emotion. • n. 1 an act of gulping.

2 a large mouthful of liquid hastily drunk.

gum n. 1 the firm area of flesh around the roots of the teeth. 2 a sticky substance produced by some trees. 3 glue. 4 chewing gum. • v. (**gumming, gummed**) cover or fasten with glue. □ **gumboot** dated a wellington boot. **gumdrop** a firm, jelly-like sweet. ■ **gummy** adj.

gumption n. informal resourcefulness.

gun n. 1 a weapon that fires shells or bullets from a metal tube. 2 a device using pressure to discharge a substance or object. • v. (**gunning, gunned**) (**gun down**) shoot with a gun. □ **gunfire** repeated firing of a gun or guns. **gunman** a man who uses a gun to commit a crime. **gunpowder** an explosive mixture of saltpetre, sulphur, and charcoal. **gunship** a heavily armed helicopter. **gunsmith** a maker and seller of small firearms. **jump the gun** informal act before the proper time.

gunge n. informal sticky and messy matter.

gung-ho adj. too eager to take part in fighting.

gunnel var. of GUNWALE.

gunner n. 1 a person who operates a gun. 2 a British artillery soldier.

gunnery n. the manufacture or firing of heavy guns.

gunrunner n. a smuggler of firearms. ■ **gunrunning** n.

gunwale (or **gunnel**) /gun-n'l/ n. the upper edge of a boat's side.

guppy n. (pl. **guppies**) a small tropical freshwater fish.

gurdwara n. a Sikh temple.

g

gurgle v. make a low bubbling sound. •n. a low bubbling sound.

Gurkha n. a member of a Nepalese regiment in the British army.

guru n. **1** a Hindu spiritual teacher. **2** an influential teacher or expert.

gush v. **1** flow in a strong, fast stream. **2** express approval very enthusiastically. •n. a strong, fast stream.

gusset n. a piece of material sewn into a garment to strengthen or enlarge a part of it.

gust n. a brief, strong rush of wind. •v. blow in gusts. ■ **gusty** adj.

gusto n. enjoyment or energy.

gut n. **1** the stomach. **2** the intestine. **3** (**guts**) informal courage and determination. •v. (**gutting, gutted**) **1** take out the internal organs of a fish. **2** remove or destroy the internal parts of. •adj. informal instinctive. ■ **gutless** adj.

gutsy adj. (**gutsier, gutsiest**) informal brave and determined.

gutter n. **1** a shallow trough round a roof, or a channel beside a road, for carrying away rainwater. **2** (**the gutter**) a very poor environment. •v. (of a flame) flicker. □ **guttersnipe** a scruffy, badly behaved child.

guttural adj. (of a speech sound) produced in the throat.

guy n. **1** informal a man. **2** a stuffed figure burnt on a bonfire on 5 November. **3** a rope fixed to the

ground to secure a tent. •v. ridicule.

guzzle v. eat or drink greedily.

gybe (US **jibe**) v. Sailing change course by swinging the sail across a following wind.

gym n. **1** a gymnasium. **2** a place with facilities for improving physical fitness. **3** gymnastics.

gymkhana n. a horse-riding competition.

gymnasium n. (pl. **gymnasiums** or **gymnasia**) a room equipped for gymnastics and other physical exercise.

gymnast n. a person trained in gymnastics.

gymnastics n. exercises involving physical agility and flexibility. ■ **gymnastic** adj.

gynaecology /gy-ni-kol-uh-ji/ (US **gynecology**) n. the branch of medicine concerned with conditions and diseases specific to women. ■ **gynaecological** adj. **gynaecologist** n.

gypsum n. a chalk-like mineral used for plaster of Paris and in building.

Gypsy (or **Gipsy**) n. (pl. **Gypsies**) a member of a travelling people.

gyrate v. move in a circle or spiral. ■ **gyration** n. **gyratory** adj.

gyroscope n. a device consisting of a disc rotating on an axis, used to maintain stability or a fixed direction.

Hh

ha *abbrev.* hectares.

habeas corpus *n.* an order requiring an arrested person to be brought to court.

haberdashery *n.* sewing materials. ■ **haberdasher** *n.*

habit *n.* **1** a thing that a person does often. **2** *informal* an addiction. **3** a long, loose garment worn by a monk or nun.

habitable *adj.* suitable to live in.

habitat *n.* the natural environment of an animal or plant.

habitation *n.* a house or home.

habitual *adj.* **1** done often. **2** usual. ■ **habitually** *adv.*

habituate *v.* make or become used to.

habitué /huh-bit-yuu-ay/ *n.* a frequent visitor to a place.

hacienda *n.* (in Spanish-speaking countries) a large estate with a house.

hack *v.* **1** cut with rough or heavy blows. **2** use a computer to gain unauthorized access to another computer system. • *n.* **1** a journalist producing dull, unoriginal work. **2** a horse for ordinary riding. □ **hacksaw** a saw with a narrow blade set in a frame. ■ **hacker** *n.*

hackles *pl. n.* hairs along an animal's back, raised in anger.

hackneyed *adj.* unoriginal and dull.

had past & past part. of HAVE.

haddock *n.* (*pl.* **haddock**) an edible sea fish.

hadn't *contr.* had not.

haematology /hee-muh-tol-uh-ji/ (*US* **hematology**) *n.* the branch of medicine concerned with the blood. ■ **haematologist** *n.*

haemoglobin /hee-muh-gloh-bin/ (*US* **hemoglobin**) *n.* a red protein transporting oxygen in the blood.

haemophilia /hee-muh-fi-li-uh/ (*US* **hemophilia**) *n.* a condition in which failure of the blood to clot properly causes heavy bleeding. ■ **haemophiliac** *n.*

haemorrhage /hem-uh-rij/ (*US* **hemorrhage**) *n.* heavy bleeding. • *v.* bleed heavily.

haemorrhoid /hem-uh-royd/ (*US* **hemorrhoid**) *n.* a swollen vein at or near the anus.

hafnium *n.* a hard metallic element.

haft *n.* the handle of a knife, axe, etc.

hag *n.* an ugly old woman.

haggard *adj.* looking exhausted and unwell.

haggis *n.* a Scottish dish made from offal mixed with suet and oatmeal.

haggle *v.* bargain over a price.

haiku /hy-koo/ *n.* (*pl.* **haiku** or **haikus**) a Japanese poem of 17 syllables.

hail *n.* **1** pellets of frozen rain falling in showers. **2** a large number of things hurled through the air. • *v.* **1** hail falls. **2** call out to. **3** describe enthusiastically. **4** (**hail from**) come from or live in. □ **hailstone** a pellet of hail.

hair n. **1** any of the fine thread-like strands growing from the skin. **2** strands of hair. □ **hairdresser** a person who cuts and styles hair. **hairdo** informal a hairstyle. **hairgrip** a flat hairpin. **hairline 1** the edge of a person's hair. **2** (of a crack) very thin. **hairpin** a U-shaped pin for fastening the hair. **hairpin bend** a sharp U-shaped bend. **hair-raising** very frightening. **hairslide** a clip for keeping hair in place. **hairstyle** a way in which the hair is cut or arranged.

hairy adj. (**hairier**, **hairiest**) **1** covered with hair. **2** informal frightening or dangerous. ■ **hairiness** n.

hajj n. a pilgrimage made by Muslims to Mecca.

haka n. a ceremonial Maori war dance.

hake n. (pl. **hake**) an edible sea fish.

halal adj. (of meat) prepared according to Muslim law.

halberd n. hist. a combined spear and battleaxe.

halcyon /hal-si-uhn/ adj. (of a past time) happy and peaceful.

hale adj. strong and healthy.

half n. (pl. **halves**) **1** either of two equal parts into which something is divided. **2** informal half a pint of beer. • adj. & pron. an amount equal to a half. • adv. **1** to the extent of half. **2** partly. □ **at half mast** (of a flag) flown halfway down its mast as a sign of mourning. **half-and-half** in equal parts. **halfback** a player between the forwards and full backs. **half board** bed, breakfast, and one main meal at a hotel etc. **half-brother** (or **sister**) a brother (or

sister) with whom you have one parent in common. **half-caste** offens. a person of mixed race. **half-hearted** not very enthusiastic. **half-life** the time taken for radioactivity to fall to half its original value. **half-term** a short holiday halfway through a school term. **half-timbered** having walls with a timber frame and a brick or plaster filling. **half-time** an interval between two halves of a sports match. **halfway** at or to a point equal in distance between two others. **half-witted** informal stupid.

halfpenny /hayp-ni/ n. (pl. **halfpennies**; **halfpence**) a former British coin worth half a penny.

halibut n. (pl. **halibut**) a large edible flatfish.

halitosis n. unpleasant-smelling breath.

hall n. **1** the room or space inside the front entrance of a house. **2** a large room or building for meetings, concerts, etc. **3** a large country house.

hallelujah (or **alleluia**) exclam. God be praised.

hallmark n. **1** an official mark stamped on gold, silver, or platinum articles to certify their purity. **2** a distinctive feature. • v. stamp with a hallmark.

hallo var. of HELLO.

hallowed adj. made holy.

Halloween (or **Hallowe'en**) n. 31 October, the eve of All Saints' Day.

hallucinate v. see something which is not actually present. ■ **hallucination** n. **hallucinatory** adj.

hallucinogen n. a drug causing hallucinations. ■ **hallucinogenic** adj.

halo n. (pl. **haloes** or **halos**) (in a painting) a circle of light round the head of a holy person.

halogen n. any of a group of elements including fluorine, chlorine, and iodine.

halt v. stop suddenly. •n. 1 a stopping of movement or activity. 2 a minor stopping place on a railway.

halter n. a strap round an animal's head, used for leading it. □ **halter neck** a style of woman's top fastened behind the neck, leaving the upper back and arms bare.

halting adj. slow and hesitant.

halve v. 1 divide into halves. 2 reduce by half.

halves pl. of **HALF**.

halyard n. a rope for raising and lowering a sail or flag.

ham n. 1 salted or smoked meat from a pig's thigh. 2 (**hams**) the thighs and buttocks. 3 a poor actor. 4 informal an amateur radio operator. •v. (**hamming**, **hammed**) informal overact. □ **ham-fisted** informal clumsy.

hamburger n. a flat cake of minced beef.

hamlet n. a small village.

hammer n. 1 a tool with a head for driving in nails etc. 2 a metal ball attached to a wire, thrown in an athletic contest. •v. 1 hit repeatedly. 2 (**hammer out**) work out the details of.

hammock n. a hanging bed of canvas or rope mesh.

hamper n. a basket with a lid, used to carry picnic items. •v. prevent or hinder the movement or progress of.

hamster n. a small domesticated rodent.

hamstring n. a tendon at the back of the knee. •v. (**hamstringing**, **hamstrung**) 1 cripple by cutting the hamstrings. 2 severely restrict.

hand n. 1 the part of the arm below the wrist. 2 a pointer on a clock etc. 3 (**hands**) power or control. 4 help. 5 a manual worker. 6 a round of applause. 7 the cards dealt to a player in a game. 8 a unit of measurement of a horse's height. •v. give or pass to. □ **at hand** near. **handbag** a small bag for personal items. **handball** 1 a game in which the ball is hit with the hand in a walled court. 2 (in football) unlawful touching of the ball with the hand or arm. **handbill** a printed advertisement distributed by hand. **handbook** a book giving basic information. **handcuff** put handcuffs on. **handcuffs** a pair of lockable linked metal rings for securing a prisoner's wrists. **handout** 1 a gift of money etc. to a needy person. 2 a piece of printed information given free of charge. **handshake** an act of shaking a person's hand. **handstand** an act of balancing upside down on the hands. **handwriting** 1 writing by hand with a pen or pencil. 2 a style of this. **on hand** available. **out of hand** out of control. **to hand** within reach.

handful n. 1 a quantity that fills the hand. 2 a small number or amount. 3 informal a person who is difficult to control.

handicap n. 1 an obstacle to progress. 2 dated a physical or mental disability. 3 a disadvantage given to a superior competitor in a sport to make the chances more equal.

4 the number of strokes by which a golfer normally exceeds par for a course. • v. (**handicapping, handicapped**) act as a handicap to.

handicraft n. a decorative object made by hand.

handiwork n. (**your handiwork**) something that you have made or done.

handkerchief n. (pl. **handkerchiefs** or **handkerchieves**) a square of material for wiping the nose.

handle v. **1** feel or move with the hands. **2** control. **3** deal with. • n. a part by which a thing is held, carried, or controlled. □ **handlebar** the steering bar of a bicycle or motorbike.

handler n. a person in charge of a trained animal.

handsome adj. **1** good-looking. **2** striking and impressive. **3** (of an amount) large. ■ **handsomely** adv.

handy adj. (**handier, handiest**) **1** useful. **2** conveniently near. □ **handyman** a person who does general building repairs. ■ **handily** adv.

hang v. (**hanging, hung** except in sense 2) **1** suspend or be suspended from above. **2** (past & past part. **hanged**) kill by suspending from a rope tied round the neck. **3** (of a garment) drape in a particular way. □ **hang-glider** a simple aircraft consisting of a framework from which a person is suspended in a harness. **hangman** a person who executes people by hanging. **hangnail** torn skin at the base of a fingernail. **hang out** informal spend time relaxing. **hang-up** informal an emotional problem.

hangar n. a building for aircraft.

hangdog adj. shamefaced.

hanger n. a curved frame with a hook at the top, for hanging clothes on.

hanging n. a decorative piece of fabric hung on a wall.

hangover n. a headache and other after-effects from drinking too much alcohol.

hank n. a coil or length of wool etc.

hanker v. feel a desire for or to do.

hanky (or **hankie**) n. (pl. **hankies**) informal a handkerchief.

Hanukkah n. a Jewish festival of lights held in December.

haphazard adj. lacking order; random. ■ **haphazardly** adv.

hapless adj. unlucky.

happen v. **1** take place; occur. **2** (**happen on**) find by chance. **3** (**happen to**) be experienced by. **4** (**happen to**) become of. ■ **happening** n.

happy adj. (**happier, happiest**) **1** feeling or showing pleasure. **2** fortunate. □ **happy-go-lucky** cheerfully unconcerned. ■ **happily** adv. **happiness** n.

hara-kiri n. (formerly, in Japan) ritual suicide by cutting open the stomach with a sword.

harangue v. criticize aggressively.

harass v. **1** subject to constant pressure or interference. **2** attack an enemy repeatedly. ■ **harassment** n.

> ❗ Only one r: harass.

harbinger /har-bin-jer/ n. a sign or herald of something.

harbour (US **harbor**) n. a place on the coast for ships to moor. • v.

1 keep a thought etc. secretly in the mind. **2** shelter.

hard adj. **1** solid, firm, and rigid. **2** requiring effort. **3** not showing weakness. **4** done with force. **5** harsh or unpleasant. **6** (of information) precise and true. **7** (of drink) strongly alcoholic. **8** (of a drug) very addictive. **9** (of water) containing mineral salts. •adv. **1** with effort or force. **2** so as to be firm. □ **hardback** a book bound in stiff covers. **hardboard** board made of compressed wood pulp. **hard-boiled 1** (of an egg) boiled until solid. **2** tough and cynical. **hard copy** a printed version of computer data. **hard core 1** the most committed members of a group. **2** very explicit pornography. **hard disk** (or **hard drive**) a rigid magnetic disk with a large data storage capacity. **hard-headed** tough and realistic. **hard shoulder** a strip of road alongside a motorway for emergency use. **hardship** poverty. **hard up** informal short of money. **hardware 1** the physical components of a computer. **2** tools and household implements. **hardwood** wood from broad-leaved trees. ■ **harden** v. **hardness** n.

hardly adv. **1** scarcely. **2** only with difficulty.

hardy adj. (**hardier**, **hardiest**) capable of surviving difficult conditions. ■ **hardiness** n.

hare n. an animal like a large rabbit. •v. run very fast. □ **harebrained** foolish and unlikely to succeed.

harebell n. a plant with blue bell-shaped flowers.

harelip n. offens. a cleft lip.

harem /hah-reem/ n. **1** the women's quarters of a Muslim household. **2** the women in a harem.

haricot /ha-ri-koh/ n. a round white bean.

hark v. **1** literary listen. **2** (**hark back to**) recall an earlier period.

harlequin n. a character in traditional pantomime with a diamond-patterned costume. •adj. in varied colours.

harlot n. old use a prostitute.

harm n. **1** deliberate injury. **2** damage. •v. cause harm to. ■ **harmful** adj. **harmless** adj.

harmonica n. a mouth organ.

harmonious adj. **1** tuneful. **2** pleasingly arranged. **3** free from conflict. ■ **harmoniously** adv.

harmonium n. a musical instrument like a small organ.

harmonize (or **-ise**) v. **1** add notes to a melody to produce harmony. **2** make or be harmonious. ■ **harmonization** n.

harmony n. (pl. **harmonies**) **1** the combination of musical notes to produce chords with a pleasing effect. **2** the quality of forming a pleasing combination. **3** agreement. ■ **harmonic** adj.

harness n. **1** a set of straps by which a horse is controlled. **2** a set of straps for attaching a person's body to something. •v. **1** control and use a resource. **2** fit with a harness.

harp n. a musical instrument with strings in a frame. •v. (**harp on**) talk persistently about. ■ **harpist** n.

harpoon n. a spear-like missile for catching whales etc. •v. spear with a harpoon.

harpsichord n. a keyboard instrument.

harpy n. (pl. **harpies**) an unpleasant woman.

harridan n. a bossy or aggressive old woman.

harrier n. **1** a hound used for hunting hares. **2** a bird of prey.

harrow n. a heavy frame with spikes for breaking up soil. •v. **1** draw a harrow over. **2** (**harrowing**) very distressing.

harry v. (**harrying, harried**) harass.

harsh adj. **1** unpleasantly bright, strong, rough, etc. **2** cruel or severe. ■ **harshly** adv. **harshness** n.

hart n. an adult male deer.

harvest n. **1** the process or period of gathering in crops. **2** the season's yield or crop. •v. gather as a harvest. ■ **harvester** n.

has 3rd person sing. present of HAVE. □ **has-been** informal a person who is no longer important.

hash n. a dish of chopped reheated meat. □ **make a hash of** informal do badly.

hashish n. cannabis.

hasn't contr. has not.

hasp n. a hinged metal plate fitted over a metal loop as part of a fastening.

hassle informal n. annoying inconvenience. •v. harass or bother.

hassock n. a cushion for kneeling on in church.

haste n. speed or urgency.

hasten v. **1** hurry. **2** cause to happen sooner.

hasty adj. (**hastier, hastiest**) hurried; rushed. ■ **hastily** adv.

hat n. a shaped covering for the head. □ **hat-trick** three successes of the same kind.

hatch n. a small opening in a floor, wall, or roof allowing access. •v. **1** come out from an egg. **2** devise a plot. **3** shade with close parallel lines. □ **hatchback** a car with a back door that opens upwards.

hatchet n. a small axe. □ **bury the hatchet** end a quarrel.

hate v. feel intense dislike for. •n. intense dislike.

hateful adj. arousing hate.

hatred n. extreme hate.

haughty adj. (**haughtier, haughtiest**) arrogant and superior towards others. ■ **haughtily** adv. **haughtiness** n.

haul v. pull or drag with effort. •n. a quantity of something obtained, esp. illegally.

haulage n. the commercial transport of goods.

haulier n. a person or company transporting goods by road.

haunch n. **1** the buttock and thigh. **2** a leg and loin of an animal.

haunt v. **1** (of a ghost) appear regularly in a place. **2** visit frequently. **3** linger disturbingly in the mind. •n. a place often visited by a particular person.

haute couture /oht kuu-**tyoor**/ n. high fashion.

haute cuisine /oht kwi-**zeen**/ n. high-quality cookery.

hauteur /oh-**ter**/ n. superiority of manner.

have v. (**has, having, had**) **1** possess. **2** experience. **3** (**have to**) be obliged to. **4** suffer from. **5** cause to be or be done. **6** place, hold, or keep. •aux. v. used with a past participle to form past tenses.

haven n. a place of safety.

haven't contr. have not.

haversack *n.* a strong bag carried on the back or over the shoulder.

havoc *n.* great destruction or disorder.

hawk *n.* 1 a bird of prey. 2 a person favouring aggressive policies in foreign affairs. • *v.* 1 offer goods for sale in the street. 2 clear the throat noisily. ■ **hawker** *n.* **hawkish** *adj.*

hawser *n.* a thick rope or cable for mooring or towing a ship.

hawthorn *n.* a thorny shrub or tree with small red berries.

hay *n.* grass cut and dried for use as fodder. □ **hay fever** an allergy to pollen or dust. **haystack** (or **hayrick**) a large packed pile of hay.

haywire *adj.* informal out of control.

hazard *n.* a danger. • *v.* 1 dare to say. 2 put at risk. ■ **hazardous** *adj.*

haze *n.* a thin mist.

hazel *n.* 1 a tree bearing small round nuts (**hazelnuts**). 2 a rich reddish-brown colour.

hazy *adj.* (**hazier, haziest**) 1 covered by a haze. 2 vague or unclear. ■ **hazily** *adv.*

H-bomb *n.* a hydrogen bomb.

he *pron.* 1 the male previously mentioned. 2 a person or animal of unspecified sex.

> **!** The use of **he** to refer to any person, male or female, is considered outdated and sexist by many. Using **he or she** can be clumsy, so **they** is often used instead, as in *everyone needs to feel that they matter.*

head *n.* 1 the part of the body containing the brain, mouth, and sense organs. 2 a person in

charge. 3 the front or top part. 4 a person or animal considered as a unit. 5 a compact mass of leaves or flowers at the top of a stem. 6 (**heads**) the side of a coin bearing the image of a head. 7 pressure of water or steam in an enclosed space. • *adj.* chief. • *v.* 1 be the head of. 2 give a heading to. 3 move in a specified direction. 4 (**head off**) obstruct and turn aside. 5 *Football* hit the ball with the head. □ **come to a head** reach a crisis. **headache** 1 a continuous pain in the head. 2 informal a worry. **headdress** a decorative covering for the head. **headgear** hats, helmets, etc. **headhunt** approach someone employed elsewhere to fill a vacant post. **headland** a promontory. **headlight** a powerful light at the front of a vehicle. **headline** a heading in a newspaper. **headlines** a summary of broadcast news. **headlong** 1 with the head first. 2 in a rush. **headmaster** (or **headmistress**) a male (or female) head teacher. **head-on** 1 involving the front of a vehicle. 2 directly confronting. **headphones** a pair of earphones. **headquarters** the place from which an organization or military operation is directed. **head start** an initial advantage. **headstone** a stone slab at the head of a grave. **headstrong** wilful and determined. **headway** progress. **headwind** a wind blowing from directly in front. ■ **headless** *adj.*

header *n.* Football an act of heading the ball.

heading *n.* 1 a title at the top of a page or section of a book etc. 2 a direction or bearing.

h

heady *adj.* (**headier, headiest**) **1** exciting or exhilarating. **2** intoxicating. ■ **healer** *n.*

heal *v.* make or become healthy again. ■ **healer** *n.*

health *n.* **1** the state of being free from illness. **2** mental or physical condition. □ **health farm** a place where people try to improve their health by dieting, exercise, etc. **health visitor** a nurse who visits patients etc. at home.

healthy *adj.* (**healthier, healthiest**) **1** having or helping towards good health. **2** sensible or desirable. **3** very satisfactory in size or amount. ■ **healthily** *adv.*

heap *n.* **1** a pile of a substance or of a number of objects. **2** *informal* a large amount or number. •*v.* **1** put in or form a heap. **2** load heavily with.

hear *v.* (**hearing, heard**) **1** perceive a sound with the ears. **2** be told or aware of. **3** (**hear from**) be contacted by. **4** listen to. **5** judge a legal case. □ **hearsay** information received which may be unreliable. ■ **hearer** *n.*

hearing *n.* **1** the ability to hear. **2** an opportunity to state your case: *a fair hearing.* **3** a formal act of listening to evidence. □ **hearing aid** a small amplifying device worn by a partially deaf person.

hearse /herss/ *n.* a vehicle for carrying the coffin at a funeral.

heart *n.* **1** the organ that pumps blood around the body. **2** the central or innermost part. **3** capacity for love or compassion. **4** courage or enthusiasm. **5** (**hearts**) one of the four suits in a pack of playing cards. □ **break someone's heart** make someone very sad. **by heart** from memory.

heartache worry or grief. **heart attack** (or **heart failure**) a sudden failure of the heart to function normally. **heartbeat** a pulsation of the heart. **heartburn** indigestion felt as a burning sensation in the chest. **heartfelt** deeply felt. **heart-rending** very distressing. **heart-searching** examination of your feelings and motives. **heart-throb** *informal* a very attractive famous man. **heart-to-heart** (of a conversation) intimate. **heart-warming** emotionally uplifting.

heartbreak *n.* extreme distress. ■ **heartbreaking** *adj.* **heart-broken** *adj.*

hearten *v.* make more cheerful or confident.

hearth *n.* the floor of a fireplace.

heartless *adj.* unfeeling. ■ **heartlessly** *adv.*

hearty *adj.* (**heartier, heartiest**) **1** enthusiastic and friendly. **2** strong and healthy. **3** heartfelt. **4** (of a meal) large. ■ **heartily** *adv.*

heat *n.* **1** the quality of being hot. **2** hot conditions. **3** strength of feeling. **4** a preliminary round in a race or contest. •*v.* **1** make or become hot. **2** (**heat up**) become more intense. **3** (**heated**) passionate. □ **heatstroke** a condition caused by excessive exposure to sun. **heatwave** a period of unusually hot weather. **on heat** (of a female mammal) ready to mate. ■ **heatedly** *adv.*

heater *n.* a device supplying heat.

heath *n.* an area of open uncultivated land covered with heather etc.

heathen *n.* a person who does not belong to a widely held religion.

heather *n.* a shrub with small purple flowers.

heating n. equipment used to provide heat.

heave v. (**heaving, heaved** or *Naut.* **hove**) 1 lift or move with great effort. 2 produce a sigh noisily. 3 rise and fall. 4 try to vomit.

heaven n. 1 (in various religions) the place where God or the gods live. 2 (**the heavens**) *literary* the sky. 3 a place or state of great happiness.

heavenly adj. 1 of heaven or the sky. 2 *informal* wonderful. □ **heavenly body** a planet, star, etc.

heavy adj. (**heavier, heaviest**) 1 of great weight. 2 thick or dense. 3 of more than the usual size, amount, or force. 4 doing something to excess. 5 done with or needing force or effort. 6 *informal* serious or difficult. □ **heavy-handed** clumsy or insensitive.

heavy industry industry producing heavy machinery and materials. **heavy metal** a type of loud rock music. **heavyweight** 1 the heaviest weight in boxing etc. 2 *informal* an influential person. ■ **heavily** adv. **heaviness** n.

Hebrew n. 1 a member of an ancient people living in what is now Israel and Palestine. 2 the language of the Hebrews. ■ **Hebraic** adj.

heckle v. interrupt a public speaker with comments or abuse. ■ **heckler** n.

hectare n. a unit of area, 10,000 sq. m (2.471 acres).

hectic adj. full of frantic activity. ■ **hectically** adv.

hector v. talk to in a bullying way.

hedge n. a barrier of closely growing bushes. •v. 1 surround with a hedge. 2 avoid making a

definite statement or decision. □ **hedgehog** a small mammal with a spiny coat. **hedgerow** bushes and trees bordering a field.

hedonism n. the belief that pleasure is most important in life. ■ **hedonist** n. **hedonistic** adj.

heed v. pay attention to. □ **pay** (or **take**) **heed** pay careful attention. ■ **heedless** adj. **heedlessly** adv.

heel n. 1 the back part of the foot below the ankle. 2 the part of a shoe supporting the heel. •v. 1 renew the heel on a shoe. 2 (of a ship) tilt to one side.

hefty adj. (**heftier, heftiest**) large, heavy, and powerful.

hegemony /hi-jem-uh-ni, hi-gem-uh-ni/ n. dominance of one group or state over another.

Hegira /hej-iruh/ n. Muhammad's departure from Mecca to Medina (AD 622).

heifer /hef-fer/ n. a young cow.

height n. 1 measurement from head to foot or from base to top. 2 distance above ground or sea level. 3 the quality of being tall or high. 4 a high place. 5 the most intense part. 6 an extreme example. ■ **heighten** v.

heinous /hay-nuhss, hee-nuhss/ adj. very wicked.

heir /air/ n. (fem. **heiress**) a person entitled to inherit property or a rank. □ **heirloom** a valuable object that has belonged to a family for several generations.

held past & past part. of **HOLD**.

helical adj. like a helix.

helicopter n. an aircraft with horizontally revolving overhead blades.

heliport n. an airport for helicopters.

helium n. a light colourless gas that does not burn.

helix n. (pl. **helices**) a spiral.

hell n. **1** (in various religions) a place of punishment for the wicked after death. **2** a state or place of great suffering. □ **hell-bent** recklessly determined. **hell-hole** a very unpleasant place. **hell for leather** as fast as possible. ■ **hellish** adj.

Hellenic adj. Greek.

hello (or **hallo, hullo**) exclam. used as a greeting or to attract attention.

helm n. a tiller or wheel for steering a ship or boat. □ **helmsman** a person who steers a boat.

helmet n. a hard or padded protective hat.

help v. **1** make something easier for someone to do. **2** improve a situation. **3** serve food or drink to. **4** (**help yourself**) take without asking first. **5** (**cannot help**) be unable to stop yourself doing. • n. a person or thing that helps. □ **helpline** a phone service providing help with problems. ■ **helper** n.

helpful adj. **1** ready to give help. **2** useful. ■ **helpfully** adv. **helpfulness** n.

helping n. a portion of food served.

helpless adj. **1** unable to manage without help. **2** uncontrollable. ■ **helplessly** adv. **helplessness** n.

helter-skelter adj. & adv. in disorderly haste. • n. a spiral slide round a tower at a fair.

hem n. the edge of a piece of cloth or clothing turned under and sewn. • v. (**hemming, hemmed**) **1** turn under and sew the edge of. **2** (**hem in**) surround and restrict.

hematology etc. US = **HAEMA-TOLOGY** etc.

hemisphere n. **1** a half of a sphere. **2** a half of the earth. ■ **hemispherical** adj.

hemlock n. a poisonous plant.

hemp n. a plant with fibres used to make rope, cloth, etc., and from which cannabis is made.

hen n. a female bird, esp. of a domestic fowl. □ **hen night** (or **hen party**) an all-female celebration held for a woman about to get married. **henpecked** (of a man) nagged by his wife.

hence adv. **1** for this reason. **2** from now. □ **henceforth** (or **henceforward**) from this or that time on.

henchman n. derog. a follower or assistant.

henna n. a reddish-brown dye. ■ **hennaed** adj.

henry n. (pl. **henries** or **henrys**) the basic unit of inductance.

hepatic adj. of the liver.

hepatitis n. a serious disease of the liver.

heptagon n. a plane figure with seven sides. ■ **heptagonal** adj.

heptathlon n. an athletic contest involving seven events. ■ **heptathlete** n.

her pron. used as the object of a verb or preposition to refer to a female previously mentioned. • adj. belonging to her.

herald n. **1** hist. a person who carried official messages and made announcements. **2** a sign of something to come. • v. be a sign of.

heraldry n. the system by which coats of arms are drawn up and regulated. ■ **heraldic** adj.

herb *n.* a plant used for flavouring or in medicine. ∎ **herbal** *adj.*

herbaceous /her-bay-shuhss/ *adj.* (of plants) soft-stemmed. □ **herbaceous border** a garden border containing plants which flower every year.

herbage *n.* herbaceous plants.

herbalism *n.* the use of plants in medicine. ∎ **herbalist** *n.*

herbicide *n.* a substance used to destroy plants.

herbivore *n.* an animal that feeds on plants. ∎ **herbivorous** *adj.*

Herculean *adj.* requiring great strength or effort.

herd *n.* **1** a large group of animals living or kept together. **2** a large crowd of people. • *v.* **1** move in a group. **2** look after livestock. □ **herdsman** the owner or keeper of a herd of animals.

here *adv.* in, at, or to this place, position, or point. □ **hereabouts** near this place. **hereafter 1** from now on. **2** (**the hereafter**) life after death. **hereby** by this means. **herein** in this document etc. **hereto** to this. **herewith** with this.

hereditary *adj.* of or by inheritance.

heredity *n.* **1** the passing on of characteristics from one generation to another. **2** the inheriting of a title etc.

heresy *n.* (*pl.* **heresies**) a belief or opinion contrary to traditional religious doctrine.

heretic *n.* a person believing in a heresy. ∎ **heretical** *adj.*

heritage *n.* valued things such as historic buildings, passed down from previous generations.

hermaphrodite *n.* a person, animal, or plant having both male and female sex organs or characteristics.

hermetic *adj.* airtight. ∎ **hermetically** *adv.*

hermit *n.* a person living in solitude, esp. for religious reasons.

hermitage *n.* the home of a hermit.

hernia *n.* a condition in which part of an organ protrudes through the wall of the cavity containing it.

hero *n.* (*pl.* **heroes**) **1** a person admired for their courage or actions. **2** the chief male character in a story. ∎ **heroism** *n.*

heroic *adj.* very brave. • *n.* (**heroics**) brave behaviour. ∎ **heroically** *adv.*

heroin *n.* a highly addictive illegal drug.

heroine *n.* **1** a woman admired for her courage or achievements. **2** the chief female character in a story.

heron *n.* a long-legged wading bird.

herpes /her-peez/ *n.* a viral disease causing blisters.

herring *n.* (*pl.* **herring** or **herrings**) an edible fish. □ **herringbone** a pattern of columns of short slanting parallel lines.

hers *possess. pron.* belonging to her.

> ! No apostrophe: hers.

herself *pron.* **1** used when a female who performs an action is also affected by it. **2** she or her personally.

hertz *n.* (*pl.* **hertz**) the basic unit of frequency.

hesitant *adj.* reluctant or uncertain. ∎ **hesitancy** *n.* **hesitantly** *adv.*

h

hesitate v. **1** pause indecisively. **2** be reluctant to do. ∎ **hesitation** n.

hessian n. a strong, coarse fabric.

heterodox adj. not following traditional standards or beliefs. ∎ **heterodoxy** n.

heterogeneous adj. varied. ∎ **heterogeneity** n.

heterosexual adj. sexually attracted to people of the opposite sex. •n. a heterosexual person. ∎ **heterosexuality** n.

heuristic adj. allowing someone to learn something for themselves.

hew v. (**hewing, hewed**, past part. **hewn** or **hewed**) chop or cut with an axe etc.

hex n. US a magic spell.

hexagon n. a plane figure with six sides. ∎ **hexagonal** adj.

hexameter n. a line of verse made up of six metrical feet.

heyday n. the period when someone is most successful or active.

HGV abbrev. heavy goods vehicle.

hiatus /hy-ay-tuhss/ n. (pl. **hiatuses**) a pause or gap in a sequence.

hibernate v. spend the winter in a sleep-like state. ∎ **hibernation** n.

Hibernian adj. Irish. •n. an Irish person.

hibiscus n. a plant with large brightly coloured flowers.

hiccup (or **hiccough**) n. **1** a gulping sound in the throat. **2** a minor setback. •v. (**hiccuping, hiccuped**) make the sound of a hiccup.

hide v. (**hiding, hid**; past part. **hidden**) **1** put or keep out of sight. **2** conceal yourself. **3** keep secret. •n. **1** a concealed shelter for observing wildlife. **2** the skin of an animal. □ **hideaway** (or **hideout**) a hiding place. **hidebound** unwilling to accept new ideas.

hideous adj. very ugly. ∎ **hideously** adv. **hideousness** n.

hiding n. a severe beating.

hierarchy n. (pl. **hierarchies**) a system ranking people or things one above the other according to status or importance. ∎ **hierarchical** adj.

hieroglyphics pl. n. a form of writing consisting of pictorial symbols. ∎ **hieroglyphic** adj.

hi-fi adj. of high fidelity. •n. (pl. **hi-fis**) a set of high-fidelity equipment.

higgledy-piggledy adv. & adj. in disorder.

high adj. **1** extending far upwards. **2** of a specified height. **3** far above ground or sea level. **4** large in amount, value, size, etc. **5** at the peak. **6** great in status. **7** (of a sound) not deep or low. **8** informal under the influence of drugs or alcohol. **9** (of food) beginning to go bad. •n. **1** a high level. **2** an area of high atmospheric pressure. **3** informal a state of high spirits. •adv. at or to a high or specified level. □ **highbrow** intellectual or refined. **higher education** education at university etc. **high fidelity** the reproduction of sound with little distortion. **high-handed** using authority arrogantly. **highland** (or **highlands**) an area of high or mountainous land. **high-rise** (of a building) with many storeys. **high school** a secondary school. **high seas** the areas of the sea not under the control of any one country. **high season** the most popular time for a holiday. **high-spirited** lively and cheerful. **high street** the main shopping street of a town. **high tea** a meal eaten in the late afternoon or early evening. **high-tech** involving advanced technology. **high tide** (or **high water**) the tide when at its highest level. **high time** at or past the time when something should have happened.

highlight n. **1** an outstanding part of an event etc. **2** a bright area in a picture. **3** (**highlights**) dyed light streaks in the hair. • v. **1** draw attention to. **2** create highlights in hair.

highly adv. **1** to a high degree. **2** favourably. □ **highly strung** nervous and easily upset.

Highness n. (**His, Your,** etc. **Highness**) a title given to a royal person.

highway n. **1** a main road. **2** a public road. □ **highwayman** hist. a man who held up and robbed travellers.

hijack v. illegally seize control of an aircraft etc. while it is travelling. • n. an act of hijacking. ■ **hijacker** n.

hike n. **1** a long walk. **2** a sharp increase. • v. **1** go on a hike. **2** increase sharply. ■ **hiker** n.

hilarious adj. very funny. ■ **hilariously** adv. **hilarity** n.

hill n. a raised area of land, lower than a mountain. ■ **hilly** adj.

hillbilly n. (pl. **hillbillies**) US informal an unsophisticated country person.

hillock n. a small hill.

hilt n. the handle of a sword or dagger. □ **to the hilt** completely.

him pron. used as the object of a verb or preposition to refer to a male previously mentioned.

himself pron. **1** used when a male who performs an action is also affected by it. **2** he or him personally.

hind adj. at the back. • n. a female deer.

hinder v. delay or obstruct.

Hindi n. a language of northern India.

hindmost adj. furthest back.

hindrance n. something that hinders.

hindsight n. understanding of something after it has happened.

Hindu n. (pl. **Hindus**) a follower of Hinduism.

Hinduism n. a major religion of the Indian subcontinent.

hinge n. a movable joint or mechanism by which a door, lid, etc. opens and closes. • v. **1** attach with a hinge. **2** (**hinge on**) depend on.

hint n. **1** a slight or indirect suggestion. **2** a slight trace. **3** a piece of practical information. • v. suggest indirectly.

hinterland n. the remote areas of a country away from the coast.

hip n. **1** the projection of the pelvis on each side of the body. **2** the fruit of a rose.

hip hop n. a style of pop music featuring rap with an electronic backing.

hippo n. (pl. **hippo** or **hippos**) a hippopotamus.

hippopotamus n. (pl. **hippopotamuses** or **hippopotami**) a large African river mammal with huge jaws.

hippy (or **hippie**) n. (pl. **hippies**) a person who rejects traditional values and dresses unconventionally.

hire v. **1** use or allow to be used temporarily in return for payment. **2** employ someone. • n. the act of hiring. □ **hireling** someone willing to do any paid work. **hire purchase** a system of buying by payment in instalments.

hirsute /her-syoot/ *adj.* hairy.

his *adj. & possess. pron.* belonging to a male previously mentioned.

Hispanic *adj.* of Spain or a Spanish-speaking country.

hiss *v.* **1** make a sharp sound as of the letter s, esp. in disapproval. **2** whisper urgently. • *n.* a hissing sound.

histamine *n.* a substance released by cells in response to an allergy or injury.

histology *n.* the study of animal or plant tissues. ∎ **histologist** *n.*

historian *n.* an expert in history.

historic *adj.* important in history, or likely to be so in the future.

historical *adj.* **1** of history. **2** belonging to or set in the past. ∎ **historically** *adv.*

history *n.* (*pl.* **histories**) **1** the study of past events. **2** the past. **3** the past events connected with someone or something. **4** a record of past events.

histrionic *adj.* excessively dramatic. • *n.* (**histrionics**) exaggerated behaviour.

hit *v.* (**hitting**, **hit**) **1** bring the hand or an object into sudden forceful contact with. **2** come into sudden forceful contact with. **3** cause harm or distress to. **4** reach a place, target, or level. • *n.* **1** an instance of hitting or being hit. **2** a success. **3** an instance of accessing a website. ∎ **hit it off** *informal* like one another. **hitman** a person paid to kill someone.

hitch *v.* **1** move with a jerk. **2** *informal* travel by hitchhiking. **3** fasten with a rope. • *n.* a temporary difficulty. ∎ **get hitched** *informal* get married. **hitchhike** travel by getting free lifts in passing vehicles.

hither *adv.* to or towards this place.

hitherto *adv.* until this time.

HIV *abbrev.* human immunodeficiency virus (causing Aids).

hive *n.* **1** a beehive. **2** (**hives**) an allergic rash. • *v.* (**hive off**) transfer part of a business to new ownership.

HM *abbrev.* Her (or His) Majesty or Majesty's.

HMS *abbrev.* Her or His Majesty's Ship.

HND *abbrev.* Higher National Diploma.

hoard *n.* a secret store of something valued. • *v.* build up a store of. ∎ **hoarder** *n.*

> **!** Don't confuse **hoard** with **horde**, which means 'a large group or crowd'.

hoarding *n.* a large board for displaying advertisements.

hoar frost *n.* a feathery frost.

hoarse *adj.* (of a voice) rough and harsh. ∎ **hoarsely** *adv.* **hoarseness** *n.*

hoary *adj.* **1** having grey hair. **2** old and unoriginal.

hoax *n.* a deception or trick, esp. an unpleasant one. • *v.* deceive with a hoax. ∎ **hoaxer** *n.*

hob *n.* the flat top of a cooker, with hotplates or burners.

hobble *v.* **1** walk with difficulty or painfully. **2** strap together the legs of a horse to limit its movement.

hobby *n.* (*pl.* **hobbies**) a leisure activity done regularly for pleasure. ∎ **hobby horse 1** a person's favourite topic. **2** a toy consisting of a stick with a model of a horse's head.

hobgoblin n. a mischievous imp.

hobnail n. a heavy-headed nail for the soles of boots. ■ **hobnailed** adj.

hobnob v. (**hobnobbing**, **hobnobbed**) informal socialize with important people.

Hobson's choice n. a choice of taking what is offered or nothing at all.

hock n. 1 the middle joint in the back leg of a four-legged animal. 2 a dry white German wine.

hockey n. a game played with curved sticks and a small hard ball.

hocus-pocus n. meaningless talk used to deceive.

hod n. 1 a V-shaped trough on a pole for carrying mortar or bricks. 2 a container for coal.

hodgepodge US = HOTCHPOTCH.

hoe n. a gardening tool with a thin metal blade. • v. use a hoe to cut through earth or weeds.

hog n. a castrated male pig reared for its meat. • v. (**hogging**, **hogged**) informal hoard or hoard selfishly.

Hogmanay n. (in Scotland) New Year's Eve.

hoick v. informal lift or pull with a jerk.

hoi polloi /hoy puh-**loy**/ pl. n. the ordinary people.

hoist v. haul or lift up. • n. a piece of equipment for hoisting.

hoity-toity adj. snobbish.

hokum n. informal 1 nonsense. 2 overused or sentimental material in a film etc.

hold v. (**holding**, **held**) 1 grasp, carry, or support. 2 contain or be able to contain. 3 have, own, or

occupy. 4 keep or detain. 5 stay or keep at a certain level. 6 arrange and take part in. 7 regard in a specified way. • n. 1 a grip. 2 a place to grip while climbing. 3 a degree of control. 4 a storage space in a ship or aircraft. □ **holdall** a large, soft bag. **hold on 1** wait. 2 keep going in difficult circumstances. **hold out 1** resist difficult circumstances. 2 continue to be sufficient. **hold up 1** delay. 2 rob with a gun. **hold-up 1** a delay. 2 an armed robbery. **no holds barred** without restrictions. ■ **holder** n.

holding n. 1 land held by lease. 2 (**holdings**) stocks and property owned by someone.

hole n. 1 a hollow space or opening in an object or surface. 2 informal an awkward or unpleasant place or situation. • v. 1 make a hole in. 2 Golf hit the ball into a hole. ■ **holey** adj.

Holi /hoh-li/ n. a Hindu spring festival.

holiday n. 1 a period spent away from home for enjoyment. 2 a day when most organizations are closed. • v. spend a holiday. ■ **holidaymaker** n.

holistic adj. treating the whole person rather than just the symptoms of a disease. ■ **holism** n.

hollow adj. 1 having empty space inside. 2 curving inwards. 3 worthless. • n. 1 a hole or sunken place. 2 a small valley. • v. form by making a hole.

holly n. an evergreen shrub with prickly leaves and red berries.

hollyhock n. a tall plant with large showy flowers.

holmium n. a soft metallic element.

h

holocaust *n.* destruction or killing on a mass scale.

hologram *n.* a three-dimensional photographic image. ■ **holographic** *adj.*

holster *n.* a holder for a handgun.

holy *adj.* (**holier**, **holiest**) **1** dedicated to God or a religious purpose. **2** morally and spiritually good. ■ **holiness** *n.*

homage *n.* a public act of respect shown to someone.

home *n.* **1** the place where someone lives. **2** an institution for people needing special care. •*adj.* **1** of a person's home or country. **2** (of a match) played on a team's own ground. •*adv.* **1** to or at a person's home. **2** to the intended position. •*v.* (of an animal) return by instinct to its territory. □ **home in on** move or be aimed towards. **homeland** a person's native land. **home page** the main page of an Internet site. **homesick** missing your home during a time away from it. **home truth** an unpleasant fact about yourself. **homework** school work to be done at home. ■ **homeless** *adj.* **homeward** *adj.* & *adv.* **homewards** *adv.*

homely *adj.* **1** simple but comfortable. **2** unsophisticated.

homeopathy (or **homoeopathy**) *n.* a system of treating diseases by tiny doses of substances that would normally produce symptoms of the disease. ■ **homeopath** *n.* **homeopathic** *adj.*

homicide *n.* the killing of another person. ■ **homicidal** *adj.*

homily *n.* (*pl.* **homilies**) a talk on a moral or religious issue.

hominid *n.* a member of a family of primates including humans and their prehistoric ancestors.

homogeneous /hom-uh-jee-ni-uhss/ *adj.* **1** alike. **2** made up of parts of the same kind. ■ **homogeneity** *n.*

homogenize (or **-ise**) *v.* **1** treat milk so that the cream does not separate. **2** make alike.

homograph *n.* a word with the same spelling as another but a different meaning.

homonym *n.* a word having the same spelling and pronunciation as another but a different meaning.

homophobia *n.* hatred or fear of homosexuality and homosexuals. ■ **homophobe** *n.* **homophobic** *adj.*

homophone *n.* a word with the same pronunciation as another.

Homo sapiens *n.* the species to which modern humans belong.

homosexual *adj.* sexually attracted to people of your own sex. •*n.* a homosexual person. ■ **homosexuality** *n.*

hone *v.* **1** make better. **2** sharpen.

honest *adj.* **1** truthful and sincere. **2** fairly earned. ■ **honesty** *n.*

honestly *adv.* **1** in an honest way. **2** really.

honey *n.* (*pl.* **honeys**) a sweet, sticky fluid made by bees from nectar. □ **honeybee** the common bee. **honeycomb** a structure of six-sided wax compartments made by bees to store honey and eggs. **honeydew** a type of melon with sweet green flesh. **honeymoon 1** a holiday taken by a newly married couple. **2** an initial period of goodwill. **honeysuckle**

a climbing shrub with scented flowers.

honk n. **1** the cry of a goose. **2** the sound of a car horn. • v. make a honk.

honorarium n. (pl. **honoraria** or **honoraria**) a voluntary payment for services offered without charge.

honorary adj. **1** given as an honour. **2** (of a position or its holder) unpaid.

honour (US **honor**) n. **1** great respect. **2** a clear sense of what is morally right. **3** a privilege. **4** an award for achievement. **5** (**honours**) a university course of a higher level than an ordinary one. • v. **1** regard or treat with great respect. **2** keep an agreement.

honourable (US **honorable**) adj. deserving or bringing honour. ■ **honourably** adv.

hood n. **1** a covering for the head and neck. **2** a folding waterproof cover of a vehicle or pram. **3** US a car bonnet. **4** informal a gangster or gunman. ■ **hooded** adj.

hoodlum n. a gangster or violent criminal.

hoodoo n. a run or cause of bad luck.

hoodwink v. deceive or trick.

hoody (or **hoodie**) n. (pl. **hoodies**) a hooded top.

hoof n. (pl. **hoofs** or **hooves**) the horny part of the foot of a horse, cow, etc. ■ **hoofed** adj.

hook n. **1** a curved object for catching hold of things or hanging things on. **2** a short punch made with the elbow bent. • v. **1** catch or fasten with a hook. **2** (**hook up**) link to electronic equipment.

□ **hookworm** an intestinal worm

with hook-like mouthparts. ■ **hooked** adj.

hookah n. an oriental tobacco pipe with a long tube to draw the smoke through water.

hooligan n. a violent young troublemaker. ■ **hooliganism** n.

hoop n. **1** a rigid circular band. **2** a large ring used as a toy. ■ **hooped** adj.

hoopla n. a game in which rings are thrown over a prize.

hoopoe n. a crested bird.

hooray exclam. hurrah.

hoot n. **1** a low sound made by owls or a hooter. **2** a short laugh or mocking shout. **3** informal an amusing person or thing. • v. make a hoot.

hooter n. a siren, steam whistle, or horn.

Hoover n. trademark a vacuum cleaner. • v. (**hoover**) clean with a vacuum cleaner.

hooves pl. of HOOF.

hop v. (**hopping**, **hopped**) **1** jump along on one foot. **2** (of an animal) jump along. **3** informal move or go quickly. • n. **1** a hopping movement. **2** a short journey. **3** a plant used to flavour beer. □ **hopscotch** a children's game of hopping into and over marked squares. **on the hop** informal unprepared.

hope n. **1** a feeling that something wanted may happen. **2** a cause for hope. **3** something wished for. • v. expect and want to happen. ■ **hopeful** adj.

hopefully adv. **1** in a hopeful way. **2** it is to be hoped that.

hopeless adj. **1** without hope. **2** very bad or unskilful. ■ **hopelessly** adv.

hopper *n.* a tapering container that empties its contents at the bottom.

horde *n.* a large group or crowd.

! Don't confuse **horde** with **hoard**, which means 'a store of something valued'.

horizon *n.* **1** the line at which the earth's surface and the sky appear to meet. **2** the limit of a person's understanding or interests.

horizontal *adj.* parallel to the horizon. ■ **horizontally** *adv.*

hormone *n.* a substance produced in the body that controls the action of cells or tissues. ■ **hormonal** *adj.*

horn *n.* **1** a hard bony growth on the heads of cattle, sheep, etc. **2** the substance of a horn. **3** a wind instrument shaped like a cone or wound into a spiral. **4** an instrument sounding a warning. □ **hornpipe** a lively solo dance traditionally performed by sailors. ■ **horned** *adj.*

hornblende *n.* a dark brown, black, or green mineral.

hornet *n.* a large wasp.

horny *adj.* (**hornier, horniest**) **1** of or like horn. **2** *informal* sexually aroused.

horology *n.* **1** the study and measurement of time. **2** the making of clocks and watches.

horoscope *n.* a forecast of events based on the positions of stars.

horrendous *adj.* very unpleasant or horrifying. ■ **horrendously** *adv.*

horrible *adj.* **1** causing horror. **2** very unpleasant. ■ **horribly** *adv.*

horrid *adj.* horrible.

horrific *adj.* causing horror. ■ **horrifically** *adv.*

horrify *v.* (**horrifying, horrified**) fill with horror.

horror *n.* **1** great fear, shock, disgust, or dismay. **2** a cause of this.

hors d'oeuvre /or derv/ *n.* a small savoury first course of a meal.

horse *n.* a four-legged mammal used for riding and for pulling heavy loads. •*v.* (**horse around/ about**) *informal* fool about. □ **horsebox** a vehicle for transporting horses. **horse chestnut** a large tree producing nuts (conkers). **horsefly** a large biting fly. **horseman** (or **horsewoman**) a rider on horseback. **horseplay** boisterous play. **horsepower** a unit measuring the power of an engine. **horseradish** a hot-tasting root used to make a sauce. **horseshoe** a U-shaped iron band attached to the base of a horse's hoof. **on horseback** mounted on a horse.

horsey (or **horsy**) *adj.* **1** of or like a horse. **2** very keen on horses.

horticulture *n.* the cultivation of gardens. ■ **horticultural** *adj.* **horticulturist** *n.*

hose *n.* **1** a flexible tube for conveying water. **2** hosiery. •*v.* wash with a hose.

hosiery *n.* stockings, socks, and tights.

hospice *n.* a home for the care of the terminally ill.

hospitable *adj.* friendly and welcoming. ■ **hospitably** *adv.*

hospital *n.* an institution for the treatment and care of sick or injured people.

hospitality *n.* friendly and generous treatment of guests or visitors.

hospitalize (or **-ise**) v. admit to hospital for treatment. ■ **hospitalization** n.

host n. **1** a person who receives or entertains guests. **2** the presenter of a television or radio programme. **3** a place holding an event to which others are invited. **4** an animal or plant on or in which a parasite lives. **5** a large number of people or things. •v. act as host at or for.

hostage n. a person held captive in an attempt to ensure that a demand is met.

hostel n. a place providing cheap food and lodging for a particular group.

hostelry n. (pl. **hostelries**) old use an inn or pub.

hostess n. a female host.

hostile adj. **1** showing dislike or opposition. **2** of a military enemy.

hostility n. **1** hostile behaviour. **2** (**hostilities**) acts of warfare.

hot adj. (**hotter, hottest**) **1** having a high temperature. **2** feeling or producing an uncomfortable sensation of heat. **3** currently popular or interesting. **4** showing strong emotion. •v. (**hotting, hotted**) (**hot up**) informal become more exciting or intense. ■ **hotly** adv.

hotbed a place where an activity happens or flourishes. **hot-blooded** passionate. **hot dog** a hot sausage served in a bread roll. **hotfoot** in eager haste. **hothead** a rash or quick-tempered person. **hothouse** **1** a heated greenhouse. **2** an environment encouraging rapid development. **hotline** a direct phone line set up for a purpose. **hotplate** a flat heated surface on an electric cooker. ■ **hotly** adv.

hotchpotch (US **hodgepodge**) n. a confused mixture.

hotel n. a place providing rooms and meals for guests.

hotelier n. a hotel owner or manager.

houmous var. of **HUMMUS**.

hound n. a hunting dog. •v. harass.

hour n. **1** a period of 60 minutes, one of the 24 parts of a day. **2** a point in time. **3** a time set aside for a purpose or activity. ■ **hourglass** a device with two connected glass bulbs containing sand that takes an hour to fall from the upper to the lower bulb. ■ **hourly** adj. & adv.

houri /hoor-i/ n. (in Islamic belief) a beautiful virgin in paradise.

house n. **1** a building for people to live in, or for a specific purpose. **2** a business. **3** a dynasty. **4** a law-making assembly. **5** a group of pupils living together at boarding school. **6** a style of fast popular dance music. •v. **1** provide accommodation or space for. **2** enclose. **house arrest** detention in a person's own house. **houseboat** a boat that people can live in. **housebound** unable to leave your house because of illness or old age. **housebreaking** breaking into a building to commit a crime. **housecoat** a woman's dressing gown. **household** a house and its occupants. **householder** a person who owns or rents a house. **housekeeper** a person employed to manage a household. **housemaster** (or **housemistress**) a teacher in charge of a house at a boarding school. **house-proud** very concerned with the appearance of your home. **house-train** train a pet to urinate and defecate outdoors. **house-warming** a

h

party celebrating a move to a new home. **housewife** a woman whose main occupation is looking after her family and the home. **housework** cleaning, cooking, etc. done in running a home. **on the house** at the management's expense.

housing n. 1 houses and flats. 2 a rigid case for a piece of equipment.

hove Naut. past of **HEAVE**.

hovel n. a small dirty or run-down house.

hover v. 1 remain in one place in the air. 2 wait about uncertainly. 3 remain at or near a particular level. □ **hovercraft** a vehicle that travels over land or water on a cushion of air.

how adv. 1 in what way or by what means. 2 in what condition. 3 to what extent or degree. 4 the way in which.

howdah n. a seat on an elephant's back.

however adv. 1 nevertheless; despite this. 2 in whatever way or to whatever extent.

howitzer n. a short gun firing shells at a high angle.

howl n. a long wailing cry or sound. •v. make a howl.

howler n. informal a stupid mistake.

hoyden n. dated a high-spirited or wild girl.

h.p. (or **HP**) abbrev. 1 hire purchase. 2 horsepower.

HQ abbrev. headquarters.

HRH abbrev. Her (or His) Royal Highness.

HRT abbrev. hormone replacement therapy.

HTML n. Hypertext Markup Language.

hub n. 1 the central part of a wheel. 2 the centre of an activity. □ **hubcap** a cover for the hub of a wheel.

hubbub n. a confused noise of a crowd.

hubris /hyoo-briss/ n. excessive pride or self-confidence.

huddle v. crowd together. •n. a close group of people or things.

hue n. a colour or shade.

hue and cry n. a strong public outcry.

huff n. a fit of annoyance. •v. (**huff and puff**) 1 breathe out noisily. 2 show annoyance. ■ **huffy** adj. **huffily** adv.

hug v. (**hugging, hugged**) 1 hold tightly in your arms. 2 keep close to. •n. an embrace.

huge adj. very large. ■ **hugely** adv.

hula hoop n. trademark a large hoop spun round the body.

hulk n. 1 a large or clumsy person or thing. 2 an old ship stripped of its fittings.

hulking adj. very large or clumsy.

hull n. 1 the main body of a ship. 2 the outer covering of a fruit or seed. 3 the cluster of leaves on a strawberry.

hullabaloo n. informal an uproar.

hullo var. of **HELLO**.

hum v. (**humming, hummed**) 1 make a low continuous sound. 2 sing with closed lips. 3 informal be very busy. •n. a low continuous sound.

human adj. 1 of people. 2 showing kindness, emotion, etc. •n. (or **human being**) a person. □ **humankind** people as a whole.

human resources the section of an organization dealing with recruitment etc. **human rights** basic rights to which all people are entitled. ■ **humanely** *adv.*

humane *adj.* kind and considerate. ■ **humanely** *adv.*

humanism *n.* the belief that people are able to live by reason rather than relying on religious faith. ■ **humanist** *n.* & *adj.*

humanitarian *adj.* concerned with human welfare. ■ **humanitarianism** *n.*

humanity *n.* (*pl.* **humanities**) **1** people as a whole. **2** the condition of being human. **3** sympathy and kindness. **4** (**humanities**) studies concerned with culture.

humanize (or **-ise**) *v.* make more pleasant or suitable for people.

humble *adj.* **1** having a low opinion of your importance. **2** of low rank. **3** not large or elaborate. •*v.* cause to seem less important. ■ **humbly** *adv.*

humbug *n.* **1** misleading or foolish talk. **2** a peppermint sweet.

humdrum *adj.* dull or ordinary.

humerus *n.* (*pl.* **humeri**) the bone in the upper arm.

humid *adj.* (of the air) damp and warm. ■ **humidity** *n.*

humidifier *n.* a device for regulating moisture in the air of a room.

humiliate *v.* cause to feel ashamed or stupid. ■ **humiliation** *n.*

humility *n.* the quality of being humble.

hummingbird *n.* a small tropical bird able to hover by beating its wings very fast.

hummock *n.* a small hill or mound.

hummus (or **houmous**) *n.* a dip made from puréed chickpeas.

humorist *n.* a writer or speaker noted for being amusing.

humorous *adj.* **1** causing amusement. **2** showing a sense of humour. ■ **humorously** *adv.*

> ❗ *-or-* not *-our-*: humorous.

humour (US **humor**) *n.* **1** the quality of being amusing. **2** a state of mind. •*v.* agree with someone to keep them happy. ■ **humourless** *adj.*

hump *n.* **1** a rounded lump or mound. **2** a rounded part projecting from the back of a camel or as an abnormality on a person's back. •*v. informal* carry with difficulty. ■ **humped** *adj.*

humus /hyoo-muhss/ *n.* a substance found in soil, formed from dead plant material.

hunch *v.* raise the shoulders and bend the top of the body forward. •*n.* an idea or feeling that is not based on evidence. □ **hunchback** *offens.* a person with a hump on their back.

hundred *adj.* & *n.* ten more than ninety; 100. □ **hundredweight 1** a unit of weight equal to 112 lb (about 50.8 kg). **2** US a unit of weight equal to 100 lb (about 45.4 kg). ■ **hundredth** *adj.* & *n.*

hung past & past part. of **HANG**. •*adj.* **1** having no political party with an overall majority. **2** (of a jury) unable to agree on a verdict. □ **hungover** suffering from a hangover.

hunger *n.* **1** a feeling of discomfort caused by lack of food. **2** a strong desire. •*v.* (**hunger after/ for**) have a strong desire for.

h

□ **hunger strike** refusal to eat as a means of protest.

hungry *adj.* (**hungrier, hungriest**) feeling hunger. ■ **hungrily** *adv.*

hunk *n.* **1** a large piece cut or broken off. **2** *informal* a strong, attractive man.

hunt *v.* **1** chase and kill a wild animal for sport or food. **2** search. **3** (**hunt down**) chase and capture. •*n.* **1** an act of hunting. **2** a group who hunt animals as a sport. ■ **hunter** *n.*

hurdle *n.* **1** an upright frame to be jumped over in a race. **2** an obstacle or difficulty. •*v.* jump over while running. ■ **hurdler** *n.*

hurl *v.* throw forcefully.

hurly-burly *n.* noisy activity.

hurrah (or **hooray, hurray**) *exclam.* used to express joy or approval.

hurricane *n.* a severe storm with a strong wind.

hurry *v.* (**hurrying, hurried**) **1** move or act quickly. **2** do too quickly. •*n.* great haste. ■ **hurriedly** *adv.*

hurt *v.* (**hurting, hurt**) **1** cause pain or harm to. **2** feel pain. **3** make upset. •*n.* injury or pain. ■ **hurtful** *adj.*

hurtle *v.* move very fast.

husband *n.* a married man in relation to his wife. •*v.* use resources carefully.

husbandry *n.* **1** farming. **2** careful use of resources.

hush *v.* **1** make or become quiet. **2** (**hush up**) prevent from becoming known. •*n.* a silence.

husk *n.* the dry outer covering of some fruits or seeds.

husky *adj.* (**huskier, huskiest**) **1** (of a voice) deep and rough. **2** big and strong. •*n.* (*pl.* **huskies**) a dog used for pulling sledges. ■ **huskily** *adv.* **huskiness** *n.*

hussy *n.* (*pl.* **hussies**) a cheeky or immoral girl or woman.

hustings *n.* the political meetings and speeches before an election.

hustle *v.* push or move roughly. •*n.* busy activity.

hut *n.* a small simple house or shelter.

hutch *n.* a box with a wire mesh front, for keeping rabbits etc.

hyacinth *n.* a plant with scented flowers.

hyaena var. of **HYENA**.

hybrid *n.* **1** the offspring of two plants or animals of different species or varieties. **2** something made by combining two different things.

hydrangea /hy-**drayn**-juh/ *n.* a shrub with white, blue, or pink flowers.

hydrant *n.* a water pipe with a nozzle for attaching a fire hose.

hydrate *v.* cause to absorb or combine with water. •*n.* a chemical compound of water and another substance. ■ **hydration** *n.*

hydraulic *adj.* operated by a liquid moving under pressure. •*n.* (**hydraulics**) the study of the use of liquids moving under pressure to provide mechanical force. ■ **hydraulically** *adv.*

hydrocarbon *n.* a compound of hydrogen and carbon.

hydrochloric acid *n.* an acid containing hydrogen and chlorine.

hydroelectric *adj.* using flowing water to generate electricity.

hydrofoil → hypocrite

hydrofoil n. a boat designed to rise above the water when travelling at speed.

hydrogen n. a highly flammable gas which is the lightest chemical element. □ **hydrogen bomb** a nuclear bomb whose power comes from the fusion of hydrogen nuclei.

hydrolysis n. the chemical breakdown of a compound due to reaction with water.

hydrophobia n. **1** extreme fear of water, esp. as a symptom of rabies. **2** rabies.

hydroplane n. a light, fast motor boat designed to skim over the water.

hydroponics n. the growing of plants in sand or liquid rather than soil.

hydrotherapy n. therapeutic exercises in water.

hydrous adj. containing water.

hyena (or **hyaena**) n. a doglike African mammal.

hygiene n. the practice of keeping yourself and your surroundings clean to prevent disease. ■ **hygienic** adj. **hygienically** adv. **hygienist** n.

hymen n. the membrane partially closing the opening of the vagina, usu. broken when a woman or girl first has sex.

hymn n. a religious song of praise.

hype informal n. excessive publicity. • v. publicize in an excessive way.

hyper- prefix **1** over; above. **2** excessively.

hyperactive adj. excessively active.

hyperbola /hy-per-buh-luh/ n. (pl. **hyperbolas**) a symmetrical curve formed when a cone is cut

by a plane nearly parallel to the cone's axis.

hyperbole /hy-per-buh-li/ n. statements that are deliberately exaggerated for effect.

hyperlink n. a link from a hypertext document to another location.

hypermarket n. a very large supermarket.

hypersonic adj. of speeds more than five times that of sound.

hypertension n. abnormally high blood pressure.

hypertext n. software enabling quick movement between documents or sections of data.

hyperventilate v. breathe at an abnormally rapid rate. ■ **hyperventilation** n.

hyphen n. the sign (-) used to join words together or to split a word at the end of a line. ■ **hyphenate** v. **hyphenation** n.

hypnosis n. the practice of causing a person to enter a state in which they respond very readily to suggestions or commands. ■ **hypnotic** adj. **hypnotically** adv.

hypnotism n. hypnosis. ■ **hypnotist** n. **hypnotize** (or **-ise**) v.

hypo- prefix **1** under. **2** below normal.

hypoallergenic adj. unlikely to cause an allergic reaction.

hypochondria n. excessive anxiety about your health. ■ **hypochondriac** n.

hypocrisy n. behaviour in which a person pretends to have higher standards than is the case.

hypocrite n. a person guilty of hypocrisy. ■ **hypocritical** adj.

h

hypodermic adj. used to inject a drug etc. beneath the skin. •n. a hypodermic syringe.

hypotension n. abnormally low blood pressure.

hypotenuse /hy-pot-uh-nyooz/ n. the longest side of a right-angled triangle.

hypothermia n. the condition of having an abnormally low body temperature.

hypothesis n. (pl. **hypotheses**) an idea or explanation that has not yet been proved to be true or correct. ■ **hypothesize** (or **-ise**) v.

hypothetical adj. based on a possible situation rather than fact. ■ **hypothetically** adv.

hysterectomy n. (pl. **hysterectomies**) an operation to remove all or part of the womb.

hysteria n. extreme or uncontrollable emotion. ■ **hysterical** adj. **hysterically** adv.

hysterics pl. n. 1 wildly emotional behaviour. 2 informal uncontrollable laughter.

Hz abbrev. hertz.

I pron. used by a speaker to refer to himself or herself. •n. (or **i**) the Roman numeral for one.

iambic /I-am-bik/ adj. (of verse) having one short syllable followed by one long syllable.

ibex n. (pl. **ibexes**) a wild mountain goat.

ibid. adv. in the book just mentioned.

ice n. 1 frozen water. 2 an ice cream. •v. 1 decorate with icing. 2 become covered with ice. □ **break the ice** start a conversation on first meeting. **ice age** a period when ice covered much of the earth's surface. **iceberg** a large mass of ice floating in the sea. **icebox** a freezing compartment in a fridge. **ice cream** a frozen dessert made with milk fat. **ice skate** a boot with a blade on the sole, for skating on ice.

ichthyology /ik-thi-ol-uh-ji/ n. the study of fish. ■ **ichthyologist** n.

icicle n. a hanging, tapering piece of ice.

icing n. a mixture of sugar with liquid or fat, used to coat cakes.

icon n. 1 a famous person who symbolizes something. 2 a symbol on a computer screen representing a program. 3 (or **ikon**) a sacred painting of a holy person. ■ **iconic** adj.

iconoclast n. a person who attacks established customs and values. ■ **iconoclastic** adj.

icy adj. (**icier**, **iciest**) 1 covered with ice. 2 very cold. 3 very unfriendly. ■ **icily** adv. **iciness** n.

ID abbrev. identification or identity.

Id n. var. of EID.

id *n.* the part of the unconscious mind consisting of basic inherited instincts and feelings.

idea *n.* **1** a thought or suggestion about a possible course of action. **2** a mental impression. **3** a belief.

ideal *adj.* most suitable; perfect. •*n.* **1** a principle or standard that is worth aiming for. **2** a person or thing regarded as perfect. ∎ **ideally** *adv.*

idealism *n.* the belief that ideals can be achieved. ∎ **idealist** *n.* **idealistic** *adj.*

idealize (or **-ise**) *v.* represent as better than in reality.

identical *adj.* **1** exactly alike. **2** the same. ∎ **identically** *adv.*

identify *v.* (**identifying, identified**) **1** prove or recognize as being a specified person or thing. **2** understand or share the feelings of. **3** consider to be the same. ∎ **identifiable** *adj.* **identification** *n.*

identikit *n. trademark* a picture of a wanted person, put together from typical facial features.

identity *n.* (*pl.* **identities**) **1** the fact of being who or what a person or thing is. **2** a close similarity.

ideology *n.* (*pl.* **ideologies**) a system of ideas forming the basis of an economic or political theory. ∎ **ideological** *adj.*

idiocy *n.* (*pl.* **idiocies**) very stupid behaviour.

idiom *n.* a phrase whose meaning is different from the meanings of the individual words.

idiomatic *adj.* using expressions natural to a native speaker.

idiosyncrasy *n.* (*pl.* **idiosyncrasies**) a person's particular way of behaving or thinking. ∎ **idiosyncratic** *adj.*

❗ The ending is *-asy*, not *-acy*: idio*syncrasy.*

idiot *n.* a stupid person. ∎ **idiotic** *adj.* **idiotically** *adv.*

idle *adj.* **1** avoiding work; lazy. **2** not working or in use. **3** having no purpose or effect. •*v.* **1** spend time doing nothing. **2** (of an engine) run slowly while out of gear. ∎ **idleness** *n.* **idler** *n.* **idly** *adv.*

idol *n.* **1** a greatly admired person. **2** a statue or picture of a god that is worshipped.

idolatry *n.* worship of idols. ∎ **idolatrous** *adj.*

idolize (or **-ise**) *v.* admire or love greatly.

idyll /I-dil/ *n.* **1** a very happy or peaceful situation. **2** a short poem describing a peaceful country scene. ∎ **idyllic** *adj.* **idyllically** *adv.*

i.e. *abbrev.* that is.

if *conj.* **1** on the condition or in the event that. **2** whether.

iffy *adj. informal* uncertain or in poor condition.

igloo *n.* a dome-shaped Eskimo house built from blocks of snow.

igneous *adj.* (of rock) formed from solidified molten rock.

ignite *v.* catch or set on fire.

ignition *n.* **1** the act of igniting. **2** the mechanism igniting the fuel in an engine.

ignoble *adj.* dishonourable.

ignominy *n.* public disgrace. ∎ **ignominious** *adj.* **ignominiously** *adv.*

ignoramus *n.* (*pl.* **ignoramuses**) an ignorant person.

ignorant *adj.* **1** lacking knowledge. **2** *informal* not polite. ∎ **ignorance** *n.*

ignore v. 1 deliberately take no notice of. 2 fail to consider.

iguana n. a large tropical lizard.

ikon var. of ICON (sense 3).

ilk n. a type.

ill adj. 1 not in good health. 2 bad or harmful. • adv. 1 badly or wrongly. 2 only with difficulty. n. 1 a problem or misfortune. 2 harm. ■ **ill-advised** unwise. **ill at ease** uncomfortable or embarrassed. **ill-gotten** obtained illegally or unfairly. **ill-starred** unlucky. **ill-treat** treat cruelly. **ill will** hostility.

illegal adj. against the law. ■ **illegality** n. **illegally** adv.

illegible adj. not clear enough to be read. ■ **illegibility** n.

illegitimate adj. 1 not allowed by law or rules. 2 born of parents not married to each other. ■ **illegitimacy** n.

illicit adj. forbidden by law, rules, or standards. ■ **illicitly** adv.

illiterate adj. 1 unable to read or write. 2 not knowledgeable about a subject. ■ **illiteracy** n.

illness n. a disease or period of being ill.

illogical adj. not sensible or based on sound reasoning. ■ **illogicality** n. **illogically** adv.

illuminate v. 1 light up. 2 help to explain. ■ **illumination** n.

illumine v. illuminate.

illusion n. 1 a false idea or belief. 2 a thing that seems to be something it is not.

illusionist n. a magician.

illusory (or **illusive**) adj. not real.

illustrate v. 1 provide a book etc. with pictures. 2 make clear by using examples etc. 3 act as an example of. ■ **illustrative** adj. **illustrator** n.

illustration n. 1 a picture in a book etc. 2 the act of illustrating. 3 an explanatory example.

illustrious adj. famous and greatly admired.

image n. 1 a picture or statue. 2 a picture seen on a screen, through a lens, or in a mirror. 3 a picture in the mind. 4 an impression presented to the public.

imagery n. language producing images in the mind.

imaginary adj. existing only in the imagination.

imagination n. 1 the part of the mind that imagines things. 2 the ability to be creative or solve problems. ■ **imaginative** adj. **imaginatively** adv.

imagine v. 1 form a mental picture of. 2 suppose; assume. 3 believe something unreal to exist. ■ **imaginable** adj.

imam n. the person who leads prayers in a mosque.

imbalance n. a lack of balance.

imbecile n. informal a stupid person. ■ **imbecilic** adj. **imbecility** n.

imbed var. of EMBED.

imbibe v. 1 drink alcohol. 2 absorb ideas.

imbroglio /im-broh-li-oh/ n. (pl. **imbroglios**) a confused or complicated situation.

imbue v. fill with a feeling or quality.

IMF abbrev. International Monetary Fund.

imitate v. 1 follow as a model. 2 copy or mimic. ■ **imitation** n. **imitative** adj. **imitator** n.

immaculate adj. 1 completely clean or tidy. 2 free from flaws or mistakes. ■ **immaculately** adv.

immanent adj. present throughout; inherent. ■ **immanence** n.

immaterial adj. not important or relevant.

immature adj. 1 not fully developed. 2 childish. ■ **immaturity** n.

immeasurable adj. too large or extreme to measure. ■ **immeasurably** adv.

immediate adj. 1 occurring or done at once. 2 nearest in time, space, or relationship. 3 most urgent; current. ■ **immediacy** n. **immediately** adv.

immemorial adj. existing for longer than can be remembered.

immense adj. very large or great. ■ **immensely** adv. **immensity** n.

immerse v. 1 dip or cover completely in a liquid. 2 involve deeply in an activity. ■ **immersion** n.

immersion heater n. an electric heating device in a water tank.

immigration n. the act of coming to live permanently in a foreign country. ■ **immigrant** n. **immigrate** v.

imminent adj. about to happen. ■ **imminence** n. **imminently** adv.

immobile adj. not moving or able to move. ■ **immobility** n. **immobilize** (or **-ise**) v.

immoderate adj. excessive.

immolate v. kill or sacrifice by burning.

immoral adj. not following accepted moral standards. ■ **morality** n.

immortal adj. 1 living forever. 2 deserving to be remembered forever. ■ **immortality** n. **immortalize** (or **-ise**) v.

immovable adj. 1 unable to be moved. 2 unable to be changed. ■ **immovably** adv.

immune adj. 1 naturally resistant to an infection. 2 not affected. 3 exempt or protected. ■ **immunity** n. **immunize** (or **-ise**) v. **immunization** n.

immunodeficiency n. failure of the body's ability to resist infection.

immunology n. the study of resistance to infection. ■ **immunological** adj. **immunologist** n.

immure v. confine or imprison.

immutable adj. unchanging or unchangeable.

imp n. 1 a small devil. 2 a mischievous child. ■ **impish** adj.

impact n. 1 an act of one object hitting another. 2 a noticeable effect. • v. 1 hit another object. 2 have a strong effect.

impair v. weaken or damage. ■ **impairment** n.

impala n. (pl. impala) an African antelope with lyre-shaped horns.

impale v. pierce with a sharp object.

impalpable adj. 1 unable to be felt by touch. 2 not easily understood.

impart v. 1 communicate information. 2 give a quality to.

impartial adj. not favouring one more than another. ■ **impartiality** n. **impartially** adv.

impassable adj. impossible to travel along or over.

impasse /am-pahss/ n. a deadlock.

impassioned adj. filled with or showing great emotion.

impassive adj. not feeling or showing emotion.

impatient adj. 1 lacking patience or tolerance. 2 restlessly eager.

i

■ **impatience** n. **impatiently** adv.

impeach v. charge a public official with serious misconduct. ■ **impeachment** n.

impeccable adj. faultless. ■ **impeccably** adv.

impecunious adj. having little or no money.

impedance n. the total resistance of an electric circuit to the flow of alternating current.

impede v. delay or block the progress of.

impediment n. **1** a hindrance. **2** a defect in a person's speech.

impel v. (**impelling, impelled**) drive or urge to do something.

impending adj. imminent.

impenetrable adj. impossible to get through or into or to understand.

imperative adj. **1** essential or vital. **2** giving or expressing a command. • n. an essential thing.

imperceptible adj. too slight to be seen or felt. ■ **imperceptibly** adv.

imperfect adj. **1** faulty or incomplete. **2** (of a tense) referring to a past action not yet completed. ■ **imperfection** n. **imperfectly** adv.

imperial adj. **1** of an empire or an emperor. **2** (of measures) in a non-metric system formerly used in the UK.

imperialism n. a policy of extending a country's power and influence by military force etc. ■ **imperialist** n. & adj.

imperil v. (**imperilling, imperilled**; US **imperiling, imperiled**) endanger.

imperious adj. expecting unquestioning obedience. ■ **imperiously** adv.

impermeable adj. not allowing fluid to pass through.

impersonal adj. **1** not influenced by personal feelings. **2** distant, unemotional, etc. ■ **impersonally** adv.

impersonate v. pretend to be another person. ■ **impersonation** n. **impersonator** n.

impertinent adj. not showing proper respect. ■ **impertinence** n. **impertinently** adv.

imperturbable adj. unable to be upset.

impervious adj. **1** impermeable. **2** (**impervious to**) unaffected by.

impetigo /im-pi-ty-goh/ n. a contagious skin infection.

impetuous adj. acting or done quickly and without thought. ■ **impetuously** adv.

impetus n. **1** the force or energy with which something moves. **2** a driving force.

impinge v. have an effect or impact.

impious adj. irreverent.

implacable adj. **1** unwilling to be reconciled. **2** (of negative feelings) unable to be changed. ■ **implacably** adv.

implant v. **1** insert tissue or a device surgically into the body. **2** establish in the mind. • n. something implanted. ■ **implantation** n.

implausible adj. not probable or convincing. ■ **implausibly** adv.

implement n. a tool. • v. put into effect. ■ **implementation** n.

implicate v. **1** show to be involved in a crime. **2** (**be implicated in**) be partly responsible for.

implication n. **1** a conclusion implied by something. **2** a possible effect. **3** involvement in something.

implicit adj. **1** suggested but not stated directly. **2** with no doubt or question. ■ **implicitly** adv.

implode v. collapse violently inwards. ■ **Implosion** n.

implore v. beg earnestly.

imply v. (**implying**, **implied**) **1** suggest rather than state directly. **2** suggest as a possible effect.

> **!** Don't confuse **imply** and **infer**. If you **imply** something, you are suggesting it though not saying it directly. If you **infer** something from a statement, you come to the conclusion that this is what was meant.

impolite adj. not having good manners.

impolitic adj. unwise.

imponderable adj. difficult or impossible to assess.

import v. bring goods into a country from abroad. •n. **1** an imported item. **2** the act of importing. **3** implied meaning. **4** importance. ■ **importation** n. **importer** n.

important adj. **1** of great value or significance. **2** having great authority or influence. ■ **importance** n. **importantly** adv.

importunate adj. very persistent.

importune v. bother with persistent requests.

impose v. **1** force something to be done or accepted. **2** (**impose on**) take unfair advantage of. ■ **imposition** n.

imposing adj. impressive.

impossible adj. **1** not able to occur, exist, or be done. **2** very difficult to deal with. ■ **impossibility** n. **impossibly** adv.

impostor (or **imposter**) n. a person who pretends to be someone else so as to deceive.

impotent adj. **1** helpless or powerless. **2** (of a man) unable to achieve an erection. ■ **impotence** n.

impound v. **1** seize and take legal possession of. **2** shut up animals in an enclosure.

impoverish v. **1** make poor. **2** make worse in quality.

impracticable adj. unable to be done.

impractical adj. not sensible or realistic.

imprecation n. a spoken curse.

imprecise adj. not exact.

impregnable adj. unable to be captured or broken into.

impregnate v. **1** saturate with a substance. **2** make pregnant. ■ **impregnation** n.

impresario n. (pl. **impresarios**) an organizer of plays, operas, etc.

impress v. **1** cause to feel admiration. **2** (**impress on**) cause to realize the importance of. **3** make a mark with a stamp etc.

impression n. **1** an idea, feeling, or opinion. **2** an effect produced on someone. **3** an imitation of a person, done to entertain. **4** a mark made by pressing.

impressionable adj. easily influenced.

Impressionism n. a style of art depicting the visual impression of a moment. ■ **Impressionist** n. & adj.

impressionist n. an entertainer who impersonates famous people.

impressionistic adj. based on personal impressions.

impressive adj. of admirable size, quality, or skill. ■ **impressively** adv. **impressiveness** n.

imprint v. make a mark on by pressure. •n. 1 a mark made by pressure. 2 a publisher's name etc. in a book.

imprison v. put or keep in prison. ■ **imprisonment** n.

improbable adj. not likely to be true or to happen. ■ **improbability** n. **improbably** adv.

impromptu adj. & adv. done without being planned or rehearsed.

improper adj. 1 not conforming to rules or standards. 2 not modest or decent. ■ **improperly** adv. **impropriety** n.

improve v. make or become better.

improvement n. 1 the act of improving. 2 a thing that improves or is better than something.

improvident adj. not providing for future needs.

improvise v. 1 invent and perform drama, music, etc. without preparation. 2 make from whatever is available. ■ **improvisation** n.

imprudent adj. not careful; rash.

impudent adj. not showing proper respect. ■ **impudence** n. **impudently** adv.

impugn /im-pyoon/ v. express doubts about the truth or honesty of.

impulse n. 1 a sudden urge to do something. 2 a driving force. ■ **impulsion** n.

impulsive adj. acting without thinking ahead. ■ **impulsively** adv.

impunity n. freedom from punishment or harm.

impure adj. 1 mixed with unwanted substances. 2 morally wrong. ■ **impurity** n.

impute v. (**impute to**) believe to have been done or caused by. ■ **imputation** n.

in prep. 1 enclosed, surrounded, or inside. 2 during or within a period of time. 3 expressing a state or quality. 4 included or involved. 5 indicating the language or medium used. •adv. 1 so as to be enclosed, surrounded, or inside. 2 present at your home or office. 3 expressing arrival. •adj. informal fashionable. □ **in-house** within an organization. **in-law** a relative by marriage. **the ins and outs** informal all the details.

in. abbrev. inches.

inability n. the state of being unable to do something.

in absentia adv. while not present.

inaccessible adj. 1 unable to be reached. 2 difficult to understand.

inaccurate adj. not accurate. ■ **inaccuracy** n. **inaccurately** adv.

inaction n. lack of action.

inactive adj. not active or working. ■ **inactivity** n.

inadequate adj. 1 not enough or not good enough. 2 unable to deal with a situation. ■ **inadequacy** n. **inadequately** adv.

inadmissible adj. (of evidence in court) not accepted as valid.

inadvertent adj. not deliberate. ■ **inadvertently** adv.

❗ -ent, not -ant: inadvertent.

inalienable adj. unable to be taken or given away.

inane adj. silly. ■ **inanely** adv. **inanity** n.

inanimate adj. not alive.

inapplicable adj. not relevant or appropriate.

inappropriate adj. unsuitable. ■ **inappropriately** adv.

inarticulate adj. 1 unable to express yourself clearly. 2 not expressed in words.

inasmuch adv. (**inasmuch as**) 1 to the extent that. 2 considering that.

inattentive adj. not paying attention.

inaudible adj. unable to be heard. ■ **inaudibly** adv.

inaugurate v. 1 begin or introduce a system etc. 2 establish someone in office or mark the opening of a building etc. with a ceremony. ■ **inaugural** adj. **inauguration** n.

inborn adj. existing from birth.

inbred adj. 1 produced by inbreeding. 2 inborn.

inbreeding n. breeding from closely related people or animals.

incalculable adj. too great to be calculated or estimated.

incandescent adj. glowing with heat. ■ **incandescence** n.

incantation n. words said as a magic spell.

incapable adj. 1 not able to do something. 2 not able to care for yourself.

incapacitate v. prevent from functioning.

incapacity n. inability to do something.

incarcerate v. imprison. ■ **incarceration** n.

incarnate adj. in human or physical form.

incarnation n. 1 a god, spirit, or quality in human form. 2 (**the Incarnation**) (in Christian belief) God as Jesus Christ.

incendiary adj. 1 (of a bomb) designed to cause fire. 2 stirring up conflict. •n. (pl. **incendiaries**) an incendiary bomb.

incense n. a substance burnt to produce a sweet smell. •v. make very angry.

incentive n. something that encourages action or effort.

inception n. the beginning of something.

incessant adj. never stopping. ■ **incessantly** adv.

incest n. sex between very closely related people. ■ **incestuous** adj.

inch n. a unit of length equal to one twelfth of a foot (2.54 cm). •v. move slowly and carefully.

inchoate adj. not fully formed or developed.

incidence n. 1 the rate of occurrence of something. 2 Physics the meeting of a line or ray with a surface.

incident n. an event, esp. a distinctive or unpleasant one.

incidental adj. 1 occurring as a result of something else. 2 minor or unimportant. ■ **incidentally** adv. □ **incidental music** background music in a film.

incinerate v. destroy by burning. ■ **incineration** n. **incinerator** n.

incipient adj. beginning to happen or develop.

incise v. make a cut in a surface. ■ **incision** n.

incisive adj. 1 showing clear thought and understanding. 2 quick and direct.

incisor n. a narrow-edged front tooth.

incite v. urge to act violently or unlawfully. ■ **incitement** n.

incivility n. rudeness.

inclement adj. (of the weather) unpleasantly cold or wet.

inclination n. **1** a tendency to act in a particular way. **2** an interest or liking. **3** a slope or slant.

incline v. **1** (**be inclined to**) tend or be willing to. **2** (**be inclined**) have a particular tendency or talent. **3** lean or bend. • n. a slope.

include v. **1** have as part of a whole. **2** make or treat as part of a whole.

inclusion n. **1** the act of including. **2** a person or thing that is included.

inclusive adj. **1** including everything expected or required. **2** including the specified limits.

incognito /in-kog-nee-toh/ adj. & adv. with your true identity concealed.

incoherent adj. **1** hard to understand. **2** not logical or well-organized. ■ **incoherence** n. **incoherently** adv.

income n. money received for work or from investments.

incoming adj. coming in.

incommunicado adj. & adv. not able to communicate with other people.

incomparable adj. so good that nothing can be compared to it. ■ **incomparably** adv.

incompatible adj. not able to exist, be used, or to live or work together. ■ **incompatibility** n.

incompetent adj. lacking the skill to do something. ■ **incompetence** n.

incomplete adj. not complete.

incomprehensible adj. unable to be understood.

inconceivable adj. unable to be believed. ■ **inconceivably** adv.

inconclusive adj. not leading to a firm conclusion.

incongruous adj. out of place. ■ **incongruity** n. **incongruously** adv.

inconsequential adj. not important.

inconsiderable adj. small in size, amount, etc.

inconsiderate adj. not thinking of others' feelings.

inconsistent adj. not consistent. ■ **inconsistency** n.

inconsolable adj. unable to be comforted. ■ **inconsolably** adv.

inconspicuous adj. not noticeable.

inconstant adj. frequently changing.

incontestable adj. unable to be disputed.

incontinent adj. unable to control your bladder or bowels. ■ **incontinence** n.

incontrovertible adj. unable to be denied or disputed. ■ **incontrovertibly** adv.

inconvenience n. slight trouble or difficulty. • v. cause inconvenience to. ■ **inconvenient** adj.

incorporate v. **1** include as part of a whole. **2** form a company into a corporation. ■ **incorporation** n.

incorrect adj. not true or accurate. ■ **incorrectly** adv.

incorrigible adj. having bad habits that cannot be changed.

incorruptible adj. too honest to take bribes.

increase v. make or become greater in size, amount, or intensity. • n. a rise in amount, size, or intensity. ■ **increasingly** adv.

incredible adj. impossible or hard to believe. ■ **incredibly** adv.

incredulous adj. unwilling or unable to believe something. ■ **incredulity** n. **incredulously** adv.

increment n. an increase in a number or amount. ■ **incremental** adj.

incriminate v. cause to appear guilty of a crime.

incubate v. 1 hatch eggs by keeping them warm. 2 (of an infectious disease) develop slowly without obvious signs. ■ **incubation** n. **incubator** n.

inculcate v. fix an idea in the mind by repetition.

incumbent adj. 1 necessary as a duty. 2 currently holding office. • n. the holder of an office.

incur v. (**incurring**, **incurred**) bring something unwelcome on yourself.

incurable adj. unable to be cured. ■ **incurably** adv.

incursion n. a sudden invasion or attack.

indebted adj. 1 grateful. 2 owing money.

indecent adj. not following accepted standards, esp. in relation to sex. □ **indecent assault** sexual assault that does not involve rape. **indecent exposure** the crime of showing the genitals in public. ■ **indecency** n. **indecently** adv.

indecipherable adj. unable to be read or understood.

indecisive adj. not decisive. ■ **indecision** n.

indeed adv. used to emphasize a statement.

indefatigable adj. never tiring.

indefensible adj. unable to be justified.

indefinable adj. unable to be defined exactly.

indefinite adj. 1 not clearly defined; vague. 2 lasting for an unknown period. □ **indefinite article** the word a or an. ■ **indefinitely** adv.

indelible adj. 1 (of ink or a mark) unable to be removed. 2 unable to be forgotten. ■ **indelibly** adv.

indelicate adj. tactless or rude.

indemnity n. (pl. **indemnities**) 1 insurance against legal responsibility for your actions. 2 compensation for damage or loss. ■ **indemnify** v.

indent v. 1 form hollows or notches in. 2 begin a line of writing further from the margin than the other lines. ■ **indentation** n.

indenture n. a formal contract, esp. of apprenticeship.

independent adj. 1 free from outside control or influence. 2 self-governing. 3 having enough money to support yourself. 4 not connected; separate. ■ **independence** n. **independently** adv.

> !!! **-ent**, not **-ant**: independent.

indescribable adj. too extreme or unusual to be described. ■ **indescribably** adv.

indestructible adj. unable to be destroyed.

indeterminate adj. not exactly known.

index n. (pl. **indexes** or **indices**) 1 an alphabetical list of names or subjects referred to in a book. 2 an alphabetical list of books or documents. **3** a sign or measure of something. **4** a number indicating the relative level of prices or wages compared with a previous level. •*v.* record in or provide with an index. □ **index finger** the forefinger.

Indian *n.* **1** a person from India. **2** an American Indian. •*adj.* of India. □ **Indian ink** deep black ink used in drawing. **Indian summer** dry, warm weather in autumn.

indicate *v.* **1** point out. **2** be a sign of. **3** state briefly. ■ **indication** *n.* **indicative** *adj.*

indicator *n.* **1** a thing that indicates a state or level. **2** a flashing light on a vehicle showing that it is about to pull out or turn.

indict /in-dyt/ *v.* formally accuse of or charge with a serious crime. ■ **indictable** *adj.* **indictment** *n.*

indifferent *adj.* **1** having no interest or sympathy. **2** not very good. ■ **indifference** *n.* **indifferently** *adv.*

indigenous *adj.* native.

indigent *adj.* very poor.

indigestible *adj.* difficult to digest.

indigestion *n.* discomfort caused by difficulty in digesting food.

indignation *n.* annoyance caused by unfair treatment. ■ **indignant** *adj.* **indignantly** *adv.*

indignity *n.* (*pl.* **indignities**) humiliating treatment.

indigo *n.* a dark blue colour or dye.

indirect *adj.* **1** not direct. **2** (of tax) charged on goods etc. rather than income or profits. □ **indirect object** a person or thing that is affected by the action of a transitive verb but is not the main object. ■ **indirectly** *adv.*

indiscreet *adj.* revealing things that should remain private. ■ **indiscretion** *n.* **indiscreetly** *adv.*

indiscriminate *adj.* done or acting without careful judgement. ■ **indiscriminately** *adv.*

indispensable *adj.* essential.

⚠ -*able*, not -*ible*: indispens*able*.

indisposed *adj.* **1** slightly unwell. **2** unwilling. ■ **indisposition** *n.*

indisputable *adj.* undeniable. ■ **indisputably** *adv.*

indistinct *adj.* not clear or sharp. ■ **indistinctly** *adv.*

indistinguishable *adj.* not identifiable as different.

indium *n.* a soft metallic element.

individual *adj.* **1** single; separate. **2** of or for one person. **3** striking or unusual. •*n.* a single person or item. ■ **individuality** *n.* **individually** *adv.*

individualism *n.* the quality of being independent in thought and action. ■ **individualist** *n.*

indivisible *adj.* unable to be divided.

indoctrinate *v.* force to accept a set of beliefs. ■ **indoctrination** *n.*

indolent *adj.* lazy. ■ **indolence** *n.*

indomitable *adj.* impossible to defeat or subdue.

indoor *adj.* situated, done, or used inside a building. •*adv.* (**indoors**) into or inside a building.

indubitable *adj.* impossible to doubt. ■ **indubitably** *adv.*

induce *v.* **1** persuade. **2** bring about. **3** bring on labour in childbirth by drugs etc.

inducement *n.* a thing that persuades someone to do something.

induct v. introduce formally to a post or organization.

inductance n. a process by which a change in the current of an electric circuit produces an electromotive force.

induction n. 1 the act of inducting. 2 reasoning in which a general rule is drawn from particular examples. 3 the passing of electricity or magnetism from one object to another without them touching. ■ **inductive** adj. **inductor** n.

indulge v. 1 (**indulge in**) allow yourself something enjoyable. 2 satisfy a desire. 3 allow someone to do or have what they want.

indulgent adj. allowing someone to do or have what they want or overlooking their faults. ■ **indulgence** n. **indulgently** adv.

industrial adj. of industry. □ **industrial action** a strike or similar protest by workers. **industrial estate** an area of land developed for factories. **industrial relations** relations between management and workers. ■ **industrially** adv.

industrialism n. a system in which industry is the basis of the economy.

industrialist n. a person who owns or controls a manufacturing business.

industrialize (or **-ise**) v. develop industries in a country or region on a wide scale. ■ **industrialization** n.

industrious adj. hard-working. ■ **industriously** adv.

industry n. (pl. **industries**) 1 the manufacture of goods in factories. 2 a branch of economic activity. 3 hard work.

inebriated adj. drunk. ■ **inebriation** n.

inedible adj. not fit for eating.

ineffable adj. too great to be described.

ineffective adj. not producing any or the desired effect. ■ **ineffectively** adv.

ineffectual adj. 1 ineffective. 2 not forceful enough to do something. ■ **ineffectually** adv.

inefficient adj. not making the best use of time or resources. ■ **inefficiency** n. **inefficiently** adv.

inelegant adj. not elegant or graceful.

ineligible adj. not eligible.

ineluctable adj. unable to be avoided.

inept adj. lacking skill. ■ **ineptitude** n.

inequality n. (pl. **inequalities**) lack of equality.

inequitable adj. unfair; unjust. ■ **inequity** n.

inert adj. 1 lacking the power to move or act. 2 without active chemical properties.

inertia /i-ner-shuh/ n. 1 a tendency to do nothing or to remain unchanged. 2 a property by which matter remains still or continues moving unless acted on by an external force.

inescapable adj. unavoidable.

inessential adj. not essential.

inestimable adj. too great to be measured.

inevitable adj. certain to happen. ■ **inevitability** n. **inevitably** adv.

inexact adj. not exact.

inexcusable adj. too bad to be justified or tolerated.

inexhaustible adj. available in unlimited quantities.

inexorable adj. impossible to stop or prevent. ■ **inexorably** adv.

inexpensive adj. cheap.

inexperience n. lack of experience. ■ **inexperienced** adj.

inexpert adj. lacking skill or knowledge.

inexplicable adj. unable to be explained. ■ **inexplicably** adv.

in extremis adv. 1 in a very difficult situation. 2 at the point of death.

inextricable adj. impossible to separate. ■ **inextricably** adv.

infallible adj. incapable of being wrong. ■ **infallibility** n. **infallibly** adv.

infamous adj. well known for something bad. ■ **infamy** n.

infancy n. 1 early childhood or babyhood. 2 an early stage of development.

infant n. a very young child or baby.

infanticide n. the killing of an infant.

infantile adj. 1 of infants. 2 childish.

infantry n. soldiers who fight on foot.

infatuated adj. feeling an intense passion for someone. ■ **infatuation** n.

infect v. 1 affect with an organism that causes disease. 2 contaminate.

infection n. 1 the process of infecting. 2 an infectious disease.

infectious adj. 1 (of a disease) able to be transmitted through the environment. 2 likely to spread infection. 3 likely to spread to others.

infer v. (**inferring**, **inferred**) work out from suggestions or evidence. ■ **inference** n.

❗ On the difference between **imply** and **infer**, see **IMPLY**.

inferior adj. lower in status or quality. •n. an inferior person. ■ **inferiority** n.

infernal adj. 1 of hell. 2 informal very annoying.

inferno n. (pl. **infernos**) a large uncontrollable fire.

infertile adj. 1 unable to bear young. 2 (of land) unable to produce crops. ■ **infertility** n.

infest v. be present in large numbers, so as to cause damage or disease. ■ **infestation** n.

infidel n. old use a person who does not believe in a religion.

infidelity n. (pl. **infidelities**) un-faithfulness to your sexual partner.

infighting n. conflict within a group.

infiltrate v. secretly and gradually gain access to a group etc. ■ **infiltration** n. **infiltrator** n.

infinite adj. 1 limitless. 2 very great or very many. ■ **infinitely** adv.

infinitesimal adj. very small. ■ **infinitesimally** adv.

infinitive n. the basic form of a verb, occurring in English with the word to.

infinity n. (pl. **infinities**) 1 the state of being infinite. 2 a very great number or amount.

infirm adj. physically weak. ■ **infirmity** n.

infirmary n. (pl. **infirmaries**) a hospital.

inflame v. 1 arouse strong feelings. 2 (**inflamed**) (of a part of the body) red, swollen, and hot.

inflammable *adj.* easily set on fire.

inflammation *n.* redness, swelling, heat, and pain in a part of the body.

inflammatory *adj.* arousing strong feeling.

inflatable *adj.* able to be inflated. • *n.* an object that is inflated before use.

inflate *v.* **1** expand by filling with air or gas. **2** increase a cost or price significantly. **3** (**inflated**) exaggerated.

inflation *n.* **1** the act of inflating. **2** a general increase in prices. ■ **inflationary** *adj.*

inflect *v.* **1** (of a word) change in form to show its grammatical function, number, etc. **2** vary the tone or pitch of the voice. ■ **inflection** *n.*

inflexible *adj.* **1** unable to be altered. **2** unwilling to change or compromise. **3** unable to be bent.

inflict *v.* cause to experience something painful or unpleasant. ■ **infliction** *n.*

inflorescence *n.* the complete flower head of a plant.

influence *n.* **1** the power or ability to affect beliefs or actions. **2** a person or thing with such ability or power. • *v.* have an influence on. ■ **influential** *adj.*

influenza *n.* a viral infection causing fever, aches, and catarrh.

influx *n.* an arrival of large numbers of people or things.

inform *v.* **1** give information to. **2** (**inform on**) reveal someone's criminal activity to the police. **3** (**informed**) showing knowledge or understanding. ■ **informant** *n.* **informer** *n.*

informal *adj.* **1** relaxed or unofficial. **2** (of clothes) casual. ■ **informality** *n.* **informally** *adv.*

information *n.* facts or knowledge provided or learned. □ **information technology** the use of computers and telecommunications for storing and sending information.

informative *adj.* providing useful information.

infraction *n.* a breaking of a law or agreement.

infrared *adj.* (of electromagnetic radiation) having a wavelength just greater than that of red light.

infrastructure *n.* the basic structures and facilities (e.g. roads or power) needed for the operation of a society or organization.

infrequent *adj.* not happening often. ■ **infrequently** *adv.*

infringe *v.* **1** break a law or agreement. **2** limit a right or privilege. ■ **infringement** *n.*

infuriate *v.* make angry.

infuse *v.* **1** spread throughout. **2** soak tea or herbs to extract the flavour. ■ **infuser** *n.* **infusion** *n.*

ingenious *adj.* clever and inventive. ■ **ingeniously** *adv.* **ingenuity** *n.*

ingenuous *adj.* innocent and unsuspecting. ■ **ingenuously** *adv.*

ingest *v.* take food or drink into the body. ■ **ingestion** *n.*

inglenook *n.* a space on either side of a large fireplace.

inglorious *adj.* causing shame.

ingot *n.* a rectangular block of metal.

ingrained *adj.* **1** (of a habit or belief) firmly established. **2** (of dirt) deeply embedded.

i

ingratiate v. (**ingratiate yourself**) gain favour by flattery or trying to please.

ingratitude n. a lack of gratitude.

ingredient n. any of the substances combined to make a dish.

ingress n. 1 the act of entering. 2 a place or means of access.

ingrown (or **ingrowing**) adj. (of a toenail) having grown into the flesh.

inhabit v. live in or occupy. ■ **inhabitable** adj.

inhabitant n. a person or animal that lives in or occupies a place.

inhalant n. a medicine that is inhaled.

inhale v. breathe in air, smoke, etc. ■ **inhalation** n.

inhaler n. a device for inhaling a drug.

inherent adj. existing in something as a permanent or essential quality. ■ **inherently** adv.

inherit v. (**inheriting**, **inherited**) 1 receive property or a title from someone when they die. 2 have a characteristic passed on from parents or ancestors. ■ **inheritance** n.

inhibit v. 1 hinder or prevent. 2 cause to feel inhibitions.

inhibition n. a feeling preventing you from acting naturally.

inhospitable adj. (of a place) harsh and difficult to live in.

inhuman adj. cruel and barbaric. ■ **inhumanity** n.

inimical adj. harmful; hostile.

inimitable adj. impossible to imitate. ■ **inimitably** adv.

iniquity n. (pl. **iniquities**) great injustice. ■ **iniquitous** adj.

initial adj. at the beginning; first. • n. the first letter of a name or word. • v. (**initialling**, **initialled**; US **initialing**, **initialed**) mark with your initials. ■ **initially** adv.

initiate v. 1 cause a process etc. to begin. 2 admit to a group with a formal ceremony. 3 introduce to a new activity. ■ **initiation** n.

initiative n. 1 the ability to act independently. 2 the opportunity to act before others do. 3 a new approach to a problem.

inject v. 1 put a drug etc. into the body with a syringe. 2 introduce a different quality. ■ **injection** n.

injudicious adj. unwise.

injunction n. a court order stating that someone must or must not do something.

injure v. 1 do physical harm to. 2 damage.

injurious adj. harmful.

injury n. (pl. **injuries**) 1 an instance of harm to the body. 2 damage or harm.

injustice n. 1 lack of justice. 2 an unjust act.

ink n. coloured liquid for writing, drawing, or printing. • v. apply ink to. ■ **inky** adj.

inkling n. a slight suspicion.

inland adj. & adv. in or into the interior of a country.

inlay v. (**inlaying**, **inlaid**) decorate by embedding pieces of a different material in a surface.

inlet n. 1 a narrow inland extension of the sea etc. 2 a way in.

in loco parentis adv. & adj. in the place of a parent.

inmate n. a person living in a prison or other institution.

inmost adj. innermost.

inn n. a pub.

innards pl. n. informal internal organs or parts.

innate adj. inborn; natural.
■ **innately** adv.

inner adj. **1** inside; close to the centre. **2** mental or spiritual. **3** private. □ **inner city** an area in or near the centre of a city.

innermost adj. **1** furthest in. **2** most private.

innings n. (pl. **innings**) (in cricket) a batsman's or side's turn at batting.

innocent adj. **1** not guilty of a crime etc. **2** having little experience of life. **3** not intended to offend. •n. an innocent person. ■ **innocence** n. **innocently** adv.

innocuous adj. harmless. ■ **innocuously** adv.

innovate v. introduce something new. ■ **innovation** n. **innovative** adj. **innovator** n.

innuendo n. (pl. **innuendoes** or **innuendos**) a remark indirectly referring to something.

innumerable adj. too many to be counted.

innumerate adj. without a basic knowledge of mathematics.

inoculate v. vaccinate. ■ **inoculation** n.

❗ One n, one c: inoculate.

inoperable adj. unable to be cured by a medical operation.

inoperative adj. not working or taking effect.

inopportune adj. occurring at an inconvenient time.

inordinate adj. unusually large; excessive. ■ **inordinately** adv.

inorganic adj. **1** not consisting of or coming from living matter. **2** not containing carbon.

inpatient n. a hospital patient staying day and night during treatment.

input n. **1** something put in or contributed. **2** the act of inputting computer data. •v. (**inputting**, **input**) put data into a computer.

inquest n. an official inquiry, esp. by a coroner into the cause of a death.

inquire v. enquire. ■ **inquiry** n.

inquisition n. a long period of intensive questioning. ■ **inquisitor** n.

inquisitive adj. eager to find things out. ■ **inquisitively** adv.

inroad n. a gradual entry into or effect on a situation.

insalubrious adj. seedy; unwholesome.

insane adj. **1** seriously mentally ill. **2** very foolish. ■ **insanely** adv. **insanity** n.

insanitary adj. dirty and unhygienic.

insatiable adj. impossible to satisfy. ■ **insatiably** adv.

inscribe v. **1** write or carve words on a surface. **2** write a dedication in a book.

inscription n. words inscribed.

inscrutable adj. impossible to interpret. ■ **inscrutably** adv.

insect n. a small invertebrate animal with six legs and a segmented body.

insecticide n. a substance for killing insects.

insectivore n. an animal that eats insects. ■ **insectivorous** adj.

insecure adj. **1** not confident. **2** not firmly fixed. ■ **insecurity** n.

inseminate v. introduce semen into. ■ **insemination** n.

insensible adj. unconscious.

insensitive adj. not sensitive. ■ **insensitively** adv. **insensitivity** n.

inseparable adj. unable to be separated or treated separately. ■ **inseparably** adv.

insert v. place, fit, or add into. • n. a loose page or section in a magazine. ■ **insertion** n.

inset n. a thing inserted. • v. (**insetting, inset**) insert.

inshore adj. & adv. at sea but close or towards the shore.

inside n. 1 an inner side, part, or surface. 2 (**insides**) informal the stomach and bowels. • adj. on or in the inside. • prep. & adv. 1 situated or moving within. 2 informal in prison. 3 within a specified time. ☐ **inside out** with the inner surface turned outwards.

insider n. a person in an organization who has information not known to those outside it.

insidious adj. developing in a gradual and harmful way. ■ **insidiously** adv.

insight n. understanding of the truth about people or situations.

insignia n. (pl. **insignia**) a badge or symbol indicating rank or office.

insignificant adj. of little or no importance or value. ■ **insignificance** n.

insincere adj. saying things that you do not mean. ■ **insincerely** adv. **insincerity** n.

insinuate v. 1 suggest something bad indirectly. 2 move yourself gradually into a favourable position. ■ **insinuation** n.

insipid adj. 1 lacking flavour. 2 dull.

insist v. 1 demand or state forcefully. 2 (**insist on**) persist in doing.

insistent adj. 1 insisting. 2 sustained and demanding attention. ■ **insistence** n. **insistently** adv.

in situ adv. & adj. in the original position.

insolent adj. rude and disrespectful. ■ **insolence** n. **insolently** adv.

insoluble adj. 1 impossible to solve. 2 unable to be dissolved.

insolvent adj. unable to pay your debts. ■ **insolvency** n.

insomnia n. inability to sleep. ■ **insomniac** n.

insouciant adj. unconcerned. ■ **insouciance** n.

inspect v. 1 look at closely. 2 visit officially to check on standards. ■ **inspection** n.

inspector n. 1 an official who inspects. 2 a police officer ranking below a chief inspector.

inspiration n. 1 the process of being inspired. 2 an inspiring person or thing. 3 a sudden clever idea. ■ **inspirational** adj.

inspire v. 1 fill with the urge to do something. 2 create a feeling in a person.

instability n. lack of stability.

install v. 1 place in position ready for use. 2 establish in a new place or role. ■ **installation** n.

instalment (US **installment**) n. 1 each of several payments made over a period of time. 2 each of the parts of a serial.

instance n. a particular example or occurrence. • v. give as an example.

instant adj. 1 immediate. 2 (of food) processed to allow quick preparation. • n. 1 a precise moment of time. 2 a very short time. ■ **instantly** adv.

instantaneous adj. instant. ■ **instantaneously** adv.

instead adv. as an alternative.

instep n. the middle part of the foot.

instigate v. cause to happen or begin. ■ **instigation** n. **instigator** n.

instil (US **instill**) v. (**instilling**, **instilled**) gradually establish in the mind.

instinct n. an inborn tendency or ability. ■ **instinctive** adj. **instinctively** adv.

institute n. an organization for the promotion of science, education, etc. • v. begin or establish.

institution n. **1** an important organization or public body. **2** a home providing care for people with special needs. **3** an established law or custom. ■ **institutional** adj.

institutionalize (or **-ise**) v. **1** establish as an accepted part of an organization etc. **2** place in a residential institution.

instruct v. **1** direct or order. **2** teach. ■ **instructor** n.

instruction n. **1** a direction or order. **2** teaching or education. ■ **instructional** adj.

instructive adj. useful and informative.

instrument n. **1** a tool or implement for precise work. **2** a measuring device. **3** a device for producing musical sounds.

instrumental adj. **1** important in achieving something. **2** performed on musical instruments. ■ **instrumentalist** n.

insubordinate adj. disobedient. ■ **insubordination** n.

insubstantial adj. not strong or solid.

insufferable adj. intolerable. ■ **insufferably** adv.

insufficient adj. not enough. ■ **insufficiency** n. **insufficiently** adv.

insular adj. **1** narrow-minded. **2** of an island.

insulate v. **1** cover or line with material to prevent heat, electricity, etc. being conducted. **2** protect from something unpleasant. ■ **insulation** n. **insulator** n.

insulin n. a hormone regulating glucose levels in the blood.

insult v. speak to or treat in a way that offends. • n. an insulting remark or act.

insuperable adj. impossible to overcome.

insupportable adj. intolerable.

insurance n. **1** an arrangement by which payments are made to a company who in return pay compensation in the event of loss, damages, death, etc. **2** money paid by or to an insurance company. **3** a safeguard.

insure v. **1** pay money to receive compensation in the event of damage, loss, death, etc. **2** ensure. ■ **insurer** n.

insurgent n. a rebel.

insurmountable adj. too great to be overcome.

insurrection n. a violent revolt.

intact adj. not damaged.

intake n. **1** an amount or number taken in. **2** an act of taking in.

intangible adj. **1** not solid or real. **2** vague and abstract.

integer n. a whole number.

integral adj. necessary to make a whole complete.

integrate v. **1** combine to form a whole. **2** make accepted within a social group. ■ **integration** n.

i

integrity n. 1 the quality of being morally good. 2 wholeness or unity.

intellect n. the ability to think logically and understand things.

intellectual adj. 1 of the intellect. 2 having a highly developed intellect. • n. an intellectual person. ■ **intellectually** adv.

intellectualize (or **-ise**) v. talk or write in an intellectual way.

intelligence n. 1 the ability to gain and apply knowledge and skills. 2 secret information obtained about an opponent.

intelligent adj. good at learning and understanding. ■ **intelligently** adv.

intelligentsia n. intellectual or highly educated people.

intelligible adj. able to be understood. ■ **intelligibility** n. **intelligibly** adv.

intend v. 1 have as an aim or plan. 2 plan a particular role, use, or meaning for.

intense adj. 1 great in force, strength, or degree. 2 very earnest. ■ **intensify** v. **intensity** n.

intensive adj. 1 involving much effort over a short time. 2 (of farming) aiming to achieve maximum yields. □ **intensive care** special medical treatment of a dangerously ill patient. ■ **intensively** adv.

intent n. an aim, plan, or purpose. • adj. 1 (**intent on**) determined to do. 2 showing concentrated attention. ■ **intently** adv.

intention n. an aim or plan.

intentional adj. deliberate. ■ **intentionally** adv.

inter v. (**interring**, **interred**) bury a dead body.

interact v. act so as to affect each other. ■ **interaction** n. **interactive** adj.

interbreed v. (**interbreeding**, **interbred**) breed with an animal of a different species.

intercede v. intervene on behalf of another.

intercept v. stop and prevent from continuing. ■ **interception** n. **interceptor** n.

intercession n. the act of interceding.

interchange v. 1 (of two people) exchange things. 2 put each of two things in the other's place. • n. 1 the act of interchanging. 2 a road junction on several levels. ■ **interchangeable** adj.

intercom n. an electrical device allowing one-way or two-way communication.

interconnect v. connect with each other.

intercontinental adj. between continents.

intercourse n. 1 dealings between people. 2 sexual intercourse.

interdependent adj. dependent on each other.

interdict n. an order forbidding something.

interdisciplinary adj. involving more than one branch of knowledge.

interest n. 1 eagerness to know about something or someone. 2 the quality of arousing such a feeling. 3 a subject arousing enthusiasm or concern. 4 money paid for the use of money lent. 5 a person's advantage. 6 a share in a business. • v. 1 make curious or attentive. 2 (**interested**) not impartial. ■ **interesting** adj.

interface n. 1 a point where two things interact. 2 a device or program enabling a user to communicate with a computer, or for connecting two items of hardware or software.

interfere v. 1 prevent from continuing or operating. 2 become involved in something without being asked. 3 (**interfere with**) handle without permission.

interference n. 1 the act of interfering. 2 disturbance to radio signals.

interferon n. a protein preventing a virus from reproducing.

intergalactic adj. moving or situated between galaxies.

interim n. the time between two events. • adj. temporary.

interior adj. inner. • n. 1 the inner part. 2 the internal affairs of a country.

interject v. say suddenly as an interruption. ■ **interjection** n.

interlace v. weave together.

interlink v. link together.

interlock v. (of two parts) fit together.

interlocutor n. a participant in a conversation.

interloper n. an intruder.

interlude n. 1 a period of time that contrasts with what goes before or after. 2 an interval.

intermarry v. (**intermarrying**, **intermarried**) (of people of different races, religions, etc.) marry each other. ■ **intermarriage** n.

intermediary n. (pl. **intermediaries**) a person who tries to settle a dispute.

intermediate adj. 1 coming between two things in time, place,

etc. 2 having more than basic knowledge or skills.

interment n. burial.

intermezzo /in-ter-**met**-zoh/ n. (pl. **intermezzi** or **intermezzos**) a short piece of music between parts of an opera etc.

interminable adj. seemingly endless. ■ **interminably** adv.

intermission n. a pause or interval.

intermittent adj. happening at irregular intervals. ■ **intermittently** adv.

intern v. confine as a prisoner. • n. US a junior doctor receiving training in a hospital. ■ **internee** n. **internment** n.

internal adj. 1 of the inside. 2 inside the body. 3 of affairs within a country. 4 used within an organization. □ **internal-combustion engine** an engine generating power by the explosion of fuel and air inside the engine. ■ **internally** adv.

internalize (or **-ise**) v. make part of your behaviour or thinking.

international adj. 1 between nations. 2 agreed on or used by all or many nations. • n. a match between teams from different countries. ■ **internationally** adv.

internecine /in-ter-**nee**-syn/ adj. (of conflict) happening between members of a group.

Internet n. a huge global computer network.

interplay n. interaction.

interpolate /in-ter-**puh**-layt/ v. 1 insert. 2 interject a remark. ■ **interpolation** n.

interpose v. 1 place between one thing and another. 2 interject a remark.

interpret v. **1** explain the meaning of. **2** translate aloud the words of a person speaking a different language. **3** understand as meaning. ▪ **interpretable** adj. **interpretation** n. **interpreter** n.

interracial adj. involving different races.

interregnum n. a period between regimes when normal government is suspended.

interrelate v. relate or connect to one other. ▪ **interrelation** n.

interrogate v. question closely or aggressively. ▪ **interrogation** n. **interrogator** n.

interrogative adj. in the form of a question or used in questions.

interrupt v. **1** break the progress or continuity of. **2** stop a speaker by saying or doing something. ▪ **interruption** n.

intersect v. divide or cross by passing or lying across. ▪ **intersection** n.

intersperse v. scatter or place among or between things.

interstate adj. between states.

interstice /in-ter-stiss/ n. a crack or small space.

interval n. **1** a period or pause between two events. **2** a pause between parts of a play etc. **3** a difference in musical pitch.

intervene v. **1** become involved in a situation to improve or control it. **2** occur between events. ▪ **intervention** n.

interview n. **1** an occasion when a journalist questions someone. **2** a formal meeting to assess a job applicant etc. ▪v. hold an interview with. ▪ **interviewee** n. **interviewer** n.

interweave v. (**interweaving**, **interwove**; past part. **interwoven**) weave together.

intestate adj. (of a dead person) not having made a will.

intestine n. the long tubular organ leading from the stomach to the anus. ▪ **intestinal** adj.

intimate[1] /in-ti-muht/ adj. **1** close and friendly. **2** private and personal. **3** having a sexual relationship. **4** (of knowledge) detailed. ▪n. a close friend. ▪ **intimacy** n. **intimately** adv.

intimate[2] /in-ti-mayt/ v. state indirectly. ▪ **intimation** n.

intimidate v. frighten into doing something. ▪ **intimidation** n.

into prep. **1** to a point on or within. **2** expressing a change or result. **3** in the direction of. **4** concerning. **5** expressing division.

intolerable adj. unable to be endured. ▪ **intolerably** adv.

intolerant adj. unwilling to accept ideas or behaviour different to your own. ▪ **intolerance** n.

intonation n. the rise and fall of the voice in speaking.

intone v. say with little intonation.

intoxicate v. **1** (of alcohol or a drug) cause to lose control. **2** excite. ▪ **intoxication** n.

intractable adj. **1** hard to deal with. **2** stubborn.

intranet n. a computer network within an organization.

intransigent adj. stubborn. ▪ **intransigence** n.

intransitive adj. (of a verb) not taking a direct object.

intrauterine adj. within the womb.

intravenous adj. within or into a vein.

intrepid adj. fearless.

intricate adj. very complicated.
■ **intricacy** n. **intricately** adv.

intrigue v. **1** arouse the curiosity of. **2** plot secretly. • n. **1** a plot. **2** a secret love affair. ■ **intriguing** adj.

intrinsic adj. forming part of the basic nature of something.
■ **intrinsically** adv.

introduce v. **1** bring into use. **2** present someone by name. **3** bring to someone's attention for the first time. **4** insert. **5** occur at the start of.

introduction n. **1** the act of introducing. **2** a thing introducing another. **3** a thing newly brought in. ■ **introductory** adj.

introspection n. examination of your thoughts or feelings. ■ **introspective** adj.

introvert n. a shy, introspective person. ■ **introverted** adj.

intrude v. enter a place or situation where you are unwelcome or uninvited. ■ **intruder** n. **intrusion** n.

intrusive adj. disturbing or unwelcome.

intuition n. the ability to understand or know something without conscious reasoning. ■ **intuitive** adj.

Inuit /in-yuu-it/ n. (pl. **Inuit** or **Inuits**) a member of a people of northern Canada and parts of Greenland and Alaska.

❗ For an explanation of **Inuit** and **Eskimo**, see **ESKIMO**.

inundate v. **1** flood. **2** overwhelm.

inure v. accustom to something unpleasant.

invade v. **1** enter a country so as to conquer or occupy it. **2** enter in large numbers. **3** intrude on.
■ **invader** n.

invalid n. a person weak or disabled by illness or injury. • adj. **1** not legally or officially recognized. **2** incorrect. ■ **invalidity** n.

invalidate v. make invalid.

invaluable adj. very useful.

invariable adj. never changing.
■ **invariably** adv.

invasion n. an act of invading.

invasive adj. **1** tending to invade. **2** (of medical procedures) involving the introduction of instruments into the body.

invective n. abusive language.

inveigh /in-vay/ v. (**inveigh against**) speak or write about with great hostility.

inveigle /in-vay-g'l/ v. persuade by trickery or flattery.

invent v. **1** create or design something new. **2** make up a false story, name, etc. ■ **inventive** adj. **inventor** n.

invention n. **1** the act of inventing. **2** something invented. **3** creative ability.

inventory n. (pl. **inventories**) **1** a complete list of items. **2** a quantity of goods in stock.

inverse adj. opposite.

invert v. put upside down or in the opposite position or order.
□ **inverted comma** a quotation mark. ■ **inversion** n.

invertebrate n. an animal without a backbone.

invest v. **1** use money or spend time so as to make a profit or achieve a result. **2** provide with a quality. **3** formally give a rank or office to. ■ **investor** n.

investigate v. **1** carry out a systematic inquiry into. **2** research.

i

■ **investigation** n. **investigative** adj. **investigator** n.

investiture n. the act or ceremony of investing a person with an office etc.

investment n. **1** the act of investing. **2** something worth buying because it will be useful.

inveterate adj. having a firmly established habit.

invidious adj. likely to cause resentment.

invigilate v. supervise exam candidates. ■ **invigilator** n.

invigorate v. give strength or energy to.

invincible adj. too powerful to be defeated. ■ **invincibility** n.

inviolable adj. never to be attacked or dishonoured.

inviolate adj. free from injury or violation.

invisible adj. unable to be seen. ■ **invisibility** n. **invisibly** adv.

invitation n. **1** a request that someone should join you in going somewhere or doing something. **2** the act of inviting.

invite v. **1** ask someone to come somewhere or do something. **2** ask for. **3** risk provoking.

inviting adj. tempting or attractive.

in vitro adj. & adv. in a test tube or elsewhere outside a living organism.

invocation n. the act of invoking.

invoice n. a bill for goods or services. •v. send an invoice to.

invoke v. **1** appeal to as an authority. **2** call on a god or spirit.

involuntary adj. **1** done without conscious control. **2** done against someone's will. ■ **involuntarily** adv.

involve v. **1** have as a necessary part or result. **2** cause to participate. ■ **involvement** n.

involved adj. **1** having a close personal relationship. **2** complicated.

invulnerable adj. impossible to harm.

inward adj. **1** towards the inside. **2** mental or spiritual. •adv. (or **inwards**) towards the inside. ■ **inwardly** adv.

iodine n. a chemical element used in solution as an antiseptic.

ion n. an electrically charged atom that has lost or gained an electron. ■ **ionic** adj.

ionize (or **-ise**) v. convert into an ion or ions.

ionosphere n. a layer of the atmosphere containing a high concentration of ions.

iota n. a very small amount.

IOU n. a signed document acknowledging a debt.

ipso facto adv. by that very fact.

IQ abbrev. intelligence quotient.

IRA abbrev. Irish Republican Army.

Iranian n. a person from Iran. •adj. of Iran.

Iraqi n. (pl. **Iraqis**) a person from Iraq. •adj. of Iraq.

irascible adj. bad-tempered.

irate adj. very angry.

ire n. anger.

iridescent adj. shimmering with many colours. ■ **iridescence** n.

iridium n. a hard metallic element.

iris n. **1** the coloured part of the eyeball, with the pupil in the centre. **2** a plant with large bright flowers.

Irish n. the language of Ireland. •adj. of Ireland.

irk v. annoy. ■ **irksome** adj.

iron n. **1** a strong magnetic metallic element. **2** an implement with a flat base heated for smoothing clothes. **3** (**irons**) fetters or handcuffs. • v. **1** smooth clothes with an iron. **2** (**iron out**) solve a problem. □ **ironmonger** a person selling tools and other hardware.

irony n. (pl. **ironies**) **1** the use of words that say the opposite of what you mean so as to amuse or to make a point. **2** aspects of a situation that are opposite to what are expected. ■ **ironic** adj. **ironical** adj. **ironically** adv.

irradiate v. **1** expose to radiation. **2** illuminate. ■ **irradiation** n.

irrational adj. not logical or reasonable. ■ **irrationally** adv.

irreconcilable adj. **1** incompatible. **2** unable to be resolved.

irredeemable adj. unable to be saved or put right.

irrefutable adj. impossible to disprove.

irregular adj. **1** not regular in shape, arrangement, or occurrence. **2** not according to a rule or standard. ■ **irregularity** n.

irrelevant adj. not relevant. ■ **irrelevance** n. **irrelevantly** adv.

> ❗ -ant, not -ent: irrelevant.

irreparable adj. impossible to put right or repair. ■ **irreparably** adv.

irreplaceable adj. impossible to replace.

irrepressible adj. unable to be restrained.

irreproachable adj. very good and unable to be criticized.

irresistible adj. too tempting or powerful to be resisted. ■ **irresistibly** adv.

> ❗ -ible, not -able: irresistible.

irresolute adj. uncertain.

irrespective adj. (**irrespective of**) regardless of.

irresponsible adj. not showing a proper sense of responsibility. ■ **irresponsibly** adv.

irretrievable adj. unable to be retrieved or set right.

irreverent adj. disrespectful. ■ **irreverence** n. **irreverently** adv.

irreversible adj. impossible to alter or undo. ■ **irreversibly** adv.

irrevocable adj. unable to be changed or reversed. ■ **irrevocably** adv.

irrigate v. supply water to land or crops by means of channels. ■ **irrigation** n.

irritable adj. easily annoyed or angered. ■ **irritability** n. **irritably** adv.

irritate v. **1** make annoyed. **2** cause inflammation in a part of the body. ■ **irritant** n. **irritation** n.

is see BE.

Islam n. the Muslim religion. ■ **Islamic** adj.

island n. a piece of land surrounded by water. ■ **islander** n.

isle n. an island.

islet n. a small island.

isn't contr. is not.

isobar n. a line on a map connecting points with the same atmospheric pressure.

isolate v. **1** place apart or alone. **2** extract a substance in a pure form. ■ **isolation** n.

isolated adj. **1** remote. **2** single; exceptional.

isolationism n. a policy of remaining apart from the political affairs of other countries. ■ **isolationist** n. & adj.

isomer n. each of two or more compounds with the same formula but a different arrangement of atoms.

isosceles /I-soss-i-leez/ adj. (of a triangle) having two sides of equal length.

isotope n. each of two or more forms of the same element that contain equal numbers of protons but different numbers of neutrons.

ISP abbrev. Internet service provider.

Israeli n. (pl. **Israelis**) a person from Israel. • adj. of Israel.

Israelite /iz-ruh-lyt/ n. a member of the people of ancient Israel.

issue n. **1** an important topic to be discussed or resolved. **2** the act of issuing. **3** each of a regular series of publications. • v. **1** supply or give out. **2** formally send out or make known. **3** come or flow out.

isthmus /iss-muhss/ n. (pl. **isthmuses**) a narrow strip of land linking two larger areas.

IT abbrev. information technology.

it pron. **1** a thing previously mentioned or easily identified. **2** an animal or child of unspecified sex. **3** used as a subject in statements about time, distance, or weather: it is raining.

Italian n. **1** a person from Italy. **2** the language of Italy. • adj. of Italy.

italic adj. (of a typeface) sloping. • n. (or **italics**) an italic typeface. ■ **italicize** v.

itch n. an uncomfortable sensation that causes a desire to scratch. • v. **1** have an itch. **2** informal impatiently desire to do. ■ **itchy** adj.

item n. an individual article or unit.

itemize (or **-ise**) v. present as a list of items.

iterate v. do or say repeatedly. ■ **iteration** n.

itinerant adj. travelling.

itinerary n. (pl. **itineraries**) a planned route or journey.

its adj. belonging to it.

> **!** Don't confuse **its** (as in turn the camera on its side) with the form **it's** (short for either **it is** or **it has**, as in it's my fault or it's been raining).

it's contr. **1** it is. **2** it has.

itself pron. **1** used when a thing which performs an action is also affected by it. **2** used to emphasize a particular thing mentioned.

ITV abbrev. Independent Television.

IUD abbrev. intrauterine device, a contraceptive fitted inside the womb.

IVF abbrev. in vitro fertilization.

ivory n. (pl. **ivories**) **1** a hard creamy-white substance forming the tusks of an elephant. **2** a creamy-white colour. □ **ivory tower** a privileged position remote from normal difficulties.

ivy n. an evergreen climbing plant.

Supplement

Quick-reference grammar guide

adjective a word, such as *heavy*, *beautiful*, or *strong*, that is used to describe a noun.

adverb a word, such as *very*, *really*, or *slowly*, that is used to give more information about an adjective, verb, or other adverb.

clause a group of words that contains a verb and usually other components and forms part of a sentence:

I went home   and fell asleep.
[clause]   [clause]

See also **main clause**, **subordinate clause**, **relative clause**, **conditional clause**.

compound a word made up of two or more existing words, such as *earring*, *left-handed*, or *credit card*.

conditional clause a clause which usually begins with *if* or *unless* and describes something that is possible, probable, or hypothetical:

If it wasn't for her,   I could be myself.
[conditional clause]   [main clause]

conjunction a word that is used to link other words or parts of sentences, such as *and*, *but*, or *if*.

defining relative clause another term for **restrictive relative clause**.

determiner a word that comes before a noun to show how the noun is being used, such as *the*, *a*, and *every*.

infinitive the basic, unchanged form of a verb, which usually occurs with the word 'to', as in 'to go', 'to ask', 'to be'.

main clause a clause that forms part of a longer sentence, but makes sense on its own:

I went to a restaurant   and treated myself to lunch.
[main clause]   [main clause]

negative a word or phrase stating that something is not the case, such as *never*, *nothing*, or *not*.

non-restrictive (or **non-defining**) **relative clause** a clause which gives extra information that could be left out without affecting the structure or meaning of the sentence. It is normally introduced by *which*, *who*, or *whose* (but never *that*), and should have a comma before it:

she held out her hand, *which Rob shook.*
[main clause]   [non-restrictive relative clause]

A non-restrictive relative clause should also be followed by a comma if it is in the middle of a sentence:

Bill,   *who was asleep,*   *roused himself.*
       [non-restrictive relative clause]

noun a word that refers to a person, place, or thing, such as *book*, *Susan*, *England*, or *electricity*.

object the person or thing affected by a verb:

She took **the boys** out for a pizza.

Joe left **the band**.

participle the **past participle** is the form of a verb which is used to form certain past tenses (e.g. *looked* in *I have looked*) and sometimes as an adjective (e.g. *lost* in *lost property*).

The **present participle** is the form of a verb, ending in -*ing*, which is used to form tenses describing something that is still happening (e.g. I'm *thinking*), nouns (e.g. good *thinking*), and adjectives (e.g. *running* water).

phrasal verb a phrase consisting of a verb plus an adverb or a preposition which together have a particular meaning (e.g. *catch on*, *stick around*).

phrase a group of words within a sentence that forms part of a clause:

I went   to the bank   and drew out   some money.
[phrase]   [phrase]   [phrase]   [phrase]

plural the form of a noun that is used to refer to more than one person or thing, such as *books* or *churches*.

possessive determiner a determiner showing that someone or something belongs to someone or something else, such as *my*, *their*, *his*, *our*, etc.

prefix a letter or group of letters placed at the beginning of a word to change its meaning, such as *un-* (*unable*) or *pre-* (*predominant*).

preposition a word that is used with a noun or pronoun to show place, time, or method:

Roadworks **on** the M3 slowed traffic to a crawl.

She ran **across** the street.

The restaurant is open **during** the day.

pronoun a word, such as *he*, *we*, *hers*, *us*, *you*, or *they*, that is used instead of a noun to indicate someone or something that has already been mentioned, especially to avoid repeating the noun again.

Kate was tired so **she** went to bed.

Don't let **it** happen again.

relative clause a clause which is connected to a main clause by a word such as *which*, *that*, *whom*, *whose*, *when*, *where* or *who*:

I first saw her in Paris, where I lived in the early nineties
[main clause]   [relative clause]

See also **restrictive relative clause, non-restrictive relative clause.**

restrictive (or **defining**) **relative clause** a clause which gives essential information about a noun that comes before it. It can be introduced by *that, which, who,* or *whose* and does not normally have a comma before it:

she held out the hand which was hurt
she held out the hand that was hurt.
[main clause]   [restrictive relative clause]

You can also leave out *that* or *which* in some restrictive relative clauses:

It reminded him of the house that he used to live in.
It reminded him of the house he used to live in.

sentence a group of words that makes complete sense, contains a main verb, and begins with a capital letter and ends with a full stop, question mark, or exclamation mark:

I drew some money from the bank.
What's wrong with her?

subject the person or thing that causes the action of the verb:

The restaurant was packed out.
Jack went to see Natasha.

subjunctive a special form (or **mood**) of a verb that expresses a wish, a possibility, or a hypothetical situation instead of a fact. In the sentences below, the verbs *wait* and *were* are in the **subjunctive**; the ordinary forms (called the **indicative**) would be *waits* and *was*.

It was suggested he wait till the next morning.

Subjunctives are often used after *if, as if, as though,* and *unless*:

If I were taller, I would have been a model.

subordinate clause a clause which depends on a main clause for its meaning. Together with a main clause, a subordinate clause or clauses form part of a longer sentence. There are two main types of subordinate clause: the **relative clause** and the **conditional clause.**

suffix a letter or group of letters placed at the end of a word to change its meaning, such as *-able* (*breakable*) or *-ful* (*helpful*).

verb a word that describes an action or state:

There are no easy answers.
She ran the last few yards.
The ham had a smoky flavour.
Three years went past.

Commonly confused pairs of words

Word 1	Meaning	Word 2	Meaning
accept	say yes to	**except**	not including
adverse	unfavourable, harmful	**averse**	strongly disliking
advice	recommendations about future action	**advise**	recommend a course of action
affect	make a difference to	**effect**	a result; bring about a result
all together	all in one place; all at once	**altogether**	in total; completely
amoral	not concerned about right or wrong	**immoral**	not following accepted moral standards
appraise	assess the quality of	**apprise**	inform
bare	not clothed; uncover	**bear**	carry; tolerate
bated	with bated breath (in great suspense)	**baited**	taunted
born	having started life	**borne**	carried
brake	a device for stopping a vehicle; stop a vehicle	**break**	separate into pieces; a pause
censure	criticize strongly	**censor**	ban parts of a book or film; an official who does this
chord	a group of musical notes	**cord**	thin string or rope; a cord-like body part
coarse	rough	**course**	a direction
complacent	smugly self-satisfied	**complaisant**	willing to please

Commonly confused pairs of words

Word 1	Meaning	Word 2	Meaning
complement	add to in a way that improves; a thing that improves something	**compliment**	politely congratulate or praise; an expression of praise
complementary	combining to form a whole or to improve something	**complimentary**	praising; given free of charge
curb	control or limit	**kerb**	(in British English) a stone edging to a pavement
currant	a dried grape	**current**	happening now; a flow of water, air, or electricity
defuse	make a situation less tense	**diffuse**	spread over a wide area
desert	a waterless, empty area	**dessert**	the sweet course of a meal
discreet	careful to keep something secret or to avoid embarrassment	**discrete**	separate and distinct
disinterested	impartial	**uninterested**	not interested
draw	produce a picture; pull; a game that ends with an even score	**drawer**	a sliding storage compartment
elicit	draw out a response	**illicit**	forbidden by law or rules
ensure	make certain that something will occur	**insure**	pay to receive compensation in the event of damage, loss, etc.
envelop	wrap up or surround	**envelope**	a paper container for a letter

Commonly confused pairs of words

Word 1	Meaning	Word 2	Meaning
faint	lose consciousness; not clearly perceived	**feint**	a pretended attack; make a feint
fawn	a young deer; light brown	**faun**	a mythical being, part man, part goat
flair	a natural ability or talent	**flare**	gradually become wider; a brief burst of flame or light
flaunt	display obviously	**flout**	openly fail to follow a rule
flounder	have difficulty doing	**founder**	fail; sink
forbear	stop yourself from doing	**forebear**	an ancestor
freeze	turn to ice	**frieze**	a decoration around a wall
grisly	causing horror or disgust	**grizzly bear**	a type of bear
historic	important in history	**historical**	relating to history
hoard	a secret store	**horde**	a large crowd
imply	suggest indirectly	**infer**	work out from suggestions
its	belonging to it	**it's**	short for *it is* or *it has*
judicial	relating to a law court or judge	**judicious**	sensible
lama	a Buddhist monk	**llama**	an animal related to the camel
licence	a permit to own or do something	**license**	grant a licence to or for
lightening	getting lighter	**lightning**	a high-voltage electrical discharge; very quick
loath	unwilling	**loathe**	feel hatred for
loose	unfasten or set free; not fixed in place	**lose**	have taken away; be unable to find
meter	a measuring device	**metre**	a unit of measurement; rhythm in poetry
militate	be a powerful factor in preventing	**mitigate**	make less severe
pain	strong physical discomfort	**pane**	a sheet of glass

Word 1	Meaning	Word 2	Meaning
palate	the roof of the mouth	palette	an artist's board for mixing paints
pedal	a foot-operated lever; work the pedals of a bicycle	peddle	sell goods etc.
peninsula	a piece of land projecting into the sea	peninsular	relating to a peninsula
perpetrate	carry out a bad or illegal act	perpetuate	cause to continue for a long time
pore	a minute opening; study closely	pour	flow or cause to flow
practice	the action rather than the theory of doing something; the business of a doctor, dentist, etc.	practise	do repeatedly to improve skill; do regularly
prescribe	recommend the use of a medicine; state officially	proscribe	forbid
principal	most important; the most important person in an organization	principle	a fundamental law; a belief
reign	rule as a monarch; a monarch's period of rule	rein	strap used to control a horse; also used in the phrase a free rein
role	an actor's part	roll	move by turning over and over; a rolling movement
sceptic	a person who tends to question accepted opinions	septic	infected with bacteria
shear	cut the wool off a sheep	sheer	nothing but; change course quickly
sight	the ability to see	site	a location
silicon	an element used in electronics	silicone	substance used in cosmetic implants
stationary	not moving	stationery	paper and writing materials
storey	a level of a building	story	an account

Commonly confused pairs of words

Word 1	Meaning	Word 2	Meaning
straight	without a curve or bend	strait	a narrow passage of water; (straits) a difficult situation
summary	a brief statement of the main points	summery	typical of summer
swat	hit with a flat object	swot	study hard
tail	the rear or end part	tale	a story
team	a group playing or working together	teem	be swarming with; pour down
their	belonging to them	there	in, at, or to that place
titillate	interest or excite, esp. sexually	titivate	make more attractive
to	in the direction of	too	excessively; also
toe	a part of the foot; also in **toe the line**	tow	pull along behind
vain	having a very high opinion of yourself	vein	a tube that carries blood towards the heart
waive	choose not to insist on a right	wave	move to and fro; a ridge of water
who's	short for *who is* or *who has*	whose	belonging to which person
your	belonging to you	you're	short for *you are*

Frequently misspelled words

word	comment	word	comment
abscess	*sc* in the middle, two *s*'s at the end	**belief, believe**	*i* before *e*
accommodate	two *c*'s, two *m*'s	**besiege**	*i* before *e*
accumulate	two *c*'s, one *m*	**biased**	only one *s*
achieve	*i* before *e*	**blatant**	not *-ent*
acquaint, acquiesce, acquire, acquit	acq-	**broccoli**	two *c*'s, one *l*
		cappuccino	two *p*'s, two *c*'s
		Caribbean	one *r*, two *b*'s
address	two *d*'s	**cemetery**	three vowels, all *e*'s
aggressive, aggression, etc.	two *g*'s, two *s*'s	**commemorate**	two *m*'s followed by one *m*
all right	two words (not *alright*)	**commitment**	one *t* in the middle
a lot	two words (not *alot*)	**committee**	two *m*'s, two *t*'s
anaesthetic	-ae-; American anesthetic	**comparative**	-rative, not -ritive
apartment	only one *p*	**compatible**	-tible, not -table
appal	two *p*'s, one *l*; American appall	**consensus**	not -census
appalling	two *p*'s, two *l*'s	**contemporary**	-porary, not -pory
apparent	ends with *-ent*	**correspondence**	not -ance
aqueduct	aque-, not aqua-	**deceive**	*e* before *i*
Arctic	remember the *c* after the *r*	**definite**	-ite, not -ate
argument	no *e* after the *u*	**desperate**	-per- not -par-
artefact	arte-; American arti-	**detach**	not -atch
attach	not -atch	**disappear**	one *s*, two *p*'s
barbecue	not -que	**disappoint**	one *s*, two *p*'s
		ecstasy	ends with -asy
		eighth	two *h*s

word	comment
embarrass	two r's, two s's
enthral	one l; American enthrall
estuary	-tuary, not -taury
exercise	not exc-
extraordinary	extraor-, not extror-
extrovert	extro-, not extra-
February	two r's
fluorescent	fluor-, not flour-
fulfil	two single l's; American fulfill
gauge	-au-, not -ua-
government	remember the n before the m
grateful	not great-
guarantee	-ua-, not -au-
guard, guardian, etc.	-ua-, not -au-
hamster	ham-, not hamp-
harass, harassment, etc.	one r, two s's
hers	no apostrophe
humorous	-or-, not -our-
hygienic	i before e
idiosyncrasy	not -cracy
independent	ends -ent (noun and adjective)
instalment	one l; American installment
introvert	-tro-, not -tra-
itinerary	ends -erary
knowledge	remember the d

word	comment
liaison	two i's: -iai-
lightning	-tn-, not -ten-
manoeuvre	-oeu-; American maneuver
medicine	medi- not mede-
Mediterranean	one t, two r's
millennium	two l's, two n's
millionaire	two l's, one n
miniature	-ia- in second syllable
minuscule	minu-, not mini-
mischievous	-vous, not -vious
misspell	two s's
necessary	one c, two s's
niece	i before e
occasion	two c's, one s
occurrence	two c's, two r's
omit	one m
ours	no apostrophe
parallel	two l's in the middle, one at the end
parliament	-ia- in second syllable
permanent	-nent, not -nant
persistent	-tent, not -tant
pharaoh	-aoh, not -oah
pigeon	no d. -igeon
Portuguese	ends with -guese
privilege	ends -ilege
pronunciation	-nunc-, not -nounc-
publicly	-cly not -cally
questionnaire	two n's

word	comment	word	comment
receive	*e* before *i*	**supersede**	not -*cede*
recommend	one *c*, two *m*'s	**suppress**	not *sur*-; two *p*'s
relevant	ends with -*ant*	**surprise**	begins *sur*-
relief, relieve	*i* before *e*	**tariff**	one *r*, two *f*'s
restaurateur	no *n* in the middle: -*ateur*	**theirs**	no apostrophe
		thief	*i* before *e*
rhythm	begins *rh*-	**threshold**	one *h*
risotto	one *s*, two *t*'s	**truly**	no *e*
sacrilege	-*rilege*, not -*relige*	**underrate**	two *r*'s in the middle
Scandinavian	-*din*- in the middle	**until**	one *l*
		veterinary	note the -*erin* in the middle
schedule	*sche*-, not *she*-		
seize	*e* before *i*	**Wednesday**	remember the *d* before the *n*
separate	-*par*-, not -*per*-	**weird**	-*ei*-, not -*ie*-
siege	*i* before *e*	**whinge**	remember the *h*
sieve	*i* before *e*	**wilful**	single *l*'s; American *willful*
skilful	single *l*'s; American *skillful*	**withhold**	two *h*'s
		yield	*i* before *e*
successful	two *c*'s, two *s*'s, one *l*	**yours**	no apostrophe

Useful words for games and puzzles

Proper names and abbreviations which are not pronounced as they are spelled (such as *Dr* or *Mr*) are not included, as most word games don't allow them.

Two-letter words

aa rough cindery lava

ab an abdominal muscle

ad an advertisement

ag (*S. African*) expressing irritation, grief, pleasure, etc.

ah expressing surprise, sympathy, pleasure, etc.

ai the three-toed sloth

am the present tense of **be**

an a form of the indefinite article 'a'

as used to convey relative extent or degree

at expressing location or time

aw expressing mild protest, entreaty, etc.

ax dialect form of **ask**; US spelling of **axe**

ay variant spelling of **aye**

ba (in Egyptian mythology) the soul

be to exist

bi bisexual

bo a kind of fig tree

by beside

da a person's father

DJ a disc jockey

do to perform an action

dy a type of sediment

ee dialect form of **oh**

eh seeking explanation or agreement

El an elevated railway or section of railway

em a measuring unit in printing

en a measuring unit in printing

er expressing doubt or hesitation

ex a former spouse or partner

fa a musical note

Ga a member of a people living in Ghana

GI a soldier in the US army

go to move or travel

ha expressing surprise, triumph, etc.

he a male person or animal previously mentioned

hi used as a greeting

ho expressing surprise, triumph, etc.

id a part of the mind

if introducing a conditional clause

in within

io a North American moth

is the present tense of **be**

it a thing previously mentioned

ja (*S. African*) yes

jo (*Scottish, old use*): a sweetheart

ju a kind of Chinese pottery

ka (in Egyptian mythology) the spirit

ki a plant of the lily family

KO a knockout in a boxing match

la a musical note

li a Chinese unit of distance

lo (*old use*) used to draw attention to something

LP a long-playing record

ma a person's mother

MD (*Brit.*) a managing director

me the objective case of I

mi a musical note

mo a moment

MP a Member of Parliament

mu the 12th letter of the Greek alphabet

my belonging to me

no not any

nu the 13th letter of the Greek alphabet

ob a type of gene

od a power once thought to pervade the natural world

of belonging to

og (*Australian, old use*) a shilling

oh expressing surprise, anger, disappointment, etc.

oi used to attract attention

OJ orange juice

OK used to express assent, agreement, etc.

om a mystic syllable which constitutes a sacred mantra

on supported by or covering

op an operation

or used to link alternatives

os a bone

ou a Hawaiian bird

ow expressing pain

ox a cow or bull

oy = oi

Oz Australia

pa a person's father

pi the 16th letter of the Greek alphabet

po a chamber pot

qi (in Chinese philosophy) the life force

ra (in Norway and Sweden) a moraine

re a musical note

ri a Japanese unit of length

se a Chinese musical instrument

si = te

so therefore

ta thank you

te a musical note

ti = te

TV television

uh expressing hesitation

um expressing hesitation

up towards a higher position

us the objective case of we

Wa a member of a people living on the borders of China and Burma

we yourself and other people

Wu a dialect of Chinese

xi the 14th letter of Greek alphabet

xu a Vietnamese unit of money

ye (*old use*) the plural form of **thou**

Yi a people living in parts of China

yo used as a greeting

yu an ancient Chinese wine container

Three-letter words containing x or z

adz US spelling of **adze**

axe a tool for chopping wood etc.

biz business

box a container

coz (*old use*) a cousin

cox the person who steers a rowing boat

dux (*Scottish*) the top pupil in a school or class

dzo a crossbreed of a cow and a yak

fax an electronic copy of a document

fez a type of hat

fix to attach something

fox an animal with a bushy tail

hex (*N. Amer.*) to cast a spell on someone

kex (*dialect*) cow parsley

lax not strict or careful enough

lox (*N. Amer.*) smoked salmon

lux a unit for measuring illumination

max maximum

Mex Mexican

mix to blend or combine

nix nothing

pax a call for a truce

pix pictures

pox a disease

pyx the container which holds the consecrated bread used in Holy Communion

Rex the reigning king

sax a saxophone

saz a musical instrument

sex being male or female

six one more than five

tax money paid to the government

tux a tuxedo

Uzi a type of sub-machine gun

vex to annoy

vox vocals; voice

wax substance used to make candles etc.

wiz = whizz

zag a sharp change of direction

zap to destroy

zax = sax

zed the letter Z

zee (*N. Amer.*) the letter Z

Zen a type of Buddhism

zho = dzo

zig a sharp change of direction

zip a fastener

zit a spot

zol (*S. African*) a hand-rolled cigarette

zoo a place where wild animals are kept

Words with a q not followed by a u

burqa a garment worn by Muslim women

fiqh the theory or philosophy of Islamic law

Iraqi a person from Iraq; relating to Iraq

niqab a Muslim woman's veil

qadi a Muslim judge

qanat an irrigation tunnel

qasida an Arabic or Persian poem

qawwal a qawwali singer

qawwali Muslim devotional music
qi (in Chinese philosophy) the life force
qibla the direction towards Mecca
qigong a Chinese system of physical exercises
qin a Chinese musical instrument
qintar a monetary unit of Albania

qiviut wool from the musk ox
qwerty the standard layout of typewriters and keyboards
suq = souk, an Arab market
talaq (in Islamic law) a type of divorce
tariqa the Sufi method of spiritual learning

Words beginning with x (of up to nine letters)

xanthan a polysaccharide
xanthate a chemical compound
xanthene a chemical compound
xanthic yellowish
xanthin a yellow colouring matter
xanthine a biochemical compound
xanthoma a yellow patch on the skin
xebec a sailing ship
xeme a fork-tailed gull
xenia gifts to a guest or guests
xenial relating to hospitality
xenograft a tissue graft or organ transplant from a different species
xenon a gas
xenophobe a person with an irrational dislike of foreigners
xeric very dry
xeriscape landscape gardening needing little or no irrigation
xeroma abnormal dryness of a body part
xerophyte a plant needing very little water

xerox to photocopy
Xhosa a South African people or their language
xi the 14th letter of the Greek alphabet
Xiang a dialect of Chinese
xiphoid sword-shaped
Xmas Christmas
xoanon a wooden image of a god
xography a photographic process
xu a Vietnamese unit of money
xylan a compound found in wood
xylary relating to xylem
xylem plant tissue
xylene a liquid hydrocarbon
xylite a volatile liquid
xylitol a chemical substance
xylol =xylene
xylophone a musical instrument
xylose: a plant sugar
xyrid a sedge-like herb
xyster a surgical instrument
xyston an ancient Greek spear
xystus an ancient Greek portico

Jj

J abbrev. joules.

jab v. (**jabbing**, **jabbed**) poke with something pointed. • n. **1** a sharp poke or blow. **2** informal an injection.

jabber v. talk quickly but unintelligibly.

jacaranda n. a tropical tree with scented wood.

jack n. **1** a device for lifting a vehicle off the ground. **2** a playing card next below a queen. **3** a connection between two pieces of electrical equipment. **4** a small ball aimed at in bowls. • v. (**jack up**) raise with a jack.

jackal n. a wild dog of Africa and Asia.

jackass n. **1** a stupid person. **2** a male ass.

jackboot n. a military boot reaching to the knee.

jackdaw n. a small grey-headed crow.

jacket n. **1** a short coat. **2** an outer covering. **3** the skin of a potato.

jackknife n. a large folding knife. • v. (of an articulated lorry) bend into a V-shape in a skid.

jackpot n. a large cash prize in a game or lottery.

Jacobean adj. of the reign of James I of England (1603–1625).

Jacobite n. a supporter of the deposed James II and his descendants.

jacquard n. a fabric with a woven pattern.

jacuzzi /juh-koo-zi/ n. (pl. **jacuzzis**) trademark a large bath with jets of water.

jade n. a green precious stone.

jaded adj. tired and bored.

jagged adj. with rough, sharp projections.

jaguar n. a large cat of Central and South America.

jail (or **gaol**) n. prison. • v. put in jail. ■ **jailer** n.

jalopy /juh-lop-i/ n. (pl. **jalopies**) informal an old car.

jam v. (**jamming**, **jammed**) **1** pack tightly into a space. **2** block through crowding. **3** become stuck. **4** block a radio transmission. • n. **1** a spread made from fruit and sugar. **2** an instance of being blocked. **3** informal a difficult situation.

jamb n. a side post of a door or window.

jamboree n. a lavish or noisy party.

jangle v. **1** make a ringing metallic sound. **2** feel upset or on edge. • n. a jangling sound.

janitor n. a caretaker.

January n. the first month.

Japanese n. (pl. **Japanese**) **1** a person from Japan. **2** the language of Japan. • adj. of Japan.

japanned adj. coated with a black glossy varnish.

jape n. a practical joke.

japonica n. a shrub with bright red flowers.

jar n. a cylindrical glass or pottery container. •v. (**jarring, jarred**) **1** hit with a painful jolt. **2** have an unpleasant effect.

jargon n. words used by a particular group and hard for others to understand.

jasmine n. a shrub with scented flowers.

jasper n. a reddish-brown quartz.

jaundice n. **1** yellowing of the skin due to a liver disorder. **2** bitterness or resentment. ■ **jaundiced** adj.

jaunt n. a short trip for pleasure.

jaunty adj. lively and self-confident. ■ **jauntily** adv.

javelin n. a long spear thrown in a sport.

jaw n. **1** the bony structures forming the framework of the mouth. **2** (**jaws**) the gripping parts of a tool. •v. informal talk at length.

jay n. a bird of the crow family.

jaywalk v. cross a road without regard for the traffic. ■ **jay-walker** n.

jazz n. a type of music characterized by improvisation. •v. (**jazz up**) make more lively.

jazzy adj. (**jazzier, jazziest**) **1** in the style of jazz. **2** colourful and showy.

jealous adj. **1** envious of someone's success. **2** resentful of someone seen as a sexual rival. **3** very protective of your possessions. ■ **jealousy** n.

jeans pl. n. denim trousers.

jeep n. trademark a sturdy four-wheel drive vehicle.

jeer v. make rude mocking remarks at. •n. a rude mocking remark.

Jehovah n. the name of God in some translations of the Bible.

jejune adj. **1** simplistic. **2** dull.

jell v. = GEL.

jelly n. (pl. **jellies**) **1** a dessert made of a flavoured liquid set with gelatin. **2** a semi-solid substance. □ **jellyfish** a sea animal with a soft body and stinging tentacles.

jemmy n. (pl. **jemmies**) a short crowbar.

jenny n. (pl. **jennies**) a female donkey.

jeopardize (or **-ise**) v. put at risk of harm or loss.

jeopardy n. danger of harm or loss.

jerk n. a sharp, sudden movement. •v. move with a jerk. ■ **jerkily** adv. **jerky** adj.

jerkin n. a sleeveless jacket.

jerry-built adj. badly or hastily built.

jerrycan n. a large flat-sided can for liquids.

jersey n. (pl. **jerseys**) **1** a knitted top with sleeves. **2** a soft knitted fabric.

Jerusalem artichoke n. a knobbly root vegetable.

jest n. a joke. •v. speak in a joking way.

jester n. a comic entertainer at a medieval court.

Jesuit n. a member of a Roman Catholic order of priests.

jet n. **1** a stream of liquid or gas forced out of a small opening. **2** an aircraft powered by jet engines. **3** a hard black mineral. **4** (or **jet black**) a glossy black colour. •v. (**jetting, jetted**) travel by jet aircraft. □ **jet engine** an aircraft engine providing propulsion by ejecting a high-speed jet of gas from burning fuel. **jet lag** extreme tiredness felt after a long flight. **jet ski** trademark a small vehicle which skims across the water.

jetsam n. unwanted material thrown from a ship and washed ashore.

jettison v. throw or drop from an aircraft or ship.

jetty n. (pl. **jetties**) a landing stage or small pier.

Jew n. a person whose religion is Judaism and who is of ancient Hebrew descent. ■ **Jewish** adj.

jewel n. **1** a precious stone cut or set as an ornament. **2** a highly valued person or thing. ■ **jewelled** (US **jeweled**) adj.

jewellery (US **jewelry**) n. personal ornaments such as necklaces or rings. ■ **jeweller** n.

Jewry n. Jews as a group.

jib n. **1** a triangular sail in front of a mast. **2** the arm of a crane. •v. (**jibbing, jibbed**) (**jib at**) be unwilling to do or accept.

jibe (or **gibe**) n. **1** an insulting remark. **2** US = GYBE. •v. **1** make jibes. **2** US = GYBE.

jiffy n. informal a moment.

jig n. **1** a lively dance. **2** a device that holds something and guides the tools working on it. •v. (**jigging, jigged**) move up and down jerkily.

jiggery-pokery n. informal suspicious behaviour.

jiggle v. rock or shake lightly.

jigsaw n. **1** a picture cut into interlocking shapes that have to be fitted together. **2** a machine saw for cutting curved lines in a material.

jihad n. (in Islam) a war or struggle against non-Muslims.

jilt v. break off a relationship with a lover.

jingle n. **1** a light ringing sound. **2** a short memorable slogan etc. •v. make a jingle.

jingoism n. excessive pride in your country. ■ **jingoistic** adj.

jinx n. a person or thing that brings bad luck. ■ **jinxed** adj.

jitters pl. n. informal nervousness. ■ **jittery** adj.

jive n. a lively dance to swing music. •v. dance the jive.

job n. **1** a paid position of employment. **2** a task. •v. (**jobbing, jobbed**) do casual work. □ **job centre** (in the UK) a government office providing information about available jobs. **job lot** a batch of articles sold or bought at one time. ■ **jobless** adj.

jockey n. (pl. **jockeys**) a professional rider in horse races. •v. struggle to gain or achieve.

jockstrap n. a support or protection for a man's genitals.

jocose adj. humorous.

jocular adj. humorous. ■ **jocularity** n.

jocund adj. cheerful.

jodhpurs pl. n. trousers worn for horse riding that fit closely below the knee.

jog v. (**jogging, jogged**) **1** run at a steady, gentle pace. **2** knock slightly. •n. **1** a period of jogging. **2** a slight knock. □ **jog someone's memory** make someone remember something. ■ **jogger** n.

joggle v. shake slightly.

joie de vivre /zhwah duh veevruh/ n. lively enjoyment of life.

join v. **1** link or become linked. **2** unite to form a whole. **3** become a member or employee of. **4** (also **join in**) take part in. **5** meet or go with someone. **6** (**join up**) enlist in the armed forces. •n. a place where things join.

joiner n. a person who makes the wooden parts of a building. ■ **joinery** n.

joint n. **1** a join. **2** a structure in the body joining two bones. **3** a large piece of meat. **4** informal a place of a specified kind. **5** informal a cannabis cigarette. · adj. shared, held, or made by two or more people. · v. cut meat into joints. ■ **jointed** adj. **jointly** adv.

joist n. a beam supporting the floor or ceiling of a building.

jojoba /hoh-hoh-buh/ n. an oil from the seeds of a shrub, used in cosmetics.

joke n. **1** something said or done to cause laughter. **2** informal a ridiculously inadequate person or thing. · v. make jokes. ■ **jokey** adj.

joker n. **1** a person who jokes. **2** a playing card used as a wild card.

jollification n. time spent having fun.

jollity n. **1** lively and cheerful activity. **2** cheerfulness.

jolly adj. (**jollier**, **jolliest**) **1** happy and cheerful. **2** lively and entertaining. · v. (**jollying**, **jollied**) informal encourage in a friendly way. · adv. informal very.

jolt v. **1** push or shake abruptly. **2** shock into action. · n. **1** an act of jolting. **2** a shock.

josh v. informal tease playfully.

joss stick n. a thin stick of incense.

jostle v. push roughly.

jot v. (**jotting**, **jotted**) write quickly. · n. a very small amount.

jotter n. a small notebook.

joule n. a unit of energy.

journal n. **1** a newspaper or magazine. **2** a diary.

journalese n. informal a clichéd style of writing.

journalist n. a person who writes for a newspaper etc. or prepares reports to be broadcast. ■ **journalism** n.

journey n. (pl. **journeys**) an act of travelling from one place to another. · v. travel.

journeyman n. a skilled worker employed by another.

joust v. (of medieval knights) fight on horseback with lances.

jovial adj. cheerful. ■ **joviality** n. **jovially** adv.

jowl n. the lower part of the cheek.

joy n. **1** great happiness. **2** a cause of joy. ■ **joyful** adj. **joyfully** adv. **joyless** adj.

joyous adj. very happy. ■ **joyously** adv.

joyriding n. informal the crime of stealing a vehicle and driving it very fast. ■ **joyride** n. **joyrider** n.

joystick n. **1** the control column of an aircraft. **2** a lever controlling the movement of an image on a screen.

JP abbrev. Justice of the Peace.

jubilant adj. happy and triumphant. ■ **jubilation** n.

jubilee n. a special anniversary.

Judaism n. the religion of the Jews. ■ **Judaic** adj.

judder v. shake noisily or violently.

judge n. **1** a public official who decides cases in a law court. **2** a person who decides who has won a competition. **3** a person able to give an opinion. · v. **1** form an opinion about. **2** decide a case in a law court. **3** decide the winner of a competition.

judgement (or **judgment**) n. **1** the ability to make sound decisions. **2** an opinion or conclusion. **3** a decision of a law court or judge.

judgemental (or **judgmental**) adj. **1** of judgement. **2** excessively critical of others.

judicial adj. of a law court or judge. ■ **judicially** adv.

judiciary n. judges as a group.

judicious adj. having or done with good judgement. ■ **judiciously** adv.

judo n. a sport of unarmed combat.

jug n. a container with a handle and a lip, for holding and pouring liquids.

juggernaut n. a large heavy vehicle.

juggle v. **1** continuously toss and catch several objects, keeping one or more in the air at any time. **2** do several things at the same time. ■ **juggler** n.

jugular n. any of several large veins in the neck.

juice n. **1** the liquid in fruit, vegetables, or meat. **2** (**juices**) fluid produced by the stomach. •v. extract the juice from.

juicy adj. (**juicier**, **juiciest**) **1** full of juice. **2** informal (of gossip) very interesting.

ju-jitsu n. a Japanese sport of unarmed combat.

jukebox n. a coin-operated machine playing musical recordings.

julep n. a sweet drink made from sugar syrup.

julienne n. a portion of vegetables cut into thin strips.

July n. the seventh month.

jumble n. an untidy collection. •v. mix up in a confused way. □ **jumble sale** a sale of second-hand goods.

jumbo informal adj. very large. •n. (pl. **jumbos**) (or **jumbo jet**) a very large airliner.

jump v. **1** push yourself off the ground with your legs and feet. **2** leap across. **3** move suddenly from surprise. **4** (**jump at**) accept eagerly. **5** pass abruptly from one thing to another. •n. **1** an act of jumping. **2** a large or sudden increase. **3** an obstacle to be jumped. □ **jump leads** a pair of cables for recharging a battery in a vehicle by connecting it to the battery in another. **jumpsuit** a one-piece garment of trousers and a top. **jump the queue** move ahead of your proper place in a queue.

jumper n. **1** a pullover. **2** a person or animal that jumps.

jumpy adj. (**jumpier**, **jumpiest**) informal anxious and uneasy.

junction n. **1** a point where things meet or join. **2** a place where roads or railway lines meet.

juncture n. **1** a point in time. **2** a join.

June n. the sixth month.

jungle n. **1** an area of thick tropical forest and tangled vegetation. **2** a bewildering or complicated situation.

junior adj. **1** of younger people. **2** of schoolchildren aged 7–11. **3** younger. **4** low or lower in status. •n. a junior person.

juniper n. an evergreen shrub.

junk n. **1** informal useless or worthless articles. **2** a flat-bottomed sailing boat used in China. □ **junk food** unhealthy food. **junk mail** unwanted advertising material sent by post.

junket n. **1** informal an official trip paid for using public funds. **2** a dish of sweetened curds of milk.

j

junkie n. informal a drug addict.

junta n. a group ruling a country after taking power by force.

jurisdiction n. **1** the official power to make legal decisions. **2** the extent of this.

jurisprudence n. the theory of law.

jurist n. an expert in law.

juror n. a member of a jury.

jury n. (pl. **juries**) a group of people required to attend a legal case and give a verdict based on the evidence presented.

just adj. **1** right and fair. **2** deserved. • adv. **1** exactly. **2** at the same moment. **3** very recently. **4** by a small amount. **5** only. ■ **justly** adv.

justice n. **1** just behaviour or treatment. **2** the administration of law. **3** a judge or magistrate.

□ **Justice of the Peace** a non-professional magistrate.

justifiable adj. able to be shown to be right or reasonable. ■ **justifiably** adv.

justify v. (**justifying**, **justified**) **1** show to be right or reasonable. **2** be a good reason for. **3** adjust lines of type to form straight edges at both sides. ■ **justification** n.

jut v. (**jutting**, **jutted**) extend out beyond.

jute n. rough fibre from the stems of a tropical plant.

juvenile adj. **1** of young people or animals. **2** childish. • n. a young person or animal. □ **juvenile delinquent** a young person who regularly commits crimes.

juxtapose v. place close together. ■ **juxtaposition** n.

Kk

K abbrev. **1** kilobytes. **2** informal thousand.

kaftan (or **caftan**) n. a long, loose dress or tunic.

kaiser n. hist. the German or Austrian Emperor.

kale n. a type of cabbage.

kaleidoscope /kuh-ly-duh-skohp/ n. a tube containing mirrors and coloured fragments whose reflections produce changing patterns when the tube is turned. ■ **kaleidoscopic** adj.

kamikaze /ka-mi-kah-zi/ n. (in the Second World War) a Japanese

aircraft loaded with explosives and deliberately crashed on its target. • adj. reckless or suicidal.

kangaroo n. a large Australian marsupial with strong hind legs for leaping. □ **kangaroo court** a court set up unofficially and intended to find someone guilty.

kaolin n. a fine white clay, used for making china and in medicine.

kapok n. a fluffy fibre used as padding.

kaput /kuh-puut/ adj. informal broken.

karaoke /ka-ri-oh-ki/ n. an entertainment in which people sing popular songs to pre-recorded backing tracks.

karate /kuh-rah-ti/ n. a Japanese system of unarmed combat.

karma n. (in Hinduism and Buddhism) a person's actions in this and previous lives, seen as affecting their future fate.

kasbah (or **casbah**) n. (in North Africa) an old fortress in a city and the narrow streets surrounding it.

kayak /ky-ak/ n. a light covered canoe.

kebab n. pieces of meat etc. cooked on a skewer.

kedgeree n. a dish of smoked fish, rice, and hard-boiled eggs.

keel n. a structure running along the base of a ship. • v. (**keel over**) **1** (of a boat) turn over on its side. **2** fall over.

keen adj. **1** eager and enthusiastic. **2** sharp. **3** quick to understand. **4** highly developed. ■ **keenly** adv. **keenness** n.

keep v. (**keeping**, **kept**) **1** continue to have. **2** continue in a specified condition, position, or activity. **3** save for future use. **4** store in a regular place. **5** do something agreed. **6** cause to be late. **7** support financially. • n. **1** food and other essentials for living. **2** the strongest or central tower of a castle. □ **keep on** continue. **keepsake** a small item kept in memory of the person who gave it. **keep up 1** move at the same rate as another. **2** continue.

keeper n. **1** a person who manages or looks after something or someone. **2** a goalkeeper or wicketkeeper.

keeping n. (**in** (or **out of**) **keeping with**) in (or not in) harmony or agreement with.

keg n. a small barrel.

kelp n. a type of seaweed.

kelvin n. a unit of temperature.

ken n. (**your ken**) your range of knowledge or experience.

kennel n. **1** a shelter for a dog. **2** (**kennels**) a boarding or breeding establishment for dogs.

kept past & past part. of **KEEP**.

keratin n. a protein forming the basis of hair, nails, horns, etc.

kerb (US **curb**) n. a stone edging to a pavement.

kerchief n. a piece of fabric worn over the head.

kerfuffle n. informal a commotion or fuss.

kernel n. **1** the softer part inside the shell of a nut, seed, or fruit stone. **2** the seed and husk of a cereal. **3** a central part.

kerosene n. US paraffin.

kestrel n. a small falcon.

ketch n. a two-masted sailing boat.

ketchup n. a thick tomato sauce.

kettle n. a container with a lid, spout, and handle, for boiling water. □ **kettledrum** a large bowl-shaped drum.

key n. **1** a piece of shaped metal for opening or closing a lock or turning a screw etc. **2** a lever pressed down by the finger on a piano etc. **3** a button on a panel for operating a typewriter or computer. **4** a thing providing access or understanding. **5** an explanatory list of the symbols in a map etc. **6** a group of related notes forming a musical scale. • adj. of central importance. • v. **1** enter data using a

k

computer keyboard. **2 (be keyed up)** be tense or excited. ▫ **keynote 1** a central theme. **2** the note on which a musical key is based.

keypad a set of buttons for operating an electronic device or phone. **key ring** a metal ring for holding keys. **keystone 1** the central part of a policy or system. **2** the central stone at the top of an arch, locking the whole together. **keyword 1** a significant word mentioned in an index. **2** a word used in a computer system to indicate a document's content.

keyboard n. **1** a set of keys on a computer, typewriter, piano, etc. **2** an electronic musical instrument with keys arranged as on a piano. •v. key data. ■ **keyboarder** n.

keyhole n. **1** a hole in a lock for a key. ▫ **keyhole surgery** surgery carried out through a very small incision.

kg abbrev. kilograms.

KGB abbrev. the secret police of the former Soviet Union.

khaki n. a dull greenish- or yellowish-brown.

kHz abbrev. kilohertz.

kibbutz n. (pl. **kibbutzim**) (in Israel) a communal farming settlement.

kibosh n. **(put the kibosh on)** informal firmly put an end to.

kick v. **1** hit or propel forcibly with the foot. **2** informal give up a habit. **3** (of a gun) spring back when fired. •n. **1** an act of kicking. **2** informal a thrill. **3** informal the strong effect of alcohol. ▫ **kick in** come into effect. **kick-off** the start of a football match. **kick out** informal force to leave. **kick-start 1** start a motorcycle engine with a

downward thrust of a pedal. **2** cause to develop more quickly.

kid n. **1** informal a child or young person. **2** a young goat. •v. **(kidding, kidded)** informal fool into believing.

kidnap v. **(kidnapping, kidnapped;** US **kidnaping, kidnaped)** take by force and hold captive for a ransom. •n. an act of kidnapping. ■ **kidnapper** n.

kidney n. (pl. **kidneys**) each of a pair of organs that remove waste products from the blood and produce urine.

kilim /ki-leem/ n. a carpet woven without a pile, made in Turkey etc.

kill v. **1** cause the death of. **2** put an end to. **3** pass time. •n. **1** an act of killing. **2** an animal or animals killed by a hunter. ▫ **killjoy** a person who spoils the enjoyment of others. ■ **killer** n.

killing n. an act of causing death. ▫ **make a killing** make a great deal of money out of something.

kiln n. a furnace for baking or drying pottery etc.

kilo n. (pl. **kilos**) a kilogram.

kilobyte n. Computing 1,024 bytes.

kilocalorie n. 1,000 calories.

kilogram n. 1,000 grams.

kilohertz n. 1,000 hertz.

kilojoule n. 1,000 joules.

kilometre (US **kilometer**) n. 1,000 metres.

kilovolt n. 1,000 volts.

kilowatt n. 1,000 watts.

kilt n. a pleated tartan skirt, traditionally worn by men as part of Scottish Highland dress.

kilter n. **(out of kilter)** out of balance.

kimono n. (pl. **kimonos**) a loose Japanese robe worn with a sash.

kin (or **kinsfolk**) pl. n. your relations. □ **kinship 1** blood relationship. **2** relationship based on similar characteristics. ■ **kinsman** n. **kinswoman** n.

kind n. a class of similar people or things. •adj. considerate and generous. □ **in kind 1** in the same way. **2** (of payment) in goods or services instead of money. ■ **kindness** n.

kindergarten n. a nursery school.

kindle v. **1** light a flame. **2** arouse an emotion.

kindling n. small sticks used for lighting fires.

kindly adv. **1** in a kind way. **2** please (used in a polite request). •adj. kind. ■ **kindliness** n.

kindred pl. n. your relatives. •adj. similar in kind.

kinetic adj. of or resulting from motion. ■ **kinetically** adv.

king n. **1** the male ruler of a country. **2** the best or most important person or thing. **3** a playing card ranking next below an ace. **4** the most important chess piece. □ **kingpin** an important person or thing. **king-size** (or **king-sized**) extra large.

kingdom n. **1** a country ruled by a king or queen. **2** each of the three divisions in which natural objects are classified.

kingfisher n. a colourful diving bird.

kink n. **1** a bend or twist in something straight. **2** a flaw. **3** a peculiar characteristic.

kinky adj. (**kinkier**, **kinkiest**) **1** informal of or liking unusual sexual activities. **2** having kinks.

kiosk /kee-ossk/ n. a booth from which newspapers, tickets, etc. are sold, or containing a public phone.

kip n. informal a sleep.

kipper n. a smoked herring.

kirk n. Sc. a church.

kismet n. fate.

kiss v. touch with the lips. •n. a touch with the lips. □ **kiss of life** mouth-to-mouth resuscitation.

kit n. a set of equipment or clothes for a specific purpose. •v. (**kitting**, **kitted**) (**kit out**) provide with appropriate clothing or equipment.

kitchen n. a room where food is prepared and cooked. □ **kitchenette** a small kitchen. **kitchen garden** a garden for vegetables, fruit, and herbs.

kite n. **1** a light frame with fabric stretched over it, flown in the wind at the end of a long string. **2** a bird of prey. □ **Kitemark** trademark an official mark on goods approved by the British Standards Institution.

kith n. (**kith and kin**) your family and relations.

kitsch n. art, objects, or design regarded as tasteless or too sentimental.

kitten n. a young cat.

kittiwake n. a type of small gull.

kitty n. (pl. **kitties**) a fund of money for use by a number of people.

kiwi n. (pl. **kiwis**) a flightless New Zealand bird. □ **kiwi fruit** a fruit with hairy skin and green flesh.

kJ abbrev. kilojoules.

klaxon n. trademark a vehicle horn or a hooter.

kleptomania n. a recurring urge to steal. ■ **kleptomaniac** n. & adj.

k

km abbrev. kilometres.

knack n. a skill at performing a task.

knacker v. informal **1** damage. **2** (**knackered**) very tired.

knapsack n. a small rucksack.

knave n. **1** old use a dishonest man. **2** (in cards) a jack.

knead v. **1** work dough or clay with the hands. **2** massage as if kneading.

knee n. **1** the joint between the thigh and the lower leg. **2** the upper surface of a sitting person's thigh. • v. (**kneeing, kneed**) hit with the knee. □ **kneecap 1** the bone in front of the knee joint. **2** shoot in the knee as a punishment. **knee-jerk** automatic and unthinking. **knees-up** informal a lively party.

kneel v. (**kneeling, knelt** or US **kneeled**) fall or rest on the knees.

knell n. the sound of a bell rung solemnly.

knew past of KNOW.

knickerbockers pl. n. loose-fitting trousers or knickers gathered at the knee or calf.

knickers pl. n. women's or girls' underpants.

knick-knack n. a cheap ornament.

knife n. (pl. **knives**) a cutting instrument with a blade fixed in a handle. • v. stab with a knife. □ **knife-edge** a very tense or dangerous situation.

knight n. **1** (in the Middle Ages) a man of noble rank with a duty to fight for his king. **2** a man awarded a title and entitled to use 'Sir' in front of his name. **3** a chess piece shaped like a horse's head. • v. give the title of knight to. ■ **knighthood** n.

knit v. (**knitting, knitted** or **knit**) **1** make a garment by looping yarn together with long blunt needles or a machine. **2** join together. **3** tighten the eyebrows in a frown. ■ **knitter** n. **knitting** n.

knob n. **1** a rounded lump. **2** a ball-shaped handle. **3** a round button on a machine. ■ **knobbly** adj.

knock v. **1** hit a surface noisily to attract attention. **2** collide with. **3** cause to move or fall by hitting. **4** make a hole etc. by hitting. **5** informal criticize. • n. **1** a short sound made by a blow. **2** a blow. **3** a setback. □ **knock-down** informal (of a price) very low. **knock-kneed** having legs that curve inwards at the knee. **knock off** informal **1** stop work. **2** produce work quickly. **knock-on effect** a secondary or indirect result of an action. **knockout 1** an act of knocking someone out. **2** a tournament in which the loser in each round is eliminated. **3** informal a very impressive person or thing. **knock out 1** make unconscious. **2** eliminate from a competition.

knocker n. a hinged object for knocking on a door.

knoll n. a small hill.

knot n. **1** a fastening made by tying a piece of string, rope, etc. **2** a tangled mass of strands. **3** a hard mass in wood at the point

where a branch joins the trunk. **4** a small group of people. **5** a unit of speed of ships, aircraft, or winds.
• *v.* (**knotting, knotted**) **1** fasten with a knot. **2** tangle.

knotty *adj.* (**knottier, knottiest**) **1** full of knots. **2** very complex.

know *v.* (**knowing, knew;** *past part.* **known**) **1** be aware of as a result of observing, asking, or being told. **2** be certain. **3** be familiar with. **4** have a good grasp of a language etc. **5** (**known as**) called or referred to as. □ **be in the know** *informal* have information known only to a few people. **know-how** practical knowledge or skill.

knowing *adj.* suggesting that you have secret knowledge.
■ **knowingly** *adv.*

knowledge *n.* **1** information or awareness gained through experience or education. **2** the total of what is known.

! Remember the d: knowledge.

knowledgeable (or **knowledgable**) *adj.* intelligent and well informed. ■ **knowledgeably** *adv.*

knuckle *n.* **1** a finger joint. **2** a joint of an animal's leg as meat. □ **knuckle down** apply yourself seriously to a task. **knuckle-duster** a metal device worn over the knuckles in fighting. **knuckle under** submit to authority.

koala *n.* a bear-like tree-dwelling Australian marsupial.

kohl *n.* a black powder used as eye make-up.

koi /koy/ *n.* (*pl.* **koi**) a large Japanese carp.

kookaburra *n.* a large, noisy, Australasian kingfisher.

kopek (or **kopeck**) *n.* a unit of money of Russia and some other countries.

Koran *n.* the sacred book of Islam.

kosher /koh-sher/ *adj.* **1** (of food) prepared according to Jewish law. **2** *informal* genuine and legitimate.

kowtow *v.* be excessively meek and obedient.

kph *abbrev.* kilometres per hour.

kraal *n. S. Afr.* **1** a traditional African village. **2** an enclosure for sheep and cattle.

krill *pl. n.* small shrimp-like crustaceans that are eaten by whales etc.

krona *n.* **1** (*pl.* **kronor**) the basic unit of money of Sweden. **2** (*pl.* **kronur**) the basic unit of money of Iceland.

krone *n.* (*pl.* **kroner**) the basic unit of money of Denmark and Norway.

krypton *n.* an inert gaseous chemical element.

kudos *n.* praise and honour.

kumquat *n.* a small orange-like fruit.

kung fu *n.* a Chinese martial art.

Kurd *n.* a member of a people of SW Asia. ■ **Kurdish** *adj.*

kV *abbrev.* kilovolts.

kW *abbrev.* kilowatts.

k

L

L (or **l**) *n.* the Roman numeral for 50. • *abbrev.* **1** learner driver. **2** (**l**) litres.

lab *n. informal* a laboratory.

label *n.* **1** a small piece of paper etc. attached to an object and giving information about it. **2** the name or trademark of a fashion company. **3** a classifying name. • *v.* (**labelling, labelled**; US **labeling, labeled**) **1** attach a label to. **2** put in a category.

labia *pl. n.* the inner and outer folds of the vulva. ■ **labial** *adj.*

laboratory *n.* (*pl.* **laboratories**) a room or building equipped for scientific work.

laborious *adj.* requiring or showing much effort. ■ **laboriously** *adv.*

labour (US **labor**) *n.* **1** work. **2** workers as a group. **3** (**Labour** or **the Labour Party**) a left-wing political party. **4** the process of childbirth. • *v.* **1** do hard physical work. **2** move or do with difficulty. **3** (**labour under**) have a mistaken belief. ⬚ **labour the point** explain at excessive length.

labourer (US **laborer**) *n.* an unskilled manual worker.

Labrador *n.* a large breed of dog.

laburnum *n.* a tree with hanging clusters of yellow flowers.

labyrinth *n.* a complicated network of passages. ■ **labyrinthine** *adj.*

lace *n.* **1** a fine open fabric made by looping thread in patterns. **2** a cord used to fasten a shoe or gar-

ment. • *v.* **1** fasten with a lace or laces. **2** entwine. **3** add alcohol to a drink or dish.

lacerate *v.* tear the flesh or skin. ■ **laceration** *n.*

lachrymose /lak-ri-mohss/ *adj.* tearful.

lack *n.* the state of being without or not having enough of something. • *v.* be without or without enough of.

lackadaisical *adj.* unenthusiastic or careless.

lackey *n.* (*pl.* **lackeys**) **1** a servant. **2** a servile person.

lacklustre (US **lackluster**) *adj.* **1** lacking energy or inspiration. **2** (of the hair or eyes) dull.

laconic *adj.* using few words. ■ **laconically** *adv.*

lacquer *n.* **1** a hard glossy varnish. **2** a substance sprayed on hair to keep it in place. • *v.* coat with lacquer.

lacrosse *n.* a team game in which a ball is thrown, carried, and caught using a stick with a net at one end.

lactate *v.* (of a female mammal) produce milk. ■ **lactation** *n.*

lactic acid *n.* an acid present in sour milk and produced in the muscles during exercise.

lactose *n.* a sugar present in milk.

lacuna /luh-kyoo-nuh/ *n.* (*pl.* **lacunae** or **lacunas**) a gap or missing part.

lacy *adj.* (**lacier, laciest**) of or like lace.

lad n. informal a boy or young man.

ladder n. **1** a set of bars or steps between two uprights, used for climbing up. **2** a series of stages by which progress can be made. **3** a strip of unravelled fabric in tights or stockings. • v. make a ladder in tights or stockings.

laden adj. heavily loaded.

ladle n. a long-handled spoon with a cup-shaped bowl. • v. serve with a ladle.

lady n. (pl. **ladies**) **1** a woman. **2** a woman of good social position. **3** (**Lady**) a title used by peeresses and the wives and widows of knights. **4** a well-mannered woman. □ **lady-in-waiting** a woman who accompanies and looks after a queen or princess. **ladylike** well-mannered. **Your/ Her Ladyship** a respectful way of referring to or addressing a Lady.

ladybird n. a small flying beetle, usu. red with black spots.

lag v. (**lagging**, **lagged**) **1** fall behind. **2** cover a water tank etc. with insulating material. • n. (or **time lag**) a period between two events.

lager n. a light fizzy beer.

laggard n. a person who lags behind others.

lagging n. insulating material for a water tank etc.

lagoon n. an area of salt water separated from the sea by a sandbank or reef.

laid past & past part. of **LAY**[1]. □ **laid-back** informal relaxed and easy-going.

lain past part. of **LIE**[1].

lair n. a wild animal's resting place.

laird n. (in Scotland) an owner of a large estate.

laissez-faire /less-ay-**fair**/ n. a policy of not interfering in the course of things.

laity n. people who do not belong to the clergy.

lake n. a large area of water surrounded by land.

lama n. a Tibetan or Mongolian Buddhist monk.

lamb n. **1** a young sheep. **2** an innocent or gentle person. • v. give birth to a lamb.

lambaste (or **lambast**) v. criticize harshly.

lambent adj. softly glowing or flickering.

lame adj. **1** walking with difficulty because of an injured leg or foot. **2** unconvincing and feeble. • v. make lame. □ **lame duck** an unsuccessful person or thing. ■ **lamely** adv. **lameness** n.

lamé /**lah**-may/ n. fabric with interwoven gold or silver threads.

lament n. **1** an emotional expression of grief. **2** a song or poem expressing grief. • v. feel or express grief or regret for. ■ **lamentation** n.

lamentable adj. very bad or regrettable. ■ **lamentably** adv.

laminate v. **1** cover with a protective layer. **2** make by sticking layers together. • n. laminated material.

lamp n. a device for giving light.

lampoon v. publicly mock or ridicule. • n. a mocking attack.

lamprey n. (pl. **lampreys**) an eel-like fish with a sucking mouth.

lance n. a weapon with a long shaft and pointed steel head. • v. prick or cut open a boil etc. □ **lance corporal** an army rank below corporal.

lancet n. a pointed two-edged knife used in surgery.

land n. 1 the part of the earth's surface not covered by water. 2 an area of ground. 3 ground or soil used for farming. 4 a country or state. •v. 1 put or go ashore. 2 come or bring down to the ground. 3 *informal* succeed in obtaining or achieving. 4 *informal* put or end up in a difficult situation. 5 *informal* inflict a blow. □ **landfall** arrival on land after a sea journey. **landfill** 1 the disposal of waste by burying it. 2 buried waste. **landlocked** surrounded by land. **landlubber** *informal* a person unfamiliar with the sea or sailing. **landmark** 1 an object or feature easily seen from a distance. 2 an event marking an important stage. **landmine** an explosive mine laid on or just under the surface of the ground. **landslide** 1 (or **landslip**) a fall of earth or rock from a mountain or cliff. 2 an overwhelming majority of votes. ■ **landward** adv. & adj. **landwards** adv.

landed adj. owning much land.

landing n. 1 a level area at the top of a staircase. 2 a place where people and goods can be landed from a boat. □ **landing stage** a platform for coming ashore from a boat.

landlord (or **landlady**) n. 1 a person who rents out property or land. 2 a person who runs a pub.

landscape n. 1 all the visible features of an area of land. 2 a picture of a country area. •v. improve the appearance of a piece of land.

lane n. 1 a narrow road. 2 a division of a road for a single line of traffic. 3 a strip of track or water for each of the competitors in a race. 4 a route followed by ships or aircraft.

language n. 1 human communication through the structured use of words. 2 a particular system or style of this. 3 a system of symbols and rules for writing computer programs.

languid adj. relaxed or lacking energy. ■ **languidly** adv.

languish v. 1 become weak or feeble. 2 be forced to remain in an unpleasant situation.

languor n. tiredness or lack of energy. ■ **languorous** adj.

lank adj. (of hair) long, limp, and straight.

lanky adj. tall, thin, and awkward.

lanolin n. a fatty substance from sheep's wool, used in cream.

lantern n. a lamp enclosed in a metal frame with transparent panels.

lanthanum n. a metallic element.

lanyard n. 1 a rope used on a ship for securing sails etc. 2 a cord for hanging a whistle etc. round the neck or shoulder.

lap n. 1 the flat area between the waist and knees of a seated person. 2 one circuit of a racetrack. 3 a part of a journey. •v. (**lapping**, **lapped**) 1 take up liquid with the tongue. 2 (**lap up**) accept with obvious pleasure. 3 (of water) move against something with a gentle sound. 4 overtake a competitor in a race to become one lap ahead. □ **lapdog** a small pampered pet dog. **laptop** a portable computer.

laparoscopy n. a surgical operation in which a fibre-optic instrument is inserted through the abdomen to view the internal organs.

lapel n. a flap folded back on each side of a coat etc. below the collar.

lapidary adj. of the cutting or polishing of stones and gems.

lapis lazuli n. a blue semi-precious stone.

Lapp n. a member of a people of the extreme north of Scandinavia.

! The people themselves prefer to be called **Sami**.

lapse n. **1** a brief failure of concentration, memory, etc. **2** a decline in standards. **3** an interval of time. •v. **1** (of a right or agreement) become invalid because not used or renewed. **2** cease to follow the rules of a religion. **3** pass gradually into a different state.

lapwing n. a dark green and white bird with a crest on the head.

larceny n. esp. US theft of personal property.

larch n. a deciduous coniferous tree.

lard n. fat from a pig, used in cooking. •v. **1** insert strips of bacon in meat before cooking. **2** add technical or obscure expressions to talk or writing.

larder n. a room or large cupboard for storing food.

large adj. of great size or extent. □ **at large 1** escaped or not yet captured. **2** as a whole. ■ **largely** adv.

largesse (or **largess**) /lar-**zhess**/ n. **1** generosity. **2** money or gifts given generously.

lariat n. a lasso.

lark n. **1** a brown bird that sings in flight. **2** something done for fun or as a joke. •v. behave playfully.

larva n. (pl. **larvae**) a form taken by certain insects before meta-morphosing into an adult. ■ **larval** adj.

laryngitis n. inflammation of the larynx.

larynx n. (pl. **larynges**) the part of the throat containing the vocal cords.

lasagne /luh-**zan**-yuh/ n. a dish of strips of pasta layered with meat and a cheese sauce.

lascivious /luh-**siv**-i-uhss/ adj. feeling or showing open or offensive sexual desire. ■ **lasciviousness** n.

laser n. a device producing an intense narrow beam of light.

lash v. **1** beat with a whip or stick. **2** beat against. **3** (**lash out**) attack verbally or physically. **4** (of an animal) move its tail quickly to and fro. **5** fasten securely with a rope. •n. **1** an eyelash. **2** a blow with a whip or stick. **3** the flexible part of a whip.

lashings pl. n. informal a large amount.

lass (or **lassie**) n. Sc. & N. Engl. a girl or young woman.

lassitude n. weariness or lack of energy.

lasso /luh-**soo**/ n. (pl. **lassos**) a rope with a noose for catching cattle. •v. (**lassoing**, **lassoed**) catch with a lasso.

last adj. **1** coming after all others in time or order. **2** most recent. **3** lowest in importance. **4** only remaining. •v. **1** continue or be enough for a specified time. **2** remain operating or usable. •adv. on the last occasion before the present. •n. **1** the last person or thing. **2** the only remaining part. **3** a foot-shaped block used in making or repairing a shoe. □ **at last** eventually. **last post** a military bugle call sounded at sunset and at military funerals. **the last straw** the final thing making a situation unbearable. **last word 1** a final statement. **2** the ultimate or most modern example. ∎ **lastly** adv.

latch n. **1** a bar with a catch and lever for fastening a door or gate. **2** a door lock which can only be opened from the outside with a key. •v. **1** fasten with a latch. **2** (**latch on to**) become very interested in.

late adj. **1** arriving or happening after the proper or usual time. **2** far on in the day or night or a period. **3** (**the late**) (of a person) dead. **4** (**latest**) most recent. •adv. **1** after the proper or usual time. **2** far on in the day or night or a period. **3** (**later**) in the near future. □ **of late** recently. ∎ **lateness** n.

lately adv. recently.

latent adj. existing but not yet developed, apparent, or active. ∎ **latency** n.

lateral adj. of, at, to, or from the side or sides. ∎ **laterally** adv.

latex n. **1** a milky fluid in some plants, esp. the rubber tree. **2** a similar synthetic product used to make coatings etc.

lath n. a thin, flat strip of wood.

lathe n. a machine for shaping pieces of wood or metal by turning them against a cutting tool.

lather n. **1** froth from soap and water. **2** heavy frothy sweat on a horse's coat. •v. form or cover with a lather.

Latin n. the language of the ancient Romans. •adj. of Latin. □ **Latin America** the parts of the American continent where Spanish or Portuguese is spoken.

latitude n. **1** the distance of a place north or south of the equator. **2** freedom of action or thought.

latrine n. a communal toilet in a camp or barracks.

latte /lat-tay/ n. a drink of frothy hot milk with an added shot of espresso coffee.

latter adj. **1** nearer to the end than to the beginning. **2** recent. **3** (**the latter**) the second-mentioned of two people or things. □ **latter-day** modern or contemporary. ∎ **latterly** adv.

lattice n. a structure of strips crossing each other.

laud /lawd/ v. praise highly.

laudable adj. deserving praise.

laudanum n. a solution of opium formerly used as a sedative.

laudatory adj. expressing praise.

laugh v. **1** make sounds that express amusement. **2** (**laugh at**) make fun of. •n. **1** an act of laughing. **2** (**a laugh**) informal a cause of laughter. □ **laughing stock** a person ridiculed by everyone.

laughable adj. ridiculous.

laughter n. the act or sound of laughing.

launch v. **1** move a boat into the water. **2** send a rocket etc. into the air. **3** start an enterprise or introduce a new product. •n. **1** an act of launching. **2** a large motorboat.

launder v. **1** wash and iron clothes etc. **2** informal pass illegally obtained money through a bank or business to conceal its origin.

launderette n. a place with coin-operated washing machines and dryers for public use.

laundry n. (pl. **laundries**) **1** clothes etc. for washing. **2** a place where clothes are laundered.

laurel n. 1 an evergreen shrub. 2 (**laurels**) honour or praise.

lava n. flowing or hardened molten rock from a volcano.

lavatory n. (pl. **lavatories**) a toilet.

lavender n. 1 a shrub with scented purple flowers. 2 a light purple colour.

lavish adj. 1 very rich, elaborate, or luxurious. 2 generous. •v. give in large quantities. ■ **lavishly** adv.

law n. 1 a rule or system of rules established by authority. 2 a statement that a particular phenomenon always occurs if certain conditions are present. □ **law court** a place where legal cases or trials are heard. **lawsuit** a claim brought to a law court to be decided.

lawful adj. allowed by or obeying the law or rules. ■ **lawfully** adv.

lawless adj. not obeying the law. ■ **lawlessness** n.

lawn n. 1 an area of mown grass in a garden or park. 2 a fine linen or cotton fabric. □ **lawnmower** a machine for cutting grass.

lawrencium n. a radioactive metallic element.

lawyer n. a person who practises law.

lax adj. not strict, severe, or careful. ■ **laxity** n.

laxative n. a medicine causing the bowels to empty.

lay[1] v. (**laying, laid**) 1 put down carefully. 2 put down in position for use. 3 assign or place. 4 (of a female bird etc.) produce an egg. •adj. 1 not belonging to the clergy. 2 non-professional or non-specialist: layman. □ **layabout** an idle person. **lay-by** a roadside area where vehicles may stop. **lay off**

1 dismiss a worker because of a shortage of work. 2 informal stop doing something. **lay on** provide. **layout** the way in which something is laid out. **lay out** arrange according to a plan. **lay up** put out of action through illness or injury.

❗ Don't confuse **lay**, 'put something down' and **lie**, 'recline on a flat surface'. The past tense and past participle of **lay** is **laid** (they laid the carpet); the past tense of **lie** is **lay** (he lay on the floor) and the past participle is **lain** (she had lain awake for hours).

lay[2] past of **LIE**[1].

layer n. 1 a sheet or thickness of material covering a surface. 2 a person or thing that lays something. •v. arrange or cut in a layer or layers.

layette n. a set of clothing etc. for a newborn child.

laze v. spend time idly.

lazy adj. (**lazier, laziest**) 1 unwilling to work or use energy. 2 showing a lack of effort or care. ■ **lazily** adv. **laziness** n.

lb abbrev. pounds (in weight).

lbw abbrev. Cricket leg before wicket.

lea n. literary an area of grassy land.

leach v. (of chemicals or minerals) be removed from soil by water passing through it.

lead[1] v. (**leading, led**) 1 cause to go with you. 2 be a route or means of access. 3 (**lead to**) result in. 4 influence. 5 be in charge of. 6 be ahead of or superior to a competitor. 7 have a particular way of life. 8 (**lead up to**) come before or result in. 9 (**lead on**) deceive into believing. •n. 1 an example for others to follow. 2 a position of advantage. **3** the chief part in a play or film. **4** a clue. **5** a strap or cord for leading a dog. **6** a wire conveying electric current. □ **leading question** a question worded to prompt the answer wanted.

lead² n. **1** a heavy grey metallic element. **2** the part of a pencil that makes a mark. ■ **leaded** adj.

leaden adj. **1** heavy or slow. **2** dull grey.

leader n. **1** a person or thing that leads. **2** a newspaper article giving the editor's opinion. ■ **leadership** n.

leaf n. (pl. **leaves**) **1** a flat green part growing from the stem of a plant. **2** a single sheet of paper. **3** very thin gold or silver foil. **4** a hinged or detachable part of a table. •v. (**leaf through**) turn over pages, reading them casually. ■ **leafy** adj.

leaflet n. **1** a printed sheet of paper giving information. **2** a small leaf. •v. (**leafleted, leafleting**) distribute leaflets to.

league n. **1** a group of people or countries united for a purpose. **2** a group of sports clubs which play each other over a period for a championship. **3** a class of quality. □ **in league** (of people) making secret plans.

leak v. **1** accidentally allow contents to pass through a gap. **2** (of liquid, gas, etc.) pass accidentally through a gap. **3** deliberately reveal secret information. •n. **1** a gap through which contents leak. **2** an instance of leaking. ■ **leakage** n. **leaky** adj.

lean v. (**leaning, leaned** or **leant**) **1** be in or put into a sloping position. **2** (**lean against/on**) rest

against. **3** (**lean on**) rely on for support. •adj. **1** (of a person) thin. **2** (of meat) with little fat. **3** (of a period) unproductive. □ **lean-to** a small building sharing a wall with a larger one.

leaning n. a tendency or preference.

leap v. (**leaping, leaped** or **leapt**) **1** jump high, suddenly, or a long way. **2** (**leap at**) accept eagerly. •n. an act of leaping. □ **leap year** a year with 366 days, occurring once every four years.

leapfrog n. a game in which players vault over others who are bending down. •v. (**leapfrogging, leapfrogged**) **1** perform such a vault. **2** overtake others to reach a leading position.

learn v. (**learning, learned** or **learnt**) **1** gain knowledge of or skill in. **2** become aware of. **3** memorize. ■ **learner** n.

learned adj. having gained much knowledge by study.

learning n. knowledge gained through study.

lease n. a contract by which one party lets land, property, etc. to another for a specified time. •v. let or rent on lease. □ **leasehold** the holding of property by a lease.

leash n. a dog's lead.

least adj. & pron. smallest in amount, extent, or significance. •adv. to the smallest extent or degree. □ **at least 1** not less than. **2** if nothing else. **3** anyway.

leather n. a material made from the skin of an animal by tanning or a similar process.

leathery adj. tough and hard in texture.

leave v. (**leaving, left**) **1** go away from. **2** stop living at or working for. **3** go away without taking. **4** (**be left**) remain to be used or dealt with. **5** allow to do without interfering. **6** deposit something to be collected or dealt with. **7** give in a will. • n. **1** time when you are permitted to be absent from work or duty. **2** permission. □ **leave out** fail to include.

leaven /lev-uhn/ n. a substance added to dough to make it ferment and rise. • v. **1** (**leavened**) fermented by adding leaven. **2** make less serious or dull.

leaves pl. of **LEAF**.

lecher n. a lecherous man. ■ **lechery** n.

lecherous adj. showing sexual desire in an offensive way.

lectern n. a stand with a sloping top from which a speaker can read while standing.

lecture n. **1** an educational talk. **2** a lengthy reprimand. • v. **1** give a lecture or lectures. **2** reprimand. ■ **lecturer** n.

led past & past part. of **LEAD**[1].

ledge n. a narrow horizontal projection or shelf.

ledger n. a book of financial accounts.

lee n. the side of something providing shelter from wind or weather. □ **leeway** the available amount of freedom to move or act. ■ **leeward** adj. & adv.

leech n. a small bloodsucking worm.

leek n. a long vegetable related to the onion.

leer v. look in a lustful or unpleasant way. • n. a lustful or unpleasant look.

lees pl. n. sediment in wine.

left[1] adj. & adv. of, on, or towards the side which is to the west when

facing north. • n. **1** (**the left**) the left-hand side or direction. **2** (**the Left**) a left-wing group or party. □ **left-handed** using or done with the left hand. **left-wing** radical, reforming, or socialist.

left[2] past & past part. of **LEAVE**. □ **leftovers** food remaining after the rest has been used.

leg n. **1** each of the limbs on which a person or animal moves and stands. **2** a part that supports a chair, table, etc. **3** a section of a journey, race, etc. □ **leg it** informal run away.

legacy n. (pl. **legacies**) **1** money etc. left to someone in a will. **2** something handed down by a predecessor.

legal adj. of or permitted by law. □ **legal aid** payment from public funds towards the cost of legal action. **legal tender** accepted methods of payment such as coins or banknotes. ■ **legality** n. **legalize** (or **-ise**) v. **legally** adv.

legate n. a representative of the Pope.

legation n. **1** a diplomatic minister and staff. **2** the official residence of a diplomat.

legato adv. & adj. Music in a smooth, flowing way.

legend n. **1** a traditional story from the past which may or may not be true. **2** a very famous person. **3** a caption or explanatory key.

legendary adj. **1** described in legends. **2** famous.

legerdemain /lej-er-di-**mayn**/ n. **1** skilful use of the hands when doing conjuring tricks. **2** trickery.

leggings pl. n. tight-fitting stretchy trousers.

legible adj. clear enough to read. ■ **legibility** n. **legibly** adv.

legion n. **1** a division of the ancient Roman army. **2** a great number. •adj. great in number.

legionnaire n. a member of the Foreign Legion, or of an association of former members of the armed forces. □ **legionnaires' disease** a form of pneumonia.

legislate v. make laws. ■ **legislative** adj. **legislator** n.

legislation n. laws as a whole.

legislature n. the law-making body of a state.

legitimate adj. **1** allowed by the law or rules. **2** justifiable. **3** (of a child) born of parents married to each other. ■ **legitimacy** n. **legitimately** adv. **legitimize** (or **-ise**) v.

legume n. a plant bearing seeds in pods. ■ **leguminous** adj.

leisure n. time free for relaxation or enjoyment. □ **at leisure 1** not busy; free. **2** in an unhurried way. ■ **leisured** adj. **leisurely** adj. & adv.

leitmotif (or **leitmotiv**) /lyt-moh-teef/ n. a frequently repeated theme in a musical or literary composition.

lemming n. a small Arctic rodent, noted for its periodic mass migrations.

lemon n. **1** a pale yellow citrus fruit with acidic juice. **2** a pale yellow colour.

lemonade n. a lemon-flavoured drink.

lemur n. a primate with a pointed snout, found in Madagascar.

lend v. (lending, lent) **1** allow someone to use something providing that they will return it. **2** give someone money under an

agreement to pay it back later. **3** add a quality to. **4** (lend itself to) be suitable for. ■ **lender** n.

length n. **1** measurement or extent from end to end. **2** the amount of time occupied by something. **3** the quality of being long. **4** a stretch or piece. **5** a degree of effort: go to great lengths. □ **lengthways** (or **lengthwise**) in a direction parallel with a thing's length. **lengthen** v.

lengthy adj. (lengthier, lengthiest) very long. ■ **lengthily** adv.

lenient adj. not strict; merciful. ■ **leniency** n. **leniently** adv.

lens n. **1** a piece of transparent curved material that concentrates or disperses light rays, used in cameras, glasses, etc. **2** the transparent part of the eye that focuses light on to the retina.

Lent n. (in the Christian Church) the period immediately before Easter.

lent past & past part. of LEND.

lentil n. a pulse (edible seed).

leonine adj. of or like a lion.

leopard n. a large spotted cat, found in Africa and Asia.

leotard n. a stretchy garment worn by dancers, gymnasts, etc.

leper n. **1** a person with leprosy. **2** a person shunned by others.

leprechaun n. (in Irish folklore) a mischievous elf.

leprosy n. a contagious disease which affects the skin and can cause deformities. ■ **leprous** adj.

lesbian n. a homosexual woman. •adj. of lesbians. ■ **lesbianism** n.

lesion n. a damaged area of the skin or a body part.

less adj. & pron. **1** a smaller amount of. **2** fewer in number. •adv. to a smaller extent. • prep. minus. ■ lessen v.

! For the difference between less and fewer, see FEW.

lessee n. a person who holds the lease of a property.

lesser adj. not so great or important as the other or the rest.

lesson n. 1 a period of learning or teaching. 2 a thing learned. 3 a thing acting as a warning or encouragement. 4 a passage from the Bible read aloud.

lessor n. a person who leases a property to another.

lest conj. to avoid the risk of.

let v. (letting, let) 1 allow. 2 used to express an intention, suggestion, or order: let's try. 3 allow someone to use a room or property in return for payment. • n. 1 a period during which a room or property is rented. 2 (in tennis etc.) a situation in which a point is not counted and is played for again. □ let alone not to mention. let down fail to support or help. let go allow to go free. let off 1 cause a gun, firework, etc. to fire or explode. 2 choose not to punish. 3 excuse. let up informal become less intense.

lethal adj. able to cause death.

lethargy n. lack of energy and enthusiasm. ■ lethargic adj. lethargically adv.

letter n. 1 a symbol representing a speech sound. 2 a written communication sent by post or messenger. 3 (letters) literature. • v. write letters on. □ letter box a slot in a door through which post is delivered. letterhead a printed heading on stationery. the letter

of the law the precise terms of a law.

lettuce n. a vegetable eaten in salads.

leucocyte /loo-koh-syt/ n. a white blood cell.

leukaemia /loo-kee-mi-uh/ (US leukemia) n. a disease in which too many white blood cells are produced.

levee /lev-i/ n. an embankment built against flooding.

level n. 1 a position on a scale of amount, quality, etc. 2 a horizontal line or surface. 3 a height from the ground or another base. 4 an instrument to test a horizontal line. • adj. 1 having a flat, horizontal surface. 2 having the same relative height or position as another. • v. (levelling, levelled; US leveling, leveled) 1 make or become level. 2 aim a gun, criticism, etc. □ level crossing a place where a railway and road cross at the same level. level-headed sensible. on the level honest. ■ leveller n. levelly adv.

lever n. 1 a bar on a pivot, used to move a load with one end when pressure is applied to the other. 2 a handle for operating a mechanism. • v. lift or move with a lever.

leverage n. 1 the exertion of force with a lever. 2 the power to influence.

leveret n. a young hare.

leviathan /li-vy-uh-thuhn/ n. a very large or powerful thing.

levitate v. rise and hover in the air. ■ levitation n.

levity n. humorous treatment of a serious matter.

levy v. (levying, levied) impose a tax or fine. • n. (pl. levies) a sum of money paid as a tax.

lewd adj. crude and offensive in a sexual way.

lexical adj. of words.

lexicography n. the writing of dictionaries. ■ **lexicographer** n.

lexicon n. **1** a vocabulary. **2** a dictionary.

liability n. (pl. **liabilities**) **1** the state of being liable. **2** a debt. **3** a cause of difficulty.

liable adj. **1** responsible by law. **2** (**liable to**) subject by law to. **3** (**liable to do**) likely to do.

liaise v. **1** cooperate on a matter. **2** act as a link.

liaison n. **1** communication and cooperation. **2** a sexual relationship.

> ! Remember the second i: liaison.

liana n. a tropical climbing plant.

liar n. a person who tells lies.

libation n. a drink poured as an offering to a god.

libel n. the crime of publishing a false statement that harms a person's reputation. •v. (**libelling**, **libelled**; US **libeling**, **libeled**) publish something false about. ■ **libellous** adj.

liberal adj. **1** willing to accept behaviour or opinions different from your own. **2** (in politics) supporting individual liberty and moderate reform. **3** (**Liberal**) of the Liberal or Liberal Democrat Party. **4** generous. •n. a person with liberal views. ■ **liberally** adv.

liberalize (or **-ise**) v. make less strict. ■ **liberalization** n.

liberate v. **1** set free. **2** (**liberated**) free from social conventions. ■ **liberation** n. **liberator** n.

libertarian n. a person believing in very limited state intervention in people's lives. ■ **libertarianism** n.

libertine n. a man who leads an immoral life.

liberty n. (pl. **liberties**) **1** freedom. **2** a right or privilege. □ **take liberties with** treat with undue familiarity or familiarity.

libidinous adj. having a strong sex drive.

libido n. (pl. **libidos**) sexual desire.

librarian n. a person who works in a library.

library n. (pl. **libraries**) **1** a building or room containing a collection of books etc. for consulting or borrowing. **2** a private collection of books.

libretto n. (pl. **libretti** or **librettos**) the words of an opera.

lice pl. of LOUSE.

licence (US **license**) n. **1** an official permit to own, use, or do something. **2** freedom to do what you want.

> ! licence is the spelling for the noun, license for the verb; in US English the -se spelling is used for both.

license v. grant a licence to or for.

licensee n. the holder of a licence.

licentiate /ly-sen-shi-uht/ n. the holder of a certificate permitting them to practise a particular profession.

licentious adj. sexually immoral.

lichen /ly-kuhn/ n. a plant resembling moss which grows on rocks, walls, and trees.

lick v. **1** pass the tongue over. **2** move lightly and quickly. •n. **1** an act of licking. **2** informal a quick application of something.

licorice US = LIQUORICE.

lid n. **1** a removable or hinged cover for a container. **2** an eyelid.

lie [1] v. (**lying**, **lay**; past part. **lain**) **1** be in a horizontal position on a supporting surface. **2** be in a particular state. **3** be found or situated. □ **lie-in** a prolonged stay in bed in the morning. **lie low** avoid attention. **the lie of the land** the features of an area.

! Don't confuse **lay** and **lie**: see **LAY** [1].

lie [2] n. a deliberately false statement. • v. (**lying**, **lied**) tell a lie or lies.

liege /leej/ n. hist. **1** a feudal lord. **2** a person who served a feudal lord.

lieu /loo/ n. (**in lieu**) instead.

lieutenant /lef-ten-uhnt/ n. **1** a deputy or substitute acting for a superior. **2** a rank of officer in the army and navy.

life n. (pl. **lives**) **1** the condition of being able to function and grow. **2** the existence of an individual. **3** a particular type or aspect of existence. **4** living things and their activity. **5** vitality or energy. □ **lifebelt** a ring of buoyant material to keep a person afloat. **lifeboat 1** a boat for rescuing people at sea. **2** a small boat on a ship for emergency use. **life cycle** the series of changes in the life of an organism. **lifeguard** a person employed to rescue swimmers in difficulty. **life jacket** an inflatable jacket for keeping a person afloat. **lifelike** exactly like a real person or thing. **lifeless 1** dead or apparently dead. **2** without living things. **3** lacking energy. **lifeline 1** a thing on which someone depends. **2** a rope thrown to rescue someone in difficulty in water. **lifelong** lasting

throughout a person's life. **lifestyle** the way in which a person lives. **life-support** (of medical equipment) keeping the body functioning after serious illness or injury. **lifetime** the length of time that a person lives or a thing lasts.

lift v. **1** raise or be raised. **2** pick up and move to a different position. **3** formally end a restriction. • n. **1** a device for moving people or things between levels of a building. **2** an act of lifting. **3** a free ride in another person's vehicle. **4** a feeling of increased cheerfulness. □ **lift-off** the vertical take-off of a spacecraft or rocket.

ligament n. a band of tissue connecting bones or cartilages.

ligature n. a cord for tying up a bleeding artery.

light n. **1** the natural form of energy that makes things visible. **2** a lamp or other device that gives light. **3** a match or cigarette lighter. **4** understanding or enlightenment. • v. (**lighting**, **lit**; past part. **lit** or **lighted**) **1** provide with light. **2** cause to start burning. **3** (**light up**) become lively or happy. **4** (**light on**) discover by chance. • adj. **1** having a lot of light. **2** (of a colour) pale. **3** of little weight. **4** not heavily built. **5** relatively low in density or amount. **6** not serious or profound. □ **bring** (or **come**) **to light** make (or become) widely known. **in the light of** taking something into consideration. **light-fingered** informal prone to steal. **light-headed** dizzy and slightly faint. **light-hearted** amusing and entertaining. **lighthouse** a tower with a powerful light to guide ships at sea. **light industry** industry producing small articles.

lightweight 1 a weight in boxing between featherweight and welterweight. **2** *informal* an unimportant or weak person. **light year** the distance light travels in one year, nearly 6 million million miles. **make light of** treat as unimportant. ∎ **lighten** *v.* **lightly** *adv.* **lightness** *n.*

lighter *n.* **1** a device for lighting cigarettes. **2** a barge used to transfer goods to and from ships in harbour.

lighting *n.* **1** equipment for producing light. **2** the effect of lights.

lightning *n.* the discharge of electricity between a cloud and the ground or within a cloud, accompanied by a bright flash. ∙*adj.* very quick.

> **!** The spelling is **lightning**, not -*tening*.

lights *pl. n.* the lungs of certain animals used as food.

lignite *n.* soft brown coal.

like *prep.* **1** similar to. **2** in a way similar or appropriate to. **3** such as. ∙*v.* **1** find pleasant or satisfactory. **2** wish for. ∙*conj. informal* **1** in the same way that. **2** as if. ∙*n.* **1** (**the like**) things of the same kind. **2** (**likes**) things that you like. ∙*adj.* similar.

likeable (or **likable**) *adj.* pleasant.

likelihood *n.* probability.

likely *adj.* (**likelier**, **likeliest**) **1** probable. **2** promising. ∙*adv.* probably.

liken *v.* (**liken to**) point out the resemblance to.

likeness *n.* **1** resemblance. **2** a portrait or representation.

likewise *adv.* **1** also. **2** similarly.

liking *n.* **1** a fondness. **2** (**your liking**) your taste.

lilac *n.* **1** a shrub with scented purple or white blossom. **2** a pale purple colour.

lilt *n.* **1** a rise and fall of the voice when speaking. **2** a gentle rhythm in a tune. ∎ **lilting** *adj.*

lily *n.* (*pl.* **lilies**) a tall plant with large flowers.

limb *n.* **1** an arm, leg, or wing. **2** a large branch of a tree.

limber *v.* (**limber up**) warm up before exercise. ∙*adj.* supple.

limbo *n.* **1** an uncertain period of waiting. **2** (*pl.* **limbos**) a West Indian dance in which the dancer bends back to pass under a bar.

lime *n.* **1** a white alkaline substance used as a building material or fertilizer. **2** a round green citrus fruit. **3** a bright green colour. **4** a tree with heart-shaped leaves. □ **limelight** the focus of public attention. **limestone** a rock composed mainly of calcium carbonate.

limerick *n.* a humorous five-line poem.

limit *n.* **1** a point beyond which something does not or may not pass. **2** a restriction on size or amount. ∙*v.* put a limit on. □ **limited company** a company whose owners have a limited responsibility for its debts. **off limits** out of bounds. ∎ **limitless** *adj.*

limitation *n.* **1** a restriction. **2** a fault.

limousine *n.* a large, luxurious car.

limp *v.* walk with difficulty because of an injured leg or foot. ∙*n.* a limping walk. ∙*adj.* not stiff or firm. ∎ **limply** *adv.*

limpet *n.* a shellfish that clings tightly to rocks.

limpid *adj.* (of a liquid or the eyes) clear.

linchpin n. **1** a very important person or thing. **2** a pin through the end of an axle keeping a wheel in position.

linctus n. thick liquid cough medicine.

line n. **1** a long, narrow mark. **2** a row or series. **3** a course or channel. **4** a length of cord, wire, etc. **5** a phone connection. **6** a railway track or route. **7** a wrinkle. **8** a series of military defences. **9** an area of activity. **10** (**lines**) the words of an actor's part. •v. **1** be positioned along. **2** (**line up**) arrange in a row. **3** (**lined**) marked with lines. **4** cover the inner surface of. □ **line dancing** country and western dancing in which a line of dancers follow set steps.

linesman (in sport) an official who assists the referee or umpire. **line-up** a group assembled for a purpose.

lineage /lin-i-ij/ n. ancestry.

lineal adj. in a line of descent.

linear adj. **1** arranged in or extending along a straight line. **2** consisting of lines. **3** progressing in stages.

linen n. **1** cloth woven from flax. **2** sheets, pillowcases, etc.

liner n. **1** a large passenger ship. **2** a lining.

ling n. **1** an edible sea fish. **2** heather.

linger v. **1** be slow or reluctant to leave. **2** (**linger over**) spend a long time over.

lingerie /lan-zhuh-ri/ n. women's underwear.

lingo n. (pl. **lingos**) informal a language.

lingua franca n. (pl. **lingua francas**) a common language used among speakers whose native languages are different.

linguist n. **1** a person skilled in foreign languages. **2** a person who studies linguistics.

linguistic adj. of language. •n. (**linguistics**) the study of language. ■ **linguistically** adv.

liniment n. an ointment to relieve pain or bruising.

lining n. a layer of material covering the inside of something.

link n. **1** a connection. **2** a means of communication. **3** a loop in a chain. •v. connect or join. ■ **linkage** n.

linnet n. a type of finch.

lino n. informal linoleum.

linoleum n. a smooth covering for floors.

linseed n. the seeds of the flax plant, used to make oil.

lint n. **1** fluff from cloth or yarn. **2** a fabric for dressing wounds.

lintel n. a horizontal support across the top of a door or window.

lion n. a large cat of Africa and NW India.

lionize (or **-ise**) v. treat as a celebrity.

lip n. **1** either of the two fleshy parts forming the edges of the mouth opening. **2** the edge of a container or opening. **3** informal cheeky talk. □ **lip-read** understand speech from watching a speaker's lips. **lipstick** a cosmetic for colouring the lips.

liposuction n. cosmetic surgery in which fat is removed from under the skin by suction.

liquefy v. (**liquefying, liquefied**) make or become liquid. ■ **liquefaction** n.

! liquefy, not -ify.

liqueur /li-kyoor/ *n.* a strong, sweet alcoholic spirit.

liquid *n.* a substance such as water or oil that flows freely. •*adj.* **1** of or like liquid. **2** (of assets) held in or easily converted into cash.

liquidate *v.* **1** close a company and sell its assets to pay its debts. **2** convert assets into cash. ■ **liquidation** *n.*

liquidity *n.* the availability of liquid assets to a market or company.

liquidize (or **-ise**) *v.* convert solid food to a liquid. ■ **liquidizer** *n.*

liquor *n.* **1** alcoholic drink. **2** liquid produced in cooking.

liquorice (US **licorice**) *n.* a black substance used as a sweet.

lira *n.* (*pl.* **lire**) the basic unit of money of Turkey and formerly of Italy.

lisp *n.* a speech defect in which s is pronounced like *th*. •*v.* speak with a lisp.

lissom *adj.* slim and supple.

list *n.* a number of connected items or names written as a series. •*v.* **1** make a list of. **2** include in a list. **3** (of a ship) lean to one side.

listen *v.* **1** pay attention to a sound. **2** take notice of advice or a request. **3** (**listen in**) listen to a private conversation. ■ **listener** *n.*

listeria *n.* a type of bacteria causing food poisoning.

listing *n.* **1** a list. **2** an item in a list.

listless *adj.* lacking energy or enthusiasm. ■ **listlessly** *adv.*

lit past & past part. of **LIGHT**.

litany *n.* (*pl.* **litanies**) **1** a series of prayers. **2** a long, boring list of complaints etc.

liter US = **LITRE**.

literal *adj.* using or interpreting words in their usual or most basic sense. ■ **literally** *adv.*

literary *adj.* of literature.

literate *adj.* **1** able to read and write. **2** knowledgeable about a particular subject. ■ **literacy** *n.*

literati *pl. n.* educated people interested in literature.

literature *n.* **1** books, plays, etc. valued as works of art. **2** books and printed information on a particular subject.

lithe /lyth/ *adj.* slim and supple.

lithium *n.* a metallic element.

lithography *n.* printing from a flat metal surface treated so that ink sticks only where required. ■ **lithograph** *n.*

litigant *n.* a person involved in a lawsuit.

litigate *v.* take a dispute to a law court. ■ **litigation** *n.*

litigious *adj.* tending to take legal action to settle disputes.

litmus *n.* a dye turned red by acids and blue by alkalis.

litre (US **liter**) *n.* a metric unit of capacity equal to 1,000 cubic centimetres (1.76 pints).

litter *n.* **1** rubbish left in a public place. **2** a number of young born to an animal at one time. **3** material to absorb a cat's excrement. **4** straw used as animal bedding. **5** *hist.* an enclosed bed or seat carried by men or animals. •*v.* make untidy with scattered articles.

little *adj.* **1** small in size, amount, or degree. **2** young or younger. •*n. & pron.* not much. •*adv.* **1** (**a little**) to a small extent. **2** hardly or not at all.

littoral *adj.* of a seashore.

liturgy n. (pl. **liturgies**) a set form of public Christian worship. ∎ **liturgical** adj.

live v. **1** be or remain alive. **2** spend your life in a particular way. **3** have your home in a place. **4** obtain the things necessary for staying alive. **5** (**live down**) succeed in making others forget something embarrassing. • adj. **1** living. **2** (of a broadcast) transmitted while it is happening. **3** (of music) played in front of an audience. **4** connected to an electric current. **5** able to explode.

livelihood n. a way of earning enough money to live on.

lively adj. (**livelier**, **liveliest**) full of energy or activity. ∎ **liveliness** n.

liven v. (**liven up**) make or become lively.

liver n. a large organ in the abdomen producing bile.

livery n. (pl. **liveries**) **1** a special uniform. **2** a distinctive design and colour scheme used on a company's vehicles or products. ∎ **liveried** adj.

lives pl. of LIFE.

livestock n. farm animals.

livid adj. **1** informal very angry. **2** dark blue-grey in colour.

living n. **1** a way or style of life. **2** an income, or the means of earning it. • adj. alive. ▫ **living room** a room for everyday use.

lizard n. a four-legged reptile with a long tail.

llama /lah-muh/ n. a South American animal related to the camel.

load n. **1** a thing or quantity carried. **2** a weight or source of pressure. **3** (**a load/loads of**) informal a lot of. **4** the amount of work to be done. • v. **1** put a load on or in. **2** put something into a device so that it will operate. **3** put ammunition into a gun. **4** (**loaded**) biased towards a particular outcome.

loaf n. (pl. **loaves**) a piece of shaped and baked bread. • v. spend time idly. ∎ **loafer** n.

loam n. a fertile soil.

loan n. **1** a sum of money lent. **2** the act of lending. • v. lend. ▫ **loan shark** informal a moneylender charging very high rates of interest.

loath adj. unwilling.

loathe v. feel hatred or disgust for. ∎ **loathsome** adj.

lob v. (**lobbing**, **lobbed**) throw or hit in a high arc. • n. a lobbed ball.

lobby n. (pl. **lobbies**) **1** an open area inside the entrance of a public building. **2** a group trying to influence politicians on an issue. • v. (**lobbying**, **lobbied**) try to influence a politician on an issue. ∎ **lobbyist** n.

lobe n. a roundish part or projection.

lobelia n. a garden plant with blue or scarlet flowers.

lobotomy n. (pl. **lobotomies**) an operation involving cutting into part of the brain.

lobster n. a shellfish with large pincers.

local adj. of a particular place or part. • n. **1** a person who lives in a particular place. **2** informal a pub near a person's home. ▫ **local anaesthetic** an anaesthetic affecting a particular part of the body. ∎ **locally** adv.

locale /loh-kahl/ n. a place where something happens.

locality n. (pl. **localities**) **1** an area or neighbourhood. **2** the position of something.

localize (or **-ise**) v. restrict to a particular place. ■ **localization** n.

locate v. **1** discover the exact place of. **2** (**be located**) be situated.

location n. **1** a place where something is located. **2** the act of locating. **3** a place outside a studio where a film etc. is made.

loch n. (in Scotland) a lake or inlet of the sea.

loci pl. of **LOCUS**.

lock n. **1** a device for keeping something fastened or for preventing something from functioning, operated by a key. **2** a section of a canal with gates at each end allowing the water level to be changed. **3** a wrestling hold. **4** a coil or hanging piece of hair. • v. **1** fasten with a lock. **2** shut in by locking a door. **3** make or become fixed. □ **lockjaw** tetanus. **lockout** the exclusion of employees from their workplace during a dispute. **locksmith** a person who makes and repairs locks. **lock-up 1** a makeshift jail. **2** a garage or small shop separate from other premises. ■ **lockable** adj.

locker n. a small lockable cupboard.

locket n. a small ornamental case worn on a chain round the neck.

locomotion n. movement from one place to another.

locomotive n. a powered railway vehicle for pulling trains. • adj. of locomotion.

locum n. a doctor or priest standing in for another who is temporarily away.

locus n. (pl. **loci**) a particular position or place.

locust n. a large destructive tropical grasshopper.

locution n. **1** a word or phrase. **2** a person's way of speaking.

lode n. a vein of metal ore. □ **lodestone** a piece of magnetic iron ore used as a magnet.

lodge n. **1** a small house at the gates of a large house with grounds. **2** a porter's room at the entrance of a building. **3** a small house where people stay while hunting or shooting. **4** a branch of certain organizations. **5** a beaver's den. • v. **1** present a complaint, appeal, etc. **2** fix in a place. **3** live as a lodger.

lodger n. a person who pays rent to live in a property with the owner.

lodging n. **1** temporary accommodation. **2** (**lodgings**) a rented room or rooms in the same house as the owner.

loft n. **1** a room or space under a roof. **2** a large, open flat in a converted building. **3** a gallery in a church or hall. • v. hit or throw a ball high into the air.

lofty adj. (**loftier**, **loftiest**) **1** very tall. **2** morally good. **3** haughty and aloof. ■ **loftily** adv.

log n. **1** a piece cut from the trunk or a branch of a tree. **2** an official record of a ship's or aircraft's journey. • v. (**logging**, **logged**) **1** enter facts in a log. **2** (**log in/on** or **out/off**) begin (or finish) using a computer system. **3** cut down trees for commercial use. □ **logbook 1** a log of a ship or aircraft. **2** a document recording details of a vehicle and its owner.

loganberry n. a red soft fruit, similar to a raspberry.

logarithm n. each of a series of numbers set out in tables, used to simplify calculations.

loggerheads pl. n. (**at loggerheads**) in strong disagreement.

logic n. **1** the science of reasoning. **2** good reasoning. ■ **logician** n.

logical adj. **1** based on logic; using sound reasoning. **2** expected or reasonable. ■ **logically** adv.

logistics n. the detailed organization of a large and complex exercise. ■ **logistical** adj.

logo n. (pl. **logos**) a design or symbol used to identify an organization.

loin n. the part of the body between the ribs and the hip bones. □ **loincloth** a cloth worn round the hips.

loiter v. stand around idly. ■ **loiterer** n.

loll v. **1** sit, lie, or stand in a relaxed way. **2** hang loosely.

lollipop n. a large boiled sweet on a stick.

lollop v. (**lolloped, lolloping**) move with clumsy bounding steps.

lolly n. (pl. **lollies**) informal **1** a lollipop. **2** money.

lone adj. solitary.

lonely adj. (**lonelier, loneliest**) **1** sad because of having no friends or company. **2** (of time) spent alone. **3** remote. ■ **loneliness** n.

loner n. a person who prefers to be alone.

lonesome adj. US lonely.

long adj. **1** of great or a particular length. **2** (of odds) reflecting a low probability. • adv. **1** for a long time. **2** throughout a specific period. • v.

have a strong wish. □ **as** (or **so**) **long as** provided that. **longhand** ordinary handwriting as opposed to shorthand etc. **long-haul** involving transport over a long distance. **long johns** informal close-fitting underpants with long legs. **long-range 1** able to travel long distances. **2** of a period far in the future. **long shot** a scheme or guess very unlikely to succeed. **long-sighted** unable to see close things clearly. **long-suffering** bearing problems or annoyance patiently. **long-term** of or for a long time. **long wave** a radio wave of a wavelength above a kilometre and a frequency below 300 kHz. **longways** lengthways. **long-winded** long and boring.

longevity /lon-jev-i-ti/ n. long life.

longing n. a strong wish. ■ **longingly** adv.

longitude n. the distance east or west of the Greenwich meridian, measured in degrees. ■ **longitudinal** adj.

loo n. informal a toilet.

loofah n. the dried inner parts of a tropical fruit, used as a bath sponge.

look v. **1** direct your eyes. **2** appear; seem. **3** face towards. • n. **1** an act of looking. **2** appearance. **3** (**looks**) a person's facial appearance. □ **look after** take care of. **lookalike** a person who looks very similar to another. **look down on** think that you are better than. **look for** try to find. **look into** investigate. **look on** watch without getting involved. **look out** be vigilant. **lookout 1** a place from which to keep watch. **2** a person keeping watch. **look up**

1 improve. **2** search for information. **3** *informal* visit or contact. □ **look up to** admire and respect.

loom *n.* a machine for weaving cloth. • *v.* **1** appear as a vague and threatening shape. **2** seem ominously close.

loony *n.* (*pl.* **loonies**) *informal* a mad person.

loop *n.* **1** a curve that bends round and crosses itself. **2** an endless strip of tape or film. • *v.* form into a loop. □ **loophole** a way of avoiding something stipulated by a law or contract. **loop the loop** fly an aircraft in a vertical circle.

loose *adj.* **1** not firmly fixed in place. **2** not tied up or shut in. **3** (of a garment) not fitting tightly. **4** not fastened or packaged together. **5** not exact. • *v.* unfasten or set free. □ **at a loose end** with nothing to do. **loose box** a stall for a horse. **loose-leaf** with each page removable. **on the loose** having escaped from being imprisoned or tied up. ■ **loosely** *adv.*

loosen *v.* **looseness** *n.*

loot *n.* goods stolen by a thief, or during a war or riot. • *v.* steal goods from a place during a war or riot. ■ **looter** *n.*

lop *v.* (**lopping**, **lopped**) cut off a branch from a tree.

lope *v.* run with a long bounding stride.

lop-eared *adj.* with drooping ears.

lopsided *adj.* with one side lower or smaller than the other.

loquacious *adj.* talkative. ■ **loquacity** *n.*

lord *n.* **1** a nobleman. **2** (**Lord**) a title given to certain British peers or high officials. **3** a master or ruler. **4** (**Lord**) a name for God or Jesus. □ **lord it over** act in an arrogant and bullying way towards. **Your/His Lordship** a form of address to a judge, bishop, or nobleman.

lordly *adj.* proud or superior.

lore *n.* traditional knowledge.

lorgnette /lor-*nyet*/ *n.* a pair of glasses held by a long handle.

lorry *n.* (*pl.* **lorries**) a large vehicle for transporting goods.

lose *v.* (**losing**, **lost**) **1** have taken away; no longer have. **2** become unable to find. **3** fail to win. **4** waste time or an opportunity. **5** (**lose yourself in**) become deeply involved in. □ **lose out** not get a fair chance or advantage. ■ **loser** *n.*

loss *n.* **1** the act of losing. **2** a person or thing lost. **3** sadness after losing a valued person or thing. □ **at a loss** uncertain or puzzled. **loss-leader** a product sold at a loss to attract customers.

lot *pron. & adv.* (**a lot/lots**) *informal* a large number or amount. • *n.* **1** an item for sale at an auction. **2** *informal* a group of people. **3** (**the lot**) *informal* the whole number or quantity. **4** a piece of paper chosen at random from a number of marked pieces as a method of deciding something. **5** a person's situation in life. **6** a plot of land.

lotion *n.* a medicinal or cosmetic liquid put on the skin.

lottery *n.* (*pl.* **lotteries**) **1** a means of raising money by selling numbered tickets and giving prizes to the holders of numbers drawn at random. **2** something whose success is controlled by luck.

lotus *n.* a large water lily.

louche /loosh/ *adj.* having a bad reputation but still attractive.

loud *adj.* **1** making a lot of noise. **2** expressed forcefully. **3** garish. □ **loudhailer** an electronic megaphone. **loudspeaker** a device that converts electrical impulses into sound. ■ **loudly** *adv.* **loudness** *n.*

lough /lok/ *n.* (in Ireland) a loch.

lounge *v.* lie, sit, or stand in a relaxed way. • *n.* **1** a sitting room. **2** a waiting room at an airport etc. □ **lounge suit** a man's ordinary suit.

lour (or **lower**) *v.* (of the sky) look dark and threatening.

louse *n.* **1** (*pl.* **lice**) a small parasitic insect. **2** (*pl.* **louses**) *informal* an unpleasant person.

lousy *adj.* (**lousier, lousiest**) **1** *informal* very bad. **2** infested with lice.

lout *n.* a rude or aggressive man or boy. ■ **loutish** *adj.*

louvre /loo-ver/ (*US* **louver**) *n.* each of a set of slanting slats fixed at intervals to allow air or light through.

lovable (or **loveable**) *adj.* inspiring love or affection.

love *n.* **1** very strong affection. **2** very strong affection and sexual attraction. **3** great liking. **4** a person or thing that you love. **5** (in tennis etc.) a score of zero. • *v.* **1** feel love for. **2** like very much. □ **love affair** a romantic or sexual relationship between two people who are not married to each other. **lovelorn** unhappy because you love someone who does not love you. **make love** have sex. ■ **loveless** *adj.* **lover** *n.* **lovingly** *adv.*

lovely *adj.* (**lovelier, loveliest**) very beautiful or pleasant. ■ **loveliness** *n.*

low *adj.* **1** not high or tall or far above the ground. **2** below average in amount or strength. **3** not good or important. **4** (of a sound) deep or quiet. **5** depressed. **6** not moral. • *n.* **1** a low point. **2** an area of low atmospheric pressure. • *adv.* at or into a low point. • *v.* (of a cow) moo. □ **lowbrow** not intellectual or cultured. **the lowdown** the important facts. **lowkey** not elaborate or showy.

lowland (or **lowlands**) low-lying country. **low season** the least popular time for a holiday. **low tide** the time when the sea is furthest out.

lower[1] *adj.* less high. • *v.* **1** make or become lower. **2** move downwards. □ **lower case** small letters as opposed to capitals.

lower[2] var. of **LOUR**.

lowly *adj.* (**lowlier, lowliest**) low in status or importance.

loyal *adj.* firm and faithful in your support. ■ **loyally** *adv.* **loyalty** *n.*

loyalist *n.* a person who remains loyal to the established ruler or government.

lozenge *n.* **1** a tablet sucked to soothe a sore throat. **2** a diamond-shaped figure.

LP *abbrev.* long-playing record.

LSD *n.* a powerful hallucinogenic drug.

Ltd *abbrev.* Limited.

lubricant *n.* a lubricating substance.

lubricate *v.* oil or grease machinery so that it moves easily. ■ **lubrication** *n.*

lubricious *adj.* lewd.

lucerne *n.* alfalfa.

lucid adj. 1 easy to understand. 2 able to think clearly. ∎ **lucidity** n. **lucidly** adv.

luck n. 1 good or bad things that happen by chance. 2 good fortune. ∎ **luckless** adj.

lucky adj. (**luckier, luckiest**) having, bringing, or resulting from good luck. ▫ **lucky dip** a game in which small prizes are hidden in a container for people to pick out at random. ∎ **luckily** adv.

lucrative adj. making a large profit.

lucre /loo-ker/ n. money.

Luddite n. a person opposed to new technology.

ludicrous adj. ridiculous. ∎ **ludicrously** adv.

lug v. (**lugging, lugged**) carry or drag with great effort. •n. 1 informal an ear. 2 a projection on an object for carrying it or fixing it in place.

luggage n. suitcases etc. for a traveller's belongings.

lugubrious adj. sad; gloomy.

lukewarm adj. 1 only slightly warm. 2 unenthusiastic.

lull v. 1 calm or send to sleep. 2 cause to feel deceptively safe or confident. •n. a period of quiet or inactivity.

lullaby n. (pl. **lullabies**) a soothing song to send a child to sleep.

lumbago n. lower back pain.

lumbar adj. of the lower back.

lumber n. 1 disused articles of furniture. 2 US timber sawn into planks. •v. 1 informal give an unwanted responsibility to. 2 move slowly and awkwardly. ▫ **lumberjack** a person who fells and cuts up trees.

luminary n. (pl. **luminaries**) an important or influential person.

luminescence n. light given off by a substance that has not been heated. ∎ **luminescent** adj.

luminous adj. giving off light, esp. in the dark. ∎ **luminosity** n.

lump n. 1 an irregular hard or solid mass. 2 a swelling under the skin. •v. treat as alike, without regard for differences. ▫ **lump sum** a single payment as opposed to several smaller payments. ∎ **lumpy** adj.

lumpectomy n. (pl. **lumpectomies**) an operation to remove a lump from the breast.

lunacy n. 1 insanity. 2 great stupidity.

lunar adj. of the moon.

lunatic n. 1 a mentally ill person. 2 a very foolish person.

lunch n. a midday meal. •v. eat lunch.

luncheon n. lunch.

lung n. either of the pair of organs in the chest into which air is drawn in breathing.

lunge n. a sudden forward movement of the body. •v. make a lunge.

lupin n. a plant with spikes of tall flowers.

lupine adj. of or like a wolf.

lurch n. a sudden unsteady movement. •v. make a lurch. ▫ **leave in the lurch** leave in a difficult situation.

lure v. tempt into doing. •n. 1 the tempting aspects of something. 2 a bait used in fishing or hunting.

lurid adj. **1** unpleasantly bright in colour. **2** vividly shocking. ■ **luridly** adv.

lurk v. wait in hiding to attack someone.

luscious adj. **1** rich and sweet in taste. **2** sexually attractive.

lush adj. **1** growing thickly and strongly. **2** luxurious. ■ **lushly** adv. **lushness** n.

lust n. **1** strong sexual desire. **2** a strong desire. • v. feel lust. ■ **lustful** adj.

lustre (US **luster**) n. **1** a soft glow or shine. **2** prestige. ■ **lustrous** adj.

lusty adj. (**lustier**, **lustiest**) healthy and strong. ■ **lustily** adv.

lute n. a guitar-like instrument with a rounded body. ■ **lutenist** n.

luxuriant adj. growing thickly and strongly. ■ **luxuriance** n. **luxuriantly** adv.

luxuriate v. take pleasure in something enjoyable.

luxurious adj. very comfortable or elegant and expensive. ■ **luxuriously** adv.

luxury n. (pl. **luxuries**) **1** comfortable and expensive living or surroundings. **2** something enjoyable but not essential.

lychee n. a fruit with sweet white flesh and rough skin.

lychgate n. a roofed gateway to a churchyard.

Lycra n. trademark an elastic fibre or fabric.

lye n. an alkaline solution used for cleaning.

lying pres. part. of LIE¹, LIE².

lymph n. a colourless fluid containing white blood cells. ▫ **lymph gland** each of a number of small swellings where lymph is filtered. ■ **lymphatic** adj.

lymphoma n. cancer of the lymph glands.

lynch v. (of a mob) kill someone for an alleged crime without a legal trial.

lynx n. a wild cat with tufted ears.

lyre n. an ancient stringed instrument like a small harp.

lyric n. (or **lyrics**) the words of a song. • adj. (of poetry) expressing the writer's emotions.

lyrical adj. (of literature or music) expressing the writer's emotions imaginatively. ■ **lyrically** adv.

lyricism n. the imaginative expression of emotion in writing or music.

lyricist n. a person who writes lyrics.

Mm

M (or **m**) *n.* the Roman numeral for 1,000. • *abbrev.* **1** (**m**) metres. **2** (**m**) miles. **3** (**m**) millions. **4** motorway.

MA *abbrev.* Master of Arts.

ma'am *n.* madam.

mac *n. informal* a mackintosh.

macabre *adj.* disturbing because concerned with death or injury.

macadam *n.* broken stone used in surfacing roads.

macadamia *n.* the nut of an Australian tree.

macaroni *n.* narrow tubes of pasta.

macaroon *n.* a biscuit made with almonds.

macaw *n.* a parrot of Central and South America.

mace *n.* **1** a ceremonial staff carried by a mayor etc. **2** a spice made from nutmeg husks.

macerate *v.* soften food by soaking. ■ **maceration** *n.*

Mach /mak/ *n.* (**Mach 1, Mach 2,** etc.) the speed of sound, twice the speed of sound, etc.

machete /muh-**shet**-i/ *n.* a broad, heavy knife.

Machiavellian /ma-ki-uh-**vel**-i-uhn/ *adj.* cunning and underhand.

machinations *pl. n.* plots and scheming.

machine *n.* **1** a mechanical device for performing a particular task. **2** an efficient group of influential people. • *v.* make or work on with a machine. □ **machine gun** an automatic gun firing bullets in rapid succession. **machine-readable** in a form that a computer can process.

machinery *n.* **1** machines, or the parts of a machine. **2** a system or structure.

machinist *n.* a person who operates a machine.

machismo /muh-**kiz**-moh/ *n.* aggressive male pride.

macho /ma-choh/ *adj.* aggressively masculine.

mackerel *n.* (*pl.* **mackerel**) an edible sea fish.

mackintosh (or **macintosh**) *n.* a waterproof coat.

macramé /muh-**krah**-may/ *n.* the craft of knotting cord in patterns.

macrobiotic *adj.* (of diet) consisting of organic unprocessed foods.

macrocosm *n.* the whole of a complex structure.

mad *adj.* (**madder, maddest**) **1** insane. **2** very foolish. **3** frantic. **4** *informal* very enthusiastic. **5** *informal* angry. □ **mad cow disease** BSE. ■ **madden** *v.* **madly** *adv.* **madness** *n.*

madam *n.* a polite form of address for a woman.

Madame /muh-**dam**/ *n.* (*pl.* **Mesdames**) a title for a French woman.

madcap *adj.* reckless.

madder *n.* a red dye.

made past & past part. of MAKE.

Madeira n. a strong sweet wine from Madeira. □ **Madeira cake** a rich sponge cake.

Mademoiselle /ma-duh-mwah-zel/ n. (pl. **Mesdemoiselles**) a title for an unmarried French woman.

Madonna n. (**the Madonna**) the Virgin Mary.

madrigal n. a song for several unaccompanied voices.

maelstrom /mayl-struhm/ n. **1** a confused situation. **2** a powerful whirlpool.

maestro /my-stroh/ n. (pl. **maestros**) a famous and talented man, esp. a classical musician.

Mafia n. **1** an international criminal organization originating in Sicily. **2** (**mafia**) a powerful, secretly influential group.

magazine n. **1** a periodical containing articles and pictures. **2** a chamber holding cartridges in a gun. **3** a store for arms or ammunition.

magenta n. a purplish crimson.

maggot n. a larva of a fly or other insect.

Magi /may-ji/ pl. n. the three wise men from the East who brought gifts to the infant Jesus.

magic n. **1** the supposed use of mysterious or supernatural powers to influence events. **2** conjuring tricks. **3** a mysterious or wonderful quality. • adj. having supernatural powers. ■ **magical** adj. **magically** adv.

magician n. **1** a person with magic powers. **2** a conjuror.

magisterial adj. **1** authoritative. **2** of a magistrate.

magistrate n. an official authorized to judge minor cases and hold preliminary hearings. ■ **magistracy** n.

magma n. molten rock under the earth's crust.

magnanimous adj. generous or forgiving. ■ **magnanimity** n.

magnate n. a wealthy and influential businessman or businesswoman.

magnesium n. a metallic element which burns with a bright white flame.

magnet n. **1** a piece of iron that attracts objects containing iron and points north and south when suspended. **2** a powerful attraction. ■ **magnetize** (or **-ise**) v.

magnetic adj. **1** having the property of a magnet. **2** very attractive. □ **magnetic pole** each of the points near the geographical North and South Poles, which the needle of a compass points to. **magnetic tape** used in recording sound, pictures, or computer data. ■ **magnetically** adv.

magnetism n. **1** the property displayed by magnets of attracting or repelling metal objects. **2** the ability to attract and charm people.

magneto /mag-nee-toh/ n. (pl. **magnetos**) a small electric generator using a magnet.

magnificent adj. **1** very attractive and impressive. **2** very good. ■ **magnificence** n. **magnificently** adv.

magnify v. (**magnifying**, **magnified**) **1** make something appear larger than it is with a lens or microscope. **2** make larger or stronger. **3** old use praise. ■ **magnification** n.

m

magnitude n. **1** great size or importance. **2** size.

magnolia n. a tree with large white or pink flowers.

magnum n. (pl. **magnums**) a wine bottle of twice the standard size.

magnum opus /mag-nuhm oh-puhss/ n. the most important work of art etc. that a person has produced.

magpie n. a black and white bird with a long tail.

maharaja (or **maharajah**) n. hist. an Indian prince.

mah-jong (or **mah-jongg**) n. a Chinese game played with small rectangular tiles.

mahogany n. hard reddish-brown wood.

mahout /muh-howt/ n. (in South and SE Asia) an elephant driver or keeper.

maid n. **1** a female servant. **2** old use a girl or young woman.

maiden n. old use a girl or young woman, esp. a virgin. • adj. **1** first of its kind. **2** (of an older woman) unmarried. □ **maiden name** the surname of a married woman before her marriage. **maiden over** an over in cricket in which no runs are scored.

mail n. **1** letters etc. sent by post. **2** email. **3** hist. armour made of linked metal rings. • v. send by post or email. □ **mail order** the buying or selling of goods by post.

mailshot a piece of advertising material sent to many people.

maim v. inflict a permanent injury on.

main adj. greatest or most important. • n. a chief water or gas pipe or electricity cable. □ **in the main** on the whole. **mainframe** a

large computer. **mainland** the main area of land of a country, not including islands. **mainspring** the most important part. **mainstay** a thing on which something depends or is based. **mainstream** the ideas, attitudes, etc. shared by most people. ■ **mainly** adv.

maintain v. **1** cause to continue in the same state. **2** regularly check and repair. **3** support financially. **4** assert.

maintenance n. **1** the act of maintaining. **2** financial support given to a former husband or wife after divorce.

maisonette n. a flat on two storeys of a larger building.

maître d'hôtel /may-truh doh-**tel**/ n. (pl. **maîtres d'hôtel**) a head waiter.

maize n. a cereal plant whose large grains are eaten as a vegetable.

majestic adj. impressively grand or beautiful. ■ **majestically** adv.

majesty n. (pl. **majesties**) **1** impressive beauty or grandeur. **2** (**His, Your,** etc. **Majesty**) a title given to a king or queen or their wife or widow.

major adj. **1** important or serious. **2** main. **3** Music (of a scale) having intervals of a semitone between the 3rd and 4th, and 7th and 8th notes. • n. the army rank above captain. • v. (**major in**) US specialize in a subject at college. □ **major general** the army rank above brigadier.

majority n. (pl. **majorities**) **1** the greater number. **2** the number of votes by which one party or candidate in an election defeats the opposition. **3** the age when a person is legally an adult.

make v. (**making, made**) **1** form by combining parts. **2** cause. **3** force to do. **4** add up to. **5** be suitable as or decide on. **7** earn money. **8** arrive at or achieve. •n. a brand of goods. □ **make-believe** fantasy or pretence. **make do** manage with something unsatisfactory. **make for** move towards. **make it** be successful. **make off** leave hurriedly. **make off with** steal. **make out 1** manage to see, hear, or understand. **2** claim or pretend. **makeover** an improvement of the appearance of a person, house, etc. **makeshift** temporary and improvised. **make-up 1** cosmetics. **2** the composition of something. **make up 1** put together from parts or ingredients. **2** invent. **3** be reconciled after a quarrel. **4** apply cosmetics to. **make up for** compensate. ■ **maker** n.

malachite n. a green mineral.

maladjusted adj. unable to cope with normal social situations.

maladministration n. bad or corrupt management of an organization.

maladroit adj. clumsy.

malady n. (pl. **maladies**) an illness.

malaise n. a feeling of unease, illness, or low spirits.

malapropism n. the mistaken use of a word in place of a similar-sounding one.

malaria n. a disease causing recurrent fever, transmitted by some mosquitoes. ■ **malarial** adj.

Malay n. **1** a member of a people inhabiting Malaysia and Indonesia. **2** the language of the Malays.

malcontent n. a dissatisfied and rebellious person.

male adj. **1** of the sex that can fertilize or inseminate the female. **2** (of a plant or flower) having stamens but not a pistil. **3** (of a fitting) for insertion into a corresponding part. •n. a male person, animal, or plant.

malediction n. a curse.

malefactor n. a wrongdoer.

malevolent /muh-lev-uh-luhnt/ adj. wishing harm to others. ■ **malevolence** n.

malformation n. the state of being abnormally shaped. ■ **malformed** adj.

malfunction v. fail to function normally. •n. such a failure.

malice n. the desire to harm someone. ■ **malicious** adj. **maliciously** adv.

malign /muh-lyn/ adj. harmful or evil. •v. say unpleasant things about.

malignant adj. **1** (of a tumour) cancerous. **2** harmful; malevolent. ■ **malignancy** n.

malinger v. pretend to be ill to avoid work. ■ **malingerer** n.

mall /mawl/ n. **1** a large enclosed shopping area. **2** a sheltered walk.

mallard n. a kind of wild duck.

malleable adj. **1** able to be hammered or pressed into shape. **2** easily influenced. ■ **malleability** n.

mallet n. **1** a hammer with a large wooden head. **2** a wooden stick with a head, used in croquet or polo.

mallow n. a plant with pink or purple flowers.

malnutrition n. poor health caused by not having enough

m

food, or not enough of the right food. ∎ **malnourished** adj.

malodorous adj. smelling very unpleasant.

malpractice n. illegal or corrupt professional behaviour.

malt n. **1** barley or other grain soaked in water then dried. **2** whisky made with malt.

maltreat v. treat cruelly. ∎ **maltreatment** n.

mamba n. a poisonous African snake.

mammal n. a warm-blooded animal that produces milk and bears live young. ∎ **mammalian** adj.

mammary adj. of the breasts.

mammography n. the use of X-rays to detect tumours in the breasts.

Mammon n. wealth regarded as being worshipped like a god.

mammoth n. a large extinct elephant. • adj. huge.

man n. (pl. **men**) **1** an adult human male. **2** a person. **3** human beings. • v. (**manning, manned**) provide a place for, with people to work in or defend it. ☐ **manhandle** move forcibly or roughly. **manhole** a covered opening giving access to a sewer etc. **manhood 1** the state or period of being a man. **2** strength, courage, etc. **mankind** human beings as a whole. **man-made** made or caused by human beings. **manpower** the number of people available for work. **manservant** a male servant. **manslaughter** the crime of killing a person without meaning to do so. ∎ **mannish** adj.

manacle n. a shackle for the wrists or ankles. • v. restrict with manacles.

manage v. **1** be in charge of. **2** succeed in doing. **3** be able to cope. **4** control the use of money or resources. ∎ **manageable** adj.

management n. **1** the act of managing. **2** the managers of an organization.

manager n. (fem. **manageress**) a person who manages staff, an organization, etc. ∎ **managerial** adj.

manatee n. a large sea mammal.

mandarin n. **1** a small citrus fruit. **2** (**Mandarin**) the official form of the Chinese language. **3** a powerful official.

mandate n. an official order or authority to do something. • v. give authority to do something.

mandatory adj. compulsory.

mandible n. a jaw or jaw-like part.

mandolin n. a musical instrument like a lute.

mandrake n. a plant with a forked fleshy root.

mandrel n. a shaft holding work in a lathe.

mane n. a growth of long hair on the neck of a horse or lion.

maneuver US = MANOEUVRE.

manful adj. brave or determined. ∎ **manfully** adv.

manganese n. a hard metallic element.

mange n. a skin disease in some animals. ∎ **mangy** adj.

manger n. a long trough from which horses etc. feed.

mangetout /monzh-too/ n. a variety of pea eaten with the pod.

mangle v. destroy or severely damage. • n. a machine with rollers for wringing out wet laundry.

mango n. (pl. **mangoes** or **mangos**) a tropical fruit.

mangrove n. a tropical tree growing in swamps.

mania n. **1** mental illness involving periods of wild excitement. **2** an extreme enthusiasm.

maniac n. **1** a person who behaves very wildly or violently. **2** informal a person with an extreme enthusiasm. ■ **maniacal** adj.

manic adj. **1** of or affected by mania. **2** showing wild excitement or energy. ■ **manically** adv.

manicure n. a cosmetic treatment of the hands and nails. • v. give a manicure to. ■ **manicurist** n.

manifest adj. clear and obvious. • v. **1** show or display. **2** become noticeable. • n. a list of the cargo, crew, or passengers of a ship or aircraft. ■ **manifestation** n. **manifestly** adv.

manifesto n. (pl. **manifestos**) a public declaration of policy.

manifold adj. many and various. • n. a pipe with several openings, esp. in an engine.

manikin n. a very small person.

Manila n. strong brown paper.

manipulate v. **1** handle skilfully. **2** control or influence in a clever or underhand way. ■ **manipulation** n. **manipulative** adj. **manipulator** n.

manly adj. (**manlier**, **manliest**) **1** brave or strong. **2** suitable for a man. ■ **manliness** n.

manna n. something unexpected and welcome.

mannequin n. a dummy used to display clothes in a shop.

manner n. **1** a way in which something is done or happens. **2** a person's behaviour towards others. **3** (**manners**) polite behaviour. **4** a kind or sort.

mannered adj. **1** behaving in a specified way. **2** artificial and affected.

mannerism n. a distinctive gesture or way of speaking.

manoeuvre /muh-noo-ver/ (US **maneuver**) n. **1** a skilful or careful movement. **2** a well-planned scheme. **3** (**manoeuvres**) a large-scale military exercise. • v. **1** move with skill or care. **2** cleverly manipulate to achieve an aim. ■ **manoeuvrable** adj.

manor n. a large country house with lands. ■ **manorial** adj.

manqué /mong-kay/ adj. having never become what you might have been: an actor manqué.

manse n. a house provided for a minister of certain Christian Churches.

mansion n. a large, impressive house.

mantelpiece (or **mantelshelf**) n. the shelf above a fireplace.

mantilla n. a lace scarf worn by Spanish women over the hair and shoulders.

mantis n. (pl. **mantis** or **mantises**) a large insect that waits motionless for its prey.

mantle n. **1** a loose cloak. **2** a cover or covering. **3** a role passed on to another person. **4** the region of very hot, dense rock between the earth's crust and its core.

mantra n. a word or sound repeated to aid concentration when meditating.

manual adj. **1** of or operated by the hands. **2** working with the hands. • n. a book giving instructions. ■ **manually** adv.

manufacture v. **1** make on a large scale with machinery.

m

2 invent a story. •n. the process of manufacturing. ■ **manufacturer** n.

manure n. animal dung used as fertilizer.

manuscript n. **1** a handwritten book etc. **2** an author's written or typed work before printing.

Manx adj. of the Isle of Man.

many pron. & adj. a large number of. •n. the majority of people.

Maori /mow-ri/ n. (pl. **Maori** or **Maoris**) a member of the aboriginal people of New Zealand.

map n. a diagram of an area showing physical features, cities, roads, etc. •v. (**mapping**, **mapped**) **1** make a map of. **2** (**map out**) plan in detail.

maple n. a tree with five-pointed leaves.

mar v. (**marring**, **marred**) spoil the appearance or quality of.

maraca n. a container filled with small beans etc., shaken as a musical instrument.

marathon n. **1** a long-distance running race. **2** a long, difficult task.

maraud v. go around stealing things or attacking people. ■ **marauder** n.

marble n. **1** a hard stone, usu. white with coloured streaks, which is polished and used in sculpture and building. **2** a small ball of coloured glass used as a toy. ■ **marbled** adj.

March n. the third month.

march v. **1** walk in time and with regular paces. **2** walk or force to walk quickly. **3** walk in an organized procession to make a protest. •n. **1** an act of marching. **2** a piece of music written to accompany

marching. **3** (**Marches**) border regions. ■ **marcher** n.

marchioness /mar-shuh-**ness**/ n. **1** the wife or widow of a marquess. **2** a woman with the rank of marquess.

mare n. the female of a horse or related animal.

margarine n. a butter substitute made from vegetable oils or animal fats.

margin n. **1** an edge or border. **2** the blank border on each side of the print on a page. **3** an amount by which something is won.

marginal adj. **1** in a margin. **2** of minor importance. ■ **marginally** adv.

marginalize (or **-ise**) v. treat as unimportant.

marguerite n. a large daisy.

marigold n. a plant with yellow or orange flowers.

marijuana /ma-ri-**hwah**-nuh/ n. cannabis.

marina n. a harbour for yachts and small boats.

marinade n. a flavoured liquid in which food is soaked before cooking. •v. marinate.

marinate v. soak in a marinade.

marine adj. of the sea or shipping. •n. a soldier trained to serve on land or sea.

mariner n. a sailor.

marionette n. a puppet worked by strings.

marital adj. of marriage.

maritime adj. **1** of shipping or other activity taking place at sea. **2** living or found in or near the sea.

marjoram n. a herb used in cooking.

mark n. **1** a small area on a surface different in colour from the rest.

2 something indicating position. **3** a sign or symbol. **4** a characteristic feature. **5** a point awarded for a correct answer or a piece of work. **6** a particular model of a vehicle or machine. **7** a Deutschmark. • v. **1** make a mark on. **2** write a word or symbol on an object to identify it. **3** indicate the position of. **4** (**mark out**) distinguish. **5** acknowledge an event. **6** give a mark to a piece of work. **7** pay attention to. **8** (in team games) stay close to an opponent to prevent them getting or passing the ball. □ **mark time** fill in time with routine activities.

markup n. an amount added to the cost price of goods to cover overheads and profit. **quick off the mark** fast in responding.

marked adj. clearly noticeable. ■ **markedly** adv.

marker n. **1** an object used to indicate a position or route. **2** a broad felt-tip pen.

market n. **1** a place or gathering for the sale of food, livestock, etc. **2** demand for a particular product or service. • v. (**marketing**, **marketed**) advertise or promote. □ **market garden** a place where produce is grown for sale. **marketplace** the world of commercial activity. **on the market** offered for sale. ■ **marketable** adj.

marking n. **1** an identifying mark. **2** a pattern of marks on an animal.

marksman n. a person skilled in shooting. ■ **marksmanship** n.

marl n. soil consisting of clay and lime.

marlin n. a large fish of warm seas.

marmalade n. a jam made from oranges.

marmoset n. a small tropical American monkey.

maroon n. a dark brownish-red colour. • v. (**be marooned**) be abandoned alone in a remote place.

marquee n. a large tent for special events.

marquess n. a nobleman ranking above an earl.

marquetry n. inlaid work made from pieces of coloured wood.

marquis n. (in some European countries) a nobleman ranking above a count.

marram grass n. a coarse grass growing on sand.

marriage n. **1** the formal union of a man and a woman as husband and wife. **2** a combination. ■ **marriageable** adj.

marrow n. **1** a long vegetable. **2** a soft fatty substance in the cavities of bones.

marry v. (**marrying**, **married**) **1** become the husband or wife of. **2** join in marriage. **3** join together.

marsh n. an area of low-lying waterlogged land. ■ **marshy** adj.

marshal n. **1** an officer of the highest rank in some armed forces. **2** an official supervising public events. **3** (in the US) a law-enforcement officer. • v. (**marshalling**, **marshalled**; US **marshaling**, **marshaled**) assemble in an organized way.

marshmallow n. a spongy sweet made from sugar, egg white, etc.

marsupial n. a mammal whose young are carried and suckled in a pouch.

mart n. a market.

marten n. a weasel-like forest animal.

m

martial adj. of war. □ **martial arts** sports which originated as forms of self-defence or attack. **martial law** government by the military forces of a country.

martin n. a small short-tailed swallow.

martinet n. a person who enforces strict discipline.

martyr n. 1 a person who is killed because of their beliefs. 2 a person who exaggerates their difficulties to gain sympathy. • v. make a martyr of. ■ **martyrdom** n.

marvel v. (**marvelling, marvelled**; US **marveling, marveled**) feel wonder. • n. a cause of wonder.

marvellous (US **marvelous**) adj. very good; wonderful. ■ **marvellously** adv.

Marxism n. the political and economic theories of Karl Marx. ■ **Marxist** n. & adj.

marzipan n. a sweet paste made with ground almonds.

mascara n. a cosmetic for darkening the eyelashes.

mascot n. a person or thing supposed to bring good luck.

masculine adj. 1 having qualities associated with men. 2 of men. ■ **masculinity** n.

mash v. crush or beat to a soft mass. • n. a soft mass made by mashing.

mask n. a covering worn over the face as a disguise or protection. • v. 1 cover with a mask. 2 conceal or disguise.

masochism n. the enjoyment of your own pain or humiliation. ■ **masochist** n. **masochistic** adj.

mason n. a person who works with stone.

masonry n. the stone parts of a building.

masque /mahsk/ n. hist. a dramatic entertainment with masked actors.

masquerade n. a pretence. • v. pretend.

mass n. 1 an amount of matter with no definite shape. 2 a large group. 3 (**the masses**) ordinary people. 4 (**masses**) a large amount. 5 the quantity of matter which a body contains. 6 (**Mass**) a Christian service of the Eucharist. • v. gather into a mass. □ **mass-produced** produced in large quantities using machinery.

massacre n. a brutal slaughter of many people. • v. brutally kill many people.

massage n. rubbing and kneading of the body to relieve tension or pain. • v. 1 give a massage to. 2 manipulate figures to give a better result.

masseur n. (fem. **masseuse**) a person who provides massage professionally.

massif n. a compact group of mountains.

massive adj. large and heavy or solid. ■ **massively** adv.

mast n. a tall upright post, esp. one carrying a boat's sail or sails.

mastectomy n. (pl. **mastectomies**) an operation to remove a breast.

master n. 1 a man in a position of authority, control, or ownership. 2 a person skilled in a particular activity. 3 a male schoolteacher. 4 a holder of a second or further degree. 5 an original recording etc. from which copies are made. • adj. 1 highly skilled. 2 main. • v. 1 gain complete knowledge or

skill in. **2** gain control of.
□ **master key** a key that opens several different locks. **mastermind 1** a person who plans and directs a complex scheme. **2** be the mastermind of. **masterpiece** a work of outstanding skill.
■ **masterly** adj.

masterful adj. **1** powerful and able to control others. **2** very skilful. ■ **masterfully** adv.

mastery n. **1** complete knowledge or command of a subject or skill. **2** control or superiority.

mastic n. **1** gum from a Mediterranean tree. **2** a putty-like substance used in building.

masticate v. chew.

mastiff n. a dog of a large, strong breed.

mastitis n. inflammation of the breast or udder.

mastoid n. a projecting part of the bone behind the ear.

masturbate v. stimulate the genitals with the hand.
■ **masturbation** n.

mat n. **1** a piece of decorative or protective material placed on the floor. **2** a piece of protective material placed on a table etc.

matador n. a bullfighter.

match n. **1** a contest in a game or sport. **2** a person or thing equal to another in quality etc. **3** an exact or near equivalent to another. **4** a potential marriage partner. **5** a short stick with a tip that ignites when rubbed on a rough surface. • v. **1** correspond. **2** be equal to. □ **matchmaker** a person who arranges marriages or relationships between others.

mate n. **1** informal a friend. **2** a fellow member or occupant: flatmate. **3** an animal's sexual

partner. **4** an officer on a merchant ship. • v. (of animals) have sex.

material n. **1** the matter from which something is or can be made. **2** items needed for creating something. **3** cloth. • adj. **1** of physical things. **2** essential or relevant. ■ **materially** adv.

materialism n. a strong interest in material possessions rather than spiritual values.
■ **materialist** n. **materialistic** adj.

materialize (or **-ise**) v. **1** happen. **2** appear suddenly.

maternal adj. **1** of or like a mother. **2** related through a person's mother. ■ **maternally** adv.

maternity n. motherhood.

mathematics n. the study of numbers, quantities, and space. ■ **mathematical** adj. **mathematically** adv. **mathematician** n.

maths (US **math**) n. mathematics.

matinee /ma-ti-nay/ n. an afternoon performance in a theatre or cinema.

matins n. a service of morning prayer.

matriarch n. a female head of a family or tribe. ■ **matriarchal** adj. **matriarchy** n.

matricide n. **1** the killing of a mother by her child. **2** a person who kills their mother.

matriculate v. enrol at a college or university. ■ **matriculation** n.

matrimony n. marriage.
■ **matrimonial** adj.

matrix n. (pl. **matrices** or **matrixes**) **1** an environment in which something develops. **2** a mould in which something is cast. **3** a grid-like array of elements.

m

matron n. **1** a woman in charge of medical and living arrangements at a school. **2** an older married woman. **3** dated a woman in charge of nursing in a hospital. ■ **matronly** adj.

matt (or **matte**) adj. not shiny.

matted adj. (of hair or fur) in a thick tangled mass.

matter n. **1** physical substance or material. **2** a situation to be dealt with. **3** (**the matter**) the reason for a problem. •v. be important. □ **matter-of-fact** unemotional and practical.

mattress n. a fabric case filled with soft, firm, or springy material for sleeping on.

mature adj. **1** fully grown. **2** like a sensible adult. **3** full-flavoured. •v. **1** become mature. **2** (of an insurance policy) reach the end of its term and so become payable. ■ **maturation** n. **maturely** adv. **maturity** n.

maudlin adj. sentimental and full of self-pity.

maul v. **1** wound by scratching and tearing. **2** treat roughly.

maunder v. talk in a rambling way.

mausoleum n. a building housing a tomb or tombs.

mauve n. a pale purple colour.

maverick n. an unconventional, independent-minded person.

maw n. the jaws or throat.

mawkish adj. sentimental in a sickly way.

maxim n. a sentence expressing a general truth or rule of behaviour.

maximize (or **-ise**) v. make as great as possible.

maximum n. (pl. **maxima** or **maximums**) the greatest amount or size possible. •adj. greatest in amount or size. ■ **maximal** adj.

May n. **1** the fifth month. **2** (**may**) the hawthorn or its blossom. □ **mayfly** a short-lived winged insect living near water. **maypole** a decorated pole for dancing round on the first day of May.

maybe adv. perhaps.

Mayday n. an international radio distress signal used by ships and aircraft.

mayhem n. violent disorder.

mayonnaise n. a dressing made from egg yolks, oil, and vinegar.

mayor n. the elected head of a city or borough council. ■ **mayoral** adj. **mayoralty** n.

mayoress n. **1** the wife of a mayor. **2** a woman elected as mayor.

maze n. a network of paths and walls or hedges through which you have to find a way.

MB (or **Mb**) abbrev. megabytes.

MBA abbrev. Master of Business Administration.

MBE abbrev. Member of the Order of the British Empire.

MC abbrev. Master of Ceremonies.

MD abbrev. **1** Doctor of Medicine. **2** Managing Director.

ME abbrev. myalgic encephalomyelitis, a medical condition causing aches and prolonged tiredness.

me pron. the form of 'I' used when the speaker or writer is the object of a verb or preposition.

! It's wrong to use *me* as the subject of a verb, as in *John and me went to the shops*; in this case use *I* instead.

mead *n.* an alcoholic drink made from honey and water.

meadow *n.* a field of grass.

meagre (US **meager**) *adj.* small in quantity. ■ **meagreness** *n.*

meal *n.* **1** a regular occasion when food is eaten. **2** the food eaten on such an occasion. **3** coarsely ground grain.

mealy *adj.* of or like meal. □ **mealy-mouthed** unwilling to speak frankly.

mean *v.* (**meaning, meant**) **1** intend. **2** (of a word) have as its explanation in the same language or its equivalent in another. **3** have as a result. **4** be of specified importance. • *adj.* **1** unwilling to give or share. **2** unkind. **3** US aggressive. **4** poor in quality or appearance. **5** calculated as a mean. **6** in the middle of two extremes. • *n.* **1** the average value of a set of quantities. **2** something in the middle of two extremes. ■ **meanly** *adv.* **meanness** *n.*

meander *v.* **1** follow a winding course. **2** wander aimlessly. • *n.* a winding bend of a river.

meaning *n.* **1** what is meant. **2** a sense of purpose. ■ **meaningful** *adj.* **meaningless** *adj.*

means *n.* **1** a thing or method for achieving a result. **2** financial resources. □ **by all means** of course. **by no means** certainly not. **means test** an official investigation of a person's finances to find out their eligibility for welfare benefits.

meantime *adv.* (**in the meantime**) meanwhile.

meanwhile *adv.* **1** in the period of time between two events. **2** at the same time.

measles *n.* an infectious disease causing fever and a red rash.

measly *adj. informal* meagre.

measure *v.* **1** find the size, amount, etc. of something in standard units. **2** be of a specified size. **3** (**measure out**) take an exact quantity of. **4** (**measure up**) reach the required standard. • *n.* **1** a course of action. **2** a proposal for a law. **3** a standard unit used in measuring. **4** a measuring device marked with such units. **5** (**a measure of**) a certain amount of. ■ **measurable** *adj.* **measurably** *adv.*

measured *adj.* **1** slow and regular in rhythm. **2** carefully considered.

measurement *n.* **1** the act of measuring. **2** a size etc. found by measuring.

meat *n.* animal flesh as food.

meaty *adj.* (**meatier, meatiest**) **1** like or full of meat. **2** substantial or satisfying.

mechanic *n.* a skilled worker who repairs and maintains machinery.

mechanical *adj.* **1** of or operated by machinery. **2** done without conscious thought. ■ **mechanically** *adv.*

mechanics *n.* **1** the study of the forces producing motion. **2** mechanical parts.

mechanism *n.* **1** a piece of machinery. **2** the way something works or happens.

mechanize (or **-ise**) *v.* equip with machinery. ■ **mechanization** *n.*

m

medal n. an inscribed metal disc awarded for achievement or to mark an event.

medallion n. a pendant shaped like a medal.

medallist (US **medalist**) n. a person awarded a medal.

meddle v. interfere in something that is not your business. ■ **meddler** n. **meddlesome** adj.

media n. 1 television, radio, and newspapers as the means of mass communication. 2 pl. of MEDIUM.

mediaeval var. of MEDIEVAL.

medial adj. situated in the middle. ■ **medially** adv.

median adj. situated in the middle.

mediate v. try to settle a dispute between two other parties. ■ **mediation** n. **mediator** n.

medic n. informal a doctor or medical student.

medical adj. of the science of medicine. •n. an examination to assess a person's physical health. ■ **medically** adv.

medicament n. a medicine.

medicate v. 1 give medicine to. 2 (**medicated**) containing a medicinal substance.

medication n. 1 a medicine. 2 treatment with medicines.

medicinal adj. having healing properties. ■ **medicinally** adv.

medicine n. 1 the science or practice of treating and preventing disease. 2 a substance taken to treat or prevent disease.

medieval (or **mediaeval**) adj. of the Middle Ages.

mediocre adj. of average or fairly low quality. ■ **mediocrity** n.

meditate v. 1 focus the mind for spiritual purposes or relaxation.

2 think carefully. ■ **meditation** n. **meditative** adj. **meditatively** adv.

Mediterranean adj. of the Mediterranean Sea.

medium n. (pl. **media** or **mediums**) 1 a means of doing or communicating something. 2 a substance through which something acts or is conveyed. 3 (pl. **mediums**) a person claiming to communicate between the dead and the living. 4 the middle state between two extremes. •adj. between two extremes. □ **medium wave** a radio wave of a frequency between 300 kHz and 3 MHz.

medlar n. a small brown apple-like fruit.

medley n. (pl. **medleys**) 1 a varied mixture. 2 various musical excerpts performed as a continuous piece.

medulla n. a separate inner region of an organ or tissue.

meek adj. quiet, gentle, and obedient. ■ **meekly** adv. **meekness** n.

meerschaum /meer-shawm/ n. a tobacco pipe with a white clay bowl.

meet v. (**meeting**, **met**) 1 come together with someone at the same place and time. 2 be introduced to or encounter for the first time. 3 touch or join. 4 experience. 5 (**meet with**) receive a reaction. 6 satisfy a requirement. •n. a meeting. •adj. old use suitable or proper.

meeting n. 1 an organized gathering for a discussion etc. 2 a situation in which people meet.

mega adj. informal 1 huge. 2 excellent.

megabyte → memory

megabyte n. a unit of information equal to 1,048,576 bytes.

megahertz n. (pl. **megahertz**) a unit of frequency equal to one million hertz.

megalith n. a large stone forming a prehistoric monument or part of one. ■ **megalithic** adj.

megalomania n. 1 the false belief that you are very powerful and important. 2 strong desire for power. ■ **megalomaniac** n. & adj.

megaphone n. a cone-shaped device for amplifying the voice.

megapixel n. a unit for measuring the resolution of a digital image, equal to 1,048,576 pixels.

megawatt n. a unit of power equal to one million watts.

melamine n. a hard plastic used for laminated coatings.

melancholia n. great sadness or depression.

melancholy n. deep and long-lasting sadness. • adj. sad.

melange /may-lonzh/ n. a varied mixture.

melanin n. a dark pigment in the hair and skin.

melanoma n. a form of skin cancer.

meld v. blend.

melee /mel-ay/ n. 1 a confused fight. 2 a disorderly crowd.

mellifluous adj. sweet-sounding.

mellow adj. 1 pleasantly smooth or soft in sound, taste, or colour. 2 relaxed and good-humoured. • v. make or become mellow.

melodeon n. a small accordion or organ.

melodic adj. 1 of melody. 2 pleasant-sounding. ■ **melodically** adv.

melodious adj. tuneful.

melodrama n. 1 a play with exciting events and exaggerated characters. 2 exaggerated behaviour. ■ **melodramatic** adj. **melodramatically** adv.

melody n. (pl. **melodies**) 1 a tune. 2 the main part in harmonized music.

melon n. a large round fruit.

melt v. 1 make or become liquid by heating. 2 gradually disappear. □ **meltdown** an accident in a nuclear reactor in which the fuel overheats and melts the core.

member n. 1 a person belonging to a group or society. 2 a part of a structure. ■ **membership** n.

membrane n. a thin flexible skin-like tissue. ■ **membranous** adj.

memento n. (pl. **mementos** or **mementoes**) an object kept as a reminder.

memo n. (pl. **memos**) a note sent within an organization.

memoir /mem-war/ n. a written account of events etc. from personal knowledge.

memorabilia pl. n. objects collected because of their links with people or events.

memorable adj. worth remembering or easy to remember. ■ **memorably** adv.

memorandum n. (pl. **memoranda** or **memorandums**) 1 a memo. 2 a formal record or report.

memorial n. an object commemorating a person or event. • adj. in memory of someone.

memorize (or **-ise**) v. learn and remember exactly.

memory n. (pl. **memories**) 1 the ability to remember things. 2 a thing remembered. 3 a computer's equipment or capacity for

m

storing data. □ **in memory of** so as to commemorate.

men pl. of **MAN**.

menace n. **1** a dangerous or troublesome person or thing. **2** a threatening quality. •v. threaten.

ménage /may-**nahj**/ n. the members of a household.

menagerie n. a small zoo.

mend v. **1** restore to the correct or working condition. **2** improve a bad situation.

mendacious adj. untruthful. ■ **mendacity** n.

mendicant adj. living by begging. •n. a beggar.

menhir /men-**heer**/ n. a tall stone set up in prehistoric times.

menial adj. (of work) unskilled and lacking status. •n. a person with a menial job.

meningitis n. inflammation of the membranes enclosing the brain and spinal cord.

meniscus n. (pl. **menisci**) **1** the curved surface of a liquid in a tube. **2** a lens convex on one side and concave on the other.

menopause n. the period in a woman's life when menstruation gradually stops. ■ **menopausal** adj.

menorah n. a large branched candlestick used in Jewish worship.

menstruate v. discharge blood from the lining of the womb each month. ■ **menstrual** adj. **menstruation** n.

mensuration n. measurement, esp. in geometry.

mental adj. **1** of the mind. **2** informal mad. □ **mental age** a person's mental ability expressed as the age at which an average

person reaches that ability. ■ **mentally** adv.

mentality n. (pl. **mentalities**) a typical way of thinking.

menthol n. a substance in peppermint oil used in decongestants etc. ■ **mentholated** adj.

mention v. refer to briefly. •n. a reference to someone or something.

mentor n. an experienced person acting as an adviser.

menu n. **1** a list of dishes available. **2** a list of options on a computer screen.

meow var. of **MIAOW**.

MEP abbrev. Member of the European Parliament.

mercantile adj. of trade.

mercenary adj. motivated by the desire to make money. •n. (pl. **mercenaries**) a professional soldier hired by a foreign army.

merchandise n. goods for sale. •v. promote the sale of.

merchant n. a trader who sells goods in large quantities. □ **merchant bank** a bank whose customers are large businesses. **merchantman** a ship carrying merchandise. **merchant navy** a country's commercial shipping.

merchantable adj. suitable for sale.

merciful adj. **1** showing mercy. **2** giving relief from suffering. ■ **mercifully** adv.

mercurial adj. **1** tending to change mood suddenly. **2** of mercury.

mercury n. a heavy liquid metallic element.

mercy n. (pl. **mercies**) **1** pity or forgiveness shown towards someone in your power. **2** something to be grateful for. □ **at the mercy of** in the power of. ■ **merciless** adj. **mercilessly** adv.

mere adj. **1** no more than what is specified. **2** (**the merest**) the slightest. • n. literary a lake. ■ **merely** adv.

meretricious adj. superficially attractive but having no real value.

merge v. **1** combine into a whole. **2** blend gradually.

merger n. a merging of two organizations into one.

meridian n. a circle passing at the same longitude through a given place on the earth's surface and the poles.

meringue /muh-rang/ n. beaten egg whites and sugar baked until crisp.

merino n. (pl. **merinos**) a soft woollen material.

merit n. **1** excellence. **2** a good point or quality. • v. (**meriting**, **merited**) deserve.

meritocracy n. (pl. **meritocracies**) a society in which power is held by those with the greatest ability.

meritorious adj. deserving reward or praise.

merlin n. a small falcon.

mermaid n. a mythical sea creature with a woman's head and body and a fish's tail.

merry adj. (**merrier**, **merriest**) **1** cheerful and lively. **2** informal slightly drunk. ■ **merry-go-round** a funfair ride consisting of a revolving platform with model horses or cars. **merrymaking** lively celebration and fun. ■ **merrily** adj. **merriment** n.

mescaline n. a hallucinogenic drug.

Mesdames pl. of MADAME.

Mesdemoiselles pl. of MADEMOISELLE.

mesh n. **1** material made of a network of wire or thread. **2** the spacing of the strands of a net. • v. **1** be in harmony. **2** become entangled. **3** (of a gearwheel) lock together with another.

mesmeric /mez-me-rik/ adj. hypnotic.

mesmerize (or **-ise**) v. completely capture the attention of.

mess n. **1** a dirty or untidy state. **2** a state of confusion or difficulty. **3** a place where members of the armed forces eat and relax. • v. **1** make untidy or dirty. **2** (**mess about/around**) behave in a silly or playful way.

message n. **1** a spoken, written, or electronic communication. **2** a significant point or central theme. • v. send a message to.

messenger n. a person who carries a message.

Messiah n. **1** (in Judaism) the person who will be sent by God as the saviour of the Jewish people. **2** Jesus regarded by Christians as this saviour. ■ **messianic** adj.

Messieurs pl. of MONSIEUR.

Messrs pl. of MR.

messy adj. (**messier**, **messiest**) **1** untidy or dirty. **2** confused and difficult. ■ **messily** adv. **messiness** n.

met past & past part. of MEET.

metabolism n. the process by which food is used for growth or energy. ■ **metabolic** adj.

metabolize (or **-ise**) v. process by metabolism.

metacarpus n. (pl. **metacarpi**) the set of bones between the wrist and fingers.

m

metal n. **1** a hard, shiny, solid material which conducts electricity and heat. **2** broken stone used in making roads. ■ **metallic** adj.

metalled adj. (of a road) having a hard surface.

metallurgy n. the study of metals. ■ **metallurgist** n.

metamorphic adj. (of rock) changed by heat, pressure, etc.

metamorphosis n. (pl. **metamorphoses**) a change in form or nature. ■ **metamorphose** v.

metaphor n. a word or phrase used to represent or stand for something else (e.g. food for thought). ■ **metaphorical** (or **metaphoric**) adj. **metaphorically** adv.

metaphysics n. philosophy concerning the nature of existence, truth, and knowledge. ■ **metaphysical** adj.

metatarsus n. (pl. **metatarsi**) the set of bones between the ankle and the toes.

mete v. (**mete out**) deal out justice, punishment, etc.

meteor n. a small body of matter from outer space appearing as a streak of light.

meteoric adj. **1** of meteors or meteorites. **2** (of progress) very rapid.

meteorite n. a meteor that has fallen to earth.

meteorology n. the study of atmospheric conditions for weather forecasting. ■ **meteorological** adj. **meteorologist** n.

meter n. **1** a device that measures and records the quantity, degree, or rate of something. **2** US = **METRE**. • v. measure with a meter.

methadone n. a powerful pain-killing drug.

methane n. a flammable gas.

methanol n. a poisonous flammable alcohol, used to make methylated spirit.

method n. **1** a way of doing something. **2** the quality of being well organized.

methodical adj. well organized and systematic. ■ **methodically** adv.

Methodist n. a member of a Protestant group originating in the 18th century. • adj. of Methodists. ■ **Methodism** n.

methodology n. (pl. **methodologies**) a system of methods used in a particular field.

meths n. informal methylated spirit.

methyl n. a chemical unit derived from methane.

methylated spirit n. a form of alcohol used as a solvent or fuel.

meticulous adj. careful and precise. ■ **meticulously** adv. **meticulousness** n.

métier /may-ti-ay/ n. a person's trade, profession, or special ability.

metre (US **meter**) n. **1** a metric unit of length equal to 100 cm (approx. 39.37 inches). **2** rhythm in poetry.

metric adj. of or using the metric system. □ **metric system** the decimal measuring system based on the metre, litre, and gram. **metric ton** a unit of weight equal to 1,000 kg (2,205 lb).

metrical adj. of poetic metre.

metricate v. convert to a metric system. ■ **metrication** n.

metro n. (pl. **metros**) an underground railway.

metronome → middle

metronome n. a device for indicating tempo while practising music.

metropolis n. the main city of a country or region.
■ **metropolitan** adj.

mettle n. spirit and strength of character.

mew v. (of a cat or gull) make a high-pitched cry. • n. a mewing cry.

mews n. (pl. mews) a row of houses converted from stables.

mezzanine n. a partial floor of a building, between two full floors.

mezzo /met-soh/ (or **mezzo-soprano**) n. (pl. mezzos) a female singer with a voice pitched between soprano and contralto.

mg abbrev. milligrams.

MHz abbrev. megahertz.

miaow (or **meow**) n. the cry of a cat. • v. make a miaow.

miasma n. an unpleasant or unhealthy atmosphere.

mica /my-kuh/ n. a mineral found as tiny shiny scales in rocks.

mice pl. of MOUSE.

microbe n. a microorganism, esp. one that causes disease.
■ **microbial** adj.

microbiology n. the study of microorganisms.

microchip n. a miniature electronic circuit made from a tiny wafer of silicon.

microclimate n. the climate of a very small area.

microcosm n. a thing representing something much larger.

microfiche (or **microfilm**) n. a piece of film containing greatly reduced photos of the pages of a book etc.

microlight n. a very small, light aircraft for one or two people.

micrometer n. an instrument for measuring small distances or thicknesses.

micron n. one millionth of a metre.

microorganism n. a microscopic organism.

microphone n. an instrument for changing sound waves into electrical energy which is then amplified or transmitted.

microprocessor n. an integrated circuit which can function as the main part of a computer.

microscope n. an instrument for magnifying very small objects.

microscopic adj. **1** so small as to be visible only with a microscope. **2** of a microscope.
■ **microscopically** adv.

microsurgery n. surgery performed using very small instruments and a microscope.

microwave n. **1** an electromagnetic wave with a wavelength in the range 0.001–0.3 m. **2** an oven that uses microwaves to cook or heat food.

mid adj. in the middle.

midday n. 12 o'clock in the day.

midden n. a heap of dung or rubbish.

middle adj. **1** at an equal distance from the edges or ends of something. **2** medium in rank, quality, etc. • n. a middle point or position.
□ **middle-aged** in the period of life between about 45 and 60. **Middle Ages** the period of European history from about 1000 to 1450. **middle class** the social class between the upper and working classes. **Middle East** an area of SW Asia and northern Africa, stretching from the Mediterranean to Pakistan.

m

middleman a person who buys goods from producers and sells them to consumers. **middle-of-the-road** (of music) popular but rather unadventurous.

middleweight a weight in boxing etc. above welterweight.

middling adj. average in size, amount, or rank.

midfield n. the central part of a sports field. ■ **midfielder** n.

midge n. a small biting fly.

midget n. a very small person.

Midlands pl. n. the inland counties of central England.

midnight n. 12 o'clock at night.

midriff n. the front of the body between the chest and the waist.

midshipman n. a low-ranking officer in the Royal Navy.

midst n. the middle.

midway adv. halfway.

midwife n. a nurse trained to assist at childbirth.

mien /meen/ n. a person's look or manner.

might aux. v. **1** used to express possibility. **2** used in polite questions and requests. • n. great power or strength.

mighty adj. (**mightier**, **mightiest**) powerful or strong. • adv. informal very. ■ **mightily** adv.

migraine n. a very severe headache.

migrant n. **1** a worker who travels to find work. **2** a migrating animal. • adj. migrating or having migrated.

migrate v. **1** (of an animal) move from one area to another according to the seasons. **2** move to a new area to find work.
■ **migration** n. **migratory** adj.

mike n. informal a microphone.

mild adj. **1** not severe, harsh, or extreme. **2** (of weather) fairly warm. **3** not strong in flavour. **4** gentle. ■ **mildly** adv. **mildness** n.

mildew n. a coating of tiny fungi on plants or damp material.
■ **mildewed** adj.

mile n. a unit of length equal to 1,760 yds (approx. 1.609 km). □ **mileage** a number of miles covered. **milestone 1** a stone showing the distance to a particular place. **2** a significant event or stage.

milieu /mee-lyer/ n. (pl. **milieux** or **milieus**) a person's social environment.

militant adj. prepared to take aggressive action in support of a cause. • n. a militant person.
■ **militancy** n.

militarism n. belief in the value of military strength. ■ **militaristic** adj.

military adj. of soldiers or the armed forces. • n. (**the military**) the armed forces. ■ **militarily** adv.

militate v. (**militate against**) be a powerful factor in preventing.

! Don't confuse **militate** with **mitigate**, which means 'make less severe'.

militia n. a military force made up of trained civilians.

milk n. **1** a white fluid produced by female mammals to feed their young. **2** cows' milk as a drink for humans. • v. **1** draw milk from. **2** exploit a person or situation. □ **milk float** an electric van for delivering milk to houses. **milkman** a man who delivers milk to houses. **milkshake** a cold drink made from milk whisked with a flavouring. **milksop** a timid person. **milk tooth** a temporary tooth in a child or young mammal. ■ **milky** adj.

mill n. **1** a building with machinery for grinding grain into flour. **2** a device for grinding a specified substance. **3** a building containing machinery for manufacturing. •v. **1** grind in a mill. **2** (**milled**) (of a coin) having ribbed markings on the edge. **3** (**mill about/around**) move around in a confused mass. □ **millstone 1** each of a pair of circular stones for grinding grain. **2** a burden of responsibility.

millennium n. (pl. **millennia** or **millenniums**) a period of a thousand years. ■ **millennial** adj.

❗ Two ls, two ns: mi**ll**e**nn**ium.

miller n. a person who owns or works in a grain mill.

millet n. a cereal plant used to make flour etc.

millibar n. a unit for measuring atmospheric pressure.

milligram (or **milligramme**) n. one thousandth of a gram.

millilitre (US **milliliter**) n. one thousandth of a litre.

millimetre (US **millimeter**) n. one thousandth of a metre.

milliner n. a person who makes or sells women's hats. ■ **millinery** n.

million n. one thousand thousand; 1,000,000. **2** (**millions**) informal very many. ■ **millionth** adj. & n.

millionaire n. a person who has more than one million pounds or dollars.

millipede n. a small invertebrate animal with many legs.

millisecond n. one thousandth of a second.

milometer n. an instrument on a vehicle recording the number of miles travelled.

mime n. the use of gestures and expressions only to tell a story or convey feelings. •v. use mime to act out.

mimic v. (**mimicking**, **mimicked**) imitate the voice or behaviour of. •n. a person skilled in mimicking. ■ **mimicry** n.

mimosa n. an acacia tree with yellow flowers.

minaret n. a slender tower on or by a mosque.

mince v. **1** cut meat into very small pieces. **2** walk in an affected way with short, quick steps. •n. minced meat. □ **mincemeat** a mixture of dried fruit, sugar, etc. **mince pie** a small pie containing mincemeat. **not mince (your) words** speak plainly. ■ **mincer** n.

mind n. **1** the faculty of consciousness and thought. **2** a person's intellect or memory. **3** a person's attention or will. •v. **1** be distressed or annoyed by. **2** remember to do. **3** watch out for. **4** take care of temporarily. **5** (**minded**) inclined to think in a particular way: liberal-minded. ■ **minder** n.

mindful adj. conscious or aware of something.

mindless adj. **1** acting or done without thought. **2** simple and repetitive. ■ **mindlessly** adv.

mine[1] possess. pron. belonging to or associated with me.

mine[2] n. **1** a hole or passage dug in the earth for extracting coal etc. **2** an abundant source. **3** a bomb placed on or in the ground or water, which explodes on contact. •v. **1** obtain from a mine. **2** lay explosive mines on. □ **minefield 1** an area planted with explosive mines. **2** a situation presenting hidden dangers.

minesweeper n. a warship equipped for detecting and removing explosive mines.

miner n. a person who works in a mine.

mineral n. an inorganic natural substance, e.g. copper. □ **mineral water** water containing dissolved mineral salts.

mineralogy n. the scientific study of minerals.
■ **mineralogical** adj.
mineralogist n.

minestrone /mi-ni-stroh-ni/ n. an Italian soup containing vegetables and pasta.

mingle v. **1** mix together. **2** move around and chat at a party.

mini adj. very small of its kind. •n. (pl. **minis**) a miniskirt.

miniature adj. much smaller than normal. •n. a miniature thing.
■ **miniaturize** (or **-ise**) v.

minibus n. a small bus for about twelve people.

minicab n. an ordinary car that is used as a taxi but which must be ordered in advance.

minidisc n. a disc similar to a small CD, used for recording and playing back sound or data.

minim n. a musical note lasting as long as two crotchets.

minimal adj. of a minimum amount, quantity, or degree.
■ **minimally** adv.

minimalist adj. **1** (of art) using simple forms and structures. **2** deliberately simple or basic in design. •n. an artist who uses

simple forms and structures.
■ **minimalism** n.

minimize (or **-ise**) v. **1** reduce to a minimum. **2** represent as less important than in reality.

minimum n. (pl. **minima** or **minimums**) the smallest amount or extent possible. •adj. smallest in amount or extent.

minion n. a lowly worker or assistant.

miniskirt n. a very short skirt.

minister n. **1** a head of a government department. **2** a senior diplomatic representative. **3** a member of the clergy. •v. (**minister to**) attend to the needs of. ■ **ministerial** adj.

ministrations pl. n. the providing of help or care.

ministry n. (pl. **ministries**) **1** a government department headed by a minister. **2** a period of government under one Prime Minister. **3** the work of a minister of religion.

mink n. a small stoat-like animal farmed for its fur.

minnow n. a small fish.

minor adj. **1** not important or serious. **2** Music (of a scale) having intervals of a semitone between the 2nd and 3rd, 5th and 6th, and 7th and 8th notes. •n. a person under the age of full legal responsibility.

minority n. (pl. **minorities**) **1** the smaller number or part. **2** a small group differing from the majority in race, religion, etc.

minster n. a large church.

minstrel n. a medieval singer or musician.

mint n. **1** a herb used in cookery. **2** the flavour of mint. **3** a mint sweet. **4** a place where money is

made. •v. make coins. □ **in mint condition** as good as new.
■ **minty** adj.

minuet n. a slow ballroom dance.

minus prep. **1** with the subtraction of. **2** falling below zero by a specific number of degrees. **3** informal lacking. •adj. **1** (before a number) below zero. **2** (after a grade) slightly below. •n. the symbol −.

minuscule adj. very tiny.

! -u-, not -i- in the middle: minuscule.

minute[1] /min-it/ n. **1** one sixtieth of an hour or degree. **2** informal a very short time. **3** (**minutes**) a written summary of the points discussed at a meeting. •v. record in the minutes of a meeting.

minute[2] /my-nyoot/ adj. **1** very small. **2** precise and careful.
■ **minutely** adv.

minutiae /mi-nyoo-shi-ee/ pl. n. small or precise details.

minx n. a cheeky girl or young woman.

miracle n. **1** a welcome event so extraordinary that it is believed to be the work of God or a saint. **2** a remarkable event or thing.

miraculous adj. very surprising and welcome. ■ **miraculously** adv.

mirage n. an effect caused by hot air, in which a sheet of water seems to appear in a desert or on a hot road.

mire n. a boggy area.

mirror n. a surface which reflects a clear image. •v. reflect.

mirth n. laughter. ■ **mirthful** adj. **mirthless** adj.

misadventure n. a mishap.
□ **death by misadventure** death

caused by accident and not involving crime.

misanthrope n. a person who dislikes other people.
■ **misanthropic** adj. **misanthropy** n.

misapprehension n. a mistaken belief.

misappropriate v. dishonestly take for your own use.
■ **misappropriation** n.

misbehave v. behave badly.

miscalculate v. calculate wrongly. ■ **miscalculation** n.

miscarriage n. the birth of a fetus before it can survive independently. □ **miscarriage of justice** a failure of a court of law to achieve justice.

miscarry v. (**miscarrying**, **miscarried**) **1** have a miscarriage. **2** (of a plan) fail.

miscellaneous adj. consisting of many different kinds.

miscellany n. (pl. **miscellanies**) a collection of different things.

mischance n. bad luck.

mischief n. **1** playful bad behaviour. **2** harm or trouble.

mischievous adj. **1** full of mischief. **2** intended to cause trouble.
■ **mischievously** adv.

! The ending is -ous, not -ious: mischievous.

misconceived adj. badly judged or planned.

misconception n. a mistaken idea or belief.

misconduct n. bad behaviour.

misconstrue v. interpret wrongly. ■ **misconstruction** n.

miscreant n. a wrongdoer.

misdeed n. a wrongful act.

m

misdemeanour (US **misde-meanor**) n. a minor wrongdoing.

miser n. a person who hoards money and spends as little as possible. ■ **miserliness** n. **miserly** adj.

miserable adj. **1** very unhappy. **2** causing unhappiness. ■ **miserably** adv.

misery n. (pl. **miseries**) **1** great unhappiness. **2** a cause of this. **3** informal a constantly miserable person.

misfire v. **1** fail to produce the intended result. **2** (of an engine) fail to ignite the fuel correctly. **3** (of a gun) fail to fire properly.

misfit n. a person whose behaviour or views set them apart from others.

misfortune n. **1** bad luck. **2** an unfortunate event.

misgivings pl. n. feelings of doubt or worry.

misguided adj. showing bad judgement.

mishandle v. handle badly or wrongly.

mishap n. an unlucky accident.

mishmash n. a confused mixture.

misinform v. give wrong information to. ■ **misinformation** n.

misinterpret v. interpret wrongly. ■ **misinterpretation** n.

misjudge v. **1** form a wrong opinion of. **2** estimate wrongly.

mislay v. (**mislaying, mislaid**) lose temporarily.

mislead v. (**misleading, misled**) give a wrong impression or wrong information to.

mismanage v. manage badly or wrongly. ■ **mismanagement** n.

mismatch n. a combination of people or things that do not

match. • v. match unsuitably or incorrectly.

misnomer n. a wrongly applied name or description.

misogynist /mi-**soj**-uh-nist/ n. a man who hates women. ■ **misogyny** n.

misplace v. **1** put in the wrong place. **2** (**misplaced**) unwise or inappropriate.

misprint n. a mistake in printed text.

misquote v. quote inaccurately.

misread v. (**misreading, misread**) read or interpret wrongly.

misrepresent v. give a misleading account of. ■ **misrepresentation** n.

misrule n. **1** bad government. **2** disorder.

Miss n. a title for an unmarried woman or girl.

miss v. **1** fail to hit or reach. **2** be too late for. **3** fail to see or hear. **4** fail to be present at. **5** avoid. **6** (**miss out**) omit. **7** feel the loss or absence of. • n. a failure to hit or reach something.

misshapen adj. not having the normal shape.

missile n. an object thrown or fired at a target.

missing adj. lost or absent.

mission n. **1** an important assignment. **2** an organization involved in a long-term assignment abroad. **3** a strongly felt aim or calling. **4** the work of teaching people about Christianity.

missionary n. (pl. **missionaries**) a person sent to teach others about Christianity.

missive n. a letter.

m

misspell v. (**misspelling, misspelt** or **misspelled**) spell wrongly.

mist n. tiny water droplets in the air or on a surface. •v. cover or become covered with mist.

mistake n. **1** a thing that is incorrect. **2** an error of judgement. •v. (**mistaking, mistook**; past part. **mistaken**) **1** be wrong about. **2** (**mistake for**) confuse with.

mister var. of **MR**.

mistletoe n. a plant with white berries, growing on trees as a parasite.

mistral n. a strong north-westerly wind in southern France.

mistreat v. treat badly or unfairly. ■ **mistreatment** n.

mistress n. **1** a woman in a position of authority. **2** a woman having a sexual relationship with a man married to someone else. **3** a female schoolteacher.

mistrial n. a trial made invalid through a mistake in proceedings.

mistrust v. have no trust in. •n. lack of trust.

misty adj. (**mistier, mistiest**) **1** covered with mist. **2** indistinct.

misunderstand v. (**misunderstanding, misunderstood**) fail to understand correctly. ■ **misunderstanding** n.

misuse v. **1** use wrongly. **2** treat badly. •n. wrong use.

mite n. **1** a tiny animal like a spider. **2** a small child or animal. **3** a very small amount.

mitigate v. make less severe or serious. ■ **mitigation** n.

> ! Don't confuse **mitigate** with **militate**: **militate against** means 'be a powerful factor in preventing'.

mitre (US **miter**) n. **1** a bishop's pointed headdress. **2** a joint between two pieces of wood cut to form a right angle.

mitt n. a mitten.

mitten n. a glove with a single section for all four fingers.

mix v. **1** combine or be combined. **2** make by mixing ingredients. **3** (**mix up**) confuse or spoil the arrangement of. **4** meet people socially. •n. a mixture. ■ **mixer** n.

mixture n. **1** a substance made by mixing. **2** (**a mixture of**) a combination of different but distinct things.

mizzen (or **mizzenmast**) n. the mast behind a ship's main mast.

ml abbrev. millilitres.

mm abbrev. millimetres.

MMR abbrev. measles, mumps, and rubella (a vaccination given to children).

mnemonic /ni-mon-ik/ n. a pattern of words or letters used to aid the memory.

moan n. **1** a low mournful sound. **2** a grumble. •v. **1** make a moan. **2** grumble.

moat n. a wide water-filled ditch round a castle or town.

mob n. **1** a disorderly crowd. **2** informal a group. •v. (**mobbing, mobbed**) crowd round in an unruly way.

mobile adj. able to move or be moved easily. •n. **1** a decorative structure hung so as to turn freely in the air. **2** (or **mobile phone**) a portable phone. ■ **mobility** n.

mobilize (or **-ise**) v. organize troops for active service. ■ **mobilization** n.

moccasin n. a soft flat shoe.

mocha /mok-uh/ n. a drink of coffee and chocolate.

m

mock v. tease or imitate in an un-kind way. • adj. not genuine or real. □ **mock-up** a model for testing or study.

mockery n. (pl. **mockeries**)
1 ridicule. 2 an absurd or worthless version of something.

mode n. 1 a way of doing something. 2 a style in clothes, art, etc.

model n. 1 a three-dimensional copy of a person or thing. 2 something used as an example. 3 an excellent example of a quality. 4 a person employed to pose for an artist or to wear and display clothes. 5 a particular version of a product. • v. (**modelling**, **modelled**; US **modeling**, **modeled**) 1 make a model of. 2 (**model on**) use as an example for. 3 work as a model.

modem n. a device connecting a computer to a phone line.

moderate adj. 1 average in amount, intensity, etc. 2 not politically extreme. • n. a person with moderate views. • v. make or become moderate. ■ **moderately** adv. **moderation** n.

moderator n. a person who helps to solve a dispute.

modern adj. 1 of the present or recent times. 2 involving up-to-date techniques or equipment. ■ **modernity** n. **modernize** (or **-ise**) v.

modernism n. modern ideas, methods, or styles. ■ **modernist** n. & adj.

modest adj. 1 not boasting about yourself. 2 relatively moderate or small. 3 not showing off the body. ■ **modestly** adv. **modesty** n.

modicum n. a small amount.

modify v. (**modifying**, **modified**) make small changes to. ■ **modification** n.

modish adj. fashionable.

modulate v. 1 regulate. 2 vary in tone or pitch. ■ **modulation** n.

module n. 1 each of a set of parts or units that can be used to create a more complex structure. 2 a unit forming part of a course of study. ■ **modular** adj.

modus operandi n. a way of doing something.

mogul n. an important or powerful person.

mohair n. a yarn made from the hair of the angora goat.

moiety /moy-it-ee/ n. (pl. **moieties**) a half.

moist adj. slightly wet; damp. ■ **moisten** v.

moisture n. tiny drops of water making something damp.

moisturize (or **-ise**) v. make the skin less dry. ■ **moisturizer** n.

molar n. a grinding tooth at the back of the mouth.

molasses n. a thick brown liquid obtained from raw sugar.

mold etc. US = **mould** etc.

mole n. 1 a small furry burrowing mammal. 2 a spy within an organization. 3 a small dark patch on the skin. 4 a pier or breakwater. □ **molehill** n. a small mound of earth thrown up by a mole.

molecule n. a group of atoms forming the smallest unit that can take part in a chemical reaction. ■ **molecular** adj.

molest v. 1 assault sexually. 2 dated harass. ■ **molestation** n. **molester** n.

mollify v. (**mollifying**, **mollified**) cause to feel less angry.

mollusc → monolingual

mollusc (*US* **mollusk**) *n.* an animal with a soft body and often an external shell.

mollycoddle *v.* pamper.

Molotov cocktail *n.* a bomb made of a bottle of flammable liquid.

molt *US* = **MOULT**.

molten *adj.* made liquid by heat.

molybdenum /muh-**lib**-duh-nuhm/ *n.* a brittle metallic element.

moment *n.* **1** an exact point or brief period of time. **2** importance.

momentary *adj.* very brief or short-lived. ■ **momentarily** *adv.*

momentous *adj.* very important.

momentum *n.* **1** the force gained by a moving object. **2** the force caused by the development of something.

monarch *n.* a king or queen. ■ **monarchical** *adj.*

monarchist *n.* a supporter of monarchy.

monarchy *n.* (*pl.* **monarchies**) **1** government by a monarch. **2** a state ruled by a monarch.

monastery *n.* (*pl.* **monasteries**) a community of monks living under religious vows.

monastic *adj.* of monks or nuns or their communities.

Monday *n.* the day before Tuesday.

monetarism *n.* the theory that inflation is best controlled by limiting the supply of money. ■ **monetarist** *n.* & *adj.*

monetary *adj.* of money.

money *n.* **1** coins and banknotes. **2** wealth. **3** payment or profit. **4** (**moneys** or **monies**) sums of money.

moneyed *adj.* wealthy.

Mongol *n.* **1** a person from Mongolia. **2** (**mongol**) *offens.* a person with Down's syndrome.

mongoose *n.* (*pl.* **mongooses**) a small carnivorous mammal of Africa and Asia.

mongrel *n.* a dog of no particular breed.

moniker *n.* informal a name.

monitor *n.* **1** a person or device that monitors something. **2** a television used to view a picture from a camera or a display from a computer. **3** a school pupil with special duties. •*v.* keep under observation.

monk *n.* a man belonging to a religious community.

monkey *n.* (*pl.* **monkeys**) **1** a small primate, usu. with a long tail and living in trees. **2** a mischievous child. •*v.* (**monkeying, monkeyed**) **1** (**monkey about/ around**) behave in a silly way. **2** (**monkey with**) tamper with. ❑ **monkey wrench** a spanner with large adjustable jaws.

mono *n.* monophonic sound.

monochrome *adj.* produced in black and white or in tones of one colour.

monocle *n.* a single lens worn at one eye.

monoculture *n.* the cultivation of only one crop in an area.

monogamy *n.* the practice of having only one husband or wife at a time. ■ **monogamous** *adj.*

monogram *n.* a design of interwoven letters, usu. a person's initials. ■ **monogrammed** *adj.*

monograph *n.* a scholarly written study about a single subject.

monolingual *adj.* speaking or expressed in one language.

m

monolith n. a large single upright block of stone. ■ **monolithic** adj.

monologue n. a long speech.

monomania n. an obsession with one thing. ■ **monomaniac** n.

monophonic adj. (of sound reproduction) using only one transmission channel.

monoplane n. an aircraft with one pair of wings.

monopolize (or **-ise**) v. dominate or take control of.

monopoly n. (pl. **monopolies**) the control of the supply of a product or service by one person or organization.

monorail n. a railway in which the track consists of a single rail.

monosodium glutamate n. a compound used to add flavour to food.

monosyllable n. a word of one syllable. ■ **monosyllabic** adj.

monotheism n. the belief that there is only one god. ■ **monotheist** n. **monotheistic** adj.

monotone n. a level unchanging tone of voice.

monotonous adj. dull because lacking in change or variety. ■ **monotonously** adv. **monotony** n.

monoxide n. an oxide with one atom of oxygen.

Monsieur /muh-**syer**/ n. (pl. **Messieurs**) a form of address for a French man.

monsoon n. **1** a seasonal wind in the Indian subcontinent and SE Asia. **2** the rainy season accompanying this.

monster n. **1** a large, frightening imaginary creature. **2** a very cruel person. • adj. informal very large.

monstrosity n. (pl. **monstrosities**) **1** a very large and ugly object. **2** an evil act.

monstrous adj. **1** very large and ugly or frightening. **2** very evil or wrong. ■ **monstrously** adv.

montage /mon-**tahzh**/ n. a picture or film made by putting together pieces from other pictures or films.

month n. **1** each of the twelve periods into which a year is divided. **2** a period of 28 days. ■ **monthly** adj. & adv.

monument n. **1** a statue or structure built to commemorate a person or event. **2** a structure or site of historical importance.

monumental adj. **1** very large or impressive. **2** acting as a monument.

moo v. (of a cow) make a long, deep sound.

mooch v. informal pass time aimlessly.

mood n. **1** a temporary state of mind. **2** a fit of bad temper.

moody adj. (**moodier**, **moodiest**) **1** having sudden changes of mood. **2** gloomy or sulky. ■ **moodily** adv.

moon n. **1** the natural satellite of the earth. **2** a natural satellite of any planet. • v. behave in a dreamy way. □ **moonscape** a rocky landscape like that of the moon. **moonshine 1** foolish ideas. **2** US illegally made alcoholic drink. **moonstone** a white semi-precious stone.

moonlight n. the light of the moon. • v. (**moonlighting**, **moonlighted**) informal do a second job without declaring it for tax purposes. ■ **moonlit** adj.

Moor n. a member of a NW African Muslim people. ∎ **Moorish** adj.

moor. n. an area of high, open uncultivated land. •v. fasten a boat to the shore or to an anchor. ◻ **moorhen** a small black waterbird. **mooring** (or **moorings**) 1 a place where a boat is moored. 2 the ropes for mooring a boat.

moose (pl. **moose**) = ELK.

moot adj. uncertain or undecided: *a moot point.*

mop n. 1 a bundle of thick strings or a sponge on a stick, used for wiping floors. 2 a thick mass of hair. •v. (**mopping, mopped**) clean or soak up by wiping.

mope v. be listless and unhappy.

moped n. a light motorcycle.

moraine n. rocks and stones deposited by a glacier.

moral adj. 1 concerned with the principles of right and wrong behaviour. 2 following accepted standards of behaviour. •n. 1 a moral lesson learned from a story or experience. 2 (**morals**) standards of good behaviour. ◻ **moral victory** a defeat that can be interpreted as a victory because you have done the right thing. ∎ **morally** adv.

morale n. a feeling of confidence and satisfaction.

moralist n. a person promoting strict moral views.

morality n. (pl. **moralities**) 1 moral principles or behaviour. 2 the extent to which an action is right or wrong.

moralize (or **-ise**) v. comment on moral matters in a disapproving way.

morass n. 1 a boggy area. 2 a complicated situation.

moratorium n. (pl. **moratoriums** or **moratoria**) a temporary ban on an activity.

morbid adj. 1 having a strong interest in death and disease. 2 of disease. ∎ **morbidity** n. **morbidly** adv.

mordant adj. (of wit) sharply sarcastic. •n. a substance combining with a dye to fix it.

more n. & pron. a greater or additional amount or degree. •adv. 1 to a greater extent. 2 again. ◻ **moreover** besides.

mores /mor-ayz/ pl. n. the customs and conventions of a community.

morgue n. a mortuary.

moribund adj. at the point of death.

Mormon n. a member of the Church of Jesus Christ of Latter-Day Saints.

morning n. the part of the day before noon. ◻ **morning sickness** nausea occurring during early pregnancy.

moron n. informal a stupid person. ∎ **moronic** adj.

morose adj. sullen and bad-tempered. ∎ **morosely** adv.

morphine n. a painkilling drug obtained from opium.

morphology n. the study of forms, esp. of words. ∎ **morphological** adj.

morris dancing n. traditional English folk dancing.

Morse code n. a code in which letters are represented by long and short sounds or flashes of light.

morsel n. a small piece of food.

m

mortal adj. 1 having to die at some time. 2 causing death. •n. a human being. ∎ **mortally** adv.

mortality n. 1 the state of being mortal. 2 death. 3 the number of deaths in a particular place or period.

mortar n. 1 a mixture of lime, cement, sand, and water for holding bricks or stones together. 2 a bowl in which substances are crushed with a pestle. 3 a short cannon. □ **mortar board** an academic cap with a flat square top.

mortgage n. 1 a legal agreement by which a person takes out a loan using their house as security. 2 the amount of money lent in a mortgage. •v. transfer a property to a creditor as security for a loan.

mortgagee n. the lender in a mortgage.

mortgagor n. the borrower in a mortgage.

mortician n. US an undertaker.

mortify v. (**mortifying, mortified**) embarrass or humiliate. ∎ **mortification** n.

mortise (or **mortice**) n. a slot cut in a piece of wood so as to hold the end of another piece of wood. □ **mortise lock** a lock set into the framework of a door.

mortuary n. (pl. **mortuaries**) a place where corpses are kept until burial or cremation.

mosaic n. a picture or pattern made with small coloured pieces of stone, tile, or glass.

Moslem var. of **MUSLIM**.

mosque n. a Muslim place of worship.

mosquito n. (pl. **mosquitoes**) a small bloodsucking fly.

moss n. a small green spreading plant growing in damp places. ∎ **mossy** adj.

most n. & pron. 1 greatest in amount or degree. 2 the majority of. •adv. 1 to the greatest extent. 2 very.

mostly adv. on the whole; mainly.

MOT n. a compulsory annual safety test of vehicles of more than a specified age.

motel n. a roadside hotel for motorists.

motet n. a short religious choral work.

moth n. an insect like a butterfly, usu. active at night. □ **mothball** a small ball of camphor for keeping moths away from stored clothes.

mother n. 1 a female parent. 2 (**Mother**) the title of the head of a convent. •v. look after kindly and protectively. □ **motherboard** a printed circuit board containing the main components of a computer. **mother-in-law** (pl. **mothers-in-law**) the mother of a person's husband or wife. **motherland** a person's native country. **mother-of-pearl** a pearly substance lining the shells of oysters. **mother tongue** a person's native language. ∎ **motherhood** n. **motherless** adj. **motherly** adj.

motif n. 1 a single or repeated image forming a design. 2 a recurring theme in an artistic work.

motion n. 1 an act of moving. 2 a formal proposal put to a meeting. 3 an emptying of the bowels. •v. direct with a gesture. □ **motion picture** a cinema film. ∎ **motionless** adj.

motivate v. 1 provide with a motive. 2 stimulate the interest of. ■ **motivation** n.

motive n. a person's reason for doing something. • adj. producing motion.

motley adj. varied or assorted.

motocross n. cross-country racing on motorcycles.

motor n. 1 a machine supplying power to drive a device. 2 informal a car. • adj. giving or producing motion. • v. travel by car. □ **motorbike** a motorcycle.

motorboat a boat powered by a motor. **motorcade** a procession of vehicles. **motor vehicle** a road vehicle powered by an engine.

motorway a road for fast long-distance traffic. ■ **motorized** (or **-ised**) adj.

motorcycle n. a two-wheeled vehicle powered by a motor. ■ **motorcyclist** n.

motorist n. a car driver.

mottled adj. marked with patches of a different colour.

motto n. (pl. **mottoes** or **mottos**) a short sentence or phrase expressing a belief or aim.

mould (US **mold**) n. 1 a container into which a liquid is poured to set in a desired shape. 2 a distinctive style or character. 3 a furry growth of tiny fungi on a damp surface. • v. 1 shape an object out of a soft substance. 2 influence the development of. ■ **mouldy** adj.

moulder (US **molder**) v. decay.

moulding (US **molding**) n. a decorative strip of wood, stone, or plaster.

moult (US **molt**) v. shed feathers, hair, or skin before new growth.

mound n. 1 a raised mass of earth. 2 a heap.

mount v. 1 climb up or on to. 2 get up on an animal or bicycle to ride it. 3 increase in number or intensity. 4 organize a course of action. 5 put or fix in place. • n. 1 a support or setting. 2 a horse for riding. 3 (in names) a mountain.

mountain n. 1 a very high, steep hill. 2 a large pile or quantity. □ **mountain bike** a sturdy bicycle with broad deep-treaded tyres.

mountaineering n. the sport or activity of climbing mountains. ■ **mountaineer** n.

mountainous adj. 1 having many mountains. 2 huge.

mourn v. feel deep sorrow about the death or loss of. ■ **mourner** n.

mournful adj. very sad or depressing. ■ **mournfully** adv.

mourning n. 1 the expression of deep sorrow for someone who has died. 2 black clothes worn in a period of mourning.

mouse n. (pl. **mice**) 1 a small rodent with a long tail. 2 a quiet, timid person. 3 (pl. also **mouses**) a small hand-held device controlling the cursor on a computer screen.

moussaka n. a Greek dish of minced lamb and aubergines.

mousse n. 1 a dish made with whipped cream or egg white. 2 a light substance for styling hair.

moustache (US **mustache**) n. a strip of hair on a man's upper lip.

mousy adj. 1 (of hair) light brown. 2 timid.

mouth n. 1 the opening in the body through which food is taken and sounds are made. 2 an opening or entrance. 3 the place where a river enters the sea. • v. 1 move the lips as if to form words. 2 say insincerely. □ **mouth organ** a small instrument played by blowing and sucking. **mouth-piece** a part of a musical instrument etc. put in or against the mouth. **mouthwash** an antiseptic liquid for rinsing the mouth. ■ **mouthful** n.

move v. **1** go or cause to go in a specified direction or way. **2** change in position, state, etc. **3** change the place where you live. **4** take action. **5** make progress. **6** provoke emotion in. •n. **1** an act of moving. **2** a purposeful action. **3** a player's turn in a board game. ■ **movable** (or **moveable**) adj.

movement n. **1** an act of moving. **2** a group with a shared cause. **3** (**movements**) a person's activities during a particular period. **4** a main division of a musical work.

movie n. US a cinema film.

moving adj. arousing sadness or sympathy. ■ **movingly** adv.

mow v. (**mowing, mowed**; past part. **mowed** or **mown**) **1** cut down or trim grass or hay. **2** (**mow down**) kill by gunfire or by knocking down with a vehicle. ■ **mower** n.

mozzarella /mot-suh-**rel**-luh/ n. a firm white Italian cheese.

MP abbrev. Member of Parliament.

mpg abbrev. miles per gallon.

mph abbrev. miles per hour.

Mr n. a title used before a man's name.

Mrs n. a title used before a married woman's name.

MS abbrev. **1** manuscript. **2** multiple sclerosis.

Ms n. a title used before a married or unmarried woman's name.

MSc abbrev. Master of Science.

Mt abbrev. Mount.

much pron. a large amount. •adv. **1** to a great extent. **2** often.

mucilage /myoo-si-lij/ n. a sticky solution taken from plants, used in adhesives.

muck n. **1** dirt or rubbish. **2** manure. •v. **1** (**muck up**) informal spoil. **2** (**muck about/around**) informal behave in a silly way. **3** (**muck out**) clean a stable. □ **muckraking** the searching out and publicizing of scandal. ■ **mucky** adj.

mucous adj. of mucus.

mucus n. a slimy substance coating the lining of many body cavities and organs.

mud n. wet, soft earth. □ **mudguard** a curved cover above a wheel to protect against spray from the road. ■ **muddy** adj.

muddle v. **1** bring into a disordered state. **2** confuse. **3** (**muddle along/through**) cope more or less satisfactorily. •n. a muddled state.

muesli /**myooz**-li/ n. a breakfast cereal consisting of oats, dried fruit, and nuts.

muezzin /moo-**ez**-zin/ n. a man who calls Muslims to prayer.

muff n. a tube-shaped furry covering for the hands.

muffin n. **1** a flat bread roll eaten toasted with butter. **2** a small cake.

muffle v. **1** wrap or cover for warmth. **2** make a sound quieter.

muffler n. a scarf.

mufti n. civilian clothes when worn by military or police staff.

mug n. **1** a large cylindrical cup with a handle. **2** informal the face. **3** informal a stupid or gullible person. •v. (**mugging, mugged**) **1** attack and rob in a public place.

2 (**mug up**) *informal* learn a subject intensively. ■ **mugger** *n.*

muggy *adj.* (of the weather) unpleasantly warm and humid.

mulberry *n.* a dark red or white fruit similar to a loganberry.

mulch *n.* leaves, bark, etc. spread around a plant for protection or to enrich the soil. •*v.* cover with mulch.

mule *n.* **1** the offspring of a male donkey and a female horse. **2** a light backless shoe.

mulish *adj.* stubborn.

mull *v.* **1** (**mull over**) think about at length. **2** heat wine with sugar and spices.

mullah *n.* a Muslim learned in Islamic theology and law.

mullet *n.* (*pl.* **mullet**) an edible sea fish.

mulligatawny *n.* a spicy meat soup.

mullion *n.* a vertical bar between the panes in a window.

multi- *comb.* form many.

multicultural *adj.* of or involving several cultural or ethnic groups.

multifarious *adj.* very varied.

multilateral *adj.* involving three or more participants.

multimedia *n.* a computer system providing video and audio material as well as text.

multinational *adj.* involving several countries. •*n.* a company operating in several countries.

multiple *adj.* having or involving several parts. •*n.* a number divisible by another a certain number of times without a remainder. □ **multiple sclerosis** a serious disease of the nervous system that can cause paralysis.

multiplex *n.* a cinema with several separate screens.

multiplicity *n.* (*pl.* **multiplicities**) a large number or variety.

multiply *v.* (**multiplying, multiplied**) **1** add a number to itself a specified number of times. **2** increase in number or quantity. ■ **multiplication** *n.* **multiplier** *n.*

multiracial *adj.* of or involving people of many races.

multitask *v.* **1** (of a computer) operate more than one program at the same time. **2** do several things at once.

multitude *n.* a large number of people or things.

multitudinous *adj.* very numerous.

mum *n. informal* a person's mother. □ **keep mum** say nothing so as not to reveal a secret.

mumble *v.* say indistinctly. •*n.* indistinct speech.

mumbo-jumbo *n. informal* complicated but meaningless language.

mummify *v.* (**mummifying, mummified**) preserve a body as a mummy. ■ **mummification** *n.*

mummy *n.* (*pl.* **mummies**) **1** *informal* a person's mother. **2** (in ancient Egypt) a body preserved for burial by embalming and wrapping in bandages.

mumps *pl. n.* a disease causing swelling of the glands at the sides of the face.

munch *v.* eat steadily and noisily.

mundane *adj.* dull or routine.

municipality *n.* (*pl.* **municipalities**) a town or district with its own local government. ■ **municipal** *adj.*

m

munificent adj. very generous. ■ **munificence** n.

munitions pl. n. weapons, ammunition, etc.

mural n. a painting done directly on a wall.

murder n. the illegal deliberate killing of one person by another. •v. kill illegally and deliberately. ■ **murderer** n. **murderous** adj.

murk n. darkness or fog.

murky adj. 1 dark or dirty. 2 dishonest and secret.

murmur v. 1 say quietly. 2 make a low continuous sound. •n. 1 something said quietly. 2 a low continuous sound.

muscle n. 1 a band of bodily tissue that can contract to move a body part. 2 power or strength. •v. (**muscle in**) informal interfere in another's affairs.

Muscovite n. a person from Moscow.

muscular adj. 1 of the muscles. 2 having well-developed muscles. □ **muscular dystrophy** a condition in which the muscles gradually get weaker. ■ **muscularity** n.

muse n. a woman who is a creative artist's inspiration. •v. be deep in thought.

museum n. a building in which objects of interest or importance are stored and displayed.

mush n. 1 a soft, wet mass. 2 excessive sentimentality. ■ **mushy** adj.

mushroom n. an edible fungus with a domed head on a stalk. •v. increase or develop rapidly.

music n. 1 vocal or instrumental sounds combined in a pleasing way. 2 the art of writing or playing music. 3 the written signs representing music.

musical adj. 1 of or accompanied by music. 2 fond of or skilled in music. 3 pleasant-sounding. •n. a play or film with singing and dancing. ■ **musically** adv.

musician n. a person who plays a musical instrument or writes music.

musicology n. the study of the history and theory of music.

musk n. a strong-smelling substance produced by a type of male deer, used in perfumes. ■ **musky** adj.

musket n. hist. a light gun with a long barrel.

Muslim (or **Moslem**) n. a follower of Islam. •adj. of Muslims or Islam.

muslin n. thin cotton cloth.

mussel n. a small shellfish with a dark shell.

must aux. v. expressing obligation, insistence, or certainty.

mustache US = MOUSTACHE.

mustang n. a small wild horse of the south-western US.

mustard n. a hot-tasting paste eaten with meat etc.

muster v. 1 summon up a feeling. 2 bring troops together. □ **pass muster** be satisfactory.

musty adj. smelling stale or mouldy. ■ **mustiness** n.

mutable adj. liable to change. ■ **mutability** n.

mutant adj. resulting from or showing the effect of mutation. •n. a mutant form.

mutate v. change in form or nature.

mutation n. 1 the process of mutating. 2 a change in genetic

structure resulting in a variant form. **3** a mutant.

mute adj. **1** not speaking. **2** unable to speak. •n. **1** dated a person who is unable to speak. **2** a device used to muffle a musical instrument. •v. **1** muffle the sound of. **2** reduce the intensity of. ■ **mutely** adv.

mutilate v. severely injure or damage. ■ **mutilation** n.

mutinous adj. rebellious.

mutiny n. (pl. **mutinies**) an open rebellion against authority, esp. by soldiers or sailors. •v. (**mutinying, mutinied**) rebel against authority. ■ **mutineer** n.

mutter v. **1** say quietly and indistinctly. **2** talk or grumble in private. •n. something muttered.

mutton n. the flesh of mature sheep as food.

mutual adj. **1** felt or done by two or more people equally. **2** shared by two or more people. ■ **mutuality** n. **mutually** adv.

muzzle n. **1** the nose and mouth of an animal. **2** a guard fitted over an animal's muzzle to stop it biting. **3** the open end of the barrel of a gun. •v. **1** put a muzzle on. **2** prevent from expressing opinions freely.

muzzy adj. **1** dazed or confused. **2** blurred.

MW abbrev. **1** medium wave. **2** megawatts.

my adj. belonging to me.

myalgia n. muscle pain.

mycology n. the study of fungi.

mynah n. an Asian or Australasian bird, some kinds of which can mimic speech.

myopia n. short-sightedness. ■ **myopic** adj.

myriad n. (or **myriads**) a very great number. •adj. countless.

myrrh /mer/ n. a scented resin used in perfumes and incense.

myrtle n. an evergreen shrub with purple berries.

myself pron. **1** used when the speaker is also the person affected by an action. **2** I or me personally.

mysterious adj. difficult or impossible to understand or explain. ■ **mysteriously** adv.

mystery n. (pl. **mysteries**) **1** something that remains unexplained. **2** secrecy. **3** a story dealing with a puzzling crime.

mystic n. a person who seeks to know God through contemplation and prayer. •adj. mystical. ■ **mysticism** n.

mystical adj. **1** having a spiritual significance beyond human understanding. **2** inspiring a sense of mystery and awe.

mystify v. (**mystifying, mystified**) utterly bewilder. ■ **mystification** n.

mystique n. an impressive quality of mystery, glamour, or power.

myth n. **1** a traditional story of early history or explaining a natural event. **2** a widely held but false belief. ■ **mythical** adj.

mythology n. a collection of myths. ■ **mythological** adj.

myxomatosis n. a highly infectious and usu. fatal disease of rabbits.

m

Nn

N *abbrev.* North or Northern.

naan var. of **NAN** (sense 2).

nab *v.* (**nabbing, nabbed**) *informal* **1** catch a wrongdoer. **2** take suddenly.

nacho /na-choh/ *n.* (pl. **nachos**) a small piece of tortilla topped with melted cheese etc.

nadir *n.* the lowest point.

naevus /nee-vuhss/ (US **nevus**) *n.* (pl. **naevi**) a birthmark.

naff *adj. informal* lacking taste or style.

nag *v.* (**nagging, nagged**) **1** harass constantly to do something. **2** be constantly worrying or painful to. • *n. informal* a horse.

naiad /ny-ad/ *n.* (in Greek mythology) a water nymph.

nail *n.* **1** a small metal spike with a flat head, used to join pieces of wood together. **2** a thin hard layer over the tip of a finger or toe. • *v.* **1** fasten with a nail or nails. **2** *informal* catch or arrest.

naive /ny-eev/ *adj.* lacking experience or judgement. ■ **naively** *adv.* **naivety** *n.*

naked *adj.* **1** without clothes. **2** without coverings. **3** not hidden; open. □ **the naked eye** the normal power of the eyes, without using a microscope etc. ■ **nakedness** *n.*

namby-pamby *adj.* feeble or cowardly.

name *n.* **1** a word or words by which someone or something is known. **2** a famous person. **3** a reputation. • *v.* **1** give a name to. **2** identify by name. **3** specify a time etc. □ **namesake** a person or thing with the same name as another.

namely *adv.* that is to say.

nan[1] *n. informal* a person's grandmother.

nan[2] /nahn/ (or **naan**) *n.* a soft flat Indian bread.

nanny *n.* (pl. **nannies**) a woman employed to look after a child in its own home.

nanosecond *n.* one thousand millionth of a second.

nanotechnology *n.* technology on an atomic or molecular scale.

nap *n.* **1** a short sleep during the day. **2** short raised fibres on the surface of some fabrics. • *v.* (**napping, napped**) have a short sleep.

napalm /nay-pahm/ *n.* a jelly-like form of petrol used in firebombs.

nape *n.* the back of the neck.

naphtha /naf-thuh/ *n.* a flammable oil.

naphthalene *n.* a strong-smelling substance used in mothballs.

napkin *n.* a piece of cloth or paper used at meals to protect clothes or wipe the lips.

nappy *n.* (pl. **nappies**) a piece of material worn by a baby to absorb urine and faeces.

narcissism *n.* excessive interest in yourself and your appearance. ■ **narcissistic** *adj.*

narcissus n. (pl. **narcissi** or **narcissuses**) a daffodil with pale outer petals.

narcotic n. **1** an addictive drug affecting mood or behaviour. **2** a drug causing drowsiness or unconsciousness. • adj. of narcotics.

narrate v. **1** tell a story. **2** provide a commentary for. ■ **narration** n. **narrator** n.

narrative n. a story. • adj. of stories or the telling of stories.

narrow adj. **1** of small width in comparison to length. **2** limited in extent, amount, or scope. • v. become or make narrower. • n. (**narrows**) a narrow channel connecting two areas of water. □ **narrowboat** a canal boat less than 7 ft (2.1 metres) wide. **narrow-minded** intolerant. ■ **narrowly** adv.

narwhal n. an Arctic whale with a spiral tusk.

NASA abbrev. (in the US) National Aeronautics and Space Administration.

nasal adj. of the nose. ■ **nasally** adv.

nascent adj. just coming into existence.

nasturtium n. a garden plant with orange, yellow, or red flowers.

nasty adj. (**nastier**, **nastiest**) **1** unpleasant. **2** spiteful. ■ **nastily** adv. **nastiness** n.

natal adj. of the place or time of a person's birth.

nation n. a large group sharing the same culture, language, or history, and inhabiting a particular state or area. ■ **nationwide** adj. & adv.

national adj. **1** of a nation. **2** owned or supported by the state. • n. a

citizen of a particular country. ■ **nationally** adv.

nationalism n. **1** patriotic feeling. **2** belief in independence for a particular country. ■ **nationalist** n. & adj. **nationalistic** adj.

nationality n. (pl. **nationalities**) **1** the status of belonging to a particular nation. **2** an ethnic group.

nationalize (or **-ise**) v. transfer from private to state ownership. ■ **nationalization** n.

native n. **1** a person born in a specified place. **2** a local inhabitant. **3** an animal or plant that lives or grows naturally in a particular area. • adj. **1** associated with a person's place of birth. **2** (of a plant or animal) occurring naturally in a place. **3** in a person's character.

Nativity n. (**the Nativity**) the birth of Jesus.

NATO abbrev. North Atlantic Treaty Organization.

natter v. & n. informal chat.

natty adj. informal smart and fashionable. ■ **nattily** adv.

natural adj. **1** of or produced by nature; not made or caused by humans. **2** born with a particular skill or quality. **3** relaxed and unaffected. • n. a person with a natural skill or talent. □ **natural gas** gas found underground, used as fuel. **natural history** the study of animals and plants. **natural selection** the evolutionary process by which organisms better adapted to their environment tend to survive and produce more offspring. ■ **naturally** adv.

naturalism n. realism in art or literature. ■ **naturalistic** adj.

naturalist n. an expert in natural history.

n

naturalize (or **-ise**) v. **1** make a foreigner a citizen of a country. **2** introduce a plant or animal in a region where it is not native. ■ **naturalization** n.

nature n. **1** the physical world, including plants, animals, and all things not made by people. **2** the typical qualities or characteristics of a person or thing. **3** a kind or sort.

naturism n. nudism. ■ **naturist** n.

naught pron. old use nothing.

naughty adj. (**naughtier**, **naughtiest**) **1** disobedient; badly behaved. **2** informal mildly indecent. ■ **naughtily** adv. **naughtiness** n.

nausea /naw-zi-uh/ n. a feeling of sickness.

nauseate v. cause to feel sick or disgusted.

nauseous adj. affected with or causing nausea.

nautical adj. of sailors or navigation. ▢ **nautical mile** a unit of 1,852 m (approx. 2,025 yds).

nautilus n. (pl. **nautiluses**) a swimming mollusc with a spiral shell.

naval adj. of a navy.

nave n. the central part of a church.

navel n. the small hollow in a person's stomach where the umbilical cord was cut at birth.

navigable adj. able to be used by boats and ships.

navigate v. **1** plan and direct the route of a ship, aircraft, etc. **2** sail or travel over. ■ **navigation** n. **navigator** n.

navvy n. (pl. **navvies**) dated a labourer employed in building a road etc.

navy n. (pl. **navies**) **1** the branch of a country's armed services which fights at sea. **2** a dark blue colour.

nay adv. old use or dialect no.

Nazi /naht-si/ n. (pl. **Nazis**) hist. a member of the far-right National Socialist German Workers' Party.

NB abbrev. note well.

NE abbrev. north-east or north-eastern.

Neanderthal /ni-an-der-tahl/ n. an extinct human living in Europe between about 120,000 and 35,000 years ago.

neap tide n. a tide when there is least difference between high and low water.

near adv. **1** at or to a short distance in space or time. **2** almost. •prep. **1** a short distance from. **2** on the verge of. •adj. **1** at a short distance away. **2** close to being: a near disaster. •v. approach. ■ **nearness** n.

nearby adj. & adv. not far away.

nearly adv. very close to; almost.

neat adj. **1** tidy or carefully arranged. **2** clever but simple. **3** not diluted. ■ **neaten** v. **neatly** adv. **neatness** n.

nebula n. (pl. **nebulae** or **nebulas**) a cloud of gas or dust in space.

nebulous adj. not clearly defined; vague.

necessarily adv. as a necessary result; unavoidably.

necessary adj. needing to be done or present; essential. •n. (**necessaries**) basic requirements.

⚠ One c, two s's: necessary.

necessitate v. make necessary.

necessity n. (pl. **necessities**) **1** the fact of being necessary. **2** something essential.

neck n. **1** the part connecting the head to the rest of the body. **2** a narrow connecting or end part. □ **neck and neck** level in a race.

necklace a piece of jewellery worn round the neck. **neckline** the edge of a dress or top at or below the neck.

necromancy n. **1** attempted communication with dead people to predict the future. **2** witchcraft or black magic. ■ **necromancer** n.

necrophilia n. sexual activity with or interest in dead bodies. ■ **necrophiliac** n.

necrosis n. the death of cells in the body.

nectar n. a sweet fluid produced by flowers and made into honey by bees.

nectarine n. a kind of peach with a smooth skin.

née /nay/ adj. born (used in giving a married woman's maiden name).

need v. **1** want something because it is essential. **2** be obliged or required to. • n. **1** a situation in which something is necessary or must be done. **2** something needed. **3** great poverty.

needful adj. necessary.

needle n. **1** a very thin pointed piece of metal used in sewing. **2** a long thin rod used in knitting. **3** the end of a hypodermic syringe. **4** a stylus for playing records. **5** a thin pointer on a dial, compass, etc. **6** the thin, stiff leaf of a fir or pine tree. • v. informal deliberately annoy. □ **needlework** sewing or embroidery.

needless adj. unnecessary. ■ **needlessly** adv.

needy adj. (**needier**, **neediest**) very poor.

ne'er-do-well n. a lazy or useless person.

nefarious adj. wicked or criminal.

negate v. **1** stop or undo the effect of. **2** deny the existence of. ■ **negation** n.

negative adj. **1** showing the absence rather than the presence of something. **2** expressing denial, disagreement, or refusal. **3** not hopeful or favourable. **4** (of a quantity) less than zero. **5** of the kind of electric charge carried by electrons. • n. **1** a negative word or statement. **2** a photo showing light and shade or colours reversed from those of the original, from which positive prints may be made. ■ **negatively** adv. **negativity** n.

neglect v. **1** fail to give proper care or attention to. **2** fail to do. • n. the act of neglecting. ■ **neglectful** adj.

negligee /neg-li-zhay/ n. a woman's light, flimsy dressing gown.

negligence n. lack of proper care and attention. ■ **negligent** adj.

negligible adj. so small or unimportant as to be not worth considering.

negotiate v. **1** try to reach an agreement by discussion. **2** bring about by discussion. **3** find a way over or through. ■ **negotiable** adj. **negotiation** n. **negotiator** n.

Negro n. (pl. **Negroes**) a black person.

> ! The term **Negro** is now regarded as old-fashioned and offensive; use **black** instead.

neigh n. a high-pitched cry made by a horse. • v. make this cry.

n

neighbour (*US* **neighbor**) *n.* a person living next or very near to another. • *v.* be next or very near to. ■ **neighbourly** *adj.*

neighbourhood (*US* **neighborhood**) *n.* **1** a district within a town or city. **2** the area surrounding a place, person, etc.

neither *adj.* & *pron.* not either. • *adv.* **1** not either. **2** not also.

nemesis /nem-i-siss/ *n.* (*pl.* **nemeses**) a means of deserved and unavoidable downfall.

neoclassical *adj.* of the revival of a classical style in the arts.

Neolithic *adj.* of the later part of the Stone Age.

neologism *n.* a new word.

neon *n.* an inert gas used in fluorescent lighting.

neonatal *adj.* of newborn children.

neophyte *n.* a novice.

nephew *n.* a son of a person's brother or sister.

nephritis *n.* inflammation of the kidneys.

nepotism *n.* favouritism shown to relatives or friends, esp. by giving them jobs.

neptunium *n.* a radioactive metallic element.

nerd *n.* *informal* an unfashionable person obsessed with a particular interest.

nerve *n.* **1** a fibre transmitting impulses of sensation between the brain or spinal cord and other parts of the body. **2** steadiness and courage. **3** (**nerves**) nervousness. **4** *informal* cheeky boldness. • *v.* (**nerve yourself**) brace yourself for a demanding situation. □ **get on someone's nerves** *informal* irritate someone. **nerve-racking** (or **nerve-wracking**) frightening or stressful.

nervous *adj.* **1** easily frightened or worried. **2** anxious. **3** of the nerves. □ **nervous breakdown** a period of mental illness resulting from severe depression or stress. ■ **nervously** *adv.* **nervousness** *n.*

nervy *adj.* (**nervier, nerviest**) nervous or tense.

nest *n.* **1** a structure made by a bird for laying eggs and sheltering its young. **2** a place where an animal or insect breeds or shelters. **3** a set of similar objects designed to fit inside each other. • *v.* **1** use or build a nest. **2** fit an object inside a larger one. □ **nest egg** a sum of money saved for the future.

nestle *v.* **1** settle comfortably within or against something. **2** (of a place) lie in a sheltered position.

nestling *n.* a bird too young to leave the nest.

net *n.* **1** a material of twine or cord woven or tied together to form small open squares. **2** a piece or structure of net for catching fish, surrounding a goal, etc. **3** (**the Net**) the Internet. • *v.* (**netting, netted**) **1** catch in a net. **2** gain as net profit. • *adj.* (or **nett**) **1** remaining after tax or expenses have been deducted. **2** (of a weight) not including packaging. □ **netball** a team game in which a ball has to be thrown into a high net.

nether *adj.* lower.

netting *n.* material made of net.

nettle *n.* a plant covered with stinging hairs. • *v.* annoy.

network *n.* **1** a system of crossing or connecting railways, lines, etc. **2** a group of interconnected broadcasting stations, computers, etc. **3** a group of people who keep in contact to exchange informa-

n

tion. • v. keep in contact with others to exchange information.

neural adj. of nerves.

neuralgia n. intense pain along a nerve. ■ **neuralgic** adj.

neurology n. the study of the nervous system. ■ **neurological** adj. **neurologist** n.

neurosis n. (pl. **neuroses**) a mental illness involving depression, anxiety, or obsessive behaviour.

neurotic adj. **1** of neurosis. **2** informal excessively sensitive, anxious, or obsessive.

neuter adj. **1** (of a noun) not masculine or feminine. **2** having no sexual or reproductive organs. • v. castrate or spay an animal.

neutral adj. **1** not supporting either side in a dispute or war. **2** lacking noticeable or strong qualities. **3** neither acid nor alkaline. • n. **1** a neutral state or person. **2** a position of a gear mechanism in which the engine is disconnected from the driven parts. ■ **neutrality** n. **neutrally** adv.

neutralize (or **-ise**) v. prevent from having an effect. ■ **neutralization** n.

neutrino n. (pl. **neutrinos**) a subatomic particle with a mass close to zero and no electric charge.

neutron n. a subatomic particle of about the same mass as a proton but without an electric charge. □ **neutron bomb** a nuclear bomb that kills people but does little harm to property.

never adv. **1** not ever. **2** not at all.

nevermore adv. never again.

nevertheless adv. in spite of that.

nevus US = NAEVUS.

new adj. **1** made, introduced, discovered, or experienced recently. **2** not previously used or owned. **3** (**new to/at**) not used to or experienced at. **4** replacing a former one of the same kind. • adv. newly. □ **New Age** a movement concerned with alternative approaches to spirituality, medicine, etc. **newcomer** a person who has recently arrived or is new to an activity. **newfangled** derog. newly developed and unfamiliar. **new moon** the moon when it appears as a thin crescent. **New Testament** the second part of the Christian Bible. **new year** the first days of January. ■ **newness** n.

newel n. the top or bottom post of a stair rail.

newly adv. **1** recently. **2** again. □ **newly-wed** a recently married person.

news n. **1** new information about recent events. **2** (**the news**) a broadcast or published news report. □ **newsagent** a shopkeeper who sells newspapers, magazines, etc. **newsflash** a brief item of important news, interrupting other radio or television programmes. **newsgroup** a group of Internet users who exchange information about a subject online. **newsletter** a bulletin issued periodically to the members of a society etc. **newspaper** a daily or weekly publication containing news and articles. **newsprint** cheap, low-quality paper used for newspapers. **newsreader** a person who reads the news on radio or television. **newsworthy** important enough to report as news.

newt n. a small lizard-like animal that can live in water or on land.

newton n. a unit of force.

next adj. nearest in position or time. • adv. **1** immediately afterwards. **2** following in the specified order. □ **next door** in or to the next house or room. **next of kin** a person's closest living relative or relatives.

nexus n. (pl. **nexus** or **nexuses**) a connection or series of connections.

NHS abbrev. National Health Service.

NI abbrev. **1** National Insurance. **2** Northern Ireland.

niacin = NICOTINIC ACID.

nib n. the pointed end part of a pen.

nibble v. take small quick or gentle bites at. • n. a small bite of food.

nice adj. **1** enjoyable or attractive; pleasant. **2** kind. **3** involving a very small detail or difference. ■ **nicely** adv. **niceness** n.

nicety n. (pl. **niceties**) **1** a very small detail. **2** accuracy.

niche n. **1** a shallow recess in a wall. **2** (**your niche**) a job or role that suits you.

nick n. **1** a small cut. **2** (**the nick**) informal prison or a police station. **3** informal condition: in good nick. • v. **1** make a nick in. **2** informal steal. **3** informal arrest. □ **in the nick of time** only just in time.

nickel n. **1** a metallic element used in alloys. **2** US a five-cent coin.

nickname n. an alternative, usu. amusing name for a person or thing. • v. give a nickname to.

nicotine n. a poisonous oily liquid found in tobacco.

nicotinic acid n. a vitamin of the B complex.

niece n. a daughter of a person's brother or sister.

niggardly adj. not generous; mean.

nigger n. offens. a black person.

niggle v. worry or annoy slightly. • n. a minor worry or criticism. ■ **niggly** adj.

nigh adv., prep., & adj. old use near.

night n. **1** the time from sunset to sunrise. **2** an evening until bedtime. □ **nightcap** a hot or alcoholic drink taken at bedtime. **nightclub** a club open at night, with a bar and music. **nightdress** (or **nightgown**) a loose garment worn by a woman or girl in bed. **nightfall** dusk. **nightjar** a nocturnal bird with a harsh cry. **nightlife** entertainment available at night. **nightshirt** a long shirt worn in bed. **nightspot** informal a nightclub. ■ **nightly** adj. & adv.

nightingale n. a small thrush with a tuneful song.

nightmare n. **1** a frightening dream. **2** a very unpleasant experience. ■ **nightmarish** adj.

nihilism n. the belief that nothing has any value. ■ **nihilist** n. **nihilistic** adj.

nil n. nothing; zero.

nimble adj. quick and agile. ■ **nimbly** adv.

nimbus n. (pl. **nimbi** or **nimbuses**) a rain cloud.

nincompoop n. a stupid person.

nine adj. & n. one less than ten; 9. ■ **ninth** adj. & n.

nineteen adj. & n. one more than eighteen; 19. ■ **nineteenth** adj. & n.

ninety adj. & n. ten less than one hundred; 90. ■ **ninetieth** adj. & n.

ninny n. (pl. **ninnies**) informal a foolish person.

niobium n. a metallic element.

nip v. (**nipping, nipped**) 1 pinch or bite sharply. 2 informal go quickly. •n. 1 an act of nipping. 2 a sharp coldness. 3 a small drink of spirits.

nipple n. a small projection in the centre of each breast.

nippy adj. (**nippier, nippiest**) informal 1 quick; nimble. 2 chilly.

nirvana n. (in Buddhism) a state of perfect happiness.

nit n. informal 1 the egg of a human head louse. 2 a stupid person. □ **nit-picking** petty criticism.

nitrate n. a substance formed from nitric acid.

nitric acid n. a very corrosive acid.

nitrogen n. a gas forming about 78 per cent of the earth's atmosphere.

nitroglycerine (or **nitroglycerin**) n. a powerful explosive.

nitrous oxide n. a gas used as an anaesthetic.

nitty-gritty n. informal the most important details.

nitwit n. informal a foolish person.

no adj. not any. •exclam. used to refuse or disagree. •adv. not at all. □ **no-man's-land** an area between two opposing armies that is not controlled by either. **no one** no person.

no. abbrev. number.

nobble v. informal try to influence by underhand methods.

nobelium n. a radioactive metallic element.

nobility n. 1 the quality of being noble. 2 the aristocracy.

noble adj. 1 belonging to the aristocracy. 2 having fine personal qualities. 3 magnificent; impressive. •n. a nobleman or noblewoman. □ **nobleman** (or

noblewoman) a member of the aristocracy. ■ **nobly** adv.

nobody pron. no person. •n. (pl. **nobodies**) an unimportant person.

nocturnal adj. done or active at night. ■ **nocturnally** adj.

nocturne n. a short romantic piece of music.

nod v. (**nodding, nodded**) 1 lower and raise the head briefly to show agreement or as a greeting or signal. 2 let the head fall forward when drowsy or asleep. 3 (**nod off**) informal fall asleep. •n. an act of nodding.

node n. 1 a point in a network where lines cross or branch. 2 the part of a plant stem from which a leaf grows. 3 a small mass of tissue in the body. ■ **nodal** adj.

nodule n. a small swelling or lump. ■ **nodular** adj.

noggin n. informal a small quantity of alcoholic drink.

noise n. 1 a sound or series of sounds, esp. a loud or unpleasant one. 2 disturbances that accompany and interfere with an electrical signal. ■ **noiseless** adj.

noisome adj. having a very unpleasant smell.

noisy adj. (**noisier, noisiest**) full of or making a lot of noise. ■ **noisily** adv.

nomad n. a member of a people that travels from place to place to find fresh pasture for its animals. ■ **nomadic** adj.

nom de plume n. (pl. **noms de plume**) a writer's pen name.

nomenclature n. a system of names used in a particular subject.

nominal adj. 1 in name but not in reality. 2 (of a fee) very small. ■ **nominally** adv.

n

nominate v. **1** put forward as a candidate for a job, award, etc. **2** formally specify something. ■ **nomination** n. **nominee** n.

nominative n. the grammatical case used for the subject of a verb.

non- prefix not.

nonagenarian n. a person between 90 and 99 years old.

non-aligned adj. not allied with a major world power.

nonchalant adj. calm and relaxed. ■ **nonchalance** n. **nonchalantly** adv.

non-commissioned adj. (of a military officer) appointed from the lower ranks.

non-committal adj. not showing what you think or which side you are on. ■ **non-committally** adv.

nonconformist n. **1** a person who does not follow accepted ideas or behaviour. **2 (Nonconformist)** a member of a Protestant Church which does not follow the beliefs of the established Church of England.

non-contributory adj. (of a pension) funded by regular payments by the employer, not the employee.

nondescript adj. lacking special or interesting features.

none pron. **1** not any. **2** no one. • adv. not at all: none the wiser. □ **nonetheless** nevertheless.

nonentity n. (pl. **nonentities**) an unimportant person or thing.

non-event n. a very disappointing or uninteresting event.

non-existent adj. not real or present.

nonplussed adj. surprised and confused.

nonsense n. **1** words that make no sense. **2** foolish ideas or behaviour. ■ **nonsensical** adj.

non sequitur /non sek-wi-ter/ n. a statement that does not follow logically from the previous one.

non-starter n. informal something that has no chance of succeeding.

non-stop adj. & adv. **1** without stopping. **2** having no stops on the way to a destination.

noodles pl. n. long, thin strips of pasta.

nook n. a sheltered or hidden place.

noon n. 12 o'clock in the day.

noose n. a loop with a knot which tightens as the rope or wire is pulled.

nor conj. & adv. and not; and not either.

Nordic adj. of Scandinavia, Finland, and Iceland.

norm n. **1 (the norm)** the usual or standard thing. **2** a required or acceptable standard.

normal adj. usual, typical, or expected. • n. the normal state or condition. ■ **normality** n. **normally** adv.

normalize (or **-ise**) v. make or become normal. ■ **normalization** n.

normative adj. relating to or setting a norm.

north n. **1** the direction on the left-hand side of a person facing east. **2** the northern part of a place. • adj. **1** lying towards or facing the north. **2** (of a wind) from the north. • adv. towards the north. ■ **northerly** adj. & adv. **northward** adj. & adv. **northwards** adv.

north-east n. the direction or region halfway between north and east. • adj. & adv. **1** towards or facing the north-east. **2** (of a wind) from the north-east. ■ **north-easterly** adj. & adv. **north-eastern** adj.

northern adj. situated in or facing the north. □ **Northern Lights** the aurora borealis.

northerner n. a person from the north of a region.

north-west n. the direction or region halfway between north and west. • adj. & adv. **1** towards or facing the north-west. **2** (of a wind) from the north-west. ■ **north-westerly** adj. & adv. **north-western** adj.

Norwegian n. **1** a person from Norway. **2** the language spoken in Norway. • adj. of Norway.

nose n. **1** the part of the face containing the nostrils, used in breathing and smelling. **2** the front end of an aircraft etc. **3** the sense of smell. **4** a talent for finding something. • v. **1** move forward slowly. **2** look around or pry. **3** thrust the nose against something. □ **nosebag** a bag of fodder hung from a horse's head. **nosedive** a steep downward plunge by an aircraft. **nosegay** a posy of flowers.

nosh n. informal food.

nostalgia n. longing for a happier or better time in the past. ■ **nostalgic** adj.

nostril n. either of the two external openings in the nose.

nostrum n. **1** a favourite method for improving something. **2** an ineffective medicine.

nosy adj. (**nosier**, **nosiest**) informal too inquisitive.

not adv. used to express a negative.

notable adj. worthy of notice. • n. a famous or important person. ■ **notably** adv.

notary n. (pl. **notaries**) a lawyer authorized to draw up and witness the signing of contracts etc.

notation n. a system of symbols used in music, mathematics, etc.

notch n. **1** a V-shaped cut or indentation. **2** a point on a scale. • v. **1** make notches in. **2** (**notch up**) score or achieve.

note n. **1** a brief written record. **2** a short written message. **3** a banknote. **4** a single musical sound of a particular pitch and length, or a symbol representing this. **5** a particular quality: a note of scorn. • v. **1** notice. **2** write down. □ **notebook** a small book for writing notes in. **notepaper** paper for writing letters on. **take note** pay attention.

noted adj. well known.

noteworthy adj. interesting or important.

nothing pron. **1** not anything. **2** something unimportant or uninteresting. **3** nought. • adv. not at all.

notice n. **1** the fact of being aware or paying attention. **2** warning that something is going to happen. **3** a formal statement that someone is going to leave a job or end an agreement. **4** a sheet or placard displaying information. **5** a short published review. • v. become aware of. □ **take notice** (**of**) pay attention (to).

noticeable adj. easily seen or noticed. ■ **noticeably** adv.

notifiable adj. (of a disease) that must be reported to the health authorities.

n

notify v. (**notifying**, **notified**) inform formally about something. ■ **notification** n.

notion n. **1** an idea or belief. **2** an understanding.

notional adj. hypothetical. ■ **notionally** adv.

notorious adj. famous for something bad. ■ **notoriety** n. **notoriously** adv.

notwithstanding prep. in spite of. • adv. nevertheless.

nougat /noo-gah/ n. a sweet made from sugar or honey, nuts, and egg white.

nought n. the figure 0. • pron. nothing.

noun n. a word referring to a person, place, or thing.

nourish v. provide with the food etc. necessary for growth and health.

nourishment n. the food and other substances necessary for life, growth, and good health.

nous /nowss/ n. informal common sense.

nouveau riche /noo-voh reesh/ n. people who have recently become rich and display their wealth in a tasteless way.

nova n. (pl. **novae** or **novas**) a star that suddenly becomes brighter for a short time.

novel n. a fictitious story of book length. • adj. new and unusual.

novelist n. a person who writes novels.

novelty n. (pl. **novelties**) **1** the quality of new and unusual. **2** a small toy or ornament.

November n. the eleventh month.

novice n. **1** a person new to and lacking experience in a job or situation. **2** a person who has entered a religious order but has not yet taken their vows.

now adv. **1** at the present time. **2** immediately. • conj. as a result of the fact. □ **nowadays** at the present time, in contrast with the past. **now and again** (or **then**) from time to time.

nowhere adv. not anywhere. • pron. no place.

noxious adj. harmful or very unpleasant.

nozzle n. a spout controlling a stream of liquid or gas.

nuance /nyoo-ahnss/ n. a slight difference in meaning or expression.

nub n. **1** the central point of a matter. **2** a small lump.

nubile adj. (of a young woman) sexually attractive.

nuclear adj. **1** of a nucleus. **2** using energy released in the fission or fusion of atomic nuclei. □ **nuclear family** a couple and their children.

nucleic acid n. either of two complex organic substances, DNA and RNA, present in all living cells.

nucleus n. (pl. **nuclei**) **1** the central and most important part of something. **2** the positively charged central core of an atom. **3** a structure in a cell containing the genetic material.

nude adj. wearing no clothes. • n. a painting or sculpture of a naked person. ■ **nudity** n.

nudge v. **1** prod with the elbow to attract attention. **2** touch or push gently. • n. a light prod or push.

nudist n. a person who goes naked wherever possible. ■ **nudism** n.

nugatory /nyoo-guh-tuh-ri/ adj. lacking purpose or value.

nugget n. a small lump of precious metal found in the earth.

nuisance n. an annoying person or thing.

nuke v. informal attack with nuclear weapons.

null adj. having the value zero. □ **null and void** having no legal force. ■ **nullity** n.

nullify v. (**nullifying, nullified**) 1 make legally invalid. 2 cancel out the effect of. ■ **nullification** n.

numb adj. 1 (of a body part) having no sensation. 2 lacking the power to feel, think, or react. • v. make numb. ■ **numbness** n. **numbly** adv.

number n. 1 a quantity or value expressed by a word or symbol. 2 a quantity. 3 (**a number of**) several. 4 a single issue of a magazine. 5 a song, dance, or other musical item. • v. 1 amount to. 2 give a number to. 3 count. □ **number plate** a sign on the front and rear of a vehicle showing its registration number. ■ **numberless** adj.

numeral n. a symbol or word representing a number.

numerate adj. having a good basic knowledge of arithmetic. ■ **numeracy** n.

numerator n. the number above the line in a fraction.

numerical adj. of a number or numbers. ■ **numerically** adv.

numerous adj. many.

numinous adj. having a religious or spiritual quality.

numismatics n. the study of coins and medals. ■ **numismatist** n.

nun n. a woman belonging to a female religious community.

nuncio n. (pl. **nuncios**) a diplomatic representative of the pope.

nunnery n. (pl. **nunneries**) a convent.

nuptial adj. of marriage or weddings. • n. (**nuptials**) a wedding.

nurse n. 1 a person trained to care for sick or injured people. 2 dated a person employed to look after young children. • v. 1 act as nurse to. 2 hold carefully. 3 harbour a belief or feeling. 4 feed a baby at the breast. □ **nursing home** a place providing accommodation and health care for old people.

nursery n. (pl. **nurseries**) 1 a room for children. 2 a nursery school. 3 a place where plants are grown for sale. □ **nurseryman** a worker in or owner of a plant nursery. **nursery rhyme** a traditional song or poem for children. **nursery school** a school for children between three and five.

nurture v. 1 care for and encourage the growth or development of. 2 have a hope or belief for a long time. • n. the act of nurturing.

nut n. 1 a fruit consisting of a hard shell around an edible kernel. 2 the kernel of such a fruit. 3 a small flat metal ring for screwing on to a bolt. 4 (or **nutcase**) informal a mad person. 5 informal the head. • adj. (**nuts**) informal mad. □ **in a nutshell** in the fewest possible words. ■ **nutty** adj.

nutmeg n. a spice made from the seed of a tropical tree.

nutrient n. a substance essential for life and growth.

nutriment n. nourishment.

nutrition n. 1 the process of eating or taking nourishment. 2 the study of this. ■ **nutritional** adj. **nutritionist** n.

nutritious adj. full of nutrients.

n

nutritive adj. **1** of nutrition. **2** nutritious.

nuzzle v. rub or push against gently with the nose.

NVQ abbrev. National Vocational Qualification.

NW abbrev. north-west or north-western.

nylon n. a strong, light, synthetic fibre.

nymph n. **1** a mythological spirit in the form of a beautiful young woman. **2** an immature form of an insect.

nymphomania n. uncontrollable sexual desire in a woman. ■ **nymphomaniac** n.

NZ abbrev. New Zealand.

Oo

oaf n. a stupid or clumsy man. ■ **oafish** adj.

oak n. a large tree producing acorns and a hard wood. ■ **oaken** adj.

OAP abbrev. old-age pensioner.

oar n. a pole with a flat blade used to row a boat.

oasis n. (pl. **oases**) **1** a fertile place in a desert where water rises to ground level. **2** a pleasant area or period in the midst of a difficult situation.

oast house n. a building with a kiln for drying hops.

oat n. **1** a hardy cereal plant. **2** (**oats**) the edible grain of this. □ **oatcake** an oatmeal biscuit. **oatmeal** ground oats.

oath n. (pl. **oaths**) **1** a solemn promise, esp. that something is true. **2** a swear word.

obdurate adj. stubborn. ■ **obduracy** n.

OBE abbrev. Officer of the Order of the British Empire.

obedient adj. willing to do what you are told. ■ **obedience** n. **obediently** adv.

obeisance n. **1** humble respect. **2** a bow or curtsy.

obelisk n. a stone pillar tapering to a point, set up as a monument.

obese adj. very fat. ■ **obesity** n.

obey v. **1** carry out the orders of. **2** behave in accordance with a law etc.

obfuscate v. make unclear or hard to understand. ■ **obfuscation** n.

obituary n. (pl. **obituaries**) a short biography of someone published in a newspaper when they die.

object n. **1** a physical thing that can be seen and touched. **2** a person or thing to which an action or feeling is directed. **3** a purpose. **4** a noun acted on by a transitive verb or by a preposition. • v. express disapproval or opposition. ■ **objection** n. **objector** n.

objectionable adj. unpleasant or offensive.

objective *adj.* 1 not influenced by personal feelings or opinions. 2 having actual existence outside the mind. 3 of a case of nouns and pronouns used for the object of a transitive verb or a preposition. •*n.* a goal or aim. □ **object lesson** a clear practical example of a principle or ideal. ■ **objectively** *adv.* **objectivity** *n.*

objet d'art /ob-zhay dar/ *n.* (*pl.* **objets d'art**) a small decorative or artistic object.

oblation *n.* an offering made to a god.

obligated *adj.* obliged or compelled.

obligation *n.* 1 something that must be done because of a law, agreement, etc. 2 the state of being obliged to do something.

obligatory *adj.* compulsory.

oblige *v.* 1 make someone do something by law, necessity, or because it is their duty. 2 perform a service or favour for. 3 (**be obliged**) be grateful.

obliging *adj.* willing to help. ■ **obligingly** *adv.*

oblique /uh-bleek/ *adj.* 1 at an angle; slanting. 2 not explicit or direct. ■ **obliquely** *adv.*

obliterate *v.* destroy or cover completely. ■ **obliteration** *n.*

oblivion *n.* 1 the state of being unaware. 2 the state of being forgotten or destroyed.

oblivious *adj.* unaware.

oblong *adj.* rectangular in shape. •*n.* an oblong shape.

obloquy /ob-luh-kwi/ *n.* 1 strong public criticism. 2 disgrace.

obnoxious *adj.* very unpleasant.

oboe *n.* a woodwind instrument of treble pitch with a double reed. ■ **oboist** *n.*

obscene *adj.* 1 dealing with sexual matters in an offensive or disgusting way. 2 (of an amount) unacceptably large. ■ **obscenely** *adv.* **obscenity** *n.*

obscure *adj.* 1 not known about or well known. 2 hard to understand or see. •*v.* hide or make unclear. ■ **obscurely** *adv.* **obscurity** *n.*

obsequies /ob-si-kwiz/ *pl. n.* funeral rites.

obsequious *adj.* excessively obedient or respectful. ■ **obsequiously** *adv.* **obsequiousness** *n.*

observance *n.* behaving in accordance with a law, rule, or ritual.

observant *adj.* quick to notice things.

observation *n.* 1 the close watching of someone or something. 2 the ability to notice important details. 3 a remark. ■ **observational** *adj.*

observatory *n.* (*pl.* **observatories**) a building equipped for observing the stars and planets.

observe *v.* 1 notice. 2 watch carefully. 3 make a remark. 4 obey a law or rule. 5 celebrate a festival. ■ **observable** *adj.* **observer** *n.*

obsess *v.* preoccupy to a disturbing extent.

obsession *n.* 1 the state of being obsessed. 2 a persistent thought. ■ **obsessional** *adj.* **obsessive** *adj.* **obsessively** *adv.*

obsolescent *adj.* becoming obsolete. ■ **obsolescence** *n.*

obsolete *adj.* no longer produced or used; out of date.

obstacle *n.* a thing that obstructs progress.

obstetrics *n.* the branch of medicine concerned with childbirth. ■ **obstetric** *adj.* **obstetrician** *n.*

o

obstinate adj. **1** stubbornly refusing to change your mind. **2** (of a problem) hard to deal with. ■ **obstinacy** n. **obstinately** adv.

obstreperous adj. noisy and unruly.

obstruct v. **1** be in the way of. **2** stop or hinder progress. ■ **obstruction** n. **obstructive** adj.

obtain v. **1** come into possession of; get. **2** be established or usual. ■ **obtainable** adj.

obtrude v. become noticeable in an unwelcome way.

obtrusive adj. noticeable in an unwelcome way.

obtuse adj. **1** annoyingly slow to understand. **2** (of an angle) more than 90˚ and less than 180˚. **3** blunt.

obverse n. **1** the side of a coin or medal bearing the head or main design. **2** the opposite.

obviate v. remove a need or difficulty.

obvious adj. **1** easily seen or understood; clear. **2** predictable. ■ **obviously** adv.

ocarina n. an egg-shaped wind instrument.

occasion n. **1** a particular event, or the time at which it happens. **2** a special event. **3** a suitable time. **4** reason or cause. •v. cause.

> ! Two c's and one s: occasion.

occasional adj. happening or done from time to time. ■ **occasionally** adv.

occidental adj. of the countries of the West.

occlude v. close up or block. □ **occluded front** a weather front produced when a cold front catches up with a warm front, so

that the warm air in between rises. ■ **occlusion** n.

occult n. (**the occult**) supernatural beliefs, practices, or events. •adj. of the occult.

occupant n. a person occupying a place or job. ■ **occupancy** n.

occupation n. **1** a job or profession. **2** the act of occupying or state of being occupied. **3** a way of spending time.

occupational adj. of a job or profession. □ **occupational therapy** the use of particular activities as an aid to recovery from illness.

occupy v. (**occupying, occupied**) **1** live or work in. **2** enter and take control of a place. **3** fill a space, time, or position. **4** keep busy. ■ **occupier** n.

occur v. (**occurring, occurred**) **1** happen. **2** be found or present. **3** (**occur to**) come into the mind of. ■ **occurrence** n.

ocean n. a very large expanse of sea. ■ **oceanic** adj.

oceanography n. the study of the sea. ■ **oceanographer** n.

ocelot n. a wild cat found in South and Central America.

ochre /oh-ker/ (US **ocher**) n. a light yellowish brown.

o'clock adv. used to specify the hour when telling the time.

octagon n. a plane figure with eight sides. ■ **octagonal** adj.

octane n. a hydrocarbon present in petrol.

octave n. **1** a series of eight musical notes occupying the interval between (and including) two notes. **2** the interval between two such notes.

octavo n. (pl. **octavos**) a size of book page formed by folding each printed sheet into eight leaves.

octet n. **1** a group of eight voices or musicians. **2** a piece of music for an octet.

October n. the tenth month.

octogenarian n. a person between 80 and 89 years old.

octopus n. (pl. **octopuses**) a sea animal with eight tentacles.

ocular adj. of, for, or by the eyes.

OD v. (**OD'ing**, **OD'd**) informal take an overdose of a drug.

odd adj. **1** unusual or unexpected; strange. **2** (of a number) having a remainder of one when divided by two. **3** occasional. **4** separated from a pair or set. □ **oddment** an item or piece left over from a larger piece or set. □ **oddly** adv. **oddness** n.

oddity n. (pl. **oddities**) **1** the quality of being strange. **2** a strange person or thing.

odds pl. n. **1** the ratio between the amount placed as a bet and the money which would be received if the bet was won. **2** the chances of something happening. □ **at odds** in conflict or disagreement. **odds and ends** various articles or remnants. **odds-on** very likely to win, succeed, or happen.

ode n. a poem addressed to a person or thing or celebrating an event.

odious adj. very unpleasant.

odium n. widespread hatred or disgust.

odometer n. a milometer.

odoriferous adj. smelly.

odour (US **odor**) n. a smell. ■ **odorous** adj.

odyssey n. (pl. **odysseys**) a long eventful journey.

oedema /i-dee-muh/ (US **edema**) n. excess fluid in the tissues of the body.

oesophagus /ee-sof-fuh-guhss/ (US **esophagus**) n. (pl. **oesophagi** or **oesophaguses**) the tube connecting the throat to the stomach.

oestrogen /ee-struh-juhn/ (US **estrogen**) n. a hormone which produces female physical and sexual characteristics.

of prep. **1** helping to form; made up from. **2** belonging to; involving. **3** indicating measurement, value, or age.

off adv. **1** away from a place. **2** so as to be separated. **3** so as to finish or be discontinued. **4** not working or connected. • prep. **1** away from. **2** so as to be separated from. **3** informal having a temporary dislike of. • adj. (of food) no longer fresh. □ **offbeat** informal unconventional. **off colour** slightly unwell. **offcut** a piece of wood, fabric, etc. left after cutting a larger piece. **offhand 1** rudely casual or abrupt. **2** without previous thought. **off-licence** a shop selling alcoholic drink to be drunk elsewhere. **offline** not connected to a computer. **offload** unload. **offputting** unpleasant or unsettling. **offset** counteract by having an equal and opposite force or effect. **offshoot** a thing that develops from something else. **offside** (in football etc.) in a position on the field where playing the ball is not allowed. **off-white** a white colour with a grey or yellow tinge.

offal n. the internal organs of an animal used as food.

offence (US **offense**) n. **1** an illegal act. **2** a feeling of hurt or annoyance.

offend v. **1** cause to feel hurt or annoyed. **2** do something illegal. ■ **offender** n.

O

offensive adj. **1** causing offence. **2** used in attack. •n. a campaign to attack or achieve something. ■ **offensively** adv.

offer v. **1** present for acceptance, rejection, or consideration. **2** express willingness to do something for someone. •n. **1** an expression of willingness to do or give something. **2** an amount of money offered. **3** a specially reduced price.

offering n. a gift or contribution.

offertory n. (pl. **offertories**) **1** the offering of the bread and wine at Holy Communion. **2** a collection of money at a Christian church service.

office n. **1** a room or building used for business or clerical work. **2** a position of authority. **3** the holding of an official position.

officer n. a person holding a position of authority, esp. in the armed services.

official adj. of or authorized by an authority or public organization. •n. a person having official duties. ■ **officially** adv.

officiate v. **1** act as an official in charge of something. **2** perform a religious ceremony.

officious adj. asserting authority in an overbearing way. ■ **officiously** adv.

offspring n. (pl. **offspring**) a person's child or children, or the young of an animal.

often adv. **1** frequently. **2** in many cases.

ogle v. stare at in a lecherous way.

ogre n. **1** (in folklore) a man-eating giant. **2** a terrifying person.

oh exclam. expressing surprise, disappointment, joy, etc.

ohm /ohm/ n. a unit of electrical resistance.

oil n. **1** a thick, sticky liquid obtained from petroleum. **2** a thick liquid which does not dissolve in water. **3** oil paint. •v. treat or coat with oil. □ **oilfield** an area where oil is found beneath the ground or the seabed. **oil paint** paint made from pigment mixed with oil. **oil rig** a structure providing a stable base above water for drilling for and extracting oil. **oilskin 1** heavy cotton cloth waterproofed with oil. **2** (**oilskins**) clothing made of oilskin. ■ **oily** adj.

ointment n. a cream rubbed on the skin for medicinal purposes.

OK (or **okay**) informal adj. satisfactory. •adv. in a satisfactory way.

okapi /oh-kah-pi/ n. (pl. **okapi** or **okapis**) a large African mammal of the giraffe family.

okra n. the long seed pods of a tropical plant, eaten as a vegetable.

old adj. **1** having lived or existed for a long time. **2** former. **3** showing signs of age. **4** of a specified age. □ **old age** the later part of normal life. **old-fashioned** no longer current or modern. **Old Testament** the first part of the Christian Bible. **old wives' tale** a traditional belief now thought to be incorrect.

oleaginous /oh-li-aj-i-nuhss/ adj. **1** oily. **2** excessively flattering.

oleander /oh-li-an-der/ n. a flowering evergreen shrub of warm countries.

olfactory adj. of the sense of smell.

oligarchy n. (pl. **oligarchies**) **1** a small group governing a state. **2** a state governed by such a group. ■ **oligarch** n. ■ **oligarchic** adj.

olive n. **1** a small oval fruit with bitter flesh which yields **olive oil**, or the tree producing this fruit. **2** a greyish-green colour. • adj. **1** grey-ish-green. **2** (of skin) yellowish brown. □ **olive branch** an offer to restore friendly relations.

Olympic adj. of the Olympic Games. •n. (**the Olympics**) the Olympic Games.

ombudsman n. an official appointed to investigate complaints against public organizations.

omelette n. a dish of beaten eggs cooked in a frying pan.

omen n. an event seen as a sign of future good or bad luck.

ominous adj. suggesting that something bad is going to happen. ■ **ominously** adv.

omit v. (**omitting, omitted**) **1** leave out or exclude. **2** fail to do. ■ **omission** n.

omnibus n. **1** a book or programme containing several works or programmes previously published or broadcast separately. **2** dated a bus.

omnipotent adj. having unlimited or very great power. ■ **omnipotence** n.

omnipresent adj. present everywhere. ■ **omnipresence** n.

omniscient /om-ni-si-uhnt/ adj. knowing everything. ■ **omniscience** n.

omnivorous adj. eating both plants and meat.

on prep. **1** (or **on to**) into contact with, or aboard. **2** about; concerning. **3** as a member of. **4** stored in or broadcast by. **5** in the course of. **6** at a point

in time. • adv. **1** in contact with or covering something. **2** with continued movement or action. **3** taking place or being presented. **4** functioning. □ **oncoming** approaching. **ongoing** still in progress. **online** controlled by or connected to a computer. □ **onward** adv. & adj. **onwards** adv.

once adv. **1** on one occasion only. **2** formerly. • conj. as soon as. □ **at once 1** immediately. **2** at the same time. **once upon a time** at some time in the past. **once-over** informal a rapid inspection or search.

oncogene n. a gene that transforms a gene into a cancer cell.

oncology n. the study and treatment of tumours.

one n. & adj. **1** the lowest cardinal number; **1**. **2** single, or a single person or thing. **3** a certain. **4** the same. • pron. **1** used to refer to a person or thing previously mentioned. **2** used to refer to the speaker or to represent people in general. □ **one-sided 1** unfairly biased. **2** very unequal. **one-upmanship** informal the technique of gaining an advantage over someone else. **one-way** allowing movement in one direction only.

onerous /oh-nuh-ruhss/ adj. involving much effort and difficulty.

oneself pron. **1** used when 'one' is the subject of the verb and is also affected by it. **2** used to emphasize 'one'.

onion n. a vegetable with a bulb having a strong taste and smell.

onlooker n. a spectator.

only adv. **1** and no one or nothing more besides. **2** no longer ago

o

than. • *adj.* **1** single or solitary. **2** alone deserving consideration. • *conj. informal* except that.

onomatopoeia /on-uh-mat-uh-pee-uh/ *n.* the formation of a word from the sound of the thing described. ■ **onomatopoeic** *adj.*

onset *n.* a beginning.

onslaught *n.* a fierce attack.

onto var. of on to (on).

ontology *n.* philosophy dealing with the nature of being. ■ **ontological** *adj.*

onus /oh-nuhss/ *n.* a responsibility.

onyx *n.* a semi-precious stone with layers of different colours.

oodles *pl. n. informal* a very great quantity.

ooze *v.* **1** slowly seep out. **2** exude. • *n.* wet mud or slime.

opal *n.* an iridescent gem.

opalescent *adj.* iridescent like an opal.

opaque *adj.* **1** impossible to see through. **2** difficult to understand. ■ **opacity** *n.*

op. cit. *adv.* in the work already mentioned.

open *adj.* **1** not closed, fastened, or restricted. **2** not covered or protected. **3** (**open to**) likely to be affected by. **4** expanded or unfolded. **5** undisguised. **6** not concealing thoughts or feelings. **7** not finally settled. • *v.* **1** make or become open. **2** formally begin or establish. • *n.* (**the open**) fresh air or open countryside. □ **in the open** not secret. **opencast** (of mining) near the surface, rather than from shafts. **open-ended** with no limit decided in advance. **open-handed** generous. **open house** a situation in which all visitors are welcome. **open letter** a letter ad-

dressed to a particular person but published in a newspaper. **open-plan** having few or no dividing walls. **open prison** a prison with the minimum of restrictions on prisoners' movements. **open verdict** a verdict that a person's death is suspicious but that the cause is unknown. ■ **opener** *n.* **openly** *adv.* **openness** *n.*

opening *n.* **1** a gap. **2** a beginning, or a ceremony marking this. **3** an opportunity.

opera *n.* **1** a play set to music for singers and musicians. **2** pl. of opus. □ **opera glasses** small binoculars for use at a theatre. ■ **operatic** *adj.*

operable *adj.* **1** able to be operated. **2** able to be treated by surgery.

operate *v.* **1** function. **2** control the functioning of a machine or the activities of an organization. **3** perform a surgical operation. □ **operating system** the software supporting a computer's basic functions.

operation *n.* **1** the act of operating. **2** an act of surgery performed on a patient. **3** an organized action involving a number of people.

operational *adj.* **1** in or ready for use. **2** of the functioning of an organization.

operative *adj.* **1** functioning. **2** of surgery. • *n.* **1** a worker. **2** a secret agent.

operator *n.* **1** a person who operates equipment or a machine. **2** a person who works at the switchboard of a phone exchange.

operetta *n.* a short opera on a light theme.

ophthalmic *adj.* of the eye and its diseases. □ **ophthalmic optician**

an optician qualified to prescribe and supply glasses etc. and to detect eye diseases.

ophthalmology /off-thal-mol-uh-ji/ n. the study of disorders and diseases of the eye.
■ **ophthalmologist** n.

opiate n. a drug containing opium.

opine v. state as your opinion.

opinion n. 1 a personal view not necessarily based on fact or knowledge. 2 a formal statement of advice from an expert.

opinionated adj. tending to put your views forward forcefully.

opium n. an addictive drug made from the juice of a poppy.

opossum n. a small tree-dwelling marsupial.

opponent n. 1 a person who competes with or fights another. 2 a person who disagrees with something.

opportune adj. occurring at an especially appropriate time.

opportunist n. a person who exploits opportunities as and when they arise, esp. unscrupulously.
■ **opportunism** n. **opportunistic** adj.

opportunity n. (pl. **opportunities**) a favourable time or situation for doing something.

oppose v. 1 disagree with and try to prevent or resist. 2 compete with or fight. 3 (**opposed**) (of two or more things) contrasting or conflicting. 4 (**opposing**) opposite.

opposite adj. 1 facing. 2 completely different. 3 being the other of a contrasted pair. •n. an opposite person or thing. •adv. & prep. in an opposite position to something.

opposition n. 1 resistance or disagreement. 2 a group of opponents. 3 (**the Opposition**) the main party in parliament opposing the one in power. 4 a contrast or opposite.

oppress v. 1 treat harshly and unfairly. 2 distress or make anxious.
■ **oppression** n. **oppressor** n.

oppressive adj. 1 harsh and unfair. 2 causing distress or anxiety. 3 (of weather) close and sultry.

opprobrious adj. highly critical.

opprobrium n. 1 harsh criticism. 2 public disgrace as a result of bad behaviour.

opt v. make a choice. □ **opt out** 1 choose not to participate. 2 (of a school or hospital) withdraw from local authority control.

optic adj. of the eye or vision.

optical adj. of vision, light, or optics. □ **optical fibre** a thin glass fibre through which light can be transmitted. ■ **optically** adv.

optician n. a person qualified to prescribe and supply glasses etc. and to detect eye diseases.

optics n. the study of vision and the behaviour of light.

optimal adj. best or most favourable. ■ **optimally** adv.

optimism n. hopefulness and confidence about the future or success of something. ■ **optimist** n. **optimistic** adj. **optimistically** adv.

optimize (or **-ise**) v. make the best use of.

optimum adj. most likely to lead to a favourable outcome. •n. (pl. **optima** or **optimums**) the most favourable conditions for growth or success.

option n. 1 a thing that is or may be chosen. 2 the freedom or right to choose. 3 a right to buy or sell something at a specified price within a set time.

optional adj. not compulsory. ■ **optionally** adv.

optometry n. the occupation of measuring eyesight, prescribing lenses, and detecting eye disease. ■ **optometrist** n.

opulent adj. ostentatiously luxurious. ■ **opulence** n. **opulently** adv.

opus n. (pl. **opuses** or **opera**) a separate musical composition or set of compositions.

or conj. **1** used to link alternatives. **2** otherwise.

oracle n. **1** (in ancient Greece or Rome) a priest or priestess who acted as a channel for prophecy from the gods. **2** an authority which is always correct.

oracular adj. **1** of an oracle. **2** hard to interpret.

oral adj. **1** spoken rather than written. **2** of or done by the mouth. •n. a spoken exam. ■ **orally** adv.

orange n. **1** a large round citrus fruit with reddish-yellow rind. **2** a bright reddish-yellow colour.

orang-utan (or **orang-utang**) n. a large ape with reddish hair.

oration n. a formal speech.

orator n. a skilful public speaker.

oratorio n. (pl. **oratorios**) a musical work on a religious theme for orchestra and voices.

oratory n. formal public speaking, esp. when inspiring. ■ **oratorical** adj.

orb n. **1** a sphere. **2** a golden globe with a cross on top, carried by a monarch.

orbit n. **1** the regularly repeated course of a planet, spacecraft, etc.

around a star or planet. **2** an area of activity or influence. •v. (**orbiting, orbited**) move in orbit round.

orbital adj. **1** of an orbit or orbits. **2** (of a road) passing round the outside of a town.

orchard n. a piece of land planted with fruit trees.

orchestra n. a large group of musicians with string, woodwind, brass, and percussion sections. ■ **orchestral** adj.

orchestrate v. **1** arrange music for performance by an orchestra. **2** direct a situation to produce a desired effect. ■ **orchestration** n.

orchid n. a plant with unusually shaped flowers.

ordain v. **1** make someone a priest or minister. **2** order officially.

ordeal n. a prolonged painful or horrific experience.

order n. **1** the arrangement of people or things according to a particular sequence or method. **2** a state in which everything is in its correct place. **3** a state in which the laws regulating public behaviour are followed. **4** a command. **5** a request for something to be supplied. **6** the set procedure followed in a court, religious service, etc. **7** a rank, kind, or quality. **8** a religious community living according to particular rules. **9** a classifying category of plants and animals. •v. **1** give a command. **2** request that something be supplied. **3** arrange methodically. □ **in order 1** in the correct condition for use. **2** suitable in the circumstances. **out of order** not functioning.

orderly adj. **1** neatly arranged. **2** well behaved. •n. (pl. **orderlies**)

1 a hospital attendant. **2** a soldier assisting an officer. ■ **orderliness** n.

ordinal number n. a number expressing order (1st, 2nd, 3rd, etc.), rather than quantity (1, 2, 3, etc.).

ordinance n. an official order.

ordinand n. a candidate for ordination.

ordinary adj. normal or usual. ■ **ordinarily** adv.

ordination n. the ordaining of someone as a priest or minister.

ordnance n. **1** large guns mounted on wheels. **2** military equipment and stores.

ordure n. dung.

ore n. naturally occurring material from which a metal or mineral can be extracted.

oregano /o-ri-gah-noh/ n. a herb.

organ n. **1** a body part with a particular function. **2** a keyboard instrument with rows of pipes supplied with air from bellows, or one producing similar sounds electronically. **3** a newspaper which puts forward particular views. ■ **organist** n.

organic adj. **1** of or derived from living matter. **2** produced without artificial chemicals such as fertilizers. **3** of a bodily organ or organs. **4** (of development or change) continuous or natural. ■ **organically** adv.

organism n. an individual animal, plant, or life form.

organization (or **-isation**) n. **1** the act of organizing. **2** a systematic arrangement or approach. **3** an organized group with a particular purpose, e.g. a business. ■ **organizational** adj.

organize (or **-ise**) v. **1** arrange in an orderly way. **2** make arrangements for. ■ **organizer** n.

orgasm n. a climax of sexual excitement.

orgy n. (pl. **orgies**) **1** a wild party with indiscriminate sexual activity. **2** excessive indulgence in a specified activity. ■ **orgiastic** adj.

orient n. (**the Orient**) the countries of the East. •v. (or **orientate**) **1** position in relation to the points of a compass. **2** (**orient yourself**) find your position in relation to unfamiliar surroundings. **3** tailor to meet particular needs. ■ **oriental** adj. **orientation** n.

orienteering n. the sport of finding your way across country with a map and compass.

orifice n. an opening in the body.

origami /o-ri-gah-mi/ n. the Japanese art of folding paper into decorative shapes.

origin n. **1** the point where something begins. **2** a person's social background or ancestry.

original adj. **1** existing from the beginning. **2** produced by an artist, author, etc. rather than copied. **3** inventive or novel. •n. the earliest form of something, from which copies can be made. ■ **originality** n. **originally** adv.

originate v. bring or come into being. ■ **origination** n. **originator** n.

ormolu n. a gold-coloured alloy of copper, zinc, and tin.

ornament n. **1** an object designed to add beauty to something. **2** decorative items as a whole. ■ **ornamental** adj. **ornamentation** n.

ornate adj. highly decorated.

o

ornithology *n.* the study of birds. ■ **ornithological** *adj.* **ornithologist** *n.*

orphan *n.* a child whose parents are dead. ▪*v.* (**be orphaned**) (of a child) be made an orphan.

orphanage *n.* a home which cares for orphans.

orthodontics *n.* the treatment of irregularities in the teeth. ■ **orthodontic** *adj.* **orthodontist** *n.*

orthodox *adj.* **1** of or holding traditional or generally accepted beliefs. **2** conventional. □ **Orthodox Church** the Christian Church in Greece and eastern Europe. ■ **orthodoxy** *n.*

orthography *n.* the conventional spelling system of a language. ■ **orthographic** *adj.*

orthopaedics (US **orthopedics**) *n.* the branch of medicine concerned with bones or muscles. ■ **orthopaedic** *adj.*

oscillate *v.* move or swing back and forth. ■ **oscillation** *n.*

osier /oh-zi-er/ *n.* a willow with long flexible shoots.

osmium *n.* a hard metallic element.

osmosis *n.* a process by which molecules pass through a membrane from a less concentrated solution to a more concentrated one. ■ **osmotic** *adj.*

osprey *n.* (*pl.* **ospreys**) a large fish-eating bird of prey.

osseous *adj.* consisting of or turned into bone.

ossify *v.* (**ossifying, ossified**) **1** turn into bone. **2** stop developing. ■ **ossification** *n.*

ostensible *adj.* apparently true, but not necessarily so. ■ **ostensibly** *adv.*

ostentation *n.* showy display intended to impress. ■ **ostentatious** *adj.* **ostentatiously** *adv.*

osteopathy *n.* a system of complementary medicine involving manipulation of bones and muscles. ■ **osteopath** *n.*

ostracize (or **-ise**) *v.* exclude from a society or group. ■ **ostracism** *n.*

ostrich *n.* a large flightless African bird.

other *adj. & pron.* **1** used to refer to a person or thing different from one already mentioned or known. **2** additional. **3** alternative of two. **4** those not already mentioned. □ **otherwise 1** in different circumstances. **2** in other respects. **3** in a different way.

otiose *adj.* serving no practical purpose.

otter *n.* a fish-eating water mammal.

ottoman *n.* (*pl.* **ottomans**) a low padded seat without a back or arms.

ought *aux. v.* **1** expressing duty, advisability, or a desired state. **2** expressing probability.

Ouija board /wee-juh/ *n.* *trademark* a board marked with letters and signs, to which a pointer moves, supposedly in answer to questions at a seance.

ounce *n.* **1** a unit of weight of one sixteenth of a pound (approx. 28 g). **2** a very small amount.

our *adj.* of or belonging to us.

ours *possess. pron.* belonging to us.

ourselves *pron.* **1** the form of 'we' used when you and another person or people are the subject of the verb and are also affected by it. **2** we or us personally.

oust *v.* force from a position of power.

out adv. **1** moving away from a place. **2** away from your home or place of work. **3** outdoors. **4** so as to be revealed, heard, or known. **5** at or to an end. **6** so as to be extinguished. **7** away from the land. •adj. **1** not possible. **2** unconscious. **3** (of the ball in tennis etc.) not in the playing area. •v. informal reveal the homosexuality of. □ **out-and-out** complete. **out of date** no longer current, valid, or fashionable.

outback n. the remote, sparsely populated part of Australia.

outboard adj. (of a motor) attached to the outside of a boat.

outbreak n. a sudden or violent occurrence of war, disease, etc.

outbuilding n. a smaller building in the grounds of a main building.

outburst n. a sudden release of emotion.

outcast n. a person rejected by their society or social group.

outclass v. be far better than.

outcome n. a consequence.

outcrop n. a part of a rock formation visible on the surface.

outcry n. (pl. **outcries**) a strong expression of public disapproval.

outdistance v. leave a pursuer far behind.

outdo v. (**outdoes, outdoing, outdid**; past part. **outdone**) do better than.

outdoor adj. done, situated, or used in the open air. ■ **outdoors** adv.

outer adj. **1** outside. **2** further from the centre or the inside. ■ **outermost** adj.

outface v. defeat someone by confronting them boldly.

outfit n. a set of clothes worn together.

outflank v. **1** move round the side of an enemy. **2** outwit.

outgoing adj. **1** friendly and confident. **2** leaving a job or position. •n. (**outgoings**) regular expenditure.

outgrow v. (**outgrowing, outgrew**; past part. **outgrown**) **1** grow too big for. **2** leave behind or cease to be interested in as you mature.

outhouse n. a smaller building attached or close to a house.

outing n. a short trip taken for pleasure.

outlandish adj. strange or unfamiliar.

outlast v. last longer than.

outlaw n. a person who has broken the law and remains at large. •v. make illegal.

outlay n. an amount of money spent.

outlet n. **1** a pipe or hole for water or gas to escape. **2** a point from which goods are sold. **3** a means of expressing your energy, emotions, etc.

outline n. **1** a sketch or diagram showing the shape of an object. **2** the outer edges of an object. **3** a summary. •v. **1** draw the outer edge or shape of. **2** summarize.

outlook n. **1** a person's attitude to life. **2** a view. **3** what is likely to happen in the future.

outlying adj. situated far from a centre.

outmoded adj. old-fashioned.

outnumber v. be more numerous than.

outpace v. go faster than.

outpatient n. a patient attending a hospital for treatment without staying overnight.

outpost n. 1 a small military camp at a distance from the main army. 2 a remote settlement.

output n. the amount of power, energy, work, etc. produced. • v. (**outputting, output** or **outputted**) (of a computer) produce data.

outrage n. 1 extreme shock and anger. 2 a very cruel, wicked, or shocking act. • v. cause to feel outrage.

outrageous adj. 1 shockingly bad or excessive. 2 very bold and unusual. ■ **outrageously** adv.

outré /oo-tray/ adj. unusual and rather shocking.

outrider n. a person in a vehicle or on horseback escorting another vehicle.

outrigger n. a float fixed parallel to a canoe or small ship to aid stability.

outright adv. 1 totally. 2 openly. 3 immediately. • adj. 1 open and direct. 2 complete.

outrun v. (**outrunning, outran;** past part. **outrun**) run faster or further than.

outset n. the beginning.

outside n. the external side, part, or surface. • adj. 1 on or near the outside. 2 not of or from a particular group. • prep. & adv. 1 situated or moving beyond the boundaries of. 2 not being a member of. □ **an outside chance** a remote possibility.

outsider n. 1 a person who does not belong to a particular group. 2 a competitor thought to have little chance of success.

outsize adj. very large.

outskirts pl. n. the outer parts of a town or city.

outsource v. arrange for work to be done outside a company.

outspoken adj. very frank.

outstanding adj. 1 very good. 2 clearly noticeable. 3 not yet dealt with or paid. ■ **outstandingly** adv.

outstrip v. (**outstripping, outstripped**) 1 move faster than and overtake. 2 surpass.

outvote v. defeat by gaining more votes.

outward adj. & adv. 1 on or from the outside. 2 out or away from a place. ■ **outwardly** adv. **outwards** adv.

outweigh v. be greater or more important than.

outwit v. (**outwitting, outwitted**) defeat by cunning or ingenuity.

ova pl. of **OVUM**.

oval adj. having a rounded and slightly elongated outline. • n. an oval object or shape.

ovary n. (pl. **ovaries**) 1 a female reproductive organ in which eggs are produced. 2 the base of the reproductive organ of a flower. ■ **ovarian** adj.

ovate adj. oval.

ovation n. a long, enthusiastic round of applause.

oven n. an enclosed compartment in which things are cooked or heated.

over prep. 1 extending upwards from or above. 2 above so as to cover or protect. 3 expressing movement across. 4 beyond and falling or hanging from. 5 expressing length of time. 6 higher or more than. 7 expressing authority or control. • adv. 1 expressing movement across an area. 2 beyond and falling or hanging from a point. **3** finished. **4** repeatedly. •*n.* Cricket a sequence of six balls bowled from one end of the pitch.

over- *prefix* **1** excessively. **2** over; above.

overall *adj. & adv.* including everything; taken as a whole. •*n.* (or **overalls**) a loose protective garment worn over ordinary clothes.

overarm *adj. & adv.* (of an arm action) made with the hand brought forward and down from above shoulder level.

overawe *v.* impress someone so much that they are silent or nervous.

overbalance *v.* fall due to loss of balance.

overbearing *adj.* unpleasantly overpowering.

overblown *adj.* pretentious.

overboard *adv.* from a ship into the water. □ **go overboard** be very or too enthusiastic.

overcast *adj.* cloudy.

overcharge *v.* charge too high a price.

overcoat *n.* a long, warm coat.

overcome *v.* (**overcoming**, **overcame**; *past part.* **overcome**) **1** succeed in dealing with a problem. **2** defeat. **3** (**be overcome**) be overwhelmed by an emotion.

overdo *v.* (**overdoes**, **overdoing**, **overdid**; *past part.* **overdone**) **1** do excessively or in an exaggerated way. **2** use too much of. **3** cook for too long.

overdose *n.* a dangerously large dose of a drug. •*v.* take an overdose.

overdraft *n.* an arrangement with a bank allowing someone to take

out more money than their account holds.

overdrawn *adj.* (of a bank account) having had more money taken out of it than it holds.

overdrive *n.* **1** a mechanism providing an extra gear above top gear. **2** a state of great activity.

overdue *adj.* not having arrived, happened, or been done by the expected or required time.

overestimate *v.* form too high an estimate of. •*n.* an estimate which is too high.

overflow *v.* **1** flow over the edge of a container. **2** be too full or crowded. •*n.* **1** an excess or surplus. **2** an outlet for excess water.

overgrown *adj.* **1** covered with weeds. **2** grown too large.

overhaul *v.* **1** examine and repair. **2** overtake. •*n.* an act of examining and repairing.

overhead *adv. & adj.* above the head. •*n.* (**overheads**) expenses incurred in running a business etc.

overhear *v.* (**overhearing**, **overheard**) hear accidentally.

overjoyed *adj.* very happy.

overkill *n.* too much of something.

overland *adj. & adv.* by land.

overlap *v.* (**overlapping**, **overlapped**) **1** extend over so as to partly cover. **2** partly coincide in time. •*n.* an overlapping part or amount.

overleaf *adv.* on the other side of the page.

overload *v.* **1** load too heavily. **2** put too great a demand on. •*n.* an excessive amount.

o

overlook v. **1** fail to notice. **2** ignore a fault. **3** have a view of from above.

overly adv. excessively.

overnight adv. & adj. during or for a night.

overpass n. a bridge by which a road crosses another.

overpower v. **1** defeat with greater strength. **2** overwhelm.

overrate v. rate more highly than is deserved.

overreach v. (**overreach yourself**) fail through being too ambitious.

overreact v. react more strongly than is justified. ■ **overreaction** n.

override v. (**overriding**, **overrode**; past part. **overridden**) **1** overrule. **2** interrupt the action of an automatic device. **3** be more important than.

overrule v. reject or disallow by using your higher authority.

overrun v. (**overrunning**, **overran**; past part. **overrun**) **1** spread over or occupy in large numbers. **2** exceed a limit.

overseas adv. & adj. in or to a foreign country.

oversee v. (**overseeing**, **oversaw**; past part. **overseen**) supervise. ■ **overseer** n.

overshadow v. **1** cast a shadow over. **2** appear more important or successful than.

overshoot v. (**overshooting**, **overshoot**) go past an intended place or limit.

oversight n. an unintentional failure to notice or do something.

overspill n. people who move from an overcrowded area to live elsewhere.

oversteer v. (of a car) tend to turn more sharply than intended.

overstep v. (**overstepping**, **overstepped**) go beyond a limit.

overt adj. done or shown openly. ■ **overtly** adv.

overtake v. (**overtaking**, **overtook**; past part. **overtaken**) **1** catch up with and pass while travelling in the same direction. **2** suddenly affect.

overthrow v. (**overthrowing**, **overthrew**; past part. **overthrown**) remove from power by force. •n. a removal from power.

overtime n. time worked in addition to normal working hours.

overtone n. a subtle or additional quality or implication.

overture n. **1** an orchestral piece at the beginning of a musical work. **2** an approach towards opening negotiations or establishing a relationship.

overturn v. **1** turn over and come to rest upside down, or cause to do this. **2** abolish or reverse a decision, system, etc.

overview n. a general review.

overweening adj. showing too much confidence or pride.

overwhelm v. **1** bury beneath a huge mass. **2** overpower. **3** have a strong emotional effect on.

overwrought adj. very worried or nervously excited.

oviduct n. the tube through which an ovum passes from an ovary.

oviparous adj. egg-laying.

ovoid adj. egg-shaped.

ovulate v. discharge ova from the ovary. ■ **ovulation** n.

ovule n. the part of the ovary of a plant that after fertilization becomes the seed.

ovum *n.* (*pl.* **ova**) a female reproductive cell, which can develop into an embryo if fertilized by a male cell.

owe *v.* (**owing, owed**) **1** be required to pay or repay money etc. in return for something received. **2** have something because of: *I owe him my life.*

owing *adj.* yet to be paid. □ **owing to** because of.

owl *n.* a bird of prey with large eyes, active at night. ■ **owlish** *adj.*

own *adj. & pron.* belonging to or done by the person specified. •*v.* **1** possess. **2** admit to be the case. **3** (**own up**) confess to a wrongdoing. ■ **owner** *n.* **ownership** *n.*

ox *n.* (*pl.* **oxen**) **1** a cow or bull. **2** a castrated bull, used for pulling heavy loads.

oxide *n.* a compound of oxygen and another element.

oxidize (or **-ise**) *v.* combine with oxygen. ■ **oxidation** *n.* **oxidization** *n.*

oxyacetylene *adj.* (of welding or cutting) using a very hot flame produced by mixing acetylene and oxygen.

oxygen *n.* a gas forming about 20 per cent of the earth's atmosphere.

oxygenate *v.* supply or treat with oxygen.

oxymoron *n.* a figure of speech in which apparently contradictory terms appear together (e.g. *a deafening silence*).

oyster *n.* an edible shellfish.

oz *abbrev.* ounces.

ozone *n.* a strong-smelling, poisonous form of oxygen. □ **ozone hole** an area of the ozone layer where the ozone is greatly reduced. **ozone layer** a layer in the earth's stratosphere containing much ozone, absorbing ultraviolet radiation.

o
p

Pp

p *abbrev.* **1** page. **2** penny or pence.

PA *abbrev.* **1** personal assistant. **2** public address.

p.a. *abbrev.* per annum.

pace *n.* **1** a single step when walking or running. **2** rate of movement or change. •*v.* **1** walk steadily or to and fro. **2** measure a distance by pacing. **3** (**pace yourself**) do something at a steady rate. □ **pacemaker 1** an artificial device for regulating the heart

muscle. **2** a runner who sets the pace for other competitors.

pachyderm /pak-i-derm/ *n.* a large thick-skinned mammal, e.g. an elephant.

pacific *adj.* **1** peaceful. **2** (**Pacific**) of the Pacific Ocean.

pacifism *n.* the belief that disputes should be settled without the use of war and violence. ■ **pacifist** *n. & adj.*

pacify v. (**pacifying**, **pacified**) 1 make less angry or upset. 2 establish peace in a country. ■ **pacification** n.

pack n. 1 a cardboard or paper container and the items in it. 2 a set of playing cards. 3 a group of dogs or wolves. •v. 1 fill a bag with items needed for travel. 2 put or cram items in a container. 3 cover or surround with something crammed tightly. □ **pack in** informal stop doing. **pack off** informal send away. ■ **packer** n.

package n. 1 something wrapped in paper or packed in a box. 2 a set of proposals offered or agreed as a whole. •v. 1 put into a box or wrapping. 2 present in an attractive way. □ **package holiday** a holiday whose price covers transport and accommodation.

packet n. 1 a small container or plastic bag in which goods are packed. 2 (**a packet**) informal a large sum of money.

pact n. a formal agreement.

pad n. 1 a piece of soft or absorbent material. 2 the fleshy underpart of an animal's foot. 3 a number of sheets of blank paper fastened together at one edge. 4 a flat surface for helicopter take-off and landing or for rocket-launching. •v. (**padding**, **padded**) 1 fill or cover with a pad. 2 lengthen a speech etc. with unnecessary material. 3 walk with soft, steady steps.

padding n. soft material used to pad or stuff something.

paddle n. a short oar with a broad blade. •v. 1 propel with a paddle. 2 walk with bare feet in shallow water.

paddock n. a small field or enclosure for horses.

padlock n. a detachable lock hanging by a hinged hook through a ring on the object fastened. •v. secure with a padlock.

padre /pah-dray/ n. a chaplain in the armed services.

paean /pee-uhn/ n. a song of praise or triumph.

paediatrics /pee-di-at-riks/ (US **pediatrics**) n. the branch of medicine concerned with children and their diseases. ■ **paediatric** adj. **paediatrician** n.

paedophile /pee-duh-fyl/ (US **pedophile**) n. a person who is sexually attracted to children. ■ **paedophilia** n.

paella /py-el-uh/ n. a Spanish dish of rice, seafood, etc.

pagan n. a person holding religious beliefs other than those of established religions. •adj. of pagans or their beliefs. ■ **paganism** n.

page n. 1 a leaf of a book etc. 2 one side of this. 3 a young male attendant in a hotel. 4 a young boy attending a bride. 5 hist. a boy in training for knighthood. •v. 1 (**page through**) leaf through. 2 summon over a public address system or by a pager.

pageant /paj-uhnt/ n. a public entertainment performed by people in elaborate or historical costumes. ■ **pageantry** n.

pager n. a radio device that bleeps or vibrates to summon the wearer.

pagoda n. a Hindu or Buddhist temple or other sacred building.

paid past & past part. of **PAY**.

pail n. a bucket.

pain n. 1 strong physical discomfort caused by illness or injury. 2 mental suffering. 3 (**pains**) great care or trouble. •v. cause pain to.

◻ **painkiller** a medicine for relieving pain. ■ **painful** adj. **painfully** adv. **painless** adj. **painlessly** adv.

painstaking adj. very careful and thorough.

paint n. a coloured substance spread over a surface to give a decorative or protective coating. •v. **1** apply paint to. **2** apply a liquid to a surface with a brush. **3** produce a picture with paint. **4** describe. ■ **painting** n.

painter n. **1** a person who paints as an artist or decorator. **2** a rope attached to a boat's bow for tying it up.

pair n. **1** a set of two things or people. **2** an article consisting of two parts: *a pair of scissors.* •v. **1** connect to form a pair. **2** (**pair off/ up**) form a couple.

paisley n. an intricate pattern of curved shapes like feathers.

pajamas US = PYJAMAS.

pal n. informal a friend.

palace n. an official residence of a monarch, archbishop, etc.

palaeography /pa-li-og-ruh-fi/ (US **paleography**) n. the study of ancient writing and manuscripts.

Palaeolithic /pa-li-uh-li-thik/ (US **Paleolithic**) adj. of the early phase of the Stone Age.

palaeontology /pa-li-on-tol-uh-ji/ (US **paleontology**) n. the study of fossil animals and plants. ■ **palaeontologist** n.

palatable adj. **1** pleasant to taste. **2** acceptable.

palate n. **1** the roof of the mouth. **2** the sense of taste.

palatial /puh-lay-sh'l/ adj. like a palace; very spacious or grand.

palaver n. informal a lengthy, boring fuss.

pale adj. **1** light in colour. **2** (of the face) having less colour than normal. •v. **1** become pale. **2** seem less important. ◻ **beyond the pale** outside the bounds of acceptable behaviour.

Palestinian n. a member of the native Arab population of Palestine. •adj. of Palestine.

palette n. **1** a board on which an artist mixes paints. **2** a range of colours used. ◻ **palette knife** a knife with a blunt, flexible blade for applying paint or smoothing soft substances.

palindrome n. a word or phrase that reads the same backwards as forwards.

paling n. **1** a fence made from stakes. **2** a stake.

palisade n. a fence of stakes or iron railings.

pall /pawl/ n. **1** a cloth spread over a coffin. **2** a dark cloud of smoke, dust, etc. •v. become less appealing through familiarity. ◻ **pall-bearer** a person helping to carry or escorting a coffin at a funeral.

palladium n. a rare silvery-white metallic element.

pallet n. **1** a straw mattress or makeshift bed. **2** a portable platform on which goods can be moved or stacked.

palliate v. **1** make the symptoms of a disease less severe. **2** make something bad less serious. ■ **palliative** adj.

pallid adj. pale, esp. from illness. ■ **pallor** n.

pally adj. informal friendly.

palm n. **1** an evergreen tree of warm regions, with a crown of long leaves. **2** the inner surface of the hand. •v. **1** hide in the hand.

p

2 (**palm off**) *informal* persuade someone to accept something by deception. □ **palmtop** a computer small enough to be held in one hand.

palmistry *n.* the prediction of a person's future by examining their hand. ■ **palmist** *n.*

palomino *n.* (*pl.* **palominos**) a pale golden horse with a white mane and tail.

palpable *adj.* able to be touched or felt. ■ **palpably** *adv.*

palpate *v.* medically examine by touch.

palpitate *v.* **1** (of the heart) beat rapidly. **2** shake; tremble. ■ **palpitations** *pl. n.*

palsy *n.* (*pl.* **palsies**) *dated* paralysis. ■ **palsied** *adj.*

paltry *adj.* **1** (of an amount) very small. **2** trivial.

pampas *n.* vast treeless plains in South America.

pamper *v.* treat very indulgently.

pamphlet *n.* a small booklet or leaflet.

pamphleteer *n.* a writer of pamphlets.

pan *n.* **1** a metal container for cooking food in. **2** the bowl of a toilet. • *v.* (**panning**, **panned**) **1** *informal* criticize severely. **2** swing a film camera to give a panoramic effect or follow a subject. **3** wash gravel in a bowl to separate out gold.

pan- *comb. form* all or whole.

panacea /pan-uh-see-uh/ *n.* a solution or remedy for all difficulties or diseases.

panache /puh-nash/ *n.* a confident stylish manner.

panama *n.* a straw hat.

pancake *n.* a thin, flat cake of fried batter.

pancreas *n.* a gland behind the stomach producing insulin. ■ **pancreatic** *adj.*

panda *n.* a large black and white bear-like mammal.

pandemic *adj.* (of a disease) occurring over a whole country or a wide area.

pandemonium *n.* uproar.

pander *v.* (**pander to**) indulge an immoral or distasteful desire or habit.

p. & p. *abbrev.* postage and packing.

pane *n.* a single sheet of glass in a window or door.

panegyric /pa-ni-ji-rik/ *n.* a speech or text in praise of someone or something.

panel *n.* **1** a section of a door, vehicle, garment, etc. **2** a small group assembled to investigate or decide on a matter. ■ **panelled** (US **paneled**) *adj.* **panellist** (US **panelist**) *n.*

panelling (US **paneling**) *n.* wooden panels as a wall covering.

pang *n.* a sudden sharp pain or painful emotion.

panic *n.* **1** sudden uncontrollable fear. **2** a frenzied hurry to do something. • *v.* (**panicking**, **panicked**) feel panic. ■ **panic-stricken** *adj.* **panicky** *adj.*

panjandrum *n.* a self-important official.

pannier *n.* **1** a bag fitted on the back of a bicycle or motorcycle. **2** a basket carried by a donkey etc.

panoply *n.* an impressive display.

panorama *n.* a view of a wide area or sequence of events. ■ **panoramic** *adj.*

p

pan pipes pl. n. a musical instrument made from a row of short pipes.

pansy n. **1** a plant with brightly coloured flowers. **2** offens. an effeminate or homosexual man.

pant v. breathe with short, quick breaths.

pantaloons pl. n. baggy trousers gathered at the ankles.

pantechnicon n. a large van for transporting furniture.

pantheism n. the belief that God is present in all things. ■ **pantheist** n. **pantheistic** adj.

pantheon n. **1** all the gods of a people or religion. **2** an ancient temple dedicated to all the gods.

panther n. a black leopard.

panties pl. n. informal women's underpants.

pantile n. a curved roof tile.

pantograph n. a device for copying a plan etc. on any scale.

pantomime n. a theatrical entertainment based on a fairy tale.

pantry n. (pl. **pantries**) a small room or cupboard for storing food, crockery, etc.

pants pl. n. **1** underpants or knickers. **2** US trousers.

pap n. **1** bland soft food suitable for babies or invalids. **2** undemanding reading matter or entertainment.

papacy n. (pl. **papacies**) the position or period of office of the pope.

papal adj. of the pope or papacy.

paparazzo /pa-puh-**rat**-zoh/ n. (pl. **paparazzi**) a freelance photographer who pursues celebrities to get photos of them.

papaya /puh-**py**-uh/ n. a tropical fruit with orange flesh.

paper n. **1** material manufactured in thin sheets from wood pulp, used for writing on, wrapping, etc. **2** a document. **3** a newspaper. **4** an essay. **5** a set of exam questions. •v. cover with wallpaper. □ **paperback** a book bound in flexible card. **paperweight** a small, heavy object for keeping loose papers in place. **paperwork** routine work involving written documents.

papier mâché /pa-pi-ay mash-ay/ n. a mixture of paper and glue that becomes hard when dry.

paprika n. a powdered spice made from red peppers.

papyrus n. (pl. **papyri** or **papyruses**) a material made in ancient Egypt from the stem of a water plant, used for writing or painting on.

par n. Golf the number of strokes required by a first-class player for a hole or course. □ **above** (or **below** or **under**) **par** above (or below) the usual or expected level. **on a par with** equal to.

parable n. a story told to illustrate a moral.

parabola n. a curve resembling the path of an object that is thrown into the air and falls back down. ■ **parabolic** adj.

paracetamol n. a drug used to reduce pain and fever.

parachute n. a cloth canopy used to slow the descent of a person or object dropping from a great height. •v. drop by parachute. ■ **parachutist** n.

parade n. **1** a public procession. **2** a formal assembly of troops. **3** an ostentatious display. **4** a public square, promenade, or row

p

of shops. •v. **1** march in a parade.
2 display ostentatiously.

paradigm /pa-ruh-dym/ n. a
typical example or model.

paradise n. **1** heaven. **2** a very
pleasant or beautiful place or
state.

paradox n. a statement that
seems to contradict itself, but may
in fact be true. ■ **paradoxical** adj.
paradoxically adv.

paraffin n. a flammable substance
obtained from petroleum or shale,
used as fuel.

paragliding n. a sport in which a
person glides with a wide parachute after jumping from or being
hauled to a height.

paragon n. a model of excellence
or of a particular quality.

paragraph n. a distinct section of
a piece of writing, begun on a new
line.

parakeet n. a small parrot.

parallax n. an apparent difference
in an object's position when
viewed from different points.

parallel adj. **1** (of lines or planes)
side by side and having the same
distance continuously between
them. **2** existing at the same time
or in a similar way. •n. **1** a person
or thing similar to another. **2** a
comparison. **3** a line of latitude. •v.
(**paralleling, paralleled**) **1** be
parallel to. **2** be similar to.

parallelogram n. a plane figure
with four straight sides and opposite sides parallel.

paralyse (US **paralyze**) v. affect
with paralysis.

paralysis n. (pl. **paralyses**) **1** the
loss of the power of movement.
2 inability to act or function.
■ **paralytic** adj.

paramedic n. a person who is
trained to do medical work but is
not a fully qualified doctor.

parameter n. a limit defining the
scope of a process or activity.

paramilitary adj. organized like a
military force.

paramount adj. more important
than anything else.

paramour n. old use a lover.

paranoia n. **1** a mental condition
in which a person has delusions of
persecution or grandeur. **2** un-
justified mistrust of others.
■ **paranoid** adj.

paranormal adj. beyond the
scope of scientific knowledge.

parapet n. a low wall along the
edge of a bridge, balcony, etc.

paraphernalia n. miscellaneous
equipment.

paraphrase v. express using different words. •n. a rewording of a
passage.

paraplegia /pa-ruh-plee-juh/ n.
paralysis of the legs and lower
body. ■ **paraplegic** adj. & n.

parapsychology n. the study of
mental phenomena such as telepathy or hypnosis.

paraquat n. a poisonous weed-
killer.

parasite n. **1** an organism living in
or on another. **2** a person living off
others. ■ **parasitic** adj.

parasol n. a light umbrella used to
give shade from the sun.

paratroops pl. n. troops trained
to parachute into an attack.
■ **paratrooper** n.

parboil v. partly cook by boiling.

parcel n. something wrapped in
paper so as to be carried or
posted. •v. (**parcelling, parcelled**)

US **parceling, parceled**) 1 wrap as a parcel. 2 divide into portions.

parched adj. 1 dried out through heat. 2 informal very thirsty.

parchment n. 1 hist. writing material made from animal skin. 2 paper treated to resemble this.

pardon n. 1 forgiveness. 2 a cancellation of the punishment for an offence. •v. (**pardoning, pardoned**) 1 forgive. 2 give an offender a pardon. ∎ **pardonable** adj.

pare v. 1 trim the edges of. 2 gradually reduce.

parent n. 1 a father or mother. 2 an organization owning or controlling subsidiary ones. ∎ **parental** adj. **parenthood** n. **parenting** n.

parentage n. the identity and origins of a person's parents.

parenthesis /puh-ren-thi-siss/ n. (pl. **parentheses**) 1 a word or phrase added as an explanation or aside. 2 (**parentheses**) a pair of round brackets (). ∎ **parenthetic** adj. **parenthetical** adj.

pariah n. an outcast.

parietal bone n. either of two bones forming part of the skull.

parings pl. n. thin strips pared off something.

parish n. 1 a district with its own church and clergy. 2 the smallest unit of local government in rural areas. ∎ **parishioner** n.

parity n. equality.

park n. 1 a large public garden in a town. 2 the enclosed land of a country house. 3 an area devoted to a specified purpose. 4 an area for parking vehicles. •v. stop and leave a vehicle temporarily.

parka n. a windproof hooded jacket.

Parkinson's disease n. a disease causing trembling and muscular rigidity.

parky adj. informal chilly.

parlance n. a particular way of using words.

parley n. (pl. **parleys**) a meeting between enemies to settle a dispute. •v. (**parleying, parleyed**) hold a parley.

parliament n. an assembly making the laws in a country. ∎ **parliamentarian** n. **parliamentary** adj.

parlour (US **parlor**) n. 1 dated a sitting room. 2 a shop providing particular goods or services.

parlous adj. precarious.

Parmesan n. a hard Italian cheese.

parochial adj. 1 of a parish. 2 having a narrow outlook. ∎ **parochialism** n.

parody n. (pl. **parodies**) a piece of writing etc. that imitates the style of another so as to be amusing. •v. (**parodying, parodied**) produce a parody of.

parole n. the release of a prisoner before the end of their sentence, on the condition of good behaviour. •v. release on parole.

paroxysm n. a sudden attack or outburst.

parquet /par-kay/ n. flooring composed of wooden blocks arranged in a geometric pattern.

parricide n. the killing of someone's own parent.

parrot n. a tropical bird with a hooked bill, some kinds of which can copy human speech. •v. (**parroting, parroted**) repeat mechanically.

p

parry v. (**parrying**, **parried**)
1 ward off a weapon or blow.
2 evade a question.

parse v. analyse a sentence in terms of grammar.

parsimony n. extreme reluctance to spend money. ■ **parsimonious** adj.

parsley n. a herb with crinkly or flat leaves.

parsnip n. a long tapering cream-coloured root vegetable.

parson n. an Anglican parish priest.

parsonage n. a parson's house.

part n. 1 a piece combining with others to make up a whole.
2 some but not all of something.
3 an acting role. 4 a person's contribution to a situation. • v. 1 separate or be separated. 2 (**part with**) give up possession of. • adv. partly. □ **in good part** without taking offence. **part of speech** a category in which a word is placed according to its grammatical function, e.g. noun, verb, etc. **part-time** for only part of the usual working day or week. **take part** join in.

partake v. (**partaking**, **partook**; past part. **partaken**) 1 (**partake in**) participate in. 2 (**partake of**) eat or drink.

partial adj. 1 not complete or whole. 2 favouring one side in a dispute. 3 (**partial to**) having a liking for. ■ **partiality** n. **partially** adv.

participate v. take part. ■ **participant** n. **participation** n.

participle n. a word formed from a verb (e.g. burning, burnt) and used in compound tenses or as an adjective or noun. ■ **participial** adj.

particle n. a tiny portion of matter.

particular adj. 1 of an individual member of a group or class.
2 more than is usual. 3 very careful or concerned about something. • n. a detail. □ **in particular** especially. ■ **particularly** adv.

parting n. 1 an act of leaving someone. 2 a line of scalp visible when the hair is combed in different directions.

partisan n. 1 a strong supporter.
2 a guerrilla. • adj. prejudiced.

partition n. 1 a structure dividing a space or room. 2 division into parts. • v. divide into parts or with a partition.

partly adv. to some extent.

partner n. 1 each of two or more people who are involved in an undertaking. 2 either of two people doing something as a pair.
3 either member of a couple having a sexual or romantic relationship. • v. be the partner of.
■ **partnership** n.

partook past of PARTAKE.

partridge n. a short-tailed game bird.

parturition n. the act of giving birth.

party n. (pl. **parties**) 1 a social gathering. 2 an organized political group. 3 a group taking part in an activity or trip. 4 one side in an agreement or dispute. □ **party line** a policy officially adopted by a political party. **party wall** a wall shared by two adjoining buildings or rooms.

parvenu n. derog. a person who has recently become wealthy or famous.

pascal n. a unit of pressure.

paschal /pass-kuhl/ adj. 1 of Easter. 2 of Passover.

pass v. **1** move or go onward, past, through, or across. **2** change from one state to another. **3** transfer. **4** kick, hit, or throw the ball to a teammate. **5** (of time) go by. **6** spend time. **7** be successful in an exam. **8** declare to be satisfactory. **9** approve a proposal etc. by voting. • n. **1** an act of passing. **2** a success in an exam. **3** a permit to enter a place. **4** a route over or through mountains. **5** informal a sexual advance. ☐ **pass away** die. **pass off as** pretend that something is something else. **pass out** become unconscious. **pass up** refrain from taking an opportunity.

password a secret word or phrase used to gain admission.

passable adj. **1** just satisfactory. **2** able to be travelled along or on. ■ **passably** adv.

passage n. **1** the act of passing. **2** a way through something. **3** a journey by sea. **4** the right to pass through. **5** a short section from a text etc. ☐ **passageway** a corridor or walled access between buildings or rooms.

passé /pas-ay/ adj. old-fashioned.

passenger n. a person travelling in a vehicle, ship, or aircraft, other than the driver, pilot, or crew.

passer-by n. (pl. **passers-by**) a person who happens to be walking past something or someone.

passim adv. at various places throughout a text.

passing adj. done or carried out quickly and casually.

passion n. **1** very strong emotion. **2** intense sexual love. **3** great enthusiasm. **4** (**the Passion**) the suffering and death of Jesus on the cross. ■ **passionate** adj. **passionately** adv.

passive adj. **1** accepting what happens without resistance. **2** (of a verb) in which the subject undergoes the action of the verb. ■ **passively** adv. **passivity** n.

Passover n. a Jewish spring festival commemorating the liberation of the Israelites from slavery in Egypt.

passport n. an official document certifying the holder's identity and citizenship and entitling them to travel abroad.

past adj. **1** gone by in time and no longer existing. **2** (of time) that has gone by. • n. **1** a past period or the events in it. **2** a person's previous experiences. • prep. **1** beyond in time or space. **2** in front of or from one side to the other of. **3** beyond the scope or power of. • adv. going past or beyond. ☐ **past master** an expert.

pasta n. dough formed into various shapes and cooked in boiling water.

paste n. **1** a soft, moist substance. **2** a glue. **3** a hard substance used in making imitation gems. • v. coat or stick with paste. ☐ **pasteboard** cardboard.

pastel n. **1** a crayon made of powdered pigments. **2** a picture drawn with pastels. **3** a pale shade of a colour.

pasteurize (or **-ise**) v. sterilize by heating. ■ **pasteurization** n.

pastiche /pa-steesh/ n. a work in the style of another artist.

pastille n. a small sweet or lozenge.

pastime n. an activity done regularly for enjoyment.

pastor n. a minister in charge of a church or congregation.

p

pastoral adj. **1** of or used for the keeping of sheep or cattle. **2** of country life. **3** of spiritual and moral guidance.

pastrami /pass-trah-mi/ n. highly seasoned smoked beef.

pastry n. (pl. **pastries**) **1** a dough of flour, fat, and water, used for making pies etc. **2** a cake of sweet pastry with a filling.

pasture n. grassy land suitable for grazing cattle or sheep. •v. put animals to graze in a pasture. ■ **pasturage** n.

pasty[1] /pass-ti/ n. (pl. **pasties**) a folded pastry case filled with meat and vegetables.

pasty[2] /pay-sti/ adj. unhealthily pale.

pat v. (**patted**, **patting**) tap quickly and gently with the flat of the hand. •n. **1** an act of patting. **2** a mass of a soft substance. •adj. too quick or easy and not convincing. □ **off pat** perfectly memorized.

patch n. **1** a piece of material used to mend a hole or strengthen a weak point. **2** a small area differing from its surroundings. **3** a small plot of land. **4** informal a period of time. **5** a cover worn over an injured eye. •v. mend with a patch. □ **patch up** informal **1** repair quickly or temporarily. **2** settle a dispute. **patchwork** needlework in which small pieces of cloth are joined to make a pattern.

patchy adj. **1** existing in small, isolated areas. **2** uneven in quality.

pâté /pa-tay/ n. a rich savoury paste of meat etc.

patella n. (pl. **patellae**) the kneecap.

patent n. a licence giving someone the sole right to make, use, or sell their invention. •adj. **1** obvious. **2** patented. •v. obtain a patent for. □ **patent leather** glossy varnished leather. ■ **patently** adv.

paternal adj. **1** of or like a father. **2** related through a person's father. ■ **paternally** adv.

paternalism n. the policy of protecting the people you have control over, but also of restricting their freedom. ■ **paternalistic** adj.

paternity n. the state or fact of being a father.

path n. **1** a way laid down for or made by walking. **2** the course along which a person or thing moves. **3** a course of action.

pathetic adj. **1** arousing pity. **2** informal completely inadequate. ■ **pathetically** adv.

pathological adj. **1** of or caused by a disease. **2** informal compulsive. ■ **pathologically** adv.

pathology n. the study of diseases. ■ **pathologist** n.

pathos n. a quality arousing pity or sadness.

patience n. **1** the ability to accept delay or trouble calmly. **2** a card game for one player.

patient adj. showing patience. •n. a person receiving medical treatment. ■ **patiently** adv.

patina n. **1** a green film on bronze. **2** a sheen on a surface produced by age and polishing.

patio n. (pl. **patios**) a paved outdoor area by a house.

patisserie n. a shop where cakes etc. are sold.

patois /pat-wah/ n. (pl. **patois**) a dialect.

patriarch n. **1** the male head of a family or tribe. **2** a high-ranking

bishop in certain Churches.
■ **patriarchal** adj. **patriarchy** n.

patricide n. **1** the killing of a father by his child. **2** a person who kills their father.

patrimony n. (pl. **patrimonies**) property inherited from a person's father or male ancestor.

patriot n. a person who strongly supports their country. ■ **patriotic** adj. **patriotism** n.

patrol v. (**patrolling, patrolled**) keep watch over an area by regularly walking or travelling around it. •n. **1** a person or group sent to patrol an area. **2** the act of patrolling an area.

patron n. **1** a person giving financial or other support to a cause. **2** a regular customer of a hotel etc. □ **patron saint** a saint believed to protect a particular place or group. ■ **patronage** n.

patronize (or **-ise**) v. **1** treat someone in a way that suggests they are inferior. **2** be a regular customer of.

patronymic n. a name derived from that of a father or ancestor.

patter v. make a repeated light tapping sound. •n. **1** a pattering sound. **2** fast continuous talk.

pattern n. **1** a repeated decorative design. **2** a regular sequence of actions or events. **3** a model, design, or set of instructions for making something. **4** an example to follow. **5** a sample of cloth etc. ■ **patterned** adj.

patty n. (pl. **patties**) a small pie or pasty.

paucity n. scarcity or lack of something.

paunch n. a protruding stomach.

pauper n. a very poor person.

pause n. a temporary stop. •v. stop temporarily.

pave v. cover a piece of ground with flat stones or bricks.
■ **paving** n.

pavement n. a raised path at the side of a road.

pavilion n. **1** a building at a sports ground for changing and taking refreshments. **2** a summer house in a park etc.

paw n. an animal's foot having claws and pads. •v. feel or scrape with a paw or hoof.

pawn n. **1** a chess piece of the smallest size and value. **2** a person used by others for their own purposes. •v. leave an item with a pawnbroker as security for money lent. □ **pawnbroker** a person licensed to lend money in exchange for an item left with them. **pawnshop** a pawnbroker's shop.

pawpaw n. a papaya.

pay v. (**paying, paid**) **1** give someone money for work or goods. **2** give a sum of money owed. **3** result in a profit or advantage. **4** suffer as a result of an action. **5** give attention etc. to. •n. money paid for work. □ **payload** an explosive warhead carried by an aircraft or missile. **pay-off** informal a payment made as a bribe or on leaving a job. **pay off 1** dismiss with a final payment. **2** informal yield good results. **payroll** a list of a company's employees and their wages.
■ **payable** adj.

PAYE abbrev. pay as you earn, a system whereby tax is deducted from wages before payment.

payee n. a person to whom money is paid.

payment n. **1** an amount that is paid. **2** the act of paying.

payola n. US bribery in return for the unofficial promotion of a product in the media.

PC abbrev. **1** personal computer. **2** police constable. **3** politically correct; political correctness.

PDF n. an electronic file which can be sent by any system and displayed on any computer.

PE abbrev. physical education.

pea n. a round green seed in a pod, eaten as a vegetable.

peace n. **1** freedom from noise or anxiety. **2** freedom from war.

peaceable adj. **1** avoiding conflict. **2** peaceful. ■ **peaceably** adv.

peaceful adj. **1** free from noise or anxiety. **2** not involving war or violence. ■ **peacefully** adv. **peacefulness** n.

peach n. **1** a round juicy fruit with a rough stone inside. **2** a pinkish-orange colour.

peacock n. a colourful bird with long tail feathers that can be fanned out in display.

peahen n. the female of the peacock.

peak n. **1** the pointed top of a mountain. **2** a stiff brim at the front of a cap. **3** the point of highest activity, achievement, etc. • v. reach a highest point. • adj. maximum. ■ **peaked** adj.

peaky adj. pale from illness or tiredness.

peal n. **1** the loud ringing sound of a bell or bells. **2** a loud sound of thunder or laughter. **3** a set of bells. • v. ring or sound loudly.

peanut n. **1** the oval edible seed of a South American plant. **2** (**peanuts**) informal a very small sum of money.

pear n. a rounded fruit tapering towards the stalk.

pearl n. a small, hard, shiny white gem formed within the shell of an oyster. ■ **pearly** adj.

peasant n. a poor smallholder or farm labourer. ■ **peasantry** n.

peat n. decomposed vegetable matter formed in boggy ground, used in gardening or as fuel. ■ **peaty** adj.

pebble n. a small, smooth, round stone. ■ **pebbly** adj.

pecan n. a smooth pinkish-brown nut.

peccadillo n. (pl. **peccadilloes** or **peccadillos**) a minor fault.

peccary n. (pl. **peccaries**) a small piglike mammal.

peck v. **1** hit or bite with the beak. **2** kiss lightly and quickly. • n. an act of pecking.

peckish adj. informal hungry.

pectin n. a substance present in fruits, used to set jam.

pectoral adj. of, in, or on the breast or chest. • n. a pectoral fin or muscle.

peculiar adj. **1** strange or odd. **2** (**peculiar to**) belonging only to. ■ **peculiarity** n. **peculiarly** adv.

pecuniary adj. of or in money.

pedagogue n. a teacher. ■ **pedagogy** n.

pedal n. a lever operated by the foot. • v. (**pedalling**, **pedalled**; US **pedaling**, **pedaled**) move a bicycle by working the pedals.

> **!** Don't confuse **pedal** with **peddle**, which means 'sell goods'.

pedalo n. (pl. **pedalos** or **pedaloes**) a small pedal-operated pleasure boat.

pedantic *adj.* excessively concerned with minor details or rules. ■ **pedant** *n.* **pedantry** *n.*

peddle *v.* **1** sell goods by going from place to place. **2** sell an illegal drug.

! Don't confuse **peddle** with **pedal**.

peddler var. of PEDLAR.

pedestal *n.* the base supporting a statue or column etc.

pedestrian *n.* a person walking rather than travelling in a vehicle. •*adj.* dull.

pediatrics etc. *US* = PAEDIATRICS etc.

pedicure *n.* a cosmetic treatment of the feet and toenails.

pedigree *n.* **1** an animal's record of descent. **2** a person's ancestry.

pediment *n.* the triangular part above the entrance of a classical building.

pedlar (or **peddler**) *n.* **1** a travelling trader who sells small goods. **2** a person who sells illegal drugs.

pedometer *n.* an instrument for estimating the distance travelled on foot.

peek *v.* look quickly. •*n.* a quick look.

peel *v.* **1** remove the skin from a fruit or vegetable. **2** remove a thin covering or layer from. **3** (of a surface) come off in small pieces. •*n.* the outer skin of a fruit or vegetable. ■ **peeler** *n.* **peelings** *pl. n.*

peep *v.* **1** look quickly or secretly. **2** (**peep out**) be just visible. •*n.* **1** a quick or secret look. **2** a glimpse. □ **peephole** a small hole in a door through which callers can be seen. **peeping Tom** a furtive voyeur.

peer *v.* look with difficulty or concentration. •*n.* **1** a member of the nobility in Britain or Ireland. **2** a person of the same age, status, etc. as another.

peerage *n.* **1** the rank of peer or peeress. **2** peers as a whole.

peeress *n.* **1** a woman holding the rank of a peer. **2** a peer's wife or widow.

peerless *adj.* better than all others.

peevish *adj.* irritable. ■ **peevishly** *adv.*

peg *n.* **1** a pin or bolt used for hanging things on or fastening something. **2** a clip for holding clothes on a line. •*v.* (**pegging**, **pegged**) **1** fix, attach, or mark with a peg or pegs. **2** fix a price etc. at a particular level. □ **off the peg** (of clothes) ready-made.

pejorative *adj.* expressing contempt or disapproval.

Pekinese *n.* (*pl.* **Pekinese**) a small dog with long hair, short legs, and a snub nose.

pelican *n.* a waterbird with a long bill and a throat pouch. □ **pelican crossing** a pedestrian crossing with traffic lights operated by pedestrians.

pellagra *n.* a disease involving inflamed skin, diarrhoea, etc., caused by an inadequate diet.

pellet *n.* **1** a small compressed mass of a substance. **2** a piece of small shot.

pell-mell *adj.* & *adv.* in a confused or rushed way.

pellucid *adj.* very clear.

pelmet *n.* a strip of wood or fabric fitted above a window to conceal curtain fittings.

pelt *v.* **1** hurl missiles at. **2** (**pelt down**) fall very heavily. •*n.* an

P

animal skin with the fur or wool still on it. □ **(at) full pelt** as fast as possible.

pelvis *n.* the bony frame at the base of the spine to which the legs are attached. ■ **pelvic** *adj.*

pen *n.* **1** an instrument for writing or drawing with ink. **2** a small enclosure for farm animals. **3** a female swan. *v.* (**penning, penned**) **1** write or compose. **2** put or keep in a pen or restricted space. □ **penfriend** a person with whom someone forms a friendship by exchanging letters. **pen name** a name used by a writer instead of their real name.

penal *adj.* of the use of punishment as part of the legal system.

penalize (or **-ise**) *v.* **1** give a penalty or punishment to. **2** put in an unfavourable position.

penalty *n.* (*pl.* **penalties**) a punishment for breaking a law, rule, or contract.

penance *n.* an act done as a punishment for or acknowledgement of wrongdoing.

pence pl. of **PENNY**.

penchant /pon-shon/ *n.* a strong liking.

pencil *n.* an instrument for writing or drawing, consisting of a stick of wood with a graphite core. *v.* (**pencilling, pencilled**; US **penciling, penciled**) write, draw, or mark with a pencil.

pendant *n.* a piece of jewellery hung from a chain around the neck.

pendent (or **pendant**) *adj.* hanging down.

pending *adj.* waiting to be decided or settled. *prep.* until.

pendulous *adj.* hanging loosely.

pendulum *n.* a weight hung from a fixed point so that it can swing freely, used to regulate a clock's mechanism.

penetrate *v.* **1** force a way into or through. **2** understand or gain insight into. **3** (**penetrating**) (of a sound) clearly heard above other sounds. ■ **penetration** *n.*

penguin *n.* a flightless seabird of the southern hemisphere.

penicillin *n.* an antibiotic.

peninsula *n.* a long piece of land projecting into the sea. ■ **peninsular** *adj.*

penis *n.* the male organ used for urinating and having sex.

penitent *adj.* feeling regret for having done wrong. *n.* a penitent person. ■ **penitence** *n.* **penitential** *adj.*

penitentiary *n.* (*pl.* **penitentiaries**) US a prison.

pennant *n.* a long, tapering flag.

penniless *adj.* without money.

pennon *n.* a pennant.

penny *n.* (*pl.* **pennies**; **pence**) **1** a British bronze coin worth one hundredth of a pound. **2** a former coin worth one twelfth of a shilling. □ **penny-farthing** an early type of bicycle with a large front wheel and small rear wheel. **penny-pinching** miserly.

pension[1] *n.* a regular payment made to retired people, widows, etc., either by the state or from an investment fund. *v.* (**pension off**) dismiss with a pension. ■ **pensionable** *adj.* **pensioner** *n.*

pension[2] /pon-syon/ *n.* a small hotel in Europe.

pensive *adj.* deep in thought. ■ **pensively** *adv.*

pentagon *n.* a plane figure with five sides.

pentagram n. a five-pointed star.

Pentateuch /pen-tuh-tyook/ n. the first five books of the Old Testament and Hebrew Scriptures.

pentathlon n. an athletic contest involving five events.

Pentecost n. a Christian festival celebrating the descent of the Holy Spirit on the disciples of Jesus.

penthouse n. a flat on the top floor of a tall building.

pent-up adj. not expressed or released.

penultimate adj. last but one.

penumbra n. (pl. **penumbrae** or **penumbras**) the partially shaded outer part of a shadow.

penury n. extreme poverty. ■ **penurious** adj.

peony n. (pl. **peonies**) a plant grown for its showy flowers.

people pl. n. **1** human beings. **2** the ordinary citizens of a country. **3** (pl. **peoples**) the members of a particular nation, community, or ethnic group. •v. fill with people.

pep informal n. liveliness. •v. (**pepping**, **pepped**) (**pep up**) make more lively. □ **pep talk** a talk intended to make someone feel braver or more enthusiastic.

pepper n. **1** a hot-tasting seasoning made from peppercorns. **2** the fruit of a tropical American plant. •v. **1** sprinkle with pepper. **2** (**pepper with**) scatter in large amounts over or through. **3** hit repeatedly with small missiles or gunshot. ■ **peppery** adj.

peppercorn n. the dried berry of a plant, ground to make pepper. □ **peppercorn rent** a very low or nominal rent.

peppermint n. **1** a plant producing an aromatic oil. **2** a sweet flavoured with peppermint oil.

pepperoni n. beef and pork sausage seasoned with pepper.

pepsin n. the chief digestive enzyme in the stomach.

peptic adj. of digestion.

per prep. **1** for each. **2** (as per) in accordance with. □ **per annum** for each year. **per capita** for each person. **per cent** in or for every hundred. **per se** by or in itself.

perambulate v. walk or travel from place to place. ■ **perambulation** n.

perambulator n. a pram.

perceive v. **1** become aware of through the senses. **2** regard as.

percentage n. **1** a rate or amount in each hundred. **2** a proportion or share, esp. of profits.

perceptible adj. able to be perceived. ■ **perceptibly** adv.

perception n. the ability to perceive, or the act of perceiving.

perceptive adj. having or showing insight. ■ **perceptively** adv.

perch n. **1** a branch, bar, etc. on which a bird rests or roosts. **2** a high or narrow seat. **3** (pl. **perch**) an edible freshwater fish. •v. **1** sit or rest somewhere. **2** place or balance somewhere.

percipient adj. perceptive. ■ **percipience** n.

percolate v. **1** filter, esp. through small holes. **2** prepare coffee in a percolator. ■ **percolation** n.

percolator n. a device for making coffee, consisting of a pot in which boiling water is circulated through ground coffee held in a small chamber.

p

percussion n. musical instruments that are played by being struck or shaken.

perdition n. eternal damnation.

peregrinations pl. n. old use travels.

peregrine n. a falcon.

peremptory adj. insisting on immediate attention or obedience. ▪ **peremptorily** adv.

perennial adj. **1** lasting for a long time or forever. **2** (of a plant) living for several years. **3** constantly recurring. • n. a perennial plant. ▪ **perennially** adv.

perestroika /pe-ri-stroy-kuh/ n. (in the former USSR) the economic and political reforms introduced during the 1980s.

perfect adj. **1** without any faults or defects. **2** complete; total: it made perfect sense. • v. make perfect. ▪ **perfection** n. **perfectly** adv.

perfectionism n. refusal to accept any standard short of perfection. ▪ **perfectionist** n.

perfidious adj. deceitful and disloyal. ▪ **perfidy** n.

perforate v. pierce and make a hole or holes in. ▪ **perforation** n.

perforce adv. necessarily; unavoidably.

perform v. **1** carry out or complete an action. **2** present entertainment to an audience. ▪ **performance** n. **performer** n.

perfume n. **1** a scented liquid for applying to the body. **2** a pleasant smell. • v. give a pleasant smell to. ▪ **perfumery** n.

perfunctory adj. done with a minimum of effort or thought. ▪ **perfunctorily** adv.

pergola n. an arched framework for climbing plants.

perhaps adv. possibly; maybe.

pericardium n. (pl. **pericardia**) the membrane enclosing the heart.

perigee n. the point in the moon's orbit when it is nearest to the earth.

peril n. serious danger. ▪ **perilous** adj. **perilously** adv.

perimeter n. the outer edge or boundary of something.

perinatal adj. of the time immediately before and after birth.

period n. **1** a length or portion of time. **2** a lesson in a school. **3** a flow of blood each month from the lining of a woman's womb. **4** a full stop. • adj. belonging to a past historical time.

periodic adj. occurring at intervals. ▫ **periodic table** a table of all the chemical elements.

periodical adj. periodic. • n. a magazine etc. published at regular intervals. ▪ **periodically** adv.

peripatetic adj. travelling from place to place.

periphery n. (pl. **peripheries**) **1** the outer limits of an area or object. **2** the less important part of a subject or group. ▪ **peripheral** adj.

periphrasis n. (pl. **periphrases**) indirect language.

periscope n. a tube attached to a set of mirrors, by which things can be seen that are above or behind something else.

perish v. **1** die. **2** be destroyed. **3** rot.

perishable adj. (of food) likely to rot quickly.

peritoneum /pe-ri-tuh-nee-uhm/ n. (pl. **peritoneums** or **peritonea**) the membrane lining the abdominal cavity.

peritonitis n. inflammation of the peritoneum.

periwinkle n. a plant with flat five-petalled flowers.

perjure v. (**perjure yourself**) commit perjury.

perjury n. the offence of deliberately telling a lie in court when under oath.

perk v. (**perk up**) make or become more cheerful or lively. • n. informal a benefit to which an employee is entitled.

perky adj. (**perkier, perkiest**) cheerful and lively. ■ **perkily** adv.

perm n. a chemical treatment giving hair a long-lasting curly style. • v. treat hair with a perm.

permafrost n. a layer of soil beneath the surface that remains frozen throughout the year.

permanent adj. lasting for a long time or forever. ■ **permanence** n. **permanently** adv.

permeable adj. allowing liquids or gases to pass through. ■ **permeability** n.

permeate v. spread throughout.

permissible adj. allowable.

permission n. the act of allowing someone to do something.

permissive adj. allowing freedom of behaviour, esp. in sexual matters. ■ **permissiveness** n.

permit v. (**permitting, permitted**) 1 give permission to or for. 2 make possible. • n. an official document giving permission to do something.

permutation n. each of several possible ways of ordering or arranging a number of things.

pernicious adj. harmful.

pernickety adj. informal fussy.

peroration n. the concluding part of a speech.

peroxide n. a chemical used to bleach hair.

perpendicular adj. at an angle of 90° to a line or surface. • n. a perpendicular line.

perpetrate v. carry out a bad or illegal action. ■ **perpetration** n. **perpetrator** n.

perpetual adj. 1 never ending or changing. 2 very frequent. ■ **perpetually** adv.

perpetuate v. cause to continue for a long time. ■ **perpetuation** n.

perpetuity n. the state of lasting forever.

perplex v. puzzle greatly. ■ **perplexity** n.

perquisite n. a special right or privilege resulting from a person's position.

perry n. an alcoholic drink made from fermented pears.

persecute v. 1 treat badly over a long period. 2 persistently harass. ■ **persecution** n. **persecutor** n.

persevere v. continue in spite of difficulty or lack of success. ■ **perseverance** n.

persimmon n. a tropical fruit.

persist v. 1 continue doing something in spite of difficulty or opposition. 2 continue to exist. ■ **persistence** n. **persistent** adj. **persistently** adv.

person n. (pl. **people** or **persons**) 1 an individual human being. 2 an individual's body. 3 Grammar a category used in classifying pronouns or verb forms according to whether they indicate the speaker (**first person**), the person spoken to (**second person**), or a third party (**third person**). □ **in person** actually present.

persona n. (pl. **personas** or **personae**) the aspect of a person's character that is presented to others.

personable adj. having a pleasant appearance and manner.

personage n. an important or famous person.

personal adj. **1** belonging to or affecting a particular person. **2** done by a particular person rather than someone else. **3** concerning a person's private life. **4** of a person's body. □ **personal organizer** a loose-leaf notebook with a diary and address section. **personal pronoun** each of the pronouns (*I, you, he, she*, etc.) that show person, gender, number, and case. ■ **personally** adv.

personality n. (pl. **personalities**) **1** the qualities that form a person's character. **2** qualities that make someone interesting or popular. **3** a celebrity.

personalize (or **-ise**) v. **1** design to suit or identify as belonging to a particular person. **2** cause an issue to be concerned with personalities or feelings.

personify v. (**personifying, personified**) **1** represent in human form or as having human characteristics. **2** be an example of a quality. ■ **personification** n.

personnel pl. n. employees; staff.

perspective n. **1** the art of drawing things so as to give an effect of solidity and relative distance. **2** a way of seeing something. **3** understanding of the relative importance of things.

perspex n. trademark a tough, light transparent plastic.

perspicacious adj. quickly gaining insight into things. ■ **perspicacity** n.

perspicuous adj. expressing things clearly. ■ **perspicuity** n.

perspire v. sweat. ■ **perspiration** n.

persuade v. cause to do or believe something by reasoning.

persuasion n. **1** the act or a means of persuading. **2** a belief or set of beliefs.

persuasive adj. **1** good at persuading. **2** providing sound reasoning. ■ **persuasively** adv.

pert adj. attractively lively or cheeky.

pertain v. be related or relevant.

pertinacious adj. persistent. ■ **pertinacity** n.

pertinent adj. relevant. ■ **pertinence** n. **pertinently** adv.

perturb v. make anxious. ■ **perturbation** n.

peruse v. read carefully. ■ **perusal** n.

pervade v. spread or be present throughout. ■ **pervasive** adj.

perverse adj. **1** deliberately choosing to behave in an unacceptable way. **2** contrary to what is accepted or expected. ■ **perversely** adv. **perversity** n.

pervert v. **1** divert from the correct or intended meaning or course. **2** lead into abnormal or unacceptable sexual behaviour. •n. a person whose sexual behaviour is abnormal or unacceptable. ■ **perversion** n.

pervious adj. allowing water to pass through.

peseta n. a former currency unit of Spain.

peso n. a currency unit of several South American countries.

pessary n. (pl. **pessaries**) a small soluble block inserted into the vagina to treat infection.

pessimism n. lack of hope or confidence in the future. ■ **pessimist** n. **pessimistic** adj. **pessimistically** adv.

pest n. a destructive insect or other animal that attacks plants, crops, etc.

pester v. trouble with persistent requests or interruptions.

pesticide n. a substance for destroying insects or other pests.

pestilence n. old use a deadly epidemic disease. ■ **pestilential** adj.

pestle n. a heavy tool with a rounded end for crushing things in a mortar.

pesto n. a sauce of basil, pine nuts, Parmesan cheese, and olive oil, served with pasta.

pet n. **1** a tame animal kept for company and pleasure. **2** a person treated with special favour. •adj. **1** of or kept as a pet. **2** favourite or particular. •v. (**petting, petted**) **1** stroke or pat an animal. **2** caress sexually.

petal n. each of the segments forming the outer part of a flower.

peter v. (**peter out**) come to an end gradually.

petite adj. small and dainty.

petition n. **1** an appeal or request, esp. a written one signed by many people. **2** an application to a law court for a writ etc. •v. present a petition to.

petrel n. a seabird.

petrify v. (**petrifying, petrified**) **1** change organic matter into stone. **2** paralyse with fear. ■ **petrifaction** n.

petrochemical n. a chemical obtained from petroleum and natural gas.

petrol n. refined petroleum used as fuel in vehicles.

petroleum n. an oil found in layers of rock and refined to produce fuels.

petticoat n. a woman's undergarment in the form of a skirt.

pettifogging adj. petty; trivial.

pettish adj. childishly sulky.

petty adj. (**pettier, pettiest**) **1** unimportant; trivial. **2** small-minded. **3** minor. ■ **petty cash** money kept in an office for small payments. ■ **pettiness** n.

petulant adj. childishly sulky or bad-tempered. ■ **petulance** n. **petulantly** adv.

petunia n. a plant with white, purple, or red funnel-shaped flowers.

pew n. a long bench with a back in a church.

pewter n. a grey alloy of tin with copper and antimony.

pfennig n. a former currency unit of Germany.

PG abbrev. (in film classification) parental guidance.

pH n. a measure of the acidity or alkalinity of a substance.

phalanx n. (pl. **phalanxes**) a group of people or things, esp. a body of troops or police officers.

phallus n. (pl. **phalli** or **phalluses**) a penis. ■ **phallic** adj.

phantom n. a ghost.

pharaoh /fair-oh/ n. a ruler in ancient Egypt.

! Remember, -aoh not -oah: phar*aoh*.

p

pharmaceutical *adj.* of medicinal drugs.

pharmacist *n.* a person qualified to prepare and dispense medicinal drugs.

pharmacology *n.* the study of the uses and effects of drugs. ■ **pharmacological** *adj.* **pharmacologist** *n.*

pharmacopoeia /far-muh-kuh-pee-uh/ *n.* an official list of medicinal drugs with their effects.

pharmacy *n.* (*pl.* **pharmacies**) **1** a place where medicinal drugs are prepared or sold. **2** the preparation and dispensing of medicinal drugs.

pharynx *n.* (*pl.* **pharynges** /fa-rin-jeez/) the cavity behind the nose and mouth.

phase *n.* a distinct stage in a process of change or development. • *v.* **1** carry out in gradual stages. **2** (**phase in/out**) gradually introduce or withdraw.

PhD *abbrev.* Doctor of Philosophy.

pheasant *n.* a long-tailed game bird.

phenomenal *adj.* excellent. ■ **phenomenally** *adv.*

phenomenon *n.* (*pl.* **phenomena**) **1** a fact or situation observed to exist or happen. **2** a remarkable person or thing.

! The plural of **phenomenon** is **phenomena**. Don't use **phenomena** as a singular form.

pheromone *n.* a chemical released by an animal and causing a response in others of its species.

phial *n.* a small bottle.

philander *v.* (of a man) have numerous sexual relationships with women. ■ **philanderer** *n.*

philanthropy *n.* the practice of helping people in need. ■ **philanthropic** *adj.* **philanthropist** *n.*

philately *n.* stamp collecting. ■ **philatelist** *n.*

philistine *n.* a person who is not interested in culture.

philology *n.* the study of languages. ■ **philological** *adj.* **philologist** *n.*

philosophical *adj.* **1** of philosophy. **2** calm in difficult circumstances. ■ **philosophically** *adv.*

philosophize (or **-ise**) *v.* theorize.

philosophy *n.* (*pl.* **philosophies**) **1** the study of the fundamental nature of knowledge, reality, and existence. **2** a set or system of beliefs. ■ **philosopher** *n.*

philtre (*US* **philter**) *n.* a love potion.

phlegm /flem/ *n.* mucus in the nose and throat.

phlegmatic /fleg-mat-ik/ *adj.* calm and unemotional.

phlox *n.* a flowering garden plant.

phobia *n.* an extreme or irrational fear. ■ **phobic** *adj.* & *n.*

phoenix /fee-niks/ *n.* a mythological bird said to burn itself and be born again from its ashes.

phone *n.* a telephone. • *v.* telephone. □ **phonecard** a prepaid card allowing calls to be made on a public phone. **phone-in** a broadcast during which listeners or viewers join in by phone.

phonetic *adj.* **1** of or representing speech sounds. **2** (of spelling) closely matching the sounds represented. • *n.* (**phonetics**) the study of speech sounds. ■ **phonetically** *adv.*

phoney (or **phony**) *informal adj.* (**phonier, phoniest**) not genuine. • *n.* (*pl.* **phoneys** or **phonies**) a phoney person or thing.

phonograph *n.* US a record player.

phosphate *n.* a compound of phosphorus.

phosphorescent *adj.* luminous. ■ **phosphorescence** *n.*

phosphorus *n.* a yellowish waxy element which glows in the dark and ignites in air.

photo *n.* (*pl.* **photos**) a photograph. □ **photo finish** a finish of a race so close that the winner has to be decided from a photo. **photofit** a picture of a person made up of separate photos of facial features. **photogenic** looking attractive in photos.

photocopy *n.* (*pl.* **photocopies**) a photographic copy of a document etc. • *v.* (**photocopying, photocopied**) make a photocopy of. ■ **photocopier** *n.*

photoelectric cell *n.* a device generating an electric current when light falls on it.

photograph *n.* a picture made with a camera. • *v.* take a photo of. ■ **photographer** *n.* **photographic** *adj.* **photography** *n.*

photon *n.* an indivisible unit of electromagnetic radiation.

photosensitive *adj.* responding to light.

photostat *n.* trademark **1** a type of photocopier. **2** a copy made by a photostat.

photosynthesis *n.* the process by which green plants use sunlight to form nutrients from carbon dioxide and water. ■ **photosynthesize** (or **-ise**) *v.*

phrase *n.* **1** a small group of words forming a unit. **2** a group of musical notes forming a distinct unit. • *v.* put into a particular form of words. ■ **phrasal** *adj.*

phraseology *n.* (*pl.* **phraseologies**) a particular form or use of words.

phrenology *n.* the study of the shape of a person's skull as a supposed indication of their character.

phylum *n.* (*pl.* **phyla**) a category used in classifying animals.

physical *adj.* **1** of the body. **2** of things that can be seen, heard, or touched. **3** of physics or the operation of natural forces. □ **physical education** instruction in physical exercise and games. **physical geography** the study of the earth's natural features. **physical sciences** the sciences studying inanimate natural objects. ■ **physically** *adv.*

physician *n.* a person qualified to practise medicine.

physics *n.* the study of the nature and properties of matter and energy. ■ **physicist** *n.*

physiognomy *n.* (*pl.* **physiognomies**) a person's face.

physiology *n.* the study of the way in which living organisms function. ■ **physiological** *adj.* **physiologist** *n.*

physiotherapy *n.* the treatment of an injury etc. by massage and exercise. ■ **physiotherapist** *n.*

physique *n.* the shape and size of a person's body.

pi *n.* the ratio of a circle's circumference to its diameter (about 3.14).

pianissimo *adv. & adj. Music* very softly.

P

piano n. (pl. **pianos**) a musical instrument with strings struck by hammers when keys are pressed. • adv. & adj. Music softly. ■ **pianist** n.

pianoforte n. formal a piano.

piazza /pi-at-zuh/ n. a public square or marketplace.

picador n. a bullfighter on horseback.

picaresque adj. of fiction dealing with the adventures of a dishonest but appealing hero.

piccalilli n. a pickle of chopped vegetables and hot spices.

piccolo n. (pl. **piccolos**) a small flute.

pick v. **1** take hold of and lift or remove from its place. **2** select. • n. **1** an act of selecting. **2** the best of a group. **3** (or **pickaxe**) a tool with a pointed iron bar at right angles to its handle, for breaking up hard ground. □ **pick holes in** criticize. **pick a lock** open a lock with something other than a key. **pick on** single out for unfair treatment. **pickpocket** a person who steals from people's pockets. **pickup 1** a small truck with low sides. **2** an act of picking up. **3** a device converting sound vibrations into electrical signals for amplification. **pick up 1** go to collect. **2** improve or increase. **3** casually get to know someone as a sexual approach. ■ **picker** n.

picket n. **1** a person or group standing outside a workplace to dissuade others from entering during a strike. **2** a pointed wooden stake driven into the ground. • v. (**picketing, picketed**) act as a picket outside a workplace.

pickings pl. n. profits or gains.

pickle n. **1** vegetables or fruit preserved in vinegar or brine. **2** (**a pickle**) informal a difficult situation. • v. preserve in vinegar or brine.

picnic n. an informal meal eaten outdoors. • v. (**picnicking, picnicked**) have a picnic. ■ **picnicker** n.

pictograph n. a picture representing a word or phrase.

pictorial adj. of or using pictures. ■ **pictorially** adv.

picture n. **1** a painting, drawing, or photo. **2** an image. **3** (**the pictures**) the cinema. • v. **1** show in a picture. **2** imagine.

picturesque adj. attractive in a quaint or charming way.

pidgin n. a simple form of a language with elements taken from local languages.

pie n. a baked dish of ingredients topped with pastry. □ **pie chart** a diagram representing quantities as sections of a circle.

piebald adj. (of a horse) having irregular patches of two colours.

piece n. **1** a portion or part. **2** an item forming part of a set. **3** a musical, literary, or artistic work. **4** a small object used in a board game. • v. (**piece together**) assemble from individual parts. □ **piecemeal** done in a gradual and inconsistent way. **piecework** work paid for according to the amount produced.

pièce de résistance /pyess duh ray-ziss-tonss/ n. the most impressive feature.

pied adj. having two or more different colours.

pied-à-terre /pyay-dah-'tair/ n. (pl. **pieds-à-terre**) a small flat or house for occasional use.

pier n. a structure built out into the sea, used as a landing stage or promenade.

pierce v. **1** make a hole in or through with a sharp object. **2** force a way through. **3** (**piercing**) very sharp, cold, or high-pitched.

piety n. (pl. **pieties**) the quality of being deeply religious.

piffle n. informal nonsense.

pig n. **1** a domestic or wild mammal with a flat snout. **2** informal a greedy or dirty person. □ **pig-headed** stubborn. **pig iron** oblong blocks of crude iron from a smelting furnace. **pigsty** or an enclosure for pigs. **pigtail** a length of hair worn in a plait at the back or on each side of the head. ■ **piglet** n.

pigeon n. a plump bird with a cooing voice.

pigeonhole n. each of a set of small compartments where letters etc. may be left. • v. place in a particular category.

piggery n. (pl. **piggeries**) a farm or enclosure where pigs are kept.

piggy adj. like a pig. □ **piggyback** a ride on someone's back and shoulders. **piggy bank** a money box shaped like a pig.

pigment n. **1** natural colouring. **2** a colouring matter. ■ **pigmentation** n.

pigmy var. of PYGMY.

pike n. **1** (pl. **pike**) a large predatory freshwater fish. **2** a spear with a long wooden shaft.

pilaf (or **pilau**) n. a dish of rice with spices, meat, etc.

pilaster n. a rectangular column projecting from a wall.

pilchard n. a small edible fish.

pile n. **1** a number of things lying one on top of another. **2** informal a large amount. **3** a heavy post driven into the ground to support foundations. **4** the surface of a carpet or fabric, consisting of many small projecting threads. **5** (**piles**) haemorrhoids. • v. **1** place in a pile. **2** (**pile up**) accumulate. □ **pile-up** informal a crash involving several vehicles.

pilfer v. steal items of little value.

pilgrim n. a person who travels to a holy place for religious reasons. ■ **pilgrimage** n.

pill n. **1** a small piece of solid medicine for swallowing whole. **2** (**the Pill**) a contraceptive pill. □ **pillbox 1** a small round hat with a flat top. **2** a small concrete fort.

pillage v. & n. plunder.

pillar n. an upright structure used as a support for a building. □ **pillar box** a red cylindrical postbox.

pillion n. a seat for a passenger behind a motorcyclist.

pillory n. (pl. **pillories**) a wooden frame with holes for the head and hands, in which offenders were formerly locked and exposed to public abuse. • v. (**pillorying, pilloried**) ridicule publicly.

pillow n. a cushion to support the head when lying down. • v. rest the head as if on a pillow. □ **pillowcase** a cloth cover for a pillow.

pilot n. **1** a person who operates an aircraft's flying controls. **2** a person qualified to steer ships into or out of a harbour. **3** something done as a test before being introduced more widely. • v. (**piloting, piloted**) **1** act as a pilot of an aircraft or ship. **2** test a project before introducing it more widely. □ **pilot light** a small gas burner

p

kept alight permanently to light a larger burner.

pimiento n. (pl. **pimientos**) a red sweet pepper.

pimp n. a man who controls prostitutes and takes a percentage of their earnings. •v. act as a pimp.

pimple n. a small inflamed spot on the skin. ■ **pimply** adj.

PIN (or **PIN number**) abbrev. personal identification number.

pin n. 1 a thin pointed piece of metal with a round head, used as a fastener. 2 a short metal rod or peg. •v. (**pinning, pinned**) 1 attach or fasten with a pin or pins. 2 hold someone firmly so they are unable to move. 3 (**pin down**) force someone to be specific. 4 (**pin on**) fix blame on. □ **pinball** a game in which small balls are propelled across a sloping board to hit targets. **pin money** a small sum of money for everyday items. **pinpoint** locate exactly. **pins and needles** a tingling sensation. **pinstripe** a very narrow pale stripe in dark cloth. **pin-up** a poster of an attractive person.

pinafore n. 1 a collarless sleeveless dress worn over a blouse or jumper. 2 an apron.

pince-nez /panss-nay/ n. a pair of glasses with a nose clip instead of earpieces.

pincer n. (**pincers**) a metal tool with blunt jaws for gripping and pulling things. 2 a front claw of a lobster or similar crustacean.

pinch v. 1 grip flesh tightly between the finger and thumb. 2 hurt by being too tight. 3 informal steal. •n. 1 an act of pinching. 2 a very small amount. □ **at a pinch** if absolutely necessary. **feel the pinch** experience financial hardship.

pine v. 1 become weak because of grief etc. 2 (**pine for**) miss someone intensely. •n. an evergreen coniferous tree with needle-shaped leaves. □ **pine marten** a dark brown weasel-like mammal.

pineapple n. a large tropical fruit.

ping n. a short high-pitched ringing sound. •v. make a pinging sound. □ **ping-pong** informal table tennis.

pinion v. tie or hold the arms or legs of. •n. 1 the outer part of a bird's wing. 2 a small cogwheel.

pink adj. pale red. •n. 1 pink colour. 2 (**the pink**) informal the best condition. 3 a plant with scented flowers. •v. 1 cut a zigzag edge on. 2 (of an engine) make rattling sounds when running imperfectly.

pinnacle n. 1 a high pointed rock. 2 a small turret. 3 the most successful point.

pint n. a liquid measure equal to one eighth of a gallon (0.568 litre).

pioneer n. 1 a person who explores or settles in a new region. 2 a person who develops a new idea or technique. •v. be a pioneer of.

pious adj. 1 deeply religious. 2 pretending to be good or religious. ■ **piously** adv.

pip n. 1 a small seed in a fruit. 2 a short high-pitched sound. 3 a star on an army officer's uniform, showing rank. •v. (**be pipped**) informal be only just defeated.

pipe n. 1 a tube through which water, gas, oil, etc. can flow. 2 a narrow tube with a bowl at one end for smoking tobacco. 3 a wind instrument. 4 (**pipes**) bagpipes. •v. 1 send through a pipe. 2 play a tune on a pipe. 3 say in a high voice. □ **pipe down** informal be quiet. **pipe dream** an unrealistic hope or scheme. **piping hot** very hot. ■ **piper** n.

pipeline n. a long pipe for carrying oil, gas, etc. over a distance. □ **in the pipeline** being developed.

pipette n. a thin tube for transferring or measuring small quantities of liquid.

piquant adj. having a pleasantly sharp or spicy taste. ■ **piquancy** n.

pique /peek/ n. resentment arising from hurt pride. • v. **1** stimulate someone's interest. **2** (**be piqued**) feel resentful.

piquet /pee-kay/ n. a card game for two players.

piranha /pi-rah-nuh/ n. a freshwater fish with very sharp teeth.

pirate n. a person who attacks and robs ships at sea. • adj. (of a film etc.) pirated. • v. reproduce a film, recording, etc. for profit without permission. ■ **piracy** n. **piratical** adj.

pirouette n. (in ballet) an act of spinning on one foot. • v. perform a pirouette.

pistachio /pi-sta-shi-oh/ n. (pl. **pistachios**) a nut with a green kernel.

piste /peest/ n. a ski run.

pistil n. the female organs of a flower.

pistol n. a small gun.

piston n. a sliding disc or cylinder inside a tube, esp. as part of an engine or pump.

pit n. **1** a large hole in the ground. **2** a coal mine. **3** a sunken area. **4** an area at the side of a track where racing cars are refuelled etc. **5** (**the pits**) informal a very bad place or situation. • v. (**pitting**, **pitted**) **1** (**pit against**) set in

competition with. **2** make a hollow in the surface of.

pitch n. **1** an area of ground for outdoor team games. **2** the extent to which a sound is high or low. **3** a level of intensity. **4** a form of words used to persuade. **5** a place where a street seller or performer is stationed. **6** the steepness of a roof. **7** a sticky black substance. • v. **1** throw roughly. **2** set at a particular musical pitch. **3** aim at a particular level, target, etc. **4** set up a tent. **5** (**pitch in**) informal join in enthusiastically. **6** (of a ship etc.) rock up and down. **7** (**pitched**) (of a roof) sloping. □ **pitch-black** (or **pitch-dark**) completely dark. **pitched battle** a fierce fight involving many people. **pitchfork** a long-handled fork for lifting hay.

pitchblende n. a mineral containing radium.

pitcher n. a large jug.

piteous adj. deserving or arousing pity. ■ **piteously** adv.

pitfall n. a hidden danger or difficulty.

pith n. spongy white tissue in stems or fruits.

pithy adj. **1** full of pith. **2** (of language or style) concise and expressive.

pitiful adj. **1** deserving or arousing pity. **2** very small or poor. ■ **pitifully** adv.

pitiless adj. showing no pity.

piton /pee-ton/ n. a peg used in rock climbing.

pitta n. a type of flat bread, hollow inside.

pittance n. a very small amount of money.

pituitary gland n. a gland at the base of the brain controlling growth and development.

pity n. (pl. **pities**) 1 a feeling of sorrow for another's suffering. 2 a cause for regret. •v. (**pitying, pitied**) feel pity for.

pivot n. a central point or shaft on which a mechanism turns or is balanced. •v. (**pivoting, pivoted**) turn on a pivot.

pivotal adj. 1 of a pivot. 2 of central importance.

pixel n. any of the tiny areas of light on a display screen making up an image.

pixelate v. divide an image into pixels.

pixie (or **pixy**) n. (pl. **pixies**) (in fairy tales etc.) a tiny being with pointed ears.

pizza n. a flat base of dough baked with a savoury topping.

pizzeria n. a pizza restaurant.

pizzicato adv. & adj. plucking the strings of a violin etc. instead of using the bow.

placard n. a sign or notice.

placate v. make less angry. ■ **placatory** adj.

place n. 1 a particular position or area. 2 a portion of space occupied by or set aside for someone or something. 3 a position in a sequence. 4 a person's status, or a right arising from this. •v. 1 put in a particular position or situation. 2 give a specified position in a sequence. 3 make an order for goods etc. □ **out of place** inappropriate or incongruous. **take place** occur.

placebo /pluh-see-boh/ n. (pl. **placebos**) a medicine prescribed for the mental benefit of the patient rather than for any physical effect.

placement n. 1 the act of placing. 2 a temporary job undertaken for work experience.

placenta n. (pl. **placentae** or **placentas**) an organ in the womb of a pregnant mammal supplying nourishment to the fetus through the umbilical cord.

placid adj. not easily upset or excited. ■ **placidity** n. **placidly** adv.

placket n. an opening in a garment, covering fastenings or for access to a pocket.

plagiarize (or **-ise**) v. take someone else's work etc. and pretend it is your own. ■ **plagiarism** n. **plagiarist** n.

plague n. 1 a very serious infectious disease. 2 an infestation of destructive insects or animals. •v. 1 cause continual trouble to. 2 pester continually.

plaice n. (pl. **plaice**) an edible flatfish.

plaid /plad/ n. tartan fabric.

plain adj. 1 simple or ordinary. 2 without a pattern. 3 easy to see or understand. 4 (of language) direct. 5 not attractive. •adv. informal used for emphasis: plain stupid. •n. a large area of flat land with few trees. □ **plain clothes** ordinary clothes rather than uniform. **plain sailing** easy progress. **plainsong** unaccompanied medieval church music for several voices. ■ **plainly** adv. **plainness** n.

plaintiff n. a person bringing a case against another in a court of law.

plaintive adj. sounding sad. ■ **plaintively** adv.

plait n. a single length of hair or rope made up of three or more intertwined strands. • v. form into a plait or plaits.

plan n. **1** a proposal for doing or achieving something. **2** an intention. **3** a map or diagram. • v. (**planning, planned**) **1** decide on and arrange in advance. **2** intend. **3** draw a plan of a proposed building etc. ■ **planner** n.

plane n. **1** a completely flat surface. **2** a level of existence or thought. **3** an aeroplane. **4** a tool for smoothing wood by cutting shavings from it. **5** a tall tree with a peeling bark. • adj. completely flat. • v. smooth with a plane.

planet n. a large round mass in space orbiting round a star. ■ **planetary** adj.

planetarium n. (pl. **planetariums** or **planetaria**) a building in which images of stars and planets are projected on to a domed ceiling.

plangent adj. loud and mournful.

plank n. a long, flat piece of timber.

plankton n. tiny organisms living in the sea or fresh water.

plant n. **1** a living thing that absorbs substances through its roots and makes nutrients in its leaves by photosynthesis. **2** a factory. **3** machinery used in manufacturing. **4** a person sent to a group as a spy. **5** a thing put among someone's belongings to incriminate them. • v. **1** place a seed, bulb, etc. in the ground to grow. **2** place in a specified position. **3** send or place as a plant. ■ **planter** n.

plantain n. **1** a low-growing plant. **2** a type of banana.

plantation n. **1** an estate on which coffee, tobacco, etc. is grown. **2** an area in which trees have been planted.

plaque n. **1** a commemorative plate fixed to a wall. **2** a sticky deposit on teeth, encouraging the growth of bacteria.

plasma n. **1** the colourless fluid part of blood. **2** a type of gas.

plaster n. **1** a mixture of lime, sand, water, etc. used for coating walls. **2** a sticky strip of material for covering wounds. **3** (or **plaster of Paris**) a white paste of gypsum and water that hardens when dry, used for making moulds and casts. • v. **1** apply plaster to. **2** coat thickly. □ **plasterboard** board made of plaster set between two sheets of paper, used to line interior walls and ceilings. ■ **plasterer** n.

plastic n. a chemically produced material that can be moulded to a permanent shape. • adj. **1** made of plastic. **2** easily shaped. □ **plastic surgery** surgery performed to repair or reconstruct parts of the body. □ **plasticity** n.

plasticine n. trademark a soft modelling material.

plate n. **1** a flat dish for holding food. **2** bowls, cups, etc. made of gold or silver. **3** a thin, flat piece of metal, glass, etc. **4** a printed photo or illustration in a book. • v. coat a metal object with a different metal. □ **plate glass** thick glass for windows and doors.

plateau /plat-oh/ n. (pl. **plateaux** or **plateaus**) **1** an area of level high ground. **2** a state of little change following a period of progress.

platelet n. a disc-shaped cell fragment in blood, involved in clotting.

p

platen n. the roller in a typewriter against which the paper is held.

platform n. 1 a raised level area on which people or things can stand. 2 the stated policy of a political party.

platinum n. a precious silvery-white metallic element.

platitude n. a remark used too often to be interesting. ■ **platitudinous** adj.

platonic adj. friendly and affectionate but not sexual.

platoon n. a subdivision of a company of soldiers.

platter n. a large flat serving dish.

platypus n. (pl. **platypuses**) an egg-laying Australian mammal with a duck-like bill.

plaudits pl. n. praise.

plausible adj. seeming reasonable or probable. ■ **plausibility** n. **plausibly** adv.

play v. 1 take part in games for enjoyment. 2 compete against in a sport or contest. 3 act the role of. 4 perform a piece of music on an instrument. 5 move a piece or display a playing card in a game. 6 make a CD, tape, etc. produce sounds. 7 move or flicker over a surface. •n. 1 a piece of writing performed by actors. 2 games taken part in for enjoyment. 3 the performing of a sports match. 4 action or operation. 5 freedom of movement. □ **playboy** n. a wealthy man who spends his time seeking pleasure. **play down** disguise the importance of. **playgroup** a regular play session for pre-school children. **playhouse** n. a theatre. **playing card** each of a set of pieces of card used in various games. **playmate** a friend with whom a child plays. **play on** exploit a weakness. **playpen** a portable enclosure for a young child to play in. **play up** informal cause problems. **playwright** a person who writes plays. ■ **player** n.

playful adj. 1 fond of games and amusement. 2 for amusement; not serious. ■ **playfully** adv. **playfulness** n.

plaza n. a public square.

plc (or **PLC**) abbrev. public limited company.

plea n. 1 an emotional request. 2 a formal statement by or on behalf of a defendant or prisoner.

plead v. (**pleading**, **pleaded** or US or Sc. **pled**) 1 make an emotional request. 2 argue in support of. 3 state formally in court whether you are guilty or not guilty of an offence. 4 present as an excuse.

pleasant adj. 1 satisfactory and enjoyable. 2 likeable. ■ **pleasantly** adv. **pleasantness** n.

pleasantry n. (pl. **pleasantries**) a friendly or humorous remark.

please v. 1 cause to feel happy and satisfied. 2 wish: do as you please. 3 (**please yourself**) consider only your own wishes. •adv. used in polite requests.

pleased adj. feeling or showing pleasure and satisfaction.

pleasurable adj. enjoyable. ■ **pleasurably** adv.

pleasure n. 1 a feeling of satisfaction and enjoyment. 2 a source of this.

pleat n. a fold in fabric, held by stitching at the top or side. •v. form into pleats.

pleb n. informal, derog. a member of the lower social classes.

plebeian /pli-bee-uhn/ adj. lower-class or unsophisticated.

plebiscite /pleb-i-syt/ n. a referendum.

plectrum n. (pl. **plectrums** or **plectra**) a small piece of plastic etc. for plucking the strings of a musical instrument.

pled US or Sc. past part. of **PLEAD**.

pledge n. **1** a solemn promise. **2** a valuable item given as a guarantee that a debt will be paid etc. **3** a token of love or loyalty. •v. **1** make a solemn promise. **2** give as a pledge.

plenary adj. (of a meeting at a conference etc.) attended by all participants.

plenipotentiary n. (pl. **plenipotentiaries**) a person given full power by a government to act on its behalf.

plenitude n. an abundance.

plentiful adj. existing in large amounts. ■ **plentifully** adv.

plenty pron. a large or sufficient amount or quantity. ■ **plenteous** adj.

plethora n. an excessive amount.

pleurisy n. inflammation of the membrane round the lungs.

pliable adj. **1** easily bent. **2** easily influenced. ■ **pliability** n.

pliant adj. pliable. ■ **pliancy** n.

pliers pl. n. pincers with flat surfaces for gripping small objects.

plight n. a dangerous or difficult situation. •v. (**plight your troth**) make a solemn promise to marry.

plimsoll n. a light rubber-soled canvas shoe.

Plimsoll line n. a mark on a ship's side showing the legal water level when loaded.

plinth n. a slab forming the base of a column, statue, etc.

plod v. (**plodding, plodded**) **1** walk with heavy slow steps. **2** work slowly and steadily.

plonk informal v. set down heavily or carelessly. •n. cheap wine.

plop n. a sound like that of a small object dropping into water. •v. (**plopping, plopped**) fall with a plop.

plot n. **1** a secret plan to do something illegal or harmful. **2** the story in a play, novel, or film. **3** a small piece of land. •v. (**plotting, plotted**) **1** secretly plan an illegal or harmful act. **2** mark a route or position on a map or graph. ■ **plotter** n.

plough (US **plow**) n. a large implement for turning over and cutting furrows in soil. •v. **1** turn soil with a plough. **2** progress with difficulty.

ploy n. a cunning act.

pluck v. **1** take hold of and quickly remove from its place. **2** pull out or at. **3** pull the feathers from a bird's carcass. •n. courage.

plucky adj. (**pluckier, pluckiest**) determined and brave. ■ **pluckily** adv.

plug n. **1** a piece of solid material tightly blocking a hole. **2** a device with metal pins that fit into holes in a socket to make an electrical connection. •v. (**plugging, plugged**) **1** block a hole. **2** (**plug in**) connect an electrical appliance to the mains by means of a socket. **3** informal promote something by mentioning it publicly. **4** (**plug away**) informal work steadily.

plum n. **1** an oval, usu. reddish-purple fruit. **2** a reddish-purple colour. •adj. informal highly desirable.

plumage n. a bird's feathers.

P

plumb v. **1** measure or test with a plumb line. **2** explore or experience fully. **3** connect an appliance etc. to water and drainage pipes. •n. a weight attached to a plumb line. •adv. informal exactly.
□ **plumb line** a cord with a weight attached to it, used to find the depth of water or test whether an upright surface is vertical.

plumber n. a person who fits and repairs plumbing.

plumbing n. the system of pipes, tanks, and fittings for the water supply, heating, and sanitation in a building.

plume n. **1** a long, soft feather. **2** a long cloud of smoke. ■ **plumed** adj.

plummet v. (**plummeting**, **plummeted**) fall steeply or rapidly.

plump adj. **1** full and rounded in shape. **2** rather fat. •v. **1** (**plump up**) make or become plump. **2** sit or set down heavily. **3** (**plump for**) decide on. ■ **plumpness** n.

P **plunder** v. enter a place by force and steal goods from it. •n. **1** the act of plundering. **2** goods obtained by plundering.

plunge v. **1** fall suddenly. **2** jump or dive quickly. **3** push or thrust quickly. •n. an act of plunging.

plunger n. a device that works with a plunging movement.

pluperfect adj. (of a tense) referring to an action completed earlier than some past point of time.

plural adj. **1** more than one in number. **2** (of a word or form) referring to more than one. •n. a plural word or form. ■ **plurality** n.

plus prep. with the addition of. •adj. **1** more than the amount indicated. **2** above zero. •n. **1** the

symbol +. **2** informal an advantage. •conj. also.

plush n. fabric with a long, soft nap. •adj. informal expensively luxurious.

plutocracy n. (pl. **plutocracies**) government by the wealthy. ■ **plutocrat** n.

plutonium n. a radioactive metallic element.

ply n. (pl. **plies**) a layer or strand of a material. •v. (**plying**, **plied**) **1** work steadily with a tool or at a job. **2** (of a ship etc.) travel regularly over a route. **3** (**ply with**) keep presenting with food etc. □ **plywood** board made of layers of wood glued together.

PM abbrev. Prime Minister.

p.m. abbrev. after noon.

PMT abbrev. premenstrual tension.

pneumatic /nyoo-mat-ik/ adj. containing or operated by air or gas under pressure.

pneumonia /nyoo-moh-ni-uh/ n. inflammation of one or both lungs.

PO abbrev. Post Office.

poach v. **1** simmer in a small amount of liquid. **2** take game or fish illegally. **3** unfairly entice customers, workers, etc. away from someone else. ■ **poacher** n.

pocket n. **1** a small bag sewn into or on clothing for carrying things. **2** an isolated group or area. **3** an opening at the corner or side of a billiard table. •v. (**pocketing**, **pocketed**) **1** put into your pocket. **2** take dishonestly. □ **out of pocket** having made a loss. **pocket money** a small regular allowance given to children by their parents.

pockmarked adj. (of the skin) marked by hollow scars.

pod n. a long narrow seed case.

podcast n. a digital recording of a radio broadcast, made available on the Internet for downloading to a personal audio player. ■ **podcasting** n.

podgy adj. informal rather fat.

podium n. (pl. **podiums** or **podia**) a small platform.

poem n. a piece of imaginative writing in verse.

poet n. a person who writes poems. □ **Poet Laureate** a poet appointed by the British monarch to write poems for important occasions.

poetic (or **poetical**) adj. of or like poetry. ■ **poetically** adv.

poetry n. **1** poems as a whole or as a form of literature. **2** a quality of beauty or emotional power.

po-faced adj. informal serious and disapproving.

pogrom n. an organized massacre of an ethnic group.

poignant adj. arousing a sense of sadness or regret. ■ **poignancy** n. **poignantly** adv.

poinsettia n. a plant with large scarlet bracts.

point n. **1** a tapered, sharp end. **2** a particular place or moment. **3** an item, detail, or idea. **4** the advantage or purpose of something. **5** a feature or quality. **6** a unit of scoring, value, or measurement. **7** a dot. **8** a promontory. **9** (**points**) a movable pair of rails at a junction of two railway lines. **10** an electrical socket. •v. **1** direct someone's attention by extending the finger. **2** aim or face in a particular direction. **3** (**point out**) make someone aware of. **4** fill the joints of brickwork with mortar. □ **beside the point** irrelevant. **point-**

blank 1 at very close range. **2** in a blunt and very direct way. **point of view** an attitude or opinion. **to the point** relevant.

pointed adj. **1** tapering to a point. **2** (of a remark or look) expressing a clear message. ■ **pointedly** adv.

pointer n. **1** a thing that points to something. **2** a dog that on scenting game stands rigid looking towards it.

pointing n. mortar used to fill the joints of brickwork.

pointless adj. having little or no purpose. ■ **pointlessly** adv.

poise n. **1** a graceful way of holding the body. **2** a calm and confident manner. •v. be or cause to be balanced.

poison n. a substance that causes death or injury when swallowed or absorbed. •v. **1** harm or kill with poison. **2** put poison on or in. **3** have a harmful effect on. ■ **poisoner** n. **poisonous** adj.

poke v. **1** push a finger or pointed object into. **2** search or pry. **3** push or stick out. •n. an act of poking.

poker n. **1** a metal rod for prodding an open fire. **2** a gambling card game. □ **poker face** a blank expression.

poky adj. (**pokier, pokiest**) small and cramped.

polar adj. **1** of or near the North or South Pole. **2** having an electrical or magnetic field. **3** completely opposite. □ **polar bear** a large white Arctic bear. ■ **polarity** n.

polarize (or **-ise**) v. **1** divide into two groups with completely opposite views. **2** restrict the vibrations of a light wave to one direction. **3** give magnetic or electric polarity to. ■ **polarization** n.

P

Polaroid n. trademark **1** a material that polarizes light passing through it, used in sunglasses. **2** a camera that produces a finished print rapidly after each exposure.

Pole n. a person from Poland.

pole n. **1** a long, thin rod or post. **2** either of the two points (**North Pole** or **South Pole**) at opposite ends of the earth's axis. **3** either of the two opposite points of a magnet. **4** the positive or negative terminal of an electric cell or battery. • v. push a boat along with a pole. □ **poles apart** having nothing in common. **pole position** the most favourable starting position in a motor race. **Pole Star** a star located in the part of the sky above the North Pole.

polecat n. **1** a dark brown weasel-like animal. **2** US a skunk.

polemic n. a strong verbal or written attack. ■ **polemical** adj.

polenta n. maize flour or a dough made from this.

police n. an official body of people employed by a state to prevent crime and keep public order. • v. keep law and order in an area. □ **police state** a country in which political police secretly watch and control citizens' activities.
■ **policeman** n. **policewoman** n.

policy n. (pl. **policies**) **1** a course of action adopted or proposed. **2** a contract of insurance.

polio (or **poliomyelitis**) n. an infectious disease causing temporary or permanent paralysis.

Polish n. the language of Poland. • adj. of Poland.

polish v. **1** make smooth and shiny by rubbing. **2** refine or improve. **3** (**polish off**) finish quickly. • n. **1** a substance used to polish something. **2** an act of polishing. **3** shiny appearance. **4** refinement or elegance. ■ **polisher** n.

polite adj. **1** respectful and considerate. **2** civilized or well bred. ■ **politely** adv. **politeness** n.

politic adj. sensible and wise in the circumstances.

political adj. **1** of the government or public affairs of a country. **2** of politics. □ **political correctness** the conscious avoidance of language or behaviour that could offend certain groups. ■ **politically** adv.

politician n. an elected political representative.

politics n. **1** the activities concerned with governing a country or area. **2** a set of political beliefs.

polity n. (pl. **polities**) **1** a form of government. **2** a society.

polka n. a lively dance for couples.

poll n. **1** the process of voting in an election. **2** a record of the number of votes cast. • v. **1** record the opinion or vote of. **2** receive a specified number of votes. □ **poll tax** a tax paid at the same rate by every adult.

pollard v. cut off the top and branches of a tree to encourage new growth.

pollen n. a powder produced by the male part of a flower, containing the fertilizing agent. □ **pollen count** a measure of the amount of pollen in the air.

pollinate v. fertilize with pollen. ■ **pollination** n.

pollster n. a person who carries out opinion polls.

pollute v. make dirty with harmful or poisonous substances. ■ **pollutant** n. **pollution** n.

polo n. a game like hockey, played on horseback. □ **polo neck** a high turned-over collar on a sweater.

polonium n. a radioactive metallic element.

poltergeist n. a ghost said to throw objects about.

polyandry n. the practice of having more than one husband at the same time.

polychromatic (or **polychrome**) adj. multicoloured.

polyester n. a synthetic fibre or resin.

polyethylene n. polythene.

polygamy n. the practice of having more than one wife or husband at the same time. ■ **polygamist** n. **polygamous** adj.

polyglot adj. knowing or using several languages.

polygon n. a figure with three or more straight sides. ■ **polygonal** adj.

polygraph n. a lie detector.

polyhedron n. (pl. **polyhedra** or **polyhedrons**) a solid with many sides. ■ **polyhedral** adj.

polymath n. a person with knowledge of many subjects.

polymer n. a substance with a molecular structure formed from many identical small molecules bonded together.

polymerize (or **-ise**) v. combine to form a polymer.

polyp n. **1** a simple sea animal which remains fixed in the same place, such as coral. **2** a small lump projecting from a mucous membrane.

polyphony n. the combination of a number of harmonizing melodies. ■ **polyphonic** adj.

polystyrene n. a light synthetic material, used esp. as packaging.

polytechnic n. hist. a college offering courses up to degree level (now called a 'university').

polytheism n. the belief in more than one god. ■ **polytheistic** adj.

polythene n. a tough, light, flexible plastic.

polyunsaturated adj. (of a fat) not associated with the formation of cholesterol in the blood.

polyurethane n. a synthetic resin used in paints and varnishes.

Pom n. Austral./NZ informal a British person. ■ **Pommy** adj. & n.

pomander n. a ball of scented substances.

pomegranate n. a round tropical fruit with many seeds in red flesh.

pommel /pum-m'l/ n. **1** the upward projecting front part of a saddle. **2** a knob on the hilt of a sword.

pomp n. splendid display and ceremony.

pompom n. a small woollen ball sewn on a garment for decoration.

pompous adj. ostentatiously or foolishly self-important. ■ **pomposity** n. **pompously** adv.

poncho n. (pl. **ponchos**) a garment made of a thick piece of cloth with a slit for the head.

pond n. a small area of still water.

ponder v. consider carefully.

ponderous adj. moving slowly and heavily. ■ **ponderously** adv.

pong informal n. a strong, unpleasant smell. • v. smell strongly and unpleasantly.

pontiff n. the Pope.

pontificate v. speak pompously and at length.

p

pontoon n. 1 a card game. 2 a flat-bottomed boat supporting a temporary bridge. 3 a bridge supported by pontoons.

pony n. (pl. **ponies**) a horse of a small breed. □ **ponytail** a hairstyle in which the hair is drawn back and tied at the back of the head.

poodle n. a dog with a curly coat.

pool n. 1 a small area of still water. 2 (or **swimming pool**) an artificial pool for swimming in. 3 a shallow patch of liquid on a surface. 4 a shared fund or supply. 5 a game resembling snooker. 6 (**the pools**) a form of gambling on the results of football matches. • v. put into a common fund; share.

poop n. a raised deck at the back of a ship.

poor adj. 1 having little money. 2 of a low standard or quality. 3 deserving sympathy.

poorly adv. badly. • adj. unwell.

pop v. (**popping, popped**) 1 make a sudden short explosive sound. 2 go or put somewhere quickly. • n. 1 a sudden short explosive sound. 2 informal a soft fizzy drink. 3 (or **pop music**) modern popular music with a strong melody and beat. • adj. 1 of pop music. 2 made intellectually accessible to the general public. □ **popcorn** maize kernels heated until they burst open.

pope n. the head of the Roman Catholic Church.

poplar n. a tall, slender tree.

poplin n. a cotton fabric.

poppadom n. a thin circular piece of Indian bread fried until crisp.

popper n. informal a press stud.

poppy n. a plant with large bright flowers.

poppycock n. informal nonsense.

populace n. the general public.

popular adj. 1 liked by many people. 2 of or for the general public. ■ **popularity** n. **popularly** adv.

popularize (or **-ise**) v. 1 make popular. 2 make accessible or interesting to the general public.

populate v. form the population of.

population n. the inhabitants of a place.

populous adj. densely populated.

porcelain n. fine china.

porch n. a covered shelter over the entrance of a building.

porcine adj. of or like a pig.

porcupine n. an animal covered with long protective spines.

pore n. a tiny opening in the skin or another surface. • v. (**pore over**) study closely.

pork n. the flesh of a pig as food.

porn n. informal pornography.

pornography n. pictures, writing, or films intended to arouse sexual excitement. ■ **pornographer** n. **pornographic** adj.

porous adj. having tiny spaces through which liquid or air may pass. ■ **porosity** n.

porpoise n. a small whale.

porridge n. a dish of oats or oatmeal boiled with water or milk.

port n. 1 a town or city with a harbour. 2 a harbour. 3 an opening for boarding or loading a ship or for firing a gun from a tank etc. 4 a socket in a computer network into which a device can be plugged. 5 a strong, sweet dark red wine. 6 the left-hand side of a ship or aircraft. □ **porthole** a small window in the side of a ship or aircraft.

portable *adj.* able to be carried. ∎ **portability** *n.*

portal *n.* a large impressive doorway or gate.

portcullis *n.* a strong grating lowered to block a castle's gateway.

portend *v.* be a portent of.

portent *n.* a sign or warning of a future event. ∎ **portentous** *adj.*

porter *n.* **1** a person employed to carry luggage or goods or move hospital equipment or patients. **2** a doorkeeper of a large building.

portfolio *n.* (*pl.* **portfolios**) **1** a thin, flat case for drawings, maps, etc. **2** a set of investments. **3** a government minister's area of responsibility.

portico *n.* (*pl.* **porticoes** or **porticos**) a roof supported by columns forming a porch.

portion *n.* **1** a part or share. **2** an amount of food for one person. •*v.* divide into portions and share out.

portly *adj.* rather fat.

portmanteau /port-man-toh/ *n.* (*pl.* **portmanteaus** or **portmanteaux**) a large travelling bag.

portrait *n.* **1** a picture of a person. **2** a description. ∎ **portraiture** *n.*

portray *v.* show or describe in a work of art or literature. ∎ **portrayal** *n.*

Portuguese *n.* (*pl.* **Portuguese**) **1** a person from Portugal. **2** the language of Portugal and Brazil. •*adj.* of Portugal. ☐ **Portuguese man-of-war** a sea animal like a jellyfish.

pose *v.* **1** present or be a problem, question, etc. **2** sit or stand in a particular position to be photographed, painted, etc. **3** (**pose as**) pretend to be. •*n.* **1** a position adopted to be photographed,

painted, etc. **2** a way of behaving intended to impress or mislead.

poser *n.* **1** a poseur. **2** a puzzling question.

poseur *n.* a person who behaves in a way intended to impress.

posh *adj. informal* **1** very elegant or luxurious. **2** upper-class.

posit *v.* (**positing**, **posited**) put forward as a basis for argument.

position *n.* **1** a place where someone or something is or should be. **2** a way in which someone or something is placed or arranged. **3** a situation. **4** a job. **5** a person's status. **6** a point of view. •*v.* place or arrange. ∎ **positional** *adj.*

positive *adj.* **1** expressing agreement or permission. **2** hopeful or favourable. **3** not allowing doubt; certain. **4** (of a test) showing the presence of something. **5** (of a quantity) greater than zero. **6** of the kind of electric charge opposite to that carried by electrons. •*n.* a positive quality. ☐ **positive discrimination** the policy of employing members of groups which suffer discrimination. ∎ **positively** *adv.* **positivity** *n.*

positron *n.* a particle with the same mass as an electron but a positive charge.

posse /poss-i/ *n.* **1** *US hist.* a body of men summoned by a sheriff to enforce the law. **2** *informal* a group or gang.

possess *v.* **1** have or own. **2** dominate or have complete power over. ∎ **possessor** *n.*

possession *n.* **1** the state of possessing something. **2** a thing owned.

possessive *adj.* **1** demanding someone's total attention and

p

love. **2** unwilling to share your possessions. **3** *Grammar* expressing possession. □ **possessive pronoun** a pronoun showing possession (e.g. *mine*). ■ **possessively** *adv.*

possible *adj.* capable of existing, happening, or being done. ■ **possibility** *n.* **possibly** *adv.*

possum *n.* an opossum.

post *n.* **1** the official service or system for delivering letters and parcels. **2** letters and parcels sent or delivered. **3** an upright piece of timber or metal used as a support or marker. **4** a place where someone is on duty or where an activity is carried out. **5** a job. •*v.* **1** send via the postal system. **2** put up a notice. **3** send to a place to take up a job or duty. □ **keep posted** keep informed. **postbox** a large public box into which letters are put for sending by post. **postcard** a card for sending a message by post without an envelope. **postcode** a group of letters and numbers in a postal address to assist the sorting of mail. **postman** (or **postwoman**) a person employed to deliver or collect post. **postmark** an official mark stamped on a letter or parcel, giving the date of posting. **post office** a building where postal business is carried on.

post- *prefix* after.

postage *n.* the charge for sending something by post.

postal *adj.* of or sent by post.

post-date *v.* **1** put a date later than the actual one on a cheque etc. **2** occur later than.

poster *n.* a large picture or notice used for decoration or advertisement.

poste restante /pohst resstuhnt/ *n.* a post office department where letters are kept until collected by the addressee.

posterior *adj.* at or nearer the back. •*n.* a person's bottom.

posterity *n.* future generations.

postern *n.* a back or side entrance.

postgraduate *n.* a person studying for a higher degree.

post-haste *adv.* with great speed.

posthumous *adj.* happening, awarded, or published after the person involved has died. ■ **posthumously** *adv.*

post-mortem *n.* **1** an examination of a dead body to find out the cause of death. **2** an analysis of an event after it has occurred.

post-natal *adj.* after childbirth.

postpone *v.* arrange for something to take place later than originally planned. ■ **postponement** *n.*

postprandial *adj.* after a meal.

postscript *n.* a remark added at the end of a letter.

postulant *n.* a candidate wishing to enter a religious order.

postulate *v.* assume to be true, as a basis for a theory or discussion. ■ **postulation** *n.*

posture *n.* the way in which a person holds their body. •*v.* behave in a way intended to impress or mislead. ■ **postural** *adj.*

posy *n.* (*pl.* **posies**) a small bunch of flowers.

pot *n.* **1** a rounded container for storage or cooking. **2** *informal* cannabis. •*v.* (**potting**, **potted**) **1** plant in a pot. **2** preserve food in a pot. **3** (**potted**) in a short, understandable form. **4** hit a billiard ball into a pocket. □ **pot belly** a large protruding stomach. **pot luck** a situation of taking a chance that whatever is available will be acceptable. **potsherd** a broken piece of earthenware. **potshot** a shot aimed at random.

potable adj. drinkable.

potash n. a compound of potassium.

potassium n. a soft silvery-white metallic element.

potato n. (pl. **potatoes**) a vegetable with starchy white flesh that grows underground as a tuber.

poteen n. illegally distilled whisky.

potent adj. **1** having great power, influence, or effect. **2** (of a man) able to achieve an erection. ■ **potency** n.

potentate n. a monarch or ruler.

potential adj. capable of becoming or developing into something. •n. qualities that may be developed. ■ **potentiality** n. **potentially** adv.

pothole n. **1** a deep underground cave. **2** a hole in a road surface. □ **potholing** exploring potholes as a sport.

potion n. a drink with healing, magical, or poisonous powers.

potpourri /poh-poor-i/ n. (pl. **potpourris**) **1** a scented mixture of dried petals and spices. **2** a mixture.

pottage n. old use soup or stew.

potter v. do minor pleasant tasks in a relaxed way. •n. a person who makes pottery.

pottery n. (pl. **potteries**) **1** articles made of baked clay. **2** the craft of making pottery.

potty adj. informal foolish; mad. •n. (pl. **potties**) a bowl for a child to use as a toilet.

pouch n. **1** a small flexible bag. **2** a pocket of skin in which certain animals carry their young.

pouffe n. a large firm cushion used as a seat.

poult n. a young chicken or game bird.

poulterer n. a person who sells poultry.

poultice n. a moist mass put on the skin to reduce inflammation.

poultry n. chickens, turkeys, ducks, and geese.

pounce v. move suddenly so as to seize or attack. •n. an act of pouncing.

pound n. **1** a unit of weight equal to 16 oz avoirdupois (0.454 kg), or 12 oz troy (0.373 kg). **2** the basic unit of money of the UK. **3** a place where stray dogs or illegally parked vehicles are kept until claimed. •v. **1** hit heavily again and again. **2** run with heavy steps. **3** beat or throb with a strong regular rhythm. **4** crush to a powder or paste.

poundage n. a charge made per pound in weight or value.

pour v. **1** flow or cause to flow. **2** rain heavily. **3** come or go in large numbers.

pout v. push out the lips. •n. a pouting expression.

poverty n. **1** the state of being very poor. **2** lack or scarcity of a quality etc.

POW abbrev. prisoner of war.

powder n. **1** a mass of fine dry particles. **2** a cosmetic in this form. •v. sprinkle or cover with powder. □ **powder room** a women's toilet. ■ **powdery** adj.

P

power n. **1** the ability to do something. **2** influence or control. **3** right or authority. **4** a country of international influence and military strength. **5** strength or force. **6** energy produced by mechanical, electrical, or other means. **7** the product of a number multiplied by itself a certain number of times. •v. supply with power. □ **power of attorney** the authority to act for another person in legal or financial matters. **power station** a building where electricity is generated. ■ **powerless** adj.

powerful adj. having power. ■ **powerfully** adv.

pp abbrev. **1** (**pp.**) pages. **2** per procurationem (used when signing a letter on someone else's behalf).

PR abbrev. **1** proportional representation. **2** public relations.

practicable adj. able to be done. ■ **practicability** n.

practical adj. **1** involving the actual doing or use of something rather than theory. **2** likely to be successful or useful. **3** skilled at making or doing things. **4** almost complete; virtual. □ **practical joke** a humorous trick played on someone. ■ **practicality** n. **practically** adv.

practice n. **1** the action rather than the theory of doing something. **2** the usual way of doing something. **3** the business of a doctor, dentist, or lawyer. **4** the doing of something repeatedly to improve your skill.

! **practice** is the spelling for the noun, and in America for the verb as well; **practise** is the British spelling for the verb.

practise (US **practice**) v. **1** do repeatedly to improve your skill. **2** do regularly. **3** be working in a particular profession. **4** (**practised**) expert or experienced.

practitioner n. a person who practises a profession.

pragmatic adj. dealing with things in a practical and sensible way. ■ **pragmatically** adv. **pragmatism** n. **pragmatist** n.

prairie n. a large open area of grassland, esp. in North America. □ **prairie dog** a North American rodent that lives in burrows.

praise v. **1** express approval of or admiration for. **2** express thanks to or respect for God. •n. the expression of approval or admiration. ■ **praiseworthy** adj.

praline n. a sweet substance made from nuts boiled in sugar.

pram n. a wheeled vehicle for a baby, pushed by a person on foot.

prance v. move with high steps.

prang v. informal crash a vehicle.

prank n. a mischievous act.

prankster n. a person fond of playing pranks.

prat n. informal a stupid person.

prattle v. chatter in a foolish or trivial way. •n. foolish or trivial talk.

prawn n. an edible shellfish like a large shrimp.

pray v. **1** say a prayer. **2** wish or hope strongly for something.

prayer n. **1** a request for help or expression of thanks made to God or a god. **2** an earnest hope or wish.

pre- prefix before.

preach v. **1** give a religious talk to a group. **2** recommend a course of action. **3** give moral advice in an annoying or self-righteous way. ■ **preacher** n.

preamble n. an introduction or opening statement.

prearrange v. arrange beforehand.

precarious adj. **1** likely to tip or fall. **2** unsafe or uncertain. ■ **precariously** adv.

precaution n. something done in advance to avoid problems or danger. ■ **precautionary** adj.

precede v. come, go, or happen before in time or order.

precedence n. the state of coming before others in order or importance.

precedent n. a previous case taken as an example to be followed in a similar situation.

precept n. a general rule of behaviour.

precinct n. **1** an area closed to traffic in a town. **2** the area around a place or building, often enclosed by a wall. **3** US each of the electoral or policing districts of a city or town.

precious adj. **1** having great value. **2** greatly loved or valued. **3** affectedly refined.

precipice n. a very steep rock face or cliff.

precipitate v. **1** cause to happen suddenly or too soon. **2** cause to move suddenly and with force. **3** cause a substance to be deposited in solid form from a solution. **4** cause vapour to condense and fall as rain, snow, etc. • adj. rash or hasty. • n. a substance precipitated from a solution.

precipitation n. **1** rain, snow, sleet, or hail. **2** the act of precipitating.

precipitous adj. very steep.

precis /pray-si/ n. (pl. **precis**) a summary. • v. make a precis of.

precise adj. **1** clear and detailed. **2** careful about details and accuracy. **3** particular. ■ **precisely** adv. **precision** n.

preclude v. prevent something from happening.

precocious adj. having developed certain abilities etc. earlier than usual. ■ **precocity** n.

precognition n. foreknowledge by paranormal means.

preconceived adj. (of an idea) formed before having full knowledge or evidence. ■ **preconception** n.

precondition n. a condition that must be fulfilled beforehand.

precursor n. a forerunner.

pre-date v. exist or occur at a date earlier than.

predator n. a predatory animal.

predatory adj. (of an animal) killing others for food.

predecease v. die before another person.

predecessor n. a person who held a job etc. before the current holder.

predestination n. the belief that everything has been decided in advance by God or fate.

predicament n. a difficult situation.

predicate n. the part of a sentence or clause containing a verb and stating something about the subject (e.g. *went home* in *we went home*). ■ **predicative** adj.

predict v. state that an event will happen in the future. ■ **predictable** adj. **predictably** adv. **prediction** n. **predictive** adj. **predictor** n.

P

predilection n. a special liking.

predispose v. make likely to be, do, or think something. ■ **predisposition** n.

predominant adj. 1 present as the main part. 2 having the greatest power. ■ **predominance** n. **predominantly** adv. **predominate** v.

pre-eminent adj. better than all others; outstanding. ■ **pre-eminence** n.

pre-empt v. 1 take action to prevent something happening. 2 prevent from saying something by speaking first. ■ **pre-emption** n. **pre-emptive** adj.

preen v. 1 (of a bird) tidy and clean its feathers with its beak. 2 attend to and admire your appearance. 3 (**preen yourself**) feel very self-satisfied.

prefabricated adj. (of a building) made in sections for easy assembly on site.

preface n. an introduction to a book. •v. say or do something to introduce a book, speech, etc.

prefect n. 1 a senior pupil in a school who has some authority over other pupils. 2 an administrative official in certain countries. ■ **prefecture** n.

prefer v. (**preferring, preferred**) 1 like better than another or others. 2 put forward a formal accusation.

preferable adj. more desirable. ■ **preferably** adv.

preference n. 1 a greater liking for one alternative over another or others. 2 a thing preferred. 3 favour shown to one person over others.

preferential adj. favouring a particular person or group. ■ **preferentially** adv.

preferment n. promotion.

prefix n. a letter or group of letters placed at the beginning of a word to alter its meaning. •v. add a prefix to.

pregnant adj. 1 having a child or young developing in the womb. 2 full of meaning. ■ **pregnancy** n.

prehensile adj. (of an animal's limb or tail) able to grasp things.

prehistoric adj. of the period before written records.

prejudge v. form a judgement before knowing all the facts.

prejudice n. 1 an opinion not based on reason or experience. 2 dislike or unfair behaviour based on such opinions. •v. 1 give rise to prejudice in. 2 cause harm to.

prejudicial adj. harmful to rights etc.

prelate n. a high-ranking member of the clergy.

preliminary adj. happening before or preparing for a main action or event. •n. (pl. **preliminaries**) a preliminary action or event.

prelude n. 1 an action or event acting as an introduction to something more important. 2 an introductory piece of music.

premarital adj. before marriage.

premature adj. occurring or done before the usual or proper time. ■ **prematurely** adv.

premeditated adj. planned in advance. ■ **premeditation** n.

premenstrual adj. occurring before menstruation.

premier adj. first in importance, order, or position. •n. a Prime Minister or other head of government. ■ **premiership** n.

premiere n. the first performance of a play, film, etc.

premise (or **premiss**) *n.* a statement or idea forming the basis for a theory or argument.

premises *pl. n.* the building and land occupied by a business.

premium *n.* (*pl.* **premiums**) **1** an amount paid for an insurance policy. **2** a sum added to a usual price or charge. □ **at a premium 1** scarce and in demand. **2** above the usual price.

premonition *n.* a feeling that something is about to happen. ■ **premonitory** *adj.*

preoccupy *v.* (**preoccupying, preoccupied**) fill the mind of completely. ■ **preoccupation** *n.*

preparation *n.* **1** the act of preparing. **2** something done to prepare for an event or undertaking. **3** a substance prepared for use.

preparatory *adj.* done so as to prepare for something. □ **preparatory school** a private school for pupils aged 7 to 13.

prepare *v.* **1** make ready for use. **2** make or get ready to do or deal with something. **3** (**prepared**) willing.

preponderance *n.* the state of being greater in number. ■ **preponderant** *adj.* **preponderate** *v.*

preposition *n.* a word used with a noun or pronoun to show place, position, time, or method. ■ **prepositional** *adj.*

prepossessing *adj.* attractive.

preposterous *adj.* completely ridiculous or outrageous. ■ **preposterously** *adv.*

prepuce /pree-pyooss/ *n.* the foreskin.

prerequisite *n.* something that must exist or happen before something else can exist or happen.

prerogative *n.* a right or privilege.

presage *v.* be an omen of. •*n.* an omen.

Presbyterian *adj.* of a Protestant Church governed by elders of equal rank. •*n.* a member of a Presbyterian Church. ■ **Presbyterianism** *n.*

presbytery *n.* (*pl.* **presbyteries**) **1** an administrative body in a Presbyterian Church. **2** the house of a Roman Catholic priest.

prescient /press-i-uhnt/ *adj.* having knowledge of events before they happen. ■ **prescience** *n.*

prescribe *v.* **1** recommend and permit the use of a medicine etc. **2** state officially that something should be done.

> ! Don't confuse **prescribe** with **proscribe**, which means 'forbid'.

prescription *n.* a doctor's written instruction stating that a patient may be issued with a medicine.

prescriptive *adj.* stating what should be done.

presence *n.* **1** the state of being present. **2** an impressive manner or appearance. **3** a person or thing that seems to be present but is not seen. □ **presence of mind** the ability to act quickly and sensibly in a crisis.

present¹ /pre-z'nt/ *adj.* **1** being or occurring in a particular place. **2** existing or occurring now. •*n.* the present time.

present² *v.* /pri-zent/ **1** give formally at a ceremony. **2** introduce and appear in a broadcast. **3** be the cause of a problem. **4** give a particular impression. •*n.*

/pre-z'nt/ a gift. ■ **presentation** n. **presenter** n.

presentable adj. clean or smart enough to be seen in public.

presentiment n. a feeling that something unpleasant is going to happen.

presently adv. **1** soon. **2** now.

preservative n. a substance used to prevent food or wood from decaying.

preserve v. **1** keep in its original or existing state. **2** keep safe from harm. **3** treat food to prevent it from decaying. • n. **1** jam. **2** something seen as reserved for a particular person or group. ■ **preservation** n. **preserver** n.

preside v. be in charge of a meeting, court, etc.

president n. **1** the elected head of a republic. **2** the head of an organization. ■ **presidency** n. **presidential** adj.

press v. **1** move into contact with something by using steady force. **2** push something to operate a device. **3** apply pressure to something to flatten or shape it. **4** move along by pushing. **5** (**press on/ahead**) continue with something. **6** forcefully put forward an opinion. **7** try hard to persuade. **8** (**be pressed for**) have too little of. • n. **1** a device for flattening or shaping something. **2** a printing press. **3** newspapers or journalists as a whole. □ **press conference** a meeting with a number of journalists. **press-gang** force into doing something. **press into service** put to a particular use as a makeshift measure. **press stud** a small fastener with two parts that fit together when pressed. **press-up** an exercise in which a person

lies on the floor and raises their body by pressing down on their hands.

pressing adj. urgent.

pressure n. **1** steady force applied to an object. **2** the use of persuasion or threats. **3** stress. **4** the force per unit area applied by a fluid against a surface. • v. pressurize. □ **pressure cooker** an airtight pot for cooking food quickly under steam pressure. **pressure group** a group that tries to influence public policy in the interest of a particular cause.

pressurize (or **-ise**) v. **1** persuade or force into doing something. **2** keep the air pressure in an aircraft cabin the same as it is at ground level.

prestige n. respect and admiration resulting from achievement, high quality, etc.

prestigious adj. having or bringing prestige.

presto adv. & adj. Music quickly.

prestressed adj. (of concrete) strengthened by rods or wires inside it.

presumably adv. as may be presumed.

presume v. **1** suppose to be true. **2** be bold enough to do something that you should not do. **3** (**presume on**) take advantage of someone's kindness, friendship, etc. ■ **presumption** n.

presumptuous adj. behaving too confidently. ■ **presumptuously** adv.

presuppose v. **1** require as a precondition. **2** assume to be the case. ■ **presupposition** n.

pretence (US **pretense**) n. **1** an act of pretending. **2** a claim to have or be something.

pretend → prima donna

pretend v. **1** make it seem that something is the case when in fact it is not. **2 (pretend to)** claim to have. ■ **pretender** n.

pretension n. **1** a claim to have or be something. **2** pretentiousness.

pretentious adj. trying to appear more important or better than you actually are. ■ **pretentiousness** n.

preternatural adj. beyond what is normal or natural. ■ **preternaturally** adv.

pretext n. a false reason used to justify an action.

prettify v. **(prettifying, prettified)** make something seem pretty.

pretty adj. **(prettier, prettiest)** attractive in a delicate way. •adv. informal to a certain extent. ■ **prettily** adv. **prettiness** n.

pretzel n. a knot-shaped salted biscuit.

prevail v. **1** be more powerful than. **2 (prevail on)** persuade. **3** be widespread or current.

prevalent adj. widespread. ■ **prevalence** n.

prevaricate v. avoid giving a direct answer. ■ **prevarication** n.

prevent v. stop something from happening or someone from doing something. ■ **preventable** adj. **prevention** n.

preventive (or **preventative**) adj. designed to prevent something.

preview n. a viewing or showing of something before it becomes widely available.

previous adj. coming before in time or order. ■ **previously** adv.

prey n. **1** an animal hunted and killed by another for food. **2** a victim. •v. **(prey on) 1** hunt and kill

for food. **2** take advantage of or cause distress to.

price n. **1** the amount of money for which something is bought or sold. **2** something unwelcome that must be done to achieve something. •v. decide the price of.

priceless adj. **1** very valuable. **2** informal very amusing.

prick v. **1** pierce slightly. **2** cause to have a slight prickling feeling. •n. a mark, hole, or pain caused by pricking. □ **prick up your ears 1** (of an animal) make the ears stand erect. **2** begin to pay attention.

prickle n. **1** a small thorn or a pointed spine. **2** a tingling feeling. •v. have a tingling feeling.

prickly adj. **1** having prickles. **2** easily offended or annoyed.

pride n. **1** pleasure or satisfaction gained from achievements, qualities, or possessions. **2** a source of this. **3** self-respect. **4** a group of lions. •v. **(pride yourself on)** be proud of. □ **pride of place** the most noticeable or important position.

priest n. **1** a member of the clergy. **2** (fem. **priestess**) a person who performs ceremonies in a non-Christian religion. ■ **priesthood** n. **priestly** adj.

prig n. a self-righteous person. ■ **priggish** adj.

prim adj. showing prudish disapproval of anything improper. ■ **primly** adv.

prima ballerina n. the chief female dancer in a ballet company.

primacy n. the fact of being most important.

prima donna n. **1** the chief female singer in an opera. **2** a temperamental self-important person.

prima facie /pry-muh fay-shi-ee/ *adj. & adv. Law* accepted as correct until proved otherwise.

primal *adj.* primitive; primeval.

primary *adj.* **1** most important. **2** earliest in time or order. **3** of education for children below the age of 11. • *n.* (*pl.* **primaries**) (in the US) a preliminary election to select delegates or candidates. □ **primary colour** each of the colours blue, red, and yellow, from which all other colours can be obtained by mixing. ■ **primarily** *adv.*

primate *n.* **1** a mammal of an order including monkeys, apes, and humans. **2** an archbishop.

prime *adj.* **1** most important. **2** excellent. **3** (of a number) that can be divided only by itself and one. • *n.* a time of greatest strength, success, etc. • *v.* **1** make ready for use or action. **2** provide with information in preparation for something. □ **prime minister** the head of a government.

primer *n.* **1** a substance painted on a surface as a base coat. **2** a book giving a basic introduction to a subject.

primeval *adj.* of the earliest times in history.

primitive *adj.* **1** of the earliest times in history or stages in development. **2** simple or crude.

primogeniture *n.* a system by which an eldest son inherits all his parents' property.

primordial *adj.* primeval.

primrose *n.* a pale yellow spring flower.

primula *n.* a kind of primrose.

prince *n.* a son or other close male relative of a monarch.

princely *adj.* **1** of or suitable for a prince. **2** (of a sum of money) generous.

princess *n.* **1** a daughter or other close female relative of a monarch. **2** a prince's wife or widow.

principal *adj.* most important; main. • *n.* **1** the most important person in an organization or group. **2** the head of a school or college. **3** a sum of money lent or invested, on which interest is paid. ■ **principally** *adv.*

! Don't confuse **principal** and **principle**, a noun meaning 'a truth or general law'.

principality *n.* (*pl.* **principalities**) a state ruled by a prince.

principle *n.* **1** a truth or general law used as a basis for a theory or system of belief. **2** (**principles**) beliefs governing someone's behaviour. **3** a general scientific law. □ **in principle** in theory. **on principle** because of your moral beliefs.

print *v.* **1** produce a book etc. by a process involving the transfer of words or pictures to paper. **2** produce a photographic print from a negative. **3** write words clearly without joining the letters. **4** mark with a coloured design. • *n.* **1** printed text. **2** a mark where something has pressed or touched a surface. **3** a printed picture, design, or fabric. **4** a photo printed on paper from a negative or transparency. □ **printed circuit** an electronic circuit with thin strips of conducting material on an insulating board. **printing press** a machine for printing from type or plates. **printout** a page of printed material from a computer's printer. ■ **printer** *n.*

437

prior → probe

prior *adj.* coming before in time, order, or importance. •*n.* (*fem.* **prioress**) **1** the person next in rank below an abbot (or abbess). **2** the head of a priory.

prioritize (or **-ise**) *v.* **1** treat as most important. **2** decide the order of importance of tasks.

priority *n.* (*pl.* **priorities**) **1** the state of being more important. **2** a thing seen as more important than others. **3** the right to go before other traffic.

priory *n.* (*pl.* **priories**) a monastery or nunnery governed by a prior or prioress.

prise (*US* **prize**) *v.* force open or apart.

prism *n.* **1** a transparent object with triangular ends, used to separate white light into colours. **2** a solid geometric figure whose ends are parallel and of the same size and shape. ■ **prismatic** *adj.*

prison *n.* a building used to confine criminals or people awaiting trial.

prisoner *n.* **1** a person kept in prison. **2** a person captured and kept confined.

prissy *adj.* prim.

pristine *adj.* in its original and unspoilt condition.

privacy *n.* a state in which you are not watched or disturbed by others.

private *adj.* **1** for or belonging to a particular person or group only. **2** not to be made known. **3** not provided or owned by the state. **4** not connected with a person's work. **5** where you will not be disturbed; secluded. •*n.* a soldier of the lowest rank. ■ **privately** *adv.*

privation *n.* lack of food and other essentials.

privatize (or **-ise**) *v.* transfer from state to private ownership. ■ **privatization** *n.*

privet *n.* a shrub with small dark green leaves.

privilege *n.* a special right or advantage for a particular person or group. ■ **privileged** *adj.*

! There's no *d*: privilege.

privy *adj.* (**privy to**) sharing in the knowledge of a secret. •*n.* (*pl.* **privies**) an outside toilet.

prize *n.* a thing given to a winner or to mark an outstanding achievement. •*adj.* **1** having been awarded a prize. **2** excellent. •*v.* **1** value highly. **2** *US* = **PRISE**.

pro *n.* (*pl.* **pros**) **1** *informal* a professional. **2** (**pros and cons**) arguments for and against something.

pro- *prefix* in favour of.

proactive *adj.* creating or controlling a situation rather than just responding to it. ■ **proactively** *adv.*

probability *n.* (*pl.* **probabilities**) **1** the extent to which something is probable. **2** a probable event.

probable *adj.* likely to happen or be the case. ■ **probably** *adv.*

probate *n.* the official process of proving that a will is valid.

probation *n.* **1** a system whereby an offender is not sent to prison subject to a period of good behaviour under supervision. **2** a period of training and testing a new employee. ■ **probationary** *adj.* **probationer** *n.*

probe *n.* **1** a blunt surgical instrument for exploring a wound etc. **2** an investigation. **3** an unmanned exploratory spacecraft. •*v.* **1** examine with a probe. **2** investigate closely.

probity /proh-bi-ti/ *n.* honesty.

problem *n.* something difficult to deal with or understand. ■ **problematic** *adj.* **problematical** *adj.*

proboscis /pruh-boss-iss/ *n. (pl.* **probosces** or **proboscises**) **1** a long, flexible nose. **2** an insect's elongated sucking mouthpart.

procedure *n.* **1** an established or official way of doing something. **2** a series of actions done in a certain way. ■ **procedural** *adj.*

proceed *v.* **1** begin a course of action. **2** go on to do. **3** continue. **4** move forward.

proceedings *pl. n.* **1** a series of activities. **2** a lawsuit.

proceeds *pl. n.* money obtained from an event or activity.

process *n.* **1** a series of actions to achieve an end. **2** a natural series of changes. •*v.* **1** perform a series of actions to change or preserve something. **2** deal with using an established procedure. ■ **processor** *n.*

procession *n.* a number of people, vehicles, etc. moving forward in an orderly line.

proclaim *v.* announce publicly. ■ **proclamation** *n.*

proclivity *n. (pl.* **proclivities**) a tendency or inclination.

procrastinate *v.* postpone action. ■ **procrastination** *n.*

procreate *v.* produce young. ■ **procreation** *n.*

procurator fiscal *n.* (in Scotland) a local coroner and public prosecutor.

procure *v.* obtain. ■ **procurement** *n.*

procurer *n.* a person who obtains a prostitute for another person.

prod *v.* (**prodding, prodded**) **1** poke. **2** prompt or remind to do something. •*n.* **1** a poke. **2** a prompt or reminder. **3** a pointed implement.

prodigal *adj.* wasteful or extravagant.

prodigious *adj.* impressively large. ■ **prodigiously** *adv.*

prodigy *n. (pl.* **prodigies**) **1** a young person with exceptional abilities. **2** an amazing or unusual thing.

produce *v.* **1** make, manufacture, or create. **2** cause to happen or exist. **3** show or provide for consideration. **4** administer the financing of a film or the staging of a play. **5** supervise the making of a recording. •*n.* things that have been produced or grown. ■ **producer** *n.* **production** *n.*

product *n.* **1** a thing produced. **2** a number obtained by multiplying.

productive *adj.* producing or achieving a great deal.

productivity *n.* the efficiency with which things are produced.

profane *adj.* **1** not holy or religious. **2** not reverent. •*v.* treat irreverently. ■ **profanity** *n.*

profess *v.* **1** claim to have, feel, or be. **2** declare your faith in a religion.

profession *n.* **1** a job requiring special training and a formal qualification. **2** a body of people engaged in this. **3** a declaration.

professional *adj.* **1** of or belonging to a profession. **2** doing something as a job rather than as a hobby. **3** competent. •*n.* a professional person. ■ **professionalism** *n.* **professionally** *adv.*

p

professor n. a university academic of the highest rank. ■ **professorial** adj.

proffer v. offer.

proficient adj. competent; skilled. ■ **proficiency** n.

profile n. **1** an outline of a person's face seen from the side. **2** a short descriptive article about someone. **3** the extent to which a person or organization attracts notice.

profit n. **1** a financial gain. **2** advantage; benefit. • v. (**profiting**, **profited**) benefit, esp. financially.

profitable adj. **1** making a profit. **2** useful. ■ **profitability** n. **profitably** adv.

profiteering n. the making of a large profit in an unfair way.

profligate adj. **1** extravagant or wasteful. **2** dissolute. • n. a profligate person. ■ **profligacy** n.

profound adj. **1** very great. **2** showing or needing great knowledge or understanding. ■ **profoundly** adv. **profundity** n.

profuse adj. plentiful. ■ **profusely** adv. **profusion** n.

progenitor n. an ancestor.

progeny n. offspring.

progesterone n. a hormone that stimulates the womb to prepare for pregnancy.

prognosis n. (pl. **prognoses**) a forecast, esp. of the likely course of an illness. ■ **prognostic** adj.

prognosticate v. forecast. ■ **prognostication** n.

programme (US **program**) n. **1** a planned series of events. **2** a radio or television broadcast. **3** a set of related measures with a long-term aim. **4** a sheet or booklet giving details about a play, concert, etc. **5** (**program**) a series of software

instructions to control the operation of a computer. • v. **1** (**program**) (**programming**, **programmed**; US **programing**, **programed**) provide a computer with a program. **2** arrange according to a plan. ■ **programmer** n.

progress n. **1** forward movement. **2** development or improvement. • v. move forward or develop. ■ **progression** n.

progressive adj. **1** happening gradually. **2** favouring new ideas or social reform. ■ **progressively** adv.

prohibit v. (**prohibiting**, **prohibited**) forbid. ■ **prohibition** n.

prohibitive adj. **1** forbidding something. **2** (of a price) too high.

project n. **1** a piece of work planned to achieve a particular aim. **2** a piece of work involving research. • v. **1** estimate. **2** plan. **3** stick out beyond something else. **4** make light or an image fall on a surface. **5** present an image of yourself to others.

projectile n. a missile.

projection n. **1** a forecast based on present trends. **2** the projecting of an image etc. **3** a thing that sticks out. ■ **projectionist** n.

projector n. a device for projecting slides or film on to a screen.

prolapse n. a condition in which an organ of the body has slipped from its normal position.

proletariat n. workers or working-class people. ■ **proletarian** adj. & n.

proliferate v. reproduce or grow rapidly. ■ **proliferation** n.

prolific adj. producing things in abundance. ■ **prolifically** adv.

P

prolix → propeller

440

prolix adj. (of speech or writing) long and boring. ▪ **prolixity** n.

prologue n. an introduction to a book, play, etc.

prolong v. cause to last longer. ▪ **prolongation** n.

prom n. **1** a promenade by the sea. **2** a promenade concert.

promenade n. **1** a paved public walk along a seafront. **2** a leisurely walk, ride, or drive. □ **promenade concert** a concert of classical music at which part of the audience stands.

prominent adj. **1** important; famous. **2** sticking out. **3** conspicuous. ▪ **prominence** n. **prominently** adv.

promiscuous adj. having many sexual relationships. ▪ **promiscuity** n.

promise n. **1** an assurance that you will do something or that something will happen. **2** potential excellence. •v. **1** make a promise. **2** give good grounds for expecting.

promising adj. showing signs of future success.

promissory note n. a written signed promise to pay a stated sum.

promontory n. (pl. **promontories**) high land jutting out into the sea.

promote v. **1** aid the progress of a cause or aim. **2** publicize a product. **3** raise to a higher rank or office. ▪ **promoter** n. **promotion** n.

prompt v. **1** cause to happen or to do. **2** tell an actor a word they have forgotten. •n. an act of prompting. •adj. done or acting without delay. •adv. punctually. ▪ **prompter** n. **promptly** adv.

promulgate v. make widely known. ▪ **promulgation** n.

prone adj. **1** likely to suffer from or do. **2** lying face downwards.

prong n. each of the projecting pointed parts of a fork.

pronoun n. a word used instead of a noun to indicate someone or something already mentioned or known, e.g. I, this.

pronounce v. **1** make the sound of a word or part of a word. **2** declare or announce. ▪ **pronouncement** n. **pronunciation** n.

❗ **pronunciation** has no o after the first n.

pronounced adj. noticeable.

proof n. **1** evidence proving that something is true. **2** a copy of printed material used for making corrections before final printing. •adj. resistant to: damp-proof. □ **proofread** read printed proofs and mark any errors.

prop n. **1** a pole or beam used as a temporary support. **2** a portable object used on the set of a play or film. •v. (**propping, propped**) support with or as if with a prop.

propaganda n. false or exaggerated information used to promote a political cause etc.

propagate v. **1** produce a new plant from a parent plant. **2** promote an idea etc. widely. ▪ **propagation** n. **propagator** n.

propane n. a gas present in natural gas, used as fuel.

propel v. (**propelling, propelled**) drive or push forwards. ▪ **propellant** n.

propeller n. a revolving shaft with angled blades, for propelling a ship or aircraft.

propensity n. (pl. **propensities**) a tendency.

proper adj. **1** deserving the description; genuine. **2** appropriate or correct. **3** very respectable. **4** (**proper to**) belonging exclusively to. □ **proper name** (or **proper noun**) a name for a person, place, or organization. ■ **properly** adv.

property n. (pl. **properties**) **1** a thing or things belonging to someone. **2** a building and the land belonging to it. **3** a quality or characteristic.

prophecy n. (pl. **prophecies**) a prediction about what will happen.

prophesy v. (**prophesying, prophesied**) predict.

prophet n. **1** a person regarded as being sent by God to teach people. **2** a person who predicts the future.

prophetic adj. **1** accurately predicting the future. **2** of a prophet or prophecy.

prophylactic adj. intended to prevent disease. • n. a preventive medicine.

propinquity n. nearness.

propitiate v. win or regain the favour of. ■ **propitiation** n. **propitiatory** adj.

propitious adj. favourable.

proponent n. a person proposing a theory or plan.

proportion n. **1** a part or share of a whole. **2** relative size or amount. **3** the correct relation between things. **4** (**proportions**) the size and shape of something.

proportional (or **proportionate**) adj. corresponding in size or amount to something else. □ **proportional representation** an electoral system in which parties gain seats in proportion to the number of votes cast for them. ■ **proportionally** adv.

proposal n. **1** a plan or suggestion. **2** the act of proposing. **3** an offer of marriage.

propose v. **1** put forward an idea for consideration. **2** nominate for a post. **3** make an offer of marriage to someone.

proposition n. **1** a statement expressing an opinion. **2** a plan of action. • v. informal ask someone to have sex with you.

propound v. put forward an idea for consideration.

proprietary adj. **1** of an owner or ownership. **2** (of a product) marketed under a registered trade name.

proprietor n. the owner of a business. ■ **proprietorial** adj.

propriety n. (pl. **proprieties**) correctness of behaviour.

propulsion n. the act of propelling.

pro rata adj. proportional. • adv. proportionally.

prorogue /pruh-rohg/ v. suspend a session of parliament without dissolving it.

prosaic adj. ordinary or unimaginative. ■ **prosaically** adv.

proscenium n. (pl. **prosceniums** or **proscenia**) the part of a stage in front of the curtain.

proscribe v. forbid.

> ! Don't confuse **proscribe** with **prescribe**.

prose n. ordinary written or spoken language.

prosecute v. **1** take legal proceedings against someone for a crime. **2** continue a course of action. ■ **prosecution** n. **prosecutor** n.

proselyte /pross-i-lyt/ n. a convert from one religion to another. ■ **proselytize** (or **-ise**) v.

prospect n. **1** the possibility of something occurring. **2** (**prospects**) chances for success. •v. search for mineral deposits. ■ **prospector** n.

prospective adj. likely to happen or be in the future.

prospectus n. (pl. **prospectuses**) a booklet giving details of a school etc. or a share offer.

prosper v. succeed or flourish.

prosperous adj. rich and successful. ■ **prosperity** n.

prostate n. a gland surrounding the neck of the bladder in male mammals.

prosthesis n. (pl. **prostheses**) an artificial body part. ■ **prosthetic** adj.

prostitute n. a person who has sex for payment. •v. **1** offer as a prostitute. **2** put your abilities to an unworthy use. ■ **prostitution** n.

prostrate adj. **1** lying stretched with the face downwards. **2** overcome with distress or exhaustion. •v. **1** (**prostrate yourself**) throw yourself flat on the ground. **2** (**be prostrated**) be overcome with distress or exhaustion. ■ **prostration** n.

protagonist n. **1** the leading character in a drama, novel, etc. **2** a supporter of a cause etc.

protean adj. able to change or adapt.

protect v. keep safe from harm or injury. ■ **protection** n. **protector** n.

protectionism n. the policy of shielding a country's industries from foreign competition by taxing imports. ■ **protectionist** n. & adj.

protective adj. serving or wishing to protect. ■ **protectively** adv.

protectorate n. a state that is controlled and protected by another.

protégé /prot-i-zhay/ n. (fem. **protégée**) a person who is guided and supported by a more experienced person.

protein n. a substance which forms part of body tissues and is an important part of the diet.

❗ **protein** is an exception to the usual rule of i before e except after c.

pro tem adv. & adj. for the time being.

protest n. a statement or action expressing disapproval or objection. •v. **1** express an objection. **2** state strongly. ■ **protestation** n. **protester** n.

Protestant n. a member of any of the Western Christian Churches that are separate from the Roman Catholic Church. ■ **Protestantism** n.

protocol n. **1** the system of rules governing formal occasions. **2** the accepted code of behaviour in a situation. **3** a draft of a treaty.

proton n. a subatomic particle with a positive electric charge.

protoplasm n. the material comprising the living part of a cell.

prototype n. a first or earlier form from which others are developed.

protozoan n. a single-celled microscopic animal.

protracted adj. lasting longer than usual or expected.

protractor n. an instrument for measuring angles.

protrude v. stick out from a surface. ■ **protrusion** n.

protuberance n. a protruding part. ■ **protuberant** adj.

proud adj. 1 feeling pride. 2 giving cause for pride. 3 slightly projecting from a surface. ■ **proudly** adv.

prove v. (**proving, proved**; past part. **proved** or **proven**) 1 show by evidence or argument that something is true or exists. 2 show or be seen to be.

provenance n. the place of origin of something.

provender n. animal fodder.

proverb n. a short saying stating a general truth or piece of advice.

proverbial adj. 1 referred to in a proverb. 2 well known.

provide v. 1 make available for use; supply. 2 (**provide for**) make enough preparation for. ■ **provider** n.

provided (or **providing**) conj. on the condition that.

providence n. 1 the protective care of God or of nature. 2 the state of being provident.

provident adj. careful in planning for the future.

providential adj. happening at a favourable time. ■ **providentially** adv.

province n. 1 a main administrative division of a country. 2 (**the provinces**) the whole of a country outside the capital. 3 an area of knowledge or responsibility.

provincial adj. 1 of a province or the provinces. 2 unsophisticated

or narrow-minded. • n. a person who lives in the provinces.

provision n. 1 the act of providing. 2 something provided. 3 (**provisions**) supplies of food and drink. 4 a condition in a legal document.

provisional adj. arranged temporarily. ■ **provisionally** adv.

proviso /pruh-vy-zoh/ n. (pl. **provisos**) a condition attached to an agreement.

provoke v. 1 cause a strong reaction. 2 deliberately annoy or anger. 3 stir up to do something. ■ **provocation** n. **provocative** adj.

provost n. the head of certain colleges and schools.

prow n. the pointed front part of a ship.

prowess n. skill or expertise.

prowl v. move about in a stealthy or restless way. ■ **prowler** n.

proximity n. nearness. ■ **proximate** adj.

proxy n. (pl. **proxies**) 1 the authority to represent someone else, esp. in voting. 2 a person authorized to act on behalf of another.

prude n. a person who is easily shocked by sexual matters. ■ **prudery** n. **prudish** adj.

prudent adj. showing thought for the future. ■ **prudence** n. **prudently** adv.

prune n. a dried plum. • v. trim a shrub etc. by cutting away dead or unwanted parts.

prurient adj. showing excessive interest in sexual matters. ■ **prurience** n.

pry v. (**prying, pried**) enquire too intrusively into a person's private affairs.

P

PS *abbrev.* postscript.

psalm /sahm/ *n.* a song or poem praising God.

psalter /sawl-ter/ *n.* a copy of the Book of Psalms in the Bible.

psephology /se-fol-uh-ji/ *n.* the study of trends in voting.

pseudo /syoo-doh/ *adj.* fake.

pseudonym /syoo-duh-nim/ *n.* a false name, esp. one used by an author. ■ **pseudonymous** *adj.*

psoriasis /suh-ry-uh-siss/ *n.* a skin condition causing itchy, scaly patches.

psyche /sy-ki/ *n.* the human soul, mind, or spirit.

psychedelic /sy-kuh-del-ik/ *adj.* **1** (of a drug) producing hallucinations. **2** having bright colours or an abstract pattern.

psychiatry /sy-ky-uh-tri/ *n.* the study and treatment of mental illness. ■ **psychiatric** *adj.* **psychiatrist** *n.*

psychic /sy-kik/ *adj.* **1** of or possessing abilities that cannot be explained by science. **2** of the mind. •*n.* a person claiming to have psychic powers. ■ **psychically** *adv.*

psychoanalyse (*US* **-yze**) *v.* treat using psychoanalysis.

psychoanalysis *n.* a method of treating mental illnesses by investigating the unconscious elements of the mind. ■ **psychoanalyst** *n.*

psychology *n.* **1** the study of the human mind and its functions. **2** a person's mental characteristics. ■ **psychological** *adj.* **psychologically** *adv.* **psychologist** *n.*

psychopath *n.* a person with a serious mental illness causing violent behaviour. ■ **psychopathic** *adj.*

psychosis *n.* (*pl.* **psychoses**) a severe mental illness in which a person loses contact with reality. ■ **psychotic** *adj.*

psychosomatic *adj.* (of a physical illness) caused or made worse by a mental factor such as stress.

psychotherapy *n.* the treatment of mental illness by psychological rather than medical means. ■ **psychotherapist** *n.*

PT *abbrev.* physical training.

Pt *abbrev.* **1** Part. **2** (**pt**) pint. **3** (**pt.**) point.

PTA *abbrev.* parent-teacher association.

ptarmigan /tar-mi-guhn/ *n.* a grouse of northern regions.

pterodactyl /te-ruh-dak-til/ *n.* an extinct reptile with wings.

PTO *abbrev.* please turn over.

pub *n.* a building licensed to serve alcoholic drinks.

puberty *n.* the period during which adolescents reach sexual maturity.

pubescence *n.* the time when puberty begins. ■ **pubescent** *adj.*

pubic *adj.* of the lower abdomen.

public *adj.* **1** of, for, or known to people in general. **2** provided by the state rather than an independent company. •*n.* (**the public**) **1** ordinary people in general. **2** a group with a particular interest. □ **public address system** a system of microphones and loudspeakers for amplifying speech or music. **public house** a pub. **public relations** the business of maintaining a good public image for an organization or famous person. **public school** (in the UK) a private fee-paying secondary school. **public servant** a person working for the state or for local government. ■ **publicly** adv.

publican n. a person who owns or manages a pub.

publication n. **1** the act of publishing. **2** a published book etc.

publicity n. **1** attention given to someone or something by the media. **2** information used for advertising.

publicize (or **-ise**) v. **1** make widely known. **2** advertise. ■ **publicist** n.

publish v. **1** produce a book etc. for public sale. **2** print in a book or newspaper. ■ **publisher** n.

puce n. a purple-brown colour.

puck n. a hard rubber disc used in ice hockey.

pucker v. gather into wrinkles. •n. a wrinkle.

pudding n. **1** a cooked dessert. **2** a savoury dish made with suet and flour. **3** a kind of sausage.

puddle n. a small pool of rainwater or other liquid.

puerile /pyoor-yl/ adj. childishly silly.

puerperal fever n. fever caused by infection of the womb after childbirth.

puff n. **1** a short amount of air or smoke blown out. **2** an act of drawing quickly on a cigarette etc. **3** a light pastry case. •v. **1** breathe in repeated short gasps. **2** move with short, noisy puffs of air or steam. **3** smoke a cigarette etc. **4** (**puff out/up**) swell or cause to swell. □ **puffball** a ball-shaped fungus. **puff pastry** light flaky pastry.

puffin n. a seabird with a large brightly coloured bill.

puffy adj. (**puffier, puffiest**) swollen. ■ **puffiness** n.

pug n. a small dog with a flat nose and wrinkled face.

pugilist n. a boxer. ■ **pugilistic** adj.

pugnacious adj. quick to argue or fight. ■ **pugnaciously** adv. **pugnacity** n.

puke v. & n. informal vomit.

pukka adj. **1** genuine. **2** informal excellent.

pull v. **1** apply force to something so as to move it towards yourself. **2** move steadily or with effort. **3** strain a muscle etc. **4** inhale deeply while smoking. •n. **1** an act of pulling. **2** a deep drink of something or a deep breath of smoke from a cigarette etc. **3** a force or attraction. □ **pull back** retreat. **pull off** informal succeed in doing. **pull out** withdraw. **pull through** recover from a serious illness or injury. **pull up** (of a vehicle) stop.

pullet n. a young hen.

pulley n. (pl. **pulleys**) a wheel around which a rope etc. passes, used in lifting things.

pullover n. a knitted garment for the upper body.

pulmonary adj. of the lungs.

pulp n. **1** a soft, wet mass of crushed material. **2** the soft fleshy part of a fruit. •v. crush into a pulp. •adj. (of writing) popular and badly written. ■ **pulpy** adj.

pulpit n. a raised platform in a church from which a preacher speaks.

pulsar n. a star emitting regular pulses of radio waves.

pulsate v. expand and contract rhythmically. ■ **pulsation** n.

pulse n. **1** the regular throbbing of the arteries as blood is sent through them. **2** a single vibration

p

or short burst of sound, light, etc. **3** the edible seeds of some plants of the pea family. • v. pulsate.

pulverize (or **-ise**) v. crush to fine particles.

puma n. a large American wild cat.

pumice /pum-iss/ n. solidified lava, used to remove fresh skin.

pummel v. (**pummelling**, **pummelled**; US **pummeling**, **pummeled**) hit repeatedly with the fists.

pump n. **1** a device for moving liquid, gas, or air. **2** a plimsoll. • v. **1** move with a pump. **2** fill with liquid, gas, etc. **3** move vigorously up and down.

pumpkin n. a large round orange fruit.

pun n. a joke that uses a word or words with more than one meaning. • v. (**punning**, **punned**) make a pun.

punch v. **1** hit with the fist. **2** press a key on a machine. **3** pierce a hole in a material. • n. **1** a blow with the fist. **2** a device for cutting holes or impressing a design. **3** a drink of wine or spirits mixed with fruit juices etc. □ **punch-drunk** dazed by a series of punches. **punchline** the final part of a joke, providing the humour.

punctilious adj. showing great attention to detail or correct behaviour.

punctual adj. happening or doing something at the appointed time. ■ **punctuality** n. **punctually** adv.

punctuate v. **1** interrupt at intervals. **2** put punctuation marks in.

punctuation n. the marks, such as full stop and comma, used in writing to separate sentences and to make meaning clear.

puncture n. a small hole made by a sharp object. • v. make a puncture in.

pundit n. an expert.

pungent adj. having a strong taste or smell. ■ **pungency** n.

punish v. impose a penalty on someone for an offence. ■ **punishment** n.

punitive adj. intended as punishment.

punk n. **1** a loud, fast form of rock music with aggressive lyrics and behaviour. **2** an admirer of punk music.

punnet n. a small container for fruit.

punt n. a long, narrow, flat-bottomed boat moved with a long pole. • v. travel in a punt.

punter n. informal **1** a person who places a bet. **2** a customer.

puny adj. (**punier**, **puniest**) small and weak.

pup n. **1** a puppy. **2** a young wolf, seal, or rat.

pupa /pyoo-puh/ n. (pl. **pupae**) an insect in the form between larva and adult.

pupate v. become a pupa.

pupil n. **1** a person who is taught by another. **2** the dark opening in the centre of the iris of the eye.

puppet n. **1** a model of a person or animal moved either by strings or by a hand inside it. **2** a person under the control of another. ■ **puppetry** n.

puppy n. (pl. **puppies**) a young dog.

purchase v. buy. • n. **1** the act of buying. **2** a thing bought. **3** firm contact or grip. ■ **purchaser** n.

purdah n. the practice in certain Muslim and Hindu societies of

pure → put

screening women from men or strangers.

pure adj. 1 not mixed with any other substance. 2 innocent or good. 3 complete; nothing but. 4 theoretical rather than practical. ■ **purely** adv. **purity** n.

purée /pyoor-ay/ n. pulped fruit or vegetables. •v. make a purée of.

purgative adj. having a strongly laxative effect. •n. a laxative.

purgatory n. (pl. **purgatories**) (in RC belief) a place of suffering inhabited by the souls of sinners making amends before going to heaven.

purge v. rid of undesirable people or things. •n. an act of purging.

purify v. (**purifying**, **purified**) make pure. ■ **purification** n. **purifier** n.

purist n. an adherent of traditional rules in language, style, etc.

puritan n. a person with strong moral beliefs who is critical of the behaviour of others. ■ **puritanical** adj.

purl n. a knitting stitch.

purlieus /per-lyooz/ pl. n. the area surrounding a place.

purloin v. steal.

purple n. a colour between red and blue.

purport v. appear to be or do, esp. falsely. •n. meaning. ■ **purportedly** adv.

purpose n. 1 the reason for an action or for existence. 2 strong determination. □ **on purpose** intentionally. ■ **purposeful** adj. **purposefully** adv.

purposely adv. on purpose.

purr v. (of a cat) make a low continuous sound of contentment. •n. a purring sound.

purse n. 1 a small pouch for carrying money. 2 US a handbag. •v. pucker the lips.

purser n. a ship's officer who keeps the accounts.

pursuance n. the carrying out of a plan etc.

pursue v. 1 follow so as to catch or attack. 2 try to achieve a goal. 3 engage in an activity. 4 continue to investigate or discuss. ■ **pursuer** n.

! *pur-*, not *per-*: pursue.

pursuit n. 1 the act of pursuing. 2 a leisure activity.

purulent adj. of or containing pus.

purvey v. supply food or drink as a business. ■ **purveyor** n.

pus n. a thick yellowish liquid produced in infected tissue.

push v. 1 apply force to something so as to move it away from yourself. 2 move forward by using force. 3 urge to greater effort. 4 informal sell an illegal drug. •n. 1 an act of pushing. 2 a great effort. □ **pushchair** n. a folding chair on wheels, in which a young child can be pushed along. ■ **pusher** n.

pushy adj. (**pushier**, **pushiest**) very self-assertive or ambitious.

pusillanimous adj. cowardly.

puss (or **pussy**) n. informal a cat. □ **pussyfoot** v. act cautiously.

pustule n. a small pimple containing pus. ■ **pustular** adj.

put v. (**putting**, **put**) 1 move or bring into a particular position or state. 2 express or phrase. 3 throw a shot or weight as a sport. □ **put down** 1 suppress by force. 2 kill a sick animal. **put off** 1 postpone. 2 discourage or cause to feel dislike. **put on** 1 organize an event.

2 gain weight. **put out** inconvenience or annoy. **put up** accommodate for a short time. **put up with** tolerate.

putative adj. reputed.

putrefy v. (**putrefying, putrefied**) rot. ■ **putrefaction** n. **putrescent** adj.

putrid adj. rotting and foul-smelling.

putt v. hit a golf ball gently so that it rolls into or near a hole. •n. a stroke of this kind. ■ **putter** n.

putty n. a soft paste that sets hard, used for sealing glass in window frames.

puzzle v. **1** confuse because hard to understand. **2** think hard about a problem. •n. **1** a toy or problem designed to test mental skills. **2** a difficult question or problem. ■ **puzzlement** n.

PVC abbrev. polyvinyl chloride, a type of plastic.

pygmy (or **pigmy**) n. (pl. **pygmies**) a member of an African people of very short stature.

pyjamas (US **pajamas**) pl. n. a jacket and loose trousers for sleeping in.

pylon n. a tall metal structure carrying electricity cables.

pyramid n. a structure with a square or triangular base and sloping sides that meet in a point at the top. ■ **pyramidal** adj.

pyre n. a large pile of wood for the ritual burning of a dead body.

pyretic adj. of or producing fever.

Pyrex n. trademark a hard heat-resistant glass.

pyrites /py-ry-teez/ n. a shiny mineral that is a compound of iron and sulphur.

pyromania n. a strong urge to set fire to things. ■ **pyromaniac** n.

pyrotechnics pl. n. a firework display, or the art of staging these. ■ **pyrotechnic** adj.

pyrrhic /pir-rik/ adj. (of a victory) won at too great a cost to have been worthwhile.

python n. a large snake that crushes its prey.

Qq

QC abbrev. Queen's Counsel.

QED abbrev. quod erat demonstrandum, used to say that something proves the truth of a claim.

qua /kway, kwah/ conj. in the capacity of.

quack n. **1** the harsh sound made by a duck. **2** a person who falsely claims to have medical knowledge. •v. (of a duck) make a quack.

quad n. **1** a quadrangle. **2** a quadruplet. □ **quad bike** a motorcycle with four large tyres, for off-road use.

quadrangle n. a square or rectangular courtyard enclosed by buildings.

quadrant n. **1** a quarter of a circle or its circumference. **2** hist. an instrument for measuring altitude in astronomy and navigation.

quadraphonic adj. (of sound reproduction) using four channels.

quadratic adj. Math. involving the second and no higher power of an unknown quantity.

quadrilateral n. a four-sided figure. • adj. having four straight sides.

quadrille n. a square dance.

quadriplegia n. paralysis of all four limbs. ■ **quadriplegic** adj. & n.

quadruped n. a four-footed animal.

quadruple adj. 1 having four parts or elements. 2 four times as much. • v. multiply by four.

quadruplet n. each of four children born at one birth.

quaff /kwoff/ v. drink heartily.

quagmire n. a bog or marsh.

quail n. a small game bird. • v. feel or show fear.

quaint adj. attractively unusual or old-fashioned. ■ **quaintly** adv.

quake v. shake or tremble.

Quaker n. a member of the Religious Society of Friends, a Christian movement rejecting set forms of worship.

qualification n. 1 the act of qualifying. 2 a pass in an exam or the completion of a course. 3 a statement limiting the meaning of another statement.

qualify v. (**qualifying, qualified**) 1 meet the necessary standard or conditions to be entitled to something. 2 become officially recognized as able to do a particular job. 3 limit the meaning of a statement. ■ **qualifier** n.

qualitative adj. of or measured by quality.

quality n. (pl. **qualities**) 1 the standard of something as measured against similar things. 2 excellence. 3 a distinctive feature.

qualm /kwahm/ n. a feeling of doubt or unease.

quandary n. (pl. **quandaries**) a state of uncertainty.

quango n. (pl. **quangos**) a semipublic organization with senior appointments made by the government.

quantify v. (**quantifying, quantified**) express or measure the quantity of. ■ **quantifiable** adj.

quantitative adj. of or measured by quantity.

quantity n. (pl. **quantities**) 1 an amount or number. 2 a large number or amount. □ **quantity surveyor** a person who calculates the amount and cost of materials needed for building work.

quantum n. (pl. **quanta**) the minimum amount of energy that can take part in a physical process. □ **quantum leap** a sudden large increase or advance.

quarantine n. a period of isolation for people or animals that have or may have a disease. • v. put in quarantine.

quark n. any of a group of subatomic particles believed to form protons, neutrons, etc.

quarrel n. 1 an angry argument. 2 a reason for disagreement. • v. (**quarrelling, quarrelled**; US **quarreling, quarreled**) have a quarrel. ■ **quarrelsome** adj.

quarry n. (pl. **quarries**) 1 a place where stone etc. is dug out of the earth. 2 a person or animal being chased or hunted. • v. (**quarrying, quarried**) take stone etc. from a quarry.

quart n. a quarter of a gallon, approx. 1.13 litres.

q

quarter n. **1** each of four equal parts of something. **2** three months. **3** fifteen minutes. **4** a particular part of a town or city. **5** a US or Canadian coin worth 25 cents. **6** (**quarters**) rooms or lodgings. **7** mercy shown to an opponent. •v. **1** divide into quarters. **2** (**be quartered**) be lodged. □ **quarterdeck** the part of a ship's upper deck near the stern. **quarter-final** a match of a competition preceding the semi-final. **quartermaster** an army officer in charge of accommodation and supplies.

quarterly adj. & adv. produced or occurring once every three months. •n. (pl. **quarterlies**) a quarterly publication.

quartet n. **1** a group of four playing music or singing together. **2** music for a quartet.

quarto n. (pl. **quartos**) a size of book page resulting from folding a sheet into four leaves.

quartz n. a hard mineral.

quasar /kway-zar/ n. a galaxy giving off enormous amounts of energy.

quash v. **1** officially declare a legal decision invalid. **2** put an end to.

quasi- /kway-zy/ comb. form seemingly.

quatrain n. a verse of four lines.

quaver v. (of a voice) tremble. •n. **1** a tremble in a voice. **2** a musical note with the value of half a crotchet. ■ **quavery** adj.

quay /kee/ n. a platform in a harbour for loading and unloading ships. □ **quayside** a quay and the area around it.

queasy adj. (**queasier, queasiest**) feeling sick. ■ **queasiness** n.

queen n. **1** the female ruler of a country. **2** a king's wife. **3** the best or most important woman or thing. **4** a playing card ranking next below a king. **5** the most powerful chess piece. **6** a reproductive bee, ant, etc. **7** informal a homosexual man who behaves like a woman. □ **queen mother** the widow of a king and mother of the sovereign. ■ **queenly** adj.

queer adj. **1** strange; odd. **2** derog. homosexual. •n. derog. a homosexual man. □ **queer someone's pitch** informal spoil someone's chances.

quell v. suppress.

quench v. **1** satisfy thirst. **2** put out a fire.

quern n. a hand mill for grinding grain.

querulous adj. complaining petulantly. ■ **querulously** adv.

query n. (pl. **queries**) a question, esp. one expressing doubt. •v. (**querying, queried**) raise a query.

quest n. a long search.

question n. **1** a sentence requesting information. **2** a matter needing to be dealt with. **3** doubt, or the raising of doubt. •v. **1** ask questions of. **2** express doubt about. □ **in question** being discussed. **out of the question** not possible. **question mark** a punctuation mark (?) indicating a question.

questionable adj. open to doubt.

questionnaire n. a set of printed questions for a survey.

queue n. a line of people or vehicles waiting their turn for something. •v. (**queuing** or **queueing**, **queued**) wait in a queue.

quibble n. a minor objection. •v. raise a minor objection.

quiche /keesh/ n. a baked flan with a savoury filling.

quick adj. **1** moving fast. **2** taking a short time. **3** intelligent or alert. •n. the tender flesh below a fingernail or toenail. □ **quicklime** = LIME (sense 1). **quicksand** loose wet sand that sucks in anything resting on it. **quicksilver** mercury. **quickstep** a fast foxtrot. **quick-tempered** easily angered. ■ **quicken** v. **quickly** adv. **quickness** n.

quid n. (pl. **quid**) informal one pound in money.

quid pro quo n. (pl. **quid pro quos**) a favour given in return for another.

quiescent adj. not active. ■ **quiescence** n.

quiet adj. **1** making little or no noise. **2** calm and tranquil. **3** discreet. •n. absence of noise or disturbance. □ **on the quiet** informal secretly. ■ **quieten** v. **quietly** adv. **quietness** n.

quietude n. calmness and quiet.

quiff n. a piece of hair brushed up and back from the forehead.

quill n. **1** a large feather. **2** a pen made from this. **3** a spine of a porcupine or hedgehog.

quilt n. a padded bed covering.

quilted adj. made of two layers of fabric filled with padding.

quin n. informal a quintuplet.

quince n. a hard yellowish fruit.

quinine n. a drug formerly used to treat malaria.

quintessence n. the perfect or most typical example. ■ **quintessential** adj. **quintessentially** adv.

quintet n. **1** a group of five playing music or singing together. **2** music for a quintet.

quintuple adj. **1** having five parts or elements. **2** five times as much.

quintuplet n. each of five children born at one time.

quip n. a witty remark. •v. (**quipping, quipped**) make a quip.

quire n. 25 sheets of paper.

quirk n. **1** a peculiar habit. **2** a strange thing happening by chance. ■ **quirky** adj.

quisling n. a traitor collaborating with an occupying force.

quit v. (**quitting, quitted** or **quit**) **1** leave a place. **2** resign from a job. **3** informal stop doing something.

quite adv. **1** to a certain extent. **2** completely.

quits adj. on equal terms because a debt or score has been settled.

quiver v. shake or vibrate slightly. •n. **1** a quivering movement. **2** a case for carrying arrows.

quixotic adj. idealistic and impractical.

quiz n. (pl. **quizzes**) a competition involving a set of questions as a test of knowledge. •v. (**quizzing, quizzed**) question.

quizzical adj. showing mild or amused puzzlement. ■ **quizzically** adv.

quoit /koyt/ n. a ring thrown to land over a peg in the game of **quoits**.

quondam /kwon-dam/ adj. former.

quorate /kwor-uht/ adj. (of a meeting) having a quorum.

quorum /kwor-uhm/ n. a minimum number of people that

q

must be present at a meeting to make it valid.

quota n. **1** a limited quantity allowed. **2** a share that is expected or needed.

quotation n. **1** a passage repeated by someone other than the originator. **2** a formal estimate of the cost of a job. □ **quotation mark** each of a set of punctuation marks, (' ' or " "), enclosing quoted words.

quote v. **1** repeat something spoken or written by another person. **2** give an estimated price. ■ **quotable** adj.

quoth v. old use said.

quotidian /kwuh-**tid**-i-uhn/ adj. daily.

quotient /**kwoh**-shuhnt/ n. a result obtained by dividing one quantity by another.

q.v. abbrev. used to direct a reader to another part of a book for further information.

Rr

R abbrev. **1** Regina or Rex. **2** (**R.**) River.

rabbi n. (pl. **rabbis**) a Jewish religious leader. ■ **rabbinical** adj.

rabbit n. a burrowing mammal with long ears and a short tail. • v. (**rabbiting**, **rabbited**) informal chatter.

rabble n. a disorderly crowd.

rabid adj. **1** fanatical. **2** affected with rabies.

rabies n. a dangerous disease of dogs etc. that can be transmitted through saliva to humans.

raccoon (or **racoon**) n. an American mammal with a black face and striped tail.

race n. **1** a competition to determine the fastest over a set course. **2** each of the major divisions of humankind. **3** a group with a common feature. **4** a subdivision of a species. • v. **1** compete in a race against. **2** move or operate at full or excessive speed. □ **racecourse**

a ground or track for horse or dog racing. **racehorse** a horse bred and trained for racing. **racetrack** **1** a racecourse. **2** a track for motor racing. ■ **racer** n.

raceme n. a flower cluster with separate flowers along a central stem.

racial adj. of or based on race. ■ **racially** adv.

racialism n. racism. ■ **racialist** n. & adj.

racism n. **1** the belief that certain races are better than others. **2** discrimination against or hostility towards other races. ■ **racist** n. & adj.

rack n. **1** a framework for holding or storing things. **2** hist. a frame on which a person was tortured by being stretched. • v. (or **wrack**) cause great pain to. □ **go to rack and ruin** fall into a bad condition. **rack up** achieve or accumulate. **rack your brains** think very hard.

racket n. **1** (or **racquet**) a bat with a stringed frame, used in tennis etc. **2** a loud unpleasant noise. **3** informal a dishonest scheme for making money.

racketeer n. a person who makes money through dishonest activities. ■ **racketeering** n.

raconteur /ra-kon-**ter**/ n. a person who tells stories in an entertaining way.

racoon var. of RACCOON.

racy adj. (**racier**, **raciest**) lively and exciting, esp. in a sexual way.

radar n. a system for detecting aircraft, ships, etc. by means of reflected radio waves.

radial adj. **1** arranged in lines coming out from a central point to the edge of a circle. **2** (of a tyre) in which fabric layers run at right angles to the tyre's circumference. ■ **radially** adv.

radiant adj. **1** shining or glowing brightly. **2** showing joy or health. **3** (of heat) transmitted by radiation. ■ **radiance** n. **radiantly** adv.

radiate v. **1** (of energy) be sent out in rays or waves. **2** spread out from a central point.

radiation n. energy sent out as electromagnetic waves or sub-atomic particles.

radiator n. **1** a metal device that radiates heat, esp. one filled with hot water pumped in through pipes. **2** a cooling device in a vehicle.

radical adj. **1** of the basic nature of something; fundamental. **2** supporting complete political or social reform. **3** Math. relating to the root of a number or quantity. •n. a person holding radical views. ■ **radically** adv.

radicchio /ra-**dee**-ki-oh/ n. (pl. **radicchios**) a dark red variety of chicory.

radicle n. an embryonic plant root.

radii pl. of RADIUS.

radio n. (pl. **radios**) **1** the sending and receiving of electromagnetic waves carrying sound messages. **2** broadcasting in sound. **3** a device for receiving radio broadcasts, or for sending and receiving radio messages. •v. (**radioing**, **radioed**) send by radio.

radioactive adj. giving out harmful radiation or particles. ■ **radioactivity** n.

radiocarbon n. a radioactive form of carbon used in carbon dating.

radiography n. the production of images by X-rays or other radiation. ■ **radiographer** n.

radiology n. the study and use of X-rays and similar radiation in medicine. ■ **radiologist** n.

radiotherapy n. the treatment of disease using X-rays or similar radiation. ■ **radiotherapist** n.

radish n. a plant with a crisp, hot-tasting root eaten raw.

radium n. a radioactive metallic element.

radius n. (pl. **radii** or **radiuses**) **1** a straight line from the centre to the circumference of a circle. **2** a specified distance from a centre in all directions. **3** the thicker of the two bones in the forearm.

radon n. a radioactive gas.

RAF abbrev. Royal Air Force.

raffia n. fibre from the leaves of a palm tree, used for hats etc.

raffish adj. slightly disreputable.

r

raffle n. a lottery with goods as prizes. • v. offer as a prize in a raffle.

raft n. 1 a flat floating structure used as a boat. 2 a large amount.

rafter n. a beam forming part of the internal framework of a roof.

rag n. 1 a piece of old cloth. 2 (**rags**) old torn clothes. 3 informal a low-quality newspaper. 4 a programme of entertainments by students in aid of charity. • v. (**ragging, ragged**) make fun of.

ragamuffin n. a person in ragged, dirty clothes.

rage n. violent anger. • v. 1 feel or express rage. 2 continue with great force. □ **all the rage** very popular or fashionable.

ragged adj. 1 (of clothes) old and torn. 2 rough or irregular.

raglan adj. (of a sleeve) continuing in one piece up to the neck.

ragout /ra-goo/ n. a stew of meat and vegetables.

ragtime n. an early form of jazz, played esp. on the piano.

raid n. 1 a sudden attack on an enemy or a building. 2 a surprise visit by police to arrest suspects or seize illegal goods. • v. make a raid on. ■ **raider** n.

rail n. 1 a fixed horizontal bar. 2 each of the two metal bars forming a railway track. 3 railways as a means of transport. • v. 1 provide or enclose with a rail or rails. 2 (**rail against/at**) complain strongly about. □ **railroad** 1 US a railway. 2 informal force into doing something. **railway** 1 a track made of rails along which trains run. 2 a transport system using trains and tracks.

railing n. a fence made of rails.

raiment n. old use clothing.

rain n. 1 condensed moisture from the atmosphere falling in separate drops. 2 (**rains**) falls of rain. • v. 1 fall as rain. 2 fall in large quantities. □ **rainbow** an arch of colours in the sky, caused by the sun shining through water droplets in the atmosphere. **raincoat** a coat made from water-resistant fabric. **rainfall** the amount of rain falling. **rainforest** a dense tropical forest with consistently heavy rainfall. ■ **rainy** adj.

raise v. 1 lift or move upwards or into an upright position. 2 increase the amount or level of. 3 cause to be heard, felt, or considered. 4 collect money. 5 bring up a child. 6 (**raise to**) multiply a quantity to a specified power. • n. US an increase in salary.

raisin n. a partially dried grape.

raison d'être /ray-zon de-truh/ n. (pl. **raisons d'être**) the most important reason for someone or something's existence.

Raj n. the period of British rule in India.

raja (or **rajah**) n. hist. an Indian king or prince.

rake n. 1 a pole with prongs at the end for collecting fallen leaves, smoothing soil, etc. 2 a fashionable, wealthy, but immoral man. • v. 1 collect or smooth with a rake. 2 scratch with a sweeping movement. 3 sweep with gunfire etc. 4 search through. 5 (**rake up**) bring up something best forgotten. 6 set at a sloping angle.

rakish adj. dashing but slightly disreputable in appearance.

rally n. (pl. **rallies**) 1 a mass meeting held as a protest or in support of a cause. 2 a long-distance driving competition over roads or rough country. **3** a recovery. **4** a long exchange of strokes in tennis etc. •v. (**rallying, rallied**) **1** bring or come together again for united action. **2** recover in health or strength.

RAM abbrev. Computing random-access memory.

ram n. **1** an adult male sheep. **2** a striking or plunging device in a machine. •v. (**ramming, rammed**) hit or push with force. □ **ram raid** a robbery in which a shop window is rammed with a vehicle. **ramrod** a rod formerly used to ram down the charge of a firearm.

Ramadan n. the ninth month of the Muslim year, during which Muslims fast from dawn to sunset.

ramble v. **1** walk for pleasure in the countryside. **2** talk in a confused way and at length. •n. a country walk for pleasure. ■ **rambler** n.

ramekin /ra-mi-kin/ n. a small individual baking dish.

ramifications pl. n. complex results of an action or event.

ramify v. (**ramifying, ramified**) branch out.

ramp n. a slope joining two levels.

rampage v. rush around in a wild, violent way. •n. a period of wild, violent behaviour.

rampant adj. **1** flourishing or spreading uncontrollably. **2** (of an animal in heraldry) standing on its left hind leg with its front legs in the air.

rampart n. a defensive wall having a broad top with a walkway.

ramshackle adj. in a very bad condition.

ran past of RUN.

ranch n. a large cattle farm in America. ■ **rancher** n.

rancid adj. smelling or tasting of stale fat.

rancour (US **rancor**) n. bitter feeling or resentment. ■ **rancorous** adj.

rand n. the basic unit of money of South Africa.

R & B abbrev. rhythm and blues.

random adj. done or happening without order, purpose, or planning. ■ **randomly** adv. **randomness** n.

randy adj. (**randier, randiest**) informal sexually excited.

rang past of RING.

range n. **1** the limits between which something varies. **2** a set of things of the same general type. **3** the distance over which a sound, missile, etc. can travel. **4** a line of mountains or hills. **5** a large open area for grazing or hunting. **6** an area for testing military equipment or for shooting practice. •v. **1** vary between particular limits. **2** arrange in order. **3** travel over or cover a wide area.

ranger n. a keeper of a park, forest, or area of countryside.

rangy adj. tall and slim.

rank n. **1** a position within the armed forces or an organization. **2** a row of people or things. **3** high social position. **4** (**the ranks**) ordinary soldiers rather than officers. •v. **1** give a rank to. **2** hold a specified rank. **3** arrange in a row or rows. •adj. **1** foul-smelling. **2** complete: a rank amateur. **3** growing too thickly. □ **rank and file** the ordinary members of an organization.

rankle v. cause continuing resentment.

ransack v. go hurriedly through a place stealing or searching for things.

ransom n. a sum of money demanded or paid for the release of a captive. • v. demand or pay a ransom for.

rant v. speak in a loud, forceful way.

rap v. (**rapping, rapped**) **1** hit sharply. **2** informal criticize sharply. • n. **1** a quick, sharp knock or blow. **2** informal criticism. **3** a type of pop music in which words are spoken rhythmically over an instrumental backing. ■ **rapper** n.

rapacious adj. very greedy. ■ **rapacity** n.

rape v. (of a man) force someone to have sex with him against their will. • n. **1** an act of raping. **2** a plant with oil-rich seeds.

rapid adj. quick. • pl. n. (**rapids**) a fast-flowing stretch of a river. ■ **rapidity** n. **rapidly** adv.

rapier n. a thin, light sword.

rapist n. a man who commits rape.

rapport /rap-por/ n. a close and harmonious relationship.

rapprochement /ra-prosh-mon/ n. a renewal of friendly relations.

rapt adj. fascinated or totally absorbed.

rapture n. great joy. ■ **rapturous** adj.

rare adj. **1** not occurring or found very often. **2** unusually good. **3** (of meat) lightly cooked, so that the inside is still red. ■ **rarely** adv. **rarity** n.

rarebit (or **Welsh rarebit**) n. a dish of melted cheese on toast.

rarefied adj. **1** (of air) of lower pressure than usual. **2** understood by only a limited group.

⚠ **-ref-**, not **-rif-**: rarefied.

raring adj. informal very eager: raring to go.

rascal n. **1** a mischievous person. **2** a dishonest man. ■ **rascally** adj.

rash adj. acting or done without considering the possible results. • n. an area of red spots or patches on the skin. ■ **rashly** adv.

rasher n. a slice of bacon.

rasp n. **1** a harsh, grating noise. **2** a coarse file. • v. **1** (of a rough surface) scrape. **2** make a rasping noise.

raspberry n. **1** an edible red soft fruit. **2** informal a rude sound made with the tongue and lips.

Rastafarian n. a member of a Jamaican religious movement which worships Haile Selassie, the former Emperor of Ethiopia. ■ **Rastafarianism** n.

rat n. **1** a rodent like a large mouse. **2** informal an unpleasant person. • v. (**ratting, ratted**) (**rat on**) informal inform on. □ **the rat race** informal a fiercely competitive way of life.

ratatouille /ra-tuh-too-i/ n. a dish of stewed courgettes, peppers, tomatoes, etc.

ratchet n. a bar or wheel with a set of angled teeth in which a cog etc. fits, allowing movement in one direction only.

rate n. **1** a measure, quantity, or frequency measured against another. **2** the speed of something. **3** a fixed price or charge. **4** (**rates**) a local tax on land and buildings paid by a business. • v. **1** give something a standard or value according to a particular scale. **2** judge to be of a certain standard. **3** be worthy of. □ **at any rate** whatever happens. ■ **rateable** (or **ratable**) adj.

rather adv. **1** (**would rather**) would prefer. **2** to some extent. **3** on the contrary or more precisely.

ratify v. (**ratifying, ratified**) confirm an agreement etc. formally. ∎ **ratification** n.

rating n. **1** a classification based on quality or standard. **2** (**ratings**) the estimated audience of a broadcast. **3** a sailor in the navy who does not hold a commission.

ratio n. (pl. **ratios**) the relationship between two amounts, showing the number of times one value contains the other.

ratiocination n. logical reasoning.

ration n. a fixed allowance of food, fuel, etc. ∙v. limit the supply of food, fuel, etc.

rational adj. **1** based on reason or logic. **2** able to think sensibly or logically. ∎ **rationality** n. **rationally** adv.

rationale /ra-shuh-nahl/ n. the reasons for a course of action or a belief.

rationalism n. the belief that opinions and actions should be based on reason rather than on religious belief or emotions. ∎ **rationalist** n.

rationalize (or **-ise**) v. **1** try to find a logical reason for. **2** reorganize so as to become more efficient. ∎ **rationalization** n.

rattan n. the thin, pliable stems of a palm, used to make furniture.

rattle v. **1** make a rapid series of short, sharp sounds. **2** informal make nervous or irritated. **3** (**rattle off**) say or do quickly. ∙n. **1** a rattling sound. **2** a device or toy that makes this. ☐ **rattlesnake** n. an American viper with horny rings

on the tail that make a rattling sound.

raucous adj. sounding loud and harsh. ∎ **raucously** adv.

raunchy adj. (**raunchier, raunchiest**) informal sexually exciting or direct.

ravage v. do great damage to. ∙n. (**ravages**) damage.

rave v. **1** talk angrily or incoherently. **2** speak or write about enthusiastically. ∙n. a very large event with dancing to fast electronic music.

raven n. a large black crow. ∙adj. (of hair) glossy black.

ravenous adj. very hungry. ∎ **ravenously** adv.

ravine n. a deep, narrow gorge.

ravioli pl. n. small pasta cases with a savoury filling.

ravish v. **1** dated rape. **2** (**ravishing**) very beautiful.

raw adj. **1** not cooked. **2** not yet processed. **3** (of the skin) red and painful from being rubbed. **4** new and inexperienced. **5** (of the weather) cold and damp. ☐ **raw deal** unfair treatment. **rawhide** untanned leather. ∎ **rawness** n.

ray n. **1** a line of light or other radiation. **2** a large flat fish.

rayon n. a synthetic fibre or fabric made from viscose.

raze v. completely destroy a building etc.

razor n. an instrument with a sharp blade for shaving.

razzmatazz n. informal noisy, showy, and exciting activity or display.

RC abbrev. Roman Catholic.

RE abbrev. religious education.

re prep. with regard to.

reach v. 1 stretch out an arm to touch or grasp something. 2 be able to touch. 3 arrive at; get as far as. 4 achieve. 5 make contact with. •n. 1 the distance over which someone or something can reach. 2 a stretch of river between two bends.

react v. 1 respond in a particular way. 2 interact and undergo a chemical or physical change. ■ **reactive** adj.

reaction n. 1 something done or experienced as a result of an event. 2 a bad response by the body to a drug etc. 3 a process in which substances interact causing chemical or physical change.

reactionary adj. opposing political or social progress or reform. •n. (pl. **reactionaries**) a reactionary person.

reactor n. a piece of equipment for producing nuclear energy.

read v. (**reading, read**) 1 understand the meaning of written or printed words or symbols. 2 speak written or printed words aloud. 3 interpret in a particular way. 4 (**read into**) think that something has a meaning that it may not possess. 5 (of an instrument) show a measurement. •n. informal a book that is interesting to read. ■ **readable** adj. **reader** n.

readership n. the readers of a publication as a group.

readjust v. 1 adjust again. 2 adapt to a changed situation. ■ **readjustment** n.

ready adj. (**readier, readiest**) 1 prepared. 2 available for immediate use. 3 easily obtained. 4 willing. 5 quick. •v. (**readying, readied**) prepare. •n. (**readies** or

the ready) informal cash. ■ **readily** adv. **readiness** n.

reagent /ri-ay-juhnt/ n. a substance that produces a chemical reaction, used in tests.

real adj. 1 actually existing or occurring. 2 not artificial; genuine. □ **real estate** US buildings or land.

realign v. change to a different position or state. ■ **realignment** n.

realism n. 1 the acceptance of a situation as it is. 2 the accurate and true representation of things. ■ **realist** n.

realistic adj. 1 sensible and practical. 2 (of representation) true to life. ■ **realistically** adv.

reality n. (pl. **realities**) 1 the state of things as they actually exist. 2 a thing that is experienced or seen.

realize (or **-ise**) v. 1 become aware of as a fact. 2 achieve a wish or plan. 3 convert property etc. into money by selling it. ■ **realization** n.

really adv. 1 in fact. 2 very. •exclam. expressing interest, surprise, doubt, etc.

realm n. 1 a kingdom. 2 a field of activity or interest.

ream n. 1 500 sheets of paper. 2 (**reams**) a large quantity.

reap v. 1 cut a crop as harvest. 2 receive as a result of your actions. ■ **reaper** n.

reappear v. appear again. ■ **reappearance** n.

rear n. the back part. •adj. at the back. •v. 1 bring up children. 2 breed animals. 3 (of an animal) raise itself upright on its hind legs. 4 extend to a great height. □ **rear admiral** a naval rank below vice admiral. **rearguard** a group of troops protecting the rear of the main force. ■ **rearward** adj. & adv. **rearwards** adv.

rearm v. arm again. ■ **rearmament** n.

rearrange v. arrange in a different way. ■ **rearrangement** n.

reason n. **1** a cause or explanation. **2** the power to think logically and draw conclusions. **3** (**your reason**) your sanity. **4** what is right or practical. • v. **1** think logically and draw conclusions. **2** (**reason with**) persuade by giving reasons.

reasonable adj. **1** fair and sensible. **2** appropriate. **3** fairly good. **4** not too expensive. ■ **reasonably** adv.

reassess v. reconsider. ■ **reassessment** n.

reassure v. cause to feel less worried or afraid. ■ **reassurance** n.

rebate n. a partial refund.

rebel v. (**rebelling, rebelled**) **1** fight against an established government or ruler. **2** oppose authority or accepted behaviour. • n. a person who rebels. ■ **rebellion** n. **rebellious** adj.

rebirth n. a return to life or activity.

rebound v. bounce back after impact. • n. a ball or shot that rebounds. □ **on the rebound** while still upset after the end of a romantic relationship.

rebuff v. reject in an abrupt or unkind way. • n. an act of rebuffing.

rebuild v. (**rebuilding, rebuilt**) build again.

rebuke v. reprimand. • n. a reprimand.

rebut v. (**rebutting, rebutted**) claim or prove to be false. ■ **rebuttal** n.

recalcitrant adj. unwilling to cooperate. ■ **recalcitrance** n.

recall v. **1** remember. **2** make someone think of. **3** order someone to return. • n. the act of recalling.

recant v. withdraw a former opinion or belief.

recap v. (**recapping, recapped**) give a summary of.

recapitulate v. give a summary of. ■ **recapitulation** n.

recapture v. **1** capture again. **2** experience a past time etc. again.

recce /rek-i/ n. a reconnaissance.

recede v. **1** move back or further away. **2** diminish. **3** (**receding**) (of the chin) sloping backwards.

receipt n. **1** a note confirming that something has been paid for or received. **2** the act of receiving.

receive v. **1** be given or paid. **2** accept or take in. **3** experience or meet with. **4** greet or welcome. **5** detect or pick up broadcast signals.

receiver n. **1** a device that converts broadcast signals into sound or images. **2** the part of a phone that converts electrical signals into sounds. **3** a person appointed to manage the financial affairs of a bankrupt business. ■ **receivership** n.

recent adj. having happened or been done shortly before the present. ■ **recently** adv.

receptacle n. a container.

reception n. **1** the act of receiving. **2** a reaction to something. **3** a formal social occasion. **4** the area in a hotel, office, etc. where visitors are greeted. **5** the quality of broadcast signals received.

receptionist n. a person who greets and deals with visitors to an office, hotel, etc.

r

receptive *adj.* willing to consider new ideas. ■ **receptivity** *n.*

receptor *n.* a nerve ending that responds to a stimulus and transmits a signal to a nerve.

recess *n.* **1** a small space set back in a wall or into a surface. **2** a break between sessions of a parliament, law court, etc. •*v.* set back into a wall etc.

recession *n.* a temporary decline in economic activity.

recessive *adj.* (of a gene) appearing in offspring only if a contrary gene is not also inherited.

recharge *v.* charge a battery etc. again. ■ **rechargeable** *adj.*

recherché /ruh-shair-shay/ *adj.* unusual and not easily understood.

recidivist *n.* a person who constantly commits crimes. ■ **recidivism** *n.*

recipe *n.* **1** a list of ingredients and instructions for preparing a dish. **2** something likely to lead to a particular outcome.

recipient *n.* a person who receives something.

r **reciprocal** *adj.* **1** given or done in return. **2** affecting two parties equally. ■ **reciprocally** *adv.* **reciprocity** *n.*

reciprocate *v.* respond to an action with a similar one.

recital *n.* **1** a musical performance. **2** a listing of facts etc.

recitative /re-si-tuh-teev/ *n.* a passage in an opera sung in a rhythm like that of ordinary speech.

recite *v.* **1** repeat aloud from memory. **2** state facts in order. ■ **recitation** *n.*

reckless *adj.* without thought or care for the results of an action. ■ **recklessly** *adv.* **recklessness** *n.*

reckon *v.* **1** have as an opinion. **2** (**reckon on**) expect. **3** calculate. **4** (**reckon with** or **without**) take (or fail to take) into account.

reclaim *v.* **1** recover possession of. **2** make waste land usable. ■ **reclamation** *n.*

recline *v.* lean or lie back in a relaxed position.

recluse *n.* a person who avoids other people. ■ **reclusive** *adj.*

recognition *n.* **1** the act of recognizing. **2** appreciation or acknowledgement.

recognize (or **-ise**) *v.* **1** know from having encountered before. **2** accept as genuine, legal, or valid. **3** show official appreciation of. ■ **recognizable** *adj.*

recoil *v.* **1** suddenly move back in fear, disgust, etc. **2** (of a gun) suddenly move back after firing. **3** (**recoil on**) have an unpleasant effect on. •*n.* the act of recoiling.

recollect *v.* remember. ■ **recollection** *n.*

recommend *v.* **1** suggest as suitable for a purpose or role. **2** make appealing or desirable.

recommendation *n.* **1** a proposal as to the best course of action. **2** the act of recommending.

recompense *v.* **1** compensate. **2** pay for work. •*n.* compensation or reward.

reconcile *v.* **1** restore friendly relations between. **2** find a satisfactory way of dealing with opposing facts, ideas, etc. **3** (**reconcile to**) cause to accept an unwelcome situation. ■ **reconciliation** *n.*

recondite *adj.* obscure and little known.

recondition v. renovate.

reconnaissance /ri-kon-ni-suhnss/ n. military observation of an area to gain information.

reconnoitre /rek-uh-**noy**-ter/ (US **reconnoiter**) v. make a reconnaissance of.

reconsider v. consider again, with a view to changing a decision. ■ **reconsideration** n.

reconstitute v. 1 change the form of an organization. 2 restore dried food to its original state by adding water. ■ **reconstitution** n.

reconstruct v. 1 construct again. 2 act out a past event. ■ **reconstruction** n.

record n. 1 a permanent account kept for evidence or information. 2 previous behaviour or performance. 3 a list of an offender's past convictions. 4 the best officially recognized performance of its kind. 5 a disc carrying recorded sound in grooves. •v. 1 make a record of. 2 convert sound etc. into permanent form so as to be reproduced later. □ **off the record** not made as an official statement.

recorder n. 1 a person or thing that records. 2 a barrister serving as a part-time judge. 3 a simple woodwind instrument.

recount[1] v. tell in detail.

recount[2] v. count again. •n. an act of recounting.

recoup v. recover money spent or lost.

recourse n. (**have recourse to**) be able to use as a source of help.

recover v. 1 return to health. 2 regain possession or control of. ■ **recovery** n.

recreate v. make or do again.

recreation n. enjoyable leisure activity. ■ **recreational** adj.

recrimination n. an accusation in response to another.

recruit v. take on someone to serve in the armed forces or work for an organization. •n. a newly recruited person. ■ **recruitment** n.

rectangle n. a plane figure with four straight sides and four right angles, and with unequal adjacent sides. ■ **rectangular** adj.

rectify v. (**rectifying, rectified**) 1 put right. 2 convert alternating current to direct current. ■ **rectification** n.

rectilinear adj. within or moving in a straight line or lines.

rectitude n. correct behaviour.

recto n. (pl. **rectos**) a right-hand page of an open book.

rector n. 1 a priest in charge of a parish. 2 the head of certain universities, colleges, and schools.

rectory n. (pl. **rectories**) the house of a rector.

rectum n. (pl. **rectums** or **recta**) the final section of the large intestine, ending at the anus. ■ **rectal** adj.

recumbent adj. lying down.

recuperate v. 1 recover from illness. 2 regain. ■ **recuperation** n. **recuperative** adj.

recur v. (**recurring, recurred**) happen again or repeatedly. ■ **recurrence** n. **recurrent** adj.

recycle v. convert waste into a reusable form. ■ **recyclable** adj.

red adj. (**redder, reddest**) 1 of the colour of blood or fire. 2 (of hair) reddish-brown. 3 informal communist. •n. 1 red colour or material. 2 informal a communist. □ **in the red** overdrawn. **redcurrant** a small edible red berry. **red-handed** in the act of doing something wrong. **redhead** a person with red hair. **red herring** a thing drawing attention away from something important. **red-hot 1** so hot as to glow red. **2** very exciting. **red-letter day** an important or memorable day. **red-light district** an area with many brothels, strip clubs, etc. **red tape** complicated official rules which hinder progress. **redwood** a giant coniferous tree with reddish wood. **see red** *informal* become very angry. ∎ **redden** v. **reddish** adj. **redness** n.

redeem v. **1** make up for the faults of. **2** save from sin. **3** pay a debt. **4** exchange a coupon for goods or money. **5** fulfil a promise. ∎ **redemption** n.

redeploy v. assign to a new place or task. ∎ **redeployment** n.

redolent adj. (**redolent of/with**) **1** strongly suggestive of. **2** smelling of. ∎ **redolence** n.

redouble v. increase or intensify.

redoubtable adj. formidable.

redound v. (**redound to**) be to a person's credit.

redress v. set right. •n. reparation or amends.

reduce v. **1** make or become less. **2** (**reduce to**) change to a simpler form. **3** (**reduce to**) bring to a particular state or condition. ∎ **reducible** adj.

reduction n. **1** the act of reducing. **2** the amount by which something is reduced.

reductive adj. presenting something in an over-simplified form.

redundant adj. **1** unemployed because your job is no longer

needed. **2** no longer needed or useful. ∎ **redundancy** n.

reed n. **1** a water or marsh plant with hollow stems. **2** a piece of thin cane or metal in certain wind instruments which vibrates to produce the sound.

reedy adj. (of a voice) high and thin in tone.

reef n. **1** a ridge of rock or coral near the surface of the sea. **2** a strip in a sail that can be reefed to reduce the area exposed to the wind. •v. take in a reef or reefs of a sail. □ **reef knot** a secure double knot.

reefer n. *informal* a cannabis cigarette.

reefer jacket n. a thick double-breasted jacket.

reek v. have an unpleasant smell. •n. a strong unpleasant smell.

reel n. **1** a cylinder on which something is wound. **2** a lively Scottish or Irish folk dance. •v. **1** (**reel in**) bring towards you by turning a reel. **2** (**reel off**) say rapidly and with ease. **3** stagger.

refectory n. (pl. **refectories**) a room for meals in a college or religious institution.

refer v. (**referring, referred**) (**refer to**) **1** mention. **2** turn to for information. **3** pass to an authority or specialist for a decision. ∎ **referral** n.

referee n. **1** an official who supervises a game to ensure that players keep to the rules. **2** a person who gives a reference for a job applicant. •v. (**refereeing, refereed**) be a referee of.

reference n. **1** the act of referring. **2** a mention of a source of information in a book etc. **3** a letter testifying to someone's suitability for a job. □ **with** (or **in**) **reference to** in relation to.

referendum n. (pl. **referendums** or **referenda**) a vote by a country's electorate on a single political issue.

refill v. fill again. • n. an act of refilling.

refine v. **1** remove unwanted substances from. **2** improve by making minor changes. **3** (**refined**) well educated and elegant. ■ **refinement** n.

refinery n. (pl. **refineries**) a factory where a substance is refined.

refit v. (**refitting**, **refitted**) replace or repair fittings in a ship, building, etc. • n. an act of refitting.

reflect v. **1** throw back heat, light, or sound from a surface. **2** (of a mirror) show an image of. **3** show the nature of. **4** think seriously. **5** (**reflect well/badly on**) give a good or bad impression of. ■ **reflector** n.

reflection n. **1** the act of reflecting. **2** a reflected image. **3** a sign. **4** a source of shame or blame.

reflective adj. **1** providing a reflection. **2** thoughtful. ■ **reflectively** adv.

reflex n. an action done without conscious thought as a response to something. • adj. **1** done as a reflex. **2** (of an angle) more than 180°.

reflexive adj. Grammar referring back to the subject of a clause or verb, e.g. *myself* in *I hurt myself*.

reflexology n. a system of massage of points on the feet used to relieve tension and treat illness. ■ **reflexologist** n.

reform v. **1** improve by making changes. **2** cause to improve behaviour. • n. the act of reforming.

■ **reformation** n. **reformer** n. **reformist** adj. & n.

refract v. (of water, air, or glass) make a ray of light change direction when it enters at an angle. ■ **refraction** n. **refractive** adj. **refractor** n.

refractory adj. **1** stubborn or difficult to control. **2** (of a disease) not responding to treatment.

refrain v. (**refrain from**) stop yourself from doing something. • n. the part of a song that is repeated at the end of each verse.

refresh v. **1** give new energy to. **2** prompt someone's memory. **3** (**refreshing**) pleasantly new or different. ■ **refreshingly** adv.

refreshment n. **1** a snack or drink. **2** the giving of new energy.

refrigerate v. chill food or drink to keep it fresh. ■ **refrigeration** n.

refrigerator n. a fridge.

! No *d* in the middle: refriger-ator, not -ridg-.

refuge n. a place or state of safety from danger or trouble.

refugee n. a person forced to leave their country because of war or persecution.

refulgent adj. literary shining.

refund v. pay back. • n. a repayment of a sum of money.

refurbish v. redecorate and improve a building or room. ■ **refurbishment** n.

refuse[1] /ri-fyooz/ v. state that you are unwilling to do or accept something. ■ **refusal** n.

refuse[2] /ref-yooss/ n. waste material; rubbish.

refute v. prove wrong. ■ **refutation** n.

r

regain v. **1** get back after loss. **2** get back to a place.

regal adj. of or like a monarch. ■ **regally** adv.

regale v. **1** entertain with stories. **2** supply generously with food or drink.

regalia n. the distinctive clothing and objects of royalty or other rank or office, used at formal occasions.

regard v. **1** think of in a particular way. **2** look steadily at. • n. **1** concern or care. **2** high opinion; respect. **3** a steady gaze. **4** (**regards**) best wishes. □ **as regards** concerning. **with** (or **in**) **regard to** concerning.

regarding prep. concerning.

regardless adv. **1** (**regardless of**) without concern for. **2** despite what is happening.

regatta n. a series of boat or yacht races.

regency n. (pl. **regencies**) a period of rule by a regent.

regenerate v. **1** bring new life or strength to. **2** grow new tissue. ■ **regeneration** n. **regenerative** adj.

regent n. a person appointed to rule while the monarch is too young or unfit to rule, or is absent.

reggae /reg-gay/ n. a style of pop music originating in Jamaica.

regicide n. **1** the killing of a king. **2** a person who kills a king.

regime /ray-zheem/ n. **1** a government. **2** a system of doing something.

regimen n. a course of medical treatment, diet, or exercise.

regiment n. a permanent unit of an army. • v. organize according to a strict system. ■ **regimental** adj. **regimentation** n.

Regina n. the reigning queen (used in referring to lawsuits).

region n. **1** an area of a country or the world. **2** an administrative district. **3** a part of the body. □ **in the region of** approximately. ■ **regional** adj.

register n. **1** an official list. **2** a part of the range of a voice or musical instrument. **3** the level and style of writing or speech (e.g. formal, informal). • v. **1** enter in a register. **2** express an opinion or emotion. **3** become aware of. **4** (of a measuring instrument) show a reading. □ **register office** a local government building where civil marriages are performed and births, marriages, and deaths are recorded. ■ **registration** n.

registrar n. **1** an official responsible for keeping official records. **2** a hospital doctor who is training to be a specialist.

registry n. (pl. **registries**) a place where official records are kept. □ **registry office** a register office.

regress v. return to an earlier or less advanced state. ■ **regression** n. **regressive** adj.

regret n. a feeling of sorrow or disappointment about something you have done or should have done. • v. (**regretting**, **regretted**) feel regret about. ■ **regretful** adj. **regretfully** adv.

regrettable adj. giving rise to regret. ■ **regrettably** adv.

regular adj. **1** following or arranged in an evenly spaced pattern or sequence. **2** done, happening, or doing something frequently. **3** following an accepted standard. **4** belonging to a country's permanent armed forces. **5** (of a geometrical figure) having all sides and all angles equal. •n. a regular customer, soldier, etc. ■ **regularity** n. **regularly** adv.

regularize (or **-ise**) v. 1 make regular. 2 make a temporary situation legal or official.

regulate v. 1 control the rate or speed of a machine or process. 2 control by rules. ■ **regulator** n. **regulatory** adj.

regulation n. 1 a rule. 2 the act of regulating.

regurgitate v. 1 bring swallowed food up again to the mouth. 2 repeat facts without understanding them. ■ **regurgitation** n.

rehabilitate v. help back to normal life after imprisonment or illness. ■ **rehabilitation** n.

rehash v. reuse old ideas or material. •n. an act of rehashing.

rehearsal n. a trial performance of a play or other work for later public performance.

rehearse v. 1 practise a play, music, etc. for later public performance. 2 state points made many times before.

reign v. 1 rule as monarch. 2 be the main quality or aspect. •n. a monarch's period of rule.

reimburse v. repay money to. ■ **reimbursement** n.

rein n. (**reins**) 1 long, narrow straps attached to a bridle, used to control a horse. 2 the power to direct and control. •v. 1 control with reins. 2 (**rein in/back**) restrain. ▢ **free rein** freedom of action.

❗ Remember: free **rein**, not **reign**.

reincarnate v. (**be reincarnated**) be born again in another body. ■ **reincarnation** n.

reindeer n. (pl. **reindeer** or **reindeers**) a deer with large antlers, found in cold northern regions.

reinforce v. 1 make stronger. 2 strengthen a military force with additional personnel. ■ **reinforcement** n.

reinstate v. restore to a former position. ■ **reinstatement** n.

reiterate v. say again or repeatedly. ■ **reiteration** n.

reject v. refuse to accept or agree to. •n. a rejected person or thing. ■ **rejection** n.

rejig v. (**rejigging**, **rejigged**) rearrange.

rejoice v. feel or show great joy.

rejoin v. 1 join again. 2 say in reply.

rejoinder n. a quick reply.

rejuvenate v. make more lively or youthful. ■ **rejuvenation** n.

relapse v. 1 become ill again after a period of improvement. 2 revert to a worse state. •n. an instance of relapsing.

relate v. 1 make or show a connection between. 2 (**relate to**) have to do with. 3 (**be related**) be connected by blood or marriage. 4 (**relate to**) feel sympathy with. 5 give an account of.

relation n. 1 a connection between people or things. 2 (**relations**) people's feelings and behaviour towards each other. 3 a relative. 4 (**relations**) sex.

relationship n. 1 the way in which people or things are connected. 2 the way in which people behave towards each other. 3 a loving and sexual association between two people.

relative adj. 1 considered in relation to something else. 2 existing only in comparison to something else. 3 Grammar referring to an

r

earlier noun or clause. • n. a person connected by blood or marriage. ■ **relatively** adv.

relativity n. **1** the state of being relative. **2** Physics a description of matter, energy, space, and time according to Einstein's theories.

relax v. **1** become less tense or rigid. **2** rest from work; do something recreational. **3** make a rule less strict. ■ **relaxation** n.

relay n. **1** a group engaged in a task for a time and then replaced by a similar group. **2** a race between teams, each team member in turn covering part of the total distance. **3** an electrical device activating a circuit. **4** a device to receive and transmit a signal. • v. receive and pass on or transmit again.

release v. **1** set free. **2** allow to move freely. **3** make information, a film, or a recording available to the public. • n. **1** the act of releasing. **2** a film or recording released to the public.

relegate v. place in a lower rank or position. ■ **relegation** n.

relent v. **1** finally agree to something after refusing it. **2** become less intense.

relentless adj. **1** never stopping or weakening. **2** harsh or inflexible. ■ **relentlessly** adv.

relevant adj. connected or appropriate to the current matter. ■ **relevance** n.

reliable adj. able to be relied on. ■ **reliability** n. **reliably** adv.

reliance n. dependence on or trust in someone or something. ■ **reliant** adj.

relic n. **1** something surviving from an earlier time. **2** a part of a holy person's body or belongings kept after their death.

relief n. **1** a feeling of relaxation after anxiety. **2** the act of relieving. **3** a break in a tense or boring situation. **4** help given to people in need. **5** a person or group replacing another on duty. **6** a carving in which the design stands out from the surface. □ **relief map** a map showing hills and valleys by shading.

relieve v. **1** lessen or remove pain, difficulty, or anxiety. **2** replace someone on duty. **3** (**relieve of**) take a responsibility from. **4** bring military support for a place under siege. **5** (**relieve yourself**) urinate or defecate.

religion n. **1** the belief in and worship of a God or gods. **2** a particular system of faith and worship.

religious adj. **1** of or believing in a religion. **2** very careful or regular. ■ **religiously** adv.

relinquish v. give up. ■ **relinquishment** n.

reliquary n. (pl. **reliquaries**) a container for holy relics.

relish v. enjoy or look forward to. • n. **1** great enjoyment. **2** a spicy sauce or pickle.

relocate v. move to a different place. ■ **relocation** n.

reluctant adj. unwilling and hesitant. ■ **reluctance** n. **reluctantly** adv.

rely v. (**relying**, **relied**) (**rely on**) **1** be dependent on. **2** trust or have faith in.

remain v. **1** still be in the same place or condition. **2** continue to be. **3** be left over.

remainder n. **1** a remaining part, number, or amount. **2** the number left over when one quantity does not exactly divide into another.

remains pl. n. **1** things remaining. **2** archaeological relics. **3** a dead body.

remand v. send a defendant to await trial, either on bail or in jail. □ **on remand** in jail awaiting trial.

remark v. **1** say as a comment. **2** notice. •n. a comment.

remarkable adj. extraordinary or striking. ■ **remarkably** adv.

remedial adj. **1** intended as a remedy. **2** for children with learning difficulties.

remedy n. (pl. **remedies**) **1** a medicine or treatment for a disease or injury. **2** a means of putting a matter right. •v. (**remedying**, **remedied**) put right.

remember v. **1** have in or bring to the mind someone or something from the past. **2** keep something to be done in mind. ■ **remembrance** n.

remind v. cause to remember. ■ **reminder** n.

reminisce v. think or talk about the past.

reminiscence n. **1** an account of something remembered. **2** the enjoyable remembering of past events.

reminiscent adj. tending to remind you of something.

remiss adj. negligent.

remission n. **1** a temporary period during which an illness becomes less severe. **2** the reduction of a prison sentence for good behaviour.

remit n. the area of responsibility officially assigned to someone. •v. (**remitting**, **remitted**) **1** send payment. **2** cancel a debt or pun-

ishment. **3** refer a matter for decision to an authority.

remittance n. a sum of money sent in payment.

remnant n. a small remaining quantity.

remonstrate v. make a protest. ■ **remonstration** n.

remorse n. deep regret or guilt for something wrong that you have done. ■ **remorseful** adj. **remorsefully** adv.

remorseless adj. **1** never ending. **2** without remorse. ■ **remorselessly** adv.

remote adj. **1** far away in space or time. **2** not closely connected. **3** (of a possibility) slight. **4** unfriendly and aloof. **5** operating or operated by means of radio or infrared signals. ■ **remotely** adv. **remoteness** n.

removal n. **1** the act of removing. **2** the transfer of furniture etc. when moving house.

remove v. **1** take off or away. **2** get rid of. **3** dismiss from a post. •n. the extent to which things are separated. ■ **removable** adj. **remover** n.

remunerate v. pay for work. ■ **remuneration** n. **remunerative** adj.

Renaissance n. **1** the revival of classical styles in art and literature in the 14th–16th centuries. **2** (**renaissance**) a revival of interest in something.

renal adj. of the kidneys.

rend v. (**rending**, **rent**) tear to pieces.

render v. **1** provide a service, help, etc. **2** present for inspection, payment, etc. **3** cause to become. **4** perform music or drama. **5** melt down fat.

rendezvous /ron-day-voo/ n. (pl. **rendezvous**) an arranged meeting or meeting place. •v. meet at an agreed time and place.

rendition n. a performance of a dramatic or musical work.

renegade n. a person who deserts and betrays a group, cause, etc.

renege /ri-nayg/ v. fail to keep a promise or agreement.

renew v. 1 begin again after an interruption. 2 give fresh life or strength to. 3 extend the period of validity of a licence etc. 4 replace something broken or worn out. ■ **renewable** adj. **renewal** n.

rennet n. a substance that curdles milk, used in making cheese.

renounce v. formally give up.

renovate v. restore to a good state of repair. ■ **renovation** n.

renown n. fame. ■ **renowned** adj.

rent¹ n. a regular payment for the use of property or land. •v. pay or receive rent for.

rent² past & past part. of **REND**. •n. a large tear in a piece of fabric.

rental n. 1 an amount paid as rent. 2 the act of renting.

renunciation n. the act of renouncing something.

reoccur v. (**reoccurring**, **reoccurred**) occur again or repeatedly. ■ **reoccurrence** n.

reorganize (or **-ise**) v. change the organization of. ■ **reorganization** n.

reorient v. 1 change the focus of. 2 (**reorient yourself**) find your bearings again.

rep n. informal a representative.

repair v. 1 restore to a good condition. 2 (**repair to**) go to a place. •n. 1 the act of repairing. 2 the

condition of something. ■ **repairer** n.

reparation n. 1 the making of amends for a wrong. 2 (**reparations**) compensation for war damage paid by a defeated state.

repartee n. quick, witty comments or replies.

repast n. a meal.

repatriate v. send someone back to their own country. ■ **repatriation** n.

repay v. (**repaying, repaid**) 1 pay back. 2 be worth spending time on. ■ **repayable** adj. **repayment** n.

repeal v. officially cancel a law. •n. the act of repealing.

repeat v. 1 say or do again. 2 (**repeat itself**) occur again in the same way. •n. a repeated broadcast. ■ **repeatedly** adv.

repel v. (**repelling, repelled**) 1 force back or away. 2 disgust. 3 (of a substance) be able to keep something out.

repellent adj. 1 causing disgust. 2 able to repel a particular thing. •n. a substance that repels insects etc.

repent v. feel or express remorse. ■ **repentance** n. **repentant** adj.

repercussions pl. n. the consequences of an event or action.

repertoire /rep-er-twar/ n. the works known or regularly performed by a performer or company.

repertory n. (pl. **repertories**) 1 the performance by a company of various plays, operas, etc. at regular intervals. 2 a repertoire.

repetition n. 1 the act of repeating. 2 a thing that repeats another.

repetitious adj. repetitive.

repetitive adj. repeated many times or too much. ■ **repetitively** adv.

repine v. literary be unhappy.

replace v. 1 provide or be a substitute for. 2 put back in place. ■ **replacement** n.

replay v. 1 play back a recording. 2 play a match again. •n. 1 a replayed match. 2 an act of replaying.

replenish v. fill up a supply again after some has been used. ■ **replenishment** n.

replete adj. 1 well supplied. 2 very full with food.

replica n. an exact copy.

replicate v. make a replica of. ■ **replication** n. **replicator** n.

reply v. (**replying, replied**) answer or respond. •n. (pl. **replies**) an answer.

report v. 1 give an account of. 2 make a formal complaint about. 3 present yourself on arrival. 4 (**report to**) be responsible to a manager. •n. 1 a spoken or written account. 2 a teacher's written assessment of a pupil's progress. 3 the sound of an explosion or gunfire.

reportage /rep-or-**tahzh**/ n. the reporting of news.

reporter n. a person who reports news for a newspaper or broadcasting company.

repose n. a state of calm or peace. •v. rest; lie.

repository n. (pl. **repositories**) a place or container for storage.

repossess v. take back goods etc. when the required payments are not made. ■ **repossession** n.

reprehensible adj. deserving condemnation.

represent v. 1 act and speak on behalf of. 2 be an example of. 3 amount to. 4 describe in a particular way. 5 depict in a work of art. 6 be a symbol of.

representation n. 1 the act of representing. 2 an image, model, etc. 3 (**representations**) an appeal or protest.

representative adj. 1 typical of a class or group. 2 consisting of people chosen to represent a wider group. •n. 1 a person chosen to represent others. 2 a person who visits potential clients to sell their company's products.

repress v. 1 bring under control by force. 2 restrain or suppress a thought or feeling. 3 (**repressed**) tending to keep your feelings or desires hidden. ■ **repression** n. **repressive** adj.

reprieve v. cancel the punishment of. •n. 1 an act of reprieving. 2 a brief delay before an undesirable event.

reprimand v. express strong disapproval to. •n. an act of reprimanding.

reprint v. print again. •n. a copy of a book that has been reprinted.

reprisal n. an act of retaliation.

reproach v. express disapproval of or disappointment with. •n. an act of reproaching. ■ **reproachful** adj. **reproachfully** adv.

reprobate n. an immoral person.

reproduce v. 1 produce a copy of. 2 produce again in a different situation. 3 produce offspring.

reproduction n. 1 the act of reproducing. 2 a copy of a work of art. ■ **reproductive** adj.

reproof n. a reprimand.

reprove v. reprimand.

r

reptile n. a cold-blooded animal of a group that includes snakes. ■ **reptilian** adj.

republic n. a state in which power is held by the people's representatives, with a president rather than a monarch.

republican adj. of or supporting the principles of a republic. •n. a person in favour of republican government.

repudiate v. **1** refuse to accept or be associated with. **2** deny the truth of. ■ **repudiation** n.

repugnant adj. disgusting or very unpleasant. ■ **repugnance** n.

repulse v. **1** force back an attacking enemy. **2** reject or rebuff.

repulsion n. **1** a feeling of intense disgust. **2** a force by which objects tend to move away from each other.

repulsive adj. highly disgusting. ■ **repulsively** adv.

reputable adj. having a good reputation.

reputation n. the opinion generally held about someone or something.

repute n. reputation, esp. when good. •v. (**be reputed**) be said or thought to be. ■ **reputedly** adv.

request n. **1** a formal or polite act of asking. **2** a thing asked for. •v. ask formally or politely.

requiem n. a musical work based on a Mass for the souls of the dead.

require v. **1** need for a purpose. **2** order or expect to do.

requirement n. something needed or compulsory.

requisite adj. necessary because of circumstances or rules. •n. something needed.

requisition n. an official order allowing property or materials to be taken and used. •v. officially take or use, esp. during a war.

rescind v. cancel a law, order, etc.

rescue v. save from danger or distress. •n. an act of rescuing. ■ **rescuer** n.

research n. the study of materials and sources to discover facts. •v. carry out research into a subject or for a book etc. ■ **researcher** n.

resemblance n. **1** the fact of resembling. **2** a way in which things resemble each other.

resemble v. look like or be similar to.

resent v. feel bitter or angry about. ■ **resentful** adj. **resentfully** adv. **resentment** n.

reservation n. **1** the act of reserving. **2** an arrangement for something to be reserved. **3** an area of land set aside for native people. **4** an expression of doubt.

reserve v. **1** keep for future use. **2** arrange for a room, seat, etc. to be kept for a particular purpose. **3** have or keep a right etc. •n. **1** a supply kept available for use if required. **2** a military force kept to reinforce others or for use in an emergency. **3** an extra player in a team, serving as a possible substitute. **4** a lack of warmth or openness. **5** an area set aside for wildlife.

reserved adj. slow to reveal emotion or opinions.

reservist n. a member of a military reserve force.

reservoir n. **1** a lake used as a source of water supply. **2** a container for a supply of fluid.

reshuffle v. change the roles or positions of government ministers. • n. an act of reshuffling.

reside v. 1 live in a particular place. 2 (**reside in/with**) (of a right or power) belong to a person or group. 3 (**reside in**) be present in.

residence n. 1 the fact of residing. 2 a person's home.

resident n. 1 a person living somewhere on a long-term basis. 2 a guest in a hotel. • adj. living somewhere on a long-term basis.

residential adj. 1 suitable for living in. 2 providing accommodation.

residue n. an amount remaining after the greater part has gone or been taken. ■ **residual** adj.

resign v. 1 voluntarily leave a job. 2 (**be resigned**) accept that something bad cannot be avoided.

resignation n. 1 an act of resigning. 2 a letter stating an intention to resign. 3 acceptance of something bad but inevitable.

resilient adj. 1 able to spring back into shape after bending, stretching, etc. 2 able to recover quickly from difficulty. ■ **resilience** n.

resin n. 1 a sticky substance produced by some trees. 2 a synthetic substance used in plastics, adhesives, etc. ■ **resinous** adj.

resist v. 1 withstand the action or effect of. 2 try to prevent or oppose. 3 refrain from something tempting.

resistance n. 1 the act of resisting or the ability to resist. 2 a secret organization that fights against an occupying enemy. 3 the degree to which a material or device opposes the passage of an electric current. ■ **resistant** adj. **resistor** n.

resolute adj. determined. ■ **resolutely** adv.

resolution n. 1 a firm decision. 2 a formal expression of opinion by a law-making body. 3 determination. 4 the solving of a problem etc. 5 the degree to which detail is visible in an image.

resolve v. 1 find a solution to. 2 firmly decide to do. 3 separate into constituent parts. • n. determination.

resonant adj. 1 deep, clear, and ringing. 2 suggesting images, a quality, etc. ■ **resonance** n.

resonate v. make a deep, clear, ringing sound.

resort n. 1 a place visited for holidays. 2 a course of action. • v. (**resort to**) adopt a strategy to solve a problem.

resound v. 1 be filled with a ringing or echoing sound. 2 (**resounding**) definite.

resource n. 1 (**resources**) a stock or supply of materials or assets. 2 a source of help or information. 3 (**resources**) personal qualities for dealing with difficult situations.

resourceful adj. quick and clever at overcoming difficulties. ■ **resourcefully** adv. **resourcefulness** n.

respect n. 1 admiration for someone because of their qualities or achievements. 2 consideration for the feelings or rights of others. 3 a particular aspect or point. • v. 1 have respect for. 2 agree to observe a law etc. ■ **respectful** adj. **respectfully** adv.

respectable adj. 1 regarded by society as proper or correct. 2 adequate or acceptable. ■ **respectability** n. **respectably** adv.

r

respective *adj.* belonging to each as an individual.

respectively *adv.* separately and in the order mentioned.

respiration *n.* the act of breathing.

respirator *n.* **1** a device worn over the face to prevent the breathing in of smoke etc. **2** a device enabling someone to breathe when they are unable to do so naturally.

respiratory *adj.* of breathing.

respire *v.* breathe.

respite *n.* rest or relief from something difficult or unpleasant.

resplendent *adj.* impressively colourful or attractive.

respond *v.* say or do in reply or as a reaction.

respondent *n.* a person against whom a legal petition is filed, esp. one in a divorce case.

response *n.* an answer or reaction.

responsibility *n.* (*pl.* **responsibilities**) **1** the state of being responsible. **2** a thing required as part of a job or legal obligation.

responsible *adj.* **1** obliged to do something or care for someone. **2** being the cause of something and so deserving blame or credit for it. **3** able to be trusted. **4** involving important duties. **5** having to report to a senior person. ■ **responsibly** *adv.*

responsive *adj.* responding readily.

rest *v.* **1** stop work or movement so as to relax or recover your strength. **2** place in a specified position. **3** remain or be left in a specified state: *rest assured.* **4** (**rest on**) depend or be based on. **5** (**rest with**) (of power etc.) belong to. • *n.* **1** a period of resting.

2 a motionless state. **3** an object used to hold or support something. **4** the remaining part, people, or things.

restaurant *n.* a place where people pay to eat meals cooked on the premises.

restaurateur /ress-tuh-ruh-**ter**/ *n.* the owner or manager of a restaurant.

! There is no *n*: restau*rateur.*

restful *adj.* relaxing.

restitution *n.* **1** the restoration of something lost or stolen to its owner. **2** payment for injury or loss.

restive *adj.* restless; impatient.

restless *adj.* unable to rest or relax. ■ **restlessly** *adv.* **restlessness** *n.*

restorative *adj.* able to restore health or strength.

restore *v.* **1** return to a previous condition, place, or owner. **2** repair or renovate. **3** bring back a previous practice, situation, etc. ■ **restoration** *n.* **restorer** *n.*

restrain *v.* **1** keep under control. **2** stop from moving or acting freely.

restraint *n.* **1** the act of restraining. **2** something that restrains. **3** self-controlled behaviour.

restrict *v.* **1** put a limit on. **2** stop from moving or acting freely. ■ **restrictive** *adj.*

restriction *n.* **1** a limiting condition or measure. **2** the act of restricting.

result *n.* **1** a thing caused or produced by something else. **2** information obtained by experiment or calculation. **3** a final score or mark in a contest or exam. • *v.* **1** occur as a result. **2** (**result in**) have as a result.

resultant adj. occurring as a result.

resume v. begin again or continue after a pause.

résumé /rez-yuu-may/ n. **1** a summary. **2** US a curriculum vitae.

resurgent adj. becoming stronger or more popular again. ■ **resurgence** n.

resurrect v. **1** restore to life. **2** revive a practice etc. ■ **resurrection** n.

resuscitate v. revive from unconsciousness. ■ **resuscitation** n.

retail n. the sale of goods to the general public. • v. sell or be sold to the public. ■ **retailer** n.

retain v. **1** keep possession of. **2** absorb and hold. **3** keep in place. **4** secure the services of.

retainer n. **1** a fee paid in advance to a barrister to secure their services. **2** a servant who has worked for a family for a long time.

retaliate v. attack in return for a similar attack. ■ **retaliation** n. **retaliatory** adj.

retard v. prevent from developing or progressing. ■ **retardation** n.

retarded adj. offens. less developed mentally than is usual at a particular age.

retch v. make the sound and movement of vomiting.

retention n. the act of retaining.

retentive adj. able to retain facts easily.

rethink v. (**rethinking, rethought**) consider again.

reticent adj. not revealing your thoughts or feelings. ■ **reticence** n.

retina n. (pl. **retinas** or **retinae**) a layer at the back of the eyeball that is sensitive to light.

retinue n. a group of assistants accompanying an important person.

retire v. **1** stop working because you have reached a particular age. **2** withdraw from a competition. **3** go to bed. ■ **retirement** n.

retiring adj. shy.

retort v. make a sharp or witty reply. • n. **1** a sharp or witty reply. **2** a glass container with a long neck, used in distilling.

retouch v. improve a painting or photo with slight alterations.

retrace v. go back over or follow a route.

retract v. **1** draw or be drawn back. **2** withdraw an accusation etc. ■ **retractable** adj. **retraction** n.

retractile adj. able to be retracted.

retreat v. **1** (of an army) withdraw from attacking enemy forces. **2** move back from a difficult situation. • n. **1** an act of retreating. **2** a quiet or secluded place.

retrench v. reduce costs or spending. ■ **retrenchment** n.

retrial n. a second or further trial.

retribution n. severe punishment inflicted as revenge.

retrieve v. **1** get or bring back. **2** extract information from a computer. **3** improve a bad situation. ■ **retrieval** n.

retriever n. a dog of a breed used to retrieve game.

retro adj. imitative of a style from the recent past.

retroactive adj. taking effect from a date in the past.

r

retrograde adj. moving backwards or to a worse state.

retrogressive adj. returning to an earlier and worse state. ■ **retrogression** n.

retrospect n. (**in retrospect**) when looking back on a past event.

retrospective adj. 1 looking back on or dealing with past events. 2 retroactive. ■ **retrospectively** adv.

retroussé /ruh-troo-say/ adj. (of a nose) turned up at the tip.

retsina n. a Greek wine flavoured with resin.

return v. 1 come or go back. 2 give, send, or put back. 3 feel, say, or do the same thing in response. 4 give a verdict. 5 yield a profit. 6 elect to office. • n. 1 an act of returning. 2 a profit. 3 a ticket allowing travel to a place and back again.

reunion n. a social gathering of people who have not seen each other for some time.

reunite v. bring or come together again.

reuse v. use again. ■ **reusable** adj.

Rev. (or **Rev**) abbrev. Reverend.

rev informal v. (**revving**, **revved**) increase the running speed of an engine. • n. a revolution of an engine.

revamp v. alter so as to improve.

reveal v. 1 make known. 2 allow something hidden to be seen.

reveille /ri-val-li/ n. a signal sounded to wake up soldiers.

revel v. (**revelling**, **revelled**; US **reveling**, **reveled**) 1 (**revel in**) gain great pleasure from. 2 enjoy yourself in a lively way. • n. (**revels**) lively celebrations. ■ **reveller** n. **revelry** n.

revelation n. 1 the act of revealing. 2 a surprising thing.

revelatory adj. revealing something previously unknown.

revenge n. something harmful done in return for an injury or wrong. • v. (**be revenged**) take revenge.

revenue n. the income received by an organization, or by a state from taxes.

reverberate v. 1 be repeated as an echo. 2 have continuing effects. ■ **reverberation** n.

revere v. respect or admire deeply.

reverence n. deep respect. ■ **reverent** adj. **reverential** adj.

reverend adj. a title given to Christian ministers.

reverie n. a daydream.

reversal n. a change to an opposite direction, course of action, etc.

reverse v. 1 move backwards. 2 make something the opposite of what it was. 3 turn the other way round. 4 cancel a judgement. • adj. opposite in direction, order, etc. • n. 1 a change of direction or action. 2 the opposite. 3 a setback. ■ **reversible** adj.

revert v. return to a previous state, practice, etc. ■ **reversion** n.

review n. 1 a formal examination so as to make changes if necessary. 2 a critical assessment of a book etc. 3 a report of events. 4 a ceremonial inspection of military forces. • v. carry out or write a review of. ■ **reviewer** n.

revile v. criticize in a scornful way.

revise v. 1 examine and alter. 2 study previous work to prepare for an exam. ■ **revision** n.

revival n. **1** an improvement in condition, strength, or popularity. **2** a new production of an old play.

revivalism n. the promotion of a revival of religious faith. ■ **revivalist** n. & adj.

revive v. **1** restore to consciousness, health, or strength. **2** start doing or using again.

revivify v. (**revivifying**, **revivified**) revive.

revoke v. make a decree, law, etc. no longer valid. ■ **revocation** n.

revolt v. **1** rebel against an authority. **2** disgust. •n. an act of rebellion.

revolution n. **1** the overthrow of a government by force, in favour of a new system. **2** a great and influential change. **3** a single movement around a central point.

revolutionary adj. **1** involving great change. **2** of or engaged in political revolution. •n. (pl. **revolutionaries**) a person who starts or supports a political revolution.

revolutionize (or **-ise**) v. change completely.

revolve v. **1** move in a circle around a central point. **2** (**revolve around**) treat as the most important aspect.

revolver n. a type of pistol.

revue n. a theatrical show with short sketches, songs, etc.

revulsion n. strong disgust.

reward n. a thing given in recognition of service, effort, or achievement. •v. give a reward to or for.

rhapsodize (or **-ise**) v. express great enthusiasm.

rhapsody n. (pl. **rhapsodies**) **1** an expression of great enthusiasm. **2** a piece of music in one extended movement. ■ **rhapsodic** adj.

rhenium n. a metallic element.

rheostat n. a device for varying the resistance in an electrical circuit.

rhesus factor n. a substance in red blood cells which can cause disease in a newborn baby.

rhesus monkey n. a small southern Asian monkey.

rhetoric n. **1** effective or persuasive public speaking. **2** persuasive but insincere language.

rhetorical adj. **1** intended to impress. **2** (of a question) asked to make a statement rather than to obtain an answer. ■ **rhetorically** adv.

rheumatism n. a disease causing inflammation and pain in the joints and muscles. ■ **rheumatic** adj.

rheumatoid adj. of or resembling rheumatism.

rhinestone n. an imitation diamond.

rhino n. (pl. **rhino** or **rhinos**) informal a rhinoceros.

rhinoceros n. (pl. **rhinoceros** or **rhinoceroses**) a large thick-skinned mammal with one or two horns on the nose.

rhizome n. an underground stem bearing both roots and shoots.

rhodium n. a metallic element.

rhododendron n. a shrub with large clusters of flowers.

rhombus n. (pl. **rhombuses** or **rhombi**) a quadrilateral whose sides are of equal length. ■ **rhomboid** adj. & n.

rhubarb n. a plant with thick red stems cooked and eaten as a fruit.

rhyme n. **1** a word that has or ends with the same sound as another. **2** similarity of sound between

r

words or the endings of words. **3** a short poem with rhyming lines. •v. have or end with the same sound.

> ! Remember the first *h*, following the *r*, in *rhyme* and *rhythm*.

rhythm n. **1** a strong, regular repeated pattern of sound or movement. **2** a regularly recurring sequence of events. □ **rhythm and blues** a type of music that is a combination of blues and jazz. ■ **rhythmic** adj. **rhythmical** adj. **rhythmically** adv.

rib n. **1** each of a series of bones curving round the chest. **2** a curved structure forming part of a boat's framework. •v. (**ribbing, ribbed**) **1** (**ribbed**) having a pattern of raised bands. **2** informal tease.

ribald adj. humorous in a coarse way. ■ **ribaldry** n.

riband n. old use a ribbon.

ribbon n. **1** a long, narrow strip of fabric, for tying or decoration. **2** a long, narrow strip.

riboflavin n. vitamin B2.

rice n. the edible grains of a cereal plant grown on wet land in warm countries.

rich adj. **1** having a great deal of money or assets. **2** plentiful. **3** having something in large amounts. **4** (of a colour, sound, or smell) pleasantly deep and strong. **5** (of soil) fertile. •pl. n. (**riches**) wealth. ■ **richness** n.

richly adv. **1** in a rich way. **2** fully.

Richter scale /rik-ter/ n. a scale for measuring the severity of an earthquake.

rick n. **1** a stack of hay etc. **2** a slight sprain or strain. •v. strain slightly.

rickets n. a bone disease of children caused by lack of vitamin D.

rickety adj. likely to collapse.

rickshaw n. a light two-wheeled vehicle pulled by a person walking or riding a bicycle.

ricochet /ri-kuh-shay/ v. (**ricocheting, ricocheted**) rebound off a surface. •n. a shot or hit that ricochets.

ricotta n. a soft white Italian cheese.

rictus n. a fixed grimace or grin.

rid v. (**ridding, rid**) **1** (**rid of**) free of something unwanted. **2** (**be/ get rid of**) be or make yourself free of.

riddance n. (**good riddance**) expressing relief at being rid of someone or something.

riddle n. **1** a cleverly worded question asked as a game. **2** a puzzling person or thing. **3** a large coarse sieve. •v. (**be riddled**) **1** have many holes. **2** be filled with something undesirable.

ride v. (**riding, rode**; past part. **ridden**) **1** sit on and control the movement of a horse, bicycle, etc. **2** travel in a vehicle. **3** be carried or supported by. •n. **1** an act of riding. **2** a roundabout etc. ridden at a fair or amusement park. □ **ride on** depend on. **ride up** (of clothing) move upwards.

rider n. **1** a person who rides a horse etc. **2** an additional condition.

ridge n. **1** a long narrow hilltop. **2** a narrow raised band. **3** a long region of high pressure. **4** the edge formed where the two slopes of a roof meet at the top. ■ **ridged** adj.

ridicule n. mockery or derision. •v. make fun of.

ridiculous adj. very silly or unreasonable. ■ **ridiculously** adv.

rife adj. **1** widespread. **2** (**rife with**) full of.

riff n. a short repeated phrase in jazz etc.

riffle v. turn over pages quickly and casually.

riff-raff n. people considered to be socially unacceptable.

rifle n. a gun with a long barrel. • v. search through hurriedly.

rift n. **1** a crack, split, or break. **2** a serious break in friendly relations. □ **rift valley** a steep-sided valley formed by subsidence of the earth's surface.

rig v. (**rigging, rigged**) **1** arrange dishonestly to gain an advantage. **2** set up a device or structure. **3** fit sails and rigging on a boat. • n. **1** a piece of equipment for a particular purpose. **2** an oil rig.

rigging n. the system of ropes etc. supporting a ship's masts.

right adj. **1** of, on, or towards the side which is to the east when facing north. **2** morally good or justified. **3** factually correct. **4** most appropriate. **5** satisfactory, sound, or normal. **6** informal complete: a right idiot. • adv. **1** on or to the right side. **2** completely. **3** exactly; directly. **4** correctly. • n. **1** what is morally right. **2** an entitlement to have or do something. **3** (**the right**) the right-hand side or direction. **4** (**the Right**) a right-wing group or party. • v. **1** restore to a normal or upright position. **2** correct or make amends for. □ **by rights** if things were fair or correct. **in your own right** as a result of your own qualifications or efforts. **right angle** an angle of 90˚. **right away** immediately.

right-handed using or done with the right hand. **right-hand man** an indispensable assistant. **right of way 1** the legal right to go through another's property. **2** a public path through another's property. **3** the right to proceed before another vehicle. **right-wing** conservative or reactionary. ■ **rightly** adv.

righteous adj. morally right. ■ **righteousness** n.

rightful adj. **1** having a right to something. **2** just; fitting. ■ **rightfully** adv.

rigid adj. **1** unable to bend. **2** strict or inflexible. ■ **rigidity** n. **rigidly** adv.

rigmarole n. a long, complicated procedure.

rigor mortis n. stiffening of the body after death.

rigorous adj. **1** very thorough or accurate. **2** (of a rule etc.) strictly applied or followed. **3** harsh or severe. ■ **rigorously** adv.

rigour (US **rigor**) n. **1** the quality of being rigorous. **2** (**rigours**) demanding conditions.

rile v. informal annoy.

rill n. a small stream.

rim n. an edge or border, esp. of something circular. • v. (**rimming, rimmed**) provide with a rim.

rime n. literary frost.

rind n. a tough outer layer on fruit, cheese, or bacon.

ring[1] n. **1** a small circular band worn on a finger. **2** a circular band, object, or mark. **3** an enclosed space in which a sport or show takes place. **4** a group working together illegally or secretly. • v. **1** surround. **2** draw a circle round. □ **ringleader** a person who leads others in crime or causing trouble.

ringlet a corkscrew-shaped curl of hair. **ringworm** a skin disease causing small circular itchy patches.

ring² v. (**ringing, rang**; past part. **rung**) **1** make a clear resonating sound. **2** (**ring with**) echo with a sound. **3** call by phone. **4** (**ring off**) end a phone call. **5** call for attention by sounding a bell. •n. **1** an act of ringing. **2** a loud clear sound or tone. **3** informal a phone call. **4** a quality conveyed by words: a ring of truth. □ **ringtone** a sound made by a mobile phone when an incoming call is received.

rink n. an enclosed area of ice for skating etc.

rinse v. wash with clean water to remove soap or dirt. •n. **1** an act of rinsing. **2** a mouthwash. **3** a liquid for conditioning or colouring the hair.

riot n. **1** a violent disturbance by a crowd. **2** a confused combination or display. **3** informal a very amusing person or thing. •v. take part in a riot. □ **run riot** behave in an uncontrolled way. ■ **rioter** n. **riotous** adj.

RIP abbrev. rest in peace (used on graves).

rip v. (**ripping, ripped**) **1** tear or become torn. **2** pull forcibly away. •n. a long tear. □ **let rip** informal act or speak without restraint.

ripcord a cord pulled to open a parachute. **rip-off** informal a very overpriced article. **rip off** informal **1** cheat someone. **2** steal.

ripe adj. **1** ready for harvesting and eating. **2** (of a cheese) fully matured. **3** (**ripe for**) ready for. **4** (of age) advanced. ■ **ripen** v. **ripeness** n.

riposte n. a quick reply.

ripple n. **1** a small wave or waves. **2** a feeling or effect that spreads through someone or something. •v. **1** form ripples. **2** (of a feeling etc.) spread through.

rise v. (**rising, rose**; past part. **risen**) **1** come or go up. **2** get up from lying, sitting, or kneeling. **3** increase. **4** (of land) slope upwards. **5** (of the sun etc.) appear above the horizon. **6** reach a higher rank or position. **7** rebel. **8** (of a river) have its source. •n. **1** an act of rising. **2** an upward slope. **3** a pay increase.

risible adj. causing laughter. ■ **risibly** adv.

rising n. a revolt.

risk n. **1** the possibility of something bad happening. **2** a person or thing causing this. •v. **1** expose to danger or loss. **2** act in such a way that something bad could happen.

risky adj. (**riskier, riskiest**) involving risk. ■ **riskily** adv. **riskiness** n.

risotto n. (pl. **risottos**) a dish of rice with meat, seafood, etc.

risqué /riss-kay/ adj. slightly indecent.

rissole n. a small cake of minced meat, coated in breadcrumbs and fried.

rite n. a ritual.

ritual n. a religious or solemn ceremony involving a set series of actions. •adj. of or done as a ritual. ■ **ritualistic** adj. **ritually** adv.

rival n. a person or thing competing with or equal to another. •v. (**rivalling, rivalled**; US **rivaling, rivaled**) be comparable to.

rivalry n. (pl **rivalries**) a situation in which two people are competing for the same thing.

riven adj. torn apart.

river n. a large natural flow of water along a channel.

rivet n. a short bolt for holding together two metal plates. • v. (**riveting, riveted**) 1 fasten with a rivet or rivets. 2 (**be riveted**) be completely engrossed.

rivulet n. a small stream.

RN abbrev. Royal Navy.

RNA n. ribonucleic acid, a substance in living cells which carries instructions from DNA.

roach n. (pl. **roach**) a freshwater fish of the carp family.

road n. 1 a wide track with a hard surface for vehicles to travel on. 2 a way leading to a particular outcome. □ **road rage** violent anger caused by conflict with another driver. **roadway** 1 a road. 2 the part of a road intended for vehicles. **roadworks** repairs to roads or to pipes under roads. **roadworthy** (of a vehicle) fit to be used on the road.

roadie n. informal a person who sets up equipment for a rock group.

roadster n. an open-top sports car.

roam v. wander.

roan adj. (of a horse) having a dark coat interspersed with white hairs.

roar n. 1 a long, deep sound made by a lion, engine, etc. 2 a loud sound expressing anger, amusement, etc. • v. 1 make a roar. 2 laugh loudly. 3 move very fast.

roaring adj. informal complete: a roaring success.

roast v. 1 cook food in an oven or over a fire. 2 make or become very warm. • adj. (of food) having been roasted. • n. a roast joint of meat.

rob v. (**robbing, robbed**) 1 steal from by force or threat of force. 2 deprive of something valued. ■ **robber** n. **robbery** n.

robe n. a long loose outer garment for formal or ceremonial occasions. • v. dress in a robe.

robin n. a red-breasted songbird.

robot n. a machine able to carry out a complex series of actions automatically. ■ **robotic** adj.

robotics n. the study of the design, construction, and use of robots.

robust adj. 1 sturdy. 2 healthy. 3 forceful.

rock n. 1 the hard material of the earth's crust. 2 a piece or mass of rock. 3 a hard sweet in the form of a cylindrical stick. 4 a type of loud pop music with a strong beat. • v. 1 move to and fro or from side to side. 2 shock or distress greatly. □ **on the rocks** informal 1 in difficulties and likely to fail. 2 (of a drink) served with ice cubes. **rock and roll** a type of popular dance music with simple melodies. **rock bottom** the lowest possible level.

rocker n. 1 a person who performs or likes rock music. 2 a curved piece of wood on which something may rock.

rockery n. (pl. **rockeries**) an arrangement of rocks in a garden with plants growing between them.

rocket n. 1 a cylindrical missile or spacecraft propelled by a stream of burning gases. 2 a firework that shoots into the air and explodes. 3 informal a severe reprimand. 4 a plant eaten in salads. • v. (**rocketing, rocketed**) move or increase very rapidly.

rocky adj. (**rockier, rockiest**) 1 of rock. 2 full of rocks. 3 unsteady or unstable.

r

rococo adj. of an ornate style of furniture or architecture of the 18th century.

rod n. 1 a thin straight bar of wood, metal, etc. 2 (or **fishing rod**) a long stick with a line and hook attached, for catching fish.

rode past of RIDE.

rodent n. a mammal of a group with large front teeth.

rodeo n. (pl. **rodeos**) a contest or entertainment in which cowboys show their skills.

roe n. 1 the eggs of a fish, eaten as food. 2 (pl. **roe** or **roes**) a small deer.

roentgen /runt-yuhn/ n. a unit of ionizing radiation.

rogue n. 1 a dishonest man. 2 an elephant living apart from the herd.

roguish adj. playfully mischievous.

roister v. enjoy yourself in a lively, noisy way.

role n. 1 an actor's part. 2 a person's or thing's function.

roll v. 1 move by turning over and over. 2 move on wheels or with a smooth motion. 3 (of a ship, aircraft, etc.) sway from side to side. 4 turn something flexible over and over on itself. 5 flatten with a roller. 6 (of a deep sound) reverberate. •n. 1 a cylinder formed by rolling material. 2 a rolling movement. 3 a very small loaf of bread. 4 a reverberating sound. 5 an official list of names. □ **roll call** the reading aloud of a list of names to check who is present. **rolled gold** a thin coating of gold on another metal. **rolling pin** a cylinder for rolling out dough. **rolling stock** locomotives, carriages, and other railway vehicles. **roll out** launch a new product.

roller n. 1 a rotating cylinder used to move, flatten, or spread something. 2 a small cylinder on which hair is wound to produce curls. 3 a long swelling wave. □ **roller coaster** a railway at a fairground with a steep, twisting track. **roller skate** a boot with wheels, for gliding across a hard surface.

rollicking adj. very lively and amusing.

roly-poly adj. informal plump.

ROM abbrev. Computing read-only memory.

Roman adj. of Rome or its ancient empire. •n. 1 an inhabitant of Rome. 2 (**roman**) plain upright type. □ **Roman Catholic** a member of the part of the Christian Church which has the Pope as its head. **Roman numeral** each of the letters used as numbers in the ancient Roman system.

romance n. 1 a love affair. 2 a feeling of excitement associated with love. 3 a book or film about a love affair. 4 a feeling of mystery and excitement: the romance of the past. 5 (**Romance**) French, Italian, and other languages descended from Latin. •v. try to gain the love of.

Romanesque adj. of a style of architecture common in Europe c.900–1200.

romantic adj. 1 of love or romance. 2 showing or regarding life in an unrealistic and idealized way. 3 (**Romantic**) of Romanticism. •n. 1 a romantic person. 2 (**Romantic**) a writer or artist of the Romantic movement. ■ **romantically** adv.

Romanticism n. a literary and artistic movement which emphasizes creative inspiration and emotion.

romanticize (or **-ise**) v. cause to seem more attractive than in reality. □ **root for** informal support enthusiastically. **root out** find and get rid of. **take root** become established. ■ **rootless** adj.

Romany n. (pl. **Romanies**) **1** the language of the Gypsies. **2** a Gypsy.

romp v. **1** play about roughly and energetically. **2** informal achieve something easily.

rondo n. (pl. **rondos**) a piece of music with a recurring theme.

rood screen n. a screen separating the nave from the chancel of a church.

roof n. (pl. **roofs**) the upper covering of a building, vehicle, etc. •v. cover with a roof. ■ **roofer** n.

rook n. **1** a bird of the crow family. **2** a chess piece that can move in any direction.

rookery n. (pl. **rookeries**) a colony of rooks.

rookie n. informal a new recruit.

room n. **1** a part of a building enclosed by walls, a floor, and a ceiling. **2** space for holding things or moving in. **3** opportunity or scope.

roomy adj. (**roomier**, **roomiest**) having plenty of space.

roost n. a place where birds regularly settle to rest. •v. (of a bird) settle to rest.

rooster n. a male domestic fowl.

root n. **1** the part of a plant below ground, which collects water and nourishment. **2** the embedded part of a hair, tooth, etc. **3** the basic cause or origin. **4** (**roots**) family, ethnic, or cultural origins. **5** a number that when multiplied by itself one or more times gives a specified number. •v. **1** (**be rooted**) be firmly established. **2** (of a plant) grow roots. **3** rummage. **4** (of an animal) turn up the ground with its snout in search of

food. □ **root for** informal support enthusiastically. **root out** find and get rid of. **take root** become established. ■ **rootless** adj.

rope n. **1** strong thick cord. **2** (**the ropes**) informal the established procedure. •v. **1** catch or tie with rope. **2** (**rope in**) persuade to take part in. □ **on the ropes** in a state of near collapse.

ropy (or **ropey**) adj. informal poor in quality or health.

rosary n. (pl. **rosaries**) **1** (in the RC Church) a set series of prayers. **2** a string of beads for keeping count of prayers said.

rose¹ n. **1** a scented flower growing on a prickly bush. **2** a warm pink colour. □ **rosewood** the dark wood of a tropical tree, used for making furniture.

rose² past of RISE.

rosé /roh-zay/ n. light pink wine.

rosemary n. an evergreen shrub with leaves used as a herb.

rosette n. a round badge made of ribbon.

Rosh Hashana /rosh huh-shah-nuh/ (or **Rosh Hashanah**) n. the Jewish New Year festival.

rosin n. a resin rubbed on the bows of stringed instruments.

roster n. a list of people's names and their turns of duty etc.

rostrum n. (pl. **rostra** or **rostrums**) a platform for standing on to make a speech, conduct an orchestra, etc.

rosy adj. (**rosier**, **rosiest**) **1** pink. **2** promising.

rot v. (**rotting**, **rotted**) decay as a result of bacterial action. •n. **1** the process of rotting. **2** informal nonsense.

r

rota n. a list showing when each of a number of people has to do a particular job.

rotary adj. **1** revolving around a central point. **2** having a rotating part or parts.

rotate v. **1** move in a circle round a central point. **2** (of a job) pass on a regular basis to each of a group in turn. **3** grow different crops one after the other on a piece of land. ■ **rotation** n. **rotatory** adj.

rote n. regular repetition of something to be learned.

rotisserie n. a rotating spit for roasting meat.

rotor n. the rotating part of a machine.

rotten adj. **1** decayed. **2** corrupt. **3** informal very bad.

Rottweiler n. a large powerful breed of dog.

rotund adj. rounded and plump. ■ **rotundity** n.

rotunda n. a round building or room.

rouble (or **ruble**) n. the basic unit of money of Russia.

roué /roo-ay/ n. a man who leads an immoral life.

rouge n. a cosmetic for colouring the cheeks.

rough adj. **1** not smooth or level. **2** not gentle. **3** (of weather or the sea) wild and stormy. **4** plain and basic. **5** not detailed; approximate. **6** harsh in sound or taste. **7** informal difficult and unpleasant. •n. **1** a basic version. **2** long grass at the edge of a golf course. •v. **1** (**rough out**) make a first version of. **2** (**rough it**) informal live with only very basic necessities. **3** (**rough up**) informal beat up. □ **rough and ready** basic but effective. **rough and tumble** a

competitive situation without rules. **rough diamond** a person of good character but lacking manners or education. ■ **roughen** v. **roughly** adv. **roughness** n.

roughage n. indigestible material in cereals, vegetables, and fruit.

roughshod adj. (**ride roughshod over**) fail to consider the wishes or feelings of.

roulette n. a gambling game in which a ball is dropped on to a revolving wheel with numbered compartments.

round adj. **1** curved, circular, cylindrical, or spherical. **2** (of a number) expressed in convenient units rather than exactly. •n. **1** a circular shape or piece. **2** a route by which a number of people or places are visited in turn. **3** a regular sequence of activities. **4** each of a sequence of stages in a sports contest. **5** a song for several voices, each singing the same theme but starting one after another. **6** the amount of ammunition needed to fire one shot. **7** a set of drinks bought for all the members of a group. •adv. **1** in a circle or curve. **2** so as to include a whole area or group. **3** so as to face in the opposite direction. **4** so as to surround. •prep. **1** on every side of. **2** so as to encircle. •v. **1** pass and go round. **2** make or become round in shape. □ **round off** complete. **round robin** a tournament in which each competitor plays in turn against every other. **round trip** a journey to a place and back again. **round-up** a summary. **round up** collect into one place. **round up/down** make a figure less exact but more convenient. **roundworm** a parasitic

worm with a rounded body.
■ **roundness** n.

roundabout n. **1** a road junction with a circular island round which traffic has to move in one direction. **2** a large revolving device in a playground. **3** a merry-go-round. • adj. indirect.

roundel n. a small disc or circular design.

rounders n. a ball game in which players run round a circuit after hitting the ball with a bat.

Roundhead n. hist. a supporter of Parliament in the English Civil War.

roundly adv. in a firm or thorough way.

rouse v. **1** wake. **2** stir up; arouse.

rout n. **1** a disorderly retreat. **2** a decisive defeat. • v. defeat decisively.

route n. a way taken in getting from a starting point to a destination. • v. (**routeing** or **routing**, **routed**) send along a route.

routine n. **1** a regular procedure. **2** a set sequence in a performance. • adj. performed as part of a regular procedure. ■ **routinely** adv.

roux /roo/ n. (pl. **roux**) a mixture of butter and flour used in making sauces.

rove v. wander. ■ **rover** n.

row[1] /roh/ n. **1** a number of people or things in a line. **2** a period of rowing. • v. propel a boat with oars.

row[2] /row/ n. **1** an angry quarrel. **2** a loud noise. • v. quarrel angrily.

rowan n. a small tree with red berries.

rowdy adj. (**rowdier**, **rowdiest**) noisy and disorderly. • n. (pl. **rowdies**) a rowdy person. ■ **rowdily** adv. **rowdiness** n.

rowlock /rol-luhk/ n. a fitting on the side of a boat for holding an oar.

royal adj. **1** of or having the status of a king or queen or a member of their family. **2** impressive in quality or size. • n. informal a member of a royal family. □ **royal blue** a deep, vivid blue. ■ **royally** adv.

royalist n. a person supporting the principle of having a king or queen.

royalty n. (pl. **royalties**) **1** people of royal status. **2** the status of a king or queen. **3** a sum paid to the author of a book for each copy sold or to a composer for each performance of a work.

rpm abbrev. revolutions per minute.

RSI abbrev. repetitive strain injury.

RSPCA abbrev. Royal Society for the Prevention of Cruelty to Animals.

RSVP abbrev. répondez s'il vous plaît; please reply.

rub v. (**rubbing**, **rubbed**) **1** move the hand, a cloth, etc. back and forth over a surface while pressing against it. **2** dry, smooth, or make sore by rubbing. **3** (**rub out**) remove pencil marks with a rubber. • n. **1** an act of rubbing. **2** an ointment for rubbing on the skin.

rubber n. **1** a tough elastic substance made from a tropical plant or from chemicals. **2** a piece of this for erasing pencil marks. **3** a unit of play in the card game bridge. □ **rubber-stamp** approve automatically without proper consideration. ■ **rubbery** adj.

rubberneck v. informal turn to stare at something as you pass.

rubbish n. **1** waste material. **2** nonsense. •v. informal criticize harshly.

rubble n. rough fragments of stone, brick, etc.

rubella n. a viral disease with symptoms like mild measles.

rubidium n. a soft silvery metallic element.

ruble var. of **ROUBLE**.

rubric n. **1** a document heading. **2** a set of instructions.

ruby n. (pl. **rubies**) **1** a deep red precious stone. **2** a deep red colour. □ **ruby wedding** the 40th anniversary of a wedding.

ruche /roosh/ n. a frill or pleat. ∎ **ruched** adj.

ruck n. **1** Rugby a loose scrum. **2** a tightly packed crowd. •v. (**ruck up**) make or form creases.

rucksack n. a bag carried on the back.

ruckus n. a row or commotion.

ructions pl. n. informal angry protests or trouble.

rudder n. a hinged upright piece of wood or metal at the back of a boat or aircraft, used for steering.

ruddy adj. (**ruddier**, **ruddiest**) of a reddish colour.

rude adj. **1** impolite or bad-mannered. **2** referring to sex in an offensive way. **3** sudden or abrupt. □ **in rude health** very healthy. ∎ **rudely** adv. **rudeness** n.

rudiment n. **1** (**rudiments**) the basic facts of a subject. **2** an undeveloped part.

rudimentary adj. **1** basic or elementary. **2** not highly developed.

rue v. bitterly regret.

rueful adj. expressing regret. ∎ **ruefully** adv.

ruff n. **1** a starched frill worn round the neck. **2** a ring of feathers or hair round the neck of a bird or mammal.

ruffian n. a violent person.

ruffle v. **1** disturb the smooth surface of. **2** upset or worry. •n. a gathered frill.

rug n. **1** a small carpet. **2** a thick blanket.

rugby n. a team game played with an oval ball that may be kicked or carried.

rugged adj. **1** rocky or uneven. **2** (of a man) having strong, attractive features. ∎ **ruggedly** adv.

rugger n. informal rugby.

ruin n. **1** the state of being destroyed or severely damaged. **2** (or **ruins**) a badly damaged building. **3** the loss of everything a person owns. •v. **1** destroy or severely damage. **2** make bankrupt or very poor. ∎ **ruination** n.

ruinous adj. **1** disastrous or destructive. **2** in ruins.

rule n. **1** a statement of what must be done or not done. **2** control over a people or country. **3** a ruler for measuring etc. •v. **1** have control over. **2** state with legal authority. **3** make lines on paper. □ **as a rule** usually. **rule of thumb** a rough guide. **rule out** exclude. **the rule** the normal state of things.

ruler n. **1** a person who rules. **2** a strip of plastic, wood, etc. for drawing straight lines or measuring distances.

ruling n. an authoritative decision or statement.

rum n. an alcoholic spirit made from sugar cane. •adj. informal, dated peculiar.

rumba n. a ballroom dance.

rumble v. **1** make a low continuous sound. **2** *informal* find out the truth about. •n. a rumbling sound.

rumbustious adj. *informal* boisterous or difficult to control.

ruminant n. a mammal that chews the cud.

ruminate v. **1** think deeply. **2** chew the cud. ∎ **rumination** n. **ruminative** adj.

rummage v. search in a disorderly way. •n. an act of rummaging.

rummy n. a card game.

rumour (US **rumor**) n. a story spread among a number of people which is not confirmed or may be false. •v. (**be rumoured**) be spread as a rumour.

rump n. the hind part of the body of a mammal or the lower back of a bird.

rumple v. make untidy.

rumpus n. (pl. **rumpuses**) a noisy disturbance.

run v. (**running, ran**; *past part.* **run**) **1** move at a speed faster than walking. **2** be in charge of. **3** continue or proceed. **4** function or cause to function. **5** be at or in a particular level or state. **6** (of a liquid) flow or spread. **7** stand as a candidate in an election. **8** (of a bus, train, etc.) travel on a particular route. **9** publish in a newspaper etc. •n. **1** an act or spell of running. **2** a journey or route. **3** a continuous period or sequence. **4** an enclosed area in which animals or birds may run freely. **5** (**the run of**) unrestricted use of or access to a place. **6** a point scored in cricket or baseball. **7** a ladder in tights etc. ∎ **in** (or **out of**) **the running** in (or no longer in) with a chance of success. **on the run** escaping. **run down**

1 criticize. **2** reduce in size or resources. **run-down 1** in a poor or neglected state. **2** tired and rather unwell. **run into** meet by chance. **run off** produce a copy on a machine. **run-of-the-mill** ordinary. **run out** use up or be used up. **run over** knock down with a vehicle. **run up** allow a bill to build up. **run-up** the period before an important event. **runway** a strip of hard ground where aircraft take off and land.

rune n. a letter of an ancient Germanic alphabet. ∎ **runic** adj.

rung¹ n. a horizontal bar on a ladder.

rung² *past part.* of RING².

runnel n. a stream.

runner n. **1** a person or animal that runs. **2** a messenger. **3** a rod, groove, or roller on which something slides. **4** a creeping shoot of a plant which can take root. **5** a long, narrow rug. ▫ **runner-up** (pl. **runners-up**) a competitor who comes second.

runny adj. (**runnier, runniest**) **1** more liquid than is usual. **2** (of the nose) producing mucus.

runt n. the smallest animal in a litter.

rupee n. the basic unit of money of India, Pakistan, etc.

rupture v. **1** break or burst suddenly. **2** suffer an abdominal hernia. •n. **1** an instance of rupturing. **2** an abdominal hernia.

rural adj. of the countryside.

ruse n. a trick or deception.

rush v. **1** move or act very quickly or too quickly. **2** produce, deal with, or transport very quickly. **3** dash towards in a sudden attack. •n. **1** a sudden quick movement. **2** a very busy spell of activity. **3** a

r

sudden strong feeling. **4** a water plant used in making baskets etc. □ **rush hour** a time at the start and end of the working day when traffic is heaviest.

rusk n. a biscuit for babies.

russet n. a reddish-brown colour.

Russian n. **1** a person from Russia. **2** the language of Russia. • adj. of Russia.

rust n. a reddish-brown flaky coating formed on iron exposed to moisture. • v. be affected with rust.

rustic adj. **1** of life in the country. **2** simple and charming.

rustle v. **1** make a soft crackling sound. **2** steal cattle, horses, or sheep. **3** (**rustle up**) informal produce food or a drink quickly. • n. a rustling sound. ■ **rustler** n.

rusty adj. **1** affected by rust. **2** (of knowledge or a skill) weakened by lack of recent practice.

rut n. **1** a deep track made by wheels. **2** a dull pattern of behaviour that is hard to change. **3** an annual period of sexual activity in deer etc., when males fight for access to the females. • v. (**rutting**, **rutted**) (of male deer etc.) be in rut.

ruthless adj. having no pity; hard and determined. ■ **ruthlessly** adv. **ruthlessness** n.

rye n. **1** a cereal plant. **2** whisky made from rye. □ **ryegrass** a grass used for fodder.

Ss

S abbrev. **1** South or Southern. **2** (**s**) seconds.

SA abbrev. **1** South Africa. **2** South Australia.

sabbath n. a day for rest and religious worship.

sabbatical n. a period of paid leave for study or travel.

sable n. a dark brown marten native to Japan and Siberia.

sabotage /sab-uh-tahzh/ v. deliberately destroy or damage. • n. the act of sabotaging. ■ **saboteur** n.

sabre (US **saber**) n. a curved sword.

sac n. a hollow, flexible bag-like structure.

saccharin n. a synthetic sugar substitute.

saccharine adj. excessively sweet or sentimental.

sacerdotal adj. of priests.

sachet /sa-shay/ n. a small sealed packet.

sack n. **1** a large strong bag for storing or carrying goods. **2** (**the sack**) informal dismissal from employment. • v. **1** informal dismiss from employment. **2** (in the past) attack, steal from, and destroy a place. □ **sackcloth** a rough fabric woven from flax or hemp.

sacrament n. (in the Christian Church) a symbolic religious ceremony. ■ **sacramental** adj.

sacred *adj.* **1** connected with God or a god or goddess, and treated as holy. **2** religious. □ **sacred cow** an established idea, custom, etc. regarded as above criticism.

sacrifice *n.* **1** the killing of an animal or person or giving up of a possession as an offering to a god or goddess. **2** an animal, person, etc. offered in this way. **3** an act of giving up something valued for the sake of something else. • *v.* give as a sacrifice. ■ **sacrificial** *adj.*

sacrilege *n.* disrespect to something sacred or highly valued. ■ **sacrilegious** *adj.*

sacristan *n.* a person in charge of a sacristy.

sacristy *n.* (*pl.* **sacristies**) a room in a church where sacred objects are kept.

sacrosanct *adj.* too important or valuable to be changed.

sacrum *n.* (*pl.* **sacra** or **sacrums**) a triangular bone between the two hip bones. ■ **sacral** *adj.*

sad *adj.* (**sadder**, **saddest**) feeling or causing sorrow: *a sad story.* ■ **sadden** *v.* **sadly** *adv.* **sadness** *n.*

saddle *n.* **1** a seat on a bicycle or motorcycle or fastened on the back of a horse. **2** a joint of meat consisting of the two loins. • *v.* **1** put a saddle on a horse. **2** burden with a task.

saddler *n.* a person who makes, repairs, or deals in equipment for horses.

sadism *n.* pleasure felt from hurting or humiliating other people. ■ **sadist** *n.* **sadistic** *adj.*

safari *n.* (*pl.* **safaris**) a trip to observe or hunt animals in their natural environment. □ **safari park** an area where animals are kept in

the open and may be observed by visitors.

safe *adj.* **1** protected from danger or risk. **2** not leading to harm. **3** giving security. • *n.* a strong cabinet with a complex lock, for storing valuables. □ **safe conduct** protection from arrest or harm. ■ **safely** *adv.*

safeguard *n.* a measure taken to protect or prevent something. • *v.* protect.

safety *n.* the condition of being safe. □ **safety belt** a seat belt. **safety pin** a pin with a point bent back to the head and held in a guard when closed. **safety valve** a valve that opens automatically to relieve excessive pressure.

saffron *n.* a yellow spice.

sag *v.* (**sagging**, **sagged**) sink or droop gradually. ■ **saggy** *adj.*

saga *n.* a long story.

sagacious *adj.* wise. ■ **sagacity** *n.*

sage *n.* **1** a herb. **2** a very wise man. • *adj.* wise. ■ **sagely** *adv.*

sago *n.* a pudding made with starchy granules from a palm tree, cooked with milk.

said past & past part. of **SAY.**

sail *n.* **1** a piece of fabric spread on a mast to catch the wind and propel a boat or ship. **2** a trip in a sailing boat. **3** a flat board attached to the arm of a windmill. • *v.* **1** travel in a ship or boat. **2** begin a voyage. **3** control a boat. **4** move smoothly. **5** (**sail through**) *informal* succeed easily at. □ **sailboard** a board with a mast and a sail, used in windsurfing. **sailcloth** strong fabric for sails. **sailing boat** (or **sailboat**) a boat with sails.

sailor *n.* a member of a ship's crew.

s

saint n. **1** a very good person who is declared to be a saint by the Church after death. **2** a very good or kind person. ∎ **sainthood** n. **saintliness** n. **saintly** adj.

sake¹ n. **(for the sake of)** **1** so as to get or keep. **2** out of consideration for.

sake² /sah-ki/ n. a Japanese alcoholic drink made from rice.

salaam /suh-lahm/ n. a low bow with the hand touching the forehead, used as a gesture of respect by Muslims.

salacious adj. containing too much sexual detail.

salad n. a cold dish of raw vegetables.

salamander n. an animal resembling a newt.

salami n. (pl. **salami** or **salamis**) a type of spicy preserved sausage.

salary n. (pl. **salaries**) a fixed regular payment made by an employer to an employee. ∎ **salaried** adj.

sale n. **1** the exchange of something for money. **2** (**sales**) the activity or profession of selling. **3** a period in which goods are sold at reduced prices. **4** a public event at which goods are sold. □ **salesman** (or **saleswoman** or **salesperson**) a person whose job is to sell goods. ∎ **saleable** (or **salable**) adj.

salient adj. most noticeable or important.

saline adj. containing salt. ∎ **salinity** n.

saliva n. a watery liquid produced in the mouth. ∎ **salivary** adj.

salivate v. produce saliva. ∎ **salivation** n.

sallow adj. (of the complexion) yellowish in colour.

sally n. (pl. **sallies**) **1** a sudden charge out of a place surrounded by an enemy. **2** a witty reply. ∎ v. (**sallying**, **sallied**) (**sally forth**) set out.

salmon n. (pl. **salmon**) a large edible fish with pink flesh.

salmonella n. a bacterium causing food poisoning.

salon n. **1** a place where a hairdresser, beautician, etc. works. **2** a reception room in a large house.

saloon n. **1** a car with a separate boot. **2** a public lounge on a ship.

salsa n. **1** a Latin American dance performed to music combining jazz and rock. **2** a spicy sauce.

salt n. **1** a white crystalline substance (sodium chloride), used for flavouring and preserving food. **2** a chemical compound of an acid and a metal. ∎ v. flavour or preserve with salt. □ **salt cellar** a container for salt. **saltpetre** (US **saltpeter**) potassium nitrate. **the salt of the earth** a very kind, reliable, or honest person. **take with a pinch** (or **grain**) **of salt** recognize as untrue or exaggerated. **worth your salt** competent. ∎ **saltiness** n. **salty** adj.

salubrious adj. good for the health.

salutary adj. (esp. of something unpleasant) producing a good effect.

salutation n. a greeting.

salute n. **1** a gesture of respect or acknowledgement. **2** a raising of a hand to the head, made as a formal military gesture of respect. ∎ v. **1** make a salute to. **2** express admiration for.

salvage v. **1** save from being lost or destroyed. **2** rescue a ship or its cargo from loss at sea. •n. **1** the act of salvaging. **2** salvaged cargo.

salvation n. the saving of someone from harm or (in Christian belief) from the consequences of sin.

salve n. **1** a soothing ointment. **2** something that reduces guilty feelings. •v. reduce guilty feelings.

salver n. a tray.

salvia n. a garden plant with scarlet flowers.

salvo n. (pl. **salvos** or **salvoes**) **1** a simultaneous firing of guns. **2** a sudden series of aggressive statements or acts.

Samaritan (or **good Samaritan**) n. a kind or helpful person.

samba n. a Brazilian dance.

same adj. **1** exactly alike. **2** referring to a person or thing already mentioned. •pron. the person or thing already mentioned. •adv. in the same way. ■ **sameness** n.

Sami pl. n. the Lapps of northern Scandinavia.

samosa n. a triangular fried Indian pastry containing spiced vegetables or meat.

samovar n. a Russian tea urn.

sampan n. a small boat used in the Far East.

sample n. **1** a small part or quantity intended to show what the whole is like. **2** a specimen. •v. **1** take a sample or samples of. **2** try out. **3** take an extract from one musical recording and use it as part of another.

sampler n. **1** a piece of embroidery showing various stitches. **2** a device for sampling music.

samurai /sam-uh-ry/ n. (pl. **samurai**) hist. a member of a powerful Japanese military class.

sanatorium n. (pl. **sanatoriums** or **sanatoria**) **1** a place for the care of people with a long-term illness or convalescents. **2** a place in a boarding school for sick pupils.

sanctify v. (**sanctifying**, **sanctified**) make or declare holy. ■ **sanctification** n.

sanctimonious adj. making a show of being morally superior.

sanction n. **1** (**sanctions**) measures taken by a state to force another into doing something. **2** a penalty for disobeying a law. **3** official permission. •v. give permission for.

sanctity n. (pl. **sanctities**) **1** holiness. **2** supreme importance.

sanctuary n. (pl. **sanctuaries**) **1** a place of safety. **2** a nature reserve. **3** a holy place.

sanctum n. (pl. **sanctums**) a sacred or private place.

sand n. **1** very fine particles of crushed rock. **2** (**sands**) a wide area of sand. •v. smooth with sandpaper or a sander. □ **sandbag** a bag of sand, used to protect against floods etc. **sandbank** a raised bank of sand in the sea or a river. **sandblast** roughen or clean with a jet of sand. **sandcastle** a model castle built out of sand. **sandpaper** paper with a coating of sand or another rough substance, for smoothing surfaces. **sandstone** rock formed from compressed sand. **sandstorm** a strong desert wind carrying clouds of sand.

sandal n. a shoe with a partly open upper part or straps.

sandalwood n. the scented wood of an Asian tree.

S

sander n. a power tool used for smoothing a surface.

sandwich n. two pieces of bread with a filling between them. •v. insert between two people or things. □ **sandwich course** a course of study which includes periods working in business or industry.

sandy adj. (**sandier, sandiest**) **1** covered in or consisting of sand. **2** light yellowish brown.

sane adj. **1** not mad. **2** sensible.

sang past of SING.

sangfroid /song-frwah/ n. calmness in difficult situations.

sangria n. a Spanish drink of red wine, lemonade, and fruit.

sanguinary adj. old use involving much bloodshed.

sanguine adj. optimistic.

sanitarium n. US a sanatorium.

sanitary adj. **1** of sanitation. **2** hygienic. □ **sanitary towel** a pad worn to absorb menstrual blood.

sanitation n. arrangements to protect public health, esp. the provision of clean drinking water and the disposal of sewage.

sanitize (or **-ise**) v. **1** make hygienic. **2** make something unpleasant seem more acceptable.

sanity n. the condition of being sane.

sank past of SINK.

Sanskrit n. an ancient language of India.

sap n. the liquid in plants, carrying food to all parts. •v. (**sapping, sapped**) gradually weaken.

sapling n. a young tree.

sapper n. a military engineer who lays or finds and defuses mines.

sapphire n. **1** a blue precious stone. **2** a bright blue colour.

saprophyte n. a plant or fungus living on decaying matter.

sarcasm n. the use of irony to mock or convey contempt.
■ **sarcastic** adj. **sarcastically** adv.

sarcoma n. a cancerous tumour found esp. in connective tissue.

sarcophagus n. (pl. **sarcophagi**) a stone coffin.

sardine n. a young pilchard or similar small fish.

sardonic adj. mocking.
■ **sardonically** adv.

sari n. (pl. **saris**) a length of fabric draped round the body, worn by women from the Indian subcontinent.

sarong n. a length of fabric wrapped round the body and tucked at the waist or armpits.

sartorial adj. of a person's style of dress.

SAS abbrev. Special Air Service.

sash n. **1** a strip of cloth worn over one shoulder or round the waist. **2** a frame holding the glass in a window. □ **sash window** a window with two sashes which can be slid up and down to open it.

sashay v. informal swing the hips from side to side when walking.

Sassenach n. Sc. & Ir. derog. an English person.

sassy adj. (**sassier, sassiest**) informal confident or cheeky.

SAT abbrev. standard assessment task.

sat past & past part. of SIT.

Satan n. the Devil.

satanic adj. of Satan or the worship of Satan.

satanism n. the worship of Satan.
■ **satanist** n. & adj.

satchel n. a bag with a long strap, worn over one shoulder.

sated adj. fully satisfied.

satellite n. **1** an artificial object placed in orbit round a planet to collect information or for communication. **2** a natural object orbiting a planet. • adj. (of a country etc.) dependent on another. □ **satellite dish** a bowl-shaped aerial for receiving satellite television. **satellite television** television in which the signals are broadcast via satellite.

satiate /say-shi-ayt/ v. satisfy fully. ■ **satiation** n. **satiety** n.

satin n. a smooth, glossy fabric. ■ **satiny** adj.

satire n. **1** the use of humour, irony, etc. to criticize or ridicule. **2** a play, novel, etc. using satire. ■ **satirical** adj. **satirically** adv. **satirist** n.

satirize (or **-ise**) v. criticize using satire.

satisfaction n. **1** pleasure arising from having what you want or need. **2** a satisfactory way of dealing with an injustice, complaint, etc.

satisfactory adj. acceptable. ■ **satisfactorily** adv.

satisfy v. (**satisfying**, **satisfied**) **1** please someone by doing what they want or giving them what they need. **2** meet a demand, desire, or need. ■ **satisfaction** n.

satsuma n. a variety of tangerine.

saturate v. **1** soak thoroughly. **2** supply a market beyond the point at which there is demand for a product. ■ **saturation** n.

Saturday n. the day before Sunday.

saturnine adj. gloomy or brooding.

satyr /sat-er/ n. a woodland god in classical mythology, with a goat's ears, legs, and tail.

sauce n. **1** a thick liquid served with food to add moistness and flavour. **2** informal impudence. □ **saucepan** a deep cooking pan with a long handle.

saucer n. a shallow dish on which a cup stands.

saucy adj. (**saucier**, **sauciest**) informal **1** cheeky. **2** sexually suggestive. ■ **saucily** adv.

sauerkraut /sow-er-krowt/ n. chopped pickled cabbage.

sauna /saw-nuh/ n. a small room used as a hot-air or steam bath.

saunter v. stroll. • n. a stroll.

sausage n. a short tube of minced meat encased in a skin.

sauté /soh-tay/ v. (**sautéing**, **sautéed** or **sautéd**) fry quickly in shallow fat.

savage adj. **1** fierce and violent. **2** cruel and vicious. **3** uncivilized or primitive. • n. a primitive and uncivilized person. • v. attack fiercely and maul. ■ **savagely** adv. **savagery** n.

savannah n. a grassy plain in tropical regions.

save v. **1** rescue or protect from harm or danger. **2** store or keep for future use. **3** avoid or guard against. **4** prevent the scoring of a goal. • n. an act of preventing a goal. ■ **saver** n.

saveloy n. a smoked pork sausage.

savings pl. n. money saved.

saviour (US **savior**) n. a person who saves someone from danger or harm.

savoir faire /sav-war **fair**/ n. the ability to act appropriately in social situations.

S

savour (US **savor**) v. **1** enjoy the taste of food or drink. **2** enjoy or appreciate fully. •n. a flavour or smell.

savoury (US **savory**) adj. **1** (of food) salty or spicy. **2** morally acceptable.

saw¹ n. **1** a cutting tool with a jagged blade. **2** a proverb or wise saying. •v. (**sawing**, **sawed**; past part. **sawn** or US **sawed**) cut with a saw.

saw² past of **SEE**.

sax n. informal a saxophone.

saxophone n. a metal wind instrument. ■ **saxophonist** n.

say v. (**saying**, **said**) **1** speak words. **2** convey or express information. **3** (**be said**) be reported. **4** suggest as an example or theory. •n. an opportunity to state your opinion.

saying n. a well-known phrase or proverb.

scab n. **1** a crust forming over a wound. **2** informal, derog. a person who refuses to take part in a strike. ■ **scabby** adj.

scabbard n. a cover for a sword or dagger.

scabies n. a skin disease causing itching.

scabrous adj. **1** indecent or sordid. **2** covered with scabs.

scaffold n. **1** a platform used formerly for public executions. **2** a structure of scaffolding.

scaffolding n. a structure of planks and metal poles, used while working on a building.

scald v. burn with very hot liquid or steam. •n. a burn caused by scalding.

scale n. **1** relative size or extent. **2** an ordered range of values for measuring or grading something.

3 (**scales**) an instrument for weighing. **4** a fixed series of notes in a system of music. **5** each of the overlapping plates protecting the skin of fish and reptiles. **6** a white deposit formed in a kettle etc. by hard water. **7** tartar on teeth. •v. **1** climb. **2** represent in proportion to the size of the original. **3** remove scale or scales from. ■ **scaly** adj.

scalene adj. (of a triangle) having unequal sides.

scallop n. **1** an edible shellfish with two hinged fan-shaped shells. **2** each of a series of small curves as a decorative edging. ■ **scalloped** adj.

scallywag n. informal a mischievous person.

scalp n. the skin covering the top and back of the head. •v. cut the scalp from.

scalpel n. a surgeon's knife with a small blade.

scam n. informal a dishonest scheme.

scamp n. informal a mischievous person.

scamper v. run with quick light steps.

scampi pl. n. the tails of large prawns, coated in breadcrumbs and fried.

scan v. (**scanning**, **scanned**) **1** look over quickly to find relevant features. **2** move a detector or beam across. **3** convert a document etc. into digital form for storing or processing on a computer. **4** analyse the metre of a line of verse. **5** (of verse) follow metrical rules. •n. an act of scanning. ■ **scanner** n.

scandal n. **1** an action or event causing outrage. **2** outrage or gossip arising from this. ■ **scandalous** adj. **scandalously** adv.

scandalize (or **-ise**) v. shock or outrage.

Scandinavian adj. of the countries of Scandinavia, esp. Norway, Sweden, and Denmark.

scandium n. a soft silvery-white metallic element.

scansion n. the rhythm of a line of verse.

scant adj. barely enough.

scanty adj. (**scantier**, **scantiest**) too little in quantity or amount. ■ **scantily** adv.

scapegoat n. a person blamed for the wrongdoings of others.

scapula n. (pl. **scapulae** or **scapulas**) the shoulder blade. ■ **scapular** adj.

scar n. **1** a mark left where a wound has healed. **2** a lasting effect of an unpleasant experience. • v. (**scarring**, **scarred**) mark or be marked with a scar.

scarab n. a beetle treated as sacred in ancient Egypt.

scarce adj. **1** available in quantities that are too small to meet demand. **2** rare. ■ **scarcity** n.

scarcely adv. **1** only just. **2** surely or probably not.

scare v. frighten or be frightened. • n. **1** a fright. **2** a period of general alarm. □ **scarecrow** a figure set up to scare birds away from crops. **scaremongering** the spreading of alarming rumours.

scarf n. (pl. **scarves** or **scarfs**) a length or square of fabric worn around the neck or head.

scarlet n. a bright red colour. □ **scarlet fever** an infectious disease causing fever and a scarlet rash.

scarp n. a steep slope.

scary adj. (**scarier**, **scariest**) informal frightening. ■ **scarily** adv.

scathing adj. harshly critical.

scatological adj. obsessed with excrement. ■ **scatology** n.

scatter v. **1** throw in various random directions. **2** separate and move off in different directions. □ **scatterbrained** (or **scatty**) disorganized and forgetful.

scavenge v. **1** search for and collect anything usable from waste. **2** (of an animal) search for dead animals as food. ■ **scavenger** n.

scenario n. (pl. **scenarios**) **1** a possible sequence of future events. **2** a written outline of a film, play, etc.

scene n. **1** the place where an incident occurs. **2** a view of a place. **3** an incident. **4** a sequence of continuous action in a play, film, etc. **5** a display of emotion or anger. **6** an area of activity or interest. □ **behind the scenes** out of public view.

scenery n. **1** the features of a landscape. **2** the background used to represent a place on a stage or film set.

scenic adj. picturesque.

scent n. **1** a pleasant smell. **2** perfume. **3** a trail left by an animal, indicated by its smell. • v. **1** give a pleasant smell to. **2** detect by smell. **3** sense the imminence of.

sceptic /skep-tik/ (US **skeptic**) n. a sceptical person. ■ **scepticism** n.

sceptical adj. not easily convinced; having doubts. ■ **sceptically** adv.

s

sceptre /sep-ter/ (*US* **scepter**) *n.* a staff carried by a monarch on ceremonial occasions.

schedule *n.* a programme or timetable of intended events. •*v.* **1** plan for a particular time. **2** (**scheduled**) (of a flight) forming part of a regular service rather than specially chartered.

schema *n.* (*pl.* **schemata** or **schemas**) an outline of a plan or theory.

schematic *adj.* (of a diagram) outlining the main features; simplified. ■ **schematically** *adv.* **schematize** (or **-ise**) *v.*

scheme *n.* **1** a systematic plan for achieving something. **2** a plot. **3** a system or pattern. •*v.* plot.

scherzo /skair-tsoh/ *n.* (*pl.* **scherzos** or **scherzi**) a lively piece of music.

schism /ski-z'm/ *n.* a strong disagreement within an organization, causing it to split into groups. ■ **schismatic** *adj.*

schist /shist/ *n.* a rock consisting of different layers of minerals.

schizoid /skit-soyd/ *adj.* having a mental condition similar to schizophrenia.

schizophrenia *n.* a mental disorder whose symptoms include withdrawal from reality into fantasy. ■ **schizophrenic** *adj. & n.*

schmaltz *n. informal* excessive sentimentality. ■ **schmaltzy** *adj.*

schnapps *n.* a strong alcoholic drink.

scholar *n.* **1** a person studying at an advanced level. **2** the holder of a scholarship. ■ **scholarly** *adj.*

scholarship *n.* **1** academic study. **2** a grant made to support a student's education.

scholastic *adj.* of schools or education.

school *n.* **1** an educational institution. **2** a group of artists, philosophers, etc. sharing similar ideas. **3** a large group of fish or sea mammals. •*v.* educate or train.

schooner *n.* **1** a sailing ship. **2** a large sherry glass.

sciatica /sy-at-ik-uh/ *n.* pain in the back, hip, and thigh.

science *n.* the study or knowledge of the physical world, based on observation and experiment. ■ **scientific** *adj.* **scientifically** *adv.*

scientist *n.* a person who studies or is an expert in science.

scimitar /sim-i-ter/ *n.* a short curved sword.

scintilla *n.* a trace.

scintillating *adj.* very impressive or skilful.

scion /sy-uhn/ *n.* **1** a plant shoot cut off for grafting. **2** a descendant of a family.

scissors *pl. n.* a cutting tool with two crossing pivoted blades.

sclerosis *n.* abnormal hardening of body tissue.

scoff *v.* **1** speak about scornfully. **2** *informal* eat greedily.

scold *v.* angrily rebuke.

sconce *n.* a candle holder attached to a wall.

scone *n.* a small plain cake.

scoop *n.* **1** a utensil resembling a spoon, with a short handle and a deep bowl. **2** *informal* a news item printed by one newspaper before its rivals. •*v.* **1** pick up or hollow out with a scoop. **2** pick up in a quick, smooth movement.

scooter *n.* **1** a light motorcycle. **2** a child's toy with two wheels and a long steering handle, moved by pushing a foot against the ground.

scope n. **1** opportunity for doing something. **2** the range of a subject, activity, etc.

scorch v. burn on the surface.

score n. **1** the number of points, goals, etc. achieved in a game. **2** (pl. **score**) a set of twenty. **3** the written music for a composition. • v. **1** gain a point, goal, etc. in a game. **2** record the score during a game. **3** cut a mark on a surface. **4** (**score out**) cross out a word or words. **5** arrange a piece of music. ■ **scorer** n.

scorn n. open contempt. • v. **1** express scorn for. **2** reject with scorn. ■ **scornful** adj. **scornfully** adv.

scorpion n. a small six-legged creature with a poisonous sting at the end of its tail.

Scot n. a person from Scotland.

Scotch n. whisky made in Scotland. • adj. dated Scottish.

! Use **Scotch** only to refer to things: people are **Scots** or **Scottish**.

scotch v. put an end to a rumour.

scot-free adv. without punishment or injury.

Scots adj. Scottish. • n. the form of English used in Scotland.

Scottish adj. of Scotland or its people.

scoundrel n. a dishonest person.

scour v. **1** clean by rubbing with something rough. **2** search thoroughly.

scourge n. a cause of great suffering. **2** hist. a whip. • v. **1** cause suffering to. **2** hist. whip.

scout n. **1** a person sent ahead to gather information about an enemy. **2** (or **talent scout**) a person whose job is searching for talented performers. • v. **1** search. **2** act as a scout.

scowl n. a bad-tempered expression. • v. make a scowl.

scrabble v. grope around with the fingers to find or hold on to something.

scraggy adj. thin and bony.

scram v. (**scramming**, **scrammed**) informal go away quickly.

scramble v. **1** move quickly and awkwardly, using hands as well as feet. **2** muddle. **3** put a transmission into a form intelligible only with a decoding device. **4** stir and cook beaten eggs. **5** (of fighter aircraft) take off immediately in an emergency. • n. **1** an act of scrambling. **2** a motorcycle race over rough ground. ■ **scrambler** n.

scrap n. **1** a small piece. **2** (**scraps**) uneaten food left after a meal. **3** waste metal that can be used again. **4** informal a short fight or quarrel. • v. (**scrapping**, **scrapped**) **1** abolish or remove from use. **2** informal have a short fight or quarrel. □ **scrapbook** a book for sticking cuttings etc. in.

scrape v. **1** drag a hard or sharp implement across a surface. **2** rub against a rough surface. **3** just manage to achieve. • n. **1** an act of scraping. **2** an injury or mark caused by scraping. **3** informal an embarrassing or difficult situation.

scrappy adj. disorganized or incomplete.

scratch v. **1** mark or wound with something sharp. **2** rub part of the body with the fingernails to relieve itching. **3** abandon a plan or withdraw from a competition. • n. a mark or wound made by

s

scratching. • adj. assembled from whatever is available. □ from scratch from the very beginning. scratch card a card with sections which may be scraped to reveal whether a prize has been won. up to scratch up to the required standard. ■ scratchy adj.

scrawl v. write in a hurried, careless way. • n. scrawled handwriting.

scrawny adj. (scrawnier, scrawniest) thin and bony.

scream v. make a loud, piercing cry. • n. 1 a loud, piercing cry or sound. 2 informal a very funny person or thing.

scree n. a mass of small loose stones on a mountain slope.

screech n. a loud, harsh cry or sound. • v. make a screech.

screed n. a long speech or piece of writing.

screen n. 1 the flat front surface of a television or computer monitor, on which images and data are displayed. 2 an upright partition used to divide a room or hide something. 3 a thing that conceals or protects. 4 a blank surface on to which films are projected. • v. 1 conceal or protect. 2 show or broadcast a film or television programme. 3 test for the presence or absence of a disease. □ screenplay the script of a film. screen saver a computer program which replaces an unchanging screen display with a moving image.

screw n. 1 a metal pin with a spiral thread, turned and pressed into a surface to join things together. 2 a propeller. 3 informal a prison warder. • v. 1 fasten or tighten with a screw or screws. 2 rotate so as to attach or remove. 3 informal

swindle. □ screwdriver a tool for turning screws. screw up 1 crush into a tight mass. 2 informal cause to go wrong. 3 informal make emotionally disturbed.

scribble v. write or draw carelessly or hurriedly. • n. something scribbled.

scribe n. (in the past) a person who copied out documents.

scrimmage n. a confused struggle.

scrimp v. economize; save.

script n. 1 the written text of a play, film, or broadcast. 2 handwriting as distinct from print. • v. write a script for.

scripture (or scriptures) n. the sacred writings of Christianity or another religion. ■ scriptural adj.

scroll n. a roll of parchment or paper. • v. move displayed data up or down on a computer screen.

Scrooge n. a person who is mean with money.

scrotum n. (pl. scrota or scrotums) the pouch of skin containing the testicles.

scrounge v. informal try to get something without paying or working for it. ■ scrounger n.

scrub v. (scrubbing, scrubbed) 1 rub hard to clean. 2 informal cancel. • n. 1 an act of scrubbing. 2 land covered mainly with bushes and small trees.

scruff n. the back of the neck.

scruffy adj. (scruffier, scruffiest) shabby and untidy. ■ scruffily adv.

scrum n. 1 (or scrummage) Rugby a formation in which players push against each other with heads down and the ball is thrown in. 2 informal a disorderly crowd.

scrumptious adj. informal delicious.

scrumpy n. strong cider made in the west of England.

scrunch v. crush or squeeze into a tight mass.

scruple n. a feeling of doubt as to whether an action is morally right. •v. (**not scruple to do**) not hesitate to do something, even if it may be wrong.

scrupulous adj. very careful and thorough. ∎ **scrupulously** adv.

scrutinize (or **-ise**) v. examine carefully.

scrutiny n. (pl. **scrutinies**) careful examination.

scuba-diving n. swimming underwater using an aqualung.

scud v. (**scudding**, **scudded**) move quickly, driven by the wind.

scuff v. mark a shoe etc. by scraping it against something.

scuffle n. a short, confused fight or struggle. •v. take part in a scuffle.

scull n. **1** each of a pair of small oars used by a single rower. **2** a light boat for a single rower. •v. row with sculls.

scullery n. (pl. **sculleries**) a room for washing dishes and other household work.

sculpt v. carve or shape.

sculpture n. **1** the art of making figures and shapes by carving or shaping stone, metal, etc. **2** a work made in this way. •v. make by sculpture. ∎ **sculptor** n. (fem. **sculptress**) n. **sculptural** adj.

scum n. **1** a layer of dirt or froth on the surface of a liquid. **2** informal a worthless person.

scupper v. **1** informal stop from working or succeeding. **2** sink a ship deliberately.

scurf n. flakes of skin.

scurrilous adj. insulting and abusive; slanderous.

scurry v. (**scurrying**, **scurried**) move hurriedly with short steps.

scurvy n. a disease caused by a lack of vitamin C.

scut n. the short tail of a hare, rabbit, or deer.

scuttle n. a metal container used to store coal for a fire. •v. **1** scurry. **2** cause a plan to fail. **3** sink a ship deliberately.

scythe n. a tool with a long curved blade, for cutting long grass.

SE abbrev. south-east or south-eastern.

sea n. **1** the salt water surrounding the land masses of the earth. **2** a particular area of sea. **3** a vast expanse. ∎ **at sea** confused. **sea anemone** a sea creature with stinging tentacles. **seabird** a bird that lives near the sea. **seaboard** the coast. **sea change** a great or remarkable change. **seafaring** travelling by sea. **seafood** shellfish and sea fish as food. **seagoing** of or for sea voyages. **seagull** a gull. **sea horse** a small sea fish that swims upright and has a horse-like head. **sea lion** a large seal. **seaman** a sailor. **seaplane** an aircraft designed to land on and take off from water. **seascape** a view or picture of the sea. **seasick** feeling nausea caused by the motion of a ship. **seaside** a beach area or holiday resort. **sea urchin** a sea animal with a round spiny shell. **seaweed** large algae growing in the sea. **seaworthy** (of a boat) in good enough condition to sail on the sea. ∎ **seaward** adj. & adv. **seawards** adv.

s

seal n. 1 a device or substance used to join things or prevent fluid passing through. 2 a piece of wax with a design stamped into it, attached to a document. 3 a confirmation or guarantee. 4 a sea mammal with flippers and a streamlined body. •v. 1 fasten or close securely. 2 coat so as to prevent fluid passing through. 3 make definite.

sealant n. material used to make something airtight or watertight.

seam n. 1 a line where two pieces of fabric are sewn together. 2 an underground layer of coal etc. ■ **seamed** adj.

seamless adj. smooth and without obvious joins. ■ **seamlessly** adv.

seamstress n. a woman who sews, esp. as a job.

seamy adj. (**seamier**, **seamiest**) immoral or sordid.

seance /say-onss/ n. a meeting at which people try to contact the dead.

sear v. burn or scorch.

search v. 1 try to find. 2 examine thoroughly so as to find. 3 (**searching**) investigating deeply. •n. an act of searching. □ **search engine** a computer program that searches the Internet for web pages containing a specified item. **searchlight** a powerful outdoor light with a movable beam. ■ **searcher** n.

season n. 1 each of the four divisions of the year (spring, summer, autumn, and winter). 2 a part of the year with particular weather, or when a particular activity takes place: *the rainy season*. •v. 1 add salt etc. to food. 2 dry wood for use as timber. 3 (**seasoned**) experienced. □ **in season** 1 (of fresh

food) plentiful and ready to eat. 2 (of a female mammal) ready to mate. **season ticket** a ticket allowing travel or admission within a particular period.

seasonable adj. usual for a particular season.

seasonal adj. 1 of a particular season. 2 changing according to the season. ■ **seasonally** adv.

seasoning n. salt or spices added to food to improve the flavour.

seat n. 1 a thing made or used for sitting on. 2 the buttocks. 3 a place in an elected parliament or council. 4 a parliamentary constituency. 5 a site or location. 6 a large country house. •v. 1 cause to sit. 2 have enough seats for. □ **seat belt** a belt used to secure a seated person in a vehicle or aircraft.

sebaceous /si-bay-shuhss/ adj. producing oil or fat.

secateurs pl. n. pruning clippers.

secede v. withdraw from an alliance or federation. ■ **secession** n.

secluded adj. (of a place) sheltered and private.

seclusion n. the state of being private and apart from others.

second[1] adj. & n. 1 that is number two in a sequence. 2 lower in position, rank, or importance. 3 (**seconds**) imperfect goods. 4 an attendant at a duel or boxing match. •v. formally support a proposal etc. □ **second class** of a lower standard or quality than first class. **second-degree** (of burns) causing blistering but not permanent scars. **second-hand** 1 having had a previous owner. 2 learned from others. **second nature** a habit that has become instinctive. **second-rate** of poor quality. **second sight** the supposed ability to foresee the future. **second thoughts** a change of opinion after reconsideration. **second wind** fresh energy for an activity. ■ **secondly** adv.

second² n. one-sixtieth of a minute.

second³ /si-kond/ v. temporarily move a worker to another job or role. ■ **secondment** n.

secondary adj. **1** coming after or less important than something primary. **2** (of education) for pupils aged 11 to 16 or 18.
■ **secondarily** adv.

secret adj. kept from or not known by others. •n. **1** something secret. **2** an effective method of achieving something. ■ **secrecy** n. **secretly** adv.

secretariat n. a government office or department.

secretary n. (pl. **secretaries**) **1** a person employed to type letters, keep records, etc. **2** an official of a society or other organization. □ **Secretary of State** (in the UK) the head of a major government department. ■ **secretarial** adj.

secrete v. **1** (of a cell, gland, etc.) produce and discharge a substance. **2** hide. ■ **secretion** n. **secretory** adj.

secretive adj. inclined to hide your feelings or withhold information. ■ **secretively** adv.

sect n. a group with different religious views from those of a larger group to which they belong.

sectarian adj. of a sect or sects. ■ **sectarianism** n.

section n. **1** any of the parts into which something is divided. **2** a distinct group within a larger one.

3 a cross section. •v. divide into sections. ■ **sectional** adj.

sector n. **1** a distinct area or part. **2** a part of a circle between two lines drawn from its centre to its circumference.

secular adj. not religious or spiritual.

secure adj. **1** certain to remain safe. **2** fixed or fastened so as not to give way or become loose. **3** free from fear or anxiety. •v. **1** make secure. **2** succeed in obtaining. ■ **securely** adv.

security n. (pl. **securities**) **1** the state of being secure. **2** the safety of a state or organization. **3** a valuable item given as a guarantee that you will repay a loan.

sedan n. **1** hist. an enclosed chair carried between two horizontal poles. **2** US a car for four or more people.

sedate adj. calm and unhurried. •v. give a sedative to. ■ **sedately** adv. **sedation** n.

sedative n. a drug that makes someone calm or sleepy.

sedentary adj. involving or taking little exercise.

sedge n. a grass-like marsh plant.

sediment n. **1** matter that settles to the bottom of a liquid. **2** material carried and deposited by water or wind. ■ **sedimentary** adj.

sedition n. actions or speech inciting rebellion. ■ **seditious** adj.

seduce v. **1** persuade someone to have sex with you. **2** persuade to do something unwise. ■ **seducer** n. **seduction** n. **seductive** adj.

sedulous adj. dedicated and careful.

see v. (**seeing**, **saw**; past part. **seen**) **1** perceive with the eyes.

S

2 experience. **3** realize or deduce. **4** think of in a particular way. **5** meet. **6** meet regularly as a boyfriend or girlfriend. **7** guide or lead to a place. • *n.* the district or position of a bishop or archbishop. □ **see off** escort to the point of departure. **see to 1** deal with. **2** ensure that.

seed *n.* **1** a small object produced by a plant, from which a new plant may grow. **2** the beginning of a feeling, process, etc. **3** any of the stronger competitors in a sports tournament who are kept from playing each other in the early rounds. **4** *old use* semen. • *v.* **1** sow with seeds. **2** remove the seeds from. **3** make a competitor a seed in a tournament.

seedling *n.* a young plant raised from seed.

seedy *adj.* (**seedier**, **seediest**) sordid or disreputable. ■ **seediness** *n.*

seek *v.* (**seeking, sought**) **1** try to find or obtain. **2** try or want to do.

seem *v.* give the impression of being.

seeming *adj.* appearing to be real or true. ■ **seemingly** *adv.*

seemly *adj.* socially appropriate.

seen past part. of **SEE**.

seep *v.* flow or leak slowly through a substance. ■ **seepage** *n.*

seer *n.* a person supposedly able to foresee the future.

seersucker *n.* a fabric with a puckered surface.

see-saw *n.* a long plank balanced on a fixed support, on which children sit at each end and move up and down. • *v.* repeatedly change between two states or positions.

seethe *v.* **1** be filled with great but unexpressed anger. **2** boil or churn.

segment *n.* each of the parts into which something is divided. • *v.* divide into segments.

segregate *v.* keep separate from others. ■ **segregation** *n.*

seine /sayn/ *n.* a fishing net which hangs vertically from floats.

seismic /syz-mik/ *adj.* of earthquakes.

seismograph *n.* an instrument for measuring and recording earthquakes.

seismology *n.* the study of earthquakes. ■ **seismologist** *n.*

seize *v.* **1** take hold of suddenly and forcibly. **2** take possession of by force or by right. **3** (**seize on**) take eager advantage of. **4** (**seize up**) become jammed.

> **!** **seize** is an exception to the usual rule of *i* before *e* except after *c*.

seizure *n.* **1** the act of seizing. **2** a stroke or an epileptic fit.

seldom *adv.* not often.

select *v.* carefully choose from a group. • *adj.* **1** carefully chosen. **2** used by or made up of wealthy people. ■ **selector** *n.*

selection *n.* **1** the act of selecting. **2** things selected. **3** a range from which to choose.

selective *adj.* **1** of selection. **2** choosing carefully. **3** affecting some things and not others. ■ **selectively** *adv.* **selectivity** *n.*

selenium *n.* a crystalline chemical element.

self *n.* (*pl.* **selves**) **1** a person's essential being that separates them from others. **2** a person's particular nature.

self- *comb. form* of or to yourself or itself.

self-assurance *n.* confidence. ■ **self-assured** *adj.*

self-centred *adj.* obsessed with yourself.

self-confidence *n.* trust in your abilities and qualities. ■ **self-confident** *adj.*

self-conscious *adj.* nervous or awkward because worried about what others think of you.

self-contained *adj.* **1** (of accommodation) having its own facilities and entrance. **2** independent.

self-control *n.* the ability to control your emotions and behaviour. ■ **self-controlled** *adj.*

self-denial *n.* not allowing yourself to have things that you like.

self-determination *n.* the right of a country to run its own affairs.

self-evident *adj.* obvious.

self-importance *n.* an exaggerated sense of your own importance. ■ **self-important** *adj.*

self-interest *n.* your own interest or advantage.

selfish *adj.* concerned mainly with your own needs or wishes. ■ **selfishly** *adv.* **selfishness** *n.*

selfless *adj.* concerned more with the needs and wishes of others than with your own.

self-made *adj.* having become successful by your own efforts.

self-possessed *adj.* confident and in control of your feelings. ■ **self-possession** *n.*

self-raising *adj.* (of flour) having baking powder added.

self-respect *n.* pride and confidence in yourself.

self-righteous *adj.* certain that you are correct or morally superior.

selfsame *adj.* (**the selfsame**) the very same.

self-satisfied *adj.* smugly pleased with yourself. ■ **self-satisfaction** *n.*

self-seeking *adj.* concerned only with your own interests.

self-service *adj.* (of a shop etc.) in which customers select goods and pay at a checkout.

self-styled *adj.* using a description or title that you have given yourself.

self-sufficient *adj.* able to do or produce what you need without outside help. ■ **self-sufficiency** *n.*

sell *v.* (**selling, sold**) **1** exchange or offer something in return for money. **2** (of goods) be bought in specified amounts. **3** persuade someone of the merits of. □ **sell out 1** sell all of your stock. **2** abandon your principles. **sell up** sell all your property etc. ■ **seller** *n.*

Sellotape *n. trademark* transparent adhesive tape.

selvedge *n.* an edge on woven fabric that prevents it from unravelling.

selves pl. of SELF.

semantic *adj.* of meaning. •*n.* (**semantics**) the study of the meaning of words. ■ **semantically** *adv.*

semaphore *n.* a system of signalling with the arms.

semblance *n.* the way something looks or seems.

semen *n.* the liquid containing sperm that is produced by males.

semester *n.* a half-year term in a school or university.

semi- *prefix* **1** half. **2** partly.

semibreve *n.* a musical note equal to four crotchets.

s

semicircle n. a half of a circle. ■ **semicircular** adj.

semicolon n. a punctuation mark (;).

semiconductor n. a solid that conducts electricity in certain conditions.

semi-detached adj. (of a house) joined to another house by a shared wall.

semi-final n. (in sport) a match or round preceding the final. ■ **semi-finalist** n.

seminal adj. 1 strongly influencing later developments. 2 of semen.

seminar n. 1 a meeting for discussion or training. 2 a small university class meeting to discuss topics with a teacher.

seminary n. (pl. **seminaries**) a training college for priests or rabbis.

semiotics n. the study of signs and symbols. ■ **semiotic** adj.

semi-precious adj. (of minerals) used as gems but less valuable than precious stones.

semiquaver n. a musical note equal to half a quaver.

Semitic adj. of the group of peoples that includes Jews and Arabs.

semitone n. half a tone in music.

semolina n. the hard grains left after flour is milled, used in puddings and pasta.

senate n. 1 the smaller but higher law-making body in the US and some other countries. 2 the governing body of a university or college.

senator n. a member of a senate.

send v. (**sending**, **sent**) 1 cause to go or be taken to a destination. 2 move sharply or quickly. 3 put in a specified state. □ **send for** order to come or be brought. **send up** informal ridicule by imitation.

senile adj. having a loss of mental abilities because of old age. ■ **senility** n.

senior adj. 1 of older people. 2 of schoolchildren above the age of about 11. 3 older. 4 high or higher in status. •n. a senior person. □ **senior citizen** an elderly person. ■ **seniority** n.

senna n. a laxative made from the dried pods of a tropical tree.

sensation n. 1 a feeling resulting from something that happens to or touches the body. 2 a vague awareness. 3 a widespread reaction of excited interest, or a cause of this.

sensational adj. causing or trying to cause great public interest and excitement. ■ **sensationalism** n. **sensationalist** adj. **sensationally** adv.

sensationalize (or **-ise**) v. present information in an exaggerated way to make it seem more interesting.

sense n. 1 any of the powers of sight, smell, hearing, taste, and touch, by which the body perceives things. 2 a feeling that something is the case. 3 awareness or sensitivity. 4 a sensible and practical attitude. 5 a meaning. •v. 1 perceive by a sense. 2 be vaguely aware of. □ **make sense** be understandable or sensible.

senseless adj. 1 lacking meaning, purpose, or common sense. 2 unconscious.

sensibility n. (pl. **sensibilities**) the ability to understand emotion or art.

sensible adj. having or showing common sense. ■ **sensibly** adv.

sensitive adj. **1** quick to detect or be affected by slight changes. **2** appreciating the feelings of others. **3** easily offended or upset. **4** secret or controversial. ■ **sensitively** adv. **sensitivity** n.

sensitize (or **-ise**) v. make sensitive or aware.

sensor n. a device for detecting or measuring heat, light, etc.

sensory adj. of sensation or the senses.

sensual adj. of the senses as a source of pleasure. ■ **sensuality** n. **sensually** adv.

sensuous adj. **1** of the senses rather than the intellect. **2** physically attractive or pleasing. ■ **sensuously** adv.

sent past & past part. of **SEND**.

sentence n. **1** a set of words that is complete in itself, conveying a statement, question, etc. **2** a punishment given to someone found guilty by a court. •v. state in a court that an offender is to receive a particular punishment.

sententious adj. making pompous comments on moral issues.

sentient adj. able to perceive or feel things. ■ **sentience** n.

sentiment n. **1** an opinion or feeling. **2** exaggerated tenderness, sadness, or nostalgia.

sentimental adj. showing or having excessive tenderness, sadness, or nostalgia. ■ **sentimentality** n. **sentimentally** adv.

sentinel n. a sentry.

sentry n. (pl. **sentries**) a soldier stationed to keep guard or control access to a place.

sepal n. each of the leaf-like parts of a flower surrounding the petals.

separate adj. forming a unit by itself. •v. **1** move, come, or keep apart. **2** stop living together as a couple. **3** divide into parts. ■ **separable** adj. **separately** adv. **separation** n.

> ! The middle is -par-, not -per-: sep**a**rate.

separatist n. a member of a group seeking independence from a larger group. ■ **separatism** n.

sepia n. a reddish-brown colour.

sepsis n. the presence in tissues of harmful bacteria.

September n. the ninth month.

septet n. a group of seven musicians.

septic adj. infected with bacteria. □ **septic tank** an underground tank in which sewage decomposes before draining into the soil.

septicaemia (US **septicemia**) n. blood poisoning caused by bacteria.

septuagenarian n. a person between 70 and 79 years old.

sepulchral adj. gloomy.

sepulchre /sep-uhl-ker/ (US **sepulcher**) n. a stone tomb.

sequel n. **1** a book, film, etc. continuing the story of an earlier one. **2** something taking place after or as a result of an earlier event.

sequence n. **1** an order in which related things follow each other. **2** a set of things following each other in a particular order.

sequential adj. following in a logical sequence. ■ **sequentially** adv.

sequester v. **1** isolate. **2** sequestrate.

s

sequestrate v. take legal possession of assets until a debt has been paid. ■ **sequestration** n.

sequin n. a small, shiny disc for decorating clothes. ■ **sequinned** adj.

sequoia n. a redwood tree.

seraglio /si-rah-li-oh/ n. (pl. **seraglios**) the women's quarters in a Muslim household.

seraph n. (pl. **seraphim** or **seraphs**) a type of angel. ■ **seraphic** adj.

serenade n. a piece of music sung or played by a man to his lover, outdoors and at night. •v. perform a serenade for.

serendipity n. the fortunate occurrence of events by chance. ■ **serendipitous** adj.

serene adj. calm and peaceful. ■ **serenely** adv. **serenity** n.

serf n. (in the feudal system) an agricultural labourer tied to working on a particular estate.

serge n. a hard-wearing fabric.

sergeant n. 1 a non-commissioned officer in the army or air force above corporal. 2 a police officer ranking below an inspector. □ **sergeant major** an army officer who helps with administrative duties.

serial adj. 1 arranged in a series. 2 repeatedly committing the same offence. •n. a story published or broadcast in regular instalments. □ **serial number** an identification number given to a manufactured item. ■ **serially** adv.

serialize (or **-ise**) v. publish or broadcast as a serial. ■ **serialization** n.

series n. (pl. **series**) 1 a number of similar things coming one after

another. 2 a sequence of related television or radio programmes.

serious adj. 1 dangerous or severe. 2 needing careful consideration or action. 3 solemn or thoughtful. 4 sincere and in earnest. ■ **seriously** adv. **seriousness** n.

sermon n. a talk on a religious or moral subject, esp. during a church service.

sermonize (or **-ise**) v. give moral advice.

serpent n. a large snake.

serpentine adj. winding or twisting.

serrated adj. having a jagged edge. ■ **serration** n.

serried adj. (of rows of people or things) standing close together.

serum n. (pl. **sera** or **serums**) the thin liquid which separates out when blood clots.

servant n. a person employed to do domestic work in a household or for a person.

serve v. 1 perform duties or services for. 2 be a member of the armed forces. 3 spend a period in a job or in prison. 4 present food or drink to. 5 attend to a customer. 6 fulfil a purpose. 7 hit the ball in tennis etc. to begin play for each point of a game. •n. an act of serving in tennis etc.

server n. 1 a person or thing that serves. 2 a computer or program that controls or supplies information to a network.

service n. 1 the act of serving. 2 a period of employment with an organization. 3 help or advice. 4 a religious ceremony. 5 a system supplying a public need. 6 a department run by the state. 7 (the **services**) the armed forces.

8 a routine inspection and maintenance of a vehicle etc. **9** a set of matching crockery. **10** a serve in tennis etc. • *v.* **1** perform maintenance on. **2** provide services for. **3** pay interest on a debt. □ **service area** (or **services**) a roadside area with a service station, cafe, etc. for motorists. **serviceman** (or **servicewoman**) a member of the armed forces. **service provider** a company which provides access to the Internet. **service road** a road parallel to a main road, giving access to houses, shops, etc. **service station** a garage selling petrol etc.

serviceable *adj.* **1** in working order. **2** useful and hard-wearing.

serviette *n.* a table napkin.

servile *adj.* excessively willing to serve or please others. ■ **servility** *n.*

serving *n.* a quantity of food for one person.

servitude *n.* the state of being a slave or of being controlled by someone more powerful.

sesame *n.* a tropical plant grown for its oil-rich seeds.

session *n.* **1** a period devoted to a particular activity. **2** a meeting of a council, court, etc. to conduct its business.

set *v.* (**setting, set**) **1** put in a specified place, position, or state. **2** give a task to. **3** decide on or fix a time, value, etc. **4** establish as an example or record. **5** adjust a device as required. **6** prepare a table for a meal. **7** harden into a solid, semi-solid, or fixed state. **8** (of the sun etc.) appear to move towards and below the earth's horizon. • *n.* **1** a number of things or people grouped together. **2** the way something is set. **3** a radio or

television receiver. **4** a group of games counting as a unit towards a match in tennis etc. **5** a collection of scenery etc. used for a scene in a play or film. • *adj.* **1** fixed or established beforehand. **2** (**set on**) determined to do. □ **set about** start doing. **set aside** temporarily stop using land for growing crops. **setback** a problem that delays progress. **set off 1** begin a journey. **2** make a bomb or alarm go off. **set out 1** begin a journey. **2** intend. **set square** a right-angled triangular drawing instrument. **set up** establish a business.

sett *n.* a badger's burrow.

settee *n.* a sofa.

setter *n.* a breed of dog trained to stand rigid on scenting game.

setting *n.* **1** the way or place in which something is set. **2** a set of crockery and cutlery laid for one person.

settle *v.* **1** resolve a dispute or problem. **2** decide or arrange finally. **3** make your home in a new place. **4** adopt a more steady lifestyle. **5** become or make calmer. **6** begin to feel at ease in a new situation. **7** sit or rest comfortably or securely. **8** pay a debt. **9** (**settle for**) accept something less than satisfactory. • *n.* a wooden bench with a high back and arms. ■ **settler** *n.*

settlement *n.* **1** the act of settling. **2** a place where people establish a community. **3** an agreement intended to settle a dispute.

seven *adj.* & *n.* one more than six; 7. ■ **seventh** *adj.* & *n.*

seventeen *adj.* & *n.* one more than sixteen; 17. ■ **seventeenth** *adj.* & *n.*

S

seventy adj. & n. (pl. **seventies**) ten less than eighty; 70. ■ **seventieth** adj. & n.

sever v. **1** cut off. **2** put an end to. ■ **severance** n.

several adj. & pron. more than two but not many. • adj. separate or respective. ■ **severally** adv.

severe adj. **1** (of something bad) very great. **2** strict or harsh. **3** very plain in style or appearance. ■ **severely** adv. **severity** n.

sew v. (**sewing, sewed**; past part. **sewn** or **sewed**) join or repair by stitching with a needle and thread.

sewage /soo-ij/ n. waste water and excrement conveyed in sewers.

sewer /soo-er/ n. an underground pipe for sewage. ■ **sewerage** n.

sex n. **1** either of the two main categories (male and female) into which living things are divided. **2** the fact of being male or female. **3** sexual intercourse.

sexagenarian n. a person between 60 and 69 years old.

sexism n. prejudice or discrimination on the basis of sex. ■ **sexist** adj. & n.

sexless adj. **1** not sexually attractive or active. **2** neither male nor female.

sextant n. an instrument for measuring angles and distances, used in navigation and surveying.

sextet n. **1** a group of six musicians. **2** music for a sextet.

sexton n. a person who looks after a church and churchyard.

sextuplet n. each of six children born at one birth.

sexual adj. **1** of sex or physical attraction or contact. **2** of the sexes. **3** (of reproduction) involving the fusion of male and female cells. □ **sexual intercourse** sexual contact in which a man puts his erect penis into a woman's vagina. ■ **sexually** adv.

sexuality n. (pl. **sexualities**) **1** capacity for sexual feelings. **2** a person's sexual preference.

sexy adj. (**sexier, sexiest**) **1** sexually attractive or exciting. **2** sexually aroused. **3** informal exciting or interesting. ■ **sexily** adv. **sexiness** n.

shabby adj. (**shabbier, shabbiest**) **1** worn out or scruffy. **2** mean and unfair. ■ **shabbily** adv. **shabbiness** n.

shack n. a roughly built hut.

shackle n. (**shackles**) a pair of rings connected by a chain, used to fasten a prisoner's wrists or ankles. • v. **1** put shackles on. **2** restrain; limit.

shade n. **1** darkness and coolness caused by shelter from direct sunlight. **2** a colour, esp. with regard to how light or dark it is. **3** a variety. **4** a slight amount. **5** a lampshade. **6** (**shades**) informal sunglasses. **7** literary a ghost. • v. **1** screen from direct light. **2** cover or reduce the light of. **3** darken parts of a drawing etc.

shadow n. **1** a dark area produced by an object coming between light rays and a surface. **2** partial or complete darkness. **3** sadness or gloom. **4** a slight trace. **5** a person who constantly accompanies or secretly follows another. • v. **1** cast a shadow over. **2** follow and observe secretly. □ **shadow-boxing** boxing against an imaginary opponent as a form of training. **Shadow Cabinet** members of the main opposition party in Parliament holding posts corresponding to

those of the government Cabinet.
■ **shadowy** adj.

shady adj. (**shadier, shadiest**)
1 giving or situated in shade.
2 informal seeming to be
dishonest or illegal.

shaft n. **1** the long, narrow handle
of a tool or body of an arrow etc.
2 a ray of light. **3** a narrow vertical
passage. **4** each of the two poles
between which a horse is har-
nessed to a vehicle. **5** a rotating
rod transmitting mechanical
power in a machine.

shag n. **1** coarse tobacco. **2** a cormorant. • adj. (of pile on a carpet)
long and rough.

shaggy adj. (**shaggier, shaggi-
est**) (of hair or fur) long, thick, and
untidy.

shah n. a title of the former king of
Iran.

shake v. (**shaking, shook**; past
part. **shaken**) **1** move quickly and
jerkily up and down or to and fro.
2 tremble. **3** shock or disturb. • n. an
act of shaking. □ **shake hands**
clasp right hands on meeting,
parting, or as a sign of agreement.
shake off get rid of. **shake
up** make major changes to.
■ **shaker** n.

shaky adj. (**shakier, shakiest**)
1 shaking; unsteady. **2** not safe or
certain. ■ **shakily** adv.

shale n. soft rock that splits easily.

shall aux. v. **1** used with I and we to
express the future tense. **2** expressing determination or an
order.

shallot n. a small onion.

shallow adj. **1** not deep. **2** not
thinking or thought out seriously.
• n. (**shallows**) a shallow area of
water. ■ **shallowness** n.

sham n. a thing that is not as good
or genuine as it seems to be. • adj.
not genuine; false. • v. (**shamming,
shammed**) pretend.

shaman /shay-muhn/ n. (in some
societies) a person believed to be
able to contact good and evil
spirits.

shamble v. walk in a slow, shuffling way.

shambles n. informal a state of
complete disorder.

shame n. **1** embarrassment or
distress arising from awareness
that you have done something
wrong or foolish. **2** loss of respect.
3 a cause of shame. **4** a cause for
regret. • v. cause to feel ashamed.
□ **shamefaced** adj. showing shame.
■ **shameful** adj. **shamefully** adv.
shameless adj.

shampoo n. **1** a liquid soap for
washing the hair. **2** a similar substance for cleaning a carpet etc.
3 an act of shampooing. • v.
(**shampooing, shampooed**)
wash or clean with shampoo.

shamrock n. a clover-like plant.

shandy n. (pl. **shandies**) beer
mixed with lemonade or ginger
beer.

shank n. **1** the lower part of the
leg. **2** the shaft of a tool.

shan't contr. shall not.

shantung n. a silk fabric with a
rough surface.

shanty n. (pl. **shanties**) **1** a small
roughly built hut. **2** a sailors' traditional song. □ **shanty town** a
settlement in or near a town
where people live in shanties.

shape n. **1** the form of something
produced by its outline. **2** a particular condition: in poor shape.
3 well-defined structure or arrangement. • v. **1** give a shape to.

s

2 influence greatly. **3** (**shape up**) develop in a particular way. ■ **shapeless** adj.

shapely adj. having an attractive shape.

shard n. a piece of broken pottery, glass, etc.

share n. **1** a part of a larger amount which is divided among or contributed by a number of people. **2** any of the equal parts into which a company's wealth is divided, entitling the holder to a proportion of the profits. • v. **1** have or give a share of. **2** have or use jointly. □ **shareholder** an owner of shares in a company. ■ **sharer** n.

shark n. **1** a large sea fish with a triangular fin on the back. **2** informal a person who exploits or swindles others.

sharp adj. **1** having a cutting or piercing edge or point. **2** tapering to a point or edge. **3** sudden and noticeable. **4** clear and definite. **5** producing a sudden, piercing feeling. **6** quick to understand, notice, or respond. **7** (of a taste or smell) strong and slightly bitter. **8** above true or normal pitch in music. • adv. **1** precisely. **2** suddenly or abruptly. • n. a musical note raised by a semitone, or the sign showing this. □ **sharp practice** dishonest business dealings. **sharpshooter** a person skilled in shooting. ■ **sharpen** v. **sharpener** n. **sharply** adv. **sharpness** n.

shatter v. **1** break violently into pieces. **2** destroy. **3** upset greatly.

shave v. **1** remove hair by cutting it off close to the skin with a razor. **2** cut a thin slice from something. **3** pass very close to. • n. an act of shaving. ■ **shaver** n.

shaven adj. shaved.

shaving n. a thin strip cut off a surface.

shawl n. a large piece of fabric worn over the shoulders or wrapped round a baby.

she pron. the female previously mentioned.

sheaf n. (pl. **sheaves**) **1** a bundle of papers. **2** a bundle of grain stalks.

shear v. (**shearing**, **sheared**; past part. **shorn** or **sheared**) **1** cut off or trim with shears. **2** break off because of strain. **3** (**be shorn of**) have something taken away from you. • pl. n. (**shears**) a cutting implement like very large scissors. ■ **shearer** n.

sheath n. (pl. **sheaths**) **1** a cover for the blade of a knife or sword. **2** a condom.

sheathe v. **1** put a sword etc. into a sheath. **2** encase in a close-fitting cover.

shed n. a simple building used for storage or to shelter animals. • v. (**shedding**, **shed**) **1** have leaves, hair, etc. fall off naturally. **2** get rid of. **3** give off light. **4** drop or let fall.

sheen n. a soft shine on a surface.

sheep n. (pl. **sheep**) a mammal with a woolly coat, kept for its wool or meat. □ **sheepdog** a dog trained to guard and herd sheep. **sheepskin** a sheep's skin with the wool on.

sheepish adj. embarrassed or shy. ■ **sheepishly** adv.

sheer adj. **1** nothing but; absolute. **2** vertical or almost vertical. **3** (of a fabric) very thin. • v. change course quickly.

sheet n. **1** a large piece of cotton or other fabric, used to cover a bed. **2** a broad thin piece of metal, glass, paper, etc. **3** an expanse of water, flame, etc. **4** a rope attached to the lower corner of a sail.

sheikh (or **sheik**) /shayk/ n. a Muslim or Arab leader.
■ **sheikhdom** n.

shekel n. the basic unit of money of Israel.

shelf n. (pl. **shelves**) **1** a flat length of wood etc. fixed horizontally for displaying or storing things. **2** a ledge of rock. □ **shelf life** the time for which an item to be sold remains fresh or usable.

shell n. **1** the hard outer covering of an egg, nut kernel, or an animal. **2** a metal case filled with explosive, fired from a large gun. **3** a hollow case or outer structure. •v. **1** fire explosive shells at. **2** remove the shell or pod from. **3** (**shell out**) informal pay a sum of money.
□ **shellfish** an edible water animal that has a shell. **shell shock** a mental condition that can affect soldiers after prolonged combat.

shellac n. a resin used in varnish.

shelter n. **1** a place giving protection from bad weather or danger. **2** protection. •v. **1** provide with shelter. **2** find or take shelter.

shelve v. **1** put on a shelf. **2** postpone or cancel. **3** slope downwards.

shenanigans pl. n. informal high-spirited or underhand behaviour.

shepherd n. a person who looks after sheep. •v. guide. □ **shepherd's pie** a dish of minced meat topped with mashed potato.
■ **shepherdess** n.

sherbet n. a sweet fizzing powder eaten alone or made into a drink.

sheriff n. **1** (in England and Wales) the chief executive officer of the Crown in a county. **2** (in Scotland) a judge. **3** US an elected officer in a county, responsible for keeping law and order.

Sherpa n. (pl. **Sherpa** or **Sherpas**) a member of a Himalayan people of Nepal and Tibet.

sherry n. (pl. **sherries**) a strong wine from southern Spain.

Shia /shi-uh/ n. (pl. **Shia** or **Shias**) **1** one of the two main branches of Islam. **2** (or **Shiite**) a Muslim who follows the Shia branch of Islam.

shiatsu /shi-at-soo/ n. a Japanese therapy in which pressure is applied with the hands to points on the body.

shibboleth n. a long-standing belief or principle, regarded by many as outdated.

shied past & past part. of SHY.

shield n. **1** a broad piece of armour held for protection against blows or missiles. **2** a person or thing acting as a barrier or screen. **3** a sporting trophy in the form of a metal plate mounted on a piece of wood. •v. protect or hide.

shift v. **1** move or change from one position to another. **2** transfer blame etc. **3** informal move quickly. •n. **1** a slight change in position or direction. **2** a period of time worked by a group of workers who start work as another group finishes. **3** a straight dress without a waist.

shiftless adj. lazy and lacking ambition.

shifty adj. informal dishonest or untrustworthy.

Shiite /shee-yt/ n. = SHIA (sense 2).

shilling n. a former British coin worth 12 old pence.

shilly-shally v. (**shilly-shallying, shilly-shallied**) be indecisive.

shimmer v. shine with a soft wavering light. •n. a soft wavering light or shine.

shimmy v. (**shimmying, shimmied**) move swiftly and smoothly.

shin n. the front of the leg below the knee. •v. (**shinning, shinned**) climb quickly up or down by gripping with the arms and legs.

shindig n. informal a lively party.

shine v. (**shone** or **shined**) 1 give out or reflect light. 2 direct a torch etc. somewhere. 3 be very good at something. 4 (past & past part. **shined**) polish. •n. brightness. □ **take a shine to** informal develop a liking for. ■ **shiny** adj.

shingle n. 1 a mass of small rounded pebbles, esp. on a beach. 2 a wooden roof tile. 3 (**shingles**) a disease with a rash of painful blisters forming along a nerve path.

Shinto n. a Japanese religion involving the worship of ancestors and nature spirits.

ship n. a large boat for transporting people or goods by sea. •v. (**shipping, shipped**) transport on a ship or by other means. □ **shipment** 1 the act of transporting goods. 2 an amount of goods shipped. **shipping** ships as a whole. **shipshape** orderly and neat. **shipwreck** the sinking or breaking up of a ship at sea. **shipwrecked** having suffered a shipwreck. **shipyard** a place where ships are built and repaired. ■ **shipper** n.

shire n. a county. □ **shire horse** a heavy powerful horse.

shirk v. avoid work or a duty. ■ **shirker** n.

shirt n. a garment for the upper body, with sleeves and buttons down the front.

shirty adj. informal angry or annoyed.

shiver v. shake slightly, esp. from fear or cold. •n. a shivering movement. ■ **shivery** adj.

shoal n. 1 a large number of fish swimming together. 2 an area of shallow water. 3 a submerged sandbank.

shock n. 1 a sudden upsetting or surprising experience. 2 sudden surprise and distress. 3 a serious medical condition caused by loss of blood, severe injury, etc. 4 a violent shaking movement caused by an impact, earthquake, etc. 5 a sudden discharge of electricity through the body. 6 a thick mass of hair. •v. 1 surprise and upset. 2 outrage or disgust. ■ **shocker** n.

shocking adj. 1 causing outrage or disgust. 2 informal very bad. ■ **shockingly** adv.

shoddy adj. 1 badly made or done. 2 dishonest or unfair. ■ **shoddily** adv.

shoe n. 1 a covering for the foot with a stiff sole. 2 a horseshoe. •v. (**shoeing, shod**) fit with a shoe or shoes. □ **on a shoestring** with only a very small amount of money. **shoehorn** a curved implement for easing the heel into a shoe. **shoe tree** a shaped block for keeping a shoe in shape.

shone past & past part. of SHINE.

shoo exclam. a word said to drive away animals. •v. drive away.

shook past of SHAKE.

shoot v. (**shooting**, **shot**) **1** kill or wound with a bullet or arrow. **2** fire a gun. **3** move suddenly and rapidly. **4** (in sport) kick, hit, or throw the ball etc. in an attempt to score. **5** film or photograph. **6** (of a plant) send out shoots. • n. **1** a new part growing from a plant. **2** an act of shooting. □ **shooting star** a small, rapidly moving meteor. **shooting stick** a walking stick with a handle that unfolds to form a seat. ■ **shooter** n.

shop n. **1** a building where goods or services are sold. **2** a workshop. • v. (**shopping**, **shopped**) **1** go to a shop or shops to buy goods. **2** (**shop around**) look for the best available price. **3** informal inform on. □ **shop floor** the part of a factory where production is carried out. **shopkeeper** the owner or manager of a shop. **shoplifter** a person who steals goods from a shop. **shop-soiled** dirty or damaged from being displayed in a shop. **shop steward** a trade union official elected by workers as their representative. **talk shop** discuss work in a social setting. ■ **shopper** n. **shopping** n.

shore n. the land along the edge of a sea, lake, etc. • v. (**shore up**) **1** support or strengthen. **2** hold up with a beam.

shorn past part. of **SHEAR**.

short adj. **1** of a small length in space or time. **2** small in height. **3** (**short of/on**) not having enough of. **4** rude and abrupt. **5** (of odds in betting) reflecting a high probability. **6** (of pastry) crumbly. • adv. not as far as expected or required. • n. **1** informal a small drink of spirits. **2** (**shorts**) short trousers reaching to the knees or thighs. • v. have a short-

circuit. □ **shortbread** (or **short-cake**) a rich, crumbly biscuit. **short-change** cheat, esp. by giving insufficient change. **short circuit** a fault in an electrical circuit when the current flows along a shorter route than it should do. **short-circuit** cause a short circuit in. **shortcoming** a fault or defect. **shortcrust pastry** crumbly pastry, esp. for making pies. **short cut** a quicker route or method. **shortfall** an amount by which something is less than what is required. **shorthand** a method of rapid writing using abbreviations and symbols. **short-handed** without enough staff. **shortlist** a list of selected candidates from which a final choice is made. **short shrift** abrupt or unsympathetic treatment. **short-sighted** unable to see things clearly unless they are close to the eyes. **2** lacking foresight. **short-tempered** losing your temper quickly. **short-term** of or for a short time. **short wave** a radio wave of a frequency of about 3 to 30 megahertz. ■ **shorten** v. **shortness** n.

shortage n. a lack of something needed.

shortening n. fat used to make pastry.

shortly adv. **1** soon. **2** abruptly or sharply.

shot past & past part. of **SHOOT**. • n. **1** the firing of a gun etc. **2** (in sport) a hit, stroke, or kick of the ball as an attempt to score. **3** informal an attempt. **4** a photo. **5** informal a small drink of spirits. **6** informal an injection. **7** tiny lead pellets used in a shotgun. **8** a heavy ball thrown in the sport of shot put. • adj. woven with different colours to give a contrasting

s

effect. □ **like a shot** *informal* without hesitation. **shotgun** a gun for firing small shot at short range. **shot put** an athletic contest in which a heavy round ball is thrown as far as possible. **shot through** with filled with.

should *aux. v.* **1** expressing duty or obligation, or a possible or probable future event. **2** expressing a polite request, opinion, or hope.

shoulder *n.* the joint between the upper arm and the main part of the body. •*v.* **1** take on a responsibility. **2** push aside with the shoulder. □ **shoulder blade** either of the flat triangular bones at the top of the back.

shout *v.* **1** speak or call out very loudly. **2** (**shout down**) prevent from speaking or being heard by shouting. •*n.* a loud cry or call.

shove *v.* **1** push roughly. **2** place carelessly or roughly. **3** (**shove off**) *informal* go away. •*n.* a strong push.

shovel *n.* a tool resembling a spade for moving earth, snow, etc. •*v.* (**shovelling, shovelled;** *US* **shoveling, shoveled**) move with a shovel.

show *v.* (**showing, showed;** *past part.* **shown** or **showed**) **1** be or make visible. **2** offer for inspection or viewing. **3** present an image of. **4** lead or guide. **5** treat in a particular way. **6** demonstrate or prove. •*n.* **1** a theatrical performance or light entertainment programme. **2** a competition involving the public display of animals, plants, etc. **3** an impressive or pleasing sight. **4** an outward display, esp. when misleading. □ **show business** theatre, films, television, etc. as a profession or industry. **showdown** a final con-

frontation intended to settle a dispute. **showjumping** the sport of riding horses over a course of obstacles in an arena. **showman** the manager or presenter of a circus, fair, etc. **show off 1** try to impress by boasting about your abilities etc. **2** display. **show-off** a person who shows off. **showpiece** an outstanding example. **showroom** a room where goods for sale are displayed. **show up 1** reveal as bad or faulty. **2** *informal* humiliate.

showcase *n.* **1** an occasion for presenting something favourably. **2** a glass display case. •*v.* put on display.

shower *n.* **1** a brief fall of rain or snow. **2** a large number of things that fall or arrive together. **3** a device producing a spray of water under which someone stands to wash. **4** a wash in a shower. •*v.* **1** fall or throw in a shower. **2** (**shower with**) give a great number of things to. **3** wash in a shower. ■ **showery** *adj.*

showy *adj.* very bright or colourful and noticeable. ■ **showily** *adv.*

shrank past of **SHRINK**.

shrapnel *n.* small metal fragments from an exploding shell or bomb.

shred *n.* **1** a strip of material torn or cut from something. **2** a very small amount. •*v.* (**shredding, shredded**) tear or cut into shreds. ■ **shredder** *n.*

shrew *n.* a small mouse-like mammal with a pointed snout.

shrewd *adj.* having or showing good judgement. ■ **shrewdly** *adv.* **shrewdness** *n.*

shrewish *adj.* (of a woman) bad-tempered.

s

shriek v. make a piercing cry. • n. a piercing cry.

shrill adj. high-pitched and piercing. ■ **shrillness** n. **shrilly** adv.

shrimp n. (pl. **shrimp** or **shrimps**) a small edible shellfish.

shrine n. a place connected with a holy person or event, where people go to pray.

shrink v. (**shrinking**, **shrank**; past part. **shrunk** or (esp. as adj.) **shrunken**) **1** become or make smaller. **2** move back or away in fear or disgust. ■ n. informal a psychiatrist. ■ **shrinkage** n.

shrivel v. (**shrivelling**, **shrivelled**; US **shriveling**, **shriveled**) wrinkle and shrink through loss of moisture.

shroud n. **1** a length of cloth in which a dead person is wrapped for burial. **2** a thing covering or hiding something. • v. cover or hide.

shrub n. a woody plant smaller than a tree. ■ **shrubby** adj.

shrubbery n. (pl. **shrubberies**) an area planted with shrubs.

shrug v. (**shrugging**, **shrugged**) **1** raise the shoulders briefly as a sign of indifference or ignorance. **2** (**shrug off**) treat as unimportant. • n. an act of shrugging.

shrunk (or **shrunken**) past part. of **SHRINK**.

shudder v. tremble or shake violently. • n. an act of shuddering.

shuffle v. **1** walk without lifting the feet clear of the ground. **2** reorder a pack of cards. **3** rearrange. • n. an act of shuffling.

shun v. (**shunning**, **shunned**) avoid or reject.

shunt v. push or pull a train from one set of tracks to another.

shut v. (**shutting**, **shut**) **1** move into place to block an opening.

2 (**shut in/out**) keep in or out by closing a door etc. **3** prevent access to. **4** (referring to a shop etc.) stop operating for business. **5** close a book, curtains, etc. □ **shut down** cease business or operation. **shut up** informal stop talking.

shutter n. **1** a pair of hinged panels that can be closed over a window. **2** a device that opens and closes to expose the film in a camera. ■ **shuttered** adj.

shuttle n. **1** a form of transport travelling regularly between two places. **2** a bobbin carrying the weft thread in weaving. • v. **1** travel regularly between places. **2** transport in a shuttle. ■ **shuttlecock** a light cone-shaped object, struck with rackets in badminton.

shy adj. nervous or timid in the company of others. • v. (**shying**, **shied**) **1** (of a horse) turn aside in fright. **2** (**shy away from**) avoid through lack of confidence. **3** throw. ■ **shyly** adv. **shyness** n.

SI abbrev. Système International, the international system of units of measurement.

Siamese adj. of Siam (the former name for Thailand). □ **Siamese cat** a breed of cat with pale fur and darker face, paws, and tail. **Siamese twins** twins whose bodies are joined at birth.

sibilant adj. making a hissing sound.

sibling n. a brother or sister.

sibyl n. (in ancient Greece and Rome) a woman believed to pass on prophecies from a god.

sic adv. written exactly as it stands in the original.

sick adj. **1** ill. **2** wanting to vomit. **3** (**sick of**) bored by or annoyed with. **4** *informal* (of humour) dealing with unpleasant subjects in an offensive way.

sicken v. **1** disgust or shock. **2** (**be sickening for**) start to develop an illness.

sickle n. a short-handled cutting tool with a curved blade.

sickly adj. (**sicklier, sickliest**) **1** often ill. **2** looking unhealthy. **3** so bright or sweet as to cause sickness.

sickness n. **1** the state of being ill. **2** an illness or disease. **3** nausea or vomiting.

side n. **1** a position to the left or right of an object, place, or central point. **2** either of the halves into which something is divided. **3** a surface of an object, esp. one that is not the top, bottom, front, or back. **4** a part near the edge of something. **5** a person or group opposing another in a dispute or contest. **6** a particular aspect. **7** each of the lines forming the boundary of a plane figure. • v. (**side with/against**) support or oppose in a conflict or dispute. • adj. additional or less important. ▫ **sideboard** a piece of furniture with cupboards and drawers for crockery, glasses, etc. **sideboards** (or **sideburns**) a strip of hair growing down each side of a man's face. **sidecar** a small passenger vehicle attached to one side of a motorcycle. **side effect** a secondary, usu. bad effect of a drug. **sidelong** to or from one side; sideways. **side-saddle** (of a rider) sitting with both feet on the same side of the horse. **sideshow** a minor show or stall at a fair etc. **sidestep 1** avoid by stepping sideways. **2** avoid dealing with or discussing. **sidetrack** distract. **sidewalk** US a

pavement. **sideways** to, towards, or from the side.

sideline n. **1** an activity done in addition to someone's main job. **2** either of the two lines along the longer sides of a sports field or court. • v. remove from an influential position. ▫ **on/from the sidelines** watching something but not involved in it.

sidereal /sy-deer-i-uhl/ adj. of the stars or their apparent positions in the sky.

siding n. a short track beside a railway, where trains are left.

sidle v. walk in a stealthy or timid way.

siege n. a military operation in which forces surround a town and cut off its supplies.

sienna n. a brownish earth used as a pigment.

sierra n. a long jagged mountain chain.

siesta n. an afternoon rest or nap.

sieve n. a piece of mesh held in a frame, used for straining solids from liquids or separating coarser from finer particles. • v. put through a sieve.

sift v. **1** sieve. **2** examine to select what is important.

sigh v. let out a long, deep, breath expressing sadness, relief, etc. • n. an act of sighing.

sight n. **1** the ability to see. **2** the act of seeing. **3** the distance within which someone can see. **4** a thing seen or worth seeing. **5** *informal* a person or thing that looks ridiculous or unattractive. **6** a device looked through to aim a gun or see with a telescope. • v. see or glimpse. ▫ **sight-read** perform music without previous study of

the score. ■ **sighted** adj.
sightless adj.

sightseeing n. visiting places of interest. ■ **sightseer** n.

sign n. **1** an indication that something exists, is occurring, or may occur. **2** a signal, gesture, or notice giving information or an instruction. **3** a symbol or word representing something in algebra, music, etc. **4** each of the twelve divisions of the zodiac. •v. **1** write your name on something to authorize it. **2** recruit or be recruited by signing a contract. **3** use gestures to give instructions. □ **sign on 1** commit yourself to a job. **2** register as unemployed.

signpost a sign on a post, giving the direction and distance to a place. **sign up** commit yourself to a course, job, etc.

signal n. **1** a gesture, action, or sound giving information or an instruction. **2** a device that indicates whether a road or railway is clear. **3** an electrical impulse or radio wave sent or received. •v. (**signalling, signalled**; US **signaling, signaled**) **1** give a signal. **2** show by means of a signal. •adj. noteworthy. □ **signal box** a building beside a railway track from which signals and points are controlled.

signatory n. (pl. **signatories**) a person who has signed an agreement.

signature n. a person's name written in a distinctive way, used in signing something. □ **signature tune** a tune announcing a particular television or radio programme.

signet ring n. a ring with an engraved design.

significance n. **1** importance. **2** meaning.

significant adj. **1** important or large enough to have an effect. **2** having a particular or secret meaning. ■ **significantly** adv.

signify v. (**signifying, signified**) **1** be a sign of; mean. **2** make known. ■ **signification** n.

Sikh /seek/ n. a follower of a religion that developed from Hinduism. ■ **Sikhism** n.

silage /sy-lij/ n. grass or green crops stored in a silo without being dried, used as animal feed.

silence n. complete lack of sound or speech. •v. make silent.

silencer n. a device for reducing the noise made by a gun or exhaust system.

silent adj. **1** without sound. **2** not speaking or not spoken aloud. ■ **silently** adv.

silhouette n. a dark shadow or outline seen against a lighter background. •v. show as a silhouette.

silica n. a compound of silicon occurring as quartz and found in sandstone.

silicon n. a non-metallic element, used to make electronic circuits. □ **silicon chip** a microchip.

silicone n. a substance made from silicon, used in implants etc.

silk n. a fine, soft shiny fibre produced by silkworms, made into thread or fabric. □ **silkworm** a caterpillar that spins a silk cocoon. ■ **silken** adj. **silky** adj.

sill n. a shelf or ledge at the foot of a window or doorway.

silly adj. (**sillier, silliest**) lacking common sense or judgement. ■ **silliness** n.

s

silo n. (pl. **silos**) **1** a tower for storing grain. **2** a pit or airtight structure for storing silage. **3** an underground chamber in which a guided missile is kept ready for firing.

silt n. fine sand or clay deposited by running water. • v. (**silt up**) fill or block with silt.

silvan var. of **SYLVAN**.

silver n. **1** a shiny greyish-white precious metal. **2** a shiny grey-white colour. **3** coins or articles made of silver or of a metal resembling silver. □ **silverfish** a small wingless insect. **silver jubilee** the 25th anniversary of an important event. **silverside** a joint of beef from the outside of the leg. **silver wedding** the 25th anniversary of a wedding. ■ **silvery** adj.

SIM card n. an electronic card in a mobile phone that stores personal data etc.

simian adj. of or like apes or monkeys.

similar adj. alike but not identical. ■ **similarity** n. **similarly** adv.

simile /sim-i-li/ n. a phrase that compares one thing to another, using as or like.

simmer v. **1** stay or keep just below boiling point. **2** be full of barely suppressed anger or excitement. **3** (**simmer down**) become calmer.

simper v. smile coyly. • n. a coy smile.

simple adj. **1** easily understood or done. **2** plain and basic. **3** composed of a single element. **4** of very low intelligence. ■ **simplicity** n. **simply** adv.

simpleton n. a foolish or unintelligent person.

simplify v. (**simplifying, simplified**) make easier to do or understand. ■ **simplification** n.

simplistic adj. treating complex issues as more simple than they really are. ■ **simplistically** adv.

simulate v. **1** imitate. **2** produce a computer model of. **3** pretend to feel. ■ **simulation** n. **simulator** n.

simultaneous adj. occurring or done at the same time. ■ **simultaneity** n. **simultaneously** adv.

sin n. an act that breaks a religious or moral law. • v. (**sinning, sinned**) commit a sin. ■ **sinner** n.

since prep. in the period between a time in the past until the present. • conj. **1** from the time that. **2** because. • adv. from the time mentioned until the present.

sincere adj. not pretending to be or feel; genuine and honest. ■ **sincerely** adv. **sincerity** n.

sine n. (in a right-angled triangle) the ratio of the side opposite a particular acute angle to the hypotenuse.

sinecure /sin-i-kyoor/ n. a paid job requiring little or no work.

sine qua non /see-nay kwah nohn/ n. a thing that is absolutely necessary.

sinew n. a band of strong tissue joining muscle to bone. ■ **sinewy** adj.

sinful adj. wicked. ■ **sinfully** adv. **sinfulness** n.

sing v. (**singing, sang**; past part. **sung**) **1** make musical sounds with the voice in the form of a song. **2** make a whistling sound. □ **sing-song 1** a rising and falling rhythm in a person's voice.

2 *informal* an informal gathering for singing. ■ **singer** *n.*

singe *v.* burn slightly. ■ *n.* a slight burn.

single *adj.* **1** one only. **2** designed for one person. **3** consisting of one part. **4** individual and distinct. **5** not involved in a romantic or sexual relationship. **6** (of a ticket) for an outward journey only. ■ *n.* **1** a single person or thing. **2** a short record or CD. **3** (**singles**) a game or contest for individual players. ■ *v.* (**single out**) choose from a group. □ **single-breasted** (of a coat) having one row of buttons at the centre of the front. **single-handed** done without help. **single market** an association of countries trading with few or no restrictions. **single-minded** concentrating on one particular aim. **single parent** a person bringing up a child or children without a partner. ■ **singly** *adv.*

singlet *n.* a sleeveless vest.

singleton *n.* a single person or thing.

singular *adj.* **1** (of a word or form) referring to just one person or thing. **2** very good; remarkable. ■ *n.* the singular form of a word. ■ **singularity** *n.* **singularly** *adv.*

sinister *adj.* seeming evil or dangerous.

sink *v.* (**sinking, sank**; *past part.* **sunk**) **1** go down below the surface of liquid. **2** go or send to the bottom of the sea. **3** move slowly downwards. **4** decrease in amount or strength. **5** force something sharp through a surface. **6** (**sink in**) be understood. **7** invest money. ■ *n.* a fixed basin with taps and a drainage pipe.

sinker *n.* a weight used to keep a fishing line beneath the water.

sinuous *adj.* **1** curving. **2** gracefully swaying.

sinus /sy-nuhss/ *n.* a hollow space in the bones of the face that connects with the nostrils.

sinusitis *n.* inflammation of a sinus.

sip *v.* (**sipping, sipped**) drink in small mouthfuls. ■ *n.* a small mouthful of liquid.

siphon *n.* a tube for transferring liquid from one container to another, using air pressure so as to maintain the flow. ■ *v.* **1** draw off by means of a siphon. **2** (**siphon off**) take small amounts of money over time.

sir *n.* **1** a polite form of address to a man. **2** used as the title of a knight or baronet.

sire *n.* **1** an animal's male parent. **2** *old use* a respectful form of address to a king. ■ *v.* be the male parent of.

siren *n.* **1** a device that makes a long loud warning sound. **2** an attractive but dangerous woman.

sirloin *n.* the best part of a loin of beef.

sirocco *n.* (*pl.* **siroccos**) a hot wind blowing from Africa to southern Europe.

sisal *n.* fibre from a tropical plant, used for ropes or matting.

sissy *n.* (*pl.* **sissies**) *informal* an effeminate or weak person.

sister *n.* **1** a woman or girl in relation to other children of her parents. **2** a female friend or colleague. **3** a nun. **4** a senior female nurse. □ **sisterhood 1** friendship and understanding between women. **2** a group of women with a shared interest.

s

sister-in-law (pl. **sisters-in-law**) the sister of a person's wife or husband, or the wife of a person's brother. ■ **sisterly** adj.

sit v. (**sitting, sat**) **1** rest your weight on your buttocks with your back upright. **2** be in a particular position or state. **3** pose for a portrait. **4** be a member of a committee etc. **5** (of a parliament, law court, etc.) be carrying on its business. **6** take an exam.

! Use **sitting** rather than **sat** with the verb 'to be': *we were sitting there for hours* not *we were sat there for hours.*

sitar n. a long-necked Indian lute.

sitcom n. informal a situation comedy.

site n. **1** a place where something is, was, or will be located. **2** a website. •v. establish or build in a particular place.

sitter n. **1** a person who sits for an artist. **2** a babysitter.

sitting n. **1** a period of time when a group are served a meal. **2** a period of time when a law court etc. is carrying on its business. **3** a period of posing for a portrait. □ **sitting room** a room for relaxing in. **sitting tenant** a tenant who has the legal right to remain living in a property.

situate v. put in a particular place.

situation n. **1** a set of circumstances. **2** the location and surroundings of a place. **3** a job. □ **situation comedy** a comedy series in which the same characters are involved in amusing situations. ■ **situational** adj.

six adj. & n. one more than five; 6. ■ **sixth** adj. & n.

sixteen adj. & n. one more than fifteen; 16. ■ **sixteenth** adj. & n.

sixty adj. & n. (pl. **sixties**) ten more than fifty; 60. ■ **sixtieth** adj. & n.

size n. **1** the overall measurements or extent of something. **2** each of the series of standard measurements in which articles are made. **3** a sticky solution used to glaze paper, stiffen textiles, etc. •v. (**size up**) assess.

sizeable (or **sizable**) adj. fairly large.

sizzle v. (of food) hiss when being fried.

skate n. **1** an ice skate or roller skate. **2** an edible flatfish. •v. **1** move on skates. **2** (**skate over**) refer only briefly to. □ **skateboard** a narrow board with wheels fixed to the bottom, for riding on while standing. ■ **skater** n.

skedaddle v. informal leave quickly.

skein /skayn/ n. a loosely coiled bundle of yarn.

skeletal adj. **1** of the skeleton. **2** very thin.

skeleton n. **1** a framework of bone or cartilage supporting or containing an animal's body. **2** a supporting structure. •adj. comprising an essential or minimum number: *a skeleton staff.* ■ **skeleton key** a key designed to fit many locks.

skeptic US = SCEPTIC.

sketch n. **1** a rough drawing. **2** a short humorous scene in a comedy show. **3** a brief account. •v. make a sketch of.

sketchy adj. not thorough or detailed. ■ **sketchily** adv.

skew v. **1** suddenly change direction or move at an angle. **2** make biased or distorted. □ **skewbald**

s

(of a horse) having patches of white and brown.

skewer n. a thin length of wood or metal for holding pieces of food during cooking. •v. hold or pierce with a skewer.

ski n. (pl. **skis**) each of a pair of long, narrow pieces of plastic etc. attached to boots for travelling over snow. •v. (**skiing**, **skied**) travel on skis. ■ **skier** n.

skid v. (**skidding**, **skidded**) slide sideways in an uncontrolled way. •n. an act of skidding.

skiff n. a light rowing boat.

skilful (US **skillful**) adj. having or showing skill. ■ **skilfully** adv.

> **!** There is only one l in the middle in British English: skilful.

skill n. **1** the ability to do something well. **2** a particular ability. ■ **skilled** adj.

skillet n. US a frying pan.

skim v. (**skimming**, **skimmed**) **1** remove a substance from the surface of a liquid. **2** glide. **3** read quickly. **4** (**skim over**) deal with briefly. □ **skimmed milk** milk from which the cream has been removed.

skimp v. spend less money, time, etc. than is really needed.

skimpy adj. (**skimpier**, **skimpiest**) **1** meagre. **2** (of clothes) short and revealing.

skin n. **1** the thin layer of tissue forming the outer covering of the body. **2** the skin of a dead animal used for clothing etc. **3** an outer layer. •v. (**skinning**, **skinned**) remove the skin from. □ **skindiving** swimming under water without a diving suit, using an aqualung and flippers. **skinflint** informal a miser. **skinhead** n. a

young person of a group with very short shaved hair.

skinny adj. (**skinnier**, **skinniest**) very thin.

skint adj. informal having little or no money.

skip v. (**skipping**, **skipped**) **1** move lightly, jumping from one foot to the other. **2** jump repeatedly over a rope turned over the head and under the feet. **3** omit or miss. •n. **1** a skipping movement. **2** a large open container for bulky refuse.

skipper n. informal a captain.

skirmish n. a short spell of fighting. •v. take part in a skirmish.

skirt n. a woman's garment hanging from the waist, or this part of a coat or dress. •v. **1** go round or past the edge of. **2** avoid dealing with. □ **skirting board** a wooden board along the base of the wall of a room.

skit n. a short comedy sketch.

skittish adj. nervous, lively, or unpredictable.

skittle n. **1** (**skittles**) a game played with wooden pins set up to be bowled down with a ball. **2** a pin used in skittles.

skive v. informal avoid work or a duty by staying away or leaving early. ■ **skiver** n.

skivvy n. (pl. **skivvies**) informal a female domestic servant.

skulduggery n. underhand behaviour.

skulk v. loiter stealthily.

skull n. the bony framework surrounding the brain. □ **skullcap** a small cap without a peak.

skunk n. a black-and-white striped mammal able to spray foul-smelling liquid.

s

sky n. (pl. **skies**) the upper atmosphere seen from the earth.
□ **skydiving** the sport of parachuting from an aircraft and performing acrobatic movements in the air. **skylark** a lark that sings while in flight. **skylight** a window set in a roof. **skyscraper** a very tall building.

slab n. a broad, flat piece of something solid.

slack adj. **1** not taut or tight. **2** not busy. **3** careless or lazy. •n. **1** a slack part of a rope. **2** (**slacks**) casual trousers. •v. **1** decrease in intensity or speed. **2** informal work slowly. ■ **slacken** v. **slacker** n. **slackness** n.

slag n. **1** stony waste left when metal has been smelted. **2** informal, derog. a promiscuous woman. •v. (**slagging**, **slagged**) (**slag off**) informal criticize rudely.

slain past part. of SLAY.

slake v. satisfy a thirst.

slalom n. a skiing or canoeing race following a winding course.

slam v. (**slamming, slammed**) **1** shut forcefully and loudly. **2** put or hit with great force. **3** informal criticize severely. •n. a noise of slamming.

slander n. the crime of making false statements that damage a person's reputation. •v. make false and harmful statements about. ■ **slanderous** adj.

slang n. very informal language used esp. in speech and by a particular group.

slant v. **1** slope. **2** present information from a particular point of view. •n. **1** a slope. **2** a point of view. ■ **slantwise** adv.

slap v. (**slapping, slapped**) **1** hit with the palm of the hand or a flat

object. **2** place quickly or carelessly. •n. an act of slapping. •adv. informal suddenly and forcefully. □ **slapdash** hurried and careless. **slapstick** comedy based on deliberately clumsy actions.

slash v. **1** cut with a sweeping stroke. **2** informal reduce greatly. •n. **1** a cut made with a sweeping stroke. **2** a slanting line (/) used between alternatives.

slat n. a thin, narrow piece of wood etc.

slate n. a greyish rock that splits into smooth, flat plates, used for roofs and formerly for writing on. •v. **1** informal criticize severely. **2** plan; schedule.

slattern n. old use a dirty, untidy woman. ■ **slatternly** adj.

slaughter n. **1** the killing of farm animals for food. **2** the killing of many people in a brutal way. •v. kill in this way. □ **slaughterhouse** a place where animals are killed for food.

Slav n. a member of a group of peoples in central and eastern Europe. ■ **Slavic** adj.

slave n. **1** hist. a person owned by another and forced to obey them. **2** a person strongly influenced or controlled by something. •v. work very hard. □ **slave-driver** informal a person who makes others work very hard. ■ **slavery** n.

slaver v. let saliva run from the mouth.

slavish adj. showing no originality. ■ **slavishly** adv.

slay v. (**slaying, slew**; past part. **slain**) old use kill. ■ **slayer** n.

sleaze n. informal immoral or dishonest behaviour.

sleazy *adj.* (**sleazier**, **sleaziest**)
1 immoral or dishonest. **2** dirty
and seedy. ■ **sleaziness** *n.*

sled *n.* US a sledge.

sledge *n.* a vehicle on runners for
travelling over snow. •*v.* ride on a
sledge.

sledgehammer *n.* a large, heavy
hammer.

sleek *adj.* **1** smooth and glossy.
2 looking wealthy and smart.

sleep *n.* a state of rest in which the
eyes are closed and the mind unconscious. •*v.* (**sleeping**, **slept**)
1 be asleep. **2** (**sleep in**) remain
asleep later than usual. **3** have
sleeping accommodation for.
□ **sleeping bag** a padded bag to
sleep in. **sleeping partner** a
partner who invests in a business
but is not involved in running it.
sleepover a night spent by children at another person's house.
sleepwalk walk around while
asleep. ■ **sleepless** *adj.*

sleeper *n.* **1** a beam on which a
railway track rests. **2** a ring or bar
worn in a pierced ear to keep the
hole from closing. **3** a train with
carriages having sleeping accommodation.

sleepy *adj.* (**sleepier**, **sleepiest**)
1 needing or ready for sleep.
2 without much activity.
■ **sleepily** *adv.* **sleepiness** *n.*

sleet *n.* rain containing snow. •*v.*
fall as sleet.

sleeve *n.* **1** the part of a garment
covering the arm. **2** a protective
cover. □ **up your sleeve** secret
but ready for use. ■ **sleeveless**
adj.

sleigh *n.* a sledge pulled by horses
or reindeer.

sleight /slyt/ *n.* (**sleight of hand**)
skilful use of the hands when
performing conjuring tricks.

slender *adj.* **1** gracefully thin.
2 barely enough.

slept past & past part. OF SLEEP.

sleuth /slooth/ *n. informal* a
detective.

slew¹ *v.* turn or slide uncontrollably.

slew² past of SLAY.

slice *n.* **1** a thin, broad piece of
food cut from a larger portion. **2** a
share. **3** a utensil for lifting food.
•*v.* **1** cut into slices. **2** (in sport) hit
a ball so that it spins and curves as
it travels.

slick *adj.* **1** smooth and efficient.
2 self-confident but insincere.
3 smooth and glossy or slippery.
•*n.* a patch of oil. •*v.* make hair
smooth and glossy. ■ **slickly** *adv.*
slickness *n.*

slide *v.* (**sliding**, **slid**) **1** move
along a smooth surface while
remaining in contact with it.
2 move smoothly or without being
noticed. •*n.* **1** a structure with a
smooth sloping surface for sliding
down. **2** a piece of glass on which
an object is placed for viewing
under a microscope. **3** a piece of
photographic film for viewing with
a projector. □ **sliding scale** a
scale of fees, wages, etc., that
varies according to particular conditions.

slight *adj.* **1** small in degree. **2** not
sturdy. **3** superficial or trivial. •*v.*
treat disrespectfully. •*n.* an insult.
■ **slightly** *adv.*

slim *adj.* (**slimmer**, **slimmest**)
1 gracefully thin. **2** small in width.
3 very small. •*v.* (**slimming**,
slimmed) become thinner.

S

□ **slimline** slender in design. ■ **slimmer** n.

slime n. an unpleasantly moist, slippery substance.

slimy adj. (**slimier, slimiest**) 1 like or covered with slime. 2 informal insincerely flattering.

sling n. 1 a loop of fabric used to support or lift something. 2 a strap or loop for hurling small missiles. •v. (**slinging, slung**) 1 hang or carry loosely. 2 informal throw.

slink v. (**slinking, slunk**) move stealthily.

slinky adj. (of a garment) close-fitting and sexy.

slip v. (**slipping, slipped**) 1 lose your balance and slide. 2 slide out of position or from someone's grasp. 3 gradually worsen. 4 (**slip up**) make a careless error. 5 move or place quietly, quickly, or secretly. 6 get free from. •n. 1 an act of slipping. 2 a minor mistake. 3 a petticoat. 4 a small piece of paper. □ **give someone the slip** informal escape from someone. **slipped disc** a displaced disc between vertebrae in the spine. **slip road** a road entering or leaving a motorway. **slipshod** careless or disorganized. **slipstream** a current of air or water driven back by a propeller or jet engine. **slipway** a slope leading into water, for launching or landing boats.

slipper n. a light indoor shoe.

slippery adj. 1 difficult to hold or stand on because smooth or wet. 2 not trustworthy. ■ **slipperiness** n.

slit n. a long, narrow cut or opening. •v. (**slitting, slit**) make a slit in.

slither v. slide unsteadily.

sliver n. a small, sharp piece.

slob n. informal a lazy, untidy person.

slobber v. slaver or dribble.

sloe n. a small sour bluish-black fruit.

slog informal v. (**slogging, slogged**) 1 work hard. 2 move with effort. 3 hit hard. •n. a period of hard work or travelling.

slogan n. a short, memorable phrase used in advertising or politics.

sloop n. a sailing boat with one mast.

slop v. (**slopping, slopped**) spill or overflow. •pl. n. (**slops**) 1 un-appetizing semi-liquid food. 2 waste liquid.

slope n. a surface with one end higher than another. •v. 1 form a slope. 2 (**slope off**) informal leave without being noticed.

sloppy adj. (**sloppier, sloppiest**) 1 careless or disorganized. 2 containing too much liquid. ■ **sloppily** adv. **sloppiness** n.

slosh v. move with a splashing sound.

slot n. 1 a long, narrow opening into which something may be inserted. 2 a place in an arrangement etc. •v. (**slotting, slotted**) fit into a slot. □ **slot machine** a fruit machine or vending machine.

sloth /slohth/ n. 1 laziness. 2 a slow-moving tropical American mammal. ■ **slothful** adj.

slouch v. stand, move, or sit in a lazy, drooping way. •n. a lazy, drooping posture.

slough[1] /slow/ n. a swamp.

slough[2] /sluf/ v. (of an animal) shed an old skin.

slovenly adj. 1 untidy. 2 careless. ■ **slovenliness** n.

slow → smear

slow adj. 1 not moving or able to move quickly. 2 taking a long time. 3 (of a clock etc.) showing a time earlier than the correct time. 4 not quick to understand or learn. • v. reduce speed. □ **slow-worm** a small lizard without legs. ▪ **slowly** adv. **slowness** n.

sludge n. thick, soft mud.

slug n. 1 a small creature like a snail without a shell. 2 a small amount of an alcoholic drink. 3 a bullet. • v. (**slugging**, **slugged**) informal hit hard.

sluggard n. a lazy person.

sluggish adj. 1 slow-moving. 2 not lively. ▪ **sluggishly** adv. **sluggishness** n.

sluice /slooss/ n. 1 a sliding gate controlling a flow of water. 2 a channel for surplus water. • v. rinse with water.

slum n. a run-down city area inhabited by very poor people.

slumber v. sleep. • n. a sleep.

slump v. 1 sit or lean heavily and limply. 2 decline greatly. • n. a sudden fall in prices or demand.

slung past & past part. of SLING.

slunk past & past part. of SLINK.

slur v. (**slurring**, **slurred**) 1 speak in an unclear way. 2 perform a group of musical notes in a flowing way. • n. 1 an insult or accusation. 2 a curved line indicating that notes are to be slurred.

slurp v. eat or drink with a loud sucking sound.

slurry n. a semi-liquid mixture of water and manure, cement, or coal.

slush n. 1 partially melted snow or ice. 2 informal sentimental talk or writing. □ **slush fund** a reserve of money for illegal purposes. ▪ **slushy** adj.

slut n. a slovenly or promiscuous woman. ▪ **sluttish** adj.

sly adj. 1 cunning and deceitful. 2 (of a remark etc.) suggesting secret knowledge. □ **on the sly** secretly. ▪ **slyly** adv. **slyness** n.

smack n. 1 a slap. 2 a loud, sharp sound. 3 a loud kiss. 4 informal heroin. 5 a sailing boat with one mast. • v. 1 slap. 2 part the lips noisily. □ **smack of 1** suggest the presence of. 2 taste of.

small adj. 1 of less than normal size. 2 not great in amount, power, or importance. 3 young. □ **smallholding** a small area of leased agricultural land. **small hours** the early hours of the morning after midnight. **smallpox** a viral disease with blisters that leave permanent scars. **small talk** polite conversation about unimportant matters. ▪ **smallness** n.

smarmy adj. informal excessively and insincerely friendly.

smart adj. 1 neat and stylish. 2 fashionable and upmarket. 3 intelligent. 4 quick. • v. 1 give a sharp, stinging pain. 2 feel annoyed. □ **smart card** a plastic card on which electronic information is stored. ▪ **smarten** v. **smartly** adv. **smartness** n.

smash v. 1 break violently into pieces. 2 hit or collide forcefully. 3 destroy or ruin. • n. 1 an act of smashing. 2 informal a very successful song, film, etc.

smashing adj. informal excellent.

smattering n. 1 a small amount. 2 a slight knowledge.

smear v. 1 coat or mark with a greasy or sticky substance. 2 damage the reputation of. • n. 1 a greasy or sticky mark. 2 a false accusation. □ **smear test** a test to detect signs of cervical cancer.

smell n. **1** the ability to sense things with the nose. **2** something sensed by the nose. **3** an act of smelling. •v. (**smelling, smelt** or **smelled**) **1** sense the smell of. **2** give off a smell. ■ **smelly** adj.

smelt v. heat and melt ore to extract metal.

smidgen (or **smidgin**) n. informal a tiny amount.

smile v. turn up the corners of the mouth to show pleasure, amusement, or friendliness. •n. an act of smiling.

smirk v. smile smugly. •n. a smug smile.

smite v. (**smiting, smote;** past part. **smitten**) **1** (**be smitten**) be strongly attracted to someone. **2** (**be smitten**) be severely affected by a disease. **3** old use hit hard.

smith n. **1** a worker in metal. **2** a blacksmith.

smithereens pl. n. informal small pieces.

smithy n. (pl. **smithies**) a blacksmith's workshop.

smock n. a loose dress, shirt, or overall.

smog n. fog or haze made worse by atmospheric pollution.

smoke n. **1** a visible vapour produced by a burning substance. **2** an act of smoking tobacco. •v. **1** give out smoke. **2** breathe smoke from a cigarette etc. in and out. **3** preserve meat or fish by exposure to smoke. □ **smokescreen** something intended to disguise your real motives etc. ■ **smokeless** adj. **smoker** n. **smoky** adj.

smolder US = SMOULDER.

smooch v. informal kiss and cuddle.

smooth adj. **1** having an even and regular surface. **2** moving without jerks. **3** without difficulties. **4** charming but possibly insincere. **5** not harsh or bitter. •v. make smooth. ■ **smoothly** adv. **smoothness** n.

smoothie n. **1** a drink made of fruit puréed with milk or ice cream. **2** informal a charming and confident man.

smorgasbord n. a meal consisting of a range of savoury items.

smote past of SMITE.

smother v. **1** suffocate. **2** cover completely. **3** prevent from happening.

smoulder (US **smolder**) v. **1** burn slowly with smoke but no flame. **2** feel strong and barely hidden anger etc.

SMS abbrev. Short Message Service, used to send and receive text messages.

smudge v. make or become blurred or smeared. •n. a smudged mark. ■ **smudgy** adj.

smug adj. (**smugger, smuggest**) irritatingly pleased with yourself. ■ **smugly** adv. **smugness** n.

smuggle v. **1** move goods illegally into or out of a country. **2** convey secretly. ■ **smuggler** n.

smut n. **1** a small flake of soot or dirt. **2** indecent writing, pictures, etc. ■ **smutty** adj.

snack n. a small or casual meal.

snaffle v. informal take quickly or secretly. •n. a simple bit on a bridle.

snag n. **1** an unexpected difficulty. **2** a jagged projection. **3** a small tear. •v. (**snagging, snagged**) catch or tear on a snag.

snail n. a mollusc with a spiral shell.

snake n. a reptile with no legs and a long slender body. •v. move with a twisting motion. ■ **snaky** adj.

snap v. (**snapping, snapped**) 1 break with a sharp crack. 2 open or close with a brisk movement or sharp sound. 3 (**snap up**) quickly buy. 4 say quickly and irritably. 5 take a snapshot of. •n. 1 an act of snapping. 2 a snapshot. •adj. done on the spur of the moment. □ **snapdragon** a plant with brightly coloured flowers that have a mouth-like opening. **snapshot** an informal photo.

snapper n. an edible sea fish.

snappy adj. (**snappier, snappiest**) informal 1 short and clever: snappy slogans. 2 neat and stylish. 3 irritable.

snare n. a trap with a loop of wire that pulls tight. •v. catch or trap.

snarl v. 1 growl with bared teeth. 2 say aggressively. 3 (**snarl up**) entangle. •n. an act of snarling. □ **snarl-up** informal a traffic jam.

snatch v. seize quickly or eagerly. •n. 1 an act of snatching. 2 a fragment of music or talk.

snazzy adj. (**snazzier, snazziest**) informal stylish.

sneak v. 1 go, do, or obtain furtively. 2 informal report another's wrongdoings. 3 (**sneaking**) (of a feeling) persisting. •n. informal a telltale. ■ **sneakily** adv. **sneaky** adj.

sneaker n. a soft shoe worn for sports or casual occasions.

sneer n. a scornful smile or remark. •v. smile or speak scornfully.

sneeze v. suddenly expel air from the nose and mouth. •n. an act of sneezing.

snicker v. & n. = SNIGGER.

snide adj. disrespectful or mocking in an indirect way.

sniff v. 1 draw in air audibly through the nose. 2 (**sniff around**) informal investigate secretly. 3 (**sniff out**) informal discover. •n. an act of sniffing. ■ **sniffer** n.

sniffle v. sniff slightly or repeatedly. •n. an act of sniffling.

snifter n. informal a small quantity of an alcoholic drink.

snigger n. a half-suppressed laugh. •v. give a snigger.

snip v. (**snipping, snipped**) cut with small, quick strokes. •n. 1 an act of snipping. 2 informal a bargain.

snipe v. 1 fire shots from a hiding place at long range. 2 criticize in a sly way. •n. (pl. **snipe** or **snipes**) a wading bird with a long bill. ■ **sniper** n.

snippet n. a small piece.

snivel v. (**snivelling, snivelled**; US **sniveling, sniveled**) 1 cry. 2 complain in a whining way.

snob n. a person who greatly respects high social status or wealth and who looks down on lower-class people. ■ **snobbery** n. **snobbish** adj.

snog informal v. (**snogging, snogged**) kiss. •n. a kiss.

snood n. a hairnet worn at the back of a woman's head.

snooker n. a game played with cues on a billiard table.

snoop v. informal investigate secretly. ■ **snooper** n.

S

snooty adj. (**snootier, snootiest**) informal superior towards others. ■ **snootily** adv.

snooze informal n. a nap. •v. have a nap.

snore n. a snorting sound made whilst asleep. •v. make such sounds.

snorkel n. a tube for a swimmer to breathe through while under water. •v. (**snorkelling, snorkelled;** US **snorkeling, snorkeled**) swim with a snorkel.

snort n. an explosive sound made by forcing breath through the nose. •v. **1** make a snort. **2** informal inhale cocaine.

snot n. informal mucus in the nose.

snout n. an animal's projecting nose and mouth.

snow n. frozen water vapour in the atmosphere that falls in light white flakes. •v. **1** fall as snow. **2** (**be snowed under**) be overwhelmed with work etc. □ **snowboarding** the sport of sliding downhill over snow on a single short, broad ski. **snowdrift** a bank of deep snow heaped up by the wind. **snowdrop** a plant bearing drooping white flowers in late winter. **snowman** a human figure made of compressed snow. **snowplough** (US **snowplow**) a device or vehicle for clearing roads of snow. ■ **snowy** adj.

snowball n. a ball of packed snow. •v. increase rapidly in size or importance.

snub v. (**snubbing, snubbed**) ignore or reject scornfully. •n. an act of snubbing. •adj. (of the nose) short and turned up at the end.

snuff v. **1** put out a candle. **2** (**snuff it**) informal die. •n. powdered tobacco for sniffing up the nostril.

snuffle v. breathe with noisy sniffs. •n. a snuffling sound.

snug adj. (**snugger, snuggest**) **1** cosy. **2** close-fitting. •n. a small, cosy bar in a pub. ■ **snugly** adv.

snuggle v. settle into a warm, comfortable position.

so adv. **1** to such a great extent. **2** to the same extent. **3** similarly. **4** thus. •conj. **1** therefore. **2** (**so that**) with the result or aim that. □ **so-and-so** informal **1** a person whose name you do not know. **2** a disliked person. **so-called** wrongly called by the name or term specified.

soak v. **1** keep immersed in liquid until thoroughly wet. **2** (of a liquid) spread throughout. **3** (**soak up**) absorb.

soap n. **1** a substance used with water for washing. **2** informal a soap opera. •v. wash with soap. □ **soap opera** a television or radio serial dealing with the lives of a group of characters. ■ **soapy** adj.

soar v. **1** rise high into the air. **2** increase rapidly.

sob v. (**sobbing, sobbed**) cry with loud gasps. •n. an act of sobbing.

sober adj. **1** not drunk. **2** serious. **3** (of a colour) not bright. •v. make or become sober. ■ **soberly** adv. **sobriety** n.

sobriquet (or **soubriquet**) /sohbri-kay/ n. a nickname.

soccer n. a form of football played with a round ball.

sociable adj. **1** enjoying the company of others. **2** friendly and welcoming. ■ **sociability** n. **sociably** adv.

social adj. **1** of society. **2** needing the company of others. **3** (of an

activity) in which people meet for pleasure. **4** (of animals) living in organized communities. • n. a social gathering. □ **social security** money provided by the state for people with little or no income.
social services services provided by the state such as medical care.
social worker a person whose job is to help people with family or financial problems. ■ **socially** adv.

socialism n. a political theory that a country's transport, resources, and industries should be owned or controlled by the state. ■ **socialist** n. & adj.

socialite n. a person who mixes in fashionable society.

socialize (or **-ise**) v. mix socially with others.

society n. (pl. **societies**) **1** people living together in an ordered community. **2** a particular community of people. **3** fashionable and wealthy people. **4** an organization or club. **5** the company of other people.

sociology n. the study of human society. ■ **sociological** adj. **sociologist** n.

sock n. a knitted garment for the foot and lower leg. **2** informal a hard blow. • v. informal hit hard.

socket n. a hollow or device into which something fits.

sod n. grass-covered ground, or a piece of this.

soda n. **1** fizzy water. **2** a compound of sodium.

sodden adj. soaked through.

sodium n. a soft silver-white metallic element. □ **sodium chloride** the chemical name for salt.

sodomy n. anal intercourse. ■ **sodomite** n.

sofa n. a long padded seat with a back and arms.

soft adj. **1** easy to mould, cut, compress, or fold. **2** not rough in texture. **3** quiet and gentle. **4** (of light or colour) not harsh. **5** not strict. **6** (of a drink) not alcoholic. **7** (of a drug) not likely to cause addiction. **8** (of water) free from mineral salts. □ **softball** a form of baseball played with a larger, softer ball. **soft fruit** fruit without a stone. **soft-hearted** kind and compassionate. **software** computer programs. **softwood** wood from coniferous trees. ■ **softly** adv. **softness** n.

soften v. make or become soft or softer. ■ **softener** n.

soggy adj. (**soggier**, **soggiest**) very wet and soft.

soigné /swun-yay/ adj. elegant and well groomed.

soil n. **1** the upper layer of the earth. **2** a nation's territory. • v. make dirty.

soirée /swah-ray/ n. an evening social gathering.

sojourn /so-juhn/ n. a temporary stay. • v. stay temporarily.

solace n. comfort in time of distress. • v. give solace to.

solar adj. of the sun or its rays. □ **solar plexus** a network of nerves at the pit of the stomach. **solar system** the sun with the planets etc. in orbit around it.

solarium n. (pl. **solariums** or **solaria**) a room equipped with sunbeds.

sold past & past part. of **SELL**.

solder n. a soft alloy for joining metals. • v. join with solder. □ **soldering iron** a tool for melting and applying solder.

soldier n. a person serving in an army. • v. **1** serve as a soldier. **2** (**soldier on**) informal keep trying.

sole n. **1** the underside of the foot. **2** the underside of a piece of footwear. **3** (pl. **sole**) an edible flatfish. • adj. **1** one and only. **2** belonging or restricted to one person or group. • v. put a sole on a shoe. ■ **solely** adv.

solecism /sol-i-si-z'm/ n. **1** a grammatical mistake. **2** an instance of incorrect behaviour.

solemn adj. **1** formal and dignified. **2** serious. ■ **solemnity** n. **solemnly** adv.

solemnize (or **-ise**) v. perform or mark with a ceremony.

solenoid n. a coil of wire which becomes magnetic when an electric current is passed through it.

solicit v. (**soliciting, solicited**) **1** try to obtain. **2** (of a prostitute) approach someone and offer sex for money. ■ **solicitation** n.

solicitor n. a lawyer who advises clients and instructs barristers.

solicitous adj. concerned about a person's well-being. ■ **solicitously** adv. **solicitude** n.

solid adj. **1** firm and stable in shape. **2** strongly built. **3** not hollow or having spaces. **4** consisting of the same substance throughout. **5** (of time) uninterrupted. **6** reliable. **7** three-dimensional. • n. a solid substance, object, or food. ■ **solidity** n. **solidly** adv.

solidarity n. agreement and support resulting from shared interests, feelings, etc.

solidify v. (**solidifying, solidified**) make or become solid. ■ **solidification** n.

soliloquy n. (pl. **soliloquies**) a speech in a play made by a character while alone.

solipsism n. the view that the self is all that can be known to exist.

solitaire n. **1** a game for one person played on a board with pegs. **2** a single gem in a piece of jewellery.

solitary adj. **1** alone. **2** isolated. **3** single.

solitude n. the state of being alone.

solo n. (pl. **solos**) a song, dance, or piece of music for or by one performer. • adj. & adv. for or done by one person. ■ **soloist** n.

solstice n. either of the two times in the year, midsummer and midwinter, when the sun reaches its highest or lowest point in the sky at noon.

soluble adj. **1** able to be dissolved. **2** able to be solved. ■ **solubility** n.

solution n. **1** a way of solving a problem. **2** the correct answer to a puzzle. **3** a mixture formed when a substance is dissolved in a liquid.

solve v. find the answer to a problem or mystery.

solvent adj. **1** having more money than you owe. **2** able to dissolve other substances. • n. a liquid used to dissolve other substances. ■ **solvency** n.

somatic adj. of the body rather than the mind.

sombre (US **somber**) adj. dark and gloomy.

sombrero n. (pl. **sombreros**) a broad-brimmed hat.

some adj. **1** an unspecified amount or number of. **2** unknown or unspecified. **3** approximately. **4** considerable. **5** expressing admiration. • pron. a certain amount or number of people or things. □ **somebody** someone. **somehow 1** by one way or another. **2** for an unknown reason. **someone 1** an unknown or unspecified person. **2** an important person. **something** an unspecified or unknown thing. **sometime** at an unspecified or unknown time. **sometimes** occasionally. **somewhat** to some extent. **somewhere** in or to an unspecified or unknown place.

somersault *n.* a movement in which a person turns head over heels and finishes on their feet. •*v.* perform a somersault.

somnambulism *n.* sleepwalking. ■ **somnambulist** *n.*

somnolent *adj.* sleepy. ■ **somnolence** *n.*

son *n.* a boy or man in relation to his parents. □ **son-in-law** (*pl.* **sons-in-law**) the husband of a person's daughter.

sonar *n.* a system for detecting objects under water by giving out sound pulses.

sonata *n.* a piece of music for a solo instrument, often with a piano accompaniment.

son et lumière /son ay loo-mi-air/ *n.* a night-time entertainment dramatizing a historical event with lighting and sound effects.

song *n.* **1** a set of words set to music. **2** singing. ■ **songbird** a bird with a musical song. **songster** (*fem.* **songstress**) a singer.

sonic *adj.* of or using sound waves. □ **sonic boom** a loud noise caused by the shock wave from an object travelling faster than the speed of sound. ■ **sonically** *adv.*

sonnet *n.* a poem of 14 lines.

sonorous *adj.* (of a sound) deep and full. ■ **sonority** *n.* **sonorously** *adv.*

soon *adv.* **1** in or after a short time. **2** (**would sooner**) would rather. □ **sooner or later** eventually.

soot *n.* a black powdery substance produced when coal, wood, etc. is burnt. ■ **sooty** *adj.*

soothe *v.* **1** calm. **2** relieve pain or discomfort.

soothsayer *n.* a prophet.

sop *n.* a thing given or done to pacify someone. •*v.* (**sopping**, **sopped**) (**sop up**) soak up liquid.

sophist *n.* a person who uses clever but specious arguments. ■ **sophism** *n.* **sophistry** *n.*

sophisticate *n.* a sophisticated person.

sophisticated *adj.* **1** having experience and taste in matters of culture or fashion. **2** highly developed and complex. ■ **sophistication** *n.*

sophomore *n.* US a second-year university or high-school student.

soporific *adj.* causing drowsiness or sleep.

sopping *adj.* wet through.

soppy *adj.* (**soppier**, **soppiest**) *informal* too sentimental. ■ **soppily** *adv.*

soprano *n.* (*pl.* **sopranos**) the highest singing voice.

sorbet /sor-bay/ *n.* a water ice.

sorcerer *n.* (*fem.* **sorceress**) a person who practises magic. ■ **sorcery** *n.*

sordid *adj.* **1** dishonest or immoral. **2** very dirty and unpleasant. ■ **sordidly** *adv.* **sordidness** *n.*

sore *adj.* painful or aching. •*n.* a sore place on the body. □ **sore point** a

S

cause of distress or annoyance. ■ **soreness** n.

sorely adv. very; badly.

sorghum n. a cereal grown for grain and animal feed.

sorrel n. 1 a sharp-tasting herb. 2 a light reddish-brown colour.

sorrow n. 1 deep distress caused by loss or disappointment. 2 a cause of this. ■ **sorrowful** adj. **sorrowfully** adv.

sorry adj. (sorrier, sorriest) 1 feeling sympathy for another's misfortune. 2 feeling regret. 3 in a bad or pitiful state.

sort n. 1 a kind or category. 2 informal a person with a specified nature. •v. 1 arrange in groups. 2 separate from a mixed group. 3 (sort out) solve a problem.

sortie n. 1 an attack by troops from a defended position. 2 a flight by an aircraft on a military operation.

SOS n. 1 an international distress signal. 2 an urgent appeal for help.

sot n. a habitual drunkard.

sotto voce /sot-toh voh-chay/ adv. & adj. in a quiet voice.

soubriquet var. of SOBRIQUET.

soufflé n. a light, spongy dish made with beaten egg whites.

sough /sow, suf/ v. make a moaning or whistling sound.

sought past & past part. of SEEK.

souk /sook/ n. an Arab market.

soul n. 1 the spiritual or immortal element of a person. 2 a person's inner nature. 3 emotional energy or power. 4 a perfect example of a quality: the soul of discretion. 5 a person. 6 a kind of music with elements of gospel and rhythm and blues. □ **soulmate** a person ideally suited to another.

soulful adj. expressing deep emotion. ■ **soulfully** adv.

soulless adj. lacking character, interest, or emotion.

sound n. 1 vibrations travelling through the air and sensed by the ear. 2 a thing that can be heard. 3 an impression. 4 a narrow stretch of water. •v. 1 make a sound. 2 make a sound to show or warn. 3 give a specified impression. 4 (sound off) express opinions forcefully. 5 (sound out) ask someone what they think. 6 find out the depth of water using sound echoes etc. •adj. 1 in good condition. 2 based on good judgement. 3 (of sleep) deep. □ **sound barrier** the point at which an aircraft reaches the speed of sound. **sound bite** a short memorable extract from a speech. **soundproof** preventing sound getting in or out. **soundtrack** the sound accompanying to a film. ■ **soundly** adv.

sounding n. 1 a measurement of the depth of water. 2 (soundings) information found out before taking action. □ **sounding board** a person used to test new ideas.

soup n. a liquid dish of meat, fish, or vegetables. •v. (soup up) informal make more powerful. □ **soup kitchen** a place where free food is served to very poor people.

soupçon /soop-son/ n. a very small quantity.

sour adj. 1 having a sharp taste. 2 unpleasantly stale. 3 resentful or angry. •v. make or become sour. ■ **sourly** adv. **sourness** n.

source n. 1 a place, person, or thing from which something originates. 2 a place where a river begins. **3** a person, book, etc. providing information.

souse v. **1** soak. **2** (**soused**) pickled.

south n. **1** the direction on the right-hand side of a person facing east. **2** the southern part of a place. • adj. **1** lying towards or facing the south. **2** (of a wind) from the south. • adv. towards the south. ■ **southerly** adj. & adv. **southward** adj. & adv. **southwards** adv.

south-east n. the direction or region halfway between south and east. • adj. & adv. **1** towards or facing the south-east. **2** (of a wind) from the south-east. ■ **south-easterly** adj. & adv. **south-eastern** adj.

southern adj. situated in or facing the south.

southerner n. a person from the south of a region.

south-west n. the direction or region halfway between south and west. • adj. & adv. **1** towards or facing the south-west. **2** (of a wind) from the south-west. ■ **south-westerly** adj. & adv. **south-western** adj.

souvenir n. a thing kept as a reminder of a person, place, or event.

sou'wester n. a waterproof hat with a broad flap at the back.

sovereign n. **1** a king or queen who is the supreme ruler of a country. **2** a former British gold coin worth one pound sterling. • adj. **1** having supreme power. **2** (of a state) independent. ■ **sovereignty** n.

Soviet n. a citizen of the former Soviet Union. • adj. of the former Soviet Union.

sow¹ /soh/ v. (**sowing**, **sowed**; past part. **sown** or **sowed**) **1** plant seed by scattering it on or in the earth. **2** spread something unwelcome.

sow² /sow/ n. an adult female pig.

soya bean n. an edible bean that is high in protein.

soy souce n. a sauce made with fermented soya beans.

sozzled adj. informal very drunk.

spa n. a place with a mineral spring believed to have health-giving properties.

space n. **1** an unoccupied expanse or area. **2** a blank between written words or characters. **3** the universe beyond the earth's atmosphere. **4** the whole expanse in which all things exist and move. **5** an interval of time. • v. **1** position items at a distance from one another. **2** (**spaced out**) informal dazed. □ **spacecraft** a vehicle for travelling in space. **spaceship** a manned spacecraft.

spacious adj. having plenty of space. ■ **spaciousness** n.

spade n. **1** a tool for digging, with a broad metal blade on a long handle. **2** (**spades**) one of the four suits in a pack of playing cards. □ **spadework** hard preparatory work.

spaghetti pl. n. pasta in long strands.

spam n. unwanted email sent to many Internet users. • v. (**spamming**, **spammed**) send unwanted email to many people.

span n. **1** extent from side to side. **2** duration. **3** a part of a bridge between the uprights supporting it. • v. (**spanning**, **spanned**) extend across or over.

spangle n. a small piece of decorative glittering material. ■ **spangled** adj.

Spaniard n. a person from Spain.

spaniel n. a dog with a long silky coat and drooping ears.

Spanish n. the main language of Spain and of much of Central and South America. • adj. of Spain.

spank v. slap on the buttocks.

spanking adj. **1** brisk. **2** informal impressive.

spanner n. a tool for gripping and turning a nut or bolt.

spar v. (**sparring, sparred**) **1** make the motions of boxing but without force, as a form of training. **2** argue without hostility. • n. a strong pole used to support a ship's sails.

spare adj. **1** additional to what is required. **2** not currently in use or occupied. **3** thin. • n. an item kept in case another is lost, broken, etc. • v. **1** give someone something that you have enough of. **2** refrain from killing or harming. □ **to spare** left over.

sparing adj. not wasteful; economical. ■ **sparingly** adv.

spark n. **1** a fiery particle. **2** a flash of light produced by an electrical discharge. **3** a small amount of a quality or feeling. • v. **1** produce sparks. **2** cause. □ **spark plug** a device which ignites the fuel in an internal-combustion engine.

sparkle v. **1** shine with flashes of light. **2** be lively and witty. **3** (**sparkling**) (of drink) fizzy. • n. a sparkling light. ■ **sparkly** adj.

sparkler n. a hand-held firework that gives out sparks.

sparrow n. a small brown and grey bird.

sparse adj. thinly scattered. ■ **sparsely** adv. **sparsity** n.

spartan adj. not comfortable or luxurious.

spasm n. **1** a sudden involuntary contraction of a muscle. **2** a sudden spell of an activity etc.

spasmodic adj. occurring or done in brief, irregular bursts. ■ **spasmodically** adv.

spastic adj. **1** of muscle spasm. **2** offens. of cerebral palsy. • n. offens. a person with cerebral palsy. ■ **spasticity** n.

> ! Say person with cerebral palsy rather than spastic, which many people find offensive.

spat[1] past and past part. of SPIT.

spat[2] n. **1** informal a petty quarrel. **2** a cloth covering formerly worn over the ankles and shoes.

spate n. **1** a large number of similar things coming one after another. **2** a sudden flood.

spatial adj. of space. ■ **spatially** adv.

spatter v. spray or splash with drops or spots.

spatula n. an implement with a broad, flat, blunt blade for mixing or spreading.

spawn v. **1** (of a fish, frog, etc.) release or deposit eggs. **2** give rise to. • n. the eggs of fish, frogs, etc.

spay v. sterilize a female animal by removing the ovaries.

speak v. (**speaking, spoke;** past part. **spoken**) **1** say something. **2** communicate or be able to communicate in a specified language. **3** (**speak for**) express the views of. **4** be evidence of.

speaker n. **1** a person who speaks. **2** (**Speaker**) the person in charge of proceedings in a parliament. **3** a loudspeaker.

spear n. **1** a weapon with a pointed tip and a long shaft. **2** a stem of asparagus or broccoli. •v. pierce with a pointed object. □ **spearhead 1** a person leading a campaign or attack. **2** lead a campaign or attack.

spearmint n. a type of mint used in cooking.

spec n. (**on spec**) *informal* without any preparation or plan.

special adj. **1** better than or different from what is usual. **2** for a particular purpose or person. □ **special effects** illusions created for films and television by computer graphics etc. ■ **specially** adv.

specialist n. an expert in a particular field. ■ **specialism** n.

speciality n. (pl. **specialities**) a subject or skill in which someone is an expert.

specialize (or **-ise**) v. **1** be a specialist. **2** (**be specialized**) be adapted for a special function. ■ **specialization** n.

species n. (pl. **species**) a group of animals or plants able to breed with each other.

specific adj. **1** clearly defined or identified. **2** precise and clear. •n. (**specifics**) precise details. ■ **specifically** adv.

specification n. **1** the act of specifying. **2** a detailed description of the design and materials used to make something.

specify v. (**specifying**, **specified**) state or identify clearly and definitely.

specimen n. **1** an individual animal, plant, etc. used as an ex-

ample for study or display. **2** a sample for medical testing.

specious adj. seeming reasonable, but actually wrong.

speck n. a tiny spot or particle.

speckle n. a small spot or patch of colour. ■ **speckled** adj.

specs pl. n. *informal* spectacles.

spectacle n. **1** a visually striking performance or display. **2** (**spectacles**) a pair of glasses.

spectacular adj. very impressive or dramatic. •n. a spectacular performance or event. ■ **spectacularly** adv.

spectator n. a person who watches a game or event.

spectral adj. **1** of or like a ghost. **2** of the spectrum.

spectre (US **specter**) n. **1** a ghost. **2** a possible unwelcome occurrence.

spectrum n. (pl. **spectra**) **1** a band of colours produced by separating light into parts with different wavelengths. **2** a range of sound waves or other types of wave. **3** a range of beliefs, qualities, etc.

speculate v. **1** form a theory without firm evidence. **2** invest in stocks, property, etc. in the hope of making a profit. ■ **speculation** n. **speculative** adj. **speculator** n.

speculum n. (pl. **specula**) a medical instrument for widening openings in the body to allow inspection.

speech n. **1** the expression of thoughts and feelings using spoken language. **2** a formal talk given to an audience. **3** a sequence of lines for one character in a play.

speechless adj. unable to speak due to shock or emotion.

S

speed n. 1 rate of movement or operation. 2 rapidity of movement or action. 3 each of the possible gear ratios of a bicycle. 4 informal an amphetamine drug. • v. (**speeding, speeded** or **sped**) 1 move quickly. 2 (**speed up**) move or work more quickly. 3 break the legal speed limit. □ **speedboat** a fast motorboat. **speedometer** a device indicating a vehicle's speed. **speedway** motorcycle racing on a dirt track.

speedy adj. (**speedier, speediest**) rapid. ■ **speedily** adv.

speleology /spee-li-ol-uh-ji/ n. the study or exploration of caves.

spell v. (**spelling, spelled** or **spelt**) 1 write or say the letters forming a word in correct order. 2 lead to. 3 (**spell out**) state explicitly. • n. 1 a short period of time. 2 words spoken to make a piece of magic work. □ **spellbound** entranced. **spellchecker** a computer program which checks spelling in an electronic document. ■ **spelling** n.

spend v. (**spending, spent**) 1 pay money to buy or hire goods or services. 2 pass time. 3 use or use up. □ **spendthrift** a person who spends money irresponsibly. ■ **spender** n.

sperm n. (pl. **sperm** or **sperms**) 1 semen. 2 a spermatozoon.

spermatozoon /sper-muh-tuh-zoh-on/ n. (pl. **spermatozoa**) the male sex cell of an animal, that fertilizes the egg.

spermicide n. a contraceptive substance that kills sperm.

spew v. 1 pour out in large quantities. 2 informal vomit.

sphere n. 1 a perfectly round solid figure. 2 an area of activity or interest. ■ **spherical** adj. **spherically** adv.

sphincter n. a ring of muscle surrounding an opening in the body.

sphinx n. an ancient Egyptian stone figure with a lion's body and a human or animal head.

spice n. 1 a strong-tasting vegetable substance for flavouring food. 2 interest and excitement. • v. 1 flavour with spice. 2 (**spice up**) make more interesting. ■ **spiciness** n. **spicy** adj.

spick and span adj. neat and clean.

spider n. an eight-legged insect-like animal. ■ **spidery** adj.

spiel /shpeel, speel/ n. informal an elaborate and insincere persuasive speech.

spigot n. a small peg or plug.

spike n. a thin, pointed piece of metal, wood, etc. • v. 1 pierce with a pointed object. 2 put an end to. 3 informal secretly add alcohol or a drug to drink or food. ■ **spiked** adj. **spiky** adj.

spill v. (**spilling, spilt** or **spilled**) 1 flow or cause to flow over the edge of a container. 2 move or empty out from a place. • n. 1 an amount spilt. 2 a fall from a horse or bicycle. 3 a thin strip of wood or paper for lighting a fire. ■ **spillage** n.

spin v. (**spinning, spun**) 1 turn round quickly. 2 draw out and twist fibres to make yarn. 3 (**spin out**) prolong. • n. 1 a spinning motion. 2 informal a short drive for pleasure. 3 a favourable slant given to a news story. □ **spin doctor** a person employed by a political party to give a favourable interpretation of events to the media. **spin-off** a product or benefit produced after the main activity. ■ **spinner** n.

spina bifida n. a condition in which part of the spinal cord is exposed, often causing paralysis.

spinach n. a vegetable with large green leaves.

spinal adj. of the spine. □ **spinal cord** the nerve fibres in the spinal cord connecting all parts of the body to the brain.

spindle n. **1** a rod with tapered ends, used in spinning wool etc. by hand. **2** a rod around which something revolves.

spindly adj. long or tall and thin.

spindrift n. sea spray.

spine n. **1** the row of bones extending from the skull to the small of the back. **2** the part of a book enclosing the inner edges of the pages. **3** a hard pointed projection on certain plants and animals. ■ **spiny** adj.

spineless adj. **1** not brave or determined. **2** having no spine.

spinet n. a small harpsichord.

spinnaker n. a large extra sail on a racing yacht.

spinney n. (pl. **spinneys**) a small wooded area.

spinster n. an unmarried woman.

spiral adj. forming a continuous curve around a central point or axis. •n. **1** a spiral curve or shape. **2** a progressive rise or fall of prices, wages, etc. •v. (**spiralling, spiralled**; US **spiraling, spiraled**) **1** follow a spiral course. **2** increase or decrease rapidly. ■ **spirally** adv.

spire n. a tall pointed structure on the top of a church tower.

spirit n. **1** a person's character and feelings, often believed to survive after the body is dead. **2** a super-

natural being. **3** typical character, quality, or mood. **4** (**spirits**) a person's mood. **5** courage and determination. **6** the intended meaning of a law etc. **7** strong distilled alcoholic drink. •v. (**spiriting, spirited**) take away rapidly and secretly. □ **spirit level** a sealed glass tube containing a bubble in liquid whose position shows whether a surface is level.

spirited adj. energetic and determined. ■ **spiritedly** adv.

spiritual adj. **1** of the human spirit. **2** of religion or religious belief. •n. a kind of religious song associated with black American Christians. ■ **spirituality** n. **spiritually** adv.

spiritualism n. the belief that it is possible to communicate with the spirits of the dead. ■ **spiritualist** n.

spirituous adj. old use strongly alcoholic.

spit v. (**spitting, spat** or **spit**) **1** forcibly eject saliva, food, or liquid from the mouth. **2** say in a hostile way. **3** rain lightly. •n. **1** saliva. **2** a metal rod for holding and turning roasting meat. **3** a narrow point of land projecting into the sea. □ **spitfire** a hot-tempered person.

spite n. a desire to annoy or upset. •v. deliberately annoy or upset. □ **in spite of** without being affected by.

spiteful adj. deliberately hurtful. ■ **spitefully** adv.

spittle n. saliva.

spittoon n. a container for spitting into.

splash v. **1** (of a liquid) fall in scattered drops. **2** wet with scattered drops. **3** move around in water, causing it to fly about. **4** display a story etc. prominently in a newspaper. **5** (**splash out**) *informal* spend money freely. • *n.* **1** an act of splashing. **2** a patch of colour.

splatter *v.* spatter.

splay *v.* spread wide apart.

spleen *n.* **1** an abdominal organ involved in producing and removing blood cells. **2** bad temper.

splendid *adj.* **1** very impressive. **2** excellent. ■ **splendidly** *adv.*

splendour (US **splendor**) *n.* magnificent and impressive appearance.

splenetic *adj.* bad-tempered.

splice *v.* join by interweaving or overlapping the ends.

splint *n.* a rigid support for a broken bone.

splinter *n.* a small, thin, sharp fragment of wood etc. • *v.* break into splinters. □ **splinter group** a small organization that has broken away from a larger one.

split *v.* (**splitting**, **split**) **1** break into parts by force. **2** divide into parts or groups. **3** (often **split up**) end a relationship. • *n.* **1** a tear or crack. **2** an act of splitting. **3** (**the splits**) a leg or seated position with the legs straight and at right angles to the body. □ **split infinitive** an infinitive with a word placed between *to* and the verb. **split second** a very brief moment.

splodge *n. informal* a spot or smear.

splurge *informal v.* spend extravagantly. • *n.* a burst of extravagance.

splutter *v.* **1** make a series of short spitting sounds. **2** say incoherently.

spoil *v.* (**spoiling**, **spoilt** or **spoiled**) **1** make less good or en-

joyable. **2** harm a child's character by being too indulgent. **3** (of food) become unfit for eating. **4** (**be spoiling for**) be very eager for. • *n.* (**spoils**) stolen goods. □ **spoilsport** a person who spoils others' enjoyment.

spoiler *n.* **1** a flap on an aircraft wing raised to create drag and so reduce speed. **2** a similar device on a vehicle to improve roadholding at speed.

spoke¹ *n.* each of the rods connecting the centre of a wheel to its rim.

spoke² past of **SPEAK**.

spoken past part. of **SPEAK**.

spokesman (or **spokeswoman** or **spokesperson**) *n.* a person who makes statements on behalf of a group.

sponge *n.* **1** an invertebrate sea creature with a soft porous body. **2** a piece of a light, absorbent substance for washing, padding, etc. **3** a very light cake. • *v.* (**sponging** or **spongeing**, **sponged**) **1** clean with a wet sponge. **2** *informal* live at the expense of others. ■ **sponger** *n.* **spongy** *adj.*

spongiform *adj.* with a porous sponge-like texture.

sponsor *n.* **1** a person or organization that contributes to the costs of an event in return for advertising. **2** a person who promises to give money to a charity after another person has taken part in a stated activity. **3** a person who proposes a new law. • *v.* be a sponsor for. ■ **sponsorship** *n.*

⚠ *-or, not -er: sponsor.*

spontaneous *adj.* **1** done or occurring as a result of an impulse or without apparent external cause. **2** natural and relaxed. ■ **spontaneity** n. **spontaneously** adv.

spoof n. informal a parody.

spook n. informal a ghost. ■ **spookily** adv. **spooky** adj.

spool n. a reel on which thread, film, etc. is wound. • v. wind on to a spool.

spoon n. an eating and cooking utensil with a small, shallow bowl on a handle. • v. scoop up with a spoon. □ **spoon-feed** give excessive help to. ■ **spoonful** n.

spoonerism n. the accidental swapping round of the initial sounds or letters of two or more words, as in you hissed the mystery lectures.

spoor n. the track or scent of an animal.

sporadic adj. occurring irregularly or only in a few places. ■ **sporadically** adv.

spore n. a tiny reproductive cell produced by ferns, fungi, etc.

sporran n. a pouch worn in front of a kilt.

sport n. **1** a competitive activity involving physical effort and skill. **2** informal a person who behaves well when teased or defeated. • v. **1** wear a distinctive item. **2** play. □ **sports car** a low-built fast car. **sports jacket** a man's informal jacket. **sportsman** (or **sportswoman**) **1** a person who takes part in a sport. **2** a fair and generous person. ■ **sporty** adj.

sporting adj. **1** connected with or interested in sport. **2** fair and generous. □ **sporting chance** a reasonable chance of success.

sportive adj. playful.

spot n. **1** a small round mark. **2** a pimple. **3** a place or position. • v.

(**spotting**, **spotted**) **1** notice or perceive. **2** mark with spots. □ **on the spot 1** immediately. **2** at the scene of an event. **spot check** a random check. **spotlight 1** a lamp projecting a strong beam of light on a small area. **2** intense public attention. ■ **spotter** n. **spotty** adj.

spotless adj. absolutely clean or pure. ■ **spotlessly** adv.

spouse n. a husband or wife.

spout n. **1** a projecting tube or lip through or over which liquid can be poured. **2** a stream of liquid. • v. **1** send out or flow in a stream. **2** express in a lengthy or emphatic way.

sprain v. injure a joint by wrenching it violently. • n. such an injury.

sprang past of **SPRING**.

sprat n. a small edible sea fish.

sprawl v. **1** sit, lie, or fall with the arms and legs spread out awkwardly. **2** spread out in a disorganized way. • n. the disorganized expansion of a city.

spray n. **1** liquid sent through the air in tiny drops. **2** a liquid or device for spraying. **3** a stem or branch with flowers and leaves. **4** a bunch of cut flowers. • v. **1** apply a spray of liquid to. **2** scatter over an area. □ **spray gun** a device for spraying paint etc.

spread v. (**spreading**, **spread**) **1** open out so as to be wider, longer, etc. **2** extend over a wide area or period. **3** reach or cause to reach more and more people. **4** apply in an even layer. • n. **1** the act of spreading. **2** extent or range. **3** a paste for spreading on bread. **4** an article covering several pages of a newspaper. **5** informal a lavish meal. □ **spreadeagled** with the arms and legs extended.

spreadsheet n. a computer program in which figures in a grid are used in calculations.

spree n. a period of unrestrained activity.

sprig n. a small stem with leaves or flowers.

sprightly adj. (**sprightlier**, **sprightliest**) lively or energetic. ■ **sprightliness** n.

spring v. (**springing**, **sprang**; past part. **sprung**) 1 jump. 2 move or do suddenly. 3 (**spring from**) come or appear from. 4 (**spring up**) suddenly develop or appear. 5 (**sprung**) having springs. ·n. 1 the season between winter and summer. 2 a spiral coil that returns to its former shape after being pressed or pulled. 3 a jump. 4 a place where water flows from an underground source. 5 elasticity. □ **springboard** a flexible board from which a diver or gymnast jumps to gain more power. **spring-clean** clean thoroughly. **spring tide** a tide when there is the greatest difference between high and low water. ■ **springy** adj.

springbok n. a southern African gazelle.

sprinkle v. scatter small drops or particles over a surface.

sprinkler n. a device for watering lawns or putting out fires.

sprinkling n. a small, thinly distributed amount.

sprint v. run at full speed. ·n. 1 a fast run. 2 a short, fast race. ■ **sprinter** n.

sprite n. an elf or fairy.

spritzer n. a drink of white wine and soda water.

sprocket n. a projection on a wheel, engaging with links on a chain etc.

sprout v. 1 produce shoots, hair, etc. 2 appear or develop suddenly. ·n. 1 a shoot of a plant. 2 a Brussels sprout.

spruce n. a coniferous tree. ·adj. neat and smart. ·v. (**spruce up**) make smarter.

sprung past part. of SPRING.

spry adj. lively.

spud n. informal a potato.

spume n. froth.

spun past & past part. of SPIN.

spunk n. informal courage and spirit.

spur n. 1 a spiked device worn on a rider's heel for urging a horse on. 2 an encouragement. 3 an area projecting from a mountain. ·v. (**spurring**, **spurred**) 1 encourage. 2 urge a horse on with spurs. □ **on the spur of the moment** on impulse.

spurious adj. false or fake. ■ **spuriously** adv.

spurn v. reject with contempt.

spurt v. 1 gush out in a stream. 2 move with a sudden burst of speed. ·n. 1 a gushing stream. 2 a sudden burst of activity or speed.

sputter v. splutter.

sputum n. saliva and mucus that is coughed up.

spy n. (pl. **spies**) a person who secretly collects information on an enemy or competitor. ·v. (**spying**, **spied**) 1 be a spy. 2 watch secretly. 3 see.

sq. abbrev. square.

squabble n. a noisy quarrel about a trivial matter. ·v. have a squabble.

squad n. 1 a division of a police force. 2 a group of sports players from which a team is chosen. **3** a small group of soldiers.

squadron *n.* **1** a unit of an air force. **2** a division of an armoured regiment. **3** a group of warships.

squalid *adj.* **1** dirty and unpleasant. **2** immoral or dishonest. ■ **squalor** *n.*

squall *n.* a sudden storm or wind. ■ **squally** *adj.*

squander *v.* waste money, time, etc.

square *n.* **1** a plane figure with four equal straight sides and four right angles. **2** an open area surrounded by buildings. **3** the product of a number multiplied by itself. **4** an instrument for testing right angles. •*adj.* **1** having the shape of a square. **2** right-angled. **3** equal to the area of a square whose side is of the unit specified. **4** level or parallel. **5** *informal* old-fashioned or conventional. •*adv.* directly; straight. •*v.* **1** make square. **2** (**squared**) marked out in squares. **3** multiply a number by itself. **4** make or be compatible. **5** settle a bill. □ **square dance** a dance in which four couples face one another in a square. **square meal** a large meal. **square root** a number which produces a specified quantity when multiplied by itself. **square up** take up the position of a person about to fight. ■ **squarely** *adv.*

squash *v.* **1** crush or squeeze so as to become flat or out of shape. **2** force into a restricted space. **3** suppress or reject. •*n.* **1** a state of being squashed. **2** a concentrated fruit-flavoured liquid, diluted to make a drink. **3** a game played with rackets and a small ball in a closed court. **4** a vegetable like a marrow. ■ **squashy** *adj.*

squat *v.* (**squatting, squatted**) **1** crouch or sit on the heels. **2** unlawfully occupy an uninhabited building. •*adj.* short and wide. •*n.* **1** a squatting position. **2** a building occupied unlawfully. ■ **squatter** *n.*

squawk *v.* make a loud, harsh noise. •*n.* a squawking sound.

squeak *n.* a short, high-pitched sound. •*v.* make a squeak. ■ **squeaky** *adj.*

squeal *n.* a long, high-pitched sound. •*v.* **1** make a squeal. **2** (**squeal on**) *informal* inform on.

squeamish *adj.* easily disgusted or made to feel sick.

squeeze *v.* **1** firmly press from opposite or all sides. **2** crush to extract liquid. **3** manage to get into or through a restricted space. •*n.* **1** an act of squeezing. **2** a hug. **3** a small amount of liquid produced by squeezing. **4** a strong financial demand or pressure.

squelch *v.* make a soft sucking sound, e.g. by treading in mud. •*n.* a squelching sound. ■ **squelchy** *adj.*

squib *n.* a small firework.

squid *n.* a sea animal with a long body and tentacles.

squiggle *n.* a short curly line. ■ **squiggly** *adj.*

squint *v.* **1** look at with partly closed eyes. **2** have a squint affecting one eye. •*n.* a condition in which one eye looks in a different direction from the other.

squire *n.* a country gentleman.

squirm *v.* **1** wriggle. **2** be embarrassed.

squirrel *n.* a bushy-tailed rodent that lives in trees.

squirt *v.* **1** force liquid out in a thin jet from a small opening. **2** wet

s

with a jet of liquid. •n. **1** a thin jet of liquid. **2** *informal* an insignificant person.

squish v. make a soft squelching sound. ■ **squishy** adj.

SS abbrev. **1** Saints. **2** steamship. •n. the Nazi special police force.

St abbrev. **1** Saint. **2** Street. **3** (**st**) stone (in weight).

stab v. (**stabbing, stabbed**) pierce, wound, or kill with a knife or other pointed object. •n. **1** an act of stabbing. **2** a sudden sharp feeling or pain. **3** *informal* an attempt.

stabilize (or **-ise**) v. make or become stable. ■ **stabilization** n. **stabilizer** n.

stable adj. **1** firmly fixed. **2** emotionally well-balanced. **3** not likely to change or fail. •n. **1** a building for housing horses. **2** an establishment where racehorses are kept and trained. •v. put or keep in a stable. ■ **stability** n. **stably** adv.

staccato adv. & adj. *Music* with each sound sharply distinct.

stack n. **1** a neat pile or heap. **2** *informal* a large quantity. **3** a chimney. •v. **1** arrange in a stack. **2** arrange a pack of cards dishonestly.

stadium n. (pl. **stadiums** or **stadia**) a sports ground with tiers of seats for spectators.

staff n. **1** the employees of an organization. **2** a long stick used as a support or sign of authority. **3** a stave in music. •v. provide with staff.

stag n. a fully adult male deer. □ **stag night** an all-male celebration for a man about to be married.

stage n. **1** a point or step in a process. **2** a raised platform on

which actors, entertainers, etc. perform. **3** the acting profession. •v. **1** present a performance of a play etc. **2** organize an event. □ **stagecoach** a horse-drawn vehicle formerly used to carry passengers along a regular route. **stage-manage** arrange carefully to create a specific effect. **stage manager** the person responsible for a play's technical arrangements. **stage whisper** a whisper intended to be overheard.

stagger v. **1** walk or move unsteadily. **2** astonish. **3** spread over a period. •n. an act of staggering.

stagnant adj. **1** not flowing and having an unpleasant smell. **2** showing little activity.

stagnate v. become stagnant. ■ **stagnation** n.

staid adj. respectable and unadventurous.

stain v. **1** mark or discolour with something that is hard to remove. **2** dye. •n. **1** a discoloured patch or mark. **2** a thing that damages a person's reputation. **3** a dye. □ **stainless steel** a form of steel resistant to tarnishing and rust.

stair n. **1** each of a set of fixed steps. **2** (**stairs**) a set of such steps. □ **staircase** (or **stairway**) a set of stairs and its surrounding structure. **stairwell** a shaft in which a staircase is built.

stake n. **1** a pointed post driven into the ground as a support, part of a fence, etc. **2** a sum of money gambled. **3** a share or interest in a business etc. •v. **1** support with a stake. **2** gamble. □ **at stake** at risk. **stake out** keep under secret observation. **2** state a claim or opinion forcefully.

stalactite *n.* a deposit of calcium salts hanging from the roof of a cave.

stalagmite *n.* a deposit of calcium salts rising from the floor of a cave.

stale *adj.* 1 not fresh. 2 no longer new and interesting. 3 no longer interested or motivated. □ **stalemate** 1 a situation in which progress seems impossible. 2 a position counting as a draw in chess. ■ **staleness** *n.*

stalk *n.* a stem or other supporting part of a plant. *v.* 1 follow stealthily. 2 harass with unwanted and obsessive attention. 3 walk stiffly or proudly. □ **stalking horse** a person or thing used to disguise a real purpose. ■ **stalker** *n.*

stall *n.* 1 a stand or booth for the sale of goods in a market. 2 a compartment in a stable, toilet, etc. 3 (**stalls**) the ground-floor seats in a theatre. 4 a seat in the choir or chancel of a church. *v.* 1 (of an engine) stop running. 2 stop making progress. 3 be vague so as to gain more time. 4 (of an aircraft) be moving too slowly to be controlled effectively.

stallion *n.* an uncastrated adult male horse.

stalwart *adj.* loyal and hard-working. *n.* a stalwart supporter.

stamen *n.* a male fertilizing organ of a flower.

stamina *n.* the ability to sustain effort over a long period.

stammer *v.* speak with difficulty, making sudden pauses and repeating the first letters of words. *n.* a tendency to stammer.

stamp *v.* 1 bring down the foot heavily. 2 (**stamp out**) put an end to decisively. 3 impress a pattern or mark on a surface. *n.* 1 a small piece of paper stuck to a posted item to show that postage has been paid. 2 an instrument for stamping a pattern or mark. 3 a mark made by this. 4 a distinctive quality. 5 an act of stamping the foot. □ **stamping ground** a place where someone regularly spends time.

stampede *n.* a sudden rush of animals or people. *v.* take part in or cause a stampede.

stance *n.* 1 the way in which someone stands. 2 a standpoint.

stanch *US* = **STAUNCH**.

stanchion *n.* an upright bar or post.

stand *v.* (**standing, stood**) 1 be or become upright, supported by the feet. 2 place or be situated in a particular position. 3 remain valid or unchanged. 4 be in a specified condition. 5 tolerate. 6 be a candidate in an election. *n.* 1 an attitude towards an issue. 2 a determined effort to resist attack etc. 3 a structure for holding or displaying something. 4 a large structure for spectators. 5 a platform. 6 a stall or booth. □ **standby** 1 readiness for action. 2 a person or thing ready to be used in an emergency. 3 (of tickets) sold only at the last minute. **stand by** 1 look on without interfering. 2 remain loyal to or abide by. 3 be ready for action. **stand down** resign or withdraw. **stand for** 1 be an abbreviation of or symbol for. 2 tolerate. **stand-in** a substitute. **stand in** deputize. **stand-off** a deadlock between two opponents. **stand-offish** *informal* distant and cold. **stand out** be noticeable. **standpipe** a vertical pipe extending from a

S

water supply. **standpoint** an attitude towards a particular issue. **standstill** a situation without movement or activity. **stand up** informal fail to keep a date with someone. **stand up for** speak or act in support of.

standard n. 1 a level of quality or achievement. 2 a measure or model used to make comparisons. 3 (**standards**) principles of good behaviour. 4 a flag. • adj. used or accepted as normal or average. ▫ **standard lamp** a tall lamp placed on the floor.

standardize (or **-ise**) v. cause to meet a standard. ▪ **standardization** n.

standing n. 1 status or reputation. 2 duration. ▫ **standing order** an instruction to a bank to make regular fixed payments to someone.

stank past of **STINK**.

stanza n. a verse of poetry.

staphylococcus n. (pl. **staphylococci**) a bacterium causing pus to be formed.

staple n. 1 a small piece of bent wire used to fasten papers together. 2 a main item of trade or production. 3 a main or important element. • adj. main or important. • v. secure with a staple or staples. ▪ **stapler** n.

star n. 1 a huge mass of burning gas visible as a glowing point in the night sky. 2 a shape representing a star, often used as a mark of excellence. 3 a famous entertainer or sports player. • v. (**starring**, **starred**) 1 have as a leading performer. 2 have a leading role in a film etc. 3 mark with a star. ▫ **starfish** a star-shaped sea animal. **star sign** a sign of the zodiac. ▪ **stardom** n.

starboard n. the right-hand side of a ship or aircraft.

starch n. 1 a carbohydrate obtained from cereals and potatoes. 2 powder or spray used to stiffen fabric. • v. stiffen with starch. ▪ **starchy** adj.

stare v. look at with great concentration. • n. an act of staring.

stark adj. 1 desolate or bare. 2 sharply clear. 3 complete; sheer. • adv. completely.

starlet n. informal a promising young female film star etc.

starling n. a bird with dark shiny plumage.

starry adj. (**starrier**, **starriest**) full of or lit by stars. ▫ **starry-eyed** full of unrealistic hopes.

start v. 1 begin to do, be, happen, or operate. 2 cause to begin or operate. 3 begin to move or travel. 4 jerk in surprise. • n. 1 a beginning, or the point at which something begins. 2 an advantage given at the beginning of a race. 3 a jerk of surprise. ▪ **starter** n.

startle v. shock or surprise.

starve v. 1 suffer or die from hunger. 2 cause to starve. 3 informal feel very hungry. 4 (**be starved of**) be deprived of. ▪ **starvation** n.

stash informal v. store secretly. • n. a secret store.

stasis /stay-sis/ n. a period or state when there is no activity or change.

state n. 1 the condition of someone or something at a particular time. 2 a country considered as an organized political unit. 3 an area forming part of a federal republic. 4 the government of a country. 5 ceremony associated with

S

monarchy or government.
6 *informal* an agitated condition.
• *v.* express in words. □ **stateroom** a private cabin on a ship. **statesman** (or **stateswoman**) an experienced and respected political leader.

stateless *adj.* not recognized as a citizen of any country.

stately *adj.* (**statelier**, **stateliest**) dignified or grand.

statement *n.* **1** a clear expression of something in words. **2** a formal account of facts or events. **3** a document listing amounts paid into and out of a bank account.

static *adj.* not moving, active, or changing. • *n.* **1** (or **static electricity**) an electric charge acquired by an object that is not a conductor of electricity. **2** crackling on a phone, radio, etc. ■ **statically** *adv.*

station *n.* **1** a place where trains stop on a railway line. **2** a place where an activity or service is based. **3** a broadcasting company. **4** the place where someone or something stands. **5** a person's social rank. • *v.* assign to a station. □ **station wagon** *US & Austral./NZ* an estate car.

stationary *adj.* not moving or changing.

❗ Don't confuse **stationary** with **stationery**, which means 'paper and other writing materials'.

stationer *n.* a seller of stationery.

stationery *n.* paper and other writing materials.

statistic *n.* **1** a fact or piece of information found by studying numerical data. **2** (**statistics**) the collection and analysis of numerical data. ■ **statistical** *adj.* **statistically** *adv.* **statistician** *n.*

statuary *n.* statues.

statue *n.* a carved or cast figure of a person or animal.

statuesque *adj.* tall and graceful.

statuette *n.* a small statue.

stature *n.* **1** a person's height. **2** importance or reputation.

status *n.* **1** a person's social or professional position. **2** high rank or social standing. **3** the situation at a particular time. □ **status quo** the existing situation.

statute *n.* a written law.

statutory *adj.* required or permitted by law.

staunch *adj.* loyal and committed. • *v.* (US **stanch**) stop the flow of blood from a wound. ■ **staunchly** *adv.*

stave *n.* **1** any of the strips of wood forming the side of a barrel etc. **2** a strong post. **3** a set of five horizontal lines on which musical notes are written. • *v.* (**staving**, **staved** or **stove**) **1** (**stave in**) dent or break a hole in. **2** (*past & past part* **staved**) (**stave off**) stop or delay.

stay *v.* **1** remain in the same place or in a specified state. **2** live temporarily. **3** stop or delay. • *n.* **1** a period of staying somewhere. **2** a brace or support. □ **stay of execution** a delay in carrying out the orders of a law court.

stead *n.* (**in someone's** or **someone's stead**) instead of someone or something. □ **stand in good stead** be useful to in the future.

steadfast *adj.* not changing in your attitudes or aims. ■ **steadfastly** *adv.*

steady *adj.* (**steadier**, **steadiest**) **1** firmly fixed or supported. **2** not wavering. **3** sensible and reliable.

S

4 regular and continuous. •v. (**steadying, steadied**) make or become steady. ■ **steadily** adv. **steadiness** n.

steak n. a thick slice of meat (esp. beef) or fish.

steal v. (**stealing, stole**; past part. **stolen**) **1** take something without permission and without intending to return it. **2** move stealthily. □ **steal the show** attract the most attention and praise.

stealth n. cautious and secretive action or movement. ■ **stealthy** adj. **stealthily** adv.

steam n. **1** the hot vapour into which water is converted when heated. **2** power derived from this. **3** momentum. •v. **1** give off steam. **2** (**steam up**) mist over with steam. **3** cook with steam. **4** move under steam power. **5** informal move quickly. □ **steam-roller** a heavy, slow vehicle with a roller, used in road construction. ■ **steamer** n. **steamy** adj.

steed n. literary a horse.

steel n. **1** a hard, strong alloy of iron with carbon. **2** strength and determination. •v. mentally prepare yourself to do something difficult. ■ **steely** adj.

steep adj. **1** rising or falling sharply. **2** informal (of a price) excessive. •v. **1** soak in liquid. **2** (**steeped in**) full of a particular quality. ■ **steeply** adv. **steepness** n.

steeple n. a church tower and spire. □ **steeplejack** a person who repairs tall structures such as chimneys.

steeplechase n. **1** a horse race with ditches and hedges as jumps. **2** a running race with hurdles and water jumps. ■ **steeplechaser** n.

steer v. **1** direct the course of a vehicle, ship, etc. **2** guide. •n. a bullock. □ **steer clear of** take care to avoid.

stellar adj. of a star or stars.

stem n. **1** the supporting part of a plant. **2** a long, thin supporting part of a wine glass etc. **3** the main part of a word, to which other elements are added. •v. (**stemming, stemmed**) **1** (**stem from**) be caused by. **2** stop the flow of.

stench n. a foul smell.

stencil n. a sheet of card etc. with a cut-out design, painted over to produce a design on the surface below. •v. (**stencilling, stencilled**; US **stenciled, stenciling**) decorate with a stencil.

stenographer n. US a shorthand typist.

stentorian adj. (of a voice) very loud.

step n. **1** an act of lifting and putting down the foot or feet in walking. **2** the distance covered by this. **3** a flat surface on which to step in moving from one level to another. **4** a position or grade in a scale. **5** a measure taken to achieve something. •v. (**stepping, stepped**) lift and put down your foot or feet. □ **step down** resign. **step in** intervene. **stepladder** a short free-standing folding ladder. **stepping stone 1** a raised stone on which to step when crossing a stream. **2** a stage in progress towards a goal. **step up** increase.

step- comb. form referring to a relationship resulting from a remarriage: stepmother, stepsister.

steppe n. a large grassy treeless plain in SE Europe or Siberia.

stereo n. (pl. **stereos**) **1** stereophonic sound. **2** a stereo CD player, record player, etc. • adj. stereophonic.

stereophonic adj. (of sound reproduction) using two or more channels so that the sound seems to come from more than one source.

stereoscopic adj. (of a photo) taken with a special device to give a three-dimensional effect.

stereotype n. an oversimplified idea of the typical characteristics of a person or thing. • v. view as a stereotype. ■ **stereotypical** adj.

sterile adj. **1** not able to produce children, young, or fruit. **2** free from bacteria etc. ■ **sterility** n. **sterilization**. **sterilize** (or **-ise**) v.

sterling n. British money. • adj. excellent.

stern adj. severe or strict. • n. the rear of a ship or aircraft. ■ **sternly** adv. **sternness** n.

sternum n. (pl. **sternums** or **sterna**) the breastbone.

steroid n. any of a class of organic compounds including certain hormones.

stertorous adj. (of breathing) noisy and laboured.

stethoscope n. a medical instrument for listening to a person's heart or breathing.

stevedore n. a docker.

stew n. a dish of meat and vegetables cooked slowly in a closed dish. • v. **1** cook slowly in a closed dish. **2** be anxious.

steward n. **1** (fem. **stewardess**) an attendant on a ship or aircraft. **2** an official who helps to organize a public event. **3** a person employed to manage an estate. **4** a

person responsible for supplies of food to a college, club, etc.

stick n. **1** a thin piece of wood. **2** an implement used to hit the ball in hockey etc. **3** a long, thin object or piece. **4** informal criticism. • v. (**sticking, stuck**) **1** push a pointed object into or through something. **2** adhere or cause to adhere. **3** (**be stuck**) be fixed or unable to move or to make progress. **4** informal put quickly or carelessly. ▫ **stick out 1** protrude or extend. **2** be conspicuous. **stick to** continue doing or using. **stick up for** support.

sticker n. a sticky label or notice.

stickleback n. a small fish with spines along its back.

stickler n. a person who insists on a certain type of behaviour.

sticky adj. (**stickier, stickiest**) **1** tending or designed to stick. **2** humid.

stiff adj. **1** not easily bent. **2** unable to move easily. **3** not relaxed or friendly. **4** severe or strong. ▫ **stiff-necked** obstinate. ■ **stiffen** v. **stiffly** adv. **stiffness** n.

stifle v. **1** prevent from breathing freely. **2** restrain or prevent.

stigma n. **1** a mark of disgrace. **2** a part of a flower pistil that receives the pollen.

stigmata pl. n. marks on a person's body corresponding to the Crucifixion marks on Christ's body.

stigmatize (or **-ise**) v. regard or treat as shameful.

stile n. a set of steps in a fence or wall allowing people to climb over.

stiletto n. (pl. **stilettos**) **1** a thin, high heel. **2** a short, narrow dagger.

still adj. **1** not moving. **2** (of a drink) not fizzy. • n. **1** deep, quiet

s

calm. **2** a photo or a single shot from a cinema film. **3** a device for distilling alcohol. • *adv.* **1** even now or at a particular time. **2** nevertheless. **3** even: *better still.* • *v.* make or become still. □ **stillborn** born dead. **still life** a painting or drawing of inanimate objects.
■ **stillness** *n.*

stilt *n.* **1** either of a pair of upright poles enabling the user to walk above the ground. **2** each of a set of posts supporting a building.

stilted *adj.* (of speech or writing) stiff and unnatural.

stimulant *n.* something that stimulates.

stimulate *v.* **1** make more active, interested, or excited. **2** raise levels of physiological or nervous activity in the body.
■ **stimulation** *n.*

stimulus *n.* (*pl.* **stimuli**) something that stimulates.

sting *n.* **1** a sharp part of an insect able to wound by injecting poison. **2** a wound from this. **3** a sharp tingling sensation. • *v.* (**stinging**, **stung**) **1** wound with a sting. **2** produce a stinging sensation. **3** upset.

stingy *adj.* (**stingier**, **stingiest**) *informal* mean.

stink *v.* (**stinking**, **stank** or **stunk**; *past part.* **stunk**) **1** have a foul smell. **2** *informal* be corrupt or bad. • *n.* **1** a foul smell. **2** *informal* a row or fuss.

stint *n.* a period of work. • *v.* (**stint on**) provide or use in a very economical or mean way.

stipend /sty-pend/ *n.* a salary paid to a priest etc.

stipendiary *adj.* receiving a stipend.

stipple *v.* mark with many small dots.

stipulate *v.* demand or specify as part of an agreement.
■ **stipulation** *n.*

stir *v.* (**stirring**, **stirred**) **1** move an implement round in a liquid etc. to mix it. **2** move slightly or begin to be active. **3** wake or get up. **4** arouse a strong feeling. • *n.* **1** an act of stirring. **2** a commotion.

stirrup *n.* each of a pair of loops attached to a horse's saddle to support the rider's foot.

stitch *n.* **1** a loop of thread or yarn resulting from a single pass of the needle in sewing, knitting, etc. **2** a method of sewing etc. that produces a particular pattern. **3** a sudden pain in the side. • *v.* make or mend with stitches. □ **in stitches** *informal* laughing uncontrollably.

stoat *n.* a small brown mammal of the weasel family.

stock *n.* **1** a supply of goods or materials available for sale or use. **2** livestock. **3** money raised by selling shares in a company. **4** (**stocks**) shares in a company. **5** water in which bones, meat, etc. have been simmered. **6** ancestry. **7** the trunk or stem of a tree or shrub. **8** (**the stocks**) *hist.* a wooden structure with holes in which a criminal's feet and hands were locked as punishment. • *adj.* common or conventional. • *v.* **1** keep a stock of. **2** provide with a supply. □ **stockbroker** a broker who buys and sells shares for clients. **stock car** a car used in a type of racing in which cars collide with each other. **stock exchange** (or **stock market**) a market in which shares are bought and sold. **stock-in-trade** the typical thing a person or company uses or deals in. **stockpile** a large stock of goods. **stock-still** completely still. **stocktaking** the recording of the amount of stock held by a business.

stockade n. an enclosure of wooden posts.

stocking n. a close-fitting covering for the foot and leg.

stockist n. a retailer stocking goods of a particular type.

stocky adj. (**stockier, stockiest**) short and sturdy.

stodge n. informal heavy, filling food. ■ **stodgy** adj.

stoic n. a stoical person. • adj. stoical. ■ **stoicism** n.

stoical adj. enduring pain and hardship without complaint. ■ **stoically** adv.

stoke v. 1 add coal to a fire etc. 2 increase a strong emotion. ■ **stoker** n.

stole[1] n. a woman's wide scarf or shawl.

stole[2] past of STEAL.

stolen past part. of STEAL.

stolid adj. calm and dependable. ■ **stolidly** adv.

stomach n. 1 the internal organ in which the first part of digestion occurs. 2 the belly. 3 appetite or desire. • v. tolerate.

stomp v. tread heavily.

stone n. 1 the hard material of which rock is made. 2 a piece of stone. 3 a gem. 4 a hard seed in certain fruits. 5 (pl. **stone**) a unit of weight equal to 14 lb (6.35 kg). • v. 1 throw stones at. 2 remove the stone from a fruit. □ **Stone Age** the prehistoric period when tools were made of stone. **stonewall** delay or block by giving evasive replies. **stonewashed** washed

with small stones to give a faded appearance.

stony adj. (**stonier, stoniest**) 1 full of stones. 2 cold and unfeeling. ■ **stonily** adv.

stood past & past part. of STAND.

stooge n. 1 derog. a person doing routine or unpleasant work for another. 2 a performer who is the butt of a comedian's jokes.

stool n. 1 a seat without a back or arms. 2 a piece of faeces. □ **stool pigeon** informal a police informer.

stoop v. 1 bend forwards and down. 2 lower your standards to do something wrong. • n. a stooping posture.

stop v. (**stopping, stopped**) 1 come or bring to an end. 2 prevent from happening or from doing something. 3 cease moving. 4 block a hole. • n. 1 an act of stopping. 2 a place where a bus stops regularly. 3 a thing preventing movement. 4 a set of organ pipes. □ **stopcock** a valve regulating the flow in a pipe. **stopgap** a temporary substitute. **stop press** late news added to a newspaper. **stopwatch** a watch that can be started and stopped, used to time races. ■ **stoppage** n.

stopper n. a plug for a bottle etc.

storage n. 1 the act of storing. 2 space for storing. □ **storage heater** an electric heater that stores up heat during the night.

store n. 1 a supply kept for use as needed. 2 a place to keep things for future use. 3 a large shop. • v. keep for future use. □ **in store** about to happen. **set store by** consider important.

storey (US **story**) n. (pl. **storeys** or **stories**) a particular level of a building.

S

stork n. a tall long-legged bird with a long bill.

storm n. 1 a disturbance of the atmosphere with strong winds and rain or snow. 2 an uproar or outburst. •v. 1 move angrily and forcefully. 2 suddenly attack and capture. ■ **stormy** adj.

story n. (pl. **stories**) an account of imaginary or real events.

stout adj. 1 rather fat. 2 sturdy and thick. 3 brave and determined. •n. strong, dark beer. ■ **stoutly** adv.

stove¹ n. a device for cooking or heating.

stove² past & past part. of **STAVE**.

stow v. 1 store tidily. 2 (**stow away**) hide on a ship, aircraft, etc. so as to travel without paying. □ **stowaway** a person who stows away.

straddle v. 1 sit or stand with one leg on either side of. 2 extend across.

strafe v. attack with gunfire from the air.

straggle v. 1 lag behind. 2 grow or spread untidily. ■ **straggler** n. **straggly** adj.

straight adj. 1 extending in one direction only; without a curve or bend. 2 level or symmetrical. 3 tidy or ordered. 4 honest and direct. 5 in continuous succession. 6 (of an alcoholic drink) undiluted. 7 informal heterosexual. •adv. 1 in a straight line or a straight way. 2 without delay. 3 clearly and logically. •n. the straight part of something. □ **straight away** immediately. **straight-faced** having a serious expression. ■ **straighten** v.

straightforward adj. 1 easy to do or understand. 2 honest and open.

strain v. 1 make an unusually great effort. 2 injure by overexertion. 3 make great or excessive demands on. 4 pour a liquid through a sieve to separate out any solid matter. •n. 1 a force pulling or stretching something. 2 an injury caused by straining. 3 a severe demand on strength or resources. 4 the sound of a piece of music. 5 a breed or variety of an animal or plant. 6 a tendency in a person's character. ■ **strainer** n.

strained adj. 1 not relaxed. 2 not spontaneous.

strait n. 1 (or **straits**) a narrow stretch of water connecting two seas. 2 (**straits**) a difficult situation.

straitened adj. without enough money; poor.

straitjacket (or **straightjacket**) n. a strong garment with long sleeves for confining the arms of a violent person.

strait-laced (or **straight-laced**) adj. strictly moral and conventional.

strand v. 1 run aground. 2 leave without the means to move from a place. •n. 1 a single length of thread etc. 2 an element in a complex whole. 3 literary a beach or shore.

strange adj. 1 unusual or odd. 2 not seen or met before. ■ **strangely** adv. **strangeness** n.

stranger n. 1 a person that you do not know. 2 a person who does not know a particular place.

strangle v. 1 kill or injure by squeezing the neck. 2 suppress or hinder. □ **stranglehold** 1 a strangling grip. 2 complete control. ■ **strangler** n.

strangulation n. the act of strangling.

strap *n.* a strip of flexible material used for fastening, carrying, or holding on to. •*v.* (**strapping**, **strapped**) fasten with a strap.

strapping *adj.* big and strong.

strata pl. of STRATUM.

stratagem *n.* a plan intended to outwit an opponent.

strategic *adj.* **1** of strategy. **2** (of weapons) for use against enemy territory rather than in battle.
■ **strategically** *adv.*

strategy *n.* (*pl.* **strategies**) **1** a plan designed to achieve a long-term aim. **2** the planning and directing of military activity in a war or battle. ■ **strategist** *n.*

stratify *v.* (**stratifying**, **stratified**) form or arrange into strata.
■ **stratification** *n.*

stratosphere *n.* the layer of the atmosphere about 10–50 km above the earth's surface.

stratum *n.* (*pl.* **strata**) a layer or level in a series.

straw *n.* **1** dried stalks of corn etc. **2** a single dried stalk. **3** a thin hollow tube for sucking up a drink. □ **straw poll** an unofficial test of opinion.

strawberry *n.* a sweet red fruit.

stray *v.* move away aimlessly from a group or from the right course or place. •*adj.* **1** not in the right place. **2** (of a domestic animal) having no home. •*n.* a stray animal.

streak *n.* **1** a long, thin mark. **2** an element in someone's character. **3** a period of specified success or luck. •*v.* **1** mark with streaks. **2** move very fast. **3** *informal* run naked in a public place.
■ **streaker** *n.* **streaky** *adj.*

stream *n.* **1** a small, narrow river. **2** a continuous flow of liquid, air, people, etc. **3** a group in which schoolchildren of the same age and ability are taught. •*v.* **1** move in a continuous flow. **2** run with tears, sweat, etc. **3** float out in the wind. **4** put schoolchildren in streams. □ **on stream** in or into operation.

streamline 1 design with a shape presenting little resistance to a flow of air or water. **2** make more efficient.

streamer *n.* a long, narrow strip of decorative material.

street *n.* a public road in a city, town, etc. □ **streetcar** US a tram.

strength *n.* **1** the quality of being strong. **2** a good or useful quality. **3** the number of people making up a group. □ **on the strength of** on the basis of. ■ **strengthen** *v.*

strenuous *adj.* requiring or using great effort. ■ **strenuously** *adv.*

streptococcus *n.* (*pl.* **streptococci**) a bacterium causing serious infections.

stress *n.* **1** pressure or tension on an object. **2** mental or emotional tension or strain. **3** emphasis. **4** emphasis given to a syllable or word in speech. •*v.* **1** emphasize. **2** subject to pressure, tension, or strain. ■ **stressful** *adj.*

stretch *v.* **1** be able to be lengthened or widened without tearing or breaking. **2** pull tightly from one point to another. **3** extend a part of the body to its full length. **4** extend over an area or period. **5** make demands on. •*n.* **1** an act of stretching. **2** the capacity to stretch. **3** a continuous area or period. ■ **stretchy** *adj.*

stretcher *n.* a framework covered with canvas, for carrying injured or dead people.

strew *v.* (**strewing**, **strewed**; *past part.* **strewn** or **strewed**)

s

1 scatter over a surface or area. **2** cover with scattered things.

striation *n.* each of a series of ridges or grooves.

stricken *adj.* affected by something unpleasant.

strict *adj.* **1** demanding that rules are obeyed. **2** (of a rule) rigidly enforced. **3** following rules or beliefs exactly. ■ **strictly** *adv.* **strictness** *n.*

stricture *n.* **1** a restriction. **2** a critical remark.

stride *v.* (**striding, strode**) walk with long steps. •*n.* a long step. □ **get into your stride** start making good progress. **take in your stride** deal calmly with.

strident *adj.* **1** loud and harsh. **2** excessively forceful. ■ **stridency** *n.* **stridently** *adv.*

strife *n.* bitter disagreement.

strike *v.* (**striking, struck**) **1** hit with force. **2** occur or attack suddenly. **3** refuse to work as a form of organized protest. **4** suddenly come into the mind of. **5** light a match by rubbing it against a rough surface. **6** find oil, gold, etc. **7** reach an agreement. **8** (of a clock) show the time by chiming. •*n.* **1** an act of striking by employees. **2** a sudden attack. □ **strike off** officially expel from a professional group. **strike up 1** begin to play a piece of music. **2** begin a friendship or conversation.

striker *n.* **1** an employee on strike. **2** a forward in football.

striking *adj.* **1** noticeable. **2** very good-looking. ■ **strikingly** *adv.*

string *n.* **1** material consisting of threads twisted together to form a thin length. **2** a length of catgut or wire on a musical instrument, producing a sound by vibration.

3 (**strings**) stringed instruments. **4** a set of things strung together. **5** a series. **6** (**strings**) *informal* conditions or restrictions. •*v.* (**stringing, strung**) **1** arrange on a string. **2** (**be strung out**) be spread out in a long line. **3** fit strings on a musical instrument etc. **4** (**string up**) kill by hanging.

stringent *adj.* strict and precise. ■ **stringency** *n.* **stringently** *adv.*

stringy *adj.* (**stringier, stringiest**) **1** like string. **2** (of food) tough and fibrous.

strip *v.* (**stripping, stripped**) **1** remove covers or clothes from. **2** deprive of rank or property. **3** remove all the contents of a room, vehicle, etc. •*n.* **1** an act of undressing. **2** the identifying outfit of a sports team. **3** a long, narrow piece or area. □ **strip light** a tubular fluorescent lamp. **striptease** an entertainment in which a performer gradually undresses.

stripe *n.* **1** a long narrow band differing in colour or texture from its surroundings. **2** a V-shaped stripe on a uniform showing rank. ■ **striped** *adj.* **stripy** *adj.*

stripling *n. old use* a young man.

stripper *n.* **1** a device or substance for removing paint etc. **2** a striptease performer.

strive *v.* (**striving, strove** or **strived**; *past part.* **striven** or **strived**) make great efforts.

strobe *n.* a bright light which flashes at rapid intervals.

strode past of **STRIDE**.

stroke *n.* **1** an act of hitting. **2** a sound of a striking clock. **3** an act of stroking. **4** a mark made by drawing a pen, paintbrush, etc. across a surface. **5** a style of swimming. **6** a sudden disabling attack caused by an interruption in the flow of blood to the brain. •v. gently move the hand over.

stroll v. walk in a leisurely way. •n. a leisurely walk.

strong adj. **1** physically powerful. **2** done with or exerting great force. **3** able to withstand pressure. **4** secure or stable. **5** great in power or ability. **6** intense. **7** full-flavoured. **8** containing much alcohol. **9** indicating the size of a group: fifty strong. □ **stronghold 1** a place of strong support for a cause or political party. **2** a place strengthened against attack. **strong language** swearing. **strongroom** a room designed for the safe storage of valuable items. ■ **strongly** adv.

strontium n. a soft silvery-white metallic element.

strop n. a leather strip used for sharpening razors.

stroppy adj. informal bad-tempered.

strove past of STRIVE.

struck past & past part. of STRIKE.

structural adj. of or forming part of a structure. ■ **structurally** adv.

structure n. **1** the way a thing is constructed or organized. **2** a building or other constructed object. •v. give structure to.

strudel n. a baked roll of flaky pastry with a fruit filling.

struggle v. **1** make great efforts to get free. **2** make your way or try to do with difficulty. •n. **1** an act of struggling. **2** a difficult task.

strum v. (**strumming**, **strummed**) play a guitar etc. by sweeping the thumb across the strings.

strumpet n. old use a promiscuous woman.

strung past & past part. of STRING.

strut n. **1** a bar supporting a structure. **2** a strutting walk. •v. (**strutting, strutted**) walk in a stiff, proud way.

strychnine /strik-neen/ n. a bitter, highly poisonous substance.

Stuart adj. of the royal family ruling Scotland 1371–1714, and Britain 1603–1649 and 1660–1714.

stub n. **1** the part of a pencil, cigarette, etc. remaining after use. **2** the counterfoil of a cheque, ticket, etc. •v. (**stubbing, stubbed**) **1** hit your toe against something. **2** extinguish a cigarette by pressing it against something. ■ **stubby** adj.

stubble n. **1** short, stiff hairs growing after shaving. **2** the cut stalks of cereal plants left in the ground after harvesting. ■ **stubbly** adj.

stubborn adj. determined not to change your mind. ■ **stubbornly** adv. **stubbornness** n.

stucco n. plaster used for coating walls or moulding into decorations. ■ **stuccoed** adj.

stuck past part. of STICK. □ **stuck-up** informal arrogantly snobbish.

stud n. **1** a piece of metal with a large head projecting from a surface. **2** a fastener for clothes. **3** a small piece of jewellery for a pierced ear etc. **4** an establishment where horses are kept for breeding. **5** a stallion. •v. (**studding, studded**) decorate with studs or other small objects.

student n. a person studying at a university, college, or school.

studio n. (pl. **studios**) **1** a room where an artist works or where dancers practise. **2** a room from

S

which programmes are broadcast or recordings are made. □ **studio flat** a flat containing one main room.

studious adj. **1** spending a lot of time studying. **2** deliberate and careful. ■ **studiously** adv.

study n. (pl. **studies**) **1** time and effort spent in reading etc. to gain knowledge. **2** a detailed analysis of a subject or situation. **3** a room for reading and writing. **4** a piece of art, esp. one done in preparation for a larger picture. •v. (**studying, studied**) **1** learn about or investigate. **2** look at closely. **3** (**studied**) done with careful effort.

stuff n. **1** material, objects, etc. of a particular or unspecified kind. **2** basic characteristics. •v. **1** fill a container or space tightly or hastily. **2** fill out the skin of a dead animal to restore its original appearance.

stuffing n. **1** a mixture put inside poultry before cooking. **2** padding used to stuff cushions etc.

stuffy adj. (**stuffier, stuffiest**) **1** lacking fresh air or ventilation. **2** narrow-minded.

stultify v. (**stultifying, stultified**) cause to feel bored or drained of energy.

stumble v. **1** trip and lose your balance. **2** walk unsteadily. **3** make a mistake in speaking. **4** (**stumble across/on**) find by chance. •n. an act of stumbling. □ **stumbling block** an obstacle.

stump n. **1** the part of a tree trunk left in the ground after the rest has fallen or been cut down. **2** a remaining piece. **3** each of the uprights of a wicket in cricket. •v. **1** baffle. **2** (**stump up**) informal

pay a sum of money. ■ **stumpy** adj.

stun v. (**stunning, stunned**) **1** knock unconscious. **2** astonish.

stung past & past part. of **STING**.

stunk past & past part. of **STINK**.

stunner n. informal a strikingly attractive or impressive person or thing.

stunning adj. very attractive or impressive. ■ **stunningly** adv.

stunt v. **1** hinder the growth or development of. **2** an action displaying skill and daring. **3** something done to attract attention.

stupefy v. (**stupefying, stupefied**) make unable to think. ■ **stupefaction** n.

stupendous adj. very impressive.

stupid adj. **1** lacking intelligence. **2** dazed. ■ **stupidity** n. **stupidly** adv.

stupor n. a state of being nearly unconscious.

sturdy adj. (**sturdier, sturdiest**) strongly built. ■ **sturdily** adv. **sturdiness** n.

sturgeon n. (pl. **sturgeon**) a large edible fish.

stutter v. stammer, esp. by repeating the first sound of a word. •n. a tendency to stutter.

sty n. (pl. **sties**) **1** a pigsty. **2** (or **stye**) an inflamed swelling on the edge of an eyelid.

Stygian /sti-ji-uhn/ adj. literary very dark.

style n. **1** a way of doing something. **2** a particular design or arrangement. **3** elegance. •v. design or arrange in a particular fashion.

stylish adj. fashionably elegant. ■ **stylishly** adv. **stylishness** n.

stylist n. a person who designs fashionable clothes or cuts hair.

stylistic adj. of literary or artistic style. ■ **stylistically** adv.

stylized (or **-ised**) adj. represented in an artificial style.

stylus n. (pl. **styli**) 1 a hard point following a groove in a record. 2 a pointed implement for scratching letters or engraving.

stymie v. (**stymying** or **stymie-ing, stymied**) informal obstruct or thwart.

styptic adj. able to make bleeding stop.

suave /swahv/ adj. charming, confident, and elegant. ■ **suavely** adv. **suavity** n.

sub informal n. 1 a submarine. 2 a substitute.

sub- prefix 1 under. 2 subordinate.

subaltern n. the army rank below captain.

subatomic adj. smaller than or occurring within an atom.

subconscious adj. of the part of the mind of which a person is not fully aware. • n. this part of the mind. ■ **subconsciously** adv.

subcontinent n. a large part of a continent considered as a particular area.

subcontract v. employ a firm or person outside your company to do work. ■ **subcontractor** n.

subculture n. a distinct group in a society having beliefs or interests different from those of the majority.

subcutaneous adj. under the skin.

subdivide v. divide into smaller parts. ■ **subdivision** n.

subdue v. 1 overcome, quieten, or make less intense. 2 bring under control.

subedit v. check and correct text before printing. ■ **subeditor** n.

subhuman adj. not behaving like a human being.

subject n. 1 a person or thing that is being discussed or dealt with. 2 a branch of knowledge studied or taught. 3 the word in a sentence naming who or what performs the action of the verb. 4 a member of a state ruled by a monarch. • adj. (**subject to**) 1 able to be affected by. 2 dependent on. 3 under the authority of. • v. (**subject to**) cause to undergo. ■ **subjection** n.

subjective adj. based on or influenced by personal opinions. ■ **subjectively** adv. **subjectivity** n.

sub judice /sub joo-di-si/ adj. being considered by a law court and so forbidden to be discussed elsewhere.

subjugate v. forcibly bring under control. ■ **subjugation** n.

subjunctive adj. (of a form of a verb) expressing what is imagined, wished, or possible.

sublet v. (**subletting, sublet**) let a property that you are already renting to another person.

sublimate v. transform into a purer or idealized form. ■ **sublimation** n.

sublime adj. 1 of great excellence. 2 very great; extreme. ■ **sublimely** adv.

subliminal adj. affecting someone's mind without their being aware of it. ■ **subliminally** adv.

sub-machine gun n. a lightweight machine gun.

submarine n. a streamlined warship operating under the sea. • adj.

existing or done under the sea's surface. ■ **submariner** n.

submerge v. **1** push or go under water. **2** cover or hide.

submerse v. submerge. ■ **submersion** n.

submersible adj. designed to operate under water.

submission n. **1** the act of submitting. **2** a proposal submitted for consideration.

submissive adj. very obedient or passive. ■ **submissively** adv.

submit v. (**submitting**, **submitted**) **1** give in to authority or greater power. **2** present for consideration.

subordinate adj. lower in rank. **2** less important. •n. a subordinate person. •v. treat as less important. ■ **subordination** n.

suborn v. pay or persuade to commit an unlawful act.

subpoena /suh-pee-nuh/ n. a writ ordering a person to attend a court. •v. (**subpoenaing**, **subpoenaed**) summon with a subpoena.

subscribe v. **1** arrange to receive something regularly by paying in advance. **2** contribute to a cause. **3** apply to take part in. **4** (**subscribe to**) agree with. ■ **subscriber** n.

subscript adj. (of a letter, figure, etc.) written below the line.

subscription n. **1** a payment to subscribe to something. **2** the act of subscribing.

subsequent adj. coming after. ■ **subsequently** adv.

subservient adj. **1** too willing to obey others. **2** less important. ■ **subservience** n.

subset n. Math. a set of which all the elements are contained in another set.

subside v. **1** become less intense. **2** sink to a lower or the normal level. ■ **subsidence** n.

subsidiary adj. **1** related but less important. **2** (of a company) controlled by another. •n. (pl. **subsidiaries**) a subsidiary company.

subsidize (or **-ise**) v. **1** pay part of the cost of producing something. **2** support financially.

subsidy n. (pl. **subsidies**) a sum of money given to help keep the price of something low.

subsist v. maintain or support yourself at a basic level. ■ **subsistence** n.

subsoil n. the soil lying under the surface soil.

subsonic adj. of or flying at speeds less than that of sound.

substance n. **1** a type of solid, liquid, or gas that has particular qualities. **2** the physical matter of which a thing consists. **3** solid basis in reality. **4** importance. **5** the most important or essential part or meaning. **6** an intoxicating or narcotic drug.

substantial adj. **1** of considerable importance or size. **2** strongly built. ■ **substantially** adv.

substantiate v. support with evidence. ■ **substantiation** n.

substantive adj. real and meaningful.

substitute n. a person or thing acting or used in place of another. •v. use or act as a substitute. ■ **substitution** n.

subsume v. include in something else.

subterfuge n. a secret or dishonest act used to achieve a goal.

subterranean *adj.* underground.

subtext *n.* an underlying theme.

subtitle *n.* **1 (subtitles)** captions at the bottom of a cinema or television screen that translate dialogue. **2** a secondary title. • *v.* provide with subtitles.

subtle *adj.* **1** so delicate or precise as to be difficult to analyse or describe. **2** able to make fine distinctions. **3** using clever and indirect methods. ■ **subtlety** *n.* **subtly** *adv.*

subtotal *n.* the total of part of a group of figures.

subtract *v.* take away a number or amount from another. ■ **subtraction** *n.*

subtropical *adj.* of regions bordering on the tropics.

suburb *n.* an outlying residential part of a city. ■ **suburban** *adj.*

suburbia *n.* suburbs and suburban life.

subversive *adj.* trying to undermine an established system or institution. • *n.* a subversive person. ■ **subversively** *adv.*

subvert *v.* damage or weaken the power of. ■ **subversion** *n.*

subway *n.* **1** a tunnel under a road for pedestrians. **2** *US* an underground railway.

succeed *v.* **1** achieve an aim. **2** take over a role, title, etc., from someone. **3** come after and take the place of.

success *n.* **1** the achievement of an aim. **2** the gaining of wealth or status. **3** a successful person or thing.

successful *adj.* **1** having achieved an aim. **2** having achieved wealth or status. ■ **successfully** *adv.*

succession *n.* **1** a number of people or things following one after the other. **2** the act or right of inheriting a position, title, etc. □ **in succession** following one another. ■ **successor** *n.*

successive *adj.* following one another or others. ■ **successively** *adv.*

succinct *adj.* concise and clear. ■ **succinctly** *adv.*

succour (*US* **succor**) *n.* help.

succulent *adj.* **1** juicy. **2** having thick fleshy leaves. • *n.* a succulent plant. ■ **succulence** *n.*

succumb *v.* give in to pressure, temptation, etc.

such *adj. & pron.* **1** of the type previously mentioned or about to be mentioned. **2** to so high a degree. □ **such as 1** for example. **2** of a kind that. **suchlike** things of the type mentioned.

suck *v.* **1** draw into the mouth by tightening the lips and breathing in. **2** hold in the mouth and pull at with the mouth muscles. **3** pull in a specified direction. **4 (suck up to)** *informal* try to please to gain advantage. • *n.* an act of sucking.

sucker *n.* **1** an organ or device that can stick to a surface by suction. **2** *informal* a person who is easily fooled. **3** a shoot springing from the base of a plant.

suckle *v.* feed from the breast or teat.

suckling *n.* a young child or animal that has not been weaned.

sucrose *n.* sugar.

suction *n.* the force produced when a partial vacuum is created by the removal of air.

sudden *adj.* occurring or done quickly and unexpectedly. ■ **suddenly** *adv.* **suddenness** *n.*

sudoku /soo-doh-koo, soo-**dok**-koo/ *n.* a type of number puzzle.

suds pl. n. froth from soap and water.

sue v. take legal action against.

suede n. leather with a velvety nap on one side.

suet n. the hard white fat from round an animal's kidneys, used in cooking.

suffer v. **1** experience something bad. **2** be affected by a disease etc. **3** become worse. **4** old use tolerate. ■ **sufferer** n.

sufferance n. toleration rather than actual approval.

suffice v. be enough.

sufficient adj. enough. ■ **sufficiency** n. **sufficiently** adv.

suffix n. a part added to the end of a word to form another word.

suffocate v. die or kill from lack of air. ■ **suffocation** n.

suffrage n. the right to vote in political elections.

suffragette n. hist. a woman who campaigned for female suffrage.

suffuse v. spread through or over. ■ **suffusion** n.

sugar n. a sweet substance obtained from various plants. ·v. sweeten or coat with sugar. □ **sugar beet** beet from which sugar is extracted. **sugar cane** a tropical grass from which sugar is extracted. ■ **sugary** adj.

suggest v. **1** put forward for consideration. **2** make you think of. **3** express indirectly.

suggestible adj. easily influenced.

suggestion n. **1** something suggested. **2** the act of suggesting. **3** a slight trace.

suggestive adj. **1** making you think of something. **2** hinting at sexual matters. ■ **suggestively** adv.

suicide n. **1** the act of killing yourself deliberately. **2** a person who does this. **3** an act which is damaging to your own interests. ■ **suicidal** adj. **suicidally** adv.

suit n. **1** a jacket and trousers or a jacket and skirt of the same fabric. **2** a set of clothes for a particular activity. **3** any of the sets into which a pack of playing cards is divided. **4** a lawsuit. ·v. **1** be convenient for or acceptable to. **2** (of clothes etc.) be right for the features or figure of. □ **suitcase** a case with a handle and a hinged lid for carrying clothes.

suitable adj. right for the purpose or occasion. ■ **suitability** n. **suitably** adv.

suite /sweet/ n. **1** a set of rooms or furniture. **2** a set of musical pieces.

suitor n. a man seeking to marry a particular woman.

sulk v. be silently bad-tempered or resentful. ·n. a period of sulking. ■ **sulkily** adv. **sulky** adj.

sullen adj. silently bad-tempered. ■ **sullenly** adv. **sullenness** n.

sully v. (**sullying**, **sullied**) spoil the purity or cleanness of.

sulphate (US **sulfate**) n. a salt of sulphuric acid.

sulphide (US **sulfide**) n. a compound of sulphur with another element.

sulphur (US **sulfur**) n. a yellow non-metallic element. □ **sulphuric acid** a strong corrosive acid. ■ **sulphurous** adj.

sultan n. a Muslim ruler. ■ **sultanate** n.

sultana n. **1** a seedless raisin. **2** the wife of a sultan.

s

sultry *adj.* **1** (of the weather) hot and humid. **2** suggesting sexual passion.

sum *n.* **1** an amount of money. **2** a total. **3** an arithmetical calculation. • *v.* (**summing, summed**) (**sum up**) describe concisely or summarize.

summarize (or **-ise**) *v.* give a brief account of.

summary *n.* (*pl.* **summaries**) a brief statement of the main points of something. • *adj.* **1** brief and without unnecessary detail. **2** without the usual legal procedures. ■ **summarily** *adv.*

summation *n.* **1** the act of adding up. **2** a summary.

summer *n.* the season between spring and autumn. ■ **summery** *adj.*

summit *n.* **1** the top of a mountain. **2** the highest level of achievement. **3** a meeting between heads of government.

summon *v.* **1** instruct to be present. **2** send for help. **3** arrange a meeting. **4** make an effort to produce a quality or reaction.

summons *n.* (*pl.* **summonses**) **1** an order to appear in a law court. **2** an act of summoning. • *v.* order to appear in a law court.

sumo *n.* Japanese wrestling.

sump *n.* a reservoir of oil in a petrol engine.

sumptuous *adj.* splendid; lavish. ■ **sumptuously** *adv.*

sun *n.* **1** the star round which the earth orbits. **2** any similar star. **3** the light or warmth from the sun. • *v.* (**sunning, sunned**) (**sun yourself**) sit or lie in the sun. □ **sunbathe** sit or lie in the sun to get a suntan. **sunbed** a device with ultraviolet lamps for acquiring an

artificial suntan. **sunburn** inflammation of the skin caused by too much exposure to the sun. **sunburnt** (or **sunburned**) suffering from sunburn. **sundial** a device showing the time by the shadow cast by a pointer. **sundown** sunset. **sunflower** a tall plant with large yellow flowers. **sunglasses** glasses tinted to protect the eyes from sunlight. **sunlight** light from the sun. **sunrise** the time when the sun rises. **sunset 1** the time when the sun sets. **2** the colours in the sky at sunset. **sunshine** sunlight unbroken by cloud. **sunspot** a dark patch on the sun's surface. **sunstroke** illness caused by excessive exposure to the sun. **suntan** a golden-brown skin colouring caused by exposure to the sun.

sundae *n.* a dish of ice cream with fruit and syrup.

Sunday *n.* the day following Saturday. □ **Sunday school** a class held on Sundays to teach children about Christianity or Judaism.

sunder *v. literary* split apart.

sundry *adj.* of various kinds. • *n.* (**sundries**) various small items.

sung past part. of **SING**.

sunk past part. of **SINK**.

sunken *adj.* **1** having sunk. **2** lower than the surrounding area.

Sunni *n.* (*pl.* **Sunni** or **Sunnis**) a follower of one of the two main branches of Islam.

sunny *adj.* (**sunnier, sunniest**) **1** bright with or receiving much sunlight. **2** cheerful.

super *adj. informal* excellent.

superannuation *n.* regular payment made by an employee towards a pension.

superb *adj.* **1** excellent. **2** magnificent. ■ **superbly** *adv.*

S

supercharger n. a device improving the efficiency of an engine by forcing more air or fuel into it. ■ **supercharged** adj.

supercilious adj. haughty and superior. ■ **superciliously** adv.

supercomputer n. a very powerful computer.

superficial adj. **1** of or on the surface. **2** apparent rather than real. **3** not thorough or deep. ■ **superficiality** n. **superficially** adv.

superfluous adj. more than is needed. ■ **superfluity** n.

superhuman adj. having exceptional ability or powers.

superimpose v. place one thing over another.

superintend v. supervise.

superintendent n. **1** a supervisor. **2** a senior police officer.

superior adj. **1** higher in status, quality, or power. **2** thinking that you are better than others. •n. a person of superior rank.
■ **superiority** n.

superlative adj. **1** of the highest quality. **2** (of an adjective or adverb) expressing the highest degree of a quality.

supermarket n. a large self-service shop selling food and household goods.

supernatural adj. not able to be explained by the laws of nature. ■ **supernaturally** adv.

supernova n. (pl. **supernovae** or **supernovas**) a star that suddenly becomes much brighter because of an explosion.

supernumerary adj. extra.

superpower n. a very powerful nation.

superscript adj. (of a letter, figure, etc.) written above the line.

supersede v. take the place of.

! -sede, not -cede.

supersonic adj. of or flying at a speed greater than that of sound.

superstition n. a belief in supernatural influences, or a practice based on this. ■ **superstitious** adj.

superstore n. a very large supermarket.

superstructure n. **1** a structure built on top of something else. **2** the upper part of a building or ship.

supervene v. occur as an interruption or change. ■ **supervention** n.

supervise v. watch and direct the performance of a task or the work of a person. ■ **supervision** n. **supervisor** n. **supervisory** adj.

supine adj. **1** lying face upwards. **2** passive or lazy.

supper n. a light or informal evening meal.

supplant v. take the place of.

supple adj. bending easily.
■ **suppleness** n.

supplement n. **1** a thing added to improve or complete something. **2** a separate additional section of a newspaper. **3** an additional charge for an extra facility. •v. provide a supplement to. ■ **supplemental** adj.

supplementary adj. completing or improving something.

suppliant n. a person making a humble request.

supplicate v. humbly ask for something. ■ **supplicant** n. **supplication** n.

supply v. (**supplying**, **supplied**) make available to; provide. •n. (pl. **supplies**) **1** a stock of something available. **2** the act of supplying. **3** (**supplies**) necessary provisions and equipment. ■ **supplier** n.

support v. **1** bear the weight of. **2** help, encourage, or approve of. **3** provide with the necessities of life. **4** confirm. •n. **1** a person or thing that supports. **2** the act of supporting. ■ **supporter** n. **supportive** adj.

suppose v. **1** think to be true or likely. **2** require as a necessary condition. **3** (**be supposed to do**) be required or expected to do. ■ **supposedly** adv.

supposition n. a belief not based on proof or certainty.

suppository n. (pl. **suppositories**) a solid medical preparation designed to dissolve after being inserted in the rectum or vagina.

suppress v. **1** forcibly put an end to. **2** prevent from developing. **3** prevent from being stated or published. ■ **suppressant** n. **suppression** n.

suppurate v. form pus. ■ **suppuration** n.

supremacy n. the state of being superior to all others.

supreme adj. **1** highest in authority or rank. **2** very great or greatest. ■ **supremely** adv.

supremo n. (pl. **supremos**) informal a person in overall charge.

surcharge n. an extra charge.

sure adj. **1** confident that you are right. **2** (**sure of/to do**) certain to get or do. **3** undoubtedly true. **4** steady and confident. •adv. informal certainly. ■ **sureness** n.

surely adv. **1** it must be true that. **2** certainly.

surety n. (pl. **sureties**) **1** a person who guarantees that someone will do something. **2** money given as a guarantee.

surf n. waves that break and form foam on a shore or reef. •v. **1** stand on a surfboard and ride on the crest of a wave. **2** move from site to site on the Internet. □ **surfboard** a long, narrow board used in surfing. ■ **surfer** n.

surface n. **1** the outside or uppermost layer of something. **2** outward appearance. •v. **1** come up to the surface. **2** become apparent. **3** provide with a surface.

surfeit n. an excess.

surge n. **1** a sudden powerful forward or upward movement. **2** a sudden increase. •v. **1** move in a surge. **2** increase suddenly.

surgeon n. a doctor qualified to practise surgery.

surgery n. (pl. **surgeries**) **1** medical treatment involving cutting open the body and removing or repairing parts. **2** a place where a doctor or nurse sees patients. **3** a time when an MP is available for consultation. ■ **surgical** adj. **surgically** adv.

surly adj. (**surlier**, **surliest**) bad-tempered and unfriendly. ■ **surliness** n.

surmise v. suppose or guess. •n. a guess.

surmount v. **1** overcome a difficulty. **2** be on top of.

surname n. a family name.

surpass v. be greater or better than.

surplice n. a white robe worn over a cassock by Christian clergy and choristers.

surplus n. an amount left over after what is needed has been used.

surprise n. 1 a feeling caused by something sudden or unexpected. 2 an unexpected or astonishing thing. •v. 1 cause to feel surprise. 2 attack or find suddenly and unexpectedly.

! Don't forget the first r.

surreal adj. strange and dream-like. ■ **surreally** adv.

surrealism n. an artistic movement combining normally unrelated images in a strange way. ■ **surrealist** n. **surrealistic** adj.

surrender v. 1 give in to an opponent. 2 give up a right or possession. •n. an act of surrendering.

surreptitious adj. done secretly. ■ **surreptitiously** adv.

surrogate n. a deputy. □ **surrogate mother** a woman who bears a child on behalf of another. ■ **surrogacy** n.

surround v. be or place all round. •n. a border.

surroundings pl. n. the conditions or area around a person or thing.

surtax n. an extra tax.

surveillance n. close observation.

survey v. 1 look carefully at. 2 record the features of an area to produce a map. 3 examine and report on the condition of a building. 4 question a group to find out their opinions. •n. 1 an act of surveying. 2 a general examination or description. 3 a map or report obtained by surveying. ■ **surveyor** n.

survival n. 1 the state of surviving. 2 something that has survived from an earlier time.

survive v. 1 continue to live or exist, esp. despite an accident or ordeal. 2 remain alive after the death of. ■ **survivor** n.

susceptible adj. easily influenced or harmed by a particular thing. ■ **susceptibility** n.

sushi n. a Japanese dish of balls of cold rice served esp. with raw seafood.

suspect v. 1 believe to be likely or possible. 2 believe to be guilty without certain proof. 3 doubt the genuineness of a crime. •n. a person suspected of a crime. •adj. possibly dangerous or false.

suspend v. 1 halt temporarily. 2 temporarily bar from a job or from attending school. 3 (**suspended**) (of a sentence) not enforced as long as no further offence is committed. 4 hang up.

suspender n. 1 an elastic strap attached to a belt and fastened to the top of a stocking to hold it up. 2 (**suspenders**) US braces for trousers.

suspense n. excited or anxious uncertainty about what may happen.

suspension n. 1 the act of suspending. 2 the mechanism by which a vehicle is supported on its wheels. 3 a mixture in which particles are spread throughout a fluid. □ **suspension bridge** a bridge suspended from cables running between towers.

suspicion n. 1 a feeling that something is possible or that someone is guilty. 2 distrust. 3 a slight trace.

suspicious adj. 1 feeling suspicion. 2 apparently dishonest or dangerous. ■ **suspiciously** adv.

suss v. informal realize the true nature of.

sustain v. 1 support. 2 keep going over time or continuously. 3 experience something unpleasant. 4 uphold the validity of.

sustainable adj. (of industry etc.) avoiding using up natural resources. ■ **sustainability** n.

sustenance n. food and drink as needed to stay alive.

suture n. a stitch holding together the edges of a wound. •v. stitch with a suture.

suzerainty /soo-zuh-rayn-ty/ n. the right of one country to rule over another country that is not fully independent.

svelte adj. slender and elegant.

SW abbrev. south-west or south-western.

swab n. 1 a pad for cleaning wounds or taking specimens from the body. 2 a specimen taken with a swab. •v. (**swabbing**, **swabbed**) clean with a swab.

swaddle v. wrap in garments or cloth.

swag n. 1 a drooping ornamental arrangement of flowers, fabric, etc. 2 informal items stolen by a burglar.

swagger v. walk or behave in a very confident way. •n. a swaggering walk.

Swahili n. a Bantu language widely used in East Africa.

swain n. old use a young male lover.

swallow v. 1 cause to pass down the throat. 2 take in or cover completely. 3 accept or believe. •n. 1 an act of swallowing. 2 a swift-flying bird with a forked tail.

swam past of **SWIM**.

swamp n. a marsh. •v. 1 flood with water. 2 overwhelm with too much of something. ■ **swampy** adj.

swan n. a large white waterbird with a long neck. □ **swansong** the final performance or activity of a person's career.

swank v. informal show off.

swanky adj. (**swankier**, **swankiest**) informal luxurious and expensive.

swap (or **swop**) v. (**swapping**, **swapped**) exchange. •n. an act of exchanging.

sward n. an area of short grass.

swarm n. a large group of flying insects, people, etc. •v. 1 move in a swarm. 2 be crowded. 3 (**swarm up**) climb by gripping with the hands and feet.

swarthy adj. (**swarthier**, **swarthiest**) dark-skinned.

swashbuckling adj. having daring and romantic adventures. ■ **swashbuckler** n.

swastika n. a symbol in the form of a cross with each arm bent at a right angle.

swat v. (**swatting**, **swatted**) hit hard with a flat object.

swatch n. a sample of fabric.

swathe n. (US **swath**) 1 a broad strip. 2 a row of grass etc. as it falls when cut down. •v. wrap in layers of fabric.

sway v. 1 move gently to and fro. 2 make someone change their opinion. •n. 1 a swaying movement. 2 power or influence.

swear v. (**swearing**, **swore**; past part. **sworn**) 1 promise solemnly or on oath. 2 use offensive or obscene language. □ **swear by** have great confidence in. **swear word** an offensive or obscene word.

S

sweat n. moisture given out through the pores of the skin. •v. **1** produce sweat. **2** make a great effort. **3** be very anxious. □ **sweatshirt** a loose cotton sweater. **sweatshop** a place employing workers for long hours in poor conditions. ■ **sweaty** adj.

sweater n. a pullover with long sleeves.

Swede n. a person from Sweden. ■ **Swedish** adj. & n.

swede n. a yellow root vegetable.

sweep v. (**sweeping, swept**) **1** clean by brushing away dirt or litter. **2** move or affect quickly or forcefully. **3** extend in a long curve. •n. **1** an act of sweeping. **2** a long curving movement. **3** a long curved stretch of road etc. **4** a person who cleans soot from chimneys. □ **sweepstake** a form of gambling in which the winner receives all the money bet by the other players. ■ **sweeper** n.

sweeping adj. **1** wide in range or effect. **2** (of a statement) too general.

sweet adj. **1** having the pleasant taste of sugar. **2** having a pleasant smell. **3** pleasant and kind. **4** charming. •n. **1** a small piece of confectionery made with sugar. **2** a sweet dish forming a course of a meal. □ **sweetbread** an animal's pancreas, eaten as food. **sweetcorn** a variety of maize with sweet kernels eaten as a vegetable. **sweetheart** a lover. **sweet-talk** informal persuade by using charm or flattery. **sweet tooth** a liking for sweet foods. ■ **sweeten** v. **sweetly** adv. **sweetness** n.

sweetener n. **1** a sweetening substance. **2** informal a bribe.

swell v. (**swelling, swelled**, past part. **swollen** or **swelled**) **1** become larger or more rounded. **2** increase in strength or amount. •n. **1** a full or rounded form. **2** a gradual increase in strength or amount. **3** a slow, regular movement of the sea.

swelling n. a swollen place on the body.

swelter v. be uncomfortably hot.

swept past & past part. of **SWEEP**.

swerve v. abruptly go off from a straight course. •n. an abrupt change of course.

swift adj. quick; fast. •n. a fast-flying bird with slender wings. ■ **swiftly** adv. **swiftness** n.

swig v. (**swigging, swigged**) informal drink quickly.

swill v. rinse out. •n. waste food mixed with water for feeding to pigs.

swim v. (**swimming, swam**; past part. **swum**) **1** move through water using your arms and legs. **2** be covered with liquid. **3** experience a dizzy feeling. •n. a period of swimming. ■ **swimmer** n.

swimmingly adv. informal smoothly and satisfactorily.

swindle v. cheat someone of money etc. •n. a dishonest scheme to obtain money. ■ **swindler** n.

swine n. **1** (pl. **swine**) a pig. **2** (pl. **swine** or **swines**) informal an unpleasant person.

swing v. (**swinging, swung**) **1** move back and forth or from side to side when suspended. **2** move by grasping a support and leaping. **3** move in a smooth, curving line. **4** change from one opinion, mood, or situation to another. **5** have a decisive influence on. •n. **1** a hanging seat on which to sit and swing. **2** an act of swinging. **3** a change in public opinion. **4** a style of jazz with a flowing rhythm. □ **in full swing** at the height of activity.

swingeing *adj.* severe or extreme.

swipe *informal v.* **1** hit with a swinging blow. **2** steal. **3** pass a swipe card through an electronic reader. • *n.* a swinging blow. □ **swipe card** a plastic card carrying coded information which is read when the card is slid through an electronic device.

swirl *v.* move in a twisting pattern. • *n.* a swirling movement or pattern.

swish *v.* move with a soft hissing sound. • *n.* a swishing sound.

Swiss *adj.* of Switzerland. □ **Swiss roll** a thin sponge cake spread with jam etc. and rolled up.

switch *n.* **1** a device operated to turn electric current on or off. **2** a change or exchange. **3** a flexible shoot cut from a tree. • *v.* **1** change in position or direction. **2** exchange. **3** (**switch off/on**) turn an electrical device off (or on). □ **switchback** a road with alternate sharp ascents and descents.

switchboard a device for routing phone calls within an organization.

swivel *v.* (**swivelling, swivelled**; *US* **swiveling, swiveled**) turn around a central point. • *n.* a link or pivot enabling one part to revolve without turning the other.

swollen past part. of SWELL.

swoon *v.* faint.

swoop *v.* **1** move rapidly downwards through the air. **2** carry out a sudden raid. • *n.* an act of swooping.

swop var. of SWAP.

sword *n.* a weapon with a long metal blade. □ **swordfish** an edible sea fish with a sword-like snout.

swore past of SWEAR.

sworn past part. of SWEAR. • *adj.* determined to remain the specified thing: *sworn enemies*.

swot *informal v.* (**swotting, swotted**) study hard. • *n.* a person who studies hard.

swum past part. of SWIM.

swung past & past part. of SWING.

sybarite *n.* a person fond of luxury and pleasure. ■ **sybaritic** *adj.*

sycamore *n.* a large tree of the maple family.

sycophant *n.* a person who tries to win favour by flattery. ■ **sycophancy** *n.* **sycophantic** *adj.*

syllable *n.* a unit of pronunciation in a word. ■ **syllabic** *adj.*

syllabub *n.* a dish of flavoured whipped cream.

syllabus *n.* (*pl.* **syllabuses** or **syllabi**) the topics in a course of study or teaching.

syllogism *n.* a form of reasoning in which a conclusion is drawn from two propositions.

sylph *n.* **1** a slender woman or girl. **2** an imaginary spirit of the air.

sylvan (or **silvan**) *adj. literary* of woods; wooded.

symbiosis *n.* (*pl.* **symbioses**) a situation in which two different organisms live with and are dependent on each other, to the advantage of both. ■ **symbiotic** *adj.*

symbol *n.* **1** a thing representing something else. **2** a mark or character used as a standard representation of something.

s

■ **symbolic** adj. **symbolically** adv.

symbolism n. the use of symbols to represent ideas or qualities. ■ **symbolist** n.

symbolize (or **-ise**) v. 1 be a symbol of. 2 represent by symbols.

symmetry n. (pl. **symmetries**) 1 the state of having exactly matching parts facing each other or round an axis. 2 the quality of being similar or equal. ■ **symmetrical** adj. **symmetrically** adv.

sympathetic adj. 1 feeling or showing sympathy. 2 showing or inspiring approval. ■ **sympathetically** adv.

sympathize (or **-ise**) v. feel or express sympathy. ■ **sympathizer** n.

sympathy n. (pl. **sympathies**) 1 the feeling of being sorry for someone. 2 understanding between people. 3 support or approval.

symphony n. (pl. **symphonies**) an elaborate musical composition for a full orchestra. ■ **symphonic** adj.

symposium n. (pl. **symposia** or **symposiums**) a conference to discuss a particular academic subject.

symptom n. 1 a change in the body or mind which is the sign of a disease. 2 a sign of an undesirable situation. ■ **symptomatic** adj.

synagogue n. a building where Jews meet for religious worship and teaching.

synapse n. a connection between two nerve cells.

sync (also **synch**) n. (**in** or **out of sync**) informal working well (or badly) together.

synchronize (or **-ise**) v. cause to happen or operate at the same time or rate.

synchronous adj. existing or occurring at the same time.

syncopate v. alter the accents in music so that strong beats become weak and vice versa. ■ **syncopation** n.

syndicate n. a group of people or firms combining to achieve a common interest. • v. 1 manage by a syndicate. 2 publish or broadcast in different media at the same time. ■ **syndication** n.

syndrome n. a group of symptoms consistently occurring together.

synergy n. cooperation of two or more things to produce a combined effect greater than the sum of their separate effects.

synod n. an official meeting of Church ministers and members.

synonym n. a word or phrase meaning the same as another in the same language. ■ **synonymous** adj.

synopsis n. (pl. **synopses**) a brief summary.

syntax n. the arrangement of words and phrases to form sentences. ■ **syntactic** adj.

synthesis n. (pl. **syntheses**) 1 the combination of parts to form a connected whole. 2 the production of chemical compounds by reaction from simpler materials.

synthesize (or **-ise**) v. make by synthesis.

synthesizer n. an electronic musical instrument.

synthetic adj. 1 made by chemical synthesis, esp. to imitate a natural product. **2** not genuine. ■ **synthetically** adv.

syphilis n. a serious sexually transmitted disease. ■ **syphilitic** adj.

syringe n. a tube with a nozzle and piston for sucking in and forcing out liquid. •v. clean with liquid sprayed from a syringe.

syrup (US **sirup**) n. a thick sweet liquid. ■ **syrupy** adj.

system n. **1** a set of things that are connected or that work together. **2** an organized scheme or method. **3** (**the system**) the laws and rules that govern society. ■ **systematize** (or **-ise**) v.

systematic adj. done according to a system. ■ **systematically** adv.

systemic adj. affecting the whole of a system.

Tt

T n. (**to a T**) informal to perfection. □ **T-bone** a piece of steak containing a T-shaped bone. **T-shirt** a short-sleeved casual top. **T-square** a T-shaped instrument for drawing or testing right angles.

ta exclam. informal thank you.

tab n. a small projecting flap or strip. □ **keep tabs on** informal monitor.

tabard n. a short sleeveless tunic.

tabby n. (pl. **tabbies**) a grey or brown cat with dark stripes.

tabernacle n. **1** a place of worship for some religions. **2** (in the RC church) a container for the Eucharist.

table n. **1** a piece of furniture with a flat top supported by legs. **2** a set of facts or figures displayed in rows or columns. •v. present formally for discussion at a meeting. □ **tableland** a plateau. **tablespoon** a large spoon for serving food. **table tennis** a game played with bats and a light hollow ball on a table.

tableau /tab-loh/ n. (pl. **tableaux**) a group of models or motionless figures representing a scene.

table d'hôte /tah-bluh **doht**/ n. a restaurant meal at a fixed price and with limited choices.

tablet n. **1** a pill. **2** a slab on which an inscription is written.

tabloid n. a small-sized newspaper written in a popular style.

taboo n. (pl. **taboos**) a ban or restriction made by social custom. •adj. banned or restricted by social custom.

tabular adj. arranged in columns or tables.

tabulate v. arrange in columns or tables. ■ **tabulation** n.

tachograph n. an instrument used in commercial road vehicles to provide a record of speed and distance travelled.

tachometer /ta-kom-i-ter/ n. an instrument measuring the speed of an engine.

s
t

tachycardia /ta-ki-kar-di-uh/ n. an abnormally rapid heart rate.

tacit adj. understood or meant without being stated. ■ **tacitly** adv.

taciturn adj. saying little. ■ **taciturnity** n.

tack n. 1 a small broad-headed nail. 2 a long stitch used to fasten fabrics together temporarily. 3 a course of action. 4 an act of tacking in sailing. 5 equipment used in horse riding. • v. 1 fasten with tacks. 2 (**tack on**) add as an extra. 3 change course by turning a sailing boat into the wind.

tackle v. 1 try to deal with a difficult task. 2 confront someone about a difficulty. 3 (in football, rugby, etc.) try to take the ball from or prevent the movement of an opponent. • n. 1 the equipment needed for a task or sport. 2 a set of ropes and pulleys for lifting heavy objects. 3 an act of tackling in sport.

tacky adj. (**tackier, tackiest**) 1 (of glue etc.) not fully dry. 2 informal lacking in taste and quality.

taco n. (pl. **tacos**) a folded tortilla filled with spicy meat or beans.

tact n. sensitivity and skill in dealing with others. ■ **tactful** adj. **tactfully** adv. **tactless** adj. **tactlessly** adv.

tactic n. 1 an action intended to achieve something. 2 (**tactics**) the directing and organizing of armed forces and equipment during a war. ■ **tactician** n.

tactical adj. 1 planned to achieve a particular end. 2 (of weapons) for use in direct support of military operations. 3 (of voting) done to prevent the leading candidate from winning by supporting

whoever is next strongest. ■ **tactically** adv.

tactile adj. 1 of the sense of touch. 2 liking to touch others.

tadpole n. the larva of a frog or toad, at the stage when it has gills and a tail.

tae kwon do /ty kwon **doh**/ n. a Korean martial art.

taffeta n. a crisp shiny fabric.

tag n. 1 a label. 2 a description by which a person or thing is widely known. 3 an electronic device attached to someone to monitor their movements. 4 a much repeated saying etc. • v. (**tagging, tagged**) 1 attach a tag to. 2 (**tag on**) add at the end. 3 (**tag along**) accompany someone without being invited.

tagliatelle /tal-yuh-**tel**-li/ pl. n. pasta in narrow ribbons.

t'ai chi /ty chee/ n. a Chinese martial art and system of exercises.

tail n. 1 the part sticking out at the rear of an animal. 2 the rear part of an aircraft. 3 the final, more distant, or weaker part. 4 (**tails**) the side of a coin without the image of a head. 5 (**tails**) informal a tailcoat. • v. 1 secretly follow and observe. 2 (**tail off**) become smaller or weaker. □ **tailback** a long queue of traffic. **tailcoat** a man's formal coat with a long divided flap at the back. **tailgate** 1 the door at the back of an estate or hatchback car. 2 a hinged flap at the back of a truck. **tailplane** a small wing at the tail of an aircraft. **tailspin** a spinning dive by an aircraft. **tailwind** a wind blowing from behind.

tailor n. a person who makes men's clothing for individual customers. •v. **1** make clothes to fit individual customers. **2** make or adapt for a particular purpose. □ **tailor-made** made for a particular purpose.

taint v. spoil the purity or quality of; contaminate. •n. a trace of an undesirable quality.

take v. (**taking**, **took**; past part. **taken**) **1** reach for and hold. **2** occupy a place or position. **3** gain possession of by force. **4** carry or bring with you. **5** remove. **6** use. **7** accept. **8** require. **9** regard or react to. **10** experience or endure. **11** perform an action etc. •n. **1** a sequence of sound or film recorded at one time. **2** an amount gained. □ **take after** resemble a parent. **takeaway** **1** a restaurant or shop selling cooked food to be eaten elsewhere. **2** a meal of such food. **take in** **1** deceive. **2** make a garment tighter. **3** understand. **take off** **1** become airborne. **2** mimic. **3** leave hastily. **take-off** an act of taking off. **take on** **1** employ. **2** undertake. **take over** assume control. **takeover** an act of taking over. **take to** **1** fall into the habit of. **2** develop a liking or ability for. **3** go to a place to escape danger. **take up** **1** adopt a pursuit. **2** occupy time or space. **3** pursue a matter. **4** accept an offer.

takings pl. n. money received for goods sold.

talc n. **1** talcum powder. **2** a soft mineral.

talcum powder n. a powder used to make the skin feel smooth and dry.

tale n. a story.

talent n. natural ability or skill. ■ **talented** adj.

talisman n. (pl. **talismans**) an object believed to bring good luck.

talk v. **1** speak so as to give information or express ideas or feelings. **2** be able to speak. •n. **1** conversation. **2** a speech or lecture. **3** (**talks**) formal discussions. □ **talk back** reply disrespectfully. **talking-to** informal a reprimand.

talkative adj. fond of talking.

tall adj. of great or specified height. □ **a tall order** a difficult task. **a tall story** an implausible account.

tallow n. animal fat used to make candles and soap.

tally n. (pl. **tallies**) a current score or amount. •v. (**tallying**, **tallied**) **1** agree or correspond. **2** calculate the total of.

Talmud n. the ancient writings on Jewish law and legend. ■ **Talmudic** adj.

talon n. a claw of a bird of prey.

tamarind n. a tropical fruit with sticky pulp used in Asian cookery.

tambourine n. a shallow drum with metal discs around the edge.

tame adj. **1** (of an animal) not dangerous or frightened of people. **2** unexciting. •v. make tame or easier to control. ■ **tamely** adv.

Tamil n. **1** a member of a people of South India and Sri Lanka. **2** their language.

tamp v. pack down firmly.

tamper v. (**tamper with**) interfere with.

tampon n. a plug of soft material inserted into the vagina to absorb menstrual blood.

tan n. **1** a suntan. **2** a yellowish-brown colour. •v. (**tanning**, **tanned**) **1** develop a suntan. **2** convert animal skin into leather.

tandem n. a bicycle for two riders, one behind the other. □ **in tandem** together or at the same time.

tandoori adj. (of Indian food) cooked in a clay oven.

tang n. a strong taste or smell. ■ **tangy** adj.

tangent n. **1** a straight line that touches a curve but does not cross it. **2** (in a right-angled triangle) the ratio of the sides opposite and adjacent to a particular angle. **3** a completely different line of thought or action. ■ **tangential** adj.

tangerine n. a small orange citrus fruit.

tangible adj. **1** able to be perceived by touch. **2** definite or real. ■ **tangibility** n. **tangibly** adv.

tangle v. **1** twist into a confused mass. **2** informal come into conflict. •n. a confused mass or muddle.

tango n. (pl. **tangos**) a Latin American ballroom dance.

tank n. **1** a large container for liquid or gas. **2** a heavy armoured fighting vehicle moving on a continuous metal track.

tankard n. a tall beer mug.

tanker n. a ship, vehicle, or aircraft for carrying liquid in bulk.

tannery n. (pl. **tanneries**) a place where animal skins are tanned.

tannin (or **tannic acid**) n. a bitter substance present in tea, grapes, etc.

tannoy n. trademark a public address system.

tantalize (or **-ise**) v. tease with the sight or promise of something unobtainable.

tantalum n. a hard silver-grey metallic element.

tantamount adj. (**tantamount to**) equivalent in seriousness to.

tantra n. a Hindu or Buddhist text on mystical practices. ■ **tantric** adj.

tantrum n. an uncontrolled outburst of anger and frustration.

tap n. **1** a device for controlling a flow of liquid or gas from a pipe or container. **2** a light blow. **3** a device for listening secretly to phone conversations. •v. (**tapping, tapped**) **1** knock gently. **2** take some of a supply. **3** draw liquid from a barrel etc. **4** connect a device to a phone to listen secretly to conversations. □ **on tap** informal readily available. **tap dancing** a style of dancing performed in shoes fitted with metal pieces on the toes and heels. **taproot** a plant's main root.

tapas pl. n. small Spanish savoury dishes.

tape n. **1** light, flexible material in a narrow strip, used to hold, fasten, or mark off something. **2** magnetic tape, used for recording. **3** a cassette or reel of magnetic tape. •v. **1** record on magnetic tape. **2** fasten or mark off with tape. □ **tape measure** a strip of tape marked for measuring length. **tape recorder** a device for recording and reproducing sounds on magnetic tape. **tapeworm** a long worm living as a parasite in the intestines.

taper v. **1** reduce in thickness towards one end. **2** (**taper off**) gradually lessen. •n. a thin candle.

tapestry n. (pl. **tapestries**) a piece of thick fabric with a design woven or embroidered on it.

tapioca n. starchy grains used for puddings etc.

tapir /tay-peer/ n. a piglike animal with a flexible snout.

tappet n. a moving part in a machine which transmits motion from one part to another.

tar n. **1** a dark, thick liquid distilled from wood or coal. **2** a similar substance formed by burning tobacco. • v. (**tarring, tarred**) coat with tar.

taramasalata n. a creamy dip made from fish roe.

tarantula n. a large hairy spider.

tardy adj. (**tardier, tardiest**) **1** late. **2** slow to act or respond. ■ **tardily** adv. **tardiness** n.

tare n. **1** the weight of a vehicle without its fuel or load. **2** a weed.

target n. **1** a person or thing that is the aim of an attack. **2** a result that you aim to achieve. • v. (**targeting, targeted**) **1** select as an object of attack. **2** aim or direct.

tariff n. **1** a tax paid on some imports or exports. **2** a list of charges in a hotel etc.

tarmac n. **1** trademark broken stone mixed with tar for surfacing roads etc. **2** a tarmacked area. • v. (**tarmacking, tarmacked**) surface with tarmac.

tarn n. a small mountain lake.

tarnish v. **1** cause metal to lose its shine. **2** damage or spoil. • n. a film or stain on metal.

tarot /ta-roh/ n. a set of cards for fortune-telling.

tarpaulin n. a sheet of heavy waterproof cloth.

tarragon n. a herb.

tarsus n. (pl. **tarsi**) the set of small bones in the ankle and upper foot.

tart n. **1** an open pastry case with a filling. **2** informal a prostitute. • v. (**tart up**) informal improve the

appearance of. • adj. **1** sour. **2** (of a remark etc.) unkind. ■ **tartly** adv. **tartness** n.

tartan n. woollen cloth woven in a pattern of coloured checks and lines.

tartar n. **1** a hard deposit forming on teeth. **2** a deposit formed during the fermentation of wine.

tartare sauce n. mayonnaise mixed with gherkins and capers.

tartrazine n. a yellow dye used to colour food.

task n. a piece of work to be done. □ **take to task** reprimand. **task force** a group organized for a special task. **taskmaster** a person who makes others work hard.

tassel n. a decorative tuft of threads knotted at one end. ■ **tasselled** adj.

taste n. **1** the sensation of flavour perceived in the mouth on contact with a substance. **2** the sense by which taste is perceived. **3** a small sample of food or drink. **4** a brief experience. **5** a liking. **6** the ability to judge what is good quality or appropriate behaviour. • v. **1** perceive or test the flavour of. **2** have a particular flavour. **3** experience briefly. ■ **taster** n.

tasteful adj. showing good judgement as to quality etc. ■ **tastefully** adv.

tasteless adj. **1** lacking flavour. **2** showing poor judgement as to quality etc. ■ **tastelessly** adv.

tasty adj. (**tastier, tastiest**) having a pleasant flavour.

tat n. informal tasteless or badly made articles.

tattered adj. old and torn.

tatters pl. n. torn pieces.

tattle n. & v. gossip.

tattoo n. (pl. **tattoos**) **1** a permanent design made on the skin with a needle and ink. **2** a military display with music and marching. **3** a rhythmic tapping. •v. mark with a tattoo. ■ **tattooist** n.

tatty adj. (**tattier, tattiest**) informal worn and shabby.

taught past & past part. of TEACH.

taunt n. a jeering or mocking remark. •v. anger or upset with taunts.

taupe /tohp/ n. a greyish brown.

taut adj. stretched tight. ■ **tauten** v. **tautly** adv.

tautology n. (pl. **tautologies**) the saying of the same thing over again in different words. ■ **tautological** adj. **tautologous** adj.

tavern n. old use an inn or pub.

taverna n. a Greek restaurant.

tawdry adj. (**tawdrier, tawdriest**) showy but cheap and of poor quality. ■ **tawdriness** n.

tawny adj. of an orange-brown or yellowish-brown colour.

tax n. money that must be paid to the state. •v. **1** impose a tax on. **2** make heavy demands on. □ **tax return** a form on which a person states their income, used for tax assessment. ■ **taxable** adj. **taxation** n.

taxi n. (or **taxicab**) (pl. **taxis**) a car licensed to transport passengers in return for payment of a fare. •v. (**taxiing, taxied**) (of an aircraft) move slowly along the ground before take-off or after landing.

taxidermy n. the art of preparing and stuffing the skins of dead animals to make them look lifelike. ■ **taxidermist** n.

taxonomy n. the scientific classification of organisms. ■ **taxonomic** adj.

TB abbrev. tuberculosis.

tbsp (or **tbs**) abbrev. tablespoonful.

tea n. **1** a drink made by soaking the dried leaves of an Asian shrub in boiling water. **2** these leaves. **3** an afternoon or evening meal. □ **tea bag** a sachet of tea leaves. **teacake** a currant bun. **teapot** a pot with a handle, spout, and lid, in which tea is made. **tea towel** (or **tea cloth**) a cloth for drying washed crockery etc. **teaspoon** a small spoon for stirring hot drinks.

teach v. (**teaching, taught**) **1** give lessons in a subject to a class or pupil. **2** show how to do something. ■ **teacher** n.

teak n. hard wood from a SE Asian tree.

team n. **1** a group of players forming one side in a game or sport. **2** two or more people or animals working together. •v. **1** (**team up**) work together. **2** (**team with**) match with. □ **teamwork** organized effort as a group.

tear¹ v. (**tearing, tore**; past part. **torn**) **1** rip a hole in. **2** pull apart or to pieces. **3** informal move very quickly. **4** (**be torn**) be unsure about which option to choose. •n. a hole or split caused by tearing. □ **tearaway** a wild or reckless person.

tear² n. a drop of clear salty liquid forming in and falling from a person's eye. □ **in tears** crying. **teardrop** a single tear. **tear gas** gas causing severe irritation to the eyes. ■ **tearful** adj. **tearfully** adv.

tease v. **1** playfully make fun of or attempt to provoke. **2** gently pull into separate strands. • n. *informal* a person who teases. ■ **teaser** n.

teasel n. a plant with spiny flower heads.

teat n. **1** a plastic device through which milk can be sucked from a bottle. **2** a nipple or similar body part.

technetium n. a radioactive metallic element.

technical adj. **1** of a particular subject, craft, etc. **2** of the practical use of machinery and methods in science and industry. **3** needing specialized knowledge. **4** according to the law or rules when applied strictly. ■ **technically** adv.

technicality n. (pl. **technicalities**) a small formal detail in a set of rules.

technician n. **1** a person employed to look after technical equipment. **2** an expert in the technique of a subject, craft, etc.

Technicolor n. *trademark* a process of producing cinema films in colour.

technique n. **1** a special way of doing something. **2** a person's level of practical skill.

technocracy n. (pl. **technocracies**) a social or political system in which technical experts have great power. ■ **technocrat** n.

technology n. (pl. **technologies**) **1** the application of scientific knowledge for practical purposes. **2** machinery developed from this. ■ **technological** adj. **technologically** adv. **technologist** n.

tectonic adj. of the earth's crust.

teddy (or **teddy bear**) n. (pl. **teddies**) a soft toy bear.

tedious adj. too long or dull. ■ **tediously** adv.

tedium n. the state of being tedious.

tee n. **1** a place from which a golf ball is struck at the start of each hole. **2** a small peg for supporting a golf ball on a tee. • v. (**teeing**, **teed**) **1** (**tee up**) place the ball on a tee. **2** (**tee off**) begin a round or hole in golf.

teem v. **1** (**teem with**) be swarming with. **2** (of rain) fall heavily.

teen *informal* adj. of teenagers. • n. **1** a teenager. **2** (**teens**) the years of age from 13 to 19.

teenager n. a person aged between 13 and 19 years. ■ **teenage** (or **teenaged**) adj.

teeny adj. (**teenier**, **teeniest**) *informal* tiny.

teepee n. var. of TEPEE.

tee shirt n. a T-shirt.

teeter v. move or sway unsteadily.

teeth pl. of TOOTH.

teethe v. (of a baby) develop its first teeth. □ **teething troubles** problems occurring in the early stages of a project.

teetotal adj. choosing not to drink alcohol. ■ **teetotaller** n.

TEFL *abbrev.* teaching of English as a foreign language.

Teflon n. *trademark* a non-stick coating for saucepans etc.

telecommunications n. the technology concerned with long-distance communication by cable, telephone, broadcasting, satellite, etc.

telegram n. a message sent by telegraph.

telegraph n. a system or device for sending messages from a dis-

t

telekinesis n. the supposed ability to move objects by mental power.

telepathy n. supposed communication by means other than the senses. ■ **telepathic** adj.

telephone n. a device for transmitting speech over a distance using wire or radio. •v. contact by telephone. ■ **telephonic** adj. **telephonically** adv. **telephony** n.

telephonist n. an operator of a phone switchboard.

telephoto lens n. a lens that produces a magnified image of a distant object.

teleprinter n. a device for transmitting telegraph messages as they are keyed.

telesales n. the selling of goods or services by phone.

telescope n. an optical instrument for making distant objects appear nearer. •v. 1 (of an object made up of several tubes) slide into itself so as to become smaller. 2 condense into less space or time. ■ **telescopic** adj.

teletext n. an information service transmitted to televisions.

televise v. show on television.

television n. 1 a system for transmitting visual images with sound and displaying them electronically on a screen. 2 a device with a screen for receiving television signals. 3 the activity or medium of broadcasting on television. ■ **televisual** adj.

telex n. 1 an international system in which printed messages are transmitted and received by teleprinters. 2 a message sent by telex.

tell v. (**telling**, **told**) 1 communicate information to. 2 order or advise. 3 express in words. 4 (**tell off**) informal reprimand. 5 determine or establish. 6 distinguish. 7 have a noticeable effect. 8 (**tell on**) informal inform about a person's wrongdoings.

teller n. 1 esp. US a bank cashier. 2 a person who counts votes. 3 a narrator.

telling adj. having a striking or revealing effect. ■ **tellingly** adv.

telltale adj. revealing something. •n. a person who reports others' wrongdoings.

tellurium n. a crystalline element.

telly n. (pl. **tellies**) informal a television.

temerity n. very confident behaviour, likely to be regarded as disrespectful.

temp informal n. a temporary employee. •v. work as a temp.

temper n. 1 a state of mind. 2 a tendency to become angry easily. 3 an angry mood. •v. 1 make less extreme; moderate. 2 harden a metal by reheating and then cooling it.

tempera n. a method of painting using colours mixed with egg.

temperament n. a person's nature in terms of the effect it has on their behaviour.

temperamental adj. 1 tending to change mood in an unreasonable way. 2 of or caused by temperament. ■ **temperamentally** adv.

temperance n. complete avoidance of alcohol.

temperate adj. 1 (of a climate) having mild temperatures. 2 self-controlled.

temperature n. **1** the degree of heat or cold. **2** a body temperature above normal.

tempest n. a violent storm.

tempestuous adj. **1** stormy. **2** full of strong and changeable emotion.

template n. a shaped piece of rigid material used as a pattern for cutting out etc.

temple n. **1** a building for the worship of a god or gods. **2** the flat part between the forehead and the ear.

tempo n. (pl. **tempos** or **tempi**) **1** the speed of a piece of music. **2** the pace of an activity or process.

temporal adj. **1** of time. **2** of worldly affairs. **3** of or situated in the temples of the head. ■ **temporally** adv.

temporary adj. lasting for a limited time. ■ **temporarily** adv.

temporize (or **-ise**) v. delay making a decision.

tempt v. entice someone to do something against their better judgement. ■ **temptation** n. **tempter** n. **tempting** adj. **temptress** n.

ten adj. & n. one more than nine; 10. ■ **tenfold** adj. & adv.

tenable adj. able to be defended or upheld.

tenacious adj. holding firmly to something. ■ **tenaciously** adv. **tenacity** n.

tenancy n. (pl. **tenancies**) use of land or property as a tenant.

tenant n. a person who rents land or property from a landlord.

tend v. **1** frequently behave in a particular way or have a certain characteristic. **2** take care of.

tendency n. (pl. **tendencies**) an inclination to behave in a particular way.

tendentious adj. promoting a particular point of view.

tender adj. **1** gentle and kind. **2** easy to cut or chew. **3** painful to the touch. **4** easily damaged. •v. **1** offer formally. **2** make a formal written offer to carry out work, supply goods, etc. for a stated fixed price. •n. **1** a tendered offer. **2** a vehicle used by a fire service for carrying equipment. **3** a wagon attached to a steam locomotive to carry fuel and water. ■ **tenderly** adv. **tenderness** n.

tendon n. a strong band of tissue attaching a muscle to a bone.

tendril n. **1** a thread-like part by which a climbing plant clings. **2** a slender curl of hair.

tenement n. a large house divided into flats.

tenet n. a central principle or belief.

tenner n. informal a ten-pound note.

tennis n. a game in which players use rackets to hit a ball over a net stretched across an open court.

tenon n. a projecting piece of wood shaped to fit into a mortise.

tenor n. **1** the highest ordinary adult male singing voice. **2** the general meaning or nature of something.

tense adj. **1** stretched tight. **2** anxious or nervous. •v. make or become tense. •n. a set of forms of a verb indicating the time of the action. ■ **tensely** adv.

tensile adj. **1** of tension. **2** able to be stretched.

tension n. **1** the state of being stretched tight. **2** mental or emo-

t

tional strain. **3** a strained political or social state. **4** voltage of specified magnitude.

tent n. a portable fabric shelter supported by poles.

tentacle n. a long, thin, flexible part of certain animals, used for feeling or grasping.

tentative adj. **1** hesitant. **2** not certain. ■ **tentatively** adv.

tenterhook n. (**on tenterhooks**) in a state of nervous suspense.

tenth adj. & n. next after ninth; 10th.

tenuous adj. very slight or weak. ■ **tenuously** adv.

tenure n. the holding of a job, or of land or buildings.

tepee (or **teepee**) n. a conical tent used by American Indians.

tepid adj. lukewarm.

tequila n. a Mexican alcoholic spirit.

tercentenary n. (pl. **tercentenaries**) a 300th anniversary.

tergiversation n. evasive or ambiguous language.

term n. **1** a word or phrase. **2** (**terms**) conditions laid down or agreed. **3** (**terms**) relations: on good terms. **4** a period for which something lasts. **5** each period in the year during which teaching is given in a school or college. **6** each quantity in a mathematical ratio, series, etc. • v. call by a specified term. □ **come to terms with** become able to accept or deal with. ■ **termly** adj. & adv.

termagant n. a bad-tempered or overbearing woman.

terminal adj. **1** of or situated at the end. **2** (of a disease) predicted to lead to death. • n. **1** the station at the end of a railway or bus route. **2** an airport building for

passengers arriving and departing. **3** a point of connection in an electric circuit. **4** a keyboard and screen connected to a central computer system. ■ **terminally** adv.

terminate v. come or bring to an end. ■ **termination** n.

terminology n. (pl. **terminologies**) the set of terms used in a subject. ■ **terminological** adj.

terminus n. (pl. **termini** or **terminuses**) a railway or bus terminal.

termite n. a small insect which eats wood.

tern n. a seabird.

ternary adj. composed of three parts.

terrace n. **1** a raised flat area, esp. forming part of a tier. **2** a patio. **3** a row of houses built in one block. ■ **terraced** adj.

terracotta n. **1** unglazed, brownish-red pottery. **2** a brownish-red colour.

terra firma n. dry land.

terrain n. land with regard to its physical features.

terrapin n. a freshwater turtle.

terrarium /ter-rair-i-uhm/ n. (pl. **terrariums** or **terraria**) an enclosed container in which small reptiles or amphibians are kept or plants are grown.

terrestrial adj. **1** of the earth. **2** living on or in the ground. **3** (of television broadcasting) not using a satellite.

terrible adj. very bad, serious, or unpleasant. ■ **terribly** adv.

terrier n. a small dog.

terrific adj. **1** very great or intense. **2** informal excellent. ■ **terrifically** adv.

t

terrify v. (**terrifying, terrified**) cause to feel terror.

terrine n. a mixture of chopped meat, fish, etc. pressed into a container and served cold.

territorial adj. of, having, or defending a territory. ■ **territorially** adv.

Territorial Army n. a voluntary military reserve force.

territory n. (pl. **territories**) **1** an area under the control of a ruler or state. **2** an area defended by an animal against others. **3** an area in which someone has rights, responsibilities, or knowledge.

terror n. **1** extreme fear. **2** a cause of this. **3** informal a very annoying person.

terrorism n. the unofficial use of violence and intimidation in the attempt to achieve political aims. ■ **terrorist** n.

terrorize (or **-ise**) v. threaten and frighten over a period of time.

terry n. a towelling fabric.

terse adj. using few words. ■ **tersely** adv. **terseness** n.

tertiary /ter-shuh-ri/ adj. third in order or level.

tessellated adj. decorated with mosaics. ■ **tessellation** n.

test n. **1** a procedure to establish the quality, performance, presence, etc. of something. **2** a short examination of skill or knowledge. **3** (or **Test match**) an international cricket or rugby match. • v. subject to a test. □ **test tube** a thin glass tube closed at one end, used to hold material in laboratory tests. **test-tube baby** informal a baby conceived by in vitro fertilization. ■ **tester** n.

testament n. **1** a will. **2** evidence or proof. **3** (**Testament**) each of the two divisions of the Bible.

testate adj. having made a valid will before dying.

testator n. (fem. **testatrix**) a person who has made a will.

testicle n. either of the two organs producing sperm in male mammals. ■ **testicular** adj.

testify v. (**testifying, testified**) **1** give evidence in a law court. **2** serve as evidence or proof.

testimonial n. **1** a formal statement of a person's good character and qualifications. **2** a public tribute to someone.

testimony n. (pl. **testimonies**) **1** a formal statement, esp. one given in a law court. **2** evidence or proof.

testis n. (pl. **testes**) a testicle.

testosterone n. a male sex hormone.

testy adj. irritable. ■ **testily** adv.

tetanus n. a disease causing muscular spasms and rigidity.

tetchy adj. bad-tempered and irritable. ■ **tetchily** adv.

tête-à-tête /tet-ah-tet/ n. a private conversation between two people.

tether v. fasten an animal to a post etc. • n. a rope or chain used to tether an animal.

tetrahedron n. (pl. **tetrahedra** or **tetrahedrons**) a solid with four triangular faces.

Teutonic adj. German.

text n. **1** a written or printed work. **2** the main body of a book as distinct from illustrations etc. **3** (or **text message**) an electronic message sent and received via mobile phone. **4** a passage from

t

the Bible as the subject of a sermon. •v. send a text message to. □ **textbook** a book used for the study of a subject. ■ **textual** adj.

textile n. a woven or knitted fabric.

texture n. the feel or consistency of a substance. •v. give a rough texture to. ■ **textural** adj.

thalidomide n. a sedative drug which was found to cause malformation of the fetus when taken during pregnancy.

thallium n. a highly toxic metallic element.

than conj. & prep. used to introduce the second part of a comparison.

thank v. express gratitude to. •n. (**thanks**) 1 an expression of gratitude. 2 thank you. □ **thanksgiving** the expression of gratitude to God. **Thanksgiving** a national holiday held in the autumn in North America. **thank you** a polite expression of gratitude.

thankful adj. pleased and relieved. ■ **thankfulness** n.

thankfully adv. 1 in a thankful way. 2 fortunately.

thankless adj. unpleasant and unlikely to be appreciated by others.

that pron. & adj. (pl. **those**) referring to a person or thing seen or heard or already mentioned or known, or to the more distant of two things. •pron. introducing a clause defining or identifying something. •adv. to such a degree. •conj. introducing a statement or suggestion.

thatch n. a roof covering of straw, reeds, etc. •v. cover with thatch. ■ **thatcher** n.

thaw v. 1 make or become unfrozen. 2 make or become friend-

lier. •n. 1 a period of warmer weather that thaws ice and snow. 2 an increase in friendliness.

the adj. used to refer to one or more people or things already mentioned or understood; the definite article.

theatre (US **theater**) n. 1 a building in which plays etc. are performed. 2 the writing and production of plays. 3 a room for lectures with seats in tiers. 4 a room where surgical operations are performed.

theatrical adj. 1 of acting, actors, or the theatre. 2 exaggerated for effect. •n. (**theatricals**) theatrical performances. ■ **theatricality** n. **theatrically** adv.

thee pron. old use you (as the singular object of a verb or preposition).

theft n. stealing.

their adj. of or belonging to them.

! Don't confuse **their** with **there**, which means 'in, at, or to that place or position'

theirs possess. pron. belonging to them.

! No apostrophe: theirs.

them pron. used as the object of a verb or preposition to refer to two or more people or things previously mentioned, or to a person of unspecified sex.

theme n. 1 a subject being discussed. 2 a prominent or frequently recurring melody in a musical piece. □ **theme park** an amusement park based around a particular idea. ■ **thematic** adj. **thematically** adv.

themselves pron. 1 used when a group of people or things or a person of unspecified sex performing an action are also affected by it. **2** they or them personally.

then adv. **1** at that time. **2** after that. **3** in that case.

thence adv. formal from that place or source. □ **thenceforth** from that time onward.

theocracy n. (pl. **theocracies**) a system of government by priests. ∎ **theocratic** adj.

theodolite n. a surveying instrument for measuring angles.

theology n. (pl. **theologies**) **1** the study of God and religious belief. **2** a system of religious beliefs. ∎ **theologian** n. **theological** adj. **theologist** n.

theorem n. a scientific or mathematical proposition that can be proved by reasoning.

theoretical adj. concerning or based on theory rather than practice. ∎ **theoretically** adv.

theorize (or -**ise**) v. form a theory or theories about something. ∎ **theorist** n.

theory n. (pl. **theories**) **1** a set of ideas intended to explain something. **2** a set of principles on which an activity is based.

theosophy n. a philosophy believing that knowledge of God is achievable through intuition and meditation. ∎ **theosophical** adj.

therapeutic adj. **1** of the curing of disease. **2** having a good effect on the body or mind. ∎ **therapeutically** adv.

therapy n. (pl. **therapies**) treatment for a physical or mental disorder. ∎ **therapist** n.

there adv. **1** in, at, or to that place or position. **2** on that issue. □ **thereabouts** near that place, time, or figure. **thereafter** after

that time. **thereby** by that means. **therefore** for that reason. **therein** formal in that place, document, or respect. **thereof** formal of that. **thereupon** formal immediately after that.

! Don't confuse **there** with **their**, which means 'belonging to them'.

thermal adj. **1** of heat. **2** (of a garment) made of a fabric providing good insulation. •n. an upward current of warm air.

thermodynamics n. the study of the relations between heat and other forms of energy.

thermometer n. an instrument for measuring temperature.

thermonuclear adj. of or using nuclear reactions occurring at very high temperatures.

thermoplastic adj. (of a substance) becoming soft when heated and hardening when cooled.

Thermos n. trademark a vacuum flask.

thermosetting adj. (of a substance) setting permanently when heated.

thermostat n. a device that regulates temperature automatically. ∎ **thermostatic** adj. **thermostatically** adv.

thesaurus n. (pl. **thesauri** or **thesauruses**) a book containing lists of synonyms.

these pl. of **THIS**.

thesis n. (pl. **theses**) **1** a theory put forward to be supported or proved. **2** a long essay written as part of a university degree.

thespian adj. of the theatre. •n. an actor or actress.

t

they pron. **1** the people or things or person of unspecified sex previously mentioned. **2** people in general.

thiamine (or **thiamin**) n. vitamin B1, found in unrefined cereals, beans, and liver.

thick adj. **1** with opposite sides or surfaces relatively far apart. **2** made up of a large number of things close together. **3** dense or difficult to see through. **4** relatively firm in consistency. **5** informal stupid. **6** informal very friendly. •n. (**the thick**) the busiest or most intense part. □ **thickset** heavily or solidly built. **thick-skinned** not sensitive to criticism etc. ■ **thicken** v. **thickly** adv. **thickness** n.

thicket n. a dense group of bushes or trees.

thief n. (pl. **thieves**) a person who steals.

thieve v. steal. ■ **thievery** n.

thigh n. the part of the leg between the hip and the knee.

thimble n. a hard cap worn to protect the end of the finger in sewing.

thin adj. (**thinner**, **thinnest**) **1** not thick. **2** having little fat on the body. **3** (of a sound) faint and high-pitched. **4** weak and inadequate. •v. (**thinning**, **thinned**) make or become thinner. ■ **thinly** adv. **thinness** n.

thine possess. pron. & adj. old use your or yours.

thing n. **1** an inanimate object. **2** an unspecified matter, action, activity, thought, etc. **3** (**things**) belongings. **4** (**the thing**) informal what is needed, acceptable, or fashionable.

think v. (**thinking**, **thought**) **1** have a particular opinion or belief. **2** use or direct the mind. **3** (**think of/about**) take into account or consideration. **4** (**think up**) informal devise. •n. an act of thinking. □ **think better of** reconsider and decide not to do. **think tank** a body of experts providing advice and ideas. ■ **thinker** n.

thinner n. a solvent used to thin paint etc.

third adj. & n. **1** next after second. **2** each of three equal parts. □ **third-degree** (of burns) affecting tissue below the skin. **the third degree** long and harsh questioning. **third party 1** a person or group besides the two main ones involved in a situation. **2** (of insurance) covering damage or injury suffered by a person other than the insured. **third-rate** of very poor quality. **Third World** the developing countries of Asia, Africa, and Latin America. ■ **thirdly** adv.

thirst n. **1** a feeling of needing or wanting to drink. **2** a strong desire. •v. (**thirst for/after**) have a strong desire for. ■ **thirstily** adv. **thirsty** adj.

thirteen adj. & n. one more than twelve; 13. ■ **thirteenth** adj. & n.

thirty adj. & n. (pl. **thirties**) ten less than forty; 30. ■ **thirtieth** adj. & n.

this pron. & adj. (pl. **these**) referring to the person or thing near, mentioned, or indicated. •adv. to the degree or extent indicated.

thistle n. a prickly plant. □ **thistledown** the light fluff on thistle seeds.

thither adv. old use to or towards that place.

thong n. **1** a narrow strip of leather etc. used as a fastening or as the lash of a whip. **2** a G-string.

thorax n. (pl. **thoraces** or **thoraxes**) the part of the body between the neck and the abdomen. ■ **thoracic** adj.

thorn n. **1** a stiff, sharp woody projection on a plant. **2** a thorny bush or tree. ■ **thorny** adj.

thorough adj. **1** complete with regard to every detail. **2** very careful and detailed. □ **thoroughbred** an animal of pure breed. **thoroughfare** a road or path between two places. ■ **thoroughly** adv. **thoroughness** n.

those pl. of THAT.

thou pron. old use singular form of 'you'.

though conj. despite the fact that. • adv. however.

thought past & past part. of THINK. • n. **1** an idea. **2** the process of thinking. **3** careful consideration.

thoughtful adj. **1** deep in thought. **2** thought out carefully. **3** considerate. ■ **thoughtfully** adv.

thoughtless adj. **1** inconsiderate. **2** without thinking of the consequences. ■ **thoughtlessly** adv.

thousand adj. & n. ten hundred; 1,000 or M. ■ **thousandth** adj. & n.

thrall n. the state of being in another's power.

thrash v. **1** beat repeatedly and violently. **2** move in a violent or uncontrolled way. **3** informal defeat heavily. **4** (**thrash out**) discuss thoroughly.

thread n. **1** a long, thin strand of cotton, nylon, etc. **2** the spiral ridge of a screw etc. **3** a theme running through a situation or piece of writing. • v. **1** pass a thread through. **2** move or weave in and out of obstacles. □ **threadbare** worn and tattered with age.

threat n. **1** a stated intention to harm someone. **2** a person or thing likely to cause harm or danger.

threaten v. **1** make a threat to or to do. **2** put at risk.

three adj. & n. one more than two; 3. □ **three-dimensional** having or appearing to have length, breadth, and depth. **threesome** a group of three people. ■ **threefold** adj. & adv.

thresh v. **1** separate grain from the husks of corn etc. **2** move about wildly.

threshold n. **1** a strip of wood or stone forming the bottom of a doorway. **2** a level or point marking the start of something.

> ! There is only one h in the middle: threshold.

threw past of THROW.

thrice adv. old use three times.

thrift n. economy in the use of resources. ■ **thrifty** adj.

thrill n. **1** a sudden feeling of excitement. **2** an exciting experience. **3** a wave of emotion. • v. have or cause to have a thrill. ■ **thrilling** adj.

thriller n. an exciting novel, play, or film, esp. involving crime.

thrive v. (**thriving**, **thrived** or **throve**; past part. **thrived** or **thriven**) **1** grow or develop well. **2** prosper.

throat n. **1** the passage from the back of the mouth to the oesophagus and lungs. **2** the front of the neck.

throaty adj. (of a voice) deep and husky. ■ **throatily** adv.

throb v. (**throbbing, throbbed**) **1** beat or sound with a strong rhythm. **2** feel regular bursts of pain. • n. a strong, regular beat or sound.

throes pl. n. severe or violent pains. □ **in the throes of** struggling in the midst of.

thrombosis n. (pl. **thromboses**) the formation of a blood clot in a blood vessel or the heart.

throne n. **1** a ceremonial chair for a monarch or bishop. **2** the power or rank of a monarch.

throng n. a densely packed crowd. • v. gather in large numbers in a place.

throttle n. a device controlling the flow of fuel or power to an engine. • v. strangle.

through prep. & adv. **1** from end to end or side to side of. **2** from start to finish. **3** by means of. • adj. **1** (of public transport) continuing to the final destination. **2** passing straight through a place. **3** having passed to the next stage of a competition. □ **throughout** all the way through. **throughput** the amount of material processed.

throve past of THRIVE.

throw v. (**throwing, threw;** past part. **thrown**) **1** send through the air from the hand. **2** move or place hurriedly or roughly. **3** direct or cast light, a look, etc. somewhere. **4** send suddenly into a particular state. **5** confuse; put off. **6** form pottery on a wheel. • n. **1** an act of throwing, or the distance thrown. **2** a light cover for furniture. □ **throw away** discard as useless.

throwback a return to an earlier ancestral type or characteristic.

throw up vomit.

thrum v. (**thrumming, thrummed**) make a rhythmic humming sound.

thrush n. **1** a brown songbird with spotted breast. **2** a fungal infection of the mouth and throat or the genitals.

thrust v. (**thrusting, thrust**) **1** push suddenly or violently. **2** make your way forcibly. • n. **1** a thrusting force or movement. **2** the main point of an argument.

thud n. a dull, heavy sound. • v. (**thudding, thudded**) move or fall with a thud.

thug n. a violent man. ■ **thuggery** n. **thuggish** adj.

thumb n. the short, thick first digit of the hand. • v. **1** turn over pages with the thumb. **2** request a lift in a passing vehicle by signalling with the thumb. □ **under someone's thumb** completely under someone's control. **thumbnail** brief or concise. **thumbscrew** an instrument of torture that crushes the thumbs.

thump v. **1** hit heavily. **2** (of the heart) beat rapidly. • n. a heavy blow or noise.

thunder n. **1** a loud rumbling or crashing noise heard after lightning. **2** a loud, deep noise. • v. **1** make the sound of thunder. **2** move noisily and forcefully. **3** speak loudly and angrily. □ **thunderbolt** a flash of lightning with a crash of thunder. **thunderclap** a crash of thunder. **thunderstorm** a storm with thunder and lightning. **thunderstruck** very surprised. ■ **thunderous** adj. **thundery** adj.

Thursday n. the day before Friday.

thus adv. formal **1** as a result of this. **2** in this way.

thwack v. hit forcefully. • n. a heavy blow.

thwart v. prevent from accomplishing something.

thy adj. old use your.

thyme /tym/ n. a herb used in cookery.

thymus n. (pl. **thymi**) a gland in the neck producing white blood cells.

thyroid n. a gland in the neck producing growth hormones.

thyself pron. old use yourself.

tiara n. a woman's jewelled semi-circular headdress.

tibia n. (pl. **tibiae**) the inner of the two bones between the knee and the ankle.

tic n. a recurring spasm in the muscles of the face.

tick n. **1** a mark (✓) used to show that something is correct or has been chosen or checked. **2** a regular clicking sound, as made by a clock etc. **3** a bloodsucking insect-like animal. **4** informal a moment. • v. **1** mark with a tick. **2** make regular ticking sounds. **3** (**tick over**) (of an engine) run slowly in neutral. **4** (**tick off**) informal reprimand. □ **on tick** on credit.

ticket n. **1** a piece of paper or card entitling the holder to enter a place or to travel on public transport. **2** an official notice of a traffic offence. **3** a label showing the price, size, etc. of an item for sale. • v. (**ticketing**, **ticketed**) give a ticket to.

ticking n. a strong fabric used to cover mattresses.

tickle v. **1** lightly touch in a way that causes itching or twitching and often laughter. **2** appeal to or amuse. • n. an act of tickling or feeling of being tickled. ■ **tickly** adj.

ticklish adj. **1** sensitive to being tickled. **2** requiring care and tact.

tidal adj. of or affected by tides. □ **tidal wave** a very large ocean wave.

tiddler n. informal a small fish.

tiddly adj. informal **1** slightly drunk. **2** tiny. □ **tiddlywinks** a game involving flicking small counters into a cup.

tide n. **1** the regular alternate rise and fall of the sea. **2** a powerful surge of feeling or trend of events. • v. (**tide over**) help through a difficult period.

tidings pl. n. literary news.

tidy adj. (**tidier**, **tidiest**) neat and orderly. • v. (**tidying**, **tidied**) make tidy. ■ **tidily** adv. **tidiness** n.

tie v. (**tying**, **tied**) **1** attach or fasten with string etc. **2** form into a knot or bow. **3** restrict. **4** connect. **5** achieve the same score as another competitor. • n. (pl. **ties**) **1** a thing that ties. **2** a strip of material worn beneath a collar and knotted at the front. **3** an equal score in a game or match. **4** a sports match in which the winners proceed to the next round. □ **tiebreak** a means of deciding a winner when competitors have tied. **tie in** link or agree. **tie-up** a link. **tie up 1** bind someone's arms and legs. **2** conclude. **3** informal occupy fully.

tied adj. **1** (of a house) for occupation only by someone working for its owner. **2** (of a pub) owned and controlled by a brewery.

t

tier n. any of a series of rows or levels placed one above and behind the other. ■ **tiered** adj.

tiff n. informal a trivial quarrel.

tiger n. a large striped member of the cat family.

tight adj. 1 closed or fastened firmly. 2 close-fitting. 3 stretched so as to leave no slack. 4 allowing little room for movement. 5 strictly imposed. 6 (of money or time) limited. •pl. n. (**tights**) a close-fitting stretchy garment covering the legs, hips, and bottom. □ **tightrope** a rope or wire stretched high above the ground, on which acrobats balance. ■ **tighten** v. **tightly** adv. **tightness** n.

tigress n. a female tiger.

tilde /til-duh/ n. an accent (˜) placed over a letter to mark a change in pronunciation.

tile n. a thin piece of baked clay etc. for covering roofs, floors, or walls. •v. cover with tiles. ■ **tiling** n.

till prep. & conj. until. •n. a cash register or drawer for money in a shop etc. •v. prepare land for crops.

tiller n. a horizontal bar fitted to a boat's rudder, used for steering.

tilt v. move into a sloping position. •n. a sloping position. □ (**at**) **full tilt** with maximum speed or force.

timber n. wood prepared for use in building and carpentry. ■ **timbered** adj.

timbre /tam-ber/ n. the quality of a voice or musical sound.

time n. 1 the continuing progress of existence and events in the past, present, and future. 2 a period of time. 3 a point of time measured in hours and minutes. 4 an instance of something happening or being done. 5 (**times**) expressing multiplication. 6 rhythm in music. •v. 1 arrange a time for. 2 do at a certain time. 3 measure the time taken by. □ **time bomb** a bomb designed to explode at a set time. **time-honoured** (of a custom) respected because of its long existence. **timepiece** a clock or watch. **timeshare** an arrangement in which joint owners use a property as a holiday home at different times. **timetable** a list of times at which events are scheduled to take place. ■ **timer** n. **timing** n.

timeless adj. not affected by the passage of time.

timely adj. done or occurring at a good time.

timid adj. lacking courage or confidence. ■ **timidity** n. **timidly** adv.

timorous adj. timid.

timpani (or **tympani**) pl. n. kettledrums. ■ **timpanist** n.

tin n. 1 a silvery-white metallic element. 2 a metal container. 3 a sealed metal container for preserving food. •v. (**tinning, tinned**) 1 coat with tin. 2 (**tinned**) preserved in a tin. □ **tinpot** informal of poor quality.

tincture n. a medicine made by dissolving a drug in alcohol.

tinder n. dry material which burns easily.

tine n. a prong or point, esp. of a fork.

tinge n. a slight trace of a colour or quality. •v. (**tinging** or **tingeing, tinged**) give a tinge to.

tingle n. a slight prickling or stinging sensation. •v. have or cause a tingle.

t

tinker v. casually try to repair or improve. •n. a travelling mender of pots, kettles, etc.

tinkle v. make a light, clear ringing sound. •n. a tinkling sound.

tinnitus n. ringing or buzzing in the ears.

tinny adj. **1** having a thin, metallic sound. **2** made of thin or poor-quality metal.

tinsel n. a decoration made of thin strips of shiny metal foil.

tint n. **1** a shade of colour. **2** a dye for colouring the hair. •v. colour slightly.

tiny adj. (**tinier**, **tiniest**) very small.

tip n. **1** the end of something thin or tapering. **2** a place where rubbish is left. **3** a small sum of money given for good service in a restaurant, taxi, etc. **4** a piece of advice. **5** a prediction as to the likely winner of a race etc. •v. (**tipping**, **tipped**) **1** overbalance so as to fall over. **2** empty out the contents of a container by holding it at an angle. **3** cover the end of something thin or tapering with a material. **4** give a tip to someone for good service. **5** predict as likely to win or achieve something. **6** (**tip off**) informal give someone secret information. ▢ **tip-off** informal a piece of secret information.

tipple v. drink alcohol regularly. •n. an alcoholic drink. ■ **tippler** n.

tipster n. a person who gives tips as to the likely winner of a race etc.

tipsy adj. slightly drunk. ■ **tipsily** adv.

tiptoe v. (**tiptoeing**, **tiptoed**) walk quietly and carefully with the heels raised.

tirade n. a long angry speech.

tire v. **1** make or become tired. **2** (**tire of**) become impatient or bored with. •n. US = TYRE.

tired adj. **1** in need of sleep or rest. **2** (**tired of**) impatient or bored with. ■ **tiredness** n.

tireless adj. having or showing great energy. ■ **tirelessly** adv.

tiresome adj. annoying or tedious.

tissue n. **1** any of the substances of which animals or plants are made. **2** a disposable paper handkerchief. ▢ **tissue paper** very thin, soft paper.

tit n. a small songbird.

titanic adj. of very great size or power.

titanium n. a silver-grey metallic element.

titbit n. **1** a small piece of tasty food. **2** an item of interesting information.

tit for tat n. a situation in which someone takes retaliation for an insult or injury.

tithe n. one tenth of annual income or produce, formerly paid to the Church.

titillate v. interest or excite, esp. sexually. ■ **titillation** n.

! Don't confuse **titillate** with **titivate**.

titivate v. informal make smarter or more attractive. ■ **titivation** n.

title n. **1** the name of a book, piece of music, etc. **2** a word describing a position or job, or used in speaking to someone with a particular rank or job. **3** the position of champion in a sports contest. **4** the legal right to ownership of property. ▢ **title role** the part in a play or film from which the title is taken.

t

titled adj. having a title indicating nobility or rank.

titter n. a short, quiet laugh. •v. give a titter.

tittle-tattle n. & v. gossip.

titular adj. holding a formal position or title but no real authority.

tizzy n. (pl. **tizzies**) informal a state of nervous excitement or worry.

TNT abbrev. trinitrotoluene, a high explosive.

to prep. **1** in the direction of. **2** so as to reach a state. **3** indicating the person or thing affected. **4** indicating that a verb is in the infinitive. •adv. so as to be closed or nearly closed. □ **to and fro** backwards and forwards or from side to side. **to-do** informal a commotion or fuss.

toad n. a short, stout, tailless amphibian.

toadstool n. a fungus with a rounded cap on a stalk.

toady n. (pl. **toadies**) an ingratiating person. •v. act in an ingratiating way.

toast n. **1** sliced bread heated until brown and crisp. **2** an act of raising glasses and drinking together in honour of a person or thing. **3** a respected or admired person. •v. **1** make bread brown and crisp by heating it. **2** drink a toast to.

toaster n. an electrical device for making toast.

tobacco n. (pl. **tobaccos**) the dried leaves of an American plant which can be smoked or chewed.

tobacconist n. a shopkeeper selling cigarettes etc.

toboggan n. a small sledge for sliding downhill. ■ **tobogganing** n.

today adv. **1** on this present day. **2** at the present time. •n. **1** this present day. **2** the present time.

toddle v. (of a young child) move with short unsteady steps.

toddler n. a young child who is just beginning to walk.

toddy n. (pl. **toddies**) a hot drink of spirits, water, and sugar.

toe n. any of the digits at the end of the foot. •v. push or touch with the toes. □ **toe the line** obey authority. **toehold** a small foothold.

toff n. informal a rich, upper-class person.

toffee n. a sweet made by boiling together sugar and butter.

tofu n. a soft food made from mashed soya beans.

tog n. **1** (**togs**) informal clothes. **2** a unit for measuring the insulating properties of duvets. •v. (**be togged out/up**) informal be dressed.

toga n. a loose outer garment worn by men in ancient Rome.

together adv. **1** in company. **2** so as to touch or combine. **3** regarded as a whole. **4** at the same time.

toggle n. **1** a narrow piece of wood etc. pushed through a loop to fasten a garment. **2** a switch or key turning a function on and off alternately.

toil v. work or move laboriously. •n. laborious work. ■ **toilsome** adj.

toilet n. **1** a large bowl for urinating into or defecating into. **2** old use the process of washing and dressing yourself. □ **toilet water** a light perfume.

toiletries pl. n. articles used in washing and grooming.

token n. **1** a thing representing a fact, quality, or feeling. **2** a voucher that can be exchanged for goods. **3** a disc used to operate a machine. • *adj.* done just for the sake of appearances.

told past & past part. of TELL.

tolerable *adj.* **1** able to be tolerated. **2** fairly good. ∎ **tolerably** *adv.*

tolerance *n.* **1** the ability to tolerate something. **2** an allowable variation in the size of a machine part. ∎ **tolerant** *adj.*

tolerate *v.* **1** allow to exist or happen without protest. **2** endure patiently. ∎ **toleration** *n.*

toll *n.* **1** a charge payable for the use of certain bridges or roads. **2** the number of casualties arising from a disaster etc. **3** a single ring of a bell. • *v.* (of a bell) sound with slow strokes, esp. to mark a death.

tom (or **tomcat**) *n.* a male cat.

tomahawk *n.* a light axe formerly used by American Indians.

tomato *n.* (*pl.* **tomatoes**) a red fruit eaten as a vegetable.

> **!** No *e* at the end in the singular: *tomato.*

tomb *n.* a stone structure forming a burial place. □ **tombstone** a flat inscribed stone marking a grave.

tombola *n.* a lottery in which tickets are drawn from a revolving drum.

tomboy *n.* a girl who enjoys rough, noisy activities.

tome *n.* a large book.

tomfoolery *n.* silly behaviour.

tomography *n.* a technique for displaying a cross section through the body using X-rays or ultrasound.

tomorrow *adv.* **1** on the day after today. **2** in the near future. • *n.* **1** the day after today. **2** the near future.

tom-tom *n.* a drum beaten with the hands.

ton *n.* **1** a unit of weight equal to 2,240 lb or 1016.05 kg (**long ton**) or (especially in the US) 2,000 lb or 907.19 kg (**short ton**). **2** (or **tonne**) a metric ton. **3** a unit of measurement of a ship's weight equal to 2,240 lb or 35 cu. ft (0.99 cu. m). **4** *informal* a great weight or large number.

tone *n.* **1** the quality of a musical sound. **2** the feeling or mood expressed in a person's voice. **3** general character. **4** a basic interval in music, equal to two semitones. **5** a shade of colour. **6** firmness in a resting muscle. • *v.* **1** give firmness to the body or a muscle. **2** (**tone down**) make less harsh or extreme. □ **tone-deaf** unable to perceive differences of musical pitch. ∎ **tonal** *adj.* **tonality** *n.* **tonally** *adv.* **toneless** *adj.*

toner *n.* **1** a liquid applied to the skin to reduce oiliness. **2** a powder used in photocopiers.

tongs *pl. n.* an implement with two joined arms for picking up and holding things.

tongue *n.* **1** the muscular organ in the mouth, used in tasting and speech. **2** a language. **3** a strip of leather or fabric under a shoe's laces. □ **tongue in cheek** not seriously meaning what you are saying. **tongue-tied** too nervous to speak.

tonic *n.* **1** a medicinal drink taken to give a feeling of energy or wellbeing. **2** (also **tonic water**) a carbonated soft drink with a bitter flavour.

tonight *adv.* on the present evening or night. • *n.* the evening or night of the present day.

tonnage n. **1** weight in tons. **2** a ship's carrying capacity measured in tons.

tonne n. a metric ton.

tonsil n. either of two small masses of tissue in the throat.

tonsillitis n. inflammation of the tonsils.

tonsure n. a circular area on a monk's or priest's head where the hair is shaved off. ■ **tonsured** adj.

too adv. **1** more than is desirable or possible. **2** also.

took past of **TAKE**.

tool n. **1** a device or implement used for a particular task. **2** a person used by another. • v. **1** impress a design on leather. **2** equip with tools. □ **toolbar** Computing a strip of icons used to perform certain functions.

toot n. a short, sharp sound made by a horn, trumpet, etc. • v. make a toot.

tooth n. (pl. **teeth**) **1** each of a set of hard white structures in the jaws, used for biting and chewing. **2** a cog on a gearwheel or a point on a saw or comb. □ **toothpaste** a paste for cleaning the teeth. **toothpick** a thin, pointed piece of wood etc. for removing food stuck between the teeth. ■ **toothed** adj. **toothless** adj.

toothy adj. having or showing large teeth.

top n. **1** the highest or uppermost point, part, or surface. **2** a thing placed on or covering the upper part of something. **3** the utmost degree. **4** a garment for the upper part of the body. **5** a toy with a pointed base, made to be made to spin. • adj. highest in position, rank, or degree. • v. (**topping**, **topped**) **1** be more or better than. **2** be at

the highest place or rank in. **3** reach the top of. **4** put a top or topping on. **5** (**top up**) fill up a partly full container. □ **topcoat 1** an overcoat. **2** an outer coat of paint. **top-dress** apply fertilizer on the top of soil. **top hat** a man's formal black hat with a high crown. **top-heavy** unstable because too heavy at the top. **topknot** a knot of hair arranged on the top of the head. **topsoil** the top layer of soil. **topspin** a fast forward spin given to a moving ball. ■ **topmost** adj.

topaz n. a colourless, yellow, or blue precious stone.

topiary n. the art of clipping shrubs or trees into attractive shapes.

topic n. a subject of a text, speech, etc.

topical adj. of or dealing with current affairs. ■ **topicality** n. **topically** adv.

topless adj. having the breasts uncovered.

topography n. the arrangement of the physical features of an area. ■ **topographical** adj.

topology n. the study of geometrical properties unaffected by changes in shape or size.

topping n. a layer of food poured or spread over another food.

topple v. overbalance or cause to overbalance and fall.

topsy-turvy adj. & adv. **1** upside down. **2** in disorder.

tor n. a hill or rocky peak.

Torah n. (in Judaism) the law of God as revealed to Moses.

torch n. **1** a portable electric lamp. **2** a burning piece of wood etc. carried as a light.

tore past of **TEAR**¹.

toreador n. a bullfighter.

torment n. **1** great suffering. **2** a cause of this. •v. **1** cause to suffer greatly. **2** annoy or tease unkindly. ■ **tormentor** n.

torn past part. of TEAR¹.

tornado n. (pl. **tornadoes** or **tornados**) a violent rotating wind storm.

torpedo n. (pl. **torpedoes**) a self-propelled underwater missile. •v. (**torpedoing, torpedoed**) attack or destroy with a torpedo.

torpid adj. sluggish and inactive. ■ **torpidity** n. **torpidly** adv. **torpor** n.

torque n. a force causing rotation.

torrent n. **1** a strong, fast-moving stream of liquid. **2** an outpouring. ■ **torrential** adj.

torrid adj. **1** very hot and dry. **2** passionate.

torsion n. the state of being twisted.

torso n. (pl. **torsos**) the trunk of the human body.

tort n. Law a wrongful act or a violation of a right for which damages may be claimed.

tortellini /tor-tuh-lee-ni/ n. stuffed pasta parcels rolled into small rings.

tortilla /tor-tee-yuh/ n. a thin, flat maize pancake.

tortoise n. a slow-moving reptile with a domed shell. ■ **tortoise-shell 1** the mottled brown and yellow shell of certain turtles, used to make ornaments. **2** a cat with markings that resemble tortoiseshell.

tortuous adj. **1** full of twists and turns. **2** lengthy and complex. ■ **tortuously** adv.

torture n. the inflicting of severe pain as a punishment or means of coercion. **2** great suffering.

•v. inflict torture on. ■ **torturer** n. **torturous** adj.

Tory n. (pl. **Tories**) a member or supporter of the British Conservative Party.

toss v. **1** throw lightly. **2** move from side to side. **3** throw a coin into the air to make a choice based on which side lands uppermost. **4** turn food in a liquid to coat it lightly. •n. an act of tossing.

tot n. **1** a very young child. **2** a small drink of spirits. •v. (**totting, totted**) add up.

total adj. **1** comprising the whole number or amount. **2** complete. •n. a total number or amount. •v. (**totalling, totalled;** US **totaling, totaled**) **1** amount to. **2** find the total of. ■ **totality** n. **totally** adv.

totalitarian adj. (of government) consisting of only one leader or party and having complete control. ■ **totalitarianism** n.

totalizator (or **totalisator**) n. a device showing the number and amount of bets staked on a race.

tote informal v. carry. •n. a system of betting using the totalizator.

totem n. a natural object or animal believed to have spiritual significance and adopted as an emblem. □ **totem pole** a pole decorated with totems.

totter v. walk or rock unsteadily.

toucan n. a tropical American bird with a massive bill.

touch v. **1** come into or be in physical contact with. **2** bring the hand or another part of the body into contact with. **3** harm or interfere with. **4** affect. **5** (**be touched**) feel gratitude or sympathy. •n. **1** an act or way of touching. **2** the ability to perceive something through physical con-

t

tact. **3** a small amount. **4** a detail or feature. **5** a way of dealing with something. □ **in touch** in communication. **touch-and-go** (of an outcome) uncertain. **touch down** (of an aircraft) land. **touchline** the boundary line on each side of a rugby or football field. **touch on** deal briefly with. **touchstone** a standard by which something is judged. **touch up** make small improvements to.

touché /too-shay/ *exclam.* used to acknowledge a good point made at your expense.

touching *adj.* arousing gratitude or sympathy; moving.

touchy *adj.* (**touchier**, **touchiest**) quick to take offence.

tough *adj.* **1** strong enough to withstand wear and tear. **2** able to endure difficulty or pain. **3** strict. **4** involving difficulty or hardship. **5** (of a person) violent. ■ **toughen** *v.* **toughness** *n.*

toupee /too-pay/ *n.* a small wig.

tour *n.* **1** a journey for pleasure in which several places are visited. **2** a series of performances or matches in several places. •*v.* make a tour of. □ **tour de force** something accomplished with great skill.

tourism *n.* the commercial organization of holidays and services for tourists.

tourist *n.* a person visiting a place for pleasure.

tourmaline *n.* a mineral used in jewellery and electrical devices.

tournament *n.* a sporting contest consisting of a number of matches.

tourniquet /toor-ni-kay/ *n.* a bandage tied tightly round a limb

to stop the flow of blood through an artery.

tousle *v.* make a person's hair untidy.

tout *v.* **1** try to sell. **2** resell a ticket for an event at a price higher than the official one. •*n.* a person who buys up tickets for an event to resell them at a profit.

tow *v.* pull along behind. •*n.* an act of towing. □ **towpath** a path beside a river or canal, originally for horses towing barges.

towards (or **toward**) *prep.* **1** in the direction of. **2** in relation to. **3** contributing to the cost of.

towel *n.* a piece of absorbent cloth or paper used for drying. •*v.* (**towelling**, **towelled**; US **toweling**, **toweled**) dry with a towel.

towelling (US **toweling**) *n.* absorbent cloth used for towels.

tower *n.* **1** a tall, narrow building or part of a building. **2** a tall structure. •*v.* be very tall. □ **tower block** a tall modern building with many storeys.

town *n.* **1** a settlement larger than a village. **2** the central business or shopping area of a town or city. □ **town hall** a building housing local government offices. **township** (in South Africa) a suburb or city mainly inhabited by black people.

toxaemia (US **toxemia**) /tok-see-mi-uh/ *n.* blood poisoning.

toxic *adj.* **1** poisonous. **2** of or caused by poison. ■ **toxicity** *n.*

toxicology *n.* the study of poisons. ■ **toxicologist** *n.*

toxin *n.* a poison produced by a living organism.

toy *n.* an object to play with. •*v.* (**toy with**) **1** consider casually.

2 move or touch idly or nervously. • *adj.* (of a breed of dog) very small.

trace *v.* **1** find or follow by careful investigation. **2** copy a design etc. by drawing over it on transparent paper. **3** draw an outline. • *n.* **1** a mark or other sign of the existence or passing of something. **2** a very small amount. **3** a slight indication. **4** each of the two straps by which a horse pulls a vehicle. □ **trace element** a chemical element that is present or required only in tiny amounts. ■ **traceable** *adj.*

tracery *n.* (*pl.* **traceries**) a decorative pattern of interlacing lines, esp. in stone.

trachea /truh-kee-uh/ *n.* (*pl.* **tracheae** or **tracheas**) the windpipe.

tracheotomy *n.* (*pl.* **tracheotomies**) a surgical incision made in the windpipe.

tracing *n.* a copy of a drawing or map made by tracing.

track *n.* **1** a rough path or road. **2** a prepared course for racing. **3** a line of marks left by a person etc. in passing. **4** a railway line. **5** a section of a record, compact disc, etc. **6** a jointed metal band around the wheels of a heavy vehicle. • *v.* **1** follow the trail or course of. **2** (**track down**) find after a thorough search. □ **track record** a person's past achievements. **tracksuit** an outfit consisting of a loose sweatshirt and trousers. ■ **tracker** *n.*

tract *n.* **1** a large area of land. **2** a major passage in the body. **3** a pamphlet on a religious or political subject.

tractable *adj.* easy to deal with or control. ■ **tractability** *n.*

traction *n.* **1** the act of pulling a thing along a surface. **2** the exertion of a sustained pull on a limb to keep a broken bone in position. **3** the grip of a tyre on a road.

tractor *n.* a powerful vehicle for pulling farm equipment.

trade *n.* **1** the buying and selling of goods and services. **2** a job requiring manual skills and training. **3** the people engaged in a particular business. • *v.* **1** buy and sell goods and services. **2** exchange. **3** (**trade in**) give a used article as partial payment for a new one. **4** (**trade on**) take advantage of. **5** (**trade off**) exchange as a compromise. ■ **trademark** a symbol, word, or words chosen to represent a company or product. **tradesman** a person engaged in trading or a trade. **trade union** an organized association of workers formed to protect and promote their rights and interests. **trade wind** a wind blowing steadily towards the equator. ■ **trader** *n.*

tradition *n.* **1** the passing on of customs or beliefs from generation to generation. **2** a long-established custom. ■ **traditional** *adj.* **traditionally** *adv.*

traditionalism *n.* the upholding of tradition, esp. to resist change. ■ **traditionalist** *n. & adj.*

traduce *v.* slander.

traffic *n.* **1** vehicles, ships, or aircraft moving along a route. **2** the act of trading in something illegal. • *v.* (**trafficking**, **trafficked**) trade in something illegal. □ **traffic warden** an official who locates and reports on vehicles breaking parking regulations. ■ **trafficker** *n.*

tragedian *n.* **1** an actor who plays tragic roles. **2** a writer of tragedies.

t

tragedy n. (pl. **tragedies**) **1** an event causing great sadness or suffering. **2** a serious play with an unhappy ending.

tragic adj. **1** very sad. **2** of dramatic tragedy. ■ **tragically** adv.

tragicomedy n. (pl. **tragicomedies**) a play or novel containing elements of both comedy and tragedy. ■ **tragicomic** adj.

trail n. **1** a series of signs left behind by a person etc. in passing. **2** a long thin part stretching behind or hanging down. **3** a line of people or animals. **4** a path. • v. **1** draw or be drawn along behind. **2** follow the trail of. **3** walk or move slowly or wearily. **4** (**trail away/off**) (of the voice) fade gradually. **5** be losing to an opponent in a contest.

trailer n. **1** an unpowered vehicle pulled by another. **2** an extract from a film etc. used to advertise it.

train v. **1** teach a particular skill to. **2** learn a particular skill. **3** become physically fit through exercise. **4** (**train on**) point at. **5** make a plant grow in a particular direction or shape. • n. **1** a series of railway carriages or wagons moved by a locomotive. **2** a line of vehicles or pack animals. **3** a series of connected events or thoughts. **4** a long piece of trailing material at the back of a dress.

trainee n. a person being trained.

trainer n. **1** a person who trains people or animals. **2** a soft shoe for sports or casual wear.

traipse v. walk or move wearily.

trait n. a characteristic.

traitor n. a person who betrays their country or a cause. ■ **traitorous** adj.

trajectory n. (pl. **trajectories**) the path of an object moving through the air.

tram (or **tramcar**) n. a passenger vehicle powered by electricity and running on rails (**tramlines**) laid in a public road.

trammel v. (**trammelling**, **trammelled**; US **trammeling**, **trammeled**) hamper or restrict.

tramp v. **1** walk heavily or noisily. **2** walk wearily over a long distance. • n. **1** a homeless person who travels around and lives by begging. **2** the sound of heavy steps. **3** a long walk. **4** a cargo vessel that does not sail a fixed route.

trample v. tread on and crush.

trampoline n. a strong fabric sheet connected by springs to a frame, used for performing acrobatic leaps. ■ **trampolining** n.

trance n. a half-conscious state.

tranquil adj. free from disturbance; calm. ■ **tranquillity** n. **tranquilly** adv.

tranquillize (or **tranquillise**; US **tranquilize**) v. give a calming or sedative drug to.

tranquillizer (or **tranquilliser**; US **tranquilizer**) n. a drug used to reduce tension or anxiety.

transact v. conduct or carry out business. ■ **transaction** n.

transatlantic adj. **1** crossing the Atlantic. **2** of or on the other side of the Atlantic.

transceiver n. a radio transmitter and receiver.

transcend v. **1** be or go beyond the range or limits of. **2** be better than. ■ **transcendence** n. **transcendent** adj.

transcendental adj. of a spiritual or mystical realm.

transcontinental adj. crossing or extending across a continent.

transcribe v. **1** put into written form, or into a different written form. **2** arrange a piece of music for a different instrument. ■ **transcription** n.

transcript n. a written version of material that was originally spoken or in another form.

transducer n. a device that converts variations in a physical medium into an electrical signal, or vice versa.

transept n. a part lying at right angles to the nave in a church.

transfer v. (**transferring, transferred**) **1** move from one place etc. to another. **2** pass property etc. to another person. • n. **1** an act of transferring. **2** a small picture which can be transferred to another surface by being pressed or heated. ■ **transferable** adj. **transference** n.

transfigure v. transform into something more beautiful or spiritual. ■ **transfiguration** n.

transfix v. **1** make motionless with fear or astonishment. **2** pierce with a sharp object.

transform v. **1** change in appearance or nature. **2** change the voltage of an electric current. ■ **transformation** n.

transformer n. a device for changing the voltage of an electric current.

transfuse v. **1** give a transfusion of blood to someone. **2** permeate or imbue.

transfusion n. a medical procedure in which blood is transferred from one person or animal to another.

transgress v. go beyond what is morally or legally acceptable.

■ **transgression** n. **transgressor** n.

transient adj. lasting only for a short time. ■ **transience** n.

transistor n. **1** a semiconductor device able to amplify or rectify an electric current. **2** a portable radio using circuits containing transistors.

transit n. **1** the carrying of people or things from one place to another. **2** an act of passing through a place.

transition n. the process of changing from one state or condition to another. ■ **transitional** adj.

transitive adj. (of a verb) taking a direct object. ■ **transitivity** n.

transitory adj. short-lived.

translate v. express or be expressed in another language. ■ **translation** n. **translator** n.

transliterate v. write a letter or word using the letters of a different alphabet or language. ■ **transliteration** n.

translucent adj. allowing light to pass through partially. ■ **translucence** (or **translucency**) n.

transmigration n. the passing of the soul into another body after death.

transmission n. **1** the act of transmitting. **2** the mechanism transmitting power from an engine to the axle in a vehicle.

transmit v. (**transmitting, transmitted**) **1** cause to pass on from one place, person, or thing to another. **2** send out an electrical signal or a radio or television programme. ■ **transmissible** adj. **transmittable** adj. **transmitter** n.

transmogrify v. (**transmogrifying, transmogrified**) trans-

t

form in a surprising or magical way.

transmute v. change in form or substance. ■ **transmutation** n.

transom n. **1** the flat surface forming the stern of a boat. **2** a crossbar above a door or window.

transparency n. (pl. **transparencies**) **1** the condition of being transparent. **2** a photographic slide.

transparent adj. **1** able to be seen through. **2** obvious or evident. ■ **transparently** adv.

transpire v. **1** become known. **2** happen. **3** (of a plant) give off water vapour from the leaves. ■ **transpiration** n.

transplant v. **1** transfer to another place or situation. **2** take living tissue and put it in another body or part of the body. •n. **1** an operation in which living tissue is transplanted. **2** something transplanted. ■ **transplantation** n.

transport v. carry people or goods from one place to another. •n. **1** a system, means, or act of transporting. **2** (**transports**) strong emotions. ■ **transportation** n. **transporter** n.

transpose v. **1** cause two or more things to change places. **2** move to a different place or situation. **3** write or play music in a different key. ■ **transposition** n.

transsexual (or **transexual**) n. a person who emotionally and psychologically feels that they belong to the opposite sex.

transubstantiation n. the doctrine that the bread and wine of the Eucharist are converted by consecration into the body and blood of Christ.

transverse adj. placed or extending across something.

transvestite n. a person who derives pleasure from dressing in clothes worn by the opposite sex. ■ **transvestism** n.

trap n. **1** a device for catching and holding animals. **2** a scheme for tricking or catching someone. **3** a curve in a waste pipe that holds liquid to prevent gases from coming up. **4** a compartment from which a dog is released at the start of a race. **5** a two-wheeled horse-drawn carriage. •v. (**trapping**, **trapped**) catch or hold in a trap. □ **trapdoor** a hinged or removable panel in a floor, ceiling, or roof.

trapeze n. a hanging horizontal bar used by circus acrobats.

trapezium n. (pl. **trapezia** or **trapeziums**) a quadrilateral with one pair of sides parallel.

trapezoid n. a quadrilateral with no sides parallel.

trapper n. a person who traps wild animals.

trappings pl. n. the signs or objects associated with a particular status or role.

trash n. **1** US waste material. **2** poor-quality writing etc. •v. informal wreck or destroy. ■ **trashy** adj.

trattoria n. an Italian restaurant.

trauma n. **1** a deeply distressing experience. **2** emotional shock following a stressful event. **3** physical injury. ■ **traumatic** adj. **traumatize** (or **-ise**) v.

travail n. old use labour.

travel v. (**travelling**, **travelled**; US **traveling**, **traveled**) **1** go from one place to another. **2** journey along or through. •n. **1** the act of travelling. **2** (**travels**) journeys over a long distance.

traveller (US **traveler**) n. **1** a person who travels. **2** a Gypsy or other nomadic person. □ **traveller's cheque** a cheque for a fixed amount that can be exchanged for cash in foreign countries.

travelogue n. a film, book, etc. about a person's travels.

traverse v. travel or extend across.

travesty n. (pl. **travesties**) an absurd or shocking misrepresentation.

trawl v. **1** catch fish with a trawl net. **2** search through thoroughly. • n. **1** an act of trawling. **2** (or **trawl net**) a large wide-mouthed fishing net.

trawler n. a boat used for trawling.

tray n. a shallow container with a rim for carrying things.

treacherous adj. **1** guilty of or involving betrayal. **2** having hidden dangers. ■ **treacherously** adv. **treachery** n.

treacle n. a thick sticky liquid produced when sugar is refined. ■ **treacly** adj.

tread v. (**treading**, **trod**; past part. **trodden** or **trod**) **1** walk in a specified way. **2** press down or crush with the feet. **3** walk on or along. • n. **1** a way or the sound of walking. **2** the top surface of a step or stair. **3** the part of a vehicle tyre that grips the road. □ **treadmill 1** a large wheel turned by the weight of people or animals treading on steps fitted into it, formerly used to drive machinery. **2** a tiring or boring job. **tread water** keep upright in deep water by making a walking movement.

treadle n. a lever worked by the foot to operate a machine.

treason n. the crime of betraying your country. ■ **treasonable** adj.

treasure n. **1** a quantity of precious metals, gems, or other valuables. **2** a very valuable object. **3** informal a highly valued person. • v. **1** look after carefully. **2** value highly. □ **treasure trove** valuables of unknown ownership, found hidden.

treasurer n. a person in charge of the finances of a society etc.

treasury n. (pl. **treasuries**) **1** the funds or revenue of a state, society, etc. **2** (**Treasury**) (in some countries) the government department responsible for the overall management of the economy.

treat v. **1** behave towards or deal with in a certain way. **2** give medical care or attention to. **3** apply a process or a substance to. **4** (**treat to**) provide with food, drink, etc. at your expense. • n. a surprise gift, event, etc. that gives great pleasure. ■ **treatment** n.

treatise n. a formal written work on a subject.

treaty n. (pl. **treaties**) a formal agreement between states.

treble adj. three times as much or as many. • n. **1** an amount three times as large as usual. **2** a high-pitched voice, esp. a boy's singing voice. • v. make or become treble.

tree n. a woody perennial plant with a single thick stem and branches that can grow to a great height.

trefoil n. **1** a plant with three-lobed leaves. **2** a design in the form of three rounded lobes.

t

trek n. a long difficult journey, esp. on foot. • v. (**trekking, trekked**) go on a trek. ■ **trekker** n.

trellis n. a framework of bars used to support climbing plants.

tremble v. 1 shake uncontrollably from fear, excitement, etc. 2 be very frightened. • n. a trembling movement.

tremendous adj. 1 very great. 2 informal very good or impressive. ■ **tremendously** adv.

tremolo n. (pl. **tremolos**) a wavering effect in singing or music.

tremor n. 1 a trembling movement. 2 a slight earthquake. 3 a sudden feeling of fear or excitement.

tremulous adj. shaking slightly.

trench n. a deep ditch.

trenchant adj. (of speech or writing) expressed strongly and clearly. ■ **trenchantly** adv.

trencher n. hist. a wooden platter.

trend n. 1 a general tendency. 2 a fashion. □ **trendsetter** a person leading the way in fashion or ideas.

trendy adj. (**trendier, trendiest**) informal fashionable. ■ **trendily** adv. **trendiness** n.

trepidation n. nervousness.

trespass v. enter land or property without permission. • n. the act of trespassing. ■ **trespasser** n.

tress n. a lock of hair.

trestle n. a framework of a horizontal bar on sloping legs, used in pairs to support a surface such as a table top.

trews pl. n. trousers.

triad n. a group or set of three.

trial n. 1 an examination of evidence in a law court to decide if a person is guilty of a crime. 2 a test of performance or quality. 3 something that tries a person's patience. • v. (**trialling, trialled**; US **trialing, trialed**) test to assess performance etc. □ **on trial** 1 being tried in a law court. 2 undergoing tests.

triangle n. 1 a figure with three straight sides and three angles. 2 a triangular steel rod used as a percussion instrument. ■ **triangular** adj.

triangulation n. the division of an area into a series of triangles to determine distances and relative positions.

triathlon n. an athletic contest involving three different events.

tribe n. a social group in a traditional society consisting of linked families. ■ **tribal** adj. **tribesman** n.

tribulation n. trouble or suffering.

tribunal n. a board of officials appointed to settle disputes.

tributary n. (pl. **tributaries**) a river flowing into a larger river or lake.

tribute n. 1 an act, statement, or gift intended to show gratitude or respect. 2 hist. a payment made by a state to a more powerful one.

trice n. (**in a trice**) in an instant.

triceps n. (pl. **triceps**) the large muscle at the back of the upper arm.

trichology /tri-kol-uh-ji/ n. the study of the hair and scalp and their diseases. ■ **trichologist** n.

trick n. 1 something done to deceive or outwit someone. 2 a skilful act performed for entertainment. 3 a mannerism. • v. deceive or outwit. ■ **trickery** n.

trickle v. **1** flow in a small stream. **2** come or go gradually. •n. a trickling flow.

tricky adj. (**trickier**, **trickiest**) **1** difficult or awkward. **2** deceitful.

tricolour /tri-kuh-ler/ (US **tricolor**) n. a flag with three bands of different colours.

tricycle n. a vehicle similar to a bicycle but with three wheels.

trident n. a three-pronged spear.

tried past & past part. of **TRY**.

triennial adj. taking place every three years.

trier n. a person who tries hard.

trifle n. **1** a thing of little value or importance. **2** a small amount. **3** a cold dessert of sponge cake and fruit covered with custard and jelly. •v. (**trifle with**) treat without seriousness or respect.

trifling adj. trivial.

trigger n. **1** a lever for releasing a spring or catch, esp. to fire a gun. **2** an event that causes something to happen. •v. **1** cause to function. **2** bring about. □ **trigger-happy** tending to shoot on the slightest provocation.

trigonometry n. the study of the relationships between the sides and angles of triangles.

trilateral adj. **1** involving three parties. **2** on or with three sides.

trilby n. (pl. **trilbies**) a soft felt hat with an indented crown.

trill n. a high warbling sound. •v. make a trilling sound.

trillion adj. & n. **1** a million million. **2** dated a million million million.

trilobite n. a fossil sea animal.

trilogy n. (pl. **trilogies**) a group of three related novels, plays, etc.

trim v. (**trimming**, **trimmed**) **1** cut away unwanted parts, esp.

to neaten. **2** decorate along the edges. **3** adjust a sail. •n. **1** decoration along the edges. **2** an act of trimming. **3** good condition. •adj. (**trimmer**, **trimmest**) neat and smart.

trimaran /try-muh-ran/ n. a yacht with three hulls side by side.

trimming n. **1** (**trimmings**) small pieces trimmed off. **2** decoration.

trinity n. (pl. **trinities**) **1** (**the Trinity**) (in Christian belief) the three persons (Father, Son, and Holy Spirit) that together make up God. **2** a group of three.

trinket n. a small inexpensive ornament or item of jewellery.

trio n. (pl. **trios**) a set or group of three.

trip v. (**tripping**, **tripped**) **1** catch the foot on something and stumble or fall. **2** (**trip up**) make a mistake. **3** move with quick light steps. **4** activate a mechanism. •n. **1** a journey or excursion. **2** an act of stumbling. **3** informal a hallucinatory experience caused by a drug. **4** a device that trips a mechanism.

tripartite adj. **1** consisting of three parts. **2** involving three parties.

tripe n. **1** the stomach of a cow or sheep used as food. **2** informal nonsense.

triple adj. **1** having or involving three parts, things, or people. **2** having three times as much or as many. •v. increase by three times the amount.

triplet n. **1** each of three children born at one birth. **2** a set of three.

triplicate adj. existing in three copies or examples.

tripod n. a three-legged stand for a camera etc.

t

triptych /trip-tik/ *n.* a picture or carving on three panels.

trite *adj.* unoriginal or overused.

tritium *n.* a radioactive isotope of hydrogen.

triumph *n.* **1** a great victory or achievement. **2** joy resulting from this. • *v.* achieve a triumph.
■ **triumphal** *adj.*

triumphant *adj.* **1** having won a battle or contest. **2** joyful after a victory or achievement.
■ **triumphantly** *adv.*

triumvirate *n.* a group of three powerful people.

trivet *n.* a metal stand for a kettle or hot dish.

trivia *pl. n.* trivial details or pieces of information.

trivial *adj.* of little value or importance. ■ **triviality** *n.* **trivialize** (or **-ise**) *v.* trivially *adv.*

trod past & past part. of TREAD.

trodden past part. of TREAD.

troglodyte *n.* a person who lives in a cave.

troika *n.* **1** a Russian vehicle pulled by a team of three horses. **2** a group of three people working together.

troll *n.* (in folklore) an ugly giant or dwarf.

trolley *n.* (*pl.* **trolleys**) **1** a large metal basket on wheels, for transporting goods. **2** a small table on wheels.

trollop *n.* dated a promiscuous woman.

trombone *n.* a large brass wind instrument with a sliding tube.
■ **trombonist** *n.*

trompe l'œil /tromp **loy**/ *n.* a painting creating the illusion of a three-dimensional object or space.

troop *n.* **1** (**troops**) soldiers or armed forces. **2** a group of people or animals. • *v.* come or go as a group.

trooper *n.* **1** a private soldier in a cavalry or armoured unit. **2** *US* a state police officer.

trophy *n.* (*pl.* **trophies**) **1** an object awarded as a prize. **2** a souvenir of an achievement.

tropic *n.* **1** a line of latitude 23°26 north or south of the equator. **2** (**the tropics**) the region between these, with a hot climate.
■ **tropical** *adj.*

trot *v.* (**trotting, trotted**) **1** (of a horse) move at a pace faster than a walk. **2** run at a moderate pace with short steps. **3** (**trot out**) *informal* give an account that has been produced many times before. • *n.* a trotting pace. □ **on the trot** *informal* one after another.

trotter *n.* a pig's foot.

troubadour /troo-buh-dor/ *n.* a medieval travelling poet.

trouble *n.* **1** difficulty or inconvenience. **2** a cause of this. **3** a situation likely to bring punishment or blame. **4** public disorder. • *v.* **1** cause worry or inconvenience to. **2** make the effort to do something. □ **troubleshooter** a person who investigates and solves problems in an organization.
■ **troublesome** *adj.*

trough *n.* **1** a long, narrow open container for animals' food or drink. **2** a long region of low pressure.

trounce *v.* defeat heavily.

troupe *n.* a group of touring entertainers.

trouper *n.* **1** an entertainer with long experience. **2** a reliable person.

t

trousers *pl. n.* an outer garment for the body from the waist down, with a separate part for each leg.

trousseau /troo-soh/ *n.* (*pl.* **trousseaux** or **trousseaus**) the clothes etc. collected by a bride for her marriage.

trout *n.* (*pl.* **trout** or **trouts**) an edible fish of the salmon family.

trowel *n.* **1** a small hand-held tool for digging. **2** a similar tool for applying and spreading mortar or plaster.

troy (or **troy weight**) *n.* a system of weights used for precious metals and gems.

truant *n.* a pupil who stays away from school without permission. • *v.* (or **play truant**) stay away as a truant. ■ **truancy** *n.*

truce *n.* an agreement to stop fighting temporarily.

truck *n.* **1** a lorry. **2** an open railway wagon.

trucker *n.* a lorry driver.

truculent *adj.* quick to argue or fight. ■ **truculence** *n.* **truculently** *adv.*

trudge *v.* walk with slow, heavy steps. • *n.* a long and tiring walk.

true *adj.* **1** in accordance with fact. **2** real or actual. **3** accurate. **4** loyal. ■ **truly** *adv.*

⚠ No *e* in **truly**.

truffle *n.* **1** an underground fungus eaten as a delicacy. **2** a soft chocolate sweet.

trug *n.* a shallow oblong wooden basket.

truism *n.* a statement that is obviously true and says nothing new.

trump *n.* (in card games) a card of a suit chosen to rank above the others. • *v.* (**trump up**) invent a false accusation or excuse.

trumpet *n.* a brass musical instrument with a flared end. • *v.* (**trumpeting, trumpeted**) **1** (of an elephant) make a loud sound through its trunk. **2** proclaim widely. ■ **trumpeter** *n.*

truncate *v.* shorten by cutting off the end. ■ **truncation** *n.*

truncheon *n.* a short thick stick carried as a weapon by a police officer.

trundle *v.* move or roll slowly.

trunk *n.* **1** the main woody stem of a tree. **2** the body apart from the limbs and head. **3** the long nose of an elephant. **4** a large box with a hinged lid for storing or transporting clothes etc. **5** *US* the boot of a car. **6** (**trunks**) men's shorts worn for swimming. □ **trunk call** a long-distance phone call. **trunk road** an important main road.

truss *n.* **1** a framework supporting a roof etc. **2** a padded belt worn to support a hernia. • *v.* bind tightly.

trust *n.* **1** firm belief in the reliability, truth, or ability of someone or something. **2** responsibility for someone or something. **3** an arrangement whereby someone manages property for the benefit of another. **4** an organization managed by trustees. • *v.* **1** have trust in. **2** entrust. **3** hope. ■ **trustful** *adj.* **trustfully** *adv.* **trustworthiness** *n.* **trustworthy** *adj.*

trustee *n.* a person given legal powers to hold and manage property for the benefit of another.

trusty *adj.* *old use* reliable or faithful.

truth *n.* **1** the state of being true. **2** something which is true.

t

truthful adj. **1** telling or expressing the truth. **2** realistic.
■ **truthfully** adv. **truthfulness** n.

try v. **(trying, tried) 1** attempt. **2** test by use. **3 (try on)** put on a garment to see if it fits or suits you. **4** make severe demands on. **5** put on trial. • n. (pl. **tries**) **1** an attempt. **2** an act of testing by use. **3** Rugby an act of touching the ball down behind the opposing goal line to score points.

trying adj. annoying.

tryst /trist/ n. a meeting between lovers.

tsar (or **czar**) /zar/ n. an emperor of Russia before 1917. ■ **tsarist** adj.

tsetse /tet-si/ n. an African bloodsucking fly which transmits diseases.

tsp abbrev. teaspoonful.

tsunami /tsoo-**nah**-mi/ n. a tidal wave caused by an earthquake.

tub n. **1** a wide, open container. **2** a small container for food.

tuba n. a large low-pitched brass wind instrument.

tubby adj. **(tubbier, tubbiest)** informal short and fat.

tube n. **1** a long, hollow cylinder. **2** a flexible container sealed at one end and having a cap at the other. **3** (the Tube) trademark the underground railway in London.

tuber n. a thick underground part of the stem or root of some plants from which new plants grow.
■ **tuberous** adj.

tubercle n. a small rounded swelling or protuberance.

tuberculosis n. a serious infectious disease in which small swellings appear, esp. in the lungs.
■ **tubercular** adj.

tubing n. tubular pieces of plastic etc.

tubular adj. tube-shaped.

TUC abbrev. Trades Union Congress.

tuck v. **1** push, fold, or turn under or between two surfaces. **2** store in a safe or secret place. **3 (tuck in)** informal eat heartily. • n. **1** a flattened, stitched fold in a garment or material. **2** informal food eaten by schoolchildren as a snack.

Tudor adj. of the English royal dynasty which ruled 1485–1603.

Tuesday n. the day before Wednesday.

tufa n. a porous rock formed as a deposit from mineral springs.

tuft n. a bunch of threads, grass, or hair, held or growing together at the base. ■ **tufted** adj. **tufty** adj.

tug v. **(tugging, tugged)** pull hard or suddenly. • n. **1** a hard or sudden pull. **2** a small, powerful boat for towing larger boats. □ **tug of war** a contest of strength in which two teams pull at opposite ends of a rope.

tuition n. teaching or instruction.

tulip n. a plant with bright cup-shaped flowers.

tulle /tyool/ n. a soft, fine net fabric.

tumble v. **1** fall suddenly, clumsily, or headlong. **2** move in a headlong way. • n. **1** a fall. **2** an untidy or confused arrangement or state. **3** an acrobatic feat.
□ **tumbledown** dilapidated.

tumble dryer a machine for drying washing in hot air inside a rotating drum.

tumbler n. **1** a drinking glass with no handle or stem. **2** an acrobat.

3 a part of a lock that holds the bolt until lifted by a key.

tumbril n. hist. an open cart used to take prisoners to the guillotine during the French Revolution.

tumescent adj. swollen.
■ **tumescence** n.

tummy n. (pl. **tummies**) informal the stomach or abdomen.

tumour (US **tumor**) n. a swelling of a part of the body caused by an abnormal growth of tissue.

tumult n. **1** a loud, confused noise. **2** confusion or disorder.
■ **tumultuous** adj.

tun n. a large cask.

tuna n. (pl. **tuna** or **tunas**) a large edible sea fish.

tundra n. a vast, flat, treeless Arctic region with permanently frozen subsoil.

tune n. a pleasant-sounding sequence of musical notes. •v. **1** adjust a musical instrument to the correct pitch. **2** adjust a radio or television to the desired frequency. **3** adjust an engine to run smoothly. □ **in** (or **out of**) **tune** (or not) in the correct musical pitch. ■ **tuneful** adj. **tunefully** adv. **tuneless** adj.

tuner n. **1** a person who tunes pianos etc. **2** a part of a stereo system that receives radio signals.

tungsten n. a hard grey metallic element.

tunic n. **1** a loose sleeveless garment reaching to the thigh or knees. **2** a close-fitting short coat worn as part of a uniform.

tunnel n. an underground passage. •v. (**tunnelling**, **tunnelled**; US **tunneling**, **tunneled**) dig or force a passage underground or through something.

tunny n. (pl. **tunny** or **tunnies**) a tuna.

turban n. a long length of material wound round a cap or the head, worn by Muslim and Sikh men.

turbid adj. (of a liquid) cloudy or muddy.

turbine n. a machine in which a wheel or rotor is driven by a flow of water or gas.

turbocharger n. a supercharger driven by a turbine powered by the engine's exhaust gases.
■ **turbocharged** adj.

turbot n. (pl. **turbot** or **turbots**) a large edible flatfish.

turbulent adj. **1** involving much conflict, disorder, or confusion. **2** (of air or water) moving unsteadily or violently.
■ **turbulence** n. **turbulently** adv.

tureen n. a deep covered dish from which soup is served.

turf n. (pl. **turfs** or **turves**) **1** grass and the layer of soil just below it. **2** a piece of turf. **3** (**the turf**) horse racing and racecourses. •v. **1** (**turf off/out**) informal force to leave. **2** cover with turf. □ **turf accountant** a bookmaker.

turgid adj. **1** swollen or full. **2** (of language) pompous. ■ **turgidity** n.

Turk n. a person from Turkey.

turkey n. (pl. **turkeys**) a large bird bred for food.

Turkish n. the language of Turkey. •adj. of Turkey. □ **Turkish bath** a period of sitting in a room filled with very hot air or steam, followed by washing and massage. **Turkish delight** a sweet made of syrup and cornflour.

turmeric n. a bright yellow spice.

t

turmoil n. a state of great disturbance or confusion.

turn v. **1** move around a central point. **2** move so as to face or go in a different direction. **3** make or become. **4** shape wood on a lathe. **5** twist or sprain an ankle. •n. **1** an act of turning. **2** a bend or branch in a road, river, etc. **3** the time when a member of a group must or is allowed to do something. **4** a time when one period ends and another begins. **5** a change in circumstances. **6** a short walk. **7** a brief feeling of illness. **8** a short performance. □ **do someone a good turn** do something helpful for someone. **turn against** make or become hostile towards. **turncoat** a person who changes sides in a dispute etc. **turn down** reject. **turn in** hand over to the authorities. **turn off** switch off. **turn on 1** switch on. **2** suddenly attack. **3** informal excite sexually. **turnout** the number of people attending or taking part in an event. **turn out 1** switch off an electric light. **2** prove to be the case. **3** be present at an event. **4 (be turned out)** be dressed in a particular way. **turnover 1** the amount of money taken by a business. **2** the rate at which employees leave or goods are sold and are replaced. **3** a small pie made of pastry folded over a filling. **turnpike** hist. & US a road on which a toll is collected. **turnstile** a revolving gate allowing only one person at a time to pass through. **turntable** a circular revolving platform. **turn up 1** increase the volume of. **2** be found. **3** appear. **turn-up 1** the end of a trouser leg folded upwards on the outside. **2** informal an unexpected event.

turning n. a place where a road branches off another.

turnip n. a round root vegetable.

turpentine n. a liquid derived from certain trees, used to thin paint and clean brushes.

turpitude n. formal wickedness.

turps n. turpentine.

turquoise n. **1** a greenish-blue semi-precious stone. **2** a greenish-blue colour.

turret n. **1** a small tower. **2** an armoured tower for a gun on a ship, aircraft, or tank. ■ **turreted** adj.

turtle n. a sea reptile with a bony or leathery shell. □ **turn turtle** capsize. **turtle dove** a small dove with a soft call. **turtleneck** a high, round, close-fitting neckline.

turves pl. of TURF.

tusk n. a long, pointed tooth protruding from the mouth of an elephant, walrus, etc.

tussle n. a struggle. •v. engage in a tussle.

tussock n. a clump or tuft of grass.

tutelage /tyoo-ti-lij/ n. **1** protection or authority. **2** tuition.

tutor n. **1** a private teacher. **2** a university or college teacher. •v. act as a tutor to.

tutorial n. a period of tuition given by a university or college tutor. •adj. of a tutor.

tutu n. a female ballet dancer's short, stiff skirt that projects from the waist.

tuxedo /tuk-see-doh/ n. (pl. **tuxedos** or **tuxedoes**) a man's dinner jacket.

TV abbrev. television.

twaddle n. informal nonsense.

twang n. **1** a strong ringing sound made by the plucked string of a musical instrument. **2** a nasal way of speaking. • v. make a twang.

tweak v. **1** twist or pull sharply. **2** informal improve by making fine adjustments. • n. an act of tweaking.

twee adj. affectedly quaint or sentimental.

tweed n. **1** a rough, flecked woollen cloth. **2** (**tweeds**) clothes made of tweed. ■ **tweedy** adj.

tweet v. give a chirp. • n. a chirping sound.

tweeter n. a loudspeaker designed to reproduce high frequencies.

tweezers pl. n. a small pair of pincers for plucking out hairs and picking up small objects.

twelve adj. & n. two more than ten; 12. ■ **twelfth** adj. & n.

twenty adj. & n. (pl. **twenties**) ten less than thirty; 20. ■ **twentieth** adj. & n.

twerp n. informal a silly person.

twice adv. **1** two times. **2** double in degree or quantity.

twiddle v. play or fiddle with idly. □ **twiddle your thumbs** have nothing to do.

twig n. a slender woody shoot growing from a branch or stem. • v. (**twigging**, **twigged**) informal understand or realize.

twilight n. **1** the soft light from the sky when the sun is below the horizon. **2** the period of this.

twill n. a woven fabric with a surface of diagonal parallel ridges. ■ **twilled** adj.

twin n. **1** one of two children born at one birth. **2** one of a pair that are exactly alike. • v. (**twinning**, **twinned**) **1** link or combine as a pair. **2** link a town with another in a different country for the purposes of cultural exchange.

twine n. strong string. • v. wind or coil.

twinge n. a brief, sharp pain or pang.

twinkle v. shine with a flickering light. • n. a twinkling light.

twirl v. spin quickly and lightly round. • n. **1** an act of twirling. **2** a spiral shape.

twist v. **1** bend or curl. **2** force out of the natural position. **3** have a winding course. **4** deliberately change the meaning of. • n. **1** an act of twisting. **2** a spiral shape. **3** an unexpected development.

twit n. informal a silly person.

twitch v. make a short, sudden jerking movement. • n. a twitching movement.

twitter v. **1** (of a bird) make a series of short high sounds. **2** talk rapidly in a nervous or trivial way. • n. a twittering sound.

two adj. & n. one less than three; 2. □ **two-dimensional** having or appearing to have length and breadth but no depth. **two-faced** insincere and deceitful. **twosome** a set of two people. **two-time** informal be unfaithful to a lover. ■ **twofold** adj. & adv.

tycoon n. a wealthy, powerful person in business or industry.

tying pres. part. of TIE.

tyke n. informal a mischievous child.

tympani var. of TIMPANI.

tympanum n. (pl. **tympanums** or **tympana**) the eardrum.

type n. **1** a kind or category. **2** informal a person of a specified nature. **3** printed characters or letters. • v. write using a typewriter or computer. □ **typecast** (of an actor) repeatedly cast in the same type of role. **typeface** a particular design of printed type.

t

typescript a typed copy of a text.

typesetter a person or machine that arranges type for printing.

typewriter a machine with keys for producing print-like characters. ■ **typist** n.

typhoid n. a serious infectious disease causing fever.

typhoon n. a tropical storm.

typhus n. an infectious disease causing a rash and fever.

typical adj. having the distinctive qualities of a particular type of person or thing. ■ **typically** adv.

typify v. (**typifying, typified**) be typical of.

typography n. the process or style of printing. ■ **typographer** n. **typographical** adj.

tyrannize (or **-ise**) v. dominate or treat cruelly.

tyrannosaurus rex n. a very large meat-eating dinosaur.

tyranny n. (pl. **tyrannies**) cruel and oppressive government or rule. ■ **tyrannical** adj. **tyrannically** adv. **tyrannous** adj.

tyrant n. a cruel and oppressive person, esp. a ruler.

tyre (US **tire**) n. a rubber covering, usu. inflated, that fits around a wheel.

tyro n. (pl. **tyros**) a beginner.

tzatziki /tsat-**see**-ki/ n. a Greek dip of yogurt, cucumber, mint, and garlic.

Uu

ubiquitous /yoo-**bi**-kwi-tuhss/ adj. appearing or found everywhere. ■ **ubiquity** n.

udder n. the bag-like milk-producing organ of female cattle, sheep, goats, etc.

UFO n. (pl. **UFOs**) a mysterious object seen in the sky, believed by some to carry beings from outer space (short for *unidentified flying object*).

ugly adj. (**uglier, ugliest**) **1** unpleasant or unattractive in appearance. **2** hostile or threatening. ■ **ugliness** n.

UHF abbrev. ultra-high frequency, a radio frequency in the range 300 to 3,000 MHz.

UHT abbrev. ultra heat treated (esp. of milk).

UK abbrev. United Kingdom.

ukulele /yoo-kuh-**lay**-li/ n. a small four-stringed guitar.

ulcer n. an open sore. ■ **ulcerated** adj. **ulceration** n.

ulna n. (pl. **ulnae** or **ulnas**) the thinner, longer bone of the human forearm.

ulterior adj. other than what is obvious or admitted.

ultimate adj. **1** final. **2** best or most extreme. **3** fundamental. ■ **ultimately** adv.

ultimatum n. (pl. **ultimatums** or **ultimata**) a final warning that action will be taken unless your demands are met.

ultra- *prefix* **1** beyond. **2** extremely.

ultramarine *n.* a brilliant deep blue.

ultrasonic *adj.* above the upper limit of human hearing.

ultrasound *n.* sound or other vibrations with an ultrasonic frequency, used in medical scans.

ultraviolet *adj.* of or using radiation with a wavelength just shorter than that of visible light rays.

ululate *v.* howl or wail. ■ **ululation** *n.*

umbel *n.* a broad flat flower cluster.

umber *n.* a brownish pigment.

umbilical *adj.* of the navel. □ **umbilical cord** a flexible tube by which a fetus is nourished while in the womb.

umbra *n.* (*pl.* **umbras** or **umbrae**) the dark central part of the shadow cast by the earth and the moon in an eclipse.

umbrage *n.* (**take umbrage**) take offence; become annoyed.

umbrella *n.* a folding dome-shaped device used as protection against rain.

umlaut /uum-lowt/ *n.* a mark (¨) placed over a vowel in some languages to indicate a change in pronunciation.

umpire *n.* (in certain sports) an official who supervises a game to ensure that the rules are observed. • *v.* act as an umpire in.

umpteen *adj. informal* very many. ■ **umpteenth** *adj.*

UN *abbrev.* United Nations.

un- *prefix* **1** not. **2** reversing the action indicated by a verb.

unable *adj.* not having the skill, means, etc. to do something.

unaccountable *adj.* **1** unable to be explained. **2** not responsible for results or consequences. ■ **unaccountably** *adv.*

unadulterated *adj.* not mixed with any different or extra elements.

unalloyed *adj.* complete; total.

unanimous /yoo-nan-i-muhss/ *adj.* **1** fully in agreement. **2** agreed by everyone involved. ■ **unanimity** *n.* **unanimously** *adv.*

unarmed *adj.* without weapons.

unassailable *adj.* unable to be attacked or defeated.

unassuming *adj.* not pretentious or arrogant.

unattended *adj.* not being supervised or looked after.

unavoidable *adj.* unable to be avoided or prevented. ■ **unavoidably** *adv.*

unaware *adj.* not aware of something. • *adv.* (**unawares**) so as to surprise; unexpectedly.

unbalanced *adj.* emotionally or mentally disturbed.

unbeknown (or **unbeknownst**) *adj.* (**unbeknown to**) without the knowledge of.

unbelievable *adj.* **1** unlikely to be true. **2** extraordinary. ■ **unbelievably** *adv.*

unbend *v.* (**unbending, unbent**) **1** straighten. **2** become less formal or strict.

unbending *adj.* unwilling to change your mind.

unbidden *adj.* without having been invited.

unborn *adj.* not yet born.

unbounded *adj.* having no limits.

unbridled *adj.* uncontrolled.

u

unburden v. (**unburden yourself**) confide in someone about a worry or problem.

uncalled adj. (**uncalled for**) undesirable and unnecessary.

uncanny adj. strange or mysterious. ■ **uncannily** adv.

unceremonious adj. impolite or abrupt. ■ **unceremoniously** adv.

uncertain adj. 1 not known, reliable, or definite. 2 not completely sure. ■ **uncertainly** adv. **uncertainty** n.

uncharitable adj. unkind or unsympathetic. ■ **uncharitably** adv.

uncharted adj. (of an area of land or sea) not mapped or surveyed.

uncle n. the brother of your father or mother or the husband of your aunt.

unclean adj. 1 dirty. 2 immoral. 3 (of food) forbidden by a religion.

uncomfortable adj. 1 not comfortable. 2 uneasy or awkward. ■ **uncomfortably** adv.

uncommon adj. unusual. ■ **uncommonly** adv.

uncompromising adj. unwilling to compromise.

unconcern n. a lack of worry or interest. ■ **unconcerned** adj.

unconditional adj. not subject to any conditions. ■ **unconditionally** adv.

unconscionable adj. not right or reasonable. ■ **unconscionably** adv.

unconscious adj. 1 not conscious. 2 done or existing without you realizing. 3 unaware. ■ **unconsciously** adv. **unconsciousness** n.

uncouth adj. lacking good manners.

uncover v. 1 remove a cover from. 2 discover something secret or unknown.

unction n. 1 the smearing of someone with oil as a religious ceremony. 2 excessive politeness.

unctuous adj. excessively polite or flattering. ■ **unctuously** adv.

undeceive v. tell someone that an idea or belief is mistaken.

undecided adj. 1 not having made a decision. 2 not settled or resolved.

undeniable adj. undoubtedly true. ■ **undeniably** adv.

under prep. 1 extending or directly below. 2 at a lower level or grade than. 3 controlled by. 4 according to the rules of. 5 undergoing. ▪ adv. extending or directly below something. □ **under way** making progress.

under- prefix 1 below; beneath. 2 insufficiently.

underarm adj. & adv. done with the arm or hand below shoulder level.

undercarriage n. 1 an aircraft's landing wheels and supporting structure. 2 the supporting framework of a vehicle.

underclass n. the lowest and poorest social class in a country.

undercoat n. a layer of paint applied before the topcoat.

undercover adj. & adv. involving secret investigative work.

undercurrent n. 1 a current of water flowing below the surface. 2 an underlying feeling or influence.

undercut v. (**undercutting**, **undercut**) 1 offer goods or services at a lower price than a competitor. 2 cut or wear away the part under. 3 weaken; undermine.

u

underdog n. a competitor thought to have little chance of winning.

underdone adj. not cooked enough.

underestimate v. 1 estimate to be smaller or less important than in reality. 2 regard as less capable than in reality.

underfoot adv. 1 on the ground. 2 getting in your way.

undergo v. (**undergoes, undergoing, underwent**; past part. **undergone**) experience something unpleasant or difficult.

undergraduate n. a university student who has not yet taken a degree.

underground adj. & adv. 1 beneath the surface of the ground. 2 in secrecy or hiding. •n. an underground railway.

undergrowth n. a dense growth of shrubs and other plants.

underhand adj. acting or done secretly or dishonestly.

underlay n. material laid under a carpet for support.

underlie v. (**underlying, underlay**; past part. **underlain**) be the cause or basis of.

underline v. 1 draw a line under. 2 emphasize.

underling n. a subordinate.

undermine v. 1 damage or weaken. 2 weaken the foundations of.

underneath prep. & adv. 1 situated directly beneath. 2 so as to be hidden by.

underpants pl. n. an article of underwear covering the lower part of the body and having two holes for the legs.

underpass n. a road or tunnel passing under another road or a railway.

underpin v. (**underpinning, underpinned**) 1 strengthen from below. 2 form the basis for an argument or theory.

underprivileged adj. not enjoying the same rights or standard of living as the majority.

underrate v. underestimate.

underscore v. underline.

undersell v. sell something at a lower price than a competitor.

undershoot v. (**undershooting, undershot**) 1 fall short of a target. 2 land short of a runway.

underside n. the bottom or lower side or surface.

undersigned n. the person or people who have signed the document in question.

underskirt n. a petticoat.

understaffed adj. having too few members of staff.

understand v. (**understanding, understood**) 1 know or realize the intended meaning or cause of. 2 interpret or view in a particular way. 3 believe to be the case from information received.

understandable adj. 1 able to be understood. 2 to be expected; normal or reasonable. ■ **understandably** adv.

understanding n. 1 the ability to understand. 2 sympathetic awareness or tolerance. 3 an agreement. •adj. sympathetically aware of others' feelings. ■ **understandingly** adv.

understate v. represent as smaller or less important than in reality. ■ **understatement** n.

understated adj. pleasingly subtle.

understudy n. (pl. **understudies**) an actor who learns another's

role so as to take their place if
needed.

undertake v. (**undertaking,
undertook;** past part. **undertaken**) **1** begin an activity. **2** formally promise.

undertaker n. a person whose
job is to prepare dead bodies for
burial or cremation and to make
arrangements for funerals.

undertaking n. **1** a formal
promise. **2** a task.

undertone n. **1** a low or subdued
tone. **2** an underlying quality or
feeling.

undertow n. an undercurrent
moving in the opposite direction
to the surface water.

underwater adj. & adv. situated
or occurring beneath the surface
of the water.

underwear n. clothing worn
under other clothes next to the
skin.

underwent past of **UNDERGO**.

underworld n. **1** the world of
criminals or of organized crime.
2 (in myths and legends) the
home of the dead, imagined as
being under the earth.

underwrite v. (**underwriting,
underwrote;** past part. **underwritten**) **1** accept legal responsibility for an insurance policy.
2 finance. ■ **underwriter** n.

undesirable adj. harmful or unpleasant.

undies pl. n. informal articles of
underwear.

undo v. (**undoes, undoing,
undid;** past part. **undone**) **1** unfasten or loosen. **2** cancel the effect of. **3** cause the ruin or
downfall of.

undoing n. a person's ruin or
downfall.

undone adj. **1** not tied or fastened. **2** not done or finished.

undoubted adj. not questioned
or doubted. ■ **undoubtedly** adv.

undreamed (or **undreamt**) adj.
(**undreamed of**) not previously
thought to be possible.

undress v. take clothes off. • n. the
state of being naked or only partially clothed.

undue adj. excessive. ■ **unduly**
adv.

undulate v. **1** move with a
smooth wave-like motion. **2** have
a wavy form or outline. ■ **undulation** n.

undying adj. everlasting.

unearth v. **1** find in the ground
by digging. **2** discover by
searching.

unearthly adj. **1** supernatural or
mysterious. **2** informal unreasonably early or inconvenient.

uneasy adj. (**uneasier, uneasiest**) troubled or uncomfortable.
■ **unease** n. **uneasily** adv. **uneasiness** n.

uneatable adj. not fit to be eaten.

uneconomic adj. not profitable.

unemployable adj. not having
enough skills or qualifications to
get paid employment.

unemployed adj. **1** without a
paid job. **2** not in use. ■ **unemployment** n.

unending adj. seeming to last for
ever.

unequalled (US **unequaled**)
adj. better or greater than all
others.

unequivocal /un-i-kwiv-uh-k'l/
adj. leaving no doubt. ■ **unequivocally** adv.

unerring adj. always right or accurate. ■ **unerringly** adv.

u

uneven *adj.* **1** not level or smooth. **2** not regular. ■ **unevenly** *adv.* **unevenness** *n.*

unexceptionable *adj.* not open to objection.

unexceptional *adj.* not out of the ordinary.

unexpected *adj.* not expected or thought likely to happen. ■ **unexpectedly** *adv.*

unfailing *adj.* reliable or constant. ■ **unfailingly** *adv.*

unfair *adj.* not based on or showing fairness. ■ **unfairly** *adv.* **unfairness** *n.*

unfaithful *adj.* **1** not faithful; disloyal. **2** having sex with a person other than your regular partner. ■ **unfaithfulness** *n.*

unfeeling *adj.* unsympathetic, harsh, or cruel.

unfit *adj.* **1** unsuitable. **2** not in good physical condition.

unflappable *adj. informal* calm in a crisis.

unfold *v.* **1** open or spread out. **2** reveal or be revealed.

unforeseen *adj.* not predicted.

unforgettable *adj.* highly memorable. ■ **unforgettably** *adv.*

unfortunate *adj.* **1** unlucky. **2** regrettable. ■ **unfortunately** *adv.*

unfounded *adj.* having no basis in fact.

unfrock *v.* defrock.

unfurl *v.* spread out or unroll.

ungainly *adj.* clumsy; awkward. ■ **ungainliness** *n.*

ungodly *adj.* **1** sinful or immoral. **2** *informal* unreasonably early or late.

ungovernable *adj.* uncontrollable.

ungrateful *adj.* not feeling or showing gratitude. ■ **ungratefully** *adv.*

unguarded *adj.* **1** not guarded. **2** not well considered; careless.

unguent /ung-gwuhnt/ *n.* an ointment or lubricant.

ungulate *n.* a mammal with hoofs.

unhand *v. old use* let go of.

unhappy *adj.* (**unhappier, unhappiest**) **1** not happy; sad. **2** unfortunate. ■ **unhappily** *adv.* **unhappiness** *n.*

unhealthy *adj.* (**unhealthier, unhealthiest**) **1** in poor health. **2** not good for health. ■ **unhealthily** *adv.*

unheard *adj.* (**unheard of**) previously unknown.

unhinged *adj.* mentally unbalanced.

unholy *adj.* **1** wicked. **2** *informal* dreadful.

unicorn *n.* a mythical animal like a horse with a single horn on its forehead.

uniform *adj.* not varying; the same in all cases and at all times. • *n.* the distinctive clothing worn by members of the same organization or school. ■ **uniformed** *adj.* **uniformity** *n.* **uniformly** *adv.*

unify *v.* (**unifying, unified**) unite. ■ **unification** *n.*

unilateral *adj.* done by or affecting only one person, group, etc. ■ **unilaterally** *adv.*

unimpeachable *adj.* beyond doubt or criticism.

uninhabited *adj.* without inhabitants.

unintelligible *adj.* impossible to understand.

uninterested *adj.* not interested or concerned.

u

! Don't confuse **uninterested** with **disinterested**, which means 'impartial'.

uninviting *adj.* not attractive; unpleasant.

union *n.* **1** the act of uniting or the fact of being united. **2** a society or association, esp. a trade union. **3** (or **Union**) a political unit consisting of a number of states or provinces with the same central government. □ **Union Jack** the national flag of the UK.

unionist *n.* **1** a member of a trade union. **2** (**Unionist**) a person in favour of the union of Northern Ireland with Great Britain.

unionize (or **-ise**) *v.* make or become members of a trade union.

unique *adj.* **1** being the only one of its kind. **2** (**unique to**) belonging only to one person, group, or place. **3** very special or unusual. ■ **uniquely** *adv.*

unisex *adj.* suitable for both sexes.

unison *n.* the fact of two or more things being said or happening at the same time.

unit *n.* **1** an individual thing, group, or person, esp. as part of a complex whole. **2** a device, item of furniture, or part of a building or organization with a specified function. **3** a fixed quantity that is used as a standard measurement. □ **unit trust** a company that invests money in a range of businesses on behalf of individuals, who can buy small units.

Unitarian *n.* a member of a Christian Church believing that God is one person and rejecting the idea of the Trinity.

unitary *adj.* **1** single. **2** of a unit or units.

unite *v.* come or bring together for a common purpose or to form a whole.

unity *n.* (*pl.* **unities**) **1** the state of being united. **2** a complex whole.

universal *adj.* of, for, or done by all. ■ **universally** *adv.*

universe *n.* all existing matter and space considered as a whole.

university *n.* (*pl.* **universities**) an educational institution where students study for a degree and where academic research is done.

unkempt *adj.* having an untidy appearance.

unkind *adj.* not caring or kind. ■ **unkindness** *n.*

unknown *adj.* not known. • *n.* an unknown person, thing, or place.

unleaded *adj.* (of petrol) without added lead.

unleash *v.* release; set loose.

unleavened *adj.* (of bread) made without yeast or other raising agent.

unless *conj.* except when; if not.

unlike *prep.* **1** not like. **2** uncharacteristic of. • *adj.* different.

unlikely *adj.* (**unlikelier, unlikeliest**) not likely to happen, be done, or be true. ■ **unlikelihood** *n.*

unlimited *adj.* not limited; infinite.

unload *v.* **1** remove goods from a vehicle, ship, etc. **2** *informal* get rid of.

unlooked *adj.* (**unlooked for**) unexpected.

unmanned *adj.* operated without a crew.

unmask *v.* reveal the true character of.

unmentionable *adj.* too shocking to be spoken about.

u

unmistakable (or **unmistakable**) *adj.* unable to be mistaken for anything else. ■ **unmistakably** *adv.*

unmitigated *adj.* absolute.

unmoved *adj.* **1** not affected by emotion. **2** not changed in purpose.

unnatural *adj.* **1** different to what is found in nature. **2** different to what is normal or expected. ■ **unnaturally** *adv.*

unnecessary *adj.* not necessary, or more than is necessary. ■ **unnecessarily** *adv.*

unnerve *v.* cause to feel nervous or frightened.

unnumbered *adj.* **1** not given a number. **2** countless.

unobtrusive *adj.* not conspicuous or attracting attention. ■ **unobtrusively** *adv.*

unorthodox *adj.* different from what is usual or accepted.

unpack *v.* open and remove the contents of a suitcase or container.

unparalleled *adj.* having no equal; exceptional.

unpick *v.* undo the stitching of.

unplaced *adj.* not placed as one of the first three in a race.

unpleasant *adj.* **1** not pleasant. **2** not friendly or kind. ■ **unpleasantly** *adv.* **unpleasantness** *n.*

unpopular *adj.* not liked or popular. ■ **unpopularity** *n.*

unprecedented *adj.* never done or known before.

unprepared *adj.* not ready or able to deal with something.

unprepossessing *adj.* unattractive.

unprincipled *adj.* unscrupulous.

unprintable *adj.* too offensive to be published.

unprofessional *adj.* not in accordance with professional standards of behaviour. ■ **unprofessionally** *adv.*

unprompted *adj.* spontaneous.

unqualified *adj.* **1** not having the necessary qualifications or skills. **2** complete; absolute.

unquestionable *adj.* unable to be denied or doubted. ■ **unquestionably** *adv.*

unravel *v.* (**unravelling**, **unravelled**; *US* **unraveling**, **unraveled**) **1** undo twisted, knitted, or woven threads. **2** become undone. **3** solve a mystery.

unreasonable *adj.* **1** not based on good sense. **2** beyond what is acceptable or achievable. ■ **unreasonably** *adv.*

unrelenting *adj.* **1** not stopping or becoming less severe. **2** not giving in to requests. ■ **unrelentingly** *adv.*

unremitting *adj.* not stopping or slackening.

unrequited *adj.* (of love) not returned.

unreserved *adj.* without doubts or reservations; complete. ■ **unreservedly** *adv.*

unrest *n.* **1** rebellious discontent and disorder. **2** uneasiness.

unrivalled (*US* **unrivaled**) *adj.* greater or better than all others.

unruly *adj.* (**unrulier**, **unruliest**) not easy to control. ■ **unruliness** *n.*

unsavoury (*US* **unsavory**) *adj.* **1** unpleasant to taste, smell, or look at. **2** not respectable.

unscathed *adj.* without suffering any injury.

unscrupulous *adj.* without moral principles; dishonest. ■ **unscrupulously** *adv.*

u

unseasonable adj. (of weather) unusual for the time of year.
■ **unseasonably** adv.

unseat v. **1** cause to fall from a saddle or seat. **2** remove from a position of power.

unselfish adj. putting other people's needs before your own.

unsettle v. make uneasy; disturb.

unsettled adj. **1** changeable. **2** uneasy. **3** not yet resolved.

unshakeable (or **unshakable**) adj. (of a belief etc.) firm.

unsightly adj. unpleasant to look at. ■ **unsightliness** n.

unskilled adj. not having or needing special skill or training.

unsociable adj. not enjoying the company of others.

unsocial adj. **1** (of hours of work) falling outside the normal working day and so inconvenient. **2** antisocial.

unsolicited adj. not asked for.

unsound adj. **1** not safe or strong. **2** not based on reliable evidence or reasoning.

unsparing adj. **1** merciless; severe. **2** giving generously.

unspeakable adj. too bad or horrific to express in words. ■ **unspeakably** adv.

unstable adj. **1** not stable. **2** prone to mental health problems or sudden mood changes.

unstinting adj. given or giving freely or generously.

unstuck adj. (**come unstuck**) informal fail.

unstudied adj. natural and unaffected.

unsung adj. not acknowledged or praised.

unsuspecting adj. not aware of the presence of danger.

unswerving adj. not changing or becoming weaker.

untenable adj. unable to be defended against criticism or attack.

unthinkable adj. too unlikely or unpleasant to be considered a possibility.

unthinking adj. without proper consideration.

untidy adj. (**untidier, untidiest**) **1** not arranged tidily. **2** not inclined to be neat. ■ **untidily** adv. **untidiness** n.

untie v. (**untying, untied**) unfasten something tied.

until prep. & conj. up to the point in time or the event mentioned.

untimely adj. **1** happening or done at an unsuitable time. **2** (of a death or end) premature. ■ **untimeliness** n.

unto prep. old use to.

untold adj. **1** too much or too many to be counted. **2** not told.

untouchable adj. **1** unable to be touched or affected. **2** unrivalled. • n. offens. a member of the lowest Hindu social class.

untoward adj. unexpected and unwanted.

untried adj. not yet tested.

untruth n. (pl. **untruths**) **1** a lie. **2** the quality of being false. ■ **untruthful** adj. **untruthfully** adv.

unusual adj. **1** not often done or occurring. **2** exceptional. ■ **unusually** adv.

unutterable adj. too great or bad to describe. ■ **unutterably** adv.

unvarnished adj. **1** not varnished. **2** plain and straightforward.

unveil v. **1** remove a veil or covering from. **2** show or announce publicly for the first time.

unwarranted *adj.* not justified.

unwell *adj.* ill.

unwieldy *adj.* hard to move or manage because of its size, shape, or weight.

unwilling *adj.* reluctant. ■ **unwillingly** *adv.* **unwillingness** *n.*

unwind *v.* (**unwinding, unwound**) **1** undo or become undone after winding. **2** relax after a period of work or tension.

unwise *adj.* foolish. ■ **unwisely** *adv.*

unwitting *adj.* **1** not aware of the full facts. **2** unintentional. ■ **unwittingly** *adv.*

unwonted *adj.* unaccustomed or unusual.

unworldly *adj.* having little awareness of the realities of life. ■ **unworldliness** *n.*

unworthy *adj.* not deserving attention, effort, or respect. ■ **unworthiness** *n.*

unwritten *adj.* (of a rule etc.) generally known about and accepted, although not made official.

up *adv.* **1** towards a higher place or position. **2** at or to a higher level or value. **3** into the desired condition or position. **4** out of bed. • *prep.* from a lower to a higher point of. • *adj.* **1** directed or moving towards a higher place or position. **2** at an end. • *v.* (**upping, upped**) increase. ❑ **uphill** going or sloping upwards. **upstairs** on or to an upper floor. **upstream** in the direction opposite to that in which a stream or river flows. **up to date** using or aware of the latest developments and trends. **upwind** into the wind. ■ **upward** *adj.* & *adv.* **upwards** *adv.*

upbeat *adj.* cheerful.

upbraid *v.* scold.

upcoming *adj.* forthcoming.

update *v.* bring up to date.

upend *v.* set on its end or upside down.

upgrade *v.* raise to a higher standard or rank.

upheaval *n.* a violent or sudden disruption.

uphold *v.* (**upholding, upheld**) confirm or support.

upholster *v.* put a soft, padded covering on furniture.

upholstery *n.* material used to upholster furniture.

uplift *v.* make more hopeful or happy. • *n.* **1** an act of uplifting. **2** hope or happiness.

upload *v.* transfer data to a larger computer system.

upmarket *adj.* expensive and of high quality.

upon *prep. formal* on.

upper *adj.* higher in place, position, or status. • *n.* the part of a boot or shoe above the sole. ❑ **have the upper hand** have an advantage or control. **upper case** capital letters. **upper class** the social group with the highest status. ■ **uppermost** *adj.* & *adv.*

uppity *adj. informal* self-important.

upright *adj.* **1** vertical; erect. **2** strictly honest or respectable. • *n.* a vertical part or support.

uprising *n.* a rebellion.

uproar *n.* **1** a loud noise or disturbance. **2** a public expression of outrage.

uproarious *adj.* **1** very noisy. **2** very funny. ■ **uproariously** *adv.*

uproot *v.* **1** pull a plant, tree, etc. out of the ground. **2** move from home or a familiar location.

u

upset v. (**upsetting, upset**) **1** distress or worry. **2** knock over. **3** disrupt or disturb. **4** disturb the digestion of. • n. a state of distress or disruption.

upshot n. an outcome.

upside down adv. & adj. **1** with the upper part where the lower part should be. **2** in or into total disorder.

upstage adv. & adj. at or towards the back of a stage. • v. divert attention from.

upstanding adj. honest and respectable.

upstart n. a person who has suddenly become important and behaves arrogantly.

upsurge n. an increase.

upswing n. an upward trend.

uptake (**quick/slow on the uptake**) informal quick (or slow) to understand something.

uptight adj. informal nervously tense or angry.

upturn n. an improvement or upward trend.

uranium n. a radioactive metallic element.

urban adj. of a town or city. ■ **urbanize** (or **-ise**) v.

urbane adj. (of a man) sophisticated and courteous. ■ **urbanity** n.

urchin n. a poor child.

Urdu n. a language related to Hindi.

ureter /yuu-ree-ter/ n. the duct from the kidney to the bladder.

urethra /yuu-ree-thruh/ n. the duct which carries urine out of the body.

urge v. **1** encourage or earnestly ask to do something. **2** strongly recommend. • n. a strong desire or impulse.

urgent adj. requiring or calling for immediate action or attention. ■ **urgency** n. **urgently** adv.

urinal n. a receptacle in a public toilet into which men urinate.

urinate v. pass urine out of the body. ■ **urination** n.

urine n. a yellowish liquid containing waste substances, stored in the bladder before being passed out of the body. ■ **urinary** adj.

URL abbrev. uniform (or universal) resource locator, the address of a World Wide Web page.

urn n. **1** a vase, esp. one for holding a cremated person's ashes. **2** a large metal container with a tap, for keeping water or tea hot.

ursine adj. of bears.

US (or **USA**) abbrev. United States of America.

us pron. the form of 'we' used when the speaker or writer and another person or people are the object of a verb or preposition.

usable (or **useable**) adj. able to be used.

usage n. the using of something.

use v. **1** do something with an object or adopt a method. **2** take or consume an amount from a supply. **3** (**use up**) consume the whole of. **4** exploit unfairly. **5** (**used to**) did repeatedly or existed in the past. **6** (**be/get used to**) be or become familiar with through experience. **7** (**used**) second-hand. • n. **1** the act of using. **2** the ability to use something. **3** a purpose. **4** value.

useful adj. able to be used for a practical purpose. ■ **usefully** adv. **usefulness** n.

useless adj. **1** serving no purpose. **2** informal having little ability or skill. ■ **uselessly** adv.

user n. a person who uses something. □ **user-friendly** easy to use or understand.

usher n. a person who shows people to their seats in a cinema, theatre, or church. •v. lead or guide.

usherette n. a woman who shows people to their seats in a cinema or theatre.

USSR abbrev. hist. Union of Soviet Socialist Republics.

usual adj. happening or done regularly or often. ■ **usually** adv.

usurp v. take a position of power illegally or by force. ■ **usurpation** n. **usurper** n.

usury n. the lending of money at unreasonably high rates of interest. ■ **usurer** n.

utensil n. a tool or container, esp. for household use.

uterus n. the womb. ■ **uterine** adj.

utilitarian adj. useful rather than decorative.

utilitarianism n. the belief that the right course of action is the one that leads to the greatest happiness of the majority.

utility n. (pl. **utilities**) **1** the state of being useful or profitable. **2** a company supplying water, electricity, gas, etc. to the public. □ **utility room** a room in which a washing machine and other domestic equipment is kept.

utilize (or **-ise**) v. make use of. ■ **utilization** n.

utmost adj. most extreme; greatest. •n. (**the utmost**) the greatest or most extreme extent or amount.

Utopia n. an imagined perfect place. ■ **Utopian** adj.

utter¹ adj. complete; absolute. ■ **utterly** adv.

utter² v. make a sound or say something. ■ **utterance** n.

uttermost adj. & n. utmost.

U-turn n. **1** the turning of a vehicle in a U-shaped course so as to face the opposite way. **2** a reversal of policy.

UV abbrev. ultraviolet.

uvula /yoo-vyuu-luh/ n. (pl. **uvulae**) the fleshy projection hanging at the back of the throat.

uxorious adj. very or excessively fond of your wife.

Vv

V (or **v**) n. the Roman numeral for five. •abbrev. **1** volts. **2** versus. **3** very. □ **V-neck** a V-shaped neckline. **V-sign** a gesture of abuse made with the first two fingers pointing up and the back of the hand facing outwards.

vacancy n. (pl. **vacancies**) **1** an unoccupied position, job, or hotel room. **2** empty space.

vacant adj. **1** not occupied or filled. **2** showing no intelligence or interest. ■ **vacantly** adv.

vacate v. cease to occupy.

u

v

vacation n. **1** a holiday period between terms in universities etc. **2** US a holiday. **3** the act of vacating.

vaccinate v. inject with a vaccine. ■ **vaccination** n.

vaccine /vak-seen/ n. a substance that causes the body to produce antibodies, so providing immunity against a disease.

vacillate /va-si-layt/ v. keep changing your mind. .
■ **vacillation** n.

vacuous adj. showing a lack of thought or intelligence.
■ **vacuity** n.

vacuum n. (pl. **vacuums** or **vacua**) **1** a completely empty space in which there is no air or other matter. **2** a gap left by the loss of someone or something important. •v. clean with a vacuum cleaner. □ **vacuum cleaner** an electrical device that collects dust by suction. **vacuum flask** a container to keep liquids hot or cold. **vacuum-packed** sealed in a pack with the air removed.

vagabond n. a vagrant.

vagary n. (pl. **vagaries**) an unpredictable change.

vagina /vuh-jy-nuh/ n. the passage leading from a woman's external genitals to the womb.
■ **vaginal** adj.

vagrant n. a person without a settled home or job. ■ **vagrancy** n.

vague adj. **1** not certain or definite. **2** not thinking or expressing yourself clearly.
■ **vaguely** adv. **vagueness** n.

vain adj. **1** having a very high opinion of yourself. **2** useless or futile. □ **in vain** without success.
■ **vainly** adv.

vainglorious adj. literary boastful or vain.

valance n. a length of fabric around the base of a bed.

vale n. literary a valley.

valediction n. a farewell.
■ **valedictory** adj.

valency (or **valence**) n. (pl. **valencies**) the combining power of an element, as measured by the number of hydrogen atoms it can displace or combine with.

valentine n. **1** a card sent to a person you love on St Valentine's Day (14 February). **2** a person to whom you send such a card.

valet /va-lay/ n. a man's personal male attendant. •v. (**valeting**, **valeted**) clean a car as a professional service.

valetudinarian /va-li-tyoo-di-nair-i-uhn/ n. a person in poor health or unduly anxious about their health.

valiant adj. brave. ■ **valiantly** adv.

valid adj. **1** (of a reason etc.) sound or logical. **2** legally or officially acceptable. ■ **validity** n.

validate v. prove or declare to be valid. ■ **validation** n.

valise /vuh-leez/ n. a small suitcase.

valley n. (pl. **valleys**) a low area between hills.

valour (US **valor**) n. great bravery.
■ **valorous** adj.

valuable adj. **1** worth a great deal of money. **2** very useful or important. •n. (**valuables**) valuable items.

valuation n. an estimate of the worth of something.

value n. **1** importance or usefulness. **2** the amount of money that something is worth. **3 (values)** standards of behaviour. • v. **1** estimate the value of. **2** consider important or beneficial. □ **value added tax** a tax on the amount by which goods rise in value at each stage of production. ■ **valuer** n.

valve n. **1** a device controlling flow through a pipe. **2** a structure allowing blood to flow in one direction only.

vamp n. *informal* a woman who uses her sexuality to control men. • v. (**vamp up**) improve by adding something interesting.

vampire n. a corpse supposed to leave its grave at night to drink the blood of the living. □ **vampire bat** a bloodsucking tropical bat.

van n. **1** a motor vehicle for moving goods or people. **2** a railway carriage for luggage, mail, etc. **3** the leading part of an advancing group.

vanadium n. a hard grey metallic element.

vandal n. a person who deliberately damages property. ■ **vandalism** n.

vandalize (or **-ise**) v. deliberately damage.

vane n. a broad blade forming part of a windmill, propeller, etc.

vanguard n. **1** a group leading the way in new ideas. **2** the leading part of an advancing army.

vanilla n. a flavouring obtained from the pods of a tropical plant.

vanish v. disappear suddenly.

vanity n. (pl. **vanities**) **1** excessive pride in yourself. **2** futility.

vanquish v. *literary* defeat thoroughly.

vantage (or **vantage point**) n. a position giving a good view.

vapid adj. not interesting or original. ■ **vapidity** n.

vaporize (or **-ise**) v. convert into vapour. ■ **vaporization** n.

vapour (US **vapor**) n. moisture suspended in the air.

variable adj. **1** often changing; not consistent. **2** able to be changed. • n. a variable situation, feature, etc. ■ **variability** n. **variably** adv.

variance n. (**at variance**) disagreeing.

variant n. a form differing from other forms of the same thing.

variation n. **1** a change or slight difference. **2** a variant. **3** a new but still recognizable version of a musical theme.

varicose adj. (of a vein) swollen and twisted.

varied adj. involving a number of different types or elements.

variegated adj. having irregular patches of a different colour. ■ **variegation** n.

variety n. (pl. **varieties**) **1** the quality of being varied. **2** a range of things of the same type that are distinct in character. **3** a sort or kind. **4** entertainment involving singing, dancing, and comedy.

various adj. **1** of different kinds. **2** several. ■ **variously** adv.

varlet n. *old use* a dishonest man.

varnish n. a liquid applied to wood etc., forming a hard, shiny surface when dry. • v. coat with varnish.

vary v. (**varying**, **varied**) make, be, or become different.

vascular adj. of or containing veins.

vase n. a container for cut flowers.

v

vasectomy n. (pl. **vasectomies**) the surgical cutting and sealing of part of the ducts carrying semen as a means of sterilization.

vassal n. (in the feudal system) a man given land by a king or lord in return for military service.

vast adj. huge. ■ **vastly** adv. **vastness** n.

VAT abbrev. value added tax.

vat n. a large tank for liquids.

vaudeville n. entertainment featuring a mixture of musical and comedy acts.

vault n. 1 a large storage room, esp. in a bank. 2 a burial chamber. 3 a roof in the form of an arch. 4 an act of vaulting. ·v. jump using the hands or a pole to push yourself. ■ **vaulted** adj.

vaunted adj. praised or boasted about.

VC abbrev. Victoria Cross.

VCR abbrev. video cassette recorder.

VDU abbrev. visual display unit.

veal n. meat from a young calf.

vector n. 1 a quantity having direction as well as magnitude. 2 the carrier of a disease or infection.

Veda /vay-duh, vee-duh/ n. the most ancient Hindu scriptures.

veer v. change direction.

vegan n. a person who does not eat or use any animal products.

vegetable n. a plant used as food.

vegetarian n. a person who does not eat meat or fish. ·adj. eating or including no meat or fish. ■ **vegetarianism** n.

vegetate v. spend time in a dull, inactive way.

vegetation n. plants.

vegetative adj. 1 of vegetation. 2 alive but showing no sign of brain activity.

vehement ■ adj. showing strong feeling. ■ **vehemence** n. **vehemently** adv.

vehicle n. 1 a car, lorry, bus, etc. for transporting people or goods on land. 2 a means of expressing something. ■ **vehicular** adj.

veil n. 1 a piece of fine fabric worn to protect or hide the face. 2 a thing that hides or disguises. ·v. 1 cover with a veil. 2 (**veiled**) partially hidden or disguised.

vein n. 1 any of the tubes by which blood is carried towards the heart. 2 (in plants) a structure carrying sap in a leaf. 3 a streak of a different colour. 4 a narrow deposit of a mineral or ore. ■ **veined** adj.

Velcro n. trademark a fastener made of two strips of fabric which cling together when pressed.

veld (or **veldt**) n. open grassland in southern Africa.

vellum n. fine parchment made from animal skin.

velocity n. (pl. **velocities**) speed.

velour n. a fabric resembling velvet.

velvet n. a fabric with a soft, short pile on one side. ■ **velvety** adj.

venal adj. open to bribery. ■ **venality** n.

vend v. sell. □ **vending machine** a machine from which drinks, snacks, etc. can be bought by inserting coins.

vendetta n. a prolonged feud.

vendor n. a person selling something.

veneer n. 1 a thin covering of fine wood. 2 an outward appearance that hides someone's or something's true nature. ■ **veneered** adj.

venerable adj. greatly respected because of wisdom, age, etc.

venerate v. respect greatly. ■ **veneration** n.

venereal disease n. a disease caught by having sex with an infected person.

Venetian adj. of Venice. □ **venetian blind** a window blind consisting of adjustable horizontal slats.

vengeance n. the act of harming or punishing someone in return for what they have done to you. □ **with a vengeance** with great intensity.

vengeful adj. wanting revenge.

venial adj. (of a fault or offence) slight and pardonable.

venison n. meat from a deer.

Venn diagram n. a diagram using overlapping circles to show relationships between mathematical sets.

venom n. **1** poisonous fluid produced by snakes, scorpions, etc. **2** hatred or bitterness. ■ **venomous** adj.

venous /vee-nuhss/ adj. of veins.

vent n. **1** an opening allowing air, gas, or liquid to pass through. **2** a slit in a garment. •v. express a strong emotion freely.

ventilate v. cause air to enter and circulate freely in. ■ **ventilation** n.

ventilator n. **1** a machine or opening for ventilating a room etc. **2** a machine that pumps air in and out of the lungs to assist breathing.

ventral adj. of the abdomen.

ventricle n. each of the two larger and lower cavities of the heart.

ventriloquist n. an entertainer who can make their voice seem to come from a puppet. ■ **ventriloquism** n.

venture n. a business project or other activity involving risk. •v. dare to do or say. ■ **venturesome** adj.

venue n. the place where an event or meeting is held.

veracious adj. truthful. ■ **veracity** n.

veranda (or **verandah**) n. a roofed platform along the outside of a house.

verb n. a word describing an action, state, or occurrence.

verbal adj. **1** of or in the form of words. **2** spoken. **3** of a verb. ■ **verbally** adv.

verbalize (or **-ise**) v. express in words.

verbatim /ver-bay-tim/ adv. & adj. in exactly the same words.

verbena n. a garden plant with showy flowers.

verbiage n. excessively long speech or writing.

verbose adj. using more words than are needed. ■ **verbosity** n.

verdant adj. green with grass etc.

verdict n. **1** a formal decision made by a jury as to a person's innocence or guilt. **2** an opinion made after testing something.

verdigris /ver-di-gree/ n. a green substance formed on copper or brass by oxidation.

verdure n. green vegetation.

verge n. **1** a grass edging by the side of a road or path. **2** a limit beyond which something will happen. •v. (**verge on**) be very close to or similar to.

verger n. a church caretaker.

v

verify v. (**verifying, verified**) check the truth or correctness of. ■ **verifiable** adj. **verification** n.

verily adv. old use truly; certainly.

verisimilitude n. the appearance of being true or real.

veritable adj. rightly so called.

verity n. (pl. **verities**) a true principle or belief.

vermicelli /ver-mi-chel-li/ n. pasta made in long thin threads.

vermilion n. a brilliant red colour.

vermin n. wild animals and birds which carry disease or harm crops etc. ■ **verminous** adj.

vermouth /ver-muhth/ n. a red or white wine flavoured with herbs.

vernacular n. the language spoken by the ordinary people of a country or region.

vernal adj. of the season of spring.

verruca /vuh-roo-kuh/ n. a contagious wart on the sole of the foot.

versatile adj. able to do or be used for many different things. ■ **versatility** n.

verse n. **1** writing arranged with a regular rhythm. **2** a group of lines forming a unit in a poem or song. **3** a numbered division of a chapter of the Bible.

versed adj. (**versed in**) experienced or skilled in.

versify v. (**versifying, versified**) write verse or express in verse. ■ **versification** n.

version n. **1** a form of something differing from other forms of the same type. **2** an account told from a particular person's point of view.

verso n. (pl. **versos**) a left-hand page of an open book.

versus prep. against.

vertebra n. (pl. **vertebrae**) each of the small bones forming the backbone. ■ **vertebral** adj.

vertebrate n. an animal having a backbone.

vertex n. (pl. **vertices** or **vertexes**) **1** the highest point. **2** a meeting point of two lines that form an angle.

vertical adj. at right angles to a horizontal line or surface. ■ **vertically** adv.

vertiginous /ver-tij-i-nuhss/ adj. very high or steep.

vertigo n. giddiness caused by looking down from a great height.

verve n. energy, spirit, and style.

very adj. in a high degree. • adv. **1** actual; precise. **2** mere.

vesicle n. a small fluid-filled sac.

vespers n. a Christian service of evening prayer.

vessel n. **1** a ship or large boat. **2** a tube or duct carrying fluid in an animal or plant. **3** a container for liquids.

vest n. **1** a sleeveless undergarment worn on the upper part of the body. **2** US & Austral. a waistcoat. • v. (**vest in**) give someone the legal right or power to do or own. ■ **vested interest** a personal reason for wanting something to happen.

vestibule n. a small entrance hall.

vestige n. **1** a last remaining trace. **2** the smallest amount. ■ **vestigial** adj.

vestment n. a robe worn by the clergy or members of a choir during services.

vestry n. (pl. **vestries**) a room in a church, used as an office and for changing into robes.

vet n. a veterinary surgeon. •v. (**vetting, vetted**) check very carefully, esp. to decide on a candidate's suitability for a job.

veteran n. a person with long experience, esp. in the armed forces.

veterinarian n. US a veterinary surgeon.

veterinary /vet-uhn-ri, vet-ri-nuh-ri/ adj. of the treatment of injuries and diseases in animals. □ **veterinary surgeon** a person qualified to treat sick or injured animals.

veto n. (pl. **vetoes**) 1 a right to reject a proposal or proposal made by others. 2 a refusal to allow something. •v. (**vetoing, vetoed**) use a veto to prevent; refuse to allow.

vex v. annoy or worry. □ **vexed question** a complex and widely discussed issue. ■ **vexation** n. **vexatious** adj.

VHF abbrev. very high frequency.

via prep. by way of; through.

viable adj. capable of working or surviving successfully. ■ **viability** n.

viaduct n. a long bridge carrying a road or railway across a valley.

vial n. a small medicine bottle.

viands pl. n. old use food.

vibe (or **vibes**) n. informal the atmosphere of a place or a mood passing among people.

vibrant adj. 1 full of energy and enthusiasm. 2 (of sound) resonant. 3 (of colour) bright. ■ **vibrancy** n. **vibrantly** adv.

vibraphone n. an electrical percussion instrument giving a vibrato effect.

vibrate v. 1 move with rapid small movements to and fro. 2 (of a sound) resonate. ■ **vibration** n.

vibrato n. (in music) a rapid, slight variation in pitch.

vibrator n. a vibrating device used for massage or sexual stimulation.

vicar n. (in the Church of England) a minister in charge of a parish.

vicarage n. the house of a vicar.

vicarious adj. experienced in the imagination rather than directly. ■ **vicariously** adv.

vice n. 1 immoral or wicked behaviour. 2 criminal activities involving prostitution, pornography, or drugs. 3 a bad habit or characteristic. 4 a tool with movable jaws for holding an object firmly.

vice- comb. form next in rank to; deputy.

viceroy n. a person sent by a monarch to govern a colony. ■ **viceregal** adj.

vice versa adv. reversing the order of the items just mentioned.

vicinity n. (pl. **vicinities**) the surrounding area.

vicious adj. 1 cruel or violent. 2 wild and dangerous. □ **vicious circle** a situation in which one problem leads to another, which then makes the first one worse. ■ **viciously** adv. **viciousness** n.

vicissitudes /vi-siss-i-tyoodz/ pl. n. changes of circumstance or fortune.

victim n. a person harmed or killed.

victimize (or **-ise**) v. single out for cruel or unfair treatment. ■ **victimization** n.

victor n. a person who defeats an opponent.

Victorian adj. of the reign of Queen Victoria (1837–1901).

v

victorious adj. having won a victory. ■ **victoriously** adv.

victory n. (pl. **victories**) an act of defeating an opponent.

victualler /vit-ler/ n. a person licensed to sell alcoholic drinks.

victuals /vi-t'lz/ n. dated food or provisions.

video n. (pl. **videos**) **1** a system of recording and reproducing moving images on magnetic tape. **2** a film on magnetic tape. ▪v. (**videoing**, **videoed**) make a video recording of. □ **video recorder** a machine for recording television programmes and playing videos.

videotape 1 magnetic tape for recording images and sound. **2** a cassette of this.

vie v. (**vying**, **vied**) compete eagerly with others.

view n. **1** the ability to see something or to be seen from a particular position. **2** something seen from a particular position, esp. natural scenery. **3** an attitude or opinion. ▪v. **1** look at or inspect. **2** regard as. **3** watch on television. □ **in view of** because or as a result of this. **viewfinder** a device on a camera showing what will appear in the picture. **viewpoint** an opinion. **with a view to** with the intention of doing. ■ **viewer** n.

vigil n. a period of staying awake to keep watch or pray.

vigilant adj. alert to possible danger or problems. ■ **vigilance** n. **vigilantly** adv.

vigilante /vi-ji-lan-ti/ n. a member of group undertaking crime prevention and punishment without legal authority.

vignette /vee-nyet/ n. a brief vivid description.

vigour (US **vigor**) n. **1** physical strength and good health. **2** energy and enthusiasm. ■ **vigorous** adj. **vigorously** adv.

Viking n. an ancient Scandinavian trader, pirate, and settler.

vile adj. very unpleasant or wicked. ■ **vilely** adv.

vilify v. (**vilifying**, **vilified**) speak or write about in abusive terms. ■ **vilification** n.

villa n. **1** a rented holiday home abroad. **2** a large country house.

village n. a small settlement in a country area. ■ **villager** n.

villain n. a bad or wicked person. ■ **villainous** adj. **villainy** n.

villein n. hist. a poor man who had to work for a lord in return for a small plot of land.

vim n. informal vigour.

vinaigrette n. salad dressing of oil and vinegar.

vindicate v. **1** clear of blame or suspicion. **2** show to be justified. ■ **vindication** n.

vindictive adj. having a strong or excessive desire for revenge. ■ **vindictively** adv. **vindictiveness** n.

vine n. a climbing plant producing grapes. □ **vineyard** a plantation of vines producing grapes for making wine.

vinegar n. a sour liquid made from wine, beer, or cider. ■ **vinegary** adj.

vintage n. **1** the year in which a wine was produced. **2** a wine of high quality from a particular district and year. **3** the time that something was produced. ▪adj. (of something from the past) of high quality.

vintner n. a wine merchant.

v

vinyl /vy-n'l/ *n.* a type of plastic.

viola[1] /vi-oh-luh/ *n.* an instrument like a violin but of lower pitch.

viola[2] /vy-uh-luh/ *n.* a plant of a group including pansies and violets.

violate *v.* **1** break a rule or agreement. **2** treat with disrespect. **3** *dated* rape. ■ **violation** *n.* **violator** *n.*

violence *n.* **1** actions using physical force intended to hurt, damage, or kill. **2** great force or intensity.

violent *adj.* **1** using or involving violence. **2** very intense.
■ **violently** *adv.*

violet *n.* **1** a small plant with purple or blue flowers. **2** a bluish-purple colour.

violin *n.* a musical instrument with four strings, played with a bow.
■ **violinist** *n.*

violoncello *n.* a cello.

VIP *abbrev.* very important person.

viper *n.* a type of poisonous snake.

virago *n.* (*pl.* **viragos** or **viragoes**) a domineering or bad-tempered woman.

viral *adj.* of a virus or viruses.

virgin *n.* **1** a person who has never had sex. **2** (**the Virgin**) Mary, the mother of Jesus. • *adj.* **1** not yet used or spoilt. **2** having had no sexual experience. ■ **virginal** *adj.* **virginity** *n.*

virile *adj.* (of a man) strong, vigorous, and having a strong sex drive. ■ **virility** *n.*

virology *n.* the study of viruses.
■ **virologist** *n.*

virtual *adj.* **1** almost as described, but not completely. **2** of or using virtual reality. □ **virtual reality** *n.* a system in which images that look like real objects are created by computer. ■ **virtually** *adv.*

virtue *n.* **1** behaviour showing high moral standards. **2** a good or desirable quality. **3** *old use* virginity or chastity. □ **by virtue of** as a result of.

virtuoso *n.* (*pl.* **virtuosi** or **virtuosos**) a person highly skilled in music or another art. ■ **virtuosity** *n.*

virtuous *adj.* having high moral standards. ■ **virtuously** *adv.*

virulent *adj.* **1** (of a disease or poison) very harmful. **2** bitterly hostile. ■ **virulence** *n.* **virulently** *adv.*

virus *n.* **1** a minute organism which can cause disease. **2** a destructive code introduced secretly into a computer system.

visa *n.* a permit on a passport allowing someone to enter, leave, or stay in a country.

visage *n.* *literary* a person's face.

vis-à-vis /veez-ah-vee/ *prep.* in relation to.

viscera /viss-uh-ruh/ *pl. n.* the internal organs of the body.
■ **visceral** *adj.*

viscid /viss-id/ *adj.* sticky.

viscose *n.* a synthetic fabric made from cellulose.

viscount /vy-kownt/ *n.* a nobleman ranking between earl and baron.

viscountess *n.* **1** the wife or widow of a viscount. **2** a woman holding the rank of viscount.

viscous *adj.* thick and sticky.
■ **viscosity** *n.*

visibility *n.* **1** the state of being able to see or be seen. **2** the distance a person can see, depending on light and weather conditions.

v

visible adj. able to be seen or noticed. ■ **visibly** adv.

vision n. **1** the ability to see. **2** the ability to think about the future with imagination or wisdom. **3** a mental image. **4** the images on a television screen.

visionary adj. thinking about the future with imagination or wisdom. • n. (pl. **visionaries**) a visionary person.

visit v. **1** go to spend time with a person or in a place. **2** view a website or web page. **3** (**visit on**) cause something unpleasant to affect. • n. an act of visiting. ■ **visitor** n.

visitation n. **1** an official or formal visit. **2** a disaster or difficulty seen as a divine punishment.

visor (or **vizor**) n. **1** a movable part of a helmet for covering the face. **2** a screen for shielding the eyes from light.

vista n. a pleasing view.

visual adj. of seeing or sight. ☐ **visual display unit** a device displaying information from a computer on a screen. ■ **visually** adv.

visualize (or **-ise**) v. form a mental image of. ■ **visualization** n.

vital adj. **1** absolutely necessary. **3** essential for life. **3** full of energy. • n. (**vitals**) the body's important internal organs. ☐ **vital statistics** informal the measurements of a woman's bust, waist, and hips. ■ **vitality** n. **vitally** adv.

vitalize (or **-ise**) v. give strength and energy to.

vitamin n. an organic compound present in food and essential for normal nutrition.

vitiate /vi-shee-ayt/ v. make less good or effective.

viticulture n. the cultivation of grapevines.

vitreous adj. like or containing glass.

vitrify v. (**vitrifying**, **vitrified**) convert into glass or a glass-like substance by exposure to heat.

vitriol n. **1** great bitterness or malice. **2** old use sulphuric acid. ■ **vitriolic** adj.

vituperation n. bitter and abusive language. ■ **vituperative** adj.

viva[1] /vee-vuh/ exclam. long live!

viva[2] /vy-vuh/ (or **viva voce** /vy-vuh voh-chi/) n. an oral university exam.

vivacious adj. attractively lively. ■ **vivaciously** adv. **vivacity** n.

vivarium n. (pl. **vivaria**) a place for keeping animals in natural conditions.

vivid adj. **1** producing strong, clear images in the mind. **2** (of colour) very deep or bright. ■ **vividly** adv. **vividness** n.

vivify v. (**vivifying**, **vivified**) make more lively.

viviparous /vi-vip-uh-ruhss/ adj. giving birth to live young.

vivisection n. the performing of operations on live animals for scientific research.

vixen n. a female fox.

viz. adv. namely; in other words.

vizor var. of **VISOR**.

vocabulary n. (pl. **vocabularies**) **1** the words used in a particular language or activity or known to a person. **2** a list of words and their meanings.

vocal adj. **1** of or for the voice. **2** expressing opinions freely. • n.

623

vocalist → voluptuous

vocalist n. (or **vocals**) a piece of sung music. □ **vocal cords** membranes in the throat that vibrate to produce the voice. ■ **vocally** adv.

vocalist n. a singer.

vocalize (or **-ise**) v. utter sounds or words.

vocation n. 1 a strong feeling that you ought to pursue a particular career. 2 a career. ■ **vocational** adj.

vociferous adj. expressing opinions forcefully and loudly. ■ **vociferously** adv.

vodka n. an alcoholic spirit made from rye, wheat, or potatoes.

vogue n. the current fashion or style.

voice n. 1 the sound produced in the larynx and uttered through the mouth, as speech or song. 2 an opinion or the right to express an opinion. •v. express in words. □ **voicemail** an electronic system for storing messages from phone callers. **voice-over** spoken information in a film provided by a person who does not appear on the screen.

void adj. 1 not valid. 2 empty. •n. an empty space. •v. 1 discharge waste from the bowels or bladder. 2 declare to be no longer valid.

voile /voyl, vwahl/ n. a thin, semi-transparent fabric.

volatile adj. 1 liable to change unpredictably. 2 easily evaporated. ■ **volatility** n.

vol-au-vent /vol-oh-von/ n. a small round case of puff pastry with a savoury filling.

volcano n. (pl. **volcanoes** or **volcanos**) a mountain with an opening through which lava, gas, etc. is forced out. ■ **volcanic** adj.

vole n. a small mouse-like rodent.

volition n. the power of choosing and deciding for yourself.

volley n. (pl. **volleys**) 1 a number of bullets, missiles, etc. fired at one time. 2 a series of questions, insults, etc. 3 (in sport) a hit of the ball made before it touches the ground. •v. hit the ball before it touches the ground. □ **volleyball** a team game in which a ball is hit by hand over a net.

volt n. a basic unit of electromotive force.

voltage n. electromotive force expressed in volts.

volte-face /volt-fass/ n. an abrupt and complete reversal of attitude or policy.

voluble adj. speaking fluently and at length. ■ **volubility** n. **volubly** adv.

volume n. 1 the amount of space occupied by something or enclosed within a container. 2 an amount or quantity. 3 degree of loudness. 4 a book.

voluminous adj. (of clothing) loose and full.

voluntary adj. 1 done or acting of your own free will. 2 working or done without payment. ■ **voluntarily** adv.

volunteer n. 1 a person who offers to do something. 2 a person who works for no pay. 3 a person who freely joins the armed forces. •v. 1 freely offer to do. 2 say without being asked.

voluptuary n. (pl. **voluptuaries**) a person who loves luxury and pleasure.

voluptuous adj. 1 (of a woman) curvaceous and sexually attract-

v

ive. **2** giving sensual pleasure. ■ **voluptuously** adv.

vomit v. (**vomiting**, **vomited**) bring up food from the stomach through the mouth. •n. vomited food.

voodoo n. a religious cult practised esp. in the Caribbean and involving sorcery and possession by spirits.

voracious adj. **1** wanting or eating great quantities of food. **2** very eager and enthusiastic. ■ **voraciously** adv. **voracity** n.

vortex n. (pl. **vortexes** or **vortices**) a whirling mass of water or air.

votary n. (pl. **votaries**) **1** a person who has dedicated themselves to God. **2** a devoted follower.

vote n. **1** a formal choice made between two or more candidates or options. **2** (**the vote**) the right to participate in an election. •v. give or register a vote. ■ **voter** n.

votive adj. offered to a god as a sign of thanks.

vouch v. (**vouch for**) confirm the truth, accuracy, or honesty of.

voucher n. a piece of paper that may be exchanged for goods or services.

vouchsafe v. give or grant.

vow n. a solemn promise. •v. solemnly promise.

vowel n. a letter of the alphabet representing a speech sound in which the mouth is open and the tongue not touching the top of the mouth, the teeth, or the lips (e.g. *a* or *e*).

vox pop n. informal popular opinion represented by informal comments from the public.

voyage n. a long journey by sea or in space. •v. go on a voyage. ■ **voyager** n.

voyeur /vwa-yer/ n. a person who gets sexual pleasure from watching others when they are naked or having sex.

vs abbrev. versus.

vulcanize (or **-ise**) v. harden rubber by treating it with sulphur at a high temperature.

vulgar adj. **1** lacking sophistication or good taste. **2** referring to sex or bodily functions in a rude way. □ **vulgar fraction** a fraction shown by numbers above and below a line, not decimally. ■ **vulgarity** n. **vulgarly** adv.

vulgarian n. a person lacking in sophistication and taste.

vulnerable adj. exposed to being attacked or harmed. ■ **vulnerability** n.

vulpine adj. of or like a fox.

vulture n. a large bird of prey that feeds on dead animals.

vulva n. the female external genitals.

vying pres. part. of **VIE**.

Ww

W abbrev. **1** watts. **2** West or Western.

wacky adj. (**wackier, wackiest**) informal odd but funny.

wad n. **1** a pad of soft material. **2** a bundle of papers or banknotes. • v. (**wadding, wadded**) press into a wad.

waddle v. walk with short steps and a swaying motion. • n. a waddling walk.

wade v. **1** walk through water or mud. **2** (**wade through**) read something very slowly or boring.

wader n. **1** a long-legged waterbird. **2** (**waders**) high waterproof boots.

wadi n. (pl. **wadis**) a valley or channel that is dry except in the rainy season.

wafer n. **1** a thin, light biscuit. **2** a very thin slice.

waffle v. informal speak or write at length in a vague or trivial way. • n. **1** informal lengthy but vague or trivial talk or writing. **2** a small crisp batter cake, eaten hot.

waft v. move easily or gently through the air. • n. a scent carried in the air.

wag v. (**wagging, wagged**) move rapidly to and fro. • n. **1** a wagging movement. **2** informal a person fond of making jokes.

wage n. (also **wages**) a fixed regular payment for work. • v. carry on a war or campaign.

wager n. & v. = **BET**.

waggle v. move rapidly from side to side or up and down.

wagon (or **waggon**) n. **1** a vehicle, esp. a horse-drawn one, for transporting goods. **2** a railway vehicle for carrying goods in bulk.

wagtail n. a small bird with a long tail that it wags up and down.

waif n. **1** a homeless child. **2** a person who is thin and pale.

wail n. a long, high-pitched cry of pain or grief. • v. make a wail.

wainscot (or **wainscoting**) n. wooden panelling on the lower part of the walls of a room.

waist n. **1** the part of the body between the ribs and hips. **2** a narrow middle part. □ **waistcoat** a waist-length garment with no sleeves or collar. **waistline** the measurement around a person's waist.

wait v. **1** stay in a place or delay action until a particular time or event. **2** be delayed or deferred. **3** (**wait on**) act as an attendant to. **4** act as a waiter or waitress. • n. a period of waiting.

waiter (or **waitress**) n. a person whose job is to serve customers in a restaurant.

waive v. choose not to insist on a right or claim. ■ **waiver** n.

wake v. (**waking, woke**; past part. **woken**) **1** stop sleeping. **2** stir; rouse. • n. **1** a party held after a funeral. **2** a watch kept beside the body of a dead person. **3** a trail of disturbed water left by a ship. □ **in the wake of** coming after.

wakeful *adj.* unable to sleep. ■ **wakefulness** *n.*

waken *v.* wake.

walk *v.* 1 move fairly slowly using the legs. 2 travel over on foot. 3 accompany on foot. •*n.* 1 a journey on foot. 2 a way of walking. 3 a path for walking. □ **walking stick** a stick used for support when walking. **walk of life** social rank. **walkout** a sudden angry departure as a protest or strike. **walkover** an easy victory. ■ **walker** *n.*

walkie-talkie *n.* a portable two-way radio.

wall *n.* 1 a continuous upright structure forming a side of a building or room, or enclosing or dividing an area of land. 2 a barrier. 3 the outer layer or lining of a body organ or cavity. •*v.* enclose or block with a wall. □ **wallflower** 1 a garden plant. 2 *informal* a girl who has no one to dance with at a party. **wallpaper** decorative paper for covering the walls of a room.

wallaby *n.* (*pl.* **wallabies**) a marsupial like a small kangaroo.

wallet *n.* a small, flat, folding holder for money etc.

wallop *informal v.* (**walloping**, **walloped**) hit hard. •*n.* a heavy blow.

wallow *v.* 1 roll in mud or water. 2 (**wallow in**) indulge in.

wally *n.* (*pl.* **wallies**) *informal* a silly person.

walnut *n.* a wrinkled edible nut.

walrus *n.* a large sea mammal with long tusks.

waltz *n.* a ballroom dance in triple time. •*v.* 1 dance a waltz. 2 move or act casually.

wan /won/ *adj.* pale and appearing ill. ■ **wanly** *adv.*

wand *n.* a slender rod, esp. one used in performing magic.

wander *v.* 1 walk or move in a leisurely or aimless way. 2 move slowly away from a fixed point. •*n.* an act of wandering. □ **wanderlust** a strong desire to travel. ■ **wanderer** *n.*

wane *v.* 1 (of the moon) gradually appear to decrease in size. 2 become weaker. □ **on the wane** waning.

wangle *v.* *informal* obtain by trickery or persuasion.

want *v.* 1 desire to have or do. 2 (**wanted**) (of a suspected criminal) sought by the police. 3 lack or be short of. •*n.* 1 lack or shortage. 2 a desire.

wanting *adj.* 1 lacking something required. 2 not good enough.

wanton *adj.* 1 deliberate and unprovoked. 2 having many sexual partners. ■ **wantonly** *adv.*

WAP *abbrev.* Wireless Application Protocol, a means of enabling mobile phones to access the Internet.

war *n.* a state of armed conflict between different nations or groups. •*v.* (**warring, warred**) take part in a war. □ **warfare** the activity of fighting a war. **warhead** the explosive head of a missile. **warlike** hostile. **warmonger** a person who tries to bring about war. **warship** an armed ship designed for warfare at sea.

warble *v.* sing with constantly changing notes.

ward *n.* 1 a room in a hospital for a patient or patients. 2 a division of a city or borough represented by a councillor. 3 a young person looked after by a guardian appointed by their parents or a court. • v. (**ward off**) prevent from doing harm.

warden n. a person supervising a place or procedure.

warder n. a prison guard.

wardrobe n. 1 a large, tall cupboard for hanging clothes in. 2 a collection of clothes.

ware n. 1 manufactured articles of a specified type. 2 (**wares**) articles offered for sale. □ **warehouse** a large building for storing goods.

warlock n. a man who practises witchcraft.

warm adj. 1 moderately hot. 2 helping the body to retain heat. 3 enthusiastic, affectionate, or kind. • v. 1 make or become warm. 2 (**warm to**) become more interested in or enthusiastic about. □ **warm-blooded** (of animals) maintaining a constant body temperature. **warm up** prepare for exercise by doing gentle stretches. ■ **warmly** adv. **warmness** n.

warmth n. 1 the quality of being warm. 2 enthusiasm, affection, or kindness.

warn v. 1 inform of a possible danger or problem. 2 advise not to do. 3 (**warn off**) order to keep away.

warning n. 1 something indicating a possible danger or problem. 2 advice against wrong or foolish actions. 3 advance notice.

warp v. 1 bend or twist out of shape. 2 make abnormal or strange. • n. 1 a distortion. 2 the lengthwise threads on a loom.

warrant n. 1 an official authorization allowing the police to make an arrest, search premises, etc. 2 justification. • v. 1 justify. 2 guarantee.

warranty n. (pl. **warranties**) a written guarantee promising to repair or replace a purchased article if necessary.

warren n. a network of interconnecting rabbit burrows.

warrior n. a brave or experienced fighter.

wart n. a small, hard growth on the skin. □ **warthog** an African wild pig with warty lumps on its face. ■ **warty** adj.

wary adj. (**warier**, **wariest**) cautious. ■ **warily** adv. **wariness** n.

was see BE.

wash v. 1 clean with water and usu. soap or detergent. 2 (of flowing water) carry or move in a particular direction. 3 (**wash over**) occur without greatly affecting. 4 informal seem convincing or genuine. • n. 1 an act of washing. 2 clothes etc. to be washed. 3 the water or air disturbed by a moving boat or aircraft. 4 a cleansing solution. 5 a thin coating of paint. □ **washbasin** a basin for washing the hands and face. **washed out** pale and tired. **washout** informal a disappointing failure. **wash your hands of** take no further responsibility for. **wash up** clean dirty crockery and cutlery. ■ **washable** adj.

washer n. a small flat ring fixed between a nut and bolt.

washing n. clothes etc. to be washed or that have just been washed. □ **washing-up** crockery, cutlery, etc. to be washed.

wasp n. a stinging winged insect with a black and yellow striped body.

waspish adj. sharply irritable. ■ **waspishly** adv.

W

wassail old use n. lively festivities involving the drinking of much alcohol. • v. 1 celebrate in this way. 2 go carol-singing.

wastage n. 1 the act of wasting. 2 an amount wasted. 3 the reduction of a workforce by resignations or retirements.

waste v. 1 use more of something than is necessary. 2 fail to make use of. 3 become weaker and thinner. • adj. 1 discarded because no longer required. 2 (of land) not used, cultivated, or built on. • n. 1 an act of wasting. 2 waste material. 3 a large area of barren, uninhabited land. ◻ **lay waste to** completely destroy. ◼ **waster** n.

wasteful adj. using more of something than is necessary. ◼ **wastefully** adv.

watch v. 1 look at attentively. 2 keep under careful observation. 3 be careful about. 4 (**watch out**) be careful. • n. 1 a small timepiece usu. worn on the wrist. 2 an act of watching. 3 a shift worked by sailors, firefighters, or police officers. ◻ **watchdog** 1 a dog kept to guard property. 2 a group monitoring the practices of companies. **watchman** a man employed to guard an empty building. **watchtower** a tower built as a high observation point. **watchword** a word or phrase expressing a central aim or belief. ◼ **watchable** adj. **watcher** n.

watchful adj. alert to possible difficulty or danger. ◼ **watchfully** adv.

water n. 1 the liquid forming the seas, lakes, rivers, and rain. 2 (**waters**) an area of sea under a particular country's authority. • v. 1 pour water over. 2 give a drink of water to. 3 produce tears or saliva.

4 dilute with water. 5 (**water down**) make less forceful. ◻ **waterbed** a bed with a water-filled mattress. **water cannon** a device that ejects a powerful jet of water to disperse a crowd. **water chestnut** the crisp edible tuber of a tropical plant. **watercolour** 1 artists' paint mixed with water. 2 a picture painted with watercolours. **watercourse** a stream or artificial water channel. **watercress** a cress which grows in running water. **waterfall** a stream of water falling from a height. **waterfront** a part of a town alongside an area of water. **water ice** a frozen dessert of fruit juice in sugar syrup. **water lily** a plant that grows in water, with broad floating leaves. **waterline** the level normally reached by the water on the side of a ship. **waterlogged** saturated with water. **watermark** a faint design made in some paper, visible when held against the light. **water meadow** a meadow periodically flooded by a stream. **watermelon** a melon with watery red pulp. **watermill** a mill worked by a waterwheel. **waterproof** unable to be penetrated by water. **watershed** 1 an area of land separating two river systems. 2 a turning point in a situation. **waterskiing** the sport of skimming over water on skis while towed by a motorboat. **waterspout** a column of water formed by a whirlwind over the sea. **water table** the level below which the ground is saturated with water. **watertight** 1 not allowing water to pass through. 2 unable to be questioned. **waterway** a river or other route for travel by water. **waterwheel** a

W

wheel driven by flowing water to work machinery.

watery adj. **1** of or like water. **2** containing too much water. **3** weak or pale.

watt n. a basic unit of electric power.

wattage n. an amount of electrical power expressed in watts.

wattle n. **1** interwoven sticks used to make fences etc. **2** a fleshy part hanging from the head or neck of a turkey etc.

wave v. **1** move your hand to and fro as a greeting or signal. **2** move to and fro. • n. **1** a moving ridge of water. **2** a sudden increase in an emotion or activity. **3** an act of waving. **4** a slightly curling lock of hair. **5** a regular to-and-fro motion of particles of matter involved in transmitting sound, light, heat, etc. □ **waveband** a range of wavelengths. **wavelength 1** the distance between successive crests of a wave of sound, light, etc. **2** a person's way of thinking.

waver v. **1** flicker. **2** begin to weaken. **3** be indecisive.

wavy adj. (**wavier, waviest**) having a series of wave-like curves.

wax n. a soft solid substance used for making candles or polishes. • v. **1** polish or treat with wax. **2** remove hair from the body by applying then peeling off wax. **3** (of the moon) gradually appear to increase in size. **4** literary speak or write in a specified way. □ **waxwork** a lifelike dummy made of wax. ■ **waxen** adj. **waxy** adj.

way n. **1** a method or manner of doing something. **2** a road or path. **3** a route or means taken to reach, enter, or leave a place. **4** a direction. **5** a distance. **6** a condition.

• adv. informal by a great deal. □ **by the way** used to introduce an incidental remark. **in the way** obstructing progress. **wayfarer** literary a traveller. **wayside** the edge of a road.

waylay v. (**waylaying, waylaid**) intercept someone so as to attack or question them.

wayward adj. unpredictable and hard to control. ■ **waywardness** n.

WC abbrev. water closet (a toilet).

we pron. **1** used by a speaker to refer to himself or herself and one or more other people. **2** people in general.

weak adj. **1** lacking strength and energy. **2** likely to break or give way. **3** not secure or stable. **4** lacking power, influence, or ability. **5** heavily diluted. ■ **weaken** v. **weakly** adv.

weakling n. a weak person or animal.

weakness n. **1** the state of being weak. **2** a fault. **3** a self-indulgent liking.

weal n. a red, swollen mark left on flesh by a blow or pressure.

wealth n. **1** a large amount of money and valuable possessions. **2** the state of being rich. **3** a large amount. ■ **wealthy** adj.

wean v. **1** make a young mammal eat food other than its mother's milk. **2** cause to give up a habit etc. gradually.

weapon n. **1** a thing used to cause harm or damage. **2** a means of gaining an advantage or defending yourself. ■ **weaponry** n.

wear v. (**wearing, wore**; past part. **worn**) **1** have on the body as clothing, decoration, or protection. **2** damage by friction or use.

W

3 withstand continued use. **4** (**wear off**) lose effectiveness or strength. **5** (**wear down**) overcome by persistence. **6** (**wear out**) exhaust. **7** (**wear on**) (of time) pass slowly. •n. **1** clothing of a particular type. **2** damage from friction or use. ■ **wearable** adj. **wearer** n.

wearisome adj. causing weariness.

weary adj. (**wearier**, **weariest**) **1** tired. **2** tiring. •v. (**wearying**, **wearied**) make or become weary. ■ **wearily** adv. **weariness** n.

weasel n. a small, slender reddish-brown mammal.

weather n. the state of the atmosphere in terms of temperature, wind, rain, etc. •v. **1** wear away through the action of the weather. **2** come safely through. □ **under the weather** informal slightly unwell. **weather-beaten** damaged or tanned by exposure to the weather. **weathercock** a weathervane in the form of a cockerel. **weathervane** a revolving pointer to show the direction of the wind.

weave v. (**weaving**, **wove**; past part. **woven** or **wove**) **1** make fabric or baskets by passing crosswise threads or strips under and over lengthwise ones. **2** form a story from different elements. **3** (past & past part **weaved**) move from side to side to avoid things. •n. a way in which fabric is woven. ■ **weaver** n.

web n. **1** a network of fine threads made by a spider. **2** a complex network of elements. **3** (**the Web**) the World Wide Web. **4** the skin between the toes of a duck, frog, etc. □ **webcam** (trademark in the US) a video camera connected to a computer, allowing images to be viewed on the Internet. **weblog** a personal website on which someone regularly records their opinions or experiences. **web page** a document that can be accessed via the Internet. **website** a location on the Internet having one or more web pages. ■ **webbed** adj.

webbing n. strong fabric used for straps and belts.

wed v. (**wedding**, **wedded** or **wed**) **1** formal marry. **2** combine two desirable elements. **3** (**be wedded to**) be completely devoted to. □ **wedlock** the state of being married.

wedding n. a marriage ceremony.

wedge n. a piece of wood, metal, etc. with a thick end that tapers to a thin edge. •v. **1** fix in position with a wedge. **2** force into a narrow space.

Wednesday n. the day before Thursday.

wee adj. Sc. little.

weed n. **1** a wild plant growing where it is not wanted. **2** informal a weak or thin person. •v. **1** remove weeds from. **2** (**weed out**) remove as unwanted. ■ **weedy** adj.

week n. **1** a period of seven days. **2** the five days from Monday to Friday, when many people work. □ **weekday** a day of the week other than Sunday or Saturday. **weekend** Saturday and Sunday. ■ **weekly** adj. & adv.

weeny adj. (**weenier**, **weeniest**) informal tiny.

weep v. (**weeping**, **wept**) **1** shed tears. **2** (of a wound) discharge liquid. •n. a period of weeping.

weepy adj. (**weepier, weepiest**) informal **1** tearful. **2** sentimental.

weevil n. a small beetle that eats crops or stored food.

weft n. the crosswise threads in weaving.

weigh v. **1** find out the weight of. **2** have a specified weight. **3** (**weigh down**) be troublesome to. **4** (often **weigh up**) assess the nature or importance of. **5** (**weigh on**) be worrying to. **6** influence a decision or action. □ **weigh anchor** take up the anchor when ready to sail. **weighbridge** a machine on to which vehicles are driven to be weighed.

weight n. **1** the heaviness of a person or thing. **2** a unit or system for expressing this. **3** a piece of metal of known weight, used in weighing. **4** a heavy object. **5** ability to influence decisions. **6** importance. • v. **1** make heavier or keep in place with a weight. **2** attach comparative importance or value to. ■ **weightless** adj.

weighting n. additional wages paid to allow for a higher cost of living in a particular area.

weightlifting n. the sport of lifting heavy weights. ■ **weightlifter** n.

weighty adj. (**weightier, weightiest**) **1** heavy. **2** serious and important. **3** influential.

weir n. a low dam built to regulate the flow of a river.

weird adj. strange; bizarre. ■ **weirdly** adv. **weirdness** n.

> **!** **weird** is an exception to the usual rule of i before e except after c.

welch var. of WELSH.

welcome n. **1** an instance or way of greeting someone. **2** an approving reaction. • v. **1** greet in a polite or friendly way. **2** be glad to receive or hear of. • adj. **1** much needed or desired. **2** gladly received. **3** allowed or invited to do something.

weld v. **1** join metal parts by heating and pressing them together. **2** combine to form a whole. • n. a welded joint. ■ **welder** n.

welfare n. **1** the health, happiness, and safety of a person or group. **2** organized help given to people in need. □ **welfare state** a system under which the state provides pensions, health care, etc.

well[1] adv. (**better, best**) **1** in a good or appropriate way. **2** thoroughly. **3** to a great extent or degree. **4** very probably. **5** without difficulty. **6** with good reason. • adj. (**better, best**) **1** in good health. **2** satisfactory. • exclam. expressing surprise, anger, etc. □ **as well 1** in addition. **2** with equal reason or an equally good result. **well advised** sensible. **well appointed** well equipped or furnished. **well-being** comfort, good health, and happiness. **well disposed** sympathetic or friendly. **well heeled** informal wealthy. **well-nigh** almost. **well off 1** wealthy. **2** in a good situation. **well read** having read many literary works. **well spoken** having an educated and refined voice. **well-to-do** wealthy.

well[2] n. **1** a shaft sunk into the ground to obtain water, oil, or gas. **2** an enclosed space in a building for stairs, a lift, etc. • v. **1** (of a liquid) rise up to the surface. **2** (of an emotion) arise and intensify.

w

wellington n. a knee-length waterproof rubber or plastic boot.

Welsh n. the language of Wales. •adj. of Wales. □ **Welsh rarebit** (or **Welsh rabbit**) melted cheese on toast.

welsh (or **welch**) v. (**welsh on**) fail to honour a debt or obligation.

welt n. **1** a leather rim to which the sole of a shoe is attached. **2** a border on a knitted garment. **3** a weal.

welter n. a large and disorganized number of items.

welterweight n. a weight in boxing etc. between lightweight and middleweight.

wench n. old use a girl or young woman.

wend v. (**wend your way**) go slowly or by an indirect route.

went past of **GO**.

wept past & past part. of **WEEP**.

were see **BE**.

werewolf n. (pl. **werewolves**) (in folklore) a person who periodically changes into a wolf.

west n. **1** the direction in which the sun sets. **2** the western part of a place. **3** (**the West**) Europe and North America. •adj. & adv. **1** towards or facing the west. **2** (of a wind) from the west. ■ **westerly** adj. & adv. **westward** adj. & adv. **westwards** adv.

western adj. situated in or facing the west. •n. a film or novel about cowboys in the western US.

westerner n. a person from the west of a region.

westernize (or **-ise**) v. bring under the influence of Europe and North America.

wet adj. (**wetter**, **wettest**) **1** covered or saturated with liquid.

2 rainy. **3** (of paint etc.) not yet dry. **4** informal feeble. •v. (**wetting**, **wet** or **wetted**) make wet. •n. **1** rainy weather. **2** liquid causing dampness. □ **wet blanket** informal a person who spoils others' enjoyment by being unenthusiastic. **wet nurse** a woman employed to breastfeed another woman's child. **wetsuit** a rubber garment worn for warmth in water sports. ■ **wetly** adv. **wetness** n.

wether n. a castrated ram.

whack informal v. **1** hit forcefully. **2** (**whacked**) exhausted. •n. **1** a sharp blow. **2** a share or contribution.

whale n. (pl. **whale** or **whales**) a very large sea mammal. □ **a whale of a time** informal a very enjoyable time. **whalebone** a horny substance from the upper jaw of whales, formerly used to stiffen corsets etc.

whaler n. **1** a whaling ship. **2** a seaman engaged in whaling.

whaling n. the hunting and killing of whales.

wharf /worf/ n. (pl. **wharves** or **wharfs**) a level area where ships are moored to load and unload.

what pron. & adj. **1** asking for information. **2** whatever. **3** emphasizing a surprising or remarkable thing. •pron. the thing or things that. •adv. to what extent? □ **whatever 1** everything or anything that. **2** at all; of any kind. **whatnot** informal an unspecified item or items. **whatsoever** whatever.

wheat n. a cereal crop whose grain is ground to make flour. □ **wheatmeal** flour made from wheat from which some of the bran has been removed.

wheaten adj. made of wheat.

wheedle v. use insincere praise etc. so as to persuade.

wheel n. **1** a revolving circular object fixed below a vehicle to enable it to move along, or forming part of a machine. **2** a turn or rotation. • v. **1** push or pull a vehicle with wheels. **2** move in a wide circle or curve. **3** turn round quickly. □ **wheel and deal** take part in commercial or political scheming. **wheelbarrow** a small cart with a single wheel at the front and two handles at the rear. **wheelbase** the distance between a vehicle's front and rear axles. **wheelchair** a chair on wheels for an ill or disabled person.

wheeze v. breathe with a whistling or rattling sound in the chest. • n. **1** a sound of wheezing. **2** informal a clever scheme. ■ **wheezy** adj.

whelk n. a shellfish with a spiral shell.

whelp n. a puppy. • v. give birth to a puppy.

when adv. **1** at what time? **2** at which time or in which situation. • conj. **1** at or during the time that. **2** whenever. **3** and just then. **4** although. □ **whenever 1** at whatever time. **2** every time that.

whence adv. formal from which or from where.

where adv. **1** in or to what place? **2** in what direction or respect? **3** at, in, or to which. **4** in or to a place or situation in which. □ **whereabouts 1** where or approximately where? **2** the place where someone or something is. **whereas** in contrast with the fact

that. **whereby** by which. **whereupon** immediately after which. **wherever 1** in or to whatever place. **2** in every case when. **wherewithal** the money etc. needed for something.

wherry n. (pl. **wherries**) a light barge or rowing boat.

whet v. (**whetting**, **whetted**) **1** sharpen a blade. **2** stimulate someone's interest or appetite. □ **whetstone** a stone for sharpening blades.

whether conj. **1** expressing a choice between alternatives. **2** expressing an enquiry or investigation.

whey n. the watery part of milk remaining after curds have formed.

which pron. & adj. **1** asking for information specifying one or more members of a set. **2** introducing a clause giving further information about something previously mentioned. □ **whichever 1** any which; that or those which. **2** regardless of which.

whiff n. **1** a smell, esp. one smelt only briefly. **2** a trace.

Whig n. hist. a member of a British political party that was succeeded by the Liberals.

while n. **1** (a while) a period of time. **2** (the while) meanwhile. • conj. **1** at the same time as. **2** whereas. **3** although. • v. (**while away**) pass time in a leisurely way. □ **worth (your) while** worth the time or effort spent.

whilst conj. while.

whim n. a sudden desire or change of mind.

whimper v. make low, feeble sounds. • n. a whimpering sound.

w

whimsical *adj.* **1** quaint or fanciful. **2** showing sudden changes of mood. ▪ **whimsically** *adv.*

whimsy *n.* playfully unusual behaviour or humour.

whine *n.* **1** a long, high-pitched complaining cry. **2** a long, shrill sound. • *v.* **1** give or make a whine. **2** complain in a sulky way. ▪ **whiny** *adj.*

whinge *v.* (**whingeing, whinged**) *informal* complain persistently.

whinny *n.* (*pl.* **whinnies**) a gentle neigh. • *v.* (**whinnying, whinnied**) neigh gently.

whip *n.* **1** a length of leather or cord on a handle, used to beat a person or urge on an animal. **2** a dessert made with whipped cream etc. **3** an official maintaining discipline in a political party. **4** a written notice from a party whip requesting attendance for voting. • *v.* (**whipping, whipped**) **1** beat with a whip. **2** move or take out fast. **3** beat into a froth. **4** (**whip up**) deliberately excite or provoke. □ **whiplash** injury caused by a severe jerk to the head. **whipping boy** a scapegoat. **whip-round** *informal* a collection of money from a group.

whippersnapper *n. informal* a young and inexperienced but overconfident person.

whippet *n.* a small dog resembling a greyhound.

whirl *v.* **1** move rapidly round and round. **2** (of the head etc.) seem to spin round. • *n.* **1** a whirling movement. **2** frantic activity. **3** a state of confusion. □ **whirlpool** a current of water whirling in a circle.

whirlwind *n.* a column of air moving rapidly round and round.

• *adj.* very quick and unexpected: *a whirlwind romance*.

whirr *v.* make a low, continuous, regular sound. • *n.* a whirring sound.

whisk *v.* **1** move or take suddenly, quickly, and lightly. **2** beat eggs etc. with a light, rapid movement. • *n.* a utensil for whisking eggs etc.

whisker *n.* **1** each of the long hairs or bristles growing from the face of an animal. **2** (**whiskers**) the hair growing on a man's face.

whisky (*Irish & US* **whiskey**) *n.* (*pl.* **whiskies**) a spirit distilled from malted grain.

whisper *v.* speak very softly. • *n.* **1** a whispered remark. **2** a very soft voice.

whist *n.* a card game in which points are scored according to the number of tricks won.

whistle *n.* **1** a clear, high-pitched sound made by forcing breath between the lips or teeth. **2** any similar sound. **3** a device producing a whistling sound. • *v.* **1** produce a whistle. **2** blow a whistle. □ **whistle-blower** *informal* a person who exposes dishonest or illicit activity. **whistle-stop** very fast and with only brief pauses.

Whit *n.* a Christian festival held on the seventh Sunday after Easter.

whit *n.* a very small part or amount.

white *adj.* **1** of the colour of fresh snow. **2** very pale. **3** of people with light-coloured skin. **4** (of coffee or tea) with milk. • *n.* **1** white colour. **2** the pale part of the eyeball around the iris. **3** the outer part around the yolk of an egg. **4** a white person. □ **whitebait** the young of herrings, sprats, etc. used as food. **white-collar** of work done in an office or other professional environment. **white**

elephant a useless or unwanted possession. **white flag** a white flag waved as a symbol of surrender. **white-hot** so hot as to glow white. **white lie** a lie told to avoid hurting someone's feelings. **white noise** noise containing many frequencies with equal intensities. **White Paper** a government report giving information or proposals. **white spirit** a colourless liquid used as a solvent. ■ **whiten** v. **whiteness** n.

whitewash n. **1** a solution of lime or chalk and water, used for painting walls white. **2** a deliberate concealment of mistakes. •v. **1** paint with whitewash. **2** conceal mistakes.

whither adv. old use to what place or state?

whiting n. (pl. **whiting**) a small edible sea fish.

Whitsun (or **Whitsuntide**) n. the weekend or week including Whit Sunday.

Whit Sunday n. a Christian festival held on the seventh Sunday after Easter.

whittle v. **1** carve wood by cutting small slices from it. **2** (**whittle away/down**) gradually reduce.

whizz (or **whiz**) v. **1** move quickly through the air. **2** move or go fast. •n. a whizzing sound. □ **whizz-kid** informal a very successful or skilful young person.

who pron. **1** what or which person or people? **2** introducing a clause giving further information about a person or people previously mentioned. □ **whodunnit** (US **whodunit**) informal a detective story or play. **whoever 1** any person who. **2** regardless of who. **whosoever** formal whoever.

whoa exclam. a command to a horse to stop or slow down.

whole adj. **1** complete; entire. **2** in one piece. •n. **1** a thing that is complete in itself. **2** all of something. □ **on the whole** taking everything into account. **wholefood** food that has been processed as little as possible. **wholehearted** completely sincere and committed. **wholemeal** made from the whole grain of wheat. **whole number** a number without fractions.

wholesale n. the selling of goods in large quantities to be sold to the public by others. •adv. & adj. **1** being sold in such a way. **2** on a large scale. ■ **wholesaler** n.

wholesome adj. **1** good for health or well-being. **2** morally good.

wholly adv. entirely; fully.

whom pron. used instead of 'who' as the object of a verb or preposition.

whoop n. a loud cry of joy or excitement. •v. give a whoop. □ **whooping cough** a disease characterized by coughs followed by a rasping breath.

whopper n. informal **1** something very large. **2** a blatant lie.

whore n. a prostitute.

whorl /worl/ n. **1** each of the turns in a spiral or coil. **2** a ring of leaves or petals. **3** a circle in a fingerprint.

who's contr. **1** who is. **2** who has.

> **!** Don't confuse **who's** with **whose**. **Who's** is short for **who is** or **who has**, as in who's there or who's taken it?; **whose** means 'belonging to which person' or 'of whom or which', as in whose is this? or a man whose opinion I respect.

w

whose adj. & pron. **1** belonging to which person. **2** of whom or which.

why adv. **1** for what reason or purpose? **2** on account of which; the reason that.

wick n. a length of cord in a candle, lamp, etc. which carries liquid fuel to the flame.

wicked adj. **1** evil. **2** playfully mischievous. **3** informal excellent. ■ **wickedly** adv. **wickedness** n.

wicker n. thin canes woven to make furniture, baskets, etc. ■ **wickerwork** n.

wicket n. (in cricket) either of the two sets of three stumps with two bails across the top that are defended by a batsman. □ **wicketkeeper** a fielder positioned close behind a batsman's wicket.

wide adj. **1** of great or specified width. **2** including a great variety of people or things. **3** at a distance from a point or mark. • adv. **1** to the full extent. **2** far from a point or target. □ **wide awake** fully awake. **widespread** spread among a large number or over a large area. ■ **widen** v. **widely** adv.

widow n. a woman whose husband has died and who has not remarried. • v. (**be widowed**) become a widow or widower.

widower n. a man whose wife has died and who has not remarried.

width n. **1** the measurement or extent of something from side to side. **2** a piece of something at its full extent from side to side.

wield v. **1** hold and use a weapon or tool. **2** have and use power.

wife n. (pl. **wives**) a married woman in relation to her husband. ■ **wifely** adj.

wig n. a covering of hair worn on the head.

wiggle v. move with short movements from side to side. • n. a wiggling movement. ■ **wiggly** adj.

wigwam n. a conical tent formerly lived in by some North American Indian peoples.

wild adj. **1** living or growing in the natural environment. **2** (of a place) not inhabited or changed by people. **3** uncontrolled. **4** not based on reason or evidence. **5** informal very enthusiastic or excited. **6** informal very angry. • n. **1** (**the wild**) a natural environment. **2** (**the wilds**) a remote area. □ **spread like wildfire** spread very fast. **wild card** a playing card that can have any value, suit, etc. that the player holding it requires. **wildcat** (of a strike) sudden and unofficial. **wildfowl** game birds. **wild goose chase** a hopeless search. **wildlife** the native animals of a region. ■ **wildly** adv. **wildness** n.

wildebeest n. a gnu.

wilderness n. an uncultivated and uninhabited area.

wiles pl. n. cunning methods used to achieve something.

wilful (US **willful**) adj. **1** deliberate. **2** stubborn and determined. ■ **wilfully** adv. **wilfulness** n.

will[1] aux. v. (past **would**) **1** expressing the future tense. **2** expressing intention, ability, or a request.

will[2] n. **1** a person's power to decide on something and take action. **2** (or **willpower**) a person's ability to control their actions. **3** a desire or intention. **4** a legal document with instructions for the disposal of someone's money and property after their death. •v. **1** intend or desire. **2** achieve by mental powers. **3** leave to someone in a will. □ **at will** whenever you like.

willing adj. **1** ready or eager to do something. **2** given or done readily. ■ **willingly** adv. **willingness** n.

will-o'-the-wisp n. **1** something impossible to obtain. **2** a dim, flickering light seen over marshy ground.

willow n. a tree with narrow leaves and catkins.

willowy adj. tall and slim.

willy-nilly adv. whether you like it or not.

wilt v. **1** (of a plant) become limp through lack of water. **2** feel tired and weak.

wily adj. clever in a cunning way. ■ **wiliness** n.

wimp n. informal a weak or timid person.

wimple n. a cloth headdress covering the head, neck, and sides of the face, worn esp. by some nuns.

win v. (**winning**, **won**) **1** be the most successful in a contest etc. **2** gain as a result of success in a contest etc. **3** gain the attention, love, etc. of. **4** (also **win over**) gain the support of. •n. a victory in a game or contest.

wince v. grimace or flinch from pain or distress.

winch n. a hauling or lifting device consisting of a cable winding round a horizontal rotating drum. •v. hoist or pull with a winch.

wind[1] n. **1** a natural movement of the air. **2** breath needed to do

exercise or play an instrument. **3** gas in the stomach and intestines. **4** wind instruments as a section of an orchestra. •v. make breathless. □ **get wind of** informal hear a rumour of.

windbag informal a person who talks at unnecessary length.

windbreak a screen providing shelter from the wind. **windfall 1** a piece of unexpected good fortune. **2** fruit blown off a tree by the wind. **wind instrument** a musical instrument sounded by the player blowing into it. **windmill** a building with sails or vanes that turn in the wind and generate power to grind corn etc. **windpipe** the tube carrying air down the throat to the lungs. **windscreen** (or US **windshield**) the glass screen at the front of a vehicle. **windsock** a light, flexible cone mounted on a mast to show the direction and strength of the wind. **windsurfing** the sport of riding on water on a sailboard. **windswept** exposed to strong winds. **wind tunnel** a tunnel-like structure in which a strong current of air is created to test the effect of wind on vehicles. ■ **windward** adj. & adv. **windy** adj.

wind[2] v. (**winding**, **wound**) **1** move in or take a twisting or spiral course. **2** pass or twist around a thing or person or itself. **3** make a clockwork device work by turning a key or handle. □ **wind down 1** draw or bring to a close. **2** informal relax. **wind up 1** bring or come to an end. **2** informal irritate.

windlass n. a winch on a ship or in a harbour.

window n. **1** an opening in a wall, fitted with glass to let in light and

w

allow people to see out. **2** a framed area on a computer screen for viewing information. □ **window dressing 1** the arrangement of a display in a shop window. **2** the presentation of something to give a misleadingly good impression. **window-shopping** looking at goods displayed in shop windows without intending to buy.

wine n. an alcoholic drink esp. from fermented grape juice.

winery n. (pl. **wineries**) a place where wine is made.

wing n. **1** a projecting part enabling a bird, insect, or bat to fly. **2** a structure projecting from both sides of an aircraft and supporting it in the air. **3** a part of a large building. **4** a group within an organization. **5** (**the wings**) the sides of a stage out of view of the audience. **6** the part of a football or rugby field close to the sidelines. **7** an attacking player near the sidelines. **8** the bodywork of a vehicle above the wheel. •v. **1** fly, or move quickly as if flying. **2** wound in the wing or arm. □ **under your wing** in or into your protective care. **wingspan** the measurement from tip to tip of the wings of a bird etc. ■ **winged** adj.

winger n. an attacking player on the wing in football etc.

wink v. **1** close and open one eye quickly as a signal. **2** shine or flash on and off. •n. an act of winking.

winkle n. a small edible shellfish. •v. (**winkle out**) take out or obtain with difficulty.

winner n. **1** a person or thing that wins. **2** informal a successful thing.

winning adj. attractive. •n. (**winnings**) money won by gambling. ■ **winningly** adv.

winnow v. **1** remove members from a group until only the best are left. **2** blow air through grain to remove the chaff.

winsome adj. charming.

winter n. the cold season between autumn and spring. •v. spend the winter in a particular place. ■ **wintry** adj.

wipe v. **1** clean or dry by rubbing with a cloth or the hand. **2** erase data from a computer, video, etc. •n. **1** an act of wiping. **2** a disposable cleaning cloth. □ **wipe out** completely destroy or eliminate. ■ **wiper** n.

wire n. **1** a thin, flexible strand of metal. **2** a length of wire used for fencing, to carry an electric current, etc. •v. **1** install electric wires in. **2** fasten or reinforce with wire. □ **wiretapping** the secret tapping of phone lines.

wireless adj. using radio, microwaves, etc. (as opposed to wires) to transmit signals. •n. dated **1** a radio. **2** broadcasting using radio signals.

wiring n. a system of electric wires in a device or building.

wiry adj. (**wirier**, **wiriest**) **1** like wire. **2** lean and strong.

wisdom n. **1** the quality of being wise. **2** a body of knowledge and experience. □ **wisdom tooth** each of the four molars at the back of the mouth, usu. appearing around the age of 20.

wise adj. **1** having or showing experience, knowledge, and good judgement. **2** (**wise to**) informal aware of. •v. (**wise up**) informal become aware. □ **wisecrack** informal a joke or witty remark. ■ **wisely** adv.

w

wish v. **1** desire something that is unlikely or impossible. **2** want to do. **3** express a hope that someone has happiness or success. •n. **1** a desire or hope. **2** (**wishes**) an expression of friendly feeling. **3** a thing wished for. □ **wishbone** a forked bone between the neck and breast of a bird.

wishful adj. based on impractical wishes rather than facts: *wishful thinking*.

wishy-washy adj. feeble.

wisp n. a small thin bunch or strand of something. ■ **wispy** adj.

wisteria n. a climbing shrub with bluish-lilac flowers.

wistful adj. having or showing vague or regretful longing. ■ **wistfully** adv.

wit n. **1** (or **wits**) the ability to think quickly and make good decisions. **2** a natural talent for using words and ideas in a quick amusing way. **3** a witty person.

witch n. a woman believed to have evil magic powers. □ **witchcraft** the practice of magic. **witch doctor** a person believed to have magic powers of healing etc. **witch hazel** an astringent lotion made from a plant. **witch-hunt** a campaign against a person with unpopular views.

with prep. **1** accompanied by. **2** in the same direction as. **3** having. **4** using. **5** in opposition to or competition with. **6** indicating manner or attitude. **7** in relation to. □ **with it** informal **1** fashionable. **2** alert.

withdraw v. (**withdrawing, withdrew**; past part. **withdrawn**) **1** remove or take away. **2** leave or cause to leave a place. **3** stop taking part in an activity.

4 retract a statement. **5** take money out of an account. **6** stop taking an addictive drug. **7** (**withdrawn**) very shy or reserved. ■ **withdrawal** n.

wither v. **1** become shrivelled and dry. **2** (**withering**) scornful.

withers pl. n. the highest part of a horse's back, at the base of the neck.

withhold v. (**withholding, withheld**) **1** refuse to give. **2** suppress a reaction etc.

within prep. **1** inside. **2** inside the range or limits of. **3** in a time no longer than. •adv. inside.

without prep. **1** not accompanied by or having. **2** not doing the action specified.

withstand v. (**withstanding, withstood**) remain undamaged or unaffected by.

witless adj. stupid.

witness n. **1** a person who sees an event take place. **2** a person giving evidence in a law court. **3** a person who is present at the signing of a document and signs to confirm this. •v. be a witness to.

witter v. informal speak trivially and at length.

witticism n. a witty remark.

witty adj. (**wittier, wittiest**) quick, inventive, and amusing with words. ■ **wittily** adv. **wittiness** n.

wives pl. of WIFE.

wizard n. **1** a man with magical powers. **2** a person who is very skilled in something. ■ **wizardry** n.

wizened adj. shrivelled or wrinkled with age.

woad n. a blue dye obtained from a plant.

w

wobble v. **1** move unsteadily from side to side. **2** (of the voice) tremble. • n. a wobbling movement or sound. ■ **wobbly** adj.

wedge n. informal a large piece or amount.

woe n. **1** sorrow or distress. **2** (**woes**) troubles. □ **woebegone** sad or miserable.

woeful adj. **1** very sad. **2** very bad. ■ **woefully** adv.

wok n. a bowl-shaped frying pan used in Chinese cookery.

woke past of **WAKE**.

woken past part. of **WAKE**.

wold n. an area of high, open land.

wolf n. (pl. **wolves**) a wild animal of the dog family. • v. eat greedily. □ **cry wolf** raise false alarms.

wolf whistle a whistle with a rising and falling pitch, expressing sexual admiration. ■ **wolfish** adj.

wolfram n. tungsten or its ore.

wolverine n. a mammal with a long brown coat, found in cold northern regions.

woman n. (pl. **women**) an adult human female. ■ **womankind** women as a group.
■ **womanhood** n. **womanly** adj.

womanize (or **-ise**) v. (of a man) have many casual affairs with women. ■ **womanizer** n.

womb n. the organ in a woman or female mammal in which offspring develop before birth.

wombat n. a burrowing Australian marsupial resembling a small bear.

won past & past part. of **WIN**.

w **wonder** v. **1** want to know something. **2** feel amazement and admiration. • n. **1** amazement and admiration. **2** a cause of this. □ **wonderland** a place full of wonderful things. ■ **wonderment** n.

wonderful adj. very good or remarkable. ■ **wonderfully** adv.

wondrous adj. inspiring wonder.

wonky adj. (**wonkier, wonkiest**) informal **1** crooked. **2** unsteady or faulty.

wont /wohnt/ formal n. (**your wont**) your normal behaviour. • adj. (**wont to**) accustomed to.

woo v. **1** try to gain a woman's love. **2** seek the support or custom of.

wood n. **1** the hard material forming the trunk and branches of a tree. **2** (or **woods**) a small forest. □ **woodcut** a print made from a design cut in a block of wood. **woodland** land covered with trees. **woodlouse** a small insect-like animal with a segmented body. **woodpecker** a bird with a strong bill that pecks at tree trunks to find insects. **woodwind** wind instruments other than brass instruments. **woodwork 1** the wooden parts of a room. **2** the activity of making things from wood. **woodworm** the larva of a kind of beetle, that bores into wood. ■ **woody** adj.

wooded adj. covered with trees.

wooden adj. **1** made of wood. **2** stiff and awkward. ■ **woodenly** adv.

woof n. the bark of a dog. • v. bark.

woofer n. a loudspeaker for reproducing low frequencies.

wool n. the soft hair forming the coat of a sheep, made into yarn or fabric.

woollen (US **woolen**) adj. made of wool. • n. (**woollens**) woollen clothing.

woolly adj. **1** made of or like wool. **2** confused or unclear.

woozy adj. informal dizzy or dazed. ■ **woozily** adv.

word *n.* **1** a single meaningful unit of language, used with others to form sentences. **2** a remark or statement. **3** (**words**) angry talk. **4** a command. **5** (**your word**) a promise. **6** news. • *v.* express in particular words. □ **word of mouth** spoken communication.

word processor a computer or program for creating and printing a piece of writing.

wording *n.* the way something is worded.

wordy *adj.* using too many words.

wore past of **WEAR**.

work *n.* **1** activity involving mental or physical effort. **2** such activity as a means of earning money. **3** a task to be done. **4** a thing or things done or made. **5** (**works**) a factory. **6** (**works**) the mechanism of a machine. • *v.* **1** do work as a job. **2** (of a machine etc.) function properly. **3** have the desired result. **4** bring into a desired state. **5** produce or create. **6** move gradually or with difficulty into another position. □ **get worked up** become stressed or angry.

workforce the people working or available for work in an area, organization, etc. **workhouse** *hist.* a place where poor people were housed and fed in return for work. **workout** a session of vigorous exercise. **work out 1** solve. **2** develop in the required way. **3** plan in detail. **4** do vigorous exercise. **workshop 1** a room or building in which goods are made or repaired. **2** a meeting for discussion and activity on a particular subject or project. **workstation** a desktop computer that is part of a network. **worktop** a flat surface for working on in a kitchen. **work-to-rule** a

form of industrial action in which workers refuse to do overtime or extra work.

workable *adj.* capable of producing the desired result.

workaday *adj.* ordinary.

worker *n.* **1** a person who works. **2** a neuter bee, wasp, ant, etc. that does the basic work of a colony.

working *n.* **1** a mine or part of a mine. **2** (**workings**) the way in which a system etc. operates. • *adj.* used as the basis for work or discussion and likely to be changed later. □ **working class** the social group consisting largely of people who do manual or industrial work. **working party** a group set up to study and report on an issue and make recommendations.

workman *n.* a man employed to do manual work. □ **workmanlike** showing efficient skill. **workmanship** the skill with which something is made or done.

world *n.* **1** the earth with all its countries and peoples. **2** all that belongs to a region, period, or area of activity. □ **worldwide** throughout the world. **World Wide Web** an information system on the Internet allowing documents to be connected to each other by hypertext links.

worldly *adj.* **1** of material rather than spiritual things. **2** experienced and sophisticated.

worm *n.* **1** an animal with a long, soft body and no backbone or limbs. **2** (**worms**) intestinal parasites. • *v.* **1** move by crawling or wriggling. **2** (**worm your way into**) gradually move into a situation. **3** (**worm out of**) obtain information from someone reluctant to give it. □ **worm cast** a spiral

W

mass of soil etc. thrown up by a burrowing worm. **wormwood** n. a bitter-tasting plant, used in vermouth etc.

worn past part. of **WEAR**. ·adj. damaged by wear. □ **worn out 1** exhausted. **2** damaged by wear and no longer usable.

worried adj. feeling or showing worry. ■ **worriedly** adv.

worrisome adj. causing anxiety or concern.

worry v. (**worrying**, **worried**) **1** feel or cause to feel concern or anxiety. **2** annoy or disturb. **3** (of a dog) tear at with the teeth. **4** (of a dog) chase and attack sheep etc. ·n. (pl. **worries**) **1** anxiety or concern. **2** a source of this. ■ **worrier** n.

worse adj. **1** less good or pleasing. **2** more serious or severe. **3** more ill or unhappy. ·adv. **1** less well. **2** more seriously or severely. ·n. something worse. ■ **worsen** v.

worship n. **1** deep respect paid to God or a god or goddess. **2** great admiration and respect. ·v. (**worshipping**, **worshipped**; US **worshiping**, **worshiped**) **1** take part in an act of worship. **2** greatly admire and respect. ■ **worshipper** n.

worst adj. most bad, severe, or serious. ·adv. **1** most severely or seriously. **2** least well. ·n. the worst event etc. ·v. defeat.

worsted /wuus-tid/ n. a smooth, fine woollen fabric.

worth adj. **1** having a specified value. **2** deserving a particular treatment. ·n. **1** value or merit. **2** an amount of something equivalent to a particular sum of money.

worthless adj. **1** having no real value or use. **2** having no good qualities.

worthwhile adj. worth the time or effort spent.

worthy adj. (**worthier**, **worthiest**) **1** deserving effort, attention, or respect. **2** (**worthy of**) deserving. ·n. (pl. **worthies**) an important person. ■ **worthily** adv. **worthiness** n.

would aux. v. **1** past of **WILL**[1]. **2** expressing possible consequence. **3** expressing a desire, polite request, or opinion. □ **would-be** wishing to be a particular type of person.

wound[1] n. **1** an injury caused by a cut, blow, or other impact. **2** an injury to a person's feelings. ·v. injure or hurt.

wound[2] past & past part. of **WIND**[2].

wove past of **WEAVE**.

woven past part. of **WEAVE**.

wow informal exclam. expressing astonishment or admiration. ·v. impress greatly.

WPC abbrev. woman police constable.

wrack n. a seaweed. ·v. var. of **RACK**.

wraith n. a ghost.

wrangle n. a long dispute. ·v. engage in a wrangle.

wrap v. (**wrapping**, **wrapped**) **1** enclose in paper or soft material. **2** encircle or wind round. ·n. a shawl. □ **under wraps** kept secret. **wrap up 1** dress in warm clothes. **2** complete a meeting or deal. **3** (**wrapped up**) totally engrossed. ■ **wrapping** n. **wrapper** n.

wrasse /rass/ n. a colourful sea fish.

wrath /roth/ n. extreme anger. ■ **wrathful** adj.

wreak v. **1** cause damage. **2** take revenge.

w

wreath n. a decorative ring of flowers and leaves.

wreathe v. 1 encircle. 2 move with a curling motion.

wreck n. 1 the destruction of a ship at sea. 2 a ship destroyed at sea. 3 a badly damaged building, vehicle, etc. 4 a person in a very bad state. • v. 1 destroy or badly damage. 2 cause a ship to sink or break up.

wreckage n. the remains of something that has been wrecked.

wren n. 1 a very small bird. 2 a member of the former Women's Royal Naval Service.

wrench v. 1 pull or twist violently. 2 twist and injure a part of the body. • n. 1 a sudden violent twist or pull. 2 distress caused by parting. 3 an adjustable tool like a spanner.

wrest v. 1 forcibly pull from a person's grasp. 2 take power after a struggle.

wrestle v. 1 take part in a fight or contest involving close grappling with an opponent. 2 struggle with a task or problem. ■ **wrestler** n.

wretch n. 1 an unfortunate person. 2 informal an unpleasant person.

wretched adj. 1 very unhappy or unfortunate. 2 very bad or annoying. ■ **wretchedly** adv.

wriggle v. 1 move with quick twisting movements. 2 (**wriggle out of**) use excuses to avoid doing. • n. a wriggling movement.

wring v. (**wringing**, **wrung**) 1 squeeze and twist, esp. to remove liquid. 2 squeeze someone's hand tightly. 3 (**wring from/out of**) obtain with difficulty.

wrinkle n. a slight line or fold in fabric or the skin. • v. form or cause to form wrinkles. ■ **wrinkly** adj.

wrist n. the joint connecting the hand and forearm.

writ n. an official written order issued by a court or other legal authority.

write v. (**writing**, **wrote**; past part. **written**) 1 mark letters, words, or other symbols on a surface with a pen, pencil, etc. 2 write and send a letter. 3 compose a written or musical work. 4 fill out a cheque. □ **write off** 1 dismiss as insignificant. 2 decide not to pursue a debt. **write-off** a vehicle too badly damaged to be repaired. **write-up** a newspaper review of a recent performance etc. ■ **writer** n.

writhe v. twist or squirm in pain or embarrassment.

writing n. 1 a sequence of letters or symbols forming words. 2 (**writings**) books or other written works.

wrong adj. 1 not correct or true; mistaken. 2 unjust, dishonest, or immoral. 3 in a bad or abnormal condition. • adv. 1 mistakenly. 2 with an incorrect result. • n. an unjust or immoral action. • v. treat unjustly. □ **in the wrong** responsible for a mistake or offence. ■ **wrongly** adv.

wrongdoing n. illegal or dishonest behaviour. ■ **wrongdoer** n.

wrongful adj. not fair, just, or legal. ■ **wrongfully** adv.

wrote past of WRITE.

wrought adj. (of metals) shaped by hammering. □ **wrought iron** a tough form of iron suitable for forging or rolling.

wrung past & past part. of WRING.

wry adj. (**wryer, wryest** or **wrier, wriest**) 1 using dry, mocking humour. 2 (of the face) expressing disappointment or annoyance. ■ **wryly** adv.

WWW abbrev. World Wide Web.

W

Xx

X (or **x**) *n.* the Roman numeral for ten.

X chromosome *n.* a sex chromosome, two of which are normally present in female cells and one in male cells.

xenon /zen-on/ *n.* an inert gas.

xenophobia /zen-uh-foh-bi-uh/ *n.* dislike or fear of people from other countries. ■ **xenophobic** *adj.*

Xerox /zeer-oks/ *n.* trademark **1** a photocopying machine.

2 a photocopy. •*v.* (**xerox**) photocopy.

Xmas *n. informal* Christmas.

X-ray *n.* **1** an electromagnetic wave able to pass through solids. **2** an image of an object's internal structure produced by passing X-rays through it.

xylophone /zy-loh-fohn/ *n.* a musical instrument played by hitting a row of wooden bars with small hammers.

Yy

yacht /yot/ *n.* **1** a medium-sized sailing boat. **2** a powered boat equipped for cruising. ■ **yachting** *n.* **yachtsman** (or **yachtswoman**) *n.*

yak *n.* a large Asian ox with shaggy hair.

yam *n.* the tuber of a tropical plant, eaten as a vegetable.

yang *n.* (in Chinese philosophy) the active male force in the universe.

Yank *n. informal* an American.

yank *informal v.* pull sharply. •*n.* a sharp pull.

yap *v.* (**yapping, yapped**) bark shrilly. •*n.* a shrill bark.

yard *n.* **1** a unit of length equal to 3 ft (0.9144 m). **2** a piece of en-

closed ground next to a building. **3** a pole slung across a ship's mast for a sail to hang from. ❑ **yardstick** a standard for comparison. ■ **yardage** *n.*

yarmulke (or **yarmulka**) /yarmuul-kuh/ *n.* a skullcap worn by Jewish men.

yarn *n.* **1** spun thread. **2** *informal* a story.

yashmak *n.* a veil concealing all of the face except the eyes, worn by some Muslim women.

yaw *v.* (of a ship or aircraft) turn unsteadily from side to side.

yawn *v.* **1** open the mouth wide and breathe in deeply due to tiredness or boredom. **2** (**yawning**) wide open. •*n.* an act of yawning.

Y chromosome n. a sex chromosome normally present only in male cells.

yd abbrev. yard.

year n. **1** (or **calendar year**) the period of 365 days (or 366 days in leap years) starting from January 1. **2** the time taken by the earth to go once around the sun. □ **yearbook** an annual publication listing events or aspects of the previous year. **yearling** an animal between one and two years old. ■ **yearly** adj. & adv.

yearn v. feel great longing.

yeast n. a fungus, or substance made from this, used to ferment beer and wine and to make dough rise. ■ **yeasty** adv.

yell n. a loud, sharp cry or call. • v. utter a yell.

yellow adj. **1** of the colour of ripe lemons. **2** informal cowardly. • n. yellow colour. • v. turn yellow with age. ■ **yellowish** adj.

yelp n. a short, sharp cry. • v. utter a yelp.

yen n. (pl. **yen**) **1** the basic unit of money of Japan. **2** informal a longing.

yeoman /yoh-muhn/ n. hist. a man owning a house and a small area of farmland.

yes exclam. **1** expressing agreement or consent. **2** used as a reply to a summons. □ **yes-man** informal a person who always agrees with their superiors.

yesterday adv. on the day before today. • n. **1** the day before today. **2** the recent past.

yet adv. **1** up until now or then. **2** this soon. **3** from now into the future. **4** still; even. • conj. nevertheless.

yeti n. a large hairy manlike animal said to live in the Himalayas.

yew n. an evergreen tree with poisonous red berries.

Y-fronts pl. n. trademark men's or boys' underpants with a seam at the front in the shape of an inverted Y.

Yiddish n. a language used by Jews from central and eastern Europe.

yield v. **1** produce or provide a natural or industrial product. **2** produce a result. **3** give way to demands or pressure. **4** give up possession of. • n. an amount yielded.

yin n. (in Chinese philosophy) the passive female presence in the universe.

yob (or **yobbo**) n. informal a rude and aggressive young man. ■ **yobbish** adj.

yodel v. (**yodelling**, **yodelled**; US **yodeling**, **yodeled**) sing in a style that alternates rapidly between a normal voice and a high-pitched voice. • n. a yodelling song or call. ■ **yodeller** n.

yoga n. a system involving breathing exercises and the holding of particular body positions, based on Hindu philosophy. ■ **yogic** adj.

yogi n. (pl. **yogis**) a person skilled in yoga.

yogurt (or **yoghurt**) n. a thick liquid food made from milk with bacteria added.

yoke n. **1** a piece of wood fastened over the necks of two animals pulling a plough etc. **2** a part of a garment fitting over the shoulders. **3** a burden or oppressive restriction. **4** a frame fitting over

y

the shoulders, used to carry buckets. • v. join with a yoke.

yokel n. an unsophisticated country person.

yolk n. the yellow inner part of a bird's egg.

Yom Kippur n. an important day in the jewish year, on which people pray and fast.

yonder adj. & adv. old use or dialect over there.

yonks pl. n. informal a very long time.

yore n. (of yore) literary long ago.

Yorkshire pudding n. a baked batter pudding eaten with roast beef or gravy.

you pron. **1** the person or people being addressed. **2** any person in general.

young adj. **1** having lived or existed for only a short time. **2** of or typical of young people. • pl. n. young children or animals; offspring.

youngster n. a young person.

your adj. of or belonging to you.

> ! Don't confuse **your** meaning 'belonging to you' (as in *your daughter*) with the form **you're**, short for **you are** (as in *you're a good cook*).

you're contr. you are.

yours possess. pron. belonging to you.

yourself pron. (pl. **yourselves**) **1** used when the person or people being addressed are affected by an action. **2** you personally.

youth n. (pl. **youths**) **1** the period between childhood and adult age. **2** the qualities associated with being young. **3** young people. **4** a young man. ▫ **youth club** a club providing leisure activities for young people. **youth hostel** a place providing cheap overnight accommodation, esp. for young people on holiday.

youthful adj. **1** young or seeming young. **2** characteristic of young people. ▪ **youthfully** adv. **youthfulness** n.

yowl n. a loud wailing cry. • v. make a yowl.

yo-yo n. (pl. **yo-yos**) trademark a toy made of a pair of joined discs with a groove between them on which a string is wound, which can be spun down and up as the string unwinds and rewinds. • v. (**yo-yoing, yo-yoed**) move up and down repeatedly.

yuan n. (pl. **yuan**) the basic unit of money of China.

yucca n. a plant with large spikes of white flowers.

yuck (or **yuk**) exclam. informal used to express disgust. ▪ **yucky** adj.

Yule (or **Yuletide**) n. old use Christmas.

yummy adj. (**yummier, yummiest**) informal delicious.

yuppie (or **yuppy**) n. (pl. **yuppies**) informal a young middle-class professional person.

Zz

zany adj. (**zanier**, **zaniest**) amusingly unconventional.

zap v. (**zapping**, **zapped**) informal **1** destroy. **2** move rapidly.

zeal n. great energy or enthusiasm for a cause or aim. ■ **zealous** adj. **zealously** adv.

zealot n. a fanatical follower of a religion, cause, etc. ■ **zealotry** n.

zebra n. an African wild horse with black and white stripes. □ **zebra crossing** a pedestrian crossing marked with broad white stripes.

zeitgeist /zyt-gysst/ n. the characteristic spirit or mood of a particular period.

Zen n. a form of Buddhism.

zenith n. **1** the point of greatest power or success. **2** the point in the sky directly overhead.

zephyr n. literary a gentle wind.

zero adj. & n. (pl. **zeros**) **1** the figure 0; nought. **2** a temperature of 0˚C (32˚F). •v. (**zeroing**, **zeroed**) (**zero in on**) take aim at or focus attention on. □ **zero hour** the time at which an important event is set to begin.

zest n. **1** great enthusiasm and energy. **2** the outer coloured part of the peel of citrus fruit.

zigzag n. a line or course having sharp alternate right and left turns. •v. (**zigzagging**, **zigzagged**) move in a zigzag.

zilch n. informal nothing.

zinc n. a white metallic element.

zing n. informal energy or enthusiasm.

Zionism n. a movement for the development of a Jewish nation in Israel. ■ **Zionist** n. & adj.

zip n. **1** (or **zipper**) a fastener consisting of two flexible interlocking metal or plastic strips, closed or opened by pulling a slide along them. **2** informal energy. •v. (**zipping**, **zipped**) **1** fasten with a zip. **2** informal move quickly. □ **zip code** US a postcode. ■ **zippy** adj.

zircon n. a brown or semi-transparent mineral.

zirconium n. a metallic element.

zit n. informal a spot on the skin.

zither n. a stringed instrument played with the fingers.

zloty n. (pl. **zloty** or **zlotys**) the basic unit of money in Poland.

zodiac n. an area of the sky in which the sun, moon, and planets appear to lie, divided by astrologers into twelve equal parts or signs. ■ **zodiacal** adj.

zombie n. **1** a person who seems only partly alive or conscious. **2** a corpse supposedly brought back to life by witchcraft.

zone n. an area with particular characteristics or a particular use. •v. divide into zones. ■ **zonal** adj.

zoo n. a place where wild animals are kept for study, conservation, or display to the public.

zoology n. the study of animals. ■ **zoological** adj. **zoologist** n.

zoom v. **1** move very quickly. **2** (of a camera) change smoothly from a long shot to a close-up or vice versa.

zucchini /zuu-kee-ni/ *n.* (*pl.* **zucchini** or **zucchinis**) *US* a courgette.

Zulu *n.* **1** a member of a South African people. **2** the language of the Zulus.

zygote *n.* a cell resulting from the joining of two gametes.